"The purpose of decision modeling is to gain insight into the problem, not the mechanics of the solution process."

Balakrishnan, Render, and Stair (BRS) believe that business students will be users of decision modeling techniques, not developers. Therefore, students need to learn (1) which modeling technique they should use in a specific situation, and why; (2) how to formulate the decision model; (3) how to solve the model using a computer; and (4) how to interpret and use the results of the model.

Throughout the textbook, the authors clearly illustrate the use of Excel as a valuable tool to solve decision models quickly and effectively. Examples in the text are clear, simple, and easy to understand. BRS offers the perfect balance between the logic and algebraic formulation of decision models, and the use of Excel to solve these models.

Here are some of the notable changes in this edition...

- **Updated from Excel 2003 to Excel 2007/2010** – All spreadsheet applications have been fully updated to Excel 2010. Likewise, the illustration of Microsoft Project and Crystal Ball has been updated to their latest versions. The software program ExcelModules that accompanies this book has also been updated to suit Excel 2010 as well as 32-bit and 64-bit systems.
- **Significant Number of Revised and New Chapter Examples and End-of-Chapter Exercises** – We have made revisions to many of the end-of-chapter exercises from the previous edition and have added several new exercises. Many of the chapter examples and end-of-chapter exercises have been revised to make them more current, rigorous, and better suited to a computer-based solution environment. On average, there are more than 45 end-of-chapter exercises per chapter. Many of these exercises include multipart questions, giving instructors a rich pool of questions from which to select.
- **Expanded Use of Color in Excel Screenshots** – Unlike the first two editions where only the first six chapters had screenshots in color, screenshots in all chapters are now in color. This allows greater clarity in our explanations of these screenshots, and their understanding by students.
- **Updated *DM in Action* Boxes** – Now includes 27 new *DM in Action* boxes that illustrate the use of decision modeling in real-world scenarios, most of them in well-known global organizations. Many of these examples are from recent issues of *Interfaces* and discuss applications that have occurred within the past few years.
- **Expanded Discussion of Several Topics** – Now includes expanded coverage of unbalanced transportation and transshipment models, the O[illegible] available in Crystal Ball for simulation models, and the Multis[illegible] in Excel 2010 to solve nonlinear programming models.

Managerial Decision Modeling with Spreadsheets

THIRD EDITION

NAGRAJ (RAJU) BALAKRISHNAN

Senior Associate Dean and Professor of Management
College of Business and Behavioral Science, Clemson University

BARRY RENDER

Charles Harwood Professor of Management Science Emeritus
Graduate School of Business, Rollins College

RALPH M. STAIR, JR.

Professor Emeritus
Florida State University

PEARSON

Boston Columbus Indianapolis New York San Francisco Upper Saddle River
Amsterdam Cape Town Dubai London Madrid Milan Munich Paris Montréal Toronto
Delhi Mexico City São Paulo Sydney Hong Kong Seoul Singapore Taipei Tokyo

Editorial Director: Sally Yagan
Editor in Chief: Donna Battista
Senior Acquisitions Editor: Chuck Synovec
Editorial Project Manager: Mary Kate Murray
Editorial Assistant: Ashlee Bradbury
Director of Marketing: Maggie Moylan
Executive Marketing Manager: Anne Fahlgren
Senior Managing Editor: Judy Leale
Production Project Manager: Jane Bonnell
Senior Operations Supervisor: Arnold Vila
Operations Specialist: Cathleen Petersen
Creative Director: Blair Brown
Senior Art Director/Supervisor: Janet Slowik
Art Director: Steve Frim
Text and Cover Designer: Wee Design Group
Cover Art: Shutterstock/Digital Genetics
Associate Media Project Manager, Editorial: Sarah Peterson
Media Project Manager, Production: John Cassar
Composition/Full-Service Project Management: PreMediaGlobal
Printer/Binder: Quebecor World Color/Versailles
Cover Printer: Lehigh-Phoenix Color/Hagerstown
Text Font: 10/12 Times

Credits and acknowledgments borrowed from other sources and reproduced, with permission, in this textbook appear on the appropriate page within text.

Library of Congress Cataloging-in-Publication Data

Balakrishnan, Nagraj.
Managerial decision modeling with spreadsheets / Nagraj (Raju) Balakrishnan, Barry Render, Ralph M. Stair. —3rd ed.
p. cm.
Includes bibliographical references and index.
ISBN-13: 978-0-13-611583-0 (alk. paper)
ISBN-10: 0-13-611583-7 (alk. paper)
1. Management—Mathematical models. 2. Management science. I. Render, Barry. II. Stair, Ralph M. III. Title.
HD30.25.R465 2012
658.4'032—dc23

2011042062

10 9 8 7 6 5 4 3 2 1

ISBN 10: 0-13-611583-7
ISBN 13: 978-0-13-611583-0

To my children, Nitin and Nandita
To my parents, Chitra and K. V. Balakrishnan
To my parents-in-law, Saraswathy and N. Krishnan
Most of all to my darling wife, Meena, my rock – N.B.

To Donna, Charlie, and Jesse – B.R.

To Ken Ramsing and Alan Eliason – R.M.S.

ABOUT THE AUTHORS

Raju Balakrishnan is Senior Associate Dean in the College of Business and Behavioral Science (CBBS) at Clemson University. Prior to his appointment in the Dean's office, Dr. Balakrishnan served on the faculty at Clemson's Department of Management, including terms as Graduate Coordinator and as Department Chair. Dr. Balakrishnan has also served on the faculty at Tulane University and has taught in the Executive MBA program at Tulane and the University of Georgia.

Dr. Balakrishnan's primary teaching interests include Spreadsheet-Based Decision Modeling, Business Statistics, Project Management, and Operations Management. His current research focuses on the impact of business process outsourcing, and he has published extensively in leading academic journals such as *Decision Sciences*, *Production and Operations Management*, *European Journal of Operational Research*, *IIE Transactions*, *Naval Research Logistics*, and *Computers & Operations Research*. He serves as senior departmental editor of *Production and Operations Management* and served as secretary of the Production and Operations Management Society during 2007-09. He has won numerous teaching awards both at Clemson and at Tulane. At Clemson, these include the MBA Professor of the Year award (twice) and the CBBS Graduate Teaching Excellence award (twice). He has also received best paper awards from the Decision Sciences Institute and the Institute of Industrial Engineers, the Department of Management Award for Scholarly Achievement, and the Clemson Board of Trustees Award for Faculty Excellence.

Dr. Balakrishnan holds Bachelors and Masters degrees in Mechanical Engineering from the University of Madras (India) and the University of Kentucky respectively, and a Ph.D. in Management from Purdue University.

Barry Render is the Charles Harwood Professor of Management Science Emeritus at the Crummer Graduate School of Business at Rollins College in Winter Park, Florida. He received his M.S. in Operations Research and his Ph.D. in Quantitative Analysis at the University of Cincinnati. He previously taught at George Washington University, the University of New Orleans, Boston University, and George Mason University, where he held the GM Foundation Professorship in Decision Sciences and was Chair of the Decision Science Department. Dr. Render has also worked in the aerospace industry for General Electric, McDonnell Douglas, and NASA.

Professor Render has co-authored ten textbooks with Prentice Hall, including *Quantitative Analysis for Management*, *Operations Management*, *Principles of Operations Management*, *Service Management*, *Introduction to Management Science*, and *Cases and Readings in Management Science*. His more than one hundred articles on a variety of management topics have appeared in *Decision Sciences*, *Production and Operations Management*, *Interfaces*, *Information and Management*, *The Journal of Management Information Systems*, *Socio-Economic Planning Sciences*, and *Operations Management Review*, among others.

Dr. Render has also been honored as an AACSB Fellow and named as a Senior Fulbright Scholar in 1982 and again in 1993. He was twice vice-president of the Decision Science Institute Southeast Region and served as Software Review Editor for Decision Line from 1989 to 1995. He has also served as Editor of the *New York Times* Operations Management special issues from 1996 to 2001 and is currently Consulting Editor for *Financial Times Press*. Finally, Professor Render has been actively involved in consulting for government agencies and for many corporations, including NASA; FBI; the U.S. Navy; Fairfax County, Virginia; and C&P Telephone.

Before retiring in 2009, he taught operations management courses in Rollins College's MBA and Executive MBA programs. In 1995 and in 2009 he was named as that school's Professor of the Year, and in 1996 was selected by Roosevelt University to receive the St. Claire Drake Award for Outstanding Scholarship.

Ralph Stair is Professor Emeritus of Management Information Systems in the College of Business at Florida State University. He received a B.S. in Chemical Engineering from Purdue University and an MBA from Tulane University. Under the guidance of Ken Ramsing and Alan Eliason, he received his Ph.D. in operations management from the University of Oregon.

He has taught at the University of Oregon, the University of Washington, the University of New Orleans, and Florida State University. He has twice taught in Florida State University's Study Abroad Program in London. Over the years, his teaching has been concentrated in the areas of information systems, operations research, and operations management.

Dr. Stair is a member of several academic organizations, including the Decision Sciences Institute and INFORMS, and he regularly participates at national meetings. He has published numerous articles and books, including *Quantitative Analysis for Management*, *Introduction to Management Science*, *Cases and Readings in Management Science*, *Production and Operations Management:* A *Self-Correction Approach*, *Fundamentals of Information Systems*, *Principles of Information Systems*, *Introduction to Information Systems*, *Computers in Today's World*, *Principles of Data Processing*, *Learning to Live with Computers*, *Programming in BASIC*, *Essentials of BASIC Programming*, *Essentials of FORTRAN Programming*, and *Essentials of COBOL Programming*.

Professor Stair divides his time between Florida and Colorado. He has funded a student scholarship at St. Johns Northwestern Military Academy and endowed a faculty prize in innovative education at Florida State University.

BRIEF CONTENTS

CONTENTS

PREFACE

MAJOR CHANGES IN THE THIRD EDITION

We have made the following major changes in this third edition of *Managerial Decision Modeling with Spreadsheets*:

- *Updated from Excel 2003 to Excel 2007/2010*—All spreadsheet applications have been fully updated to Excel 2010. Likewise, the illustration of Microsoft Project and Crystal Ball has been updated to their latest versions. The software program ExcelModules that accompanies this book has also been updated to suit Excel 2010 as well as 32-bit and 64-bit systems.
- *Significant number of revised and new end-of-chapter exercises*—We have made revisions to many of the end-of-chapter exercises from the previous edition and have added several new exercises. On average, there are more than 45 end-of-chapter exercises per chapter. Many of these exercises include multipart questions, giving instructors a rich pool of questions from which to select.
- *More challenging chapter examples and end-of-chapter exercises*—Many of the chapter examples and end-of-chapter exercises have been revised to make them more current, rigorous, and better suited to a computer-based solution environment.
- *Expanded use of color in Excel screenshots*—Unlike the first two editions where only the first six chapters had screenshots in color, screenshots in all chapters are now in color. This allows greater clarity in our explanations of these screenshots and their understanding by students.
- *Updated* DM in Action *Boxes*—Now includes 27 new *DM in Action* boxes that illustrate the use of decision modeling in real-world scenarios, most of them in well-known global organizations. Many of these examples are from recent issues of *Interfaces* and discuss applications that have occurred within the past few years.
- *Expanded coverage of unbalanced transportation and transshipment models (Chapter 5)*—This edition includes discussion of a larger transshipment example with pure transshipment nodes. We have also discussed how dummy nodes can be used to convert unbalanced models into equivalent balanced models for ease of use.
- *Coverage of OptQuest in simulation (Chapter 10)*—The textbook now discusses the use of the OptQuest procedure available in Crystal Ball to automatically identify the best combination of values for decision variables that optimizes a desired output measure in a simulation model.
- *Expanded discussion of nonlinear programming (Chapter 6)*—The textbook now illustrates how the Multistart option available in Excel 2010 when using the GRG procedure to solve nonlinear programming models can be used to increase the likelihood of identifying a global optimal solution for these models.

OVERVIEW

In recent years, the use of spreadsheets to teach decision modeling (alternatively referred to as *management science*, *operations research*, and *quantitative analysis*) has become standard practice in many business programs. This emphasis has revived interest in the field significantly, and several textbooks have attempted to discuss spreadsheet-based decision modeling.

However, some of these textbooks have become too spreadsheet oriented, focusing more on the spreadsheet commands to use than on the underlying decision model. Other textbooks have maintained their algorithmic approach to decision modeling, adding spreadsheet instructions almost as an afterthought. In the third edition of *Managerial Decision Modeling with Spreadsheets*, we have continued to build on our success with the first two editions in trying to achieve the perfect balance between the decision modeling process and the use of spreadsheets to set up and solve decision models.

It is important that textbooks that support decision modeling courses try to combine the student's power to logically model and analyze diverse decision-making scenarios with software-based solution procedures. Therefore, this third edition continues to focus on teaching the reader the skills needed to apply decision models to different kinds of organizational decision-making situations. The discussions are very application oriented and software based, with a view toward how a manager can effectively apply the models learned here to improve the decision-making process. The primary target audiences for this textbook are students in undergraduate- and graduate-level introductory decision modeling courses in business schools. However, this textbook will also be useful to students in other introductory courses that cover some of the core decision modeling topics, such as linear programming, network modeling, project management, decision analysis, and simulation.

Although the emphasis in this third edition continues to be on using spreadsheets for decision modeling, the textbook remains, at heart, a *decision modeling* textbook. That is, while we use spreadsheets as a tool to quickly set up and solve decision models, our aim is not to teach students how to blindly use a spreadsheet without understanding how and why it works. To accomplish this, we discuss the fundamental concepts, assumptions, and limitations behind each decision modeling technique, show how each decision model works, and illustrate the real-world usefulness of each technique with many applications from both for-profit and not-for-profit organizations.

We have kept the notation, terminology, and equations standard with other textbooks, and we have tried to write a textbook that is easy to understand and use. Basic knowledge of algebra and Excel are the only prerequisites. For your convenience, we have included a brief introduction to Excel 2010 as an appendix.

This textbook's chapters, supplements, and software packages cover virtually every major topic in the decision modeling field and are arranged to provide a distinction between techniques that deal with deterministic environments and those that deal with probabilistic environments. Even though we have produced a somewhat smaller textbook that covers only the most important topics, we have still included more material than most instructors can cover in a typical first course. We hope that the resulting flexibility of topic selection is appreciated by instructors who need to tailor their courses to different audiences and curricula.

OVERALL APPROACH

While writing this third edition, we have continued to adhere to certain themes that have worked very well in the first two editions:

- First, we have tried to separate the discussion of each decision modeling technique into three distinct issues:

  1. Formulation or problem setup
  2. Model solution
  3. Interpretation of the results and what-if analysis

  In this three-step framework, steps 1 and 3 (formulation and interpretation) call upon the manager's expertise. Mastering these steps now will give students a competitive advantage later, in the marketplace, when it is necessary to make business decisions. We therefore emphasize these steps.

- Second, we recognize that business students are primarily going to be users of these decision modeling techniques rather than their developers. Hence, to deal with step 2 (model solution), we have integrated our discussions with software packages so that students can take full advantage of their availability. In this regard, the textbook exploits the wide availability and acceptability of spreadsheet-based software for decision modeling techniques.

Excel is a very important part of what most instructors consider the two main topics in any *basic* decision modeling textbook: linear programming and simulation. However, we recognize that some topics are not well suited for spreadsheet-based software. A case in point is project management, where Excel is generally not the best choice. In such cases, rather than try to force the topic to suit Excel, we have discussed the use of more practical packages, such as Microsoft Project.

- Third, although we use software packages as the primary vehicle to deal with step 2, we try to ensure that students focus on *what* they are doing and *why* they are doing it, rather than just mechanically learning which Excel formula to use or which Excel button to press. To facilitate this, and to avoid the "black box syndrome," we also *briefly* discuss the steps and rationale of the solution process in many cases.
- Fourth, we recognize that in this introductory textbook, the material does not need to be (and should not be) too comprehensive. Our aim here is to inform students about what is available with regard to decision modeling and pique their interest in the subject material. More detailed instruction can follow, if the student chooses, in advanced elective courses that may use more sophisticated software packages.
- Finally, we note that most of the students in decision modeling courses are likely to specialize in *other* functional areas, such as finance, marketing, accounting, operations, and human resources. We therefore try to integrate decision modeling techniques with problems drawn from these different areas so that students can recognize the importance of what they are learning and the potential benefits of using decision modeling in real-world settings. In addition, we have included summaries of selected articles from journals such as *Interfaces* that discuss the actual application of decision modeling techniques to real-world problems.

FEATURES IN THIS TEXTBOOK

The features of the first two editions of this textbook that have been well received as effective aids to the learning process have been updated and expanded in this third edition. We hope that these features will continue to help us to better adhere to the themes listed previously and help students better understand the material. These include the following features:

- *Consistent layout and format for creating effective Excel models*—We use a consistent layout and format for creating spreadsheet models for all linear, integer, goal, and nonlinear programming problems. We strongly believe such a consistent approach is best suited to the beginning student of these types of decision models.
- *Functional use of color in the spreadsheets to clarify and illustrate good spreadsheet modeling*—As part of the consistent layout and format for the spreadsheet models, we have standardized the use of colors so that the various components of the models are easily identifiable. For an excellent illustration of this feature, please see the front end papers of this edition.
- *Description of the algebraic formulation and its spreadsheet implementation for all examples*—For each model, we first discuss the algebraic formulation so that the student can understand the logic and rationale behind the decision model. The spreadsheet implementation then closely follows the algebraic formulation for ease of understanding.
- *Numerous screen captures of Excel outputs, with detailed callouts explaining the important entries*—We have included numerous screen captures of Excel files. Each screenshot has been annotated with detailed callouts explaining the important entries and components of the model. The front end papers of this edition provide a detailed illustration of this feature. Excel files are located at www.pearsonhighered.com/balakrishnan and, for your convenience, the callouts are shown as comments on appropriate cells in these Excel files.
- *Ability to teach topics both with and without the use of additional add-ins or software*—We have discussed several topics so that they can be studied either using Excel's standard built-in commands or using additional Excel add-ins or other software.

For example, we have discussed how Excel's built-in Data Table and Scenario Manager procedures can be used to analyze and replicate even large simulation models. We have also discussed how Crystal Ball can be used to develop models in a more convenient manner, for students who want to install and use this software. Likewise, we have discussed how Microsoft Project can be used to effectively manage large projects.

- *Extensive discussion of linear programming sensitivity analysis, using the Solver report*— The discussion of linear programming sensitivity analysis in this textbook is more comprehensive than that in any competing textbook.
- *Decision Modeling in Action boxes*—These boxes summarize published articles that illustrate how real-world organizations have used decision models to solve problems. This edition includes 27 new *DM in Action* boxes, mostly from recent issues of *Interfaces* that discuss applications that have occurred within the past few years.
- *History boxes*—These boxes briefly describe how some decision modeling techniques were developed.
- *Margin notes*—These notes make it easier for students to understand and remember important points.
- *Glossaries*—A glossary at the end of each chapter defines important terms.
- *ExcelModules*—This program from Professor Howard Weiss of Temple University solves problems and examples in the queuing models (Chapter 9), forecasting models (Chapter 11), and inventory control models (Chapter 12) chapters in this textbook. Students can see the power of this software package in modeling and solving problems in these chapters. ExcelModules is menu driven and easy to use, and it is available at www.pearsonhighered.com/balakrishnan.
- *Microsoft Project*—This software is featured in the project management (Chapter 7) chapter to set up and manage projects. Readers can go to www.microsoft.com to get more information about this popular software.

COMPANION WEBSITE

The following items can be downloaded at www.pearsonhighered.com/balakrishnan:

1. **Data Files**—Excel files for all examples discussed in the textbook (For easy reference, the relevant file names are printed in the margins at appropriate places in the textbook.)
2. **Online Chapter**—The electronic-only Chapter 12: Inventory Control Models in PDF format
3. **Software**—The following software can be downloaded directly from the Companion Website or will link you to the company's website where you can download the free trial version.

   ExcelModules—This program from Professor Howard Weiss of Temple University solves problems and examples in the queuing models (Chapter 9), forecasting models (Chapter 11), and inventory control models (Chapter 12) chapters in this textbook. Students can see the power of this software package in modeling and solving problems in these chapters. ExcelModules is menu driven and easy to use. This can be downloaded directly from the Companion Website.

   TreePlan—This program helps you build a decision tree diagram in an Excel worksheet using dialog boxes. Decision trees are useful for analyzing sequential decision problems under uncertainty. TreePlan automatically includes formulas for summing cash flows to obtain outcome values and for calculating rollback values for determining optimal strategy. This can be downloaded directly from the Companion Website.

   Crystal Ball—This program is a spreadsheet-based application suite for predictive modeling, forecasting, simulation, and optimization. There is a link to the company's website where you can download a free 30-day trial version.

   Risk Solver Platform— This program is a tool for risk analysis, simulation, and optimization in Excel. There is a link to the company's website where you can download a free 15-day trial version.

Subscription Content—a Companion Website Access Code is located on the inside back cover of this book. This code gives you access to the following software:

- *Crystal Ball*— Free 140-day Trial of Crystal Ball Software Compliments of the Crystal Ball Education Alliance.
- *Risk Solver Platform for Education (RSPE)*—This is a special version of Frontline Systems' Risk Solver Platform software for Microsoft Excel.

After redeeming the access code on the back cover of this book you will find a link to each company's website, where you can download the upgrade version.

To redeem the subscription content:

- Visit www.pearsonhighered.com/balakrishnan
- Click on the Companion Website link
- Click on the Subscription Content link
- First-time users will need to register, while returning users may log-in. Enter your access code found on the back cover of this book.
- Once you are logged in you will be brought to a page that will instruct you on how to download the software from the corresponding software company's website.

4. **Key equations**—Files list all the mathematical equations in a chapter.
5. **Internet Case Studies**—There are several additional case studies.

INSTRUCTOR'S SUPPLEMENTS

The supplements to this textbook reflect the spreadsheet emphasis of the textbook and provide students and instructors with the best teaching and resource package available.

- *Companion Website* at www.pearsonhighered.com/balakrishnan—See the detailed list of the contents for the Companion Website above. Instructors can also access solutions to cases on the Website.
- *Instructor's Solutions Manual*—The Instructor's Solutions Manual, prepared by Raju Balakrishnan, includes solutions (along with relevant Excel files) for all end-of-chapter exercises and cases. Also available are the solutions to the Internet Study Cases. The Instructor's Solutions Manual is available for download by visiting the Companion Website.
- *PowerPoint presentations*—An extensive set of PowerPoint slides is available for download by visiting www.pearsonhighered.com/balakrishnan. The slides are oriented toward the learning objectives listed for each chapter and build on key concepts in the textbook.
- *Test Item File*—The Test Item File is available for download by visiting the Companion Website.
- *TestGen*— Pearson Education's test-generating software is available from www.pearsonhighered.com/irc. The software is PC/MAC compatible and preloaded with all the Test Item File questions. You can manually or randomly view questions and drag and drop to create a test. You can add or modify questions as needed.
- *Subscription Content*—A Companion Website Access Code is located on the inside back cover of this book. This code gives you access to the following software:
  - *Crystal Ball*— Free 140-day Trial of Crystal Ball Software Compliments of the Crystal Ball Education Alliance
  - *Risk Solver Platform for Education (RSPE)*—This is a special version of Frontline Systems' Risk Solver Platform software for Microsoft Excel. For further information on **Risk Solver Platform for Education**, contact Frontline Systems at (888) 831-0333 (U.S. and Canada), 775-831-0300, or academic@solver.com. They will be pleased to provide **free evaluation licenses** to faculty members considering adoption of the software. They can help you with conversion of simulation models you might have created with other software to work with Risk Solver Platform (it's very straightforward).

ACKNOWLEDGMENTS

The authors are thrilled to have partnered with Professor Howard Weiss of Temple University, who did an outstanding job in developing ExcelModules. Professors Jerry Kinard, Mark McKnew, Judith McKnew, F. Bruce Simmons III, Khala Chand Seal, Victor E. Sower, Michael Ballot, Curtis P. McLaughlin, and Zbigniew H. Przasnyski contributed excellent cases and exercises.

The authors would like to thank Judith McKnew of Clemson University for her assistance in revising the end-of-chapter exercises in the textbook. Raju Balakrishnan would like to thank Dean Claude Lilly and the Dean's office staff in the College of Business and Behavioral Science at Clemson University who provided support and encouragement during the writing of this textbook.

We would also like to express our sincere appreciation to the following reviewers, whose valuable comments on the first two editions have helped us greatly in writing this revision:

Mohammad Ahmadi, University of Tennessee at Chattanooga
Anne Alexander, University of Wyoming
Susan Cholette, San Francisco State University
Anne Davey, Northeastern State University
Avi Dechter, California State University-Northridge
Kathy Dhanda, DePaul University
Robert Donnelly, Goldey-Beacom College
Michael Douglas, Millersville University
Isaac Gottlieb, Rutgers University
Raj Jagannathan, University of Iowa
Pamela Keystone, Bridgewater College
Larry J. Leblanc, Vanderbilt University
David Lewis, University of Massacusetts—Lowell
Haitao Li, University of Missouri—St. Louis
Danny Meyers, Bowling Green State University
Susan W. Palocsay, James Madison University
Gary Reeves, University of South Carolina
Chris Rump, Bowling Green State University
David A. Schilling, Ohio State University
Sylvia Shafto, College of Notre Dame
Emad Abu Shanab, University of Iowa
Brian Smith, McGill University
Nabil Tamimi, University of Scranton
Liz Umble, Baylor University
John Wang, Montclair State University
Rick Wilson, Oklahoma State University

Several people worked very hard to bring the textbook through the publication process. We would like to gratefully acknowledge the outstanding help provided by Chuck Synovec, Senior Acquisitions Editor; Mary Kate Murray, Senior Editorial Project Manager; Jane Bonnell, Senior Production Project Manager; Haylee Schwenk, PreMediaGlobal Project Manager; Ashlee Bradbury, Editorial Assistant; Anne Fahlgren, Executive Marketing Manager; and Sarah Peterson, Associate Media Project Manager. Thank you all!

It is no secret that unlike courses in functional areas such as finance, marketing, and accounting, decision modeling courses always face an uphill battle in getting students interested and excited about the material. We hope that this textbook will be an ally to all in this endeavor.

Raju Balakrishnan
864-656-3177 (phone)
nbalak@clemson.edu (e-mail)

Barry Render
brender@rollins.edu (e-mail)

Ralph Stair
ralphmstair@cs.com (e-mail)

CHAPTER 1

Introduction to Managerial Decision Modeling

LEARNING OBJECTIVES

After completing this chapter, students will be able to:

1. Define *decision model* and describe the importance of such models.
2. Understand the two types of decision models: deterministic and probabilistic models.
3. Understand the steps involved in developing decision models in practical situations.
4. Understand the use of spreadsheets in developing decision models.
5. Discuss possible problems in developing decision models.

CHAPTER OUTLINE

1.1 What Is Decision Modeling?

Decision modeling *is a scientific approach to decision making.*

Although there are several definitions of **decision modeling**, we define it here as a scientific approach to managerial decision making. Alternatively, we can define it as the development of a **model** (usually mathematical) of a real-world problem scenario or environment. The resulting model should typically be such that the decision-making process is not affected by personal bias, whim, emotions, and guesswork. This model can then be used to provide insights into the solution of the managerial problem. Decision modeling is also commonly referred to as *quantitative analysis*, *management science*, or *operations research*. In this textbook, we prefer the term *decision modeling* because we will discuss all modeling techniques in a managerial decision-making context.

Organizations such as American Airlines, United Airlines, IBM, Google, UPS, FedEx, and AT&T frequently use decision modeling to help solve complex problems. Although mathematical tools have been in existence for thousands of years, the formal study and application of quantitative (or mathematical) decision modeling techniques to practical decision making is largely a product of the twentieth century. The decision modeling techniques studied here have been applied successfully to an increasingly wide variety of complex problems in business, government, health care, education, and many other areas. Many such successful uses are discussed throughout this textbook.

It isn't enough, though, just to know the mathematical details of how a particular decision modeling technique can be set up and solved. It is equally important to be familiar with the limitations, assumptions, and specific applicability of the model. The correct use of decision modeling techniques usually results in solutions that are timely, accurate, flexible, economical, reliable, easy to understand, and easy to use.

1.2 Types of Decision Models

Decision models can be broadly classified into two categories, based on the type and nature of the decision-making problem environment under consideration: (1) deterministic models and (2) probabilistic models. We define each of these types of models in the following sections.

Deterministic Models

Deterministic *means with complete certainty.*

Deterministic models assume that all the relevant input data values are known with certainty; that is, they assume that all the information needed for modeling a decision-making problem environment is available, with fixed and known values. An example of such a model is the case of Dell Corporation, which makes several different types of PC products (e.g., desktops, laptops), all of which compete for the same resources (e.g., labor, hard disks, chips, working capital). Dell knows the specific amounts of each resource required to make one unit of each type of PC, based on the PC's design specifications. Further, based on the expected selling price and cost prices of various resources, Dell knows the expected profit contribution per unit of

HISTORY **The Origins of Decision Modeling**

Decision modeling has been in existence since the beginning of recorded history, but it was Frederick W. Taylor who, in the early 1900s, pioneered the principles of the scientific approach to management. During World War II, many new scientific and quantitative techniques were developed to assist the military. These new developments were so successful that after World War II, many companies started using similar techniques in managerial decision making and planning. Today, many organizations employ a staff of operations research or management science personnel or consultants to apply the principles of scientific management to problems and opportunities. The terms *management science*, *operations research*, and *quantitative analysis* can be used interchangeably, though here we use *decision modeling*.

The origins of many of the techniques discussed in this textbook can be traced to individuals and organizations that have applied the principles of scientific management first developed by Taylor; they are discussed in *History* boxes scattered throughout the textbook.

each type of PC. In such an environment, if Dell decides on a specific production plan, it is a simple task to compute the quantity required of each resource to satisfy that production plan. For example, if Dell plans to ship 50,000 units of a specific laptop model, and each unit includes a pair of 2.0GB SDRAM memory chips, then Dell will need 100,000 units of these memory chips. Likewise, it is easy to compute the total profit that will be realized by this production plan (assuming that Dell can sell all the laptops it makes).

The most commonly used deterministic modeling technique is linear programming.

Perhaps the most common and popular deterministic modeling technique is linear programming (LP). In Chapter 2, we first discuss how small LP models can be set up and solved. We extend our discussion of LP in Chapter 3 to more complex problems drawn from a variety of business disciplines. In Chapter 4, we study how the solution to LP models produces, as a by-product, a great deal of information that is useful for managerial interpretation of the results. Finally, in Chapters 5 and 6, we study a few extensions to LP models. These include several different network flow models (Chapter 5), as well as integer, nonlinear, and multi-objective (goal) programming models (Chapter 6).

As we demonstrate during our study of deterministic models, a variety of important managerial decision-making problems can be set up and solved using these techniques.

Probabilistic Models

Some input data are unknown in probabilistic models.

In contrast to deterministic models, **probabilistic models** (also called *stochastic models*) assume that some *input data* values are not known with certainty. That is, they assume that the values of some important variables will not be known *before* decisions are made. It is therefore important to incorporate this "ignorance" into the model. An example of this type of model is the decision of whether to start a new business venture. As we have seen with the high variability in the stock market during the past several years, the success of such ventures is unsure. However, investors (e.g., venture capitalists, founders) have to make decisions regarding this type of venture, based on their expectations of future performance. Clearly, such expectations are not guaranteed to occur. In recent years, we have seen several examples of firms that have yielded (or are likely to yield) great rewards to their investors (e.g., Google, Facebook, Twitter) and others that have either failed (e.g., eToys.com, Pets.com) or been much more modest in their returns.

Another example of probabilistic modeling to which students may be able to relate easily is their choice of a major when they enter college. Clearly, there is a great deal of uncertainty regarding several issues in this decision-making problem: the student's aptitude for a specific major, his or her actual performance in that major, the employment situation in that major in four years, etc. Nevertheless, a student must choose a major early in his or her college career. Recollect your own situation. In all likelihood, you used your own assumptions (or expectations) regarding the future to evaluate the various alternatives (i.e., you developed a "model" of the decision-making problem). These assumptions may have been the result of information from various sources, such as parents, friends, and guidance counselors. The important point to note here is that none of this information is guaranteed, and no one can predict with 100% accuracy what exactly will happen in the future. Therefore, decisions made with this information, while well thought out and well intentioned, may still turn out to not be the best choices. For example, how many of your friends have changed majors during their college careers?

Because their results are not guaranteed, does this mean that probabilistic decision models are of limited value? As we will see later in this textbook, the answer is an emphatic no. Probabilistic modeling techniques provide a structured approach for managers to incorporate uncertainty into their models and to evaluate decisions under alternate expectations regarding this uncertainty. They do so by using probabilities on the "random," or unknown, variables. Probabilistic modeling techniques discussed in this textbook include decision analysis (Chapter 8), queuing (Chapter 9), simulation (Chapter 10), and forecasting (Chapter 11). Two other techniques, project management (Chapter 7) and inventory control (Chapter 12), include aspects of both deterministic and probabilistic modeling. For each modeling technique, we discuss what kinds of criteria can be used when there is uncertainty and how to use these models to identify the preferred decisions.

Probabilistic models use probabilities to incorporate uncertainty.

Because uncertainty plays a vital role in probabilistic models, some knowledge of basic probability and statistical concepts is useful. Appendix A provides a brief overview of this topic. It should serve as a good refresher while studying these modeling techniques.

Quantitative versus Qualitative Data

The decision modeling process starts with data.

Any decision modeling process starts with data. Like raw material for a factory, these data are manipulated or processed into information that is valuable to people making decisions. This processing and manipulating of raw data into meaningful information is the heart of decision modeling.

Both qualitative and quantitative factors must be considered.

In dealing with a decision-making problem, managers may have to consider both qualitative and quantitative factors. For example, suppose we are considering several different investment alternatives, such as certificates of deposit, the stock market, and real estate. We can use *quantitative* factors such as rates of return, financial ratios, and cash flows in our decision model to guide our ultimate decision. In addition to these factors, however, we may also wish to consider *qualitative* factors such as pending state and federal legislation, new technological breakthroughs, and the outcome of an upcoming election. It can be difficult to quantify these qualitative factors.

Due to the presence (and relative importance) of qualitative factors, the role of quantitative decision modeling in the decision-making process can vary. When there is a lack of qualitative factors, and when the problem, model, and input data remain reasonably stable and steady over time, the results of a decision model can automate the decision-making process. For example, some companies use quantitative inventory models to determine automatically when to order additional new materials and how much to order. In most cases, however, decision modeling is an aid to the decision-making process. The results of decision modeling should be combined with other (qualitative) information while making decisions in practice.

Using Spreadsheets in Decision Modeling

Spreadsheet packages are capable of handling many decision modeling techniques.

In keeping with the ever-increasing presence of technology in modern times, computers have become an integral part of the decision modeling process in today's business environments. Until the early 1990s, many of the modeling techniques discussed here required specialized software packages in order to be solved using a computer. However, spreadsheet packages such as Microsoft Excel have become increasingly capable of setting up and solving most of the decision modeling techniques commonly used in practical situations. For this reason, the current trend in many college courses on decision modeling focuses on spreadsheet-based instruction. In keeping with this trend, we discuss the role and use of spreadsheets (specifically Microsoft Excel) during our study of the different decision modeling techniques presented here.

Several add-ins for Excel are included on the Companion Website for this textbook, www.pearsonhighered.com/balakrishnan.

In addition to discussing the use of some of Excel's built-in functions and procedures (e.g., Goal Seek, Data Table, Chart Wizard), we also discuss several add-ins for Excel. The Data Analysis and Solver add-ins come standard with Excel; others are included on the Companion Website. Table 1.1 lists the add-ins included on the Companion Website and indicates the chapter(s) and topic(s) in which each one is discussed and used.

Because a knowledge of basic Excel commands and procedures facilitates understanding the techniques and concepts discussed here, we recommend reading Appendix B, which provides a brief overview of the Excel features that are most useful in decision modeling. In addition, at appropriate places throughout this textbook, we discuss several Excel functions and procedures specific to each decision modeling technique.

IN ACTION IBM Uses Decision Modeling to Improve the Productivity of Its Sales Force

IBM is a well-known multinational computer technology, software, and services company with over 380,000 employees and revenue of over $100 billion. A majority of IBM's revenue comes from services, including outsourcing, consulting, and systems integration. At the end of 2007, IBM had approximately 40,000 employees in sales-related roles.

Recognizing that improving the efficiency and productivity of this large sales force can be an effective operational strategy to drive revenue growth and manage expenses, IBM Research developed two broad decision modeling initiatives to facilitate this issue. The first initiative provides a set of analytical models designed to identify new sales opportunities at existing IBM accounts and at noncustomer companies. The second initiative allocates sales resources optimally based on field-validated analytical estimates of future revenue opportunities in market segments. IBM estimates the revenue impact of these two initiatives to be in the several hundreds of millions of dollars each year.

Source: Based on R. Lawrence et al. "Operations Research Improves Sales Force Productivity at IBM," *Interfaces* 40, 1 (January-February 2010): 33–46.

TABLE 1.1
Excel Add-ins Included on This Textbook's Companion Website

EXCEL ADD-IN	USED IN	TOPIC(S)
Tree Plan	Chapter 8	Decision Analysis
Crystal Ball	Chapter 10	Simulation Models
ExcelModules (custom software provided with this textbook)	Chapters 9, 11, and 12	Queuing Models, Forecasting Models, and Inventory Control Models

1.3 Steps Involved in Decision Modeling

The decision modeling process involves three steps.

Regardless of the size and complexity of the decision-making problem at hand, the decision modeling process involves three distinct steps: (1) formulation, (2) solution, and (3) interpretation. Figure 1.1 provides a schematic overview of these steps, along with the components, or parts, of each step. We discuss each of these steps in the following sections.

It is common to iterate between the three steps.

It is important to note that it is common to have an iterative process between these three steps before the final solution is obtained. For example, testing the solution (see Figure 1.1) might reveal that the model is incomplete or that some of the input data are being measured incorrectly. This means that the formulation needs to be revised. This, in turn, causes all the subsequent steps to be changed.

Step 1: Formulation

Formulation *is the most challenging step in decision modeling.*

Formulation is the process by which each aspect of a problem scenario is translated and expressed in terms of a mathematical model. This is perhaps the most important and challenging step in decision modeling because the results of a poorly formulated problem will almost surely be incorrect. It is also in this step that the decision maker's ability to analyze a problem rationally comes into play. Even the most sophisticated software program will not automatically formulate a problem. The aim in formulation is to ensure that the mathematical model completely

FIGURE 1.1
The Decision Modeling Approach

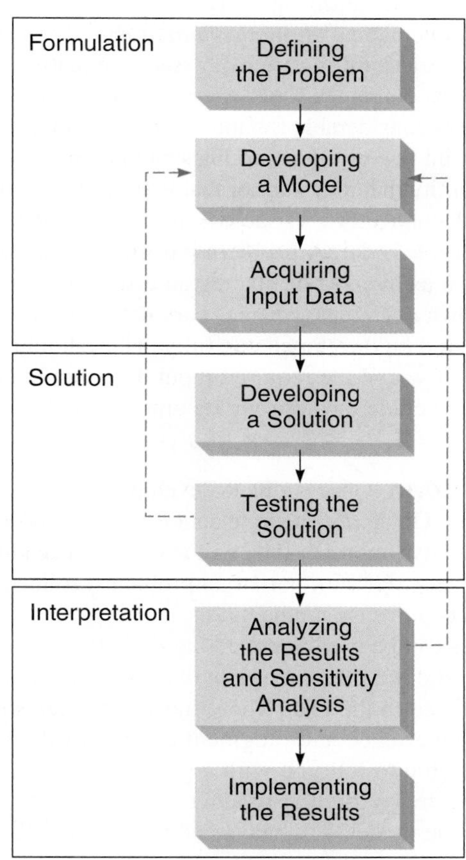

addresses all the issues relevant to the problem at hand. Formulation can be further classified into three parts: (1) defining the problem, (2) developing a model, and (3) acquiring input data.

DEFINING THE PROBLEM The first part in formulation (and in decision modeling) is to develop a clear, concise statement of the problem. This statement gives direction and meaning to all the parts that follow it.

Defining the problem can be the most important part of formulation.

In many cases, defining the problem is perhaps the most important, and the most difficult, part. It is essential to go beyond just the symptoms of the problem at hand and identify the true causes behind it. One problem may be related to other problems, and solving a problem without regard to its related problems may actually make the situation worse. Thus, it is important to analyze how the solution to one problem affects other problems or the decision-making environment in general. Experience has shown that poor problem definition is a major reason for failure of management science groups to serve their organizations well.

When a problem is difficult to quantify, it may be necessary to develop *specific, measurable* objectives. For example, say a problem is defined as inadequate health care delivery in a hospital. The objectives might be to increase the number of beds, reduce the average number of days a patient spends in the hospital, increase the physician-to-patient ratio, and so on. When objectives are used, however, the real problem should be kept in mind. It is important to avoid obtaining specific and measurable objectives that may not solve the real problem.

DEVELOPING A MODEL Once we select the problem to be analyzed, the next part is to develop a decision model. Even though you might not be aware of it, you have been using models most of your life. For example, you may have developed the following model about friendship: Friendship is based on reciprocity, an exchange of favors. Hence, if you need a favor, such as a small loan, your model would suggest that you ask a friend.

The types of models include physical, scale, schematic, and mathematical models.

Of course, there are many other types of models. An architect may make a physical model of a building he or she plans to construct. Engineers develop scale models of chemical plants, called pilot plants. A schematic model is a picture or drawing of reality. Automobiles, lawn mowers, circuit boards, typewriters, and numerous other devices have schematic models (drawings and pictures) that reveal how these devices work.

What sets decision modeling apart from other modeling techniques is that the models we develop here are mathematical. A *mathematical model* is a set of mathematical relationships. In most cases, these relationships are expressed as equations and inequalities, as they are in a spreadsheet model that computes sums, averages, or standard deviations.

A variable *is a measurable quantity that is subject to change.*

A parameter *is a measurable quantity that usually has a known value.*

Although there is considerable flexibility in the development of models, most of the models presented here contain one or more variables and parameters. A **variable**, as the name implies, is a measurable quantity that may vary or that is subject to change. Variables can be controllable or uncontrollable. A controllable variable is also called a *decision variable*. An example is how many inventory items to order. A **problem parameter** is a measurable quantity that is inherent in the problem, such as the cost of placing an order for more inventory items. In most cases, variables are unknown quantities, whereas parameters (or input data) are known quantities.

All models should be developed carefully. They should be solvable, realistic, and easy to understand and modify, and the required input data should be obtainable. A model developer has to be careful to include the appropriate amount of detail for the model to be solvable yet realistic.

ACQUIRING INPUT DATA Once we have developed a model, we must obtain the **input data** to be used in the model. Obtaining accurate data is essential because even if the model is a perfect representation of reality, improper data will result in misleading results. This situation is called *garbage in, garbage out* (GIGO). For larger problems, collecting accurate data can be one of the most difficult aspects of decision modeling.

Garbage in, garbage out means that improper data will result in misleading results.

Several sources can be used in collecting data. In some cases, company reports and documents can be used to obtain the necessary data. Another source is interviews with employees or other persons related to the firm. These individuals can sometimes provide excellent information, and their experience and judgment can be invaluable. A production supervisor, for example, might be able to tell you with a great degree of accuracy the amount of time that it takes to manufacture a particular product. Sampling and direct measurement provide other sources of data for the model. You may need to know how many pounds of a raw material are used in producing a new photochemical product. This information can be obtained by going to the plant and actually measuring the amount of raw material that is being used. In other cases, statistical sampling procedures can be used to obtain data.

Step 2: Solution

In the solution step, we solve the mathematical expressions in the formulation.

The solution step is when the mathematical expressions resulting from the formulation process are actually solved to identify the optimal solution. Until the mid-1990s, typical courses in decision modeling focused a significant portion of their attention on this step because it was the most difficult aspect of studying the modeling process. As stated earlier, thanks to computer technology, the focus today has shifted away from the detailed steps of the solution process and toward the availability and use of software packages. The solution step can be further classified into two parts: (1) developing a solution and (2) testing the solution.

An **algorithm** *is a series of steps that are repeated.*

The input data and model determine the accuracy of the solution.

DEVELOPING A SOLUTION Developing a solution involves manipulating the model to arrive at the best (or optimal) solution to the problem. In some cases, this may require that a set of mathematical expressions be solved to determine the best decision. In other cases, you can use a trial-and-error method, trying various approaches and picking the one that results in the best decision. For some problems, you may wish to try all possible values for the variables in the model to arrive at the best decision; this is called *complete enumeration*. For problems that are quite complex and difficult, you may be able to use an algorithm. An *algorithm* consists of a series of steps or procedures that we repeat until we find the best solution. Regardless of the approach used, the accuracy of the solution depends on the accuracy of the input data and the decision model itself.

Analysts test the data and model before analyzing the results.

TESTING THE SOLUTION Before a solution can be analyzed and implemented, it must be tested completely. Because the solution depends on the input data and the model, both require testing. There are several ways to test input data. One is to collect additional data from a different source and use statistical tests to compare these new data with the original data. If there are significant differences, more effort is required to obtain accurate input data. If the data are accurate but the results are inconsistent with the problem, the model itself may not be appropriate. In this case, the model should be checked to make sure that it is logical and represents the real situation.

Step 3: Interpretation and Sensitivity Analysis

Assuming that the formulation is correct and has been successfully implemented and solved, how does a manager use the results? Here again, the decision maker's expertise is called upon because it is up to him or her to recognize the implications of the results that are presented. We discuss this step in two parts: (1) analyzing the results and sensitivity analysis and (2) implementing the results.

ANALYZING THE RESULTS AND SENSITIVITY ANALYSIS Analyzing the results starts with determining the implications of the solution. In most cases, a solution to a problem will result in some kind of action or change in the way an organization is operating. The implications of these actions or changes must be determined and analyzed before the results are implemented.

Sensitivity analysis *determines how the solutions will change with a different model or input data.*

Because a model is only an approximation of reality, the sensitivity of the solution to changes in the model and input data is an important part of analyzing the results. This type of analysis is called sensitivity, postoptimality, or what-if analysis. **Sensitivity analysis** is used to determine how much the solution will change if there are changes in the model or the input data. When the optimal solution is very sensitive to changes in the input data and the model specifications, additional testing must be performed to make sure the model and input data are accurate and valid.

The importance of sensitivity analysis cannot be overemphasized. Because input data may not always be accurate or model assumptions may not be completely appropriate, sensitivity analysis can become an important part of decision modeling.

IMPLEMENTING THE RESULTS The final part of interpretation is to *implement* the results. This can be much more difficult than one might imagine. Even if the optimal solution will result in millions of dollars in additional profits, if managers resist the new solution, the model is of no value. Experience has shown that a large number of decision modeling teams have failed in their efforts because they have failed to implement a good, workable solution properly.

The solution should be closely monitored even after implementation.

After the solution has been implemented, it should be closely monitored. Over time, there may be numerous changes that call for modifications of the original solution. A changing economy, fluctuating demand, and model enhancements requested by managers and decision makers are a few examples of changes that might require an analysis to be modified.

1.4 Spreadsheet Example of a Decision Model: Tax Computation

A decision modeling example.

Now that we have discussed what a decision model is, let us develop a simple model for a real-world situation that we all face each year: paying taxes. Sue and Robert Miller, a newly married couple, will be filing a joint tax return for the first time this year. Because both work as independent contractors (Sue is an interior decorator, and Rob is a painter), their projected income is subject to some variability. However, because their earnings are not taxed at the source, they know that they have to pay estimated income taxes on a quarterly basis, based on their estimated taxable income for the year. To help calculate this tax, the Millers would like to set up a spreadsheet-based decision model. Assume that they have the following information available:

- Their only source of income is from their jobs.
- They would like to put away 5% of their total income in a retirement account, up to a maximum of $6,000. Any amount they put in that account can be deducted from their total income for tax purposes.
- They are entitled to a personal exemption of $3,700 each. This means that they can deduct $7,400 (= 2 × $3,700) from their total income for tax purposes.
- The standard deduction for married couples filing taxes jointly this year is $11,600. This means that $11,600 of their income is free from any taxes and can be deducted from their total income.
- They do not anticipate having any other deductions from their income for tax purposes.
- The tax brackets for this year are 10% for the first $17,000 of taxable income, 15% between $17,001 and $69,000 and 25% between $69,001 and $139,350. The Millers don't believe that tax brackets beyond $139,350 are relevant for them this year.

Excel Notes

- The Companion Website for this textbook, at www.pearsonhighered.com/balakrishnan, contains the Excel file for each sample problem discussed here. The relevant file name is shown in the margin next to each example.
- In each of our Excel layouts, for clarity, we color code the cells as follows:
  - Variable input cells, in which we enter specific values for the variables in the problem, are shaded yellow.
  - Output cells, which show the results of our analysis, are shaded green.
- We have used callouts to annotate the screenshots in this textbook to highlight important issues in the decision model.
- Wherever necessary, many of these callouts are also included as comments in the Excel files themselves, making it easier for you to understand the logic behind each model.

File: 1-1.xls, sheet: 1-1A

Screenshot 1-1A shows the formulas that we can use to develop a decision model for the Millers. Just as we have done for this Excel model (and all other models in this textbook), we strongly recommend that you get in the habit of using descriptive titles, labels, and comments in any decision model that you create. The reason for this is very simple: In many real-world settings, decision models that you create are likely to be passed on to others. In such cases, the use of comments will help them understand your thought process. Perhaps an appropriate question you should always ask yourself is "Will I understand this model a year or two after I first write it?" If appropriate labels and comments are included in the model, the answer should always be yes.

Wherever possible, titles, labels, and comments should be included in the model to make them easier to understand.

In Screenshot 1-1A, the known problem parameter values (i.e., constants) are shown in the box labeled Known Parameters. Rather than use these known constant values directly in the formulas, we recommend that you develop the habit of entering each known value in a cell and then using that cell reference in the formulas. In addition to being more "elegant," this way of modeling has the advantage of making any future changes to these values easy.

Rather than use constants directly in formulas, it is preferable to make them cell references.

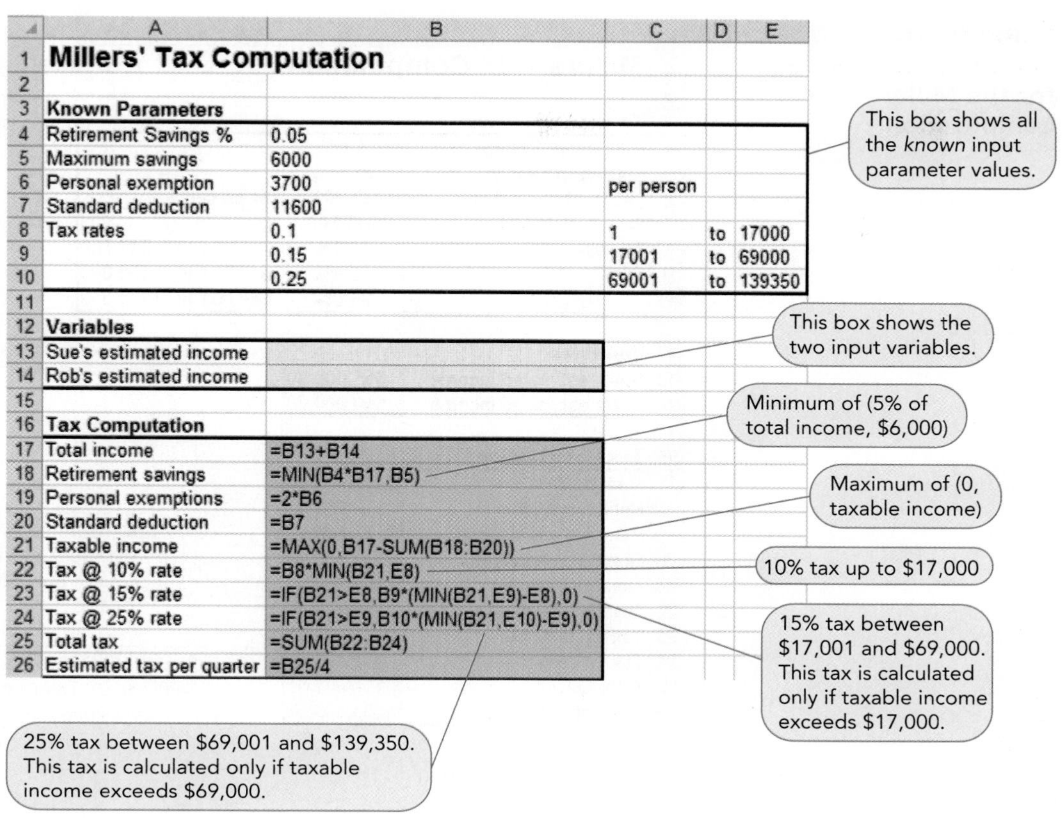

	A	B	C	D	E
1	**Millers' Tax Computation**				
2					
3	**Known Parameters**				
4	Retirement Savings %	0.05			
5	Maximum savings	6000			
6	Personal exemption	3700	per person		
7	Standard deduction	11600			
8	Tax rates	0.1	1	to	17000
9		0.15	17001	to	69000
10		0.25	69001	to	139350
11					
12	**Variables**				
13	Sue's estimated income				
14	Rob's estimated income				
15					
16	**Tax Computation**				
17	Total income	=B13+B14			
18	Retirement savings	=MIN(B4*B17,B5)			
19	Personal exemptions	=2*B6			
20	Standard deduction	=B7			
21	Taxable income	=MAX(0,B17-SUM(B18:B20))			
22	Tax @ 10% rate	=B8*MIN(B21,E8)			
23	Tax @ 15% rate	=IF(B21>E8,B9*(MIN(B21,E9)-E8),0)			
24	Tax @ 25% rate	=IF(B21>E9,B10*(MIN(B21,E10)-E9),0)			
25	Total tax	=SUM(B22:B24)			
26	Estimated tax per quarter	=B25/4			

SCREENSHOT 1-1A
Formula View of Excel Layout for the Millers' Tax Computation

Cells B13 and B14 denote the only two variable data entries in this decision model: Sue's and Rob's estimated incomes for this year. When we enter values for these two variables, the results are computed in cells B17:B26 and presented in the box labeled Tax Computation.

Excel's MAX, MIN, and IF functions have been used in this decision model.

Cell B17 shows the total income. The MIN function is used in cell B18 to specify the tax-deductible retirement contribution as the smaller value of 5% of total income and $6,000. Cells B19 and B20 set the personal exemptions and the standard deduction, respectively. The net taxable income is shown in cell B21, and the MAX function is used here to ensure that this amount is never below zero. The taxes payable at the 10%, 15%, and 25% rates are then calculated in cells B22, B23, and B24, respectively. In each of these cells, the MIN function is used to ensure that only the incremental taxable income is taxed at a given rate. (For example, in cell B23, only the portion of taxable income above $17,000 is taxed at the 15% rate, up to an upper limit of $69,000.) The IF function is used in cells B23 and B24 to check whether the taxable income exceeds the lower limit for the 15% and 25% tax rates, respectively. If the taxable income does not exceed the relevant lower limit, the IF function sets the tax payable at that rate to zero. Finally, the total tax payable is computed in cell B25, and the estimated quarterly tax is computed in cell B26.

File: 1-1.xls, sheet: 1-1B

Now that we have developed this decision model, how can the Millers actually use it? Suppose Sue estimates her income this year at $55,000 and Rob estimates his at $50,000. We enter these values in cells B13 and B14, respectively. The decision model immediately lets us know that the Millers have a taxable income of $80,750 and that they should pay estimated taxes of $3,109.38 each quarter. These input values, and the resulting computations, are shown in Screenshot 1-1B. We can use this decision model in a similar fashion with any other estimated income values for Sue and Rob.

Observe that the decision model we have developed for the Millers' example does not optimize the decision in any way. That is, the model simply computes the estimated taxes for a given income level. It does not, for example, determine whether these taxes can be reduced in some way through better tax planning. Later in this textbook, we discuss decision models that not only help compute the implications of a particular specified decision but also help identify the optimal decision, based on some objective or goal.

SCREENSHOT 1-1B Excel Decision Model for the Millers' Tax Computation

	A	B	C	D	E
1	**Millers' Tax Computation**				
2					
3	**Known Parameters**				
4	Retirement Savings %	5.0%			
5	Maximum savings	$6,000			
6	Personal exemption	$3,700	per person		
7	Standard deduction	$11,600			
8	Tax rates	10.0%	$1	to	$17,000
9		15.0%	$17,001	to	$69,000
10		25.0%	$69,001	to	$139,350
11					
12	**Variables**				
13	Sue's estimated income	$55,000.00			
14	Rob's estimated income	$50,000.00			
15					
16	**Tax Computation**				
17	Total income	$105,000.00			
18	Retirement savings	$5,250.00			
19	Personal exemptions	$7,400.00			
20	Standard deduction	$11,600.00			
21	Taxable income	$80,750.00			
22	Tax @ 10% rate	$1,700.00			
23	Tax @ 15% rate	$7,800.00			
24	Tax @ 25% rate	$2,937.50			
25	Total tax	$12,437.50			
26	Estimated tax per quarter	$3,109.38			

Estimated income

Total income of $105,000 has been reduced to taxable income of only $80,750.

The Millers should pay $3,109.38 in estimated taxes each quarter.

IN ACTION Using Decision Modeling to Combat Spread of Hepatitis B Virus in the United States and China

Hepatitis B is a vaccine-preventable viral disease that is a major public health problem, particularly among Asian populations. Left untreated, it can lead to death from cirrhosis and liver cancer. Over 350 million people are chronically infected with the hepatitis B virus (HBV) worldwide. In the United States (US), although about 10% of Asian and Pacific Islanders are chronically infected, about two thirds of them are unaware of their infection. In China, HBV infection is a leading cause of death.

During several years of work conducted at the Asian Liver Center at Stanford University, the authors used combinations of decision modeling techniques to analyze the cost effectiveness of various intervention schemes to combat the spread of the disease in the US and China. The results of these analyses have helped change US public health policy on hepatitis B screening, and have helped encourage China to enact legislation to provide free vaccination for millions of children.

These policies are an important step in eliminating health disparities and ensuring that millions of people can now receive the hepatitis B vaccination they need. The Global Health Coordinator of the Asian Liver Center states that this research "has been incredibly important to accelerating policy changes to improve health related to HBV."

Source: Based on D. W. Hutton, M. L. Brandeau, and S. K. So. "Doing Good with Good OR: Supporting Cost-Effective Hepatitis B Interventions," *Interfaces* 41, 3 (May-June 2011): 289–300.

1.5 Spreadsheet Example of a Decision Model: Break-Even Analysis

Expenses include fixed and variable costs.

Let us now develop another decision model—this one to compute the total profit for a firm as well as the associated break-even point. We know that profit is simply the difference between revenue and expense. In most cases, we can express revenue as the selling price per unit multiplied by the number of units sold. Likewise, we can express expense as the sum of the total fixed and variable costs. In turn, the total variable cost is the variable cost per unit multiplied by the number of units sold. Thus, we can express profit using the following mathematical expression:

$$\text{Profit} = (\text{Selling price per unit}) \times (\text{Number of units}) - (\text{Fixed cost}) \\ - (\text{Variable cost per unit}) \times (\text{Number of units}) \quad \text{(1-1)}$$

Let's use Bill Pritchett's clock repair shop as an example to demonstrate the creation of a decision model to calculate profit and the associated break-even point. Bill's company, Pritchett's Precious Time Pieces, buys, sells, and repairs old clocks and clock parts. Bill sells rebuilt springs for a unit price of \$10. The fixed cost of the equipment to build the springs is \$1,000. The variable cost per unit is \$5 for spring material. If we represent the number of springs (units) sold as the variable X, we can restate the profit as follows:

$$\text{Profit} = \$10X - \$1{,}000 - \$5X$$

File: 1-2.xls, sheets: 1-2A and 1-2B

Screenshot 1-2A shows the formulas used in developing the decision model for Bill Pritchett's example. Cells B4, B5, and B6 show the known problem parameter values—namely, revenue per unit, fixed cost, and variable cost per unit, respectively. Cell B9 is the lone variable in the model, and it represents the number of units sold (i.e., X). Using these entries, the total revenue, total variable cost, total cost, and profit are computed in cells B12, B14, B15, and B16, respectively. For example, if we enter a value of 1,000 units for X in cell B9, the profit is calculated as \$4,000 in cell B16, as shown in Screenshot 1-2B.

The BEP results in \$0 profit.

In addition to computing the profit, decision makers are often interested in the **break-even point (BEP)**. The BEP is the number of units sold that will result in total revenue equaling total costs (i.e., profit is \$0). We can determine the BEP analytically by setting profit equal to \$0 and solving for X in Bill Pritchett's profit expression. That is

SCREENSHOT 1-2A
Formula View of Excel Layout for Pritchett's Precious Time Pieces

	A	B
1	**Bill Pritchett's Shop**	
2		
3	**Known Parameters**	
4	Selling price per unit	10
5	Fixed cost	1000
6	Variable cost per unit	5
7		
8	**Variables**	
9	Number of units, X	
10		
11	**Results**	
12	Total revenue	=B4*B9
13	Fixed cost	=B5
14	Total variable cost	=B6*B9
15	Total cost	=B13+B14
16	Profit	=B12-B15

Input variable

Profit is revenue – fixed cost – variable cost.

SCREENSHOT 1-2B
Excel Decision Model for Pritchett's Precious Time Pieces

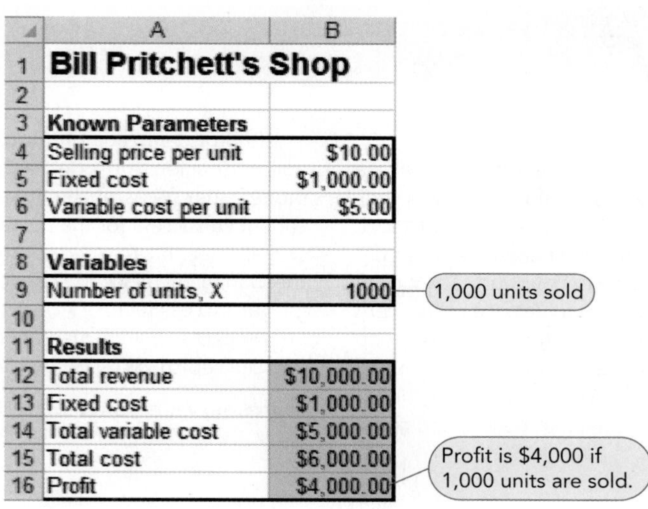

	A	B
1	**Bill Pritchett's Shop**	
2		
3	**Known Parameters**	
4	Selling price per unit	\$10.00
5	Fixed cost	\$1,000.00
6	Variable cost per unit	\$5.00
7		
8	**Variables**	
9	Number of units, X	1000
10		
11	**Results**	
12	Total revenue	\$10,000.00
13	Fixed cost	\$1,000.00
14	Total variable cost	\$5,000.00
15	Total cost	\$6,000.00
16	Profit	\$4,000.00

1,000 units sold
Profit is \$4,000 if 1,000 units are sold.

$$0 = (\text{Selling price per unit}) \times (\text{Number of units}) - (\text{Fixed cost}) - (\text{Variable cost per unit}) \times (\text{Number of units})$$

which can be mathematically rewritten as

$$\text{Break even point (BEP)} = \text{Fixed cost}/(\text{Selling price per unit} - \text{Variable cost per unit}) \quad \textbf{(1-2)}$$

For Bill Pritchett's example, we can compute the BEP as \$1,000/(\$10 – \$5) = 200 springs. The **BEP in dollars** (which we denote as $BEP_\$$) can then be computed as

$$\text{BEP}_\$ = \text{Fixed cost} + \text{Variable costs} \times \text{BEP} \quad \textbf{(1-3)}$$

For Bill Pritchett's example, we can compute $\text{BEP}_\$$ as \$1,000 + \$5 × 200 = \$2,000.

Using Goal Seek to Find the Break-Even Point

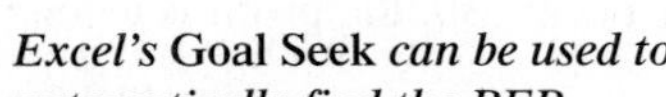

Excel's Goal Seek *can be used to automatically find the BEP.*

While the preceding analytical computations for BEP and $\text{BEP}_\$$ are fairly simple, an advantage of using computer-based models is that many of these results can be calculated automatically. For example, we can use a procedure in Excel called Goal Seek to calculate the BEP and $\text{BEP}_\$$ values in the decision model shown in Screenshot 1-2B. The Goal Seek procedure allows us to specify a desired value for a *target cell*. This target cell should contain a formula that involves a different cell, called the *changing cell*. Once we specify the target cell, its desired value, and the changing cell in Goal Seek, the procedure automatically manipulates the changing cell value to try and make the target cell achieve its desired value.

In our case, we want to manipulate the value of the number of units X (in cell B9 of Screenshot 1-2B) such that the profit (in cell B16 of Screenshot 1-2B) takes on a value of zero. That is, cell B16 is the target cell, its desired value is zero, and cell B9 is the changing cell. Observe that the formula of profit in cell B16 is a function of the value of X in cell B9 (see Screenshot 1-2A).

File: 1-2.xls, sheet: 1-2C

Screenshot 1-2C shows how the Goal Seek procedure is implemented in Excel. As shown in Screenshot 1-2C(a), we invoke Goal Seek by clicking the Data tab on Excel's main menu bar, followed by the What-If Analysis button (found in the Data Tools group within the Data tab), and then finally on Goal Seek. The window shown in Screenshot 1-2C(b) is displayed. We specify cell B16 in the Set cell box, a desired value of zero for this cell in the To value box, and cell B9 in the By changing cell box. When we now click OK, the Goal Seek Status window shown in Screenshot 1-2C(c) is displayed, indicating that the target of \$0 profit has been achieved. Cell B9 shows the resulting BEP value of 200 units. The corresponding $\text{BEP}_\$$ value of \$2,000 is shown in cell B15.

Observe that we can use Goal Seek to compute the sales level needed to obtain any desired profit. For example, see if you can verify that in order to get a profit of \$10,000, Bill Pritchett would have to sell 2,200 springs. We will use the Goal Seek procedure again in Chapter 9.

DM IN ACTION The Management Science Group Is Bullish at Merrill Lynch

Management science groups at corporations can make a huge difference in reducing costs and increasing profits. At Merrill Lynch, the management science group was established in 1986. Its overall mission is to provide high-quality quantitative (or mathematical) analysis, modeling, and decision support. The group analyzes a variety of problems and opportunities related to client services, products, and the marketplace. In the past, this group has helped Merrill Lynch develop asset allocation models, mutual fund portfolio optimization solutions, investment strategy development and research tools, financial planning models, and cross-selling approaches.

To provide meaningful assistance to Merrill Lynch, the management science group has concentrated on mathematical models that focus on client satisfaction. What are the keys to continued success for the management science group? Although skill and technical expertise in decision modeling are essential, the management science group has identified the following four critical success factors: (1) objective analysis, (2) focus on business impact and implementation, (3) teamwork, and (4) adopting a disciplined consultative approach.

Source: From R. Nigam et al. "Bullish on Management Science," *OR/MS Today*, Vol. 27, No. 3 (June 2000): 48-51. Reprinted with permission.

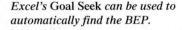

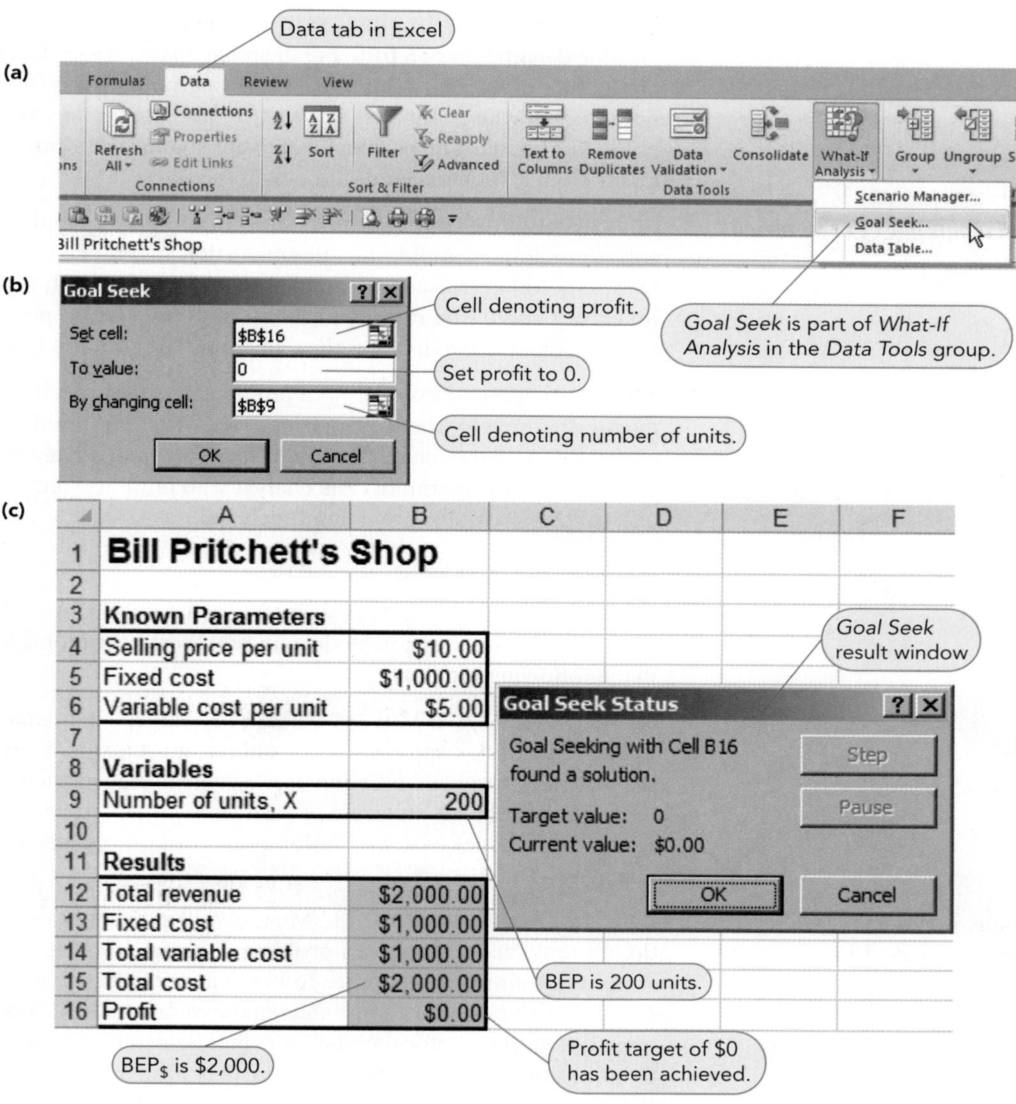

SCREENSHOT 1-2C
Using Excel's Goal Seek to Compute the Break-Even Point for Pritchett's Precious Time Pieces

1.6 Possible Problems in Developing Decision Models

We present the decision modeling approach as a logical and systematic means of tackling decision-making problems. Even when these steps are followed carefully, however, many difficulties can hurt the chances of implementing solutions to real-world problems. We now look at problems that can occur during each of the steps of the decision modeling approach.

Defining the Problem

Real-world problems are not easily identifiable.

In the worlds of business, government, and education, problems are, unfortunately, not easily identified. **Decision analysts** typically face four roadblocks in defining a problem. We use an application, inventory analysis, throughout this section as an example.

The problem needs to be examined from several viewpoints.

CONFLICTING VIEWPOINTS Analysts may often have to consider conflicting viewpoints in defining a problem. For example, in inventory problems, financial managers usually feel that inventory is too high because inventory represents cash not available for other investments. In contrast, sales managers often feel that inventory is too low because high levels of inventory may be needed to fill unexpected orders. If analysts adopt either of these views as the problem definition, they have essentially accepted one manager's perception. They can, therefore, expect resistance from the other manager when the "solution" emerges. So it's important to consider both points of view before stating the problem.

IMPACT ON OTHER DEPARTMENTS Problems do not exist in isolation and are not owned by just one department of a firm. For example, inventory is closely tied with cash flows and various production problems. A change in ordering policy can affect cash flows and upset production schedules to the point that savings on inventory are exceeded by increased financial and production costs. The problem statement should therefore be as broad as possible and include inputs from all concerned departments.

All inputs must be considered.

BEGINNING ASSUMPTIONS People often have a tendency to state problems in terms of solutions. For example, the statement that inventory is too low implies a solution: that its levels should be raised. An analyst who starts off with this assumption will likely find that inventory should be raised! From an implementation perspective, a "good" solution to the right problem is much better than an "optimal" solution to the wrong problem.

SOLUTION OUTDATED Even if a problem has been specified correctly at present, it can change during the development of the model. In today's rapidly changing business environment, especially with the amazing pace of technological advances, it is not unusual for problems to change virtually overnight. The analyst who presents solutions to problems that no longer exist can't expect credit for providing timely help.

Developing a Model

Even with a well-defined problem statement, a decision analyst may have to overcome hurdles while developing decision models for real-world situations. Some of these hurdles are discussed in the following sections.

FITTING THE TEXTBOOK MODELS A manager's perception of a problem does not always match the textbook approach. For example, most textbook inventory models involve minimizing the sum of holding and ordering costs. Some managers view these costs as unimportant; instead, they see the problem in terms of cash flow, turnover, and levels of customer satisfaction. The results of a model based on holding and ordering costs are probably not acceptable to such managers.

Managers do not use the results of a model they do not understand.

UNDERSTANDING A MODEL Most managers simply do not use the results of a model they do not understand. Complex problems, though, require complex models. One trade-off is to simplify assumptions in order to make a model easier to understand. The model loses some of its reality but gains some management acceptance. For example, a popular simplifying assumption in inventory modeling is that demand is known and constant. This allows analysts to build simple, easy-to-understand models. Demand, however, is rarely known and constant, so these models lack some reality. Introducing probability distributions provides more realism but may put comprehension beyond all but the most mathematically sophisticated managers. In such cases, one approach is for the decision analyst to start with the simple model and make sure that it is completely understood. More complex models can then be introduced slowly as managers gain more confidence in using these models.

Acquiring Input Data

Gathering the data to be used in the decision modeling approach to problem solving is often not a simple task. Often, the data are buried in several different databases and documents, making it very difficult for a decision analyst to gain access to the data.

USING ACCOUNTING DATA One problem is that most data generated in a firm come from basic accounting reports. The accounting department collects its inventory data, for example, in terms of cash flows and turnover. But decision analysts tackling an inventory problem need to collect data on holding costs and ordering costs. If they ask for such data, they may be shocked to find that the data were simply never collected for those specified costs.

Professor Gene Woolsey tells a story of a young decision analyst sent down to accounting to get "the inventory holding cost per item per day for part 23456/AZ." The accountant asked the young man if he wanted the first-in, first-out figure; the last-in, first-out figure; the lower of cost or market figure; or the "how-we-do-it" figure. The young man replied that the inventory model required only one number. The accountant at the next desk said, "Heck, Joe, give the kid a number." The analyst was given a number and departed.

The results of a model are only as good as the input data used.

VALIDITY OF DATA A lack of "good, clean data" means that whatever data are available must often be distilled and manipulated (we call it "fudging") before being used in a model. Unfortunately, the validity of the results of a model is no better than the validity of the data that go into the model. You cannot blame a manager for resisting a model's "scientific" results when he or she knows that questionable data were used as input.

Developing a Solution

An analyst may have to face two potential pitfalls while developing solutions to a decision model. These are discussed in the following sections.

HARD-TO-UNDERSTAND MATHEMATICS The first concern in developing solutions is that although the mathematical models we use may be complex and powerful, they may not be completely understood. The aura of mathematics often causes managers to remain silent when they should be critical. The well-known management scientist C. W. Churchman once cautioned that "because mathematics has been so revered a discipline in recent years, it tends to lull the unsuspecting into believing that he who thinks elaborately thinks well."[1]

Hard-to-understand mathematics and having only one answer can be problems in developing a solution.

THE LIMITATION OF ONLY ONE ANSWER The second problem in developing a solution is that decision models usually give just one answer to a problem. Most managers would like to have a range of options and not be put in a take-it-or-leave-it position. A more appropriate strategy is for an analyst to present a range of options, indicating the effect that each solution has on the objective function. This gives managers a choice as well as information on how much it will cost to deviate from the optimal solution. It also allows problems to be viewed from a broader perspective because it means that qualitative factors can also be considered.

Testing the Solution

Assumptions should be reviewed.

The results of decision modeling often take the form of predictions of how things will work in the future if certain changes are made in the present. To get a preview of how well solutions will really work, managers are often asked how good a solution looks to them. The problem is that complex models tend to give solutions that are not intuitively obvious. And such solutions tend to be rejected by managers. Then a decision analyst must work through the model and the assumptions with the manager in an effort to convince the manager of the validity of the results. In the process of convincing the manager, the analyst has to review every assumption that went into the model. If there are errors, they may be revealed during this review. In addition, the manager casts a critical eye on everything that went into the model, and if he or she can be convinced that the model is valid, there is a good chance that the solution results are also valid.

Analyzing the Results

Once a solution has been tested, the results must be analyzed in terms of how they will affect the total organization. You should be aware that even small changes in organizations are often difficult to bring about. If results suggest large changes in organizational policy, the decision analyst can expect resistance. In analyzing the results, the analyst should ascertain who must change and by how much, if the people who must change will be better or worse off, and who has the power to direct the change.

1.7 Implementation—Not Just the Final Step

We have just presented some of the many problems that can affect the ultimate acceptance of decision modeling in practice. It should be clear now that implementation isn't just another step that takes place after the modeling process is over. Each of these steps greatly affects the chances of implementing the results of a decision model.

Even though many business decisions can be made intuitively, based on hunches and experience, there are more and more situations in which decision models can assist. Some managers, however, fear that the use of a formal analytical process will reduce their

[1] Churchman, C. W. "Reliability of Models in the Social Sciences," *Interfaces* 4, 1 (November 1973): 1–12.

decision-making power. Others fear that it may expose some previous intuitive decisions as inadequate. Still others feel uncomfortable about having to reverse their thinking patterns with formal decision making. These managers often argue against the use of decision modeling.

Many action-oriented managers do not like the lengthy formal decision-making process and prefer to get things done quickly. They prefer "quick and dirty" techniques that can yield immediate results. However, once managers see some quick results that have a substantial payoff, the stage is set for convincing them that decision modeling is a beneficial tool.

Management support and user involvement are important.

We have known for some time that management support and user involvement are critical to the successful implementation of decision modeling processes. A Swedish study found that only 40% of projects suggested by decision analysts were ever implemented. But 70% of the modeling projects initiated by users, and fully 98% of projects suggested by top managers, were implemented.

Summary

Decision modeling is a scientific approach to decision making in practical situations faced by managers. Decision models can be broadly classified into two categories, based on the type and nature of the problem environment under consideration: (1) deterministic models and (2) probabilistic models. Deterministic models assume that all the relevant input data and parameters are known with certainty. In contrast, probabilistic models assume that some input data are not known with certainty. The decision modeling approach includes three major steps: (1) formulation, (2) solution, and (3) interpretation. It is important to note that it is common to iterate between these three steps before the final solution is obtained. Spreadsheets are commonly used to develop decision models.

In using the decision modeling approach, however, there can be potential problems, such as conflicting viewpoints, disregard of the impact of the model on other departments, outdated solutions, misunderstanding of the model, difficulty acquiring good input data, and hard-to-understand mathematics. In using decision models, implementation is not the final step. There can be a lack of commitment to the approach and resistance to change.

Glossary

Break-Even Point (BEP) The number of units sold that will result in total revenue equaling total costs (i.e., profit is $0).

Break-Even Point in Dollars ($BEP_{\$}$) The sum of fixed and total variable cost if the number of units sold equals the break-even point.

Decision Analyst An individual who is responsible for developing a decision model.

Decision Modeling A scientific approach that uses quantitative (mathematical) techniques as a tool in managerial decision making. Also known as *quantitative analysis*, *management science*, and *operations research*.

Deterministic Model A model which assumes that all the relevant input data and parameters are known with certainty.

Formulation The process by which each aspect of a problem scenario is translated and expressed in terms of a mathematical model.

Goal Seek A feature in Excel that allows users to specify a goal or target for a specific cell and automatically manipulate another cell to achieve that target.

Input Data Data that are used in a model in arriving at the final solution.

Model A representation (usually mathematical) of a practical problem scenario or environment.

Probabilistic Model A model which assumes that some input data are not known with certainty.

Problem Parameter A measurable quantity that is inherent in a problem. It typically has a fixed and known value (i.e., a constant).

Sensitivity Analysis A process that involves determining how sensitive a solution is to changes in the formulation of a problem.

Variable A measurable quantity that may vary or that is subject to change.

Discussion Questions and Problems

Discussion Questions

1-1 Define *decision modeling*. What are some of the organizations that support the use of the scientific approach?

1-2 What is the difference between deterministic and probabilistic models? Give several examples of each type of model.

1-3 What are the differences between quantitative and qualitative factors that may be present in a decision model?

1-4 Why might it be difficult to quantify some qualitative factors in developing decision models?

1-5 What steps are involved in the decision modeling process? Give several examples of this process.

1-6 Why is it important to have an iterative process between the steps of the decision modeling approach?

1-7 Briefly trace the history of decision modeling. What happened to the development of decision modeling during World War II?

1-8 What different types of models are mentioned in this chapter? Give examples of each.

1-9 List some sources of input data.

1-10 Define *decision variable*. Give some examples of variables in a decision model.

1-11 What is a problem parameter? Give some examples of parameters in a decision model.

1-12 List some advantages of using spreadsheets for decision modeling.

1-13 What is implementation, and why is it important?

1-14 Describe the use of sensitivity analysis, or postoptimality analysis, in analyzing the results of decision models.

1-15 Managers are quick to claim that decision modelers talk to them in a jargon that does not sound like English. List four terms that might not be understood by a manager. Then explain in nontechnical terms what each of them means.

1-16 Why do you think many decision analysts don't like to participate in the implementation process? What could be done to change this attitude?

1-17 Should people who will be using the results of a new modeling approach become involved in the technical aspects of the problem-solving procedure?

1-18 C. W. Churchman once said that "mathematics tends to lull the unsuspecting into believing that he who thinks elaborately thinks well." Do you think that the best decision models are the ones that are most elaborate and complex mathematically? Why?

Problems

1-19 A Website has a fixed cost $15,000 per day. The revenue is $0.06 each time the Website is accessed. The variable cost of responding to each hit is $0.02.
(a) How many times must this Website be accessed each day to break even?
(b) What is the break-even point, in dollars?

1-20 An electronics firm is currently manufacturing an item that has a variable cost of $0.60 per unit and selling price of $1.10 per unit. Fixed costs are $15,500. Current volume is 32,000 units. The firm can substantially improve the product quality by adding a new piece of equipment at an additional fixed cost of $8,000. Variable cost would increase to $0.70, but volume is expected to jump to 50,000 units due to the higher quality of the product.
(a) Should the company buy the new equipment?
(b) Compute the profit with the current equipment and the expected profit with the new equipment.

1-21 A manufacturer is evaluating options regarding his production equipment. He is trying to decide whether he should refurbish his old equipment for $70,000, make major modifications to the production line for $135,000, or purchase new equipment for $230,000. The product sells for $10, but the variable costs to make the product are expected to vary widely, depending on the decision that is to be made regarding the equipment. If the manufacturer refurbishes, the variable costs will be $7.20 per unit. If he modifies or purchases new equipment, the variable costs are expected to be $5.25 and $4.75, respectively.
(a) Which alternative should the manufacturer choose if it the demand is expected to be between 30,000 and 40,000 units?
(b) What will be the manufacturer's profit if the demand is 38,000 units?

1-22 St. Joseph's School has 1,200 students, each of whom currently pays $8,000 per year to attend. In addition to revenues from tuition, the school receives an appropriation from the church to sustain its activity. The budget for the upcoming year is $15 million, and the church appropriation will be $4.8 million. By how much will the school have to raise tuition per student to keep from having a shortfall in the upcoming year?

1-23 Refer to Problem 1-22. Sensing resistance to the idea of raising tuition from members of St. Joseph's Church, one of the board members suggested that the 960 children of church members could pay $8,000 as usual. Children of nonmembers would pay more. What would the nonmember tuition per year be if St. Joseph's wanted to continue to plan for a $15 million budget?

1-24 Refer to Problems 1-22 and 1-23. Another board member believes that if church members pay $8,000 in tuition, the most St. Joseph's can increase nonmember tuition is $1,000 per year. She suggests that another solution might be to cap nonmember tuition at $9,000 and attempt to recruit more nonmember students to make up the shortfall. Under this plan, how many new nonmember students will need to be recruited?

1-25 Great Lakes Automotive is considering producing, in-house, a gear assembly that it currently purchases from Delta Supply for $6 per unit. Great Lakes estimates that if it chooses to manufacture the gear assembly, it will cost $23,000 to set up the process and then $3.82 per unit for labor and materials. At what volume would these options cost Great Lakes the same amount of money?

1-26 A start-up publishing company estimates that the fixed costs of its first major project will be $190,000, the variable cost will be $18, and the selling price per book will be $34.

(a) How many books must be sold for this project to break even?

(b) Suppose the publishers wish to take a total of $40,000 in salary for this project. How many books must be sold to break even, and what is the break-even point, in dollars?

1-27 The electronics firm in Problem 1-20 is now considering purchasing the new equipment and increasing the selling price of its product to $1.20 per unit. Even with the price increase, the new volume is expected to be 50,000 units. Under these circumstances, should the company purchase the new equipment and increase the selling price?

1-28 A distributer of prewashed shredded lettuce is opening a new plant and considering whether to use a mechanized process or a manual process to prepare the product. The manual process will have a fixed cost of $43,400 per month and a variable cost of $1.80 per 5-pound bag. The mechanized process would have a fixed cost of $84,600 per month and a variable cost of $1.30 per bag. The company expects to sell each bag of shredded lettuce for $2.50.

(a) Find the break-even point for each process.

(b) What is the monthly profit or loss if the company chooses the manual process and sells 70,000 bags per month?

1-29 A fabrication company must replace its widget machine and is evaluating the capabilities of two available machines. Machine A would cost the company $75,000 in fixed costs for the first year. Each widget produced using Machine A would have a variable cost of $16. Machine B would have a first-year fixed cost of $62,000, and widgets made on this machine would have a variable cost of $20. Machine A would have the capacity to make 18,000 widgets per year, which is approximately double the capacity for Machine B.

(a) If widgets sell for $28 each, find the break-even point for each machine. Consider first-year costs only.

(b) If the fabrication company estimates a demand of 6,500 units in the next year, which machine should be selected?

(c) At what level of production do the two production machines cost the same?

1-30 Bismarck Manufacturing intends to increase capacity through the addition of new equipment. Two vendors have presented proposals. The fixed cost for proposal A is $65,000, and for proposal B, $34,000. The variable cost for A is $10, and for B, $14. The revenue generated by each unit is $18.

(a) What is the break-even point for each proposal?

(b) If the expected volume is 8,300 units, which alternative should be chosen?

CHAPTER 2

Linear Programming Models: Graphical and Computer Methods

LEARNING OBJECTIVES

After completing this chapter, students will be able to:

1. Understand the basic assumptions and properties of linear programming (LP).
2. Use graphical procedures to solve LP problems with only two variables to understand how LP problems are solved.
3. Understand special situations such as redundancy, infeasibility, unboundedness, and alternate optimal solutions in LP problems.
4. Understand how to set up LP problems on a spreadsheet and solve them using Excel's Solver.

CHAPTER OUTLINE

2.1 Introduction

Management decisions in many organizations involve trying to make the most effective use of resources. Resources typically include machinery, labor, money, time, warehouse space, and raw materials. These resources can be used to manufacture products (e.g., computers, automobiles, furniture, clothing) or provide services (e.g., package delivery, health services, advertising policies, investment decisions).

In all resource allocation situations, the manager must sift through several thousand decision choices or alternatives to identify the best, or optimal, choice. The most widely used decision modeling technique designed to help managers in this process is called **mathematical programming**. The term *mathematical programming* is somewhat misleading because this modeling technique requires no advanced mathematical ability (it uses just basic algebra) and has nothing whatsoever to do with computer software programming! In the world of decision modeling, *programming* refers to setting up and solving a problem mathematically.

Linear programming helps in resource allocation decisions.

Within the broad topic of mathematical programming, the most widely used modeling technique designed to help managers in planning and decision making is **linear programming (LP)**. We devote this and the next two chapters to illustrating how, why, and where LP works. Then, in Chapter 5, we explore several special LP models called *network flow problems*. We follow that with a discussion of a few other mathematical programming techniques (i.e., integer programming, goal programming, and nonlinear programming) in Chapter 6.

When developing LP (and other mathematical programming)–based decision models, we assume that all the relevant input data and parameters are known with certainty. For this reason, these types of decision modeling techniques are classified as *deterministic* models.

We focus on using Excel to set up and solve LP models.

Computers have, of course, played an important role in the advancement and use of LP. Real-world LP problems are too cumbersome to solve by hand or with a calculator, and computers have become an integral part of setting up and solving LP models in today's business environments. As noted in Chapter 1, over the past decade, spreadsheet packages such as Microsoft Excel have become increasingly capable of handling many of the decision modeling techniques (including LP and other mathematical programming models) that are commonly encountered in practical situations. So throughout the chapters on mathematical programming techniques, we discuss the role and use of Microsoft Excel in setting up and solving these models.

2.2 Developing a Linear Programming Model

Since the mid-twentieth century, LP has been applied extensively to medical, transportation, operations, financial, marketing, accounting, human resources, and agricultural problems. Regardless of the size and complexity of the decision-making problem at hand in these diverse applications, the development of all LP models can be viewed in terms of the three distinct steps, as defined in Chapter 1: (1) formulation, (2) solution, and (3) interpretation. We now discuss each with regard to LP models.

HISTORY How Linear Programming Started

Linear programming was conceptually developed before World War II by the outstanding Soviet mathematician A. N. Kolmogorov. Another Russian, Leonid Kantorovich, won the Nobel Prize in Economics for advancing the concepts of optimal planning. An early application of linear programming, by George Stigler in 1945, was in the area we today call "diet problems."

Major progress in the field, however, took place in 1947 and later, when George D. Dantzig developed the solution procedure known as the *simplex algorithm*. Dantzig, then a U.S. Air Force mathematician, was assigned to work on logistics problems. He noticed that many problems involving limited resources and more than one demand could be set up in terms of a series of equations and inequalities. Although early LP applications were military in nature, industrial applications rapidly became apparent with the spread of business computers. In 1984, Narendra Karmarkar developed an algorithm that appears to be superior to the simplex method for many very large applications.

Formulation

Formulation *involves expressing a problem scenario in terms of simple mathematical expressions.*

Formulation is the process by which each aspect of a problem scenario is translated and expressed in terms of simple mathematical expressions. The aim in LP formulation is to ensure that the set of mathematical equations, taken together, completely addresses all the issues relevant to the problem situation at hand. We demonstrate a few examples of simple LP formulations in this chapter. Then we introduce several more comprehensive formulations in Chapter 3.

Solution

Solution *involves solving mathematical expressions to find values for the variables.*

The *solution* step is where the mathematical expressions resulting from the formulation process are solved to identify *an* optimal (or best) solution to the model.[1] In this textbook, the focus is on solving LP models using spreadsheets. However, we briefly discuss graphical solution procedures for LP models involving only two variables. The graphical solution procedure is useful in that it allows us to provide an intuitive explanation of the procedure used by most software packages to solve LP problems of any size.

Interpretation and Sensitivity Analysis

Sensitivity analysis *allows a manager to answer "what-if" questions regarding a problem's solution.*

Assuming that a formulation is correct and has been successfully implemented and solved using an LP software package, how does a manager use the results? In addition to just providing the solution to the current LP problem, the computer results also allow the manager to evaluate the impact of several different types of what-if questions regarding the problem. We discuss this subject, called *sensitivity analysis*, in Chapter 4.

In this textbook, our emphasis is on formulation (Chapters 2 and 3) and interpretation (Chapter 4), along with detailed descriptions of how spreadsheets can be used to efficiently set up and solve LP models.

Properties of a Linear Programming Model

All LP models have the following properties in common:

First LP property: Problems seek to maximize or minimize an objective.

1. All problems seek to maximize or minimize some quantity, usually profit or cost. We refer to this property as the **objective function** of an LP problem. For example, the objective of a typical manufacturer is to maximize profits. In the case of a trucking or railroad distribution system, the objective might be to minimize shipping costs. In any event, this objective must be stated clearly and defined mathematically. It does not matter whether profits and cost are measured in cents, dollars, euros, or millions of dollars. An *optimal solution* to the problem is the solution that achieves the best value (maximum or minimum, depending on the problem) for the objective function.

Second LP property: Constraints limit the degree to which the objective can be obtained.

2. LP models usually include restrictions, or **constraints**, that limit the degree to which we can pursue our objective. For example, when we are trying to decide how many units to produce of each product in a firm's product line, we are restricted by the available machinery time. Likewise, in selecting food items for a hospital meal, a dietitian must ensure that minimum daily requirements of vitamins, protein, and so on are satisfied. We want, therefore, to maximize or minimize a quantity (the objective) subject to limited resources (the constraints).

   An LP model usually includes a set of constraints known as **nonnegativity constraints**. These constraints ensure that the variables in the model take on only nonnegative values (i.e., ≥ 0). This is logical because negative values of physical quantities are impossible; you simply cannot produce a negative number of chairs or computers.

Third LP property: There must be alternatives available.

3. There must be alternative courses of action from which we can choose. For example, if a company produces three different products, management could use LP to decide how to allocate its limited production resources (of personnel, machinery, and so on) among these products. Should it devote all manufacturing capacity to make only the first product, should it produce equal numbers or amounts of each product, or should it allocate the resources in some other ratio? If there were no alternative to select from, we would not need LP.

[1] We refer to the best solution as *an* optimal solution rather than as *the* optimal solution because, as we shall see later, the problem could have more than one optimal solution.

Fourth LP property: Mathematical relationships are linear.

4. The objective and constraints in LP problems must be expressed in terms of *linear* equations or inequalities. In linear mathematical relationships, all terms used in the objective function and constraints are of the first degree (i.e., not squared, or to the third or higher power, or appearing more than once). Hence, the equation $2A + 5B = 10$ is a valid linear function, whereas the equation $2A^2 + 5B^3 + AB = 10$ is not linear because the variable A is squared, the variable B is cubed, and the two variables appear as a product in the third term.

An inequality has a ≤ or ≥ sign.

You will see the term **inequality** quite often when we discuss LP problems. By *inequality* we mean that not all LP constraints need be of the form $A + B = C$. This particular relationship, called an equation, implies that the sum of term A and term B exactly equals term C. In most LP problems, we see inequalities of the form $A + B \leq C$ or $A + B \geq C$. The first of these means that A plus B is less than or equal to C. The second means that A plus B is greater than or equal to C. This concept provides a lot of flexibility in defining problem limitations.

Basic Assumptions of a Linear Programming Model

Four technical requirements are certainty, proportionality, additivity, and divisibility.

Technically, there are four additional requirements of an LP problem of which you should be aware:

1. We assume that conditions of *certainty* exist. That is, numbers used in the objective function and constraints are known with certainty and do not change during the period being studied.
2. We also assume that *proportionality* exists in the objective function and constraints. This means that if production of 1 unit of a product uses 3 hours of a particular resource, then making 10 units of that product uses 30 hours of the resource.
3. The third assumption deals with *additivity*, meaning that the total of all activities equals the sum of the individual activities. For example, if an objective is to maximize profit = $8 per unit of the first product made plus $3 per unit of the second product made, and if 1 unit of each product is actually produced, the profit contributions of $8 and $3 must add up to produce a sum of $11.
4. We make the *divisibility* assumption that solutions need not necessarily be in whole numbers (integers). That is, they may take any fractional value. If a fraction of a product cannot be produced (e.g., one-third of a submarine), an integer programming problem exists. We discuss integer programming in more detail in Chapter 6.

2.3 Formulating a Linear Programming Problem

Product mix problems use LP to decide how much of each product to make, given a series of resource restrictions.

One of the most common LP applications is the **product mix problem**. In many manufacturing firms, two or more products are usually produced using limited resources, such a personnel, machines, raw materials, and so on. The profit that the firm seeks to maximize is based on the profit contribution per unit of each product. (Profit contribution, you may recall, is the selling price per unit minus the variable cost per unit.[2]) The firm would like to determine how many units of each product it should produce so as to maximize overall profit, given its limited resources.

Problems with only two variables are uncommon in practice.

We begin our discussion of LP formulation with a simple product mix problem that involves only two variables (one for each product, in this case). We recognize that in most real-world situations, there is very little chance we will encounter LP models with just two variables. Such LP models therefore have little *real-world* value. We nevertheless consider it worthwhile to study these models here for two reasons. First, the compact size of these models makes it easier for a beginning student to understand the structure of LP models and the logic behind their formulation. As we will see, the same structure and logic carry forward even to problems of larger size. Second, and more importantly, as we will see in section 2.4, we can represent a two-variable model in a graphical form, which allows us to visualize the interaction between various issues in the problem.

---

[2] Technically, we maximize total contribution margin, which is the difference between unit selling price and costs that vary in proportion to the quantity of the item produced. Depreciation, fixed general expense, and advertising are excluded from calculations.

Linear Programming Example: Flair Furniture Company

Flair Furniture Company produces inexpensive tables and chairs. The production process for each is similar in that both require a certain number of labor hours in the carpentry department and a certain number of labor hours in the painting department. Each table takes 3 hours of carpentry work and 2 hours of painting work. Each chair requires 4 hours of carpentry and 1 hour of painting. During the current month, 2,400 hours of carpentry time and 1,000 hours of painting time are available. The marketing department wants Flair to make no more than 450 new chairs this month because there is a sizable existing inventory of chairs. However, because the existing inventory of tables is low, the marketing department wants Flair to make at least 100 tables this month. Each table sold results in a profit contribution of \$7, and each chair sold yields a profit contribution of \$5.

Flair Furniture's problem is to determine the best possible combination of tables and chairs to manufacture this month in order to attain the maximum profit. The firm would like this product mix situation formulated (and subsequently solved) as an LP problem.

To provide a structured approach for formulating this problem (and any other LP problem, irrespective of size and complexity), we present a three-step process in the following sections.

Decision Variables

Decision variables *are the unknown entities in a problem. The problem is solved to find values for decision variables.*

Decision variables (or choice variables) represent the unknown entities in a problem—that is, what we are solving for in the problem. For example, in the Flair Furniture problem, there are two unknown entities: the number of tables to be produced this month and the number of chairs to be produced this month. Note that all other unknowns in the problem (e.g., the total carpentry time needed this month) can be expressed as linear functions of the number of tables produced and the number of chairs produced.

Decision variables are expressed in the problems using alphanumeric symbols. When writing the formulation on paper, it is convenient to express the decision variables using simple names that are easy to understand. For example, the number of tables to be produced can be denoted by names such as T, *Tables*, or X_1, and the number of chairs to be produced can be denoted by names such as C, *Chairs*, or X_2.

Throughout this textbook, to the extent possible, we use self-explanatory names to denote the decision variables in our formulations. For example, in Flair Furniture's problem, we use T and C to denote the number of tables and chairs to be produced this month, respectively.

Different decision variables in the same model can be measured in different units.

Although the two decision variables in Flair's model define similar entities (in the sense that they both represent the number of units of a product to make), this need not be the case in all LP (and other) decision models. It is perfectly logical for different decision variables in the same model to define completely different entities and be measured in different units. For example, variable X can denote the amount of labor to use (measured in hours), while variable Y can denote the amount of paint to use (measured in gallons).

The Objective Function

The **objective function** *represents the motivation for solving a problem.*

The objective function states the goal of a problem—that is, why we are trying to solve the problem. An LP model must have a single objective function. In most business-oriented LP models, the objective is to either maximize profit or minimize cost. The goal in this step is to express the profit (or cost) in terms of the decision variables defined earlier. In Flair Furniture's problem, the total profit can be expressed as

$$\begin{aligned} \text{Profit} = {} & (\$7 \text{ profit per table}) \times (\text{number of tables produced}) \\ & + (\$5 \text{ profit per chair}) \times (\text{number of chairs produced}) \end{aligned}$$

Using the decision variables T and C defined earlier, the objective function can be written as

$$\text{Maximize } \$7T + \$5C$$

Constraints

Constraints *represent restrictions on the values the decision variables can take.*

Constraints denote conditions that prevent us from selecting any value we please for the decision variables. An LP model can have as many constraints as necessary for a problem scenario. Each constraint is expressed as a mathematical expression and can be independent of the other constraints in the model.

In Flair's problem, we note that there are four restrictions on the solution. The first two have to do with the carpentry and painting times available. The third and fourth constraints deal with marketing-specified production conditions on the numbers of chairs and tables to make, respectively.

With regard to the carpentry and painting times, the constraints must ensure that the amount of the resource (time) required by the production plan is less than or equal to the amount of the resource (time) available. For example, in the case of carpentry, the total time used is

$$(3 \text{ hour per table}) \times (\text{number of tables produced}) + (4 \text{ hours per chair}) \times (\text{number of chairs produced})$$

There are 2,400 hours of carpentry time available. Using the decision variables T and C defined earlier, this constraint can be stated as

$$3T + 4C \leq 2{,}400$$

The resource constraints put limits on the carpentry time and painting time needed mathematically.

Likewise, the second constraint specifies that the painting time used is less than or equal to the painting time available. This can be stated as

$$2T + 1C \leq 1{,}000$$

Next, there is the marketing-specified constraint that no more than 450 chairs be produced. This can be expressed as

$$C \leq 450$$

It is common for different constraints to have different signs in an LP model.

Finally, there is the second marketing-specified constraint that at least 100 tables must be produced. Note that unlike the first three constraints, this constraint involves the $\geq$ sign because 100 is a minimum requirement. It is very common in practice for a single LP model to include constraints with different signs (i.e., $\leq$, $\geq$, and $=$). The constraint on the production of tables can be expressed as

$$T \geq 100$$

A key principle of LP is that interactions exist between variables.

All four constraints represent restrictions on the numbers that we can make of the two products and, of course, affect the total profit. For example, Flair cannot make 900 tables because the carpentry and painting constraints are both violated if $T = 900$. Likewise, it cannot make 500 tables and 100 chairs, because that would require more than 1,000 hours of painting time. Hence, we note one more important aspect of LP models: Certain interactions exist between variables. The more units of one product that a firm produces, the fewer it can make of other products. We show how this concept of interaction affects the solution to the model as we tackle the graphical solution approach in the next section.

Nonnegativity Constraints and Integer Values

Nonnegativity constraints specify that decision variables cannot have negative values.

Before we consider the graphical solution procedure, there are two other issues we need to address. First, because Flair cannot produce negative quantities of tables or chairs, the nonnegativity constraints must be specified. Mathematically, these can be stated as

$$T \geq 0 \qquad (\text{number of tables produced} \geq 0)$$
$$C \geq 0 \qquad (\text{number of chairs produced} \geq 0)$$

In LP models, we do not specify that decision variables should only have integer values.

Second, it is possible that the optimal solution to the LP model will result in fractional values for T and C. Because the production plan in Flair's problem refers to a month's schedule, we can view fractional values as work-in-process inventory that is carried over to the next month. However, in some problems, we may require the values for decision variables to be whole numbers (integers) in order for the solution to make practical sense. A model in which some or all of the decision variables are restricted only to integer values is called an **integer programming (*IP*)** model. We will study IP models in detail in Chapter 6. In general, as we will see in Chapter 6, it is considerably more difficult to solve an IP problem than an LP problem. Further, LP model solutions allow detailed sensitivity analysis (the topic of Chapter 4) to be undertaken, whereas IP model solutions do not. For these reasons, we do not specify the integer requirement in LP models, and we permit fractional values in the solution. Fractional values can then be rounded off appropriately, if necessary.

Guidelines to Developing a Correct LP Model

We have now developed our first LP model. Before we proceed further, let us address a question that many students have, especially at the early stages of their experience with LP formulation: "How do I know my LP model is right?" There is, unfortunately, no simple magical answer for this question. Instead, we offer the following guidelines that students can use to judge on their own whether their model does what it is intended to do. Note that these guidelines do not guarantee that your model is correct. Formulation is still an art that you master only through repeated application to several diverse problems. (We will practice this over the next few chapters.) However, by following these guidelines, you can hopefully avoid the common errors that many beginners commit:

Here are a few guidelines to developing a correct LP model.

- Recognizing and defining the decision variables is perhaps the most critical step in LP formulation. In this endeavor, one approach we have often found useful and effective is to assume that you have to communicate your result to someone else. When you tell that person "The answer is to do ————," what exactly do you need to know to fill in the blank? Those entities are usually the decision variables.
- Remember that it is perfectly logical for different decision variables in a single LP model to be measured in different units. That is, all decision variables in an LP model need not denote similar entities.
- All expressions in the model (the objective function and each constraint) must use *only* the decision variables that have been defined for the model. For example, in the Flair Furniture problem, the decision variables are T and C. Notice that all expressions involve only T and C. It is, of course, permissible for a decision variable to not be part of a specific expression. For example, the variable T is not part of the constraint $C \leq 450$.
- At any stage of the formulation, if you find yourself unable to write a specific expression (the objective function or a constraint) using the defined decision variables, it is a pretty good indication that you either need more decision variables or you've defined your decision variables incorrectly.
- All terms within the same expression must refer to the same entity. Consider, for example, the expression for the carpentry constraint $3T + 4C \leq 2{,}400$. Notice that each term (i.e., $4T$, $3C$, and 2,400) measures an amount of carpentry time. Likewise, in the objective function, each term (i.e., $\$7T$ and $\$5C$) in the expression measures profit.
- All terms within the same expression must be measured in the same units. That is, if the first term in an expression is in hours, all other terms in that expression must also be in hours. For example, in the carpentry constraint $3T + 4C \leq 2{,}400$, the $4T$, $3C$, and 2,400 are each measured in hours.
- Address each constraint separately. That is, there is no single "mega" expression that will take care of all constraints in the model at one time. Each constraint is a separate issue,

IN ACTION Linear Programing Helps General Electric Units to Optimize Portfolios

General Electric Asset Management Incorporated (GEAM) manages investment portfolios worth billions of dollars on behalf of various General Electric (GE) units and other clients worldwide, including Genworth Financial and GE Insurance (GEI). GEAM, a wholly owned subsidiary of GE, invests portfolios of assets primarily in corporate and government bonds, taking into account risk and regulatory constraints. The objective is to identify the portfolios' risk/return trade-offs by maximizing the return or minimizing the risk. While risk is widely represented by variance or volatility, it is usually a nonlinear measure and portfolio managers typically use linear risk sensitivities for computational tractability.

To address this problem, a multidisciplinary team from GE Global Research Center worked with GEAM, Genworth, and GEI to develop a sequential linear-programming algorithm that handles the risk nonlinearity iteratively but efficiently. The team determined that the optimal solution for the portfolio management problem would result in improved financial performance and better understanding of the risk/return trade-off. GE initially used the algorithm on a limited basis to optimize portfolios valued at over $30 billion. It is now in broader use at GEAM, GEI, and Genworth. It is estimated that for every $100 billion of assets, the present value of potential benefits is around $75 million over five years.

Source: Based on K. C. Chalermkraivuth et al. "GE Asset Management, Genworth Financial, and GE Insurance Use a Sequential-Linear-Programming Algorithm to Optimize Portfolios," *Interfaces* 35, 5 (September-October 2005): 370–380.

and you must write a separate expression for each one. While writing one constraint (e.g., carpentry time), do not worry about other constraints (e.g., painting time).

- Try "translating" the mathematical expression back to words. After all, writing a constraint is just a matter of taking a problem scenario that is in words (e.g., "the amount of the carpentry time required by the production plan should be less than or equal to the carpentry time available") and translating it to a simple linear mathematical expression (e.g., $3T + 4C \leq 2{,}400$). To make sure the translation has been done correctly, do the reverse process. That is, try explaining in words (to yourself) what the expression you have just written is saying. While doing so, make sure you remember the previous guidelines about all terms in an expression dealing with the same issue and being measured in the same units. If your "reverse translation" yields exactly the situation that you were trying to express in mathematical form, chances are your expression is correct.

2.4 Graphical Solution of a Linear Programming Problem with Two Variables

The graphical method works only when there are two decision variables, but it provides valuable insight into how larger problems are solved.

As noted earlier, there is little chance of encountering LP models with just two variables in real-world situations. However, a major advantage of two-variable LP models (such as Flair Furniture's problem) is that they can be graphically illustrated using a two-dimensional graph. This graph can then be used to identify the optimal solution to the model. Although this graphical solution procedure has limited value in real-world situations, it is invaluable in two respects. First, it provides insights into the properties of solutions to *all* LP models, regardless of their size. Second, even though we use a computerized spreadsheet based procedure to solve LP models in this textbook, the graphical procedure allows us to provide an intuitive explanation of how this more complex solution procedure works for LP models of any size. For these reasons, we first discuss the solution of Flair's problem using a graphical approach.

Graphical Representation of Constraints

Here is a complete mathematical statement of the Flair LP problem.

The complete LP model for Flair's problem can be restated as follows:

$$\text{Maximize profit} = \$7T + \$5C$$

subject to the constraints

$$\begin{aligned} 3T + 4C &\leq 2{,}400 && \text{(carpentry time)} \\ 2T + 1C &\leq 1{,}000 && \text{(painting time)} \\ C &\leq 450 && \text{(maximum chairs allowed)} \\ T &\geq 100 && \text{(minimum tables required)} \\ T, C &\geq 0 && \text{(nonnegativity)} \end{aligned}$$

Nonnegativity constraints mean we are always in the graphical area where T ≥ 0 *and* C ≥ 0.

To find an optimal solution to this LP problem, we must first identify a set, or region, of feasible solutions. The first step in doing so is to plot each of the problem's constraints on a graph. We can plot either decision variable on the horizontal (X) axis of the graph, and the other variable on the vertical (Y) axis. In Flair's case, let us plot T (tables) on the X-axis and C (chairs) on the Y-axis. The nonnegativity constraints imply that we are working only in the first (or positive) quadrant of a graph.

CARPENTRY TIME CONSTRAINT To represent the carpentry constraint graphically, we first convert the expression into a linear equation (i.e., $3T + 4C = 2{,}400$) by replacing the inequality sign ($\leq$) with an equality sign ($=$).

Plotting the first constraint involves finding points at which the line intersects the T*-axis and* C*-axis.*

As you may recall from elementary algebra, the solution of a linear equation with two variables represents a straight line. The easiest way to plot the line is to find any two points that satisfy the equation and then draw a straight line through them. The two easiest points to find are generally the points at which the line intersects the horizontal (T) and vertical (C) axes.

If Flair produces no tables (i.e., $T = 0$), then $3(0) + 4C = 2{,}400$, or $C = 600$. That is, the line representing the carpentry time equation crosses the vertical axis at $C = 600$. This indicates that if the entire carpentry time available is used to make only chairs, Flair could make 600 chairs this month.

FIGURE 2.1
Graph of the Nonnegativity Constraint and the Carpentry Constraint Equation

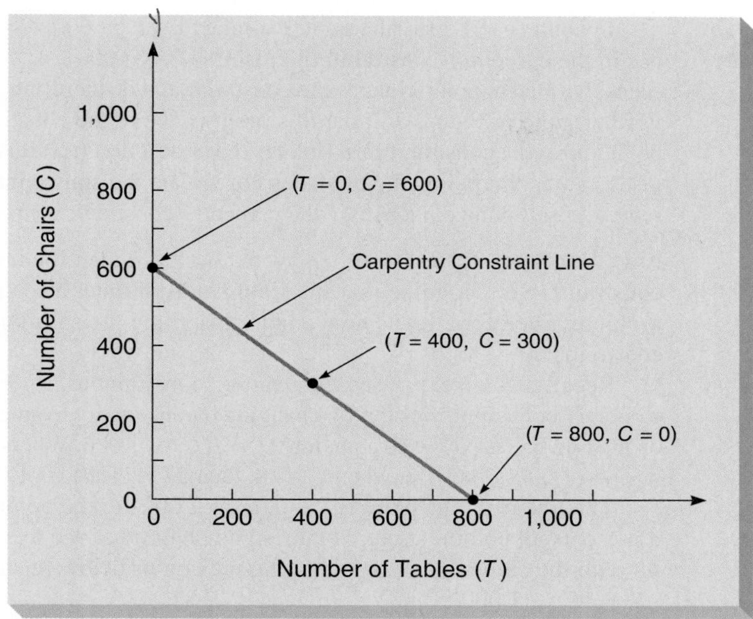

To find the point at which the line $3T + 4C = 2{,}400$ crosses the horizontal axis, let us assume that Flair uses all the carpentry time available to make only tables. That is, $C = 0$. Then $3T + 4(0) = 2{,}400$, or $T = 800$.

The nonnegativity constraints and the carpentry constraint line are illustrated in Figure 2.1. The line running from point ($T = 0, C = 600$) to point ($T = 800, C = 0$) represents the carpentry time equation $3T + 4C = 2{,}400$. We know that any combination of tables and chairs represented by points on this line (e.g., $T = 400, C = 300$) will use up all 2,400 hours of carpentry time.[3]

Recall, however, that the actual carpentry constraint is the inequality $3T + 4C \leq 2{,}400$. How do we identify all the points on the graph that satisfy this inequality? To do so, we check any possible point in the graph. For example, let us check ($T = 300, C = 200$). If we substitute these values in the carpentry constraint, the result is $3 \times 300 + 4 \times 200 = 1{,}700$. Because 1,700 is less than 2,400, the point ($T = 300, C = 200$) satisfies the inequality. Further, note in Figure 2.2 that this point is below the constraint line.

FIGURE 2.2
Region That Satisfies the Carpentry Constraint

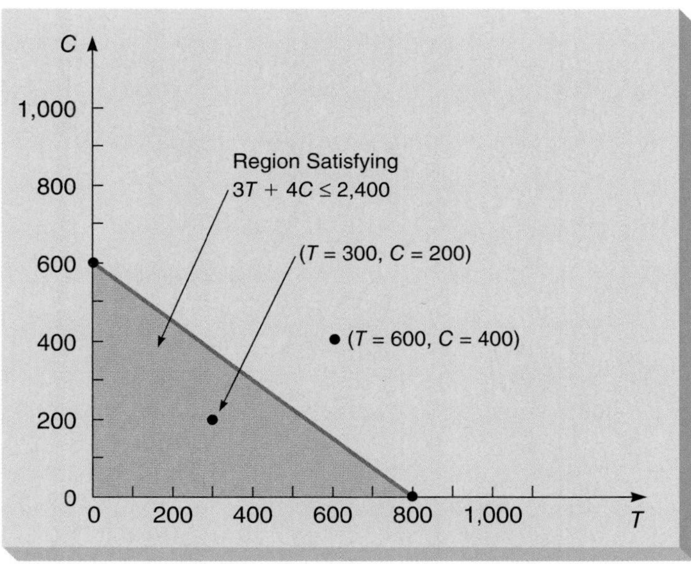

[3] Thus, we have plotted the carpentry constraint equation in its most binding position (i.e., using all of the resource).

There is a whole region of points that satisfies the first inequality constraint.

In contrast, let's say the point we select is ($T = 600$, $C = 400$). If we substitute these values in the carpentry constraint, the result is $3 \times 600 + 4 \times 400 = 3{,}400$. Because 3,400 exceeds 2,400, this point violates the constraint and is, therefore, an unacceptable production level. Further, note in Figure 2.2 that this point is above the constraint line. As a matter of fact, any point above the constraint line violates that restriction (test this yourself with a few other points), just as any point below the line does not violate the constraint. In Figure 2.2, the shaded region represents all points that satisfy the carpentry constraint inequality $3T + 4C \leq 2{,}400$.

PAINTING TIME CONSTRAINT Now that we have identified the points that satisfy the carpentry constraint, we recognize that the final solution must also satisfy all other constraints in the problem. Therefore, let us now add to this graph the solution that corresponds to the painting constraint.

Recall that we expressed the painting constraint as $2T + 1C \leq 1{,}000$. As we did with the carpentry constraint, we start by changing the inequality to an equation and identifying two points on the line specified by the equation $2T + 1C = 1{,}000$. When $T = 0$, then $2(0) + 1C = 1{,}000$, or $C = 1{,}000$. Likewise, when $C = 0$, then $2T + 1(0) = 1{,}000$, or $T = 500$.

The line from the point ($T = 0$, $C = 1{,}000$) to the point ($T = 500$, $C = 0$) in Figure 2.3 represents all combinations of tables and chairs that use exactly 1,000 hours of painting time. As with the carpentry constraint, all points on or below this line satisfy the original inequality $2T + 1C \leq 1{,}000$.

In Figure 2.3, some points, such as ($T = 300$, $C = 200$), are below the lines for both the carpentry equation and the painting equation. That is, we have enough carpentry and painting time available to manufacture 300 tables and 200 chairs this month. In contrast, there are points, such as ($T = 500$, $C = 200$) and ($T = 100$, $C = 700$), that satisfy one of the two constraints but violate the other. (See if you can verify this statement mathematically.) Because we need the solution to satisfy both the carpentry and painting constraints, we will consider only those points that satisfy both constraints simultaneously. The region that contains all such points is shaded in Figure 2.3.

PRODUCTION CONSTRAINT FOR CHAIRS We have to make sure the final solution requires us to make no more than 450 chairs ($C \leq 450$). As before, we first convert this inequality to an equation ($C = 450$). This is relatively easy to draw because it is just a horizontal line that intersects the vertical (C) axis at 450. This line is shown in Figure 2.4, and all points below this line satisfy the original inequality ($C \leq 450$).

PRODUCTION CONSTRAINT FOR TABLES Finally, we have to ensure that the final solution makes at least 100 tables ($T \geq 100$). In this case, the equation ($T = 100$) is just a vertical line

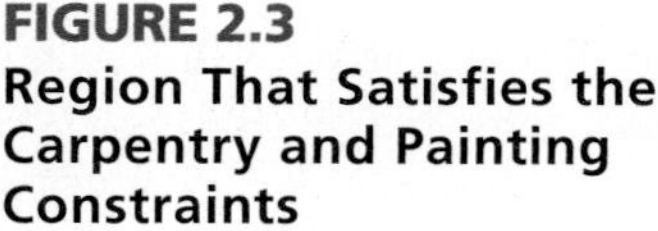

FIGURE 2.3
Region That Satisfies the Carpentry and Painting Constraints

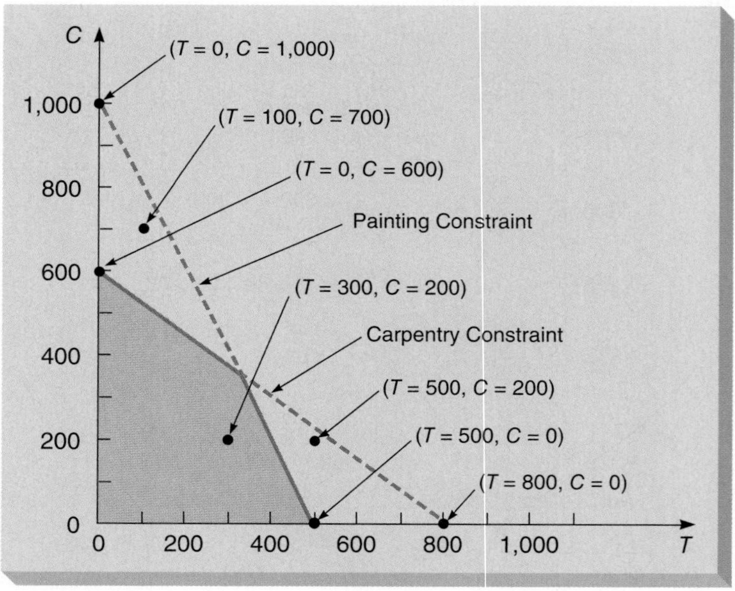

FIGURE 2.4
Feasible Solution Region for the Flair Furniture Company Problem

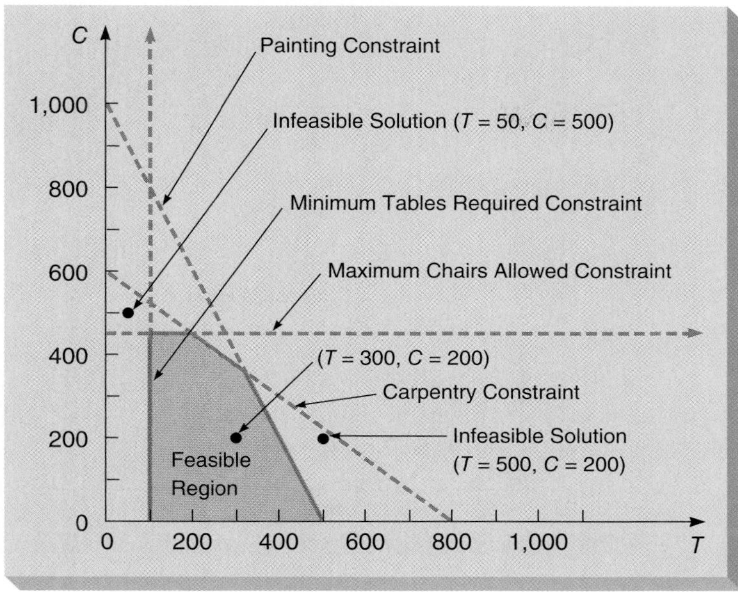

that intersects the horizontal (T) axis at 100. This line is also shown in Figure 2.4. However, because this constraint has the $\geq$ sign, it should be easy to verify that all points to the *right* of this line satisfy the original inequality ($T \geq 100$).

Feasible Region

In all problems, we are interested in satisfying all constraints at the same time.

The feasible region *is the overlapping area of all constraints.*

The **feasible region** of an LP problem consists of those points that simultaneously satisfy all constraints in the problem; that is, it is the region where all the problem's constraints overlap.

Consider a point such as ($T = 300, C = 200$) in Figure 2.4. This point satisfies all four constraints, as well as the nonnegativity constraints. This point, therefore, represents a **feasible solution** to Flair's problem. In contrast, points such as ($T = 500, C = 200$) and ($T = 50, C = 500$) each violate one or more constraints. They are, therefore, not feasible solutions. The shaded area in Figure 2.4 represents the feasible region for Flair Furniture's problem. Any point outside the shaded area represents an **infeasible solution** (or production plan).

Identifying an Optimal Solution by Using Level Lines

When the feasible region has been identified, we can proceed to find the optimal solution to the problem. In Flair's case, the *optimal solution* is the point in the feasible region that produces the highest profit. But there are many, many possible solution points in the feasible region. How do we go about selecting the optimal one, the one that yields the highest profit? We do this by essentially using the objective function as a "pointer" to guide us toward an optimal point in the feasible region.

We use the objective function to point us toward the optimal solution.

DRAWING LEVEL LINES In the **level, or iso, lines** method, we begin by plotting the line that represents the objective function (i.e., $\$7T + \$5C$) on the graph, just as we plotted the various constraints.[4] However, note that we do not know what $\$7T + \$5C$ equals in this function. In fact, that's what we are trying to find out. Without knowing this value, how do we plot this equation?

To get around this problem, let us first write the objective function as $\$7T + \$5C = Z$. We then start the procedure by selecting *any* arbitrary value for Z. In selecting this value for Z, the only recommended guideline is to select a value that makes the resulting equation easy to plot on the graph. For example, for Flair's problem, we can choose a profit of \$2,100. We can then write the objective function as $\$7T + \$5C = \$2{,}100$.

Clearly, this expression is the equation of a line that represents all combinations of (T, C) that would yield a total profit of \$2,100. That is, it is a *level line* corresponding to a profit of \$2,100.

[4] Iso means "equal" or "similar." Thus, an isoprofit line represents a line with all profits the same, in this case \$2,100.

FIGURE 2.5
Level Profit Lines for $Z = \$2{,}100$ and $Z = \$2{,}800$

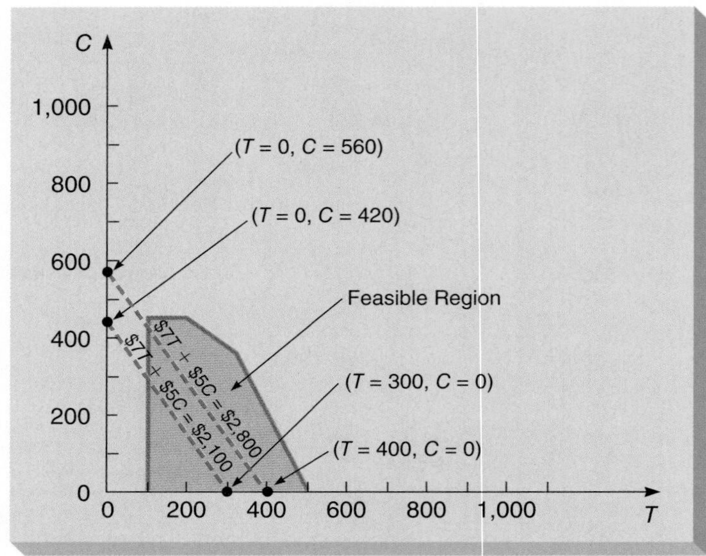

To plot this line, we proceed exactly as we do to plot a constraint line. If we let $T = 0$, then $\$7(0) + \$5C = \$2{,}100$, or $C = 420$. Likewise, if we let $C = 0$, then $\$7T + \$5(0) = \$2{,}100$, or $T = 300$.

The objective function line corresponding to $Z = \$2{,}100$ is illustrated in Figure 2.5 as the line between $(T = 0, C = 420)$ and $(T = 300, C = 0)$. Observe that if any points on this line lie in the feasible region identified earlier for Flair's problem, those points represent *feasible production plans* that will yield a profit of \$2,100.

What if we had selected a different Z value, such as \$2,800, instead of \$2,100? In that case, the objective function line corresponding to $Z = \$2{,}800$ would be between the points $(T = 0, C = 560)$ and $(T = 400, C = 0)$, also shown in Figure 2.5. Further, because there are points on this line that lie within the feasible region for Flair's problem, it is possible for Flair to find a production plan that will yield a profit of \$2,800 (obviously, better than \$2,100).

Observe in Figure 2.5 that the level lines for $Z = \$2{,}100$ and $Z = \$2{,}800$ are parallel to each other. This is a very important point. It implies that regardless of which value of Z we select, the objective function line that we draw will be parallel to the two level lines shown in Figure 2.5. The exact location of the parallel line on the graph will, of course, depend on the value of Z selected.

We draw a series of parallel level lines until we find the one that corresponds to the optimal solution.

We know now that Flair can obtain a profit of \$2,800. However, is \$2,800 the highest profit that Flair can get? From the preceding discussion, we note that as the value we select for Z gets larger (which is desirable in Flair's problem because we want to maximize profit), the objective function line moves in a *parallel* fashion away from the origin. Therefore, we can "draw" a series of parallel level lines (by carefully moving a ruler in a plane parallel to the $Z = \$2{,}800$ line). However, as we visualize these parallel lines, we need to ensure that at least one point on each level line lies within the feasible region. The level line that corresponds to the highest profit but still touches some point of the feasible region pinpoints an optimal solution.

From Figure 2.6, we can see that the level profit line that corresponds to the highest achievable profit value will be tangential to the shaded feasible region at the point denoted by ④. Any level line corresponding to a profit value higher than that of this line will have no points in the feasible region. For example, note that a level line corresponding to a profit value of \$4,200 is entirely outside the feasible region (see Figure 2.6). This implies that a profit of \$4,200 is not possible for Flair to achieve.

Observe that point ④ defines the intersection of the carpentry and painting constraint equations. Such points, where two or more constraints intersect, are called **corner points, or extreme points**. In Figure 2.6, note that the other corner points in Flair's problem are points ①, ②, ③, and ⑤.

An optimal solution to an LP model must lie at one of the corner points in the feasible region.

CORNER POINT PROPERTY The preceding discussion reveals an important property of LP problems, known as the *corner point property*. This property states that an optimal solution to an LP problem will always occur at a corner point of the feasible region. In Flair's problem,

FIGURE 2.6
Optimal Corner Point Solution to the Flair Furniture Company Problem

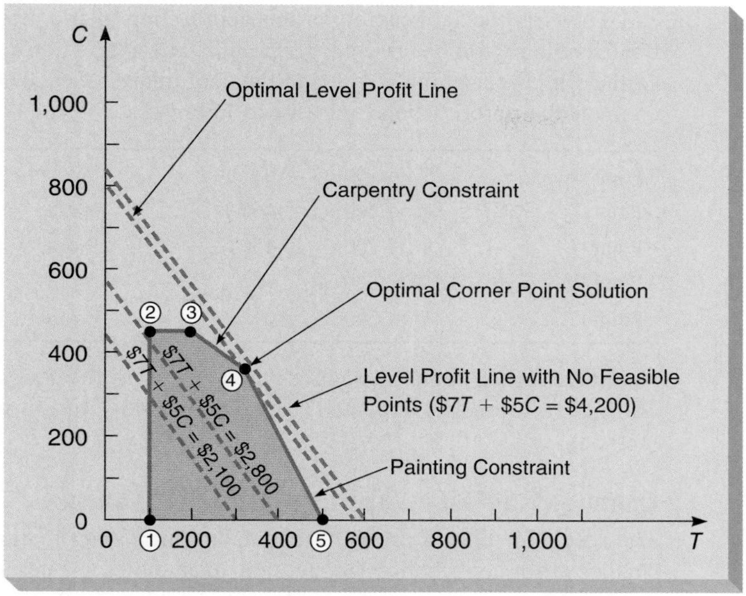

this means that the optimal solution has to be one of the five corner points (i.e., ①, ②, ③, ④, or ⑤). For the specific objective function considered here (Maximize $7T + 5C$), corner point ④ turns out to be optimal. For a different objective function, one of the other corner points could be optimal.

CALCULATING THE SOLUTION AT AN OPTIMAL CORNER POINT Now that we have identified point ④ in Figure 2.6 as an optimal corner point, how do we find the values of T and C, and the profit at that point? Of course, if a graph is perfectly drawn, you can always find point ④ by carefully examining the intersection's coordinates. Otherwise, the algebraic procedure shown here provides more precision.

Solving for the coordinates of a corner point requires the use of simultaneous equations, an algebraic technique.

To find the coordinates of point ④ accurately, we have to solve for the intersection of the two constraint equations intersecting at that point. Recall from your last course in algebra that you can apply the **simultaneous equations method** to the two constraint equations:

$$3T + 4C = 2{,}400 \qquad \text{(carpentry time equation)}$$
$$2T + 1C = 1{,}000 \qquad \text{(painting time equation)}$$

To solve these equations simultaneously, we need to eliminate one of the variables and solve for the other. One way to do this would be to first multiply the first equation by 2 and the second equation by 3. If we then subtract the modified second equation from the modified first equation, we get

$$\begin{array}{r} 6T + 8C = 4{,}800 \\ \underline{-(6T + 3C = 3{,}000)} \\ 5C = 1{,}800 \end{array} \qquad \text{implies } C = 360$$

We can now substitute 360 for C in either of the original equations and solve for T. For example, if $C = 360$ in the first equation, then $3T + (4)(360) = 2{,}400$, or $T = 320$. That is, point ④ has the coordinates $(T = 320, C = 360)$. Hence, in order to maximize profit, Flair Furniture should produce 320 tables and 360 chairs. To complete the analysis, we can compute the optimal profit as $\$7 \times 320 + \$5 \times 360 = \$4{,}040$.

Identifying an Optimal Solution by Using All Corner Points

Because an optimal solution to any LP problem always occurs at a corner point of the feasible region, we can identify an optimal solution by evaluating the objective function value at every corner point in the problem. While this approach, called the **corner point method**, eliminates the need for graphing and using level objective function lines, it is somewhat tedious because we end up unnecessarily identifying the coordinates of many corner points. Nevertheless, some people prefer this approach because it is conceptually much simpler than the level lines approach.

To verify the applicability of this approach to Flair's problem, we note from Figure 2.6 that the feasible region has five corner points: ①, ②, ③, ④, and ⑤. Using the procedure discussed earlier for corner point ④, we find the coordinates of each of the other four corner points and compute their profit levels. They are as follows:

Point ①	$(T = 100, C = 0)$	Profit $= \$7 \times 100 + \$5 \times 0 = \$700$
Point ②	$(T = 100, C = 450)$	Profit $= \$7 \times 100 + \$5 \times 450 = \$2{,}950$
Point ③	$(T = 200, C = 450)$	Profit $= \$7 \times 200 + \$5 \times 450 = \$3{,}650$
Point ④	$(T = 320, C = 360)$	Profit $= \$7 \times 320 + \$5 \times 360 = \$4{,}040$
Point ⑤	$(T = 500, C = 0)$	Profit $= \$7 \times 500 + \$5 \times 0 = \$3{,}500$

Note that corner point ④ produces the highest profit of any corner point and is therefore the optimal solution. As expected, this is the same solution we obtained using the level lines method.

Comments on Flair Furniture's Optimal Solution

The result for Flair's problem reveals an interesting feature. Even though chairs provide a smaller profit contribution ($5 per unit) than tables ($7 per unit), the optimal solution requires us to make more units of chairs (360) than tables (320). This is a common occurrence in such problems. We cannot assume that we will always produce greater quantities of products with higher profit contributions. We need to recognize that products with higher profit contributions may also consume larger amounts of resources, some of which may be scarce. Hence, even though we may get smaller profit contributions per unit from other products, we may more than compensate for this by being able to make more units of these products.

Notice, however, what happens if the profit contribution for chairs is only $3 per unit instead of $5 per unit. The objective is to now maximize $\$7T + \$3C$ instead of $\$7T + \$5C$. Although Figure 2.6 does not show the profit line corresponding to $\$7T + \$3C$, you should be able to use a straight edge to represent this revised profit line in this figure and verify that the optimal solution will now correspond to corner point ⑤. That is, the optimal solution is to make 500 tables and 0 chairs, for a total profit of $3,500. Clearly, in this case, the profit contributions of tables and chairs are such that we should devote all our resources to making only the higher profit contribution product, tables.

The key point to note here is that in either situation (i.e., when the profit contribution of chairs is $5 per unit and when it is $3 per unit), there is no easy way to predict *a priori* what the optimal solution is going to be with regard to the numbers of tables and chairs to make. We are able to determine these values only after we have formulated the LP model and solved it in each case. This clearly illustrates the power and usefulness of such types of decision models. As you can well imagine, this issue is going to become even more prominent when we deal in subsequent chapters with models that have more than two decision variables.

Extension to Flair Furniture's LP Model

As noted in Chapter 1, the decision modeling process is iterative in most real-world situations. That is, the model may need to be regularly revised to reflect new information. With this in mind, let us consider the following revision to the Flair Furniture model before we move on to the next example.

Suppose the marketing department has now informed Flair that all customers purchasing tables usually purchase at least two chairs at the same time. While the existing inventory of chairs may be enough to satisfy a large portion of this demand, the marketing department would like the production plan to ensure that at least 75 more chairs are made this month than tables. Does this new condition affect the optimal solution? If so, how?

Using the decision variables T and C we have defined for Flair's model, we can express this new condition as

$$C \geq T + 75$$

Notice that unlike all our previous conditions, this expression has decision variables on both sides of the inequality. This is a perfectly logical thing to have in an expression, and it does not

FIGURE 2.7
Optimal Corner Point Solution to the Extended Flair Furniture Company Problem

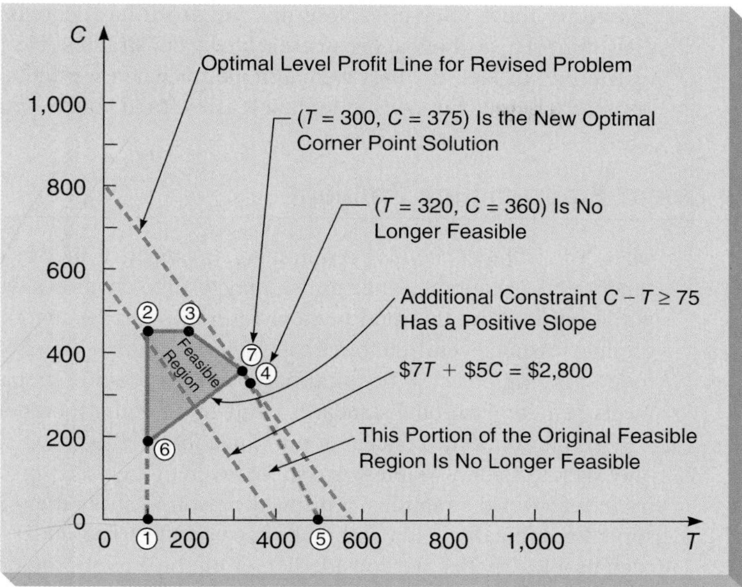

affect the validity of the model in any way. We can, of course, manipulate this expression algebraically if we wish and rewrite it as

$$C - T \geq 75$$

The revised graphical representation of Flair's model due to the addition of this new constraint is shown in Figure 2.7. The primary issue that is noticeably different in drawing the new constraint when compared to the carpentry and painting constraints is that it has a positive slope. All points above this line satisfy the inequality $(C - T \geq 75)$.

Notice the dramatic change in the shape and size of the feasible region just because of this single new constraint. This is a common feature in LP models, and it illustrates how each constraint in a model is important because it can affect the feasible region (and hence, the optimal solution) in a significant manner. In Flair's model, the original optimal corner point ④ $(T = 320, C = 360)$ is no longer even feasible in the revised problem. In fact, of the original corner points, only points ② and ③ are still feasible. Two new corner points, ⑥ and ⑦, now exist.

To determine which of these four corner points (②, ③, ⑥, and ⑦ is the new optimal solution, we use a level profit line as before. Figure 2.7 shows the level line for a profit value of $2,800. Based on this line, it appears that corner point ⑦ is the new optimal solution. The values at this corner point can be determined to be $T = 300$ and $C = 375$, for a profit of $3,975. (See if you

IN ACTION Using Linear Programming to Improve Capacity Management at Indian Railways

Indian Railways (IR) operates more than 1,600 long distance trains and carries more than 7 million passengers daily. Reserved tickets are booked through IR's passenger reservation system, which reserves a specific seat in a specific class on a specific train per booking. A major problem is deciding how many seats to allocate in a given class of a train to multiple travel segments, including segments on which en route passengers (i.e., those who are not traveling from the train's origin to its destination) travel. A train's capacity must therefore be distributed among various intermediate stations by allocating specific quotas to ensure that the twin objectives of maximizing the number of confirmed seats and increasing the seat utilization are met.

IR personnel used a linear programming model to determine the optimal capacity allocation on multiple travel segments. The model, which uses a simple, effective capacity management tool, has helped IR reduce its overall seat requirements and has increased the availability of confirmed seats for the various en route passenger demands on several trains. A spokesperson for IR notes that "The model and software developed have been used in over 50 long-distance trains originating on Western Railway with considerable success."

Source: Based on R. Gopalakrishnan and N. Rangaraj. "Capacity Management on Long-Distance Passenger Trains of Indian Railways," *Interfaces* 40, 4 (July-August 2010): 291–302.

can verify these yourself.) Note that the profit has decreased due to the addition of this new constraint. This is logical because each new constraint could make the feasible region a bit more restrictive. In fact, the best we can hope for when we add a new constraint is that our current optimal solution continues to remain feasible (and hence, optimal).

2.5 A Minimization Linear Programming Problem

Many LP problems involve minimizing an objective such as cost instead of maximizing a profit function. A restaurant, for example, may wish to develop a work schedule to meet staffing needs while minimizing the total number of employees. A manufacturer may seek to distribute its products from several factories to its many regional warehouses in such a way as to minimize total shipping costs. A hospital may want to provide its patients with a daily meal plan that meets certain nutritional standards while minimizing food purchase costs.

Minimization LP problems typically deal with trying to reduce costs.

To introduce the concept of minimization problems, we first discuss a problem that involves only two decision variables. As before, even though such problems may have limited applicability in real-world situations, a primary reason to study them is that they can be represented and solved graphically. This will make it easier for us to understand the structure and behavior of such problems when we consider larger minimization problems in subsequent chapters.

Let's take a look at a common LP problem, referred to as the *diet problem*. This situation is similar to the one that the hospital faces in feeding its patients at the least cost.

Holiday Meal Turkey Ranch

The Holiday Meal Turkey Ranch is planning to use two different brands of turkey feed—brand A and brand B—to provide a good diet for its turkeys. Each feed contains different quantities (in units) of the three nutrients (protein, vitamin, and iron) essential for fattening turkeys. Table 2.1 summarizes this information and also shows the minimum unit of each nutrient required per month by a turkey. Brand A feed costs $0.10 per pound, and brand B feed costs $0.15 per pound. The owner of the ranch would like to use LP to determine the quantity of each feed to use in a turkey's diet in order to meet the minimum monthly requirements for each nutrient at the lowest cost.

Here is a complete mathematical formulation of the Holiday Meal LP problem.

If we let A denote the number of pounds of brand A feed to use per turkey each month and B denote the number of pounds of brand B feed to use per turkey each month, we can proceed to formulate this LP problem as follows:

$$\text{Minimize cost} = \$0.10A + \$0.15B$$

subject to the constraints

$$\begin{aligned} 5A + 10B &\geq 45 && \text{(protein required)} \\ 4A + 3B &\geq 24 && \text{(vitamin required)} \\ 0.5A &\geq 1.5 && \text{(iron required)} \\ A, B &\geq 0 && \text{(nonnegativity)} \end{aligned}$$

Before solving this problem, note two features that affect its solution. First, as the problem is formulated presently, we will be solving for the optimal amounts of brands A and B to use per month *per turkey*. If the ranch houses 5,000 turkeys in a given month, we can simply multiply the A and B quantities by 5,000 to decide how much feed to use overall. Second, we

TABLE 2.1
Data for Holiday Meal Turkey Ranch

NUTRIENT	NUTRIENTS PER POUND OF FEED: BRAND A FEED	BRAND B FEED	MINIMUM REQUIRED PER TURKEY PER MONTH
Protein (units)	5	10	45.0
Vitamin (units)	4	3	24.0
Iron (units)	0.5	0	1.5
Cost per pound	$0.10	$0.15	

FIGURE 2.8
Feasible Region for the Holiday Meal Turkey Ranch Problem

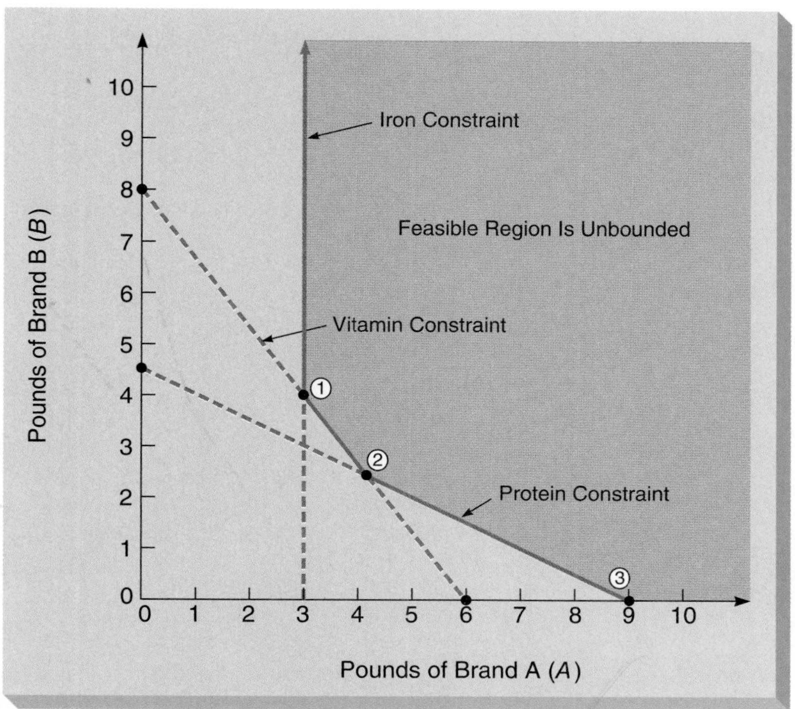

are now dealing with a series of greater than or equal to constraints. These cause the feasible solution area to be above the constraint lines, a common situation when handling minimization LP problems.

Graphical Solution of the Holiday Meal Turkey Ranch Problem

We plot the three constraints to develop a feasible solution region for the minimization problem.

We first construct the feasible solution region. To do so, we plot each of the three constraint equations as shown in Figure 2.8. In plotting constraint such as $0.5A \geq 1.5$, if you find it more convenient to do so, you can multiply both sides by 2 and rewrite the inequality as $A \geq 3$. Clearly, this does not change the position of the constraint line in any way.

Note that the feasible region of minimization problems is often unbounded (i.e., open outward).

The feasible region for Holiday Meal's problem is shown by the shaded space in Figure 2.8. Notice that the feasible region has explicit boundaries inward (i.e., on the left side and the bottom) but is unbounded outward (i.e., on the right side and on top). Minimization problems often exhibit this feature. However, this causes no difficulty in solving them as long as an optimal corner point solution exists on the bounded side. (Recall that an optimal solution will lie at one of the corner points, just as it did in a maximization problem.)

As in maximization problems, we can use the level lines method in a minimization problem to identify an optimal solution.

In Figure 2.8, the identifiable corner points for Holiday Meal's problem are denoted by points ①, ②, and ③. Which, if any, of these corner points is an optimal solution? To answer this, we write the objective function as $\$0.10A + 0.15B = Z$ and plot this equation for *any* arbitrary value of Z. For example, we start in Figure 2.9 by drawing the level cost line corresponding to $Z = \$1.00$. Obviously, there are many points in the feasible region that would yield a lower total cost. As with the parallel level lines we used to solve the Flair Furniture maximization problem, we can draw a series of parallel level cost lines to identify Holiday Meal's optimal solution. The lowest level cost line to touch the feasible region pinpoints an optimal corner point.

Because Holiday Meal's problem involves minimization of the objective function, we need to move our level cost line toward the lower left in a plane parallel to the \$1.00 level line. Note that we are moving toward the bounded side of the feasible region and that there are identifiable corner points on this side. Hence, even though the feasible region is unbounded, it is still possible to identify an optimal solution for this problem.

As shown in Figure 2.9, the last feasible point touched by a level cost line as we move it in a parallel fashion toward the lower left is corner point ②. To find the coordinates of this point algebraically, we proceed as before by eliminating one of the variables from the two equations that intersect at this point (i.e., $5A + 10B = 45$ and $4A + 3B = 24$) so that we can solve for

FIGURE 2.9
Graphical Solution to the Holiday Meal Turkey Ranch Problem Using the Level Cost Line Method

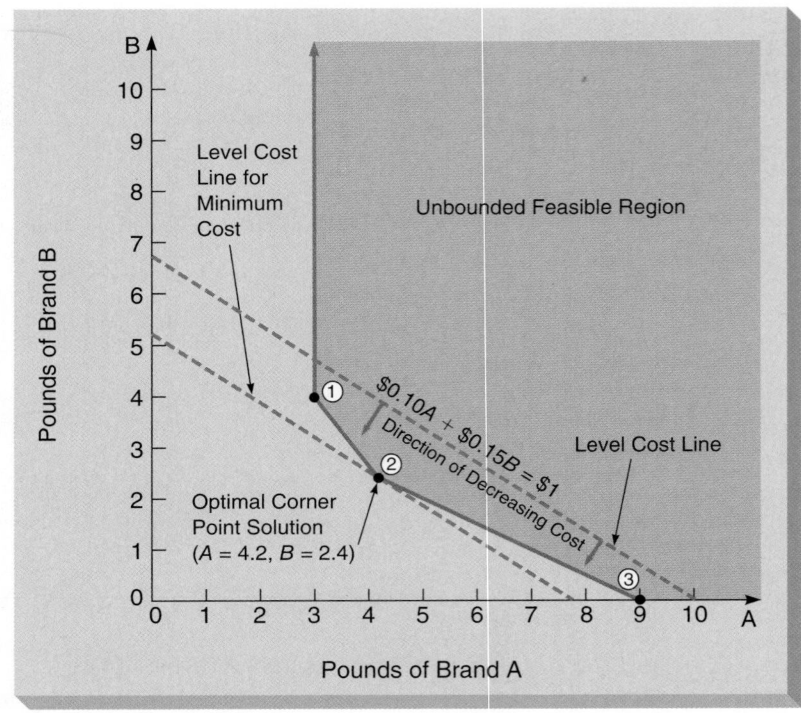

the other. One way would be to multiply the first equation by 4, multiply the second equation by 5, and subtract the second equation from the first equation, as follows:

$$\begin{aligned} 4(5A + 10B = 45) &\text{ implies} & 20A + 40B &= 180 \\ -5(4A + 3B = 24) &\text{ implies} & -(20A + 15B &= 120) \\ & & 25B &= 60 \quad \text{implies } B = 2.40 \end{aligned}$$

Substituting $B = 2.40$ into the first equation yields $4A + (3)(2.40) = 24$, or $A = 4.20$. The cost at corner point ② is $\$0.10 \times 4.20 + \$0.15 \times 2.40 = \$0.78$. That is, Holiday Meal should use 4.20 pounds of brand A feed and 2.40 pounds of brand B feed, at a cost of $0.78 per turkey per month. Observe that this solution has fractional values. In this case, however, this is perfectly logical because turkey feeds can be measured in fractional quantities.

As with the Flair Furniture example, we could also identify an optimal corner point in this problem by using the corner point method (i.e., evaluating the cost at all three identifiable corner points ①, ② , and ③).

2.6 Special Situations in Solving Linear Programming Problems

In each of the LP problems discussed so far, all the constraints in the model have affected the shape and size of the feasible region. Further, in each case, there has been a *single* corner point that we have been able to identify as the optimal corner point. There are, however, four special situations that may be encountered when solving LP problems: (1) redundant constraints, (2) infeasibility, (3) alternate optimal solutions, and (4) unbounded solutions. We illustrate the first three situations using the Flair Furniture example as the base model and the last one using the Holiday Meal Turkey Ranch example as the base model.

Redundant Constraints

A **redundant constraint** *is one that does not affect the feasible solution region.*

A **redundant constraint** is a constraint that does not affect the feasible region in any way. In other words, other constraints in the model are more restrictive and thereby negate the need to even consider the redundant constraint. The presence of redundant constraints is quite common in large LP models with many variables. However, it is typically impossible to determine whether a constraint is redundant just by looking at it.

Let's consider the LP model for the Flair Furniture problem again. Recall that the original model is

$$\text{Maximize profit} = \$7T + \$5C$$

subject to the constraints

$3T + 4C \leq 2{,}400$		(carpentry time)
$2T + 1C \leq 1{,}000$		(painting time)
C	≤ 450	(maximum chairs allowed)
T	≥ 100	(minimum tables required)
T, C	≥ 0	(nonnegativity)

Now suppose that the demand for tables has become quite weak. Instead of specifying that at least 100 tables need to be made, the marketing department is now specifying that a *maximum* of 100 tables should be made. That is, the constraint should be $T \leq 100$ instead of $T \geq 100$, as originally formulated. The revised feasible region for this problem due to this modified constraint is shown in Figure 2.10. From this figure, we see that the production limit constraints on chairs and tables are so restrictive that they make the carpentry and painting constraints redundant. That is, these two time constraints have no effect on the feasible region.

Infeasibility

Lack of a feasible solution region can occur if constraints conflict with one another.

Maximize $\$7T + \$5C$
subject to

$3T + 4C \leq 2{,}400$
$2T + 1C \leq 1{,}000$
$C \leq 450$
$T \geq 100$
$T, C \geq 0$

Infeasibility is a condition that arises when no single solution satisfies all of an LP problem's constraints. That is, no feasible solution region exists. Such a situation might occur, for example, if the problem has been formulated with conflicting constraints. As a graphical illustration of infeasibility, let us consider the Flair Furniture problem again (see the formulation in the margin note). Now suppose that Flair's marketing department has found that the demand for tables has become very strong. To meet this demand, it is now specifying that at least 600 tables should be made. That is, the constraint should now be $T \geq 600$ instead of $T \geq 100$. The revised graph for this problem due to this modified constraint is shown in Figure 2.11. From this figure, we see that there is no feasible solution region for this problem because of the presence of conflicting constraints.

Infeasibility is not uncommon in real-world, large-scale LP problems that involve hundreds of constraints. In such situations, the decision analyst coordinating the LP problem must resolve the conflict between the constraints causing the infeasibility and get them revised appropriately.

FIGURE 2.10
Problem with a Redundant Constraint

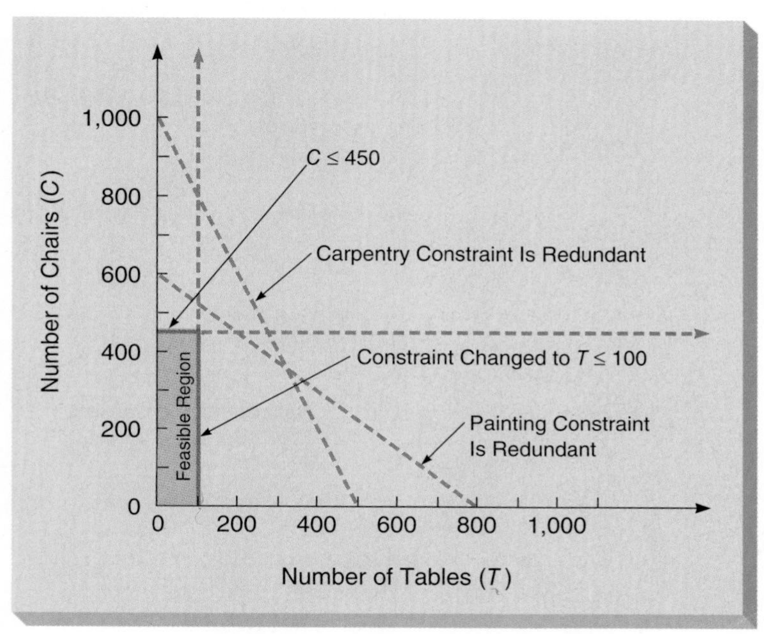

FIGURE 2.11
Example of an Infeasible Problem

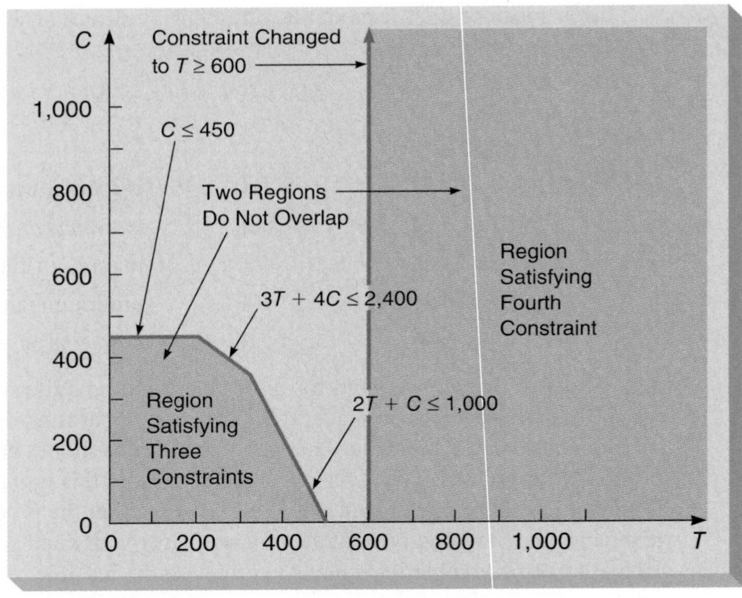

Alternate Optimal Solutions

Alternate optimal solutions *are possible in LP problems.*

An LP problem may, on occasion, have **alternate optimal solutions** (i.e., more than one optimal solution). Graphically, this is the case when the level profit (or cost) line runs parallel to a constraint in the problem that lies in the direction in which the profit (or cost) line is being moved—in other words, when the two lines have the same slope. To illustrate this situation, let us consider the Flair Furniture problem again.

Now suppose the marketing department has indicated that due to increased competition, profit contributions of both products have to be revised downward to \$6 per table and \$3 per chair. That is, the objective function is now $\$6T + \$3C$ instead of $\$7T + \$5C$. The revised graph for this problem is shown in Figure 2.12. From this figure, we note that the level profit line (shown here for a profit of \$2,100) runs parallel to the painting constraint equation. At a profit level of \$3,000, the level profit line will rest directly on top of this constraint line. This means that any point along the painting constraint equation between corner points ④ ($T = 320, C = 360$) and ⑤ ($T = 500, C = 0$) provides an optimal T and C combination.

FIGURE 2.12
Example of a Problem with Alternate Optimal Solutions

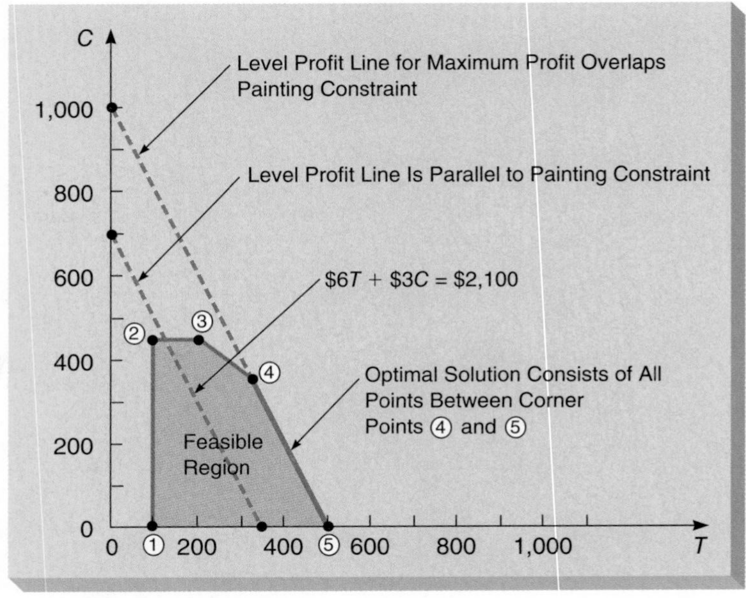

Far from causing problems, the presence of more than one optimal solution actually allows management greater flexibility in deciding which solution to select. The optimal objective function value remains the same at all alternate solutions.

Unbounded Solution

When a problem has an unbounded feasible region, it may not have a finite solution.

When an LP model has a bounded feasible region, as in the Flair Furniture example (i.e., it has an explicit boundary in every direction), it has an identifiable optimal corner point solution. However, if the feasible region is unbounded in one or more directions, as in the Holiday Meal Turkey Ranch example, depending on the objective function, the model may or may not have a finite solution. In the Holiday Meal problem, for example, we were able to identify a finite solution because the optimal corner point existed on the bounded side (refer to Figure 2.9 on page 36). However, what happens if the objective function is such that we have to move our level profit (or cost) lines away from the bounded side?

Minimize \$0.10*A* + \$0.15*B*
subject to

$$5A + 10B \geq 45$$
$$4A + 3B \geq 24$$
$$0.5A \geq 1.5$$
$$A, B \geq 0$$

To study this, let us again consider the Holiday Meal example (see the formulation in the margin note). Now suppose that instead of minimizing cost, the owner of the ranch wants to use a different objective function. Specifically, based on his experience with the feeds and their fattening impact on his turkeys, assume that the owner estimates that brand A feed yields a "fattening value" of 8 per pound, while brand B feed yields a fattening value of 12 per pound. The owner wants to find the diet that maximizes the total fattening value.

When the solution is unbounded in a maximization problem, the objective function value can be made infinitely large without violating any constraints.

The objective function now changes from "Minimize \$0.10A + \$0.15B" to "Maximize $8A + 12B$." Figure 2.13 shows the graph of this problem with the new objective function. As before, the feasible region (which has not changed) is unbounded, with three identifiable corner points on the bounded side. However, because this is now a maximization problem and the feasible region is unbounded in the direction in which profit increases, the solution itself is unbounded. That is, the profit can be made infinitely large without violating any constraints. In real-world situations, the occurrence of an **unbounded solution** usually means the problem has been formulated improperly. That is, either one or more constraints have the wrong sign or values, or some constraints have been overlooked. In Holiday Meal's case, it would indeed be wonderful to achieve an infinite fattening value, but that would have serious adverse implications for the amount of feed that the turkeys must eat each month!

FIGURE 2.13
Example of a Problem with an Unbounded Solution

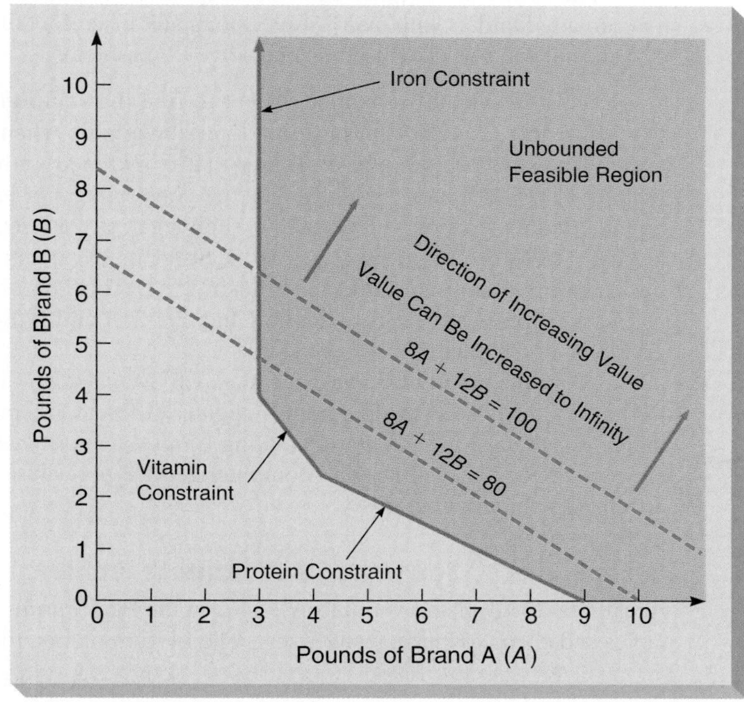

IN ACTION Resource Allocation at Pantex

Companies often use optimization techniques such as Linear Programming to allocate limited resources to maximize profits or minimize costs. One of the most important resource allocation problems faced by the United States is dismantling old nuclear weapons and maintaining the safety, security, and reliability of the remaining systems. This problem is a primary concern of Pantex, which is responsible for disarming, evaluating, and maintaining the U.S. nuclear stockpile. The company is also responsible for storing critical weapons components that relate to U.S.–Russian nonproliferation agreements. Pantex constantly makes trade-offs in meeting the requirements of disarming some nuclear weapons versus maintaining existing nuclear weapons systems, while effectively allocating limited resources. Like many manufacturers, Pantex must allocate scarce resources among competing demands, all of which are important.

The team charged with solving the resource allocation problem at Pantex developed the Pantex Process Model (PPM). PPM is a sophisticated optimization system capable of analyzing nuclear needs over different time horizons. Since its development, PPM has become the primary tool for analyzing, planning, and scheduling issues at Pantex. PPM also helps to determine future resources. For example, it was used to gain government support for $17 million to modify an existing plant with new buildings and $70 million to construct a new plant.

Source: Based on E. Kjeldgaard et al. "Swords into Plowshares: Nuclear Weapon Dismantlement, Evaluation, and Maintenance at Pantex," *Interfaces* 30, (January–February, 2000): 57–82.

2.7 Setting Up and Solving Linear Programming Problems Using Excel's Solver

Although graphical solution approaches can handle LP models with only two decision variables, more complex solution procedures are necessary to solve larger LP models. Fortunately, such solution procedures exist. (We briefly discuss them in section 2.8.) However, rather than use these procedures to solve large LP models by hand, the focus in this textbook is on using Excel to set up and solve LP problems. Excel and other spreadsheet programs offer users the ability to analyze large LP problems by using built-in problem-solving tools.

Excel has a built-in solution tool for solving LP problems.

There are two main reasons why this textbook's focus on Excel for setting up and solving LP problems is logical and useful in practice:

- The use of spreadsheet programs is now very common, and virtually every organization has access to such programs.
- Because you are likely to be using Excel in many of your other courses, you are probably already familiar with many of its commands. Therefore, there is no need to learn any specialized software to set up and solve LP problems.

Excel uses an add-in named Solver to find the solution to LP-related problems. Solver is a Microsoft Excel add-in program that is available when you install Microsoft Office or Excel. The standard version of Solver that is included with Excel can handle LP problems with up to 200 decision variables and 100 constraints, not including simple lower and upper bounds on the decision variables (e.g., nonnegativity constraints). Larger versions of Solver are available for commercial use from Frontline Systems, Inc. (www.solver.com) which has developed and marketed this add-in for Excel (and other spreadsheet packages). We use Solver to solve LP problems in Chapters 2–5 and integer and nonlinear programming problems in Chapter 6.

The standard version of Solver is included with all versions of Excel.

Several other software packages (e.g., LINDO, GAMS) are capable of handling very large LP models. Although each program is slightly different in terms of its input and output formats, the approach each takes toward handling LP problems is basically the same. Hence, once you are experienced in dealing with computerized LP procedures, you can easily adjust to minor differences among programs.

Using Solver to Solve the Flair Furniture Problem

Recall that the decision variables T and C in the Flair Furniture problem denote the number of tables and chairs to make, respectively. The LP formulation for this problem is as follows:

$$\text{Maximize profit} = \$7T + \$5C$$

subject to the constraints

$$3T + 4C \le 2{,}400 \quad \text{(carpentry time)}$$
$$2T + 1C \le 1{,}000 \quad \text{(painting time)}$$
$$C \le 450 \quad \text{(maximum chairs allowed)}$$
$$T \ge 100 \quad \text{(minimum tables required)}$$
$$T, C \ge 0 \quad \text{(nonnegativity)}$$

Just as we discussed a three-step process to formulate an LP problem (i.e., decision variables, objective function, and constraints), setting up and solving a problem using Excel's Solver also involves three parts: changing variable cells, objective cell, and constraints. We discuss each of these parts in the following sections.

There is no prescribed layout for setting up LP problems in Excel.

In practice, there are no specific guidelines regarding the layout of an LP model in Excel. Depending on your personal preference and expertise, any model that satisfies the basic requirements discussed subsequently will work. However, for purposes of convenience and ease of explanation, we use (to the extent possible) the same layout for all problems in this textbook. Such a consistent approach is more suited to the beginning student of LP. As you gain experience with spreadsheet modeling of LP problems, we encourage you to try alternate layouts.

We represent all parameters associated with a decision variable in the same column.

In our suggested layout, we use a separate column to represent all the parameters (e.g., solution value, profit contribution, constraint coefficients) associated with each decision variable in the problem. The objective function and each constraint in the problem is then modeled on separate rows of the Excel worksheet. Although not required to solve the model, we also add several labels in our spreadsheet to make the entries as self-explanatory as possible.

Excel Note

The Companion Website for this textbook, at www.pearsonhighered.com/balakrishnan, contains the Excel file for each sample problem discussed here. The relevant file name appears in the margin next to each example.

Changing Variable Cells

Changing variable cells *are the decision variables in the problem.*

File: 2-1.xls, sheet: 2-1A

Solver refers to decision variables as **changing variable cells**. Each decision variable in a formulation is assigned to a unique cell in the spreadsheet. Although there are no rules regarding the relative positions of these cells, it is typically convenient to use cells that are next to each other.

In the Flair Furniture example, two decision variables need to be assigned to any two cells in the spreadsheet. In Screenshot 2-1A, we use cells B5 and C5 to represent the number of tables to make (T) and the number of chairs to make (C), respectively.

The initial entries in these two cells can be blank or any value of our choice. At the conclusion of the Solver run, the optimal values of the decision variables will automatically be shown here (if an optimal solution is found).

It is possible, and often desirable, to format these cells using any of Excel's formatting features. For example, we can choose to specify how many decimal points to show for these values. Likewise, the cells can be assigned any name (instead of B5 and C5), using the naming option in Excel. Descriptive titles for these cells (such as those shown in cells A5, B4, and C4 of Screenshot 2-1A) are recommended to make the model as self-explanatory as possible, but they are not required to solve the problem.

Excel Notes

- In all our Excel layouts, for clarity, the changing variable cells (decision variables) are shaded yellow.
- In all our Excel layouts, we show the decision variable names (such as T and C) used in the written formulation of the model (see cells B3 and C3). These names have no role or relevance in using Solver to solve the model and can therefore be ignored. We show these decision variable names in our models in this textbook so that the equivalence of the written formulation and the Excel layout is clear.

SCREENSHOT 2-1A Formula View of the Excel Layout for Flair Furniture

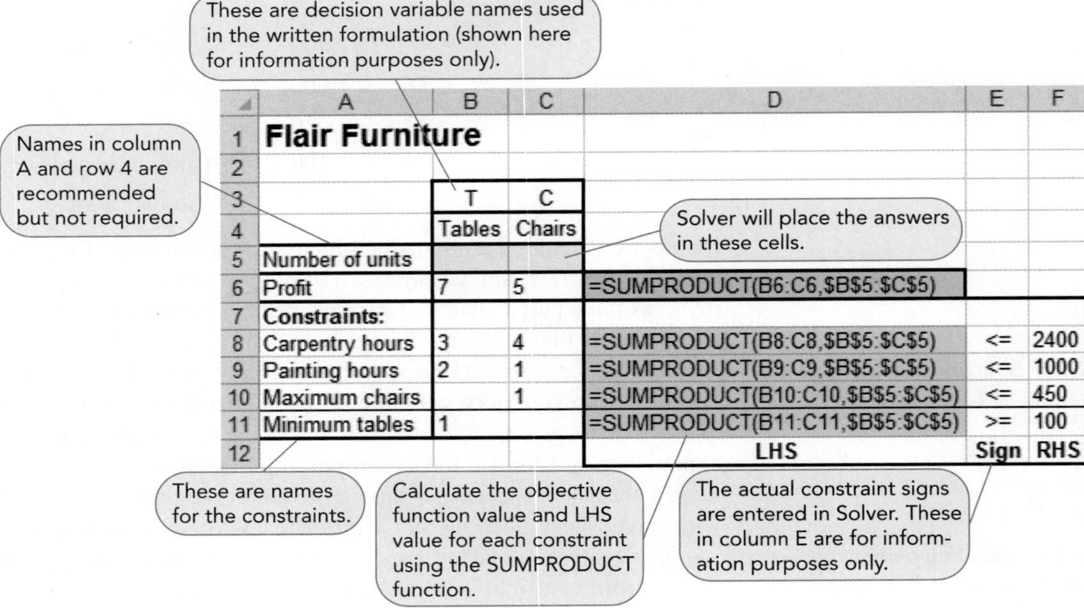
These are decision variable names used in the written formulation (shown here for information purposes only).
Names in column A and row 4 are recommended but not required.
Solver will place the answers in these cells.
These are names for the constraints.
Calculate the objective function value and LHS value for each constraint using the SUMPRODUCT function.
The actual constraint signs are entered in Solver. These in column E are for information purposes only.

	A	B	C	D	E	F
1	Flair Furniture					
2						
3		T	C			
4		Tables	Chairs			
5	Number of units					
6	Profit	7	5	=SUMPRODUCT(B6:C6,$B$5:$C$5)		
7	Constraints:					
8	Carpentry hours	3	4	=SUMPRODUCT(B8:C8,$B$5:$C$5)	<=	2400
9	Painting hours	2	1	=SUMPRODUCT(B9:C9,$B$5:$C$5)	<=	1000
10	Maximum chairs		1	=SUMPRODUCT(B10:C10,$B$5:$C$5)	<=	450
11	Minimum tables	1		=SUMPRODUCT(B11:C11,$B$5:$C$5)	>=	100
12				LHS	Sign	RHS

The Objective Cell

The **objective cell** *contains the formula for the objective function.*

We can now set up the objective function, which Solver refers to as the **objective cell**. We select any cell in the spreadsheet (other than the cells allocated to the decision variables). In that cell, we enter the formula for the objective function, referring to the two decision variables by their cell references (B5 and C5 in this case). In Screenshot 2-1A, we use cell D6 to represent the objective function. Although we could use the unit profit contribution values ($7 per table and $5 per chair) directly in the formula, it is preferable to make the $7 and $5 entries in some cells in the spreadsheet and refer to them by their cell references in the formula in cell D6. This is a more elegant way of setting up the problem and is especially useful if subsequent changes in parameter values are necessary.

In Screenshot 2-1A, we have entered the 7 and 5 in cells B6 and C6, respectively. The formula in cell D6 can therefore be written as

$$=B6*B5+C6*C5$$

The = at the start of the equation lets Excel know that the entry is a formula. This equation corresponds exactly to the objective function of the Flair Furniture problem. If we had left cells B5 and C5 blank, the result of this formula would initially be shown as 0. As with cells B5 and C5, we can format the objective cell (D6) in any manner. For example, because D6 denotes the profit, in dollars, earned by Flair Furniture, we can format it to show the result as a dollar value.

Excel's SUMPRODUCT function makes it easy to enter even long expressions.

If there are several decision variables in a problem, however, formulas can become somewhat long, and typing them can become quite cumbersome. In such cases, you can use Excel's SUMPRODUCT function to express the equation efficiently. The syntax for the SUMPRODUCT function requires specifying two cell ranges of equal size, separated by a comma.[5] One of the ranges defines the cells containing the profit contributions (cells B6:C6), and the other defines the cells containing the decision variables (cells B5:C5). The SUMPRODUCT function computes the products of the first entries in each range, second entries in each range, and so on. It then sums these products.

Based on the preceding discussion, as shown in Screenshot 2-1A, the objective function for Flair Furniture can be expressed as

$$=SUMPRODUCT(B6:C6,\$B\$5:\$C\$5)$$

[5] The SUMPRODUCT function can also be used with more than two cell ranges. See Excel's help feature for more details on this function.

Note that this is equivalent to =B6*B5+C6*C5. Also, the use of the $ symbol while specifying the cell references (in the second cell range) keeps those cell references fixed in the formula when we copy this cell to other cells. This is especially convenient because, as we show next, the formula for each constraint in the model also follows the same structure as the objective function.

Excel Note

In each of our Excel layouts, for clarity, the objective cell (objective function) has been shaded green.

Constraints

Constraints in Solver include three entries: LHS, RHS, and sign.

We must now set up each constraint in the problem. To achieve this, let us first separate each constraint into three parts: (1) a *left-hand-side (LHS)* part consisting of every term to the left of the equality or inequality sign, (2) a *right-hand-side (RHS)* part consisting of all terms to the right of the equality or inequality sign, and the (3) equality or inequality sign itself. The RHS in most cases may just be a fixed number—that is, a constant.

CREATING CELLS FOR CONSTRAINT LHS VALUES We now select a unique cell for each **constraint LHS** in the formulation (one for each constraint) and type in the relevant formula for that constraint. As with the objective function, we refer to the decision variables by their cell references. In Screenshot 2-1A, we use cell D8 to represent the LHS of the carpentry time constraint. We have entered the coefficients (i.e., 3 and 4) on the LHS of this constraint in cells B8 and C8, respectively. Then, either of the following formulas would be appropriate in cell D8:

=B8*B5+C8*C5

or

=SUMPRODUCT(B8:C8,$B$5:$C$5)

Here again, the SUMPRODUCT function makes the formula compact in situations in which the LHS has many terms. Note the similarity between the objective function formula in cell D6 [=SUMPRODUCT(B6:C6,$B$5:$C$5)] and the LHS formula for the carpentry constraint in cell D8 [=SUMPRODUCT(B8:C8,$B$5:$C$5)]. In fact, because we have anchored the cell references for the decision variables (B5 and C5) using the $ symbol in cell D6, we can simply copy the formula in cell D6 to cell D8.

Formula in cell D9: =SUMPRODUCT(B9:C9, $B$5:$C$5

The LHS formula for the painting hours constraint (cell D9), chairs production limit constraint (cell D10), and tables minimum production constraint (cell D11) can similarly be copied from cell D6. As you have probably recognized by now, the LHS cell for virtually every constraint in an LP formulation can be created in this fashion.

Excel Note

In each of our Excel layouts, for clarity, cells denoting LHS formulas of constraints have been shaded blue.

In Solver, the RHS of a constraint can also include a formula.

CREATING CELLS FOR CONSTRAINT RHS VALUES When all the LHS formulas have been set up, we can pick unique cells for each **constraint RHS** in the formulation. Although the Flair Furniture problem has only constants (2,400, 1,000, 450, and 100, respectively) for the four constraints, it is perfectly valid in Solver for the RHS to also have a formula like the LHS. In Screenshot 2-1A, we show the four RHS values in cells F8:F11.

The actual sign for each constraint is entered directly in Solver.

CONSTRAINT TYPE In Screenshot 2-1A, we also show the sign ($\leq$, $\geq$, or $=$) of each constraint between the LHS and RHS cells for that constraint (see cells E8:E11). Although this makes each constraint easier to understand, note that the inclusion of these signs here is for information purposes only. As we show next, the actual sign for each constraint is entered directly in Solver.

NONNEGATIVITY CONSTRAINTS It is not necessary to specify the nonnegativity constraints (i.e., $T \geq 0$ and $C \geq 0$) in the model using the previous procedure. As we will see shortly, there is a simple option available in Solver to automatically enforce these constraints.

Entering Information in Solver

After all the constraints have been set up, we invoke the Solver Parameters window in Excel by clicking the Data tab and then selecting Solver in the Analysis group, as shown in Screenshot 2-1B(a).[6] The Solver Parameters window is shown in Screenshot 2-1B(b).

The default in Solver is to maximize the objective cell.

SPECIFYING THE OBJECTIVE CELL We first enter the relevant cell reference (i.e., cell D6) in the Set Objective box. The default in Solver is to maximize the objective value. (Note that the Max option is already selected.) For a minimization problem, we must click the Min option to specify that the objective function should be minimized. The third option (Value Of) allows

SCREENSHOT 2-1B
Solver Parameters Window for Flair Furniture

(a)

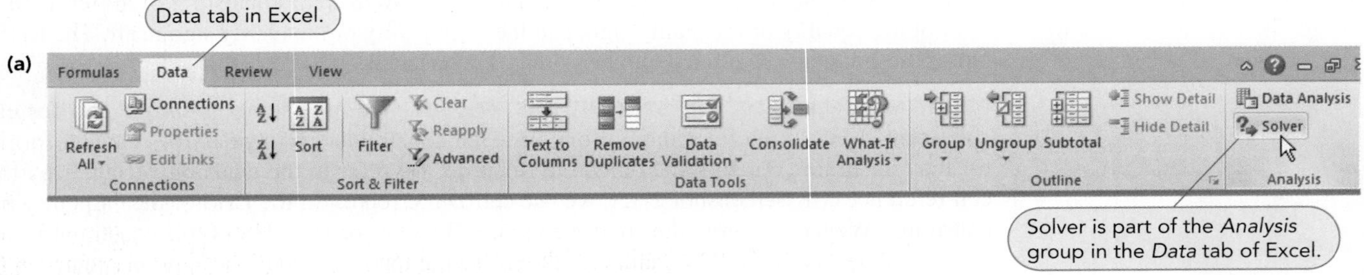

(b)

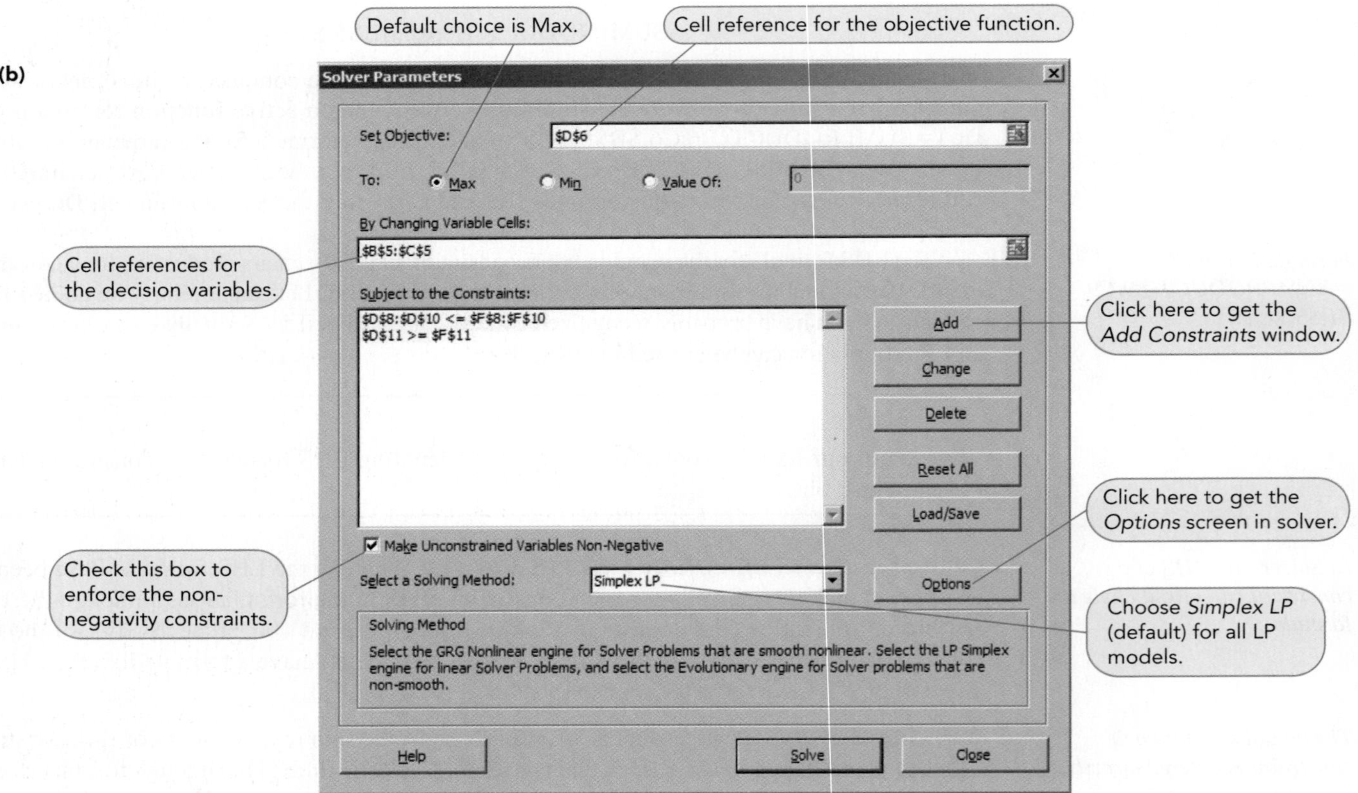

[6] If you do not see Solver in the Analysis group within the Data tab in Excel, refer to Appendix B, section B.6, *Installing and Enabling Excel Add-Ins*, for instructions on how to fix this problem. Alternatively, type *Solver* in Excel's help feature and select Load the Solver Add-in for detailed instructions.

us to specify a value that we want the objective cell to achieve, rather than obtain the optimal solution. (We do not use this option in our study of LP and other mathematical programming models.)

Changing variable cells can be entered as a block or as individual cell references separated by commas.

SPECIFYING THE CHANGING VARIABLE CELLS We now move the cursor to the box labeled By Changing Variable Cells. We enter the cell references for the decision variables in this box. If the cell references are next to each other, we can simply enter them as one block. For example, we could enter B5:C5 for Flair Furniture's problem. (If we use the mouse or keyboard to highlight and select cells B5 and C5, Excel automatically puts in the $ anchors, as shown in Screenshot 2-1B.) If the cells are not contiguous (i.e., not next to each other), we can enter the changing variable cells by placing a comma between noncontiguous cells (or blocks of cells). So, for example, we could enter B5,C5 in the By Changing Variable Cells window for this specific problem.

The Add Constraint window is used to enter constraints.

SPECIFYING THE CONSTRAINTS Next, we move to the box labeled Subject to the Constraints and click the Add button to enter the relevant cell references for the LHS and RHS of each constraint. The Add Constraint window (shown in Screenshot 2-1C) has a box titled Cell Reference in which we enter the cell reference of the constraint's LHS, a drop-down menu in which we specify the constraint's sign, and a second box titled Constraint in which we enter the cell reference of the constraint's RHS. The drop-down menu has six choices: $\leq$, $\geq$, $=$, Int (for integer), Bin (for binary), and dif (for all different). (We discuss the last three choices in Chapter 6.)

We can either add constraints one at a time or add blocks of constraints that have the same sign ($\leq$, $\geq$, or $=$) at the same time. For instance, we could first add the carpentry constraint by entering D8 in the LHS input box, entering F8 in the RHS input box, and selecting the $\leq$ sign from the drop-down menu. As noted earlier, the $\leq$ sign shown in cell E8 is not relevant in Solver, and we must enter the sign of each constraint by using the Add Constraint window. We can now add the painting constraint by entering D9 and F9 in the LHS and RHS input boxes, respectively. Next, we can add the chairs limit constraint by entering D10 and F10 in the LHS and RHS input boxes, respectively. Finally, we can add the minimum table production constraint by entering D11 and F11 in the LHS and RHS input boxes, respectively. Note that in this constraint's case, we should select the $\geq$ sign from the drop-down menu.

Constraints with the same sign can be entered as a block.

Alternatively, because the first three constraints have the same sign ($\leq$), we can input cells D8 to D10 in the LHS input box (i.e., enter D8:D10) and correspondingly enter F8:F10 in the RHS input box. We select $\leq$ as the sign between these LHS and RHS entries. Solver interprets this as taking each entry in the LHS input box and setting it $\leq$ to the corresponding entry in the RHS input box (i.e., D8 $\leq$ F8, D9 $\leq$ F9, and D10 $\leq$ F10).

Using the latter procedure, note that it is possible to have just three entries in the constraints window: one for all the $\leq$ constraints in the model, one for all the $\geq$ constraints in the model, and one for all the $=$ constraints in the model. This, of course, requires that the spreadsheet layout be such that the LHS and RHS cells for all constraints that have the same sign are in

SCREENSHOT 2-1C Solver Add Constraint Window

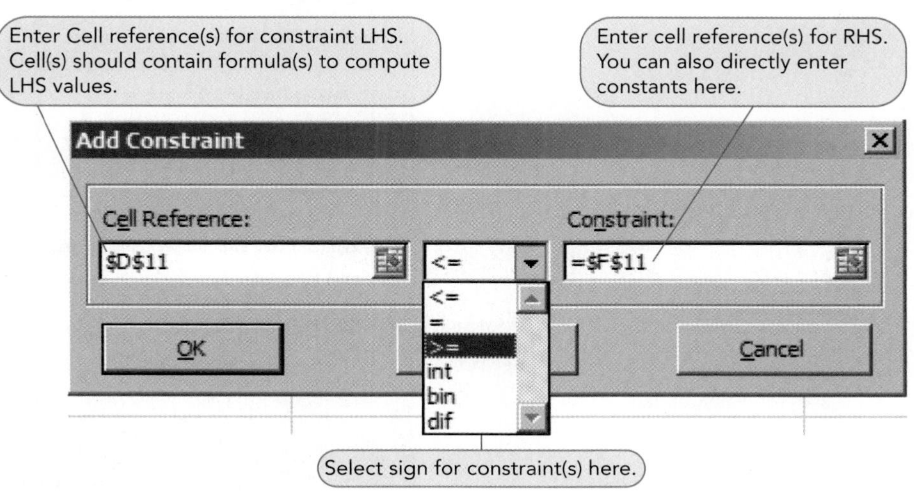

contiguous blocks, as in Screenshot 2-1A. However, as we demonstrate in several examples in Chapter 3, this is quite easy to do.

At any point during or after the constraint input process, we can use the Change or Delete buttons in the Subject to the Constraints box to modify one or more constraints, as necessary. It is important to note that we *cannot* enter the formula for the objective function and the LHS and/or RHS of constraints from within the Solver Parameters window. The formulas must be created in appropriate cells in the spreadsheet before using the Solver Parameters window. Although it is possible to directly enter constants (2,400, 1,000, 450, and 100 in our model) in the RHS input box while adding constraints, it is preferable to make the RHS also a cell reference (F8, F9, F10, and F11 in our model).

Check the **Make Unconstrained Variables Non-Negative** *box in Solver to enforce the nonnegativity constraints.*

SPECIFYING THE NONNEGATIVITY CONSTRAINTS Directly below the box labeled Subject to the Constraints (see Screenshot 2-1B), there is a box labeled Make Unconstrained Variables Non-Negative. This box is checked by default in Excel; for most LP models, it should remain this way. The checked box automatically enforces the nonnegativity constraint for all the decision variables in the model.

Select **Simplex LP** *as the solving method in Solver.*

SOLVING METHOD Next, we move to the box labeled Select a Solving Method. To solve LP problems, we should leave this option at its default setting of Simplex LP. Selecting this setting directs Solver to solve LP models efficiently and provide a detailed Sensitivity Report, which we cover in Chapter 4. Clicking the down arrow in this box reveals two other method choices: GRG Nonlinear and Evolutionary. We will discuss the GRG Nonlinear procedure in Chapter 6.

SOLVER OPTIONS After all constraints have been entered, we are ready to solve the model. However, before clicking the Solve button on the Solver Parameters window, we click the Options button to open the Solver Options window (shown in Screenshot 2-1D) and focus on the choices available in the All Methods tab. (The options in the GRG Nonlinear and Evolutionary tabs are not relevant for LP models.) For solving most LP problems, we do not have to change

SCREENSHOT 2-1D
Solver Options Window

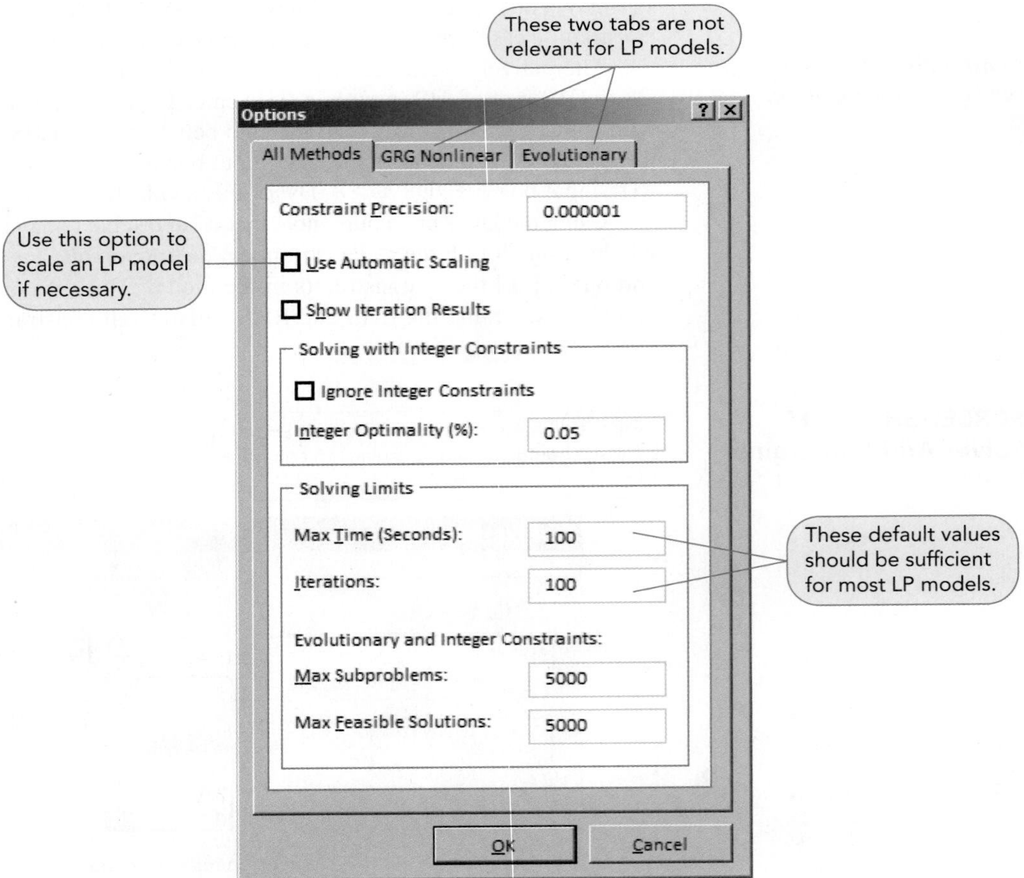

any of the default parameters for these options. The defaults of 100 seconds and 100 iterations should be adequate. The options related to Evolutionary and Integer Constraints are not relevant for LP models. To see details of each iteration taken by Solver to go from the initial solution to the optimal solution (if one exists), we can check the Show Iterations Results box.

It is a good idea to scale coefficient values in LP models.

With regard to the option called Use Automatic Scaling (see Screenshot 2-1D), it is a good idea in practice to scale problems in which values of the objective function coefficients and constraint coefficients of different constraints differ by several orders of magnitude. For instance, a problem in which some coefficients are in millions while others have fractional values would be considered a poorly scaled model. Due to the effects of a computer's finite precision arithmetic, such poorly scaled models could cause difficulty for Solver, leading to fairly large rounding errors. Checking the automatic scaling box directs Solver to scale models that it detects as poorly scaled and possibly avoid such rounding problems.

File: 2-1.xls, sheet: 2-1E

SOLVING THE MODEL When the Solve button is clicked, Solver executes the model and displays the results, as shown in Screenshot 2-1E. Before looking at the results, it is important to read the message in the Solver Results window to verify that Solver found an optimal solution. In some cases, the window indicates that Solver is unable to find an optimal solution (e.g., when the formulation is infeasible or the solution space is unbounded). Table 2.2 shows several different Solver messages that could result when an LP model is solved, the meaning of each message, and a possible cause for each message.

Solver provides options to obtain different reports.

The Solver Results window also indicates that there are three reports available: Answer, Sensitivity, and Limits. We discuss the Answer Report in the next section and the Sensitivity Report in Chapter 4. The Limits Report is not useful for our discussion here, and we therefore ignore it. Note that in order to get these reports, we must select them by clicking the relevant report names to highlight them before clicking OK on the Solver Results window.

SCREENSHOT 2-1E
Excel Layout and Solver Solution for Flair Furniture (Solver Results Window Also Shown)

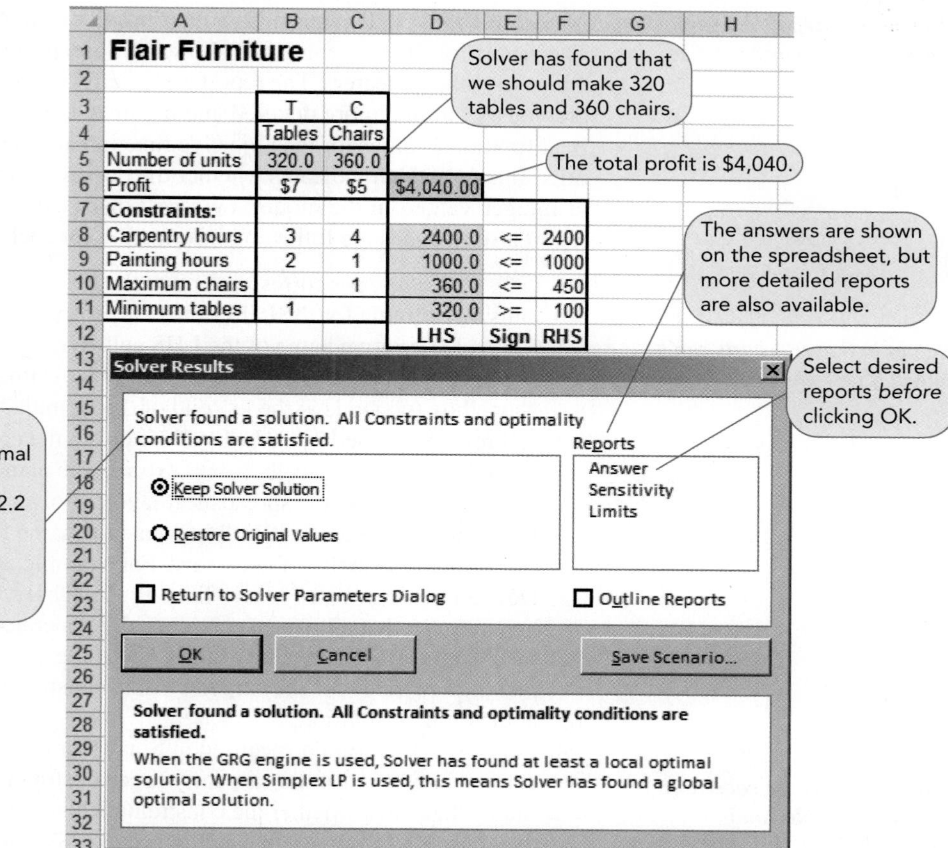

TABLE 2.2
Possible Messages in the Solver Results Window

MESSAGE	MEANING	POSSIBLE CAUSE
Solver found a solution. All Constraints and optimality conditions are satisfied.	Ideal message!	*Note:* This does *not* mean the formulation and/or solution is correct. It just means there are no syntax errors in the Excel formulas and Solver entries.
Solver could not find a feasible solution.	There is no feasible region.	Incorrect entries in LHS formulas, signs, and/or RHS values of constraints.
The Objective Cell values do not converge.	Unbounded solution.	Incorrect entries in LHS formulas, signs, and/or RHS values of constraints.
Solver encountered an error value in the Objective Cell or a Constraint cell.	Formula error in the objective cell or a constraint cell. At least one of the cells in the model becomes an error value when Solver tries different values for the changing variable cells.	Most common cause is division by zero in some cell.
The linearity conditions required by this LP Solver are not satisfied.	The Simplex LP method has been specified in Solver to solve this model, but one or more formulas in the model are not linear.	Multiplication or division involving two or more variables in some cell. *Note:* Solver sometimes gives this error message even when the formulas are linear. This occurs especially when both the LHS and RHS of a constraint have formulas. In such cases, we should manipulate the constraint algebraically to make the RHS a constant.

Cells B5 and C5 show the optimal quantities of tables and chairs to make, respectively, and cell D6 shows the optimal profit. Cells D8 to D11 show the LHS values of the four constraints. For example, cell D8 shows the number of carpentry hours used.

The Answer Report presents the results in a more detailed manner.

ANSWER REPORT If requested, Solver provides the **Answer Report** in a separate worksheet. The report for Flair's problem is shown in Screenshot 2-1F. (We have added grid lines to this report to make it clearer.) The report essentially provides the same information as that discussed previously but in a more detailed and organized manner. In addition to showing the initial and final (optimal) values for the objective function and each decision variable, it includes a column titled Integer, which indicates whether the decision variable was specified as continuous valued or integer valued in the model. (We will discuss integer valued variables in Chapter 6). The report also includes the following information for each constraint in the model:

File: 2-1.xls, sheet: 2-1F

Names in Solver reports can be edited, if desired.

1. Cell. Cell reference corresponding to the LHS of the constraint. For example, cell D8 contains the formula for the LHS of the carpentry constraint.
2. Name. Descriptive name of the LHS cell. We can use Excel's naming feature to define a descriptive name for any cell (or cell range) simply by typing the desired name in the Name box (which is at the left end of the formula bar in any Excel worksheet and has the cell reference listed by default). If we do so, the cell name is reported in this column. If no name is defined for a cell, Solver extracts the name shown in this column from the information provided in the spreadsheet layout. Solver simply combines labels (if any) to the left of and above the LHS cell to create the name for that cell. Note that these labels can be overwritten manually, if necessary. For example, the name Profit for the objective cell (cell D6) can be overwritten to say Total Profit. Observe that the Excel layout we have used here ensures that all names automatically generated by Solver are logical.
3. Cell Value. The final value of the LHS of the constraint at the optimal solution. For example, the cell value for the carpentry time constraint indicates that we are using 2,400 hours at the optimal solution.
4. Formula. The formula specified in Solver for the constraint. For example, the formula entered in Solver for the carpentry time constraint is D8 $\leq$ F8.
5. Status. Indicates whether the constraint is binding or nonbinding. *Binding* means that the constraint becomes an equality (i.e., LHS = RHS) at the optimal solution. For a $\leq$

Binding *means the constraint is exactly satisfied and LHS = RHS.*

SCREENSHOT 2-1F
Solver's Answer Report for Flair Furniture

Microsoft Excel 14.0 Answer Report
Worksheet: [2-1.xls]2-1D
Result: Solver found a solution. All Constraints and optimality conditions are satisfied.
Solver Engine
Engine: Simplex LP
Solution Time: 0.015 Seconds.
Iterations: 3 Subproblems: 0
Solver Options
Max Time 100 sec, Iterations 100, Precision 0.000001
Max Subproblems 5000, Max Integer Sols 5000, Integer Tolerance 0.05%, Assume NonNegative

Objective Cell (Max)

Cell	Name	Original Value	Final Value
$D$6	Profit	$0.00	$4,040.00

Variable Cells

Cell	Name	Original Value	Final Value	Integer
$B$5	Number of units Tables	0.0	320.0	Contin
$C$5	Number of units Chairs	0.0	360.0	Contin

Constraints

Cell	Name	Cell Value	Formula	Status	Slack
$D$8	Carpentry hours	2400.0	$D$8<=$F$8	Binding	0.0
$D$9	Painting hours	1000.0	$D$9<=$F$9	Binding	0.0
$D$10	Maximum chairs	360.0	$D$10<=$F$10	Not Binding	90.0
$D$11	Minimum tables	320.0	$D$11>=$F$11	Not Binding	220.0

The initial and final solution values are shown here.

Indicates decision variables are continuous valued in this LP model.

Calculate slack as the difference between the RHS and LHS of a ≤ constraint.

All names can be overwritten if desired.

These are the final values of the constraint LHS.

Calculate surplus as the difference between the LHS and RHS of a ≥ constraint.

constraint, this typically means that all the available amounts of that resource are fully used in the optimal solution. In Flair's case, the carpentry and painting constraints are both binding because we are using all the available hours in either case.

For a ≥ constraint, *binding* typically means we are exactly satisfying the minimum level required by that constraint. In Flair's case, the minimum tables required constraint is nonbinding because we plan to make 320 as against the required minimum of 100.

Slack *typically refers to the amount of unused resource in a ≤ constraint.*

6. Slack. Magnitude (absolute value) of the difference between the RHS and LHS values of the constraint. Obviously, if the constraint is binding, **slack** is zero (because LHS = RHS). For a nonbinding ≤ constraint, slack typically denotes the amount of resource that is left unused at the optimal solution. In Flair's case, we are allowed to make up to 450 chairs but are planning to make only 360. The absolute difference of 90 between the RHS and LHS ($=|450 - 360|$) is the slack in this constraint.

Surplus *typically refers to the amount of oversatisfaction of a ≥ constraint.*

For a nonbinding ≥ constraint, we call this term **surplus** (even though Solver refers to this difference in all cases as slack). A surplus typically denotes the extent to which the ≥ constraint is oversatisfied at the optimal solution. In Flair's case, we are planning to make 320 tables even though we are required to make only 100. The absolute difference of 220 between the RHS and LHS ($=|100 - 320|$) is the surplus in this constraint.

Using Solver to Solve Flair Furniture Company's Modified Problem

Recall that after solving Flair Furniture's problem using a graphical approach, we added a new constraint specified by the marketing department. Specifically, we needed to ensure that the number of chairs made this month is at least 75 more than the number of tables made. The constraint was expressed as

$$C - T \geq 75$$

File: 2-2.xls

The Excel layout and Solver entries for Flair's modified problem are shown in Screenshot 2-2. Note that the constraint coefficient for T is entered as –1 in cell B12 to reflect the fact that the

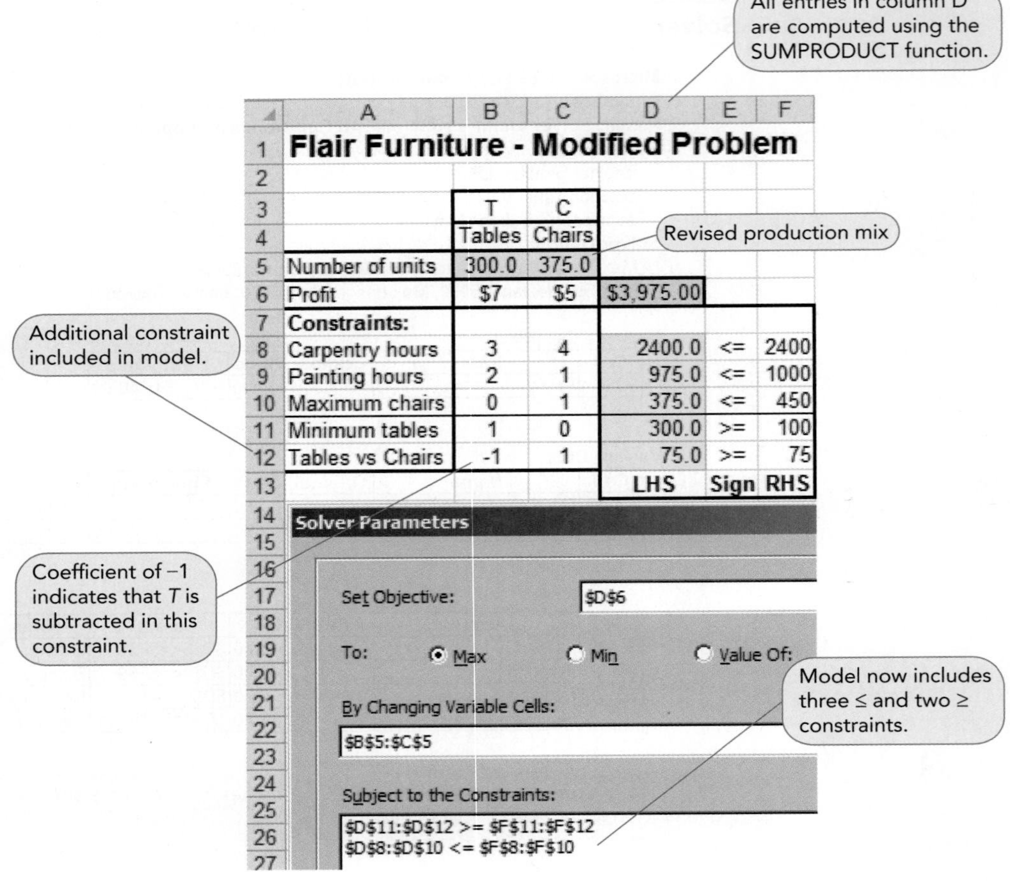

SCREENSHOT 2-2
Excel Layout and Solver Entries for Flair Furniture—Revised Problem

variable T is subtracted in the expression. The formula in cell D12 is the same SUMPRODUCT function used in cells D8:D11. The optimal solution now is to make 300 tables and 375 chairs, for a profit of $3,975, the same solution we obtained graphically in Figure 2.7 on page 33.

Using Solver to Solve the Holiday Meal Turkey Ranch Problem

Now that we have studied how to set up and solve a maximization LP problem using Excel's Solver, let us consider a minimization problem—the Holiday Meal Turkey Ranch example. Recall that the decision variables A and B in this problem denote the number of pounds of brand A feed and brand B feed to use per month, respectively. The LP formulation for this problem is as follows:

$$\text{Minimize cost} = \$0.10A + \$0.15B$$

subject to the constraints

$$\begin{aligned} 5A + 10B &\geq 45 && \text{(protein required)} \\ 4A + 3B &\geq 24 && \text{(vitamin required)} \\ 0.5A &\geq 1.5 && \text{(iron required)} \\ A, B &\geq 0 && \text{(nonnegativity)} \end{aligned}$$

WWW

File: 2-3.xls

The formula view of the Excel layout for the Holiday Meal Turkey Ranch LP problem is shown in Screenshot 2-3A. The solution values and the Solver Parameters window are shown in Screenshot 2-3B. Note that Solver shows the problem as being solved as a Min problem. As with the Flair Furniture example, all problem parameters are entered as entries in different cells of the spreadsheet, and Excel's SUMPRODUCT function is used to compute the objective function as well as the LHS values for all three constraints (corresponding to protein, vitamin, and iron).

SCREENSHOT 2-3A
Formula View of the Excel Layout for Holiday Meal

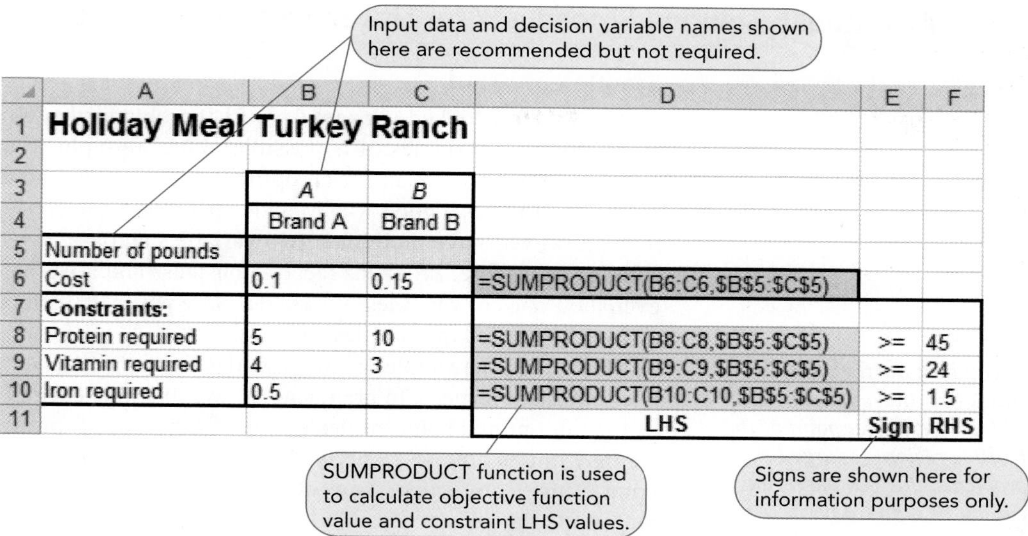

Input data and decision variable names shown here are recommended but not required.
Holiday Meal Turkey Ranch
Use 4.2 pounds of A and 2.4 pounds of B.
A
B
Brand A
Brand B
Number of pounds
Minimum cost is $0.78.
Cost
0.1
0.15
=SUMPRODUCT(B6:C6,$B$5:$C$5)
Constraints:
Protein required
5
10
=SUMPRODUCT(B8:C8,$B$5:$C$5)
>=
45
Vitamin required
4
3
=SUMPRODUCT(B9:C9,$B$5:$C$5)
>=
24
Iron required
0.5
=SUMPRODUCT(B10:C10,$B$5:$C$5)
>=
1.5
LHS
Sign
RHS
SUMPRODUCT function is used to calculate objective function value and constraint LHS values.
Signs are shown here for information purposes only.

SCREENSHOT 2-3B
Excel Layout and Solver Entries for Holiday Meal

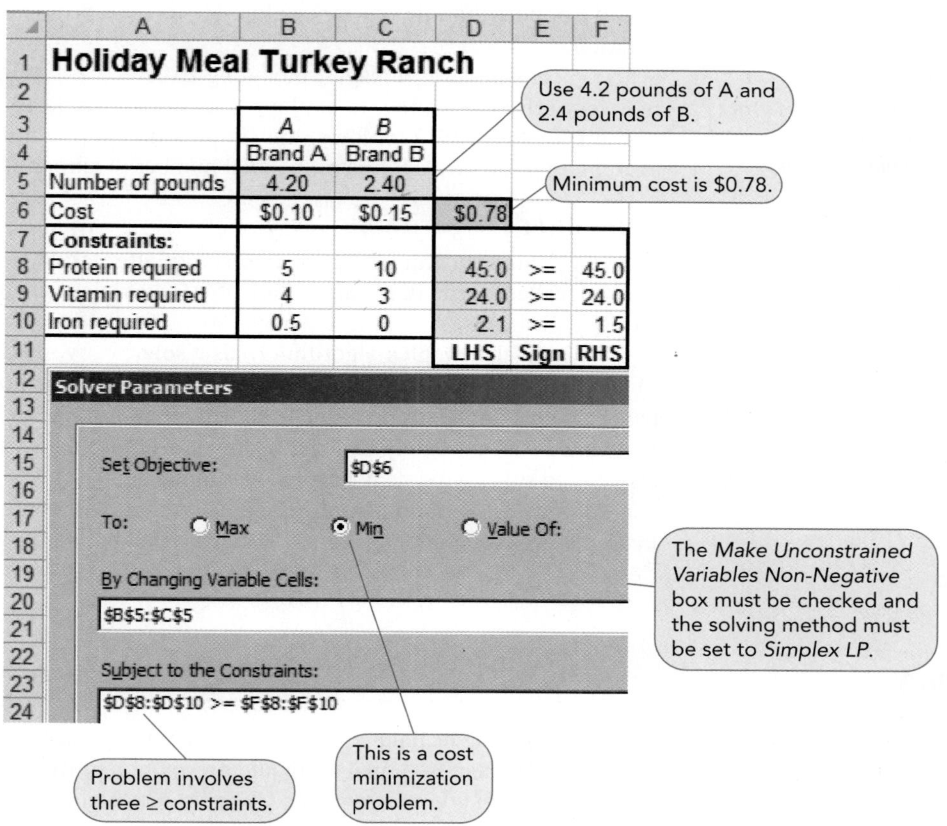

As expected, the optimal solution is the same as the one we obtained using the graphical approach. Holiday Meal should use 4.20 pounds of brand A feed and 2.40 pounds of brand B feed, at a cost of $0.78 per turkey per month. The protein and vitamin constraints are binding at the optimal solution. However, we are providing 2.1 units of iron per turkey per month even though we are required to provide only 1.5 units (i.e., an oversatisfaction, or *surplus*, of 0.6 units).

2.8 Algorithmic Solution Procedures for Linear Programming Problems

Simplex Method

So far, we have looked at examples of LP problems that contain only two decision variables. With only two variables, it is possible to use a graphical approach. We plotted the feasible region and then searched for an optimal corner point and corresponding profit or cost. This approach provides a good way to understand the basic concepts of LP. Most real-life LP problems, however, have more than two variables and are thus too large for the simple graphical solution procedure. Problems faced in business and government can have dozens, hundreds, or even thousands of variables. We need a more powerful method than graphing; for this we turn to a procedure called the **simplex method**.

Recall that the theory of LP states that the optimal solution will lie at a corner point of the feasible region. In large LP problems, the feasible region cannot be graphed because it has many dimensions, but the concept is the same.

How does the simplex method work? The concept is simple and similar to graphical LP in one important respect: In graphical LP, we examine each of the corner points; LP theory tells us that an optimal solution lies at one of them. In LP problems containing several variables, we may not be able to graph the feasible region, but an optimal solution still lies at a corner point of the many-sided, many-dimensional figure (called an n-dimensional polyhedron) that represents the area of feasible solutions. The simplex method examines the corner points in a systematic fashion, using basic algebraic concepts. It does so as an **iterative process**—that is, repeating the same set of steps time after time until an optimal solution is reached. Each iteration of the simplex method brings a value for the objective function that is no worse (and usually better) than the current value. Hence, we progressively move closer to an optimal solution.

The **simplex method** *systematically examines corner points, using algebraic steps, until an optimal solution is found.*

In most software packages, including Excel's Solver, the simplex method has been coded in a very efficient manner to exploit the computational capabilities of modern computers. As a result, for most LP problems, the simplex method identifies an optimal corner point after examining just a tiny fraction of the total number of corner points in the feasible region.

Karmarkar's Algorithm

Karmarkar's method follows a path of points inside the feasible region.

In 1984, Narendra Karmarkar developed an alternative to the simplex algorithm. The new method, called Karmarkar's algorithm, often takes significantly less computer time to solve very large LP problems.[7]

Whereas the simplex algorithm finds a solution by moving from one adjacent corner point to the next, following the outside edges of the feasible region, Karmarkar's method follows a path of points on the inside of the feasible region. Karmarkar's method is also unique in its ability to handle an extremely large number of constraints and variables, thereby giving LP users the capacity to solve previously unsolvable problems.

Although it is likely that the simplex method will continue to be used for many LP problems, a newer generation of LP software has been built around Karmarkar's algorithm.

Summary

In this chapter we introduce a mathematical modeling technique called linear programming (LP). Analysts use LP models to find an optimal solution to problems that have a series of constraints binding the objective value. We discuss how to formulate LP models and then show how models with only two decision variables can be solved graphically. The graphical solution approach of this chapter provides a conceptual basis for tackling larger, more complex real-life problems. However, solving LP models that have numerous decision variables and constraints requires a solution procedure such as the simplex algorithm.

The simplex algorithm is embedded in Excel's Solver add-in. We describe how LP models can be set up on Excel and solved using Solver. The structured approach presented in this chapter for setting up and solving LP problems with just two variables can be easily adapted to problems of larger size. We address several such problems in Chapter 3.

[7] For details, see N. Karmarkar. "A New Polynomial Time Algorithm for Linear Programming," *Combinatorica* 4, 4 (1984): 373–395; or J. N. Hooker. "Karmarkar's Linear Programming Algorithm," *Interfaces* 16, 4 (July–August 1986): 75–90.

Glossary

Alternate Optimal Solution A situation in which more than one optimal solution is possible. It arises when the angle or slope of the objective function is the same as the slope of the constraint.

Answer Report A report created by Solver when it solves an LP model. This report presents the optimal solution in a detailed manner.

Changing Variable Cells Cells that represent the decision variables in Solver.

Constraint A restriction (stated in the form of an inequality or an equation) that inhibits (or binds) the value that can be achieved by the objective function.

Constraint LHS The cell that contains the formula for the left-hand side of a constraint in Solver. There is one such cell for each constraint in a problem.

Constraint RHS The cell that contains the value (or formula) for the right-hand side of a constraint in Solver. There is one such cell for each constraint in a problem.

Corner (or Extreme) Point A point that lies on one of the corners of the feasible region. This means that it falls at the intersection of two constraint lines.

Corner Point Method The method of finding the optimal solution to an LP problem that involves testing the profit or cost level at each corner point of the feasible region. The theory of LP states that the optimal solution must lie at one of the corner points.

Decision Variables The unknown quantities in a problem for which optimal solution values are to be found.

Feasible Region The area that satisfies all of a problem's resource restrictions—that is, the region where all constraints overlap. All possible solutions to the problem lie in the feasible region.

Feasible Solution Any point that lies in the feasible region. Basically, it is any point that satisfies all of the problem's constraints.

Inequality A mathematical expression that contains a greater-than-or-equal-to relation ($\geq$) or a less-than-or-equal-to relation ($\leq$) between the left-hand side and the right-hand side of the expression.

Infeasible Solution Any point that lies outside the feasible region. It violates one or more of the stated constraints.

Infeasibility A condition that arises when there is no solution to an LP problem that satisfies all of the constraints.

Integer Programming A mathematical programming model in which some or all decision variables are restricted only to integer values.

Iterative Process A process (algorithm) that repeats the same steps over and over.

Level (or Iso) Line A straight line that represents all nonnegative combinations of the decision variables for a particular profit (or cost) level.

Linear Programming (LP) A mathematical technique used to help management decide how to make the most effective use of an organization's resources.

Make Unconstrained Variables Non-Negative An option available in Solver that automatically enforces the nonnegativity constraint.

Mathematical Programming The general category of mathematical modeling and solution techniques used to allocate resources while optimizing a measurable goal; LP is one type of programming model.

Nonnegativity Constraints A set of constraints that requires each decision variable to be nonnegative; that is, each decision variable must be greater than or equal to 0.

Objective Cell The cell that contains the formula for the objective function in Solver.

Objective Function A mathematical statement of the goal of an organization, stated as an intent to maximize or minimize some important quantity, such as profit or cost.

Product Mix Problem A common LP problem that involves a decision about which products a firm should produce, given that it faces limited resources.

Redundant Constraint A constraint that does not affect the feasible solution region.

Simplex Method An iterative procedure for solving LP problems.

Simplex LP An option available in Solver that forces it to solve the model as a linear program by using the simplex procedure.

Simultaneous Equation Method The algebraic means of solving for the intersection point of two or more linear constraint equations.

Slack The difference between the right-hand side and left-hand side of a $\leq$ constraint. Slack typically represents the unused resource.

Solver An Excel add-in that allows LP problems to be set up and solved in Excel.

SUMPRODUCT An Excel function that allows users to easily model formulas for the objective function and constraints while setting up a linear programming model in Excel.

Surplus The difference between the left-hand side and right-hand side of a $\geq$ constraint. Surplus typically represents the level of oversatisfaction of a requirement.

Unbounded Solution A condition that exists when the objective value can be made infinitely large (in a maximization problem) or small (in a minimization problem) without violating any of the problem's constraints.

Solved Problems

Solved Problem 2-1

Solve the following LP model graphically and then by using Excel:

$$\text{Maximize profit} = \$30X + \$40Y$$

subject to the constraints

$$\begin{aligned} 4X + 2Y &\leq 16 \\ Y &\leq 2 \\ 2X - Y &\geq 2 \\ X, Y &\geq 0 \end{aligned}$$

Solution

Figure 2.14 shows the feasible region as well as a level profit line for a profit value of \$60. Note that the third constraint ($2X - Y \geq 2$) has a positive slope. As usual, to find the optimal corner point, we need to move the level profit line in the direction of increased profit—that is, up and to the right. Doing so indicates that corner point Ⓒ yields the highest profit. The values at this point are calculated to be $X = 3$ and $Y = 2$, yielding an optimal profit of \$170.

File: 2-4.xls

The Excel layout and Solver entries for this problem are shown in Screenshot 2-4. As expected, the optimal solution is the same as the one we found by using the graphical approach ($X = 3$, $Y = 2$, profit $= \$170$).

FIGURE 2.14
Graph for Solved Problem 2-1

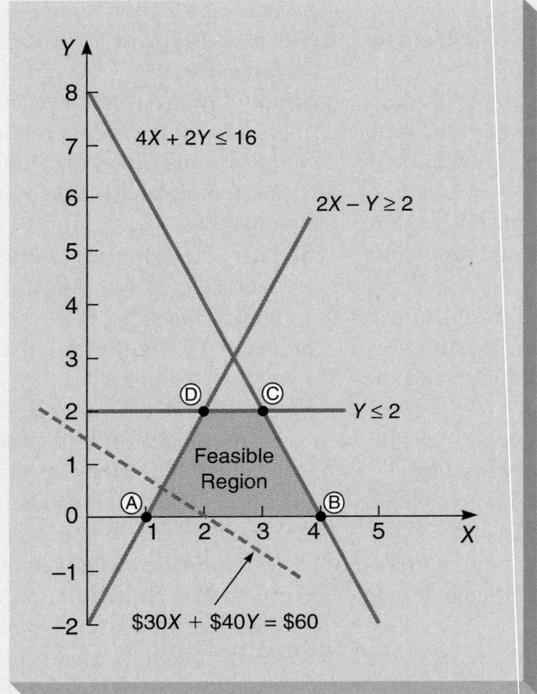

SCREENSHOT 2-4
Excel Layout and Solver Entries for Solved Problem 2-1

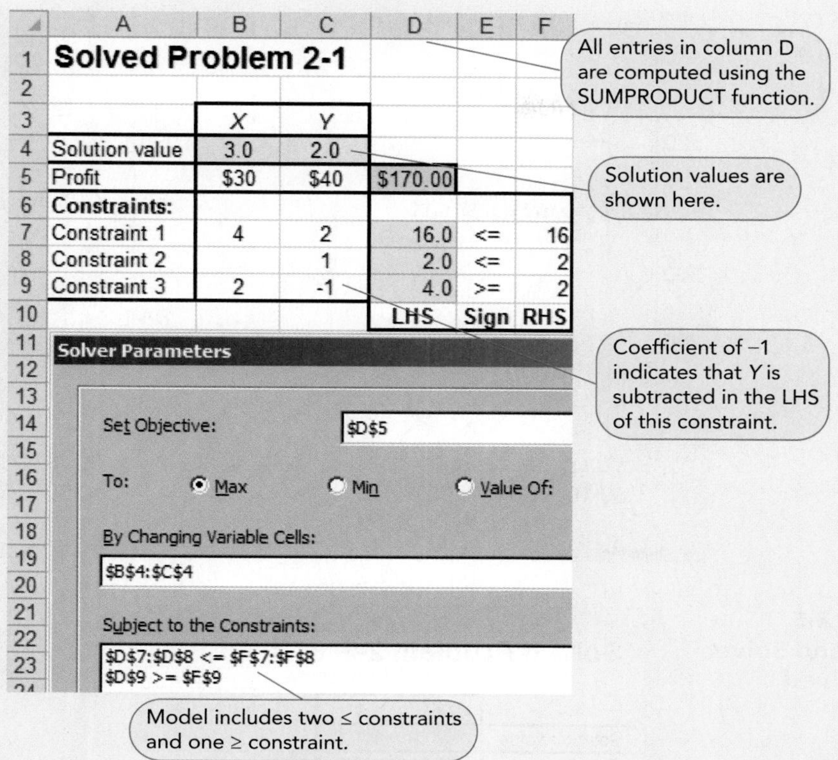

Solved Problem 2-2

Solve the following LP formulation graphically and then by using Excel:

$$\text{Minimize cost} = \$24X + \$28Y$$

subject to the constraints

$$\begin{aligned} 5X + 4Y &\leq 2{,}000 \\ X + Y &\geq 300 \\ X &\geq 80 \\ Y &\geq 100 \\ X, Y &\geq 0 \end{aligned}$$

Solution

Figure 2.15 shows a graph of the feasible region along with a level line for a cost value of \$10,000. The arrows on the constraints indicate the direction of feasibility for each constraint. To find the optimal corner point, we need to move the cost line in the direction of lower cost—that is, down and to the left. The last point where a level cost line touches the feasible region as it moves toward the origin is corner point Ⓓ. Thus Ⓓ, which represents $X = 200$, $Y = 100$, and a cost of \$7,600, is the optimal solution.

File: 2-5.xls

The Excel layout and Solver entries for this problem are shown in Screenshot 2-5. As expected, we get the same optimal solution as we do by using the graphical approach ($X = 200$, $Y = 100$, cost $= \$7{,}600$).

FIGURE 2.15
Graphs for Solved Problem 2-2

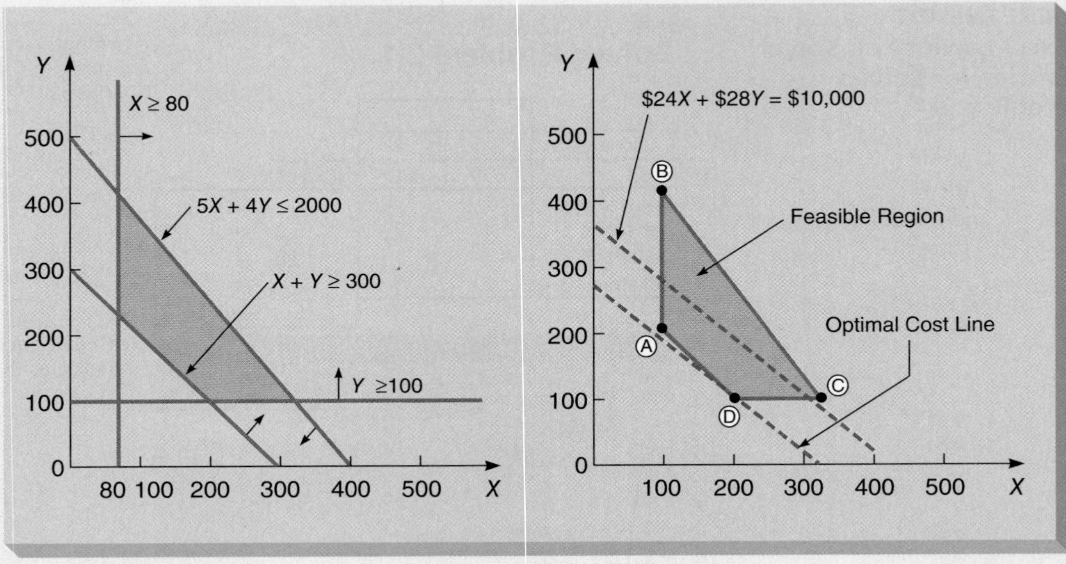

SCREENSHOT 2-5
Excel Layout and Solver Entries for Solved Problem 2-2

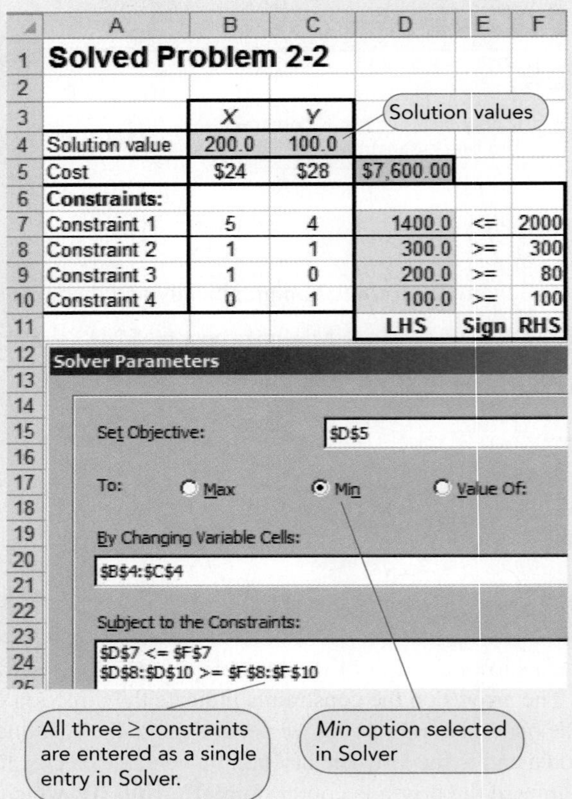

	A	B	C	D	E	F
3		X	Y			
4	Solution value	200.0	100.0			
5	Cost	$24	$28	$7,600.00		
6	Constraints:					
7	Constraint 1	5	4	1400.0	<=	2000
8	Constraint 2	1	1	300.0	>=	300
9	Constraint 3	1	0	200.0	>=	80
10	Constraint 4	0	1	100.0	>=	100
11				LHS	Sign	RHS

Discussion Questions and Problems

Discussion Questions

2-1 It is important to understand the assumptions underlying the use of any quantitative analysis model. What are the assumptions and requirements for an LP model to be formulated and used?

2-2 It has been said that each LP problem that has a feasible region has an infinite number of solutions. Explain.

2-3 Under what condition is it possible for an LP problem to have more than one optimal solution?

2-4 Under what condition is it possible for an LP problem to have an unbounded solution?

2-5 Develop your own set of constraint equations and inequalities and use them to illustrate graphically each of the following conditions:
(a) An unbounded problem
(b) An infeasible problem
(c) A problem containing redundant constraints

2-6 The production manager of a large Cincinnati manufacturing firm once made the statement, "I would like to use LP, but it's a technique that operates under conditions of certainty. My plant doesn't have that certainty; it's a world of uncertainty. So LP can't be used here." Do you think this statement has any merit? Explain why the manager may have said it.

2-7 The mathematical relationships that follow were formulated by an operations research analyst at the Smith-Lawton Chemical Company. Which ones are invalid for use in an LP problem? Why?

$$\text{Maximize profit} = 4X_1 + 3X_1X_2 + 8X_2 + 5X_3$$

subject to the constraints

$$\begin{aligned} 2X_1 + X_2 + 2X_3 &\leq 50 \\ X_1 - 4X_2 &\geq 6 \\ 1.5X_1^2 + 6X_2 + 3X_3 &\geq 21 \\ 19X_2 - 0.33X_3 &= 17 \\ 5X_1 + 4X_2 + 3\sqrt{X_3} &\leq 80 \end{aligned}$$

2-8 How do computers aid in solving LP problems today?

2-9 Explain why knowing how to use Excel to set up and solve LP problems may be beneficial to a manager.

2-10 What are the components of defining a problem in Excel so that it can be solved using Solver?

2-11 How is the slack (or surplus) calculated for a constraint? How is it interpreted?

2-12 What is an unbounded solution? How does Solver indicate that a problem solution is unbounded?

Problems

2-13 Solve the following LP problem by using the graphical procedure and by using Excel:

$$\text{Maximize profit} = 2X + Y$$

subject to the constraints

$$\begin{aligned} 3X + 6Y &\leq 32 \\ 7X + Y &\leq 20 \\ 3X - Y &\geq 3 \\ X, Y &\geq 0 \end{aligned}$$

2-14 Solve the following LP problem by using the graphical procedure and by using Excel:

$$\text{Maximize profit} = 4X + 5Y$$

subject to the constraints

$$\begin{aligned} 5X + 2Y &\leq 40 \\ 3X + 6Y &\leq 30 \\ X &\leq 7 \\ 2X - Y &\geq 3 \\ X, Y &\geq 0 \end{aligned}$$

2-15 Solve the following LP problem by using the graphical procedure and by using Excel:

$$\text{Maximize profit} = 4X + 3Y$$

subject to the constraints

$$\begin{aligned} 2X + 4Y &\leq 72 \\ 3X + 6Y &\geq 27 \\ -3X + 10Y &\geq 0 \\ X, Y &\geq 0 \end{aligned}$$

2-16 Solve the following LP problem by using the graphical procedure and by using Excel:

$$\text{Minimize cost} = 4X + 7Y$$

subject to the constraints

$$\begin{aligned} 2X + 3Y &\geq 60 \\ 4X + 2Y &\geq 80 \\ X &\leq 24 \\ X, Y &\geq 0 \end{aligned}$$

2-17 Solve the following LP problem by using the graphical procedure and by using Excel:

$$\text{Minimize cost} = 3X + 7Y$$

subject to the constraints

$$\begin{aligned} 9X + 3Y &\geq 36 \\ 4X + 5Y &\geq 40 \\ X - Y &\leq 0 \\ 2X &\leq 6 \\ X, Y &\geq 0 \end{aligned}$$

2-18 Solve the following LP problem by using the graphical procedure and by using Excel:

$$\text{Minimize cost} = 4X + 7Y$$

subject to the constraints

$$\begin{aligned} 3X + 6Y &\geq 100 \\ 10X + 2Y &\geq 160 \\ 2Y &\geq 40 \\ 2X &\leq 75 \\ X, Y &\geq 0 \end{aligned}$$

2-19 Solve the following LP problem, which involves three decision variables, by using Excel:

$$\text{Maximize profit} = 20A + 25B + 30C$$

subject to the constraints

$$\begin{aligned} 10A + 15B - 8C &\leq 45 \\ 0.5(A + B + C) &\leq A \\ A &\leq 3B \\ B &\geq C \\ A, B, C &\geq 0 \end{aligned}$$

2-20 Consider the following four LP formulations. Using a graphical approach in each case, determine
(a) which formulation has more than one optimal solution.
(b) which formulation has an unbounded solution.
(c) which formulation is infeasible.
(d) which formulation has a unique optimal solution.

Formulation 1

maximize: $3X + 7Y$

subject to:
$$\begin{aligned} 2X + Y &\leq 6 \\ 4X + 5Y &\leq 20 \\ 2Y &\leq 7 \\ 2X &\geq 7 \\ X, Y &\geq 0 \end{aligned}$$

Formulation 2

maximize: $3X + 6Y$

subject to:
$$\begin{aligned} 7X + 6Y &\leq 42 \\ X + 2Y &\leq 10 \\ X &\leq 4 \\ 2Y &\leq 9 \\ X, Y &\geq 0 \end{aligned}$$

Formulation 3

maximize: $2X + 3Y$

subject to:
$$\begin{aligned} X + 2Y &\geq 12 \\ 8X + 7Y &\geq 56 \\ 2Y &\geq 5 \\ X &\leq 9 \\ X, Y &\geq 0 \end{aligned}$$

Formulation 4

maximize: $3X + 4Y$

subject to:
$$\begin{aligned} 3X + 7Y &\leq 21 \\ 2X + Y &\leq 6 \\ X + Y &\geq 2 \\ 2X &\geq 2 \\ X, Y &\geq 0 \end{aligned}$$

Note: ***Problems 2-21 to 2-36 each involve only two decision variables. Therefore, at the discretion of the instructor, they can be solved using the graphical method, Excel, or both.***

2-21 A decorating store specializing in do-it-your-self home decorators must decide how many information packets to prepare for the summer decorating season. The store managers know they will require at least 400 copies of their popular painting packet. They believe their new information packet on specialty glazing techniques could be a big seller, so they want to prepare at least 300 copies. Their printer has given the following information: The painting packet will require 2.5 minutes of printing time and 1.8 minutes of collating time. The glazing packet will require 2 minutes for each operation. The store has decided to sell the painting packet for \$5.50 a copy and to price the glazing packet at \$4.50. At this time, the printer can devote 36 hours to printing and 30 hours to collation. He will charge the store \$1 for each packet prepared. How many of each packet should the store order to maximize the revenue associated with information packets, and what is the store's expected revenue?

2-22 The Coastal Tea Company sells 60-pound bags of blended tea to restaurants. To be able to label the tea as South Carolina Tea, at least 55% of the tea (by weight) in the bag must be Carolina grown. For quality, Coastal requires that the blend achieve an average aroma rating of at least 1.65. Carolina tea, which costs Coastal \$1.80 per pound, has an aroma rating of 2; other teas likely to be blended with Carolina tea are only rated at 1.2, but they are available for only \$0.60 per pound. Determine the best mix of Carolina and regular tea to achieve Coastal's blending goals, while keeping the costs as low as possible.

2-23 The advertising agency promoting a new product is hoping to get the best possible exposure in terms of the number of people the advertising reaches. The agency will use a two-pronged approach: focused Internet advertising, which is estimated to reach 200,000 people for each burst of advertising, and print media, which is estimated to reach 80,000 people each time an ad is placed. The cost of each Internet burst is \$3,000, as opposed to only \$900 for each print media ad. It has been agreed that the number of print media ads will be no more than five times the number of Internet bursts. The agency hopes to launch at least 5 and no more than 15 Internet bursts of advertising. The advertising budget is \$75,000. Given these constraints, what is the most effective advertising strategy?

2-24 A small motor manufacturer makes two types of motor, models A and B. The assembly process for each is similar in that both require a certain amount of wiring, drilling, and assembly. Each model A takes 3 hours of wiring, 2 hours of drilling, and 1.5 hours of assembly. Each model B must go through 2 hours of wiring, 1 hour of drilling, and 0.5 hours of assembly. During the next production period, 240 hours of wiring time, 210 hours of drilling time, and 120 hours of assembly time are available. Each model A sold yields a profit of \$22. Each model B can be sold for a \$15 profit. Assuming that all motors that are assembled can be sold, find the best combination of motors to yield the highest profit.

2-25 The manufacturer in Problem 2-24 now has a standing order of 24 model A motors for each production period. Resolve Problem 2-24 to include this additional constraint.

2-26 A furniture cabinet maker produces two types of cabinets that house and hide plasma televisions. The Mission-style cabinet requires \$340 in materials and 15 labor hours to produce, and it yields a profit of \$910 per cabinet. The Rustic-style cabinet requires \$430 in materials and 20 hours to produce, and it yields a profit of \$1,200. The firm has a budget of \$30,000 to spend on materials. To ensure full employment, the firm wishes to plan to maximize its profit but at the same time to keep all 30 workers fully employed, so all 1,200 available labor hours available must be used. What is the best combination of furniture cabinets to be made?

2-27 Members of a book club have decided, after reading an investment book, to begin investing in the stock market. They would like to achieve the following: Their investment must grow by at least $6,000 in the long term (over three years) and at least $900 in the short term, and they must earn a dividend of at least $300 per year. They are consulting with a stock broker, who has narrowed their search to two stocks: Carolina Solar Power and South West Steel. The data on each stock, per $1 invested, are as follows:

	CAROLINA SOLAR POWER	SOUTH WEST STEEL
Short-term appreciation	$0.46	$0.26
Long-term appreciation	$1.72	$1.93
Dividend income	9%	13%

Assuming that these data are indicative of what will happen to these stocks over the next three years, what is the smallest investment, in dollars, that the members would have to make in one or both of these two stocks to meet their investment goals?

2-28 Treetops Hammocks produces lightweight nylon hammocks designed for campers, scouts, and hikers. The hammocks come in two styles: double and single. The double hammocks sell for $225 each. They incur a direct labor cost of $101.25 and a production cost of $38.75, and they are packed with hanging apparatus and storage bags, which cost $20. The single hammocks sell for $175 each. Their direct labor costs are $70 and production costs are $30, and they too are packed with the same hanging apparatus and storage bags, which cost $20. Each double hammock uses 3.2 hours of production time; each single hammock uses 2.4 hours of production time. Treetops plans for no more than 960 labor hours per production cycle. Treetops wants to maximize its profit while making no more than 200 single hammocks and no more than 400 total hammocks per production cycle.

(a) How many of each hammock should Treetops make?

(b) If the restriction on single hammocks were removed, what would be the optimal production plan?

2-29 A commuter airline makes lattes in the galley and sells them to passengers. A regular latte contains a shot of espresso, 1 cup of 2% milk, frothed, and 0.5 cup of whipped cream. The low-fat latte contains a shot of espresso, 1.25 cups of skim milk, frothed, and no whipped cream. The plane begins its journey with 100 shots of espresso, 60 cups of skim milk, 60 cups of 2% milk, and 30 cups of whipped cream. The airline makes a profit of $1.58 on each regular latte and $1.65 on each low-fat latte. Assuming that all lattes that are made can be sold, what would be the ideal mix of regular and low-fat lattes to maximize the profit for the airline?

2-30 A warehouse storage building company must determine how many storage sheds of each size—large or small—to build in its new 8,000-square-foot facility to maximize rental income. Each large shed is 150 square feet in size, requires $1 per week in advertising, and rents for $50 per week. Each small shed is 50 square feet in size, requires $1 per week in advertising, and rents for $20 per week. The company has a weekly advertising budget of $100 and estimates that it can rent no more than 40 large sheds in any given week.

2-31 A bank is retrofitting part of its vault to hold safety deposit boxes. It plans to build safety deposit boxes approximately 6 feet high along the walls on both sides of a 20-foot corridor. Hence, the bank will have 240 square feet of wall space to use. It plans to offer two sizes of safety deposit box: large and small. Large boxes (which consume 122.4 square inches of wall space) will rent for $40 per year. Small boxes (which consume 72 square inches of wall space) will rent for $30 per year. The bank believes it will need at least 350 total boxes, at least 80 of which should be large. It hopes to maximize revenue for safety deposit boxes. How many boxes of each size should the bank's design provide?

2-32 An investment broker has been given $250,000 to invest in a 12-month commitment. The money can be placed in Treasury notes (with a return of 8% and a risk score of 2) or in municipal bonds (with a return of 9% and a risk score of 3). The broker's client wants diversification to the extent that between 50% and 70% of the total investment must be placed in Treasury notes. Also, because of fear of default, the client requests that the average risk score of the total investment should be no more than 2.42. How much should the broker invest in each security so as to maximize return on investment?

2-33 A wooden furniture company manufactures two products, benches and picnic tables, for use in yards and parks. The firm has two main resources: its carpenters (labor force) and a supply of redwood for use in the furniture. During the next production cycle, 1,000 hours of labor are available. The firm also has a stock of 3,500 board-feet of good-quality redwood. Each bench that Outdoor Furniture produces requires 4 labor hours and 10 board-feet of redwood; each picnic table takes 6 labor hours and 35 board-feet of redwood. Completed benches will yield a profit of $9 each, and tables will result in a profit of $20 each. Since most customers usually buy tables and benches at the same time, the number of benches made should be at least twice as many as the number of tables made. How many benches and tables should be produced to obtain the largest possible profit?

2-34 A plumbing manufacturer makes two lines of bathtubs, model A and model B. Every tub requires blending a certain amount of steel and zinc; the company has available a total of 24,500 pounds of steel and 6,000 pounds of zinc. Each model A bathtub requires a mixture of 120 pounds of steel and 20 pounds of zinc, and each yields a profit of $90. Each model B tub produced can be sold for a profit of $70; it requires 100 pounds of steel and 30 pounds of zinc. To maintain an adequate supply of both models, the manufacturer would like the number of model A tubs made to be no more than 5 times the number of model B tubs. Find the best product mix of bathtubs.

2-35 A technical college department head must plan the course offerings for the next term. Student demands make it necessary to offer at least 20 core courses (each of which counts for 3 credit hours) and 20 elective courses (each of which counts for 4 credit hours) in the term. Faculty contracts dictate that a total of at least 60 core and elective courses and at least 205 total credit hours be offered. Each core course taught costs the college an average of $2,600 in faculty salaries and each elective course costs $3,000. How many each of core and elective courses should be scheduled so that total faculty salaries are kept to a minimum?

2-36 The size of the yield of olives in a vineyard is greatly influenced by a process of branch pruning. If olive trees are pruned, trees can be planted more densely, and output is increased. (However, olives from pruned trees are smaller in size.) Obtaining a barrel of olives in a pruned vineyard requires 5 hours of labor and 1 acre of land. Obtaining a barrel of olives by the normal process requires only 2 labor hours but takes 2 acres of land. A barrel of olives produced on pruned trees sell for $20, whereas a barrel of regular olives has a market price of $30. An olive grower has 250 hours of labor available and a total of 150 acres available to plant. He has determined that because of uncertain demand, no more than 40 barrels of pruned olives should be produced. Find the combination of barrels of pruned and regular olives that will yield the maximum possible profit. Also, how many acres should the olive grower devote to each growing process?

Note: ***Problems 2-37 to 2-43 are straightforward extensions of the two-variable problems we have seen so far and involve more than two variables. They therefore cannot be solved graphically. They are intended to give you an excellent opportunity to get familiar with formulating larger LP problems and solving them using Excel.***

2-37 Cattle are sent to a feedlot to be grain-fed before being processed into beef. The owners of a feedlot seek to determine the amounts of cattle feed to buy so that minimum nutritional standards are satisfied to ensure proper weight gain, while total feed costs are minimized. The feed mix used is made up of three grains that contain the following nutrients per pound of feed:

	NUTRIENT (OUNCES PER POUND OF FEED)			
FEED	**A**	**B**	**C**	**D**
Feed mix X	3	2	1	6
Feed mix Y	2	3	0	8
Feed mix Z	4	1	2	4

Feed mixes X, Y, and Z cost $3, $4, and $2.25 per pound, respectively. The minimum requirement per cattle per day is 4 pounds of nutrient A, 5 pounds of nutrient B, 1 pound of nutrient C, and 8 pounds of nutrient D. The ranch faces one additional restriction: it can only obtain 500 pounds of feed mix Z per day from the feed supplier regardless of its need. Because there are usually 100 cattle at the feed lot at any given time, this means that no more than 5 pounds of stock Z can be counted on for use in the feed of each cattle per day. Formulate this problem as a linear program and solve it by using Excel.

2-38 The production department for an aluminum valve plant is scheduling its work for next month. Each valve must go through three separate machines during the fabrication process. After fabrication, each valve is inspected by a human being, who spends 15 minutes per valve. There are 525 inspection hours available for the month. The time required (in hours) by each machine to work on each valve is shown in the following table. Also shown are the minimum number of valves that must be produced for the month and the unit profit for each valve.

PRODUCT	V231	V242	V784	V906	CAPACITY (HOURS)
Drilling	0.40	0.30	0.45	0.35	700
Milling	0.60	0.65	0.52	0.48	890
Lathe	1.20	0.60	0.5	0.70	1,200
Unit profit	$16	$12	$13	$8	
Minimum needed	200	250	600	450	

Determine the optimal production mix for the valve plant to make the best use of its profit potential.

2-39 The bank in Problem 2-31 now wants to add a mini-size box, which will rent for $17 per year and consume 43.2 square inches of wall space. The bank still wants a total of at least 350 total boxes; of these, at least 100 should be mini boxes and at least 80 should be large boxes. However, the bank wants the total area occupied by large and mini boxes to be at most 50% of the available space. How many boxes of each type should be included to maximize revenue? If all the boxes can be rented, would the bank make more money with the addition of the mini boxes?

2-40 A photocopy machine company produces three types of laser printers—the Print Jet, the Print Desk, and the Print Pro—the sale of which earn profits of $60, $90, and $73, respectively. The Print Jet requires 2.9 hours of assembly time and 1.4 hours of testing time. The Print Desk requires 3.7 hours of assembly time and 2.1 hours of testing time. The Print Pro requires 3 hours of assembly time and 1.7 hours of testing time. The company wants to ensure that Print Desk constitutes at least 15% of the total production and Print Jet and Print Desk together constitute at least 40% of the total production. There are 3,600 hours of assembly time and 2,000 hours of testing time available for the month. What combination of printers should be produced to maximize profits?

2-41 An electronics corporation manufactures four highly technical products that it supplies to aerospace firms. Each of the products must pass through the following departments before being shipped: wiring, drilling, assembly, and inspection. The time requirement (in hours) for each unit produced, the available time in each department each month, minimum production levels for each product, and unit profits for each product are summarized in the following table:

PRODUCT	EC221	EC496	NC455	NC791	CAPACITY (HOURS)
Wiring	0.5	1.5	1.5	1.0	15,000
Drilling	0.3	1.0	2.0	3.0	17,000
Assembly	0.2	4.0	1.0	2.0	10,000
Inspection	0.5	1.0	0.5	0.5	12,000
Unit profit	$9	$12	$15	$11	
Minimum needed	150	100	300	400	

Formulate this problem and solve it by using Excel. Your solution should honor all constraints and maximize the profit.

2-42 A snack company packages and sells three different 1-pound canned party mixes: Plain Nuts, Mixed Nuts, and Premium Mix. Plain Nuts sell for $2.25 per can, Mixed Nuts sell for $3.37, and Premium Nuts sell for $6.49 per can. A can of Plain Nuts contains 0.8 pound of peanuts and 0.2 pound of cashews. A can of Mixed Nuts consists of 0.5 pound of peanuts, 0.3 pound of cashews, 0.1 pound of almonds, and 0.1 pound of walnuts. A can of Premium Nuts is made up of 0.3 pound of cashews, 0.4 pound of almonds, and 0.4 pound of walnuts. The company has on hand 500 pounds of peanuts, 225 pounds of cashews, 100 pounds of almonds, and 80 pounds of walnuts. Past demand indicates that customers purchase at least twice as many cans of Plain Nuts as Premium Nuts. What production plan will maximize the total revenue?

2-43 An investor is considering three different television news stocks to complement his portfolio: British Broadcasting Company (BBC), Canadian Broadcasting Company (CBC), and Australian Broadcasting Company (ABC). His broker has given him the following information:

	SHORT-TERM GROWTH (PER $ INVESTED)	INTERMEDIATE GROWTH (PER $ INVESTED)	DIVIDEND RATE
BBC	0.39	1.59	8%
CBC	0.26	1.70	4%
ABC	0.42	1.45	6%

The investor's criteria are as follows: (1) The investment should yield short-term growth of at least $1,000; (2) the investment should yield intermediate-term growth of at least $6,000; and (3) the dividends should be at least $250 per year. Determine the least amount the investor can invest and how that investment should be allocated between the three stocks.

Case Study

Mexicana Wire Winding, Inc.

Ron Garcia felt good about his first week as a management trainee at Mexicana Wire Winding, Inc. He had not yet developed any technical knowledge about the manufacturing process, but he had toured the entire facility, located in the suburbs of Mexico City, and had met many people in various areas of the operation.

Mexicana, a subsidiary of Westover Wire Works, a Texas firm, is a medium-sized producer of wire windings used in making electrical transformers. Carlos Alverez, the production control manager, described the windings to Garcia as being of standardized design. Garcia's tour of the plant, laid out by process type (see Figure 2.16), followed the manufacturing sequence for the windings: drawing, extrusion, winding, inspection, and packaging. After inspection, good product is packaged and sent to finished product storage; defective product is stored separately until it can be reworked.

FIGURE 2.16 Mexicana Wire Winding Inc.

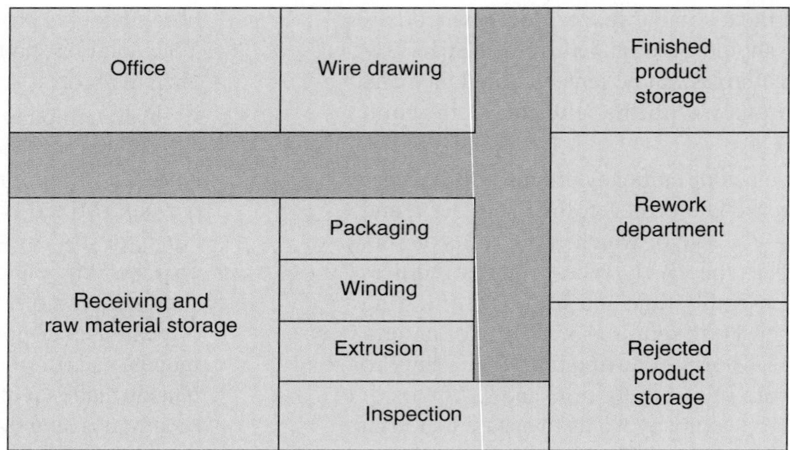

On March 8, Vivian Espania, Mexicana's general manager, stopped by Garcia's office and asked him to attend a staff meeting at 1:00 P.M.

"Let's get started with the business at hand," Vivian said, opening the meeting. "You all have met Ron Garcia, our new management trainee. Ron studied operations management in his MBA program in southern California, so I think he is competent to help us with a problem we have been discussing for a long time without resolution. I'm sure that each of you on my staff will give Ron your full cooperation."

Vivian turned to José Arroyo, production control manager, "José, why don't you describe the problem we are facing?"

"Well," José said, "business is very good right now. We are booking more orders than we can fill. We will have some new equipment on line within the next several months, which will take care of our capacity problems, but that won't help us in April. I have located some retired employees who used to work in the drawing department, and I am planning to bring them in as temporary employees in April to increase capacity there. Because we are planning to refinance some of our long-term debt, Vivian wants our profits to look as good as possible in April. I'm having a hard time figuring out which orders to run and which to back-order so that I can make the bottom line look as good as possible. Can you help me with this?"

Garcia was surprised and apprehensive to receive such an important, high-profile assignment so early in his career. Recovering quickly, he said, "Give me your data and let me work with them for a day or two."

April Orders

Product W0075C	1,400 units
Product W0033C	250 units
Product W0005X	1,510 units
Product W0007X	1,116 units

Note: Vivian Espania has given her word to a key customer that Mexicana will manufacture 600 units of product W0007X and 150 units of product W0075C for him during April.

Standard Cost

PRODUCT	MATERIAL	LABOR	OVERHEAD	SELLING PRICE
W0075C	$33.00	$9.90	$23.10	$100.00
W00033C	25.00	7.50	17.50	80.00
W0005X	35.00	10.50	24.50	130.00
W0007X	75.00	11.25	63.75	175.00

Selecting Operating Data

Average output per month = 2,400 units

Average machine utilization = 63%

Average percentage of production sent to rework department = 5% (mostly from winding department)

Average no. of rejected units awaiting rework = 850 (mostly from winding department)

Plant Capacity (HOURS)

DRAWING	EXTRUSION	WINDING	PACKAGING
4,000	4,200	2,000	2,300

Note: Inspection capacity is not a problem: Employees can work overtime as necessary to accommodate any schedule.

Bill of Labor (HOURS/UNIT)

PRODUCT	DRAWING	EXTRUSION	WINDING	PACKAGING
W0075C	1.0	1.0	1.0	1.0
W0033C	2.0	1.0	3.0	0.0
W0005X	0.0	4.0	0.0	3.0
W0007X	1.0	1.0	0.0	2.0

Discussion Questions

1. What recommendations should Ron Garcia make, with what justification? Provide a detailed analysis, with charts, graphs, and Excel printouts included.
2. Discuss the need for temporary workers in the drawing department.
3. Discuss the plant layout.

Source: Copyright © Victor E. Sower. Reprinted by permission of Victor E. Sower, Sam Houston State University. This case material is based on an actual situation, with name and data altered for confidentiality.

Case Study

Golding Landscaping and Plants, Inc.

Kenneth and Patricia Golding spent a career as a husband-and-wife real estate investment partnership in Washington, DC. When they finally retired to a 25-acre farm in northern Virginia's Fairfax County, they became ardent amateur gardeners. Kenneth planted shrubs and fruit trees, and Patricia spent her hours potting all sizes of plants. When the volume of shrubs and plants reached the point that the Goldings began to think of their hobby in a serious vein, they built a greenhouse adjacent to their home and installed heating and watering systems.

By 2005, the Goldings realized that their retirement from real estate had really only led to a second career—in the plant and shrub business—and they filed for a Virginia business license. Within a matter of months, they asked their attorney to file incorporation documents and formed the firm Golding Landscaping and Plants, Inc.

Early in the new business's existence, Kenneth Golding recognized the need for a high-quality commercial fertilizer that he could blend himself, both for sale and for his own nursery. His goal was to keep his costs to a minimum while producing a top-notch product that was especially suited to the northern Virginia climate.

Working with chemists at George Mason University, Golding blended "Golding-Grow." It consists of four chemical compounds: C-30, C-92, D-21, and E-11. The cost per pound for each compound is indicated in the following table:

CHEMICAL COMPOUND	COST PER POUND ($)
C-30	0.12
C-92	0.09
D-21	0.11
E-11	0.04

The specifications for Golding-Grow are as follows:

a. Chemical E-11 must comprise at least 15% of the blend.
b. C-92 and C-30 must together constitute at least 45% of the blend.
c. D-21 and C-92 can together constitute no more than 30% of the blend.
d. Golding-Grow is packaged and sold in 50-pound bags.

Discussion Questions

1. Formulate an LP problem to determine what blend of the four chemicals will allow Golding to minimize the cost of a 50-pound bag of the fertilizer.
2. Solve by using Excel to find the best solution.

Source: J. Heizer and B. Render. *Operations Management* Eighth Edition, p. 720, © 2006. Reprinted by permission of Pearson Education, Inc., Upper Saddle River, NJ.

Internet Case Studies

See the Companion Website for this textbook, at www.pearsonhighered.com/balakrishnan, for additional case studies.

CHAPTER 3

Linear Programming Modeling Applications with Computer Analyses in Excel

LEARNING OBJECTIVES

After completing this chapter, students will be able to:

1. Model a wide variety of linear programming (LP) problems.
2. Understand major business application areas for LP problems, including manufacturing, marketing, finance, employee staffing, transportation, blending, and multiperiod planning.
3. Gain experience in setting up and solving LP problems using Excel's Solver.

CHAPTER OUTLINE

3.1 Introduction

The purpose of this chapter is to illustrate how linear programming (LP) can be used to model real-world problems in several managerial decision-making areas. In our discussion, we use examples from areas such as product mix, make–buy decisions, media selection, marketing research, financial portfolio selection, labor planning, shipping and transportation, allocation decisions, ingredient blending, and multiperiod scheduling.

It is a good idea to always develop a written LP model on paper before attempting to implement it on Excel.

For each example discussed, we first briefly describe the development of the written mathematical model and then illustrate its solution using Excel's Solver. Although we use Solver to solve these models, it is critical that you understand the logic behind a model before implementing it on the computer. Remember that the solution is only as good as the model itself. If the model is incorrect or incomplete from a logical perspective (even if it is correct from a mathematical perspective), Excel has no way of recognizing the logical error. Too many students, especially those at the early stages of instruction in LP, hit roadblocks when they try to implement an LP problem directly in Excel without conceptualizing the model on paper first. So we highly recommend that, until you become very comfortable with LP formulations (which takes many hours of practice), you sketch out the layout for each problem on paper first. Then, you can translate your written model to the computer.

We first identify decision variables and then write linear equations for the objective function and each of the constraints.

In developing each written mathematical model, we use the approach discussed in Chapter 2. This means first identifying the decision variables and then writing out linear equations for the objective function and each constraint in terms of these decision variables. Although some of the models discussed in this chapter are relatively small numerically, the principles developed here are definitely applicable to larger problems. Moreover, the structured formulation approach used here should provide enough practice in "paraphrasing" LP model formulations and help in developing skills to apply the technique to other, less common applications.

We use a consistent layout in our Excel implementation of all models for ease of understanding.

When implementing these models in Excel, to the extent possible, we employ the same layout presented in Chapter 2. That is, all parameters (i.e., the solution value, objective coefficient, and constraint coefficients) associated with a specific decision variable are modeled in the same column. The objective function and each constraint in the problem are shown on separate rows of the worksheet. Later in this chapter (section 3.8), however, we illustrate an alternate implementation that may be more compact and efficient for some problems. As noted in Chapter 2, we encourage you to try alternate layouts based on your personal preference and expertise with Excel.

Excel Notes

- The Companion Website for this textbook, at www.pearsonhighered.com/balakrishnan, contains the Excel file for each sample problem discussed here. The relevant file name is shown in the margin next to each example.
- In each of our Excel layouts, for clarity, changing variable cells are shaded yellow, the objective cell is shaded green, and cells denoting left-hand-side formulas of constraints are shaded blue. If the right-hand side of a constraint also includes a formula, that cell is also shaded blue.
- To make the equivalence of the written formulation and the Excel layout clear, the Excel layouts show the decision variable names used in the written formulation of the model. Note that these names have no role in using Solver to solve the model.

3.2 Manufacturing Applications

Product Mix Problem

A popular use of LP is in solving product mix problems.

A fertile field for the use of LP is in planning for the optimal mix of products that a company should produce. A company must meet a myriad of constraints, ranging from financial concerns to sales demands to material contracts to union labor demands. Its primary goal is either to generate the largest profit (or revenue) possible or to keep the total manufacturing costs as low as possible. We have already studied a simple version of a product mix problem (the Flair

Improved Handling of Time-Sensitive Returns at Hewlett-Packard Using Linear Programming

Reverse supply chain operations at Hewlett-Packard Company (HP) include organizing product returns, identifying their best reuse option and reconditioning them accordingly, and finally marketing and selling the reconditioned products. HP estimates the cost of product returns at 2 percent of total outbound sales for North America. Managers are therefore increasingly aware of the value of product returns, especially for products that lose their value rapidly with time. Products such as PCs, printers, computer peripherals, and mobile phones have very short life cycles and in order to convert these returns to potential sources of revenue, the time between return and resale must be short.

Focusing on HP's notebooks and desktops because they constituted about 60 percent of the return flows and contributed more than 80 percent of revenue, the authors developed innovative linear programming models to explore alternative refurbishment options and improve reuse and reconditioning decisions. A spokesperson at HP notes that the "result of this project was really eye opening for my organization and delivered tremendous value towards improving our existing business model." He adds, "the results are applicable to a wide range of product returns for HP and we are exploring how to extend the results from this pilot study to other HP groups for other product lines and other regions."

Source: Based on V. D. R. Guide, Jr., L. Muyldermans, and L. N. Van Wassenhove. "Hewlett-Packard Company Unlocks the Value Potential from Time-Sensitive Returns," *Interfaces* 35, 4 (July–August 2005): 281–293.

Furniture problem) involving just two products in Chapter 2. Let us now look at a more detailed version of a product mix problem.

Fifth Avenue Industries, a nationally known manufacturer of menswear, produces four varieties of ties. One is an expensive, all-silk tie, one is an all-polyester tie, and two are blends of polyester and cotton. Table 3.1 illustrates the cost and availability (per monthly production planning period) of the three materials used in the production process.

The firm has fixed contracts with several major department store chains to supply ties each month. The contracts require that Fifth Avenue Industries supply a minimum quantity of each tie but allow for a larger demand if Fifth Avenue chooses to meet that demand. (Most of the ties are not shipped with the name Fifth Avenue on their label, incidentally, but with "private stock" labels supplied by the stores.) Table 3.2 summarizes the contract demand for each of the four styles of ties, the selling price per tie, and the fabric requirements of each variety. The production process for all ties is almost fully automated, and Fifth Avenue uses a standard labor cost of \$0.75 per tie (for any variety). Fifth Avenue must decide on a policy for product mix in order to maximize its monthly profit.

TABLE 3.1 Material Data for Fifth Avenue Industries

MATERIAL	COST PER YARD	MATERIAL AVAILABLE PER MONTH (YARDS)
Silk	\$20	1,000
Polyester	\$ 6	2,000
Cotton	\$ 9	1,250

TABLE 3.2 Product Data for Fifth Avenue Industries

VARIETY OF TIE	SELLING PRICE PER TIE	MONTHLY CONTRACT MINIMUM	MONTHLY DEMAND	TOTAL MATERIAL REQUIRED PER TIE (YARDS)	MATERIAL REQUIREMENTS
All silk	\$6.70	6,000	7,000	0.125	100% silk
All polyester	\$3.55	10,000	14,000	0.08	100% polyester
Poly–cotton blend 1	\$4.31	13,000	16,000	0.10	50% polyester/50% cotton
Poly–cotton blend 2	\$4.81	6,000	8,500	0.10	30% polyester/70% cotton

Decision variables in product mix problems usually represent the number of units to make of each product.

FORMULATING THE PROBLEM As is usual with product mix problems, in this case, the decision variables represent the number of units to make of each product. Let

$$S = \text{number of all-silk ties to make per month}$$
$$P = \text{number of all-polyester ties to make per month}$$
$$B_1 = \text{number of poly–cotton blend 1 ties to make per month}$$
$$B_2 = \text{number of poly–cotton blend 2 ties to make per month}$$

Unlike the Flair Furniture example in Chapter 2, where the unit profit contribution for each product was directly given (e.g., \$7 per table and \$5 per chair), the unit profits must be first calculated in this example. We illustrate the net profit calculation for all-silk ties (S). Each all-silk tie requires 0.125 yards of silk, at a cost of \$20 per yard, resulting in a material cost of \$2.50. The selling price per all-silk tie is \$6.70, and the labor cost is \$0.75, leaving a net profit of \$6.70 − \$2.50 − \$0.75 = \$3.45 per tie. In a similar fashion, we can calculate the net unit profit for all-polyester ties (P) to be \$2.32, for poly–cotton blend 1 ties (B_1) to be \$2.81, and for poly–cotton blend 2 ties (B_2) to be \$3.25. Try to verify these calculations for yourself.

The objective function can now be stated as

$$\text{Maximize profit} = \$3.45S + \$2.32P + \$2.81B_1 + \$3.25B_2$$

subject to the constraints

$$\begin{array}{lll}
0.125S & \leq 1{,}000 & \text{(yards of silk)} \\
0.08P + 0.05B_1 + 0.03B_2 & \leq 2{,}000 & \text{(yards of polyester)} \\
0.05B_1 + 0.07B_2 & \leq 1{,}250 & \text{(yards of cotton)} \\
S & \geq 6{,}000 & \text{(contract minimum for all silk)} \\
S & \leq 7{,}000 & \text{(maximum demand for all silk)} \\
P & \geq 10{,}000 & \text{(contract minimum for all polyester)} \\
P & \leq 14{,}000 & \text{(maximum demand for all polyester)} \\
B_1 & \geq 13{,}000 & \text{(contract minimum for blend 1)} \\
B_1 & \leq 16{,}000 & \text{(maximum demand for blend 1)} \\
B_2 & \geq 6{,}000 & \text{(contract minimum for blend 2)} \\
B_2 & \leq 8{,}500 & \text{(maximum demand for blend 2)} \\
S, P, B_1, B_2 & \geq 0 & \text{(nonnegativity)}
\end{array}$$

Instead of profit contributions, the objective function can include selling prices and cost components.

Instead of writing the objective function by using the profit coefficients directly, we can optionally choose to split the profit into its three components: a revenue component, a labor cost component, and a material cost component. For example, the objective (profit) coefficient for all-silk ties (S) is \$3.45. However, we know that the \$3.45 is obtained by subtracting the labor cost (\$0.75) and material cost (\$2.50) from the revenue (\$6.70) for S. Hence, we can rewrite the objective function as

$$\begin{aligned}\text{Maximize profit} = {} & (\$6.70S + \$3.55P + \$4.31B_1 + \$4.81B_2) \\ & - \$0.75(S + P + B_1 + B_2) - (\$2.50S + \$0.48P + \$0.75B_1 + \$0.81B_2)\end{aligned}$$

It is preferable to have the Excel layout show as much detail as possible for a problem.

Whether we model the objective function by using the profit coefficients directly or by using the selling prices and cost coefficients, the final solution will be the same. However, in many problems it is convenient, and probably preferable, to have the model show as much detail as possible.

File: 3-1.xls, sheet: 3-1A

SOLVING THE PROBLEM The formula view of the Excel layout for this problem is shown in Screenshot 3-1A. Cell F6 defines the revenue component, cell F7 defines the labor cost component, and cell F8 defines the material cost component of the objective function. Cell F9 (the objective cell in Solver) is the difference between cell F6 and cells F7 and F8.

Most formulas in our Excel layout are modeled using the SUMPRODUCT function.

Observe that in this spreadsheet (as well as in all other spreadsheets discussed in this chapter), the primary Excel function we have used to model all formulas is the SUMPRODUCT function (discussed in section 2.7, on page 42). We have used this function to compute the objective function components (cells F6:F8) as well as the LHS values for all constraints (cells F11:F21).

SCREENSHOT 3-1A Formula View of the Excel Layout for Fifth Avenue Industries

Titles, such as the ones shown in row 4 and column A, are included to clarify the model. They are recommended but not required.

These are the decision variable names used in the written LP formulation. They are shown here for information purposes only.

	A	B	C	D	E	F	G	H	I
1	**Fifth Avenue Industries**								
2									
3		S	P	B_1	B_2				
4		All silk	All poly	Blend-1	Blend-2				
5	Number of units								
6	Selling price	6.7	3.55	4.31	4.81	=SUMPRODUCT(B6:E6,$B$5:$E$5)			
7	Labor cost	0.75	0.75	0.75	0.75	=SUMPRODUCT(B7:E7,$B$5:$E$5)			
8	Material cost	2.5	0.48	0.75	0.81	=SUMPRODUCT(B8:E8,$B$5:$E$5)			
9	Profit	=B6-B7-B8	=C6-C7-C8	=D6-D7-D8	=E6-E7-E8	=F6-F7-F8			
10	**Constraints:**								**Cost/Yd**
11	Yards of silk	0.125				=SUMPRODUCT(B11:E11,$B$5:$E$5)	<=	1000	20
12	Yards of polyester		0.08	0.05	0.03	=SUMPRODUCT(B12:E12,$B$5:$E$5)	<=	2000	6
13	Yards of cotton			0.05	0.07	=SUMPRODUCT(B13:E13,$B$5:$E$5)	<=	1250	9
14	Maximum all silk	1				=SUMPRODUCT(B14:E14,$B$5:$E$5)	<=	7000	
15	Maximum all poly		1			=SUMPRODUCT(B15:E15,$B$5:$E$5)	<=	14000	
16	Maximum blend-1			1		=SUMPRODUCT(B16:E16,$B$5:$E$5)	<=	16000	
17	Maximum blend-2				1	=SUMPRODUCT(B17:E17,$B$5:$E$5)	<=	8500	
18	Minimum all silk	1				=SUMPRODUCT(B18:E18,$B$5:$E$5)	>=	6000	
19	Minimum all poly		1			=SUMPRODUCT(B19:E19,$B$5:$E$5)	>=	10000	
20	Minimum blend-1			1		=SUMPRODUCT(B20:E20,$B$5:$E$5)	>=	13000	
21	Minimum blend-2				1	=SUMPRODUCT(B21:E21,$B$5:$E$5)	>=	6000	
22						LHS	Sign	RHS	

Objective function terms and constraint LHS values are computed using the SUMPRODUCT function.

The signs are shown here for information purposes only. Actual signs will be entered in Solver.

As noted earlier, we have adopted this type of Excel layout for our models in order to make it easier for the beginning student of LP to understand them. Further, an advantage of this layout is the ease with which all the formulas in the spreadsheet can be created. Observe that we have used the $ sign in cell F6 to anchor the cell references for the decision variables (i.e., $B$5:$E$5). This allows us to simply copy this formula to cells F7:F8 for the other components of the objective function, and to cells F11:F21 to create the corresponding LHS formulas for the constraints.

File: 3-1.xls, sheet: 3-1B

INTERPRETING THE RESULTS The Solver entries and optimal solution values for this model are shown in Screenshot 3-1B. As discussed in Chapter 2, before solving the LP model using Solver, we ensure that the box labeled Make Unconstrained Variables Non-Negative is checked and the Select a Solving Method box is set to Simplex LP; both are set this way by default in Solver.

The results indicate that the optimal solution is to produce 7,000 all-silk ties, 13,625 all-polyester ties, 13,100 poly–cotton blend 1 ties, and 8,500 poly–cotton blend 2 ties. This results in total revenue of $192,614.75, labor cost of $31,668.75, and total material cost of $40,750, yielding a net profit of $120,196. Polyester and cotton availability are binding constraints, while 125 yards $(= 1{,}000 - 875)$ of silk will be left unused. Interestingly, the availability of the two cheaper resources (polyester and cotton) is more critical to Fifth Avenue than the availability of the more expensive resource (silk). Such occurrences are common in practice. That is, the more expensive resources need not necessarily be the most important or critical resources from an availability or need point of view. Fifth Avenue will satisfy the full demand for all silk and poly–cotton blend 2 ties, and it will satisfy a little over the minimum contract level for the other two varieties.

Make–Buy Decision Problem

The make–buy decision problem is an extension of the product mix problem.

An extension of the product mix problem is the make–buy decision problem. In this situation, a firm can satisfy the demand for a product by making some of it in-house ("make") and by subcontracting or outsourcing the remainder to another firm ("buy"). For each product, the firm

SCREENSHOT 3-1B Excel Layout and Solver Entries for Fifth Avenue Industries

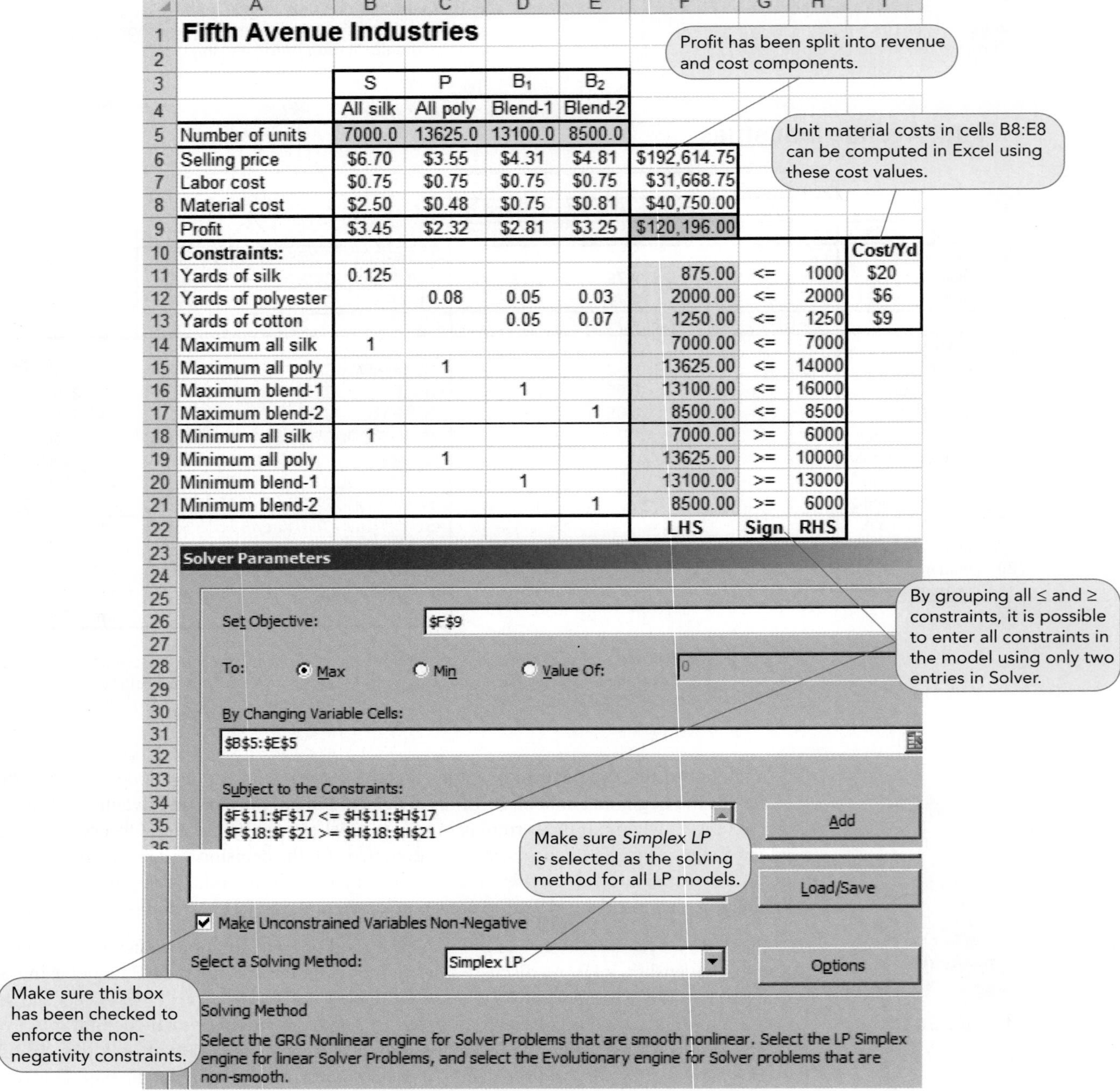

	A	B	C	D	E	F	G	H	I
1	Fifth Avenue Industries								
2									
3		S	P	B_1	B_2				
4		All silk	All poly	Blend-1	Blend-2				
5	Number of units	7000.0	13625.0	13100.0	8500.0				
6	Selling price	$6.70	$3.55	$4.31	$4.81	$192,614.75			
7	Labor cost	$0.75	$0.75	$0.75	$0.75	$31,668.75			
8	Material cost	$2.50	$0.48	$0.75	$0.81	$40,750.00			
9	Profit	$3.45	$2.32	$2.81	$3.25	$120,196.00			
10	Constraints:								Cost/Yd
11	Yards of silk	0.125				875.00	<=	1000	$20
12	Yards of polyester		0.08	0.05	0.03	2000.00	<=	2000	$6
13	Yards of cotton			0.05	0.07	1250.00	<=	1250	$9
14	Maximum all silk	1				7000.00	<=	7000	
15	Maximum all poly		1			13625.00	<=	14000	
16	Maximum blend-1			1		13100.00	<=	16000	
17	Maximum blend-2				1	8500.00	<=	8500	
18	Minimum all silk	1				7000.00	>=	6000	
19	Minimum all poly		1			13625.00	>=	10000	
20	Minimum blend-1			1		13100.00	>=	13000	
21	Minimum blend-2				1	8500.00	>=	6000	
22						LHS	Sign	RHS	

needs to determine how much of the product to make in-house and how much of it to outsource to another firm. (*Note:* Under the scenario considered here, it is possible for the firm to use *both* the in-house and outsourcing options simultaneously for a product. That is, it is not necessary for the firm to choose either the in-house option or the outsourcing option exclusively. The situation where the firm has to choose only one of the two options for a given product is an example of a binary integer programming model, which we will address in Chapter 6.)

To illustrate this type of problem, let us consider the Fifth Avenue Industries problem again. As in the product mix example, Tables 3.1 and 3.2 show the relevant data for this problem. However, let us now assume that the firm *must* satisfy all demand exactly. That is, the monthly contract minimum numbers in Table 3.2 are now the same as the monthly demands. In addition, assume that Fifth Avenue now has the option to outsource part of its tie production to Ties

Unlimited, another tie maker. Ties Unlimited has enough surplus capacity to handle any order that Fifth Avenue may place. It has provided Fifth Avenue with the following price list per tie: all silk, \$4.25; all polyester, \$2.00; poly-cotton blend 1, \$2.50; and poly-cotton blend 2, \$2.20. (Ties Unlimited is selling poly-cotton blend 2 for a lower price than poly-cotton blend 1 because it has obtained its cotton at a much cheaper cost than Fifth Avenue.) What should Fifth Avenue do under this revised situation to maximize its monthly profit?

FORMULATING THE PROBLEM As before, let

$$S = \text{number of all-silk ties to make (in-house) per month}$$
$$P = \text{number of all-polyester ties to make (in-house) per month}$$
$$B_1 = \text{number of poly–cotton blend 1 ties to make (in-house) per month}$$
$$B_2 = \text{number of poly–cotton blend 2 ties to make (in-house) per month}$$

In this case, however, Fifth Avenue must decide on a policy for the product mix that includes both the make and buy options. To accommodate this feature, let

$$S_o = \text{number of all-silk ties to outsource (buy) per month}$$
$$P_o = \text{number of all-polyester ties to outsource (buy) per month}$$
$$B_{1o} = \text{number of poly–cotton blend 1 ties to outsource (buy) per month}$$
$$B_{2o} = \text{number of poly–cotton blend 2 ties to outsource (buy) per month}$$

Note that the total number of each variety of tie equals the sum of the number of ties made in-house and the number of ties outsourced. For example, the total number of all-silk ties equals $S + S_o$. The total revenue from all ties can now be written as

$$\text{Revenue} = \$6.70(S + S_o) + \$3.55(P + P_o) + \$4.31(B_1 + B_{1o}) + \$4.81(B_2 + B_{2o})$$

To compute the profit, we need to subtract the labor cost, material cost, and outsourcing cost from this revenue. As in the previous product mix example, the total labor and material costs may be written as

$$\text{Labor cost} = \$0.75(S + P + B_1 + B_2)$$
$$\text{Material cost} = \$2.50S + \$0.48P + \$0.75B_1 + \$0.81B_2$$

Note that the labor and material costs are relevant only for the portion of the production that occurs in-house. The total outsourcing cost may be written as

$$\text{Outsourcing cost} = \$4.25S_o + \$2.00P_o + \$2.50B_{1o} + \$2.20B_{2o}$$

The objective function can now be stated as

The objective function now also includes the outsourcing cost.

$$\text{Maximize profit} = \text{revenue} - \text{labor cost} - \text{material cost} - \text{outsourcing cost}$$

subject to the constraints

$0.125S$	$\leq$	1,000	(yards of silk)
$0.08P + 0.05B_1 + 0.03B_2$	$\leq$	2,000	(yards of polyester)
$0.05B_1 + 0.07B_2$	$\leq$	1,250	(yards of cotton)
$S + S_o$	$=$	7,000	(required demand for all-silk)
$P + P_o$	$=$	14,000	(required demand for all-polyester)
$B_1 + B_{1o}$	$=$	16,000	(required demand for blend 1)
$B_2 + B_{2o}$	$=$	8,500	(required demand for blend 2)
$S, P, B_1, B_2, S_o, P_o, B_{1o}, B_{2o}$	$\geq$	0	(nonnegativity)

File: 3-2.xls

Because all demand must be satisfied in this example, we write a single demand constraint for each tie variety. Note that we have written all the demand constraints as = constraints in this model. Could we have used the ≤ sign for the demand constraints without affecting the solution? In this case, the answer is yes because we are trying to maximize profit, and the profit contribution of each tie is positive, regardless of whether it is made in-house or outsourced (as shown in cells B10:I10 in the Excel layout for this model in Screenshot 3-2).

SCREENSHOT 3-2 Excel Layout Solver Entries for Fifth Avenue Industries—Make–Buy Problem

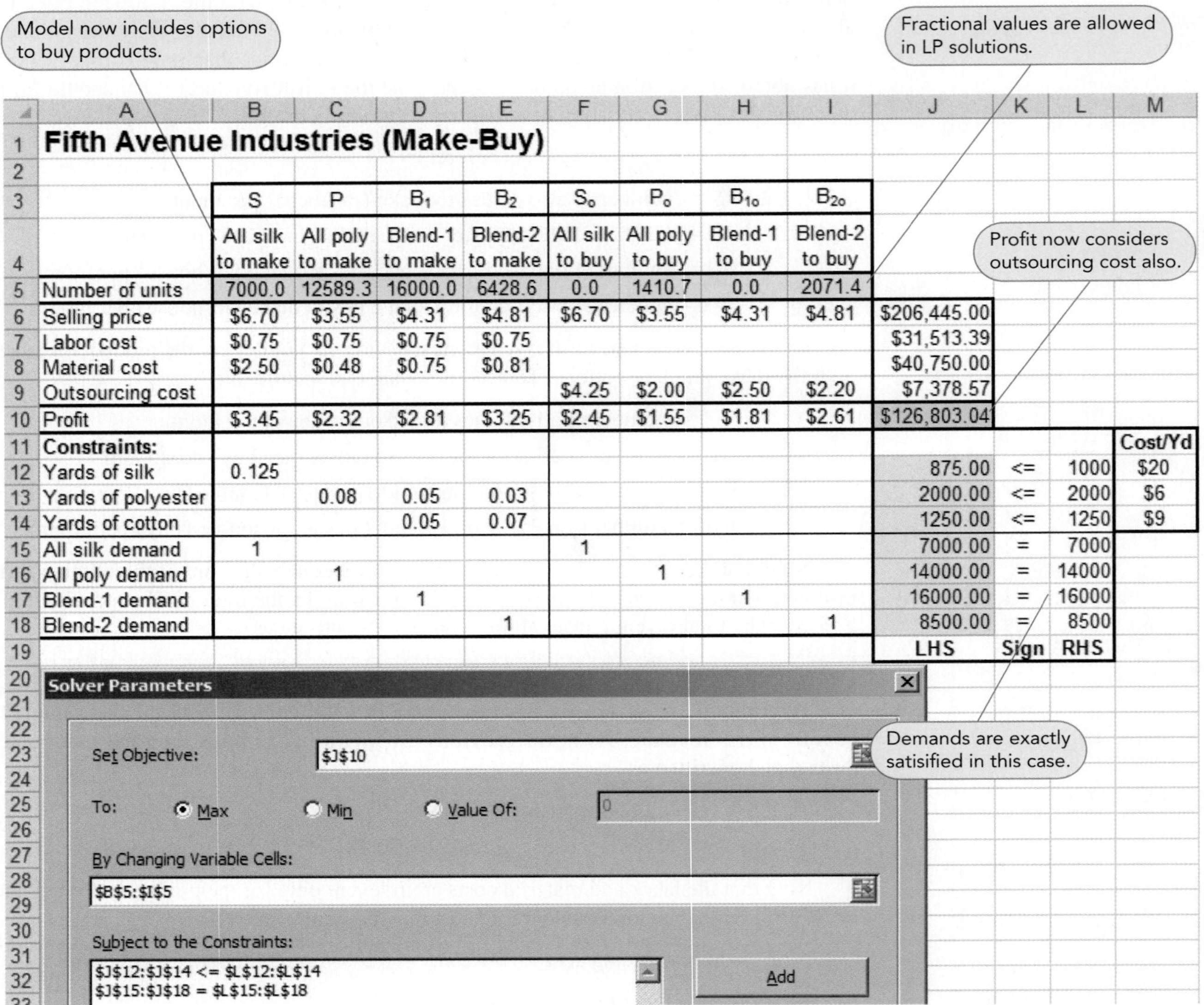

	A	B	C	D	E	F	G	H	I	J	K	L	M
1	**Fifth Avenue Industries (Make-Buy)**												
2													
3		S	P	B_1	B_2	S_o	P_o	B_{1o}	B_{2o}				
4		All silk to make	All poly to make	Blend-1 to make	Blend-2 to make	All silk to buy	All poly to buy	Blend-1 to buy	Blend-2 to buy				
5	Number of units	7000.0	12589.3	16000.0	6428.6	0.0	1410.7	0.0	2071.4				
6	Selling price	$6.70	$3.55	$4.31	$4.81	$6.70	$3.55	$4.31	$4.81	$206,445.00			
7	Labor cost	$0.75	$0.75	$0.75	$0.75					$31,513.39			
8	Material cost	$2.50	$0.48	$0.75	$0.81					$40,750.00			
9	Outsourcing cost					$4.25	$2.00	$2.50	$2.20	$7,378.57			
10	Profit	$3.45	$2.32	$2.81	$3.25	$2.45	$1.55	$1.81	$2.61	$126,803.04			
11	**Constraints:**												Cost/Yd
12	Yards of silk	0.125								875.00	<=	1000	$20
13	Yards of polyester		0.08	0.05	0.03					2000.00	<=	2000	$6
14	Yards of cotton			0.05	0.07					1250.00	<=	1250	$9
15	All silk demand	1				1				7000.00	=	7000	
16	All poly demand		1				1			14000.00	=	14000	
17	Blend-1 demand			1				1		16000.00	=	16000	
18	Blend-2 demand				1				1	8500.00	=	8500	
19										LHS	Sign	RHS	

Likewise, could we have used the ≥ sign for the demand constraints? In this case, the answer is no. Why? (*Hint:* Because the selling price of each tie variety is greater than its outsourcing cost, what will the solution suggest if we write the demand constraints as ≥ equations?)

SOLVING THE PROBLEM The Solver entries and optimal solution values for this model are shown in Screenshot 3-2. Cell J6 defines the revenue component of the profit, cells J7 and J8 define the labor and material cost components, respectively, and cell J9 defines the outsourcing cost component. The profit shown in cell J10 (the objective cell in Solver) is the difference between cell J6 and cells J7, J8, and J9.

INTERPRETING THE RESULTS The results show that the optimal solution is to make in-house 7,000 all-silk ties, 12,589.30 all-polyester ties, 16,000 poly–cotton blend 1 ties, and 6,428.60 poly–cotton blend 2 ties. The remaining demand (i.e., 1,410.70 all-polyester ties and 2,071.40 poly–cotton blend 2 ties) should be outsourced from Ties Unlimited. This results in total revenue of $206,445, total labor cost of $31,513.39, total material cost of $40,750, and total outsourcing cost of $7,378.57, yielding a net profit of $126,803.04. It is interesting to note that the presence of the outsourcing option changes the product mix for the in-house production (compare Screenshot 3-1B with Screenshot 3-2). Also, Fifth Avenue's total profit increases as a result of the outsourcing because it is now able to satisfy more of the demand (profit is now \$126,803.04 versus only \$120,196 earlier).

Because integer programming models are much more difficult to solve than LP models, we solve many problems as LP models and round off any fractional values.

Observe that this solution turns out to have some fractional values. As noted in Chapter 2, because it is considerably more difficult to solve an integer programming model than an LP model, it is quite common to not specify the integer requirement in many LP models. We can then round the resulting solution appropriately if it turns out to have fractional values. In product mix problems that have many ≤ constraints, the fractional values for production variables should typically be rounded down. If we round up these values, we might potentially violate a binding constraint for a resource. In Fifth Avenue's case, the company could probably round down P and B_2 to 12,589 and 6,428, respectively, and it could correspondingly round up the outsourced values P_o and B_{2o} to 1,411 and 2,072, respectively, without affecting the profit too much.

Rounding may be a difficult task in some situations.

In some situations, however, rounding may not be an easy task. For example, there is likely to be a huge cost and resource impact if we round a solution that suggests making 10.71 Boeing 787 aircraft to 10 versus rounding it to 11. In such cases, we need to solve the model as an integer programming problem. We discuss such problems (i.e., problems that require integer solutions) in Chapter 6.

3.3 Marketing Applications

Media Selection Problem

Media selection problems can be approached with LP from two perspectives: maximizing audience exposure or minimizing advertising costs.

LP models have been used in the advertising field as a decision aid in selecting an effective media mix. Sometimes the technique is employed in allocating a fixed or limited budget across various media, which might include radio or television commercials, newspaper ads, direct mailings, magazine ads, and so on. In other applications, the objective is to maximize audience exposure. Restrictions on the allowable media mix might arise through contract requirements, limited media availability, or company policy. An example follows.

Win Big Gambling Club promotes gambling junkets from a large Midwestern city to casinos in The Bahamas. The club has budgeted up to \$8,000 per week for local advertising. The money is to be allocated among four promotional media: TV spots, newspaper ads, and two types of radio advertisements. Win Big's goal is to reach the largest possible high-potential audience through the various media. Table 3.3 presents the number of potential gamblers reached by making use of an advertisement in each of the four media. It also provides the cost per advertisement placed and the maximum number of ads that can be purchased per week.

Win Big's contractual arrangements require that at least five radio spots be placed each week. To ensure a broad-scoped promotional campaign, management also insists that no more than \$1,800 be spent on radio advertising every week.

FORMULATING AND SOLVING THE PROBLEM This is somewhat like the product mix problem we discussed earlier in this chapter, except that the "products" here are the various media that are available for use. The decision variables denote the number of times each of these media choices should be used. Let

T = number of 1-minute television spots taken each week
N = number of full-page daily newspaper ads taken each week
P = number of 30-second prime time radio spots taken each week
A = number of 1-minute afternoon radio spots taken each week

TABLE 3.3
Data for Win Big Gambling Club

MEDIUM	AUDIENCE REACHED PER AD	COST PER AD	MAXIMUM ADS PER WEEK
TV spot (1 minute)	5,000	\$800	12
Daily newspaper (full-page ad)	8,500	\$925	5
Radio spot (30 seconds, prime time)	2,400	\$290	25
Radio spot (1 minute, afternoon)	2,800	\$380	20

Objective:

$$\text{Maximize audience coverage} = 5{,}000T + 8{,}500N + 2{,}400P + 2{,}800A$$

subject to the constraints

$$
\begin{array}{lll}
T & \leq 12 & \text{(maximum TV spots/week)} \\
N & \leq 5 & \text{(maximum newspaper ads/week)} \\
P & \leq 25 & \text{(maximum 30-second radio spots/week)} \\
A & \leq 20 & \text{(maximum 1-minute radio spots/week)} \\
800T + 925N + 290P + 380A & \leq 8{,}000 & \text{(weekly advertising budget)} \\
P + A & \geq 5 & \text{(minimum radio spots contracted)} \\
290P + 380A & \leq 1{,}800 & \text{(maximum dollars spent on radio)} \\
T, N, P, A & \geq 0 & \text{(nonnegativity)}
\end{array}
$$

The Excel layout and Solver entries for this model, and the resulting solution, are shown in Screenshot 3-3.

File: 3-3.xls

INTERPRETING THE RESULTS The optimal solution is found to be 1.97 television spots, 5 newspaper ads, 6.21 30-second prime time radio spots, and no 1-minute afternoon radio spots. This produces an audience exposure of 67,240.30 contacts. Here again, this solution turns out to have fractional values. Win Big would probably round down P to 6 spots and correspondingly round up T to 2 spots. A quick check indicates that the rounded solution satisfies all constraints even though T has been rounded up.

Marketing Research Problem

Selection of survey participants for consumer research is another popular use of LP.

LP has been applied to marketing research problems and the area of consumer research. The next example illustrates how LP can help statistical pollsters make strategic decisions.

SCREENSHOT 3-3
Excel Layout and Solver Entries for Win Big Gambling Club

	A	B	C	D	E	F	G	H
1	Win Big Gambling Club							
2								
3		T	N	P	A			
4		TV spots	Newspaper ads	Prime-time radio spots	Afternoon radio spots			
5	Number of units	1.97	5.00	6.21	0.00			
6	Audience	5000	8500	2400	2800	67240.30		
7	Constraints:							
8	Maximum TV	1				1.97	<=	12
9	Maximum newspaper		1			5.00	<=	5
10	Max prime-time radio			1		6.21	<=	25
11	Max afternoon radio				1	0.00	<=	20
12	Total budget	$800	$925	$290	$380	$8,000.00	<=	$8,000
13	Maximum radio $			$290	$380	$1,800.00	<=	$1,800
14	Minimum radio spots			1	1	6.21	>=	5
15						LHS	Sign	RHS

Fractional values can be rounded off appropriately, if desired.

Solver Parameters

Set Objective: $F$6

To: (•) Max ( ) Min ( ) Value Of: 0

By Changing Variable Cells: $B$5:$E$5

Subject to the Constraints:
$F$14 >= $H$14
$F$8:$F$13 <= $H$8:$H$13

Add

All six ≤ constraints are entered as a single entry in Solver.

Management Sciences Associates (MSA) is a marketing and computer research firm based in Washington, DC, that handles consumer surveys. One of its clients is a national press service that periodically conducts political polls on issues of widespread interest. In a survey for the press service, MSA determines that it must fulfill several requirements in order to draw statistically valid conclusions on the sensitive issue of new U.S. immigration laws aimed at countering terrorism:

1. Survey at least 2,300 people in total in the United States.
2. Survey at least 1,000 people who are 30 years of age or younger.
3. Survey at least 600 people who are between 31 and 50 years of age.
4. Ensure that at least 15% of those surveyed live in a state that borders Mexico.
5. Ensure that at least 50% of those surveyed who are 30 years of age or younger live in a state that does not border Mexico.
6. Ensure that no more than 20% of those surveyed who are 51 years of age or over live in a state that borders Mexico.

MSA decides that all surveys should be conducted in person. It estimates that the costs of reaching people in each age and region category are as shown in Table 3.4. MSA's goal is to meet the six sampling requirements at the least possible cost.

FORMULATING THE PROBLEM The first step is to decide what the decision variables are. We note from Table 3.4 that people have been classified based on their ages (three categories) and regions (two categories). There is a separate cost associated with a person based on his or her age as well as his or her region. That is, for example, the cost for all persons from the ≤ 30 group is not the same and depends explicitly on whether the person is from a border state ($7.50) or from a non-border state ($6.90). The decision variables therefore need to identify each person surveyed based on his or her age as well as his or her region. Because we have three age categories and two regions, we need a total of 6 $(= 3 \times 2)$ decision variables. We let

B_1 = number surveyed who are $\leq$ 30 years of age and live in a border state

B_2 = number surveyed who are 31–50 years of age and live in a border state

B_3 = number surveyed who are $\geq$ 51 years of age and live in a border state

N_1 = number surveyed who are $\leq$ 30 years of age and do not live in a border state

N_2 = number surveyed who are 31–50 years of age and do not live in a border state

N_3 = number surveyed who are $\geq$ 51 years of age and do not live in a border state

Objective function:

$$\text{Minimize total interview cost} = \$7.50B_1 + \$6.80B_2 + \$5.50B_3 + \$6.90N_1 + \$7.25N_2 + \$6.10N_3$$

subject to the constraints

$B_1 + B_2 + B_3 + N_1 + N_2 + N_3 \geq 2{,}300$ (total number surveyed)

$B_1 + N_1 \geq 1{,}000$ (persons 30 years or younger)

$B_2 + N_2 \geq 600$ (persons 31–50 in age)

$B_1 + B_2 + B_3 \geq 0.15(B_1 + B_2 + B_3 + N_1 + N_2 + N_3)$ (border states)

$N_1 \geq 0.5(B_1 + N_1)$ ($\leq$30 years and not border state)

$B_3 \leq 0.2(B_3 + N_3)$ (51+ years and border state)

$B_1, B_2, B_3, N_1, N_2, N_3 \geq 0$ (nonnegativity)

TABLE 3.4
Data for Management Sciences Associates

	COST PER PERSON SURVEYED		
REGION	AGE ≤ 30	AGE 31–50	AGE ≥ 51
State bordering Mexico	$7.50	$6.80	$5.50
State not bordering Mexico	$6.90	$7.25	$6.10

SCREENSHOT 3-4 Excel Layout and Solver Entries for Management Sciences Associates

	A	B	C	D	E	F	G	H	I	J
1	**Management Science Associates**									
2										
3		B_1	B_2	B_3	N_1	N_2	N_3			
4		<= 30 and border	31-50 and border	>= 51 and border	<= 30 and not border	31-50 and not border	>= 51 and not border			
5	Number of households	0.00	600.00	140.00	1000.00	0.00	560.00			
6	Interview cost	$7.50	$6.80	$5.50	$6.90	$7.25	$6.10	$15,166.00		
7	**Constraints:**									
8	Total households	1	1	1	1	1	1	2300.00	>=	2300
9	<= 30 households	1			1			1000.00	>=	1000
10	31-50 households		1			1		600.00	>=	600
11	Border Mexico	1	1	1				740.00	>=	345
12	<= 30 and not border				1			1000.00	>=	500
13	>= 51 and border			1				140.00	<=	140
14								**LHS**	**Sign**	**RHS**

Cell has been formatted to show cost in dollars.

These three constraints include formulas on both the LHS and RHS.

Solver Parameters

Set Objective: $H$6

To: Max / Min (selected) / Value Of: 0

By Changing Variable Cells: $B$5:$G$5

Subject to the Constraints:
$H$13 <= $J$13
$H$8:$H$12 >= $J$8:$J$12

Add

The SUMPRODUCT function is used to compute all entries in column H.

File: 3-4.xls

SOLVING THE PROBLEM The Excel layout and Solver entries for this model are shown in Screenshot 3-4. In implementing this model for constraints 4 (border states), 5 ($\leq$30 years and not border state), and 6 (51+ years and border state), we have chosen to include Excel formulas for both the left-hand-side (LHS) and right-hand-side (RHS) entries. For example, for the border states constraint (4), cell H11 in Screenshot 3-4 represents the formula $(B_1 + B_2 + B_3)$ and is implemented in Excel by using the SUMPRODUCT function, as usual:

=SUMPRODUCT(B11:G11,$B$5:$G$5)

Cell J11 represents the formula $0.15(B_1 + B_2 + B_3 + N_1 + N_2 + N_3)$ in the RHS of constraint 4. For this cell, we can write the Excel formula as

=0.15*SUM(B5:G5) or =0.15*H8

To be consistent with our layout format, we have colored both cells H11 and J11 blue to indicate the presence of Excel formulas in both cells. In a similar fashion, the formula in cells J12 (RHS for constraint 5) and J13 (RHS for constraint 6) would be

Cell J12: =0.5*(B5+E5)
Cell J13: =0.2*(D5+G5)

If desired, constraints can be algebraically modified to bring all variables to the LHS.

Alternatively, if we prefer, we can algebraically modify constraints 4, 5, and 6 to bring all the variables to the LHS and just leave a constant on the RHS. For example, constraint 4 is presently modeled as

$$B_1 + B_2 + B_3 \geq 0.15(B_1 + B_2 + B_3 + N_1 + N_2 + N_3)$$

This can be rewritten as

$$B_1 + B_2 + B_3 - 0.15(B_1 + B_2 + B_3 + N_1 + N_2 + N_3) \geq 0$$

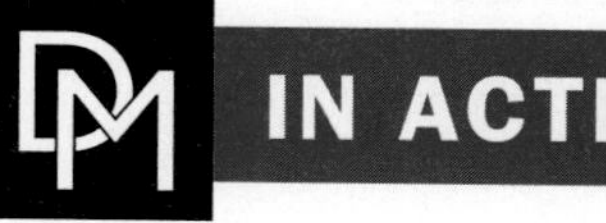

Nestlé Uses Linear Programming to Improve Financial Reporting

Nestlé's executive information system (EIS) department provides top management with operational, financial, and strategic information gathered from the firm's subsidiaries. In an effort to improve its service, the EIS department developed four business-analytics modules that use decision modeling techniques including linear programming. These four modules are integrated within a financial analysis framework that financial managers can use as needed to evaluate the economic profitability of new projects and develop strategies for its subsidiaries.

This approach has been effectively disseminated within the Nestlé group resulting in an increasing awareness among managers of the usefulness of decision modeling techniques. Interestingly, the linear programming module at Nestle focuses on the use of Solver, its answer report, and its sensitivity report–topics that are discussed in detail in Chapters 2–4 of this textbook.

Source: Based on C. Oggier, E. Fragnière, and J. Stuby. "Nestlé Improves Its Financial Reporting with Management Science," *Interfaces* 35, 4 (July–August 2005): 271–280.

which simplifies to

$$0.85B_1 + 0.85B_2 + 0.85B_3 - 0.15N_1 - 0.15N_2 - 0.15N_3 \geq 0$$

Likewise, constraints 5 and 6 would be

Constraint 5:	$-0.5B_1 + 0.5N_1 \geq 0$	($\leq$30 years and not border state)
Constraint 6:	$0.8B_3 - 0.2N_3 \leq 0$	(51+ years and border state)

Algebraic modifications of constraints are not required for implementation in Excel.

Note that such algebraic manipulations are not required to implement this model in Excel. In fact, in many cases it is probably not preferable to make such modifications because the meaning of the revised constraint is not intuitively obvious. For example, the coefficient 0.85 for B_1 in the modified form for constraint 4 has no direct significance or meaning in the context of the problem.

INTERPRETING THE RESULTS The optimal solution to MSA's marketing research problem costs \$15,166 and requires the firm to survey people as follows:

People who are 31–50 years of age and live in a border state	=	600
People who are $\geq$ 51 years of age and live in a border state	=	140
People who are $\leq$ 30 years of age and do not live in a border state	=	1,000
People who are $\geq$ 51 years of age and do not live in a border state	=	560

3.4 Finance Applications

Portfolio Selection Problem

A problem frequently encountered by managers of banks, mutual funds, investment services, and insurance companies is the selection of specific investments from among a wide variety of alternatives. A manager's overall objective is usually to maximize expected return on investment, given a set of legal, policy, or risk constraints.

Maximizing return on investment subject to a set of risk constraints is a popular financial application of LP.

Consider the example of International City Trust (ICT), which invests in trade credits, corporate bonds, precious metal stocks, mortgage-backed securities, and construction loans. ICT has \$5 million available for immediate investment and wishes to maximize the interest earned on its investments over the next year. The specifics of the investment possibilities are shown in Table 3.5. For each type of investment, the table shows the expected return over the next year as well as a score that indicates the risk associated with the investment. (A lower score implies less risk.)

To encourage a diversified portfolio, the board of directors has placed several limits on the amount that can be committed to any one type of investment: (1) No more than 25% of the total amount invested may be in any single type of investment, (2) at least 30% of the funds invested must be in precious metals, (3) at least 45% must be invested in trade credits and corporate bonds, and (4) the average risk score of the total investment must be 2 or less.

TABLE 3.5
Data for International City Trust

INVESTMENT	INTEREST EARNED	RISK SCORE
Trade credits	7%	1.7
Corporate bonds	10%	1.2
Gold stocks	19%	3.7
Platinum stocks	12%	2.4
Mortgage securities	8%	2.0
Construction loans	14%	2.9

Decision variables in financial planning models usually define the amounts to be invested in each investment choice.

FORMULATING THE PROBLEM The decision variables in most investment planning problems correspond to the amount that should be invested in each investment choice. In ICT's case, to model the investment decision as an LP problem, we let

$$
\begin{aligned}
T &= \text{dollars invested in trade credit}\\
B &= \text{dollars invested in corporate bonds}\\
G &= \text{dollars invested in gold stocks}\\
P &= \text{dollars invested in platinum stocks}\\
M &= \text{dollars invested in mortgage securities}\\
C &= \text{dollars invested in construction loans}
\end{aligned}
$$

The objective function may then be written as

$$\text{Maximize dollars of interest earned} = 0.07T + 0.10B + 0.19G + 0.12P + 0.08M + 0.14C$$

The constraints control the amounts that may be invested in each type of investment. ICT has \$5 million available for investment. Hence the first constraint is

$$T + B + G + P + M + C \leq 5{,}000{,}000$$

Could we express this constraint by using the = sign rather than ≤? Because any dollar amount that is not invested by ICT does not earn any interest, it is logical to expect that, under normal circumstances, ICT would invest the entire \$5 million. However, it is possible in some unusual cases that the conditions placed on investments by the board of directors are so restrictive that it is not possible to find an investment strategy that allows the entire amount to be invested. To guard against this possibility, it is preferable to write the preceding constraint using the ≤ sign. Note that if the investments conditions do permit the entire amount to be invested, the optimal solution will automatically do so because this is a maximization problem.

The other constraints are

$$
\begin{aligned}
T &\leq 0.25\,(T + B + G + P + M + C)\\
B &\leq 0.25\,(T + B + G + P + M + C)\\
G &\leq 0.25\,(T + B + G + P + M + C)\\
P &\leq 0.25\,(T + B + G + P + M + C)\\
M &\leq 0.25\,(T + B + G + P + M + C)\\
C &\leq 0.25\,(T + B + G + P + M + C)
\end{aligned}
$$

If we are sure that the investment conditions will permit the entire \$5 million to be invested, we can write the RHS of each of these constraints as a constant \$1,250,000 (=0.25 × \$5,000,000). However, for the same reason discussed for the first constraint, it is preferable to write the RHS for these constraints (as well as all other constraints in this problem) in terms of the sum of the decision variables rather than as constants.

As in the marketing research problem, we can, if we wish, algebraically modify these constraints so that all variables are on the LHS and only a constant is on the RHS. (*Note:* Such algebraic manipulations are not required for Excel to solve these problems, and we do not recommend that they be done.) For example, the constraint regarding trade credits would then be written as

$$0.75T - 0.25B - 0.25G - 0.25P - 0.25M - 0.25C \leq 0 \qquad \text{(no more than 25\% in trade credits)}$$

The constraints that at least 30% of the funds invested must be in precious metals and that at least 45% must be invested in trade credits and corporate bonds are written, respectively, as

$$G + P \geq 0.30\,(T + B + G + P + M + C)$$
$$T + B \geq 0.45\,(T + B + G + P + M + C)$$

Next, we come to the risk constraint which states that the average risk score of the total investment must be 2 or less. To calculate the average risk score, we need to take the weighted sum of the risk and divide it by the total amount invested. This constraint may be written as

$$\frac{1.7T + 1.2B + 3.7G + 2.4P + 2.0M + 2.9C}{T + B + G + P + M + C} \leq 2$$

Excel Notes

- Although the previous expression for the risk constraint is a valid linear equation, Excel's Solver sometimes misinterprets the division sign in the expression as an indication of nonlinearity and gives the erroneous message "The linearity conditions required by this LP Solver are not satisfied."
- Likewise, if Solver sets all decision variable values to zero at any stage during the solution process, the denominator in the previous expression becomes zero. This causes a division-by-zero error, which could sometimes lead to a "Solver encountered an error value in the Objective Cell or a Constraint cell" message.
- If a constraint with a denominator that is a function of the decision variables causes either of these situations to occur in your model, we recommend that you algebraically modify the constraint before implementing it in Excel. For example, in ICT's problem, the risk constraint could be implemented as

$$1.7T + 1.2B + 3.7G + 2.4P + 2.0M + 2.9C \leq 2(T + B + G + P + M + C)$$

Finally, we have the nonnegativity constraints:

$$T, B, G, P, M, C \geq 0$$

File: 3-5.xls, sheet: 3-5A

SOLVING THE PROBLEM The Excel layout and Solver entries for this model are shown in Screenshot 3-5A. Because we have chosen to express the RHS values for most constraints in terms of the decision variables rather than as constants, we have formulas on both sides for all but one of the constraints. The only exception is the constraint which specifies that \$5 million is available for investment. As usual, cells representing the LHS values of constraints (cells H8:H17) use the SUMPRODUCT function. Cells representing RHS values are modeled using simple Excel formulas, as in the marketing research problem. For example, the RHS (cell J9) for the constraint specifying no more than 25% in trade credits would contain the formula

=0.25*SUM(B5:G5) or =0.25*H8

Likewise, the RHS (cell J15) for the risk score constraint would contain the formula =2*H8 to reflect the algebraic manipulation of this constraint (see *Excel Notes* above).

INTERPRETING THE RESULTS The optimal solution is to invest \$1.25 million each in trade credits, corporate bonds, and platinum stocks; \$500,000 each in mortgage-backed securities and construction loans; and \$250,000 in gold stocks—earning a total interest of \$520,000. In this case, the investment conditions do allow the entire \$5 million to be invested, meaning that we could have expressed the RHS values of all constraints by using constants without affecting the optimal solution.

SCREENSHOT 3-5A Excel Layout and Solver Entries for International City Trust

	A	B	C	D	E	F	G	H	I	J
1	**International City Trust**									
2										
3		T	B	G	P	M	C			
4		Trade credits	Corp bonds	Gold	Platinum	Mortgages	Const loans			
5	Dollars Invested	$1,250,000.00	$1,250,000.00	$250,000.00	$1,250,000.00	$500,000.00	$500,000.00			
6	Interest	0.07	0.10	0.19	0.12	0.08	0.14	$520,000.00		
7	**Constraints:**									
8	Total funds	1	1	1	1	1	1	$5,000,000.00	<=	$5,000,000
9	Max trade credits	1						$1,250,000.00	<=	$1,250,000
10	Max corp bonds		1					$1,250,000.00	<=	$1,250,000
11	Max gold			1				$250,000.00	<=	$1,250,000
12	Max platinum				1			$1,250,000.00	<=	$1,250,000
13	Max mortgages					1		$500,000.00	<=	$1,250,000
14	Max const loans						1	$500,000.00	<=	$1,250,000
15	Risk score	1.7	1.2	3.7	2.4	2.0	2.9	10,000,000.00	<=	10,000,000
16	Precious metals			1	1			$1,500,000.00	>=	$1,500,000
17	Trade credits & bonds	1	1					$2,500,000.00	>=	$2,250,000
18								**LHS**	**Sign**	**RHS**

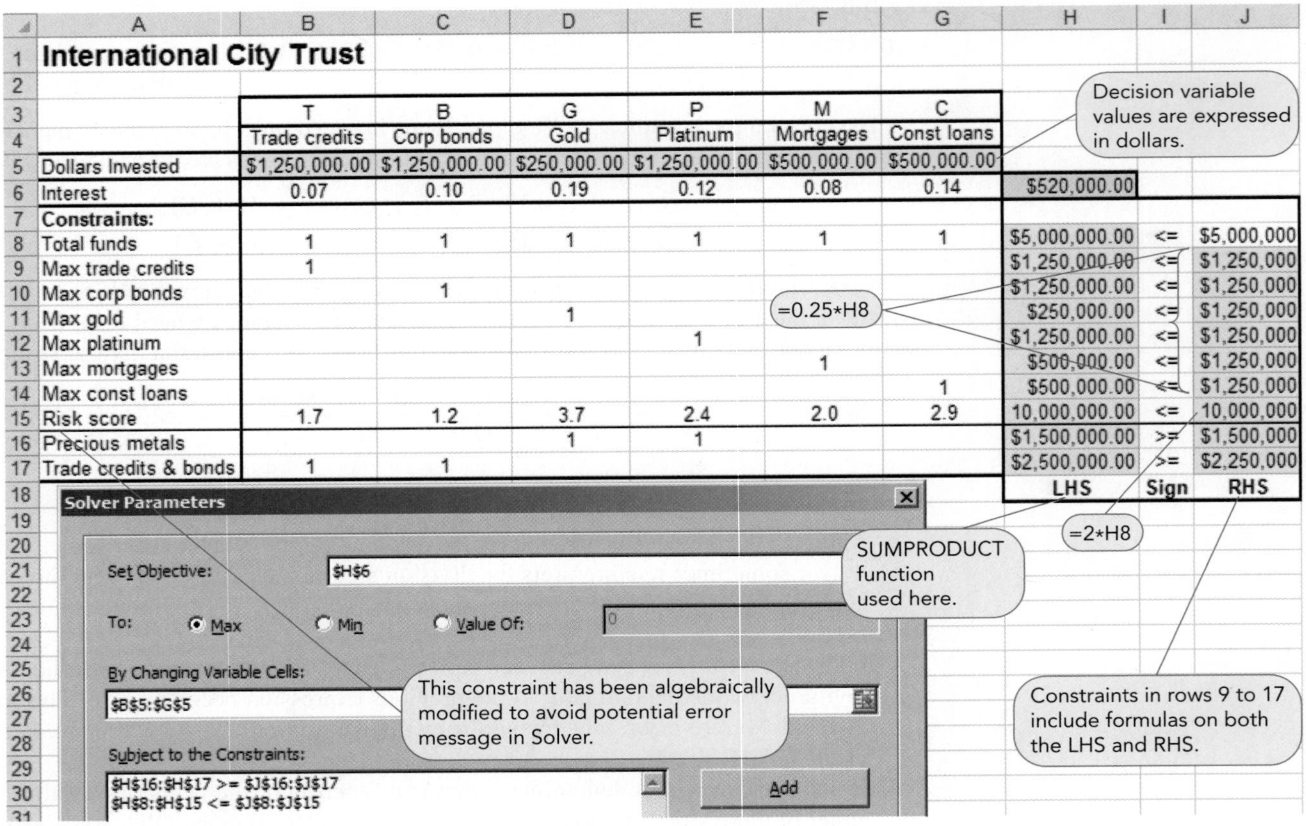

Solver Parameters

Set Objective: $H$6

To: Max Min Value Of: 0

By Changing Variable Cells: $B$5:$G$5

Subject to the Constraints:
$H$16:$H$17 >= $J$16:$J$17
$H$8:$H$15 <= $J$8:$J$15

Add

Decision variable values are expressed in dollars.

=0.25*H8

=2*H8

SUMPRODUCT function used here.

This constraint has been algebraically modified to avoid potential error message in Solver.

Constraints in rows 9 to 17 include formulas on both the LHS and RHS.

Alternate Formulations of the Portfolio Selection Problem

Alternate formulations are possible for some LP problems.

Problems with large variability in the magnitudes of parameter and/or variable values should be scaled.

In our discussion of the portfolio selection problem, we have chosen to express the decision variables as the number of dollars invested in each choice. However, for this problem (as well as many other problems), we can define the decision variables in alternate fashions. We address two alternatives here.

First, we could set up the decision variables to represent the number of dollars invested in *millions*. As noted in Chapter 2, it is usually a good idea in practice to scale problems in which values of the objective function coefficients and constraint coefficients of different constraints differ by several orders of magnitude. One way to do so would be to click the Use Automatic Scaling option available in Solver, discussed in Chapter 2. In ICT's problem, observe that the only impact of this revised definition of the decision variables on the written formulation would be to replace the $5,000,000 in the total funds available constraint by $5. Likewise, cell J8 in Screenshot 3-5A would show a value of $5. Because all other RHS values are functions of the decision variables, they will automatically reflect the revised situation. The optimal solution will show values of $1.25 each for trade credits, corporate bonds, and platinum stocks; $0.50 each for mortgage-backed securities and construction loan; and $0.25 for gold stocks—earning a total interest of $0.52.

Second, if we assume that the $5 million represents 100% of the money available, we could define the decision variables as the portion (or percentage) of this amount invested in each investment choice. For example, we could define

$$T = \text{portion (or percentage) of the \$5 million invested in trade credit}$$

We could do likewise for the other five decision variables (B, G, P, M, and C). The interesting point to note in this case is that the actual amount available ($5 million) is not really relevant and does not figure anywhere in the formulation. Rather, the idea is that if we can decide how to distribute 100% of the funds available among the various choices, we can apply those percentage allocations to any available amount.

SCREENSHOT 3-5B Excel Layout and Solver Entries for International City Trust—Alternate Model

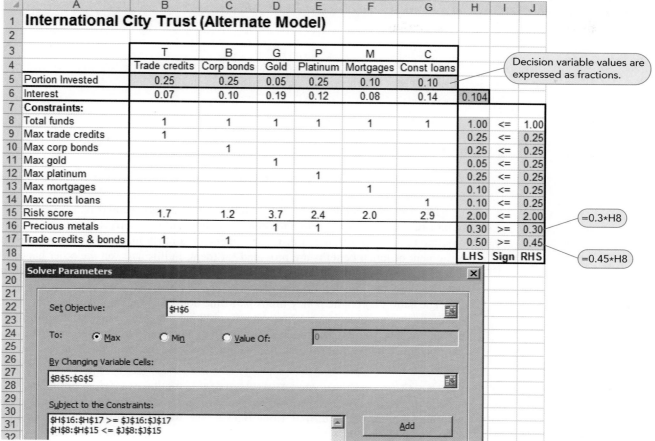

	A	B	C	D	E	F	G	H	I	J
1	**International City Trust (Alternate Model)**									
2										
3		T	B	G	P	M	C			
4		Trade credits	Corp bonds	Gold	Platinum	Mortgages	Const loans			
5	Portion Invested	0.25	0.25	0.05	0.25	0.10	0.10			
6	Interest	0.07	0.10	0.19	0.12	0.08	0.14	0.104		
7	**Constraints:**									
8	Total funds	1	1	1	1	1	1	1.00	<=	1.00
9	Max trade credits	1						0.25	<=	0.25
10	Max corp bonds		1					0.25	<=	0.25
11	Max gold			1				0.05	<=	0.25
12	Max platinum				1			0.25	<=	0.25
13	Max mortgages					1		0.10	<=	0.25
14	Max const loans						1	0.10	<=	0.25
15	Risk score	1.7	1.2	3.7	2.4	2.0	2.9	2.00	<=	2.00
16	Precious metals			1	1			0.30	>=	0.30
17	Trade credits & bonds	1	1					0.50	>=	0.45
18								**LHS**	**Sign**	**RHS**

Decision variable values are expressed as fractions.

=0.3*H8

=0.45*H8

Solver Parameters

Set Objective: $H$6

To: (•) Max ( ) Min ( ) Value Of: 0

By Changing Variable Cells: $B$5:$G$5

Subject to the Constraints:

$H$16:$H$17 >= $J$16:$J$17
$H$8:$H$15 <= $J$8:$J$15

Add

File: 3-5.xls, sheet: 3-5B

The revised Excel layout and solution for this problem is shown in Screenshot 3-5B. In ICT's problem, we note that the only impact of this revised definition of decision variables is to replace the $5 million in the total funds available constraint by 1 (or 100%). Other constraint RHS values (cells J9:J14 and J16:J17) no longer show dollar values but instead show total portions invested. The RHS for the constraint in row 15 (cell J15) shows the average risk score of the investment strategy. Screenshot 3-5B indicates that the optimal solution now shows 0.25 each for trade credits, corporate bonds, and platinum stocks; 0.10 each for mortgage-backed securities and construction loans; and 0.05 for gold stocks—earning a total return of 0.104. If we multiply each of these portions by the amount available ($5 million), we get the same dollar values as in the solution to the original formulation (Screenshot 3-5A).

It is important to define the decision variables in an LP problem as precisely as possible.

The preceding discussion reinforces the need to define the decision variables in an LP problem as precisely as possible. As we observed, depending on how the decision variables have been defined, the constraints and, hence, the resulting optimal solution values will be different.

3.5 Employee Staffing Applications

Labor Planning Problem

Labor staffing is a popular application of LP, especially when there is wide fluctuation in labor needs between various periods.

Labor planning problems address staffing needs over a specific planning horizon, such as a day, week, month, or year. They are especially useful when staffing needs are different during different time periods in the planning horizon and managers have some flexibility in assigning workers to jobs that require overlapping or interchangeable talents. Large banks frequently use LP to tackle their labor staffing problem.

Hong Kong Bank of Commerce and Industry is a busy bank that has requirements for between 10 and 18 tellers, depending on the time of day. The afternoon time, from noon to

TABLE 3.6
Tellers Required for Hong Kong Bank

TIME PERIOD	NUMBER REQUIRED
9 A.M.–10 A.M.	10
10 A.M.–11 A.M.	12
11 A.M.–Noon	14
Noon–1 P.M.	16
1 P.M.–2 P.M.	18
2 P.M.–3 P.M.	17
3 P.M.–4 P.M.	15
4 P.M.–5 P.M.	10

3 P.M., is usually heaviest. Table 3.6 indicates the workers needed at various hours that the bank is open.

The bank now employs 12 full-time tellers but also has several people available on its roster of part-time employees. A part-time employee must put in exactly 4 hours per day but can start anytime between 9 A.M. and 1 P.M. Part-timers are a fairly inexpensive labor pool because no retirement or lunch benefits are provided for them. Full-timers, on the other hand, work from 9 A.M. to 5 P.M. but are allowed 1 hour for lunch. (Half of the full-timers eat at 11 A.M. and the other half at noon.) Each full-timer thus provides 35 hours per week of productive labor time.

The bank's corporate policy limits part-time hours to a maximum of 50% of the day's total requirement. Part-timers earn \$7 per hour (or \$28 per day) on average, and full-timers earn \$90 per day in salary and benefits, on average. The bank would like to set a schedule that would minimize its total personnel costs. It is willing to release one or more of its full-time tellers if it is cost-effective to do so.

FORMULATING AND SOLVING THE PROBLEM In employee staffing problems, we typically need to determine how many employees need to start their work at the different starting times permitted. For example, in Hong Kong Bank's case, we have full-time tellers who all start work at 9 A.M. and part-timers who can start anytime between 9 A.M. and 1 P.M. Let

F = number of full-time tellers to use (all starting at 9 A.M.)
P_1 = number of part-timers to use, starting at 9 A.M. (leaving at 1 P.M.)
P_2 = number of part-timers to use, starting at 10 A.M. (leaving at 2 P.M.)
P_3 = number of part-timers to use, starting at 11 A.M. (leaving at 3 P.M.)
P_4 = number of part-timers to use, starting at noon (leaving at 4 P.M.)
P_5 = number of part-timers to use, starting at 1 P.M. (leaving at 5 P.M.)

The objective function is

$$\text{Minimize total daily personnel cost} = \$90F + \$28(P_1 + P_2 + P_3 + P_4 + P_5)$$

Next, we write the constraints. For each hour, the available number of tellers must be at least equal to the required number of tellers. This is a simple matter of counting which of the different employees (defined by the decision variables) are working during a given time period and which are not. It is also important to remember that half the full-time tellers break for lunch between 11 A.M. and noon and the other half break between noon and 1 P.M.:

$$F + P_1 \geq 10 \quad \text{(9 A.M.–10 A.M. requirement)}$$
$$F + P_1 + P_2 \geq 12 \quad \text{(10 A.M.–11 A.M. requirement)}$$
$$0.5F + P_1 + P_2 + P_3 \geq 14 \quad \text{(11 A.M.–12 noon requirement)}$$
$$0.5F + P_1 + P_2 + P_3 + P_4 \geq 16 \quad \text{(12 noon–1 P.M. requirement)}$$
$$F + P_2 + P_3 + P_4 + P_5 \geq 18 \quad \text{(1 P.M.–2 P.M. requirement)}$$
$$F + P_3 + P_4 + P_5 \geq 17 \quad \text{(2 P.M.–3 P.M. requirement)}$$
$$F + P_4 + P_5 \geq 15 \quad \text{(3 P.M.–4 P.M. requirement)}$$
$$F + P_5 \geq 10 \quad \text{(4 P.M.–5 P.M. requirement)}$$

Only 12 full-time tellers are available, so

$$F \leq 12$$

Part-time worker hours cannot exceed 50% of total hours required each day, which is the sum of the tellers needed each hour. Hence

$$4(P_1 + P_2 + P_3 + P_4 + P_5) \leq 0.5(10 + 12 + 14 + 16 + 18 + 17 + 15 + 10)$$

or

$$4P_1 + 4P_2 + 4P_3 + 4P_4 + 4P_5 \leq 56$$
$$F, P_1, P_2, P_3, P_4, P_5 \geq 0$$

File: 3-6.xls

The Excel layout and Solver entries for this model are shown in Screenshot 3-6.

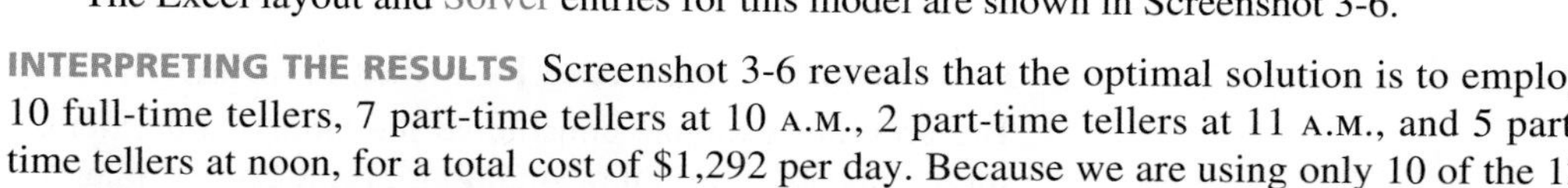

INTERPRETING THE RESULTS Screenshot 3-6 reveals that the optimal solution is to employ 10 full-time tellers, 7 part-time tellers at 10 A.M., 2 part-time tellers at 11 A.M., and 5 part-time tellers at noon, for a total cost of \$1,292 per day. Because we are using only 10 of the 12 available full-time tellers, Hong Kong Bank can choose to release up to 2 of the full-time tellers.

Alternate optimal solutions are common in many LP applications.

It turns out that there are several alternate optimal solutions that Hong Kong Bank can employ. In practice, the sequence in which you present constraints in a model can affect the specific solution that is found. We revisit this example in Chapter 4 (Solved Problem 4-1) to

SCREENSHOT 3-6 Excel Layout and Solver Entries for Hong Kong Bank

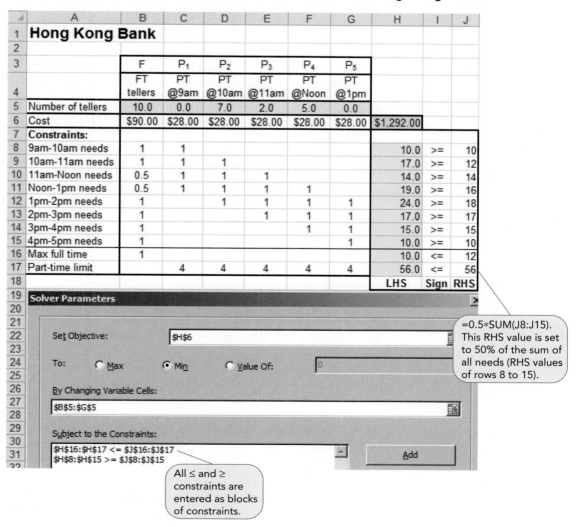

	A	B	C	D	E	F	G	H	I	J
1	**Hong Kong Bank**									
2										
3		F	P1	P2	P3	P4	P5			
4		FT tellers	PT @9am	PT @10am	PT @11am	PT @Noon	PT @1pm			
5	Number of tellers	10.0	0.0	7.0	2.0	5.0	0.0			
6	Cost	\$90.00	\$28.00	\$28.00	\$28.00	\$28.00	\$28.00	\$1,292.00		
7	**Constraints:**									
8	9am-10am needs	1	1					10.0	>=	10
9	10am-11am needs	1	1	1				17.0	>=	12
10	11am-Noon needs	0.5	1	1	1			14.0	>=	14
11	Noon-1pm needs	0.5	1	1	1	1		19.0	>=	16
12	1pm-2pm needs	1		1	1	1	1	24.0	>=	18
13	2pm-3pm needs	1			1	1	1	17.0	>=	17
14	3pm-4pm needs	1				1	1	15.0	>=	15
15	4pm-5pm needs	1					1	10.0	>=	10
16	Max full time	1						10.0	<=	12
17	Part-time limit		4	4	4	4	4	56.0	<=	56
18								**LHS**	**Sign**	**RHS**

Solver Parameters

Set Objective: \$H\$6

To: Max / Min (selected) / Value Of: 0

By Changing Variable Cells: \$B\$5:\$G\$5

Subject to the Constraints:
\$H\$16:\$H\$17 <= \$J\$16:\$J\$17
\$H\$8:\$H\$15 >= \$J\$8:\$J\$15

Add

=0.5*SUM(J8:J15). This RHS value is set to 50% of the sum of all needs (RHS values of rows 8 to 15).

All ≤ and ≥ constraints are entered as blocks of constraints.

study how we can use the Sensitivity Report generated by Solver to detect and identify alternate optimal solutions.

For this problem, one alternate solution is to employ 10 full-time tellers, 6 part-time tellers at 9 A.M., 1 part-time teller at 10 A.M., 2 part-time tellers at 11 A.M., and 5 part-time tellers at noon. The cost of this policy is also $1,292.

Note that we are setting up the teller requirement constraints as ≥ constraints rather than as = constraints. The reason for this should be obvious by now: If we try to *exactly* satisfy the teller requirements every period, the fact that each teller (full or part time) works more than one hour at a stretch may make it impossible to simultaneously satisfy all requirements as = constraints. In fact, if you replace the ≥ sign with = for the teller requirement constraints in Hong Kong Bank's model (rows 8 to 15) and resolve the problem, Solver returns a "Solver could not find a feasible solution" message.

Extensions to the Labor Planning Problem

The previous example considered the labor requirements during different time periods of a single day. In other labor planning problems, the planning horizon may consist of a week, a month, or a year. In this case, the decision variables will correspond to the different work schedules that workers can follow and will denote the number of workers who should follow a specific work schedule. Solved Problem 3-1 at the end of this chapter illustrates an example where the planning horizon is a week and the time periods are days of the week. The worker requirements are specified for each of the seven days of the week.

Labor staffing problems involving multiple shifts per period can be modeled by using LP.

In extended versions of this problem, the time periods may also include specific shifts. For example, if there are two shifts per day (day shift and night shift), there are then 14 time periods (seven days of the week, two shifts per day) in the problem. Worker requirements need to be specified for each of these 14 time periods. In this case, the work schedules need to specify the exact days and shifts that the schedule denotes. For example, an available work schedule could be "Monday to Friday on shift 1, Saturday and Sunday off." Another available work schedule could be "Tuesday to Saturday on shift 2, Sunday and Monday off." The decision analyst would need to specify all available work schedules before setting up the problem as an LP model.

Assignment Problem

Assigning people to jobs, jobs to machines, and so on is an application of LP called the assignment problem.

Assignment problems involve determining the most efficient assignment of people to jobs, machines to tasks, police cars to city sectors, salespeople to territories, and so on. The assignments are done on a one-to-one basis. For example, in a people-to-jobs assignment problem, each person is assigned to exactly one job, and, conversely, each job is assigned to exactly one person. Fractional assignments are not permitted. The objective might be to minimize the total cost of the assignments or maximize the total effectiveness or benefit of the assignments.

The assignment problem is an example of a special type of LP problem known as a network flow problem, and we study this type of problem in greater detail in Chapter 5.

3.6 Transportation Applications

Vehicle Loading Problem

Vehicle loading problems involve deciding which items to load on a vehicle (e.g. truck, ship, aircraft) to maximize the total value of the load shipped. The items loaded may need to satisfy several constraints, such as weight and volume limits of the vehicle, minimum levels of certain items that may need to be accepted, etc. As an example, we consider Goodman Shipping, an Orlando firm owned by Steven Goodman. One of his trucks, with a weight capacity of 15,000 pounds and a volume capacity of 1,300 cubic feet, is about to be loaded. Awaiting shipment are the items shown in Table 3.7. Each of these six items, we see, has an associated total dollar value, available weight, and volume per pound that the item occupies. The objective is to maximize the total value of the items loaded onto the truck without exceeding the truck's weight and volume capacities.

FORMULATING AND SOLVING THE PROBLEM The decision variables in this problem define the number of pounds of each item that should be loaded on the truck. There would be six decision

TABLE 3.7
Shipments for Goodman Shipping

ITEM	VALUE	WEIGHT (POUNDS)	VOLUME (CU. FT. PER POUND)
1	\$15,500	5,000	0.125
2	\$14,400	4,500	0.064
3	\$10,350	3,000	0.144
4	\$14,525	3,500	0.448
5	\$13,000	4,000	0.048
6	\$ 9,625	3,500	0.018

variables (one for each item) in the model. In this case, the dollar value of each item needs to be appropriately scaled for use in the objective function. For example, if the total value of the 5,000 pounds of item 1 is \$15,500, the value per pound is then 3.10 (=15,500/5,000 pounds). Similar calculations can be made for the other items to be shipped.

Let W_i be the weight (in pounds) of each item i loaded on the truck. The LP model can then be formulated as follows:

$$\text{Maximize load value} = \$3.10W_1 + \$3.20W_2 + \$3.45W_3 + \$4.15W_4 + \$3.25W_5 + \$2.75W_6$$

subject to the constraints

$$\begin{array}{lll}
W_1 + W_2 + W_3 + W_4 + W_5 + W_6 & \leq 15{,}000 & \text{(weight limit of truck)} \\
0.125\ W_1 + 0.064\ W_2 + 0.144\ W_3 + & & \\
\quad 0.0448\ W_4 + 0.048\ W_5 + 0.018\ W_6 & \leq 1{,}300 & \text{(volume limit of truck)} \\
W_1 & \leq 5{,}000 & \text{(item 1 availability)} \\
W_2 & \leq 4{,}500 & \text{(item 2 availability)} \\
W_3 & \leq 3{,}000 & \text{(item 3 availability)} \\
W_4 & \leq 3{,}500 & \text{(item 4 availability)} \\
W_5 & \leq 4{,}000 & \text{(item 5 availability)} \\
W_6 & \leq 3{,}500 & \text{(item 6 availability)} \\
W_1, W_2, W_3, W_4, W_5, W_6 & \geq 0 & \text{(nonnegativity)}
\end{array}$$

Screenshot 3-7A shows the Excel layout and Solver entries for Goodman Shipping's LP model.

File: 3-7.xls, sheet: 3-7A

INTERPRETING THE RESULTS The optimal solution in Screenshot 3-7A yields a total value of \$48,438.08 and requires Goodman to ship 3,037.38 pounds of item 1; 4,500 pounds of item 2; 3,000 pounds of item 3; 4,000 pounds of item 5; and 462.62 pounds of item 6. The truck is fully loaded from both weight and volume perspectives. As usual, if shipments have to be integers, Goodman can probably round down the totals for items 1 and 6 without affecting the total dollar value too much. Interestingly, the only item that is not included for loading is item 4, which has the highest dollar value per pound. However, its relatively high volume (per pound loaded) makes it an unattractive item to load.

File: 3-7.xls, sheet: 3-7B

ALTERNATE FORMULATIONS As in the portfolio selection problem we studied previously, there are alternate ways in which we could define the decision variables for this problem. For example, the decision variables could denote the portion (or percentage) of each item that is accepted for loading. Under this approach, let P_i be the portion of each item i loaded on the truck. Screenshot 3-7B on page 87 shows the Excel layout and solution for the alternate model, using these revised decision variables. The layout for this model is identical to that shown in Screenshot 3-7A, and you should be able to recognize its written formulation easily. The coefficients in the volume constraint show the volume occupied by the entire quantity of an item. For example, the volume coefficient for item 1 is 625 cubic feet (= 0.125 cubic feet per pound × 5,000 pounds). Likewise, the coefficient for item 2 is 288 cubic feet (= 0.064 cubic feet per pound × 4,500 pounds).

The final six constraints reflect the fact that at most one "unit" (i.e., a proportion of 1) of an item can be loaded onto the truck. In effect, if Goodman can load a *portion* of an item (e.g., item

SCREENSHOT 3-7A Excel Layout and Solver Entries for Goodman Shipping

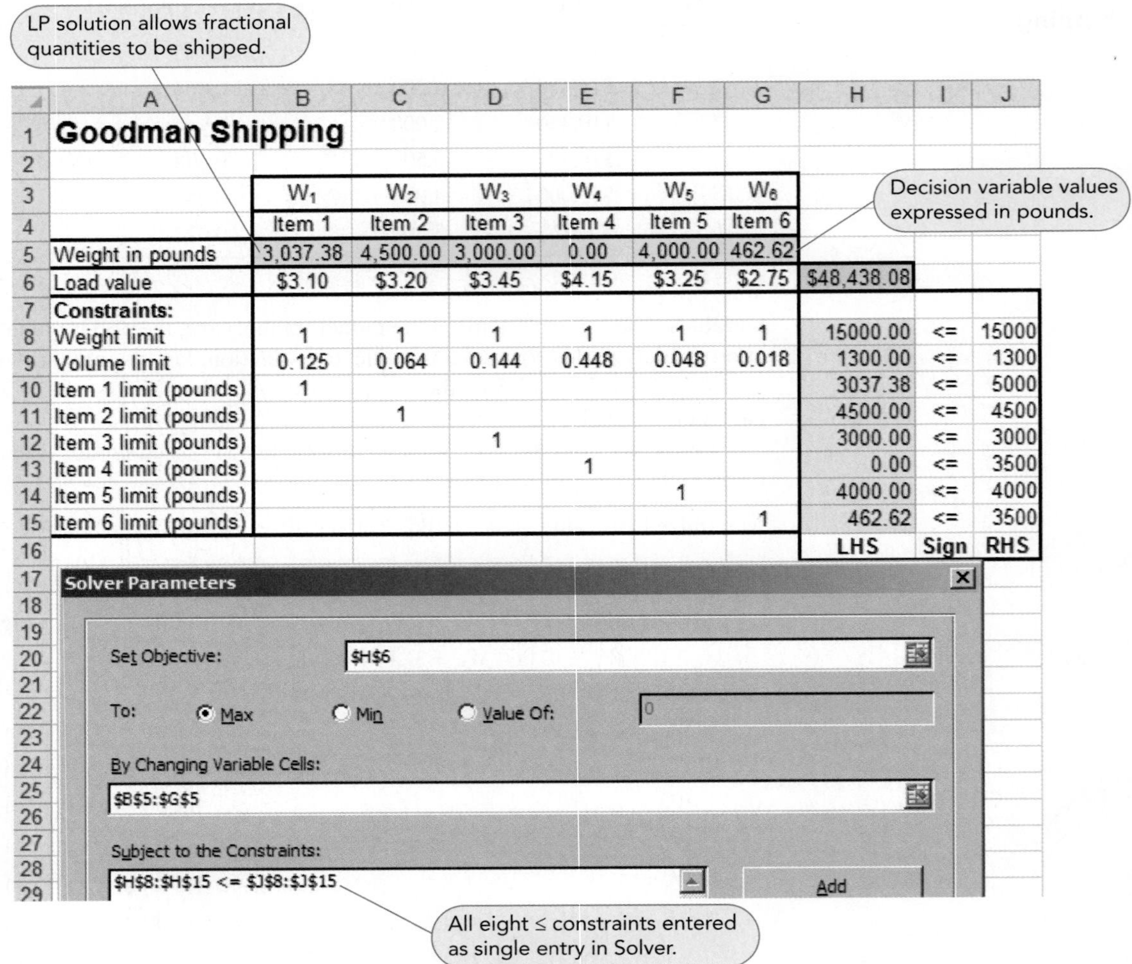

	A	B	C	D	E	F	G	H	I	J
1	**Goodman Shipping**									
2										
3		W_1	W_2	W_3	W_4	W_5	W_6			
4		Item 1	Item 2	Item 3	Item 4	Item 5	Item 6			
5	Weight in pounds	3,037.38	4,500.00	3,000.00	0.00	4,000.00	462.62			
6	Load value	$3.10	$3.20	$3.45	$4.15	$3.25	$2.75	$48,438.08		
7	**Constraints:**									
8	Weight limit	1	1	1	1	1	1	15000.00	<=	15000
9	Volume limit	0.125	0.064	0.144	0.448	0.048	0.018	1300.00	<=	1300
10	Item 1 limit (pounds)	1						3037.38	<=	5000
11	Item 2 limit (pounds)		1					4500.00	<=	4500
12	Item 3 limit (pounds)			1				3000.00	<=	3000
13	Item 4 limit (pounds)				1			0.00	<=	3500
14	Item 5 limit (pounds)					1		4000.00	<=	4000
15	Item 6 limit (pounds)						1	462.62	<=	3500
16								**LHS**	**Sign**	**RHS**

1 is a batch of 1,000 folding chairs, not all of which need to be shipped together), the proportions P_i will all have values ranging from 0 (none of that item is loaded) to 1 (all of that item is loaded).

The solution to this model shows that the maximum load value is $48,438.08. This load value is achieved by shipping 60.748% of item 1 ($0.60748 \times 5{,}000 = 3{,}037.4$ pounds) of item 1; all available quantities (i.e., 100%) of items 2, 3, and 5; and 13.218% (462.63 pounds) of item 6. As expected, this is the same solution we obtained in Screenshot 3-7A, using the original model for this problem.

Expanded Vehicle Loading Problem—Allocation Problem

In the previous example, Goodman had only a single truck and needed to load all items on the same truck. Let us now assume that Goodman has the option of replacing his single truck (with a weight capacity of 15,000 pounds and a volume capacity of 1,300 cubic feet) with two smaller trucks (each with a weight capacity of 10,000 pounds and a volume capacity of 900 cubic feet). Item availabilities and other data are still as shown in Table 3.7. If he uses two trucks, Goodman wants to ensure that they are loaded in an equitable manner. That is, the same total weight should be loaded on both trucks. Total volumes loaded in the two trucks can, however, be different. If the fixed cost of operating the two smaller trucks is $5,000 more than the current cost of operating just a single truck, should Goodman go with the two trucks?

Allocation problems involve deciding how much of an item to allocate to the different choices that are available.

In this revised model, Goodman has to decide how to allocate the six items between the two trucks. Note that it is possible for the total quantity of an item to be split between the two trucks. That is, we can load a portion of an item in the first truck and load part or all of the remaining

SCREENSHOT 3-7B Excel Layout and Solver Entries for Goodman Shipping—Alternate Model

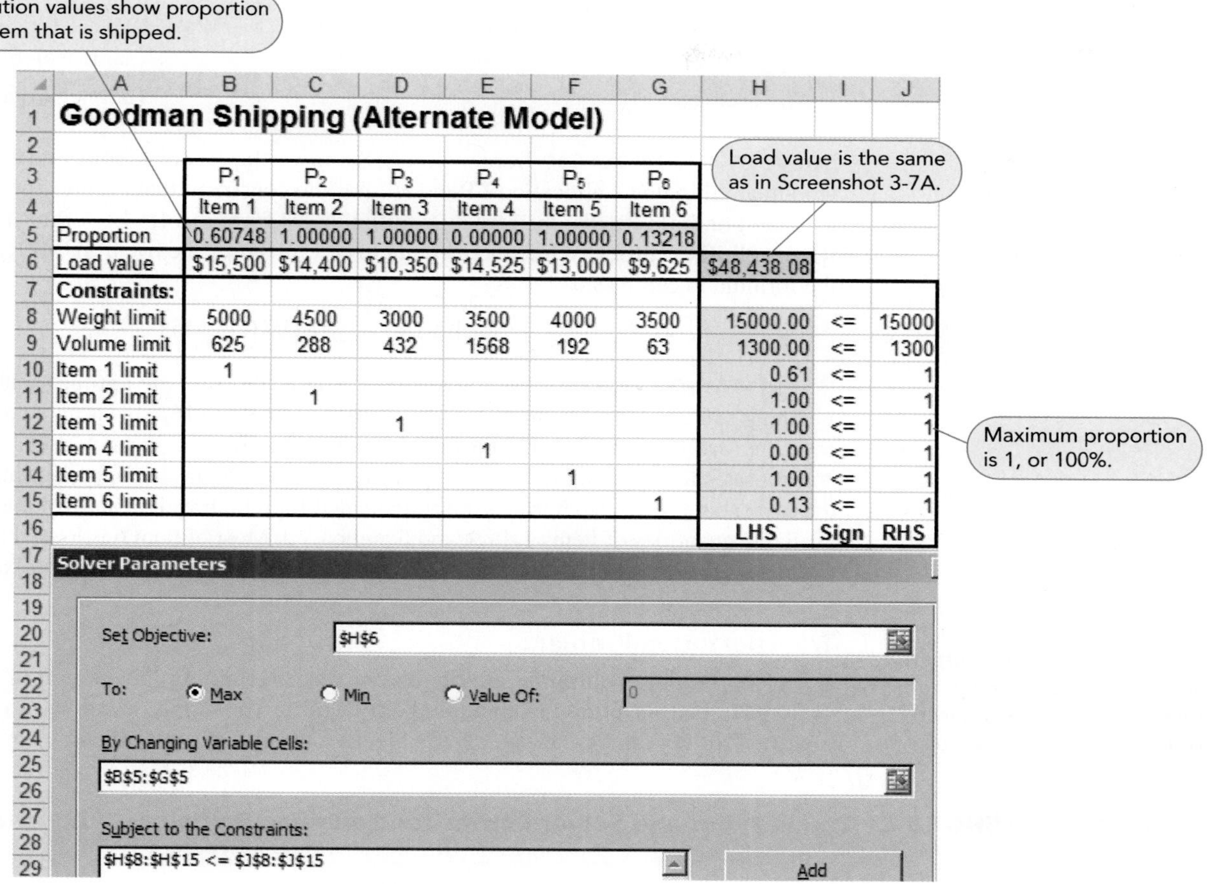

	P1	P2	P3	P4	P5	P6			
	Item 1	Item 2	Item 3	Item 4	Item 5	Item 6			
Proportion	0.60748	1.00000	1.00000	0.00000	1.00000	0.13218			
Load value	$15,500	$14,400	$10,350	$14,525	$13,000	$9,625	$48,438.08		
Constraints:									
Weight limit	5000	4500	3000	3500	4000	3500	15000.00	<=	15000
Volume limit	625	288	432	1568	192	63	1300.00	<=	1300
Item 1 limit	1						0.61	<=	1
Item 2 limit		1					1.00	<=	1
Item 3 limit			1				1.00	<=	1
Item 4 limit				1			0.00	<=	1
Item 5 limit					1		1.00	<=	1
Item 6 limit						1	0.13	<=	1
							LHS	**Sign**	**RHS**

portion in the other truck. Because the decision involves an allocation (of items to trucks, in Goodman's case), this type of problem is called an *allocation* problem.

Using double-subscripted variables is a convenient way of formulating many LP models.

FORMULATING THE PROBLEM The decision variables here need to specify how much of each item should be loaded on each truck. Let the double-subscripted variable W_{i1} be the weight (in pounds) of each item i loaded on the first truck and W_{i2} be the weight (in pounds) of each item i loaded on the second truck. The LP model for this expanded vehicle loading problem can then be formulated as follows:

$$\text{Maximize load value} = \$3.10(W_{11} + W_{12}) + \$3.20(W_{21} + W_{22}) + \$3.45(W_{31} + W_{32}) + \$4.15(W_{41} + W_{42}) + \$3.25(W_{51} + W_{52}) + \$2.75(W_{61} + W_{62})$$

subject to the constraints

$$W_{11} + W_{21} + W_{31} + W_{41} + W_{51} + W_{61} \leq 10{,}000 \quad \text{(weight limit of truck 1)}$$

$$0.125\,W_{11} + 0.064\,W_{21} + 0.144\,W_{31} + 0.448\,W_{41} + 0.048\,W_{51} + 0.018\,W_{61} \leq 900 \quad \text{(volume limit of truck 1)}$$

$$W_{12} + W_{22} + W_{32} + W_{42} + W_{52} + W_{62} \leq 10{,}000 \quad \text{(weight limit of truck 2)}$$

$$0.125\,W_{12} + 0.064\,W_{22} + 0.144\,W_{32} + 0.448\,W_{42} + 0.048\,W_{52} + 0.018\,W_{62} \leq 900 \quad \text{(volume limit of truck 2)}$$

$$W_{11} + W_{12} \leq 5{,}000 \quad \text{(item 1 availability)}$$

$$W_{21} + W_{22} \leq 4{,}500 \quad \text{(item 2 availability)}$$

$$W_{31} + W_{32} \leq 3{,}000 \quad \text{(item 3 availability)}$$

$$W_{41} + W_{42} \leq 3{,}500 \quad \text{(item 4 availability)}$$

$$
\begin{array}{lll}
W_{51} + W_{52} & \leq 4{,}000 & \text{(item 5 availability)} \\
W_{61} + W_{62} & \leq 3{,}500 & \text{(item 6 availability)} \\
W_{11} + W_{21} + W_{31} + W_{41} + W_{51} + W_{61} & = W_{12} + W_{22} + W_{32} + W_{42} + W_{52} + W_{62} & \\
 & & \text{(same weight in both trucks)} \\
\text{All variables} & \geq 0 & \text{(nonnegativity)}
\end{array}
$$

File: 3-8.xls

SOLVING THE PROBLEM Screenshot 3-8 shows the Excel layout and Solver entries for Goodman Shipping's allocation LP model. For the constraint that ensures the same total weight is loaded on both trucks, the Excel layout includes formulas for both the LHS (cell N18) and RHS (cell P18) entries. While the formula in cell N18 uses the usual SUMPRODUCT function, the formula in cell P18 is

Cell P18: =SUM(H5:M5)

INTERPRETING THE RESULTS Screenshot 3-8 indicates that the optimal solution to Goodman Shipping's allocation problem yields a total value of $63,526.16. This is an increase of $15,088.08 over the load value of $48,438.08 realizable with just the single truck. Because this more than compensates for the increased $5,000 operating cost, Goodman should replace his single truck with the two smaller ones. Both trucks are fully loaded from both weight and volume perspectives. All available quantities of items 1, 2, 3, and 5 are loaded. Most of item 6 is loaded (3,034.88 of 3,500 pounds available), while only about 13.29% (465.12 of 3,500 pounds available) of item 4 is loaded.

Transportation Problem

A problem involving transporting goods from several origins to several destinations efficiently is called a transportation problem.

A transportation, or shipping, problem involves determining the amount of goods or number of items to be transported from a number of origins (or supply locations) to a number of destinations (or demand locations). The objective usually is to minimize total shipping costs or

SCREENSHOT 3-8 Excel Layout and Solver Entries for Goodman Shipping—Allocation

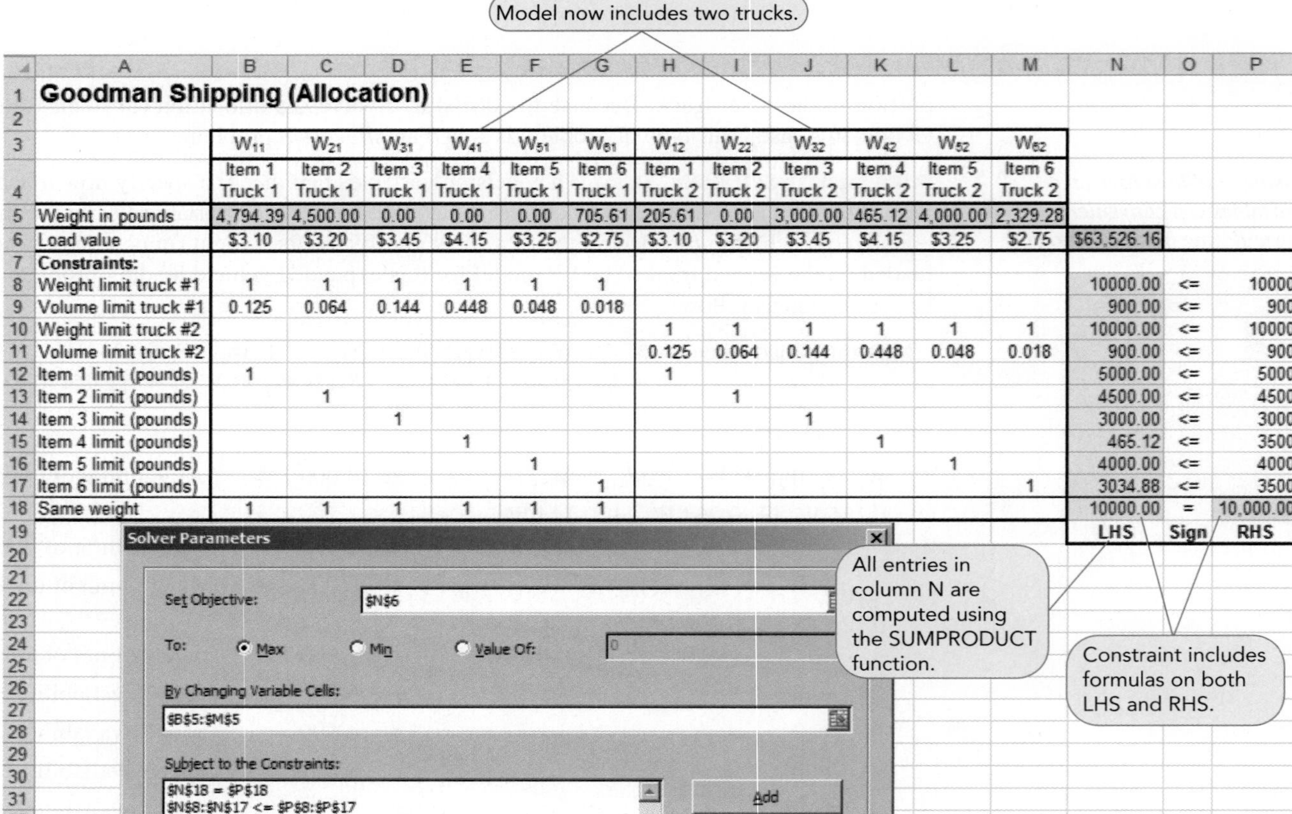

	A	B	C	D	E	F	G	H	I	J	K	L	M	N	O	P
1	Goodman Shipping (Allocation)															
2																
3		W_{11}	W_{21}	W_{31}	W_{41}	W_{51}	W_{61}	W_{12}	W_{22}	W_{32}	W_{42}	W_{52}	W_{62}			
4		Item 1 Truck 1	Item 2 Truck 1	Item 3 Truck 1	Item 4 Truck 1	Item 5 Truck 1	Item 6 Truck 1	Item 1 Truck 2	Item 2 Truck 2	Item 3 Truck 2	Item 4 Truck 2	Item 5 Truck 2	Item 6 Truck 2			
5	Weight in pounds	4,794.39	4,500.00	0.00	0.00	0.00	705.61	205.61	0.00	3,000.00	465.12	4,000.00	2,329.28			
6	Load value	$3.10	$3.20	$3.45	$4.15	$3.25	$2.75	$3.10	$3.20	$3.45	$4.15	$3.25	$2.75	$63,526.16		
7	Constraints:															
8	Weight limit truck #1	1	1	1	1	1	1							10000.00	<=	10000
9	Volume limit truck #1	0.125	0.064	0.144	0.448	0.048	0.018							900.00	<=	900
10	Weight limit truck #2							1	1	1	1	1	1	10000.00	<=	10000
11	Volume limit truck #2							0.125	0.064	0.144	0.448	0.048	0.018	900.00	<=	900
12	Item 1 limit (pounds)	1						1						5000.00	<=	5000
13	Item 2 limit (pounds)		1						1					4500.00	<=	4500
14	Item 3 limit (pounds)			1						1				3000.00	<=	3000
15	Item 4 limit (pounds)				1						1			465.12	<=	3500
16	Item 5 limit (pounds)					1						1		4000.00	<=	4000
17	Item 6 limit (pounds)						1						1	3034.88	<=	3500
18	Same weight	1	1	1	1	1	1							10000.00	=	10,000.00
19														LHS	Sign	RHS

Swift & Company Uses Linear Programming to Schedule Operations at Five Plants

Swift & Company, a privately held Colorado based protein-processing company, has three business segments: Swift Beef, Swift Pork, and Swift Australia. Beef and related products constitute the largest portion of the company's annual sales of over $8 billion. Swift operates five plants with each plant capable of processing approximately 18,000 to 25,000 head of cattle per plant per week, which translates to over 6 billion pounds of beef delivered annually.

Because beef is highly perishable, Swift's customers specify a 10 to 14 day maximum age for the beef upon delivery. Production schedulers must therefore be aware of inventory quantities and age. Tight margins means that optimizing cattle procurement and product mix is essential to improving profitability. With over 1,500 stock keeping units, 30,000 shipping locations, and the high costs and many sources of variability in raw material, Swift's optimization problem is both complex and difficult.

Working in cooperation with Swift, analysts at Aspen Technology developed an integrated system of 45 linear programming models that address Swift's four critical needs: (1) provide near real time information on product availability, (2) accurately control inventories, (3) provide the ability to sell unsold production with maximum margins, and (4) provide the ability to reoptimize the use of raw material to satisfy changes in demand. The scheduling models produce shift-level and daily schedules for each plant over a 28-day planning horizon. Swift realized total audited benefits of $12.74 million in just the first year after this new system was implemented.

Source: Based on A. Bixby, B. Downs, and M. Self. "A Scheduling and Capable-to-Promise Application for Swift & Company," *Interfaces*, 36, 1 (January–February 2006): 69–86.

distances. Constraints in this type of problem deal with capacities or supplies at each origin and requirements or demands at each destination.

Like the assignment problem, the transportation problem is also an example of a network flow problem. We will study this type of problem in greater detail in Chapter 5.

3.7 Blending Applications

Diet Problem

The diet problem, one of the earliest applications of LP, was originally used by hospitals to determine the most economical diet for patients. Known in agricultural applications as the feed mix problem, the diet problem involves specifying a food or feed ingredient combination that satisfies stated nutritional requirements at a minimum cost level. An example follows.

The Whole Food Nutrition Center uses three different types of bulk grains to blend a natural breakfast cereal that it sells by the pound. The store advertises that each 2-ounce serving of the cereal, when taken with $^1/_2$ cup of whole milk, meets an average adult's minimum daily requirement for protein, riboflavin, phosphorus, and magnesium. The cost of each bulk grain and the protein, riboflavin, phosphorus, and magnesium units per pound of each are shown in Table 3.8.

The minimum adult daily requirement (called the U.S. Recommended Daily Allowance [USRDA]) for protein is 3 units, for riboflavin is 2 units, for phosphorus is 1 unit, and for magnesium is 0.425 units. Whole Food wants to select the blend of grains that will meet the USRDA at a minimum cost.

In blending applications, the decision variables typically denote the amount of each ingredient that should be used to make the product(s).

FORMULATING AND SOLVING THE PROBLEM The decision variables in blending applications typically define the amount of each ingredient that should be used to make the product(s). It is interesting to contrast this with product mix problems, where the decision variables define the

TABLE 3.8 Requirements for Whole Food's Natural Cereal

GRAIN	COST PER POUND (CENTS)	PROTEIN (UNITS/LB)	RIBOFLAVIN (UNITS/LB)	PHOSPHORUS (UNITS/LB)	MAGNESIUM (UNITS/LB)
A	33	22	16	8	5
B	47	28	14	7	0
C	38	21	25	9	6

number of units to make of each product. That is, blending problems typically make decisions regarding amounts of each *input* (resource) to use, while product mix problems make decisions regarding numbers of each *output* to make.

In Whole Food Nutrition's case, the ingredients (inputs) are the three different types of bulk grains. We let

A = pounds of grain A to use in one 2-ounce serving of cereal
B = pounds of grain B to use in one 2-ounce serving of cereal
C = pounds of grain C to use in one 2-ounce serving of cereal

This is the objective function:

$$\text{Minimize total cost of mixing a 2-ounce serving of cereal} = \$0.33A + \$0.47B + \$0.38C$$

subject to the constraints

$$22A + 28B + 21C \geq 3 \quad \text{(protein units)}$$
$$16A + 14B + 25C \geq 2 \quad \text{(riboflavin units)}$$
$$8A + 7B + 9C \geq 1 \quad \text{(phosphorus units)}$$
$$5A + 6C \geq 0.425 \quad \text{(magnesium units)}$$
$$A + B + C = 0.125 \quad \text{(total mix is 2 ounces, or 0.125 pound)}$$
$$A, B, C \geq 0$$

Screenshot 3-9 shows the Excel layout and Solver entries for this LP model.

File: 3-9.xls

INTERPRETING THE RESULTS The solution to Whole Food Nutrition Center's problem requires mixing together 0.025 pounds of grain A, 0.050 pounds of grain B, and 0.050 pounds of grain C. Another way of stating this solution is in terms of a 2-ounce serving of each grain: 0.4 ounces of grain A, 0.8 ounces of grain B, and 0.8 ounces of grain C in each 2-ounce serving of cereal. The cost per serving is $0.05.

SCREENSHOT 3-9
Excel Layout and Solver Entries for Whole Food Nutrition Center

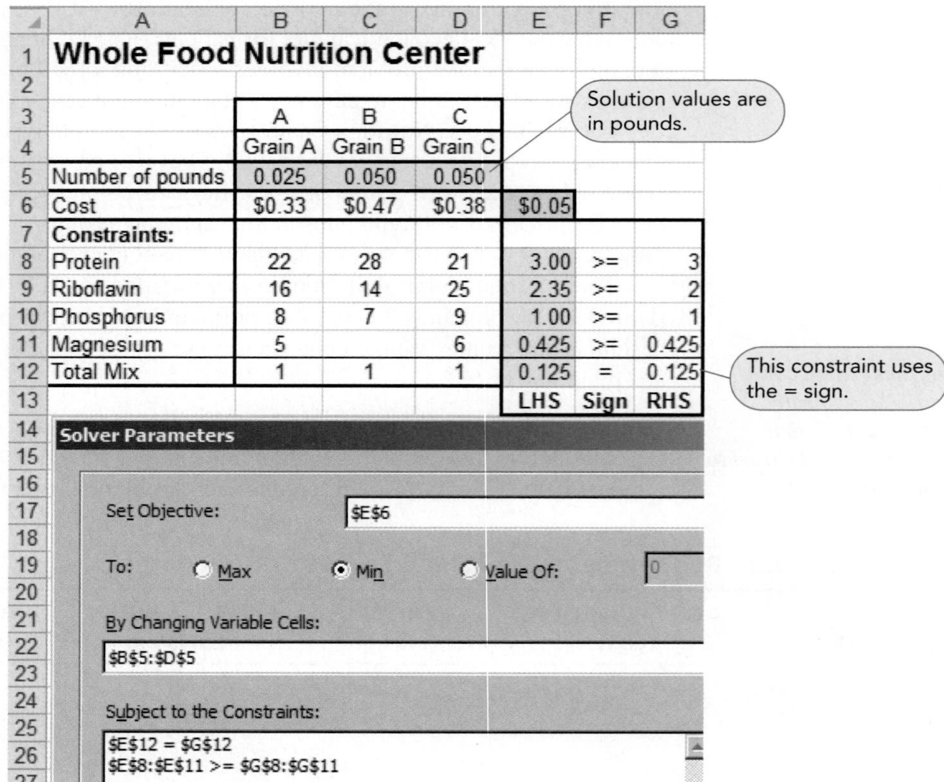

	A	B	C	D	E	F	G
1	Whole Food Nutrition Center						
2							
3		A	B	C			
4		Grain A	Grain B	Grain C			
5	Number of pounds	0.025	0.050	0.050			
6	Cost	$0.33	$0.47	$0.38	$0.05		
7	Constraints:						
8	Protein	22	28	21	3.00	>=	3
9	Riboflavin	16	14	25	2.35	>=	2
10	Phosphorus	8	7	9	1.00	>=	1
11	Magnesium	5		6	0.425	>=	0.425
12	Total Mix	1	1	1	0.125	=	0.125
13					LHS	Sign	RHS

TABLE 3.9 Ingredient Data for Low Knock Oil

CRUDE OIL TYPE	COMPOUND A (%)	COMPOUND B (%)	COMPOUND C (%)	COST/BARREL ($)	AVAIL. (BARRELS)
*X*100	35	25	35	86	15,000
*X*200	50	30	15	92	32,000
*X*300	60	20	15	95	24,000

Blending Problem

In most practical blending problems, the ingredients are usually used to make more than one product.

In the preceding diet problem, the ingredients (grains) had to be mixed to create just a single product (cereal). Diet and feed mix problems are actually special cases of a more general class of LP problems known as *blending problems*. Blending problems are very common in chemical industries, and they arise when a decision must be made regarding the blending of two or more ingredients (or resources) to produce two or more products (or end items). The ingredients must be blended in such a manner that each final product satisfies specific requirements regarding its composition. In addition, ingredients may have limitations regarding their availabilities, and products may have conditions regarding their demand. The following example deals with an application frequently seen in the petroleum industry: the blending of crude oils to produce different grades of gasoline.

Major oil refineries use LP for blending crude oils to produce gasoline grades.

The Low Knock Oil Company produces three grades of gasoline for industrial distribution. The three grades—premium, regular, and economy—are produced by refining a blend of three types of crude oil: type *X*100, type *X*200, and type *X*300. Each crude oil differs not only in cost per barrel but in its composition as well. Table 3.9 indicates the percentage of three crucial compounds found in each of the crude oils, the cost per barrel for each, and the maximum weekly availability of each.

Table 3.10 indicates the weekly demand for each grade of gasoline and the specific conditions on the amounts of the different compounds that each grade of gasoline should contain. The table shows, for example, that in order for gasoline to be classified as premium grade, it must contain at least 55% compound A. Low Knock's management must decide how many barrels of each type of crude oil to buy each week for blending to satisfy demand at minimum cost.

FORMULATING THE PROBLEM As noted in the diet problem, the decision variables in blending applications typically denote the amount of each ingredient that should be used to make the product(s). In Low Knock's case, the ingredients are the crude oils, and the products are the grades of gasoline. Because there are three ingredients that are blended to create three products, we need a total of 9 $(= 3 \times 3)$ decision variables. We let

P_1 = barrels of *X*100 crude blended to produce the premium grade
P_2 = barrels of *X*200 crude blended to produce the premium grade
P_3 = barrels of *X*300 crude blended to produce the premium grade
R_1 = barrels of *X*100 crude blended to produce the regular grade
R_2 = barrels of *X*200 crude blended to produce the regular grade
R_3 = barrels of *X*300 crude blended to produce the regular grade
E_1 = barrels of *X*100 crude blended to produce the economy grade
E_2 = barrels of *X*200 crude blended to produce the economy grade
E_3 = barrels of *X*300 crude blended to produce the economy grade

TABLE 3.10 Gasoline Data for Low Knock Oil

GASOLINE TYPE	COMPOUND A	COMPOUND B	COMPOUND C	DEMAND (BARRELS)
Premium	$\geq$ 55%	$\leq$ 23%		14,000
Regular		$\geq$ 25%	$\leq$ 35%	22,000
Economy	$\geq$ 40%		$\leq$ 25%	25,000

We can calculate the total amount produced of each gasoline grade by adding the amounts of the three crude oils used to create that grade. For example,

$$\text{Total amount of premium grade gasoline produced} = P_1 + P_2 + P_3$$

Likewise, we can calculate the total amount used of each crude oil type by adding the amounts of that crude oil used to create the three gasoline grades. For example,

$$\text{Total amount of crude oil type } X100 \text{ used} = P_1 + R_1 + E_1$$

The objective is to minimize the total cost of the crude oils used and can be written as

$$\text{Minimize total cost} = \$86(P_1 + R_1 + E_1) + \$92(P_2 + R_2 + E_2) + \$95(P_3 + R_3 + E_3)$$

subject to the constraints

$$\begin{aligned}
P_1 + R_1 + E_1 &\leq 15{,}000 && \text{(availability of } X100 \text{ crude oil)}\\
P_2 + R_2 + E_2 &\leq 32{,}000 && \text{(availability of } X200 \text{ crude oil)}\\
P_3 + R_3 + E_3 &\leq 24{,}000 && \text{(availability of } X300 \text{ crude oil)}\\
P_1 + P_2 + P_3 &\geq 14{,}000 && \text{(demand for premium gasoline)}\\
R_1 + R_2 + R_3 &\geq 22{,}000 && \text{(demand for regular gasoline)}\\
E_1 + E_2 + E_3 &\geq 25{,}000 && \text{(demand for economy gasoline)}
\end{aligned}$$

Observe that we have written the demand constraints as $\geq$ conditions in this problem. The reason is that the objective function in this problem is to minimize the total cost. If we write the demand constraints also as $\leq$ conditions, the optimal solution could result in a trivial "don't make anything, don't spend anything" situation.[1] As we have seen in several examples before now, if the objective function is a minimization function, there must be at least one constraint in the problem that forces the optimal solution away from the origin (i.e., zero values for all decision variables).

Blending constraints specify the compositions of each product.

Next, we come to the blending constraints that specify the amounts of the different compounds that each grade of gasoline can contain. First, we know that at least 55% of each barrel of premium gasoline must be compound A. To write this constraint, we note that

$$\text{Amount of compound A in premium grade gasoline} = 0.35P_1 + 0.50P_2 + 0.60P_3$$

If we divide this amount by the total amount of premium grade gasoline produced $(= P_1 + P_2 + P_3)$, we get the total portion of compound A in this grade of gasoline. Therefore, the constraint may be written as

$$(0.35P_1 + 0.50P_2 + 0.60P_3)/(P_1 + P_2 + P_3) \geq 0.55 \qquad \text{(compound A in premium grade)}$$

The other compound specifications may be written in a similar fashion, as follows:

$$\begin{aligned}
(0.25P_1 + 0.30P_2 + 0.20P_3)/(P_1 + P_2 + P_3) &\leq 0.23 && \text{(compound B in premium grade)}\\
(0.25R_1 + 0.30R_2 + 0.20R_3)/(R_1 + R_2 + R_3) &\geq 0.25 && \text{(compound B in regular grade)}\\
(0.35R_1 + 0.15R_2 + 0.15R_3)/(R_1 + R_2 + R_3) &\leq 0.35 && \text{(compound C in regular grade)}\\
(0.35E_1 + 0.50E_2 + 0.60E_3)/(E_1 + E_2 + E_3) &\geq 0.40 && \text{(compound A in economy grade)}\\
(0.35E_1 + 0.15E_2 + 0.15E_3)/(E_1 + E_2 + E_3) &\leq 0.25 && \text{(compound C in economy grade)}
\end{aligned}$$

Finally, we have the nonnegativity constraints:

$$P_1, P_2, P_3, R_1, R_2, R_3, E_1, E_2, E_3 \geq 0 \qquad \text{(nonnegativity)}$$

File: 3-10.xls

SOLVING THE PROBLEM Screenshot 3-10 shows the Excel layout and Solver entries for this LP model. As in the portfolio selection problem, to avoid potential error messages from Solver (see the *Excel Notes* on page 79), we have algebraically modified all the compound specification

[1] This, of course, assumes that the total availability of the three crude oils is sufficient to satisfy the total demand for the three gasoline grades. If total availability is less than total demand, we need to write the demand constraints as $\leq$ expressions and the availability constraints as $\geq$ expressions.

SCREENSHOT 3-10 Excel Layout and Solver Entries for Low Knock Oil

	A	B	C	D	E	F	G	H	I	J	K	L	M
1	**Low Knock Oil Company**												
2													
3		P_1	P_2	P_3	R_1	R_2	R_3	E_1	E_2	E_3			
4		X100 in premium	X200 in premium	X300 in premium	X100 in regular	X200 in regular	X300 in regular	X100 in economy	X200 in economy	X300 in economy			
5	Number of barrels	2,500.00	0.00	11,500.00	0.00	22,000.00	0.00	12,500.00	10,000.00	2,500.00			
6	Cost	$86.00	$92.00	$95.00	$86.00	$92.00	$95.00	$86.00	$92.00	$95.00	$5,564,000.00		
7	**Constraints:**												
8	Premium demand	1	1	1							14000.00	>=	14000
9	Regular demand				1	1	1				22000.00	>=	22000
10	Economy demand							1	1	1	25000.00	>=	25000
11	A in premium	0.35	0.50	0.60							7775.00	>=	7700
12	B in regular				0.25	0.30	0.20				6600.00	>=	5500
13	A in economy							0.35	0.50	0.60	10875.00	>=	10000
14	X100 available	1			1			1			15000.00	<=	15000
15	X200 available		1			1			1		32000.00	<=	32000
16	X300 available			1			1			1	14000.00	<=	24000
17	B in premium	0.25	0.30	0.20							2925.00	<=	3220
18	C in regular				0.35	0.15	0.15				3300.00	<=	7700
19	C in economy							0.35	0.15	0.15	6250.00	<=	6250
20											**LHS**	**Sign**	**RHS**

Optimal blending values

=0.55*SUM(B5:D5)

Constraints in rows 11 to 13 and 17 to 19 include formulas on RHS also.

Solver Parameters

Set Objective: $K$6

To: Max Min Value Of: 0

By Changing Variable Cells:

$B$5:$J$5

Subject to the Constraints:

$K$14:$K$19 <= $M$14:$M$19
$K$8:$K$13 >= $M$8:$M$13

Add

Constraints in rows 11 to 13 and 17 to 19 have been algebraically modified to avoid potential error message in Solver.

constraints in our Excel implementation of this model. For example, the constraint specifying the portion of compound A in premium grade gasoline is modified as

$$0.35P_1 + 0.50P_2 + 0.60P_3 \geq 0.55(P_1 + P_2 + P_3)$$

The six compound specification constraints therefore have Excel formulas in both the LHS cells (K11:K13, K17:K19) and RHS cells (M11:M13, M17:M19). The LHS cells use the usual SUMPRODUCT function.

INTERPRETING THE RESULTS Screenshot 3-10 indicates that the blending strategy will cost Low Knock Oil $5,564,000 and require it to mix the three types of crude oil as follows:

P_1 = 2,500 barrels of $X100$ crude oil to make premium grade gasoline
P_3 = 11,500 barrels of $X300$ crude oil to make premium grade gasoline
R_2 = 22,000 barrels of $X200$ crude oil to make regular grade gasoline
E_1 = 12,500 barrels of $X100$ crude oil to make economy grade gasoline
E_2 = 10,000 barrels of $X200$ crude oil to make economy grade gasoline
E_3 = 2,500 barrels of $X300$ crude oil to make economy grade gasoline

The entire demand for the three gasoline grades is met. Low Knock should buy all available barrels of crude oil types $X100$ and $X200$ and only 14,000 barrels of the 24,000 barrels available of type $X300$. (Note: This model has multiple optimal solutions.)

3.8 Multiperiod Applications

Multiperiod problems are perhaps the most challenging application of LP.

Perhaps the most challenging application of LP is in modeling multiperiod scenarios. These are situations in which the decision maker has to determine the optimal decisions for several periods (e.g., weeks, months). What makes these problems especially difficult is that the decision choices in later periods are directly dependent on the decisions made in earlier periods. We discuss two examples in the following sections to illustrate this feature. The first example deals with a multiperiod production scheduling problem. The second example involves the establishment of a multiperiod financial sinking fund.

Production Scheduling Problem

Models for multiperiod production planning typically have to include several, often conflicting, factors.

Setting a low-cost production schedule over a period of weeks or months is a difficult and important management problem in most plants. Because most companies produce more than one product, the scheduling process is often quite complex. The production manager has to consider several factors, such as labor capacity, inventory and storage costs, space limitations, product demand, and labor relations. These factors often conflict with each other. For example, it is desirable to produce the same number of each product each period in order to simplify planning and scheduling of workers and machines. However, the need to keep inventory carrying costs down suggests producing in each period only what is needed that period. As we shall see in the following problem, LP is an effective tool for resolving such conflicts and identifying a production schedule that will minimize the total cost of production and inventory holding. Production scheduling is especially amenable to solution by LP because it is a problem that must be solved on a regular basis. When the objective function and constraints for a firm are established, the inputs can easily be changed each period to provide an updated schedule.

Production decisions in later periods are directly dependent on decisions made in earlier periods.

Basically, a multiperiod problem resembles the product mix model for each period in the planning horizon, with the additional issue of inventory from one period to the next to be considered. The objective is to either maximize profit or to minimize the total cost (production plus inventory) of carrying out the task. As noted earlier, production decision choices in later periods are directly affected by decisions made in earlier periods. An example follows.

Greenberg Motors, Inc., manufactures two different electrical motors for sale under contract to Drexel Corp., a well-known producer of small kitchen appliances. Its model GM3A is found in many Drexel food processors, and its model GM3B is used in the assembly of blenders.

Three times each year, the procurement officer at Drexel contracts Irwin Greenberg, the founder of Greenberg Motors, to place a monthly order for each of the coming four months. Drexel's demand for motors varies each month, based on its own sales forecasts, production capacity, and financial position. Greenberg has just received the January–April order and must begin his own four-month production plan. The demand for motors is shown in Table 3.11.

The following additional data are available regarding Greenberg's problem:

1. Production costs are currently $10 per GM3A motor produced and $6 per GM3B unit. However, a planned wage increase going into effect on March 1 will raise each figure by 10%.
2. Each GM3A motor held in stock costs $0.18 per month, and each GM3B has a holding cost of $0.13 per month. Greenberg's accountants allow monthly ending inventories as an acceptable approximation to the average inventory levels during the month.
3. Greenberg is starting the new four-month production cycle with a change in design specifications that has left no old motors of either type in stock on January 1.
4. Greenberg wants to have ending inventories of 450 GM3As and 300 GM3Bs at the end of April.
5. The storage area can hold a maximum of 3,300 motors of either type (they are similar in size) at any one time. Additional storage space is very expensive and is therefore not available as an option.

TABLE 3.11 Four-Month Order Schedule for Greenberg Motors

MODEL	JANUARY	FEBRUARY	MARCH	APRIL
GM3A	800	700	1,000	1,100
GM3B	1,000	1,200	1,400	1,400

6. Greenberg has a no-layoff policy, which has been effective in preventing unionization of the shop. The company has a base employment level of 2,240 labor hours per month, and, by contract, this level of labor must be used each month. In busy periods, however, the company has the option of bringing on board two skilled former employees who are now retired. Each of these employees can provide up to 160 labor hours per month.
7. Each GM3A motor produced requires 1.3 hours of labor, and each GM3B takes a worker 0.9 hours to assemble.

Double-subscripted variables are very convenient in formulating multiperiod problems.

FORMULATING THE PROBLEM Just as in the product mix problem, the primary decision variables here define the number of units of each product (motors) to make. However, because production of motors occurs in four separate months, we need to define decision variables to define the production of each motor in each month. Using double-subscripted variables is a convenient way of defining the decision variables in this LP model. We let

P_{At} = number of model GM3A motors produced in month t (t = 1, 2, 3, 4 for January–April)

P_{Bt} = number of model GM3B motors produced in month t

Using these variables, the total production cost may be written as follows (recall that unit costs go up 10% in March):

$$\text{Cost of production} = \$10P_{A1} + \$10P_{A2} + \$11P_{A3} + \$11P_{A4} + \$6P_{B1} + \$6P_{B2} + \$6.60P_{B3} + \$6.60P_{B4}$$

To keep track of the inventory carried over from one month to the next, we introduce a second set of decision variables. Let

I_{At} = level of on-hand inventory for GM3A motors at end of month t (t = 1, 2, 3, 4)

I_{Bt} = level of on-hand inventory for GM3B motors at end of month t (t = 1, 2, 3, 4)

Using these variables, the total inventory carrying costs may be written as

$$\text{Cost of carrying inventory} = \$0.18I_{A1} + 0.18I_{A2} + 0.18I_{A3} + 0.18I_{A4} + 0.13I_{B1} + 0.13I_{B2} + 0.13I_{B3} + 0.13I_{B4}$$

The objective function is then

$$\begin{aligned}\text{Minimize total costs} &= \text{cost of production} + \text{cost of carrying inventory}\\ &= 10P_{A1} + 10P_{A2} + 11P_{A3} + 11P_{A4} + 6P_{B1} + 6P_{B2} + 6.60P_{B3}\\ &\quad + 6.60P_{B4} + 0.18I_{A1} + 0.18I_{A2} + 0.18I_{A3} + 0.18I_{A4} + 0.13I_{B1}\\ &\quad + 0.13I_{B2} + 0.13I_{B3} + 0.13I_{B4}\end{aligned}$$

Balance constraints specify the relationship between the previous period's closing inventory, this period's production, this period's sales, and this period's closing inventory.

In all multiperiod problems, we need to write a *balance equation*, or *constraint*, for each product for each period. Each balance equation specifies the relationship between the previous period's ending inventory, the current period's production, the current period's sales, and the current period's ending inventory. Specifically, the balance equation states that the inventory at the end of the current period is given by

$$\begin{pmatrix}\text{inventory}\\ \text{at end}\\ \text{of previous}\\ \text{period}\end{pmatrix} + \begin{pmatrix}\text{current}\\ \text{period's}\\ \text{production}\end{pmatrix} - \begin{pmatrix}\text{current}\\ \text{period's}\\ \text{sales}\end{pmatrix} = \begin{pmatrix}\text{inventory}\\ \text{at end}\\ \text{of current}\\ \text{period}\end{pmatrix}$$

In Greenberg's case, we are starting with no old motors in stock on January 1. Recalling that January's demand for GM3As is 800 and for GM3Bs is 1,000, we can write the balance constraints for January as

$$0 + P_{A1} - 800 = I_{A1} \qquad \text{(GM3A motors in January)}$$
$$0 + P_{B1} - 1{,}000 = I_{B1} \qquad \text{(GM3B motors in January)}$$

In a similar fashion, the balance constraints for February, March, and April may be written as follows:

$$I_{A1} + P_{A2} - 700 = I_{A2} \qquad \text{(GM3A motors in February)}$$
$$I_{B1} + P_{B2} - 1{,}200 = I_{B2} \qquad \text{(GM3B motors in February)}$$

$$I_{A2} + P_{A3} - 1{,}000 = I_{A3} \quad \text{(GM3A motors in March)}$$
$$I_{B2} + P_{B3} - 1{,}400 = I_{B3} \quad \text{(GM3B motors in March)}$$
$$I_{A3} + P_{A4} - 1{,}100 = I_{A4} \quad \text{(GM3A motors in April)}$$
$$I_{B3} + P_{B4} - 1{,}400 = I_{B4} \quad \text{(GM3B motors in April)}$$

If Greenberg wants to have ending inventories of 450 GM3As and 300 GM3Bs at the end of April, we add the constraints

$$I_{A4} = 450$$
$$I_{B4} = 300$$

Although the balance constraints address demand, they do not consider storage space or labor requirements. First, we note that the storage area for Greenberg Motors can hold a maximum of 3,300 motors of either type. Therefore, we write

$$I_{A1} + I_{B1} \le 3{,}300$$
$$I_{A2} + I_{B2} \le 3{,}300$$
$$I_{A3} + I_{B3} \le 3{,}300$$
$$I_{A4} + I_{B4} \le 3{,}300$$

Employment constraints are specified for each period.

Second, we note that Greenberg must use at least 2,240 labor hours per month and could potentially have up to 2,560 labor hours ($= 2{,}240 + 160 \times 2$) per month. Because each GM3A motor produced requires 1.3 hours of labor and each GM3B takes a worker 0.9 hours to assemble, we write the labor constraints as

$$1.3P_{A1} + 0.9P_{B1} \ge 2{,}240 \quad \text{(January labor minimum)}$$
$$1.3P_{A1} + 0.9P_{B1} \le 2{,}560 \quad \text{(January labor maximum)}$$
$$1.3P_{A2} + 0.9P_{B2} \ge 2{,}240 \quad \text{(February labor minimum)}$$
$$1.3P_{A2} + 0.9P_{B2} \le 2{,}560 \quad \text{(February labor maximum)}$$
$$1.3P_{A3} + 0.9P_{B3} \ge 2{,}240 \quad \text{(March labor minimum)}$$
$$1.3P_{A3} + 0.9P_{B3} \le 2{,}560 \quad \text{(March labor maximum)}$$
$$1.3P_{A4} + 0.9P_{B4} \ge 2{,}240 \quad \text{(April labor minimum)}$$
$$1.3P_{A4} + 0.9P_{B4} \le 2{,}560 \quad \text{(April labor maximum)}$$

Finally, we have the nonnegativity constraints:

$$\text{All variables} \ge 0$$

File: 3-11.xls, sheet: 3-11A

SOLVING THE PROBLEM There are several ways of setting up the Greenberg Motors problem in Excel. The setup shown in Screenshot 3-11A follows the usual logic we have used in all problems so far; that is, all parameters associated with a specific decision variable are modeled in the same column.

In setting up the balance constraints in Screenshot 3-11A, we have algebraically modified each equation by moving all variables to the LHS of the equation and the constants to the RHS. This is a convenient way of implementing these constraints. For example, the balance constraint for GM3A motors in February, which currently reads

$$I_{A1} + P_{A2} - 700 = I_{A2}$$

is modified as

$$I_{A1} + P_{A2} - I_{A2} = 700$$

INTERPRETING THE RESULTS The solution to Greenberg's problem, summarized in Table 3.12, indicates that the four-month total cost is $76,301.62. The solution requires Greenberg to use the two former employees to their maximum extent (160 hours each; 320 hours total) in three of the four months and for 115 hours in March (labor usage in March is 2,355 hours as compared to the base employment level of 2,240 hours). This suggests that perhaps Greenberg should consider increasing the base employment level. Storage space is not an issue (at least during the

SCREENSHOT 3-11A Excel Layout and Solver Entries for Greenberg Motors

All entries in column R are computed using the SUMPRODUCT function.

	A	B	C	D	E	F	G	H	I	J	K	L	M	N	O	P	Q	R	S	T
1	**Greenberg Motors**																			
2																				
3		P_{A1}	I_{A1}	P_{A2}	I_{A2}	P_{A3}	I_{A3}	P_{A4}	I_{A4}	P_{B1}	I_{B1}	P_{B2}	I_{B2}	P_{B3}	I_{B3}	P_{B4}	I_{B4}			
4		GM3A Jan prod	GM3A Jan inv	GM3A Feb prod	GM3A Feb inv	GM3A Mar prod	GM3A Mar inv	GM3A Apr prod	GM3A Apr inv	GM3B Jan prod	GM3B Jan inv	GM3B Feb prod	GM3B Feb inv	GM3B Mar prod	GM3B Mar inv	GM3B Apr prod	GM3B Apr inv			
5	Number of Units	1,276.92	476.92	1,138.46	915.38	842.31	757.69	792.31	450.00	1,000.00	0.00	1,200.00	0.00	1,400.00	0.00	1,700.00	300.00			
6	Cost	$10.00	$0.18	$10.00	$0.18	$11.00	$0.18	$11.00	$0.18	$6.00	$0.13	$6.00	$0.13	$6.60	$0.13	$6.60	$0.13	$76,301.62		
7	**Constraints:**																			
8	GM3A Jan balance	1	-1															800.00	=	800
9	GM3B Jan balance									1	-1							1000.00	=	1000
10	GM3A Feb balance		1	1	-1													700.00	=	700
11	GM3B Feb balance										1	1	-1					1200.00	=	1200
12	GM3A Mar balance				1	1	-1											1000.00	=	1000
13	GM3B Mar balance												1	1	-1			1400.00	=	1400
14	GM3A Apr balance						1	1	-1									1100.00	=	1100
15	GM3B Apr balance														1	1	-1	1400.00	=	1400
16	GM3A Apr Inventory								1									450.00	=	450
17	GM3B Apr Inventory																1	300.00	=	300
18	Jan storage cap		1								1							476.92	<=	3300
19	Feb storage cap				1								1					915.38	<=	3300
20	Mar storage cap						1								1			757.69	<=	3300
21	Apr storage cap								1								1	750.00	<=	3300
22	Jan labor max	1.3								0.9								2560.00	<=	2560
23	Feb labor max			1.3								0.9						2560.00	<=	2560
24	Mar labor max					1.3								0.9				2355.00	<=	2560
25	Apr labor max							1.3								0.9		2560.00	<=	2560
26	Jan labor min	1.3								0.9								2560.00	>=	2240
27	Feb labor min			1.3								0.9						2560.00	>=	2240
28	Mar labor min					1.3								0.9				2355.00	>=	2240
29	Apr labor min							1.3								0.9		2560.00	>=	2240
30																		LHS	Sign	RHS

Solver Parameters

Set Objective: $R$6

To: Max Min (selected) Value Of:

By Changing Variable Cells: $B$5:$Q$5

Subject to the Constraints:
$R$18:$R$25 <= $T$18:$T$25
$R$26:$R$29 >= $T$26:$T$29
$R$8:$R$17 = $T$8:$T$17

Solver includes three entries: One for each type of constraints ≤, ≥, and =.

TABLE 3.12 Solution to Greenberg Motors Problem

PRODUCTION SCHEDULE	JANUARY	FEBRUARY	MARCH	APRIL
Units of GM3A produced	1,276.92	1,138.46	842.31	792.31
Units of GM3B produced	1,000.00	1,200.00	1,400.00	1,700.00
Inventory of GM3A carried	476.92	915.38	757.69	450.00
Inventory of GM3B carried	0.00	0.00	0.00	300.00
Labor hours required	2,560.00	2,560.00	2,355.00	2,560.00

File: 3-11.xls, sheet: 3-11B

four months in consideration here), with less than one-third of the available space being used each month. The solution does include several fractional values, which may need to be rounded off appropriately before implementation. Alternatively, in such problem scenarios, it may be possible to view fractional production values as work-in-process (WIP) inventories.

For many multiperiod problems, it may often be convenient to group all the variables for a given month in the same column. Screenshot 3-11B shows the Excel layout of an alternate model for the Greenberg Motors problem.

Ending inventory is not set as a decision variable in this alternate Excel layout for the Greenberg Motors problem.

Note that in this alternate model, the only decision variables are the production variables (P_{A1} to P_{A4}, P_{B1} to P_{B4}). The inventory variables are no longer explicitly stated as decision variables,

SCREENSHOT 3-11B Excel Layout and Solver Entries for Greenberg Motors—Alternate Model

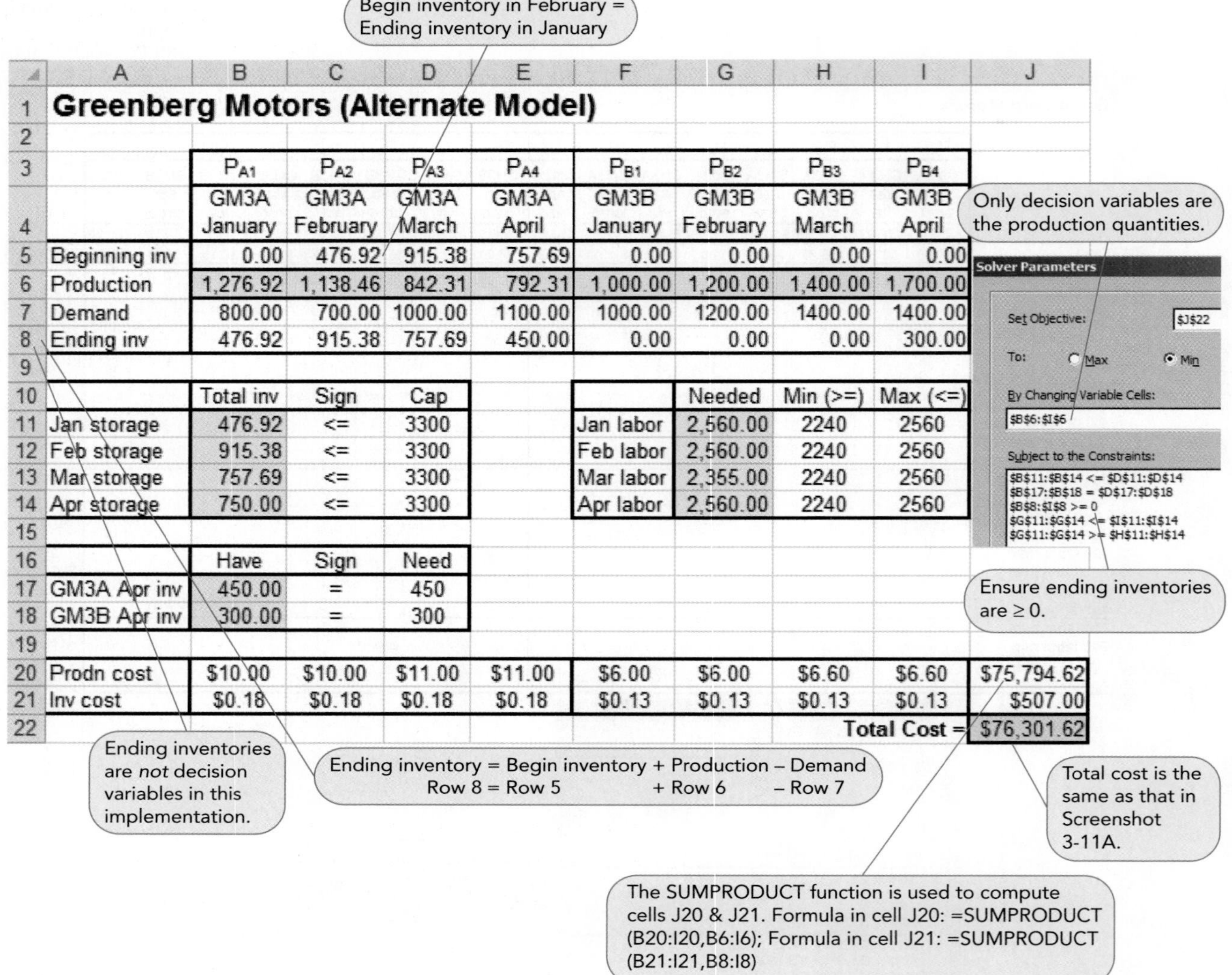

	P_{A1}	P_{A2}	P_{A3}	P_{A4}	P_{B1}	P_{B2}	P_{B3}	P_{B4}	
	GM3A January	GM3A February	GM3A March	GM3A April	GM3B January	GM3B February	GM3B March	GM3B April	
Beginning inv	0.00	476.92	915.38	757.69	0.00	0.00	0.00	0.00	
Production	1,276.92	1,138.46	842.31	792.31	1,000.00	1,200.00	1,400.00	1,700.00	
Demand	800.00	700.00	1000.00	1100.00	1000.00	1200.00	1400.00	1400.00	
Ending inv	476.92	915.38	757.69	450.00	0.00	0.00	0.00	300.00	
Prodn cost	$10.00	$10.00	$11.00	$11.00	$6.00	$6.00	$6.60	$6.60	$75,794.62
Inv cost	$0.18	$0.18	$0.18	$0.18	$0.13	$0.13	$0.13	$0.13	$507.00
								Total Cost =	$76,301.62

	Total inv	Sign	Cap
Jan storage	476.92	<=	3300
Feb storage	915.38	<=	3300
Mar storage	757.69	<=	3300
Apr storage	750.00	<=	3300

	Needed	Min (>=)	Max (<=)
Jan labor	2,560.00	2240	2560
Feb labor	2,560.00	2240	2560
Mar labor	2,355.00	2240	2560
Apr labor	2,560.00	2240	2560

	Have	Sign	Need
GM3A Apr inv	450.00	=	450
GM3B Apr inv	300.00	=	300

and they are not specified as changing variable cells in Solver. Rather, they are calculated as simple by-products of the other parameters in the problem. Using the standard inventory constraints, the ending inventory each month is calculated as follows:

$$\begin{pmatrix}\text{inventory}\\\text{at the}\\\text{end of}\\\text{last month}\end{pmatrix} + \begin{pmatrix}\text{current}\\\text{month's}\\\text{production}\end{pmatrix} - \begin{pmatrix}\text{current}\\\text{month's}\\\text{sales}\end{pmatrix} = \begin{pmatrix}\text{inventory}\\\text{at the}\\\text{end of}\\\text{this month}\end{pmatrix}$$

$$\text{Row 5} \quad + \quad \text{Row 6} \quad - \quad \text{Row 7} \quad = \quad \text{Row 8}$$

Because they are no longer decision variables, however, we need to add constraints to ensure that the ending inventories for all products have nonnegative values in each month. Depending on individual preferences and expertise, we can design other layouts for setting up and solving this problem using Excel.

The Greenberg Motors example illustrates a relatively simple production planning problem in that only two products were considered for a four-month planning horizon. The LP model discussed here can, however, be applied successfully to problems with dozens of products, hundreds of constraints, and longer planning horizons.

Sinking Fund Problem

Another excellent example of a multiperiod problem is the sinking fund problem. In this case, an investor or a firm seeks to establish an investment portfolio, using the least possible initial investment, that will generate specific amounts of capital at specific time periods in the future.

Consider the example of Larry Fredendall, who is trying to plan for his daughter Susan's college expenses. Based on current projections (it is now the start of year 1), Larry anticipates that his financial needs at the start of each of the following years is as shown in Table 3.13.

Larry has several investment choices to choose from at the present time, as listed in Table 3.14. Each choice has a fixed known return on investment and a specified maturity date. Assume that each choice is available for investment at the start of every year and also assume that returns are tax free if used for education. Because choices C and D are relatively risky choices, Larry wants no more than 20% of his total investment in those two choices at any point in time.

Larry wants to establish a sinking fund to meet his requirements. Note that at the start of year 1, the entire initial investment is available for investing in the choices. However, in subsequent years, only the amount maturing from a prior investment is available for investment.

FORMULATING THE PROBLEM Let us first define the decision variables. Note that in defining these variables, we need to consider only those investments that will mature by the end of year 5, at the latest, because there is no requirement after 6 years:

$$
\begin{aligned}
A_1 &= \$ \text{ amount invested in choice A at the start of year 1} \\
B_1 &= \$ \text{ amount invested in choice B at the start of year 1} \\
C_1 &= \$ \text{ amount invested in choice C at the start of year 1} \\
D_1 &= \$ \text{ amount invested in choice D at the start of year 1} \\
A_2 &= \$ \text{ amount invested in choice A at the start of year 2} \\
B_2 &= \$ \text{ amount invested in choice B at the start of year 2} \\
C_2 &= \$ \text{ amount invested in choice C at the start of year 2} \\
D_2 &= \$ \text{ amount invested in choice D at the start of year 2} \\
A_3 &= \$ \text{ amount invested in choice A at the start of year 3} \\
B_3 &= \$ \text{ amount invested in choice B at the start of year 3} \\
C_3 &= \$ \text{ amount invested in choice C at the start of year 3} \\
A_4 &= \$ \text{ amount invested in choice A at the start of year 4} \\
B_4 &= \$ \text{ amount invested in choice B at the start of year 4} \\
A_5 &= \$ \text{ amount invested in choice A at the start of year 5}
\end{aligned}
$$

The objective is to minimize the initial investment and can be expressed as

$$\text{Minimize } A_1 + B_1 + C_1 + D_1$$

TABLE 3.13
Financial Needs for Larry Fredendall

YEAR	$ NEEDED
3	$20,000
4	$22,000
5	$24,000
6	$26,000

TABLE 3.14
Investment Choices for Larry Fredendall

CHOICE	ROI	MATURITY
A	5%	1 year
B	13%	2 years
C	28%	3 years
D	40%	4 years

As in the multiperiod production scheduling problem, we need to write balance constraints for each period (year). These constraints recognize the relationship between the investment decisions made in any given year and the investment decisions made in all prior years. Specifically, we need to ensure that the amount used for investment at the start of a given year is restricted to the amount maturing at the end of the previous year *less* any payments made for Susan's education that year. This relationship can be modeled as

$$\begin{pmatrix}\text{amount}\\ \text{invested at}\\ \text{start of}\\ \text{year } t\end{pmatrix} + \begin{pmatrix}\text{amount}\\ \text{paid for}\\ \text{education at}\\ \text{start of year } t\end{pmatrix} = \begin{pmatrix}\text{amound}\\ \text{maturing}\\ \text{at end}\\ \text{of year } (t-1)\end{pmatrix}$$

This equation is analogous to the inventory equations in the production scheduling problem.

At the start of year 2, the total amount maturing is $1.05A_1$ (investment in choice A in year 1 plus 5% interest). The constraint at the start of year 2 can therefore be written as

$$A_2 + B_2 + C_2 + D_2 = 1.05A_1 \qquad \text{(year 2 cash flow)}$$

These are the cash flow constraints.

Constraints at the start of years 3 through 6 are as follows and also include the amounts payable for Susan's education each year:

$$\begin{aligned} A_3 + B_3 + C_3 + 20{,}000 &= 1.13B_1 + 1.05A_2 && \text{(year 3 cash flow)}\\ A_4 + B_4 + 22{,}000 &= 1.28C_1 + 1.13B_2 + 1.05A_3 && \text{(year 4 cash flow)}\\ A_5 + 24{,}000 &= 1.4D_1 + 1.28C_2 + 1.13B_3 + 1.05A_4 && \text{(year 5 cash flow)}\\ 26{,}000 &= 1.4D_2 + 1.28C_3 + 1.13B_4 + 1.05A_5 && \text{(year 6 cash flow)} \end{aligned}$$

These five constraints address the cash flow issues. However, they do not account for Larry's risk preference with regard to investments in choices C and D in any given year. To satisfy these requirements, we need to ensure that total investment in choices C and D in any year is no more than 20% of the total investment in *all* choices that year. In keeping track of these investments, it is important to also account for investments in *prior* years that may have still not matured. At the start of year 1, this constraint can be written as

$$C_1 + D_1 \le 0.2(A_1 + B_1 + C_1 + D_1) \qquad \text{(year 1 risk)}$$

These are the risk preference constraints.

In writing this constraint at the start of year 2, we must take into account the fact that investments B_1, C_1, and D_1 have still not matured. Therefore,

$$C_1 + D_1 + C_2 + D_2 \le 0.2(B_1 + C_1 + D_1 + A_2 + B_2 + C_2 + D_2) \qquad \text{(year 2 risk)}$$

Constraints at the start of years 3 through 5 are as follows. Note that there is no constraint necessary at the start of year 6 because there are no investments that year:

$$\begin{aligned} C_1 + D_1 + C_2 + D_2 + C_3 &\le 0.2(C_1 + D_1 + B_2 + C_2 + D_2 + A_3 + B_3 + C_3) && \text{(year 3 risk)}\\ D_1 + C_2 + D_2 + C_3 &\le 0.2(D_1 + C_2 + D_2 + B_3 + C_3 + A_4 + B_4) && \text{(year 4 risk)}\\ D_2 + C_3 &\le 0.2(D_2 + C_3 + B_4 + A_5) && \text{(year 5 risk)} \end{aligned}$$

Finally, we have the nonnegativity constraints:

All variables ≥ 0

File: 3-12.xls

SOLVING THE PROBLEM AND INTERPRETING THE RESULTS Screenshot 3-12 shows the Excel layout and Solver entries for this model. As with the production scheduling problem, there are several alternate ways in which the Excel layout could be structured, depending on the preference and expertise of the analyst. In our implementation of this model, we have algebraically modified the cash flow constraints for each year so that all variables are on the LHS and the education cash outflows are on the RHS. We have, however, implemented the risk constraints as written in the formulation above. The modified cash flow constraints are as follows:

$$\begin{aligned} 1.05A_1 - A_2 - B_2 - C_2 - D_2 &= 0 && \text{(year 2 cash flow)}\\ 1.13B_1 + 1.05A_2 - A_3 - B_3 - C_3 &= 20{,}000 && \text{(year 3 cash flow)}\\ 1.28C_1 + 1.13B_2 + 1.05A_3 - A_4 - B_4 &= 22{,}000 && \text{(year 4 cash flow)}\\ 1.4D_1 + 1.28C_2 + 1.13B_3 + 1.05A_4 - A_5 &= 24{,}000 && \text{(year 5 cash flow)}\\ 1.4D_2 + 1.28C_3 + 1.13B_4 + 1.05A_5 &= 26{,}000 && \text{(year 6 cash flow)} \end{aligned}$$

SCREENSHOT 3-12 Excel Layout and Solver Entries for Larry Fredendall's Sinking Fund

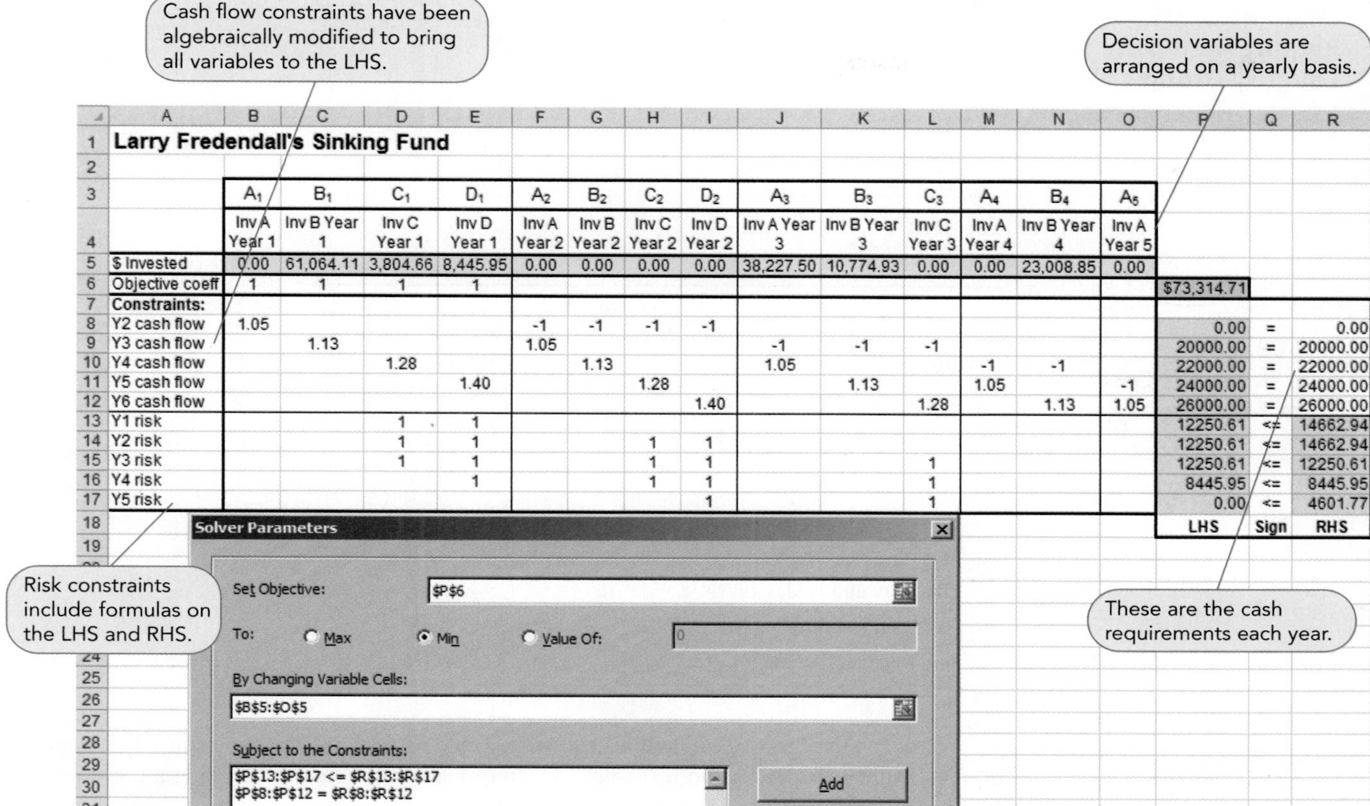
Cash flow constraints have been algebraically modified to bring all variables to the LHS.
Decision variables are arranged on a yearly basis.
Larry Fredendall's Sinking Fund
Risk constraints include formulas on the LHS and RHS.
These are the cash requirements each year.
Solver Parameters
Set Objective: $P$6
To: Max Min Value Of: 0
By Changing Variable Cells:
$B$5:$O$5
Subject to the Constraints:
$P$13:$P$17 <= $R$13:$R$17
$P$8:$P$12 = $R$8:$R$12
Add

	A_1	B_1	C_1	D_1	A_2	B_2	C_2	D_2	A_3	B_3	C_3	A_4	B_4	A_5			
	Inv A Year 1	Inv B Year 1	Inv C Year 1	Inv D Year 1	Inv A Year 2	Inv B Year 2	Inv C Year 2	Inv D Year 2	Inv A Year 3	Inv B Year 3	Inv C Year 3	Inv A Year 4	Inv B Year 4	Inv A Year 5			
$ Invested	0.00	61,064.11	3,804.66	8,445.95	0.00	0.00	0.00	0.00	38,227.50	10,774.93	0.00	0.00	23,008.85	0.00			
Objective coeff	1	1	1	1											$73,314.71		
Constraints:																	
Y2 cash flow	1.05				-1	-1	-1	-1							0.00	=	0.00
Y3 cash flow		1.13			1.05				-1	-1	-1				20000.00	=	20000.00
Y4 cash flow			1.28			1.13			1.05			-1	-1		22000.00	=	22000.00
Y5 cash flow				1.40			1.28			1.13		1.05		-1	24000.00	=	24000.00
Y6 cash flow								1.40			1.28		1.13	1.05	26000.00	=	26000.00
Y1 risk			1	1											12250.61	<=	14662.94
Y2 risk			1	1			1	1							12250.61	<=	14662.94
Y3 risk			1	1			1	1			1				12250.61	<=	12250.61
Y4 risk				1			1	1			1				8445.95	<=	8445.95
Y5 risk								1			1				0.00	<=	4601.77
															LHS	**Sign**	**RHS**

The optimal solution requires Larry to invest a total of $73,314.71 at the start of year 1, putting $61,064.11 in choice B, $3,804.66 in choice C, and $8,445.95 in choice D. There is no money maturing for investment at the start of year 2. At the start of year 3, using the maturing amounts, Larry should pay off $20,000 for Susan's education, invest $38,227.50 in choice A, and invest $10,774.93 in choice B. At the start of year 4, Larry should use the maturing amounts to pay off $22,000 for Susan's education and invest $23,008.85 in choice B. The investments in place at that time will generate $24,000 at the start of year 5 and $26,000 at the start of year 6, meeting Larry's requirements in those years.

Summary

This chapter continues the discussion of LP models. To show ways of formulating and solving problems from a variety of disciplines, we examine applications from manufacturing, marketing, finance, employee scheduling, transportation, ingredient blending, and multiperiod planning. We also consider an example with a special type of objective function. For each example, we illustrate how to set up and solve all these models by using Excel's Solver add-in.

Solved Problem

Solved Problem 3-1

The Loughry Group has opened a new mall in Gainesville, Florida. Mark Loughry, the general manager of the mall, is trying to ensure that enough support staff are available to clean the mall before it opens each day. The mall operates seven days a week, and the cleaning staff work between 12:30 A.M. and 8:30 A.M. each night. Based on projected mall traffic data for the upcoming week, Mark estimates that the number of cleaning staff required each day will be as shown in Table 3.15.

TABLE 3.15 Cleaning Staff Requirement Data for Loughry Group's Mall

DAY OF WEEK	NUMBER OF STAFF REQUIRED
Monday	22
Tuesday	13
Wednesday	15
Thursday	20
Friday	18
Saturday	23
Sunday	27

TABLE 3.16 Schedule and Cost Data for Loughry Group's Mall

WORK SCHEDULE	WAGES PER WEEK
1. Saturday and Sunday off	\$350
2. Saturday and Tuesday off	\$375
3. Tuesday and Wednesday off	\$400
4. Monday and Thursday off	\$425
5. Tuesday and Friday off	\$425
6. Thursday and Friday off	\$400
7. Sunday and Thursday off	\$375
8. Sunday and Wednesday off	\$375

Mark can use the work schedules shown in Table 3.16 for the cleaning staff. The wages for each schedule are also shown in Table 3.16. In order to be perceived as being a fair employer, Mark wants to ensure that at least 75% of the workers have two consecutive days off and that at least 50% of the workers have at least one weekend day off. How should Mark schedule his cleaning staff in order to meet the mall's requirements?

Solution

FORMULATING AND SOLVING THE PROBLEM As noted in the previous labor staffing problem, the decision variables typically determine how many employees need to start their work at the different starting times permitted. In Mark's case, because there are eight possible work schedules, we have eight decision variables in the problem. Let

S_1 = number of employees who need to follow schedule 1 (Saturday and Sunday off)
S_2 = number of employees who need to follow schedule 2 (Saturday and Tuesday off)
S_3 = number of employees who need to follow schedule 3 (Tuesday and Wednesday off)
S_4 = number of employees who need to follow schedule 4 (Monday and Thursday off)
S_5 = number of employees who need to follow schedule 5 (Tuesday and Friday off)
S_6 = number of employees who need to follow schedule 6 (Thursday and Friday off)
S_7 = number of employees who need to follow schedule 7 (Sunday and Thursday off)
S_8 = number of employees who need to follow schedule 8 (Sunday and Wednesday off)

This is the objective function:

$$\text{Minimize total weekly wages} = \$350\,S_1 + \$375\,S_2 + \$400\,S_3 + \$425\,S_4 + \$425\,S_5 + \$400\,S_6 + \$375\,S_7 + \$375\,S_8$$

Subject to the constraints

$$S_1 + S_2 + S_3 + S_5 + S_6 + S_7 + S_8 \geq 22 \quad \text{(Monday requirement)}$$
$$S_1 + S_2 + S_4 + S_6 + S_7 + S_8 \geq 13 \quad \text{(Tuesday requirement)}$$
$$S_1 + S_2 + S_4 + S_5 + S_6 + S_7 \geq 15 \quad \text{(Wednesday requirement)}$$

$$S_1 + S_2 + S_3 + S_5 + S_8 \geq 20 \quad \text{(Thursday requirement)}$$
$$S_1 + S_2 + S_3 + S_4 + S_7 + S_8 \geq 18 \quad \text{(Friday requirement)}$$
$$S_3 + S_4 + S_5 + S_6 + S_7 + S_8 \geq 23 \quad \text{(Saturday requirement)}$$
$$S_2 + S_3 + S_4 + S_5 + S_6 \geq 27 \quad \text{(Sunday requirement)}$$

At least 75% of workers must have two consecutive days off each week, and at least 50% of workers must have at least one weekend day off each week. These constraints may be written, respectively, as

$$S_1 + S_3 + S_6 \geq 0.75\,(S_1 + S_2 + S_3 + S_4 + S_5 + S_6 + S_7 + S_8)$$
$$S_1 + S_2 + S_7 + S_8 \geq 0.5\,(S_1 + S_2 + S_3 + S_4 + S_5 + S_6 + S_7 + S_8)$$

Finally,

$$S_1, S_2, S_3, S_5, S_6, S_7, S_8 \geq 0$$

File: 3-13.xls

The Excel layout and Solver entries for this model are shown in Screenshot 3-13. For the last two constraints, the Excel layout includes formulas for both the LHS (cells J15:J16) and RHS (cells L15:L16) entries. While the formulas in cells J15:J16 use the usual SUMPRODUCT function, the formulas in cells L15:L16 are

Cell L15: =0.75*SUM($B$5:$I$5)
Cell L16: =0.50*SUM($B$5:$I$5)

SCREENSHOT 3-13 Excel Layout and Solver Entries for Loughry Group Mall

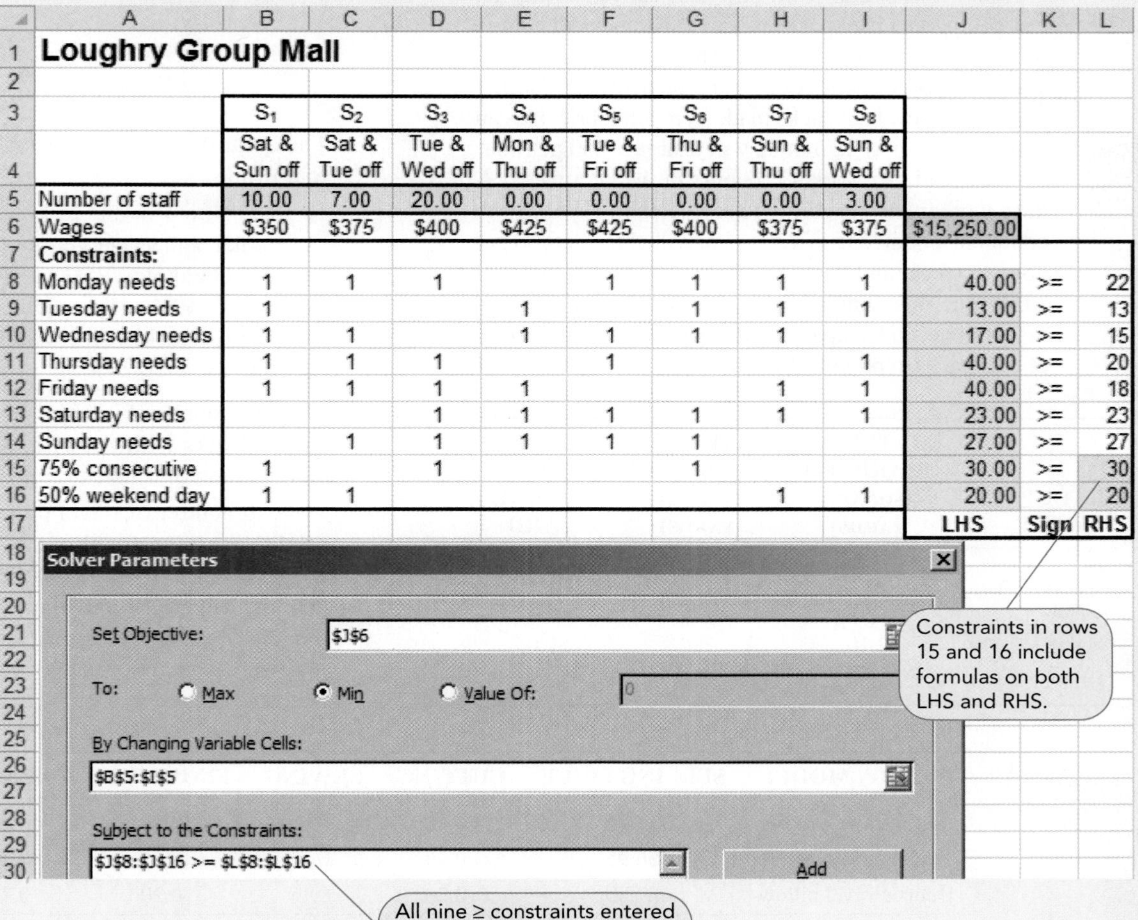

	A	B	C	D	E	F	G	H	I	J	K	L
1	**Loughry Group Mall**											
2												
3		S_1	S_2	S_3	S_4	S_5	S_6	S_7	S_8			
4		Sat & Sun off	Sat & Tue off	Tue & Wed off	Mon & Thu off	Tue & Fri off	Thu & Fri off	Sun & Thu off	Sun & Wed off			
5	Number of staff	10.00	7.00	20.00	0.00	0.00	0.00	0.00	3.00			
6	Wages	$350	$375	$400	$425	$425	$400	$375	$375	$15,250.00		
7	**Constraints:**											
8	Monday needs	1	1	1		1	1	1	1	40.00	>=	22
9	Tuesday needs	1			1		1	1	1	13.00	>=	13
10	Wednesday needs	1	1		1	1	1	1		17.00	>=	15
11	Thursday needs	1	1	1		1			1	40.00	>=	20
12	Friday needs	1	1	1	1			1	1	40.00	>=	18
13	Saturday needs			1	1	1	1	1	1	23.00	>=	23
14	Sunday needs		1	1	1	1	1			27.00	>=	27
15	75% consecutive	1		1			1			30.00	>=	30
16	50% weekend day	1	1					1	1	20.00	>=	20
17										**LHS**	**Sign**	**RHS**

INTERPRETING THE RESULTS Screenshot 3-13 reveals that the optimal solution is to employ 10 people on schedule 1; 7 people on schedule 2; 20 people on schedule 3; and 3 people on schedule 8, for a total cost of $15,250 per week. As in the solution for the Hong Kong Bank problem (see Screenshot 3-6 on page 83), it turns out that this problem has alternate optimal solutions, too. For example, we can satisfy the staff requirements at the same cost by employing 10 people on schedule 1; 7 people on schedule 2; 3 people on schedule 3; 17 people on schedule 6; and 3 people on schedule 7.

The solution indicates that while exactly meeting staffing needs for Tuesday, Saturday, and Sunday, Mark is left with way more than he needs on Monday, Thursday, and Friday. He should perhaps consider using part-time help to alleviate this mismatch in his staffing needs.

Problems

3-1 A small backpack manufacturer carries four different models of backpacks, made of canvas, plastic, nylon, and leather. The bookstore, which will exclusively sell the backpacks, expects to be able to sell between 15 and 40 of each model. The store has agreed to pay $35.50 for each canvas backpack, $39.50 for each plastic backpack, $42.50 for each nylon backpack, and $69.50 for each leather backpack that can be delivered by the end of the following week.

One worker can work on either canvas or plastic, can complete a backpack in 1.5 hours, and will charge $7.00 per hour to do the work. This worker can work a maximum of 90 hours during the next week. Another worker can sew backpacks made of nylon fabric. He can complete a bag in 1.7 hours, will charge $8.00 per hour to work, and can work 42.5 hours in the next week. A third worker has the ability to sew leather. He each can complete a book bag in 1.9 hours, will charge $9.00 per hour to work, and can work 80 hours during the next week. The following table provides additional information about each backpack. What is the best combination of backpacks to provide the store to maximize the profit?

BACKPACK MODEL	MATERIAL REQUIRED (SQUARE YARDS)	MATERIAL AVAILABLE (SQUARE YARDS)	COST/ SQUARE YARD
Canvas	2.25	200	$4.50
Plastic	2.40	350	$4.25
Nylon	2.10	700	$7.65
Leather	2.60	550	$9.45

3-2 A contestant on the hit reality television show Top Bartender was asked to mix a variety of drinks, each consisting of 4 fluid ounces. No other ingredients were permitted. She was given the following quantities of liquor:

LIQUOR	QUANTITY
Bourbon	128 ounces
Brandy	128 ounces
Vodka	128 ounces
Dry Vermouth	32 ounces
Sweet Vermouth	32 ounces

The contestant is considering making the following four drinks:

- The New Yorker: 25% each of bourbon, brandy, vodka, and sweet vermouth
- The Garaboldi: 25% each of brandy and dry vermouth; 50% sweet vermouth
- The Kentuckian: 100% bourbon
- The Russian: 75% vodka and 25% dry vermouth

The contestant's objective is to make the largest number of drinks with the available liquor. What is the combination of drinks to meet her objective?

3-3 A manufacturer of travel pillows must determine the production plan for the next production cycle. He wishes to make at least 300 of each of the three models that his firm offers and no more than 1,200 of any one model. The specifics for each model are shown in the following table. How many pillows of each type should be manufactured in order to maximize total profit?

PILLOW MODEL	SELLING PRICE	CUTTING	SEWING	FINISHING	PACKING
Junior travel pillow	$5.75	0.10	0.05	0.18	0.20
Travel pillow	$6.95	0.15	0.12	0.24	0.20
Deluxe travel pillow	$7.50	0.20	0.18	0.20	0.20
Available hours		450	550	600	450
Cost per hour		$7.00	$9.00	$8.50	$7.25

Table for Problem 3-5

CABINET STYLE	CARPENTRY	PAINTING	FINISHING	PROFIT
Italian	3.00	1.50	0.75	$72
French	2.25	1.00	0.75	$65
Caribbean	2.50	1.25	0.85	$78
Available hours	1,360	700	430	

3-4 Students who are trying to raise funds have an agreement with a local pizza chain. The chain has agreed to sell them pizzas at a discount, which the students can then resell to families in the local community for a profit. It is expected that of the 500 families in the community, at most 70% will buy pizza. Based on a survey of their personal preferences, the students believe that they should order no more than 120 cheese pizzas, no more than 150 pepperoni pizzas, and no more than 100 vegetarian pizzas. They also want to make sure that at least 20% of the total pizzas are cheese and at least 50% of the pizzas are pepperoni. They make a profit of $1.45, $1.75, and $1.98, respectively, for each cheese, pepperoni, and vegetarian pizza they resell. How many pizzas of each type should they buy?

3-5 A furniture maker sells three different styles of cabinets, including an Italian model, a French Country model, and a Caribbean model. Each cabinet produced must go through three departments: carpentry, painting, and finishing. The table at the top of this page contains all relevant information concerning production times (hours per cabinet), production capacities for each operation per day, and profit ($ per unit). The owner has an obligation to deliver a minimum of 60 cabinets in each style to a furniture distributor. He would like to determine the product mix that maximizes his daily profit. Formulate the problem as an LP model and solve using Excel.

3-6 An electronics manufacturer has an option to produce six styles of cell phones. Each of these devices requires time, in minutes, on three types of electronic testing equipment, as shown in the table at the bottom of this page. The first two test devices are each available for 120 hours per week. Test device 3 requires more preventive maintenance and may be used only for 100 hours each week. The market for all six cell phones is vast, so the manufacturer believes that it can sell as many cell phones as it can manufacture. The table also summarizes the revenues and material costs for each type of phone.

In addition, variable labor costs are $15 per hour for test device 1, $12 per hour for test device 2, and $18 per hour for test device 3. Determine the product mix that would maximize profits. Formulate the problem as an LP model and solve it by using Excel.

3-7 A company produces three different types of wrenches: W111, W222, and W333. It has a firm order for 2,000 W111 wrenches, 3,750 W222 wrenches, and 1,700 W333 wrenches. Between now and the order delivery date, the company has only 16,500 fabrication hours and 1,600 inspection hours. The time that each wrench requires in each department is shown in the table at the bottom of this page. Also shown are the costs to manufacture the wrenches in-house and the costs to outsource them. For labeling considerations, the company wants to manufacture in-house at least 60% of each type of wrench that will be shipped. How many wrenches of each type should be made in-house and how many should be

Table for Problem 3-6

	SMARTPHONE	BLUEBERRY	MOPHONE	BOLDPHONE	LUXPHONE4G	TAP3G
Test device 1	7	3	12	6	18	17
Test device 2	2	5	3	2	15	17
Test device 3	5	1	3	2	9	2
Revenue per unit	$200	$120	$180	$200	$430	$260
Material cost per unit	$35	$25	$40	$45	$170	$60

Table for Problem 3-7

WRENCH	FABRICATION HOURS	INSPECTION HOURS	IN-HOUSE COST	OUTSOURCE COST
W111	2.50	0.25	$17.00	$20.40
W222	3.40	0.30	$19.00	$21.85
W333	3.80	0.45	$23.00	$25.76

outsourced? What will be the total cost to satisfy the order?

3-8 A gear manufacturer is planning next week's production run for four types of gears. If necessary, it is possible to outsource any type of gear from another gear company located nearby. The following table and the table at the bottom of this page show next week's demand, revenue per unit, outsource cost per unit, time (in hours) required per unit in each production process, and the availability and costs of these processes. The nearby company can supply a maximum of 300 units of each type of gear next week. What should be the production and/or outsource plan for the next week to maximize profit?

GEAR TYPE	GEAR A	GEAR B	GEAR C	GEAR D
Demand	400	500	450	600
Revenue	$12.50	$15.60	$17.40	$19.30
Outsource	$7.10	$8.10	$8.40	$9.00

3-9 A political polling organization is to conduct a poll of likely voters prior to an upcoming election. Each voter is to be interviewed in person. It is known that the costs of interviewing different types of voters vary due to the differences in proportion within the population. The costs to interview males, for example, are $10 per Democrat, $9 per Republican, and $13.50 per Independent voter. The costs to interview females are $12, $11 and $13.50 for Democrat, Republican, and Independent voters, respectively. The polling service has been given certain criteria to which it must adhere:

- There must be at least 4,500 total interviews.
- At least 1,000 independent voters must be polled.
- At least 2,000 males must be polled.
- At least 1,750 females must be polled.
- No more than 40% of those polled may be Democrats.
- No more than 40% of those polled may be Republicans.
- No more than one-quarter of those polled may be Republican males.
- Each of the six categories of voters must be represented in the poll by at least 10% of the total interviews.

Determine the least expensive sampling plan and the total cost to carry out the plan.

3-10 The advertising director a large retail store in Columbus, Ohio, is considering three advertising media possibilities: (1) ads in the Sunday *Columbus Dispatch* newspaper, (2) ads in a local trade magazine that is distributed free to all houses in the city and northwest suburbs, and (3) ads on Columbus' WCC-TV station. She wishes to obtain a new-customer exposure level of at least 50% within the city and 60% in the northwest suburbs. Each TV ad has a new-customer exposure level of 5% in the city and 3% in the northwest suburbs. The *Dispatch* ads have corresponding exposure levels per ad of 3.5% and 3%, respectively, while the trade magazine has exposure levels per ad of 0.5% and 1%, respectively. The relevant costs are $1,000 per *Dispatch* ad, $300 per trade magazine ad, and $2,000 per TV ad. The advertising policy is that no single media type should consume more than 45% of the total amount spent. Find the advertising strategy that will meet the store's objective at minimum cost.

3-11 A grocery chain wants to promote the sale of a new flavor of ice cream by issuing up to 15,000 coupons by mail to preferred customers. The budget for this promotion has been limited to $12,000. The following table shows the expected increased sales per coupon and the probability of coupon usage for the various coupon amounts under consideration.

COUPON AMOUNT	INCREASED SALES PER COUPON (CARTONS)	PROBABILITY COUPON WILL BE USED
$1.00	1.50	0.80
$0.85	1.40	0.75
$0.70	1.25	0.60
$0.55	1.00	0.50
$0.40	0.90	0.42

For example, every $1-off coupon issued will stimulate sales of 1.5 additional cartons. However, since the probability that a $1-off coupon will actually be used is only 0.80, the expected increased sales per coupon issued is 1.2 (= 0.8 × 1.5) cartons.

The selling price per carton of ice cream is $3.50 before the coupon value is applied. The chain wants at least 20% of the coupons issued to be of the $1-off variety and at least 10% of the coupons issued to be

Table for Problem 3-8

PROCESS	GEAR A	GEAR B	GEAR C	GEAR D	HOURS AVAILABLE	COST PER HOUR
Forming	0.30	0.36	0.38	0.45	500	$9.00
Hardening	0.20	0.30	0.24	0.33	300	$8.00
Deburring	0.30	0.30	0.35	0.25	310	$7.50

of each of the other four varieties. What is the optimal combination of coupons to be issued, and what is the expected net increased revenue from this promotion?

3-12 A political candidate is planning his media budget for an upcoming election. He has $90,500 to spend. His political consultants have provided him with the following estimates of additional votes as a result of the advertising effort:

- For every small sign placed by the roadside, he will garner 10 additional votes.
- For every large sign placed by the roadside, he will garner 30 additional votes.
- For every thousand bumper stickers placed on cars, he will garner 10 additional votes.
- For every hundred personal mailings to registered voters, he will garner 40 additional votes, and
- For every radio ad heard daily in the last month before the election, he will garner 485 additional votes.

The costs for each of these advertising devices, along with the practical minimum and maximum that should be planned for each, are shown on the following table. How should the candidate plan to spend his campaign money?

ADVERTISING MEDIUM	COST	MINIMUM	MAXIMUM
Bumper stickers (thousands)	$30	40	100
Personal mailings (hundreds)	$81	500	800
Radio ads (per day)	$1,000	3	12
Small road side signs	$25	100	500
Large road side signs	$60	50	300

3-13 A brokerage firm has been tasked with investing $500,000 for a new client. The client has asked that the broker select promising stocks and bonds for investment, subject to the following guidelines:

- At least 20% in municipal bonds
- At least 10% each in real estate stock and pharmaceutical stock
- At least 40% in a combination of energy and domestic automobile stocks, with each accounting for at least 15%
- No more than 50% of the total amount invested in energy and automobile stocks in a combination of real estate and pharmaceutical company stock

Subject to these constraints, the client's goal is to maximize projected return on investments. The broker has prepared a list of high-quality stocks and bonds and their corresponding rates of return, as shown in the following table.

INVESTMENT	ANNUAL RATE OF RETURN
City of Miami (municipal) bonds	5.3%
American Smart Car	8.8%
GreenEarth Energy	4.9%
Rosslyn Pharmaceuticals	8.4%
RealCo (real estate)	10.4%

Formulate this portfolio selection problem by using LP and solve it by using Excel.

3-14 An investor wishes to invest some or all of his $12.5 million in a diversified portfolio through a commercial lender. The types of investments, the expected interest per year, and the maximum allowed percentage investment he will consider are shown on the following table. He wants at least 35% of his investments to be in nonmortgage instruments and no more than 60% to be in high-yield (and high-risk) instruments (i.e., expected interest >8%). How should his investment be diversified to make the most interest income?

INVESTMENT	EXPECTED INTEREST	MAXIMUM ALLOWED
Low-income mortgage loans	7.00%	20%
Conventional mortgage loans	6.25%	40%
Government sponsored mortgage loans	8.25%	25%
Bond investments	5.75%	12%
Stock investments	8.75%	15%
Futures trading	9.50%	10%

3-15 A finance major has inherited $200,000 and wants to invest it in a diversified portfolio. Some of the investments she is considering are somewhat risky. These include international mutual funds, which should earn 12.25% over the next year, and U.S. stocks, which should earn 11.5% over the next year. She has therefore decided that she will put no more than 30% of her money in either of these investments and no more than a total of 50% in both investments.

She also wants to keep some of her investment in what is considered a liquid state, so that she can divest quickly if she so chooses. She believes school bonds, which return 5% interest, short-term certificates of deposit, which return 6.25% interest, and tax-free municipal bonds, which return 8.75%, to be reasonably liquid. She will keep no more than 40% of her money in these investments and no more than 15% in any one of these investments. She believes that T-bills are also considered liquid and less risky and that they will return 7.5%. However, she has decided to invest no more than 25% of her investment in T-bills.

She wishes to have experience investing in different types of instruments, so she will invest at least 10% of her money in each of the six types of investment choices. What is the optimal investment strategy for her to follow?

3-16 A couple has agreed to attend a "casino night" as part of a fundraiser for the local hospital, but they believe that gambling is generally a losing proposition. For the sake of the charity, they have decided to attend and to allocate $300 for the games. There are to be four games, each involving standard decks of cards.

The first game, called *Jack in 52*, is won by selecting a Jack of a specific suit from the deck. The probability of actually doing this is, of course, 1 in 52 (= 0.0192). Gamblers may place a bet of $1, $2, or $4 on this game. If they win, the payouts are $12 for a $1 bet, $24.55 for a $2 bet, and $49 for a $4 bet.

The second game, called *Red Face in 52*, is won by selecting from the deck a red face card (i.e., red Jack, red Queen, or red King). The probability of winning is 6 in 52 (= 0.1154). Again, bets may be placed in denominations of $1, $2, and $4. Payouts are $8.10, $16.35, and $32.50, respectively.

The third game, called *Face in 52*, is won by selecting one of the 12 face cards from the deck. The probability of winning is 12 in 52 (= 0.2308). Payouts are $4, $8.15, and $16 for $1, $2, and $4 bets.

The last game, called *Red in 52*, is won by selecting a red card from the deck. The probability of winning is 26 in 52 (= 0.50). Payouts are $1.80, $3.80, and $7.50 for $1, $2, and $4 bets.

Given that they can calculate the expected return (or, more appropriately, loss) for each type of game and level of wager, they have decided to see if they can minimize their total expected loss by planning their evening using LP. For example, the expected return from a $1 bet in the game *Jack in 52* is equal to $0.2308 (= $12 × 1/52 + $0 × 51/52). Since the amount bet is $1, the expected loss is equal to $0.7692 (= $1 − $0.2308). All other expected losses can be calculated in a similar manner.

They want to appear to be sociable and not as if they are trying to lose as little as possible. Therefore, they will place at least 20 bets (of any value) on each of the four games. Further, they will spend at least $26 on $1 bets, at least $50 on $2 bets, and at least $72 on $4 bets. They will bet no more than (and no less than) the agreed-upon $300. What should be their gambling plan, and what is their expected loss for the evening?

3-17 A hospital emergency room is open 24 hours a day. Nurses report for duty at 1 A.M., 5 A.M., 9 A.M., 1 P.M., 5 P.M., or 9 P.M., and each works an 8-hour shift. Nurses are paid the same, regardless of the shift they work. The following table shows the minimum number of nurses needed during the six periods into which the day is divided. How should the hospital schedule the nurses so that the total staff required for one day's operation is minimized?

SHIFT	TIME	NURSES NEEDED
1	1–5 A.M.	4
2	5–9 A.M.	13
3	9 A.M.–1 P.M.	17
4	1–5 P.M.	10
5	5–9 P.M.	12
6	9 P.M.–1 A.M.	5

3-18 A nursing home employs attendants who are needed around the clock. Each attendant is paid the same, regardless of when his or her shift begins. Each shift is 8 consecutive hours. Shifts begin at 6 A.M., 10 A.M., 2 P.M., 6 P.M., 10 P.M., and 2 A.M. The following table shows the nursing home's requirements for the numbers of attendants to be on duty during specific time periods.

SHIFT	TIME	NUMBER OF ATTENDANTS
A	2–6 A.M.	8
B	6–10 A.M.	27
C	10 A.M.–2 P.M.	12
D	2–6 P.M.	23
E	6–10 P.M.	29
F	10 P.M.–2 A.M.	23

(a) What is the minimum number of attendants needed to satisfy the nursing home's requirements?

(b) The nursing home would like to use the same number of attendants determined in part (a) but would now like to minimize the total salary paid. Attendants are paid $16 per hour during 8 A.M.–8 P.M., and a 25% premium per hour during 8 P.M.–8 A.M. How should the attendants now be scheduled?

3-19 A hospital is moving from 8-hour shifts for its lab techs to 12-hour shifts. Instead of working five 8-hour days, the lab techs would work three days on and four days off in the first week followed by four days on and three days off in the second week, for a total of 84 hours every two weeks.

Because the peak demand times in the hospital appear to be between 5 A.M. and 7 A.M. and between 5 P.M. and 7 P.M., four 12-hour shifts will be arranged according to the table at the top of p. 109.

SHIFTS	WORK TIMES	PAY RATE/ WEEK
A and A (alt)	5 A.M.–5 P.M.	$756
B and B (alt)	7 A.M.–7 P.M.	$840
C and C (alt)	5 P.M.–5 A.M.	$882
D and D (alt)	7 P.M.–7 A.M.	$924

The shift pay differentials are based on the most and least desirable times to begin and end work. In any one week, techs on shift A might work Sunday through Tuesday, while techs on shift A (alt) would work at the same times but on Wednesday through Saturday. In the following week, techs on shift A would work Sunday through Wednesday, while techs on shift A (alt) would work the corresponding Thursday through Saturday. Therefore, the same number of techs would be scheduled for shift A as for shift A (alt).

The requirements for lab techs during the 24-hour day are shown in the following table. What is the most economical schedule for the lab techs?

	5 A.M.– 7 A.M.	7 A.M.– 5 P.M.	5 P.M.– 7 P.M.	7 P.M.– 5 A.M.
Lab techs needed	12	8	14	10

3-20 An airline with operations in San Diego, California, must staff its ticket counters inside the airport. Ticket attendants work 6-hour shifts at the counter. There are two types of agents: those who speak English as a first language and those who are fully bilingual (English and Spanish). The requirements for the number of agents depend on the numbers of people expected to pass through the airline's ticket counters during various hours. The airline believes that the need for agents between the hours of 6 A.M. and 9 P.M. are as follows:

	6 A.M.– 9 A.M.	9 A.M.– NOON	NOON– 3 P.M.	3 P.M.– 6 P.M.	6 P.M.– 9 P.M.
Agents needed	12	20	16	24	12

Agents begin work either at 6 A.M., 9 A.M., noon, or 3 P.M. The shifts are designated as shifts A, B, C, and D, respectively. It is the policy of the airline that at least half of the agents needed in any time period will speak English as the first language. Further, at least one-quarter of the agents needed in any time period should be fully bilingual.

(a) How many and what type of agents should be hired for each shift to meet the language and staffing requirements for the airline, so that the total number of agents is minimized?

(b) What is the optimal hiring plan from a cost perspective if English-speaking agents are paid $25 per hour and bilingual agents are paid $29 per hour? Does the total number of agents needed change from that computed in part (a)?

3-21 A small trucking company is determining the composition of its next trucking job. The load master has his choice of seven different types of cargo, which may be loaded in full or in part. The specifications of the cargo types are shown in the following table. The goal is to maximize the amount of freight, in terms of dollars, for the trip. The truck can hold up to 900 pounds of cargo in a 2,500-cubic-foot space. What cargo should be loaded, and what will be the total freight charged?

CARGO TYPE	FREIGHT PER POUND	VOLUME PER POUND (CU. FT.)	POUNDS AVAILABLE
A	$8.00	3.0	210
B	$6.00	2.7	150
C	$3.50	6.3	90
D	$5.75	8.4	120
E	$9.50	5.5	130
F	$5.25	4.9	340
G	$8.60	3.1	250

3-22 The load master for a freighter wants to determine the mix of cargo to be carried on the next trip. The ship's volume limit for cargo is 100,000 cubic meters, and its weight capacity is 2,310 tons. The master has five different types of cargo from which to select and wishes to maximize the value of the selected shipment. However, to make sure that none of his customers are ignored, the load master would like to make sure that at least 20% of each cargo's available weight is selected. The specifications for the five cargoes are shown in the following table.

CARGO TYPE	TONS AVAILABLE	VALUE PER TON	VOLUME PER TON (CU. M.)
A	970	$1,350	26
B	850	$1,675	54
C	1,900	$1,145	28
D	2,300	$ 850	45
E	3,600	$1,340	37

3-23 A cargo transport plane is to be loaded to maximize the revenue from the load carried. The plane may carry any combination and any amount of cargoes A, B, and C. The relevant values for these cargoes are shown in the table at the top of p. 110.

CARGO TYPE	TONS AVAILABLE	REVENUE PER TON	VOLUME PER TON (CU. FT.)
A	10	$700	2,000
B	12	$725	3,500
C	17	$685	3,000

The plane can carry as many as 32 tons of cargo. The plane is subdivided into compartments, and there are weight and volume limitations for each compartment. It is critical for safety reasons that the weight ratios be strictly observed. The requirements for cargo distribution are shown in the following table.

COMPARTMENT	MAXIMUM VOLUME (CU. FT.)	COMPARTMENT WEIGHT/TOTAL WEIGHT RATIO
Right fore	16,000	Must equal 18% of total weight loaded
Right center	20,000	Must equal 25% of total weight loaded
Right aft	14,000	Must equal 7% of total weight loaded
Left fore	10,000	Must equal 18% of total weight loaded
Left center	20,000	Must equal 25% of total weight loaded
Left aft	12,000	Must equal 7% of total weight loaded

Which cargoes should be carried, and how should they be allocated to the various compartments?

3-24 The owner of a private freighter is trying to decide which cargo he should carry on his next trip. He has two choices of cargo, which he can agree to carry in any combination. He may carry up to 15 tons of cargo A, which takes up 675 cubic feet per ton and earns revenue of $85 per ton. Or, he may carry up to 54 tons of cargo B, with a volume of 450 cubic feet per ton and revenue of $79 per ton.

The freighter is divided into two holds, starboard and port. The starboard hold has a volume of 14,000 cubic feet and a weight capacity of 26 tons. The port hold has a volume of 15,400 cubic feet and a weight capacity of 32 tons. For steering reasons, it is necessary that the weight be distributed equally between the two sides of the freighter. However, the freighter engines and captain's bridge, which together weight 6 tons, are on the starboard side of the freighter. This means that the port side is usually loaded with 6 tons more cargo to equalize the weight. The owner may carry any combination of the two cargoes in the same hold without a problem. How should this freighter be loaded to maximize total revenue?

3-25 A farmer is making plans for next year's crop. He is considering planting corn, tomatoes, potatoes and okra. The data he has collected, along with the availability of resources, are shown in the table at the bottom of this page. He can plant as many as 60 acres of land. Determine the best mix of crops to maximize the farm's revenue.

3-26 The farmer in Problem 3-25 has an opportunity to take over the neighboring 80-acre farm. If he acquires this farm, he will be able to increase the amounts of time available to 1,600 hours for planting, 825 hours for tending, and 1,400 hours for harvesting. Between the two farms, there are 510 units of water and 6,000 pounds of fertilizer available. However, the neighboring farm has not been cultivated in a while. Therefore, each acre of this farm will take an additional 4 hours to plant and an additional 2 hours to tend. Because of the condition of the new farm, the farmer expects the yields per acre planted there to be only 46 bushels, 37 bushels, 42 bushels, and 45 bushels, respectively, for corn, tomato, potato, and okra. In order to make sure that both farms are used effectively, the farmer would like at least 80% of each farm's acreage to be planted. What is the best combination of crops to plant at each farm in order to maximize revenue?

3-27 A family farming concern owns five parcels of farmland broken into a southeast sector, north sector, northwest sector, west sector, and southwest sector. The farm concern is involved primarily in growing wheat, alfalfa, and barley crops and is currently preparing the production plan for next year.

Table for Problem 3-25

CROP	YIELD (BUSHELS/ACRE)	REVENUE/ BUSHEL	PLANTING (HOURS/ACRE)	TENDING (HOURS/ACRE)	HARVEST (HOURS/ACRE)	WATER (UNITS/ACRE)	FERTILIZER (POUNDS/ACRE)
Corn	50	$55	10	2	6	2.5	50
Tomato	40	$85	15	8	20	3.0	60
Potato	46	$57	12	2	9	2.0	45
Okra	48	$52	18	12	20	3.0	35
Available			775	550	775	300	2,500

The Water Authority has just announced its yearly water allotment, with this farm receiving 7,500 acre-feet. Each parcel can tolerate only a certain amount of irrigation per growing season, as specified in the following table.

PARCEL	AREA (ACRES)	WATER IRRIGATION LIMIT (ACRE-FEET)
Southeast	2,000	3,200
North	2,300	3,400
Northwest	600	800
West	1,100	500
Southwest	500	600

Each crop needs a minimum amount of water per acre, and there is a projected limit on sales of each crop, as noted in the following table.

CROP	MAXIMUM SALES	WATER NEEDED PER ACRE (ACRE-FEET)
Wheat	110,000 bushels	1.6
Alfalfa	1,800 tons	2.9
Barley	2,200 tons	3.5

Wheat can be sold at a net profit of $2 per bushel, alfalfa at $40 per ton, and barley at $50 per ton. One acre of land yields an average of 1.5 tons of alfalfa and 2.2 tons of barley. The wheat yield is approximately 50 bushels per acre. What is the best planting plan for this farm?

3-28 A farmer has subdivided his land into three plots and wants to plant three crops in each plot: corn, rice, and soy. Plot sizes, crop acreage, profit per acre, and manure needed (pounds per acre) are given in the table at the bottom of this page.

The maximum acreage for each crop denotes the total acres of that crop that can be planted over all three plots. Currently there are 450,000 pounds of manure available. To ensure that the plots are used equitably, the farmer wants the same proportion of each plot to be under cultivation. (The proportion of each plot under cultivation must be the same for all three plots.) How much of each crop should be planted at each plot to maximize total profit?

3-29 A fuel cell manufacturer can hire union, non-union permanent, or temporary help. She has a contract to produce at the rate of 2,100 fuel cells per day and would like to achieve this at minimum cost. Union workers work 7 hours per day and can make up to 10 fuel cells per hour. Their wages and benefits cost the company $15.00 and $7.00 per hour, respectively. Union workers are assured that there will be no more than 80% of their number working in non-union permanent positions and that there will be no more than 20% of their number working in temporary positions.

Non-union permanent workers work 8 hours per day and can also make up to 10 fuel cells per hour. Their wages are the same as the union employees, but their benefits are worth only $3.00 per hour. Temporary workers work 6 hours per day, can make up to 5 fuel cells per hour, and earn only $10 per hour. They do not receive any benefits.

How many union, non-union, and temporary workers should be hired to minimize the cost to the manufacturer? What is the average cost of producing a fuel cell?

3-30 A chemical company wishes to mix three elements (E, F, and G) to create three alloys (X, Y, and Z). The costs of the elements are as shown in the following table.

ELEMENT	COST PER TON
E	$3.00
F	$4.00
G	$3.50

To maintain the required quality for each alloy, it is necessary to specify certain maximum or minimum percentages of the elements. These are as shown in the following table.

ALLOY	SPECIFICATIONS	SELLING PRICE PER TON
X	No more than 30% of E, at least 40% of F, no more than 50% of G	$5.50
Y	No more than 50% of E, at least 10% of F	$4.00
Z	No more than 70% of E, at least 20% of G	$6.00

Table for Problem 3-28

PLOT	ACREAGE
A	500
B	800
C	700

CROP	MAXIMUM ACREAGE	PROFIT PER ACRE	MANURE PER ACRE (POUNDS)
Corn	900	$600	200
Wheat	700	$450	300
Soy	1,000	$300	150

Table for Problem 3-31

	INGREDIENT					
NUTRIENT	BEEF	PORK	CORN	LAMB	RICE	CHICKEN
Protein (%)	16.9	12.0	8.5	15.4	8.5	18.0
Fat (%)	26.0	4.1	3.8	6.3	3.8	17.9
Fiber (%)	29.0	8.3	2.7	2.4	2.7	28.8
Cost ($/lb)	0.52	0.49	0.20	0.40	0.17	0.39

The usage of each element is limited to 5,000 tons, and the total usage of all three elements is limited to 10,000 tons. Further, due to the relatively uncertain demand for alloy Z, the company would like to ensure that Z constitutes no more than 30% of the total quantity of the three alloys produced. Determine the mix of the three elements that will maximize profit under these conditions.

3-31 An animal feed company is developing a new puppy food. Their nutritionists have specified that the mixture must contain the following components by weight: at least 16% protein, 13% fat, and no more than 15% fiber. The percentages of each nutrient in the available ingredients, along with their cost per pound, are shown in the table at the top of this page.

What is the mixture that will have the minimum cost per pound and meet the stated nutritional requirements?

3-32 A boarding stable feeds and houses work horses used to pull tourist-filled carriages through the streets of a historic city. The stable owner wishes to strike a balance between a healthy nutritional standard for the horses and the daily cost of feed. This type of horse must consume exactly 5 pounds of feed per day. The feed mixes available are an oat product, a highly enriched grain, and a mineral product. Each of these mixes contains a predictable amount of five ingredients needed daily to keep the average horse healthy. The table at the bottom of this page shows these minimum requirements, units of each nutrient per pound of feed mix, and costs for the three mixes.

Formulate this problem and solve for the optimal daily mix of the three feeds.

3-33 Clint Hanks has decided to try a new diet that promises enhanced muscle tone if the daily intake of five essential nutrients is tightly controlled. After extensive research, Clint has determined that the recommended daily requirements of these nutrients for a person of his age, height, weight, and activity level are as follows: between 69 grams and 100 grams of protein, at least 700 milligrams of phosphorus, at least 420 milligrams of magnesium, between 1,000 milligrams and 1,750 milligrams of calcium, and at least 8 milligrams of iron. Given his limited finances, Clint has identified seven inexpensive food items that he can use to meet these requirements. The cost per serving for each food item and its contribution to each of the five nutrients are given in the table at the top of p. 113.

(a) Use LP to identify the lowest cost combination of food items that Clint should use for his diet.
(b) Would you characterize your solution in (a) as a well-balanced diet? Explain your answer.

3-34 A steel company is producing steel for a new contract. The contract specifies the information in the following table for the steel.

MATERIAL	MINIMUM	MAXIMUM
Manganese	2.10%	3.10%
Silicon	4.30%	6.30%
Carbon	1.05%	2.05%

The steel company mixes batches of eight different available materials to produce each ton of steel

Table for Problem 3-32

	FEED MIX			
NUTRIENT	OAT (UNITS/LB.)	GRAIN (UNITS/LB.)	MINERAL (UNITS/LB.)	NEEDED (UNITS/DAY)
A	2.0	3.0	1.0	6
B	0.5	1.0	0.5	2
C	3.0	5.0	6.0	9
D	1.0	1.5	2.0	8
E	0.5	0.5	1.5	5
Cost/lb.	$0.33	$0.44	$0.57	

Table for Problem 3-33

FOOD ITEM (SERVING SIZE)	PROTEIN (G)	PHOSPHORUS (MG)	MAGNESIUM (MG)	CALCIUM (MG)	IRON (MG)	COST PER SERVING ($)
Chicken Patty (0.25 pound)	17.82	250	29	23	1.14	0.50
Lasagna (300 grams)	24.53	223	56	303	2.52	0.58
2% Milk (1 cup)	8.05	224	27	293	0.05	0.42
Mixed Vegetables (1 cup)	5.21	93	40	46	1.49	0.24
Fruit Cocktail (1 cup)	1.01	26	11	15	0.62	0.37
Orange Juice (1 cup)	1.69	42	27	27	0.32	0.36
Oatmeal (1 packet)	4.19	136	46	142	10.55	0.18

according to the specification. The table at the bottom of this page details these materials.

Formulate and solve the LP model that will indicate how much of each of the eight materials should be blended into a 1-ton load of steel so that the company can meet the specifications under the contract while minimizing costs.

3-35 A meat packing house is creating a new variety of hot dog for the low-calorie, low-fat, low-cholesterol market. This new hot dog will be made of beef and pork, plus either chicken, turkey, or both. It will be marketed as a 2-ounce all-meat hot dog, with no fillers. Also, it will have no more than 6 grams of fat, no more than 27 grams of cholesterol, and no more than 100 calories. The cost per pound for beef, pork, chicken, and turkey, plus their calorie, fat, and cholesterol counts are shown in the following table.

	COST/ POUND	CALORIES/ POUND	FAT (G/LB.)	CHOLESTEROL (G/LB.)
Beef	$0.76	640	32.5	210
Pork	$0.82	1,055	54.0	205
Chicken	$0.64	780	25.6	220
Turkey	$0.58	528	6.4	172

The packer would like each 2-ounce hot dog to be at least 25% beef and at least 25% pork. What is the most economical combination of the four meats to make this hot dog?

3-36 A distributor imports olive oil from Spain and Italy in large casks. He then mixes these oils in different proportions to create three grades of olive oil that are sold domestically in the United States. The domestic grades include (a) commercial, which must be no more than 35% Italian; (b) virgin, which may be any mix of the two olive oils; and (c) extra virgin, which must be at least 55% Spanish. The cost to the distributor for Spanish olive oil is $6.50 per gallon. Italian olive oil costs him $5.75 per gallon. The weekly demand for the three types of olive oils is 700 gallons of commercial, 2,200 gallons of virgin, and 1,400 gallons of extra virgin. How should he blend the two olive oils to meet his demand most economically?

3-37 A paint company has two types of bases from which it blends two types of paints: Tuffcoat and Satinwear. Each base has a certain proportion of ingredients X, Y, and Z, as shown in the table at the top of p. 114, along with their costs.

Table for Problem 3-34

MATERIAL AVAILABLE	MANGANESE	SILICON	CARBON	POUNDS AVAILABLE	COST PER POUND
Alloy 1	70.0%	15.0%	3.0%	No limit	$0.12
Alloy 2	55.0%	30.0%	1.0%	300	$0.13
Alloy 3	12.0%	26.0%	0%	No limit	$0.15
Iron 1	1.0%	10.0%	3.0%	No limit	$0.09
Iron 2	5.0%	2.5%	0%	No limit	$0.07
Carbide 1	0%	24.0%	18.0%	50	$0.10
Carbide 2	0%	25.0%	20.0%	200	$0.12
Carbide 3	0%	23.0%	25.0%	100	$0.09

Table for Problem 3-37

	INGREDIENT X	INGREDIENT Y	INGREDIENT Z	COST/GALLON
Paint base A	25%	34%	10%	$4.50
Paint base B	35%	42%	15%	$6.50

The specifications for the two paints are shown in the following table.

TUFFCOAT	SATINWEAR
Must contain at least 33% ingredient X	Must contain at least 30% ingredient X
Must contain at least 35% ingredient Y	Must contain at least 38% ingredient Y
Must contain no more than 14% ingredient Z	Must contain no more than 13% ingredient Z
Demand = 1,600 gallons	Demand = 1,250 gallons

How should the two bases be blended to manufacture the two paints at a minimum cost? What is the cost per gallon for each paint?

3-38 The military has requested a new ready-to-eat meal (MRE) that will provide to troops in the field a very high-protein, low-carbohydrate instant canned breakfast. The can will contain 11 fluid ounces, or 325 mL, of the product. The design specifications are as follows: The drink should have at least 15 grams of protein, no more than 3 grams of fat, no more than 38 grams of carbohydrates, and no more than 310 mg of sodium. To make the drink, a food contractor plans to mix two ingredients it already makes, liquid A and liquid B, together with a new ingredient, liquid protein. The table at the bottom of this page describes the costs and the nutritional makeup of the three ingredients. Determine the least-cost mixture for the new MRE.

3-39 A commercial food for caged reptiles is made in 40-pound bags from five potential feeds. For labeling purposes, feed A must constitute at least 20% of each bag by weight, and each of feeds B to E must be at least 5% of the total weight. Further, feeds B and D must together constitute at least 30% by weight, and feeds B, C, and E together must be no more than 50% by weight. The costs per pound for feeds A to E are, respectively, $0.96, $0.85, $0.775, $0.45, and $0.375. How shall this reptile food be made, and what is the cost per bag?

3-40 A power company has just announced the August 1 opening of its second nuclear power-generation facility. The human resources department has been directed to determine how many nuclear technicians will need to be hired and trained over the remainder of the year. The plant currently employs 350 fully trained technicians and projects personnel needs as shown in the following table.

MONTH	HOURS NEEDED
August	40,000
September	45,000
October	35,000
November	50,000
December	45,000

By law, a reactor employee can actually work no more than 130 hours per month (Slightly over 1 hour per day is used for check-in and check-out, record keeping, and daily radiation health scans.) Company policy at the power company also dictates that layoffs are not acceptable in months when the nuclear power plant is overstaffed. So, if more trained employees are available than are needed in any month, each worker is still fully paid, even though he or she is not required to work the 130 hours.

Training new employees is an important and costly procedure. It takes one month of one-on-one classroom instruction before a new technician is permitted to work alone in the reactor facility. Therefore, trainees must be hired one month before they are actually needed. Each trainee teams up with a skilled nuclear technician and requires 90 hours of that employee's time, meaning that 90 hours less of the technician's time is available that month for actual reactor work.

Table for Problem 3-38

	COMPOSITION OF THE INGREDIENTS (PER LITER)				
	PROTEIN (G)	FAT (G)	CARBOHYDRATE (G)	SODIUM (MG)	COST/LITER
Liquid A	6	8	147	1770	$3.25
Liquid B	9	12	96	720	$4.50
Liquid protein	230	2	24	320	$28.00

Human resources department records indicate a turnover rate of trained technicians of 2% per month. In other words, 2% of the skilled technicians at the start of any month resign by the end of that month. A trained technician earns a monthly salary of $4,500, and trainees are paid $2,000 during their one month of instruction.

Formulate this staffing problem by using LP and solve it by using Excel.

3-41 A manufacturer of integrated circuits is planning production for the next four months. The forecast demand for the circuits is shown in the following table.

CIRCUIT	SEP	OCT	NOV	DEC
IC341	650	875	790	1,100
IC256	900	350	1,200	1,300

At the beginning of September, the warehouse is expected to be completely empty. There is room for no more than 1,800 integrated circuits to be stored. Holding costs for both types is $0.05 per unit per month. Because workers are given time off during the holidays, the manufacturer wants to have at least 800 IC341s and 850 IC256s already in the warehouse at the beginning of January.

Production costs are $1.25 per unit for IC341 and $1.35 per unit for IC256. Because demand for raw materials is rising, production costs are expected to rise by $0.05 per month through the end of the year.

Labor to make model IC341 is 0.45 hours per unit; making model IC256 takes 0.52 hours of labor. Management has agreed to schedule at least 1,000 hours per month of labor. As many as 200 extra hours per month are available to management at the same cost, except during the month of December, when only 100 extra hours are possible. What should be the production schedule for IC341 and IC256 for the four months?

3-42 A woman inherited $356,000. As she had no immediate need for the money at the time she inherited, she decided to invest some or all of it on January 1, 201*n*, with a goal of making the money grow to $500,000 by December 31, 201*n* + 5. She is considering the investments in the following table.

	RATE	MATURES
Fund A	7%	December 31 (at the end of one year)
Fund B	16%	December 31 (at the end of the second year after investment)
Fund C	24%	December 31 (at the end of the third year after investment)
Fund D	32%	December 31 (at the end of the fourth year after investment)

She wants to set up her investment strategy at the start of year 1. If she does not need to invest all of the inheritance to have $500,000 at the end of year 6, she will find another purpose for the remainder. She may choose to place a sum of money in any or all of the investments available at the start of year 1. From that point, however, all subsequent investments should come from the matured investments of previous years. To ensure that funds are spread over different investment choices, she does not want any single *new* investment in any year to be over $120,000. (Note that prior investments in a fund do not count toward this limit.)

How much money will she have to invest on January 1, 201*n*, to meet her goal of $500,000 at the end of the sixth year?

3-43 The Transportation Security Administration (TSA) at a large airport has 175 agents hired and trained for the month of January. Agents earn an average of $3,300 per month and work 160 hours per month. The projection is that 26,400 agent-hours will be required in February, 29,040 agent hours will be required in March, and 31,994 agent hours will be required in each of the months of April and May. Attrition during the month of January is anticipated to be 5%, so only 95% of the agents trained and working in January will be available for work in February. Efforts are being made to improve attrition: The TSA expects to lose only 4% of agents during February, 3% in March, and 2% in May. To ensure that enough agents will be available to meet the demand, new agents must be hired and trained. During the one-month training period, trainees are paid $2,600. Existing agents, who normally work 160 hours per month, are able to work only 80 hours during the months they are training new people. How many agents should be hired during the months of January to May?

3-44 A paper mill sells rolls of paper to newspapers, which usually place orders for rolls of different widths. The mill has just received a large order for 1.5 million feet of 4-foot-wide paper, 6 million feet of 9-foot-wide paper, and 3 million feet of 12-foot-wide paper. It produces rolls of two sizes: (1) 3,000 feet long and 14 feet wide, at a cost of $600 per roll, and (2) 3,000 feet long and 20 feet wide, at a cost of $1,100 per roll. Large cutting machines are then used to cut these rolls to rolls of desired widths.

(a) What should the paper mill do to satisfy this order at minimum cost? *Hint:* You need to first identify the different ways in which 14-foot-wide and 20-foot-wide rolls can be cut into 4-, 9-, and 12-foot-wide rolls.

(b) The paper mill is very concerned about the environment. Rather than determine the cheapest way of satisfying the current order, the firm

Table for Problem 3-45

	CUSTOMERS ($ PER UNIT SHIPPED)			
PLANT	SAVANNAH	MOBILE	ROANOKE	AVAILABLE
Columbia	$13	$42	$38	450
Greensboro	$25	$48	$17	290
Required	250	225	210	

would like to determine the least wasteful way (i.e., minimize the amount of paper wasted). What is the solution with this revised objective, and what is the new cost?

3-45 A company that manufactures products in two plants ships locally using its own transportation system, but it has orders that must be sent to customers too far away to be serviced by the local fleet. It therefore contracts with a middle-distance carrier to complete its shipping. The locations of the two manufacturing plants, amounts available at each plant to be shipped per week, locations of the three customers, their weekly requirements, and shipping costs ($ per unit) between each plant and customer are shown in the table at the top of this page.

What is the optimal shipping plan to satisfy the demand at the lowest total shipping cost?

3-46 A school district must determine which students from each of the four attendance zones will attend which of the three high schools. The north attendance zone is 8 miles from Central High School, 4 miles from Northwestern High School, and 16 miles from Southeastern High School. All of the distances (in miles) are shown in the following table.

ATTENDANCE ZONE	NORTH	SOUTH	EAST	WEST
Central High School	8	5	5	11
Northwestern High School	4	17	15	6
Southeastern High School	16	6	6	18
Number of Students	903	741	923	793

Each school can have as many as 1,200 students enrolled. The school district would like to make the allocation of students to schools that will minimize the number of miles necessary to transport the students.

3-47 The school district in Problem 3-46 wishes to impose an additional constraint on the problem: It wants to enroll the same number of students in each of the three schools. Solve for the revised allocation of students to schools that will minimize the number of miles necessary to transport the students.

Case Study

Chase Manhattan Bank

The workload in many areas of bank operations has the characteristics of a non-uniform distribution with respect to time of day. For example, at Chase Manhattan Bank in New York, the number of domestic money transfer requests received from customers, if plotted against time of day, would appear to have the shape of an inverted U curve, with the peak around 1 P.M. For efficient use of resources, the personnel available should, therefore, vary correspondingly. Figure 3.1 shows a typical workload curve and corresponding personnel requirements at different hours of the day.

A variable capacity can be achieved effectively by employing part-time personnel. Because part-timers are not entitled to all the fringe benefits, they are often more economical than full-time employees. Other considerations, however, may limit the extent to which part-time people can be hired in a given department. The problem is to find an optimum workforce schedule that would meet personnel requirements at any given time and also be economical.

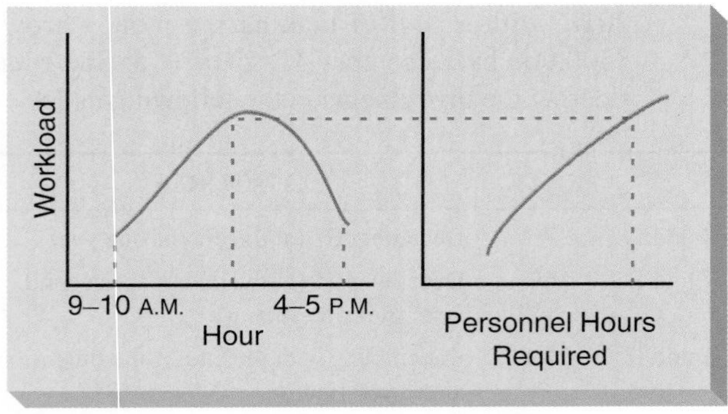

FIGURE 3.1 Figure for Case Study: Chase Manhattan Bank

Some of the factors affecting personnel assignment are listed here:

a. Full-time employees work for 8 hours per day, with a 1 hour break for lunch included.
b. Fifty percent of the full-timers go to lunch between 11 A.M. and noon, and the remaining 50% go between noon and 1 P.M.
c. Part-timers work for at least 4 continuous hours but no more than 7 continuous hours per day and are not allowed a lunch break.
d. By corporate policy, part-time personnel hours are limited to a maximum of 40% of the day's total requirement.
e. The shift starts at 9 A.M. and ends at 7 P.M. (i.e., overtime is limited to 2 hours). Any work left over at 7 P.M. is considered holdover for the next day.
f. A full-time employee is not allowed to work more than 1 hour of overtime per day. He or she is paid at the normal rate even for overtime hours—*not* at one and one-half times the normal rate typically applicable to overtime hours. Fringe benefits are not applied to overtime hours.

In addition, the following costs are pertinent:

a. The average normal rate per full-time personnel hour is $24.08.
b. The fringe benefit rate per full-time personnel hour is charged at 25% the normal rate.
c. The average rate per part-time personnel hour is $17.82.

The personnel hours required, by hour of day, are given in Table 3.17. The bank's goal is to achieve the minimum possible personnel cost subject to meeting or exceeding the hourly workforce requirements as well as the constraints on the workers listed earlier.

TABLE 3.17 Data for Chase Manhattan Bank

TIME PERIOD	HOURS REQUIRED
9–10 A.M.	14
10–11	25
11–12	26
12–1 P.M.	38
1–2	55
2–3	60
3–4	51
4–5	29
5–6	14
6–7	9

Discussion Questions

1. What is the minimum-cost schedule for the bank?
2. What are the limitations of the model used to answer question 1?

Source: Based on Shyam L. Moondra. "An L. P. Model for Work Force Scheduling for Banks," *Journal of Bank Research* (Winter 1976), 299–301.

Internet Case Studies

See the Companion Website for this textbook, at www.pearsonhighered.com/balakrishnan, for additional case studies.

CHAPTER 4

Linear Programming Sensitivity Analysis

LEARNING OBJECTIVES

After completing this chapter, students will be able to:

1. Understand, using graphs, the impact of changes in objective function coefficients, right-hand-side values, and constraint coefficients on the optimal solution of a linear programming problem.
2. Generate Answer and Sensitivity Reports using Excel's Solver.
3. Interpret all parameters of these reports for maximization and minimization problems.
4. Analyze the impact of simultaneous changes in input data values using the 100% rule.
5. Analyze the impact of the addition of a new variable using the pricing-out strategy.

CHAPTER OUTLINE

4.1 Introduction

We have solved LP models under deterministic assumptions.

Optimal solutions to linear programming (LP) problems have thus far been found under what are called *deterministic* assumptions. This means that we assume complete certainty in the data and relationships of a problem—namely, prices are fixed, resources' availabilities are known, production time needed to make a unit are exactly set, and so on. That is, we assume that all the coefficients (constants) in the objective function and each of the constraints are fixed and do not change. But in most real-world situations, conditions are dynamic and changing. This could mean, for example, that just as we determine the optimal solution to an LP model that has the profit contribution for a given product set at $10 per unit, we find out that the profit contribution has changed to $9 per unit. What does this change mean for our solution? Is it no longer optimal?

Managers are often interested in studying the impact of changes in the values of input parameters.

In practice, such changes to input data values typically occur for two reasons. First, the value may have been estimated incorrectly. For example, a firm may realize that it has overestimated the selling price by $1, resulting in an incorrect profit contribution of $10 per unit, rather than $9 per unit. Or it may determine during a production run that it has only 175 pumps in inventory, rather than 200, as specified in the LP model. Second, management is often interested in getting quick answers to a series of what-if questions. For example, what if the profit contribution of a product decreases by 10%? What if less money is available for advertising? What if workers can each stay one hour longer every day at 1.5-times pay to provide increased production capacity? What if new technology will allow a product to be wired in one-third the time it used to take?

Why Do We Need to Study Sensitivity Analysis?

Sensitivity analysis, also known as *postoptimality analysis*, is a procedure that allows us to answer questions such as those posed above, using the current optimal solution itself, without having to resolve the LP model each time. Before we discuss this topic in more detail, let us first address a question that may arise commonly: Why do we need to study sensitivity analysis when we can use the computer to make the necessary changes to the model and quickly solve it again? The answer is as follows.

If the change in an input data value is certain, the easiest approach is to change it in the formulation and resolve the model.

If, in fact, we know that a change in an input data value is definite (e.g., we know *with certainty* that the profit contribution has decreased from $10 to $9 per unit), the easiest and logical course of action is to do just what the question suggests. That is, we should simply change the input data value in the formulation and solve the model again. Given the ease with which most real-world models can be solved using computers today, this approach should not be too difficult or time-consuming. Clearly, this same approach can be used even if we are making *definite* changes to more than one input data value at the same time.

In contrast, what if changes in input data values are just hypothetical, such as in the various what-if scenarios listed earlier? For example, assume that we are just considering lowering the selling price of a product but have not yet decided to what level it should be lowered. If we are considering 10 different selling price values, changing the input data value and resolving the LP model for every proposed value results in 10 separate models. If we expand this argument to consider 10 selling price levels each for two different products, we now have 100 ($= 10 \times 10$) LP models to solve. Clearly, this approach (i.e., changing and resolving the LP model) quickly becomes impractical when we have many input data values in a model and we are considering what-if multiple changes in each of their values.

Sensitivity analysis involves examining how sensitive the optimal solution is to changes in profits, resources, or other input parameters.

In such situations, the preferred approach is to formulate and solve a *single* LP model with a given set of input data values. However, after solving this model, we conduct a sensitivity analysis of the optimal solution to see just how *sensitive* it is to changes in each of these input data values. That is, for each input data value, we attempt to determine a *range of values* within which the current optimal solution will remain optimal. For example, if the current selling price for a product is $10 per unit, we identify the extent to which this value can change (both on the higher side and on the lower side) without affecting the optimality of the current solution. We can obtain this information, as we shall see, from the current solution itself, without resolving the LP model each time.

As we did previously with LP formulations and solutions, we first study LP sensitivity analysis using a two-variable product mix problem. We recognize here again that we are unlikely

DM IN ACTION The Right Stuff at NASA

There are many areas at NASA where decision modeling tools such as linear programming have been applied successfully. With the culture of the U.S. space program changing because of an increasing pressure to develop missions under rigid schedule and budget constraints, NASA has to work in an environment of faster–better–cheaper. After its highly publicized Mars failure, NASA addresses the issue of scarce resources with a technique called *sensitivity analysis* and a measure of marginal costs called the *shadow price*.

For example, at the margin, money is sometimes spent on tests that are not justified by the value of information. In other cases, more funds would yield risk-reduction benefits that would justify the costs and greatly improve the scientific benefit of a space mission. The shadow prices of the resource constraints in such a case provide valuable insights into the cost–benefit trade-off.

When NASA looks at a project that is critical to the success of new missions, the costs of losing the project will include marginal values of the delays and loss of data incurred by these future missions. Linear programming doesn't just provide optimal solutions; it provides the ability to conduct sensitivity analysis on these solutions as well.

Source: From M. E. Pate-Cornell and R. L. Dillon. "The Right Stuff," *OR/MS Today* 27, 1 (February 2000): 36–39, reprinted with permission.

Excel's Solver can be used to generate Sensitivity Reports.

to encounter two-variable problems in real-world situations. Nevertheless, a big advantage of studying such models is that we can demonstrate the concepts of sensitivity analysis using a graphical approach. This experience will be invaluable in helping understand the various issues in sensitivity analysis even for larger problems. For these larger problems, because we cannot view them graphically, we will rely on Excel's Solver to generate a Sensitivity Report. We discuss three separate Solver Sensitivity Reports in this chapter: (1) a report for the two-variable product mix problem that we also first analyze graphically, (2) a report for a larger problem (i.e., more than two variables) with a maximization objective function, and (3) a report for a larger problem with a minimization objective function. The two larger problems allow us to illustrate fully the various types of information we can obtain by using sensitivity analysis.

We will first study the impact of only one change at a time.

We will initially study sensitivity analysis by varying only one input data value at a time. Later, we will expand our discussion to include simultaneous changes in several input data values.

4.2 Sensitivity Analysis Using Graphs

To analyze LP sensitivity analysis by using graphs, let us revisit the Flair Furniture problem that we first used in Chapter 2 to introduce LP formulation and solution. Our motivation for using the same problem here is that you are hopefully already familiar with that problem and its graphical solution. Nevertheless, you might want to briefly review sections 2.3 and 2.4 in Chapter 2 before proceeding further.

Recall that the Flair Furniture Company problem involved two products: tables and chairs. The constraints dealt with the hours available in the carpentry and painting departments, production limits on chairs, and the minimum production level on tables. If we let T denote the number of tables to make and C denote the number of chairs to make, we can formulate the following LP problem to determine the best product mix:

$$\text{Maximize profit} = \$7T + \$5C$$

subject to the constraints

$$\begin{aligned}
3T + 4C &\le 2{,}400 && \text{(carpentry time)}\\
2T + 1C &\le 1{,}000 && \text{(painting time)}\\
C &\le 450 && \text{(maximum chairs allowed)}\\
T &\ge 100 && \text{(minimum tables required)}\\
T, C &\ge 0 && \text{(nonnegativity)}
\end{aligned}$$

FIGURE 4.1
Optimal Corner Point Solution for Flair Furniture

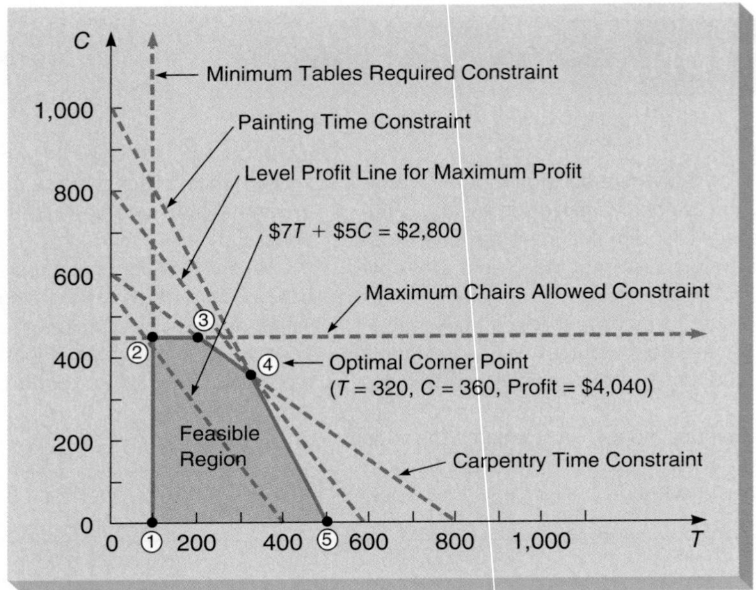

The solution to this problem is illustrated graphically in Figure 4.1 (which is essentially the same information as in Figure 2.6 on page 31 in Chapter 2). Recall from Chapter 2 that we can use the level profit lines method to identify the optimal corner point solution. (The level profit line for a profit value of $2,800 is shown in Figure 4.1.) It is easy to see that Flair's optimal solution is at corner point ④. At this corner point, the optimal solution is to produce 320 tables and 360 chairs, for a profit of $4,040.

Types of Sensitivity Analysis

In the preceding LP formulation, note that there are three types of input parameter values:

1. ***Objective function coefficient (OFC).*** The **OFCs** are the coefficients for the decision variables in the objective function (such as the $7 and $5 for *T* and *C*, respectively, in Flair's model). In many business-oriented LP models, OFCs typically represent unit profits or costs, and they are measured in monetary units such as dollars, euros, and rupees.

   Are OFCs likely to have any uncertainty in their values? Clearly, the answer is yes because in many real-world situations, selling and cost prices are seldom likely to be static or fixed. For this reason, we will study how the optimal solution may be affected by changes in OFC values.
2. ***Right-hand-side (RHS) value of a constraint.*** The **RHS values** are constants, such as the 2,400 and 1,000 in Flair's model, that typically appear on the RHS of a constraint (i.e., to the right of the equality or inequality sign). For $\leq$ constraints, they typically represent the amount available of a resource, and for $\geq$ constraints, they typically represent the minimum level of satisfaction needed.

   Are these types of input data subject to uncertainty in practice? Here again, the answer is a clear yes. In many practical situations, companies may find that their resource availability has changed due to, for example, miscounted inventory, broken-down machines, absent labor, etc. For this reason, we will study how the optimal solution may be affected by changes in RHS values.
3. ***Constraint coefficient.*** The constraint coefficients are the coefficients for the decision variables in a model's constraints (such as the 3 and 4 in the carpentry constraint in Flair's model). In many problems, these represent design issues with regard to the decision variables. For example, needing three hours of carpentry per table is a product design issue that has probably been specified by design engineers.

   Although we could think of specific situations where these types of input parameters could also be subject to uncertainty in their values, such changes are less likely here than in OFC and RHS values. For this reason, we do not usually study the impact of changes in constraint coefficient values on the optimal solution.

Most computer-based LP software packages, including Excel's Solver, provide Sensitivity Reports only for analyzing the effect of changes in OFC and RHS values.

Impact of Changes in an Objective Function Coefficient

We examine changes in OFCs first.

When the value of an OFC changes, the feasible solution region remains the same (because it depends only on the constraints). That is, we have the same set of corner points, and their locations do not change. All that changes is the slope of the level profit (or cost) line.

Let us consider the impact of changes in the profit contribution of tables (T). First, what if the demand for tables becomes so high that the profit contribution can be raised from \$7 to \$8 per table? Is corner point ④ still the optimal solution? The answer is definitely yes, as shown in Figure 4.2. In this case, the slope of the level profit line accentuates the optimality of the solution at corner point ④. However, even though the decision variable values did not change, the new optimal objective function value (i.e., the profit) does change and is now \$4,360 (= \$8 × 320 + \$5 × 360).

In a similar fashion, let us analyze what happens if the demand for tables forces us to reduce the profit contribution from \$7 to \$6 per table. Here again, we see from the level profit line in Figure 4.2 that corner point ④ continues to remain the optimal solution, and the production plan does not change. The optimal profit, however, is now only \$3,720 (= \$6 × 320 + \$5 × 360).

If the OFC changes too much, a new corner point could become optimal.

On the other hand, what if a table's profit contribution can be raised all the way to \$11 per table? In such a case, the level profit line, shown in Figure 4.3, indicates that the optimal solution is now at corner point ⑤, instead of at corner point ④. The new solution is to make 500 tables and 0 chairs, for a profit of \$5,500. That is, tables are now so profitable compared to chairs that we should devote all our resources to making only tables.

Likewise, what if a table's profit contribution was highly overestimated and should only have been \$3 per table? In this case also, the slope of the level profit line changes enough to cause a new corner point ③ to become optimal (as shown in Figure 4.3). That is, tables have now become relatively unattractive compared to chairs, and so we will make fewer tables and more chairs. In fact, the only reason we even make any tables in this case is because we are explicitly constrained in the problem to make at least 100 tables, and from making more than 450 chairs. At corner point ③, the solution is to make 200 tables and 450 chairs, for a profit of \$2,850 (= \$3 × 200 + \$5 × 450).

There is a range for each OFC over which the current solution remains optimal.

From the preceding discussion regarding the OFC for a table, it is apparent that there is a range of possible values for this OFC for which the *current* optimal corner point solution remains optimal. Any change in the OFC value beyond this range (either on the higher end or the lower end) causes a *new* corner point to become the optimal solution. Clearly, we can repeat the same discussion with regard to the OFC for chairs.

FIGURE 4.2
Small Changes in Profit Contribution of Tables

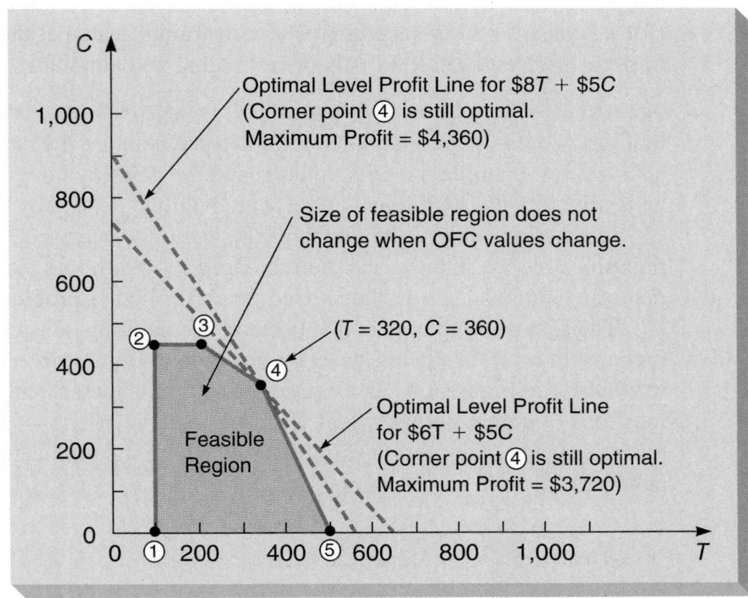

FIGURE 4.3
Larger Changes in Profit Contribution of Tables

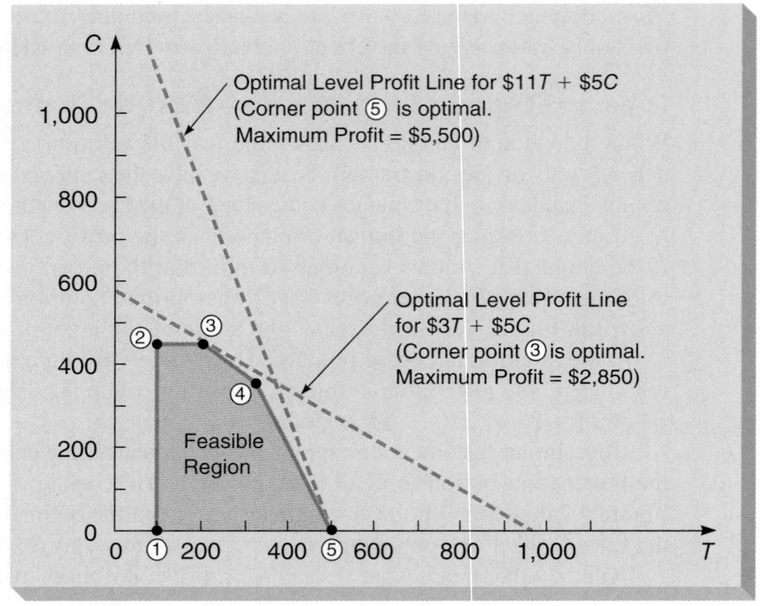

It is algebraically possible to use the graphical solution procedure to determine the allowable range for each OFC within which the current optimal solution remains optimal. However, we use the information provided in the Solver Sensitivity Report to discuss this issue further in the next section.

Changes in OFC values do not affect the size of the feasible region.

Again, whenever changes occur in OFC values, the feasible region of the problem (which depends only on the constraints) does not change. Therefore, there is no change in the physical location of each corner point. To summarize, only two things can occur due to a change in an OFC: (1) If the current optimal corner point continues to remain optimal, the decision variable values do not change, even though the objective function value may change; and (2) if the current corner point is no longer optimal, the values of the decision variables change, as does the objective function value.

Impact of Changes in a Constraint's Right-Hand-Side Value

Changes in RHS values could affect the size of the feasible region.

Unlike changes in OFC values, a change in the RHS value of a nonredundant constraint results in a change in the size of the feasible region.[1] Hence, one or more corner points may physically shift to new locations. Recall from Chapter 2 that at the optimal solution, constraints can either be binding or nonbinding. Binding constraints intersect at the optimal corner point and are, hence, exactly satisfied at the optimal solution. Nonbinding constraints have a nonzero slack (for $\leq$ constraints) or surplus (for $\geq$ constraints) value at the optimal solution. Let us analyze impacts of changes in RHS values for binding and nonbinding constraints separately.

IMPACT OF CHANGE IN RHS VALUE OF A BINDING CONSTRAINT From Figure 4.1, we know that the two binding constraints in Flair's problem are the carpentry and painting hours. Let us analyze, for example, potential changes in the painting hours available. Flair currently projects an availability of 1,000 hours, all of which will be needed by the current production plan.

Let us first analyze the impact if this value is increased. What happens if, for example, the painting time availability can be increased by 300 hours (to 1,300 hours) by adding an extra painter? Figure 4.4 shows the revised graph for Flair's problem under this scenario.

The location of the optimal corner point changes if the RHS of a binding constraint changes.

The first point to note is that because the painting constraint is a binding $\leq$ constraint, any increase in its RHS value causes the feasible region to become larger, as shown by the region marked R1 in Figure 4.4. As a consequence of this increase in the size of the feasible region, the locations of corner points ④ and ⑤ shift to new locations—(4A) and (5A), respectively. However, the level profit lines approach (shown in Figure 4.4) indicates that the intersection of the carpentry and painting constraints (i.e., corner point (4A)) is still the optimal solution. That is, the

[1] Recall from section 2.6 in Chapter 2 that a *redundant* constraint does not affect the feasible region in any way.

FIGURE 4.4
Increase in Availability of Painting Hours to 1,300 Hours

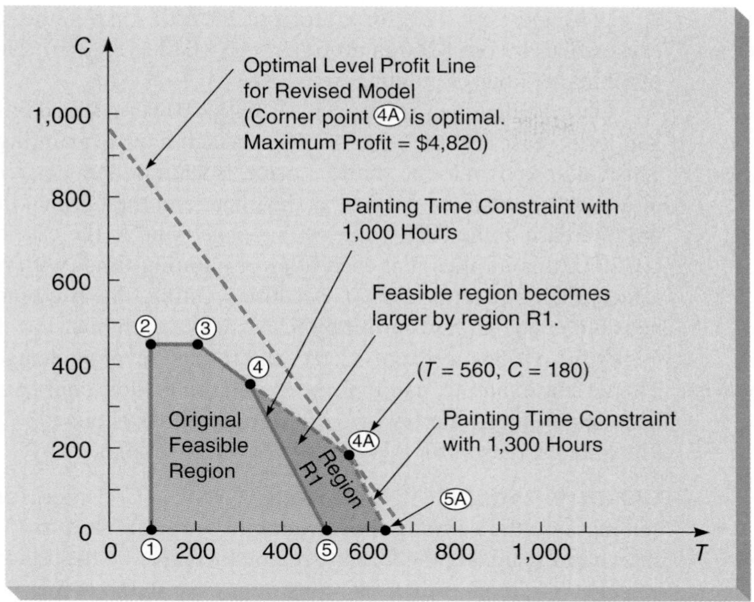

"same" corner point (in the sense that the same two constraints intersect at this point) is still optimal. But it now has a new location and, hence, there are new values for T, C, and profit. The values at corner point ④Ⓐ can be computed to be $T = 560$ and $C = 180$, for a profit of \$4,820. This implies that if Flair is able to obtain an additional 300 hours of painting time, it can increase profit by \$780 (from \$4,040 to \$4,820) by revising the production plan. This profit increase of \$780 for 300 additional hours of painting time translates to a profit increase of \$2.60 per additional hour of painting time.

The feasible region becomes smaller if the RHS value of a binding ≤ constraint is decreased.

Next, let us analyze the impact if the painting time availability is decreased. What happens if, for example, this value is only 900 hours instead of 1,000 hours? The revised graph, shown in Figure 4.5, indicates that this decrease in the RHS value of a binding ≤ constraint shrinks the size of the feasible region (as shown by the region marked R2 in Figure 4.5). Here again, the locations of corner points ④ and ⑤ have shifted to new locations, (4B) and (5B), respectively. However, as before, the level profit lines approach indicates that the "same" corner point (i.e., intersection of the carpentry and painting constraints, point (4B)) is still optimal. The values of the decision variables and the resulting profit at corner point (4B) can be computed to be

FIGURE 4.5
Decrease in Availability of Painting Hours to 900 Hours

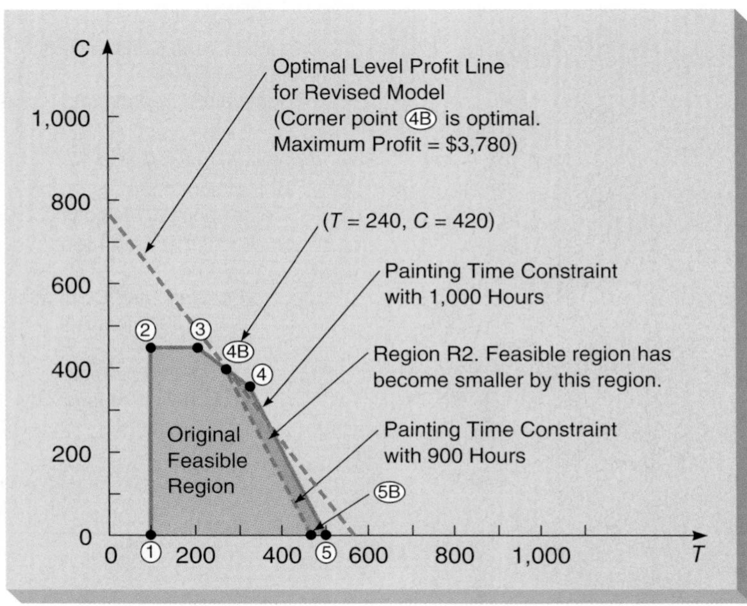

$T = 240$ and $C = 420$, for a profit of \$3,780. That is, the loss of 100 hours of painting time causes Flair to lose \$260 in profit (from \$4,040 to \$3,780). This translates to a decrease in profit of \$2.60 per hour of painting time lost.

The shadow price *is the change in objective function value for a one-unit increase in a constraint's RHS value.*

Observe that the profit increases by \$2.60 per each additional hour of painting time gained, and it decreases by the *same* \$2.60 per each hour of painting time lost from the current level. This value, known as the **shadow price**, is an important concept in LP models. The shadow price of a constraint can be defined as the change in the optimal objective function value for a one-unit increase in the RHS value of that constraint. In the case of painting time, the shadow price is \$2.60; this implies that each hour of painting time (with respect to the current availability) affects Flair's profit by \$2.60. Because painting time is a binding $\leq$ constraint, each additional hour obtained increases profit by \$2.60, while each hour lost decreases profit by \$2.60.

The shadow price is valid only for a certain range of change in a constraint's RHS value.

Is this shadow price of \$2.60 valid for any level of change in the painting time availability? That is, for example, can Flair keep obtaining additional painting time and expect its profit to keep increasing endlessly by \$2.60 for each hour obtained? Clearly, this cannot be true, and we illustrate the reason for this in the following section.

Increasing the RHS of a $\leq$ constraint endlessly will eventually make it a redundant constraint.

VALIDITY RANGE FOR THE SHADOW PRICE Consider, for example, what happens if Flair can increase the painting time availability even further, to 1,700 hours. Under this scenario, as shown in Figure 4.6, the feasible region increases by the region marked R3. However, due to the presence of the nonnegativity constraint $C \geq 0$, the corner point defined by the intersection of the carpentry and painting constraints is no longer feasible. In fact, the painting constraint has now become a redundant constraint. Obviously, in such a case, the optimal solution has shifted to a new corner point. The level profit lines approach indicates that the optimal solution is now at corner point 5C ($T = 800$, $C = 0$, profit $=$ \$5,600). Note that this translates to a profit increase of \$1,560 ($=$ \$5,600 $-$ \$4,040) for 700 additional hours, or \$2.23 per hour, which is different from the shadow price of \$2.60. That is, the shadow price of \$2.60 is not valid for an increase of 700 hours in the painting time availability.

Decreasing the RHS of a $\leq$ constraint endlessly will eventually make some other constraint a redundant constraint.

What happens if the painting time availability is decreased all the way down to 700 hours? Here again, as shown in Figure 4.7, the intersection point of the carpentry and painting constraints is no longer even feasible. The carpentry constraint is now redundant, and the optimal solution has switched to a new corner point given by corner point 3A ($T = 125$, $C = 450$, profit $=$ \$3,125). This translates to a profit decrease of \$915 ($=$ \$4,040 $-$ \$3,125) for a decrease of 300 hours, or \$3.05 per hour, which is again different from the shadow price of \$2.60. That is, the shadow price of \$2.60 is not valid for a decrease of 300 hours in the painting time availability.

There is a range of values for each RHS for which the current corner points exist.

The preceding discussion based on Figures 4.4 to 4.7 shows that for a certain range of change in the RHS value of a binding constraint, the "same" corner point will continue to remain optimal.

FIGURE 4.6
Increase in Availability of Painting Hours to 1,700 Hours

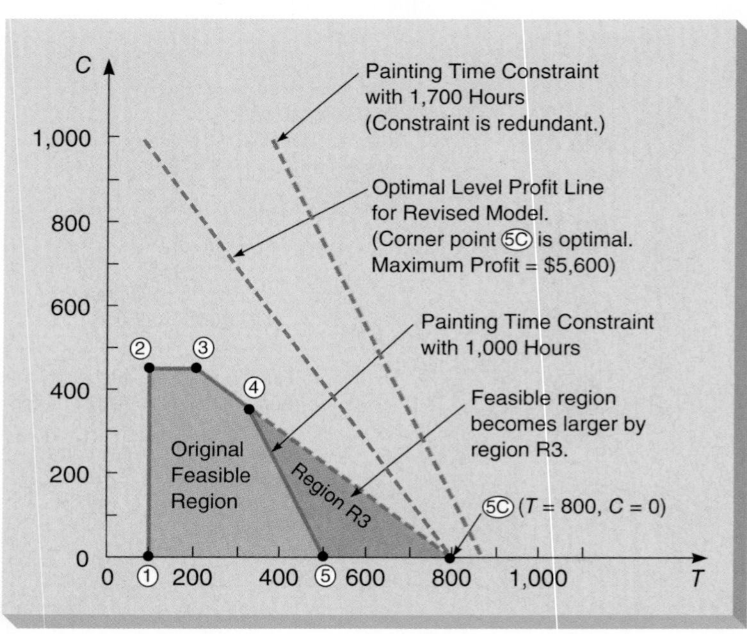

FIGURE 4.7
Decrease in Availability of Painting Hours to 700 Hours

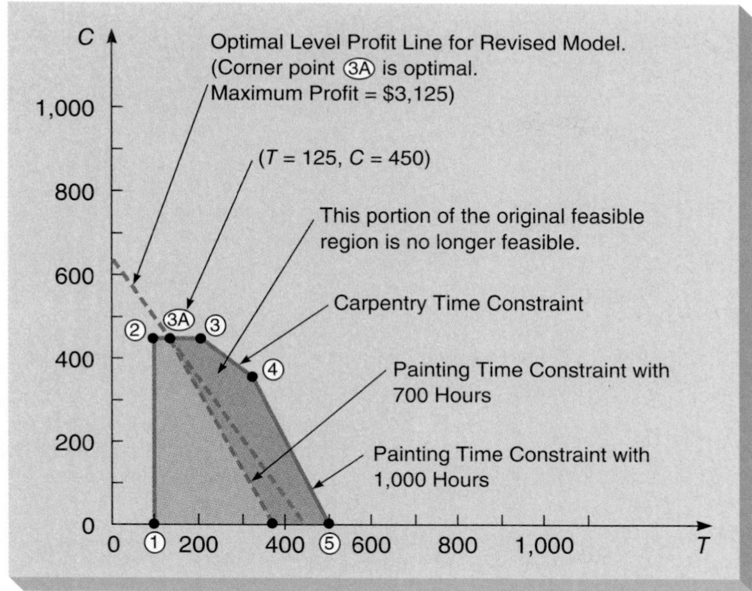

That is, the constraints that are currently binding at the optimal solution will continue to remain the binding constraints. The location of this optimal corner point will, however, change, depending on the change in the RHS value. In fact, it turns out that as long as this corner point exists in the feasible region, it will continue to remain optimal. In Flair's case, this means that the corner point where the carpentry and painting constraints intersect will remain the optimal solution *as long as it exists in the feasible region.* Also, the shadow price of \$2.60 measures the impact on profit for a unit change in painting time availability as long as this corner point continues to exist in the feasible region. Once this RHS value changes to such an extent that the current binding constraints no longer intersect in the feasible region, the shadow price of \$2.60 is no longer valid and changes to a different value. It is algebraically possible to use the graphical solution to determine the RHS range within which the current optimal corner point continues to exist, albeit at a new location. We will, however, use the information provided in the Solver Sensitivity Report to further discuss this issue in a subsequent section.

A similar analysis can be conducted with the RHS value for the other binding constraint in Flair's example—the carpentry constraint.

Increasing the RHS value of a nonbinding ≤ constraint does not affect the optimality of the current solution.

IMPACT OF CHANGES IN RHS VALUE OF A NONBINDING CONSTRAINT Let us now consider a nonbinding constraint such as the production limit on chairs ($C \leq 450$). As shown in Figure 4.8, the gap between corner point ④ and the chairs constraint represents the amount of **slack** in this nonbinding constraint. At the present solution, the slack is 90 ($= 450 - 360$). What happens now if the marketing department allows more chairs to be produced (i.e., the 450 limit is increased)? As we can see in Figure 4.8, such a change only serves to increase the slack in this constraint and does not affect the optimality of corner point ④ in any way. How far can we raise the 450 limit? Clearly, the answer is infinity.

The RHS value of a nonbinding ≤ constraint can be decreased up to its slack without affecting the optimality of the current solution.

Now consider the case where the marketing department wants to make this production limit even more restrictive (i.e., the 450 limit is decreased). As long as we are permitted to make at least 360 chairs, Figure 4.8 indicates that corner point ④ is feasible and still optimal. That is, as long as the change in the RHS value for the chairs constraint is within the slack of 90 units, the current optimal corner point continues to exist and remains optimal. However, if the chairs production limit is reduced below 360, corner point ④ is no longer feasible, and a new corner point becomes optimal. A similar analysis can be conducted with the other nonbinding constraint in the model (i.e., $T \geq 100$).

The preceding discussion illustrates that for nonbinding constraints, the allowable change limit on one side is infinity. On the opposite side, the allowable change limit equals the slack (or surplus).

FIGURE 4.8
Change in RHS Value of a Nonbinding Constraint

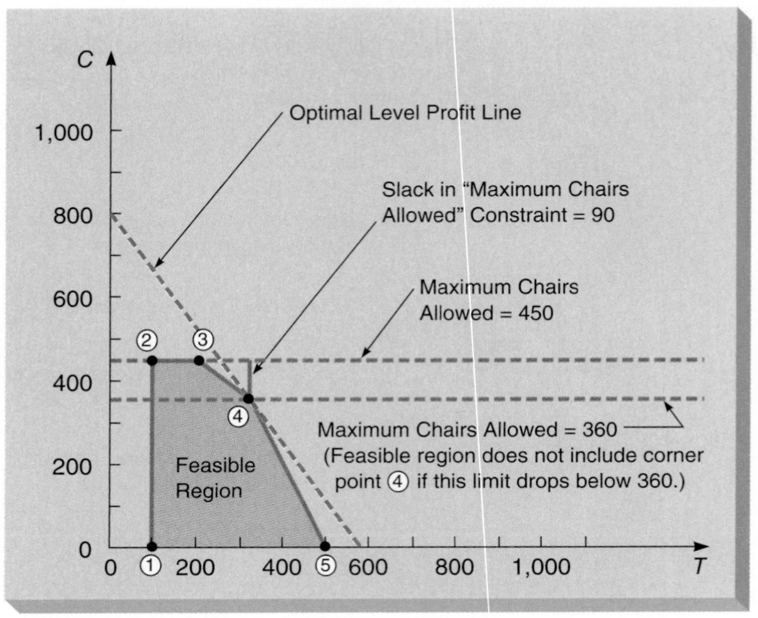

4.3 Sensitivity Analysis Using Solver Reports

Maximize $\$7T + \$5C$
subject to
$3T + 4C \leq 2{,}400$
$2T + 1C \leq 1{,}000$
$C \leq 450$
$T \geq 100$
$T, C \geq 0$

Let us consider Flair Furniture's LP model again (for your convenience, the formulation is shown in the margin note). Screenshot 4-1A shows the Excel layout and Solver entries for this model. Recall that we saw the same information in Chapter 2. Cells B5 and C5 are the entries in the By Changing Variable Cells box and denote the optimal quantities of tables and chairs to make, respectively. Cell D6 is the entry in the Set Objective box and denotes the profit. Cells D8 to D11 contain the formulas for the left-hand sides of each of the four constraints.

File: 4-1.xls, sheet: 4-1A

Excel Notes

- The Companion Website for this textbook, at www.pearsonhighered.com/balakrishnan, contains the Excel file for each problem in the examples discussed here. The relevant file name is shown in the margin next to each example.
- In each of our Excel layouts, for clarity, changing variable cells are shaded yellow, the objective cell is shaded green, and cells denoting left-hand-side (LHS) formulas of constraints are shaded blue. If the RHS of a constraint also includes a formula, that cell is also shaded blue.
- Also, to make the equivalence of the *written* formulation and the Excel layout clear, our Excel layouts show the decision variable names used in the written formulation of the model. Note that these names have no role in using Solver to solve the model.

Solver Reports

We must select the Simplex LP method as the solving method in the Solver Parameters window to obtain LP Sensitivity Reports.

Before solving the LP model, we need to ensure that the Simplex LP has been selected in the Select a Solving Method box in the Solver Parameters window to solve the problem (see Screenshot 4-1A). If a different method is selected, Solver does not solve the model as a linear program, and the resulting Sensitivity Report will look very different from the report we discuss here. Also, recall that we must check the Make Unconstrained Variables Non-Negative option to enforce the nonnegativity constraints.

The desired Solver reports must be selected in order for them to be created.

When Solver finds the optimal solution for a problem, the Solver Results window provides options to obtain three reports: Answer, Sensitivity, and Limits. Note that to obtain the desired reports, we must select them *before* we click OK. In our case, we select Answer and Sensitivity from the available choices in the box labeled Reports, and then click OK

SCREENSHOT 4-1A
Excel Layout and Solver Entries for Flair Furniture

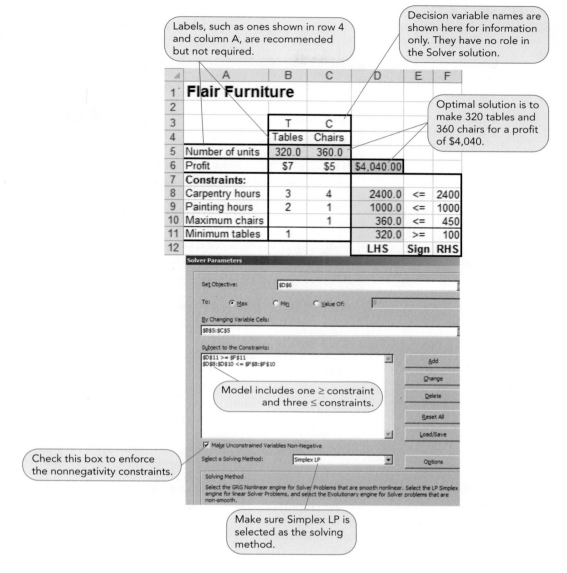

Labels, such as ones shown in row 4 and column A, are recommended but not required.

Decision variable names are shown here for information only. They have no role in the Solver solution.

	A	B	C	D	E	F
1	**Flair Furniture**					
2						
3		T	C			
4		Tables	Chairs			
5	Number of units	320.0	360.0			
6	Profit	$7	$5	$4,040.00		
7	**Constraints:**					
8	Carpentry hours	3	4	2400.0	<=	2400
9	Painting hours	2	1	1000.0	<=	1000
10	Maximum chairs		1	360.0	<=	450
11	Minimum tables	1		320.0	>=	100
12				**LHS**	**Sign**	**RHS**

Optimal solution is to make 320 tables and 360 chairs for a profit of $4,040.

Solver Parameters

Set Objective: $D$6

To: (•) Max ( ) Min ( ) Value Of: 0

By Changing Variable Cells: $B$5:$C$5

Subject to the Constraints:
$D$11 >= $F$11
$D$8:$D$10 <= $F$8:$F$10

Add / Change / Delete / Reset All / Load/Save

Model includes one ≥ constraint and three ≤ constraints.

[✓] Make Unconstrained Variables Non-Negative

Check this box to enforce the nonnegativity constraints.

Select a Solving Method: Simplex LP

Options

Solving Method
Select the GRG Nonlinear engine for Solver Problems that are smooth nonlinear. Select the LP Simplex engine for linear Solver Problems, and select the Evolutionary engine for Solver problems that are non-smooth.

Make sure Simplex LP is selected as the solving method.

(see Screenshot 4-1B). The Limits Report is relatively less useful, and we therefore do not discuss it here.

We discussed the **Answer Report** extensively in section 2.7 of Chapter 2 (see page 40) and urge you to read that section again at this time. Recall that this report provides essentially the same information as the original Excel layout (such as in Screenshot 4-1A) but in a more descriptive manner.

We are analyzing only one change at a time.

We now turn our attention to the information in the Sensitivity Report. Before we do so, it is important to note once again that while using the information in this report to answer what-if questions, we assume that we are considering a change to only a *single* input data value. Later, in section 4.5, we will expand our discussion to include simultaneous changes in several input data values.

Sensitivity Report

File: 4-1.xls, sheet: 4-1C

The Sensitivity Report for the Flair Furniture example is shown in Screenshot 4-1C. We have added grid lines to this report to make it clearer and have also formatted all values to display a consistent number of decimal points. The Sensitivity Report has two distinct tables, titled Variable Cells and Constraints. These tables permit us to answer several what-if questions regarding the problem solution.

SCREENSHOT 4-1B
Solver Results Window

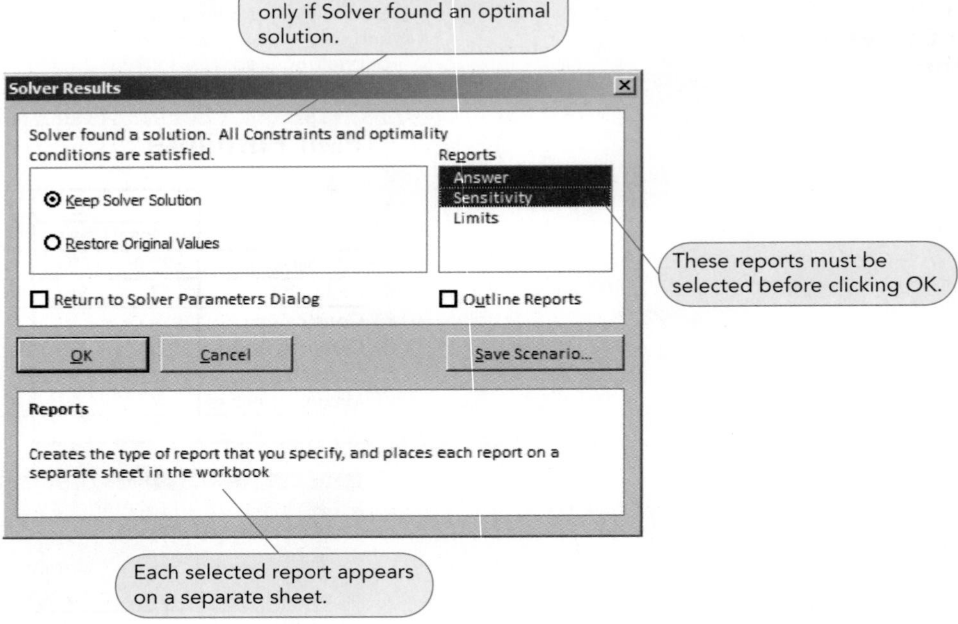

Excel Note

Solver does a rather poor job of formatting the Sensitivity Report. There is no consistency in the number of decimal points shown. While some values are displayed with no decimal points, others are displayed with many decimal points. This could sometimes cause a value such as 0.35 to be displayed (and erroneously interpreted) as 0. For this reason, we urge you to format the Sensitivity Report as needed to display a consistent number of decimal points.

The Sensitivity Report has two parts: Variable Cells and Constraints.

The Variable Cells table presents information regarding the impact of changes to the OFCs (i.e., unit profits of $7 and $5) on the optimal solution. The Constraints table presents information related to the impact of changes in constraint RHS values (such as the 2,400 and 1,000 availabilities in carpentry and painting times, respectively) on the optimal solution. Although

SCREENSHOT 4-1C Solver Sensitivity Report for Flair Furniture

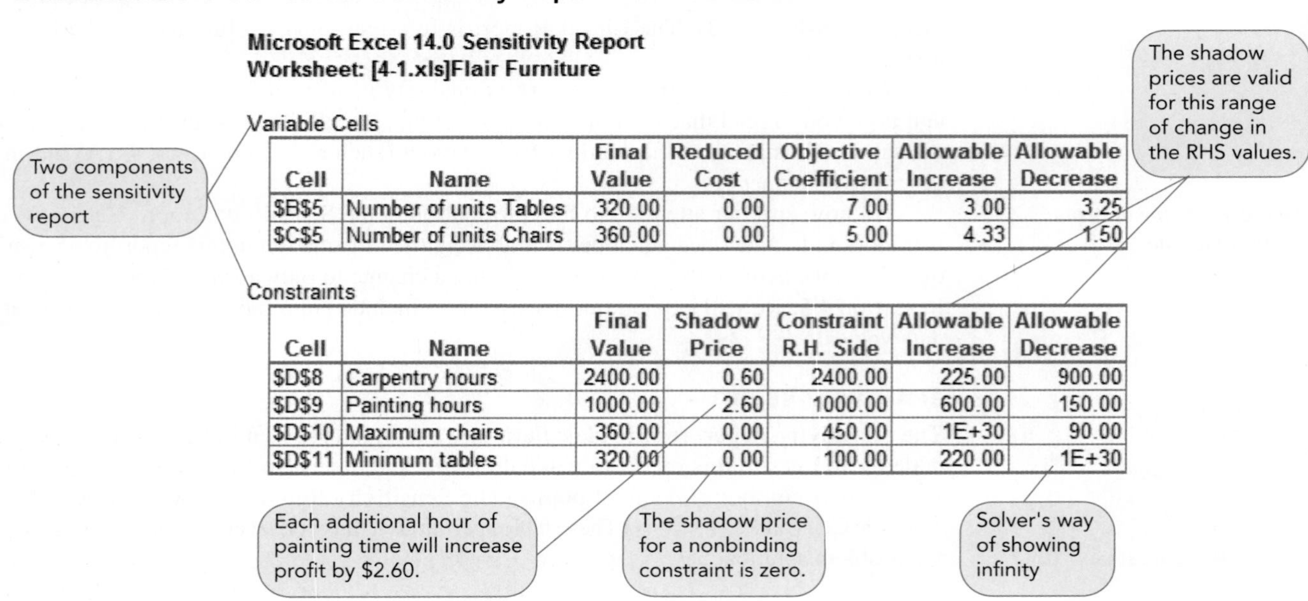

Microsoft Excel 14.0 Sensitivity Report
Worksheet: [4-1.xls]Flair Furniture

Variable Cells

Cell	Name	Final Value	Reduced Cost	Objective Coefficient	Allowable Increase	Allowable Decrease
$B$5	Number of units Tables	320.00	0.00	7.00	3.00	3.25
$C$5	Number of units Chairs	360.00	0.00	5.00	4.33	1.50

Constraints

Cell	Name	Final Value	Shadow Price	Constraint R.H. Side	Allowable Increase	Allowable Decrease
$D$8	Carpentry hours	2400.00	0.60	2400.00	225.00	900.00
$D$9	Painting hours	1000.00	2.60	1000.00	600.00	150.00
$D$10	Maximum chairs	360.00	0.00	450.00	1E+30	90.00
$D$11	Minimum tables	320.00	0.00	100.00	220.00	1E+30

different LP software packages may format and present these tables differently, the programs all provide essentially the same information.

Impact of Changes in a Constraint's RHS Value

Let us first discuss the impact on the optimal solution of a change in the RHS value of a constraint. As with the graph-based analysis earlier, we study this issue separately for binding and nonbinding constraints.

If the size of the feasible region increases, the optimal objective function value could improve.

IMPACT OF CHANGES IN THE RHS VALUE OF A BINDING CONSTRAINT Recall from the graph-based analysis in section 4.2 that if the RHS value of a binding constraint changes, the size of the feasible region also changes. If the change causes the feasible region to *increase* in size, the optimal objective function value could potentially improve. In contrast, if the change causes the feasible region to *decrease* in size, the optimal objective function value could potentially worsen. The magnitude of this change in the objective function value is given by the shadow price of the constraint, provided that the RHS change is within a certain range. In the Solver Sensitivity Report, this information is shown in the Constraints table in Screenshot 4-1C.

The shadow price is the change in objective function value for a one-unit increase in a constraint's RHS value.

Recall from section 4.2 that the shadow price can be defined as the change in the optimal objective function value for a one-unit increase in the RHS value of a constraint. In Screenshot 4-1C, the entry labeled Shadow Price for the painting constraint shows a value of \$2.60. This means that for each *additional* hour of painting time that Flair can obtain, its total profit changes by \$2.60. What is the direction of this change? In this specific case, the change is an increase in profit because the additional painting time causes the feasible region to become larger and, hence, the solution to improve.

VALIDITY RANGE FOR THE SHADOW PRICE For what level of increase in the RHS value of the painting constraint is the shadow price of \$2.60 valid? Once again, recall from our discussion in section 4.2 that there is a specific range of possible values for the RHS value of a binding constraint for which the current optimal corner point (i.e., the intersection point of the current binding constraints) exists, even if its actual location has changed. Increasing or decreasing the RHS value beyond this range causes this corner point to be no longer feasible and causes a new corner point to become the optimal solution.

The shadow price is valid only as long as the change in the RHS is within the Allowable Increase *and* Allowable Decrease *values.*

The information to compute the upper and lower limits of this range is given by the entries labeled Allowable Increase and Allowable Decrease in the Sensitivity Report. In Flair's case, these values show that the shadow price of \$2.60 for painting time availability is valid for an increase of up to 600 hours from the current value and a decrease of up to 150 hours. That is, the painting time available can range from a low of 850 (= 1,000 − 150) to a high of 1,600 (= 1,000 + 600) for the shadow price of \$2.60 to be valid. Note that the Allowable Decrease value implies that for each hour of painting time that Flair loses (up to 150 hours), its profit decreases by \$2.60. Likewise, the Allowable Increase value implies that for each hour of painting time that Flair gains (up to 600 hours), its profit increases by \$2.60.

The preceding discussion implies that if Flair can obtain an additional 300 hours of painting time, its profit will increase by 300 × \$2.60 = \$780, to \$4,820. In contrast, if it loses 100 hours of painting time, its profit will decrease by 100 × \$2.60 = \$260, to \$3,780. If the painting time availability increases by more than 600 hours (for example, increases by 700 hours, to 1,700 hours) or decreases by more than 150 hours (for example, decreases by 300 hours, to 700 hours) the current corner point is no longer feasible, and the solution has switched to a new corner point. Recall that we made these same observations earlier graphically using Figures 4.4 to 4.7.

For carpentry time, the shadow price is \$0.60, with a validity range of 1,500 (= 2,400 − 900) to 2,625 (= 2,400 + 225) hours. This means for every hour of carpentry time in this range, Flair's profit changes by \$0.60.

The shadow price of a nonbinding constraint is zero.

IMPACT OF CHANGES IN THE RHS VALUE OF A NONBINDING CONSTRAINT We note that Flair is planning to make only 360 chairs even though it is allowed to make as many as 450. Clearly, Flair's solution would not be affected in any way if we increased this production limit. Therefore, the shadow price for the chairs limit constraint is zero.

Solver displays infinity as 1E+30.

In Screenshot 4-1C, the allowable increase for this RHS value is shown to be infinity (displayed as 1E+30 in Solver). This is logical because any addition to the chair production limit will only cause the slack in this constraint to increase and will have no impact on profit. In contrast, once

SCREENSHOT 4-1D
Partial Solver Sensitivity Report for Flair Furniture

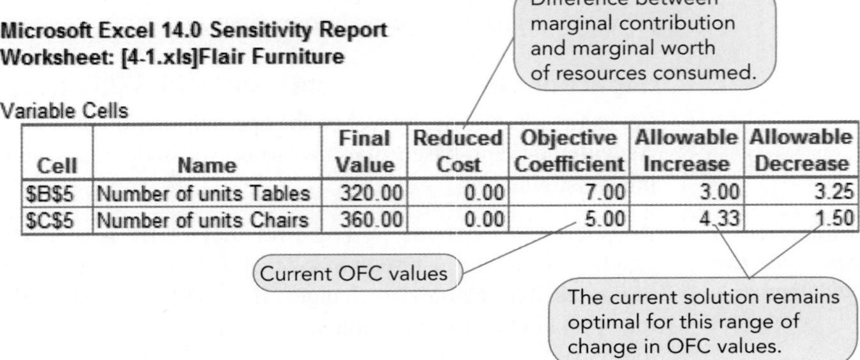

Microsoft Excel 14.0 Sensitivity Report
Worksheet: [4-1.xls]Flair Furniture

Variable Cells

Cell	Name	Final Value	Reduced Cost	Objective Coefficient	Allowable Increase	Allowable Decrease
$B$5	Number of units Tables	320.00	0.00	7.00	3.00	3.25
$C$5	Number of units Chairs	360.00	0.00	5.00	4.33	1.50

we decrease this limit by 90 chairs (our current slack), this constraint also becomes binding. Any further reduction in this limit will clearly have an adverse effect on profit. This is revealed by the value of 90 for the allowable decrease in the RHS of the chairs limit constraint. To evaluate the new optimal solution if the production limit decreases by more than 90 chairs from its current value, the problem would have to be solved again.

In a similar fashion, we note that Flair is planning to make 320 tables even though it is required to make only 100. Clearly, Flair's solution would not be affected in any way if we decreased this requirement from 100. This is indicated by the infinity in the Allowable Decrease column for this RHS. The current optimal solution will also not be affected as long as the increase in this RHS value is below 220. However, if Flair increases the RHS by more than 220 (and specifies that more than 320 tables must be made), the current optimal solution is no longer valid, and the model must be resolved to find the new solution.

Impact of Changes in an Objective Function Coefficient

Let us now focus on the information provided in the table titled Variable Cells. For your convenience, we repeat that part of Screenshot 4-1C here as Screenshot 4-1D. Each row in the Variable Cells table contains information regarding a decision variable in the model.

ALLOWABLE RANGES FOR OFCS In Figure 4.2, repeated here as Figure 4.9, we saw that as the unit profit contribution of either product changes, the slope of the isoprofit line changes. The size of the feasible region, however, remains the same. That is, the locations of the corner points do not change.

FIGURE 4.9
Changes in Profit Contribution of Tables

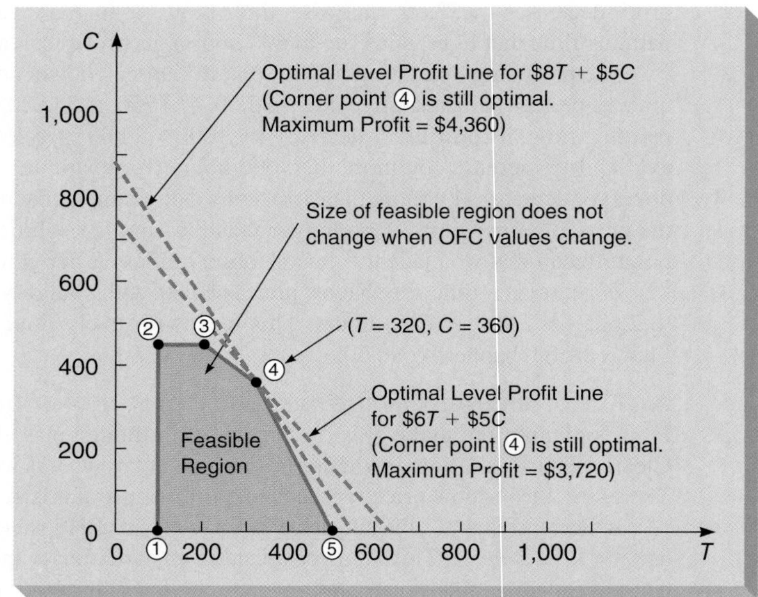

In the case of tables, as the unit profit increases from the current value of $7, the slope of the profit line in Figure 4.9 changes in a manner that makes corner point ④ an even more attractive optimal point. On the other hand, as the unit profit decreases, the slope of the profit line changes in a manner that makes corner point ③ become more and more attractive. At some point, the unit profit of tables is so low as to make corner point ③ the optimal solution.

There is an allowable decrease and an allowable increase for each OFC over which the current optimal solution remains optimal.

The limits to which the profit coefficient of tables can be changed without affecting the optimality of the current solution (corner point ④) is revealed by the values in the Allowable Increase and Allowable Decrease columns of the Sensitivity Report in Screenshot 4-1D. In the case of tables, their profit contribution per table can range anywhere from a low of $3.75 (= $7 − $3.25) to a high of $10 (= $7 + $3), and the current production plan ($T = 320$, $C = 360$) will continue to remain optimal. The total profit will, of course, change, depending on the actual profit contribution per table. For example, if the profit contribution is $6 per table, the total profit is $3,720 (= $6 × 320 + $5 × 360). This is the same result we saw earlier in Figure 4.2. Any profit contribution below $3.75 or over $10 per table will result in a different corner point solution being optimal.

For chairs, the profit contribution per chair can range anywhere from a low of $3.50 (= $5 − $1.50) to a high of $9.33 (= $5 + $4.33), and the current production plan will continue to remain optimal. Here again, the total profit will depend on the actual profit contribution per chair. For example, if the profit contribution is $8 per chair, the total profit is $5,120 (= $7 × 320 + $8 × 360). Any profit contribution below $3.50 or over $9.33 per chair will result in a different corner point solution being optimal.

Reduced cost *is the difference between the marginal contribution of a variable and the marginal worth of the resources it uses.*

REDUCED COST The **Reduced Cost** values in Screenshot 4-1D show the difference between the marginal contribution of a decision variable to the objective function value (profit, in Flair's example) and the marginal worth of the resources it would consume if produced. A property of LP models is that if a variable has a nonzero value at optimality, its marginal contribution to the objective function value will equal the marginal worth of the resources it consumes. For instance, each table we produce uses 3 hours of carpentry time, uses 2 hours of painting time, counts 1 unit toward the 100-unit minimum tables requirement, and counts 0 units toward the 450-unit maximum chairs limit. Based on the preceding discussion of the shadow price, the marginal worth of these resources can be calculated as

$$\begin{aligned}&= 3 \times \text{shadow price of carpentry constraint} + \\ &\quad 2 \times \text{shadow price of painting constraint} + \\ &\quad 1 \times \text{shadow price of minimum tables required constraint} + \\ &\quad 0 \times \text{shadow price of maximum chairs allowed constraint} \\ &= 3 \times \$0.6 + 2 \times \$2.6 + 1 \times \$0 + 0 \times \$0 \\ &= \$7\end{aligned}$$

Note that this is equal to the profit contribution per table. The same calculation will hold for chairs also. The profit contribution per chair is $5, and the marginal worth of the resources it consumes is calculated as

$$\begin{aligned}&= 4 \times \text{shadow price of carpentry constraint} + \\ &\quad 1 \times \text{shadow price of painting constraint} + \\ &\quad 0 \times \text{shadow price of minimum tables required constraint} + \\ &\quad 1 \times \text{shadow price of maximum chairs allowed constraint} \\ &= 4 \times \$0.6 + 1 \times \$2.6 + 0 \times \$0 + 1 \times \$0 \\ &= \$5\end{aligned}$$

There is an alternate interpretation for the reduced cost that is relevant especially for decision variables with zero values in the current optimal solution. Because both variables in the Flair example had nonzero values at optimality, this interpretation was not relevant here. We will, however, see this alternate interpretation in the larger example we consider next.

4.4 Sensitivity Analysis for a Larger Maximization Example

Now that we have explained some of the basic concepts in sensitivity analysis, let us consider a larger production mix example that will allow us to discuss some further issues.

Anderson Home Electronics Example

This is a larger product mix example.

Anderson Home Electronics is considering the production of four inexpensive products for the low-end consumer market: an MP3 player, a satellite radio tuner, an LCD TV, and a Blu-Ray DVD player. For the sake of this example, let us assume that the input for all products can be viewed in terms of just three resources: electronic components, nonelectronic components, and assembly time. The composition of the four products in terms of these three inputs is shown in Table 4.1, along with the unit selling prices of the products.

Electronic components can be obtained at $7 per unit; nonelectronic components can be obtained at $5 per unit; assembly time costs $10 per hour. Each resource is available in limited quantities during the upcoming production cycle, as shown in Table 4.1. Anderson believes the market demand is strong enough that it can sell all the quantities it makes of each product.

By subtracting the total cost of making a product from its unit selling price, the profit contribution of each product can be easily calculated. For example, the profit contribution of each MP3 player is $29 (= selling price of $70 less the total cost of $3 \times \$7 + 2 \times \$5 + 1 \times \$10$). Using similar calculations, see if you can confirm that the profit contribution of each satellite radio tuner is $32, each LCD TV is $72, and each Blu-Ray DVD player is $54.

Let M, S, T, and B denote the number of MP3 players, satellite radio tuners, LCD TVs, and Blu-Ray DVD players to make, respectively. We can then formulate the LP model for this problem as follows:

$$\text{Maximize profit} = \$29M + \$32S + \$72T + \$54B$$

subject to the constraints

$$\begin{aligned} 3M + 4S + 4T + 3B &\leq 4{,}700 && \text{(electronic components)} \\ 2M + 2S + 4T + 3B &\leq 4{,}500 && \text{(nonelectronic components)} \\ M + S + 3T + 2B &\leq 2{,}500 && \text{(assembly time, in hours)} \\ M, S, T, B &\geq 0 && \text{(nonnegativity)} \end{aligned}$$

File: 4-2.xls

Screenshots 4-2A, 4-2B, and 4-2C show the Excel layout and Solver entries, Answer Report, and Sensitivity Report, respectively, for Anderson's problem. The results show that Anderson should make 380 satellite radio tuners, 1,060 Blu-Ray DVD players, and no MP3 players or LCD TVs, for a total profit of $69,400 in the upcoming production cycle.

Some Questions We Want Answered

We now ask and answer several questions that will allow us to understand the shadow prices, reduced costs, and allowable ranges information in the Anderson Home Electronics Sensitivity Report. Each question is independent of the other questions and assumes that only the change mentioned in that question is being considered.

Q: What is the impact on profit of a change in the supply of nonelectronic components?

Nonelectronic components are a nonbinding constraint.

A: The slack values in the Answer Report (Screenshot 4-2B) indicate that of the potential supply of 4,500 units of nonelectronic components, only 3,940 units are used, leaving 560 units unused.

TABLE 4.1 Data for Anderson Home Electronics

	MP3 PLAYER	SATELLITE RADIO TUNER	LCD TV	BLU-RAY DVD PLAYER	SUPPLY
Electronic components	3	4	4	3	4,700
Nonelectronic components	2	2	4	3	4,500
Assembly time (hours)	1	1	3	2	2,500
Selling price (per unit)	$70	$80	$150	$110	

SCREENSHOT 4-2A Excel Layout and Solver Entries for Anderson Home Electronics

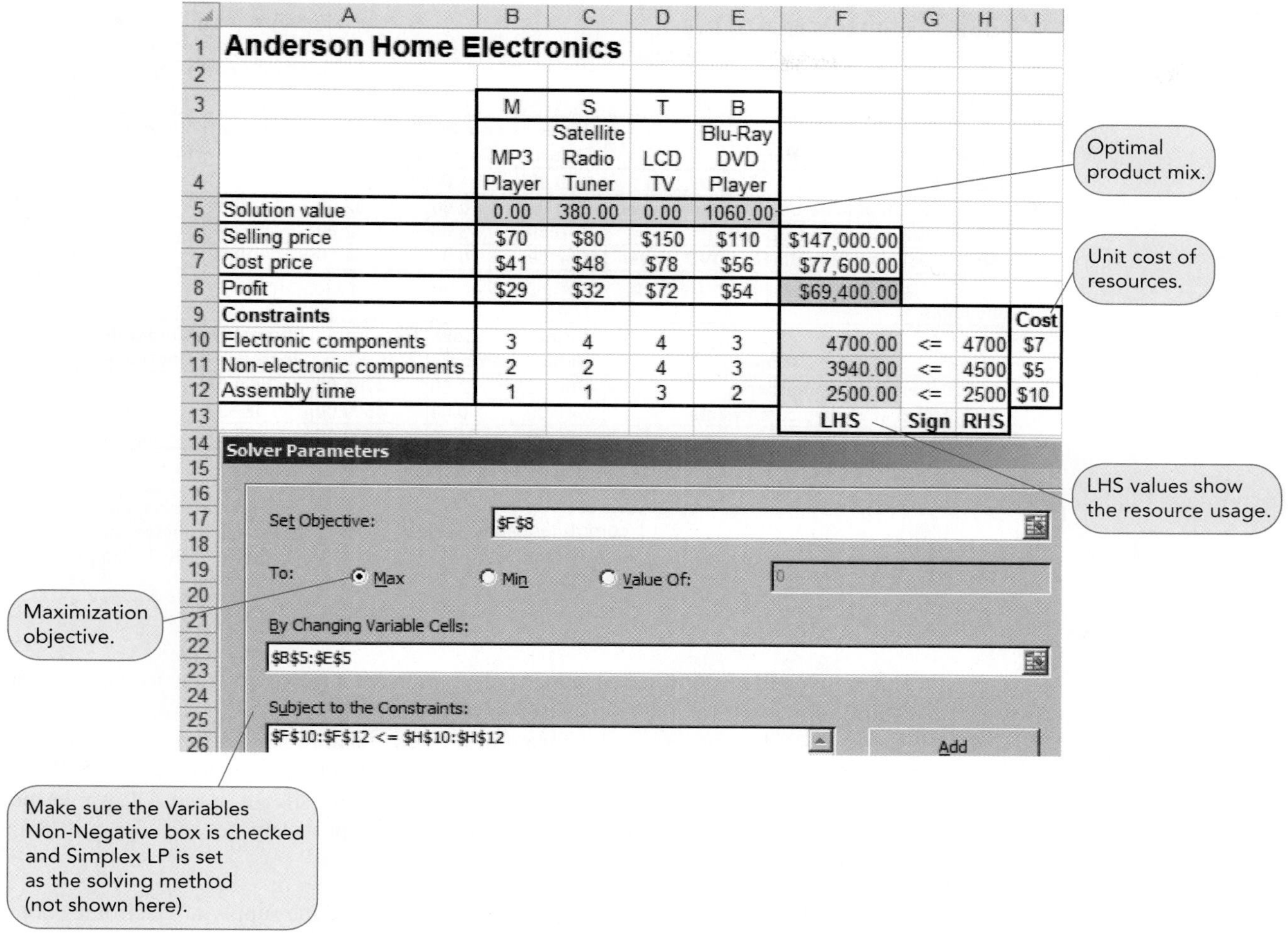

Anderson Home Electronics	M MP3 Player	S Satellite Radio Tuner	T LCD TV	B Blu-Ray DVD Player				
Solution value	0.00	380.00	0.00	1060.00				
Selling price	$70	$80	$150	$110	$147,000.00			
Cost price	$41	$48	$78	$56	$77,600.00			
Profit	$29	$32	$72	$54	$69,400.00			
Constraints								Cost
Electronic components	3	4	4	3	4700.00	<=	4700	$7
Non-electronic components	2	2	4	3	3940.00	<=	4500	$5
Assembly time	1	1	3	2	2500.00	<=	2500	$10
					LHS	Sign	RHS	

SCREENSHOT 4-2B Solver Answer Report for Anderson Home Electronics

Microsoft Excel 14.0 Answer Report
Worksheet: [4-2.xls]Anderson Home Electronics
Result: Solver found a solution. All Constraints and optimality conditions are satisfied.
Solver Engine
Engine: Simplex LP
Solution Time: 0.016 Seconds.
Iterations: 3 Subproblems: 0
Solver Options
Max Time 100 sec, Iterations 100, Precision 0.000001
Max Subproblems 5000, Max Integer Sols 5000, Integer Tolerance 0.05%, Assume NonNegative

Objective Cell (Max)

Cell	Name	Original Value	Final Value
$F$8	Profit	$0.00	$69,400.00

Optimal profit

Variable Cells

Cell	Name	Original Value	Final Value	Integer
$B$5	Solution value MP3 Player	0.00	0.00	Contin
$C$5	Solution value Satellite Radio Tuner	0.00	380.00	Contin
$D$5	Solution value LCD TV	0.00	0.00	Contin
$E$5	Solution value Blu-Ray DVD Player	0.00	1060.00	Contin

Optimal solution does not include MP3 players or LCD TVs.

Constraints

Cell	Name	Cell Value	Formula	Status	Slack
$F$10	Electronic components	4700.00	$F$10<=$H$10	Binding	0.00
$F$11	Non-electronic components	3940.00	$F$11<=$H$11	Not Binding	560.00
$F$12	Assembly time	2500.00	$F$12<=$H$12	Binding	0.00

There are 560 units of nonelectronic components unused.

SCREENSHOT 4-2C Solver Sensitivity Report for Anderson Home Electronics

Microsoft Excel 14.0 Sensitivity Report
Worksheet: [4-2.xls]Anderson Home Electronics

Variable Cells

Cell	Name	Final Value	Reduced Cost	Objective Coefficient	Allowable Increase	Allowable Decrease
$B$5	Solution value MP3 Player	0.00	-1.00	29.00	1.00	1E+30
$C$5	Solution value Satellite Radio Tuner	380.00	0.00	32.00	40.00	1.67
$D$5	Solution value LCD TV	0.00	-8.00	72.00	8.00	1E+30
$E$5	Solution value Blu-Ray DVD Player	1060.00	0.00	54.00	10.00	5.00

Constraints

Cell	Name	Final Value	Shadow Price	Constraint R.H. Side	Allowable Increase	Allowable Decrease
$F$10	Electronic components	4700.00	2.00	4700.00	2800.00	950.00
$F$11	Non-electronic components	3940.00	0.00	4500.00	1E+30	560.00
$F$12	Assembly time	2500.00	24.00	2500.00	466.67	1325.00

For changes to OFC values in this range, current solution remains optimal.

Allowable decrease is infinity since product is not attractive even at current OFC value.

Since nonelectronic components are nonbinding, shadow price is zero.

The allowable increase is infinity since there are already 560 units of slack.

This implies that additional nonelectronic components are of no value to Anderson in terms of contribution to profit; that is, the shadow price is zero.

This shadow price is valid for an unlimited (infinite) increase in the supply of nonelectronic components. Further, Anderson would be willing to give up as many as 560 units of these components with no impact on profit. These values are shown in the Allowable Increase and Allowable Decrease columns in Screenshot 4-2C, respectively, for the supply of nonelectronic components.

Q: What is the impact on profit if we could increase the supply of electronic components by 400 units (to a total of 5,100 units)?

Electronic components are a binding constraint.

A: We first look at the Allowable Increase column for electronic components in Screenshot 4-2C to verify whether the current shadow price is valid for an increase of 400 units in this resource. Because the Allowable Increase column shows a value of 2,800, the shadow price is valid.

Next, we look at the shadow price for electronic components, which is $2 per unit. That is, each additional unit of electronic components (up to 2,800 additional units) will allow Anderson to increase its profit by $2. The impact of 400 units will therefore be a net increase in profit of $800. The new profit will be $70,200 (= $69,400 + $800).

A change in the RHS value of a binding constraint causes the coordinates of the optimal corner point to change.

It is important to remember that whenever the RHS value of a nonredundant constraint changes, the size of the feasible region changes. Hence, some of the corner points shift locations. In the current situation, because the proposed change is within the allowable change, the current corner point is still *optimal*. That is, the constraints that are binding at present will continue to remain the binding constraints. However, the corner point itself has shifted from its present location. What are the values of the decision variables at the new location of this corner point? Because we know which constraints are binding at the optimal point, we can answer this question by solving those equations simultaneously. Alternatively, we can resolve the LP model.

Q: In the previous question, what would happen if we could increase the supply of electronic components by 4,000 units (to a total of 8,700 units)?

Changes beyond the allowable increase or decrease cannot be analyzed using the current report.

A: From Screenshot 4-2C, we see that the shadow price of $2 per unit is valid only up to 2,800 additional units. This means that the first 2,800 units will cause the total profit to increase by $5,600 (= $2 × 2,800). However, the impact of the last 1,200 units (assuming that we are forced to accept all or nothing of the 4,000 units) cannot be analyzed by using the current report. The problem would have to be resolved using Solver to measure its impact.

The fact that the potential additional supply (4,000) of electronic components is beyond the allowable increase value (2,800) does *not* mean that Anderson's management cannot implement this change. It just means that the total impact of the change cannot be evaluated from the *current* Sensitivity Report in Screenshot 4-2C.

Q: Refer to the question about getting an additional 400 units of electronic components. What would happen if the supplier of these 400 units wanted \$8 per unit rather than the current cost of \$7 per unit?

We must correct the shadow price for any premium that we pay.

A: We know that the shadow price of \$2 for electronic components represents the increase in total profit from each additional unit of this resource. This value is net after the cost of this additional unit has been taken into account. That is, it is actually beneficial for Anderson to pay a premium of up to \$2 per additional unit of electronic components. In the current situation, getting 400 additional units of electronic components would cost Anderson \$8 per unit. This represents a premium of \$1 per unit over the current rate of \$7 per unit. However, it would still be beneficial to get these units because each additional unit would increase the total profit by \$1 (= shadow price of \$2 less the premium of \$1). The total profit would therefore increase by \$400, to a new value of \$69,800.

This adjusted value of \$1 represents the actual increase in profit and can be referred to as the *adjusted shadow price*.

Q: Assume that we have an opportunity to get 250 additional hours of assembly time. However, this time will cost us time and a half (i.e., \$15 per hour rather than the current \$10 per hour). Should we take it?

We must calculate the adjusted shadow price here.

A: From Screenshot 4-2C, the shadow price of \$24 per hour of assembly time is valid for an increase of up to 466.67 hours. This shadow price, however, assumes that the additional time costs only \$10 per hour. The \$5 per hour premium paid on the additional time therefore results in an increase of only \$19 (= \$24 − \$5) per each additional hour of assembly time obtained.

The net impact on profit of the additional 250 hours of assembly time is an increase of \$4,750 (= 250 × \$19). Anderson should definitely accept this opportunity.

Q: If we force the production of MP3 players, what would be the impact on total profit?

The impact of forcing MP3 players to be produced is shown by the reduced cost.

A: MP3 players are currently not being recommended for production because they are not profitable enough. You may recall from our discussion in section 4.3 that the reduced cost shows the difference between the marginal contribution of a product to the objective function (profit contribution is \$29 per MP3 player, in Anderson's case) and the marginal worth of resources it would consume if produced. As an exercise, see if you can verify that this value is \$30 per MP3 player. The reduced cost for MP3 player is therefore −\$1 (= \$29 − \$30), as shown in Screenshot 4-2C. This implies that the net impact of producing one MP3 player will be to decrease total profit by \$1 (to \$69,399).

Q: How profitable must MP3 players become before Anderson would consider producing them?

A: We know that each MP3 player produced will cause Anderson's profit to decrease by \$1. This implies that if Anderson can find a way of increasing the profit contribution of MP3 players by \$1, MP3 players would then become an attractive product. This can be achieved either by increasing the selling price of MP3 players by \$1 (to \$71 per unit) or by reducing their cost price by \$1, or a combination of the two.

Reduced cost is also the minimum amount by which the OFC of a variable should change in order to affect the optimal solution.

This is an alternate interpretation of reduced cost. That is, the magnitude of the reduced cost is the minimum amount by which the OFC of a variable should change in order for it to affect the optimal solution. For MP3 players, if their OFC increases by more than \$1 per unit, MP3 players will then have a nonzero value in the new optimal solution.

This information is also seen from the \$1 in the Allowable Increase column for the OFC for MP3 players. Not surprisingly, the Allowable Decrease column shows a value of infinity (shown as 1E+30 in Excel) for the OFC of MP3 players. This is logical because if MP3 players are not attractive at a unit profit of \$29, they are clearly not going to be attractive at unit profit values lower than \$29.

Q: Assume that there is some uncertainty in the price for Blu-Ray DVD players. For what range of prices will the current production be optimal? If Blu-Ray DVD players sold for \$106, what would be Anderson's new total profit?

Even though the production values do not change, the total profit will decrease.

A: Blu-Ray DVD players currently sell for $110, yielding a profit of $54 per unit. The allowable ranges for the OFC of Blu-Ray DVD players in Screenshot 4-2C shows that this value can increase by up to $10 (to $64; selling price of $120) or decrease by up to $5 (to $49; selling price of $105) for the current production plan to remain optimal.

If Blu-Ray DVD players actually sold for $106, the profit per unit would drop to $50. The current values of the decision variables would remain optimal. However, the new total profit would decrease by $4,240 (= $4 per Blu-Ray DVD player for 1,060 players), to $65,160.

Alternate Optimal Solutions

Is the optimal solution identified in Screenshot 4-2A for Anderson Home Electronics (380 satellite radio tuners and 1,060 Blu-Ray DVD players, for a total profit of $69,400) unique? Are there alternate production mixes that will also yield a profit of $69,400?

Recall that in Chapter 2 (section 2.6, on page 38) we saw a graphical example of a situation in which a problem with only two variables had alternate optimal solutions (also referred to as *multiple optimal solutions*). How can we detect a similar condition from the Solver Sensitivity Report for problems involving more than two variables?

Zeros in the Allowable Increase or Allowable Decrease columns for OFC values may indicate alternate optimal solutions.

In most cases, when the Allowable Increase or Allowable Decrease value for the OFC of a variable is zero in the Variable Cells table, this indicates the presence of alternate optimal solutions. In Anderson's problem, we see from Screenshot 4-2C that this is not the case.

Note also from Screenshot 4-2C that the reduced costs for both products currently not being produced in the optimal solution (MP3 players and LCD TVs) are nonzero. This indicates that if Anderson is forced to produce either of these products, the net impact will be a reduction in total profit (as discussed earlier). That is, there is no solution possible involving products other than satellite radio tuners and Blu-Ray DVD players that will yield a profit as high as the current solution ($69,400). The current optimal solution is, therefore, unique.

In Solved Problem 4-1 at the end of this chapter, we discuss a problem for which the Solver Sensitivity Report indicates the presence of alternate optimal solutions. We also discuss how Solver can be used to identify these alternate optimal solutions.

4.5 Analyzing Simultaneous Changes by Using the 100% Rule

Until now, we have analyzed the impact of a change in just a single parameter value on the optimal solution. That is, when we are studying the impact of one item of the input data (OFC or RHS value), we assume that all other input data in the model stay constant at their current values. What happens when there are *simultaneous* changes in more than one OFC value or more than one RHS value? Is it possible to analyze the impact of such simultaneous changes on the optimal solution with the information provided in the Sensitivity Report?

The answer is yes, albeit under only a specific condition, as discussed in the following section. It is important to note that the condition is valid only for analyzing simultaneous changes in either OFC values or RHS values, but not a mixture of the two types of input data.

Simultaneous Changes in Constraint RHS Values

Consider a situation in which Anderson Home Electronics realizes that its available number of electronic components is actually only 4,200 and, *at the same time*, also finds that it has an opportunity to obtain an additional 200 hours of assembly time. What is the impact of these *simultaneous* changes on the optimal solution? To answer this question, we first use a condition called the **100% rule**. This condition can be stated as follows:

$$\sum_{\text{changes}} (\text{change}/\text{allowable change}) \leq 1 \qquad \textbf{(4-1)}$$

The 100% rule can be used to check whether simultaneous changes in RHS or OFC values can be analyzed by using the current Sensitivity Report.

That is, we compute the ratio of each proposed change in a parameter's value to the maximum allowable change in its value, as given in the Sensitivity Report. The sum of these ratios must not exceed 1 (or 100%) in order for the information given in the current Sensitivity Report to be valid. If the sum of the ratios does exceed 1, the current information may still be valid; we just cannot guarantee its validity. However, if the ratio does not exceed 1, the information is definitely valid.

To verify this rule for the proposed change in Anderson's problem, consider each change in turn. First, there is a decrease of 500 units (i.e., from 4,700 to 4,200) in the number of electronic components. From the Sensitivity Report (see Screenshot 4-2C), we see that the allowable decrease in this RHS value is 950. The ratio is therefore

$$500/950 = 0.5263$$

Next, there is an increase of 200 hours (from 2,500 to 2,700) in the assembly time available. From the Sensitivity Report, we see that the allowable increase for this RHS value is 466.67. This ratio is, therefore,

$$200/466.67 = 0.4285$$

The sum of these ratios is

$$\text{Sum of ratios} = 0.5263 + 0.4285 = 0.9548 < 1$$

If the sum of ratios does not exceed 1, the information in the Sensitivity Report is valid.

Because this sum does not exceed 1, the information provided in the Sensitivity Report is valid for analyzing the impact of these changes. First, the decrease of 500 units in electronic component availability reduces the size of the feasible region and will therefore cause profit to decrease. The magnitude of this decrease is \$1,000 (= 500 units of electronic components, at a shadow price of \$2 per unit).

In contrast, the additional 200 hours of assembly time will result in a larger feasible region and a net increase in profit of \$4,800 (= 200 hours of assembly time, at a shadow price of \$24 per hour). The net impact of these simultaneous changes is therefore an increase in profit of \$3,800 (= \$4,800 − \$1,000).

Simultaneous Changes in OFC Values

The 100% rule can also be used to analyze simultaneous changes in OFC values in a similar manner. For example, what is the impact on the optimal solution if Anderson decides to drop the selling price of Blu-Ray DVD players by \$3 per unit but, at the same time, increase the selling price of satellite radio tuners by \$8 per unit?

Once again, we calculate the appropriate ratios to verify the 100% rule. For the current solution to remain optimal, the allowable decrease in the OFC for Blu-Ray DVD players is \$5, while the allowable increase in the OFC for satellite radio tuners is \$40. The sum of ratios is therefore

$$\text{Sum of ratios} = (\$3/\$5) + (\$8/\$40) = 0.80 < 1$$

Because the sum of ratios does not exceed 1, the current production plan is still optimal. The \$3 decrease in profit per Blu-Ray DVD player causes total profit to decrease by \$3,180 (= \$3 × 1,060). However, the \$8 increase in the unit profit of each satellite radio tuner results in an increase of \$3,040 (= \$8 × 380) in total profit. The net impact is, therefore, a decrease in profit of only \$140, to a new value of \$69,260.

4.6 Pricing Out New Variables

Pricing out analyzes the impact of adding a new variable to the existing LP model.

The information given in the Sensitivity Report can also be used to study the impact of the introduction of new decision variables (products, in the Anderson example) in the model. For example, if Anderson's problem is solved again with a new product also included in the model, will we recommend that the new product be made? Or will we recommend not to make the new product and continue to make the same products (i.e., satellite radio tuners and Blu-Ray DVD players) Anderson is making now?

Anderson's Proposed New Product

Suppose Anderson Home Electronics wants to introduce a new product, the Digital Home Theater Speaker System (DHTSS), to take advantage of the hot market for that product. The design department estimates that each DHTSS will require five units of electronic components, four units of nonelectronic components, and four hours of assembly time. The marketing department estimates that it can sell each DHTSS for \$175, a slightly higher selling price than any of the other four products being considered by Anderson.

The question now is whether the DHTSS will be a profitable product for Anderson to produce. That is, even though the new product would have a higher selling price per unit, is it worthwhile from an overall profit perspective to divert resources from Anderson's existing products to make this new product? Alternatively, we could pose the question as this: What is the minimum price at which Anderson would need to sell each DHTSS in order to make it a viable product?

The answer to such a question involves a procedure called **pricing out**. Assume that Anderson decides to make a single DHTSS. Note that the resources required to make this system (five units of electronic components, four units of nonelectronic components, and four hours of assembly time) will no longer be available to meet Anderson's existing production plan (380 satellite radio tuners and 1,060 Blu-Ray DVD players, for a total profit of $69,400).

CHECKING THE VALIDITY OF THE 100% RULE Clearly, the loss of these resources is going to reduce the profit that Anderson could have made from its existing products. Using the shadow prices of these resources, we can calculate the exact impact of the loss of these resources. However, we must first use the 100% rule to check whether the shadow prices are valid by calculating the ratio of the reduction in each resource's availability to the allowable decrease for that resource (given in Screenshot 4-2C on page 136). The resulting calculation is as follows:

$$\text{Sum of ratios} = (5/950) + (4/560) + (4/1{,}325) = 0.015 < 1$$

REQUIRED PROFIT CONTRIBUTION OF EACH DHTSS Because the total ratio is less than 1, the shadow prices are valid to calculate the impact on profit of using these resources to produce a DHTSS, rather than the existing products. We can determine this impact as

We first calculate the worth of the resources that would be consumed by the new product, if produced.

$$\begin{aligned} &= 5 \times \text{shadow price of electronic components constraint} + \\ &\quad 4 \times \text{shadow price of nonelectronic components constraint} + \\ &\quad 4 \times \text{shadow price of assembly time constraint} \\ &= 5 \times \$2 + 4 \times \$0 + 4 \times \$24 \\ &= \$106 \end{aligned}$$

Hence, in order for DHTSS to be a viable product, the profit contribution of each DHTSS has to at least make up this shortfall in profit. That is, the OFC for DHTSS must be at least $106 in order for the optimal solution to have a nonzero value for DHTSS. Otherwise, the optimal solution of Anderson's model with a decision variable for DHTSS included will be the same as the current one, with DHTSS having a value of zero.

FINDING THE MINIMUM SELLING PRICE OF EACH DHTSS UNIT The actual cost of the resources used to make one DHTSS unit can be calculated as

We calculate the actual cost of making the new product, if produced.

$$\begin{aligned} &= 5 \times \text{unit price of electronic components constraint} + \\ &\quad 4 \times \text{unit price of nonelectronic components constraint} + \\ &\quad 4 \times \text{unit price of assembly time constraint} \\ &= 5 \times \$7 + 4 \times \$5 + 4 \times \$10 \\ &= \$95 \end{aligned}$$

The minimum selling price for DHTSS units is then calculated as the sum of the cost of making a DHTSS unit and the marginal worth of resources diverted from existing products. In Anderson's case, this works out to $201 (= $106 + $95). Because Anderson's marketing department estimates that it can sell each DHTSS unit for only $175, this product will not be profitable for Anderson to produce.

What happens if Anderson *does* include DHTSS as a variable in its model and solves the expanded formulation again? In this case, from the discussion so far, we can say that the optimal solution will once again recommend producing 380 satellite radio tuners and 1,060 Blu-Ray DVD players, for a total profit of $69,400. DHTSS will have a final value of zero (just as MP3 players and LCD TVs do in the current solution). What will be the reduced cost of DHTSS in this revised solution? We have calculated that the minimum selling price required for DHTSS to be a viable product is $201, while the actual selling price is only $175. Therefore, the reduced cost will be –$26, indicating that each DHTSS unit produced will cause Anderson's profit to decrease by $26.

SCREENSHOT 4-3A
Excel Layout and Solver Entries for Anderson Home Electronics—Revised Model

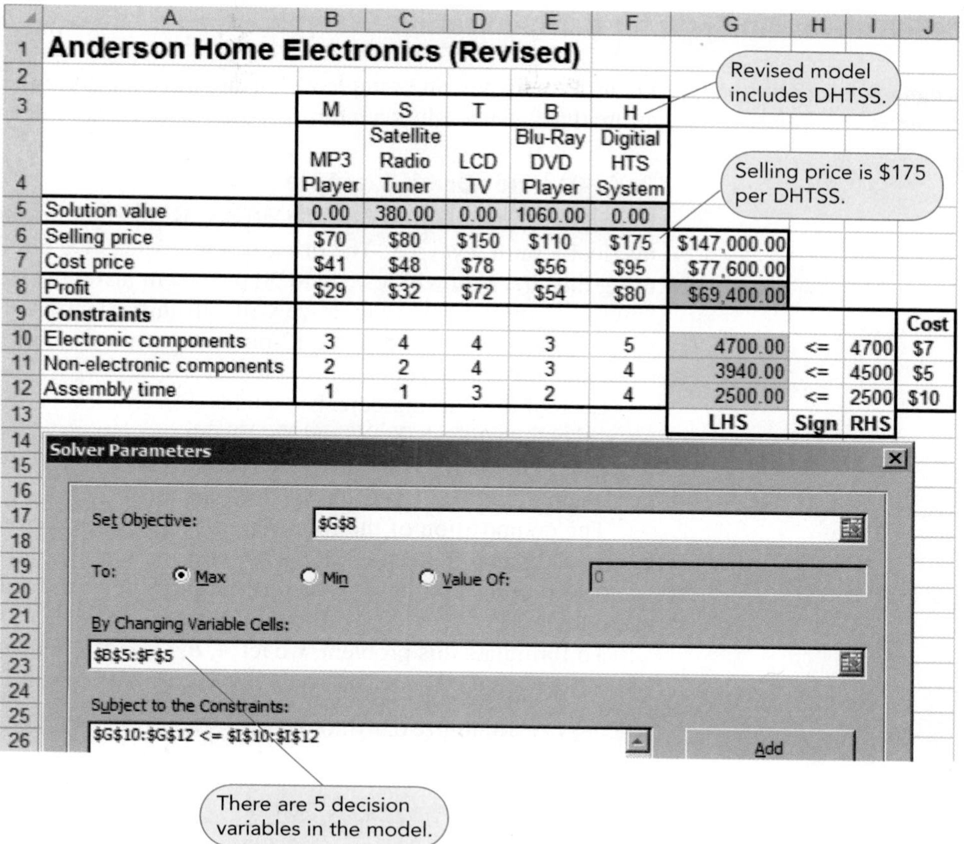

File: 4-3.xls

To verify our conclusions, let us revise the LP model for Anderson Home Electronics to include the new product, DHTSS. The Excel layout and Solver entries for this revised model are shown in Screenshot 4-3A. The Sensitivity Report for this model is shown in Screenshot 4-3B.

The results show that it continues to be optimal for Anderson to produce 380 satellite radio tuners and 1,060 Blu-Ray DVD players, for a total profit of $69,400. Further, the magnitude of the reduced cost for HTS is $26, as we had already calculated.

SCREENSHOT 4-3B Solver Sensitivity Report for Anderson Home Electronics—Revised Model

Microsoft Excel 14.0 Sensitivity Report
Worksheet: [4-3.xls]Anderson Home Electronics (Revised)

This is the same product mix as in Screenshot 4-2C.

Variable Cells

Cell	Name	Final Value	Reduced Cost	Objective Coefficient	Allowable Increase	Allowable Decrease
$B$5	Solution value MP3 Player	0.00	-1.00	29.00	1.00	1E+30
$C$5	Solution value Satellite Radio Tuner	380.00	0.00	32.00	40.00	1.67
$D$5	Solution value LCD TV	0.00	-8.00	72.00	8.00	1E+30
$E$5	Solution value Blu-Ray DVD Player	1060.00	0.00	54.00	10.00	5.00
$F$5	Solution value Digitial HTS System	0.00	-26.00	80.00	26.00	1E+30

DHTSS is not included in the optimal product mix.

Reduced cost for DHTSS is −$26.

Constraints

Cell	Name	Final Value	Shadow Price	Constraint R.H. Side	Allowable Increase	Allowable Decrease
$G$10	Electronic components	4700.00	2.00	4700.00	2800.00	950.00
$G$11	Non-electronic components	3940.00	0.00	4500.00	1E+30	560.00
$G$12	Assembly time	2500.00	24.00	2500.00	466.67	1325.00

These are the same shadow prices as in Screenshot 4-2C.

4.7 Sensitivity Analysis for a Minimization Example

Minimization problems typically involve some ≥ constraints.

Let us now analyze an example with a minimization objective. For such problems, we need to be aware that when a solution *improves*, the objective value decreases rather than increases.

Burn-Off Diet Drink Example

Burn-Off, a manufacturer of diet drinks, is planning to introduce a miracle drink that will magically burn away fat. The drink is a bit expensive, but Burn-Off guarantees that a person using this diet plan will lose up to 50 pounds in just three weeks. The drink is made up of four "mystery" ingredients (which we will call ingredients A, B, C, and D). The plan calls for a person to consume at least three 12-ounce doses per day (i.e., at least 36 ounces per day) but no more than 40 ounces per day.

Each of the four ingredients contains different levels of three chemical compounds (which we will call chemicals X, Y, and Z). Health regulations mandate that the dosage consumed per day should contain minimum prescribed levels of chemicals X and Y and should not exceed maximum prescribed levels for the third chemical, Z.

The composition of the four ingredients in terms of the chemical compounds (units per ounce) is shown in Table 4.2, along with the unit cost prices of the ingredients. Burn-Off wants to find the optimal way to mix the ingredients to create the drink, at minimum cost per daily dose.

To formulate this problem, we let A, B, C, and D denote the number of ounces of ingredients A, B, C, and D to use, respectively. The problem can then be formulated as follows:

$$\text{Minimize daily dose cost} = \$0.40A + \$0.20B + \$0.60C + \$0.30D$$

subject to the constraints

$$
\begin{array}{llll}
A + B + C + D & \geq & 36 & \text{(daily dosage minimum)} \\
3A + 4B + 8C + 10D & \geq & 280 & \text{(chemical X requirement)} \\
5A + 3B + 6C + 6D & \geq & 200 & \text{(chemical Y requirement)} \\
10A + 25B + 20C + 40D & \leq & 1{,}050 & \text{(chemical Z max limit)} \\
A + B + C + D & \leq & 40 & \text{(daily dosage maximum)} \\
A, B, C, D & \geq & 0 & \text{(nonnegativity)}
\end{array}
$$

Burn-Off's Excel Solution

File: 4-4.xls

Screenshots 4-4A and 4-4B show the Excel layout and Solver entries, and the Sensitivity Report, respectively, for Burn-Off's problem. The output shows that the optimal solution is to use 10.25 ounces of ingredient A, 4.125 ounces of ingredient C, and 21.625 ounces of ingredient D, to make exactly 36 ounces of the diet drink per day. Interestingly, ingredient B is not used, even though it is the least expensive ingredient. The total cost is $13.06 per day.

The difference between the LHS and RHS values of a ≥ constraint is called **surplus.**

The solution also indicates that the constraints for chemical Y and the maximum daily dosage are nonbinding. Although the minimum requirement is for only 200 units of chemical Y, the final drink actually provides 205.75 units of this chemical. The extra 5.75 units denote the level of oversatisfaction of this requirement. You may recall from Chapter 2 that we refer to this quantity as **surplus**, even though the Solver Answer Report always titles this value *slack*.

TABLE 4.2 Data for Burn-Off Diet Drink

	INGREDIENT A	INGREDIENT B	INGREDIENT C	INGREDIENT D	REQUIREMENT
Chemical X	3	4	8	10	At least 280 units
Chemical Y	5	3	6	6	At least 200 units
Chemical Z	10	25	20	40	At most 1,050 units
Cost per ounce	$0.40	$0.20	$0.60	$0.30	

SCREENSHOT 4-4A
Excel Layout and Solver Entries for Burn-Off Diet Drink

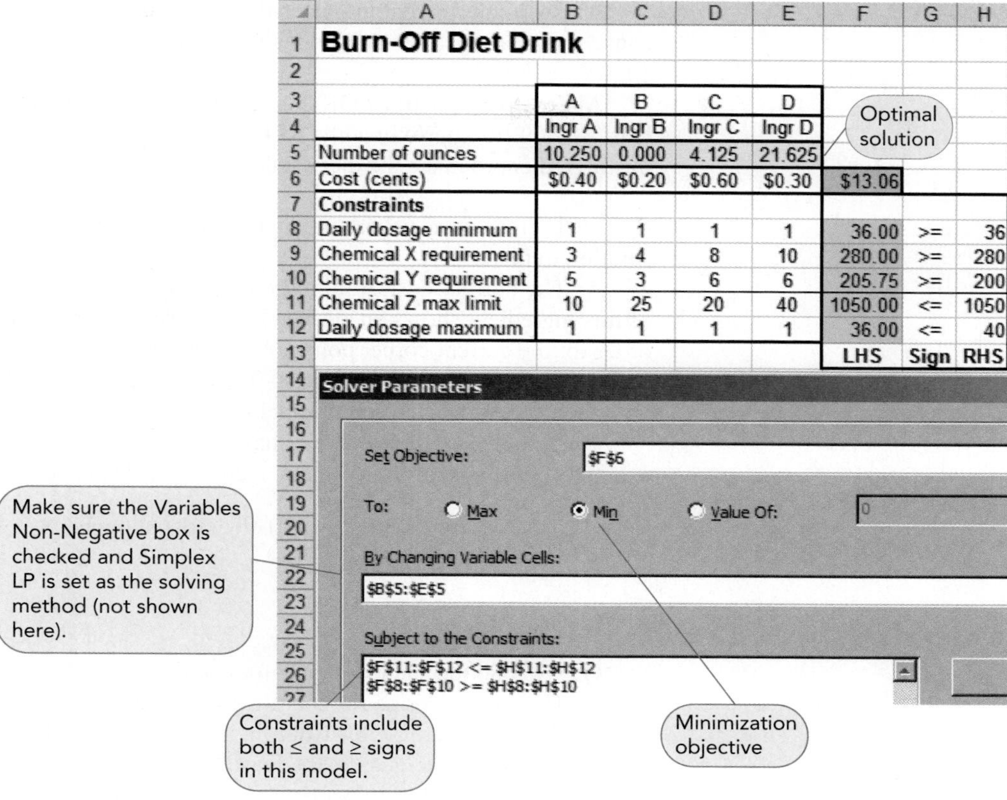

	A	B	C	D	E	F	G	H
1	Burn-Off Diet Drink							
2								
3		A	B	C	D			
4		Ingr A	Ingr B	Ingr C	Ingr D			
5	Number of ounces	10.250	0.000	4.125	21.625			
6	Cost (cents)	$0.40	$0.20	$0.60	$0.30	$13.06		
7	Constraints							
8	Daily dosage minimum	1	1	1	1	36.00	>=	36
9	Chemical X requirement	3	4	8	10	280.00	>=	280
10	Chemical Y requirement	5	3	6	6	205.75	>=	200
11	Chemical Z max limit	10	25	20	40	1050.00	<=	1050
12	Daily dosage maximum	1	1	1	1	36.00	<=	40
13						LHS	Sign	RHS

Optimal solution
Solver Parameters
Set Objective: $F$6
To: Max Min Value Of: 0
By Changing Variable Cells:
$B$5:$E$5
Subject to the Constraints:
$F$11:$F$12 <= $H$11:$H$12
$F$8:$F$10 >= $H$8:$H$10
Make sure the Variables Non-Negative box is checked and Simplex LP is set as the solving method (not shown here).
Constraints include both ≤ and ≥ signs in this model.
Minimization objective

Answering Sensitivity Analysis Questions for Burn-Off

As with the Anderson Home Electronics example, we use several questions to interpret the information given in the Sensitivity Report (Screenshot 4-4B) for Burn-Off.

Q: What is the impact on cost if Burn-Off insists on using 1 ounce of ingredient B to make the drink?

SCREENSHOT 4-4B
Solver Sensitivity Report for Burn-Off Diet Drink

Microsoft Excel 14.0 Sensitivity Report
Worksheet: [4-4.xls]Burn-Off Diet Drink

Variable Cells

Cell	Name	Final Value	Reduced Cost	Objective Coefficient	Allowable Increase	Allowable Decrease
$B$5	Number of ounces Ingr A	10.250	0.000	0.400	0.061	0.250
$C$5	Number of ounces Ingr B	0.000	0.069	0.200	1E+30	0.069
$D$5	Number of ounces Ingr C	4.125	0.000	0.600	1.500	0.073
$E$5	Number of ounces Ingr D	21.625	0.000	0.300	0.085	1E+30

Constraints

Cell	Name	Final Value	Shadow Price	Constraint R.H. Side	Allowable Increase	Allowable Decrease
$F$8	Daily dosage minimum	36.000	0.375	36.00	16.500	1.278
$F$9	Chemical X requirement	280.000	0.088	280.000	41.000	11.000
$F$10	Chemical Y requirement	205.750	0.000	200.000	5.750	1E+30
$F$11	Chemical Z max limit	1050.000	-0.024	1050.000	47.143	346.000
$F$12	Daily dosage maximum	36.000	0.000	40.000	1E+30	4.000

Reduced cost shows increase in total cost if ingredient B is used.

Infinity

The shadow price for chemical X is positive, indicating that total cost increases as the requirement for chemical X increases.

The shadow price shows amount of decrease in total cost if chemical Z's limit is increased.

A: The reduced cost indicates that each ounce of ingredient B used to make the drink will cause the total cost per daily dosage to increase by $0.069 (~$0.07). The new cost will be $13.06 + $0.07 = $13.13.

Alternatively, if Burn-Off can find a way of reducing ingredient B's cost per ounce by at least $0.069 (to approximately $0.13 or less per ounce), then it becomes cost-effective to use this ingredient to make the diet drink.

Q: There is some uncertainty in the cost of ingredient C. How sensitive is the current optimal solution to this cost?

A: The current cost of ingredient C is $0.60 per ounce. The range for the cost coefficient of this ingredient shows an allowable increase of $1.50 and an allowable decrease of $0.073 in order for the current corner point solution to remain optimal. The cost per ounce of ingredient C could therefore fluctuate between $0.527 (= $0.60 − $0.073) and $2.10 (= $0.60 + $1.50) without affecting the current optimal mix.

The total cost will, however, change, depending on the actual unit cost of ingredient C. For example, if the cost of ingredient C increases to $1.00 per ounce, the new total cost will be

$$= \$13.06 + (\$0.40 \text{ extra per ounce} \times 4.125 \text{ ounces of C})$$
$$= \$13.06 + \$1.65$$
$$= \$14.71$$

Q: What do the shadow prices for chemical X and chemical Z imply in this problem?

A: The shadow price for chemical X is $0.088. Because the constraint for chemical X is a ≥ constraint, an increase by 1 unit in the RHS (from 280 to 281) makes the problem solution even more restrictive. That is, the feasible region becomes smaller. The optimal objective function value could, therefore, worsen. The shadow price indicates that for each additional unit of chemical X required to be present in the drink, the overall cost will increase by $0.088. This value is valid for an increase of up to 41 units and a decrease by 11 units in the requirement for chemical X.

A negative value for shadow price implies that cost will decrease if the RHS value increases.

In contrast, the constraint for chemical Z is a ≤ constraint. An increase in the RHS of the constraint (from 1,050 to 1,051) will cause the feasible region to become bigger. Hence, the optimal objective function value could possibly improve. The negative value of the shadow price for this constraint indicates that each unit increase in the maximum limit allowed for chemical Z will cause the total cost to decrease by $0.024. This value is valid for an increase of up to 47.143 units. Likewise, the total cost will *increase* by $0.024 for each unit *decrease* in the maximum limit allowed for chemical Z. This is valid for a decrease of up to 346 units in the maximum limit for chemical Z.

Q: Burn-Off can decrease the minimum requirement for chemical X by 5 units (from 280 to 275), provided that the maximum limit allowed for chemical Z is reduced to 1,000 units (i.e., reduced by 50 units). Is this trade-off cost-effective for Burn-Off to implement?

Analyzing simultaneous changes requires the use of the 100% rule.

A: Because we are dealing with simultaneous changes in RHS values, we first verify whether the 100% rule is satisfied. To do so, we take the ratio of each proposed change to its maximum allowable change. The calculation is

$$\text{Sum of ratios} = (5/11) + (50/346) = 0.599 < 1$$

Because the sum does not exceed 1, we can use the shadow price information in the Sensitivity Report (Screenshot 4-4B). The reduction of 5 units in the requirement for chemical X will cause the feasible region to increase in size. The total cost will therefore improve (i.e., go down) by $0.44 (= 5 units, at a shadow price of $0.088 per unit).

In contrast, the reduction of 50 units in the maximum allowable limit for chemical Z makes the feasible region shrink in size. The total cost will therefore be adversely affected (i.e., go up) by $1.20 (= 50 units, at a shadow price of $0.024 per unit).

The net impact of this trade-off is therefore an increase in total cost of $0.76 (= $1.20 − $0.44). The new cost will be $13.82. Clearly, this trade-off is not cost-effective from Burn-Off's perspective and should be rejected.

Summary

In this chapter we present the important concept of sensitivity analysis. Sometimes referred to as postoptimality analysis, sensitivity analysis is used by management to answer a series of what-if questions about inputs to an LP model. It also tests just how sensitive the optimal solution is to changes in (1) objective function coefficients and (2) constraint RHS values.

We first explore sensitivity analysis graphically (i.e., for problems with only two decision variables). We then discuss how to interpret information in the Answer and Sensitivity Reports generated by Solver. We also discuss how the information in these reports can be used to analyze simultaneous changes in model parameter values and determine the potential impact of a new variable in the model.

Glossary

Allowable Decrease for an OFC The maximum amount by which the OFC of a decision variable can decrease for the current optimal solution to remain optimal.

Allowable Decrease for a RHS Value The maximum amount by which the RHS value of a constraint can decrease for the shadow price to be valid.

Allowable Increase for an OFC The maximum amount by which the OFC of a decision variable can increase for the current optimal solution to remain optimal.

Allowable Increase for a RHS Value The maximum amount by which the RHS value of a constraint can increase for the shadow price to be valid.

Answer Report A report created by Solver when it solves an LP model. This report presents the optimal solution in a detailed manner.

Objective Function Coefficient (OFC) The coefficient for a decision variable in the objective function. Typically, this refers to unit profit or unit cost.

100% Rule A rule used to verify the validity of the information in a Sensitivity Report when dealing with simultaneous changes to more than one RHS value or more than one OFC value.

Pricing Out A procedure by which the shadow price information in a Sensitivity Report can be used to gauge the impact of the addition of a new variable in an LP model.

Reduced Cost The difference between the marginal contribution to the objective function value from the inclusion of a decision variable and the marginal worth of the resources it consumes. In the case of a decision variable that has an optimal value of zero, it is also the minimum amount by which the OFC of that variable should change before it would have a nonzero optimal value.

Right-Hand Side (RHS) Value The amount of resource available (for a ≤ constraint) or the minimum requirement of some criterion (for a ≥ constraint). Typically expressed as a constant for sensitivity analysis.

Sensitivity Analysis The study of how sensitive an optimal solution is to model assumptions and to data changes. Also referred to as postoptimality analysis.

Shadow Price The magnitude of the change in the objective function value for a one-unit increase in the RHS of a constraint.

Slack The difference between the RHS and LHS of a ≤ constraint. Typically represents the unused resource.

Surplus The difference between the LHS and RHS of a ≥ constraint. Typically represents the level of oversatisfaction of a requirement.

Solved Problem

Solved Problem 4-1

Consider the Hong Kong Bank of Commerce and Industry example we first studied in Chapter 3 (section 3.5, on page 81). How can we use the Sensitivity Report for that example to detect the presence of alternate optimal solutions for an LP problem? Also, how can we use Excel to possibly identify those alternate optimal solutions?

Solution

For your convenience, we repeat the formulation portion of the Hong Kong Bank problem here. Define

F = number of full-time tellers to use (all starting at 9 A.M.)

P_1 = number of part-timers to use starting at 9 A.M. (leaving at 1 P.M.)

P_2 = number of part-timers to use starting at 10 A.M. (leaving at 2 P.M.)

P_3 = number of part-timers to use starting at 11 A.M. (leaving at 3 P.M.)

P_4 = number of part-timers to use starting at noon (leaving at 4 P.M.)

P_5 = number of part-timers to use starting at 1 P.M. (leaving at 5 P.M.)

Objective function:

Minimize total daily personnel cost = $\$90F + \$28(P_1 + P_2 + P_3 + P_4 + P_5)$

subject to the constraints:

$$
\begin{array}{lll}
F + P_1 & \geq 10 & \text{(9 A.M.–10 A.M. requirement)} \\
F + P_1 + P_2 & \geq 12 & \text{(10 A.M.–11 A.M. requirement)} \\
0.5F + P_1 + P_2 + P_3 & \geq 14 & \text{(11 A.M.–12 noon requirement)} \\
0.5F + P_1 + P_2 + P_3 + P_4 & \geq 16 & \text{(12 noon–1 P.M. requirement)} \\
F + P_2 + P_3 + P_4 + P_5 & \geq 18 & \text{(1 P.M.–2 P.M. requirement)} \\
F + P_3 + P_4 + P_5 & \geq 17 & \text{(2 P.M.–3 P.M. requirement)} \\
F + P_4 + P_5 & \geq 15 & \text{(3 P.M.–4 P.M. requirement)} \\
F + P_5 & \geq 10 & \text{(4 P.M.–5 P.M. requirement)} \\
F & \leq 12 & \text{(full-time tellers)} \\
4P_1 + 4P_2 + 4P_3 + 4P_4 + 4P_5 & \leq 56 & \text{(part-time workers limit)} \\
F, P_1, P_2, P_3, P_4, P_5 & \geq 0 & \text{(nonnegativity)}
\end{array}
$$

File: 4-5.xls

The Excel layout and Solver entries for this model are shown in Screenshot 4-5A. The Sensitivity Report is shown in Screenshot 4-5B.

SCREENSHOT 4-5A Excel Layout and Solver Entries for Hong Kong Bank

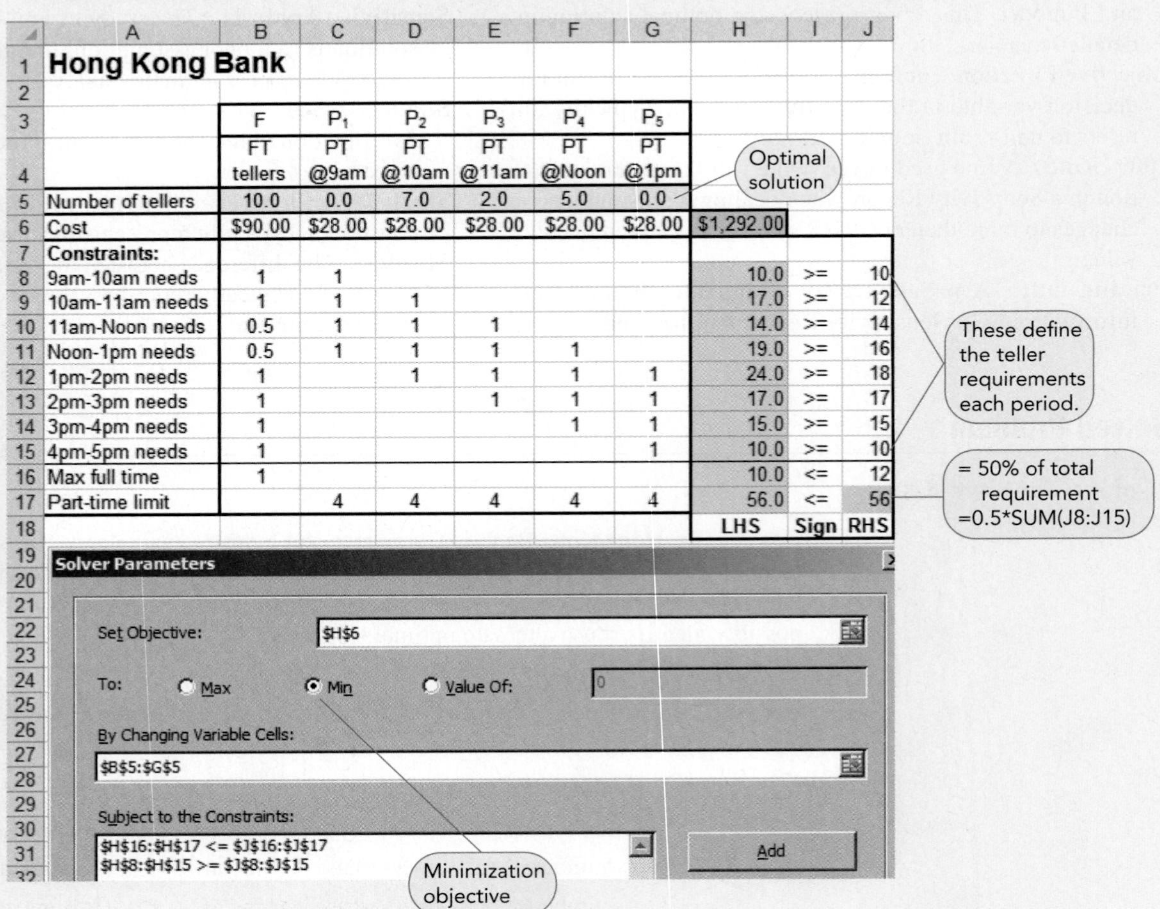

	A	B	C	D	E	F	G	H	I	J
1	**Hong Kong Bank**									
2										
3		F	P_1	P_2	P_3	P_4	P_5			
4		FT tellers	PT @9am	PT @10am	PT @11am	PT @Noon	PT @1pm			
5	Number of tellers	10.0	0.0	7.0	2.0	5.0	0.0			
6	Cost	\$90.00	\$28.00	\$28.00	\$28.00	\$28.00	\$28.00	\$1,292.00		
7	Constraints:									
8	9am-10am needs	1	1					10.0	>=	10
9	10am-11am needs	1	1	1				17.0	>=	12
10	11am-Noon needs	0.5	1	1	1			14.0	>=	14
11	Noon-1pm needs	0.5	1	1	1	1		19.0	>=	16
12	1pm-2pm needs	1		1	1	1	1	24.0	>=	18
13	2pm-3pm needs	1			1	1	1	17.0	>=	17
14	3pm-4pm needs	1				1	1	15.0	>=	15
15	4pm-5pm needs	1					1	10.0	>=	10
16	Max full time	1						10.0	<=	12
17	Part-time limit		4	4	4	4	4	56.0	<=	56
18								LHS	Sign	RHS

SCREENSHOT 4-5B Solver Sensitivity Report for Hong Kong Bank

Microsoft Excel 14.0 Sensitivity Report
Worksheet: [4-5.xls]Hong Kong Bank

Reduced cost of zero indicates that a solution that uses part-time tellers at 9 A.M. exists, with no change in the optimal objective value.

Variable Cells

Cell	Name	Final Value	Reduced Cost	Objective Coefficient	Allowable Increase	Allowable Decrease
$B$5	Number of tellers FT tellers	10.00	0.00	90.00	1E+30	48.00
$C$5	Number of tellers PT @9am	0.00	0.00	28.00	48.00	0.00
$D$5	Number of tellers PT @10am	7.00	0.00	28.00	0.00	45.00
$E$5	Number of tellers PT @11am	2.00	0.00	28.00	60.00	0.00
$F$5	Number of tellers PT @Noon	5.00	0.00	28.00	0.00	60.00
$G$5	Number of tellers PT @1pm	0.00	0.00	28.00	48.00	0.00

These zeros indicate that there are alternate optimal solutions.

Constraints

Cell	Name	Final Value	Shadow Price	Constraint R.H. Side	Allowable Increase	Allowable Decrease
$H$8	9am-10am needs	10.00	0.00	10.00	6.00	0.00
$H$9	10am-11am needs	17.00	0.00	12.00	5.00	1E+30
$H$10	11am-Noon needs	14.00	60.00	14.00	0.00	3.00
$H$11	Noon-1pm needs	19.00	0.00	16.00	3.00	1E+30
$H$12	1pm-2pm needs	24.00	0.00	18.00	6.00	1E+30
$H$13	2pm-3pm needs	17.00	0.00	17.00	5.00	2.00
$H$14	3pm-4pm needs	15.00	60.00	15.00	0.00	3.00
$H$15	4pm-5pm needs	10.00	0.00	10.00	3.00	0.00
$H$16	Max full time	10.00	0.00	12.00	1E+30	2.00
$H$17	Part-time limit	56.00	-8.00	56.00	60.00	0.00

Screenshot 4-5A reveals that the optimal solution is to employ 10 full-time tellers, 7 part-time tellers at 10 A.M., 2 part-time tellers at 11 A.M., and 5 part-time tellers at noon, for a total cost of $1,292 per day.

In Screenshot 4-5B, the shadow price of −$8 for the part-time limit of 56 hours indicates that each additional hour (over the 56-hour limit) that part-time tellers are allowed to work will allow the bank to reduce costs by $8. This shadow price is valid for a limit of 60 more hours (i.e., up to 116 hours).

Examining the Allowable Increase and Allowable Decrease columns for the OFCs, we see that there are several values of zero in these columns. This indicates that there are alternate optimal solutions to this problem.

Likewise, consider the reduced cost for variables P_1 (part-timers starting at 9 A.M.) and P_5 (part-timers starting at 1 P.M.). These are zero, even though these variables have values of zero (their lower limit). This implies that, for example, it is possible to force P_1 (or P_5) to have a nonzero value at optimality and not affect the total cost in any way. This is another indication of the presence of alternate optimal solutions to this problem.

We can force Excel to identify alternate optimal solutions.

How can we identify these optimal solutions by using Excel's Solver? There are at least a couple ways of doing so. First, simply rearranging the order in which the variables and/or constraints are included in the Excel layout may make Solver identify an alternate optimal solution. That is, we can just swap the order in which some of the rows and/or columns are included in the model. There is, however, no guarantee that this approach will always identify an alternate optimal solution.

The second approach, which will definitely find an alternate optimal solution (if one exists), is as follows. From the preceding discussion, we know that variable P_1 (which currently has a zero value) can have a nonzero value at an optimal solution. To force this to happen, we include the current objective function as a constraint, as follows:

$$\$90F + \$28(P_1 + P_2 + P_3 + P_4 + P_5) = \$1{,}292$$

This will force the new solution to have the same optimal cost (i.e., it is also an optimal solution). Then, the new objective for the model would be

$$\text{Max } P_1$$

Note that this will find a solution that costs $1,292 but has a nonzero value for P_1. We can repeat the same approach with the variable P_5 to find yet another optimal solution.

Using these approaches, we can identify two alternate solutions for Hong Kong Bank, as follows:

1. 10 full-time tellers, 6 part-time tellers at 9 A.M., 1 part-time teller at 10 A.M., 2 part-time tellers at 11 A.M., and 5 part-time tellers at noon.
2. 10 full-time tellers, 6 part-time tellers at 9 A.M., 1 part-time teller at 10 A.M., 2 part-time tellers at 11 A.M., 2 part-time tellers at noon, and 3 part-time tellers at 10 A.M.

The cost of each of these employment policies is also $1,292.

Discussion Questions and Problems

Discussion Questions

4-1 Discuss the role of sensitivity analysis in LP. Under what circumstances is it needed, and under what conditions do you think it is not necessary?

4-2 Is sensitivity analysis a concept applied to LP only, or should it also be used when analyzing other techniques (e.g., break-even analysis)? Provide examples to prove your point.

4-3 Explain how a change in resource availability can affect the optimal solution of a problem.

4-4 Explain how a change in an OFC can affect the optimal solution of a problem.

4-5 Are simultaneous changes in input data values logical? Provide examples to prove your point.

4-6 Explain the 100% rule and its role in analyzing the impact of simultaneous changes in model input data values.

4-7 How can a firm benefit from using the pricing out procedure?

4-8 How do we detect the presence of alternate optimal solutions from a Solver Sensitivity Report?

4-9 Why would a firm find information regarding the shadow price of a resource useful?

Problems

4-10 A graphical approach was used to solve the following LP model in Problem 2-14:

$$\text{Maximize profit} = \$4X + \$5Y$$

Subject to the constraints

$$\begin{aligned} 5X + 2Y &\le 40 \\ 3X + 6Y &\le 30 \\ X &\le 7 \\ 2X - Y &\ge 3 \\ X, Y &\ge 0 \end{aligned}$$

Use the graphical solution to answer the following questions. Each question is independent of the others. Determine if (and how) the following changes would affect the optimal solution values and/or profit.

(a) A technical breakthrough raises the profit per unit of Y to $10.
(b) The profit per unit of X decreases to only $2.
(c) The first constraint changes to $5X + 2Y \le 54$.

4-11 A graphical approach was used to solve the following LP model in Problem 2-16:

$$\text{Minimize cost} = \$4X + \$7Y$$

Subject to the constraints

$$\begin{aligned} 2X + 3Y &\ge 60 \\ 4X + 2Y &\ge 80 \\ X &\le 24 \\ X, Y &\ge 0 \end{aligned}$$

Use the graphical solution to answer the following questions. Each question is independent of the others. Determine if (and how) the following changes would affect the optimal solution values and/or cost.

(a) The cost per unit of Y increases to $9.
(b) The first constraint changes to $2X + 3Y \ge 90$.
(c) The third constraint changes to $X \le 15$.

4-12 A graphical approach was used to solve the following LP model in Problem 2-15:

$$\text{Maximize profit} = \$4X + \$3Y$$

Subject to the constraints

$$\begin{aligned} 2X + 4Y &\le 72 \\ 3X + 6Y &\ge 27 \\ -3X + 10Y &\ge 0 \\ X, Y &\ge 0 \end{aligned}$$

Use the graphical solution to answer the following questions. Each question is independent of the others. Determine if (and how) the following changes would affect the optimal solution values and/or profit.

(a) The profit per unit of X decreases to \$1.
(b) The first constraint changes to $2X + 4Y \leq 80$.
(c) The third constraint changes to $-3X + 10Y \leq 0$.

4-13 Consider the Win Big Gambling Club media selection example discussed in section 3.3 (page 73) of Chapter 3. Use the Sensitivity Report for this LP model (shown in Screenshot 4-6) to answer the following questions. Each question is independent of the others.
What is the impact on the audience coverage under the following scenarios?
(a) Management approves spending \$200 more on radio advertising each week.
(b) The contractual agreement to place at least five radio spots per week is eliminated.
(c) The audience reached per ad increases to 3,100.
(d) There is some uncertainty in the audience reached per TV spot. For what range of values for this OFC will the current solution remain optimal?

4-14 Consider the MSA marketing research example discussed in Section 3.3 (page 74) of Chapter 3. Use the Sensitivity Report for this LP model (shown in Screenshot 4-7 on page 150) to answer the following questions. Each question is independent of the others.
(a) What is the maximum unit cost that will make it worthwhile to include in the survey persons 30 years of age or younger who live in a border state?
(b) What is the impact if MSA wants to increase the sample size to 3,000?
(c) What is the impact if MSA insists on including people 31–50 years of age who do not live in a border state?
(d) What is the impact if we can reduce the minimum 30 or younger persons required to 900, provided that we raise the persons 31–50 years of age to 650?

4-15 Consider the Whole Food Nutrition Center diet problem example discussed in Section 3.7 (page 89) of Chapter 3. Use the Sensitivity Report for this LP model (shown in Screenshot 4-8 on page 150) to answer the following questions. Each question is independent of the others.
(a) What is the impact if the daily allowance for protein can be reduced to 2.9 units?
(b) Whole Food believes the unit price of grain A could be 5% overestimated and the unit price of grain B could be 10% underestimated. If these turn out to be true, what is the new optimal solution and optimal total cost?
(c) What is the impact if the reduction in the daily allowance for protein in (a) requires Whole Food to simultaneously increase the daily allowance of riboflavin to 2.20 units?

4-16 Consider the cell phone manufacturing problem presented in Chapter 3 as Problem 3-6 on page 105. Use Solver to create the Sensitivity Report for this LP problem. Use this report to answer the following questions. Each question is independent of the others.
(a) Interpret the reduced costs for the products that are not currently included in the optimal production plan.

SCREENSHOT 4-6 Solver Sensitivity Report for Problem 4-13: Win Big Gambling Club

Microsoft Excel 14.0 Sensitivity Report
Problem 4-13. Win Big Gambling Club

Variable Cells

Cell	Name	Final Value	Reduced Cost	Objective Coefficient	Allowable Increase	Allowable Decrease
\$B\$5	Number of units TV spots	1.97	0.00	5000.00	1620.69	5000.00
\$C\$5	Number of units Newspaper ads	5.00	0.00	8500.00	1E+30	2718.75
\$D\$5	Number of units Prime-time radio spots	6.21	0.00	2400.00	1E+30	263.16
\$E\$5	Number of units Afternoon radio spots	0.00	-344.83	2800.00	344.83	1E+30

Constraints

Cell	Name	Final Value	Shadow Price	Constraint R.H. Side	Allowable Increase	Allowable Decrease
\$F\$8	Maximum TV	1.97	0.00	12.00	1E+30	10.03
\$F\$9	Maximum newspaper	5.00	2718.75	5.00	1.70	5.00
\$F\$10	Max prime-time radio	6.21	0.00	25.00	1E+30	18.79
\$F\$11	Max afternoon radio	0.00	0.00	20.00	1E+30	20.00
\$F\$12	Total budget	8,000.00	6.25	8000.00	8025.00	1575.00
\$F\$13	Maximum radio \$	1,800.00	2.03	1800.00	1575.00	350.00
\$F\$14	Minimum radio spots	6.21	0.00	5.00	1.21	1E+30

SCREENSHOT 4-7 Solver Sensitivity Report for Problem 4-14: MSA Marketing Research

Microsoft Excel 14.0 Sensitivity Report
Problem 4-14. Management Science Associates

Variable Cells

Cell	Name	Final Value	Reduced Cost	Objective Coefficient	Allowable Increase	Allowable Decrease
$B$5	Number of households <= 30 and border	0.00	0.60	7.50	1E+30	0.60
$C$5	Number of households 31-50 and border	600.00	0.00	6.80	0.45	0.82
$D$5	Number of households >= 51 and border	140.00	0.00	5.50	0.6	29.90
$E$5	Number of households <= 30 and not border	1000.00	0.00	6.90	0.6	0.92
$F$5	Number of households 31-50 and not border	0.00	0.45	7.25	1E+30	0.45
$G$5	Number of households >= 51 and not border	560.00	0.00	6.10	1.025	0.60

Constraints

Cell	Name	Final Value	Shadow Price	Constraint R.H. Side	Allowable Increase	Allowable Decrease
$H$8	Total households	2300.00	5.98	2300.00	1E+30	700.00
$H$9	<= 30 households	1000.00	0.92	1000.00	700.00	1000.00
$H$10	31-50 households	600.00	0.82	600.00	700.00	493.75
$H$11	Border Mexico	740.00	0.00	0.00	395.00	1E+30
$H$12	<= 30 and not border	1000.00	0.00	0.00	500.00	1E+30
$H$13	>= 51 and border	140.00	-0.60	0.00	560.00	140.00

(b) Another part of the corporation wants to take 35 hours of time on test device 3. How does this affect the optimal solution?

(c) The company has the opportunity to obtain 20 additional hours on test device 1 at a cost of $25 per hour. Would this be worthwhile?

(d) The company has the opportunity to give up 20 hours of time on device 1 and obtain 40 hours of time on device 2 in return. Would this be worthwhile? Justify your answer.

4-17 Consider the family farm planning problem presented in Chapter 3 as Problem 3-27 on page 110. Use Solver to create the Sensitivity Report for this LP problem. Use this report to answer the following questions. Each question is independent of the others.

(a) Is this solution a unique optimal solution? Why or why not?

(b) If there are alternate solutions, use Solver to identify at least one other optimal solution.

(c) Would the total profit increase if barley sales could be increased by 10%? If so, by how much?

(d) Would the availability of more water increase the total profit? If so, by how much?

4-18 Consider the boarding stable feed problem presented in Chapter 3 as Problem 3-32 on page 112. Use Solver to create the Sensitivity Report for this LP problem. Use this report to answer the

SCREENSHOT 4-8 Solver Sensitivity Report for Problem 4-15: Whole Food Nutrition Center

Microsoft Excel 14.0 Sensitivity Report
Problem 4-15. Whole Food Nutrition Center

Variable Cells

Cell	Name	Final Value	Reduced Cost	Objective Coefficient	Allowable Increase	Allowable Decrease
$B$5	Number of pounds Grain A	0.025	0.000	0.330	0.063	1E+30
$C$5	Number of pounds Grain B	0.050	0.000	0.470	1E+30	0.190
$D$5	Number of pounds Grain C	0.050	0.000	0.380	1E+30	0.073

Constraints

Cell	Name	Final Value	Shadow Price	Constraint R.H. Side	Allowable Increase	Allowable Decrease
$E$8	Protein	3.000	0.038	3.000	0.000	0.250
$E$9	Riboflavin	2.350	0.000	2.000	0.350	1E+30
$E$10	Phosphorus	1.000	0.088	1.000	0.018	0.000
$E$11	Magnesium	0.425	0.000	0.425	0.000	1E+30
$E$12	Total Mix	0.125	-1.210	0.125	0.004	0.000

following questions. Each question is independent of the others.

(a) If the price of grain decreases by \$0.01 per pound, will the optimal solution change?
(b) Which constraints are binding? Interpret the shadow price for the binding constraints.
(c) What would happen to the total cost if the price of mineral decreased by 20% from its current value?
(d) For what price range of oats is the current solution optimal?

4-19 Consider the campus dietitian's problem presented in Chapter 3 as Problem 3-33 on page 112. Use Solver to create the Sensitivity Report for this LP problem. Use this report to answer the following questions. Each question is independent of the others.

(a) Interpret the shadow prices for the carbohydrates and iron constraints.
(b) What would happen to total cost if the dietitian chooses to use milk in the diet?
(c) What would be the maximum amount the dietitian would be willing to pay for beans to make it a cost-effective item for inclusion in the diet?
(d) Is the solution to this problem a unique optimal solution? Justify your answer.

4-20 Consider the following LP problem, in which X and Y denote the number of units of products X and Y to produce, respectively:

$$\text{Maximize profit} = \$4X + \$5Y$$

subject to the constraints

$$\begin{aligned} X + 2Y &\le 10 \quad \text{(labor available, in hours)} \\ 6X + 6Y &\le 36 \quad \text{(material available, in pounds)} \\ 8X + 4Y &\le 40 \quad \text{(storage available, in square feet)} \\ X, Y &\ge 0 \quad \text{(nonnegativity)} \end{aligned}$$

The Excel Sensitivity Report for this problem is shown in Screenshot 4-9. Calculate and explain what happens to the optimal solution for each of the following situations. Each question is independent of the other questions.

(a) You acquire 2 additional pounds of material.
(b) You acquire 1.5 additional hours of labor.
(c) You give up 1 hour of labor and get 1.5 pounds of material.
(d) The profit contributions for both products X and Y are changed to \$4.75 each.
(e) You decide to introduce a new product that has a profit contribution of \$2. Each unit of this product will use 1 hour of labor, 1 pound of material, and 2 square feet of storage space.

4-21 Consider the following LP problem, in which X and Y denote the number of units of products X and Y to produce, respectively:

$$\text{Maximize profit} = \$5X + \$5Y$$

subject to the constraints

$$\begin{aligned} 2X + 3Y &\le 60 \quad \text{(resource 1)} \\ 4X + 2Y &\le 80 \quad \text{(resource 2)} \\ X &\le 18 \quad \text{(resource 3)} \\ X, Y &\ge 0 \quad \text{(nonnegativity)} \end{aligned}$$

The Excel Sensitivity Report for this problem is shown in Screenshot 4-10 on page 152. Calculate and explain what happens to the optimal solution for each of the following situations. Each question is independent of the other questions.

(a) What is the optimal solution to this problem?
(b) For what ranges of values, holding all else constant, could each of the objective function coefficients be changed without changing the optimal solution?
(c) If we could obtain one additional unit of resource 1, how would it impact profit? Over what range of RHS values could we rely upon this value?
(d) If we were to give up one unit of resource 2, how would it impact profit? Over what range of RHS values could we rely upon this value?

SCREENSHOT 4-9
Solver Sensitivity Report for Problem 4-20

Microsoft Excel 14.0 Sensitivity Report
Problem 4-20

Variable Cells

Cell	Name	Final Value	Reduced Cost	Objective Coefficient	Allowable Increase	Allowable Decrease
\$B\$4	Solution value X	2.00	0.00	4.00	1.00	1.50
\$C\$4	Solution value Y	4.00	0.00	5.00	3.00	1.00

Constraints

Cell	Name	Final Value	Shadow Price	Constraint R.H. Side	Allowable Increase	Allowable Decrease
\$D\$7	Labor	10.00	1.00	10.00	2.00	2.00
\$D\$8	Material	36.00	0.50	36.00	4.00	6.00
\$D\$9	Storage	32.00	0.00	40.00	1E+30	8.00

SCREENSHOT 4-10
Solver Sensitivity Report for Problem 4-21

Microsoft Excel 14.0 Sensitivity Report
Problem 4-21

Variable Cells

Cell	Name	Final Value	Reduced Cost	Objective Coefficient	Allowable Increase	Allowable Decrease
$B$4	Solution value X	15.00	0.00	5.00	5.00	1.67
$C$4	Solution value Y	10.00	0.00	5.00	2.50	2.50

Constraints

Cell	Name	Final Value	Shadow Price	Constraint R.H. Side	Allowable Increase	Allowable Decrease
$D$7	Resource 1	60.00	1.25	60.00	60.00	12.00
$D$8	Resource 2	80.00	0.63	80.00	8.00	40.00
$D$9	Resource 3	15.00	0.00	18.00	1E+30	3.00

(e) If we were to increase the profit for product X by $4, how would the solution change? What would be the new solution values and the new profit?
(f) If we were to decrease the profit for product Y by $2, how would the solution change? What would be the new solution values and the new profit?
(g) Suppose that two units of resource 3 were found to be unusable, how would the solution change?
(h) If we were able to obtain five more units of resource 3, would you be interested in the deal? Why or why not?
(i) If the profit for product X was increased to $7 while at the same time the profit for product Y was reduced to $4, what would be the new solution values and the new profit?
(j) Suppose you were to be offered 50 units of resource 1 at a premium of $1 each over the existing cost price for that resource. Would you purchase this? If so, by how much would your profit increase?

4-22 The Good-to-Go Suitcase Company makes three kinds of suitcases: (1) Standard, (2) Deluxe, and (3) Luxury styles. Each suitcase goes through four production stages: (1) cutting and coloring, (2) assembly, (3) finishing, and (4) quality and packaging. The total number of hours available in each of these departments is 630, 600, 708, and 135, respectively.

Each Standard suitcase requires 0.7 hours of cutting and coloring, 0.5 hours of assembly, 1 hour of finishing, and 0.1 hours of quality and packaging. The corresponding numbers for each Deluxe suitcase are 1 hour, 5/6 hours, 2/3 hours, and 0.25 hours, respectively. Likewise, the corresponding numbers for each Luxury suitcase are 1 hour, 2/3 hours, 0.9 hours, and 0.4 hours, respectively.

The sales revenue for each type of suitcase is as follows: Standard $36.05, Deluxe $39.50, and Luxury $43.30. The material costs are Standard $6.25, Deluxe $7.50, and Luxury $8.50. The hourly cost of labor for each department is cutting and coloring $10, assembly $6, finishing $9, and quality and packaging $8.

The Excel layout and LP Sensitivity Report of Good-to-Go's problem are shown in Screenshots 4-11A and 4-11B, respectively. Each of the following questions is independent of the others.

SCREENSHOT 4-11A
Excel Layout for Good-to-Go Suitcase Company

	A	B	C	D	E	F	G	H
1	Good-to-Go Suitcase Company							
2								
3		Standard	Deluxe	Luxury				
4	Solution value	540.00	252.00	0.00				
5	Selling price per unit	$36.05	$39.50	$43.30	$29,421.00			
6	Material cost per unit	$6.25	$7.50	$8.50	$5,265.00			
7	Labor cost per unit	$19.80	$23.00	$25.30	$16,488.00			
8	Profit	$10.00	$9.00	$9.50	$7,668.00			
9	Constraints							Cost
10	Cutting & Coloring	0.70	1.00	1.00	630.00	<=	630	$10
11	Assembly	0.50	0.83	0.67	480.00	<=	600	$6
12	Finishing	1.00	0.67	0.90	708.00	<=	708	$9
13	Quality & Packaging	0.10	0.25	0.40	117.00	<=	135	$8
14					LHS	Sign	RHS	

SCREENSHOT 4-11B Solver Sensitivity Report for Good-to-Go Suitcase Company

Microsoft Excel 14.0 Sensitivity Report
Problems P4-22&23. Good-to-Go Suitcase Company

Variable Cells

Cell	Name	Final Value	Reduced Cost	Objective Coefficient	Allowable Increase	Allowable Decrease
$B$4	Solution value Standard	540.00	0.00	10.00	3.50	2.56
$C$4	Solution value Deluxe	252.00	0.00	9.00	5.29	1.61
$D$4	Solution value Luxury	0.00	-1.12	9.50	1.12	1E+30

Constraints

Cell	Name	Final Value	Shadow Price	Constraint R.H. Side	Allowable Increase	Allowable Decrease
$E$10	Cutting & Coloring	630.00	4.38	630	52.36	134.40
$E$11	Assembly	480.00	0.00	600	1E+30	120.00
$E$12	Finishing	708.00	6.94	708	192.00	128.00
$E$13	Quality & Packaging	117.00	0.00	135	1E+30	18.00

(a) What is the optimal production plan? Which of the resources are scarce?

(b) Suppose Good-to-Go is considering including a polishing process, the cost of which would be added directly to the price. Each Standard suitcase would require 10 minutes of time in this treatment, each Deluxe suitcase would need 15 minutes, and each Luxury suitcase would need 20 minutes. Would the current production plan change as a result of this additional process if 170 hours of polishing time were available? Explain your answer.

(c) Now consider the addition of a waterproofing process where each Standard suitcase would use 1 hour of time in the process, each Deluxe suitcase would need 1.5 hours, and each Luxury suitcase would require 1.75 hours. Would this change the production plan if 900 hours were available? Why or why not?

Source: Professors Mark and Judith McKnew, Clemson University.

4-23 Suppose Good-to-Go (Problem 4-22) is considering the possible introduction of two new products to its line of suitcases: the Compact model (for teenagers) and the Kiddo model (for children). Market research suggests that Good-to-Go can sell the Compact model for no more than $30, whereas the Kiddo model would go for as much as $37.50 to specialty toy stores. The amount of labor and the cost of raw materials for each possible new product are as follows:

COST CATEGORY	COMPACT	KIDDO
Cutting and coloring (hr.)	0.50	1.20
Assembly (hr.)	0.75	0.75
Finishing (hr.)	0.75	0.50
Quality and packaging (hr.)	0.20	0.20
Raw materials	$5.00	$4.50

Use a pricing out strategy to check if either model would be economically attractive to make.

4-24 The Strollers-to-Go Company makes lightweight umbrella-type strollers for three different groups of children. The TiniTote is designed specifically for newborns who require extra neck support. The ToddleTote is for toddlers up to 30 pounds. Finally, the company produces a heavy-duty model called TubbyTote, which is designed to carry children up to 60 pounds. The stroller company is in the process of determining its production for each of the three types of strollers for the upcoming planning period.

The marketing department has forecast the following maximum demand for each of the strollers during the planning period: TiniTote 180, TubbyTote 70, and ToddleTote 160. Strollers-to-Go sells TiniTotes for $63.75, TubbyTotes for $82.50, and ToddleTotes for $66. As a matter of policy, it wants to produce no less than 50% of the forecast demand for each product. It also wants to keep production of ToddleTotes to a maximum of 40% of total stroller production.

The production department has estimated that the material costs for TiniTote, TubbyTote, and ToddleTote strollers will be $4, $6, and $5.50 per unit, respectively. The strollers are processed through fabrication, sewing, and assembly workstations. The metal and plastic frames are made in the fabrication station. The fabric seats are cut and stitched together in the sewing station. Finally, the frames are put together with the seats in the assembly station. In the upcoming planning period, there will be 620 hours available in fabrication, where the direct labor cost is $8.25 per hour. The sewing station has 500 hours available, and the direct labor cost is $8.50 per hour. The assembly station has 480 hours available, and the direct labor cost is $8.75 per hour.

The standard processing rate for TiniTotes is 3 hours in fabrication, 2 hours in sewing, and

SCREENSHOT 4-12A
Excel Layout for Strollers-to-Go Company

	A	B	C	D	E	F	G	H
1	**Strollers-to-Go Company**							
2								
3		TiniTote	TubbyTote	ToddleTote				
4	Solution value	100.00	35.00	90.00				
5	Selling price per unit	$63.75	$82.50	$66.00	$15,202.50			
6	Material cost per unit	$4.00	$6.00	$5.50	$1,105.00			
7	Labor cost per unit	$50.50	$67.75	$51.00	$12,011.25			
8	Profit	$9.25	$8.75	$9.50	$2,086.25			
9	**Constraints**							**Cost**
10	Fabrication	3.0	4.0	2.0	620.00	<=	620	$8.25
11	Sewing	2.0	1.0	2.0	415.00	<=	500	$8.50
12	Assembly	1.0	3.0	2.0	385.00	<=	480	$8.75
13	Tinitote demand	1.0			100.00	<=	180	
14	Tubbytote demand		1.0		35.00	<=	70	
15	Toddletote demand			1.0	90.00	<=	160	
16	Toddletote max prod ratio	-0.4	-0.4	0.6	0.00	<=	0	
17	Tinitote min prod	1.0			100.00	>=	90	
18	Tubbytote min prod		1.0		35.00	>=	35	
19	Toddletote min prod			1.0	90.00	>=	80	
20					**LHS**	**Sign**	**RHS**	

1 hour in assembly. TubbyTotes require 4 hours in fabrication, 1 hour in sewing and 3 hours in assembly, whereas ToddleTotes require 2 hours in each station.

The Excel layout and LP Sensitivity Report for Strollers-to-Go's problem are shown in Screenshots 4-12A and 4-12B, respectively. Each of the following questions is independent of the others.

(a) How many strollers of each type should Strollers-to-Go make? What is the profit? Which constraints are binding?

(b) How much labor time is being used in the fabrication, sewing, and assembly areas?

(c) How much would Strollers-to-Go be willing to pay for an additional hour of fabrication time? For an additional hour of sewing time?

(d) Is Strollers-to-Go producing any product at its maximum sales level? Is it producing any product at its minimum level?

Source: Professors Mark and Judith McKnew, Clemson University.

4-25 Consider the Strollers-to-Go production problem (Problem 4-24).

(a) Over what range of costs could the TiniTote materials vary and the current production plan

SCREENSHOT 4-12B
Solver Sensitivity Report for Strollers-to-Go Company

Microsoft Excel 14.0 Sensitivity Report
Problems 4-24to27. Strollers-to-Go Company

Variable Cells

Cell	Name	Final Value	Reduced Cost	Objective Coefficient	Allowable Increase	Allowable Decrease
$B$4	Solution value TiniTote	100.00	0.00	9.25	5.00	3.33
$C$4	Solution value TubbyTote	35.00	0.00	8.75	4.10	1E+30
$D$4	Solution value ToddleTote	90.00	0.00	9.50	1E+30	3.33

Constraints

Cell	Name	Final Value	Shadow Price	Constraint R.H. Side	Allowable Increase	Allowable Decrease
$E$10	Fabrication	620.00	3.60	620.00	110.50	43.33
$E$11	Sewing	415.00	0.00	500.00	1E+30	85.00
$E$12	Assembly	385.00	0.00	480.00	1E+30	95.00
$E$13	Tinitote demand	100.00	0.00	180.00	1E+30	80.00
$E$14	Tubbytote demand	35.00	0.00	70.00	1E+30	35.00
$E$15	Toddletote demand	90.00	0.00	160.00	1E+30	70.00
$E$16	Toddletote max prod ratio	0.00	3.85	0.00	13.00	8.67
$E$17	Tinitote min prod	100.00	0.00	90.00	10.00	1E+30
$E$18	Tubbytote min prod	35.00	-4.10	35.00	8.13	35.00
$E$19	Toddletote min prod	90.00	0.00	80.00	10.00	1E+30

remain optimal? (*Hint*: How are material costs reflected in the problem formulation?)

(b) Suppose that Strollers-to-Go decided to polish each stroller prior to shipping. The process is fast and would require 10, 15, and 12 minutes, respectively, for TiniTote, TubbyTote, and ToddleTote strollers. Would this change the current production plan if 48 hours of polishing time were available?

4-26 Consider the Strollers-to-Go production problem (Problem 4-24).

(a) Suppose that Strollers-to-Go could purchase additional fabrication time at a cost of $10.50 per hour. Should it be interested? Why or why not? What is the most that it would be willing to pay for an additional hour of fabrication time?

(b) Suppose that Strollers-to-Go could only purchase fabrication time in multiples of 40-hour bundles. How many bundles should it be willing to purchase then?

4-27 Suppose that Strollers-to-Go (Problem 4-24) is considering the production of TwinTotes for families who are doubly blessed. Each TwinTote would require $7.10 in materials, 4 hours of fabrication time, 2 hours of sewing time, and 2 hours to assemble. Would this product be economically attractive to manufacture if the sales price were $86? Why or why not?

4-28 The Classic Furniture Company is trying to determine the optimal quantities to make of six possible products: tables and chairs made of oak, cherry, and pine. The products are to be made using the following resources: labor hours and three types of wood. Minimum production requirements are as follows: at least 3 each of oak and cherry tables, at least 10 each of oak and cherry chairs, and at least 5 pine chairs.

The Excel layout and LP Sensitivity Report for Classic Furniture's problem are shown in Screenshots 4-13A and 4-13B, respectively. The objective function coefficients in the Screenshots refer to unit profit per item. Each of the following questions is independent of the others.

(a) What is the profit represented by the objective function, and what is the production plan?
(b) Which constraints are binding?
(c) What is the range over which the unit profit for oak chairs can change without changing the production plan?
(d) What is the range over which the amount of available oak could range without changing the combination of binding constraints?
(e) Does this Sensitivity Report indicate the presence of multiple optima? How do you know?
(f) After production is over, how many pounds of cherry wood will be left over?
(g) According to this report, how many more chairs were made than were required?

4-29 Consider the Classic Furniture product mix problem (Problem 4-28). For each of the following situations, what would be the impact on the production plan and profit? If it is possible to compute the new profit or production plan, do so.

(a) The unit profit for oak tables increases to $83.
(b) The unit profit for pine chairs decreases to $13.
(c) The unit profit for pine tables increases by $20.
(d) The unit profit for cherry tables decreases to $85.
(e) The company is required to make at least 20 pine chairs.
(f) The company is required to make no more than 55 cherry chairs.

4-30 Consider the Classic Furniture product mix problem (Problem 4-28). For each of the following situations,

SCREENSHOT 4-13A
Excel Layout for Classic Furniture Company

	A	B	C	D	E	F	G	H	I	J
1	**Classic Furniture Company**									
2										
3		Oak tables	Oak chairs	Cherry tables	Cherry chairs	Pine tables	Pine chairs			
4	Number of units	3.00	51.67	3.00	85.56	42.26	33.08			
5	Profit	$75	$35	$90	$60	$45	$20	$10,000.00		
6	**Constraints**									
7	Labor hours	7.5	3.5	9.0	6.0	4.5	2.0	1000.00	<=	1,000
8	Oak (pounds)	200	30					2150.00	<=	2,150
9	Cherry (pounds)			240	36			3800.00	<=	3,800
10	Pine (pounds)					180	27	8500.00	<=	8,500
11	Min oak tables	1						3.00	>=	3
12	Min cherry tables			1				3.00	>=	3
13	Min oak chairs		1					51.67	>=	10
14	Min cherry chairs				1			85.56	>=	10
15	Min pine chairs						1	33.08	>=	5
16								**LHS**	**Sign**	**RHS**

SCREENSHOT 4-13B Solver Sensitivity Report for Classic Furniture Company

Microsoft Excel 14.0 Sensitivity Report
Problems 4-28to32. Classic Furniture Company

Variable Cells

Cell	Name	Final Value	Reduced Cost	Objective Coefficient	Allowable Increase	Allowable Decrease
$B$4	Number of units Oak tables	3.00	0.00	75.00	0.00	1E+30
$C$4	Number of units Oak chairs	51.67	0.00	35.00	1E+30	0.00
$D$4	Number of units Cherry tables	3.00	0.00	90.00	0.00	1E+30
$E$4	Number of units Cherry chairs	85.56	0.00	60.00	1E+30	0.00
$F$4	Number of units Pine tables	42.26	0.00	45.00	88.33	0.00
$G$4	Number of units Pine chairs	33.08	0.00	20.00	0.00	13.25

Constraints

Cell	Name	Final Value	Shadow Price	Constraint R.H. Side	Allowable Increase	Allowable Decrease
$H$7	Labor hours	1000.00	10.00	1000.00	373.30	37.21
$H$8	Oak (pounds)	2150.00	0.00	2150.00	318.93	1250.00
$H$9	Cherry (pounds)	3800.00	0.00	3800.00	223.25	2239.78
$H$10	Pine (pounds)	8500.00	0.00	8500.00	1488.33	5039.50
$H$11	Min oak tables	3.00	0.00	3.00	6.25	2.35
$H$12	Min cherry tables	3.00	0.00	3.00	11.33	1.20
$H$13	Min oak chairs	51.67	0.00	10.00	41.67	1E+30
$H$14	Min cherry chairs	85.56	0.00	10.00	75.56	1E+30
$H$15	Min pine chairs	33.08	0.00	5.00	28.08	1E+30

what would be the impact on the production plan and profit? If it is possible to compute the new profit or production plan, do so.

(a) The number of labor hours expands to 1,320.
(b) The amount of cherry wood increases to 3,900.
(c) The number of labor hours decreases to 950.
(d) The company does not have a minimum requirement for cherry chairs.

4-31 Consider the Classic Furniture product mix problem (Problem 4-28). For each of the following situations, what would be the impact on the production plan and profit? If it is possible to compute the new profit or production plan, do so.

(a) OFCs for oak tables and cherry tables each decreases by $15.
(b) OFCs for oak tables and oak chairs are reversed.
(c) OFCs for pine tables and pine chairs are reversed.
(d) $OFC_{\text{Pine Table}}$ increases by $20 while at the same time the $OFC_{\text{Pine Chair}}$ decreases by $10.
(e) Unit profits for all three types of chairs are increased by $6 each.

4-32 Consider the Classic Furniture product mix problem (Problem 4-28). In answering each of the following questions, be as specific as possible. If it is possible to compute a new profit or production plan, do so.

(a) A part-time employee who works 20 hours per week decided to quit his job. How would this affect the profit and production plan?
(b) Classic has been approached by the factory next door, CabinetsRUs, which has a shortage of both labor and oak. CabinetsRUs proposes to take one full-time employee (who works 30 hours) plus 900 pounds of oak. It has offered $560 as compensation. Should Classic make this trade?
(c) Classic is considering adding a new product, a cherry armoire. The armoire would consume 200 pounds of cherry wood and take 16 hours of labor. Cherry wood costs $9 per pound, and labor costs $12 per hour. The armoire would sell for $2,180. Should this product be made?
(d) What would happen to the solution if a constraint were added to make sure that for every table made, at least two matching chairs were made?

4-33 The Tiger Catering Company is trying to determine the most economical combination of sandwiches to make for a tennis club. The club has asked Tiger to provide 70 sandwiches in a variety to include tuna, tuna and cheese, ham, ham and cheese, and cheese. The club has specified a minimum of 10 each of tuna and ham and 12 each of tuna/cheese and ham/cheese. Tiger makes the sandwiches using the following resources: bread, tuna, ham, cheese, mayonnaise, mustard, lettuce, tomato, packaging material, and labor hours.

The Excel layout and LP Sensitivity Report for Tiger Catering's problem are shown in Screenshots 4-14A and 4-14B, respectively. The objective function coefficients in the screenshots refer to unit cost per item. Each of the following questions is independent of the others.

(a) What is the optimal cost represented by the objective function and what is the optimal sandwich-making plan?
(b) Which constraints are binding?

SCREENSHOT 4-14A Excel Layout for Tiger Catering Company

	A	B	C	D	E	F	G	H	I
1	**Tiger Catering Company**								
2									
3		Tuna	Tuna/Ch	Ham	Ham/Ch	Cheese			
4	Number to make	10.00	30.00	10.00	12.00	8.00			
5	Cost	$2.42	$2.12	$3.35	$3.02	$2.36	$176.42		
6	**Constraints**								
7	Bread (slices)	2	2	2	2	2	140.00	<=	140
8	Tuna (oz.)	4	3				130.00	<=	130
9	Ham (oz.)			4	3		76.00	<=	100
10	Cheese (oz.)		1		1	4	74.00	<=	80
11	Mayo (oz.)	1.2	0.9	0.5	0.5	0.5	54.00	<=	72
12	Mustard (oz.)			0.2	0.2		4.40	<=	8
13	Lettuce (oz.)	0.25	0.25	0.25	0.25	0.25	17.50	<=	20
14	Tomato (oz.)	0.5	0.5	0.5	0.5	0.5	35.00	<=	40
15	Package (unit)	1	1	1	1	1	70.00	<=	72
16	Labor (hrs)	0.08	0.08	0.08	0.08	0.08	5.60	<=	8
17	Min total	1	1	1	1	1	70.00	>=	70
18	Min Tuna	1					10.00	>=	10
19	Min Tuna/Ch		1				30.00	>=	12
20	Min Ham			1			10.00	>=	10
21	Min Ham/Ch				1		12.00	>=	12
22							LHS	Sign	RHS

(c) What is the range over which the cost for cheese sandwiches could vary without changing the production plan?

(d) What is the range over which the quantity of tuna could vary without changing the combination of binding constraints?

(e) Does this Sensitivity Report indicate the presence of multiple optimal solutions? How do you know?

(f) After the sandwiches are made, how many labor hours remain?

4-34 Consider the Tiger Catering problem (Problem 4-33). For each of the following situations, what would be

SCREENSHOT 4-14B Solver Sensitivity Report for Tiger Catering Company

Microsoft Excel 14.0 Sensitivity Report
Problems 4-33to37. Tiger Catering Company

Variable Cells

Cell	Name	Final Value	Reduced Cost	Objective Coefficient	Allowable Increase	Allowable Decrease
$B$4	Number to make Tuna	10.00	0.00	2.42	1E+30	0.38
$C$4	Number to make Tuna/Ch	30.00	0.00	2.12	0.24	1E+30
$D$4	Number to make Ham	10.00	0.00	3.35	1E+30	0.99
$E$4	Number to make Ham/Ch	12.00	0.00	3.02	1E+30	0.66
$F$4	Number to make Cheese	8.00	0.00	2.36	0.66	0.24

Constraints

Cell	Name	Final Value	Shadow Price	Constraint R.H. Side	Allowable Increase	Allowable Decrease
$G$7	Bread (slices)	140.00	0.00	140.00	1E+30	0.00
$G$8	Tuna (oz.)	130.00	-0.08	130.00	24.00	6.00
$G$9	Ham (oz.)	76.00	0.00	100.00	1E+30	24.00
$G$10	Cheese (oz.)	74.00	0.00	80.00	1E+30	6.00
$G$11	Mayo (oz.)	54.00	0.00	72.00	1E+30	18.00
$G$12	Mustard (oz.)	4.40	0.00	8.00	1E+30	3.60
$G$13	Lettuce (oz.)	17.50	0.00	20.00	1E+30	2.50
$G$14	Tomato (oz.)	35.00	0.00	40.00	1E+30	5.00
$G$15	Package (unit)	70.00	0.00	72.00	1E+30	2.00
$G$16	Labor (hrs)	5.60	0.00	8.00	1E+30	2.40
$G$17	Min total	70.00	2.36	70.00	0.00	8.00
$G$18	Min Tuna	10.00	0.38	10.00	13.50	10.00
$G$19	Min Tuna/Ch	30.00	0.00	12.00	18.00	1E+30
$G$20	Min Ham	10.00	0.99	10.00	6.00	1.50
$G$21	Min Ham/Ch	12.00	0.66	12.00	8.00	2.00

the impact on the sandwich-making plan and total cost? If it is possible to compute the new cost or sandwich-making plan, do so.

(a) The unit cost for tuna sandwiches decreases by $0.30.
(b) The unit cost for tuna and cheese sandwiches increases to $2.40.
(c) The unit cost for ham sandwiches increases to $3.75.
(d) The unit cost for ham and cheese sandwiches decreases by $0.70.
(e) The club does not want any more than 12 ham sandwiches.
(f) The unit cost for cheese sandwiches decreases to $2.05.

4-35 Consider the Tiger Catering problem (Problem 4-33). For each of the following situations, what would be the impact on the sandwich-making plan and total cost? If it is possible to compute the new cost or sandwich-making plan, do so.

(a) The quantity of tuna available decreases to 120 ounces.
(b) The quantity of ham available increases to 115 ounces.
(c) The quantity of cheese available decreases to 72 ounces.
(d) Tiger is required to deliver a minimum of 13 tuna sandwiches.
(e) Tiger is required to deliver only a minimum of 10 tuna and cheese sandwiches.
(f) Tiger is asked to bring a minimum of only 66 sandwiches.

4-36 Consider the Tiger Catering problem (Problem 4-33). For each of the following situations, what would be the impact on the sandwich-making plan and total cost? If it is possible to compute the new cost or sandwich-making plan, do so.

(a) The cost of ham sandwiches and the cost of ham and cheese sandwiches each decreases by $0.35.
(b) The cost of both ham and cheese sandwiches and cheese sandwiches increases by $0.60.
(c) The cost of tuna decreases by $0.10 per ounce. (*Hint:* Note that tuna sandwiches use 4 ounces of tuna and tuna/cheese sandwiches use 3 ounces of tuna.)
(d) The availability of tuna increases by 10 ounces and the availability of ham decreases by 10 ounces.
(e) A 16-oz jar of mustard is sent by mistake instead of a 16-oz jar of mayonnaise. (*Hint:* This would decrease the quantity of mayonnaise by 16 ounces and increase the quantity of mustard by 16 ounces.)

4-37 Consider the Tiger Catering problem (Problem 4-33). In answering each of the following questions, be as specific as possible. If it is possible to compute a new cost or sandwich-making plan, do so.

(a) An additional pound of tuna can be obtained for a premium of $1.50. Should this tuna be purchased?
(b) The tennis club is willing to accept fewer ham and ham and cheese sandwiches. How many of these sandwiches would Tiger try to substitute with other types before they would not be able to predict their new total cost?
(c) The tennis club wants to include a dill pickle slice with each meat sandwich order. If Tiger finds an average of 18 slices in a 2-pound pickle jar, how many jars should be included with the club's order?

Case Study

Coastal States Chemicals and Fertilizers

In December 2005, Bill Stock, general manager for the Louisiana Division of Coastal States Chemicals and Fertilizers, received a letter from Fred McNair of the Cajan Pipeline Company, which notified Coastal States that priorities had been established for the allocation of natural gas. The letter stated that Cajan Pipeline, the primary supplier of natural gas to Coastal States, might be instructed to curtail natural gas supplies to its industrial and commercial customers by as much as 40% during the ensuing winter months. Moreover, Cajan Pipeline had the approval of the Federal Power Commission (FPC) to curtail such supplies.

Possible curtailment was attributed to the priorities established for the use of natural gas:

First priority:	residential and commercial heating
Second priority:	commercial and industrial users that use natural gas as a source of raw material
Third priority:	commercial and industrial users whereby natural gas is used as boiler fuel

Almost all of Coastal States' uses of natural gas were in the second and third priorities. Hence, its plants were certainly subject to brownouts, or natural gas curtailments. The occurrence and severity of the brownouts depended on a number of complex factors. First, Cajan Pipeline was part of an interstate transmission network that delivered natural gas to residential and commercial buildings on the Atlantic coast and in Northeastern regions of the United States. Hence, the severity of the forthcoming winter in these regions would have a direct impact on the use of natural gas.

Second, the demand for natural gas was soaring because it was the cleanest and most efficient fuel. There were almost no environmental problems in burning natural gas. Moreover, maintenance problems due to fuel-fouling in fireboxes and boilers were negligible with natural gas systems. Also, burners were much easier to operate with natural gas than with oil or coal.

Finally, the supply of natural gas was dwindling. The traditionally depressed price of natural gas had discouraged new exploration for gas wells; hence, shortages appeared imminent.

Stock and his staff at Coastal States had been aware of the possibility of shortages of natural gas and had been investigating ways of converting to fuel oil or coal as a substitute for natural gas. Their plans, however, were still in the developmental stages. Coastal States required an immediate contingency plan to minimize the effect of a natural gas curtailment on its multiplant, operations. The obvious question was, what operations should be curtailed, and to what extent could the adverse effect upon profits be minimized? Coastal States had approval from the FPC and Cajan Pipeline to specify which of its plants would bear the burden of the curtailment if such cutbacks were necessary. McNair, of Cajan Pipeline, replied, "It's your 'pie': we don't care how you divide it if we make it smaller."

The Model

Six plants of Coastal States Louisiana Division were to share in the "pie." They were all located in the massive Baton Rouge–Geismar–Gramercy industrial complex along the Mississippi River between Baton Rouge and New Orleans. Products manufactured at those plants that required significant amounts of natural gas were phosphoric acid, urea, ammonium phosphate, ammonium nitrate, chlorine, caustic soda, vinyl chloride monomer, and hydrofluoric acid.

Stock called a meeting of members of his technical staff to discuss a contingency plan for allocation of natural gas among the products if a curtailment developed. The objective was to minimize the impact on profits. After detailed discussion, the meeting was adjourned. Two weeks later, the meeting reconvened. At this session, the data in Table 4.3 were presented.

Coastal States' contract with Cajan Pipeline specified a maximum natural gas consumption of 36,000,000 cubic feet per day for all six member plants. With these data, the technical staff proceeded to develop a model that would specify changes in production rates in response to a natural gas curtailment. (Curtailments are based on contracted consumption and not current consumption.)

Discussion Questions

1. Develop a contingency model and specify the production rates for each product for
   (a) a 20% natural gas curtailment.
   (b) a 40% natural gas curtailment.
2. What impact will the natural gas shortage have on company profits?
3. Develop the Sensitivity Report for the 20% natural gas curtailment model. Use this report to answer the following questions. Each question is independent of the others.
   (a) Interpret the shadow prices for the natural gas availability constraint and for the two constraints that limit the maximum phosphoric acid and chlorine that Coastal can produce.
   (b) Brenda Lamb, Bill Stock's marketing manager, believes that due to increased competition she may have to decrease the unit profit contributions for all products by 3.5% each. What is the impact of this decrease on the production values? On the total profit?
   (c) Jose Fernandez, Bill Stock's production manager, thinks that he can increase the maximum production rate for chlorine and vinyl chloride monomer to 80% of capacity. For all other products, he thinks he can increase the maximum production rate to 100% of capacity. What would be the impact of this change on the total profit?

TABLE 4.3 Contribution to Profit and Overhead

PRODUCT	CONTRIBUTION ($ PER TON)	CAPACITY (TONS PER DAY)	MAXIMUM PRODUCTION RATE (PERCENTAGE OF CAPACITY)	NATURAL GAS CONSUMPTION (1,000 CU. FT. PER TON)
Phosphoric acid	60	400	80	5.5
Urea	80	250	80	7.0
Ammonium phosphate	90	300	90	8.0
Ammonium nitrate	100	300	100	10.0
Chlorine	50	800	60	15.0
Caustic soda	50	1,000	60	16.0
Vinyl chloride monomer	65	500	60	12.0
Hydrofluoric acid	70	400	80	11.0

(d) Bill Stock thinks he can persuade Coastal's Mississippi Division to give him 1,000,000 cubic feet of its allotment of natural gas from Cajan Pipeline. However, due to the Mississippi Division's pricing contract with Cajan Pipeline, this additional amount of natural gas will cost Stock an additional $1.50 per 1,000 cubic feet (over current costs). Should Stock pursue this option? If so, what is the impact of this additional gas on his total profit? What is the impact if Bill Stock can persuade the Mississippi Division to give him 3,000,000 cubic feet of its allotment of natural gas from Cajan Pipeline?

4. Redo question 3 using the Sensitivity Report for the 40% natural gas curtailment model. In addition, interpret the reduced cost for caustic soda.

Source: Jerry Kinard, Western Carolina University, and Brian Kinard, University of North Carolina - Wilmington.

CHAPTER 5

Transportation, Assignment, and Network Models

LEARNING OBJECTIVES

After completing this chapter, students will be able to:

1. Structure special LP network flow models.
2. Set up and solve transportation models, using Excel's Solver.
3. Set up and solve transportation models with Max-Min and Min-Max objectives.
4. Extend the basic transportation model to include transshipment points.
5. Set up and solve maximal-flow network models, using Excel's Solver.
6. Set up and solve shortest-path network models, using Excel's Solver.
7. Connect all points of a network while minimizing total distance, using the minimal-spanning tree model.

CHAPTER OUTLINE

5.1 Introduction

In this chapter, we examine six different examples of special linear programming (LP) models, called *network flow models*: (1) transportation, (2) transshipment, (3) assignment, (4) maximal-flow, (5) shortest-path, and (6) minimal-spanning tree models. Networks consist of nodes (or points) and arcs (or lines) that connect the nodes together. Roadways, telephone systems, and citywide water systems are all examples of networks.

Transportation Model

Transportation models *deal with distribution of goods from supply points to demand points at minimum cost.*

The **transportation model** deals with the distribution of goods from several supply points (also called **origins**, or **sources**) to a number of demand points (also called **destinations**, or **sinks**). Usually, we have a given capacity of goods at each source and a given requirement for the goods at each destination. The most common objective of a transportation model is to schedule shipments from sources to destinations so that total production and transportation costs are minimized. Occasionally, transportation models can have a maximization objective (e.g., maximize total profit of shipping goods from sources to destinations).

Transportation models can also be used when a firm is trying to decide where to locate a new facility. Before opening a new warehouse, factory, or office, it is good practice to consider a number of alternative sites. Good financial decisions concerning facility location also involve minimizing total production and transportation costs for the entire system.

Transshipment Model

In **transshipment models**, *some points can have shipments that arrive as well as leave.*

In a basic transportation model, shipments either leave a supply point or arrive at a demand point. An extension of the transportation model is called the **transshipment model**, in which a point can have shipments that both arrive and leave. An example would be a warehouse where shipments arrive from factories and then leave for retail outlets. It may be possible for a firm to achieve cost savings (economies of scale) by consolidating shipments from several factories at the warehouse and then sending them together to retail outlets. This type of approach is the basis for the *hub-and-spoke* system of transportation employed by most major U.S. airlines. For example, most travel on Delta Air Lines from the Western U.S. to the Eastern U.S. (or vice versa) involves a connection through Delta's hub in Atlanta, Georgia.

Assignment Model

An **assignment model** *seeks to find the optimal one-to-one assignment of people to projects, jobs to machines, and so on.*

The **assignment model** refers to the class of LP problems that involve determining the most efficient assignment of people to projects, salespeople to territories, contracts to bidders, jobs to machines, and so on. The typical objective is to minimize total cost or total time of performing the tasks at hand, although a maximization objective is also possible. An important characteristic of assignment models is that each job or worker can be assigned to at most one machine or project, and vice versa.

Maximal-Flow Model

A **maximal-flow model** *finds the maximum flow possible through a network.*

Consider a network that has a specific starting point (called the *origin*) and a specific ending point (called the *destination*). The arcs in the network have capacities that limit the amounts of flow that can occur on them. These capacities can be different for different arcs. The **maximal-flow model** finds the maximum flow that can occur from the origin to the destination through this network. This model can be used to determine, for example, the maximum number of vehicles (cars, trucks, and so forth) that can go through a network of roads from one location to another.

Shortest-Path Model

A **shortest-path model** *finds the shortest route from an origin to a destination.*

Consider a network that has a specified origin and a specified destination. The arcs in the network are such that there are many paths available to go from the origin to the destination. The **shortest-path model** finds the shortest path or route through this network from the origin to the destination. For example, this model can be used to find the shortest distance and route from one city to another through a network of roads. The *length* of each arc can be a function of its distance, travel time, travel cost, or any other measure.

Minimal-Spanning Tree Model

A **minimal-spanning tree model** *connects all nodes in a network while minimizing total distance.*

The **minimal-spanning tree model** determines the path through the network that connects all the points. The most common objective is to minimize total distance of all arcs used in the path. For example, when the points represent houses in a subdivision, the minimal-spanning tree model can be used to determine the best way to connect all the houses to electrical power, water systems, and so on, in a way that minimizes the total distance or length of power lines or water pipes.

All the examples used to describe the various network models in this chapter are rather small (compared to real problems), to make it easier for you to understand the models. In some cases, the small size of these network examples may make them solvable by inspection or intuition. For larger real-world problems, however, finding a solution can be very difficult and requires the use of computer-based modeling approaches, as discussed here.

5.2 Characteristics of Network Models

A **node** *is a specific point or location in a network.*

An **arc** *connects two nodes to each other.*

Each of the circles (numbered 1 to 5) in Figure 5.1 is called a *node*. A node can be defined as the location of a specific point on the network. For example, nodes could represent cities on a road network, Ethernet ports on a campus computer network, houses in a city's water supply network, etc. An *arc* is a line that connects two nodes to each other. Arcs could represent roads that connect cities, computer network cables between various Ethernet ports, pipes that carry water to each house, etc. Figure 5.1 shows a network that has 5 nodes and 10 arcs.

Types of Arcs

Arcs can be one way or two way.

As shown in Figure 5.1, it is not necessary for an arc to exist between every pair of nodes in a network. A network that does have arcs between all pairs of nodes is called a *fully connected* network. Arcs can be either *unidirectional* (meaning that flow can occur only in one direction, as in a one-way road) or *bidirectional* (meaning that flow can occur in either direction). From a modeling perspective, it is convenient to represent a bidirectional arc with a pair of unidirectional arcs with opposite flow directions. This concept is illustrated in Figure 5.1 by the pairs of arcs between nodes 1 and 3, nodes 3 and 5, and nodes 2 and 4. Flows between all other pairs of nodes in Figure 5.1 are unidirectional.

Arcs can also be classified as capacitated or uncapacitated. A *capacitated* arc has a limited capacity, as in the case of a water pipe or a road. An *uncapacitated* arc, in contrast, can support an unlimited flow. In practice, this does not necessarily mean that the arc has infinite capacity. Rather, it means that the arc's capacity is so high that it is not a constraint in the model. An example could be a road in a small, rural area. The road rarely encounters traffic congestion because its capacity is far greater than the number of vehicles traveling on it at any one time.

Types of Nodes

Nodes can be **origins, destinations,** *or* **transshipment** *nodes.*

Nodes can be classified as *supply nodes*, *demand nodes*, or *transshipment* nodes. A supply node, also known as an origin or a source, denotes a location such as a factory that creates goods. That is, goods enter the network at that node.

FIGURE 5.1
Example of a Network
Note: Nodes are circles; arcs are lines.

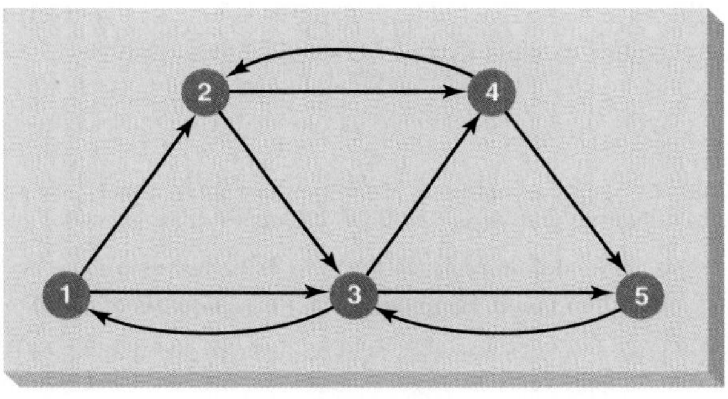

A demand node, also known as a destination or a sink, denotes a location such as a retail outlet that consumes goods. That is, goods leave the network at that node.

A transshipment node denotes a location through which goods pass on their way to or from other locations. In many practical networks, the same node can be a combination of a supply node, a demand node, and a transshipment node. For example, in the case of Delta Air Lines, Atlanta is a supply node for people starting their trip from Atlanta, a demand node for people ending their trip in Atlanta, and a transshipment node for people taking connecting flights through Atlanta.

Why are transportation models (and other network flow models) a special case of LP models? The reason is that many network models share some common characteristics, as follows:

1. In *all* network models, the decision variables represent the amounts of flows (or shipments) that occur on the unidirectional arcs in the network. For example, the LP model for the network shown in Figure 5.1 will have 10 decision variables representing the amounts of flows on the 10 unidirectional arcs.
2. Second, there will be a *flow balance* constraint written for each node in the network. These flow balance constraints calculate the *net flow* at each node (i.e., the difference between the total flow on all arcs entering a node and the total flow on all arcs leaving the node):

$$\text{Net flow} = (\text{total flow } \textit{in} \text{ to node}) - (\text{Total flow } \textit{out} \text{ of node}) \quad \textbf{(5-1)}$$

The net flow at a node is the difference between the total flow in to the node and the total flow out of the node.

At supply nodes, the total flow *out* of the node will exceed the total flow *in* to the node because goods are created at the node. In fact, at a pure supply node, there will only be flows out of the node (i.e., the total flow out will be a positive quantity) and no flows in to the node (i.e., the total flow in will be zero). The net flow represents the amount of goods created (i.e., the supply) at that node. Note that because the flow out is larger than the flow in at supply nodes, the resulting net flow will be a *negative* quantity. For this reason, as we will see shortly, we will express supply values (i.e., net flows at supply nodes) as negative numbers in our model.

On the other hand, at demand nodes, the total flow *out* of the node will be less than the total flow *in* to the node because goods are consumed at the node. At a pure demand node, there will only be flows in to the node (i.e., the total flow in will be a positive quantity) and no flows out of the node (i.e., the total flow out will be zero). The net flow, which represents the amount of goods consumed (i.e., the demand) at that node, will therefore be a *positive* quantity. For this reason, as we will again see shortly, we will express demand values (i.e., net flows at demand nodes) as positive numbers in our model.[1]

At pure transshipment nodes, goods are neither created nor consumed. The total flow *out* of such a node equals the total flow *in* to the node, and the net flow is therefore zero.
3. The constraint coefficients (i.e., the coefficients in front of decision variables in a constraint) for all flow balance constraints and most other problem-specific constraints in network models equal either 0 or 1. That is, if a decision variable exists in a constraint in a network model, its constraint coefficient is usually 1. This special trait allows network flow models to be solved very quickly, using specialized algorithms. However, we use Solver in the same manner as in Chapters 2 and 3 to solve these models here.

If all supplies and demands are integers, all flows in a network will also be integer values.

4. If all supply values at the supply nodes and all demand values at the demand nodes are whole numbers (i.e., integer values), the solution to a network model will automatically result in integer values for the decision variables, even if we don't impose an explicit condition to this effect. This property is especially useful in modeling the assignment and shortest-path models discussed later in this chapter.

---

[1] Some students may find it confusing, and somewhat counterintuitive, to write supply values as negative numbers. To avoid this, you may prefer to define net flows differently at supply nodes and demand nodes, as follows:

$$\text{Net flow at demand nodes} = (\text{Total flow } \textit{in} \text{ to node}) - (\text{Total flow } \textit{out} \text{ of node})$$
$$\text{Net flow at supply nodes} = (\text{Total flow } \textit{out} \text{ of node}) - (\text{Total flow } \textit{in} \text{ to node})$$

In this textbook, however, we have chosen to use a single definition of net flow at both these types of nodes. We will therefore express supply values as negative numbers and demand values as positive numbers in our models.

IN ACTION Improving Freight Car Assignment at Union Pacific Railroad

Union Pacific Railroad (UP), the largest railroad in North America, has about 32,300 miles of track, 8,500 locomotives, 104,700 freight cars, 50,000 employees, and an annual payroll of $3.7 billion. UP faces a difficult problem in assigning empty freight cars to customers since these assignments depend on many factors including the location of empty cars, the demand urgency, and whether or not cars can be substituted. Working with researchers at Purdue University, UP developed a transportation optimization model to address this problem, with the objective of reducing transportation costs while improving delivery time and customer satisfaction. The resulting real-time decision system is compatible with UP's operational practices, and can be used to assign and reassign empty freight cars in a short time.

UP has achieved significant savings in transportation costs due to the implementation of this system. In addition, UP experienced a 35% ROI due to reductions in demand fulfillment personnel that was made possible by this project. As an added benefit, this project also helped UP obtain a better understanding of the importance and the accuracy required for many of the data elements, and gain valuable insight into some of the issues and tradeoff that arise in automating the assignment of empty freight cars.

Source: Based on A. K. Narisetty et al. "An Optimization Model for Empty Freight Car Assignment at Union Pacific Railroad," *Interfaces* 38, 2 (March–April 2008): 89–102.

5.3 Transportation Model

Let us begin to illustrate the transportation model with an example dealing with the Executive Furniture Company. This company manufactures office desks at three locations: Des Moines, Evansville, and Fort Lauderdale. The firm distributes the desks through regional warehouses located in Albuquerque, Boston, and Cleveland (see Figure 5.2). Estimates of the monthly supplies available at each factory and the monthly desk demands at each of the three warehouses are shown in Figure 5.3.

Our goal is to select the shipping routes and units to be shipped to minimize total transportation cost.

The firm has found that production costs per desk are identical at each factory, and hence the only relevant costs are those of shipping from each factory to each warehouse. These costs, shown in Table 5.1, are assumed to be constant, regardless of the volume shipped.[2] The transportation problem can now be described as *determining the number of desks to be shipped on each route so as to minimize total transportation cost*. This, of course, must be done while observing the restrictions regarding factory supplies and warehouse demands.

FIGURE 5.2 Geographic Locations of Executive Furniture's Factories and Warehouses

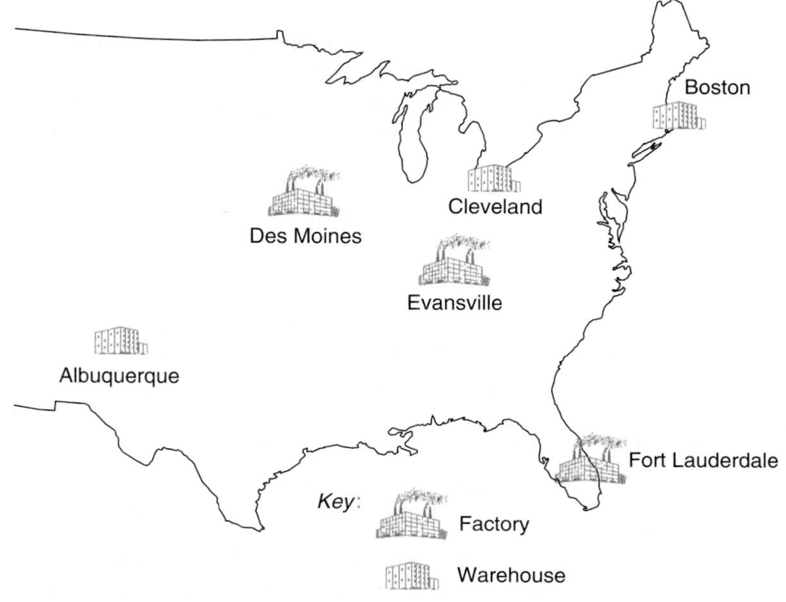

[2] The other assumptions that held for LP problems (see Chapter 2) are still applicable to transportation problems.

FIGURE 5.3
Network Model for Executive Furniture—Transportation

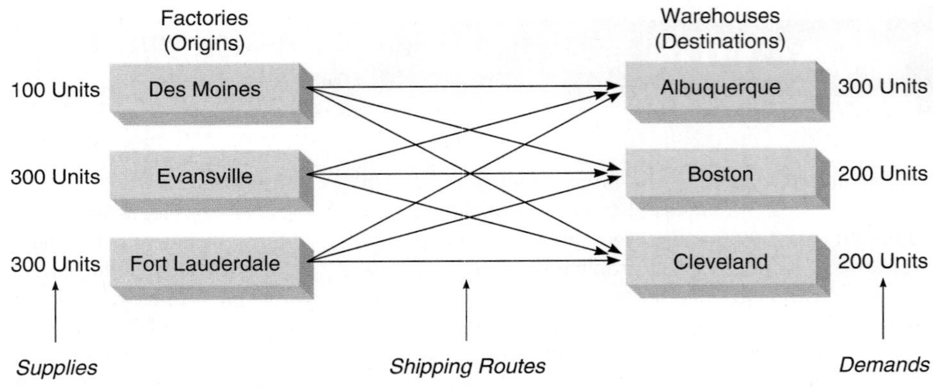

TABLE 5.1
Transportation Costs per Desk for Executive Furniture

	TO		
FROM	ALBUQUERQUE	BOSTON	CLEVELAND
Des Moines	\$5	\$4	\$3
Evansville	\$8	\$4	\$3
Fort Lauderdale	\$9	\$7	\$5

Balanced supply and demand occurs when total supply equals total demand.

We see in Figure 5.3 that the total factory supply available (700) is exactly equal to the total warehouse demand (700). When this situation of equal total demand and total supply occurs (something that is rather unusual in real life), a **balanced model** is said to exist. Later in this section we look at how to deal with *unbalanced* models—namely, those in which total demands are greater than or less than total supplies.

LP Formulation for Executive Furniture's Transportation Model

Because there are three factories (Des Moines, Evansville, and Fort Lauderdale) and three warehouses (Albuquerque, Boston, and Cleveland), there are nine potential shipping routes. We therefore need nine decision variables to define the number of units that would be shipped from each supply node (factory) to each demand node (warehouse). In general, the number of decision variables in a basic transportation model is the number of supply nodes multiplied by the number of demand nodes.

It is convenient to express all network flows by using double-subscripted variables.

Recall from section 5.2 that in the transportation model (as well as in other network flow models), decision variables denote the flow between two nodes in the network. Therefore, it is convenient to represent these flows by using double-subscripted decision variables. We let the first subscript represent the supply node and the second subscript represent the demand node of the flow. Hence, for the Executive Furniture example, let

$$X_{ij} = \text{number of desks shipped from factory } i \text{ to warehouse } j$$

where

$$i = \text{D (for Des Moines), E (for Evansville), or F (for Fort Lauderdale)}$$
$$j = \text{A (for Albuquerque), B (for Boston), or C (for Cleveland)}$$

OBJECTIVE FUNCTION The objective function for this model seeks to minimize the total transportation cost and can be expressed as

$$\text{Minimize total shipping costs} = 5X_{DA} + 4X_{DB} + 3X_{DC} + 8X_{EA} + 4X_{EB} + 3X_{EC} + 9X_{FA} + 7X_{FB} + 5X_{FC}$$

We write a flow balance *constraint for each node in the network.*

CONSTRAINTS As discussed earlier, we need to write *flow balance* constraints for each node in the network. Because the Executive Furniture example is a balanced model, we know that all desks will be shipped from the factories and all demand will be satisfied at the warehouses. The number of desks shipped from each factory will therefore be equal to the number of desks available, and the number of desks received at each warehouse will be equal to the number of desks required.

We write a supply constraint *for each factory.*

SUPPLY CONSTRAINTS The *supply constraints* deal with the supplies available at the three factories. At all factories, the total flow *in* is zero because there are no arcs coming into these nodes. The net flow at the Des Moines factory (for example) can therefore be expressed as

$$\begin{aligned}\text{Net flow at Des Moinse} &= (\text{Total flow } in \text{ to Des Moines}) - (\text{Total flow } out \text{ of Des Moines})\\ &= (0) - (X_{DA} + X_{DB} + X_{DC})\end{aligned}$$

Supplies are usually written as negative quantities.

This net flow is equal to the total number of desks available (supply) at Des Moines. Recall from section 5.2 that we express supply values as negative numbers in our network flow balance constraints. Therefore, the right-hand side (RHS) is written as -100 in this equation:

$$\text{Net flow at Des Moines} = -X_{DA} - X_{DB} - X_{DC} = -100 \qquad \text{(Des Moines supply)}$$

Likewise, the flow balance constraints at the other factories can be expressed as

$$\begin{aligned}-X_{EA} - X_{EB} - X_{EC} &= -300 \qquad \text{(Evansville supply)}\\ -X_{FA} - X_{FB} - X_{FC} &= -300 \qquad \text{(Fort Lauderdale supply)}\end{aligned}$$

As noted earlier, if you prefer not to have negative quantities on the RHS of the supply constraints, you can redefine the net flow at *supply nodes* as equal to (Total flow *out* of node – Total flow *in* to node), and rewrite these equations as

$$\begin{aligned}X_{DA} + X_{DB} + X_{DC} &= 100 \qquad \text{(Des Moines supply)}\\ X_{EA} + X_{EB} + X_{EC} &= 300 \qquad \text{(Evansville supply)}\\ X_{FA} + X_{FB} + X_{FC} &= 300 \qquad \text{(Fort Lauderdale supply)}\end{aligned}$$

We write a demand constraint for each warehouse.

DEMAND CONSTRAINTS Now, let us model the *demand constraints* that deal with the warehouse demands. At all warehouses, the total flow *out* is zero because there are no arcs leaving from these nodes. The net flow at the Albuquerque warehouse, for example, can therefore be expressed as

$$\begin{aligned}\text{Net flow at Albuquerque} &= (\text{Total flow } in \text{ to Albuquerque}) - (\text{Total flow } out \text{ of Albuquerque})\\ &= (X_{DA} + X_{EA} + X_{FA}) - (0)\end{aligned}$$

Net flow at a demand node is written as a positive number.

This net flow is equal to the total number of desks required (demand) at Albuquerque. Recall from section 5.2 that we express demand values at demand nodes as positive numbers in our network flow balance constraints. Therefore,

$$\text{Net flow at Albuquerque} = (X_{DA} + X_{EA} + X_{FA}) = 300 \qquad \text{(Albuquerque demand)}$$

Likewise, the flow balance constraints at the other warehouses can be expressed as

$$\begin{aligned}X_{DB} + X_{EB} + X_{FB} &= 200 \qquad \text{(Boston demand)}\\ X_{DC} + X_{EC} + X_{FC} &= 200 \qquad \text{(Cleveland demand)}\end{aligned}$$

In general, the number of constraints in the basic transportation model is the sum of the number of supply nodes and the number of demand nodes. There could, however, be other problem-specific constraints that restrict shipments in individual routes. For example, if we wished to ensure that no more than 100 desks are shipped from Evansville to Cleveland, an additional constraint in the model would be $X_{EC} \leq 100$.

Solving the Transportation Model Using Excel

WWW

File: 5-1.xls

Screenshot 5-1 shows the Excel setup and Solver entries for Executive Furniture's transportation model. Consistent with our choice of using the same definition of net flow at all types of nodes, all supply values are expressed here as negative values (cells M8:M10). The Excel layout in Screenshot 5-1 follows the same logic as in Chapter 3. This means that (1) each decision variable is modeled in a separate column of the worksheet, and (2) the objective function and left-hand side (LHS) formulas for all constraints are computed using Excel's SUMPRODUCT function.

SCREENSHOT 5-1 Excel Layout and Solver Entries for Executive Furniture—Transportation

	A	B	C	D	E	F	G	H	I	J	K	L	M
1	**Executive Furniture (Transportation)**												
2													
3		X_{DA}	X_{DB}	X_{DC}	X_{EA}	X_{EB}	X_{EC}	X_{FA}	X_{FB}	X_{FC}			
4		DM to Albuq	DM to Bost	DM to Clev	Evan to Albuq	Evan to Bost	Evan to Clev	FL to Albuq	FL to Bost	FL to Clev			
5	Desks shipped	100.0	0.0	0.0	0.0	200.0	100.0	200.0	0.0	100.0			
6	Cost	$5	$4	$3	$8	$4	$3	$9	$7	$5	$3,900		
7	**Constraints:**												
8	Des Moines supply	-1	-1	-1							-100.0	=	-100
9	Evansville supply				-1	-1	-1				-300.0	=	-300
10	Fort Lauderdale supply							-1	-1	-1	-300.0	=	-300
11	Albuquerque demand	1			1			1			300.0	=	300
12	Boston demand		1			1			1		200.0	=	200
13	Cleveland demand			1			1			1	200.0	=	200
14											**LHS**	**Sign**	**RHS**

Solver Parameters

Set Objective: $K$6

To: Max Min Value Of: 0

By Changing Variable Cells: $B$5:$J$5

Subject to the Constraints: $K$8:$K$13 = $M$8:$M$13

Add

Decision variable names are shown here for information purposes only.

Supplies are shown as negative numbers.

All entries in column K are computed using the SUMPRODUCT function.

All constraints are = since the problem is balanced.

Excel Notes

- The Companion Website for this textbook, at www.pearsonhighered.com/balakrishnan, contains the Excel file for each sample problem discussed here. The relevant file name is shown on the margin next to each example.
- In each of our Excel layouts, for clarity, changing variable cells are shaded yellow, the objective cell is shaded green, and cells containing the LHS formula for each constraint are shaded blue.

The optimum solution for Executive Furniture Company is to ship 100 desks from Des Moines to Albuquerque, 200 desks from Evansville to Boston, 100 desks from Evansville to Cleveland, 200 desks from Fort Lauderdale to Albuquerque, and 100 desks from Fort Lauderdale to Cleveland. The total shipping cost is $3,900. Observe that because all supplies and demands were integer values, all shipments turned out to be integer values as well.

Alternate Excel Layout for the Transportation Model

The alternate Excel layout for network flow models uses a tabular form to model the flows.

File: 5-2.xls

For many network models, the number of arcs (and, hence, decision variables) could be quite large. Modeling the problem by using the layout used in Screenshot 5-1 can therefore become quite cumbersome. For this reason, it may be more convenient to model network flow models in Excel in such a way that decision variables are in a *tabular* form, with rows (for example) denoting supply nodes and columns denoting demand nodes. The formula view of the alternate Excel layout for Executive Furniture's transportation model is shown in Screenshot 5-2A, and the optimal solution is shown in Screenshot 5-2B.

By adding the row (or column) entries, we can easily calculate the appropriate total flows *out* and total flows *in* at each node. It is then possible to model a flow balance constraint for each node by calculating each net flow as the difference between the total flow *in* to the node and the

SCREENSHOT 5-2A Formula View of Alternate Excel Layout for Executive Furniture—Transportation

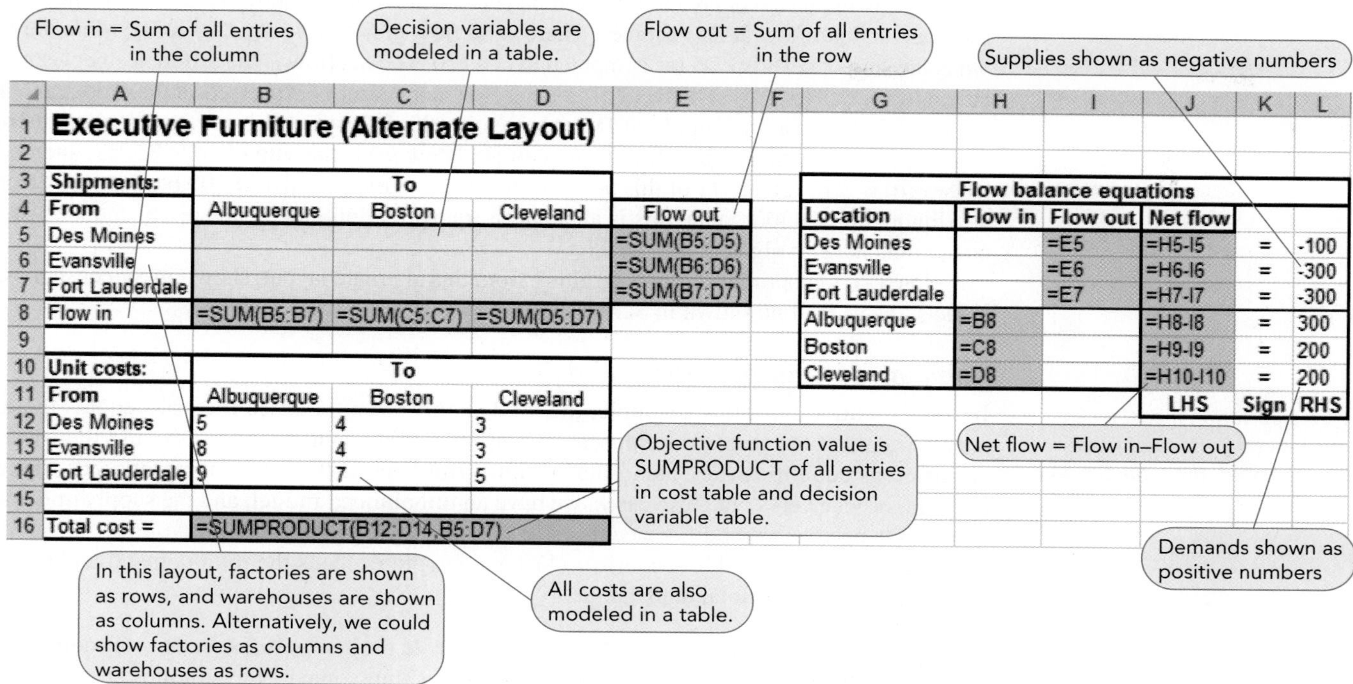
Flow in = Sum of all entries in the column
Decision variables are modeled in a table.
Flow out = Sum of all entries in the row
Supplies shown as negative numbers
Objective function value is SUMPRODUCT of all entries in cost table and decision variable table.
Net flow = Flow in–Flow out
Demands shown as positive numbers
In this layout, factories are shown as rows, and warehouses are shown as columns. Alternatively, we could show factories as columns and warehouses as rows.
All costs are also modeled in a table.

Executive Furniture (Alternate Layout)

Shipments:	To			
From	Albuquerque	Boston	Cleveland	Flow out
Des Moines				=SUM(B5:D5)
Evansville				=SUM(B6:D6)
Fort Lauderdale				=SUM(B7:D7)
Flow in	=SUM(B5:B7)	=SUM(C5:C7)	=SUM(D5:D7)	

Unit costs:	To		
From	Albuquerque	Boston	Cleveland
Des Moines	5	4	3
Evansville	8	4	3
Fort Lauderdale	9	7	5

Total cost = =SUMPRODUCT(B12:D14,B5:D7)

Flow balance equations					
Location	Flow in	Flow out	Net flow		
Des Moines		=E5	=H5-I5	=	-100
Evansville		=E6	=H6-I6	=	-300
Fort Lauderdale		=E7	=H7-I7	=	-300
Albuquerque	=B8		=H8-I8	=	300
Boston	=C8		=H9-I9	=	200
Cleveland	=D8		=H10-I10	=	200
			LHS	Sign	RHS

SCREENSHOT 5-2B Solver Entries for Alternate Layout of Executive Furniture—Transportation

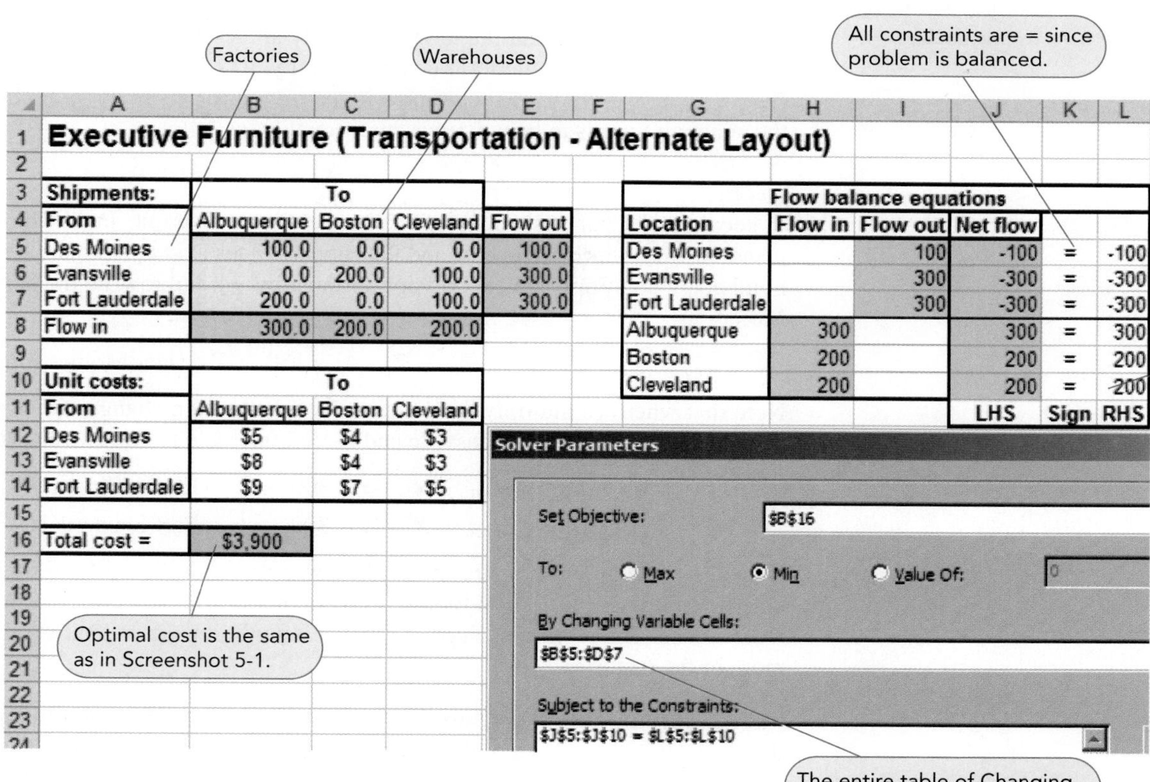
Factories
Warehouses
All constraints are = since problem is balanced.
Optimal cost is the same as in Screenshot 5-1.
The entire table of Changing Variable Cells can be specified as one block in Solver.
Solver Parameters
Set Objective: $B$16
To: Max Min Value Of: 0
By Changing Variable Cells: $B$5:$D$7
Subject to the Constraints: $J$5:$J$10 = $L$5:$L$10

Executive Furniture (Transportation - Alternate Layout)

Shipments:	To			
From	Albuquerque	Boston	Cleveland	Flow out
Des Moines	100.0	0.0	0.0	100.0
Evansville	0.0	200.0	100.0	300.0
Fort Lauderdale	200.0	0.0	100.0	300.0
Flow in	300.0	200.0	200.0	

Unit costs:	To		
From	Albuquerque	Boston	Cleveland
Des Moines	$5	$4	$3
Evansville	$8	$4	$3
Fort Lauderdale	$9	$7	$5

Total cost = $3,900

Flow balance equations					
Location	Flow in	Flow out	Net flow		
Des Moines		100	-100	=	-100
Evansville		300	-300	=	-300
Fort Lauderdale		300	-300	=	-300
Albuquerque	300		300	=	300
Boston	200		200	=	200
Cleveland	200		200	=	200
			LHS	Sign	RHS

total flow *out* of the node. To make this easy to understand, we have arranged these entries in a separate box in our Excel layout. For example, cells H5, I5, and J5 show, respectively, the flow *in*, flow *out*, and net flow at Des Moines. There is no flow *in* (i.e., it is equal to zero), while the flow *out* is the sum of cells B5:D5 (as computed in cell E5). The net flow is the difference between cells H5 and I5 (i.e., H5 – I5). The RHS of this net flow constraint is expressed in the model as −100 (in cell L5) because the supply at Des Moines is 100. Likewise, the net flow at Albuquerque (cell J8) is computed as (H8 – I8), where cell H8 (flow *in*) is the sum of cells B5:B7, and cell I8 (flow *out*) is zero. The RHS of this net flow constraint is expressed as +300 because the demand at Albuquerque is 300. Since this is a balanced transportation model, all supply and all demand constraints have = signs in the model.

Note that the optimal solution resulting from this alternate layout, shown in Screenshot 5-2B, is the same as the one shown in Screenshot 5-1.

Unbalanced Transportation Models

A transportation model is **unbalanced** *if the total supply does not equal the total demand.*

In the Executive Furniture example, the total supply from the three factories equals the total requirements at the three warehouses. All supply and demand constraints could therefore be specified as equalities (i.e., using the = sign). But what if the total supply exceeds the total demand, or vice versa? In these cases, we have an **unbalanced model**, and the supply or demand constraints need to be modified accordingly.

There are two possible scenarios: (1) Total supply exceeds the total demand and (2) total supply is less than the total demand.

TOTAL SUPPLY EXCEEDS THE TOTAL DEMAND If total supply exceeds total demand, all demands will be fully satisfied at the demand nodes, but some of the supplies at one or more supply nodes will not need to be shipped out. That is, they will remain at the supply nodes. To allow for this possibility, the total flow *out* of each supply node should be permitted to be smaller than the supply at that node. The total flow *in* to the demand nodes will, however, continue to be written with = signs.

If total supply exceeds total demand, the supply constraints are written as inequalities.

Assume that the supply and demand values in the Executive Furniture example are altered so that the total supply at the three factories exceeds the total demand at the three warehouses. For example, assume that the monthly supply at Des Moines is 150 desks. The total supply is now 750 desks, while the total demand is only 700 desks. The total flow out of Des Moines (i.e., $X_{DA} + X_{DB} + X_{DC}$) should now be permitted to be smaller than the total supply. That is, the constraint needs to be written as an inequality, as follows:

$$X_{DA} + X_{DB} + X_{DC} \leq 150$$

In keeping with our convention of writing net flow constraints in which flows *out* of nodes have negative constraint coefficients and the supply values at supply nodes are expressed as negative numbers, we multiply this expression through by −1 and rewrite the supply constraint for Des Moines as

$$-X_{DA} - X_{DB} - X_{DC} \geq -150 \qquad \text{(Des Moines supply)}$$

Note that when we multiply the equation by −1, the sign changes from ≤ to ≥. Likewise, the supply constraints at the Evansville and Fort Lauderdale factories would need to be revised as

$$-X_{EA} - X_{EB} - X_{EC} \geq -300 \qquad \text{(Evansville supply)}$$
$$-X_{FA} - X_{FB} - X_{FC} \geq -300 \qquad \text{(Fort Lauderdale supply)}$$

Because the demand constraints at the three warehouses will continue to be written as = constraints, the solution will show movements of 700 desks between the factories and the warehouses. The remaining supply of 50 desks will remain at their original locations at one or more of the factories.

TOTAL SUPPLY IS LESS THAN THE TOTAL DEMAND When total supply is less than total demand, all items at the supply nodes will be shipped out, but demands at one or more demand nodes will remain unsatisfied. To allow for this possibility, the total flow *in* at demand nodes should be permitted to be smaller than the requirement at those nodes. The total flow *out* of supply nodes will, however, continue to be written with = signs.

If total demand exceeds total supply, the demand constraints are written as inequalities.

Assume that the supply and demand values in the Executive Furniture example are altered so that the total supply at the three factories is now *less* than the total demand at the three warehouses. For example, assume that the monthly demand at the Albuquerque warehouse is 350 desks. The total flow *in* to Albuquerque (i.e., $X_{DA} + X_{EA} + X_{FA}$) should now be permitted to be smaller than the total demand. The demand constraint for this warehouse should therefore be written as

$$X_{DA} + X_{EA} + X_{FA} \leq 350 \qquad \text{(Albuquerque demand)}$$

Likewise, the demand constraints at the Boston and Cleveland warehouses would need to be written as

$$X_{DB} + X_{EB} + X_{FB} \leq 200 \qquad \text{(Boston demand)}$$
$$X_{DC} + X_{EC} + X_{FC} \leq 200 \qquad \text{(Cleveland demand)}$$

In this case, because the supply constraints at the three factories will continue to be written as = constraints, the solution will show movements of 700 desks between the factories and the warehouses. The remaining demand of 50 desks will remain unsatisfied, and one or more of the warehouses will not get its full share of desks.

Use of a Dummy Location to Balance an Unbalanced Model

Some students may find it confusing to deal with ≤ and ≥ signs in the net flow constraints for unbalanced models. One way to avoid this is to use a dummy location to transform an unbalanced model into a balanced model. We illustrate this by revisiting the situation we just considered, where the total supply is 750 desks while the total demand is only 700 desks. We can covert this to a balanced model by creating a dummy demand node with a demand of 50 desks (i.e., the excess supply). Likewise, if the total demand is larger than the total supply, we can covert this to a balanced model by creating a dummy supply node with a supply value equal to the excess demand. All supply and demand constraints can then be written with = signs in the model.

What about the unit objective coefficients (e.g., shipping costs) from the dummy location? Since the dummy location doesn't actually exist, we need to make sure the solution focuses on flows from or to locations that actually exist and that it uses the dummy location only as a last resort to balance the flows. An easy way to accomplish this is to assign an objective coefficient of ∞ (for minimization models) or $-\infty$ (for maximization models) to flows from or to the dummy location.[3]

Alternate Optimal Solutions

It is quite common for transportation models to have alternate optimal solutions.

Just as with regular LP problems, it is possible for a transportation model to have alternate or multiple optimal solutions. In fact, having multiple optimal solutions is quite common in transportation models. Practically speaking, multiple optimal solutions provide management with greater flexibility in selecting and using resources. Chapter 4 (section 4.4, on page 138) indicates that if the allowable increase or allowable decrease for the objective coefficient of a variable has a value of zero (in the Variable Cells table of the Solver Sensitivity Report), this usually indicates the presence of alternate optimal solutions. In Solved Problem 4-1 (see page 145), we saw how Solver can be used to identify alternate optimal solutions.

An Application of the Transportation Model: Facility Location

Deciding where to locate a new facility within an overall distribution system is aided by the transportation model.

The transportation model has proved to be especially useful in helping firms decide where to locate a new factory or warehouse. Because a new location has major financial implications for a firm, several alternative locations must usually be considered and evaluated. Even though a firm may consider a wide variety of subjective factors, including quality of labor supply, presence of labor unions, community attitude, utilities, and recreational and educational facilities,

---

[3] ∞ here simply means a value that is very large when compared to other objective coefficients in the model. For example, if the other objective coefficients have values such as \$4, \$5, etc., an objective coefficient of \$200 will be sufficient to represent ∞.

IN ACTION Answering Warehousing Questions at San Miguel Corporation

San Miguel Corporation, based in the Philippines, faces unique distribution challenges. With more than 300 products, including beer, alcoholic drinks, juices, bottled water, feeds, poultry, and meats to be distributed to every corner of the Philippine archipelago, shipping and warehousing costs make up a large part of total produce cost.

The company grappled with these questions:

- Which products should be produced in each plant, and in which warehouse should they be stored?
- Which warehouses should be maintained and where should new ones be located?
- When should warehouses be closed or opened?
- Which demand centers should each warehouse serve?

Turning to the transportation model, San Miguel was able to answer these questions. The firm used these types of warehouses: company owned and staffed, rented but company staffed, and contracted out (i.e., not company owned or staffed).

San Miguel's Operations Research Department computed that the firm saves $7.5 million annually with optimal beer warehouse configurations over the existing national configurations. In addition, analysis of warehousing for ice cream and other frozen products indicated that the optimal configuration of warehouses, compared with existing setup, produced a $2.17 million savings.

Source: Based on E. del Rosario. "Logistical Nightmare," *OR/MS Today* 26, 2 (April 1999): 44–46. Reprinted with permission.

a final decision also involves minimizing total production and shipping costs. This means that the **facility location analysis** should analyze each location alternative within the framework of the overall distribution system. The new location that will yield the minimum cost for the entire system should be the one recommended.

We solve a separate transportation model with each location to find the location with the lowest system cost.

How do we use the transportation model to help in this decision-making process? Consider a firm that is trying to decide between several competing locations for a new factory. To determine which new factory yields the lowest total systemwide cost, we solve separate transportation models: one for each of the possible locations. We illustrate this application of the transportation model in Solved Problem 5-1 at the end of this chapter, with the case of the Hardgrave Machine Company, which is trying to decide between Seattle, Washington, and Birmingham, Alabama, as a site to build a new factory.

5.4 Transportation Models with Max-Min and Min-Max Objectives

Max-Min ***and*** **Min-Max** ***models seek to reduce the variability in the values of the decision variables.***

In all LP models discussed so far (starting in Chapter 2), the objective function has sought to either maximize or minimize some function of the decision variables. However, there are some situations, especially in transportation settings, where we may be interested in a special type of objective function. The objective in these situations may be to *maximize the minimum value* of the decision variables (**Max-Min model**), or, alternatively, *minimize the maximum value* of the decision variables (**Min-Max model**). These types of objective functions are applicable when we want to reduce the variability in the values of the decision variables. Let us illustrate this issue by revisiting Executive Furniture's transportation example and formulating it as a Min-Max model.

Managers at Executive Furniture noticed that the optimal solution to their transportation problem (Screenshot 5-2B) recommends the use of only five of the nine available shipping routes. Further, the entire demand at Boston is being satisfied by the factory at Evansville. This means that if, for any reason, the Evansville factory has a production problem in a given month, the Boston warehouse is severely affected. To avoid this situation, the managers would like to distribute the shipments among all shipping routes, to the extent possible. They would like to achieve this by minimizing the maximum amount shipped on any specific route. Note that because the total number of desks available is fixed, if we reduce the number shipped on any route, shipments on some other route(s) will automatically increase. This implies that the difference between the largest and smallest shipments will be lowered to the extent allowed by the other constraints in the model.

To achieve this new objective, the managers are willing to allow an increase of up to 5% in the current total transportation cost. Because the current plan costs \$3,900 (Screenshot 5-2B), this implies that the maximum transportation cost allowed is $1.05 \times \$3{,}900 = \$4{,}095$.

FORMULATING THE PROBLEM To formulate this Min-Max model, we define a new decision variable as follows:

$$S = \text{maximum quantity shipped on any route}$$

The objective function is to minimize the value of S. We then set S to be greater than or equal to all the other decision variables (i.e., the nine shipping quantities) in the model. Note that doing so implies that S will be greater than the largest of the nine shipping amounts. Further, because S is being minimized in the objective function, S will automatically equal the maximum quantity shipped on any route. The complete LP model may be written as

$$\text{Minimize } S$$

subject to the constraints

$$
\begin{aligned}
-X_{DA} - X_{DB} - X_{DC} &= -100 && \text{(Des Moines supply)}\\
-X_{EA} - X_{EB} - X_{EC} &= -300 && \text{(Evansville supply)}\\
-X_{FA} - X_{FB} - X_{FC} &= -300 && \text{(Fort Launderdale supply)}\\
X_{DA} + X_{EA} + X_{FA} &= 300 && \text{(Albuquerque demand)}\\
X_{DB} + X_{EB} + X_{FB} &= 200 && \text{(Boston demand)}\\
X_{DC} + X_{EC} + X_{FC} &= 200 && \text{(Cleveland demand)}\\
5X_{DA} + 4X_{DB} + 3X_{DC} & && \\
+ 8X_{EA} + 4X_{EB} + 3X_{EC} & && \\
+ 9X_{FA} + 7X_{FB} + 5X_{FC} &\leq 4{,}095 && \text{(Cost contraint)}
\end{aligned}
$$

$$
\begin{array}{lll}
S \geq X_{DA} & S \geq X_{DB} & S \geq X_{DC}\\
S \geq X_{EA} & S \geq X_{EB} & S \geq X_{EC}\\
S \geq X_{FA} & S \geq X_{FB} & S \geq X_{FC}
\end{array}
$$

All variables ≥ 0

File: 5-3.xls

SOLVING THE PROBLEM The Excel layout and Solver entries for Executive Furniture's revised transportation model are shown in Screenshot 5-3. Notice that the objective cell (B16) is also a decision variable (i.e., changing variable cell). The flow balance equations are the same as in Screenshot 5-2B. However, we now have a new constraint on the total cost, as well as constraints specifying that cell B16 should be greater than or equal to each of the nine shipping routes (cells B5:D7).

The addition of constraints other than supply and demand constraints may cause the optimal solution in network flow models to no longer be integers.

INTERPRETING THE RESULTS The revised optimal solution costs \$4,095 and uses seven of the nine available shipping routes. The maximum number shipped on any route drops from 200 (in Screenshot 5-2B) to only 102.50. This solution reveals an interesting point. Recall that if all supply and demand values are integers, all flows are also integer values in network flow models. However, when we add additional constraints (i.e., other than supply and demand constraints), this integer solution property is destroyed, and the resulting solution can have fractional values. In Executive Furniture's case, the managers would need to round up and round down values appropriately to achieve an integer-valued shipping plan.

The LP model can be set up in a similar manner if the objective is to maximize the minimum value of the decision variables (i.e., Max-Min model). The only modifications needed to the Min-Max model discussed previously are to (1) change the objective from Max to Min and (2) change the sign in the constraints linking the variable S to the decision variables from $\geq$ to $\leq$.

SCREENSHOT 5-3 Excel Layout and Solver Entries for Executive Furniture—Min-Max

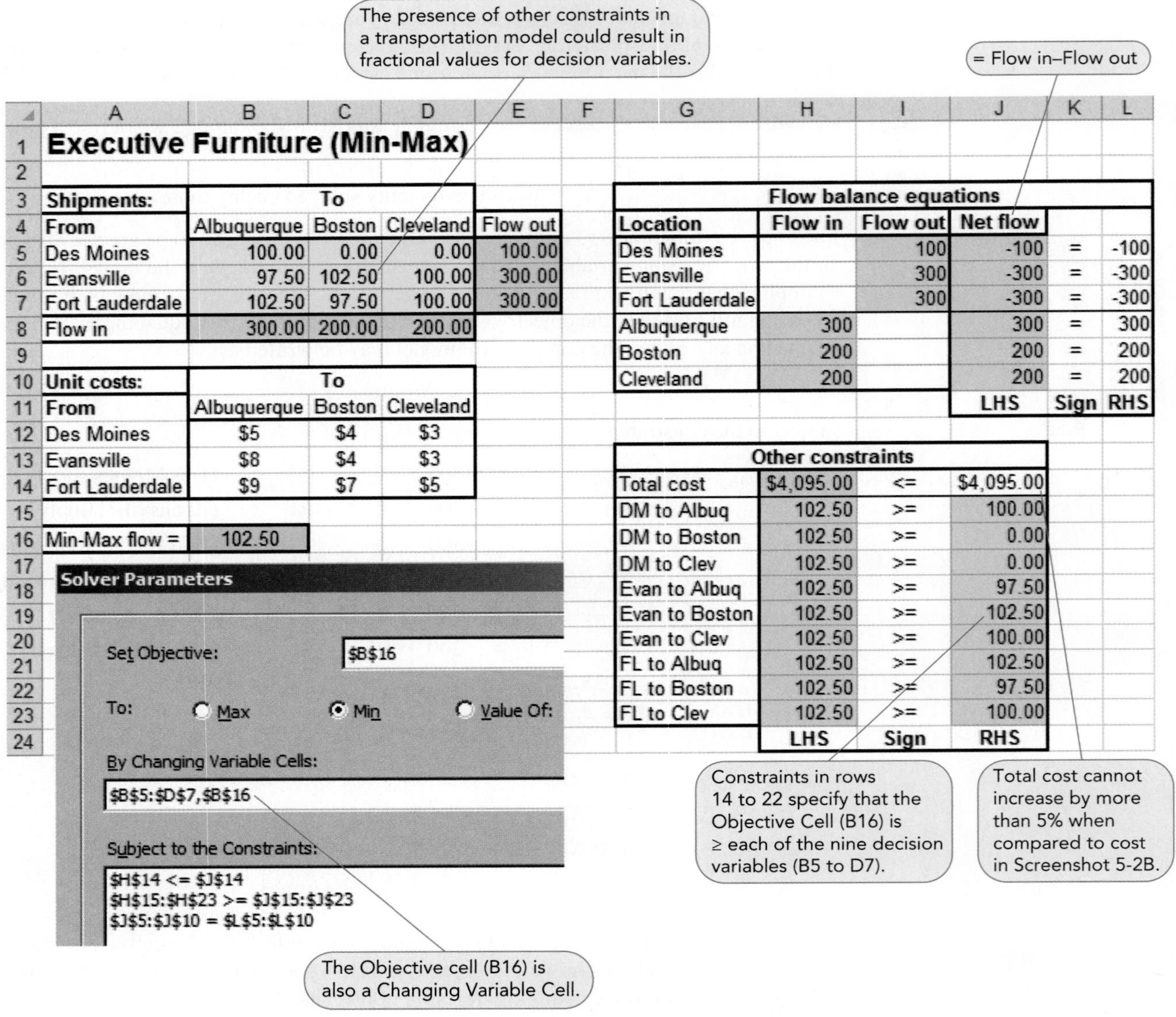

Executive Furniture (Min-Max)

Shipments:	To			
From	Albuquerque	Boston	Cleveland	Flow out
Des Moines	100.00	0.00	0.00	100.00
Evansville	97.50	102.50	100.00	300.00
Fort Lauderdale	102.50	97.50	100.00	300.00
Flow in	300.00	200.00	200.00	

Unit costs:	To		
From	Albuquerque	Boston	Cleveland
Des Moines	$5	$4	$3
Evansville	$8	$4	$3
Fort Lauderdale	$9	$7	$5

Min-Max flow = 102.50

Flow balance equations					
Location	Flow in	Flow out	Net flow		
Des Moines		100	-100	=	-100
Evansville		300	-300	=	-300
Fort Lauderdale		300	-300	=	-300
Albuquerque	300		300	=	300
Boston	200		200	=	200
Cleveland	200		200	=	200
			LHS	Sign	RHS

Other constraints			
Total cost	$4,095.00	<=	$4,095.00
DM to Albuq	102.50	>=	100.00
DM to Boston	102.50	>=	0.00
DM to Clev	102.50	>=	0.00
Evan to Albuq	102.50	>=	97.50
Evan to Boston	102.50	>=	102.50
Evan to Clev	102.50	>=	100.00
FL to Albuq	102.50	>=	102.50
FL to Boston	102.50	>=	97.50
FL to Clev	102.50	>=	100.00
	LHS	Sign	RHS

The presence of other constraints in a transportation model could result in fractional values for decision variables.
= Flow in–Flow out
Solver Parameters
Set Objective: $B$16
To: Max Min Value Of:
By Changing Variable Cells:
$B$5:$D$7,$B$16
Subject to the Constraints:
$H$14 <= $J$14
$H$15:$H$23 >= $J$15:$J$23
$J$5:$J$10 = $L$5:$L$10
Constraints in rows 14 to 22 specify that the Objective Cell (B16) is ≥ each of the nine decision variables (B5 to D7).
Total cost cannot increase by more than 5% when compared to cost in Screenshot 5-2B.
The Objective cell (B16) is also a Changing Variable Cell.

5.5 Transshipment Model

Transshipment models include nodes that can have shipments arrive as well as leave.

In the basic transportation model, shipments either flow *out* of supply nodes or flow *in* to demand nodes. That is, it is possible to explicitly distinguish between supply nodes and demand nodes for flows. In the more general form of the transportation model, called the transshipment model, flows can occur both *out* of and *in* to the same node in three ways:

1. If the total flow *in* to a node is less than the total flow *out* of the node, the node then represents a net creator of goods—that is, a supply node. The flow balance equation for this type of node will therefore have a negative RHS value.
2. If the total flow *in* to a node exceeds the total flow *out* of the node, the node then represents a net consumer of goods—that is, a demand node. The flow balance equation for this type of node will therefore have a positive RHS value.
3. If the total flow *in* to a node is equal to the total flow *out* of the node, the node then represents a pure transshipment node. The flow balance equation for this type of node will therefore have a zero RHS value.

We use two examples in the following sections to illustrate transshipment models. The first is a simple extension of the Executive Furniture Company's transportation model. The second is a larger example that includes some pure transshipment nodes.

Executive Furniture Company Example—Revisited

Transshipment example: A modified form of the Executive Furniture example.

Let us consider a modified version of the Executive Furniture Company example from section 5.3. As before, the company has factories in Des Moines, Evansville, and Fort Lauderdale and warehouses in Albuquerque, Cleveland, and Boston. Recall that the supply at each factory and demand at each warehouse are shown in Figure 5.3 on page 166.

Now suppose that due to a special contract with an Evansville-based shipping company, it is possible for Executive Furniture to ship desks from its Evansville factory to its three warehouses at very low unit shipping costs. These unit costs are so attractive that Executive Furniture is considering shipping all the desks produced at its other two factories (Des Moines and Fort Lauderdale) to Evansville and then using this new shipping company to move desks from Evansville to all its warehouses.

The revised unit shipping costs are shown in Table 5.2. Note that the Evansville factory now shows up both in the "From" and "To" entries because it is possible for this factory to receive desks from other factories and then ship them out to the warehouses. There are therefore two additional shipping routes available: Des Moines to Evansville and Fort Lauderdale to Evansville.

LP Formulation for Executive Furniture's Transshipment Model

The LP formulation for this model follows the same logic and structure as the formulation for Executive Furniture's transportation model (see section 5.3). However, we now have two *additional* decision variables for the two new shipping routes. We define these as follows:

$$X_{DE} = \text{number of desks shipped from Des Moines to Evansville}$$
$$X_{FE} = \text{number of desks shipped from Fort Lauderdale to Evansville}$$

OBJECTIVE FUNCTION The objective function for this transshipment model, including the two additional decision variables and using the unit costs shown in Table 5.2, can be written as follows:

$$\text{Minimize total shipping costs} = 5X_{DA} + 4X_{DB} + 3X_{DC} + 2X_{DE} + 3X_{EA} + 2X_{EB} + X_{EC} + 9X_{FA} + 7X_{FB} + 5X_{FC} + 3X_{FE}$$

CONSTRAINTS Once again, we need to write flow balance constraints for each node in the network. Let us first consider the net flows at the Des Moines and Fort Lauderdale factories. After taking into account the desks shipped from either of these locations to the Evansville factory (rather than directly to the warehouses), the relevant flow balance equations can be written as

$$(0) - (X_{DA} + X_{DB} + X_{DC} + X_{DE}) = -100 \qquad \text{(Des Moines supply)}$$
$$(0) - (X_{FA} + X_{FB} + X_{FC} + X_{FE}) = -300 \qquad \text{(Fort Lauderdale supply)}$$

As usual, supplies have been expressed as negative numbers on the RHS. Now, let us model the flow equation at Evansville:

$$\begin{aligned}\text{New flow at Evansville} &= (\text{Total flow } \textit{in} \text{ to Evansville}) - (\text{Total flow } \textit{out} \text{ of Evansville})\\ &= (X_{DE} + X_{FE}) - (X_{EA} + X_{EB} + X_{EC})\end{aligned}$$

TABLE 5.2
Revised Transportation Costs per Desk for Executive Furniture

	TO			
	ALBUQUERQUE	BOSTON	CLEVELAND	EVANSVILLE
Des Moines	\$5	\$4	\$3	\$2
Evansville	\$3	\$2	\$1	—
Fort Lauderdale	\$9	\$7	\$5	\$3

This net flow is equal to the total number of desks produced—namely, the supply, at Evansville (which would also appear as a negative number in the flow balance constraint). Therefore,

$$\text{New flow at Evansville} = (X_{DE} + X_{FE}) - (X_{EA} + X_{EB} + X_{EC}) = -300$$

There is no change in the demand constraints that represent the warehouse requirements. So, as discussed in section 5.3, they are

$$X_{DA} + X_{EA} + X_{FA} = 300 \qquad \text{(Albuquerque demand)}$$
$$X_{DB} + X_{EB} + X_{FB} = 200 \qquad \text{(Boston demand)}$$
$$X_{DC} + X_{EC} + X_{FC} = 200 \qquad \text{(Cleveland demand)}$$

File: 5-4.xls

EXCEL SOLUTION Screenshot 5-4, which uses the tabular layout for representing the network flows, shows the Excel layout and Solver entries for Executive Furniture's transshipment model. Note that the net flow at Evansville (cell K6) is calculated as (cell I6 – cell J6), where cell I6 (= cell E8) is the total flow *in* to the Evansville factory, and cell J6 (= cell F6) represents the total flow *out* of Evansville. The difference of 300 is the supply of desks created at the Evansville factory.

In the revised solution, which now has a total transportation cost of $2,600, Executive should ship the 300 desks made at Fort Lauderdale to Evansville and then ship the consolidated load to the warehouses. It continues, though, to be cost beneficial to ship desks made at the Des Moines factory directly to a warehouse.

Lopez Custom Outfits—A Larger Transshipment Example

Paula Lopez makes and sells custom outfits for theme parties hosted by her wealthy clients. She uses three tailoring shops located in the Northeastern United States (in Albany, Boston, and Hartford) to make the outfits. These are then shipped to her finishing facilities in Charlotte and Richmond, where they are further customized to suit the clients' specifications and inspected before being shipped to the clients. Paula's clients are based primarily in four cities: Dallas, Louisville, Memphis, and Nashville.

SCREENSHOT 5-4 Excel Layout and Solver Entries for Executive Furniture—Transshipment

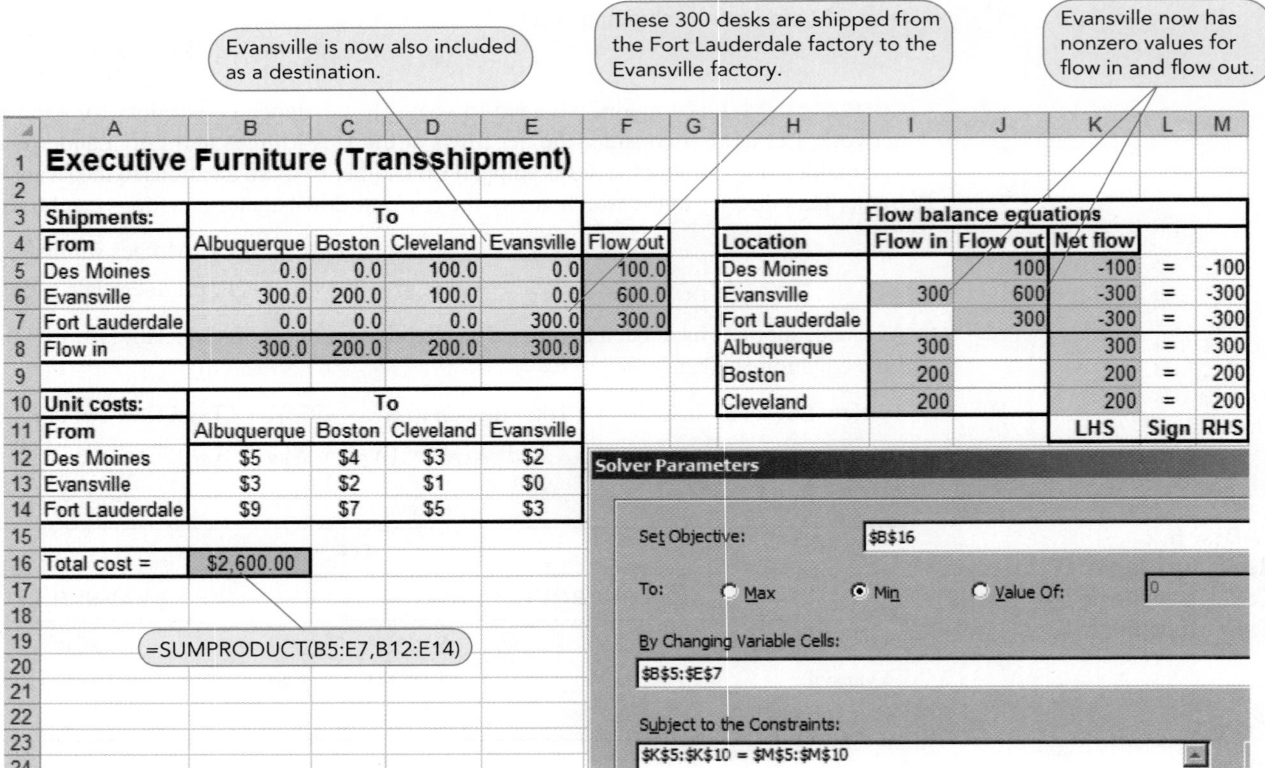

Shipments:	To				
From	Albuquerque	Boston	Cleveland	Evansville	Flow out
Des Moines	0.0	0.0	100.0	0.0	100.0
Evansville	300.0	200.0	100.0	0.0	600.0
Fort Lauderdale	0.0	0.0	0.0	300.0	300.0
Flow in	300.0	200.0	200.0	300.0	

Unit costs:	To			
From	Albuquerque	Boston	Cleveland	Evansville
Des Moines	$5	$4	$3	$2
Evansville	$3	$2	$1	$0
Fort Lauderdale	$9	$7	$5	$3

Total cost = $2,600.00

Flow balance equations					
Location	Flow in	Flow out	Net flow		
Des Moines		100	-100	=	-100
Evansville	300	600	-300	=	-300
Fort Lauderdale		300	-300	=	-300
Albuquerque	300		300	=	300
Boston	200		200	=	200
Cleveland	200		200	=	200
			LHS	Sign	RHS

TABLE 5.3 TRANSPORTATION COSTS PER OUTFIT FOR LOPEZ CUSTOM OUTFITS

	TO	
FROM	CHARLOTTE	RICHMOND
Albany	$40	$55
Boston	$43	$46
Hartford	$50	$50

	TO			
FROM	DALLAS	LOUISVILLE	MEMPHIS	NASHVILLE
Charlotte	$38	$40	$51	$40
Richmond	$30	$47	$41	$45

Paula has received the following firm orders for custom outfits: 450 from Dallas, 300 from Louisville, 275 from Memphis, and 400 from Nashville. Her tailoring shop in Albany can make up to 450 outfits, the Boston shop can handle up to 500 outfits, and the Hartford shop has the capacity to make 580 outfits. Therefore, Paula's total tailoring capacity exceeds the total demand for outfits. She therefore knows that she will be able to fully satisfy all her clients' needs.

There is no production cost difference between the three tailoring shops, and Paula sells all her outfits at the same fixed price to her clients. There is also no cost difference between Charlotte and Richmond with regard to the customization and inspection processes at these locations. Further, since these processes do not consume too much time or space, Paula need not be concerned about both these locations with regard to capacity. Paula's cost difference between the various locations arises primarily from the shipping costs per outfit, which are summarized in Table 5.3.

LP Formulation for Lopez Custom Outfits Transshipment Model

Before we discuss the LP formulation for this model, it is useful to draw it as a network so that we can visualize the various flows that could occur. Figure 5.4 shows the network for Paula's transshipment model. We note that there are arcs both coming into and going out of the transshipment nodes, Charlotte and Richmond.

The LP formulation for this model involves 14 decision variables, 1 for each of the arcs shown in Figure 5.4. Let us define these decision variables as

$$X_{ij} = \text{number of outfits shipped from location } i \text{ to location } j$$

where

i = A (for Albany), B (for Boston), H (for Hartford), C (for Charlotte), or R (for Richmond)

j = C (for Charlotte), R (for Richmond), D (for Dallas), L (for Louisville), M (for Memphis), or N (for Nashville)

OBJECTIVE FUNCTION The objective function for this problem seeks to minimize the total transshipment cost and can be expressed as

$$\text{Minimize } \$40X_{AC} + \$55X_{AR} + \$43X_{BC} + \$46X_{BR} + \$50X_{HC} + \$50X_{HR} + \$38X_{CD} + \$40X_{CL} + \$51X_{CM} + \$40X_{CN} + \$30X_{RD} + \$47X_{RL} + \$41X_{RM} + \$45X_{RN}$$

FIGURE 5.4 Network Model for Lopez Custom Outfits—Transshipment

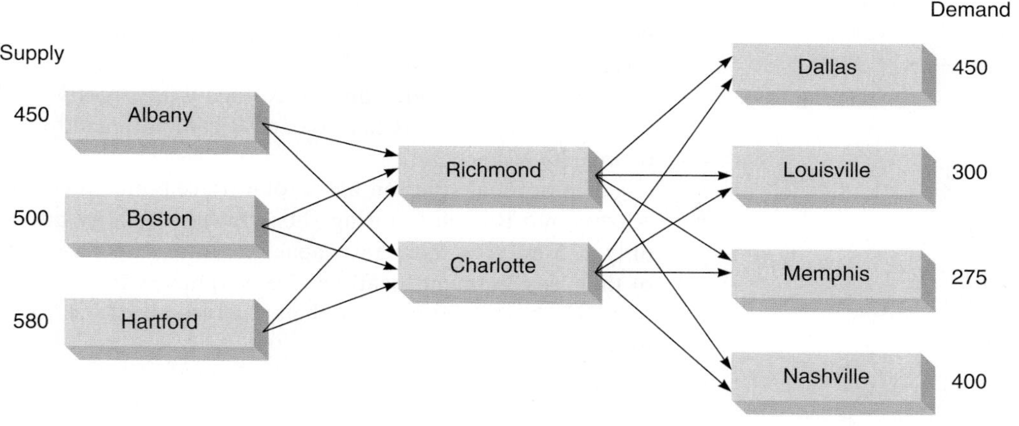

CONSTRAINTS Here again, we need to write flow balance constraints for each of the nine nodes in the network (see Figure 5.4). For the three tailoring shops, the net flow equations can be expressed as

$$(0) - (X_{AC} + X_{AR}) \geq -450 \quad \text{(Albany supply)}$$
$$(0) - (X_{BC} + X_{BR}) \geq -500 \quad \text{(Boston supply)}$$
$$(0) - (X_{HC} + X_{HR}) \geq -580 \quad \text{(Hartford supply)}$$

As usual, supplies have been expressed as negative numbers on the RHS. Also, because total supply exceeds total demand, this is an unbalanced model in which not all tailoring shops will be used to their full capacity. The supply constraints therefore need to be written as inequalities. Recall from our discussion of unbalanced models on page 170 that based on the definition of net flows being used in this textbook, we should express the supply constraints in such situations using the $\geq$ sign.

Now, let us model the flow equation at the two transshipment locations, Charlotte and Richmond:

$$(X_{AC} + X_{BC} + X_{HC}) - (X_{CD} + X_{CL} + X_{CM} + X_{CN}) = 0 \quad \text{(net flow at Charlotte)}$$
$$(X_{AR} + X_{BR} + X_{HR}) - (X_{RD} + X_{RL} + X_{RM} + X_{RN}) = 0 \quad \text{(net flow at Richmond)}$$

Note that the RHS of both these equations is zero since Charlotte and Richmond are pure transshipment locations and all outfits simply pass through these locations (i.e., no outfit is created there, and none are consumed there).

Finally, we model the net flow equations at the four demand locations as

$$(X_{CD} + X_{RD}) - (0) = 450 \quad \text{(Dallas demand)}$$
$$(X_{CL} + X_{RL}) - (0) = 300 \quad \text{(Louisville demand)}$$
$$(X_{CM} + X_{RM}) - (0) = 275 \quad \text{(Memphis demand)}$$
$$(X_{CN} + X_{RN}) - (0) = 400 \quad \text{(Nashville demand)}$$

Since all demands will be met in this model, we can express all four demand constraints using $=$ signs.

File: 5-5.xls

EXCEL SOLUTION Screenshot 5-5 shows the Excel layout and Solver entries for Lopez's transshipment model. Note that Charlotte and Richmond appear both in the rows and in the columns. Also, even though the table of flows contains 30 cells (i.e., cells B5:G9), only 14 of these are actual routes that exist (shown in yellow in Screenshot 5-5).

How do we enter these changing variable cells in Solver? There are two simple ways of doing this. First, we can specify only the 14 shaded cells as changing variable cells. Recall that to do this in Solver, we must separate entries for nonadjacent cells by using commas (i.e., B5:C7, D8:G9). Although this approach is quite straightforward, it could be cumbersome, especially if there are many nonadjacent decision variables in the model.

The second (and easier) approach is to specify the entire cell range B5:G9 in the By Changing Variable Cells box in Solver. Then, for all routes that do not exist (e.g., Albany to Dallas), we simply set the unit cost to artificially high values ($2,000 in this case). We have illustrated this approach in Screenshot 5-5.

The model includes three locations with negative RHS values (tailors), two locations with zero RHS values (Charlotte and Richmond), and four locations with positive RHS values (demands).

The optimal solution has a total transshipment cost of $116,775. Paula should use the Albany and Boston tailoring shops to full capacity but use the Hartford tailoring shop for only 475 units of their 580 capacity. Shipments from Albany and Hartford go to just one of the transshipment locations, but shipments from Boston are split between the two locations. Each demand location then receives all its outfits from one of the two transshipment locations.

SCREENSHOT 5-5 Excel Layout and Solver Entries for Lopez Custom Outfits—Transshipment

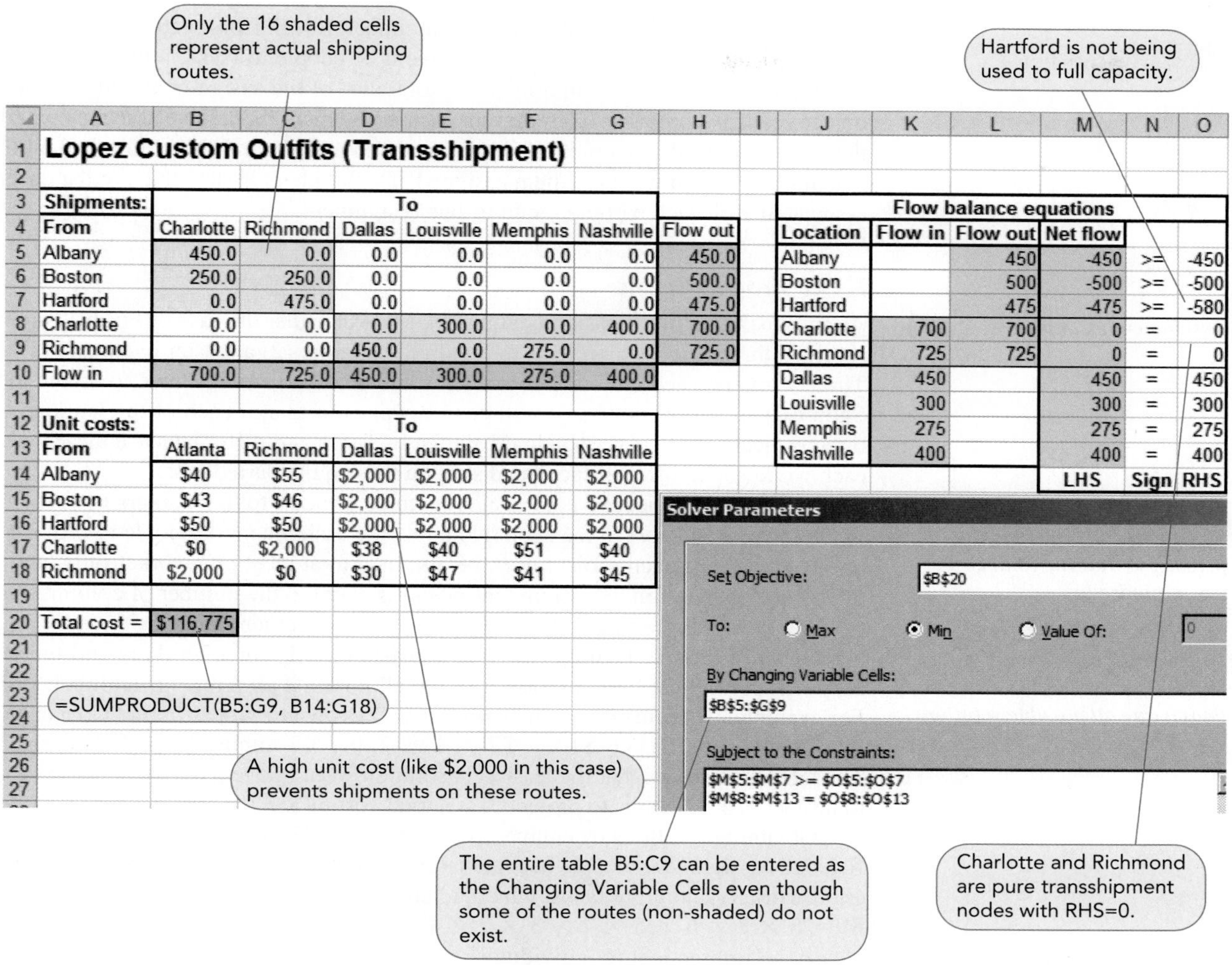

Only the 16 shaded cells represent actual shipping routes.

Hartford is not being used to full capacity.

Lopez Custom Outfits (Transshipment)

Shipments:	To						
From	Charlotte	Richmond	Dallas	Louisville	Memphis	Nashville	Flow out
Albany	450.0	0.0	0.0	0.0	0.0	0.0	450.0
Boston	250.0	250.0	0.0	0.0	0.0	0.0	500.0
Hartford	0.0	475.0	0.0	0.0	0.0	0.0	475.0
Charlotte	0.0	0.0	0.0	300.0	0.0	400.0	700.0
Richmond	0.0	0.0	450.0	0.0	275.0	0.0	725.0
Flow in	700.0	725.0	450.0	300.0	275.0	400.0	

Unit costs:	To					
From	Atlanta	Richmond	Dallas	Louisville	Memphis	Nashville
Albany	$40	$55	$2,000	$2,000	$2,000	$2,000
Boston	$43	$46	$2,000	$2,000	$2,000	$2,000
Hartford	$50	$50	$2,000	$2,000	$2,000	$2,000
Charlotte	$0	$2,000	$38	$40	$51	$40
Richmond	$2,000	$0	$30	$47	$41	$45

Total cost = $116,775

=SUMPRODUCT(B5:G9, B14:G18)

A high unit cost (like $2,000 in this case) prevents shipments on these routes.

Flow balance equations					
Location	Flow in	Flow out	Net flow		
Albany		450	-450	>=	-450
Boston		500	-500	>=	-500
Hartford		475	-475	>=	-580
Charlotte	700	700	0	=	0
Richmond	725	725	0	=	0
Dallas	450		450	=	450
Louisville	300		300	=	300
Memphis	275		275	=	275
Nashville	400		400	=	400
			LHS	Sign	RHS

Solver Parameters

Set Objective: $B$20

To: Max / Min (selected) / Value Of: 0

By Changing Variable Cells: $B$5:$G$9

Subject to the Constraints:
$M$5:$M$7 >= $O$5:$O$7
$M$8:$M$13 = $O$8:$O$13

The entire table B5:C9 can be entered as the Changing Variable Cells even though some of the routes (non-shaded) do not exist.

Charlotte and Richmond are pure transshipment nodes with RHS=0.

IN ACTION British Telecommunications Uses the Assignment Model to Schedule Field Engineers

British Telecommunications PLC (BT) employs over 50,000 field engineers across the UK to repair network faults, maintain networks, and provide other services to customers. It is critical for BT to optimize its field workforce scheduling, which involves sending the right engineer to the right customer at the right time and place with the right equipment. BT's ability to provide high quality service while achieving maximum productivity and low operational costs is vital to its success.

BT's automated work-management and field-communication system, called Work Manager, is equipped with a real-time allocation algorithm that uses an assignment model to determine the minimal-cost assignment set, The model considers the skill requirements of individual engineers as well as the geographic distribution of the available engineers and job sites. BT runs an extended version of Work Manager every 5 to 15 minutes, with a typical problem consisting of 50 to 100 engineers and 300 to 500 tasks. The model usually returns a good schedule within one minute.

BT estimates that the use of Work Manager has saved them $150 million annually even with only 28,000 engineers scheduled using the model. The amount would exceed $250 million annually when it fully covers all engineers. BT has also improved its performance with regards to due dates, appointment windows, and skill requirements.

Source: Based on D. Lesaint, C. Voudouris, and N. Azarmi. "Dynamic Workforce Scheduling for British Telecommunications PLC," *Interfaces* 30, 1 (January–February 2000): 45–56.

5.6 Assignment Model

The next model we study is the assignment model. Recall from section 5.1 that this model seeks to identify an optimal one-to-one assignment of people to tasks, jobs to machines, and so on. The typical objective is to minimize the total cost of the assignment, although a maximization objective is also possible. To represent each assignment model, we associate a table. Generally, the rows denote the people or jobs we want to assign, and the columns denote the tasks or machines to which we want them assigned. The numbers in the table are the costs (or benefits) associated with each particular one-to-one assignment.

Fix-It Shop Example

Assignment example: Fix-It Shop

As an illustration of the assignment model, let us consider the case of Fix-It Shop, which has just received three new rush projects to repair: (1) a radio, (2) a toaster oven, and (3) a coffee table. Three workers, each with different talents and abilities, are available to do the jobs. The Fix-It Shop owner estimates what it will cost in wages to assign each of the workers to each of the three projects. The costs, which are shown in Table 5.4, differ because the owner believes that each worker will differ in speed and skill on these quite varied jobs.

The objective is to assign projects to people (one project to one person) so that the total costs are minimized.

The owner's objective is to assign the three projects to the workers in a way that will result in the lowest total cost to the shop. Note that the assignment of people to projects must be on a one-to-one basis; each project must be assigned to at most one worker only, and vice versa. If the number of rows in an assignment model is equal to the number of columns (as in the Fix-It example), we refer to this problem as a *balanced* assignment model.

One way to solve (small) assignment models is to enumerate all possible solutions.

Because the Fix-It Shop example consists of only three workers and three projects, one easy way to find the best solution is to list all possible assignments and their respective costs. For example, if Adams is assigned to project 1, Brown to project 2, and Cooper to project 3, the total cost will be \$11 + \$10 + \$7 = \$28. Table 5.5 summarizes all six assignment options. The table also shows that the least-cost solution would be to assign Cooper to project 1, Brown to project 2, and Adams to project 3, at a total cost of \$25.

Obtaining solutions by enumeration works well for small models but quickly becomes inefficient as assignment models become larger. For example, a model involving the assignment of eight workers and eight tasks, which actually is not that large in a real-world situation, yields $8!(= 8 \times 7 \times 6 \times 5 \times 4 \times 3 \times 2 \times 1)$, or 40,320 possible solutions! Because it would clearly be impractical to individually examine so many alternatives, a more efficient solution approach is needed.

TABLE 5.4
Estimated Project Repair Costs for Fix-It Shop

	PROJECT		
PERSON	1	2	3
Adams	\$11	\$14	\$ 6
Brown	\$ 8	\$10	\$11
Cooper	\$ 9	\$12	\$ 7

TABLE 5.5
Summary of Fix-It Shop's Assignment Alternatives and Costs

PROJECT ASSIGNMENT					
1	2	3	LABOR COSTS (\$)		TOTAL COSTS
Adams	Brown	Cooper	\$11 + \$10 + \$ 7	=	\$28
Adams	Cooper	Brown	\$11 + \$12 + \$11	=	\$34
Brown	Adams	Cooper	\$ 8 + \$14 + \$ 7	=	\$29
Brown	Cooper	Adams	\$ 8 + \$12 + \$ 6	=	\$26
Cooper	Adams	Brown	\$ 9 + \$14 + \$11	=	\$34
Cooper	Brown	Adams	\$ 9 + \$10 + \$ 6	=	\$25

Solving Assignment Models

Each supply and each demand in an assignment model equals one unit.

A straightforward approach to solving assignment models is to formulate them as a transportation model. To do so for the Fix-It Shop problem, let us view each worker as a supply node in a transportation network with a supply of one unit. Likewise, let us view each project as a demand node in the network with a demand of one unit. The arcs connecting the supply nodes to the demand nodes represent the possible assignment of a supply (worker) to a demand (project). The network model is illustrated in Figure 5.5.

We see that this network looks identical to a transportation model with three supply nodes and three demand nodes. But here, each supply and each demand is equal to one unit. The objective is to find the least-cost solution that uses the one-unit supplies at the origin nodes to satisfy the one-unit demands at the demand nodes. However, we need to also ensure that each worker *uniquely* gets assigned to just one project, and vice versa. That is, the *entire* supply of one unit at an origin node (worker) should flow to the same demand node (project), indicating the assignment of a worker to a project. How do we ensure this? The answer lies in the special property of network models stated earlier: When all the supplies and demands in a network model are whole numbers (as in this case), the resulting solution will automatically have integer-valued flows on the arcs.

The special integer flow property of network models automatically ensures unique assignments.

Consider the "flow" out of the supply node for Adams in the Fix-It Shop example. The three arcs (to projects 1, 2, and 3) denote the assignment of Adams to these projects. Due to the integer property of the resulting network flows, the only possible solutions will have a flow of 1 on one of the three arcs and a flow of 0 on the other two arcs. This is the only way in which a total flow of 1 (equal to the "supply" at the node representing Adams) can flow on these arcs and have integer values. The arc that has a flow of 1 in the optimal solution will indicate the project to which Adams should be assigned. Likewise, arcs that have flows of 1 and originate from the other two supply nodes will show the optimal assignments for those two workers.

Even without us constraining it to be so, the solution to the assignment model yields a solution in which the optimal values of the decision variables are either 1 (indicating the assignment of a worker to a project) or 0 (indicating that the worker should not be assigned to the project). In fact, there are several situations in which such decision variables, known as *binary*, or 0–1, variables must have values of zero or one in the formulation itself. We study these types of models in more detail in Chapter 6.

LP Formulation for Fix-It Shop's Assignment Model

We now develop the LP model for Fix-It Shop's example. Let

X_{ij} = "Flow" on arc from node denoting worker i to node denoting project j. The solution value will equal 1 if worker i is assigned to project j, and will equal 0 otherwise.

where

$$i = \text{A (for Adams), B (for Brown), C (for Cooper)}$$
$$j = \text{1 (for project 1), 2 (for project 2), 3 (for project 3)}$$

FIGURE 5.5 Network Model for Fix-It Shop—Assignment

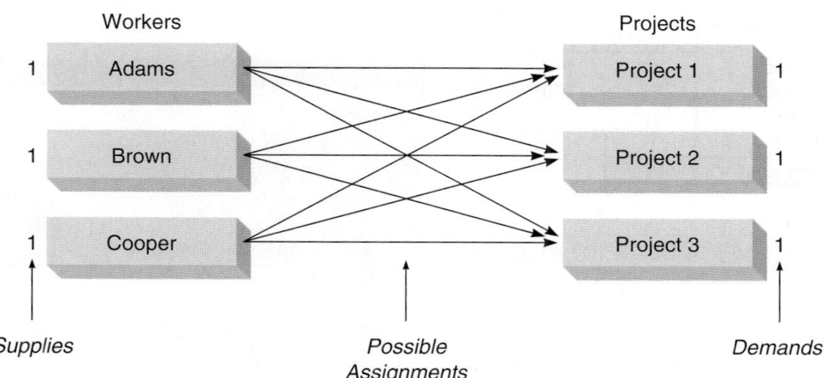

OBJECTIVE FUNCTION The objective is to minimize the total cost of assignment and is expressed as

$$\text{Minimize total assignment costs} = \$11X_{A1} + \$14X_{A2} + \$6X_{A3} + \$8X_{B1} + \$10X_{B2} + \$11X_{B3} + \$9X_{C1} + \$12X_{C2} + \$7X_{C3}$$

Here again, we write supply constraints and demand constraints.

CONSTRAINTS As in the transportation model, we have supply constraints at each of the three supply nodes (workers) and demand constraints at each of the three demand nodes (projects). Using the standard convention we have adopted for all flow balance equations, these can be written as

$$-X_{A1} - X_{A2} - X_{A3} = -1 \quad \text{(Adams availability)}$$
$$-X_{B1} - X_{B2} - X_{B3} = -1 \quad \text{(Brown availability)}$$
$$-X_{C1} - X_{C2} - X_{C3} = -1 \quad \text{(Cooper availability)}$$
$$X_{A1} + X_{B1} + X_{C1} = 1 \quad \text{(project 1 requirement)}$$
$$X_{A2} + X_{B2} + X_{C3} = 1 \quad \text{(project 2 requirement)}$$
$$X_{A3} + X_{B3} + X_{C3} = 1 \quad \text{(project 3 requirement)}$$

File: 5-6.xls

EXCEL SOLUTION Screenshot 5-6 shows the Excel layout and Solver entries for Fix-It Shop's assignment model. The optimal solution identified by the model indicates that Adams should be assigned to project 3, Brown to project 2, and Cooper to project 1, for a total cost of \$25.

An assignment model can sometimes involve a maximization objective.

SOLVING MAXIMIZATION ASSIGNMENT MODELS The model discussed here can be very easily modified to solve *maximization* assignment models, in which the objective coefficients represent profits or benefits rather than costs. The only change needed would be in the statement of the objective function (which would be set to maximize instead of minimize).

UNBALANCED ASSIGNMENT MODELS In the Fix-It Shop example, the total number of workers equaled the total number of projects. All supply and demand constraints could therefore

SCREENSHOT 5-6 Excel Layout and Solver Entries for Fix-It Shop—Assignment

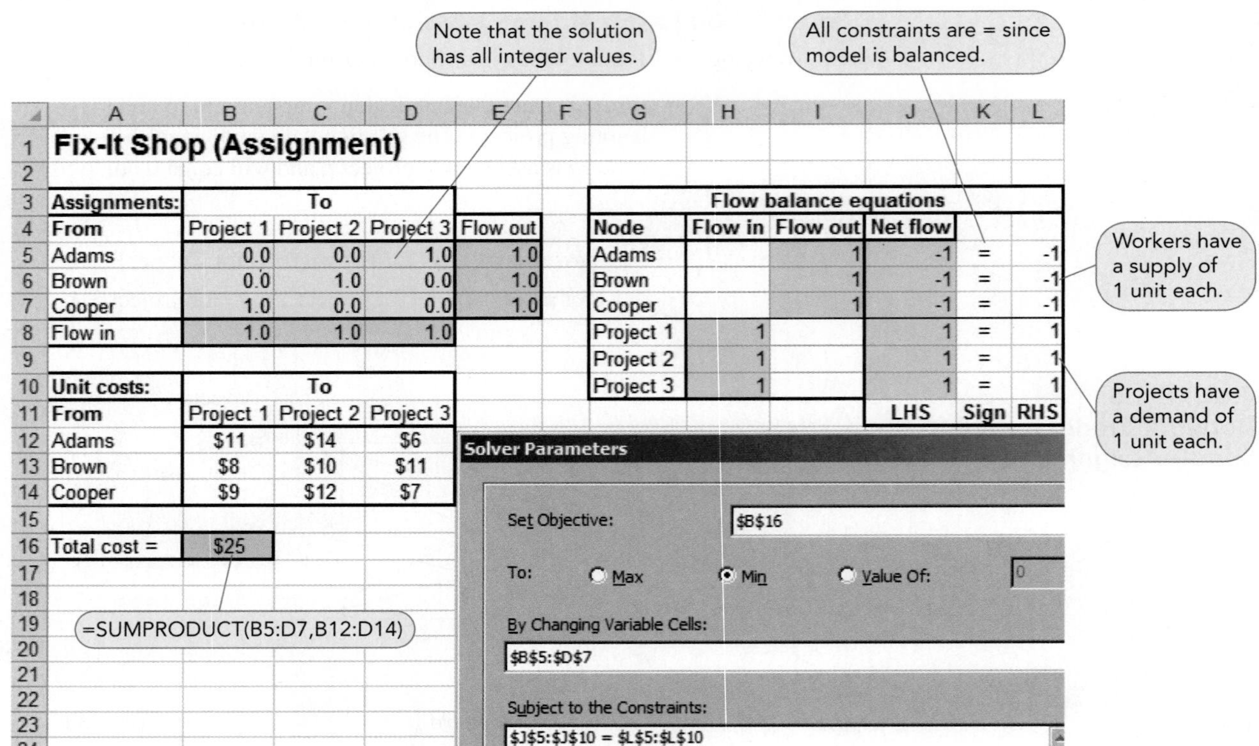

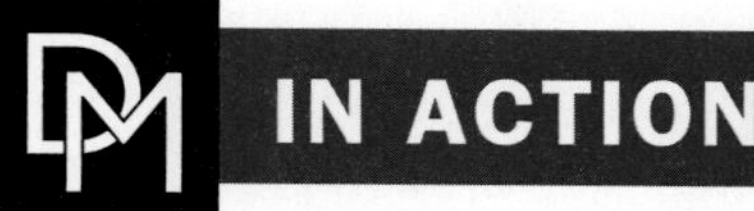

Scheduling the Belgian Soccer League with the Assignment Model

Worldwide interest in soccer has increased significantly over the past several years and Belgian soccer is no exception. Belgacom TV pays millions of Euros each year for the soccer broadcasting rights and there is a great deal of interest in ensuring that the league's schedule is properly designed. In addition to the obvious influence on the results of the sports competition, the schedule also affects game attendance, public interest, and the league's profitability and attractiveness to broadcasters, sponsors, and advertisers in subsequent years.

Until the 2005–2006 season schedules were created manually, which resulted in several teams viewing the schedules as being unbalanced and unfair. There were even accusations that the chairman of the calendar committee was favoring his own team. For the 2006–2007 season, the authors used an assignment model to develop the schedule for the Jupiler league, the highest division in Belgian Soccer. The league is organized as a double round-robin tournament with 18 teams with several constraints such as no team can play more than two consecutive home or away matches, the total number of breaks is minimal, and no team should start or end the season with a break. The authors expanded their model to a two-phased approach starting with the 2007–2008 season. In the first phase, each team is assigned a home-away pattern; in the second phase, the actual opponents are determined.

A spokesperson for the Belgian soccer league states that due to the use of this two-phased assignment model, "we have been able to come up with schedules that are much more satisfying for our partners (the police, Belgacom TV, and the clubs). In addition, the transparency of the process of agreeing upon a schedule has improved considerably as well."

Source: Based on D. Goossens and F. Spieksma. "Scheduling the Belgian Soccer League," *Interfaces* 39, 2 (March–April 2009): 109–118.

be specified as equalities (i.e., using the = sign). What if the number of workers exceeds the number of projects, or vice versa? In these cases, we have *unbalanced* assignment models and, just as in the case of unbalanced transportation models, the supply or demand constraints need to be modified accordingly. For example, if the number of workers exceeds the number of projects, the supply constraints would become inequalities, and the demand constraints would remain equality constraints. In contrast, if the number of projects exceeds the number of workers, the supply constraints would remain equality constraints, and the demand constraints would become inequalities. Solved Problem 5-2 at the end of this chapter shows an example of an unbalanced assignment model.

5.7 Maximal-Flow Model

A maximal-flow model finds the most that can flow through a network.

The *maximal-flow* model allows us to determine the maximum amount that can flow from a given origin node to a given destination node in a network with capacitated arcs. It has been used, for example, to find the maximum number of automobiles that can flow through a state highway road system.

Road System in Waukesha, Wisconsin

Waukesha, a small town in Wisconsin, is in the process of developing a road system for the downtown area. Bill Blackstone, a city planner, would like to determine the maximum number of cars that can flow through the town from west to east. The road network is shown in Figure 5.6, where the arcs represent the roads.

Traffic can flow in both directions.

The numbers by the nodes indicate the maximum number of cars (in hundreds of cars per hour) that can flow (or travel) *from* the various nodes. For example, the number 3 by node 1 (on the road from node 1 to node 2) indicates that 300 cars per hour can travel from node 1 to node 2. Likewise, the numbers 1, 1, and 2 by node 2 indicate that 100, 100, and 200 cars can travel per hour on the roads from node 2 to nodes 1, 4, and 6, respectively. Note that traffic can flow in both directions down a road. A zero (0) means no flow in that direction, or a one-way road.

Unlike the transportation and assignment models, in which there are multiple origin nodes and multiple destination nodes, the typical maximal-flow model has a single starting node (origin) and a single ending node (destination).

FIGURE 5.6
Road Network for Waukesha—Maximal-Flow

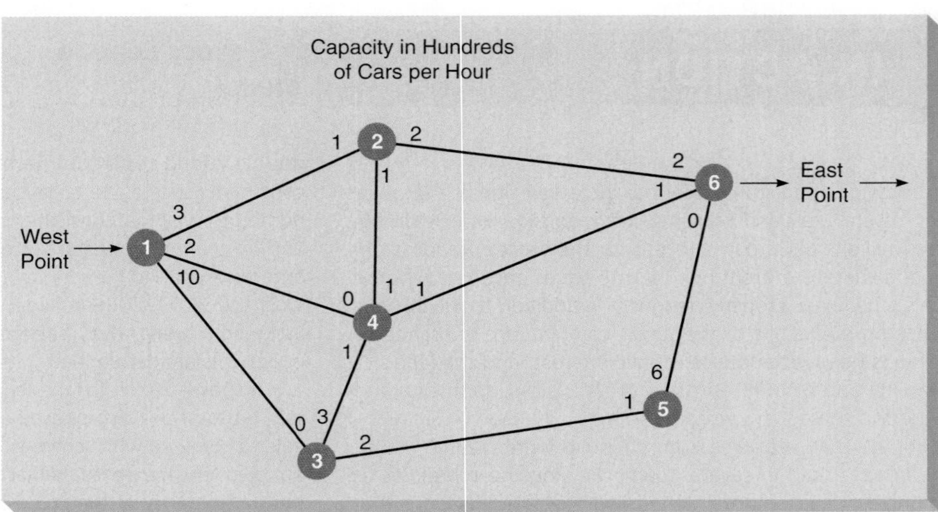

LP Formulation for Waukesha Road System's Maximal-Flow Model

We replace each two-way road (arc) with a pair of one-way roads.

To formulate this example as an LP model, we first replace each two-way (bidirectional) road in the network with two one-way (unidirectional) roads with flows in opposite directions. Note that some of the unidirectional roads (e.g., the road from node 4 to node 1, the road from node 6 to node 5) are not needed because the maximum flow permissible in that direction is zero (i.e., it is a one-way road). The revised network for Waukesha therefore has 15 unidirectional roads (i.e., roads $1 \rightarrow 2$, $1 \rightarrow 3$, $1 \rightarrow 4$, $2 \rightarrow 1$, $2 \rightarrow 4$, $2 \rightarrow 6$, $3 \rightarrow 4$, $3 \rightarrow 5$, $4 \rightarrow 2$, $4 \rightarrow 3$, $4 \rightarrow 6$, $5 \rightarrow 3$, $5 \rightarrow 6$, $6 \rightarrow 2$, and $6 \rightarrow 4$).

There is a decision variable associated with each arc in the network.

As with the transportation and assignment models, the presence of 15 unidirectional arcs in the network implies that there are 15 decision variables in Waukesha's maximal-flow model—1 for each arc (road) in the network. Let

$$X_{ij} = \text{Number of cars that flow (or travel) per hour on road from node } i \text{ to node } j$$

where i and j each equal 1, 2, 3, 4, 5, or 6. Of course, flow variables are defined only on roads that actually exist. For example, X_{12} (i.e., $i = 1, j = 2$) is defined, while X_{15} (i.e., $i = 1, j = 5$) is not defined.

We need to determine the maximum number of cars that can originate at node 1 and terminate at node 6. Hence, node 1 is the origin node in this model, and node 6 is the destination node. All other nodes (nodes 2 to 5) are transshipment nodes, where flows of cars neither start nor end. However, unlike in the transportation and assignment models, there is neither a known quantity of "supply" of cars available at node 1, nor is there a known quantity of "demand" for cars required at node 6. For this reason, we need to slightly modify the network to set up and solve the maximal-flow model using LP.

We add a one-way dummy road (arc) from the destination node to the source node.

The modification consists of creating a unidirectional *dummy* arc (road) going *from* the destination node (node 6) *to* the origin node (node 1). We call this a dummy arc because the arc (road) really does not exist in the network and has been created only for modeling purposes. The capacity of this dummy arc is set at infinity (or any artificially high number, such as 1,000 for the Waukesha example). The modified network is shown in Figure 5.7.

OBJECTIVE FUNCTION Let us consider the objective function first. The objective is to maximize the total number of cars flowing *in* to node 6. Assume that there are an unknown number of cars flowing on the dummy road from node 6 to node 1. However, because there is no supply at node 6 (i.e., no cars are created at node 6), the entire number of cars flowing *out* of node 6 (on road $6 \rightarrow 1$) must consist of cars that flowed *in* to node 6. Likewise, because there is no demand at node 1 (i.e., no cars are consumed at node 1), the entire number of cars on road $6 \rightarrow 1$ must consist of cars that originally flowed *out* of node 1 (to nodes 2, 3, and 4).

The objective is to maximize the flow on the dummy arc.

These two issues imply that if we maximize the number of cars flowing on the dummy road $6 \rightarrow 1$, this is equivalent to maximizing the total number of cars flowing *out* of node 1 as well

FIGURE 5.7 Modified Road Network for Waukesha—Maximal-Flow

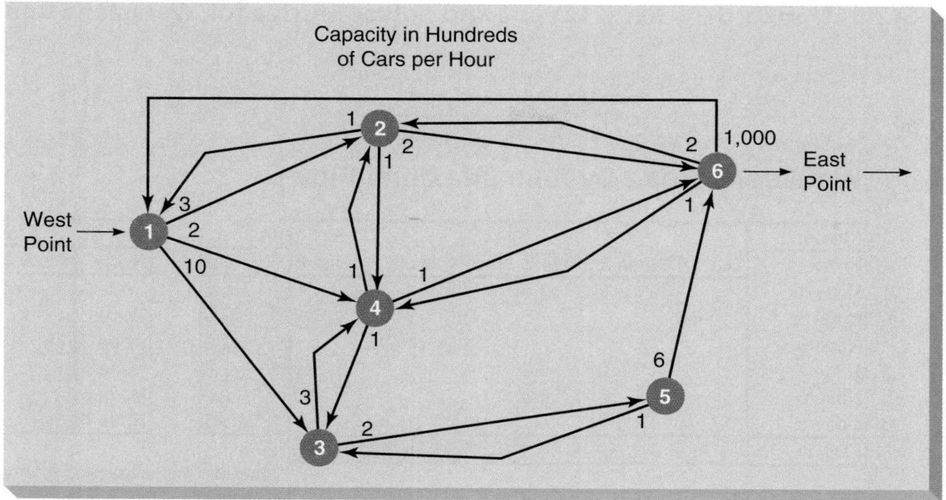

as the total number of cars flowing *in* to node 6. The objective for Waukesha's maximal-flow model can therefore be written as

$$\text{Maximize } X_{61}$$

CONSTRAINTS Because all nodes in the network are transshipment nodes with no supplies or demands, the flow balance equations need to ensure that the net flow (i.e., number of cars) at each node is zero. Hence,

All net flows are zero.

$$(X_{61} + X_{21}) - (X_{12} + X_{13} + X_{14}) = 0 \quad \text{(net flow at node 1)}$$
$$(X_{12} + X_{42} + X_{62}) - (X_{21} + X_{24} + X_{26}) = 0 \quad \text{(net flow at node 2)}$$
$$(X_{13} + X_{43} + X_{53}) - (X_{34} + X_{35}) = 0 \quad \text{(net flow at node 3)}$$
$$(X_{14} + X_{24} + X_{34} + X_{64}) - (X_{42} + X_{43} + X_{46}) = 0 \quad \text{(net flow at node 4)}$$
$$(X_{35}) - (X_{53} + X_{56}) = 0 \quad \text{(net flow at node 5)}$$
$$(X_{26} + X_{46} + X_{56}) - (X_{61} + X_{62} + X_{64}) = 0 \quad \text{(net flow at node 6)}$$

Capacity constraints limit the flows on the arcs.

Finally, we have capacity constraints on the maximum number of cars that can flow on each road. These are written as

$$\begin{array}{lll} X_{12} \leq 3 & X_{13} \leq 10 & X_{14} \leq 2 \\ X_{21} \leq 1 & X_{24} \leq 1 & X_{26} \leq 2 \\ X_{34} \leq 3 & X_{35} \leq 2 & \\ X_{42} \leq 1 & X_{43} \leq 1 & X_{46} \leq 1 \\ X_{53} \leq 1 & X_{56} \leq 6 & \\ X_{61} \leq 1{,}000 & X_{62} \leq 2 & X_{64} \leq 1 \end{array}$$

File: 5-7.xls

EXCEL SOLUTION Screenshot 5-7 shows the Excel layout and Solver entries for Waukesha's maximal-flow model. To be consistent with earlier models, flows on arcs have been modeled here using a tabular layout (cells B5:G10). As noted earlier, a big advantage of the tabular layout is that it greatly simplifies the calculations of the total flows in and total flows out of each node in the network.

However, of the 36 (= 6 × 6) arcs represented by cells B5:G10, only 16 of them actually exist in Waukesha's network. That is, the decision variables in this model refer only to selected entries in the table. These entries have been shaded yellow in Screenshot 5-7.

Entries for nonadjacent cells are separated by commas in Solver.

As with the Lopez Custom Outfits transshipment model we discussed in section 5.5, there are two ways of specifying the variables for a maximal-flow model in Solver. First, we could enter only the shaded cells, as illustrated in the By Changing Variable Cells box in Screenshot 5-7. Note that we separate entries for nonadjacent cells by using commas (i.e., B6:B8, B10, C5, etc.). As you can see, this approach could be cumbersome especially if there are many nonadjacent decision variables in the model.

SCREENSHOT 5-7 Excel Layout and Solver Entries for Waukesha Road System—Maximal-Flow

All values are in 100s of cars per hour.

Only the shaded cells represent roads that actually exist.

RHS = 0 since all nodes are transshipment nodes.

Waukesha Road System (Maximal-Flow)

Flows:	To						
From	Node 1	Node 2	Node 3	Node 4	Node 5	Node 6	Flow out
Node 1		2.0	2.0	1.0			5.0
Node 2	0.0			0.0		2.0	2.0
Node 3				0.0	2.0		2.0
Node 4		0.0	0.0			1.0	1.0
Node 5			0.0			2.0	2.0
Node 6	5.0	0.0		0.0			5.0
Flow in	5.0	2.0	2.0	1.0	2.0	5.0	

Flow balance equations					
Node	Flow in	Flow out	Net flow		
Node 1	5	5	0	=	0
Node 2	2	2	0	=	0
Node 3	2	2	0	=	0
Node 4	1	1	0	=	0
Node 5	2	2	0	=	0
Node 6	5	5	0	=	0
			LHS	Sign	RHS

Capacities:	To					
From	Node 1	Node 2	Node 3	Node 4	Node 5	Node 6
Node 1		3	10	2		
Node 2	1			1		2
Node 3				3	2	
Node 4		1	1			1
Node 5			1			6
Node 6	1000	2		1		

Maximal flow = 5.0

=B10

Table shows road capacities.

Solver Parameters

Set Objective: $C$22

To: Max Min Value Of: 0

By Changing Variable Cells:

$B$6:$B$8,$B$10,$C$5,$C$8,$C$10,$D$5,$D$8:$D$9,$E$5:$E$7,E

Subject to the Constraints:

$B$5:$G$10 <= $B$15:$G$20

$M$5:$M$10 = $O$5:$O$10

Road capacity constraints

Changing Variable Cells that are not contiguous are separated by commas.

Arc capacities of zero will prevent flows on arcs.

In the second (and easier) approach, we specify the entire cell range B5:G10 in the By Changing Variable Cells box in Solver.[4] Then, for all roads that do not exist (e.g., road $1 \rightarrow 5$, road $2 \rightarrow 3$), we set the flow capacity to zero. Solved Problem 5-3 at the end of this chapter shows an example of this approach for a maximal-flow model.

The solution to Waukesha's problem shows that 500 cars (recall that all numbers are in hundreds of cars) can flow through the town from west to east. The values of the decision variables indicate the actual car flow on each road. Total flow in (column K) and total flow out (column L) at each node are also shown. For example, the total flow out of node 1 is 500 cars, split as 200 cars on $1 \rightarrow 2$, 200 cars on $1 \rightarrow 3$, and 100 cars on $1 \rightarrow 4$.

5.8 Shortest-Path Model

A shortest-path model finds the path with the minimum distance through a network.

The *shortest-path model* finds how a person or an item can travel from one location to another through a network while minimizing the total distance traveled, time taken, or some other measure. In other words, it finds the shortest path or route from an origin to a series of destinations.

[4] If there are more than 14 nodes in the network, we cannot use this approach with the standard version of Solver (included with Excel) because that version can handle a maximum of only 200 decision variables.

IN ACTION Maximal-Flow Model Facilitates Improved Natural Gas Production and Transport

Norwegian gas covered three percent of the worldwide production in 2007, and its export is expected to increase by nearly 50 percent within the next decade. With over 7,800 km of subsea pipelines, the natural gas transport network on the Norwegian Continental Shelf (NCS) is the world's largest offshore pipeline network. The network has an annual capacity of 120 billion standard cubic meters, which represents about 15 percent of European consumption.

In order to ensure the most effective usage of this complex network, StatoilHydro, Norway's main shipper of natural gas, and Gassco, an independent network operator, use a maximum flow model embedded within a decision support tool named GassOpt to optimize the network configuration and routing. The primary decision variables in this model are the total flow and component flow between different nodes in the network. The objective function is to maximize the gas flow with some penalty terms for pressure increases, etc. The constraints include such issues as field capacities, market demands, mass balance, and pressure and flow restrictions.

GassOpt has been used extensively for the development of the dry-gas network on the NCS for the past decade, and is expected to remain an important part of infrastructure development. StatoilHydro estimates that its accumulated savings related to the use of GassOpt were approximately US$2 billion during the period 1995–2008.

Source: Based on F. Rømo et al. "Optimizing the Norwegian Natural Gas Production and Transport," *Interfaces* 39, 1 (January–February 2009): 46–56.

Ray Design Inc. Example

Every day, Ray Design Inc. must transport beds, chairs, and other furniture items from the factory to the warehouse. This involves going through several cities (nodes). Ray would like to find the path with the shortest distance, in miles. The road network is shown in Figure 5.8.

A shortest-path model has a unique starting node and a unique ending node.

The shortest-path model is another example of a network model that has a unique starting node (origin) and a unique ending node (destination). If we assume that there is a supply of one unit at node 1 (factory) and a demand of one unit at node 6 (warehouse), the shortest-path model for the Ray Design example is identical to a transshipment model with a single origin node (node 1), a single destination node (node 6), and four transshipment nodes (node 2 through node 5).

Each flow in a shortest-path model will equal one unit.

Because the supply and demand both equal one unit, which is a whole number, the solution to the model will have integer-valued flows on all arcs. Hence, the supply of one unit at node 1 will flow in its entirety on either road $1 \rightarrow 2$ or road $1 \rightarrow 3$. Further, because the net flow is zero at each of the transshipment nodes (cities), a flow of one unit on an incoming arc (road) at any of these cities automatically has to result in a flow of one unit on an outgoing road from that city.

LP Formulation for Ray Design Inc.'s Shortest-Path Model

Because all 9 arcs (roads) in the network are bidirectional, we first replace each one with a pair of unidirectional roads. There are, therefore, 18 decision variables in the model. As usual, let

X_{ij} = Flow on road from node i to node j. The solution value will equal 1 if travel occurs on the road from node i to node j and will equal 0 otherwise.

where i and j each equal 1, 2, 3, 4, 5, or 6. As with the maximal-flow model, flow variables are defined only on roads that actually exist. For example, X_{12} (i.e., $i = 1, j = 2$) is defined, while X_{14} (i.e., $i = 1, j = 4$) is not defined.

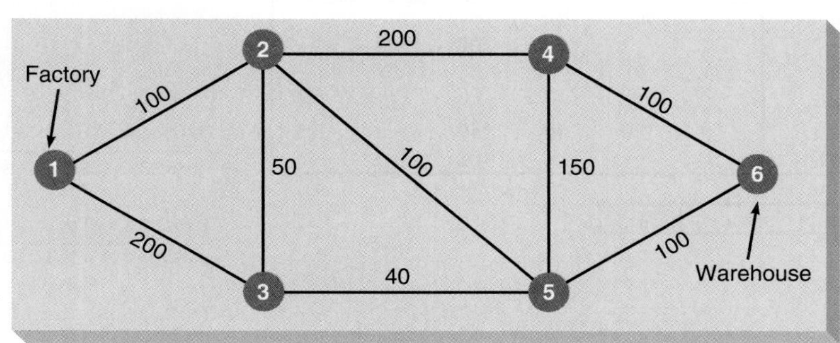

FIGURE 5.8
Roads from Ray Design's Factory to Warehouse—Shortest-Path

OBJECTIVE FUNCTION The objective is to minimize the distance between node 1 and node 6 and can be expressed as

$$\begin{aligned}\text{Minimize}z\ & 100X_{12} + 200X_{13} + 100X_{21} + 50X_{23} + 200X_{24} + 100X_{25}\\ & + 200X_{31} + 50X_{32} + 40X_{35} + 200X_{42} + 150X_{45} + 100X_{46}\\ & + 100X_{52} + 40X_{53} + 150X_{54} + 100X_{56} + 100X_{64} + 100X_{65}\end{aligned}$$

The optimal value for each variable will be 0 or 1, depending on whether travel occurs on that road. So the objective function is the sum of road distances on which travel (flow) actually occurs.

CONSTRAINTS We write the flow balance constraints at each node as follows:

$$\begin{aligned}
(X_{21} + X_{31}) - (X_{12} + X_{13}) &= -1 && \text{(supply of one unit at node 1)}\\
(X_{12} + X_{32} + X_{42} + X_{52}) - (X_{21} + X_{23} + X_{24} + X_{25}) &= 0 && \text{(transshipment at node 2)}\\
(X_{13} + X_{23} + X_{53}) - (X_{31} + X_{32} + X_{35}) &= 0 && \text{(transshipment at node 3)}\\
(X_{24} + X_{54} + X_{64}) - (X_{42} + X_{45} + X_{46}) &= 0 && \text{(transshipment at node 4)}\\
(X_{25} + X_{35} + X_{45} + X_{65}) - (X_{52} + X_{53} + X_{54} + X_{56}) &= 0 && \text{(transshipment at node 5)}\\
(X_{46} + X_{56}) - (X_{64} + X_{65}) &= 1 && \text{(demand of one unit at node 6)}
\end{aligned}$$

File: 5-8.xls

EXCEL SOLUTION Screenshot 5-8 shows the Excel layout and Solver entries for Ray Design's shortest-path model. Once again, we use the tabular layout to represent flows on roads. However, only 18 of the 36 cells in the range B5:G10 actually represent roads that exist (indicated by the cells shaded yellow in Screenshot 5-8). As with the maximal-flow model, roads that do not exist need to be excluded when specifying entries for the changing variable cells in Solver.

SCREENSHOT 5-8 Excel Layout and Solver Entries for Ray Design Inc.—Shortest-Path

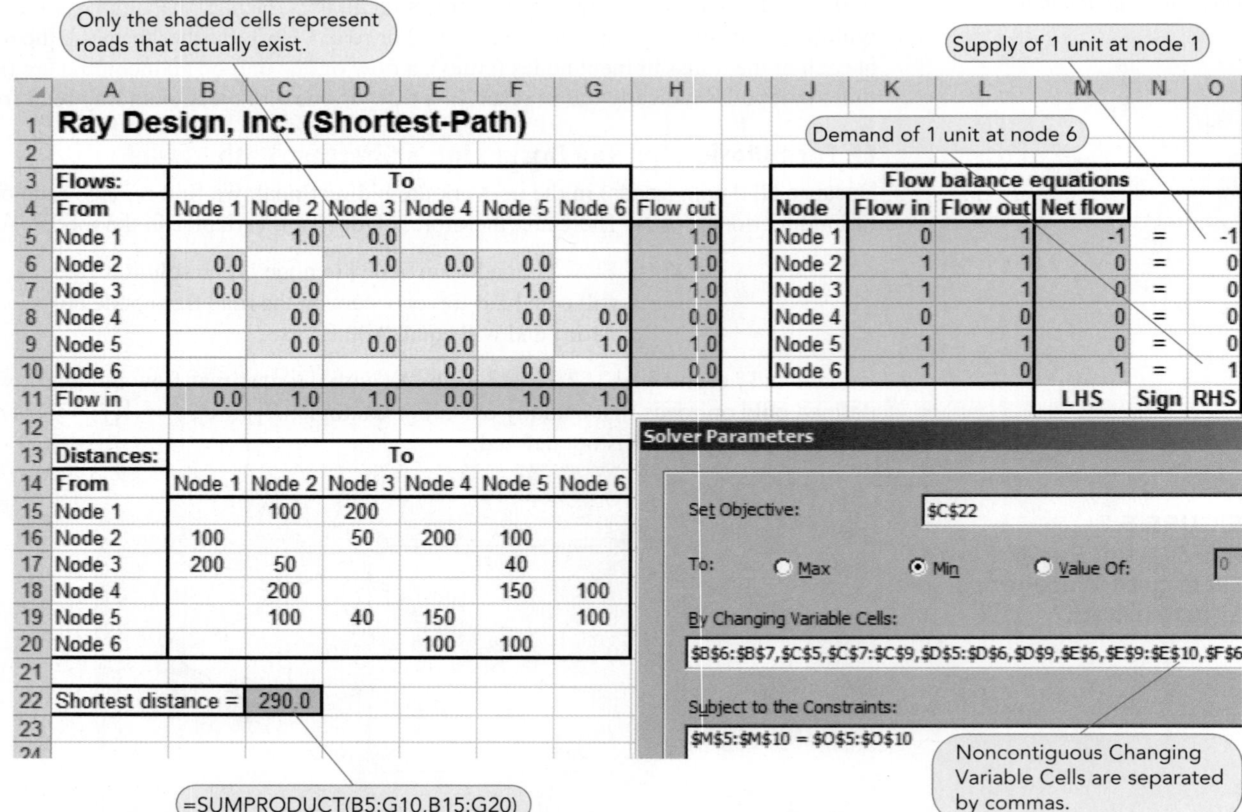

Flows: From	Node 1	Node 2	Node 3	Node 4	Node 5	Node 6	Flow out
Node 1		1.0	0.0				1.0
Node 2	0.0		1.0	0.0	0.0		1.0
Node 3	0.0	0.0			1.0		1.0
Node 4		0.0			0.0	0.0	0.0
Node 5		0.0	0.0	0.0		1.0	1.0
Node 6				0.0	0.0		0.0
Flow in	0.0	1.0	1.0	0.0	1.0	1.0	

Node	Flow in	Flow out	Net flow		
Node 1	0	1	-1	=	-1
Node 2	1	1	0	=	0
Node 3	1	1	0	=	0
Node 4	0	0	0	=	0
Node 5	1	1	0	=	0
Node 6	1	0	1	=	1
			LHS	Sign	RHS

Distances: From	Node 1	Node 2	Node 3	Node 4	Node 5	Node 6
Node 1		100	200			
Node 2	100		50	200	100	
Node 3	200	50			40	
Node 4		200			150	100
Node 5		100	40	150		100
Node 6				100	100	

IN ACTION Spanning Tree Analysis of a Telecommunications Network

Network models have been used to solve a variety of problems of many different companies. In telecommunications, there is always a need to connect computer systems and devices together in an efficient and effective manner. Digital Equipment Corporation (DEC), for example, was concerned about how computer systems and devices were connected to a local area network (LAN) using Ethernet. The DEC net routing department was responsible for this and other network and telecommunications solutions.

Because of a number of technical difficulties, it was important to have an effective way to transport packets of information throughout the LAN. The solution was to use a spanning tree algorithm. The success of this approach can be seen in a poem written by one of the developers:

"I think I shall never see a graph more lovely than a tree.
A tree whose critical property is loop-free connectivity.
A tree that must be sure to span, so packets can reach every LAN.
First the route must be selected, by ID it is elected.
Least-cost paths from the root are traced.
In the tree these paths are placed.
A mesh is made for folks by me, then bridges find a spanning tree."

Source: Based on R. Perlman et al. "Spanning the LAN," Data Communications (October 21, 1997): 68.

One way of achieving this is to separate noncontiguous cell entries by using commas, as shown in Screenshot 5-8. That is, we specify only cells B6:B7, C5, C7:C9, etc. in the By Changing Variables Cells box in Solver.

Arcs with large (infinite) distances will have zero flows.

Alternatively, we can specify the entire cell range (cells B5:G10) as the changing variable cells.[5] However, to prevent travel on roads that do not exist (e.g., $1 \rightarrow 4$, $1 \rightarrow 5$), the distance of these roads can be set to a large number (compared to other distances in the problem) in the corresponding cells in B15:G20. For example, we could specify a large distance such as 2,000 for road $1 \rightarrow 4$ in cell E15. Clearly, no travel will occur on this road because the objective is to minimize total distance. Solved Problem 5-4 at the end of this chapter shows an example of this approach.

The solution to Ray's problem shows that the shortest distance from the factory to the warehouse is 290 miles and involves travel through cities 2, 3, and 5.

5.9 Minimal-Spanning Tree Model

A minimal-spanning tree model connects nodes at a minimum total distance.

The *minimal-spanning tree model* can be used to connect all the nodes of a network to each other while minimizing the total distance of all the arcs used for this connection. It has been applied, for example, by telephone companies to connect a number of phones (nodes) together while minimizing the total length of telephone cable (arcs).

Lauderdale Construction Company Example

Let us consider the Lauderdale Construction Company, which is currently developing a luxurious housing project in Panama City, Florida. Melvin Lauderdale, owner of Lauderdale Construction, must determine the minimum total length of water pipes needed to provide water to each house. The network of eight houses is shown in Figure 5.9, along with the distances between the houses (in hundreds of feet).

Unlike the other network flow models studied so far in this chapter, in a minimal-spanning tree model, it is difficult to classify nodes *a priori* as origins, destinations, and transshipment nodes. For this reason, we do not formulate these models as LP problems using the flow balance

[5] As with the maximal-flow model, the standard version of Solver cannot handle this approach on networks with more than 14 nodes.

FIGURE 5.9
Network for Lauderdale Construction—Minimal-Spanning Tree

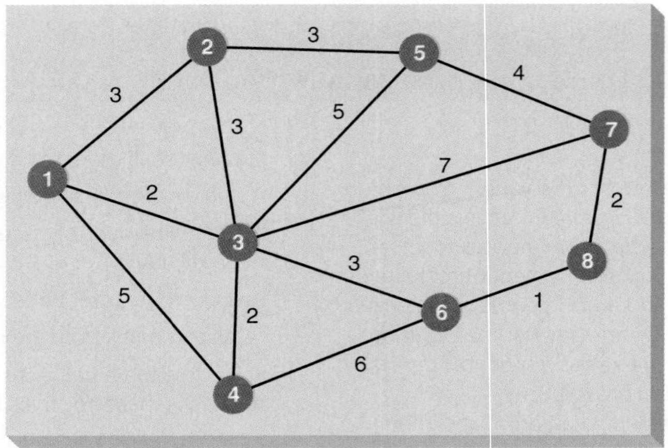

equations. However, the minimal-spanning tree model is very easy to solve by hand, using a simple solution procedure. The procedure is outlined as follows:

There are four steps in the solution procedure for minimal-spanning tree problems.

Steps for Solving the Minimal-Spanning Tree Model

1. Select any node in the network.
2. Connect this node to its nearest node.
3. Considering all the connected nodes, find the nearest *unconnected* node and then connect it. If there is a tie, and two or more unconnected nodes are equally near, select one arbitrarily. A tie suggests that there may be more than one optimal solution.
4. Repeat step 3 until all the nodes are connected.

Step 1: We select node 1.

Step 2: We connect node 1 to node 3.

Step 3: We connect the next nearest node (node 4).

Step 4: We repeat step 3 until all nodes are connected.

We can now solve the network in Figure 5.9 for Melvin Lauderdale. We start by arbitrarily selecting any node (house). Let's say we select house 1. Because house 3 is the nearest one to house 1, at a distance of 2 (200 feet), we connect these two houses. That is, we select arc $1 \rightarrow 3$ for inclusion in the spanning tree. This is shown in Figure 5.10.

Next, considering connected houses 1 and 3, we look for the unconnected house that is closest to either house. This turns out to be house 4, which is 200 feet from house 3. We connect houses 3 and 4 by selecting arc $3 \rightarrow 4$ (see Figure 5.11(a)).

We continue, looking for the nearest unconnected house to houses 1, 3, and 4. This is either house 2 or house 6, both at a distance of 300 feet from house 3. We arbitrarily pick house 2 and connect it to house 3 by selecting arc $3 \rightarrow 2$ (see Figure 5.11(b)).

FIGURE 5.10
First Iteration for Lauderdale Construction

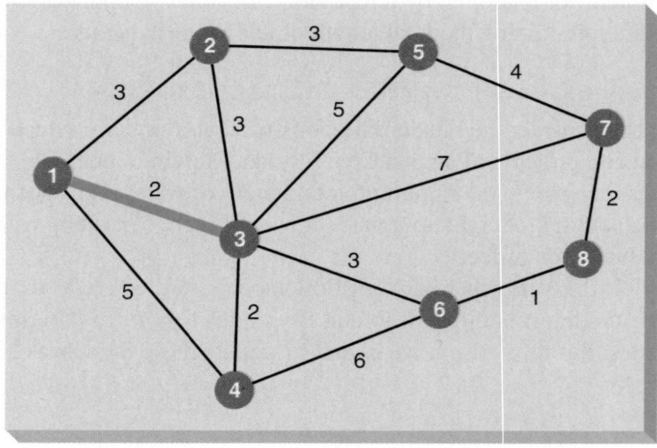

FIGURE 5.11 Second and Third Iterations for Lauderdale Construction

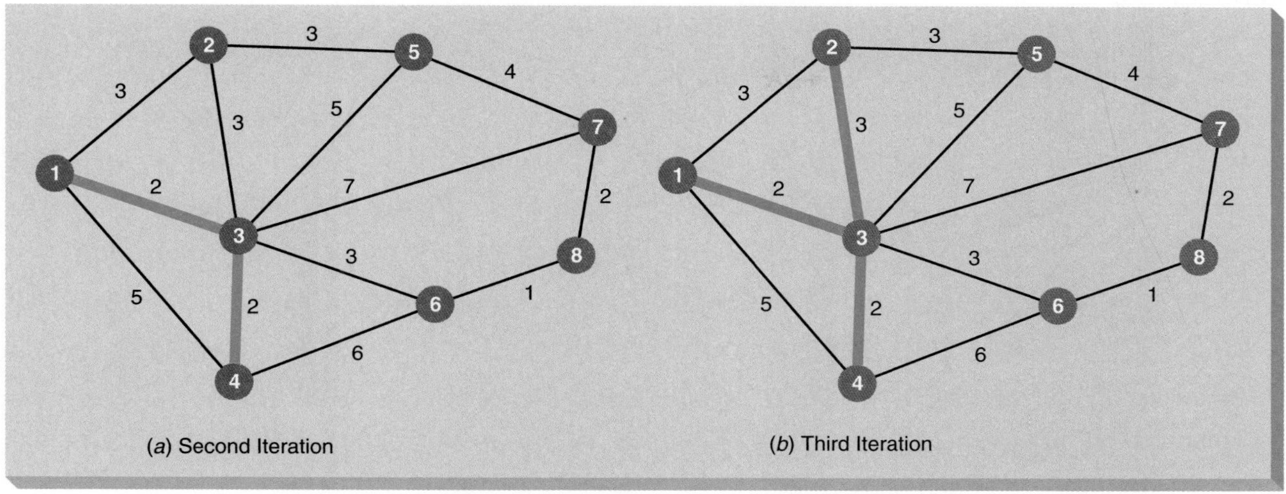

We continue the process. There is another tie for the next iteration, with a minimum distance of 300 feet (house 2 to house 5 and house 3 to house 6). Note that we do not consider house 1 to house 2, with a distance of 300 feet, at this iteration because both houses are already connected. We arbitrarily select house 5 and connect it to house 2 by selecting arc $2 \rightarrow 5$ (see Figure 5.12(a)). The next nearest house is house 6, and we connect it to house 3 by selecting arc $3 \rightarrow 6$ (see Figure 5.12(b)).

At this stage, we have only two unconnected houses left. House 8 is the nearest one to house 6, with a distance of 100 feet, and we connect it by using arc $6 \rightarrow 8$ (see Figure 5.13(a). Then the remaining house, house 7, is connected to house 8 using arc $8 \rightarrow 7$ (see Figure 5.13(b)).

Because there are no more unconnected houses, Figure 5.13(b) shows the final solution. Houses 1, 2, 4, and 6 are all connected to house 3. House 2 is connected to house 5. House 6 is connected to house 8, and house 8 is connected to house 7. The total distance is 1,600 feet.

FIGURE 5.12 Fourth and Fifth Iterations for Lauderdale Construction

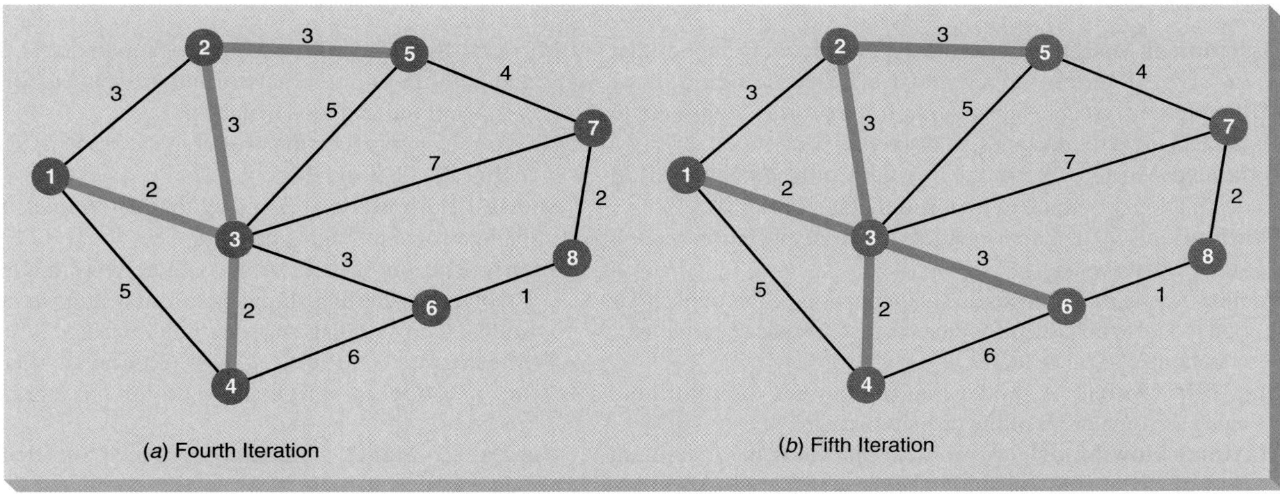

FIGURE 5.13 Sixth and Seventh (Final) Iterations for Lauderdale Construction

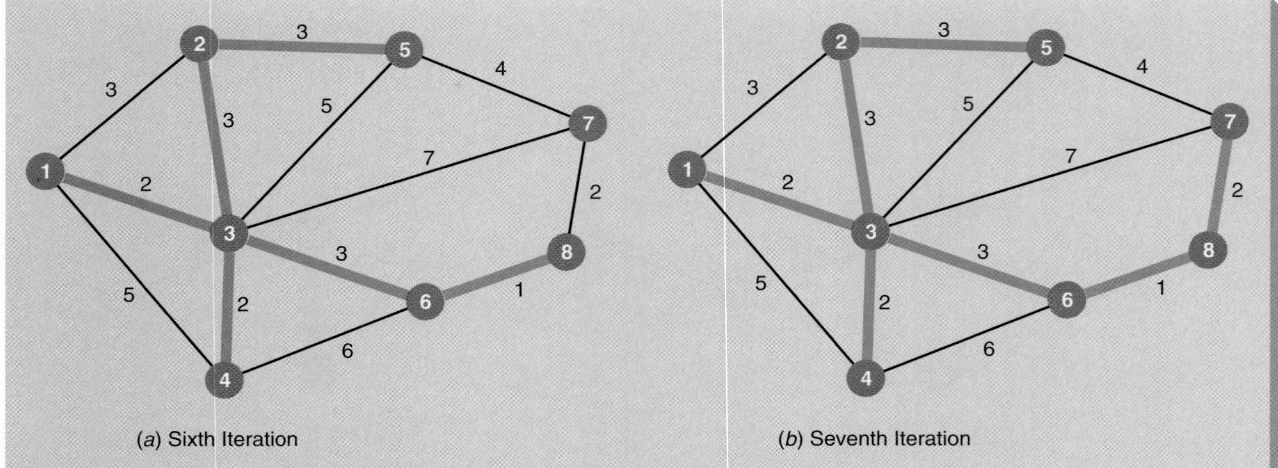

Summary

This chapter presents six important network flow models. First, we discuss the transportation model, which deals with the distribution of goods from several supply points to a number of demand points. We also consider transportation models with Max-Min and Min-Max objectives. We then extend the discussion to the transshipment model, which includes points that permit goods to both flow in and flow out of them. Next, we discuss the assignment model, which deals with determining the most efficient assignment of issues such as people to projects.

The fourth model covered is the maximal-flow model, which finds the maximum flow of any quantity or substance that can go through a network. This is followed by a discussion of the shortest-path model, which finds the shortest path through a network. Finally, we introduce the minimal-spanning tree model, which determines the path through the network that connects all the nodes while minimizing total distance.

Glossary

Assignment Model A specific type of network model that involves determining the most efficient assignment of people to projects, salespeople to territories, contracts to bidders, jobs to machines, and so on.

Balanced Model A model in which total demand (at all destinations) is equal to total supply (at all origins).

Destination A demand location in a transportation model. Also called a *sink*.

Facility Location Analysis An application of the transportation model to help a firm decide where to locate a new factory, warehouse, or other facility.

Max-Min Model A model that maximizes the minimum value of some or all of the decision variables.

Maximal-Flow Model A problem that finds the maximum flow of any quantity or substance through a network.

Min-Max Model A model that minimizes the maximum value of some or all of the decision variables.

Minimal-Spanning Tree Model A model that determines the path through the network that connects all the nodes while minimizing total distance.

Origin A supply location or source in a transportation model. Also called a *source*.

Shortest-Path Model A model that determines the shortest path or route through a network.

Transportation Model A specific network model case that involves scheduling shipments from origins to destinations so that total shipping costs are minimized.

Transshipment Model An extension of the transportation model in which some points have both flows in and out.

Unbalanced Model A situation in which total demand is not equal to total supply.

Solved Problems

Solved Problem 5-1

The Hardgrave Machine Company produces computer components at its factories in Cincinnati, Kansas City, and Pittsburgh. These factories have not been able to keep up with demand for orders at Hardgrave's four warehouses in Detroit, Houston, New York, and Los Angeles. As a result, the firm has decided to build a new factory to expand its productive capacity. The two sites being considered are Seattle, Washington, and Birmingham, Alabama. Both cities are attractive in terms of labor supply, municipal services, and ease of factory financing.

Table 5.6 presents the production costs and monthly supplies at each of the three existing factories, monthly demands at each of the four warehouses, and estimated production costs at the two proposed factories. Transportation costs from each factory to each warehouse are summarized in Table 5.7. Where should Hardgrave locate the new factory?

Solution

File: 5-9.xls

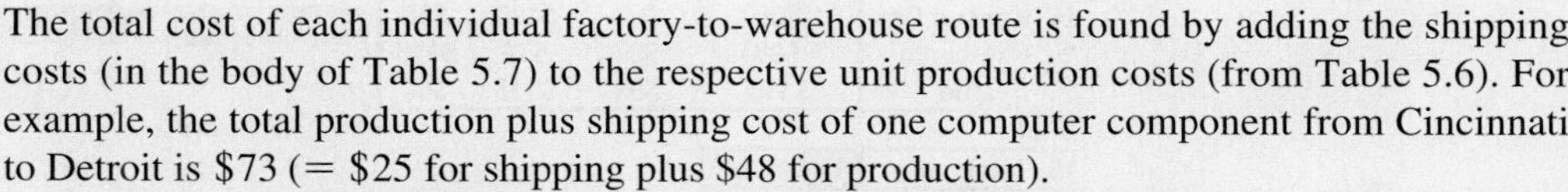

The total cost of each individual factory-to-warehouse route is found by adding the shipping costs (in the body of Table 5.7) to the respective unit production costs (from Table 5.6). For example, the total production plus shipping cost of one computer component from Cincinnati to Detroit is $73 (= $25 for shipping plus $48 for production).

To determine which new factory (Seattle or Birmingham) yields the lowest total system cost, we solve two transportation models: one for each of the two possible locations. In each case, there are 4 factories and 4 warehouses. Hence, there are 16 decision variables.

Screenshots 5-9A and 5-9B on page 194 show the resulting optimum solutions with the total cost for each of the two locations. From these solutions, it appears that Seattle should be selected as the new factory site. Its total cost of $3,704,000 is less than the $3,741,000 cost at Birmingham.

TABLE 5.6
Hardgrave Machine's Demand and Supply Data

WAREHOUSE	MONTHLY DEMAND (UNITS)	PRODUCTION PLANT	MONTHLY SUPPLY	COST TO PRODUCE ONE UNIT
Detroit	10,000	Cincinnati	15,000	$48
Houston	12,000	Kansas City	6,000	$50
New York	15,000	Pittsburgh	14,000	$52
Los Angeles	9,000		35,000	
	46,000			

Supply needed from new plant = 46,000 − 35,000 = 11,000 units per month

ESTIMATED PRODUCTION COST PER UNIT AT PROPOSED PLANTS	
Seattle	$53
Birmingham	$49

TABLE 5.7
Hardgrave Machine's Shipping Costs

	TO			
FROM	DETROIT	HOUSTON	NEW YORK	LOS ANGELES
Cincinnati	$25	$55	$40	$60
Kansas City	$35	$30	$50	$40
Pittsburgh	$36	$45	$26	$66
Seattle	$60	$38	$65	$27
Birmingham	$35	$30	$41	$50

SCREENSHOT 5-9A
Excel Layout and Solver Entries for Hardgrave Machine—New Facility in Seattle

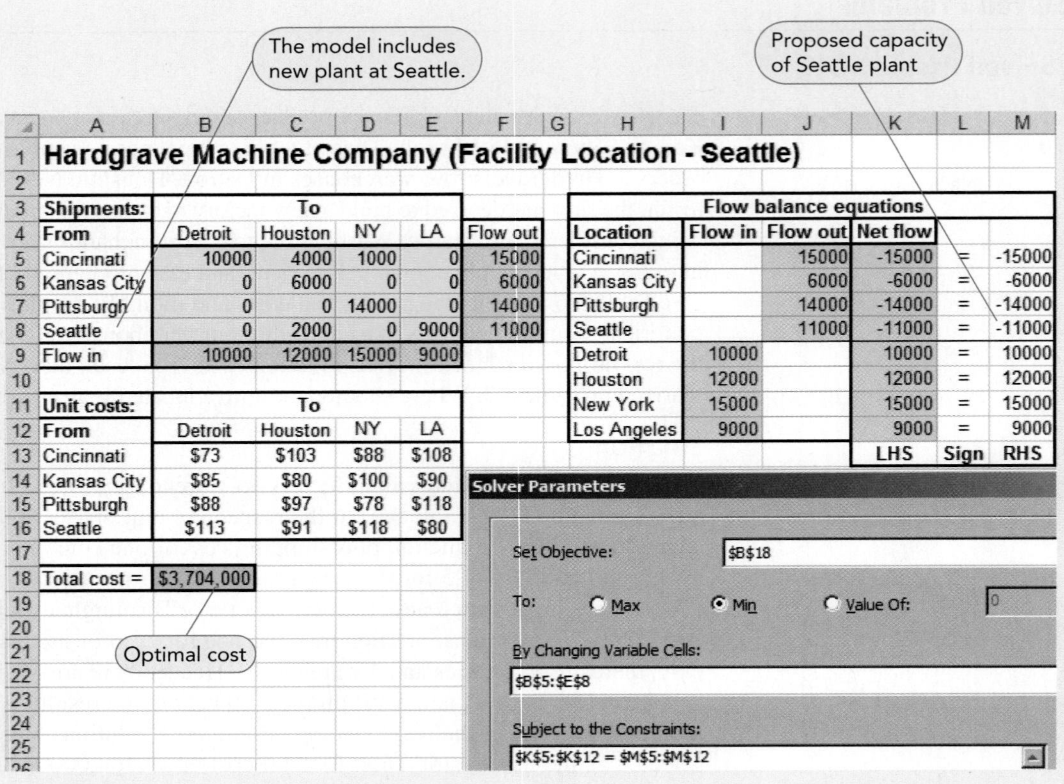

Hardgrave Machine Company (Facility Location - Seattle)

Shipments: From	Detroit	Houston	NY	LA	Flow out
Cincinnati	10000	4000	1000	0	15000
Kansas City	0	6000	0	0	6000
Pittsburgh	0	0	14000	0	14000
Seattle	0	2000	0	9000	11000
Flow in	10000	12000	15000	9000	

Unit costs: From	Detroit	Houston	NY	LA
Cincinnati	$73	$103	$88	$108
Kansas City	$85	$80	$100	$90
Pittsburgh	$88	$97	$78	$118
Seattle	$113	$91	$118	$80

Total cost = $3,704,000

Location	Flow in	Flow out	Net flow		
Cincinnati		15000	-15000	=	-15000
Kansas City		6000	-6000	=	-6000
Pittsburgh		14000	-14000	=	-14000
Seattle		11000	-11000	=	-11000
Detroit	10000		10000	=	10000
Houston	12000		12000	=	12000
New York	15000		15000	=	15000
Los Angeles	9000		9000	=	9000
			LHS	Sign	RHS

Solver Parameters
Set Objective: $B$18
To: Max / Min (selected) / Value Of: 0
By Changing Variable Cells: $B$5:$E$8
Subject to the Constraints: $K$5:$K$12 = $M$5:$M$12

SCREENSHOT 5-9B
Excel Layout and Solver Entries for Hardgrave Machine—New Facility in Birmingham

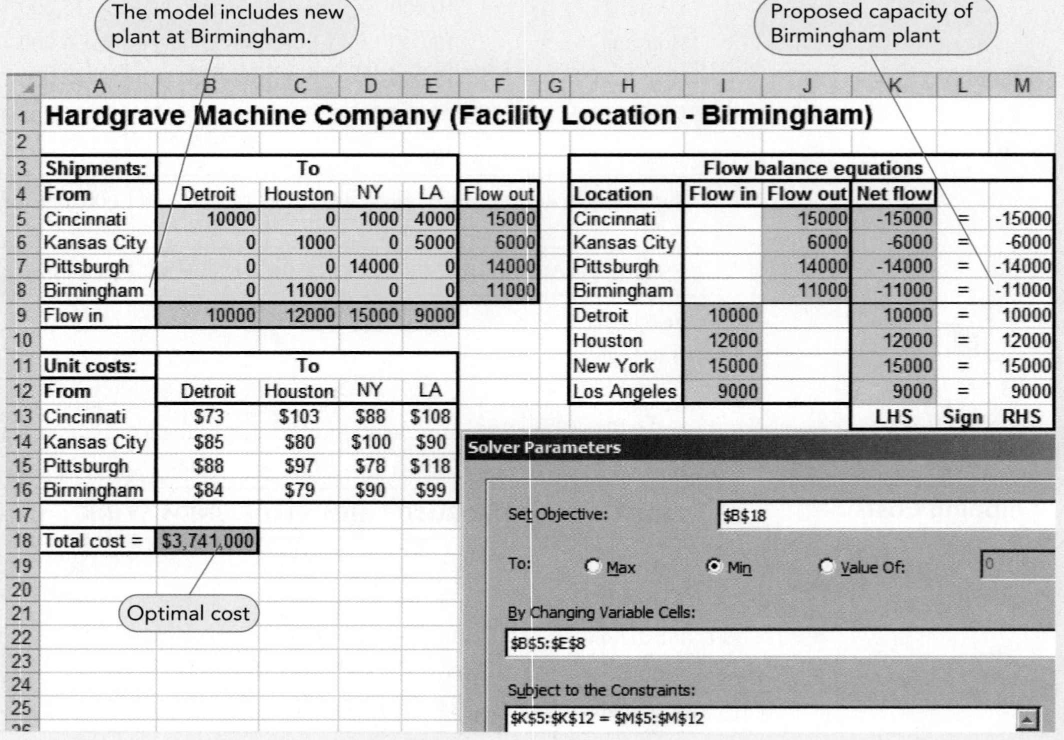

Hardgrave Machine Company (Facility Location - Birmingham)

Shipments: From	Detroit	Houston	NY	LA	Flow out
Cincinnati	10000	0	1000	4000	15000
Kansas City	0	1000	0	5000	6000
Pittsburgh	0	0	14000	0	14000
Birmingham	0	11000	0	0	11000
Flow in	10000	12000	15000	9000	

Unit costs: From	Detroit	Houston	NY	LA
Cincinnati	$73	$103	$88	$108
Kansas City	$85	$80	$100	$90
Pittsburgh	$88	$97	$78	$118
Birmingham	$84	$79	$90	$99

Total cost = $3,741,000

Location	Flow in	Flow out	Net flow		
Cincinnati		15000	-15000	=	-15000
Kansas City		6000	-6000	=	-6000
Pittsburgh		14000	-14000	=	-14000
Birmingham		11000	-11000	=	-11000
Detroit	10000		10000	=	10000
Houston	12000		12000	=	12000
New York	15000		15000	=	15000
Los Angeles	9000		9000	=	9000
			LHS	Sign	RHS

Solver Parameters
Set Objective: $B$18
To: Max / Min (selected) / Value Of: 0
By Changing Variable Cells: $B$5:$E$8
Subject to the Constraints: $K$5:$K$12 = $M$5:$M$12

Solved Problem 5-2

Prentice Hall Inc., a publisher headquartered in New Jersey, wants to assign three recently hired college graduates, Jones, Smith, and Wilson, to regional sales offices in Omaha, Miami, and Dallas. But the firm also has an opening in New York and would send one of the three there if it were more economical than a move to Omaha, Miami, or Dallas. It will cost $1,000 to relocate Jones to New York, $800 to relocate Smith there, and $1,500 to move Wilson. The other relocation costs are as follows:

	OFFICE		
HIREE	OMAHA	MIAMI	DALLAS
Jones	$800	$1,100	$1,200
Smith	$500	$1,600	$1,300
Wilson	$500	$1,000	$2,300

What is the optimal assignment of personnel to offices?

File: 5-10.xls

Solution

Because this is an unbalanced assignment model with three supply points (hirees) and four demand points (offices), note that the demand constraints should be expressed as inequalities (i.e., they should have ≤ signs).

Screenshot 5-10 shows the Excel layout and solution for Prentice Hall's assignment model. The optimal solution is to assign Wilson to Omaha, Smith to New York, and Jones to Miami. Nobody is assigned to Dallas. The total cost is $2,400.

SCREENSHOT 5-10 Excel Layout and Solver Entries for Prentice Hall Inc.—Assignment

Prentice Hall, Inc. (Assignment)

Assignments:	Office				
Hiree	Omaha	Miami	Dallas	New York	Flow out
Jones	0.0	1.0	0.0	0.0	1.0
Smith	0.0	0.0	0.0	1.0	1.0
Wilson	1.0	0.0	0.0	0.0	1.0
Flow in	1.0	1.0	0.0	1.0	

Unit costs:	Office			
Hiree	Omaha	Miami	Dallas	New York
Jones	$800	$1,100	$1,200	$1,000
Smith	$500	$1,600	$1,300	$800
Wilson	$500	$1,000	$2,300	$1,500

Total cost = $2,400

Flow balance equations					
Node	Flow in	Flow out	Net flow		
Jones		1	-1	=	-1
Smith		1	-1	=	-1
Wilson		1	-1	=	-1
Omaha	1		1	<=	1
Miami	1		1	<=	1
Dallas	0		0	<=	1
New York	1		1	<=	1
			LHS	Sign	RHS

Optimal solution has no one assigned to Dallas.

Demand flow balance constraints are ≤ since number of locations exceeds number of hirees.

Solver Parameters

Set Objective: $B$16

To: Max Min Value Of: 0

By Changing Variable Cells: $B$5:$E$7

Subject to the Constraints:
$K$5:$K$7 = $M$5:$M$7
$K$8:$K$11 <= $M$8:$M$11

Solved Problem 5-3

PetroChem, an oil refinery located on the Mississippi River south of Baton Rouge, Louisiana, is designing a new plant to produce diesel fuel. Figure 5.14 shows the network of the main processing centers along with the existing rate of flow (in thousands of gallons of fuel). The management at PetroChem would like to determine the maximum amount of fuel that can flow through the plant, from node 1 to node 7.

Solution

Node 1 is the origin node, and node 7 is the destination node. As described in Section 5.7, we convert all bidirectional arcs into unidirectional arcs, and we introduce a dummy arc from node 7 to node 1. The modified network is shown in Figure 5.15. The capacity of the dummy arc from node 7 to node 1 is set at a large number such as 1,000.

Screenshot 5-11 on page 197 shows the Excel layout and solution for this model. Unlike our earlier maximal-flow example in Screenshot 5-7, the entire cell range B5:H11 has been specified as the changing variable cells in Solver. However, the capacity of all arcs that do not exist (shown by the non-yellow cells in B5:H11) has been set to zero (in cells B16:H22) to prevent any fuel flows on these pipes (arcs).

The optimal solution shows that it is possible to have 10,000 gallons flow from node 1 to node 7 using the existing network.

Solved Problem 5-4

The network in Figure 5.16 shows the roads and cities surrounding Leadville, Colorado. Leadville Tom, a bicycle helmet manufacturer, must transport his helmets to a distributor based in Dillon, Colorado. To do this, he must go through several cities. Tom would like to find the shortest way to get from Leadville to Dillon. What do you recommend?

FIGURE 5.14 Network for PetroChem—Maximal-Flow

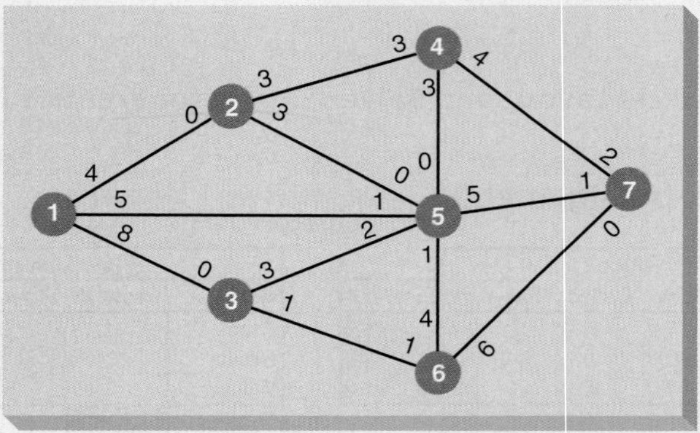

FIGURE 5.15 Modified Network for PetroChem—Maximal-Flow

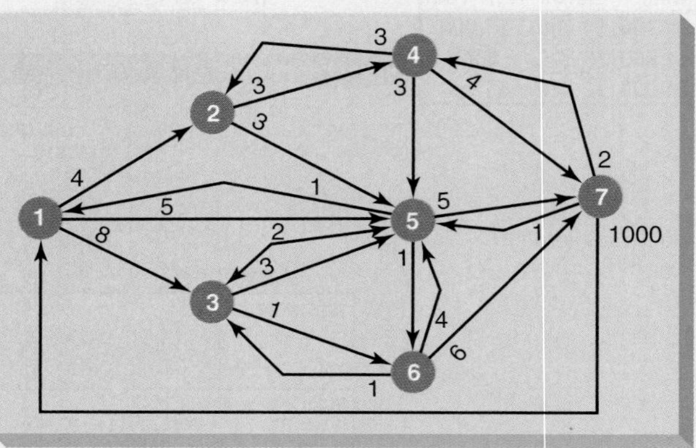

SCREENSHOT 5-11 Excel Layout and Solver Entries for PetroChem—Maximal-Flow

Table shows the flows between all pairs of nodes.

Only the shaded cells denote pipes that actually exist.

PetroChem (Maximal-Flow)

Flows:	To							
From	Node 1	Node 2	Node 3	Node 4	Node 5	Node 6	Node 7	Flow out
Node 1	0.0	4.0	1.0	0.0	5.0	0.0	0.0	10.0
Node 2	0.0	0.0	0.0	3.0	1.0	0.0	0.0	4.0
Node 3	0.0	0.0	0.0	0.0	0.0	1.0	0.0	1.0
Node 4	0.0	0.0	0.0	0.0	0.0	0.0	3.0	3.0
Node 5	0.0	0.0	0.0	0.0	0.0	1.0	5.0	6.0
Node 6	0.0	0.0	0.0	0.0	0.0	0.0	2.0	2.0
Node 7	10.0	0.0	0.0	0.0	0.0	0.0	0.0	10.0
Flow in	10.0	4.0	1.0	3.0	6.0	2.0	10.0	

Flow balance equations					
Node	Flow in	Flow out	Net flow		
Node 1	10	10	0	=	0
Node 2	4	4	0	=	0
Node 3	1	1	0	=	0
Node 4	3	3	0	=	0
Node 5	6	6	0	=	0
Node 6	2	2	0	=	0
Node 7	10	10	0	=	0
			LHS	Sign	RHS

Capacities:	To						
From	Node 1	Node 2	Node 3	Node 4	Node 5	Node 6	Node 7
Node 1	0	4	8	0	5	0	0
Node 2	0	0	0	3	3	0	0
Node 3	0	0	0	0	3	1	0
Node 4	0	3	0	0	3	0	4
Node 5	1	0	2	0	0	1	5
Node 6	0	0	1	0	4	0	6
Node 7	1000	0	0	2	1	0	0

Maximal flow = 10.0

Solver Parameters

Set Objective: $C$24

To: Max Min Value Of: 0

By Changing Variable Cells: $B$5:$H$11

Subject to the Constraints:
$B$5:$H$11 <= $B$16:$H$22
$N$5:$N$11 = $P$5:$P$11

This is an artificially high capacity for the dummy pipe from node 7 to node 1.

Capacities of pipes that do not exist are set to zero.

All cells in the table of decision variables (B5:H11) are specified as Changing Variable Cells. No flow occurs on pipes that do not exist since their capacities are zero.

Pipe capacity constraint

FIGURE 5.16 Network for Leadville Tom—Shortest-Path

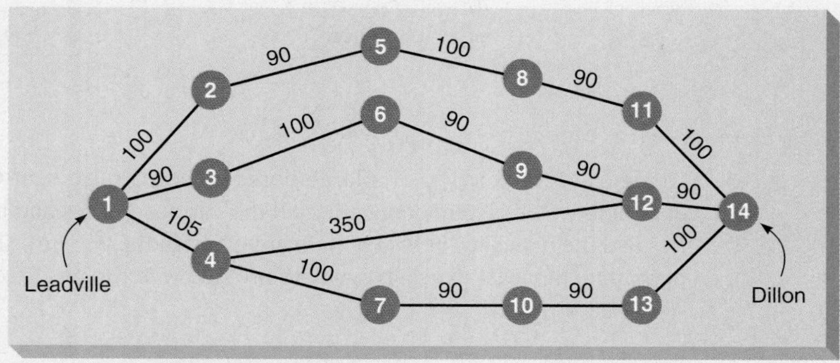

WWW

File: 5-11.xls

Solution

We associate a supply of one unit at Leadville (node 1) and a demand of one unit at Dillon (node 14). Screenshot 5-12 shows the Excel layout and solution for this model. Unlike our earlier shortest-path example in Screenshot 5-8, the entire cell range B5:O18 has been specified as the changing variable cells in Solver. However, we prevent flow (travel) on all roads that do not exist (shown by the non-yellow cells in B5:O18) by setting their distances to high values (in cells B23:O36).

The optimal solution shows that the shortest distance from Leadville to Dillon is 460 miles and involves travel through nodes 3, 6, 9, and 12.

SCREENSHOT 5-12 Excel Layout and Solver Entries for Leadville Tom—Shortest-Path

Only the shaded cells denote roads that actually exist.

Table shows the flows between all pairs of nodes.

Demand of 1 unit at node 14

Supply of 1 unit at node 1

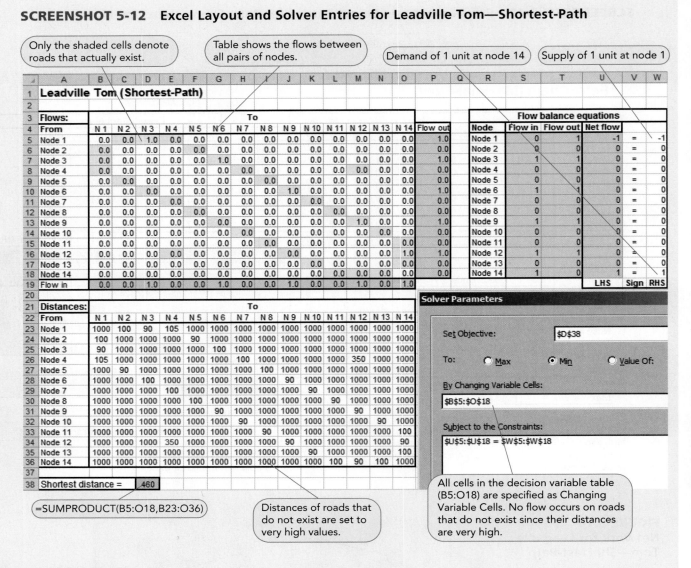

Leadville Tom (Shortest-Path)

Flows: From	N 1	N 2	N 3	N 4	N 5	N 6	N 7	N 8	N 9	N 10	N 11	N 12	N 13	N 14	Flow out
Node 1	0.0	0.0	1.0	0.0	0.0	0.0	0.0	0.0	0.0	0.0	0.0	0.0	0.0	0.0	1.0
Node 2	0.0	0.0	0.0	0.0	0.0	0.0	0.0	0.0	0.0	0.0	0.0	0.0	0.0	0.0	0.0
Node 3	0.0	0.0	0.0	0.0	0.0	1.0	0.0	0.0	0.0	0.0	0.0	0.0	0.0	0.0	1.0
Node 4	0.0	0.0	0.0	0.0	0.0	0.0	0.0	0.0	0.0	0.0	0.0	0.0	0.0	0.0	0.0
Node 5	0.0	0.0	0.0	0.0	0.0	0.0	0.0	0.0	0.0	0.0	0.0	0.0	0.0	0.0	0.0
Node 6	0.0	0.0	0.0	0.0	0.0	0.0	0.0	0.0	1.0	0.0	0.0	0.0	0.0	0.0	1.0
Node 7	0.0	0.0	0.0	0.0	0.0	0.0	0.0	0.0	0.0	0.0	0.0	0.0	0.0	0.0	0.0
Node 8	0.0	0.0	0.0	0.0	0.0	0.0	0.0	0.0	0.0	0.0	0.0	0.0	0.0	0.0	0.0
Node 9	0.0	0.0	0.0	0.0	0.0	0.0	0.0	0.0	0.0	0.0	0.0	1.0	0.0	0.0	1.0
Node 10	0.0	0.0	0.0	0.0	0.0	0.0	0.0	0.0	0.0	0.0	0.0	0.0	0.0	0.0	0.0
Node 11	0.0	0.0	0.0	0.0	0.0	0.0	0.0	0.0	0.0	0.0	0.0	0.0	0.0	0.0	0.0
Node 12	0.0	0.0	0.0	0.0	0.0	0.0	0.0	0.0	0.0	0.0	0.0	0.0	0.0	1.0	1.0
Node 13	0.0	0.0	0.0	0.0	0.0	0.0	0.0	0.0	0.0	0.0	0.0	0.0	0.0	0.0	0.0
Node 14	0.0	0.0	0.0	0.0	0.0	0.0	0.0	0.0	0.0	0.0	0.0	0.0	0.0	0.0	0.0
Flow in	0.0	0.0	1.0	0.0	0.0	1.0	0.0	0.0	1.0	0.0	0.0	1.0	0.0	1.0	

Flow balance equations					
Node	Flow in	Flow out	Net flow		
Node 1	0	1	-1	=	-1
Node 2	0	0	0	=	0
Node 3	1	1	0	=	0
Node 4	0	0	0	=	0
Node 5	0	0	0	=	0
Node 6	1	1	0	=	0
Node 7	0	0	0	=	0
Node 8	0	0	0	=	0
Node 9	1	1	0	=	0
Node 10	0	0	0	=	0
Node 11	0	0	0	=	0
Node 12	1	1	0	=	0
Node 13	0	0	0	=	0
Node 14	1	0	1	=	1
			LHS	Sign	RHS

Distances: From	N 1	N 2	N 3	N 4	N 5	N 6	N 7	N 8	N 9	N 10	N 11	N 12	N 13	N 14
Node 1	1000	100	90	105	1000	1000	1000	1000	1000	1000	1000	1000	1000	1000
Node 2	100	1000	1000	1000	90	1000	1000	1000	1000	1000	1000	1000	1000	1000
Node 3	90	1000	1000	1000	1000	100	1000	1000	1000	1000	1000	1000	1000	1000
Node 4	105	1000	1000	1000	1000	1000	100	1000	1000	1000	1000	350	1000	1000
Node 5	1000	90	1000	1000	1000	1000	1000	100	1000	1000	1000	1000	1000	1000
Node 6	1000	1000	100	1000	1000	1000	1000	1000	90	1000	1000	1000	1000	1000
Node 7	1000	1000	1000	100	1000	1000	1000	1000	1000	90	1000	1000	1000	1000
Node 8	1000	1000	1000	1000	100	1000	1000	1000	1000	1000	90	1000	1000	1000
Node 9	1000	1000	1000	1000	1000	90	1000	1000	1000	1000	1000	90	1000	1000
Node 10	1000	1000	1000	1000	1000	1000	90	1000	1000	1000	1000	1000	90	1000
Node 11	1000	1000	1000	1000	1000	1000	1000	90	1000	1000	1000	1000	1000	100
Node 12	1000	1000	1000	350	1000	1000	1000	1000	90	1000	1000	1000	1000	90
Node 13	1000	1000	1000	1000	1000	1000	1000	1000	1000	90	1000	1000	1000	100
Node 14	1000	1000	1000	1000	1000	1000	1000	1000	1000	1000	100	90	100	1000

Shortest distance = 460

=SUMPRODUCT(B5:O18,B23:O36)

Distances of roads that do not exist are set to very high values.

Solver Parameters

Set Objective: $D$38

To: Max / Min (selected) / Value Of:

By Changing Variable Cells: $B$5:$O$18

Subject to the Constraints: $U$5:$U$18 = $W$5:$W$18

All cells in the decision variable table (B5:O18) are specified as Changing Variable Cells. No flow occurs on roads that do not exist since their distances are very high.

Solved Problem 5-5

Roxie LaMothe, owner of a large horse breeding farm near Orlando, is planning to install a complete water system connecting all the various stables and barns. The locations of the facilities and the distances between them are given in the network shown in Figure 5.17. Roxie must determine the least expensive way to provide water to each facility. What do you recommend?

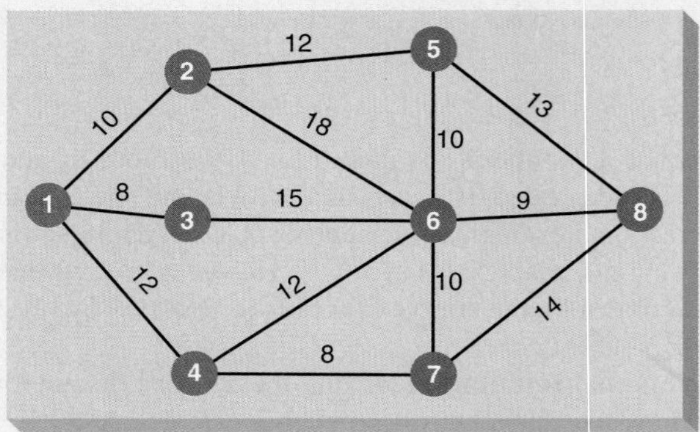

FIGURE 5.17 Network for Roxie LaMothe—Minimal-Spanning Tree

FIGURE 5.18
Minimal-Spanning Tree for Roxie LaMothe

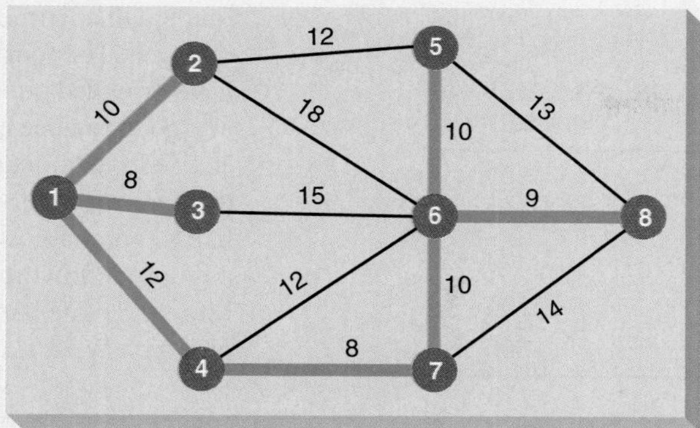

Solution

This is a typical minimal-spanning tree problem that can be solved by hand. We begin by selecting node 1 and connecting it to the nearest node, which is node 3. Nodes 1 and 2 are the next to be connected, followed by nodes 1 and 4. Now we connect node 4 to node 7 and node 7 to node 6. At this point, the only remaining points to be connected are node 6 to node 8 and node 6 to node 5. The final solution is shown in Figure 5.18.

Discussion Questions and Problems

Discussion Questions

5-1 Is the transportation model an example of decision making under certainty or decision making under uncertainty? Why?

5-2 What is a balanced transportation model? Describe the approach you would use to solve an unbalanced model.

5-3 What is the enumeration approach to solving assignment models? Is it a practical way to solve a 5 row × 5 column model? a 7 × 7 model? Why?

5-4 What is the minimal-spanning tree model? What types of problems can be solved using this type of model?

5-5 Give several examples of problems that can be solved using the maximal-flow model.

5-6 Describe a problem that can be solved by using the shortest-path model.

5-7 What is a flow balance constraint? How is it implemented at each node in a network model?

5-8 How can we manipulate a maximal-flow network model in order to set it up as a linear program?

5-9 Why might it be more convenient to set up network models in Excel by using a tabular form?

5-10 How can we manipulate a maximal-flow network model in order to specify all arcs between each pair of nodes (i.e., the entire table) as the changing variable cells in Solver?

5-11 How can we manipulate a shortest-path network model in order to specify all arcs between each pair of nodes (i.e., the entire table) as the changing variable cells in Solver?

Problems

Note: The networks for all problems given here involve no more than 14 nodes. If we arrange the decision variables in tabular form, the total number of entries will be no more than 196 (= 14 × 14). Therefore, it should be possible to specify the entire table as changing variable cells even in the standard version of Solver.

5-12 The Oconee County, South Carolina, superintendent of education is responsible for assigning students to the three high schools in his county. A certain number of students have to travel to and from school by bus, as several sectors of the county are beyond walking distance from a school. The superintendent partitions the county into five geographic sectors as he attempts to establish a plan that will minimize the total number of student miles traveled by bus. Of course, if a student happens to live in a certain sector and is assigned to the high school in that sector, there is no need to bus that student because he or she can walk to school. The three schools are located in sectors B, C, and E. The table at the top of the next page reflects the number of high-school-age students living in each sector and the distance, in miles, from each sector to each school. Assuming that each high school has a capacity of 1,100 students, set up and solve Oconee County's problem as a transportation model.

	DISTANCE TO SCHOOLS, IN MILES			
SECTOR	SECTOR B	SECTOR C	SECTOR E	NUMBER OF STUDENTS
A	6	7	11	800
B	0	3	10	600
C	9	0	6	400
D	8	3	5	700
E	15	8	0	500

5-13 Marc Hernandez's construction firm currently has three projects in progress. Each requires a specific supply of gravel. There are three gravel pits available to provide for Hernandez's needs, but shipping costs differ from location to location. The following table summarizes the transportation costs:

	TO			
FROM	JOB 1	JOB 2	JOB 3	TONNAGE ALLOWANCE
Central pit	$9	$ 8	$ 7	3,000
Rock pit	$7	$11	$ 6	4,000
Acme pit	$4	$ 3	$12	6,000
Job requirements (tons)	2,500	3,750	4,850	

(a) Determine Hernandez's optimal shipping quantities so as to minimize total transportation costs.

(b) It is the case that Rock Pit and Central Pit can send gravel by rail to Acme for $1 per ton. Once the gravel is relocated, it can be trucked to the jobs. Reformulate this problem to determine how shipping by rail could reduce the transportation costs for the gravel.

5-14 The Southern Rail Company ships coal by rail from three coal mines to meet the demand requirements of four coal depots. The following table shows the distances from the mines to the various depots and the availabilities and requirements for coal. Determine the best shipment of coal cars to minimize the total miles traveled by the cars.

5-15 The Piedmont Investment Corporation has identified four small apartment buildings in which it would like to invest. The four banks generally used by Piedmont have provided quotes on the interest rates they would charge to finance each purchase. The banks have also advised Piedmont of the maximum amount of money they are willing to lend at this time. Piedmont would like to purchase as many buildings as possible while paying the lowest possible amount in total interest. More than one bank can be used to finance the same property. What should Piedmont do?

	PROPERTY (INTEREST RATES)				
SAVINGS AND LOAN COMPANY	HILL ST.	BANKS ST.	PARK AVE.	DRURY LANE	MAX CREDIT LINE
First Homestead	8%	8%	10%	11%	$80,000
Commonwealth	9%	9%	12%	10%	$100,000
Washington Federal	9%	11%	10%	9%	$120,000
Loan required	$60,000	$40,000	$130,000	$70,000	

5-16 The manager of the O'Brian Glass Company is planning the production of automobile windshields for the next four months. The demand for the next four months is projected to be as shown in the following table.

MONTH	DEMAND FOR WINDSHIELDS
1	130
2	140
3	260
4	120

O'Brian can normally produce 100 windshields in a month. This is done during regular production hours at a cost of $100 per windshield. If demand in any one month cannot be satisfied by regular production, the production manager has three other choices: (1) He can produce up to 50 more windshields per month in

Table for Problem 5-14

	TO				
FROM	COLUMBIA	ALBANY	SPRINGFIELD	PLEASATANBURG	SUPPLY OF CARS
Parris	50	30	60	70	35
Butler	20	80	10	90	60
Century	100	40	80	30	25
Demand for cars	30	45	25	20	

overtime but at a cost of $130 per windshield; (2) he can purchase a limited number of windshields from a friendly competitor for resale at a cost of $150 each (the maximum number of outside purchases over the four-month period is 450 windshields); or (3) he can fill the demand from his on-hand inventory. The inventory carrying cost is $10 per windshield per month. Back orders are not permitted. Inventory on hand at the beginning of month 1 is 40 windshields. Set up and solve this "production smoothing" problem as a transportation model to minimize cost. *Hint:* Set the various production options (e.g., regular production, outside purchase, etc.) as supply nodes and the monthly demands as the demand nodes.

5-17 Maurice's Pump Manufacturing Company currently maintains plants in Atlanta and Tulsa that supply major distribution centers in Los Angeles and New York. Because of an expanding demand, Maurice has decided to open a third plant and has narrowed the choice to one of two cities—New Orleans or Houston. The pertinent production and distribution costs, as well as the plant capacities and distribution center demands, are shown in the following table.

	DISTRIBUTION CENTERS			
PLANTS	LOS ANGELES	NEW YORK	CAPACITY	PRODUCTION COST (PER UNIT)
Atlanta (existing)	$8	$5	600	$6
Tulsa (existing)	$4	$7	900	$5
New Orleans (proposed)	$5	$6	500	$4 (*anticipated*)
Houston (proposed)	$4	$6	500	$3 (*anticipated*)
Forecast demand	800	1,200		

Which of the new possible plants should be opened?

5-18 A food distribution company ships fresh [illegible] from its four packing plants to large East-coast cities. The shipping costs per crate, the supply and demand are shown in the table at the bottom of this page.
(a) Formulate a model that will permit the company to meet its demand at the lowest possible cost.
(b) The company wishes to spread out the source for each of its markets to the maximum extent possible. To accomplish this, it will accept a 5% increase in its total transportation cost from part (a). What is the new transportation plan, and what is the new cost?

5-19 The Lilly Snack Company is considering adding an additional plant to its three existing facilities in Wise, Virginia; Humbolt, Tennessee; and Cleveland, Georgia to serve three large markets in the Southeast. Two locations—Brevard, North Carolina, and Laurens, South Carolina—are being considered. The transportation costs per pallet are shown in the table at the top of the next page.
(a) Which site would you recommend? Why?
(b) Suppose that the Brevard location has been selected. Due to the perishable nature of the goods involved, management wishes to restrict the maximum number of pallets shipped from any one plant to any single market. To accomplish this, management is willing to accept a 10% surcharge on their optimal transportation costs from part (a). What is the new transportation plan, and what is the new cost?

5-20 Meg Bishop, vice president of supply chain at the Lilly Snack Company (see Problem 5-19) has been able to secure shipping from the proposed plant in Brevard to its plants in Wise and Cleveland for $6 and $5 per pallet, respectively. If Lilly chooses to place a new plant in Brevard, what would be the new shipping plan and cost? Ignore part (b) of Problem 5-19 in answering this question.

5-21 The distribution system for the Smith Company consists of three plants (A, B, and C), two warehouses (D and E), and four customers (W, X, Y, and Z). The relevant supply, demand, and unit shipping cost information are given in the table for Problem 5-21 near the top of the next page. Set up and solve the transshipment model to minimize total shipping costs.

Table for Problem 5-18

	MARKETS				
PACKING PLANTS	ATLANTA	BOSTON	CHARLESTOWN	DOVER	SUPPLY
Eaglestown	$6.00	$7.00	$7.50	$7.50	8,000
Farrier	$5.50	$5.50	$4.00	$7.00	10,000
Guyton	$6.00	$5.00	$6.50	$7.00	5,000
Hayesville	$7.00	$7.50	$8.50	$6.50	9,000
Demand	8,000	9,000	10,000	5,000	

Table for Problem 5-19

	FROM					
TO	WISE	HUMBOLT	CLEVELAND	BREVARD	LAURENS	DEMAND
Charlotte	$20	$17	$21	$29	$27	250
Greenville	$25	$27	$20	$30	$28	200
Atlanta	$22	$25	$22	$30	$31	350
Capacity	300	200	150	150	150	

Table for Problem 5-21

PLANT	SUPPLY
A	450
B	500
C	380

CUSTOMER	DEMAND
W	450
X	300
Y	300
Z	400

	TO	
FROM	D	E
A	$4	$7
B	$8	$5
C	$5	$6

	TO			
FROM	W	X	Y	Z
D	$6	$4	$8	$4
E	$3	$6	$7	$7

5-22 A supply chain consists of three plants (A, B, and C), three distributors (J, K, and L), and three stores (X, Y, and Z). The relevant supply, demand, and unit shipping cost information are given in the table at the bottom of this page. Set up and solve the transshipment model to minimize total shipping costs.

5-23 In a job shop operation, four jobs can be performed on any of four machines. The hours required for each job on each machine are presented in the following table:

	MACHINE			
JOB	W	X	Y	Z
A	16	14	10	13
B	15	13	12	12
C	12	12	9	11
D	18	16	14	16

The plant supervisor would like to assign jobs so that total time is minimized. Use the assignment model to find the best solution.

5-24 Greg Pickett, coach of a little-league baseball team, is preparing for a series of four games against four good opponents. Greg would like to increase the probability of winning as many games as possible by carefully scheduling his pitchers against the teams they are each most likely to defeat. Because the games are to be played back to back in less than one week, Greg cannot count on any pitcher to start in more than one game.

Greg knows the strengths and weaknesses not only of his pitchers but also of his opponents, and he believes he can estimate the probability of winning each of the four games with each of the four starting pitchers. Those probabilities are listed in the table at the top of the next column.

Table for Problem 5-22

PLANT	SUPPLY
A	400
B	500
C	350

STORE	DEMAND
X	400
Y	325
Z	400

	TO		
FROM	J	K	L
A	$4	$7	$5
B	$8	$5	$4
C	$5	$6	$7

	TO					
FROM	X	Y	Z	J	K	L
J	$6	$4	$8		$6	$5
K	$3	$6	$7	$6		$7
L	$2	$4	$5	$5	$7	

STARTING PITCHER	OPPONENT: DES MOINES	DAVEN-PORT	OMAHA	PEORIA
Jones	0.40	0.80	0.50	0.60
Baker	0.30	0.40	0.80	0.70
Parker	0.80	0.80	0.70	0.90
Wilson	0.20	0.30	0.40	0.50

What pitching rotation should Greg set to provide the highest sum of the probabilities of winning each game for his team?

5-25 Cindy Jefferson, hospital administrator at Anderson Hospital must appoint head nurses to four newly established departments: urology, cardiology, orthopedics, and pediatrics. Believing in the decision modeling approach to problem solving, Cindy has interviewed four nurses—Morris, Richards, Cook, and Morgan—and developed an index scale ranging from 0 to 100 to be used in the assignment. An index of 0 implies that the nurse would be perfectly suited to that task. A value close to 100, on the other hand, implies that the nurse is not at all suited to head that unit. The following table gives the complete set of index scales that Cindy feels represent all possible assignments.

NURSE	DEPARTMENT: UROLOGY	CARDIO-LOGY	ORTHO-PEDICS	PEDIATRICS
Morris	15	18	28	75
Richards	23	48	32	38
Cook	24	36	51	36
Morgan	55	38	25	12

Which nurse should be assigned to which unit?

5-26 A trauma center keeps ambulances at locations throughout the east side of a city in an attempt to minimize the response time in the event of an emergency. The times, in minutes, from the ambulance locations to the population centers are given in the table at the top of the next column.

AMBULANCE LOCATIONS	POPULATION CENTERS: EAST	NORTH-EAST	SOUTH-EAST	CENTRAL
Site 1	12	8	9	13
Site 2	10	9	11	10
Site 3	11	12	14	11
Site 4	13	11	12	9

Find the optimal assignment of ambulances to population centers that will minimize the total emergency response time.

5-27 The Central Police Department has five detective squads available for assignment to five open crime cases. The chief of detectives wishes to assign the squads so that the total time to conclude the cases is minimized. The average number of days, based on past performance, for each squad to complete each case is shown in following table.

SQUAD	CASE: A	B	C	D	E
1	27	7	3	7	14
2	30	6	12	7	20
3	21	5	4	3	10
4	21	12	7	12	8
5	8	26	24	25	13

Use the assignment model to find the best solution.

5-28 Kelly Spaugh, course scheduler of a technical college's business department, needs to assign instructors to courses next semester. As a criterion for judging who should teach each course, Kelly reviews the student evaluations of teaching for the past two years. Because each of the four professors taught each of the four courses at one time or another during the two-year period, Kelly is able to determine a course rating for each instructor. These ratings are shown in the table at the bottom of this page.

Find the best assignment of professors to courses to maximize the overall teaching ratings.

Table for Problem 5-28

PROFESSOR	COURSE: STATISTICS	MANAGEMENT	FINANCE	ECONOMICS
Strausbaugh	70	60	80	75
Kelley	80	60	80	75
Davidson	65	55	80	60
Merkle	95	40	65	55

5-29 Coogan Construction is in the process of installing power lines to a large housing development. Rob Coogan wants to minimize the total length of wire used, which will minimize his costs. The housing development is shown as a network in Figure 5.19. Each house has been numbered, and the distance between houses is given in hundreds of feet. What do you recommend?

5-30 The city of Six Mile, South Carolina, is considering making several of its streets one way. What is the maximum number of cars per hour that can travel from east (node 1) to west (node 8)? The network is shown in Figure 5.20.

5-31 Two Chaps and a Truck Movers have been hired to move the office furniture and equipment of Wray Properties to the company's new headquarters. What route do you recommend? The network of roads is shown in Figure 5.21.

5-32 A security firm needs to connect alarm systems to the firm's main control site from five potential trouble locations. Since the systems must be fail-safe, the cables must be run in special pipes. These pipes are very expensive but large enough to simultaneously handle five cables (the maximum that might be needed). Use the minimal-spanning tree model to find the minimum total length of pipes needed to

FIGURE 5.19
Network for Problem 5-29: Coogan Construction

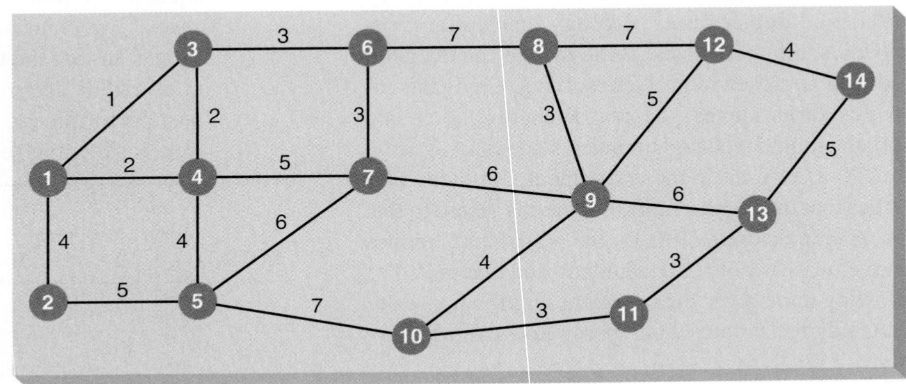

FIGURE 5.20
Network for Problem 5-30: Six Mile, South Carolina

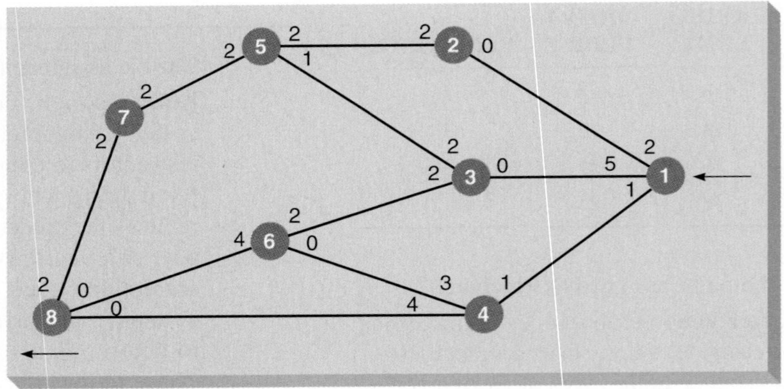

FIGURE 5.21
Network for Problem 5-31: Two Chaps and a Truck Movers

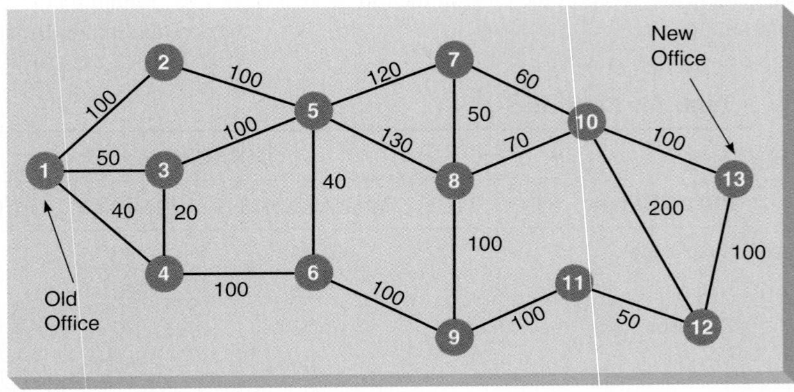

connect the locations shown in Figure 5.22. Node 6 represents the main control site.

5-33 Figure 5.23 shows a network of nodes. Any sequence of activities that takes a flow of one unit from node 1 to node 6 will produce a widget. For example, one unit flowing from node 1 to node 4 to node 6 would create a widget. Other paths are possible. Quantities given are numbers of widgets per day.
   (a) How many widgets could be produced in one day?
   (b) Suppose we want to ensure that no more than 100 widgets are processed along any of the arcs in the production facility. How many widgets are now possible?

5-34 The road system around the hotel complex (node 1) near a large amusement park (node 11) is shown in Figure 5.24. The numbers by the nodes represent the traffic flow in hundreds of cars per hour. What is the maximum flow of cars from the hotel complex to the park?

5-35 The network in Figure 5.25 shows the pipeline transportation system for treated water from the treatment plant (node 1) to a city water supply system (node 14). The arc capacities represent millions of gallons per hour. How much water can be transported per hour from the plant to the city using this network?

5-36 In Problem 5-35, two of the terminals in the water supply network (see Figure 5.25), represented by nodes 10 and 11, are to be taken offline for routine maintenance. No material can flow in to or out of these nodes. What impact does this have on the capacity of the network? By how much, if any, will the capacity of this network be decreased during the maintenance period?

5-37 The network shown in Figure 5.26 represents the major roads between Port Huron (node 1) and Dearborn (node 14). The values on the arcs represent the distance, in miles. Find the shortest route between the two cities.

5-38 In Problem 5-37, all roads leading into and out of nodes 4 and 9 (see Figure 5.26) have been closed because of bridge repairs. What impact (if any) will this have on the shortest route between Port Huron and Dearborn?

FIGURE 5.22 Network for Problem 5-32

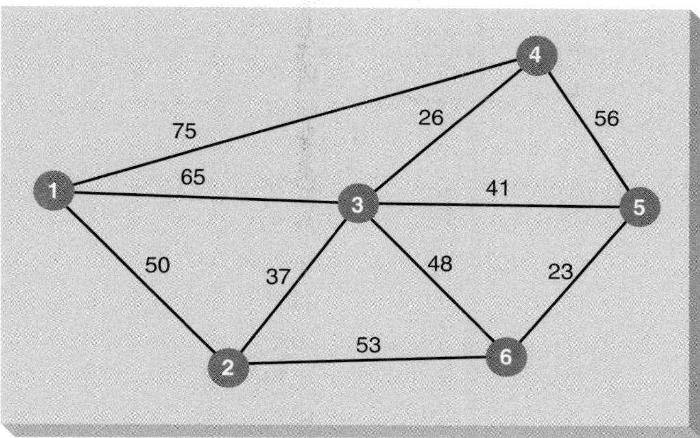

FIGURE 5.23 Network for Problem 5-33

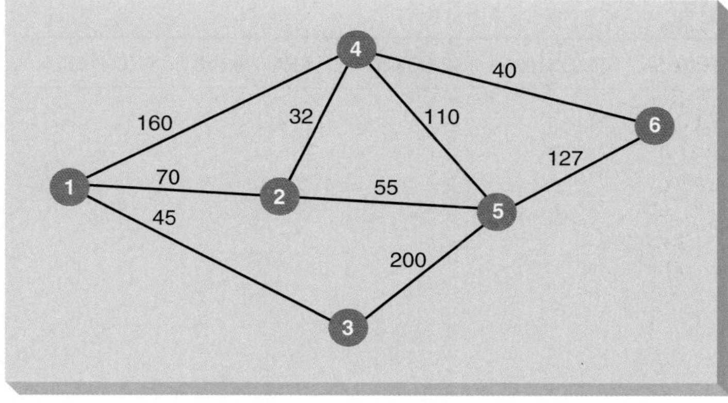

FIGURE 5.24 Network for Problem 5-34

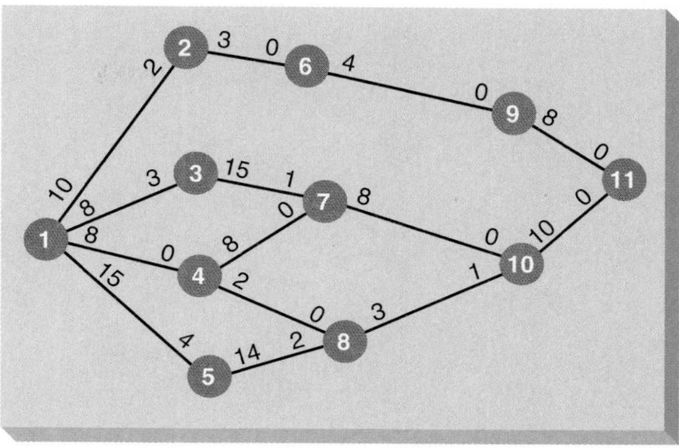

FIGURE 5.25 Network for Problem 5-35

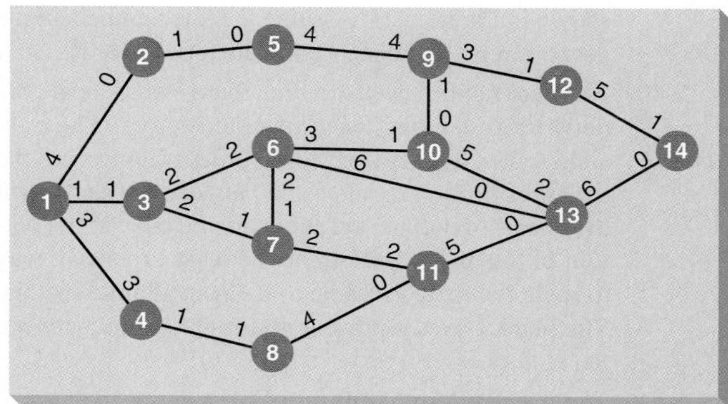

FIGURE 5.26 Network for Problem 5-37

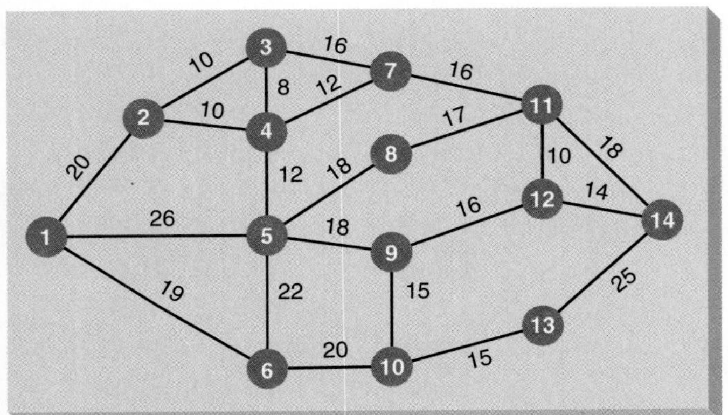

FIGURE 5.27 Network for Problem 5-39

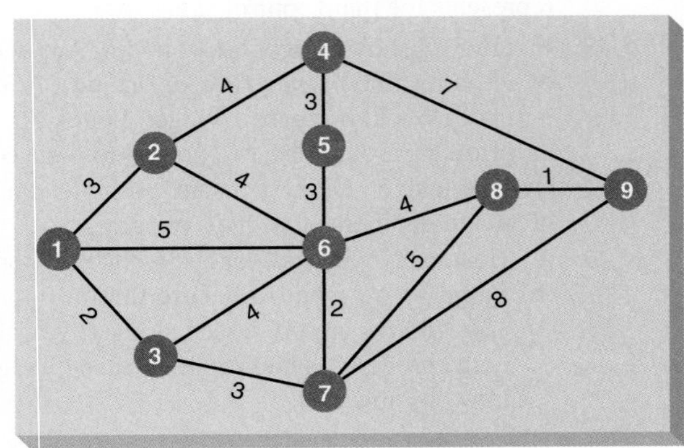

5-39 Solve the minimal-spanning tree model in the network shown in Figure 5.27. Assume that the numbers in the network represent distance in hundreds of yards.

5-40 A secure facility needs to run a hard-wired local area network to connect each of nine sectors. The possible routes the network could utilize, along with the expenses of running the cable between the sectors, in thousands of dollars, are shown in the table at the bottom of this page. Determine the least expensive way to route the network cable to connect all nine sectors. The blank boxes represent no feasible route between the sectors.

5-41 The Kimten Manufacturing Company needs to process 18 jobs. Kimten can process each job on any of the six machines it has available. Iqbal Ahmed, production supervisor at Kimten, wants to allocate jobs to machines in such a manner that all machines have total loads that are as close as possible to each other. For purposes of solving this problem, assume that a single job can be split between multiple machines and that jobs can be moved from one machine to another with no loss of time. The machine hours required for each job are shown in the table in the next column.

JOB	MACHINE HOURS
1	39.43
2	27.94
3	40.27
4	18.27
5	12.72
6	35.20
7	27.94
8	17.20
9	17.20
10	17.20
11	21.50
12	16.74
13	28.29
14	6.07
15	16.01
16	18.49
17	12.16
18	36.67

Table for Problem 5-40

FROM/TO	SECTOR 2	SECTOR 3	SECTOR 4	SECTOR 5	SECTOR 6	SECTOR 7	SECTOR 8	SECTOR 9
Sector 1	6			3	6			
Sector 2		7	6		4			4
Sector 3				4	5	3		8
Sector 4					8		9	3
Sector 5							7	
Sector 6						8	10	
Sector 7								9
Sector 8								2

Case Study

Old Oregon Wood Store

In 2005, George Brown started the Old Oregon Wood Store to manufacture Old Oregon tables. Each table is carefully constructed by hand, using the highest-quality oak. An Old Oregon table can support more than 500 pounds, and since the start of the Old Oregon Wood Store, not one table has been returned because of faulty workmanship or structural problems. In addition to being rugged, each table is beautifully finished, using a urethane varnish that George developed during 20 years of working with wood-finishing materials.

The manufacturing process consists of four steps: preparation, assembly, finishing, and packaging. Each step is performed by one person. In addition to overseeing the entire operation, George does all the finishing. Tom Surowski performs the preparation step, which involves cutting and forming the basic components of the tables. Leon Davis is in charge of the assembly, and Cathy Stark performs the packaging.

Although each person is responsible for only one step in the manufacturing process, everyone can perform any one of the steps. It is George's policy that occasionally everyone should complete several tables on his or her own, without any help or assistance. A small competition is used to see who can complete an entire table in the least amount of time. George maintains average total and intermediate completion times. The data are shown in Figure 5.28.

It takes Cathy longer than the other employees to construct an Old Oregon table. In addition to being slower than the other employees, Cathy is also unhappy about her current responsibility of packaging, which leaves her idle most of the day. Her first preference is finishing, and her second preference is preparation.

In addition to quality, George is concerned about costs and efficiency. When one of the employees misses a day, it causes major scheduling problems. In some cases, George assigns another employee overtime to complete the necessary work. At other times, George simply waits until the employee returns to work to complete his or her step in the manufacturing process. Both solutions cause problems. Overtime is expensive, and waiting causes delays and sometimes stops the entire manufacturing process.

To overcome some of these problems, Randy Lane was hired. Randy's major duties are to perform miscellaneous jobs and to help out if one of the employees is absent. George has given Randy training in all phases of the manufacturing process, and he is pleased with the speed at which Randy has been able to learn how to completely assemble Old Oregon tables. Total and intermediate completion times are given in Figure 5.29.

FIGURE 5.28 Manufacturing Time, in Minutes

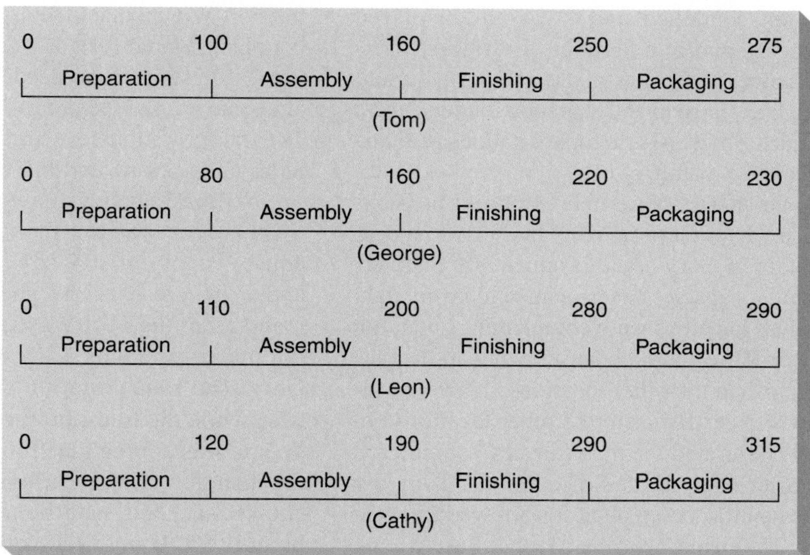

FIGURE 5.29 Randy's Completion Times, in Minutes

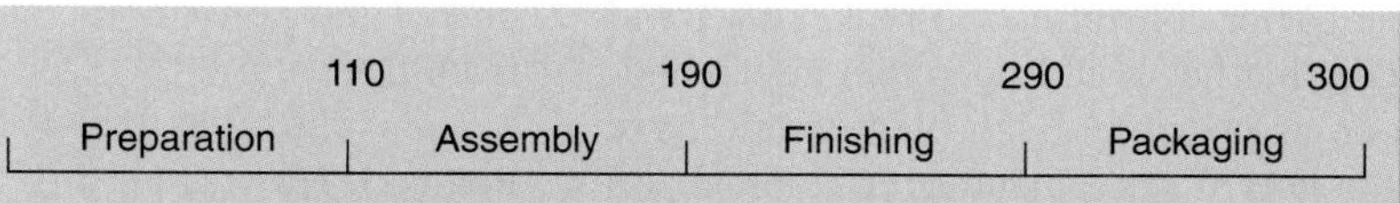

Discussion Questions

1. What is the fastest way to manufacture Old Oregon tables using the original crew? How many tables could be made per day?
2. Would production rates and quantities change significantly if George would allow Randy to perform one of the four functions and make one of the original crew members the backup person?
3. What is the fastest time to manufacture a table with the original crew if Cathy is moved to either preparation or finishing?
4. Whoever performs the packaging function is severely underutilized. Can you find a better way of utilizing the four- or five-person crew than either giving each a single job or allowing each to manufacture an entire table? How many tables could be manufactured per day with this new scheme?

Case Study

Custom Vans Inc.

Custom Vans Inc. specializes in converting standard vans into campers. Depending on the amount of work and customizing to be done, the customizing could cost less than $1,000 to more than $5,000. In less than four years, Tony Rizzo was able to expand his small operation in Gary, Indiana, to other major outlets in Chicago, Milwaukee, Minneapolis, and Detroit.

Innovation was the major factor in Tony's success in converting a small van shop into one of the largest and most profitable custom van operations in the Midwest. Tony seemed to have a special ability to design and develop unique features and devices that were always in high demand by van owners. An example was Shower-Rific, which Tony developed only six months after he started Custom Vans Inc. These small showers were completely self-contained, and they could be placed in almost any type of van and in a number of different locations within a van. Shower-Rific was made of fiberglass and contained towel racks, built-in soap and shampoo holders, and a unique plastic door. Each Shower-Rific took 2 gallons of fiberglass and 3 hours of labor to manufacture.

Most of the Shower-Rifics were manufactured in Gary, in the same warehouse where Custom Vans Inc. was founded. The manufacturing plant in Gary could produce 300 Shower-Rifics in a month, but that capacity never seemed to be enough. Custom Vans shops in all locations were complaining about not getting enough Shower-Rifics, and because Minneapolis was farther away from Gary than the other locations, Tony was always inclined to ship Shower-Rifics to the other locations before Minneapolis. This infuriated the manager of Custom Vans at Minneapolis, and after many heated discussions, Tony decided to start another manufacturing plant for Shower-Rifics at Fort Wayne, Indiana. The manufacturing plant at Fort Wayne could produce 150 Shower-Rifics per month.

The manufacturing plant at Fort Wayne was still not able to meet current demand for Shower-Rifics, and Tony knew that the demand for his unique camper shower would grow rapidly in the next year. After consulting with his lawyer and banker, Tony concluded that he should open two new manufacturing plants as soon as possible. Each plant would have the same capacity as the Fort Wayne manufacturing plant. An initial investigation into possible manufacturing locations was made, and Tony decided that the two new plants should be located in Detroit, Michigan; Rockford, Illinois; or Madison, Wisconsin. Tony knew that selecting the best location for the two new manufacturing plants would be difficult. Transportation costs and demands for the various locations were important considerations.

The Chicago shop was managed by Bill Burch. This Custom Vans shop was one of the first established by Tony, and it continued to outperform the other locations. The manufacturing plant at Gary was supplying the Chicago shop with 200 Shower-Rifics each month, although Bill knew that the demand for the showers in Chicago was 300 units. The transportation cost per unit from Gary was $10, and although the transportation cost from Fort Wayne was double that amount, Bill was always pleading with Tony to get an additional 50 units from the Fort Wayne manufacturer. The two additional manufacturing plants would certainly be able to supply Bill with the additional 100 showers he needed. The transportation costs would, of course, vary, depending on which two locations Tony picked. The transportation cost per shower would be $30 from Detroit, $5 from Rockford, and $10 from Madison.

Wilma Jackson, manager of the Custom Vans shop in Milwaukee, was the most upset about not getting an adequate supply of showers. She had a demand for 100 units, and at the present time, she was getting only half of that demand from the Fort Wayne manufacturing plant. She could not understand why Tony didn't ship her all 100 units from Gary. The transportation cost per unit from Gary was only $20, while the transportation cost from Fort Wayne was $30. Wilma was hoping that Tony would select Madison as one of the manufacturing locations. She would be able to get all the showers needed, and the transportation cost per unit would be only $5. If not Madison, a new plant in Rockford would be able to supply her total needs, but the transportation cost per unit would be twice as much as it would be from Madison. Because the transportation cost per unit from Detroit would be $40, Wilma speculated that even if Detroit became one of the new plants, she would not be getting any units from Detroit.

Custom Vans Inc. of Minneapolis was managed by Tom Poanski. He was getting 100 showers from the Gary plant. Demand was 150 units. Tom faced the highest transportation costs of all locations. The transportation cost from Gary was

$40 per unit. It would cost $10 more if showers were sent from the Fort Wayne location. Tom was hoping that Detroit would not be one of the new plants, as the transportation cost would be $60 per unit. Rockford and Madison would have costs of $30 and $25, respectively, to ship one shower to Minneapolis.

The Detroit shop's position was similar to Milwaukee's—getting only half of the demand each month. The 100 units that Detroit did receive came directly from the Fort Wayne plant. The transportation cost was only $15 per unit from Fort Wayne, whereas it was $25 from Gary. Dick Lopez, manager of Custom Vans Inc. of Detroit, placed the probability of having one of the new plants in Detroit fairly high. The factory would be located across town, and the transportation cost would be only $5 per unit. He could get 150 showers from the new plant in Detroit and the other 50 showers from Fort Wayne. Even if Detroit was not selected, the other two locations were not intolerable. Rockford had a transportation cost per unit of $35, and Madison had a transportation cost of $40.

Tony pondered the dilemma of locating the two new plants for several weeks before deciding to call a meeting of all the managers of the van shops. The decision was complicated, but the objective was clear—to minimize total costs. The meeting was held in Gary, and everyone was present except Wilma.

Tony: Thank you for coming. As you know, I have decided to open up two new plants at Rockford, Madison, or Detroit. The two locations, of course, will change our shipping practices, and I sincerely hope that they will supply you with the Shower-Rifics that you have been wanting. I know you could have sold more units, and I want you to know that I am sorry for this situation.

Dick: Tony, I have given this situation a lot of consideration, and I feel strongly that at least one of the new plants should be located in Detroit. As you know, I am now getting only half of the showers that I need. My brother, Leon, is very interested in running the plant, and I know he would do a good job.

Tom: Dick, I am sure that Leon could do a good job, and I know how difficult it has been since the recent layoffs by the auto industry. Nevertheless, we should be considering total costs and not personalities. I believe that the new plants should be located in Madison and Rockford. I am farther away from the other plants than any other shop, and these locations would significantly reduce transportation costs.

Dick: That may be true, but there are other factors. Detroit has one of the largest suppliers of fiberglass, and I have checked prices. A new plant in Detroit would be able to purchase fiberglass for $2 per gallon less than any of the other existing or proposed plants.

Tom: At Madison, we have an excellent labor force. This is due primarily to the large number of students attending the University of Madison. These students are hard workers, and they will work for $1 less per hour than the other locations that we are considering.

Bill: Calm down, you two. It is obvious that we will not be able to satisfy everyone in locating the new plants. Therefore, I would like to suggest that we vote on the two best locations.

Tony: I don't think that voting would be a good idea. Wilma was not able to attend, and we should be looking at all these factors together in some type of logical fashion.

Discussion Question

Where would you locate the two new plants?

Case Study

Binder's Beverage

Bill Binder's business nearly went under when Colorado almost passed the bottle bill. Binder's Beverage produced soft drinks for many of the large grocery stores in the area. After the bottle bill failed, Binder's Beverage flourished. In a few short years, the company had a major plant in Denver and a warehouse in east Denver. The problem was getting the finished product to the warehouse. Although Bill was not good with distances, he was good with times. Denver is a big city with numerous roads that can be taken from the plant to the warehouse. Figure 5.30 shows the road network.

The soft drink plant is located at the corner of North Street and Columbine Street. High Street also intersects North Street and Columbine Street at the plant. Twenty minutes due north of the plant on North Street is I-70, the major east–west highway in Denver.

North Street intersects I-70 at Exit 135. It takes 5 minutes driving east on I-70 to reach Exit 136. This exit connects I-70 with High Street and 6th Avenue. Ten minutes east on I-70 is Exit 137. This exit connects I-70 with Rose Street and South Avenue.

From the plant, it takes 20 minutes on High Street, which goes in a northeast direction, to reach West Street. It takes another 20 minutes on High Street to reach I-70 and Exit 136.

It takes 30 minutes on Columbine Street to reach West Street from the plant. Columbine Street travels east and slightly north.

West Street travels east and west. From High Street, it takes 15 minutes to get to 6th Avenue on West Street. Columbine Street also comes into this intersection. From this intersection, it takes an additional 20 minutes on West Street to get to Rose Street, and it takes another 15 minutes to get to South Avenue.

From Exit 136 on 6th Avenue, it takes 5 minutes to get to West Street. Sixth Avenue continues to Rose Street, requiring 25 minutes. Sixth Avenue then goes directly to the warehouse.

FIGURE 5.30
Road Map for Binder's Beverage

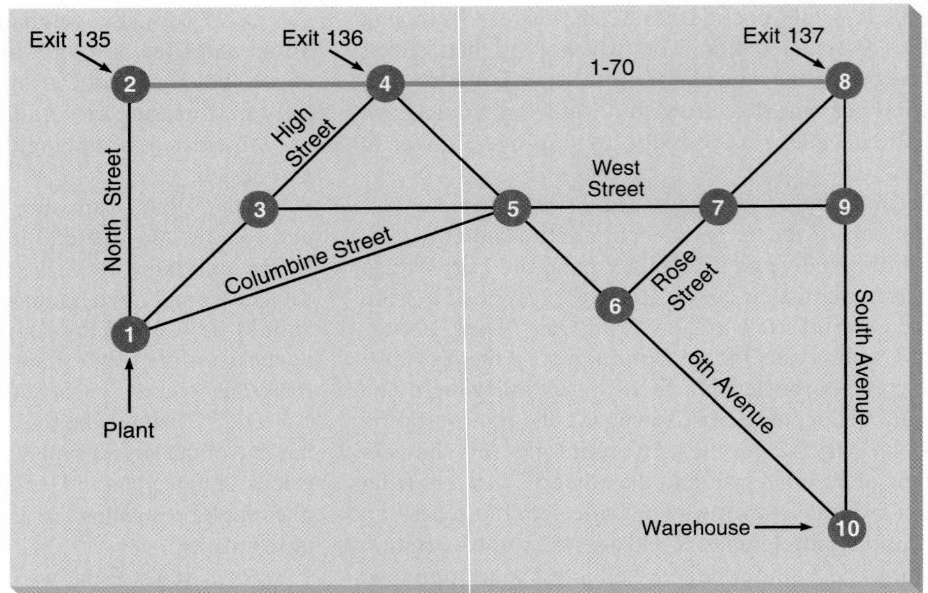

From Rose Street, it takes 40 minutes to get to the warehouse on 6th Avenue.

At Exit 137, Rose Street travels southwest. It takes 20 minutes to intersect with West Street, and it takes another 20 minutes to get to 6th Avenue. From Exit 137, South Street goes due south. It takes 10 minutes to get to West Street and another 15 minutes to get to the warehouse.

Discussion Question

What route do you recommend?

Internet Case Studies

See the Companion Website for this textbook, at www.pearsonhighered.com/balakrishnan, for additional case studies.

CHAPTER 6

Integer, Goal, and Nonlinear Programming Models

LEARNING OBJECTIVES

After completing this chapter, students will be able to:

1. Formulate integer programming (IP) models.
2. Set up and solve IP models using Excel's Solver.
3. Understand the difference between general integer and binary integer variables.
4. Understand the use of binary integer variables in formulating problems involving fixed costs.
5. Formulate goal programming (GP) problems and solve them using Excel's Solver.
6. Formulate nonlinear programming (NLP) problems and solve them using Excel's Solver.

CHAPTER OUTLINE

6.1 Introduction

Earlier chapters focus on the linear programming (LP) category of mathematical programming models. These LP models have three characteristics:

- The decision variables are allowed to have fractional values.
- There is a unique objective function.
- All mathematical expressions (objective function and constraints) have to be linear.

This chapter presents a series of other important mathematical models that allow us to relax each of these basic LP conditions. The new models—integer programming, goal programming, and nonlinear programming—are introduced here and then discussed in detail in the remainder of this chapter.

Integer Programming Models

Integer programming *is an extension of LP that solves problems that require integer solutions.*

General integer variables *can take on any nonnegative integer value.*

Binary variables *must equal either 0 or 1.*

Although fractional values such as $X = 0.33$ and $Y = 109.4$ may be valid for decision variables in many problems, a large number of business problems can be solved only if variables have *integer* values. For example, when an airline decides how many flights to operate on a given sector, it can't decide to operate 5.38 flights; it must operate 5, 6, or some other integer number.

In sections 6.2 and 6.3, we present two types of integer variables: general integer variables and binary variables. **General integer variables** are variables that can take on any nonnegative integer value that satisfies all the constraints in a model (e.g., 5 submarines, 8 employees, 20 insurance policies). **Binary variables** are a special type of integer variables that can take on only either of two values: 0 or 1. In this chapter we examine how problems involving both of these types of integer variables can be formulated and solved using Excel's Solver.

Integer programming (IP) problems can also be classified as *pure* and *mixed* types of problems, as follows:

- *Pure IP problems.* These are problems in which all decision variables must have integer solutions (general integer, binary, or a combination of the two).
- *Mixed IP problems.* These are problems in which some, but not all, decision variables must have integer solutions (i.e., general integer, binary, or a combination of the two). The noninteger variables can have fractional optimal values. We discuss an example of these types of problems in section 6.4.

Goal Programming Models

Goal programming *is an extension of LP that permits more than one objective to be stated.*

LP forces a decision maker to state only one objective. But what if a business has several objectives? Management may indeed want to minimize costs, but it might also simultaneously want to maximize market share, maximize machine utilization, maintain full employment, and minimize environmental impacts. These objectives can often conflict with each other. For example, minimizing costs may be in direct conflict with maintaining full employment. Goal programming is an extension to LP that permits multiple objectives such as these to be considered simultaneously. We discuss goal programming in detail in section 6.5.

Nonlinear Programming Models

With **nonlinear programming**, *objectives and/or constraints are nonlinear.*

Linear programming can, of course, be applied only to cases in which the objective function and all constraints are linear expressions. Yet in many situations, this may not be the case. For example, consider a price curve that relates the unit price of a product to the number of units made. As more units are made, the price per unit may decrease in a nonlinear fashion. Hence, if X and Y denote the number of units of two products to make, the objective function could be

$$\text{Maximize profit} = 25X - 0.4X^2 + 30Y - 0.5Y^2$$

Because of the squared terms, this is a nonlinear objective function. In a similar manner, we could have one or more nonlinear constraints in the model. We discuss nonlinear programming models in detail in section 6.6.

Now let's examine each of these extensions of LP—integer, goal, and nonlinear programming—one at a time.

6.2 Models with General Integer Variables

Models with general integer variables are similar to LP models—except that variables must be integer valued.

A model with general integer variables (which we will call an *IP model*) has an objective function and constraints identical to those of LP models. There is no real difference in the basic procedures for formulating an IP model and an LP model. The only additional requirement in an IP model is that one or more of the decision variables must take on integer values in the optimal solution. The actual value of this integer variable is, however, limited only by the constraints in the model. That is, values such as 0, 1, 2, 3, and so on are perfectly valid for these variables, as long as these values satisfy all constraints in the model.

Let us look at a simple two-variable example of an IP problem and see how to formulate it. We recognize that you are unlikely to ever encounter such small problems in real-world situations. However, as discussed in Chapter 2, a primary advantage of two-variable models is that we can easily represent them on a two-dimensional graph and use them effectively to illustrate how IP models behave. Let us then also look at how this two-variable IP model can be set up and solved by using Excel's Solver. The Excel setup can be extended to handle much larger IP models. In fact, thanks to the continued significant advances in computing technology, researchers have successfully modeled and solved IP models involving thousands of decision variables and constraints in just a few minutes (or even seconds).

Harrison Electric Company

Example of an IP model: Harrison Electric

Harrison Electric Company, located in Chicago's Old Town area, produces two expensive products that are popular with renovators of historic old homes: ornate lamps and old-fashioned ceiling fans. Both lamps and ceiling fans require a two-step production process involving wiring and assembly time. It takes about 2 hours to wire each lamp and 3 hours to wire a ceiling fan. Final assembly of each lamp and fan requires 6 and 5 hours, respectively. The production capability this period is such that only 12 hours of wiring time and 30 hours of assembly time are available. Each lamp produced nets the firm \$600 and each fan nets \$700 in profit.

FORMULATING THE PROBLEM If we let L denote the number of lamps to make and F denote the number of ceiling fans to make, Harrison's product mix decision can be formulated using LP as follows:

$$\text{Maximize profit} = \$600L + \$700F$$

subject to the constraints

$$\begin{aligned} 2L + 3F &\leq 12 \quad &\text{(wiring hours)} \\ 6L + 5F &\leq 30 \quad &\text{(assembly hours)} \\ L, F &\geq 0 \end{aligned}$$

SOLVING THE PROBLEM GRAPHICALLY Because there are only two decision variables, let us employ the graphical approach to visualize the feasible region. The shaded region in Figure 6.1 shows the feasible region for the LP problem. The optimal corner point solution turns out to be $L = 3.75$ lamps and $F = 1.50$ ceiling fans, for a profit of \$3,300.

Rounding is one way to reach integer solution values, but it often does not yield the optimal IP solution.

INTERPRETING THE RESULTS Because Harrison cannot produce and sell a fraction of a product, the production planner, Wes Wallace, recognized that he was dealing with an IP problem. It seemed to Wes that the simplest approach was to round off the optimal fractional LP solutions for L and F to integer values. Unfortunately, rounding can produce two problems. First, if we use the traditional rounding rule (i.e., round down if the fraction is below 0.5 and round up otherwise), the resulting integer solution may not even be in the feasible region. For example, using this rule, we would round Harrison's LP solution to $L = 4$ lamps and $F = 2$ fans. As we can see from Figure 6.1, that solution is not feasible. It is, hence, not a practical answer. Second, even if we manage to round the LP solution in such a way that the resulting integer solution is feasible, there is no guarantee that it is the optimal IP solution. For example, suppose Wes considers all possible integer solutions to Harrison's problem (shown in Figure 6.1) and rounds the LP solution to its nearest feasible IP solution (i.e., $L = 4$ lamps and $F = 1$ fan). As we will see later, it turns out that this IP

FIGURE 6.1
Graph for Harrison Electric—General IP

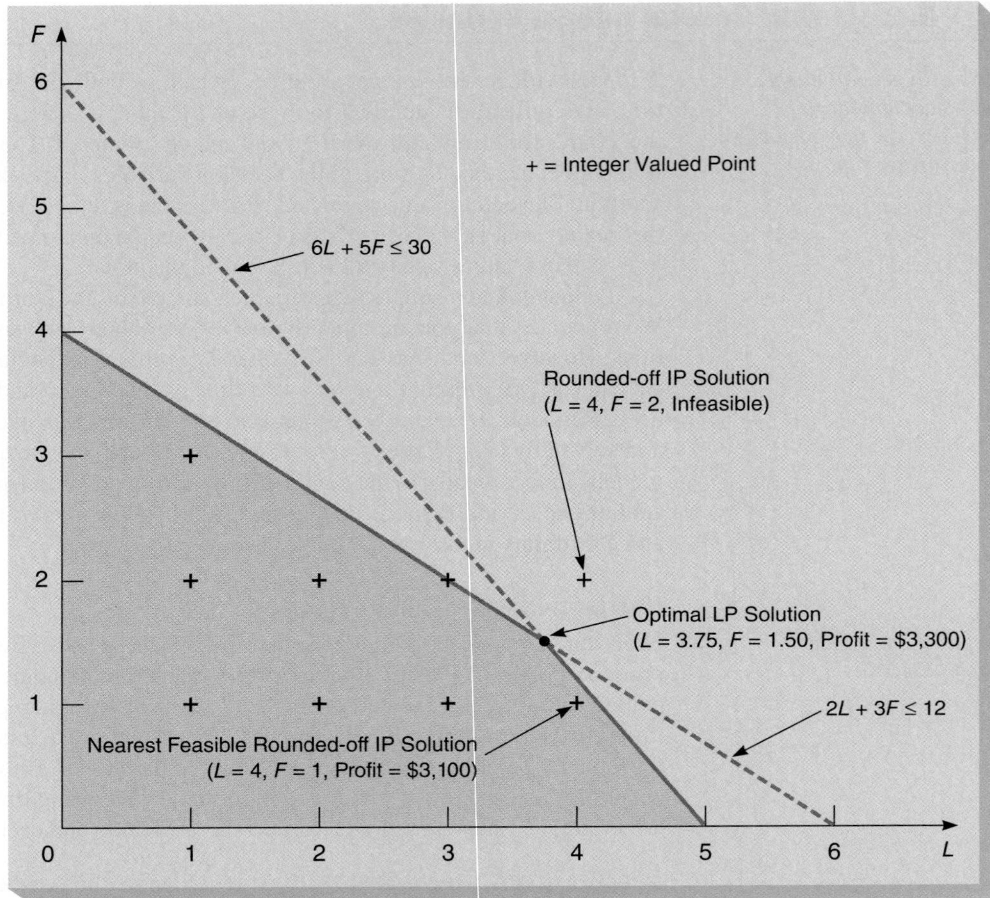

solution is not the optimal solution. Also, note that because this problem involves only two variables, we are able to at least visualize which IP solutions are feasible and round off the LP solution appropriately. Obviously, even the process of rounding the LP solution to obtain a feasible IP solution could be very cumbersome to do if there are more variables in the model.

What is the optimal integer solution in Harrison's case? Table 6.1 lists the entire set of integer-valued solutions for this problem. By inspecting the right-hand column, we see that the optimal integer solution is $L = 3$ lamps and $F = 2$ ceiling fans, for a total profit $= \$3{,}200$. The IP solution of $L = 4$ lamps and $F = 1$ fan yields a profit of only \$3,100.

An important concept to understand is that an IP solution can never be better than the solution to the same LP problem. The integer problem is usually worse in terms of higher cost or lower profit.

PROPERTIES OF OPTIMAL INTEGER SOLUTIONS We note two important properties of the optimal integer solution. First, the optimal point $L = 3$ and $F = 2$ is not a corner point (i.e., a point where two or more constraints intersect) in the LP feasible region. In fact, unlike LP problems, in which the optimal solution is always a corner point of the feasible region, the optimal solution in an IP model need not be a corner point. As we will discuss shortly, this is what makes it difficult to solve IP models in practice.

Second, the integer restriction results in an objective function value that is no better (and is usually worse) than the optimal LP solution. The logic behind this occurrence is quite simple. The feasible region for the original LP problem includes *all* IP solution points, in addition to several LP solution points. That is, the optimal IP solution will always be a feasible solution for the LP problem, *but not vice versa*. We call the LP equivalent of an IP problem (i.e., the IP model with the integer requirement deleted) the *relaxed* problem. As a rule, the IP solution can never produce a better objective value than its LP relaxed problem. At best, the two solutions can be equal (if the optimal LP solution turns out to be integer valued).

TABLE 6.1
Integer Solutions for Harrison Electric—General IP

LAMPS (L)	CEILING FANS (F)	PROFIT (600L$ + 700F$)	
0	0	$ 0	
1	0	$ 600	
2	0	$1,200	
3	0	$1,800	
4	0	$2,400	
5	0	$3,000	
0	1	$ 700	
1	1	$1,300	
2	1	$1,900	
3	1	$2,500	
4	1	$3,100	← *Nearest feasible rounded-off IP solution*
0	2	$1,400	
1	2	$2,000	
2	2	$2,600	
3	2	$3,200	← *Optimal IP solution*
0	3	$2,100	
1	3	$2,700	
0	4	$2,800	

Although using enumeration is feasible for some small IP problems, it can be difficult or impossible for large ones.

Although it is possible to solve simple IP problems such as Harrison Electric's by inspection or enumeration, larger problems cannot be solved in this manner. There would simply be too many points to enumerate. Fortunately, most LP software packages, including Excel's Solver, are capable of handling models with integer variables.

The Excel layout for IP models is similar to that used for LP models.

Using Solver to Solve Models with General Integer Variables

We can set up Harrison Electric's IP problem in Excel in exactly the same manner as we have done for several LP examples in Chapters 2 and 3. For clarity, we once again use the same Excel

IN ACTION Improving Disaster Response Times at CARE International Using Integer Programming

Each year natural disasters kill about 70,000 people and affect another 200 million people worldwide. When a disaster strikes, large quantities of supplies are needed to provide relief aid to the affected areas. However, unavailability of supplies or slowness in mobilizing them may cause emergency responses to be ineffective, resulting in increased human suffering and loss of life.

CARE International, with programs in 65 countries, is one of the largest humanitarian organizations that provide relief aid to disaster survivors. To improve disaster response times, CARE collaborated with researchers from Georgia Institute of Technology to develop a model that evaluates the effect of pre-positioning relief items on average response times.

The model focuses on up-front investment (initial inventory stocking and warehouse setup) and average response time and seeks to answer the following question: Given an initial investment, which network configuration minimizes the average response time? To answer this question, the researchers developed a mixed-integer programming model. The model included about 470,000 variables, 12 of which are binary, about 56,000 constraints, and yielded optimal solutions in under four hours.

The model's results helped CARE determine a desired configuration for its pre-positioning network. Based in part on the results of the study, CARE has pre-positioned relief supplies in three facilities around the world—Dubai, Panama, and Cambodia.

Source: Based on S. Duran, M. A. Gutierrez, and P. Keskinocak. "Pre-Positioning of Emergency Items for CARE International," *Interfaces* 41, 3 (May–June 2011): 223–237.

layout here as in those chapters; that is, all parameters (solution value, objective coefficients, and constraint coefficients) associated with a decision variable are modeled in the same column. The objective function and each constraint in the model are shown on separate rows of the worksheet.

Excel Notes

- The Companion Website for this textbook, at www.pearsonhighered.com/balakrishnan, contains the Excel file for each sample problem discussed here. The relevant file name is shown in the margin next to each example.
- In each of the Excel layouts, for clarity, changing variable cells are shaded yellow, the objective cell is shaded green, and cells containing the left-hand-side (LHS) formula for each constraint are shaded blue.
- Also, to make the equivalence of the *written* formulation and the Excel layout clear, the Excel layouts show the decision variable names used in the written formulation of the model. Note that these names have no role in using Solver to solve the model.

File: 6-1.xls

The Excel layout for Harrison Electric's problem is shown in Screenshot 6-1. As usual, we specify the objective cell (objective function), changing variable cells (decision variables), and constraint LHS and right-hand-side (RHS) cell references in the Solver Parameters window.

The integer requirement is specified as an additional constraint in Solver.

SPECIFYING THE INTEGER REQUIREMENT Before we solve the model, we need to specify the integer value requirement for the two decision variables. We specify this in Solver as a constraint, as follows:

- Use the Add option to include a new constraint. In the LHS entry for the new constraint (see Screenshot 6-1), enter the cell reference for a decision variable that must be integer valued. If there are several decision variables in the model that must be integer valued and they are in contiguous cells (i.e., next to each other), the entire cell range may be entered in the LHS entry. For Harrison's problem, the entry in this box would be B5:C5, corresponding to the number of lamps and fans to make, respectively.
- Next, click the drop-down box in the Add Constraint window. Note that this box has six choices, of which three (i.e., <=, >=, and =) have been used so far. The remaining three are int (for Integer), bin (for Binary), and dif (for AllDifferent).[1] Click the choice int. The word *integer* is displayed automatically in the box for the RHS entry. This indicates to Solver that all variables specified in the LHS box must be integer valued in the optimal solution.

The int *option is used in Solver to specify general integer variables.*

SOLVING THE IP MODEL We are now ready to solve the IP model. Before we click Solve, we need to verify that the Make Unconstrained Variables Non-Negative box is checked and that Simplex LP is specified in the Select a Solving Method box, as shown in Screenshot 6-1. The result, also shown in Screenshot 6-1, indicates that 3 lamps and 2 fans, for a profit of $3,200, is identified as the optimal solution.

As noted previously, thanks to advances in computing technology, Solver (and other decision modeling software packages) can identify optimal solutions very quickly, even for IP models involving thousands of decision variables and constraints. However, when compared to an LP model, the computational effort required to solve an IP model (of the same size) grows rapidly with problem size. We now briefly discuss the reason for this phenomenon.

How Are IP Models Solved?

Solver uses the **branch-and-bound** *procedure to solve IP problems.*

As shown in Figure 6.1 on page 214, the optimal solution to an IP model need not be at a corner point of the feasible region. Unfortunately, the simplex method evaluates only corner points as candidates for the optimal solution. In order to use the simplex method to identify an integer-valued optimal point that may *not* be a corner point, we employ a procedure called the **branch-and-bound (B&B) method**. The B&B method is used by most software packages, including Solver, to solve IP models.

[1] We illustrate only the *int* and *bin* choices in this textbook. The third choice, *dif*, is relevant for special types of sequencing models that are not discussed here.

SCREENSHOT 6-1 Excel Layout and Solver Entries for Harrison Electric—General IP

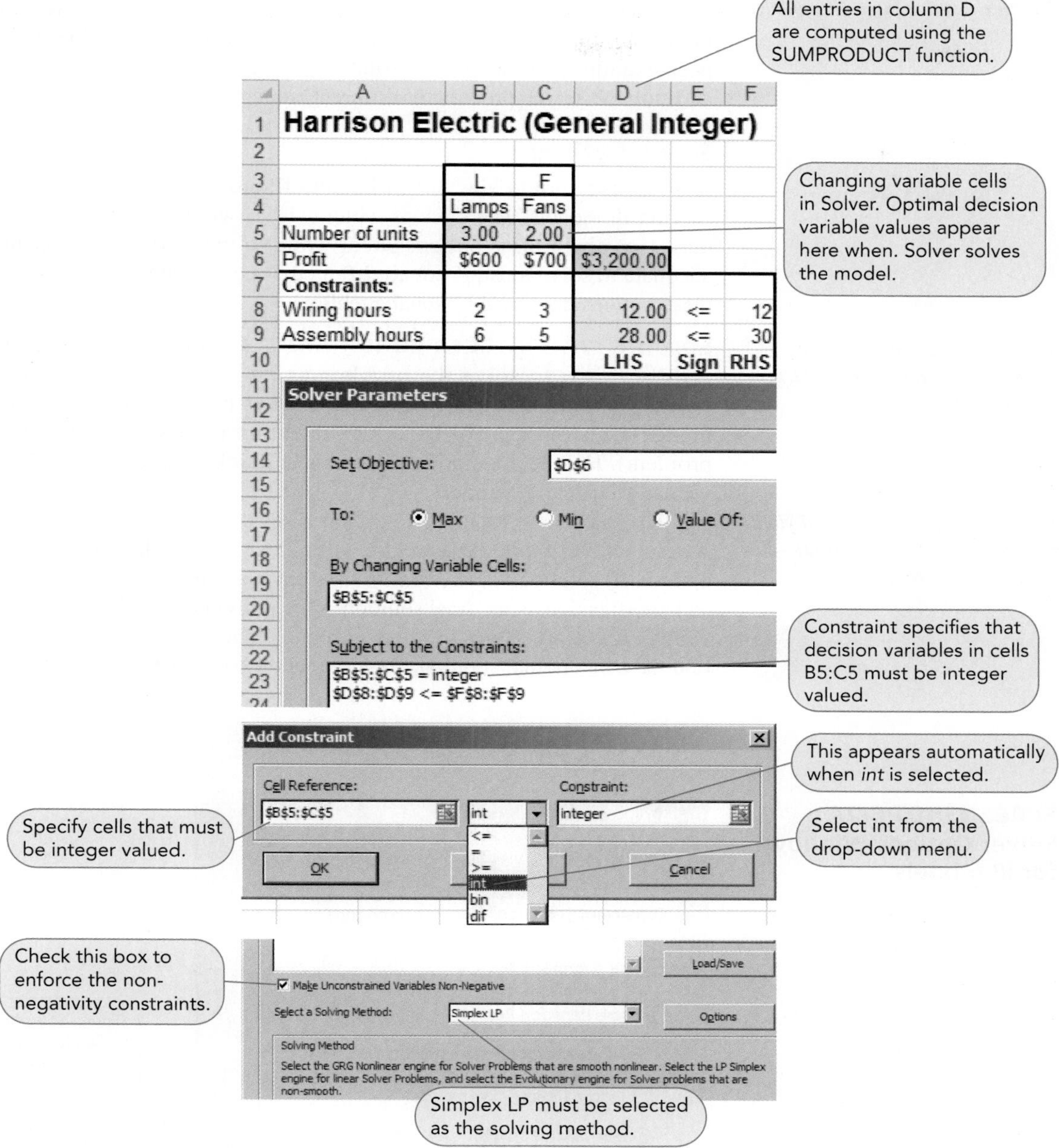

Although we do not discuss the details of the B&B procedure in this textbook, we provide a brief description of how it works.[2] Essentially, the B&B procedure uses a "divide and conquer" strategy. Rather than try to search for the optimal IP solution over the entire feasible region at one time, the B&B procedure splits the feasible region into progressively smaller and smaller subregions. It then searches each subregion in turn. Clearly, the best IP solution over all subregions will be the optimal IP solution over the entire feasible region.

Solving a single IP problem can involve solving several LP problems.

In creating each subregion, the B&B procedure forces a corner point of the new subregion to have integer values for at least one of the variables in the model. This procedure is called *branching*. Finding the optimal solution for each subregion involves the solution of an LP model, referred to in Solver as a subproblem. Hence, in order to solve a single IP model, we may have to solve several LP subproblems. Clearly, this could become computationally quite

[2] Details of the B&B procedure can be found in B. Render, R. Stair, and M. Hanna. *Quantitative Analysis for Management*, 11th ed. Upper Saddle River, NJ: Prentice Hall, 2012.

Computer time and memory requirements may make it difficult to solve large IP models.

burdensome, depending on the number of subregions that need to be created and examined for an IP model. The computer memory needed could also become extensive, especially for models with a large number of integer variables, because we need to store detailed information regarding each subregion (e.g., what part of the LP feasible region does this subregion occupy, has it been examined, is the optimal solution integer). Stopping rules are used to efficiently conduct and stop the search process for different subregions.

Solver Options

Now let us return to how Solver handles IP problems and examine the options available when solving IP models. The Options window is shown in Screenshot 6-2A. We have not concerned ourselves about these options so far while solving LP models because the default values are adequate to solve most, if not all, LP models considered here. However, for IP models, some of these options deserve additional attention.

The maximum time allowed could become an issue for large IP problems.

SOLVING WITH INTEGER CONSTRAINTS Checking the Ignore Integer Constraints box causes Solver to solve the problem as an LP model. As discussed earlier, the optimal objective value of an IP model will always be *worse* than that for the corresponding LP model (i.e., lower profit for a maximization problem and higher cost for a minimization problem). Hence, this option allows us to quickly get an idea about the best IP solution that we can find for the model.

Reducing the tolerance will yield a more accurate IP solution—but could take more time.

The Integer Optimality (%) option is set at a default value of 5% (shown as 0.05 in Solver). A value of 5% implies that we are willing to accept an IP solution that is within 5% of the true optimal IP solution value. When Solver finds a solution within the allowable tolerance, it stops and presents that as the final solution. When this occurs, it is explicitly indicated by the message "Solver found an integer solution within tolerance," as shown in Screenshot 6-2B. If we wish to find the *true* optimal solution, we must set the tolerance to 0%.

SCREENSHOT 6-2A
Solver Options Window for IP Models

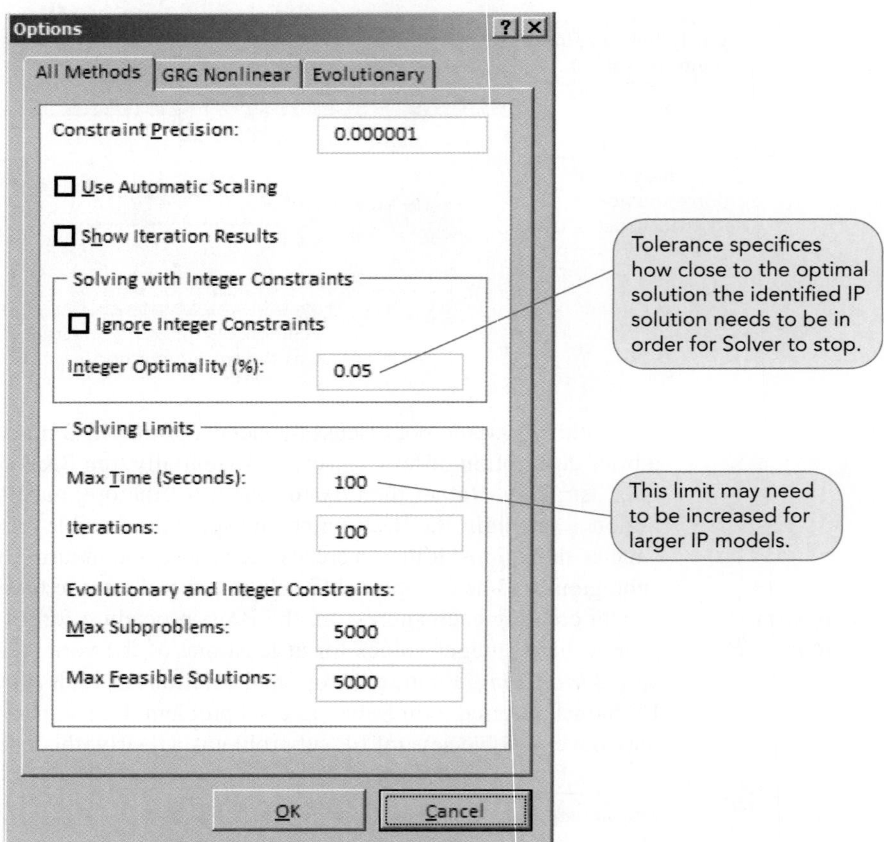

SCREENSHOT 6-2B
Solver Results Window for IP Models

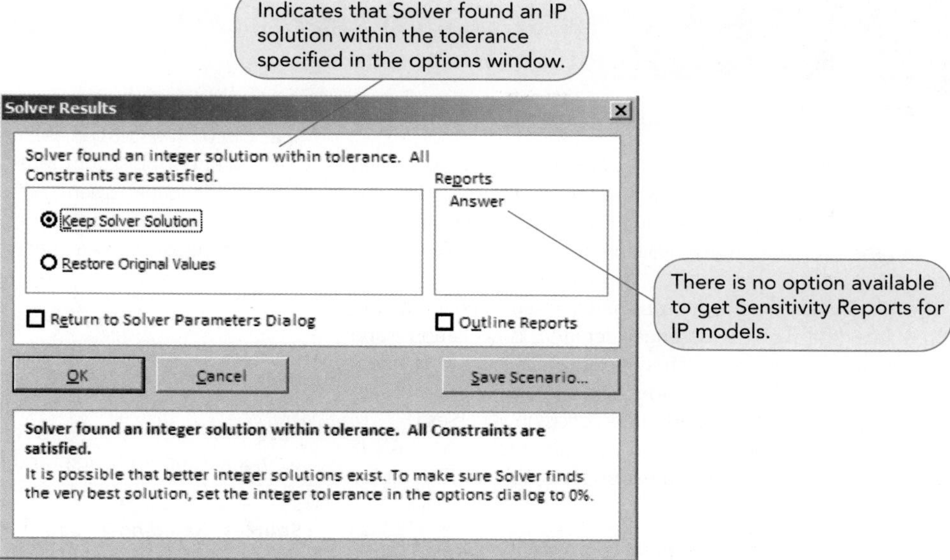

SOLVING LIMITS In Screenshot 6-2A, note that the Max Time (Seconds) option is set to a default value of 100 seconds. As the number of integer-valued decision variables increases in an IP model, this time limit may be exceeded and will need to be extended. In practice, however, it is a good idea to keep the limit at its default value and run the problem. Solver will warn you when the limit is reached and give you the opportunity to allow more time for an IP problem to solve.

Likewise, the default values of 5,000 for the Max Subproblems and Max Feasible Solutions options should be sufficient for most, if not all, IP models considered here. Recall from our brief discussion of the B&B method that in order to solve a single IP model, Solver may need to solve several LP subproblems.

Should We Include Integer Requirements in a Model?

We have already discussed one reason we should be cautious about including integer requirements in a model—namely, the possible computational burden involved in solving large IP models. A second reason for this caution has to do with Sensitivity Reports.

Sensitivity Reports are not available for IP models.

Recall from Chapter 4 that after solving an LP model, we can generate a Sensitivity Report that provides a wealth of information regarding how sensitive the current optimal solution is to changes in input data values. The information in this report allows us to even analyze issues such as the impact of acquiring additional resources, pricing out new products, etc. However, as soon as we specify that one or more decision variables in the model are integers, we lose the ability to obtain a Sensitivity Report. In fact, as shown in Screenshot 6-2B, Solver does not even give you an option to get a Sensitivity Report for an IP model.

Do these two reasons mean that we should not include the integer requirements in a model? For many real-world IP models (and all the models discussed in this textbook), the computational issue is probably not relevant due to the available computing technology. However, in practice, it is a good idea to ask ourselves the following question, especially when the model includes a large number of integer decision variables: "Do we definitely need to find the optimal integer solution, or would it be acceptable to solve the problem as an LP problem and then round off, even if that may lead to a slightly suboptimal solution?" Obviously, there is no single easy answer to this question, and the ultimate answer would depend on the cost (or profit) implications for that specific problem. The answer to this question could also be influenced by the desirability of being able to have a Sensitivity Report for the particular problem scenario.

IN ACTION Selling Seats at American Airlines Using Integer Programming

American Airlines (AA) describes *yield management* as "selling the right seats to the right customers at the right prices." The role of yield management is to determine how much of each product to put on the shelf (i.e., make available for sale) at a given point in time.

The AA yield-management problem is a mixed-integer program that requires data such as passenger demand, cancellations, and other estimates of passenger behavior that are subject to frequent changes. To solve the systemwide yield-management problem would require approximately 250 million decision variables.

To bring this problem down to a manageable size, AA's IP model creates three smaller and easier subproblems. The airline looks at

1. Overbooking, which is the practice of intentionally selling more reservations for a flight than there are actual seats on the aircraft
2. Discount allocation, which is the process of determining the number of discount fares to offer on a flight
3. Traffic management, which is the process of controlling reservations by passenger origin and destination to provide the mix of markets that maximizes revenue

Yield management has been a big winner not only for AA and other airlines, but for other service providers such as hotels. Each year, airlines estimate that profits increase by several million dollars due to the use of this approach. Since its introduction over twenty years ago, airlines and large hotel chains have continually worked to refine the yield management process to make it more efficient and profitable for their operations.

Sources: Based on T. Cook. "SABRE Soars," *OR/MS Today* 25, 3 (June 1998): 26–31; and B. Smith, J. Leimkuhler, and R. Darrow. "Yield Management at American Airlines," *Interfaces* 22, 1 (January–February 1992): 8–31.

6.3 Models with Binary Variables

Binary variables are restricted to values of 0 or 1.

As discussed earlier, binary variables are restricted to values of 0 and 1. Recall that the assignment model and shortest-path model in Chapter 5 both involve variables that ultimately take on values of either 0 or 1 at optimality. However, in both of those models, we do not have to explicitly specify that the variables were binary. The integer property of network flow models, along with the supply and demand values of one unit each, automatically ensure that the optimal solution has a value of 0 or 1.

We associate a value of 1 with one of the choices and a value of 0 with the other choice.

In contrast, we now examine models in which we will explicitly specify that the variables are binary. A binary variable is a powerful modeling tool that is applicable whenever we want to model a *yes* or *no* decision between exactly two choices. That is, the decision has to select either choice 1 or choice 2 in its entirety, and partial or fractional selections are not allowed. When we are faced with such a decision, we associate a binary variable with it. With one of the two choices, we associate a value of 1 for the binary variable. A value of 0 for the binary variable is then associated with the other choice. Now, we write the objective function and constraints in a manner that is consistent with this definition of the binary variable.

Two popular applications of binary models are selection and set covering.

A popular application of binary variables is in *selection* problems, which involve the selection of an optimal subset of items from a larger set of items. Typical examples include decisions such as introducing new products (e.g., introduce a specific product or not), building new facilities (e.g., build a specific facility or not), selecting team members (e.g., select a specific individual or not), and investing in projects (e.g., invest in a specific project or not). Another popular application of binary variables is in a class of problems known as *set covering* problems. These problems typically deal with trying to identify the optimal set of locations to cover or serve a specified set of customers. Examples include locating fire stations, police precincts, or medical clinics to serve a community, locating cell phone towers to provide uninterrupted signal over a region, etc.

Let us consider simple examples to illustrate both types of problems—selection and set covering—that use binary variables.

Portfolio Selection at Simkin and Steinberg

Here is an example of stock portfolio selection with 0–1 programming.

The Houston-based investment firm of Simkin and Steinberg specializes in recommending oil stock portfolios for wealthy clients. One such client has up to $3 million available for investments and insists on purchasing large blocks of shares of each company in which he invests. Table 6.2

TABLE 6.2
Oil Investment Opportunities

COMPANY NAME (LOCATION)	EXPECTED ANNUAL RETURN (THOUSANDS)	COST FOR BLOCK OF SHARES (THOUSANDS)
Trans-Texas Oil (Texas)	\$ 50	\$ 480
British Petro (Foreign)	\$ 80	\$ 540
Dutch Shell (Foreign)	\$ 90	\$ 680
Houston Drilling (Texas)	\$120	\$1,000
Lone Star Petro (Texas)	\$110	\$ 700
San Diego Oil (California)	\$ 40	\$ 510
California Petro (California)	\$ 75	\$ 900

describes the various companies that are under consideration. The objective is to maximize annual return on investment, subject to the following specifications made by the client:

- At least two Texas companies must be in the portfolio.
- No more than one investment can be made in foreign companies.
- Exactly one of the two California companies must be included.
- If British Petro stock is included in the portfolio, then Trans-Texas Oil stock must also be included.

FORMULATING THE PROBLEM Note that the decision with regard to each company has to be one of two choices. That is, the investment firm either buys a large block of shares in the company or it doesn't buy the company's shares. To formulate this problem, let us therefore associate a binary variable with each of the seven companies. For example, we define a binary variable, T, for Trans-Texas Oil as follows:

$$\begin{aligned} T &= 1 \text{ if Trans-Texas Oil is included in the portfolio} \\ &= 0 \text{ if Trans-Texas Oil is not included in the portfolio} \end{aligned}$$

In a similar manner, we define binary variables B (British Petro), D (Dutch Shell), H (Houston Oil), L (Lone Star Petro), S (San Diego Oil), and C (California Petro).

We now need to express the objective function and constraints in a manner that is consistent with the previous definition of the binary variables. The objective function can be written as

$$\begin{aligned} \text{Maximize return on investment} = {} & \$50T + \$80B + \$90D + \$120H \\ & + \$110L + \$40S + \$75C \end{aligned}$$

All figures are in thousands of dollars. In the previous expression, if T has an optimal value of 1 (implying that we include Trans-Texas Oil in the portfolio), this would contribute \$50,000 to the total return. In contrast, if T has an optimal value of 0 (implying that we *not* include Trans-Texas Oil in the portfolio), this would contribute \$0 to the total return.

Next, we model the constraints. The constraint regarding the \$3 million investment limit can be expressed in a similar manner to that of the objective function. That is,

$$\$480T + \$540B + \$680D + \$1{,}000H + \$700L + \$510S + \$900C \leq \$3{,}000$$

Again, all figures are in thousands of dollars. Depending on whether the optimal value of a binary variable is 0 or 1, the corresponding investment cost will be calculated in the LHS of the previous expression.

Binary variables can be used to write different types of constraints.

The other constraints in the problems are special ones that exploit the binary nature of these variables. These types of constraints are what make the use of binary variables a powerful modeling tool. We discuss these special constraints in the following sections.

Selecting k out of n choices

***k* OUT OF *n* CHOICES** The requirement that at least two Texas companies must be in the portfolio is an example of a "k out of n choices" constraint. There are three (i.e., $n = 3$) Texas companies (denoted by the variables T, H, and L), of which at least two (i.e., $k = 2$) must be selected. We can model this constraint as

$$T + H + L \geq 2$$

Avoiding incompatible selections

MUTUALLY EXCLUSIVE CHOICES The condition that no more than one investment can be made in foreign companies is an example of a *mutually exclusive* constraint. Note that the inclusion of one foreign company means that the other must be excluded. We can model this constraint as

$$B + D \leq 1$$

The condition regarding the two California companies is also an example of having mutually exclusive variables. The sign of this constraint is, however, an equality rather than an inequality because Simkin and Steinberg *must* include a California company in the portfolio. That is,

$$S + C = 1$$

Enforcing dependencies

IF–THEN (OR LINKED) CHOICES The condition that if British Petro is included in the portfolio then Trans-Texas Oil must also be included in the portfolio is an example of an *if–then* constraint. We can model this relationship as

$$B \leq T$$

or, if you prefer to have only a constant on the RHS,

$$B - T \leq 0$$

Note that if B equals 0 (i.e., British Petro is not included in the portfolio), this constraint allows T to equal either 0 or 1. However, if B equals 1, then T must also equal 1.

The relationship discussed here is a one-way linkage in that Trans-Texas Oil must be included if British Petro is included, but not vice versa. If the relationship is two way (i.e., either include both or include neither), we then rewrite the constraint as

$$B = T$$

or, once again if you prefer to have only a constant on the RHS,

$$B - T = 0$$

SOLVING THE PROBLEM The complete formulation of Simkin and Steinberg's problem is as follows:

$$\text{Maximize return} = \$50T + \$80B + \$90D + \$120H + \$110L + \$40S + \$75C$$

subject to the constraints

$$
\begin{array}{lll}
\$480T + \$540B + \$680D & & \\
\quad + \$1{,}000H + \$700L & & \\
\quad + \$510S + \$900C & \leq \$3{,}000 & \text{(investment limit)} \\
T + H + L & \geq 2 & \text{(Texas companies)} \\
B + D & \leq 1 & \text{(foreign companies)} \\
S + C & = 1 & \text{(California companies)} \\
B & \leq T & \text{(Trans-Texas and British petro)} \\
\text{All variables} & = 0 \text{ or } 1 &
\end{array}
$$

File: 6-3.xls

The Excel layout and Solver entries for Simkin and Steinberg's 0–1 problem are shown in Screenshot 6-3. The specification of the objective cell, changing variable cells, and constraint LHS and RHS cell references in the Solver Parameters window is similar to that used for LP and general IP models.

The binary requirement is specified as an additional constraint in Solver.

SPECIFYING THE BINARY REQUIREMENT To specify the binary requirement for all variables, we again use the Add option to include a new constraint. In the LHS entry for the new constraint (see Screenshot 6-3), we enter the cell reference for a decision variable that must

SCREENSHOT 6-3 Excel Layout and Solver Entries for Simkin and Steinberg—Binary IP

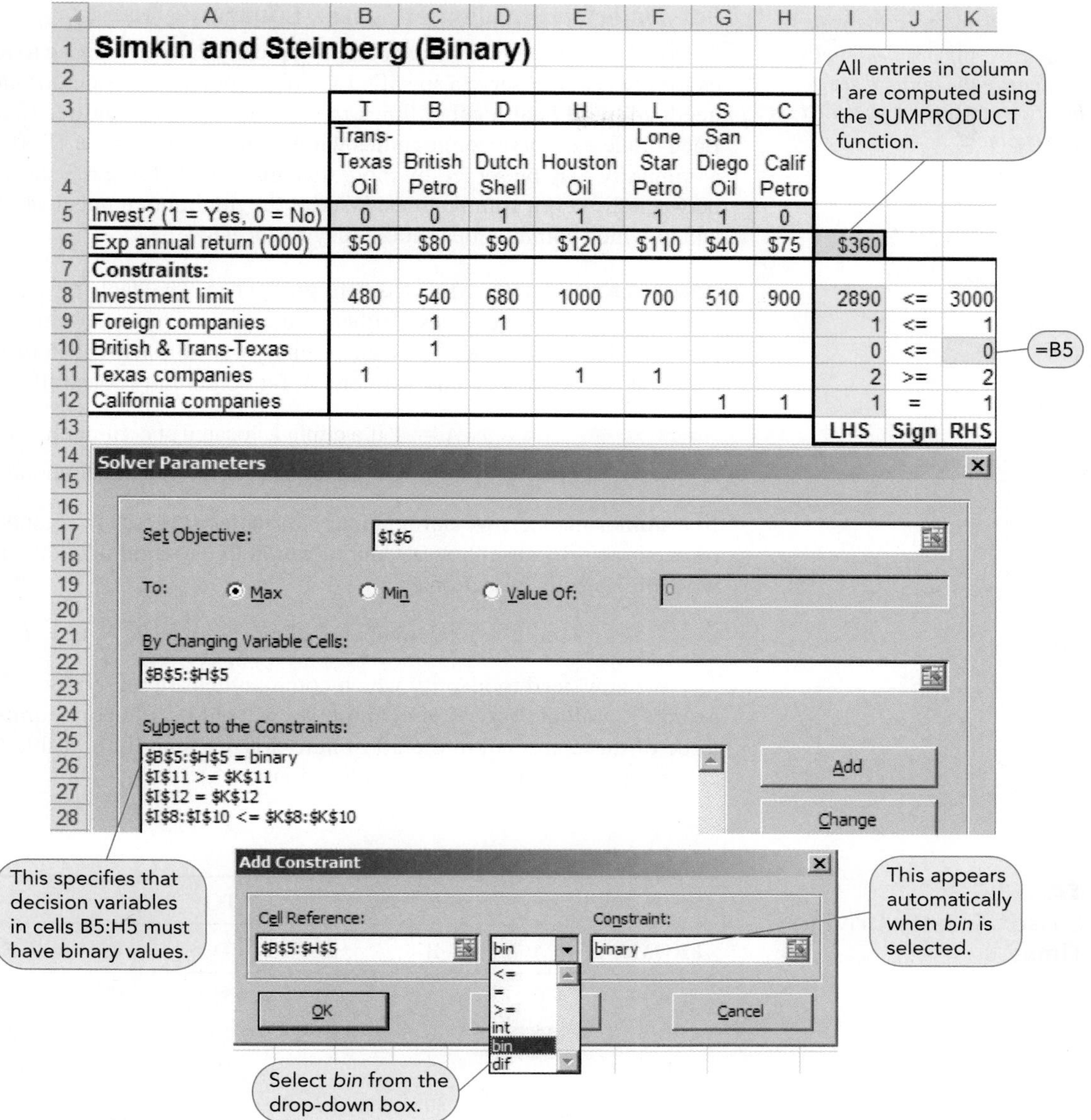

	T	B	D	H	L	S	C			
	Trans-Texas Oil	British Petro	Dutch Shell	Houston Oil	Lone Star Petro	San Diego Oil	Calif Petro			
Invest? (1 = Yes, 0 = No)	0	0	1	1	1	1	0			
Exp annual return ('000)	$50	$80	$90	$120	$110	$40	$75	$360		
Constraints:										
Investment limit	480	540	680	1000	700	510	900	2890	<=	3000
Foreign companies		1	1					1	<=	1
British & Trans-Texas		1						0	<=	0
Texas companies	1			1	1			2	>=	2
California companies						1	1	1	=	1
								LHS	Sign	RHS

be binary valued. If there are several decision variables that must be binary valued, we can enter the entire cell range, provided that these variables are in contiguous cells. For Simkin and Steinberg's problem, we enter B5:H5 in this box, corresponding to binary variables T through C, respectively.

We then click the drop-down box in the Add Constraint window and click the choice bin. The word *binary* is automatically displayed in the box for the RHS entry. This indicates to Solver that all variables specified in the LHS box are binary variables.

INTERPRETING THE RESULTS Screenshot 6-3 shows that the optimal solution is for Simkin and Steinberg to recommend that the client invest in Dutch Shell (D), Houston Oil (H), Lone Star Petro (L), and San Diego Oil (S). The expected return is $360,000 (all values are in units of $1,000). Note that the solution invests only $2.89 million of the available $3 million. Why did this happen? There are two reasons for this: (1) Company stocks can only be bought in fixed blocks, and (2) specifications made by the client are possibly too restrictive.

Set Covering Problem at Sussex County

A set covering problem seeks to identify the optimal set of locations to cover a specified set of customers.

As noted earlier, set covering problems typically deal with trying to identify the optimal set of locations to cover or serve a specified set of customers. Consider the case of Sussex County, which needs to build health care clinics to serve seven communities (named A to G) in the region. Each clinic can serve communities within a maximum radius of 30 minutes' driving time, and a community may be served by more than one clinic. Table 6.3 shows the times it takes to travel between the seven communities. What is the minimum number of clinics that would be needed, and in which communities should they be located?

FORMULATING AND SOLVING THE PROBLEM The decision with regard to each community has to be one of two choices—either locate a clinic in that community or not. To formulate this problem, let us therefore associate a binary variable with each of the seven communities. For example, we define a binary variable, A, for community A as follows:

$$\begin{aligned} A &= 1 \text{ if a clinic is located at community A} \\ &= 0 \text{ if a clinic is not located at community A} \end{aligned}$$

In a similar manner, we define binary variables B, C, D, E, F, and G for communities B to G, respectively. Because Sussex County would like to minimize the number of clinics needed, we write the objective function as

$$\text{Minimize total number of clinics} = A + B + C + D + E + F + G$$

We now need to identify which communities are served by a clinic at a given location. For example, a clinic located at community A would serve communities A, B, and C because all three of these are within the 30-minute driving time limit. Table 6.4 shows the communities covered by the clinics at all seven locations.

TABLE 6.3
Sussex County Driving Times

	TO						
FROM	A	B	C	D	E	F	G
A	0	15	20	35	35	45	40
B	15	0	35	20	35	40	40
C	20	35	0	15	50	45	30
D	35	20	15	0	35	20	20
E	35	35	50	35	0	15	40
F	45	40	45	20	15	0	35
G	40	40	30	20	40	35	0

TABLE 6.4
Sussex County Community Coverage

COMMUNITY	COMMUNITIES WITHIN 30 MINUTES
A	A, B, C
B	A, B, D
C	A, C, D, G
D	B, C, D, F, G
E	E, F
F	D, E, F
G	C, D, G

The constraints need to ensure that each community is served (or covered) by at least one clinic. For this reason, they are called *covering constraints*. For Sussex County's problem, these constraints are as follows:

$A + B + C$	≥ 1	(community A is covered)
$A + B + D$	≥ 1	(community B is covered)
$A + C + D + G$	≥ 1	(community C is covered)
$B + C + D + F + G$	≥ 1	(community D is covered)
$E + F$	≥ 1	(community E is covered)
$D + E + F$	≥ 1	(community F is covered)
$C + D + G$	≥ 1	(community G is covered)
All variables	$= 0$ or 1	

There are no other constraints in Sussex County's problem. However, if necessary, we could use the three types of constraints described earlier—k out of n choices, mutually exclusive, and if–then—in Simkin and Steinberg's portfolio selection problem, to model any other specifications. For example, if Sussex does not want to locate clinics at both B and D, this would be modeled as a mutually exclusive constraint (i.e., $B + D \leq 1$).

File: 6-4.xls

The Excel layout and Solver entries for Sussex County's set covering problem are shown in Screenshot 6-4.

SCREENSHOT 6-4 Excel Layout and Solver Entries for Sussex County—Set Covering

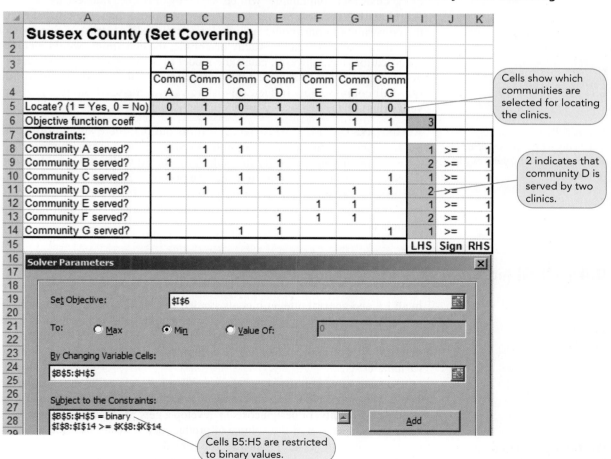

	A	B	C	D	E	F	G	H	I	J	K
1	**Sussex County (Set Covering)**										
2											
3		A	B	C	D	E	F	G			
4		Comm A	Comm B	Comm C	Comm D	Comm E	Comm F	Comm G			
5	Locate? (1 = Yes, 0 = No)	0	1	0	1	1	0	0			
6	Objective function coeff	1	1	1	1	1	1	1	3		
7	**Constraints:**										
8	Community A served?	1	1	1					1	>=	1
9	Community B served?	1	1		1				2	>=	1
10	Community C served?	1		1	1			1	1	>=	1
11	Community D served?		1	1	1		1	1	2	>=	1
12	Community E served?					1	1		1	>=	1
13	Community F served?				1	1	1		2	>=	1
14	Community G served?			1	1			1	1	>=	1
15									**LHS**	**Sign**	**RHS**

Cells show which communities are selected for locating the clinics.

2 indicates that community D is served by two clinics.

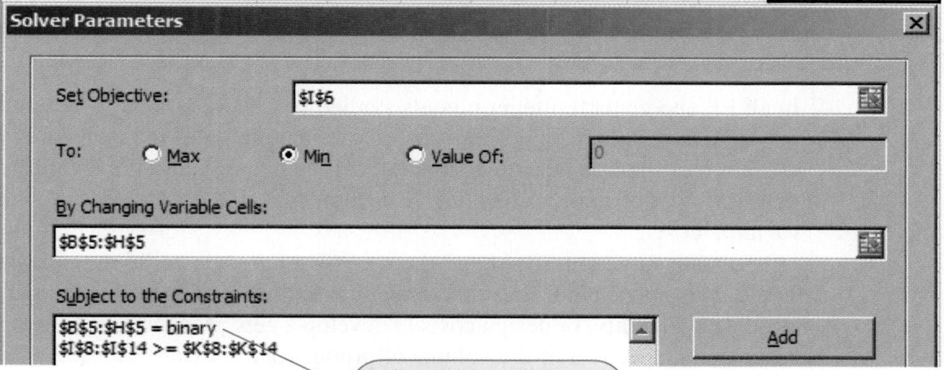

Solver Parameters

Set Objective: $I$6

To: Max | Min (selected) | Value Of: 0

By Changing Variable Cells: $B$5:$H$5

Subject to the Constraints:
$B$5:$H$5 = binary
$I$8:$I$14 >= $K$8:$K$14

Add

Cells B5:H5 are restricted to binary values.

IN ACTION Binary Integer Programming Facilitates Better Course Scheduling at the Universidad de Chile

In its simplest form, the course and examination scheduling problem can be defined as the assignment of a set of courses to different time slots and classrooms while satisfying certain requirements. These requirements can vary widely based on factors such as the institution's policies, room availabilities, level of classes being scheduled, etc.

The Executive Education Unit (EEU) of the Universidad de Chile offers courses primarily for professionals and high-level executives. Ensuring proper schedules for this high-profile audience is critical because any perception of disorganization would affect the EEU adversely. Between 2003 and 2008, about 7,000 students attended EEU courses.

The eClasSkeduler decision support system used at EEU consists of four modules: (1) input information module that stores all information relating to courses, classrooms, and instructors, (2) user interface module that transforms the input data to the format necessary for the binary integer programming (BIP) optimization model, (3) optimization module that contains the source code for the BIP model, and (4) report module that transforms the BIP model's results to an user-friendly management report with various performance indicators.

The use of eClasSkeduler has benefited all EEU participants by curtailing operating costs, lowering unused classroom capacity, and producing fewer schedule conflicts and off-premise classroom assignments.

Sources: Based on J. Miranda. "eClasSkeduler: A Course Scheduling System for the Executive Education Unit at the Universidad de Chile," *Interfaces* 40, 3 (May–June 2010): 196–207.

INTERPRETING THE RESULTS The results indicate that Sussex County will need to open three clinics, one each at communities B, D, and E, to serve the seven communities. Residents of three of the seven communities (B, D, and F) will be served by two clinics each, while residents of the other four communities will be served by only one clinic each.

Note that because Sussex County permits more than one clinic to serve a community, the constraints in our model included the $\geq$ sign. In contrast, if Sussex County wants each community to be served by exactly one clinic, the constraints would include the $=$ sign. This specification may, however, cause the model to be infeasible in some cases. For example, the driving times could be such that it would be impossible to find a set of locations that uniquely serve all communities. In fact, this is the case in Sussex County's problem (see if you can verify this).

In general, there is no easy way to detect the presence of alternate optimal solutions for IP models.

ALTERNATE OPTIMAL SOLUTIONS It turns out that there are multiple optimal solutions to Sussex County's model. For example, locating clinics in communities A, C, and F is also optimal (see if you can verify this solution). Recall that in Chapter 4 we studied how to use the Solver Sensitivity Report to detect the presence of alternate optimal solutions. However, because we cannot obtain Sensitivity Reports for IP models, we cannot adopt that strategy here. In general, there is no easy way to detect the presence of alternate optimal solutions for IP models.

6.4 Mixed Integer Models: Fixed-Charge Problems

In all LP and general integer models studied so far, we typically deal with situations in which the total cost is directly proportional to the magnitude of the decision variable. For example, if X denotes the number of toasters we will be making, and if each toaster costs \$10 to make, the total cost of making toasters is written as \$10X. Such costs per unit are referred to as *variable* costs.

In many situations, however, there are fixed costs in addition to the per-unit variable costs. These costs may include the costs to set up machines for the production run, construction costs to build a new facility, or design costs to develop a new product. Unlike variable costs, these fixed costs are independent of the volume of production. They are incurred whenever the decision to go ahead with a project or production run is made.

Fixed-charge problems *include fixed costs in addition to variable costs.*

Problems that involve both fixed and variable costs are a classic example of **mixed integer programming** models. We call such problems **fixed-charge problems**.

We use binary variables to model the fixed cost issue (e.g., whether we will incur the setup cost or not). Either linear or integer variables can be used to deal with the variable costs issue, depending on the nature of these variables. In formulating the model, we need to ensure that whenever the decision variable associated with the variable cost is nonzero, the binary variable associated with the fixed cost takes on a value of 1 (i.e., the fixed cost is also incurred).

To illustrate this type of situation, let us revisit the Hardgrave Machine Company facility location example that we first studied as Solved Problem 5-1 in Chapter 5 (see page 193).

Locating a New Factory for Hardgrave Machine Company

Hardgrave Machine Company produces computer components at its factories in Cincinnati, Kansas City, and Pittsburgh. These factories have not been able to keep up with demand for orders at Hardgrave's four warehouses in Detroit, Houston, New York, and Los Angeles. As a result, the firm has decided to build a new factory to expand its productive capacity. The two sites being considered are Seattle, Washington, and Birmingham, Alabama. Both cities are attractive in terms of labor supply, municipal services, and ease of factory financing.

Table 6.5 presents the production costs and monthly supplies at each of the three existing factories, monthly demands at each of the four warehouses, and estimated production costs at the two proposed factories. Transportation costs from each factory to each warehouse are summarized in Table 6.6.

Sunk costs are not considered in the optimization model.

In addition to this information, Hardgrave estimates that the monthly fixed cost of operating the proposed facility in Seattle would be $400,000. The Birmingham plant would be somewhat cheaper, due to the lower cost of living at that location. Hardgrave therefore estimates that the monthly fixed cost of operating the proposed facility in Birmingham would be $325,000. Note that the fixed costs at *existing* plants need not be considered here because they will be incurred regardless of which new plant Hardgrave decides to open—that is, they are sunk costs.

As in Chapter 5, the question facing Hardgrave is this: Which of the new locations, in combination with the existing plants and warehouses, will yield the lowest cost? Note that the

TABLE 6.5 Hardgrave Machine's Demand and Supply Data

WAREHOUSE	MONTHLY DEMAND (UNITS)	PRODUCTION PLANT	MONTHLY SUPPLY	COST TO PRODUCE ONE UNIT
Detroit	10,000	Cincinnati	15,000	$48
Houston	12,000	Kansas City	6,000	$50
New York	15,000	Pittsburgh	14,000	$52
Los Angeles	9,000		35,000	
	46,000			

Supply needed from new plant = 46,000 − 35,000 = 11,000 units per month

ESTIMATED PRODUCTION COST PER UNIT AT PROPOSED PLANTS	
Seattle	$53
Birmingham	$49

TABLE 6.6 Hardgrave Machine's Shipping Costs

FROM	TO: DETROIT	HOUSTON	NEW YORK	LOS ANGELES
Cincinnati	$25	$55	$40	$60
Kansas City	$35	$30	$50	$40
Pittsburgh	$36	$45	$26	$66
Seattle	$60	$38	$65	$27
Birmingham	$35	$30	$41	$50

unit cost of shipping from each plant to each warehouse is found by adding the shipping costs (Table 6.6) to the corresponding production costs (Table 6.5). In addition, the solution needs to consider the monthly fixed costs of operating the new facility.

Recall that we handled this problem in Solved Problem 5-1 by setting up and solving two separate transportation models—one for each of the two new locations. In the following pages, we show how we can use binary variables to model Hardgrave's problem as a single mixed, binary integer programming model.

DECISION VARIABLES There are two types of decisions to be made in this problem. The first involves deciding which of the new locations (Seattle or Birmingham) to select for the new plant. The second involves trying to decide the shipment quantities from each plant (including the new plant) to each of the warehouses.

We use binary variables to model the opening of a plant.

To model the first decision, we associate a binary variable with each of the two locations. Let

$$Y_S = 1 \text{ if Seattle is selected for the new plant}$$
$$= 0 \text{ otherwise}$$
$$Y_B = 1 \text{ if Birmingham is selected for the new plant}$$
$$= 0 \text{ otherwise}$$

We use regular variables (continuous-valued or general integer) to model the shipping quantities.

To model the shipping quantities, we once again use double-subscripted variables, as discussed in Chapter 5. Note that there are 5 plants (3 existing and 2 proposed) and 4 warehouses in the problem. Therefore, the model will include 20 decision variables denoting the shipping quantities (one variable for each possible shipping route). Let

$$X_{ij} = \text{Number of units shipped from plant } i \text{ to warehouse } j$$

where

$$i = \text{C (Cincinnati), K (Kansas City), P (Pittsburgh), S (Seattle), or } B \text{ (Birmingham)}$$
$$j = \text{D (Detroit), H (Houston), N (New York), or L (Los Angeles)}$$

OBJECTIVE FUNCTION Let us first model the objective function. We want to minimize the total cost of producing and shipping the components and the monthly fixed costs of maintaining the new facility. This can be written as

$$\begin{aligned}\text{Minimize total costs} = {} & \$73X_{CD} + \$103X_{CH} + \$88X_{CN} + \$108X_{CL} \\ & + \$85X_{KD} + \$80X_{KH} + \$100X_{KN} + \$90X_{KL} \\ & + \$88X_{PD} + \$97X_{PH} + \$78X_{PN} + \$118X_{PL} \\ & + \$113X_{SD} + \$91X_{SH} + \$118X_{SN} + \$80X_{SL} \\ & + \$84X_{BD} + \$79X_{BH} + \$90X_{BN} + \$99X_{BL} \\ & + \$400{,}000Y_S + \$325{,}000Y_B\end{aligned}$$

The last two terms in the expression for the objective function represent the fixed costs. Note that these costs will be incurred only if the plant is built at the location (i.e., the variable Y_S or Y_B has a value of 1).

CONSTRAINTS We need to write flow balance constraints for each of the plants and warehouses. Recall that at each node, the flow balance constraint ensures that

$$\text{Net flow} = (\text{Total flow } \textit{in} \text{ to node}) - (\text{Total flow } \textit{out} \text{ of node})$$

At source nodes, the net flow is a negative quantity and represents the amount of goods (flow) created at that node. In contrast, at destination nodes, the net flow is a positive quantity and represents the amount of goods (flow) consumed at that node. Because this is a balanced problem, all flow balance constraints can be written as equalities.

The flow balance constraints at the existing plants (Cincinnati, Kansas City, and Pittsburgh) are straightforward and can be written as

$$(0) - (X_{CD} + X_{CH} + X_{CN} + X_{CL}) = -15{,}000 \quad \text{(Cincinnati supply)}$$
$$(0) - (X_{KD} + X_{KH} + X_{KN} + X_{KL}) = -\ 6{,}000 \quad \text{(Kansas City supply)}$$
$$(0) - (X_{PD} + X_{PH} + X_{PN} + X_{PL}) = -14{,}000 \quad \text{(Pittsburgh supply)}$$

Supply is available at a plant only if the plant is opened.

However, when writing the flow balance constraint for a new plant (Seattle or Birmingham), we need to ensure that a supply is available at that plant *only* if the plant is actually built. For example, the supply at Seattle is 11,000 units if the new plant is built there and 0 otherwise. We can model this as follows:

$$(0) - (X_{SD} + X_{SH} + X_{SN} + X_{SL}) = -11{,}000Y_S \qquad \text{(Seattle supply)}$$
$$(0) - (X_{BD} + X_{BH} + X_{BN} + X_{BL}) = -11{,}000Y_B \qquad \text{(Birmingham supply)}$$

Note that if Seattle is selected for the new plant, Y_S equals 1. Hence, a supply of 11,000 is available there. In contrast, if Seattle is not selected for the new plant, Y_S equals 0. Hence, the supply in the flow balance constraint becomes 0; that is, all flows from Seattle have to equal 0. The flow balance constraint for Birmingham works in a similar manner.

The flow balance constraints at the four existing warehouses (Detroit, Houston, New York, and Los Angeles) can be written as

$$X_{CD} + X_{KD} + X_{PD} + X_{SD} + X_{BD} = 10{,}000 \qquad \text{(Detroit supply)}$$
$$X_{CH} + X_{KH} + X_{PH} + X_{SH} + X_{BH} = 12{,}000 \qquad \text{(Houston supply)}$$
$$X_{CN} + X_{KN} + X_{PN} + X_{SN} + X_{BN} = 15{,}000 \qquad \text{(New York supply)}$$
$$X_{CL} + X_{KL} + X_{PL} + X_{SL} + X_{BL} = 9{,}000 \qquad \text{(Los Angeles supply)}$$

Only one of the two sites can be selected.

Finally, we need to ensure that exactly one of the two sites is selected for the new plant. This is another example of the mutually exclusive variables discussed in section 6.3. We can express this as

$$Y_S + Y_B = 1$$

File: 6-5.xls

SOLVING THE PROBLEM AND INTERPRETING THE RESULTS The formula view of the Excel layout for Hardgrave's fixed-charge problem is shown in Screenshot 6-5A. The Solver entries and optimal solution are shown in Screenshot 6-5B.

Referring to Solved Problem 5-1 on page 193, we see that the cost of shipping was \$3,704,000 if the new plant was built in Seattle. This cost was \$3,741,000 if the new plant was built in Birmingham. With the fixed costs included, these costs would be

Seattle:	\$3,704,000 + \$400,000 = \$4,104,000
Birmingham:	\$3,741,000 + \$325,000 = \$4,066,000

SCREENSHOT 6-5A Formula View of Excel Layout for Hardgrave Machine—Fixed Charge

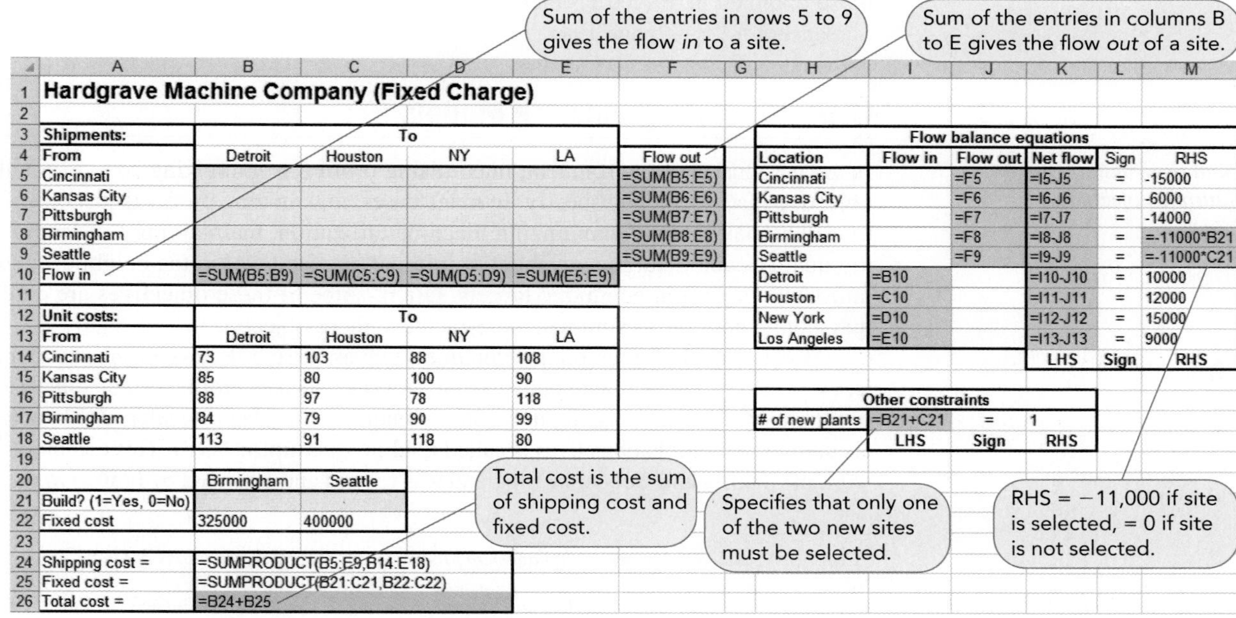

Shipments:	To				
From	Detroit	Houston	NY	LA	Flow out
Cincinnati					=SUM(B5:E5)
Kansas City					=SUM(B6:E6)
Pittsburgh					=SUM(B7:E7)
Birmingham					=SUM(B8:E8)
Seattle					=SUM(B9:E9)
Flow in	=SUM(B5:B9)	=SUM(C5:C9)	=SUM(D5:D9)	=SUM(E5:E9)	

Unit costs:	To			
From	Detroit	Houston	NY	LA
Cincinnati	73	103	88	108
Kansas City	85	80	100	90
Pittsburgh	88	97	78	118
Birmingham	84	79	90	99
Seattle	113	91	118	80

	Birmingham	Seattle
Build? (1=Yes, 0=No)		
Fixed cost	325000	400000

Shipping cost =	=SUMPRODUCT(B5:E9,B14:E18)
Fixed cost =	=SUMPRODUCT(B21:C21,B22:C22)
Total cost =	=B24+B25

Flow balance equations					
Location	Flow in	Flow out	Net flow	Sign	RHS
Cincinnati		=F5	=I5-J5	=	-15000
Kansas City		=F6	=I6-J6	=	-6000
Pittsburgh		=F7	=I7-J7	=	-14000
Birmingham		=F8	=I8-J8	=	=-11000*B21
Seattle		=F9	=I9-J9	=	=-11000*C21
Detroit	=B10		=I10-J10	=	10000
Houston	=C10		=I11-J11	=	12000
New York	=D10		=I12-J12	=	15000
Los Angeles	=E10		=I13-J13	=	9000
			LHS	Sign	RHS

Other constraints			
# of new plants	=B21+C21	=	1
	LHS	Sign	RHS

SCREENSHOT 6-5B Solver Entries and Solution for Hardgrave Machine—Fixed Charge

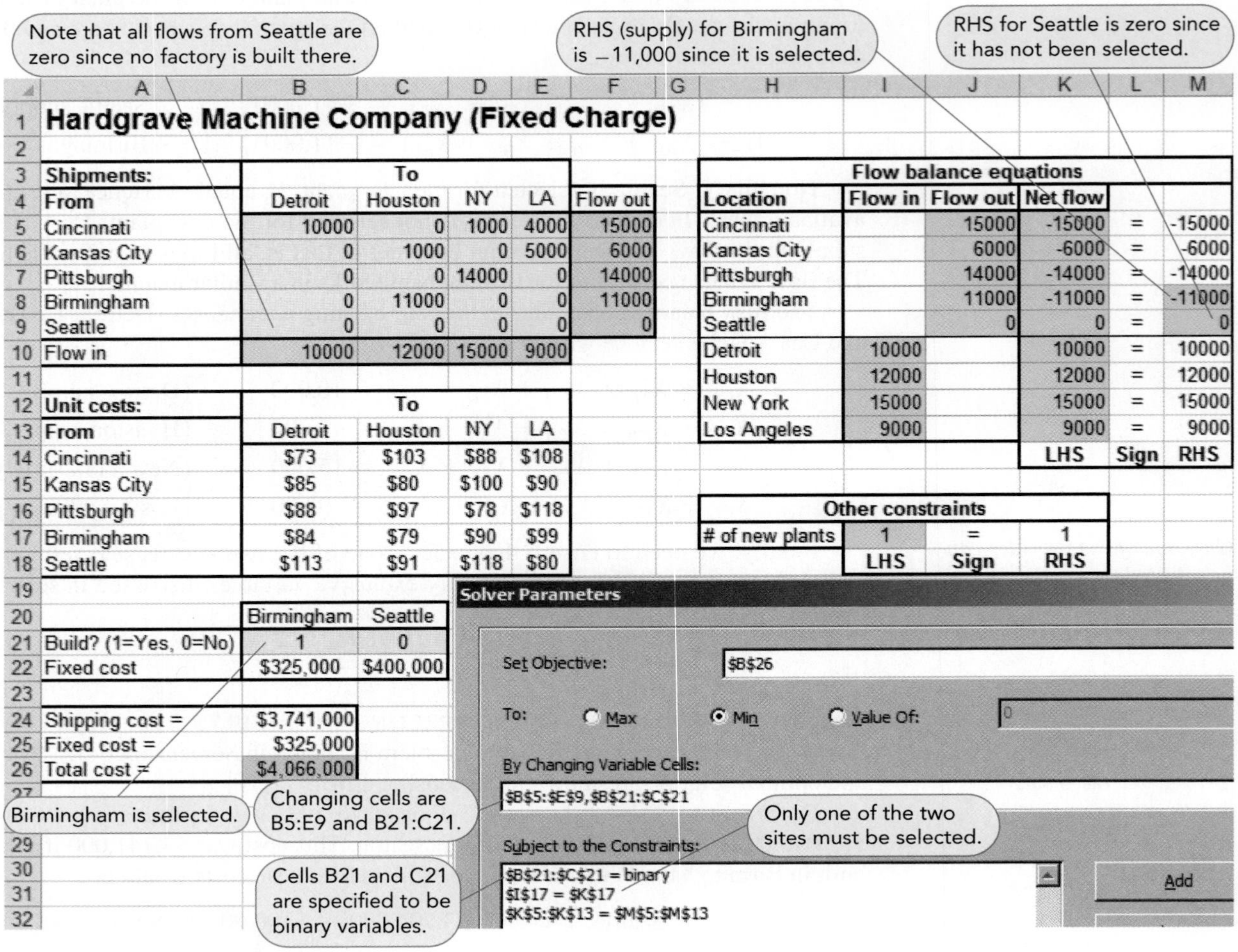

Note that all flows from Seattle are zero since no factory is built there.

RHS (supply) for Birmingham is −11,000 since it is selected.

RHS for Seattle is zero since it has not been selected.

Hardgrave Machine Company (Fixed Charge)

Shipments:	To				
From	Detroit	Houston	NY	LA	Flow out
Cincinnati	10000	0	1000	4000	15000
Kansas City	0	1000	0	5000	6000
Pittsburgh	0	0	14000	0	14000
Birmingham	0	11000	0	0	11000
Seattle	0	0	0	0	0
Flow in	10000	12000	15000	9000	

Flow balance equations					
Location	Flow in	Flow out	Net flow		
Cincinnati		15000	-15000	=	-15000
Kansas City		6000	-6000	=	-6000
Pittsburgh		14000	-14000	=	-14000
Birmingham		11000	-11000	=	-11000
Seattle		0	0	=	0
Detroit	10000		10000	=	10000
Houston	12000		12000	=	12000
New York	15000		15000	=	15000
Los Angeles	9000		9000	=	9000
			LHS	Sign	RHS

Unit costs:	To			
From	Detroit	Houston	NY	LA
Cincinnati	$73	$103	$88	$108
Kansas City	$85	$80	$100	$90
Pittsburgh	$88	$97	$78	$118
Birmingham	$84	$79	$90	$99
Seattle	$113	$91	$118	$80

Other constraints			
# of new plants	1	=	1
	LHS	Sign	RHS

	Birmingham	Seattle
Build? (1=Yes, 0=No)	1	0
Fixed cost	$325,000	$400,000

Shipping cost =	$3,741,000
Fixed cost =	$325,000
Total cost =	$4,066,000

Birmingham is selected.

Changing cells are B5:E9 and B21:C21.

Cells B21 and C21 are specified to be binary variables.

Only one of the two sites must be selected.

Solver Parameters

Set Objective: $B$26

To: Max ● Min Value Of: 0

By Changing Variable Cells: $B$5:$E$9,$B$21:$C$21

Subject to the Constraints:
$B$21:$C$21 = binary
$I$17 = $K$17
$K$5:$K$13 = $M$5:$M$13

Add

Total cost includes fixed costs and shipping costs.

That is, Hardgrave should select Birmingham as the site for the new plant. Screenshot 6-5B shows this solution. Note that the shipping quantities in this solution are the same as those obtained in Solved Problem 5-1 for the solution with the Birmingham plant (as shown in Screenshot 5-9B on page 194).

6.5 Goal Programming Models

Goal programming permits multiple objectives.

In today's business environment, maximizing profit (or minimizing cost) is not always the only objective that a firm may specify. In many cases, maximizing profits is just one of several objectives that may include maximizing machine utilization, maintaining full employment, providing quality ecological management, minimizing noise level in the neighborhood, and meeting numerous other non-economic targets. Often, some of these objectives are conflicting (i.e., it may not be possible to simultaneously achieve these objectives).

Mathematical programming techniques such as LP and IP have the shortcoming that their objective function can deal with only a single criterion, such as profit, cost, or some such measure. To overcome this shortcoming, an important technique that has been developed to handle decision models involving multiple objectives is called **goal programming (GP)**. This technique began with the work of Charnes and Cooper in 1961 and was refined and extended by Ignizio in the 1970s.[3]

---

[3] Charnes, A., and W. W. Cooper. *Management Models and Industrial Applications of Linear Programming*. New York: Wiley, 1961.

Ignizio, J. P. *Goal Programming and Extensions*. Lexington, MA: D.C. Heath and Company, 1976.

Whereas LP optimizes, GP satisfices.

How do LP/IP and GP models differ? In LP/IP models, we try to find the best possible value for a single objective. That is, the aim is to *optimize* a single measure. In GP models, on the other hand, we first set a goal (or desired target) for each objective. In most decision modeling situations, some of these goals may be achievable only at the expense of other goals. We therefore establish a hierarchy or rank of importance among these goals so that lower-ranked goals are given less prominence than higher-ranked goals. Based on this hierarchy, GP then attempts to reach a "satisfactory" level for each goal. That is, GP tries to **satisfice** the multiple objectives (i.e., come as close as possible to their respective goals) rather than optimize them. Nobel laureate Herbert A. Simon of Carnegie-Mellon University states that modern managers may not be able to optimize but may instead have to satisfice to reach goals.

In GP we want to minimize deviation variables, which are the only terms in the objective function.

How does GP satisfice the goals? Instead of trying to maximize or minimize the objective functions directly, as in LP/IP, with GP we try to minimize *deviations* between the specified goals and what we can actually achieve for the multiple objective functions within the given constraints. Deviations can be either positive or negative, depending on whether we overachieve or underachieve a specific goal. These deviations are not only real decision variables in the GP model, but they are also the only terms in the objective function. The objective is to minimize some function of these **deviation variables**.

Goal Programming Example: Wilson Doors Company

To illustrate the formulation of a GP problem, let us consider the product mix problem faced by the Wilson Doors Company. The company manufactures three styles of doors—exterior, interior, and commercial. Each door requires a certain amount of steel and two separate production steps: forming and assembly. Table 6.7 shows the material requirement, forming and assembly times, and selling price per unit of each product, along with the monthly availability of all resources.

FORMULATING AND SOLVING THE LP MODEL Let us denote E = number of exterior doors to make, I = number of interior doors to make, and C = number of commercial doors to make. If Wilson's management had just a single objective (i.e., to maximize total sales), the LP formulation for the problem would be written as

$$\text{Maximize total sales} = \$70E + \$110I + \$110C$$

subject to the constraints

$$\begin{aligned} 4E + 3I + 7C &\leq 9{,}000 && \text{(steel usage)} \\ 2E + 4I + 3C &\leq 6{,}000 && \text{(forming time)} \\ 2E + 3I + 4C &\leq 5{,}200 && \text{(assembly time)} \\ E, I, C &\leq 0 \end{aligned}$$

The optimal LP solution turns out to be $E = 1{,}400$, $I = 800$, and $C = 0$, for a total sales of \$186,000. At this stage, you should be able to easily verify this yourself. However, for your convenience, this LP solution is included in the Excel file *6-6.xls* on the Companion Website for this textbook; see the worksheet named *6-6 LP*.

WWW

File: 6-6.xls, sheet: 6-6 LP

SPECIFYING THE GOALS Now suppose that Wilson is not happy with this LP solution because it generates no sales from commercial doors. In contrast, exterior doors generate

TABLE 6.7
Data for Wilson Doors

	EXTERIOR	INTERIOR	COMMERCIAL	AVAILABILITY
Steel (lb./door)	4	3	7	9,000 pounds
Forming (hr./door)	2	4	3	6,000 hours
Assembly (hr./door)	2	3	4	5,200 hours
Selling price/door	\$70	\$110	\$110	

IN ACTION The Use of Goal Programming for TB Drug Allocation in Manila

Allocation of resources is critical when applied to the health industry. It is a matter of life and death when neither the right supply nor the correct quantity is available to meet patient demand. This was the case faced by the Manila (Philippines) Health Center, whose drug supply to patients afflicted with Category 1 tuberculosis (TB) was not being efficiently allocated to its 45 regional health centers. When the TB drug supply does not reach patients on time, the disease becomes worse and can result in death. Only 74% of TB patients were being cured in Manila, 11% short of the 85% target cure rate set by the government. Unlike other diseases, TB can be treated only with four medicines and cannot be cured by alternative drugs.

Researchers at the Mapka Institute of Technology set out to create a model, using GP, to optimize the allocation of resources for TB treatment while considering supply constraints. The objective function of the model was to meet the target cure rate of 85% (which is the equivalent of minimizing the underachievement in the allocation of anti-TB drugs to the 45 centers). Four goal constraints considered the interrelationships among variables in the distribution system. Goal 1 was to satisfy the medication requirement (a six-month regimen) for each patient. Goal 2 was to supply each health center with the proper allocation. Goal 3 was to satisfy the cure rate of 85%. Goal 4 was to satisfy the drug requirements of each health center.

The GP model successfully dealt with all these goals and raised the TB cure rate to 88%, a 13% improvement in drug allocation over the previous distribution approach. This means that 335 lives per year were saved through this thoughtful use of GP.

Source: Based on G. J. C. Esmeria. "An Application of Goal Programming in the Allocation of Anti-TB Drugs in Rural Health Centers in the Philippines," *Proceedings of the 12th Annual Conference of the Production and Operations Management Society* (March 2001), Orlando, FL.

98,000 (=70 × 1,400) and interior doors generate 88,000 (=110 × 800) in sales. This would imply that while the sales agents for exterior and interior doors get sales bonuses this month, the sales agent for commercial doors gets nothing. To alleviate this situation, Wilson would prefer that each type of door contribute a certain level of sales. Wilson is, however, not willing to compromise too much on the *total* sales. Further, it does not want to be unduly unfair to the sales agents for exterior and interior doors by taking away too much of their sales potential (and hence, their sales bonus). Considering all issues, suppose Wilson sets the following goals:

Goal 1: Achieve total sales of at least $180,000

Goal 2: Achieve exterior doors sales of at least $70,000

Goal 3: Achieve interior doors sales of at least $60,000

Goal 4: Achieve commercial doors sales of at least $35,000

Goals look similar to constraints except that goals may remain unsatisfied in the final solution.

Notice that these goals look somewhat similar to constraints. However, there is a key difference. Constraints are restrictions that *must* be satisfied by the solution. Goals, on the other hand, are specifications that we would *like* to satisfy. However, it is acceptable to leave one or more goals unsatisfied in the final solution if it is impossible to satisfy them (because of other, possibly conflicting, goals and constraints in the model). We now have a GP problem in which we want to find the product mix that achieves these four goals as much as possible, given the production resource constraints.

We must first define two deviation variables for each goal in a GP problem.

FORMULATING THE GP MODEL To formulate any problem as a GP problem, we must first define two deviation variables for each goal. These two deviation variables represent, respectively, the extent to which a goal is underachieved or overachieved. Because there are four goals in Wilson's problem, we define eight deviation variables, as follows:

d_T^- = amount by which the total sales goal is underachieved
d_T^+ = amount by which the total sales goal is overachieved
d_E^- = amount by which the exterior doors sales goal is underachieved
d_E^+ = amount by which the exterior doors sales goal is overachieved
d_I^- = amount by which the interior doors sales goal is underachieved
d_I^+ = amount by which the interior doors sales goal is overachieved

$d_C^- =$ amount by which the commercial doors sales goal is underachieved

$d_C^+ =$ amount by which the commercial doors sales goal is overachieved

We use the deviation variables to express goals as equations.

Using these deviation variables, we express the four goals mathematically as follows:

$70E + 110I + 110C + d_T^- - d_T^+$	$= 180{,}000$	(total sales goal)
$70E + d_E^- - d_E^+$	$= 70{,}000$	(exterior doors sales goal)
$110I + d_I^- - d_I^+$	$= 60{,}000$	(interior doors sales goal)
$110C + d_C^- - d_C^+$	$= 35{,}000$	(commercial doors sales goal)

The first equation states that the total sales (i.e., $\$70E + \$110I + \$110C$) plus any underachievement of total sales minus any overachievement of total sales has to equal the goal of \$180,000. For example, the LP solution ($E = 1{,}400$, $I = 800$, and $C = 0$) yields total sales of \$186,000. Because this exceeds the goal of \$180,000 by \$6,000, d_T^+ would equal \$6,000, and d_T^{--} would equal \$0. Note that it is not possible for both d_T^+ and d_T^- to be nonzero at the same time because it is not logical for a goal to be both underachieved and overachieved at the same time. The second, third, and fourth equations specify a similar issue with regard to sales from exterior, interior, and commercial doors, respectively.

We are concerned only about minimizing the underachievement of goals here.

Because all four of Wilson's goals specify that their targets should be *at least* met, we want to minimize only the level of underachievement in each goal. That is, we are not concerned if any or all goals are overachieved. With this background information, we can now formulate Wilson's problem as a single GP model, as follows:

$$\text{Minimize total underachievement of goals} = d_T^- + d_E^- + d_I^- + d_C^+$$

subject to the constraints

$70E + 110I + 110C + d_T^- + d_T^+$	$= 180{,}000$	(total sales goal)
$70E + d_E^- + d_E^+$	$= 70{,}000$	(exterior doors sales goal)
$110I + d_I^- + d_I^+$	$= 60{,}000$	(interior doors sales goal)
$110C + d_C^- + d_C^+$	$= 35{,}000$	(commercial doors sales goal)
$4E + 3I + 7C$	$\leq 9{,}000$	(steel usage)
$2E + 4I + 3C$	$\leq 6{,}000$	(forming time)
$2E + 3I + 4C$	$\leq 5{,}200$	(assembly time)

$$E, I, C, d_T^-, d_T^+, d_E^-, d_E^+, d_I^-, d_I^+, d_C^-, d_C^+ \geq 0$$

Deviation variables are 0 if a goal is fully satisfied.

If Wilson were just interested in *exactly* achieving all four goals, how would the objective function change? In that case, we would specify it to minimize the total underachievement and overachievement (i.e., the sum of all eight deviation variables). This, of course, is probably not a reasonable objective in practice because Wilson is not likely to be upset with an overachievement of any of its sales goals.

In general, once all the goals have been defined in a GP problem, management should analyze each goal to see if it wishes to include only one or both of the deviation variables for that goal in the minimization objective function. In some cases, the goals could even be one-sided in that it is not even feasible for one of the deviation variables to be nonzero. For example, if Wilson specifies that the \$180,000 target for total sales is an absolute minimum (i.e., it cannot be violated), the underachievement deviation variable d_T^- can be completely eliminated from the GP model.

There are approaches to solve GP models: using (1) **weighted goals** *and (2)* **ranked goals**.

Now that we have formulated Wilson's GP model with the four goals, how do we solve it? There are two approaches commonly used in practice: (1) using **weighted goals** and (2) using **ranked goals** (or prioritized goals). Let us now discuss each of these approaches.

Solving Goal Programming Models with Weighted Goals

Weights can be used to distinguish between different goals.

As currently formulated, Wilson's GP model assumes that all four goals are equally important to its managers. That is, because the objective function is just the sum of the four deviation variables (d_T^-, d_E^-, d_I^-, *and* d_C^-) a unit underachievement in the total sales goal (d_T^-) has the same impact on the objective function value as a unit underachievement in any of the other three sales goals (d_E^-, d_I^-, or d_C^-) If that is indeed the case in Wilson's problem, we can simply solve the model as currently formulated. However, as noted earlier, it is common in practice for managers to rank different goals in some hierarchical fashion.

FORMULATING THE WEIGHTED GP MODEL Suppose Wilson specifies that the total sales goal is five times as important as each of the other three sales goals. To include this specification in the weighted goal approach for solving GP models, we assign numeric weights to each deviation variable in the objective function. These weights serve as the objective coefficients for the deviation variables. The magnitude of the weight assigned to a specific deviation variable would depend on the relative importance of that goal. In Wilson's case, because minimizing d_T^- is five times as important as minimizing d_E^-, d_I^-, d_C^-, or d_C^-, we could assign the following weights to the four goals:

Goal 1: Achieve total sales of at least $180,000 — Weight $= 5$

Goal 2: Achieve exterior doors sales of at least $70,000 — Weight $= 1$

Goal 3: Achieve interior doors sales of at least $60,000 — Weight $= 1$

Goal 4: Achieve commercial doors sales of at least $35,000 — Weight $= 1$

With this information, we can now write the objective function with weighted goals for Wilson's model as

$$\text{Minimize total } \textit{weighted} \text{ underachievement of goals} = 5d_T^- + d_E^- + d_I^- + d_C^-$$

In the weighted goals approach, the problem reduces to an LP model with a single objective function.

The constraints are as listed earlier for the model. The problem now reduces to an LP model with a single objective function. Setting up this model on Excel and solving it by using Solver therefore become rather straightforward tasks.

File: 6-6.xls, sheet: 6-6A

SOLVING THE WEIGHTED GP MODEL The Excel layout and Solver entries for Wilson's problem with weighted goals are shown in Screenshot 6-6A. Note that the model includes 11 decision variables (3 product variables associated with the three types of doors and 8 deviation variables associated with the four goals). The results also show the extent to which each goal has been achieved (shown in cells P8:P11).

INTERPRETING THE RESULTS The optimal weighted GP solution is for Wilson to produce 1,000 exterior doors, 800 interior doors, and 200 commercial doors. This results in total revenue of $180,000, which exactly satisfies that goal (i.e., d_T^+ and d_T^- are both equal to 0). Regarding the goals for the different types of doors, the exterior doors sales goal is also exactly satisfied, while the interior doors sales goal is overachieved by $28,000. In contrast, sales from commercial doors is only $22,000 (=$110 × 200), which underachieves the goal of $35,000 by $13,000. Wilson should, however, be willing to accept this result because it is more concerned about the total sales goal (and hence, assigned it a larger weight) than with the commercial doors sales goal. That is, in trying to satisfy Wilson's *stronger* desire to generate at least $180,000 in total sales, the weighted GP solution continues to leave the commercial doors sales goal underachieved to a certain extent.

The weighted goals approach has two major drawbacks.

DRAWBACKS OF THE WEIGHTED GOALS APPROACH Although the weighted goals approach is rather easy to use, it suffers from two major drawbacks. First, it is appropriate to use only if all the goals (and hence, the deviation variables) are being measured in the same units (such as dollars). This is indeed the case in Wilson's problem, where all four goals are measured in dollars. However, what happens if different goals are measured in different units? For example, the first goal could be about sales (measured in dollars), and the second goal could be about steel usage (measured in pounds). In such cases, it is very difficult to assign appropriate weights because different deviation variables in the same objective function are measured in different units.

It is not always easy to assign suitable weights for the different deviation variables.

Second, even if all goals are measured in the same units, it is not always easy to assign suitable weights for the different deviation variables. For example, in Wilson's problem, how does management decide that the total sales goal is exactly 5 times as important as the other three goals? What if it is only 2.5 times as important? Clearly, this would affect the choice of weights, which, in turn, could affect the optimal solution.

SCREENSHOT 6-6A Excel Layout and Solver Entries for Wilson Doors—Weighted Goals Solution 1

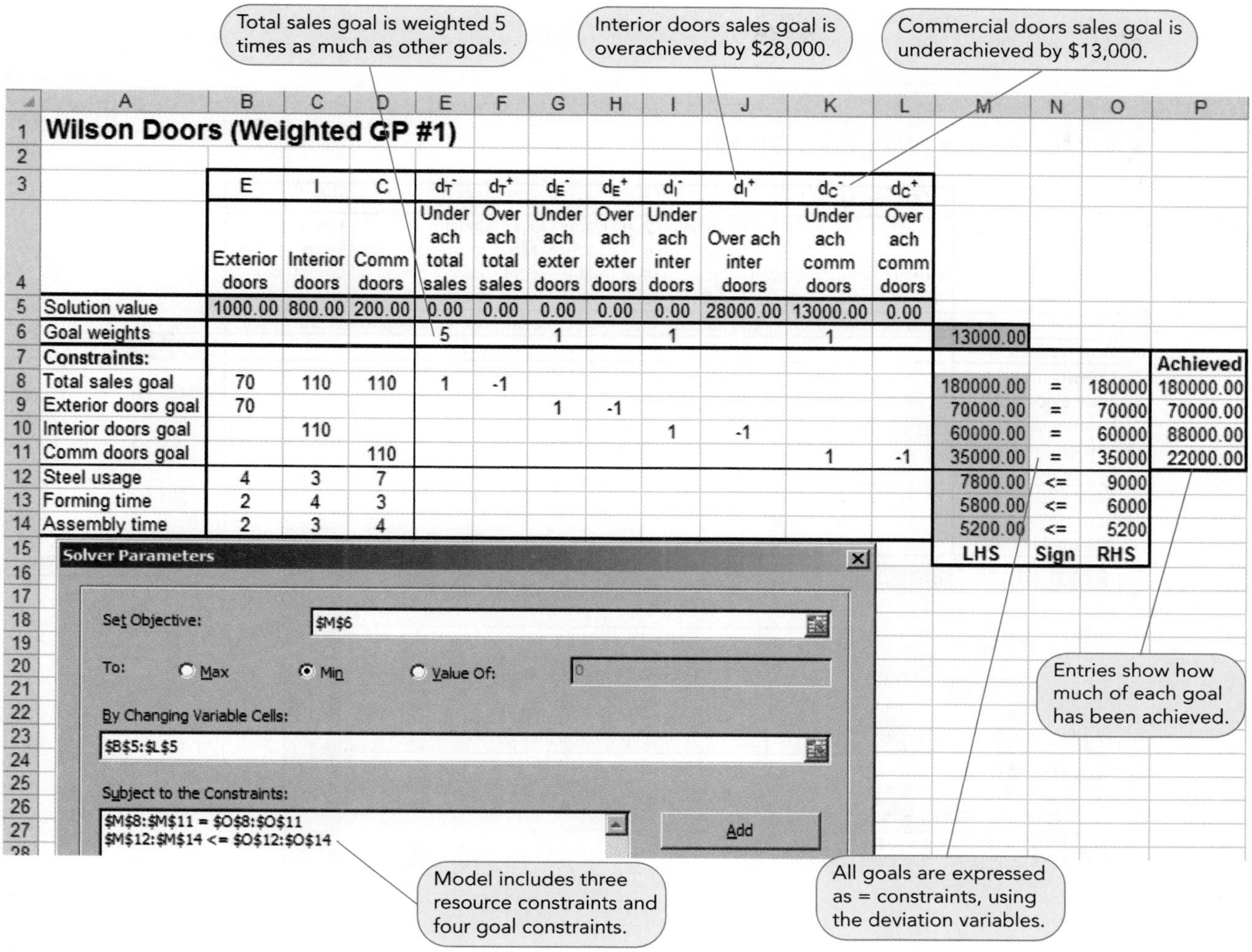

Total sales goal is weighted 5 times as much as other goals.

Interior doors sales goal is overachieved by $28,000.

Commercial doors sales goal is underachieved by $13,000.

	A	B	C	D	E	F	G	H	I	J	K	L	M	N	O	P
1	**Wilson Doors (Weighted GP #1)**															
2																
3		E	I	C	d_T^-	d_T^+	d_E^-	d_E^+	d_I^-	d_I^+	d_C^-	d_C^+				
4		Exterior doors	Interior doors	Comm doors	Under ach total sales	Over ach total sales	Under ach exter doors	Over ach exter doors	Under ach inter doors	Over ach inter doors	Under ach comm doors	Over ach comm doors				
5	Solution value	1000.00	800.00	200.00	0.00	0.00	0.00	0.00	0.00	28000.00	13000.00	0.00				
6	Goal weights				5		1		1		1		13000.00			
7	**Constraints:**															**Achieved**
8	Total sales goal	70	110	110	1	-1							180000.00	=	180000	180000.00
9	Exterior doors goal	70					1	-1					70000.00	=	70000	70000.00
10	Interior doors goal		110						1	-1			60000.00	=	60000	88000.00
11	Comm doors goal			110							1	-1	35000.00	=	35000	22000.00
12	Steel usage	4	3	7									7800.00	<=	9000	
13	Forming time	2	4	3									5800.00	<=	6000	
14	Assembly time	2	3	4									5200.00	<=	5200	
15													LHS	Sign	RHS	

Solver Parameters

Set Objective: $M$6

To: Max Min Value Of: 0

By Changing Variable Cells: $B$5:$L$5

Subject to the Constraints:
$M$8:$M$11 = $O$8:$O$11
$M$12:$M$14 <= $O$12:$O$14

Add

Entries show how much of each goal has been achieved.

Model includes three resource constraints and four goal constraints.

All goals are expressed as = constraints, using the deviation variables.

File: 6-6.xls, sheet: 6-6B

In fact, as shown in Screenshot 6-6B, if we assign a weight of only 2.5 (instead of 5) to the total sales goal in Wilson's weighted GP model and continue to assign a weight of 1 to each of the other three goals, the optimal solution changes completely. Interestingly, the total sales goal, which Wilson has specified as the most important goal, now turns out to be the only goal that is underachieved (by $4,333.33). The exterior and commercial doors sales goals are fully satisfied, while the interior doors sales goal is actually overachieved by $10,666.67. This clearly illustrates the importance of properly selecting weights.

By the way, the LP solution shown in Screenshot 6-6B has fractional solution values for interior and commercial doors. Wilson can fix this either by solving the problem as a general IP model or by rounding off the fractional values appropriately. For your convenience, the IP solution (obtained by constraining variables E, I, and C to be integer valued in Solver) for this problem is included in the Excel file *6-6.xls* on the Companion Website for this textbook; see the worksheet named *6-6B IP*. The total sales goal turns out to be underachieved by $4,290 in the IP solution.

We use ranks when it is difficult to assign weights for deviation variables.

To overcome these two drawbacks with the weighted GP approach, we examine an alternate approach—the ranked, or prioritized, goals approach—for solving GP problems.

SCREENSHOT 6-6B Excel Layout and Solver Entries for Wilson Doors—Weighted Goals Solution 2

	A	B	C	D	E	F	G	H	I	J	K	L	M	N	O	P
1	**Wilson Doors (Weighted GP #2)**															
2																
3		E	I	C	d_T^-	d_T^+	d_E^-	d_E^+	d_I^-	d_I^+	d_C^-	d_C^+				
4		Exterior doors	Interior doors	Comm doors	Under ach total sales	Over ach total sales	Under ach exter doors	Over ach exter doors	Under ach inter doors	Over ach inter doors	Under ach comm doors	Over ach comm doors				
5	Solution value	1000.00	642.42	318.18	4333.33	0.00	0.00	0.00	0.00	10666.67	0.00	0.0				
6	Goal weights				2.5		1		1		1		10833.33			
7	**Constraints:**															**Achieved**
8	Total sales goal	70	110	110	1	-1							180000.00	=	180000	175666.67
9	Exterior doors goal	70					1	-1					70000.00	=	70000	70000.00
10	Interior doors goal		110						1	-1			60000.00	=	60000	70666.67
11	Comm doors goal			110							1	-1	35000.00	=	35000	35000.00
12	Steel usage	4	3	7									8154.55	<=	9000	
13	Forming time	2	4	3									5524.24	<=	6000	
14	Assembly time	2	3	4									5200.00	<=	5200	
15													**LHS**	**Sign**	**RHS**	

IN ACTION Goal Programming Helps NBC Increase Revenues and Productivity

In 2000, the National Broadcasting Company's (NBC) television and cable networks, TV stations, and Internet divisions generated more than $5 billion in revenues for its parent company General Electric. Of these, the television network business was by far the largest, contributing more than $4 billion in revenues.

Recognizing the need for a system that would generate sales plans quickly to meet all client requirements and make optimal use of the available inventory, researchers modeled NBC's sales planning problem as a goal program. The system was designed to help management adjust pricing dynamically based on the current market and inventory situations. Client requests were modeled as goal constraints, with penalties associated with missing these goals. Penalties were linearly proportional to the magnitude of deviation from the goals, and varied also based on the importance of the client requirements.

These systems have now become an integral part of sales processes at NBC, and it is estimated that from May 1996 to June 2000, NBC used them to generate sales plans and manage inventory worth more than $9 billion, resulting in net gains of over $200 million.

Source: Based on S. Bollapragada et al. "NBC's Optimization Systems Increase Revenues and Productivity," *Interfaces* 32, 1 (January–February 2002): 47–60.

Solving Goal Programming Models with Ranked Goals

Lower-ranked goals are considered only after higher-ranked goals are met.

In the ranked goals approach to solving GP models, we assign ranks (or priorities), rather than weights, to goals. The idea is that goals can be ranked based on their importance to management. Lower-ranked goals are considered only after higher-ranked goals are met. Note that it is possible to assign the same rank to two or more goals.

Let us discuss this approach by revisiting Wilson Doors Company's problem. Recall that Wilson's management has currently specified the following four goals:

Goal 1: Achieve total sales of at least \$180,000

Goal 2: Achieve exterior doors sales of at least \$70,000

Goal 3: Achieve interior doors sales of at least \$60,000

Goal 4: Achieve commercial doors sales of at least \$35,000

The ranked goals approach can handle goals that are measured in different units.

Because in the ranked goals approach we are no longer restricted to measuring all goals in the same units, let us expand Wilson's problem by adding another goal. Suppose Wilson plans to switch to a different type of steel for the next production period. Management would therefore like to ensure that the production plan this period uses up as much of the current availability of steel (9,000 pounds) as possible. This is formally stated in the following goal:

Goal 5: Achieve steel usage of as close to 9,000 pounds as possible

Wilson's management has examined these five goals and has decided to rank, them in decreasing order of rank, as follows:

Rank R_1: Goal 1

Rank R_2: Goal 5

Rank R_3: Goals 2, 3, and 4

This means, in effect, that meeting the total sales goal is much more important than meeting the steel usage goal which, in turn, is much more important than meeting the sales goals for each of the three types of doors. If we wish, we can further distinguish between goals within the same rank by assigning appropriate weights. For example, we can assign appropriate weights to any of the three goals with rank R_3 (i.e., goals 2, 3, and 4) to make that goal more important than the other two.

FORMULATING THE RANKED GP MODEL In addition to the eight deviation variables that we have already defined earlier (i.e., d_T^-, d_T^+, d_E^-, d_E^+, d_I^-, d_C^+, d_C^-, and d_C^+), we define a ninth deviation variable, as follows:

$$d_S^- = \text{amount by which the steel usage goal is underachieved}$$

Note that we do not have to define a deviation variable for overachievement of steel usage (i.e., d_s^+) because steel is a resource constraint. That is, steel usage can never exceed 9,000 pounds. Also, unlike the eight deviation variables associated with the four sales goals, which are measured in dollars, the deviation variable d_S^- is measured in pounds.

Using the deviation variable d_S^- we can express the steel usage goal mathematically, as follows, just as we expressed the other four goals:

$$4E + 3I + 7C + d_S^- = 9{,}000 \qquad \text{(steel usage goal)}$$

Based on the specified ranking of goals (recall that goals with rank R_1 are the most important, goals with rank R_2 are the next most important, then R_3, and so on), Wilson's ranked GP problem can be stated as

$$\text{Minimize ranked deviations} = R_1(d_T^-) + R_2(d_S^-) + R_3(d_E^- + d_I^- + d_C^-)$$

subject to the constraints

$$\begin{aligned}
70E + 110I + 110C + d_T^- - d_T^+ &= 180{,}000 && \text{(total sales goal)}\\
4E + 3I + 7C + d_S^- &= 9{,}000 && \text{(steel usage goal)}\\
70E + d_E^- - d_E^+ &= 70{,}000 && \text{(exterior doors sales goal)}
\end{aligned}$$

$$
\begin{array}{lcrl}
110I + d_I^- - d_I^+ & = & 60{,}000 & \text{(interior doors sales goal)} \\
110C + d_C^- - d_C^+ & = & 35{,}000 & \text{(commercial doors sales goal)} \\
2E + 4I + 3C & \leq & 6{,}000 & \text{(forming time)} \\
2E + 3I + 4C & \leq & 5{,}200 & \text{(assembly time)} \\
E, I, C, d_T^-, d_T^+, d_S^-, d_E^-, d_E^+, d_I^-, d_I^+, d_C^-, d_C^+ & \geq & 0 & \text{(nonnegativity)}
\end{array}
$$

Note that within each rank, the objective function in this model includes only the underachievement deviation variable because all four sales goals specify that the goals should be "at least" met, and the steel usage goal can never be overachieved.

Solving a model with ranked goals requires us to solve a series of LP models.

Rank R_1 *goals are considered first.*

SOLVING THE RANK R_1 GP MODEL AND INTERPRETING THE RESULTS To find the optimal solution for a GP model with ranked goals, we need to set up and solve a series of LP models. In the first of these LP models, we consider only the highest ranked (rank R) goals and ignore all other goals (ranks R_2 and R_3). The objective function then includes only the deviation variable with rank R_1. In Wilson's problem, the objective of the first LP model is

$$\text{Minimize rank } R_1 \text{ deviation} = d_T^-$$

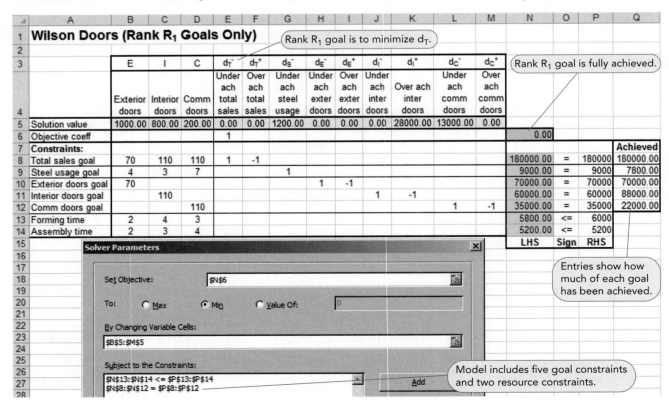

File: 6-7.xls, sheet: 6-7A

Solving this LP model using Solver is a rather simple task, and Screenshot 6-7A shows the relevant information. The results show that it is possible to fully achieve the rank R_1 goal (i.e., the total sales goal can be fully satisfied and the optimal value of d_T^- is 0). However, at the present time, the steel usage goal is underachieved by 1,200 pounds, the interior doors sales goal is overachieved by $28,000, and the commercial doors sales goal is underachieved by $13,000.

Rank R_2 *goals are considered next. Optimal values of rank* R_1 *goals are explicitly specified in the model.*

SOLVING THE RANK R_2 GP MODEL AND INTERPRETING THE RESULTS Now that we have optimally solved the model with the rank R_1 goal, we consider all goals with the next-highest rank (R_2) in the second LP model. In Wilson's problem, this is the steel usage goal. However, in setting up this LP model, we explicitly specify the optimal value of the total sales goal from

SCREENSHOT 6-7A Excel Layout and Solver Entries for Wilson Doors—Rank R_1 Goals Only

	A	B	C	D	E	F	G	H	I	J	K	L	M	N	O	P	Q
1	**Wilson Doors (Rank R_1 Goals Only)**																
2																	
3		E	I	C	d_T^-	d_T^+	d_S^-	d_E^-	d_E^+	d_I^-	d_I^+	d_C^-	d_C^+				
4		Exterior doors	Interior doors	Comm doors	Under ach total sales	Over ach total sales	Under ach steel usage	Under ach exter doors	Over ach exter doors	Under ach inter doors	Over ach inter doors	Under ach comm doors	Over ach comm doors				
5	Solution value	1000.00	800.00	200.00	0.00	0.00	1200.00	0.00	0.00	0.00	28000.00	13000.00	0.00				
6	Objective coeff				1									0.00			
7	**Constraints:**																**Achieved**
8	Total sales goal	70	110	110	1	-1								180000.00	=	180000	180000.00
9	Steel usage goal	4	3	7			1							9000.00	=	9000	7800.00
10	Exterior doors goal	70						1	-1					70000.00	=	70000	70000.00
11	Interior doors goal		110							1	-1			60000.00	=	60000	88000.00
12	Comm doors goal			110								1	-1	35000.00	=	35000	22000.00
13	Forming time	2	4	3										5800.00	<=	6000	
14	Assembly time	2	3	4										5200.00	<=	5200	
15														**LHS**	**Sign**	**RHS**	

Rank R_1 goal is to minimize d_T.

Rank R_1 goal is fully achieved.

Entries show how much of each goal has been achieved.

Solver Parameters

Set Objective: $N$6

To: Max / Min (selected) / Value Of: 0

By Changing Variable Cells: $B$5:$M$5

Subject to the Constraints:

$N$13:$N$14 <= $P$13:$P$14

$N$8:$N$12 = $P$8:$P$12

Add

Model includes five goal constraints and two resource constraints.

the rank R_1 model. To do so, we set the value of the relevant deviation variable (i.e., d_T^-) to its optimal value of 0 in the LP model.

For Wilson's second LP model, the objective function and *additional* constraint are as follows:

$$\text{Minimize rank } R_2 \text{ deviation} = d_S^-$$

and

$$d_T^- = 0 \qquad \text{(optimal value of rank } R_1 \text{ goal)}$$

File: 6-7.xls, sheet: 6-7B

Screenshot 6-7B shows the Excel layout and Solver entries for this LP model. The results show that it is possible to fully achieve the rank R_2 goal also. That is, it is possible to reduce the value of the deviation variable d_S^- also to 0, while maintaining the value of the rank R_1 deviation variable d_T^- at its optimal value of 0. In fact, the total sales goal is now overachieved by \$4,333.33, and the exterior doors sales goal is overachieved by \$63,000.

However, this emphasis on reducing the value of d_S^- results in the value of d_C^- ballooning up from \$13,000 in the rank R_1 solution (Screenshot 6-7A) to \$35,000 in the rank R_2 solution (Screenshot 6-7B). This implies that the commercial doors sales goal is fully unsatisfied and that no commercial doors should be made. Likewise, the interior doors sales goal is also underachieved by \$8,666.67. While this solution may seem unfair to the sales agents for interior and commercial doors, it is still perfectly logical because Wilson has ranked the steel usage goal higher than the sales goals for all three door types.

The LP solution shown in Screenshot 6-7B has a fractional solution value for interior doors. Interestingly, the IP solution for this problem (which is included in the Excel file *6-7.xls* on the Companion Website for this textbook; see the worksheet named *6-7B IP*) is considerably different from the LP solution in Screenshot 6-7B. The steel usage goal is still fully satisfied. However, while overachievements d_T^+ and d_E^+d and underachievement d_C^- all decrease from their corresponding LP solution values, underachievement d_T^- increases from \$8,666.67 to \$13,580.

SCREENSHOT 6-7B Excel Layout and Solver Entries for Wilson Door—Rank R_2 Goals Only

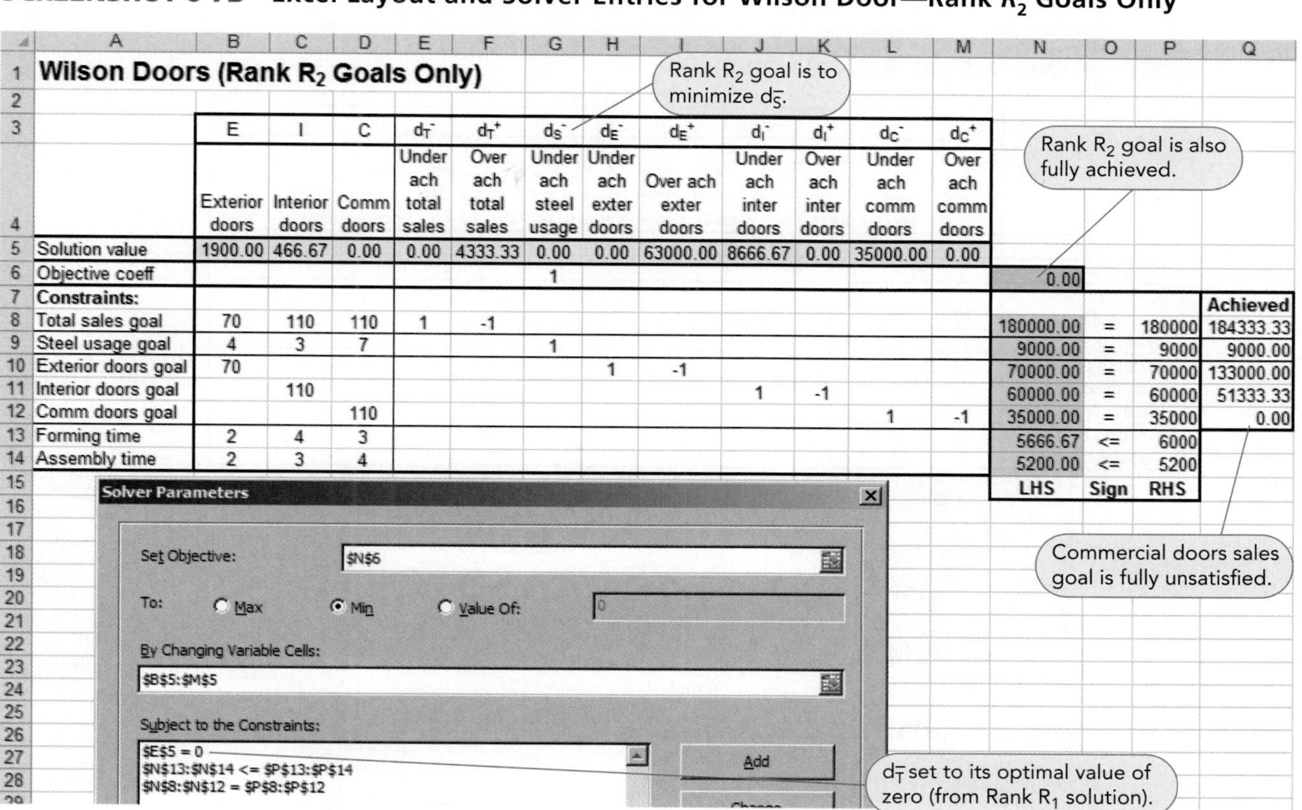

Wilson Doors (Rank R_2 Goals Only)

	E	I	C	d_T^-	d_T^+	d_S^-	d_E^-	d_E^+	d_I^-	d_I^+	d_C^-	d_C^+				
	Exterior doors	Interior doors	Comm doors	Under ach total sales	Over ach total sales	Under ach steel usage	Under ach exter doors	Over ach exter doors	Under ach inter doors	Over ach inter doors	Under ach comm doors	Over ach comm doors				
Solution value	1900.00	466.67	0.00	0.00	4333.33	0.00	0.00	63000.00	8666.67	0.00	35000.00	0.00				
Objective coeff						1							0.00			
Constraints:																**Achieved**
Total sales goal	70	110	110	1	-1								180000.00	=	180000	184333.33
Steel usage goal	4	3	7			1							9000.00	=	9000	9000.00
Exterior doors goal	70						1	-1					70000.00	=	70000	133000.00
Interior doors goal		110							1	-1			60000.00	=	60000	51333.33
Comm doors goal			110								1	-1	35000.00	=	35000	0.00
Forming time	2	4	3										5666.67	<=	6000	
Assembly time	2	3	4										5200.00	<=	5200	
													LHS	**Sign**	**RHS**	

That is, the IP solution pulls three of the four goals closer to their target while moving one further away from its target, when compared to the LP solution.

R_3 goals are now considered. Optimal values of rank R_1 and R_2 goals are explicitly specified in the model.

SOLVING THE RANK R_3 GP MODEL AND INTERPRETING THE RESULTS Now that the goals with ranks R_1 and R_2 have been optimized, we now consider all goals with the next-highest rank (R_3) in the third LP model. As before, in setting up this model, we explicitly specify the optimal values of the rank R_1 and R_2 goals obtained from the first two LP models.

For Wilson's third LP model, the objective function and *additional* constraints are as follows:

$$\text{Minimize rank } R_3 \text{ deviation} = d_E^- + d_I^- + d_C^-$$

and

$$d_T^- = 0 \qquad \text{(optimal value of rank } R_1 \text{ goal)}$$

$$d_S^- = 0 \qquad \text{(optimal value of rank } R_2 \text{ goal)}$$

File: 6-7.xls, sheet: 6-7C

Screenshot 6-7C shows the Excel layout and Solver entries for this LP model. The results show that after fully optimizing the rank R_1 and R_2 goals, the best we can do is to achieve a total underachievement of $33,631.58 in the rank R_3 goals. In the final solution, the total sales goal is exactly satisfied while the exterior doors sales goal is overachieved by $48,631.58. In contrast, the interior doors and commercial doors sales goals are underachieved by $13,684.21 and $19,947.37, respectively.

As with the second LP model, this solution too has fractional values for the production variables. The IP solution for this problem (which is included in the Excel file *6-7.xls* on the Companion Website for this textbook; see the worksheet named *6-7C IP*) turns out to be the

SCREENSHOT 6-7C Excel Layout and Solver Entries for Wilson Doors—Rank R_3 Goals Only

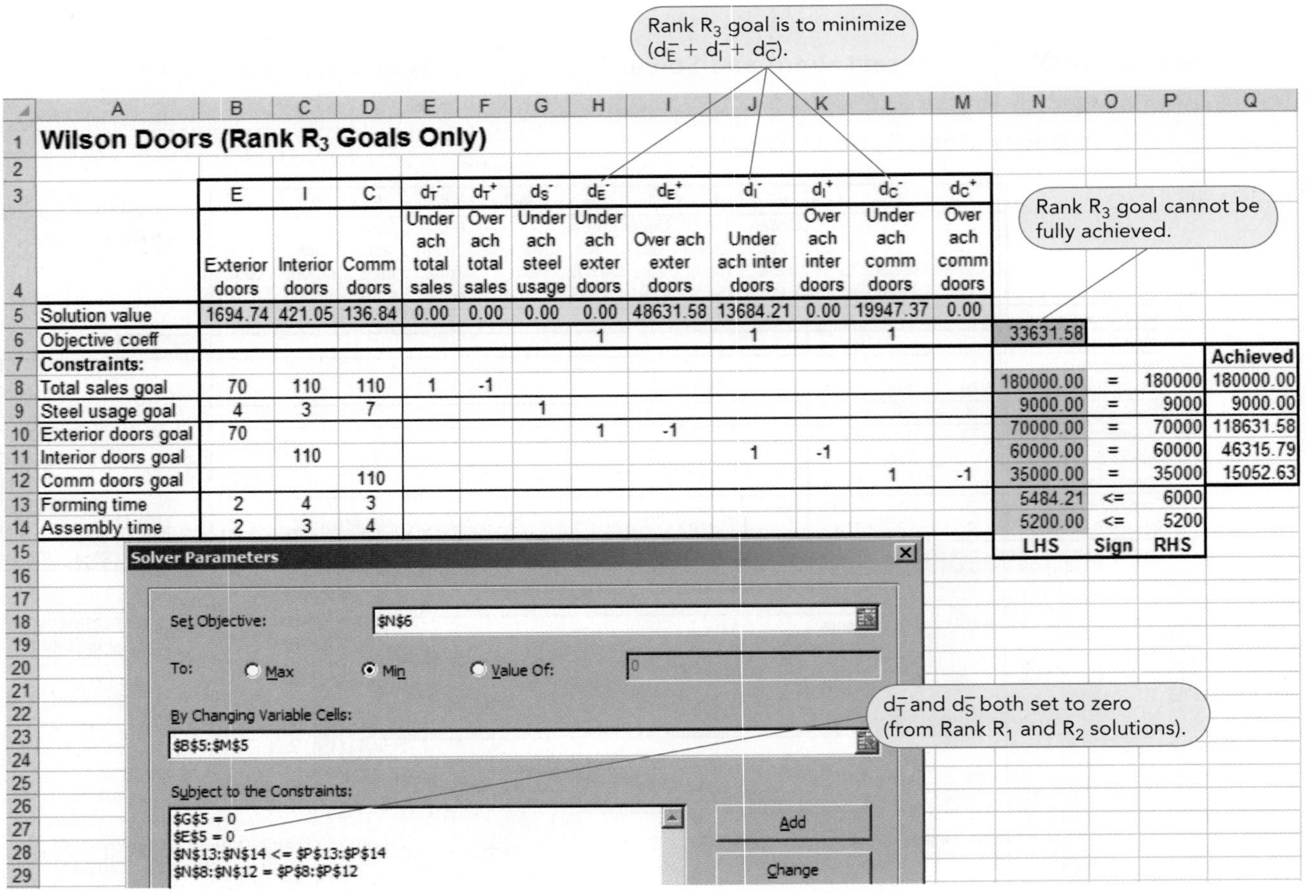

Rank R_3 goal is to minimize ($d_E^- + d_I^- + d_C^-$).

Rank R_3 goal cannot be fully achieved.

Wilson Doors (Rank R_3 Goals Only)

	A	B	C	D	E	F	G	H	I	J	K	L	M	N	O	P	Q
3		E	I	C	d_T^-	d_T^+	d_S^-	d_E^-	d_E^+	d_I^-	d_I^+	d_C^-	d_C^+				
4		Exterior doors	Interior doors	Comm doors	Under ach total sales	Over ach total sales	Under ach steel usage	Under ach exter doors	Over ach exter doors	Under ach inter doors	Over ach inter doors	Under ach comm doors	Over ach comm doors				
5	Solution value	1694.74	421.05	136.84	0.00	0.00	0.00	0.00	48631.58	13684.21	0.00	19947.37	0.00				
6	Objective coeff							1		1		1		33631.58			
7	Constraints:																Achieved
8	Total sales goal	70	110	110	1	-1								180000.00	=	180000	180000.00
9	Steel usage goal	4	3	7			1							9000.00	=	9000	9000.00
10	Exterior doors goal	70						1	-1					70000.00	=	70000	118631.58
11	Interior doors goal		110							1	-1			60000.00	=	60000	46315.79
12	Comm doors goal			110								1	-1	35000.00	=	35000	15052.63
13	Forming time	2	4	3										5484.21	<=	6000	
14	Assembly time	2	3	4										5200.00	<=	5200	
15														LHS	Sign	RHS	

Solver Parameters

Set Objective: $N$6

To: Max / Min (selected) / Value Of: 0

By Changing Variable Cells: $B$5:$M$5

Subject to the Constraints:

$G$5 = 0
$E$5 = 0
$N$13:$N$14 <= $P$13:$P$14
$N$8:$N$12 = $P$8:$P$12

Add

Change

d_T^- and d_S^- both set to zero (from Rank R_1 and R_2 solutions).

same as the IP solution we obtained for the rank R_2 model. That is, if we solve Wilson's problem as IP models, the rank R_3 model is not able to improve on the solution obtained in the rank R_2 model.

Comparing the Two Approaches for Solving GP Models

The weighted goals approach considers all goals simultaneously, and the optimal solution depends to a great extent on the weights assigned for different goals. In contrast, the ranked goals approach considers goals in a hierarchical manner. Optimal values for all higher-ranked goal deviation variables are *explicitly* specified while considering LP models with lower-ranked goals as objective functions. Which approach should we then use for a specific problem? If all goals are measured in the same units, and if it is possible to assign appropriate weights for each goal, using the weighted goals approach is clearly the easier option. In all other situations, we would need to use the ranked goals approach.

6.6 Nonlinear Programming Models

In many real-world problems, the objective function and/or one or more constraints may be nonlinear.

LP, IP, and GP all assume that a problem's objective function and constraints are linear. That means that they cannot contain nonlinear terms, such as X^3, $1/X$, $\log X$, or $5XY$. Yet in many real-world situations, the objective function and/or one or more constraints may be nonlinear. Here are two simple examples:

- We have assumed in all models so far that the profit contribution per unit of a product is fixed, regardless of how many units we make of the product. That is, if Y denotes the number of units made of a specific product and the product has a profit contribution of \$6 per unit, the total profit is \$6Y, for *all* values of Y. However, it is likely that the unit profit contribution of a product decreases as its supply (i.e., number of units made) increases. Suppose this relationship turns out to be

$$\text{Profit contribution per unit} = \$6 - \$0.02Y$$

Then, the total profit from this product is given by the following nonlinear expression:

$$\text{Total profit} = (\$6 - \$0.02Y) \times Y = \$6Y - \$0.02Y^2$$

- Likewise, we have assumed in all models so far that the relationship between resource usage and production level is linear. For example, if each patient requires 5 minutes of nursing time and there are P patients, the total time needed is $5P$ minutes, for all values of P. This term would be included in the LHS of the nursing time constraint. However, it is quite possible that the efficiency of nurses decreases as the patient load increases. Suppose the time required per patient is actually $(5 + 0.25P)$. That is, the time per patient increases as the number of patients increases. The term to be included in the nursing time constraint's LHS would now be $(5 + 0.25P) \times P = (5P + 0.25P^2)$, which would make the constraint nonlinear.

In such situations, the resulting model is called a **nonlinear programming (NLP)** model. By definition, an NLP model has a nonlinear objective function, or at least one nonlinear constraint, or both. In this section, we examine NLP models and also illustrate how Excel's Solver can often be used to solve these models. In practice, NLP models are difficult to solve and should be used with a lot of caution. Let us first examine the reason for this difficulty.

Why Are NLP Models Difficult to Solve?

In every LP, IP, and GP model, the objective function and all constraints are linear. This implies, for example, that with two variables, each equation in the model corresponds to a straight line. In contrast, as shown in Figure 6.2, a nonlinear expression in two variables is a curve. Depending on the extent of nonlinearity in the expression, the curve could be quite pronounced in that it could have many twists and turns.

The optimal solution to an NLP model need not be at a corner point of the feasible region.

You may recall from Chapter 2 that a feature of all LP models is that an optimal solution always occurs at a corner point (i.e., point where two or more linear constraints intersect).

FIGURE 6.2
Model with Nonlinear Constraints and a Nonlinear Objective Function

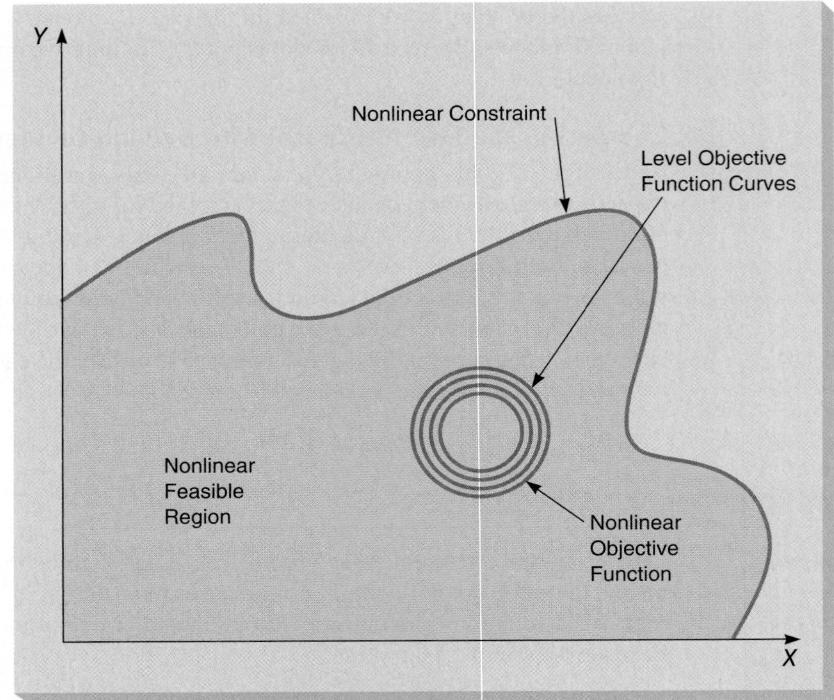

Software packages (including Solver) exploit this feature to find optimal solutions quickly even for large linear models. Unfortunately, if one or more constraints are nonlinear, an optimal solution need not be at a corner point of the feasible region. Further, as you can see from Figure 6.2, if the objective function itself is nonlinear (as in the equation of an ellipse or a sphere), it is not even easy to visualize at which feasible point the solution is optimized. This is one major reason why many NLP models are so difficult to solve in practice. As you can well imagine, this issue becomes even more difficult for NLP models that involve more decision variables.

LOCAL VERSUS GLOBAL OPTIMAL SOLUTIONS A second reason for the difficulty in solving NLP models is the concept of local versus global optimal solutions. Perhaps a simple analogy will help you understand this concept. A local optimal solution is like the peak of a specific mountain in a mountain range. The global optimal solution, in contrast, is the peak of the highest mountain in that range. If you are on a specific mountain, it is likely that you can easily see the peak of that mountain—and possibly even find your way to it. However, unless you are able to see all the mountains in the entire range from your current location, you have no way of knowing if the peak of your specific mountain is just a local peak or whether it is the global peak.

An NLP model can have both local and global optimal solutions.

Figure 6.3 illustrates this phenomenon with respect to NLP models. For the linear objective function shown in the figure, point Ⓐ is a local optimal solution, whereas point Ⓑ is a global optimal solution. The difficulty with all NLP solution procedures (including the procedure available in Solver) is that depending on where the procedure starts the search process, it could terminate the search at either a global or a local optimal solution. For example, if the procedure starts at point Ⓓ, the search process could in fact lead it to the global optimal solution, point Ⓑ, first. In contrast, if it starts at point Ⓒ, the search process could find the local optimal solution, point Ⓐ, first. Because there are no better solutions in the immediate vicinity of point Ⓐ, the procedure will erroneously terminate and yield point Ⓐ as the optimal solution.

There is no precise way to know where to start the solution search process for an NLP model.

Unfortunately, there is no precise way of knowing where to start the search process for a given NLP problem. Hence, it is usually a good idea to try different starting solutions for NLP models. Hopefully, at least one of them will result in the global optimal solution.

FIGURE 6.3
Local versus Global Optimal Solutions in an NLP Model

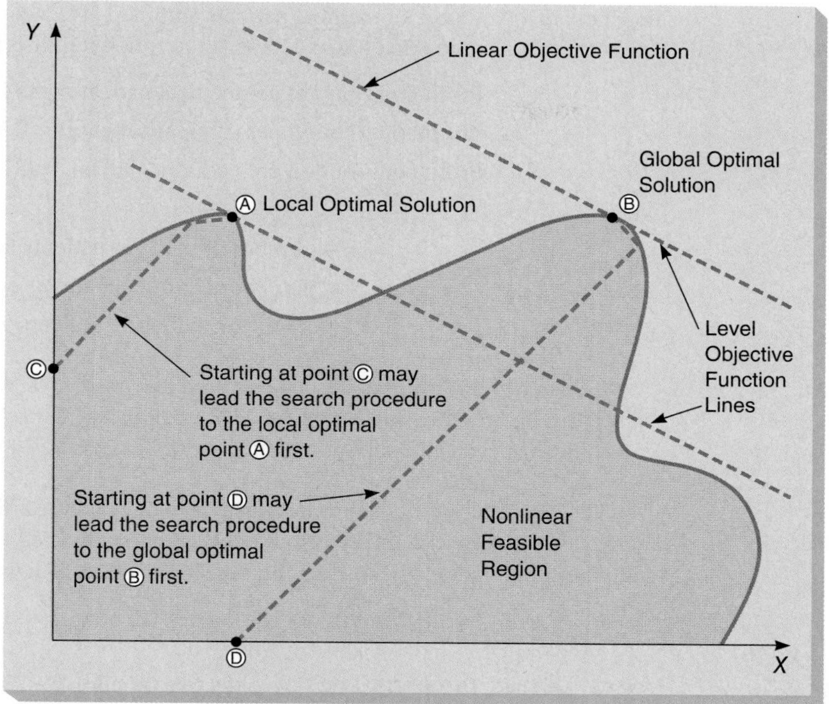

Solving Nonlinear Programming Models Using Solver

To illustrate how NLP models can be set up and solved using Solver, let us consider an example in which the objective function and some of the constraints are nonlinear. The weekly profit at Pickens Memorial Hospital depends on the number of patients admitted in three separate categories: medical, surgical, and pediatric. The hospital can admit a total of 200 patients (regardless of category) each week. However, because Pickens Memorial serves a large community, patient demand in each category by itself far exceeds the total patient capacity.

Due to a fixed overhead, the profit per patient in each category actually increases as the number of patients increases. Further, some patients who are initially classified as medical patients then get reclassified as surgical patients. As a result, the profit per surgical patient also

IN ACTION **Using Quadratic Programming to Improve Water-Release Policies on the Delaware River**

The Delaware River provides half of the drinking water for New York City (NYC). The water releases from three NYC dams on the river's headwaters impact the reliability of the water supply, the flood potential, and the quality of the aquatic habitat. Changes in release policies are, however, restricted due to two US Supreme Court decrees and the need for unanimity among NYC as well as the four states (New York, New Jersey, Pennsylvania, and Delaware) affected by these changes.

In January 2006, a coalition of four conservation organizations undertook a decision modeling–based project to study and suggest revisions to the release policies. A key component of this analysis was a quadratic nonlinear programming allocation model. The primary objective was to benefit river habitat and fisheries without increasing NYC's drought risk. The strategy was to quantify the risk-benefit trade-offs from increased conservation releases and create a simple algorithm that would explicitly link release quantities to reservoir levels.

It is estimated that the use of this model has increased critical summertime fish habitats by about 200 percent, while increasing NYC's drought risk by only 3 percent. The new release rules also mitigate flood risk and are significantly simpler to administer than prior approaches.

Source: Based on P. Kolesar and J. Serio. "Breaking the Deadlock: Improving Water-Release Policies on the Delaware River Through Operations Research," *Interfaces* 41, 1 (January–February 2011): 18–34.

depends on the number of medical patients admitted. The accountants at Pickens Memorial have analyzed this situation and have identified the following information:

$$\text{Profit contribution per medical patient} = \$45 + \$2M$$
$$\text{Profit contribution per surgical patient} = \$70 + \$3S + \$2M$$
$$\text{Profit contribution per pediatric patient} = \$60 + \$3P$$

where

$$M = \text{number of medical patients admitted}$$
$$S = \text{number of surgical patients admitted}$$
$$P = \text{number of pediatric patients admitted}$$

Pickens Memorial has identified three main constraints for this model: x-ray capacity, marketing budget, and lab capacity. Table 6.8 shows the relevant weekly data for these three constraints for each category of patient. The table also shows the weekly availabilities of each of these three resources.

The hospital's chief laboratory supervisor has noted that the time required per lab test increases as the total number of medical patients admitted (M) increases. Based on historical data, the supervisor estimates this relationship to be as follows

$$\text{Time required per lab test (in hours)} = 0.2 + 0.001M$$

In this NLP example, the objective function as well as some of the constraints are nonlinear.

FORMULATING THE PROBLEM The objective function for Pickens Memorial seeks to maximize the total profit and can be written as

$$\begin{aligned}\text{Maximize profit} &= (\$45 + \$2M) \times M + (\$70 + \$3S + \$2M) \times S + (\$60 + \$3P) \times P \\ &= \$45M + \$2M^2 + \$70S + \$3S^2 + \$2MS + \$60P + \$3P^2\end{aligned}$$

Clearly, this is a nonlinear expression. The constraints correspond to the total patient capacity of 200 and to the three limiting resources (i.e., x-ray capacity, marketing budget, and lab capacity). They may be expressed as follows:

$$\begin{aligned}
M + S + P &\leq 200 && \text{(total patient capacity)} \\
M + 3S + P &\leq 560 && \text{(x-ray capacity)} \\
3M + 5S + 3.5P &\leq 1{,}000 && \text{(marketing budger, \$)} \\
(0.2 + 0.001M) \times (3M + 3S + 3P) &\leq 140 && \text{(lab capacity, hours)} \\
M, S, P &\geq 0
\end{aligned}$$

The total patient capacity, x-ray capacity, and marketing budget constraints are linear. However, the lab capacity constraint is nonlinear because it includes terms involving multiplication of variables. We can simplify and rewrite this constraint as

$$0.6M + 0.6S + 0.6P + 0.003M^2 + 0.003MS + 0.003MP \leq 140 \text{ (lab capacity, hours)}$$

WWW

File: 6-8.xls, sheet: 6-8A

SOLVING THE PROBLEM USING EXCEL'S SOLVER We now illustrate how Excel's Solver can be used to solve this NLP model. Solver uses the **generalized reduced gradient (GRG) procedure**, sometimes called the *steepest ascent* (or *steepest descent*) *procedure*. This is an iterative procedure that moves from one feasible solution to the next in improving the value of the objective function. The GRG procedure can handle problems with both nonlinear constraints and nonlinear objective functions.

Solver uses the GRG procedure *to solve NLP models.*

TABLE 6.8
Data for Pickens Memorial Hospital

	MEDICAL	SURGICAL	PEDIATRIC	AVAILABILITY
Number of x-rays per patient	1	3	1	560 x-rays
Marketing budget per patient	\$3	\$5	\$3.5	\$1,000
Number of lab tests per patient	3	3	3	140 hours

The Excel layout includes several nonlinear terms involving the decision variables.

There are only three decision variables (i.e., M, S, and P) in Pickens Memorial's NLP model. These are denoted by cells B5, C5, and D5, respectively, in Screenshot 6-8A. However, the model includes several nonlinear terms involving these three variables: M^2, S^2, P^2, MS, and MP. There are several ways in which we can include these terms in our Excel layout. Here are two simple approaches (*Note:* Screenshot 6-8A illustrates the second approach):

- We can directly type the nonlinear formula in the appropriate cell. For example, for the nonlinear objective function in this model, the formula in the objective cell can be directly entered as follows:

  = 45*B5 + 2*B5^2 + 70*C5 + 3*C5^2 + 2*B5*C5 + 60*D5 + 3*D5^2

  In a similar manner, we can enter the nonlinear formula for the lab capacity constraint directly in the cell corresponding to the LHS of that constraint, as follows:

  = 0.6*B5 + 0.6*C5 + 0.6*D5 + 0.003*B5^2
  + 0.003*B5*C5 + 0.003*B5*D5

The SUMPRODUCT function is again used to calculate all constraint LHS values and the objective function value.

- Alternatively, as illustrated in Screenshot 6-8A, we can use the same Excel layout that we have used in all LP and IP models so far. This means that (1) each decision variable is modeled in a separate column of the worksheet and (2) the objective function and LHS formulas for all constraints are computed using Excel's SUMPRODUCT function. To use this layout for NLP models, we create a cell entry for each linear or nonlinear term involving the decision variables. In Pickens Memorial's case, we need cells for M, S, P, M^2, S^2, P^2, MS, and MP. These terms are represented by cells B8 to I8, respectively, in Screenshot 6-8A. (For clarity, we have shaded these cells blue in this NLP model.) The formulas for these cells are

= B5	(entry for M in cell B8)
= C5	(entry for S in cell C8)
= D5	(entry for P in cell D8)
= B5^2	(entry for M^2 in cell E8)
= C5^2	(entry for S^2 in cell F8)
= D5^2	(entry for P^2 in cell G8)
= B5*C5	(entry for MS in cell H8)
= B5*D5	(entry for MP in cell I8)

SCREENSHOT 6-8A Formula View of Excel Layout for Pickens Memorial—NLP

These are the only three decision variables in the model.

Entries in columns E to I are nonlinear terms.

Entries in this row are functions of the decision variables.

	A	B	C	D	E	F	G	H	I	J	K	L
1	**Pickens Memorial Hospital (NLP)**											
2												
3		M	S	P								
4		Medical	Surgical	Pediatric								
5	Number of patients											
6												
7		M	S	P	M²	S²	P²	MS	MP			
8	Variable terms	=B5	=C5	=D5	=B5^2	=C5^2	=D5^2	=B5*C5	=B5*D5			
9	Profit	45	70	60	2	3	3	2		=SUMPRODUCT(B9:I9,$B$8:$I$8)		
10	**Constraints:**											
11	Total patients	1	1	1						=SUMPRODUCT(B11:I11,$B$8:$I$8)	<=	200
12	X-ray capacity	1	3	1						=SUMPRODUCT(B12:I12,$B$8:$I$8)	<=	560
13	Marketing budget	3	5	3.5						=SUMPRODUCT(B13:I13,$B$8:$I$8)	<=	1000
14	Lab hours	0.6	0.6	0.6	0.003			0.003	0.003	=SUMPRODUCT(B14:I14,$B$8:$I$8)	<=	140
15										**LHS**	**Sign**	**RHS**

All entries in column J are computed using the SUMPRODUCT function.

GRG Nonlinear must be selected as the solving method in Solver.

The layout for this model now looks similar to all other Excel layouts we have used so far. Hence, we can use the SUMPRODUCT function to model the objective function as well as the constraint LHS values. Note, however, that even though cells B8:I8 are used in computing the objective function and constraint LHS values in column J, only cells B5:D5 are specified in the By Changing Variable Cells box in Solver (as shown in Screenshot 6-8B). The entries in row 8 are simply calculated from the final values for M, S, and P in cells B5:D5, respectively.

Screenshot 6-8B also shows the other Solver entries and solution for Pickens Memorial's NLP model. We note that in addition to ensuring that the Make Unconstrained Variables Non-Negative box is checked, we must now specify GRG Nonlinear in the Select a Solving Method, instead of Simplex LP, as we have done so far for all LP, IP, and GP models.

File: 6-8.xls, sheet: 6-8B

INTERPRETING THE RESULTS In obtaining the solution shown in Screenshot 6-8B, we set the initial values of all three decision variables (i.e., cells B5:D5) to zero. The final result indicates that Pickens Memorial should admit 20 medical patients, 180 surgical patients, and no pediatric patients each week, for a total weekly profit of $118,700.

It is usually a good idea to try different starting solutions for NLP models.

Is this a local optimal solution or a global optimal solution? As noted earlier, it is usually a good idea to try different starting solutions for NLP models. Hence, let us solve Pickens Memorial's NLP model again using Solver, but with different starting values for the decision variables. Screenshot 6-8C shows the final result obtained by Solver when we start with initial

SCREENSHOT 6-8B Excel Layout and Solver Entries for Pickens Memorial—NLP Solution 1

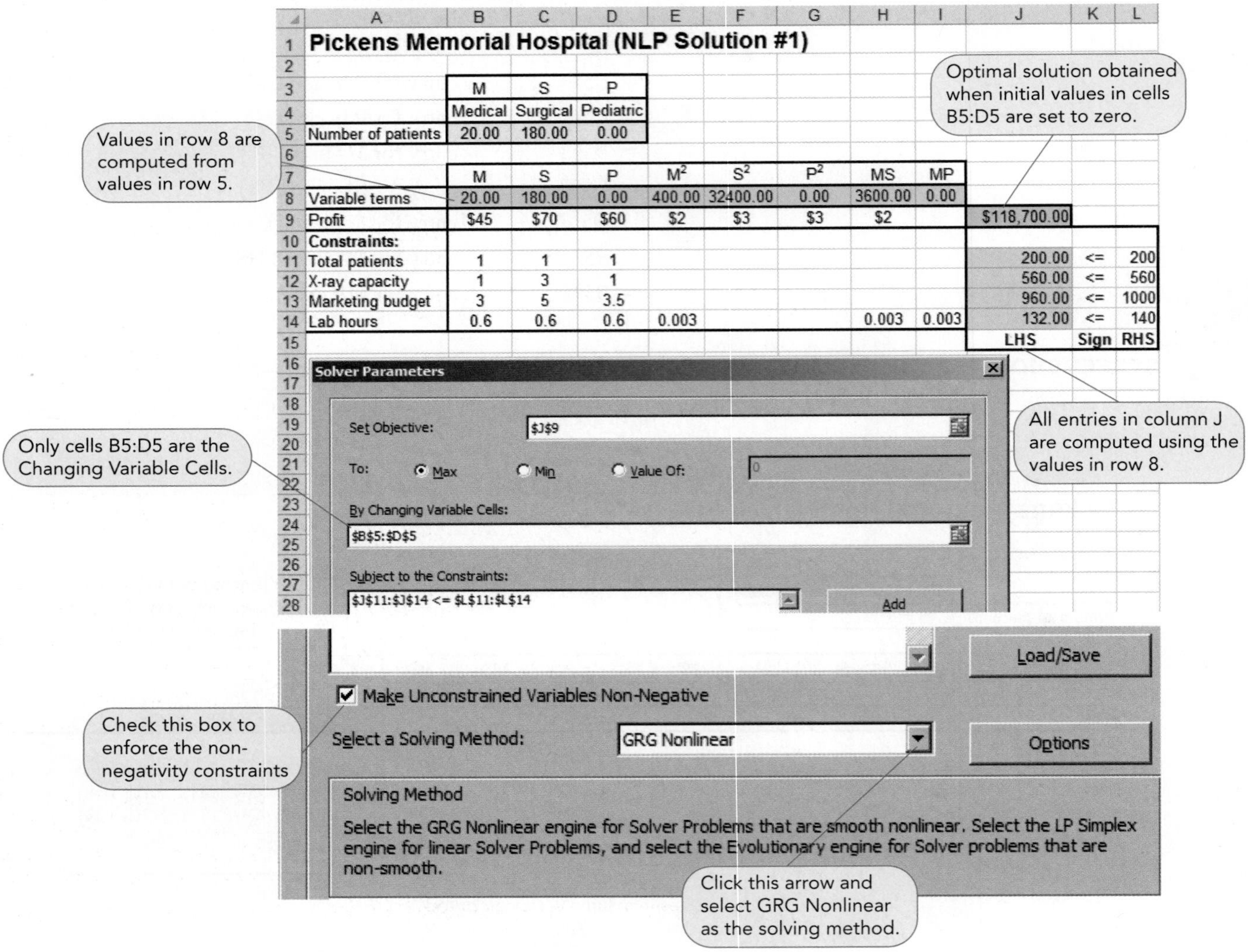

Pickens Memorial Hospital (NLP Solution #1)

	B	C	D	E	F	G	H	I	J	K	L
	M	S	P								
	Medical	Surgical	Pediatric								
Number of patients	20.00	180.00	0.00								
	M	S	P	M^2	S^2	P^2	MS	MP			
Variable terms	20.00	180.00	0.00	400.00	32400.00	0.00	3600.00	0.00			
Profit	$45	$70	$60	$2	$3	$3	$2		$118,700.00		
Constraints:											
Total patients	1	1	1						200.00	<=	200
X-ray capacity	1	3	1						560.00	<=	560
Marketing budget	3	5	3.5						960.00	<=	1000
Lab hours	0.6	0.6	0.6	0.003			0.003	0.003	132.00	<=	140
									LHS	**Sign**	**RHS**

Optimal solution obtained when initial values in cells B5:D5 are set to zero.

Values in row 8 are computed from values in row 5.

All entries in column J are computed using the values in row 8.

Solver Parameters

Set Objective: $J$9

To: Max Min Value Of: 0

By Changing Variable Cells: $B$5:$D$5

Only cells B5:D5 are the Changing Variable Cells.

Subject to the Constraints: $J$11:$J$14 <= $L$11:$L$14

Add

Load/Save

Make Unconstrained Variables Non-Negative

Check this box to enforce the non-negativity constraints

Select a Solving Method: GRG Nonlinear

Options

Solving Method

Select the GRG Nonlinear engine for Solver Problems that are smooth nonlinear. Select the LP Simplex engine for linear Solver Problems, and select the Evolutionary engine for Solver problems that are non-smooth.

Click this arrow and select GRG Nonlinear as the solving method.

SCREENSHOT 6-8C Excel Layout and Solver Entries for Pickens Memorial—NLP Solution 2

	A	B	C	D	E	F	G	H	I	J	K	L
1	**Pickens Memorial Hospital (NLP Solution #2)**											
2												
3		M	S	P								
4		Medical	Surgical	Pediatric								
5	Number of patients	0.00	0.00	200.00								
6												
7		M	S	P	M^2	S^2	P^2	MS	MP			
8	Variable terms	0.00	0.00	200.00	0.00	0.00	40000.00	0.00	0.00			
9	Profit	$45	$70	$60	$2	$3	$3	$2		$132,000.00		
10	**Constraints:**											
11	Total patients	1	1	1						200.00	<=	200
12	X-ray capacity	1	3	1						200.00	<=	560
13	Marketing budget	3	5	3.5						700.00	<=	1000
14	Lab hours	0.6	0.6	0.6	0.003			0.003	0.003	120.00	<=	140
15										**LHS**	**Sign**	**RHS**

Solution now recommends admitting only pediatric patients.

Optimal solution obtained when initial values in cells B5:D5 are set to M = 100, S = 0, and P = 100.

File: 6-8.xls, sheet: 6-8C

values of $M = 100$, $S = 0$, and $P = 100$. Interestingly, we get a different final solution now: Pickens Memorial should admit no medical and surgical patients but admit 200 pediatric patients each week, for a total weekly profit of $132,000.

Because this profit is higher than the $118,700 profit shown in Screenshot 6-8B, it is clear that the earlier solution is only a local optimal solution. We can of course manually experiment with other starting values for the decision variables to see if we can get a solution better than $132,000. Solver, however, has an option to automatically try different starting points. We should note, though, that while this approach will identify the best solution from a range of possible local optimal solutions, it does not guarantee that it will find the global optimal solution. In fact, as we will see later, when we use this approach, Solver will explicitly include the message "Solver converged in probability to a global solution" rather than say it found a global optimal solution (as it does when we use the Simplex LP method).

We can use the Multistart option in Solver to automatically try different starting values for the decision variables in an NLP problem.

SOLVER OPTIONS FOR NLP MODELS We click the Options button in Solver and select the GRG Nonlinear tab to get the window shown in Screenshot 6-8D. We focus our attention primarily on the box labeled Multistart. To get Solver to automatically try different starting values for the decision variables, we check not only the box labeled Use Multistart but also the box labeled Require Bounds on Variables. What are the bounds on the decision variables? Clearly, the nonnegativity constraints provide a lower bound for each variable. We can easily specify upper bounds for each decision variable by adding them as constraints in Solver. The likelihood of finding a global solution increases as the bounds we specify on variables become tighter, and the longer Solver runs. We illustrate the use of bounds on variables in Solved Problem 6-3 at the end of this chapter.

In the case of Pickens Memorial, it is clear that none of the variables can exceed a value of 200, and we can therefore specify this as the upper bound for all variables. If we do so and solve the model with the options specified as shown in Screenshot 6-8D, we get the same solution shown in Screenshot 6-8C. (We urge you to try this out yourself, using the Excel file *6-8.xls* on the Companion Website for this textbook.) It is therefore likely that this solution is, in fact, the global optimal solution. If so, perhaps Pickens Memorial should consider renaming itself the Pickens Memorial Pediatric Hospital!

Quadratic programming contains squared terms in the objective function.

QUADRATIC PROGRAMMING MODELS When the only nonlinear terms in an objective function are squared terms (such as M^2) and the problem's constraints are all linear, this is a special type of NLP model called a **quadratic programming (QP)** model. A number of useful problems in the field of portfolio selection fall into this category. QP problems can be solved by using a modified version of the simplex method. Such work, however, is beyond the scope of this textbook.

SCREENSHOT 6-8D
Solver Options Window for NLP Models

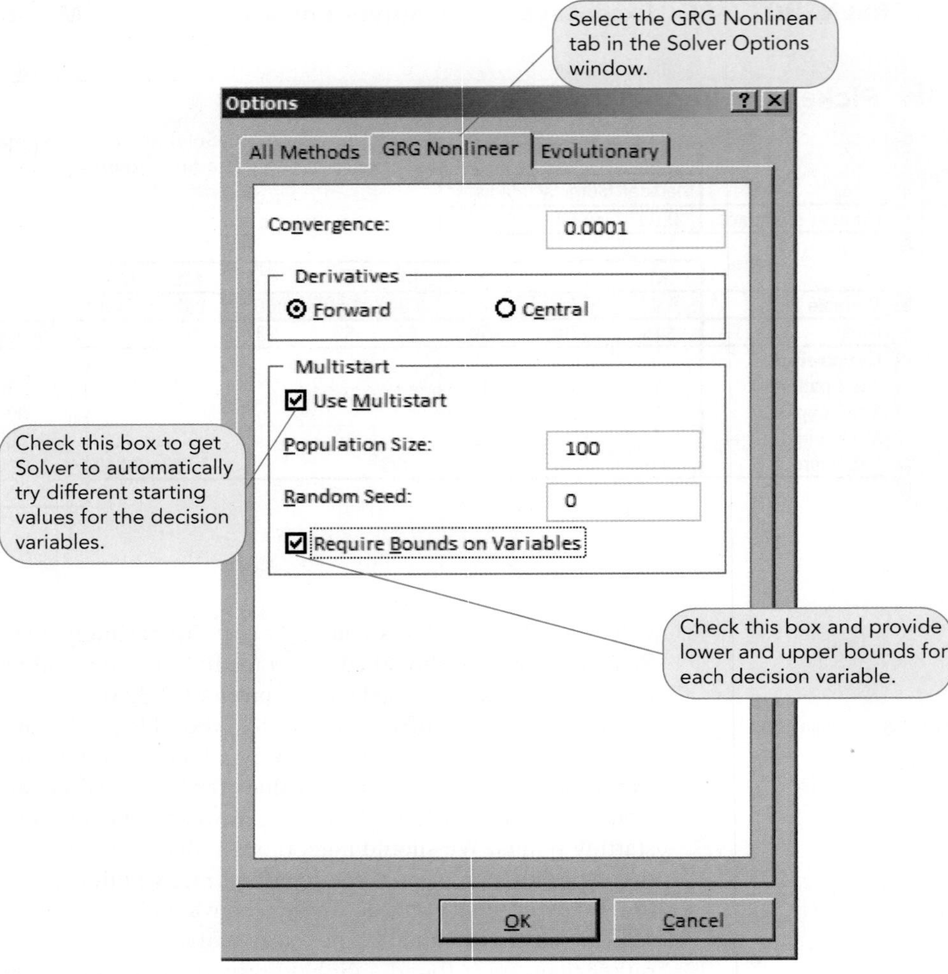
Select the GRG Nonlinear tab in the Solver Options window.
Options
All Methods
GRG Nonlinear
Evolutionary
Convergence:
0.0001
Derivatives
Forward
Central
Multistart
Use Multistart
Population Size:
100
Random Seed:
0
Require Bounds on Variables
Check this box to get Solver to automatically try different starting values for the decision variables.
Check this box and provide lower and upper bounds for each decision variable.
OK
Cancel

Computational Procedures for Nonlinear Programming Problems

We cannot always find an optimal solution to an NLP problem.

Although we have used Solver to find an optimal solution for Pickens Memorial's NLP example, there is no general method that guarantees an optimal solution for all NLP problems in a finite number of steps. As noted earlier, NLP problems are inherently more difficult to solve than LP problems.

Perhaps the best way to deal with nonlinear problems is to try to reduce them into a form that is linear or almost linear. One such approach, called *separable programming*, deals with a class of problems in which the objective and constraints are approximated by linear functions. In this way, the powerful procedures (such as the simplex algorithm) for solving LP problems can again be applied. In general, however, work in the area of NLP is the least charted and most difficult of all the decision models.

Summary

This chapter addresses three special types of LP problems. The first, integer programming, examines LP problems that cannot have fractional answers. We note that there are two types of integer variables: general integer variables, which can take on any nonnegative integer value that satisfies all the constraints in a model, and binary variables, which can only take on either of two values: 0 or 1. We illustrate how models involving both types of integer variables can be set up in Excel and solved using Solver.

The second special type of LP problem studied is goal programming. This extension of LP allows problems to have multiple objective functions, each with its own goal. We show how to model such problems using weighted goals as well as ranked goals. In either case, we use Excel's Solver to obtain optimal solutions.

Finally, we introduce the advanced topic of NLP as a special mathematical programming problem. Excel's Solver can be a useful tool in solving simple NLP models.

Glossary

Binary Variables Decision variables that are required to have integer values of either 0 or 1. Also called *0–1 variables*.

Branch-and-Bound (B&B) Method An algorithm used by Solver and other software to solve IP problems. It divides the set of feasible solutions into subregions that are examined systematically.

Deviation Variables Terms that are minimized in a goal programming problem. They are the only terms in the objective function.

Fixed-Charge Problem A problem in which there is a fixed cost in addition to variable costs. Fixed costs need to be modeled using binary (or 0–1) variables.

General Integer Variables Decision variables that are required to be integer valued. Actual values of these variables are restricted only by the constraints in the problem.

Generalized Reduced Gradient (GRG) Procedure A procedure used by Solver to solve NLP problems.

Goal Programming (GP) A mathematical programming technique that permits decision makers to set and rank multiple objective functions.

Integer Programming (IP) A mathematical programming technique that produces integer solutions to LP problems.

Mixed Integer Programming A category of problems in which some decision variables must have integer values (either general integer or binary) and other decision variables can have fractional values.

Nonlinear Programming (NLP) A category of mathematical programming techniques that allow the objective function and/or constraints to be nonlinear.

Quadratic Programming (QP) An NLP model in which the objective function includes only quadratic nonlinear terms and the constraints are all linear.

Ranked Goals An approach in which a decision maker ranks goals based on their relative importance to the decision maker. Lower-ranked goals are considered only after higher-ranked goals have been optimized. Also known as *prioritized goals*.

Satisfice To come as close as possible to reaching a set of objectives.

Weighted Goals An approach in which the decision maker assigns weights to deviation variables based on their relative importance to the decision maker.

Solved Problems

Solved Problem 6-1

Consider the 0–1 integer programming problem that follows:

$$\text{Maximize profit} = 50X_1 + 45X_2 + 48X_3$$

subject to the constraints

$$19X_1 + 27X_2 + 34X_3 \leq 80$$
$$22X_1 + 13X_2 + 12X_3 \leq 40$$
$$X_1, X_2, X_3 = 0 \text{ or } 1$$

Now reformulate this problem with additional constraints so that no more than two of the three variables can take on a value equal to 1 in the solution. Further, make sure that if $X_1 = 1$, then $X_2 = 1$ also, and vice versa. Then solve the new problem using Excel.

Solution

We need two new constraints to handle the reformulated problem:

$$X_1 + X_2 + X_3 \leq 2$$

and

File: 6-9.xls

$$X_1 - X_2 = 0$$

The Excel layout and Solver entries for this problem are shown in Screenshot 6-9. The optimal solution is $X_1 = 1, X_2 = 1, X_3 = 0$, with an objective value of 95.

SCREENSHOT 6-9 Excel Layout and Solver Entries for Solved Problem 6-1

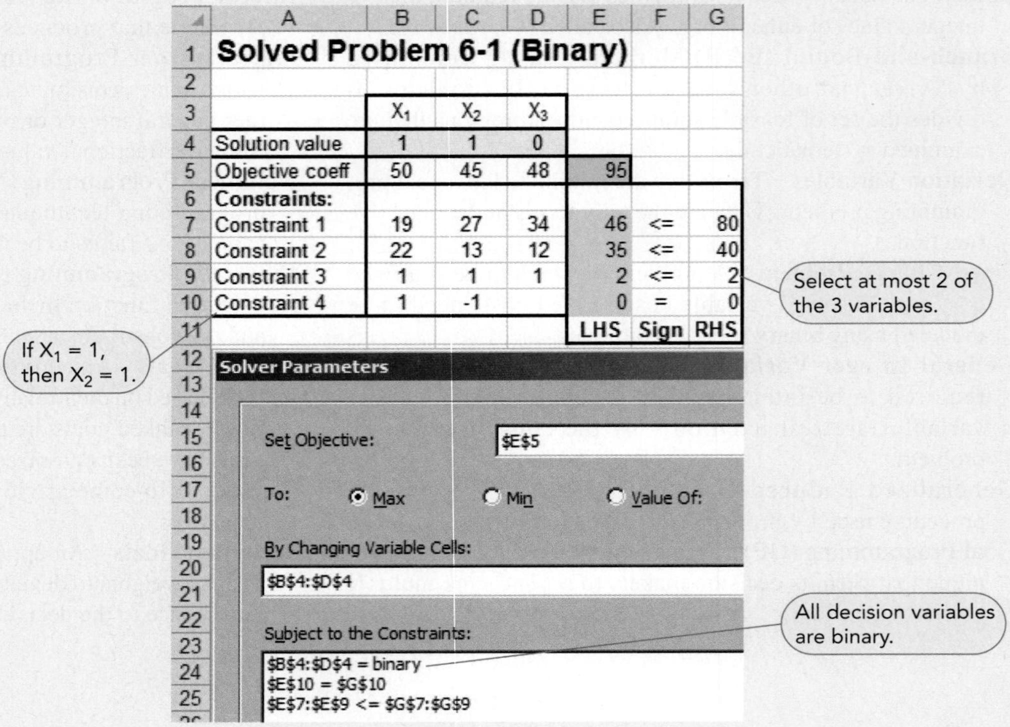

Solved Problem 6-1 (Binary)

	X_1	X_2	X_3			
Solution value	1	1	0			
Objective coeff	50	45	48	95		
Constraints:						
Constraint 1	19	27	34	46	<=	80
Constraint 2	22	13	12	35	<=	40
Constraint 3	1	1	1	2	<=	2
Constraint 4	1	-1		0	=	0
				LHS	**Sign**	**RHS**

Select at most 2 of the 3 variables.

If $X_1 = 1$, then $X_2 = 1$.

Solver Parameters

Set Objective: $E$5

To: (•) Max ( ) Min ( ) Value Of:

By Changing Variable Cells:

$B$4:$D$4

Subject to the Constraints:

$B$4:$D$4 = binary
$E$10 = $G$10
$E$7:$E$9 <= $G$7:$G$9

All decision variables are binary.

Solved Problem 6-2

Recall the Harrison Electric Company general IP problem discussed in section 6.2. Its IP model is

$$\text{Maximize profit} = \$600L + \$700F$$

subject to the constraints

$$2L + 3F \leq 12 \quad \text{(wiring hours)}$$
$$6L + 5F \leq 30 \quad \text{(assembly hours)}$$
$$L, F \geq 0, \text{ and integer}$$

where L = number of lamps produced and F = number of ceiling fans produced. Reformulate and solve Harrison Electric's problem as a GP model, with the following goals in rank order. (Note that more than one goal has been assigned the same rank.) Remember that both L and F need to be integer valued.

Rank R_1: Produce at least 4 lamps (goal 1) and 3 ceiling fans (goal 2).
Rank R_2: Limit overtime in the assembly department to 10 hours (goal 3) and in the wiring department to 6 hours (goal 4).
Rank R_3: Maximize profit (goal 5).

Solution

Let us define d_i^- and d_i^+ as the underachievement and overachievement deviation variables, respectively, for the ith goal. Then, the GP model can be formulated as follows:

$$\text{Minimize} = R_1(d_1^- + d_2^-) + R_2(d_3^+ + d_4^+) + R_3(d_5^-)$$

subject to the constraints

$$\left.\begin{aligned} L + d_1^- - d_1^+ &= 4 \\ F + d_2^- - d_2^+ &= 3 \end{aligned}\right\} \quad \text{Rank 1}$$

$$\left.\begin{aligned} 2L + 3F + d_3^- - d_3^+ &= 18 \\ 6L + 5F + d_4^- - d_4^+ &= 40 \end{aligned}\right\} \quad \text{Rank 2}$$

$$600L + 700F + d_5^- - d_5^+ = 99{,}999 \} \quad \text{Rank 3}$$

$$L, F, \text{all } d_i \geq 0$$

$$L, F \text{ integer}$$

The time availabilities in the wiring and assembly departments (rank R_2 goals) have been adjusted to include the permissible overtime. The target of \$99,999 for the rank R_3 goal represents an unrealistically high profit. It is just a mathematic trick to use as a target so that we can get as close as possible to the maximum profit.

Note that for the rank R_1 goals, we need to minimize only the underachievement deviation variables d_1^- and d_2^-. Likewise, for the rank R_2 goals, we must minimize only the overachievement deviation variables d_3^+ and d_4^+. Finally, for the rank R_3 goal, we must minimize only the underachievement deviation variable d_5^-.

File: 6-10.xls

Screenshots 6-10A, 6-10B, and 6-10C show the Excel layout and Solver entries for this problem when each goal is considered in order of its rank. In each case, optimal values of the deviation variables for a higher-ranked goal are explicitly specified while solving the problem for a lower-ranked goal. For example, while solving the GP problem with the rank R_2 goals (Screenshot 6-10B), the optimal values of the rank R_1 deviation variables (namely $d_1^- = 0$ and $d_2^- + 0$) from Screenshot 6-10A are explicitly specified in Solver.

SCREENSHOT 6-10A Excel Layout and Solver Entries for Harrison Electric—Rank R_1 Goals Only

Rank R_1 goal is to minimize $d_1^- + d_2^-$.

Harrison Electric (Rank R_1 Goals Only)

	A	B	C	D	E	F	G	H	I	J	K	L	M	N	O	P	Q
3		L	F	d_1^-	d_1^+	d_2^-	d_2^+	d_3^-	d_3^+	d_4^-	d_4^+	d_5^-	d_5^+				
4		Lamps	Fans	Under ach lamps	Over ach lamps	Under ach fans	Over ach fans	Under ach wiring	Over ach wiring	Under ach asmbly	Over ach asmbly	Under ach profit	Over ach profit				
5	Solution value	4.0	140.0	0.0	0.0	0.0	137.0	0.0	410.0	0.0	684.0	0.0	401.0				
6	Obj coeff			1		1								0.0			
7	Constraints:																Achieved
8	Lamps goal	1		1	-1									4.0	=	4	4.0
9	Fans goal		1			1	-1							3.0	=	3	140.0
10	Wiring goal	2	3					1	-1					18.0	=	18	428.0
11	Assembly goal	6	5							1	-1			40.0	=	40	724.0
12	Profit goal	600	700									1	-1	99999.0	=	99999	100400.0
13														LHS	Sign	RHS	

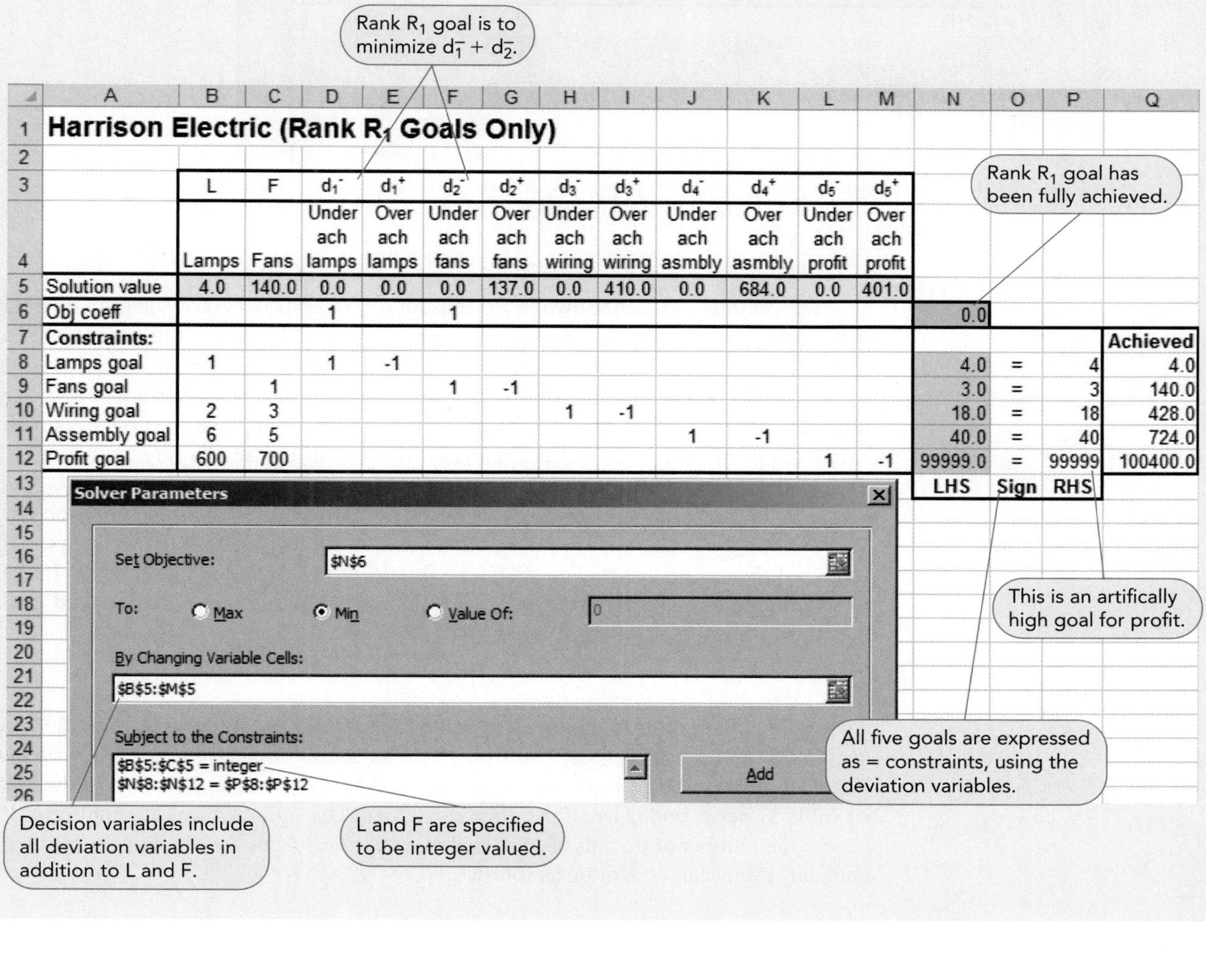

Rank R_1 goal has been fully achieved.

This is an artifically high goal for profit.

Solver Parameters

Set Objective: \$N\$6

To: Max / **Min** / Value Of: 0

By Changing Variable Cells: \$B\$5:\$M\$5

Subject to the Constraints:

\$B\$5:\$C\$5 = integer
\$N\$8:\$N\$12 = \$P\$8:\$P\$12

Add

All five goals are expressed as = constraints, using the deviation variables.

Decision variables include all deviation variables in addition to L and F.

L and F are specified to be integer valued.

SCREENSHOT 6-10B Excel Layout and Solver Entries for Harrison Electric—Rank R_2 Goals Only

Rank R_2 goal is to minimize $d_3^+ + d_4^+$.
Rank R_2 goal has also been fully achieved.
These values show to what extent each goal has been achieved.
d_1^- and d_2^- have been set to their optimal values of zero (from R_1).

Harrison Electric (Rank R_2 Goals Only)

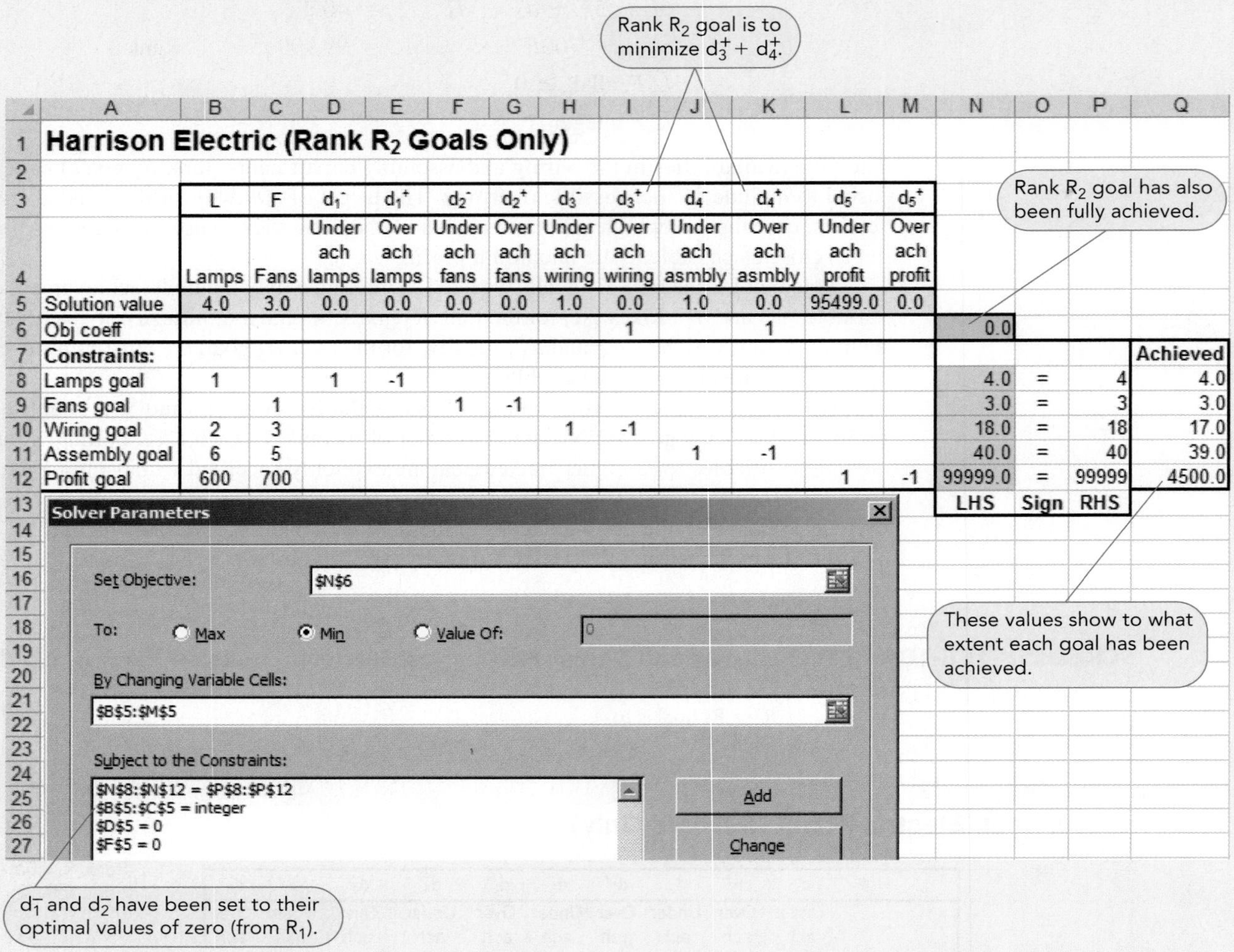

	A	B	C	D	E	F	G	H	I	J	K	L	M	N	O	P	Q
3		L	F	d_1^-	d_1^+	d_2^-	d_2^+	d_3^-	d_3^+	d_4^-	d_4^+	d_5^-	d_5^+				
4		Lamps	Fans	Under ach lamps	Over ach lamps	Under ach fans	Over ach fans	Under ach wiring	Over ach wiring	Under ach asmbly	Over ach asmbly	Under ach profit	Over ach profit				
5	Solution value	4.0	3.0	0.0	0.0	0.0	0.0	1.0	0.0	1.0	0.0	95499.0	0.0				
6	Obj coeff								1		1			0.0			
7	Constraints:																Achieved
8	Lamps goal	1		1	-1									4.0	=	4	4.0
9	Fans goal		1			1	-1							3.0	=	3	3.0
10	Wiring goal	2	3					1	-1					18.0	=	18	17.0
11	Assembly goal	6	5							1	-1			40.0	=	40	39.0
12	Profit goal	600	700									1	-1	99999.0	=	99999	4500.0
13														LHS	Sign	RHS	

Solver Parameters

Set Objective: \$N\$6

To: Max ● Min Value Of: 0

By Changing Variable Cells: \$B\$5:\$M\$5

Subject to the Constraints:

\$N\$8:\$N\$12 = \$P\$8:\$P\$12
\$B\$5:\$C\$5 = integer
\$D\$5 = 0
\$F\$5 = 0

Add

Change

The optimal solution shown in Screenshot 6-10A considers only the rank R_1 goals. Therefore, restricting overtime in assembly and wiring is not an issue in this problem. The solution therefore uses a large amount of overtime (note the values for d_3^+ and d_4^+ in Screenshot 6-10A).

However, when we now solve the rank R_2 GP problem in Screenshot 6-10B, the solution minimizes the use of excessive overtime. As a consequence, the deviation variable for underachieving profit (d_5^-) now has a large value (due to the artificially large value of \$99,999 we used as the target for profit).

When we now try to minimize this deviation variable in the rank R_3 GP problem (Screenshot 6-10C), we obtain the overall optimal solution for this GP problem. The optimal solution is $L = 4, F = 3, d_1^- = 0, d_2^- = 0, d_3^+ = 0$, and $d_4^+ = 0$, and $d_5^- = 95{,}499$. In effect, this means that the maximum profit we can get while achieving our higher-ranked goals is only \$4,500 $(= \$600 \times 4 + \$700 \times 3)$.

Solved Problem 6-3

Thermolock Corporation produces massive rubber washers and gaskets like the type used to seal joints on the NASA space shuttles. To do so, it combines two ingredients, rubber and oil. The cost of the industrial-quality rubber used is \$5 per pound, and the cost of the high-viscosity oil is \$7 per pound. Two of the three constraints Thermolock faces are nonlinear. If R and O denote the number of pounds used of rubber and oil, respectively, the firm's objective function and constraints can be written as follows:

SCREENSHOT 6-10C Excel Layout and Solver Entries for Harrison Electric—Rank R_3 Goals Only

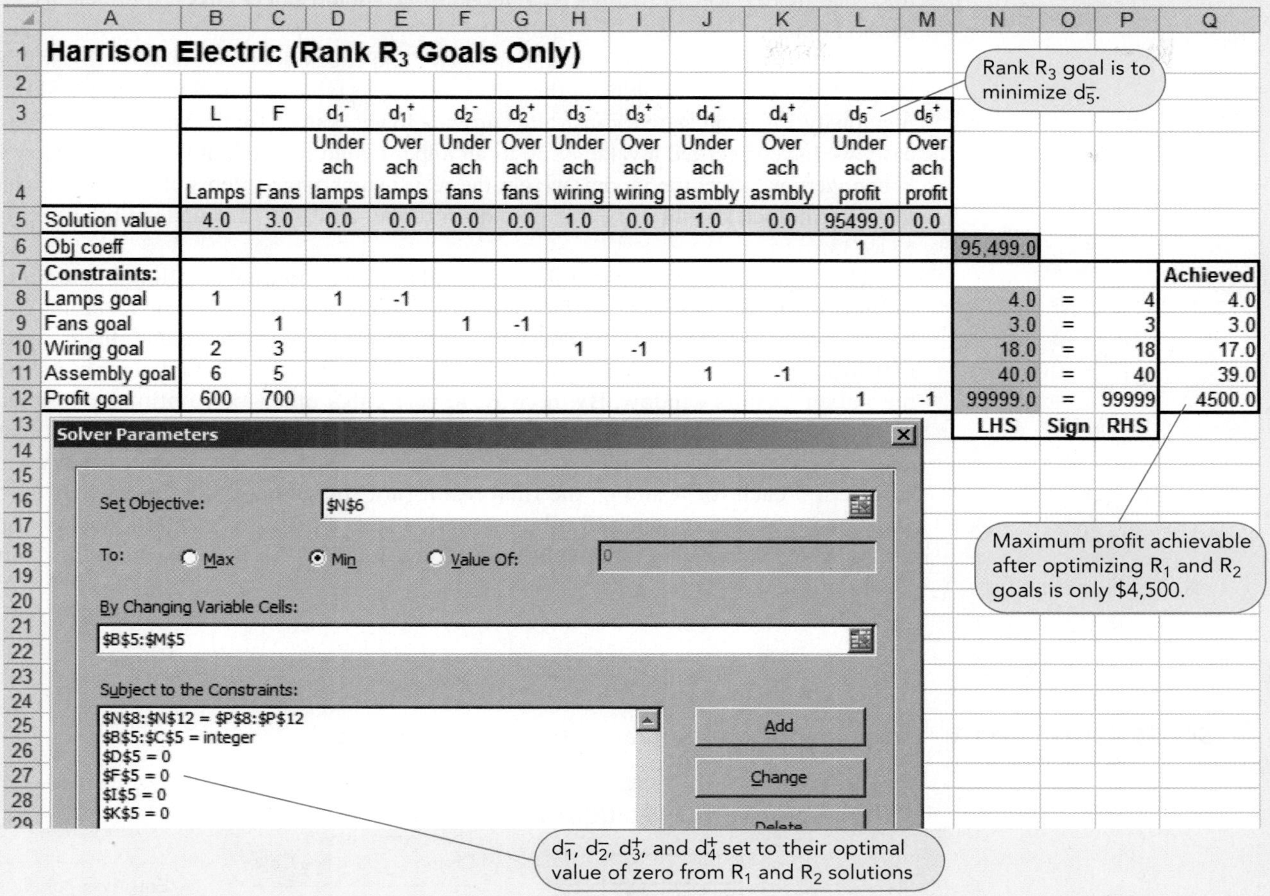

	A	B	C	D	E	F	G	H	I	J	K	L	M	N	O	P	Q
1	**Harrison Electric (Rank R_3 Goals Only)**																
2																	
3		L	F	d_1^-	d_1^+	d_2^-	d_2^+	d_3^-	d_3^+	d_4^-	d_4^+	d_5^-	d_5^+				
4		Lamps	Fans	Under ach lamps	Over ach lamps	Under ach fans	Over ach fans	Under ach wiring	Over ach wiring	Under ach asmbly	Over ach asmbly	Under ach profit	Over ach profit				
5	Solution value	4.0	3.0	0.0	0.0	0.0	0.0	1.0	0.0	1.0	0.0	95499.0	0.0				
6	Obj coeff											1		95,499.0			
7	**Constraints:**																**Achieved**
8	Lamps goal	1		1	-1									4.0	=	4	4.0
9	Fans goal		1			1	-1							3.0	=	3	3.0
10	Wiring goal	2	3					1	-1					18.0	=	18	17.0
11	Assembly goal	6	5							1	-1			40.0	=	40	39.0
12	Profit goal	600	700									1	-1	99999.0	=	99999	4500.0
13														**LHS**	**Sign**	**RHS**	

Solver Parameters

Set Objective: $N$6

To: Max / Min (selected) / Value Of: 0

By Changing Variable Cells: $B$5:$M$5

Subject to the Constraints:
$N$8:$N$12 = $P$8:$P$12
$B$5:$C$5 = integer
$D$5 = 0
$F$5 = 0
$I$5 = 0
$K$5 = 0

Add | Change | Delete

Rank R_3 goal is to minimize d_5^-.

Maximum profit achievable after optimizing R_1 and R_2 goals is only $4,500.

d_1^-, d_2^-, d_3^+, and d_4^+ set to their optimal value of zero from R_1 and R_2 solutions

$$\text{Minimize cost} = \$5R + \$7O$$

subject to the constraints

$$3R + 0.25R^2 + 4O + 0.3O^2 \geq 125 \quad \text{(hardness constraint)}$$
$$13R + R^3 \geq 80 \quad \text{(tensile strength constraint)}$$
$$0.7R + O \geq 17 \quad \text{(elasticity constraint)}$$
$$R, O \geq 0$$

Set up and solve Thermolock's NLP model using Solver.

Solution

WWW

File: 6-11.xls, sheet: 6-11A

The Excel layout and Solver entries for Thermolock's problem are shown in Screenshot 6-11A. As in the Pickens Memorial NLP example, the only decision variables (i.e., changing variable cells) are in cells B5 and C5. The entries in row 8 (cells B8:F8) represent all linear and nonlinear terms involving these decision variables. The formulas for these cells are

$= B5$ (entry for R in cell B8)
$= C5$ (entry for O in cell C8)
$= B5\text{^}2$ (entry for R^2 in cell D8)
$= C5\text{^}2$ (entry for O^2 in cell E8)
$= B5\text{^}2$ (entry for R in cell F8)

Let us use the Multistart option available in the GRG Nonlinear method in Solver to solve this NLP model. Recall that for NLP models, we should select GRG Nonlinear as the solving method to use.

We then click the Options button in Solver and check the boxes labeled Use Multistart and Require Bounds on Variables in the GRG Nonlinear tab (refer to Screenshot 6-8D). As noted previously, the nonnegative constraints provide lower bounds for the variables. In Thermolock's case, we have specified a value of 50 as an upper bound for each of the two decision variables. When we now solve the model, we get the result shown in Screenshot 6-11A, which specifies that Thermolock should use 3.325 pounds of rubber and 14.672 pounds of oil, at a total cost of $119.33.

Here again, we ask whether this is a local or global optimal solution. Since we have used Solver to automatically try different starting values for the decision variables (within the bounds we have specified), it is probable, although not guaranteed, that this is a global optimal solution. As shown in Screenshot 6-11B, Solver makes this fact clear in its message in the Solver Results window. By the way, to verify that other local optimal solutions are possible, we urge you to use the Excel file *6-11.xls* on the Companion Website for this textbook and experiment with different starting values for R and O. For example, when we start with values of 5 each for R and O, the final result (not shown here) obtained by Solver is to use 10 pounds each of rubber and oil, at a total cost of $120. Because this cost is higher than the $119.33 cost in the earlier solution (Screenshot 6-11A), it is clear that this solution is a local optimal solution.

File: 6-11.xls, sheet: 6-11B

SCREENSHOT 6-11A Excel Layout and Solver Entries for Thermolock

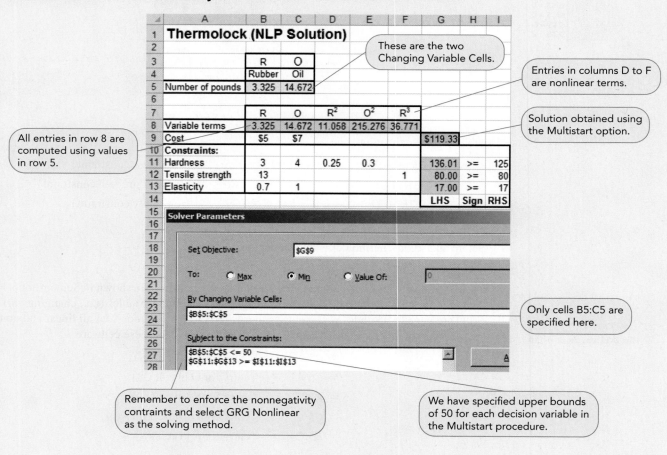

	A	B	C	D	E	F	G	H	I
1	**Thermolock (NLP Solution)**								
2									
3		R	O						
4		Rubber	Oil						
5	Number of pounds	3.325	14.672						
6									
7		R	O	R^2	O^2	R^3			
8	Variable terms	3.325	14.672	11.058	215.276	36.771			
9	Cost	$5	$7				$119.33		
10	**Constraints:**								
11	Hardness	3	4	0.25	0.3		136.01	>=	125
12	Tensile strength	13				1	80.00	>=	80
13	Elasticity	0.7	1				17.00	>=	17
14							**LHS**	**Sign**	**RHS**

SCREENSHOT 6-11B Solver Results Window When Using the Multistart Option for NLP Models

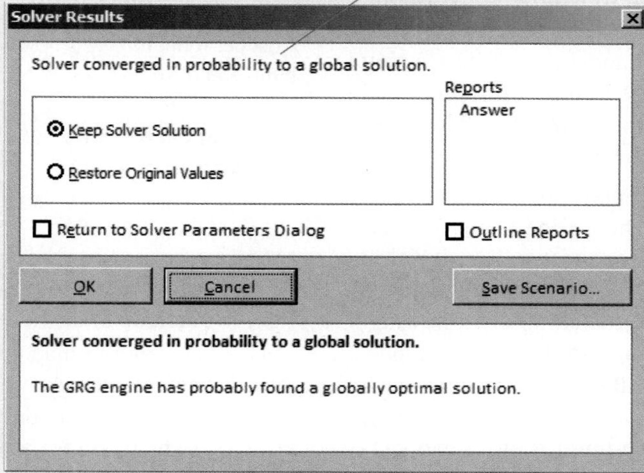

Discussion Questions and Problems

Discussion Questions

6-1 Compare the similarities and differences of LP and GP.

6-2 Provide your own examples of five applications of IP.

6-3 What is the difference between pure and mixed IP models? Which do you think is most common, and why?

6-4 What is meant by *satisficing*, and why is the term often used in conjunction with GP?

6-5 What are deviation variables? How do they differ from decision variables in traditional LP problems?

6-6 If you were the president of the college you are attending and were employing GP to assist in decision making, what might your goals be? What kinds of constraints would you include in your model?

6-7 What does it mean to rank goals in GP? How does this affect the problem's solution?

6-8 Provide your own examples of problems where (a) the objective is nonlinear and (b) one or more constraints are nonlinear.

6-9 Explain in your own words why IP problems are more difficult to solve than LP problems.

6-10 Explain the difference between assigning weights to goals and ranking goals.

6-11 What does the term *quadratic programming* mean?

6-12 Which of the following are NLP models, and why? Are any of these quadratic programming models?

(a) Maximize profit $= 3X_1 + 5X_2 + 99X_3$

subject to the contraints

$$X_1 \geq 10$$
$$X_2 \leq 5$$
$$X_3 \geq 18$$

(b) Maximize profit $= 25X_1 + 30X_2 + 8X_1X_2$

subject to the contraints

$$X_1 \geq 8$$
$$X_1 + X_2 \geq 12$$
$$X_1 - X_2 = 11$$

(c) Maximize profit $= 3X_1 + 4X_2$

subject to the contraints

$$X_1^2 - 5X_2 \geq 8$$
$$3X_1 + 4X_2 \geq 12$$

(d) Maximize profit $= 18X_1 + 5X_2 + X_2^2$

subject to the contraints

$$4X_1 - 3X_2 \geq 8$$
$$X_1 + X_2 \geq 18$$

Problems

6-13 A cleaning crew currently spends 6 hours per house cleaning eight houses every day, for a profit of $15 per hour. The crew now wants to offer its services to other houses, as well as small professional offices. The crew believes it will take 7 hours to clean the office of a lawyer and that the profit for doing so will be $19 per hour. It will take 10 hours to clean a doctor's office and that the profit for doing so will be $25 per hour. The crew can make 120 hours of labor available per day and does not want to cancel any of its existing house contracts. What is the best mix of homes and offices to clean per day to maximize profit? Remember that your solution must be in whole numbers.

6-14 An airline is preparing to replace its old planes with three new styles of jets. The airline needs 17 new planes to service its current routes. The decision regarding which planes to purchase should balance cost with capability factors, including the following: (1) The airline can finance up to $700 million in purchases; (2) each 7A7 jet will cost $38 million, each 7B7 jet will cost $27 million, and each 7C7 jet will cost $22 million; (3) at least one-third of the planes purchased should be the longer-range 7A7; (4) the annual maintenance budget is to be no more than $12 million; (5) the annual maintenance cost per 7A7 is estimated to be $800,000, $600,000 for each 7B7, and $500,000 for each 7C7; and (6) annually, each 7A7 can carry 125,000 passengers, each 7B7 can fly 95,000 passengers, and each 7C7 can fly 80,000 passengers. Formulate this as an IP problem to maximize the annual passenger-carrying capability. Solve it by using Excel.

6-15 The Gaubert Marketing Company needs the following number of telemarketers on the phones during the upcoming week: Monday 23, Tuesday 16, Wednesday 21, Thursday 17, Friday 20, Saturday 12, and Sunday 15. Each employee works five consecutive days followed by 2 days off per week. How many telemarketers should be scheduled each day of the week to begin their five-day work week? The objective is to minimize the total number of employees needed to fulfill the daily requirements.

(a) Solve as an IP model.

(b) Additional information is now available for Gaubert. Daily pay from Monday through Friday is $90, pay for Saturday is $110, and Sunday workers earn $125. In addition, up to four people can be hired who will work Friday, Saturday, and Sunday. Their pay for this three-day week is $250. The new objective is to minimize total weekly labor costs. Revise the IP model and solve it.

6-16 A hospital is planning an $8 million addition to its existing facility. The architect has been asked to consider the following design parameters: (1) There should be at least 10 and no more than 20 intensive care unit (ICU) rooms; (2) there should be at least 10 and no more than 20 cardiac care unit (CCU) rooms; (3) there should be no more than 50 double rooms; (4) there should be at least 35 single rooms; and (5) all patient rooms should fit inside the allotted 40,000-square-foot space (not including hallways). The following table summarizes the relevant room data:

	SINGLE	DOUBLE	ICU	CCU
Cost per room to build and furnish ($thousands)	$45	$54	$110	$104
Minimum square feet required	300	360	320	340
Profit per room per month ($thousands)	$21	$28	$ 48	$ 41

How many rooms of each type should the architect include in the new hospital design?

6-17 A vending machine is programmed to count out the correct change for each transaction. Formulate and solve an IP model that will determine how change is to be made for a purchase of $4.43, when a $10 bill is inserted into the machine. The model's solution should be based on the availability of coins in the machine, with the objective of minimizing the total number of coins used to make the change.

DENOMINATION	AVAILABILITY
$1 coin	8
Quarter ($0.25)	9
Dime ($0.10)	7
Nickel ($0.05)	11
Penny ($0.01)	10

6-18 Stockbroker Susan Drexler has advised her client as shown in the following table.

INVESTMENT	COST (THOUSANDS)	EXPECTED RETURN (THOUSANDS)
Andover municipal bonds	$ 400	$ 35
Hamilton city bonds	$1,000	$100
East Power & Light Co.	$ 350	$ 30
Nebraska Electric Service	$ 700	$ 65
Southern Gas and Electric	$ 490	$ 45
Manuel Products Co.	$ 270	$ 20
Builders Paint Co.	$ 800	$ 90
Rest Easy Hotels Co.	$ 500	$ 50

The client agrees to this list but provides several conditions: (1) No more than $3,000,000 can be invested, (2) the money is to be spread among at least five investments, (3) no more than one type of bond can be purchased, (4) at least two utility stocks must be purchased, and (5) at least two regular stocks must be purchased. Formulate this as a 0–1 IP problem for Ms. Drexler to maximize expected return. Solve it by using Excel.

6-19 Porter Investments needs to develop an investment portfolio for Mrs. Singh from the following list of possible investments:

INVESTMENT	COST	EXPECTED RETURN
A	$ 10,000	$ 700
B	$ 12,000	$ 1,000
C	$ 3,500	$ 390
D	$ 5,000	$ 500
E	$ 8,500	$ 750
F	$ 8,000	$ 640
G	$ 4,000	$ 300

Mrs. Singh has a total of $60,000 to invest. The following conditions must be met: (1) If investment F is chosen, then investment G must also be part of the portfolio, (2) at least four investments should be chosen, and (3) of investment A and B, exactly one must be included. What stocks should be included in Mrs. Singh's portfolio?

6-20 A truck with the capacity to load 2,200 cubic feet of cargo is available to transport items selected from the following table.

ITEM	VALUE	VOLUME (CU. FT.)
A	$1,800	700
B	$1,400	600
C	$1,100	450
D	$ 900	400
E	$1,600	650
F	$1,100	350
G	$1,200	600

If selected, an item must be shipped in its entirety (i.e., partial shipments are not allowed). Of items B, C, and D, at least two items must be selected. If item B is selected, then item G cannot be selected. Which items should be selected to maximize the value of the shipment?

6-21 The Greenville Ride have $19 million available to sign free agent pitchers for the next season. The following table provides the relevant information for eight pitchers who are available for signing, such as whether each throws right or left handed, whether each is a starter or reliever, the cost in millions of dollars to sign each, and the relative value of each on the market on a scale of 1 to 10 (10 = highest).

PITCHER	THROWS	START/ RELIEF	COST (MILLIONS)	VALUE
A	L	R	$9	8
B	R	S	$4	5
C	R	S	$5	6
D	L	S	$5	5
E	R	R	$6	8
F	R	R	$3	5
G	L	S	$8	7
H	R	S	$2	4

The Ride feel the following needs exist for next season: (1) at least two right-handed pitchers, (2) at least one left-handed pitcher, (3) at least two starters, and (4) at least one right-handed reliever. Who should the Ride try to sign, if their objective is to maximize total value?

6-22 Allied Products has six R&D projects that are potential candidates for selection during the upcoming fiscal year. The table at the bottom of the page provides the expected net present value (NPV) and capital requirements over the next five years for each project.

The table also indicates the planned budget expenditures for the entire R&D program during each of the next five years. Which projects should be selected?

Table for Problem 6-22

		CAPITAL REQUIRED (THOUSANDS)				
PROJECT	NPV (THOUSANDS)	YEAR 1	YEAR 2	YEAR 3	YEAR 4	YEAR 5
1	$140	$ 80	$25	$22	$18	$10
2	$260	$ 95	$40	$ 5	$10	$35
3	$ 88	$ 58	$17	$14	$12	$12
4	$124	$ 32	$24	$10	$ 6	$ 7
5	$176	$115	$25	$25	$10	$ 0
6	$192	$ 48	$20	$12	$32	$40
R&D Budget		$225	$80	$60	$50	$50

Table for Problem 6-23

	ATLANTA	BOSTON	CHICAGO	DALLAS	DENVER	LA	PHILADELPHIA	SEATTLE
Atlanta	—	1,108	717	783	1,406	2,366	778	2,699
Boston		—	996	1,794	1,990	3,017	333	3,105
Chicago			—	937	1,023	2,047	767	2,108
Dallas				—	794	1,450	1,459	2,112
Denver					—	1,026	1,759	1,313
Los Angeles						—	2,723	1,141
Philadelphia							—	2,872

6-23 I-Go Airlines has operations in eight cities throughout the United States. It is searching for the best location(s) to designate as a hub, which would then serve other cities within a 1,400-mile radius. For economic reasons, I-Go would like to operate no more hubs than necessary to cover all eight cities. Which of the cities in the table at the top of the page should be designated as hubs?

6-24 Laurens County has six communities that need to be served by fire stations. The number of minutes it takes to travel between the communities is shown in the following table. The county would like to establish the minimum number of fire stations so that each community can get a response in five minutes or less. How many stations will be needed, and what communities will each station serve?

	A	B	C	D	E	F
A	—	4	6	3	5	8
B		—	4	10	6	5
C			—	9	3	5
D				—	6	3
E					—	10

6-25 Georgia Atlantic Corporation needs to decide on the locations for two new warehouses. The candidate sites are Philadelphia, Tampa, Denver, and Chicago. The following table provides the monthly capacities and the monthly fixed costs for operating warehouses at each potential site.

WAREHOUSE	MONTHLY CAPACITY (UNITS)	MONTHLY FIXED COST
Philadelphia	250	$1,000
Tampa	260	$ 800
Chicago	280	$1,200
Denver	270	$ 700

The warehouses will need to ship to three marketing areas: North, South, and West. Monthly requirements are 200 units for North, 180 units for South, and 120 units for West. The following table provides the cost to ship one unit between each location and destination.

WAREHOUSE	NORTH	SOUTH	WEST
Philadelphia	$4	$ 7	$ 9
Tampa	$6	$ 3	$11
Chicago	$5	$ 6	$ 5
Denver	$8	$10	$ 2

In addition, the following conditions must be met by the final decision: (1) A warehouse must be opened in either Philadelphia or Denver, and (2) if a warehouse is opened in Tampa, then one must also be opened in Chicago. Which two sites should be selected for the new warehouses to minimize total fixed and shipping costs?

6-26 A manufacturer has acquired four small assembly plants, located in Charlotte, Tulsa, Memphis, and Buffalo. The plan is to remodel and keep two of the plants and close the other two. The table at the top of the next page provides the anticipated monthly capacities and the monthly fixed costs for operating plants at each potential site. It is estimated that the costs to remodel and/or close the plants are equivalent.

Because of union considerations, if the plant in Buffalo is kept open, the plant in Tulsa must also be kept open. If the objective is to minimize total fixed and shipping costs, which two sites should be selected to continue assembly?

6-27 A hospital in a large city plans to build two satellite trauma centers to provide improved emergency service to areas, such as highways and high-crime districts, that have historically demonstrated an increased need for critical care services. The city council has identified four potential locations for these centers. The table for Problem 6-27 near the top of the next page shows the locations (1–4), and the mileage from each center to each of the eight high-need areas (A–H). Assume that the cost of building the trauma centers will be the same, regardless of which locations are chosen.

Table for Problem 6-26

	CHARLOTTE	TULSA	MEMPHIS	BUFFALO
Monthly capacity (units)	7,000	6,500	7,250	7,500
Monthly fixed cost ($)	$30,000	$35,000	$34,000	$32,000
Shipping to Region 1 ($/unit)	$ 5	$ 8	$ 3	$ 2
Shipping to Region 2 ($/unit)	$ 4	$ 5	$ 3	$ 9
Shipping to Region 3 ($/unit)	$ 5	$ 3	$ 4	$ 10

	REGION 1	REGION 2	REGION 3
Monthly demand (units)	3,000	4,000	6,500

Table for Problem 6-27

	A	B	C	D	E	F	G	H
1	25	5	55	5	35	15	65	45
2	5	25	15	35	25	45	35	55
3	25	55	5	35	35	75	5	35
4	35	15	25	5	55	35	45	25

(a) Which two locations will minimize the total mileage from the trauma centers to the high-need areas? Which locations should be designated to receive injured persons from each of the high-need locations?

(b) Now solve this as a set covering model, assuming that the hospital wants to keep the distance between a high-need location and a trauma center to no more than 35 miles.

6-28 The Columbia Furniture Mart manufactures desks, tables, and chairs. In order to manufacture these products, Columbia must rent the appropriate equipment at a weekly cost of $2,000 for desks, $2,500 for tables, and $1,500 for chairs. The labor and material requirements for each product are shown in the following table, along with the selling price and variable cost to manufacture.

	LABOR HOURS	LUMBER (SQ. FT.)	SALES PRICE	VARIABLE COST
Desks	4	12	$135	$97
Tables	3	8	$110	$82
Chairs	2	6	$ 50	$32

There are 2,500 labor hours and 8,000 square feet of lumber available each week. Determine the product mix that maximizes weekly profit.

6-29 Rollins Publishing needs to decide what textbooks from the table at the top of the next column to publish.

Table for Problem 6-29

	DEMAND	FIXED COST	VARIABLE COST	SELLING PRICE
Book 1	9,000	$12,000	$19	$40
Book 2	8,000	$21,000	$28	$60
Book 3	5,000	$15,000	$30	$52
Book 4	6,000	$10,000	$20	$34
Book 5	7,000	$18,000	$20	$45

For each book, the maximum demand, fixed cost of publishing, variable cost, and selling price are provided. Rollins has the capacity to publish a total of 20,000 books. Which books should be selected, and how many of each should be published?

6-30 Sandy Edge is president of Edge File Works, a firm that manufactures two types of metal file cabinets. The demand for the two-drawer model is 650 cabinets per week; demand for the three-drawer cabinet is 400 per week. Edge has a weekly operating capacity of 1,600 hours, with the two-drawer cabinet taking 1.5 hours to produce and the three-drawer cabinet requiring 2 hours. Each two-drawer model sold yields a $12 profit, and the profit for the three-drawer model is $14. Edge has listed the following goals, in rank order:

Rank 1: Attain a profit as close to $12,000 as possible each week.
Rank 2: Avoid underutilization of the firm's production capacity.
Rank 3: Sell as many two- and three-drawer cabinets as the demand indicates.

Set up and solve this problem as a goal programming model.

6-31 Eric Weiss, marketing director for Charter Power and Light, is about to begin an advertising campaign promoting energy conservation. Each TV ad costs

$10,000, while each newspaper ad costs $4,000. Weiss has set the following goals, in rank order:

Rank 1: The total advertising budget of $240,000 should not be exceeded.
Rank 2: There should be at least 10 TV ads and at least 20 newspaper ads.
Rank 3: The total number of people reached by the ads should be at least 9 million.

Each television spot reaches approximately 300,000 people. A newspaper advertisement is read by about 150,000 people. Set up and solve this goal programming problem to find out how many of each type of ad Weiss should place.

6-32 Consider the staffing situation faced by the Gaubert Marketing Company in Problem 6-15. Ignore the salary and part-time information given in part (b) of that problem. Develop a schedule that meets the daily employee requirements and satisfices the following three weighted goals:

Goal 1: Use at most 27 total employees weight = 50
Goal 2: Minimize the excess employees scheduled on Saturday weight = 30
Goal 3: Minimize the excess employees scheduled on Sunday weight = 20

6-33 White & Becker Tools (W&B) requires 2,000 electric motors next month for its product line of weed trimmers. Each motor is composed of three components: a coil, a shaft, and housing. W&B has the capability to produce these components or purchase them from an outside vendor. The costs of producing them and purchasing them are shown in the following table.

COMPONENT	PRODUCTION COST PER UNIT	PURCHASE COST PER UNIT
Coil	$2.60	$3.12
Shaft	$1.80	$2.16
Housing	$1.40	$1.68

The components that are produced by W&B must pass through three departments: fabrication, molding, and inspection. The number of hours each component requires in each department and the total number of hours available next month in each department are shown in the following table:

DEPARTMENT	COIL (HR.)	SHAFT (HR.)	HOUSING (HR.)	AVAILABILITY (HR.)
Fabrication	0.5	0.2	0.6	3,000
Molding	0.4	0.7	0.3	3,000
Inspection	0.2	0.3	0.4	1,800

In order to determine the number of components that will be produced and the number that will be purchased, W&B has set the following goals, in rank order:

Rank 1: The total costs to produce and purchase components next month should not exceed $14,000.
Rank 2: Idle time in the fabrication department should be minimized.
Rank 3: At least 200 coils should be purchased from the vendor next month.

Determine the number of components produced and purchased next month, according to these ranked goals.

6-34 Pendelton County plans to develop several new recreational facilities that must be completed within the $3.5 million budget. A survey of county residents has resulted in information about the types of facilities that county residents would like to see built, as described in the following table. The table also shows the cost to construct and maintain each facility, the acres each facility will require, and the average monthly usage of each facility. The county has decided that at least 15 facilities will be built and has set aside 55 acres to be used for construction.

FACILITY	COST PER FACILITY	ACRES PER FACILITY	PEOPLE PER MONTH	ANNUAL MAINTENANCE
Basketball courts	$300,000	3	700	$3,000
Baseball fields	$250,000	5	1,000	$6,000
Playgrounds	$ 75,000	2	800	$3,000
Soccer fields	$175,000	3	1,200	$7,000

The county has also established the following list of ranked goals:

Rank 1: It would like to spend the entire budget.
Rank 2: It would like to build enough facilities so that 15,000 people or more each month can use them.
Rank 3: It wants to avoid using more than the 55 acres that have been set aside for the project.
Rank 4: It would like to avoid spending more than $80,000 per year on maintenance costs for the new facilities.

How many of each type of facility should be constructed?

6-35 Theo Harris earns $55,000 a year and has $9,000 to invest in a portfolio. His investment alternatives and their expected returns are shown in the table at the top of the next column.

INVESTMENT	DESCRIPTION	EXPECTED RETURN
A	IRA (retirement)	3.5%
B	Employer's retirement plan	4.5%
C	Deferred income (retirement)	8.0%
D	Unity mutual fund	7.0%
E	Liberty mutual fund	7.5%
F	Money market	5.5%

Theo's investment goals are as follows and can be ranked according to the weights shown in parenthesis. Which investments should be included in Theo's portfolio, and how much should he invest in each?

Goal 1: (25) Invest all funds available.
Goal 2: (20) Maximize the total annual return in dollars, with a target of $1,000.
Goal 3: (15) Invest at least 3% of salary in employer's retirement plan.
Goal 4: (15) Invest at least 10% of the total investment in the money market.
Goal 5: (10) Invest at most 25% of the total investment in retirement plans.
Goal 6: (10) Invest at least 50% of the total investment in non-retirement plans.
Goal 7: (5) Invest at most 50% of the total investment in mutual funds.

Which investments should be included in John's portfolio?

6-36 A hospital kitchen needs to make a fruit salad that contains at least 6,500 units of vitamin A and 1,800 units of vitamin C. Data on five available fruits are shown in the following table.

FRUIT TYPE	VITAMIN A (UNITS/LB.)	VITAMIN C (UNITS/LB.)	COST PER LB.	MAXIMUM AVAILABLE (LB.)
Apple	330	36	$1.49	No limit
Banana	367	41	$0.49	11
Grape	453	18	$1.69	8
Pear	91	18	$0.99	No limit
Strawberry	122	254	$2.99	14

It is estimated that at least 24 pounds, but no more than 32 pounds, of fruit salad will be necessary. The following goals (in rank order) need to be considered for the mix:

Rank 1: The salad should cost no more than $30.
Rank 2: At least 6 pounds of bananas should be in the salad.
Rank 3: At least 3 pounds of pears should be in the salad.

6-37 Consider the following NLP problem:

$$\text{Maximize } 10X_1 + 15X_2 + 25X_3$$

subject to the constraints

$$\begin{aligned} X_1 + X_2 + X_3 &\le 12 \\ X_1^2 + X_2^2 &\le 32 \\ 2X_1 + X_3^3 &\le 44 \\ X_1, X_2, X_3 &\ge 0 \end{aligned}$$

(a) Set up and solve the model by using Solver. Use a starting value of zero for each decision variable.
(b) Is the solution obtained a local optimal or global optimal solution? How do you know?

6-38 Consider the following NLP problem:

$$\text{Maximize } 2X_1 + X_2 - 2X_3 + 3X_1X_2 + 7X_3^3$$

subject to the constraints

$$\begin{aligned} 2X_1 + 4X_2 + 3X_3 &\ge 34 \\ 3X_1 + X_2 &\ge 10 \\ X_1 + X_2 + X_3 &\le 12 \\ X_1, X_2, X_3 &\ge 0 \end{aligned}$$

(a) Set up and solve the model by using Solver. Use a starting value of zero for each decision variable.
(b) Is the solution obtained a local optimal or global optimal solution? How do you know?

6-39 Hinkel Rotary Engine, Ltd., produces four-, six-, and eight-cylinder models of automobile engines. The firm's profit for each four-cylinder engine sold during its quarterly production cycle is $\$1{,}800 - \$50X_1$, where X_1 is the number of four-cylinder engines sold. Hinkel makes a profit of $\$2{,}400 - \$70X_2$ for each of the six-cylinder engines sold, with X_2 equal to the number of six-cylinder engines sold. The profit associated with each eight-cylinder engine is $\$1{,}950 - \$65X_3^3$, where X_3 is equal to the number of eight-cylinder engines sold. There are 5,000 hours of production time available during each production cycle. A four-cylinder engine requires 100 hours of production time, a six-cylinder engine takes 130 hours, and an eight-cylinder model takes 140 hours to manufacture. Formulate this production problem for Hinkel and solve it by using Excel. Use several different starting values for the decision variables to try to identify a global optimal solution.

6-40 A snowmobile manufacturer produces three models, the XJ6, the XJ7, and the XJ8. In any given production-planning week, the company has 40 hours available in its final testing bay. Each XJ6 requires 1 hour of testing, each XJ7 requires 1.5 hours, and each XJ8 takes 1.6 hours. The revenue (in $thousands) per unit of each model is defined as ($\$4 - \$0.1X_1$) for XJ6, ($\$5 - \$0.2X_2$) for XJ7, and ($\$6 - \$0.2X_3$) for XJ8, where X_1, X_2, and X_3 are the numbers of XJ6, XJ7, and XJ8 models made, respectively. Formulate this problem to maximize revenue and solve it by using Excel. Use several different starting values for the decision variables to try to identify a global optimal solution.

6-41 Susan Jones would like her investment portfolio to be selected from a combination of three stocks—Alpha, Beta, and Gamma. Let variables A, B, and G denote the percentages of the portfolio devoted to Alpha, Beta, and Gamma, respectively. Susan's objective is to minimize the variance of the portfolio's return, given by the following function:

$$3A^2 + 2B^2 + 2G^2 + 2AB - 1.1AG - 0.7BG$$

The expected returns for Alpha, Beta, and Gamma are 15%, 11%, and 9%, respectively. Susan wants the expected return for the total portfolio to be at least 10%. No individual stock can constitute more than 70% of the portfolio. Formulate this portfolio selection problem and solve using Excel. Use several different starting values for the decision variables to try to identify a global optimal solution.

6-42 Ashworth Industries would like to make a price and production decision on two of its products. Define Q_A and Q_B as the quantities of products A and B to produce and P_A and P_B as the price for products A and B. The weekly quantities of A and B that are sold are functions of the price, according to the following expressions:

$$Q_A = 5{,}500 - 200P_A$$
$$Q_B = 4{,}500 - 225P_B$$

The variable costs per unit of A and B are \$18 and \$12, respectively. The weekly production capacity for A and B are 275 and 350 units, respectively. Each unit of A requires 1 hour of labor, while each unit of B requires 2 hours. There are 700 hours of labor available each week. What quantities and price of products A and B will maximize weekly profit? (*Hint:* Set up the objective function in terms of profit per unit multiplied by the number of units produced for both products.) Use several different starting values for the decision variables to try to identify a global optimal solution.

6-43 The Kimten Manufacturing Company needs to process 18 jobs. Kimten can process each job on any of the six machines it has available, but each job must be allocated to only one machine. Iqbal Ahmed, production supervisor at Kimten, wants to allocate jobs to machines in such a manner that all machines have total loads that are as close as possible to each other. The machine hours required for each job are shown in the following table.

JOB	MACHINE HOURS
1	39.43
2	27.94
3	40.27
4	18.27
5	12.72
6	35.20
7	27.94
8	17.20
9	17.20
10	17.20
11	21.50
12	16.74
13	28.29
14	6.07
15	16.01
16	18.49
17	12.16
18	36.67

Case Study

Schank Marketing Research

Schank Marketing Research has just signed contracts to conduct studies for four clients. At present, three project managers are free for assignment to the tasks. Although all are capable of handling each assignment, the times and costs to complete the studies depend on the experience and knowledge of each manager. Using his judgment, John Schank, the president, has been able to establish a cost for each possible assignment. These costs are summarized in the following table.

	CLIENT			
PROJECT MANAGER	HINES CORP.	NBT INC.	GENERAL FOUNDRY	CBT TV
Gardener	\$320,000	\$300,000	\$280,000	\$290,000
Ruthman	\$270,000	\$320,000	\$300,000	\$310,000
Hardgraves	\$190,000	\$210,000	\$330,000	\$210,000

Schank is hesitant about neglecting NBT, which has been an important customer in the past. In addition, Schank has promised to try to assign Ruthman to a study worth at least $300,000. From previous contracts, Schank also knows that Gardener does not get along well with the management at CBT Television, so he hopes to avoid assigning him to CBT. Finally, because Hines Corporation is also an old and valued client, Schank feels that it is twice as important to assign a project manager immediately to Hines's task as it is to provide one to General Foundry, a brand-new client. Schank wants to minimize the total costs of all projects while considering each of these goals. He feels that all these goals are important, but if he had to rank them, he would put his concern about NBT first, his worry about Gardener second, his need to keep Hines Corporation happy third, his promise to Ruthman fourth, and his concern about minimizing all costs last.

Each project manager can handle, at most, one new client.

Discussion Questions

1. If Schank were not concerned about non-cost goals, how would he formulate this problem so that it could be solved quantitatively?
2. Develop a formulation that will incorporate all five objectives.
3. Solve this problem by using Excel.

Case Study

Oakton River Bridge

The Oakton River had long been considered an impediment to the development of a certain medium-sized metropolitan area in the Southeast. Lying to the east of the city, the river made it difficult for people living on its eastern bank to commute to jobs in and around the city and to take advantage of the shopping and cultural attractions that the city had to offer. Similarly, the river inhibited those on its western bank from access to the ocean resorts lying one hour to the east. The bridge over the Oakton River was built prior to World War II and was grossly inadequate to handle the existing traffic, much less the increased traffic that would accompany the forecasted growth in the area. A congressional delegation from the state prevailed upon the federal government to fund a major portion of a new toll bridge over the Oakton River, and the state legislature appropriated the rest of the needed monies for the project.

Progress in construction of the bridge has been in accordance with what was anticipated at the start of construction. The state highway commission, which will have operational jurisdiction over the bridge, has concluded that opening of the bridge for traffic is likely to take place at the beginning of the next summer, as scheduled. A personnel task force has been established to recruit, train, and schedule the workers needed to operate the toll facility.

The personnel task force is well aware of the budgetary problems facing the state. It has taken as part of its mandate the requirement that personnel costs be kept as low as possible. One particular area of concern is the number of toll collectors that will be needed. The bridge is scheduling three shifts of collectors: shift A from midnight to 8 A.M., shift B from 8 A.M. to 4 P.M., and shift C from 4 P.M. to midnight. Recently, the state employees' union negotiated a contract with the state which requires that all toll collectors be permanent, full-time employees. In addition, all collectors must work a five-on, two-off schedule on the same shift. Thus, for example, a worker could be assigned to work Tuesday, Wednesday, Thursday, Friday, and Saturday on shift A, followed by Sunday and Monday off. An employee could not be scheduled to work, say, Tuesday on shift A followed by Wednesday, Thursday, Friday, and Saturday on shift B or on any other mixture of shifts during a five-day block. The employees would choose their assignments in order of their seniority.

The task force has received projections of traffic flow on the bridge by day and hour. These projections are based on extrapolations of existing traffic patterns—the pattern of commuting, shopping, and beach traffic currently experienced, with growth projections factored in. Standards data from other state-operated toll facilities have allowed the

	MINIMUM NUMBER OF TOLL COLLECTORS REQUIRED PER SHIFT						
SHIFT	SUN.	MON.	TUE.	WED.	THU.	FRI.	SAT.
A	8	13	12	12	13	13	15
B	10	10	10	10	10	13	15
C	15	13	13	12	12	13	8

task force to convert these traffic flows into toll collector requirements—that is, the minimum number of collectors required per shift, per day, to handle the anticipated traffic load. These toll collector requirements are summarized in the table at the bottom of the previous page.

The numbers in the table include one or two extra collectors per shift to fill in for collectors who call in sick and to provide relief for collectors on their scheduled breaks. Note that each of the eight collectors needed for shift A on Sunday, for example, could come from any of the A shifts scheduled to begin on Wednesday, Thursday, Friday, Saturday, or Sunday.

Discussion Questions

1. Determine the minimum number of toll collectors that would have to be hired to meet the requirements expressed in the table.
2. The union had indicated that it might lift its opposition to the mixing of shifts in a five-day block in exchange for additional compensation and benefits. By how much could the numbers of toll collectors required be reduced if this were done?

Source: B. Render, R. M. Stair, and I. Greenberg. *Cases and Readings in Management Science*, 2nd ed. 1990, pp. 55–56. Reprinted by permission of Pearson Education, Inc., Upper Saddle River, NJ.

Case Study

Easley Shopping Center

The town of Easley, South Carolina, has experienced tremendous growth over the past few years. After a long and spirited discussion, the town council has unanimously decided to build Easley's first big shopping center. On the recommendation of the town planner, Jimmy Barnes, the council has decided to hire the Ray Development Company (RDC) to help in the shopping center's planning and construction. RDC has a great deal of experience in building malls and shopping centers in the southeastern U.S., and the town council is confident they will help Easley identify the right stores for its new shopping center.

Jennifer Ray, president of RDC, has quickly identified and signed two major anchor stores as well as several other attractive tenants for the shopping center. After assigning suitable spaces to these tenants, Jennifer has 32,000 square feet of space still available for allocation. She and Jimmy are now tasked with deciding which stores to locate in this available space. Due to the significant market interest in Easley's new shopping center, Jennifer and Jimmy are confident that they will not have any trouble finding tenants to suit whatever allocation plan they decide to use.

After extensive study, Jennifer has drawn up a list of 20 different stores she thinks she and Jimmy should consider for the

TABLE 6.9 Details of Possible Stores at Easley Shopping Center

STORE	STORE TYPE	SQ. FT. NEEDED	ANNUAL RENT	ANNUAL SALES	UPFIT COST
Bath & Body Products	Specialty	2,000	$ 35,000	$ 650,000	$40,000
Beauty Parlor	Service	3,000	$ 50,000	$ 500,000	$35,000
Children's Clothing	Apparel	4,800	$ 70,000	$1,750,000	$35,000
Chinese Fast Food	Food	2,400	$ 40,000	$ 800,000	$27,000
Electronics Store	Specialty	6,400	$ 80,000	$1,300,000	$75,000
Game Arcade	Service	6,000	$ 70,000	$1,250,000	$40,000
Hardware Store	Housewares	7,200	$ 95,000	$1,200,000	$55,000
Hobby Store	Specialty	3,600	$ 50,000	$ 550,000	$29,000
Ice Cream Store	Food	1,600	$ 30,000	$ 500,000	$20,000
Kitchen Store	Housewares	6,400	$ 80,000	$ 900,000	$42,000
Lingerie Store	Apparel	3,600	$ 55,000	$1,250,000	$30,000
Luggage Store	Housewares	4,000	$ 70,000	$ 650,000	$34,000
Men's Clothing	Apparel	7,000	$100,000	$2,000,000	$40,000
Pizza Parlor	Food	4,800	$ 62,000	$1,200,000	$31,000
Shoe Store	Apparel	4,800	$ 60,000	$1,400,000	$40,000
Sports Bar	Food	4,000	$ 80,000	$1,300,000	$50,000
Tex-Mex Fast Food	Food	2,400	$ 35,000	$1,100,000	$35,000
Toy Store	Specialty	4,800	$ 70,000	$1,000,000	$50,000
Travel Agency	Service	2,000	$ 30,000	$ 400,000	$15,000
Women's Clothing	Apparel	7,000	$120,000	$2,250,000	$65,000

available space. Table 6.9 on the previous page lists these stores in alphabetical order, along with the floor space required by each store, the annual rent the store would pay for the space, the expected annual sales at the store, and the expected upfit cost to renovate the allotted space to make it suitable for the store.

As per the leasing agreement developed by RDC, each store would pay the town an annual rent for its allotted space. The town council has mandated that the total rent payments each year must be sufficient to cover the annual fixed cost of maintaining the shopping center. This cost, which includes items such as security, janitorial services, maintenance, and utilities, is estimated to be $500,000 per year. In addition, the town council has specified that the total upfit amount spent on renovating the space to suit these stores cannot exceed 60% of the actual total annual rent that would be collected.

In order to make the shopping center attractive to a broad range of customers, Jennifer believes it must adhere to certain conditions in terms of the mix of stores. Taking into account the tenants that have already been signed for the shopping center, she thinks the remaining space should contain at least two stores each in the apparel, food, and specialty types, and at least one store each in the housewares and service types. She also thinks that there should be no more than three stores of any type, and that the number of food and service stores should not exceed the total number of stores in the other three types.

RDC has proposed an arrangement under which the town would receive a fixed percentage of the total annual sales generated by the stores. The town council therefore wants to identify the solution that would generate the maximum total sales from these stores.

Discussion Question

How should the remaining space in Easley's new shopping center be allotted?

Internet Case Studies

See the Companion Website for this textbook, at www.pearsonhighered.com/balakrishnan, for additional case studies.

CHAPTER 7

Project Management

LEARNING OBJECTIVES

After completing this chapter, students will be able to:

1. Understand how to plan, monitor, and control projects using PERT/CPM.
2. Determine earliest start, earliest finish, latest start, latest finish, and slack times for each activity.
3. Understand the impact of variability in activity times on the project completion time.
4. Develop resource loading charts to plan, monitor, and control the use of various resources during a project.
5. Use LP to find the least-cost solution to reduce total project time and solve these LP models using Excel's Solver.
6. Understand the important role of software such as Microsoft Project in project management.

CHAPTER OUTLINE

7.1 Introduction

Every organization at one time or another will take on a large and complex project. For example, when Microsoft Corporation sets out to develop a major new operating system (e.g., Windows 7), a program costing hundreds of millions of dollars, and has hundreds of programmers working on millions of lines of code, immense stakes ride on the project being delivered properly and on time. Likewise, whenever STX Europe AS, a leading builder of cruise and offshore vessels headquartered in Oslo, Noway undertakes the construction of a cruise ship, this large, expensive project requires the coordination of tens of thousands of steps. Companies in almost every industry worry about how to manage similar large-scale complicated projects effectively.[1]

Project management techniques can be used to manage large, complex projects.

Scheduling large projects is a difficult challenge for most managers, especially when the stakes are high. There are numerous press reports of firms that have incurred millions of dollars in cost overruns in their projects for various reasons; one prominent recent example is Boeing's Dreamliner project. Unnecessary delays have occurred in many projects due to poor scheduling, and companies have gone bankrupt due to poor controls. How can such problems be solved? The answers lie in a popular decision modeling approach known as **project management**.

Phases in Project Management

There are three phases in managing large projects.

A *project* can be defined as a series of related tasks (or activities) directed toward a major well-defined output. A project can consist of thousands of specific activities, each with its own set of requirements of time, money, and other resources, such as labor, raw materials, and machinery. Regardless of the scope and nature of the project, the management of large projects involves the three phases discussed in the following sections (see Figure 7.1). Each phase addresses specific questions regarding the project.

Project planning is the first phase.

PROJECT PLANNING Project planning is the first phase of project management and involves considering issues such as goal setting, defining the project, and team organization. Specific questions that are considered in this phase include the following:

1. What is the goal or objective of the project?
2. What are the various activities (or tasks) that constitute the project?
3. How are these activities linked? That is, what are the precedence relationships between the activities?
4. What is the time required for each activity?
5. What other resources (e.g., labor, raw materials, machinery) are required for each activity?

Project scheduling is the second phase.

PROJECT SCHEDULING The second phase of project management involves developing the specific time schedule for each activity and assigning people, money, and supplies to specific activities. The questions addressed in this phase should be considered soon after the project has been planned but *before* it is actually started. These questions include the following:

1. When will the entire project be completed?
2. What is the schedule (start and finish time) for each activity?
3. What are the critical activities in the project? That is, what activities will delay the entire project if they are late?
4. What are the noncritical activities in the project? That is, what activities can run late without delaying the completion time of the entire project?
5. By how much can a noncritical activity be delayed without affecting the completion time of the entire project?
6. If we take the variability in activity times into consideration, what is the probability that a project will be completed by a specific deadline?

Gantt charts are useful for project scheduling.

One popular project scheduling approach is to use a **Gantt chart**. Gantt charts are low-cost means of helping managers make sure that (1) all activities are planned for, (2) their order of

[1] Portions of sections 7.1 and 7.2 have been adapted from J. Heizer and B. Render. *Operations Management*, Tenth Edition, © 2011. Adapted by permission of Pearson Eduction, Inc., Upper Saddle River, NJ.

FIGURE 7.1
Project Planning, Scheduling, and Controlling

Source: Adapted from J. Heizer and B. Render. *Operations Management*, Eighth Edition, © 2006. Reprinted by permission of Pearson Education, Inc., Upper Saddle River, NJ.

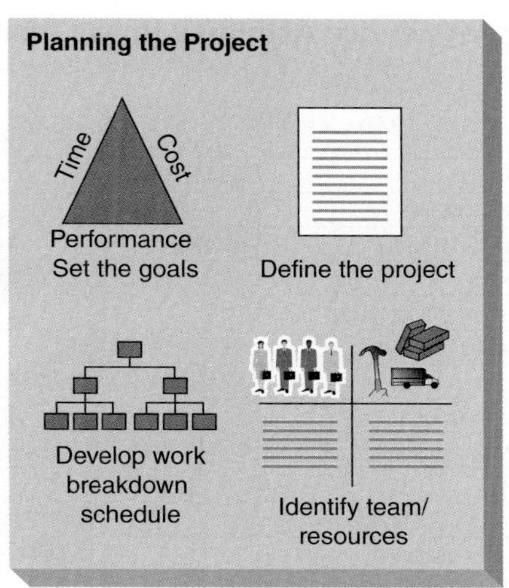

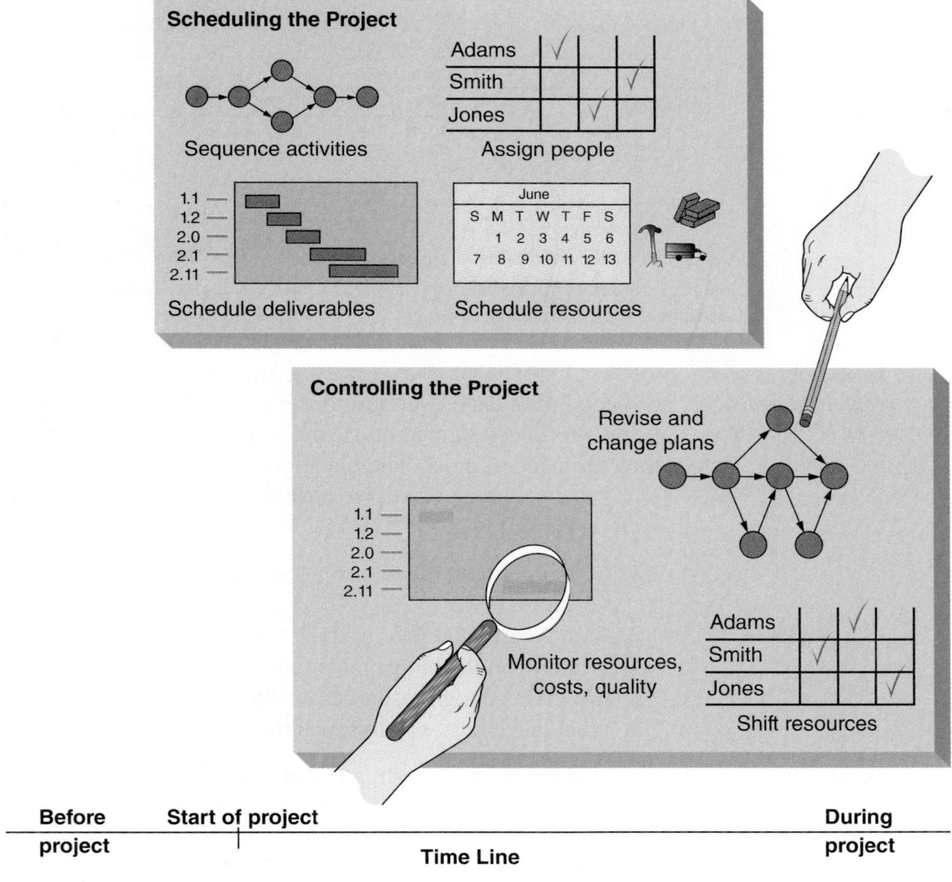

performance is accounted for, (3) the activity time schedules are recorded, and (4) the overall project time is developed. Gantt charts are easy to construct and understand, and they permit managers to plan and track the progress of each activity. For example, Figure 7.2 shows the Gantt chart for a routine servicing of a Delta jetliner during a 60-minute layover. Horizontal bars are drawn for each project activity along a time line.

For large projects, Gantt charts are used mainly to provide project summaries.

On simple projects, Gantt charts such as the one in Figure 7.2 can be used alone. Gantt charts, though, do not adequately illustrate the interrelationships between the activities and the resources. For this reason, on most large projects, Gantt charts are used mainly to provide summaries of a project's status. Projects are planned and scheduled using other network-based approaches, as discussed in subsequent sections.

FIGURE 7.2 Gantt Chart of Service Activities for a Commercial Aircraft During a Layover

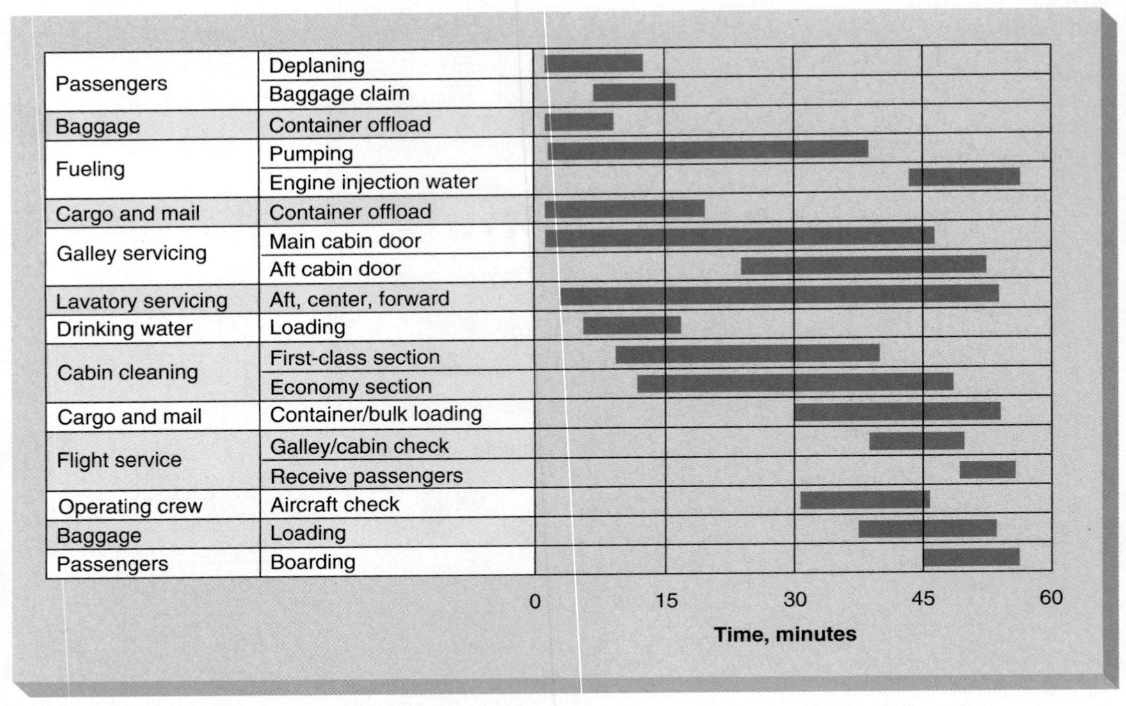

Source: J. Heizer and B. Render. *Operations Management*, Eighth Edition, © 2006. Adapted by permission of Pearson Education, Inc., Upper Saddle River, NJ.

Projects must be monitored and controlled at regular intervals. Project controlling is the third phase.

PROJECT CONTROLLING Like the control of any other management system, the control of large projects involves close monitoring of schedules, resources, and budgets. Control also means using a feedback loop to revise the project plan and having the ability to shift resources to where they are needed most. The questions addressed in this phase should be considered at regular intervals during the project to ensure that it meets all time and cost schedules. These questions include the following:

1. At any particular date or time, is the project on schedule, behind schedule, or ahead of schedule?
2. At any particular date or time, is the money spent on the project equal to, less than, or greater than the budgeted amount?
3. Are there enough resources available to finish the project on time?
4. What is the best way to finish the project in a shorter amount of time and at the least cost?

In this chapter, we investigate how project management techniques can be used to answer all these questions.

Use of Software Packages in Project Management

Software packages automate many of the routine calculations in project management.

In recent times, managing large and complex projects has become considerably easier due to the availability and capabilities of specialized project management software packages. These programs typically have simple interfaces for entering the project data, and they automate many of the routine calculations required for effective project management. In addition, they are capable of efficiently presenting the status of a project, using comprehensive graphs and tables. Some of these programs are Microsoft Project (by Microsoft Corp.), Primavera Project Planner (by Primavera Systems, Inc.), Turboproject (by OfficeWork Software), and Prochain Project Management (by Prochain Solutions, Inc.).

These programs produce a broad variety of reports, including (1) detailed cost breakdowns for each task, (2) total program labor curves, (3) cost distribution tables, (4) functional cost and hour summaries, (5) raw material expenditure forecasts, (6) variance reports, (7) time analysis reports, and (8) work status reports.

Excel is not a convenient software tool to use for project management.

Although it is possible to set up spreadsheets to perform many of the routine calculations involved, Excel is not the ideal choice for such tasks. So, in this chapter, we illustrate how Microsoft Project can be used to plan, schedule, and monitor projects.

There are, however, some issues that Microsoft Project does not handle. One such issue is question 4 posed in the section "Project Controlling" (What is the best way to finish the project in a shorter amount of time and at the least cost?) We can best answer this question by setting up and solving the problem as a linear programming (LP) model. For this question, we describe using Excel's Solver to solve the LP model.

7.2 Project Networks

Once a project's mission or goal has been clearly specified, the first issues we need to address deal with *project planning*. That is, we need to identify the activities that constitute the project, the precedence relationships between those activities, and the time and other resources required for each **activity**.

Identifying Activities

A project can be subdivided into several activities.

Almost any large project can be subdivided into a series of smaller activities or tasks. Identifying the activities involved in a project and the precedence relationships that may exist between these activities is the responsibility of the project team. In subdividing a project into various activities, however, the project team must be careful to ensure the following:

- Each activity has clearly identifiable starting and ending points. In other words, we should be able to recognize when an activity has started and when it has ended. For example, if the project goal is to build a house, an activity may be to lay the foundation. It is possible to clearly recognize when we start this activity and when we finish this activity.
- Each activity is clearly distinguishable from every other activity. That is, we should be able to associate every action we take and every dollar we spend with a specific (and unique) activity. For example, while building a house, we need to be able to recognize which actions and expenses are associated with laying the foundation.

An activity in a project may be a project of its own.

The number of activities in a project depends on the nature and scope of the project. It also depends on the level of detail with which the project manager wants to monitor and control the project. In a typical project, it is common for each activity in the project to be a project of its own. That is, a project may actually be a master project that, in turn, consists of several miniprojects. In practice, it is convenient to develop a work breakdown structure to identify the activities in a project.

A work breakdown structure details the activities in a project.

WORK BREAKDOWN STRUCTURE A **work breakdown structure (WBS)** defines a project by dividing it into its major subcomponents, which are then subdivided into more detailed subcomponents, and so on. Gross requirements for people, supplies, and equipment are also estimated in this planning phase. The WBS typically decreases in size from top to bottom and is indented like this:

Level	
1	Project
2	Major tasks in the project
3	Subtasks in major tasks
4	Activities to be completed

This hierarchical framework can be illustrated with the development of Microsoft's next operating system, internally code-named Windows 8. As we see in Figure 7.3, the project, creating a new operating system, is labeled 1.0. The first step is to identify the major tasks in the project (level 2). Two examples would be development of graphical user interfaces (GUIs) (1.1) and creating compatibility with previous versions of Windows (1.2). The major subtasks for 1.2 would be creating a team to handle compatibility with Windows 7 (1.21), Windows Vista

FIGURE 7.3
Work Breakdown Structure

Source: Adapted from J. Heizer and B. Render. *Operations Management*, Eighth Edition, © 2006. Reprinted by permission of Pearson Education, Inc., Upper Saddle River, NJ.

Level	Level ID Number	Activity
1	1.0	Develop/launch Windows 8 operating system
2	1.1	Development of GUIs
2	1.2	Ensure compatibility with earlier Windows versions
3	1.21	Compatibility with Windows 7
3	1.22	Compatibility with Windows Vista
3	1.23	Compatibility with Windows XP
4	1.231	Ability to import files

(1.22), Windows XP (1.23), and so on. Then each major subtask is broken down into level 4 activities that need to be done, such as importing files created in the previous version (1.231), saving files to work with the previous version (1.232), etc. There are usually many level 4 activities.

Identifying Activity Times and Other Resources

Activity times need to be estimated.

Once the activities of a project have been identified, the time required and other resources (e.g., money, labor, raw materials) for each activity are determined. In practice, identifying this input data is a complicated task involving a fair amount of expertise and competence on the project leader's part. For example, many individuals automatically present inflated time estimates, especially if their job is on the line if they fail to complete the activity on time. The project leader has to be able to recognize these types of issues and adjust the time estimates accordingly.

Project Management Techniques: PERT and CPM

PERT and CPM are two popular project management techniques.

When the questions in the project planning phase have been addressed, we move on to the project scheduling phase. The **program evaluation and review technique (PERT)** and the **critical path method (CPM)** are two popular decision modeling procedures that help managers answer the questions in the scheduling phase, even for large and complex projects. They were developed because there was a critical need for a better way to manage projects (see the *History* box).

Although some people still view PERT and CPM as separate techniques and refer to them by their original names, the two are similar in basic approach. The growing practice, therefore, is to refer to PERT and CPM simply as *project management* techniques.

HISTORY How PERT and CPM Started

Managers have been planning, scheduling, monitoring, and controlling large-scale projects for hundreds of years, but it has only been in the past 50 years that decision modeling techniques have been applied to major projects. One of the earliest techniques was the *Gantt chart*. This type of chart shows the start and finish times of one or more activities, as shown in the accompanying chart.

In 1958, the Special Projects Office of the U.S. Navy developed the program evaluation and review technique (PERT) to plan and control the Polaris missile program. This project involved the coordination of thousands of contractors. Today, PERT is still used to monitor countless government contract schedules. At about the same time (1957), the critical path method (CPM) was developed by J. E. Kelly of Remington Rand and M. R. Walker of du Pont. Originally, CPM was used to assist in the building and maintenance of chemical plants at du Pont.

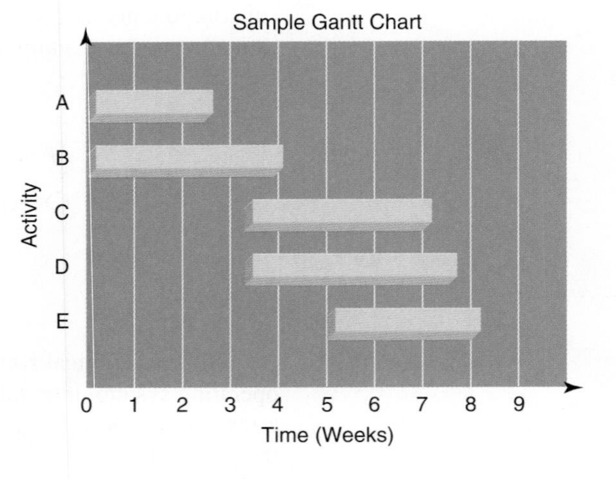

PERT is a probabilistic technique, whereas CPM is a deterministic technique.

PERT VERSUS CPM The primary difference between PERT and CPM is in the way the time needed for each activity in a project is estimated. In PERT, each activity has three time estimates that are combined to determine the expected activity completion time and its variance. PERT is considered a *probabilistic* technique; it allows us to find the probability that the entire project will be completed by a specific due date.

In contrast, CPM is a *deterministic* approach. It estimates the completion time of each activity using a single time estimate. This estimate, called the *standard* or *normal* time, is the time we estimate it will take under typical conditions to complete the activity. In some cases, CPM also associates a second time estimate with each activity. This estimate, called the *crash time*, is the shortest time it would take to finish an activity if additional funds and resources were allocated to the activity.

As noted previously, identifying these time estimates is a complicated task in most real-world projects. In our discussions in this chapter, however, we will assume that the time estimates (a single time estimate in CPM and three time estimates in PERT) are available for each activity.

Project Management Example: General Foundry, Inc.

General Foundry, Inc., a metal works plant in Milwaukee, has long tried to avoid the expense of installing air pollution control equipment. The local environmental protection agency has recently given the foundry 16 weeks to install a complex air filter system on its main smokestack. General Foundry has been warned that it may be forced to close unless the device is installed in the allotted period. Lester Harky, the managing partner, wants to make sure that installation of the filtering system progresses smoothly and on time.

Activities in the General Foundry project

General Foundry has identified the eight activities that need to be performed in order for the project to be completed. When the project begins, two activities can be simultaneously started: building the internal components for the device (activity A) and making the modifications necessary for the floor and roof (activity B). The construction of the collection stack (activity C) can begin when the internal components are completed. Pouring the concrete floor and installing the frame (activity D) can be started as soon as the internal components are completed and the roof and floor have been modified.

After the collection stack has been constructed, two activities can begin: building the high-temperature burner (activity E) and installing the pollution control system (activity F). The air pollution device can be installed (activity G) after the concrete floor has been poured, the frame has been installed, and the high-temperature burner has been built. Finally, after the control system and pollution device have been installed, the system can be inspected and tested (activity H).

All these activities and precedence relationships seem rather confusing and complex when they are presented in a descriptive form, as here. It is therefore convenient to list all the activity information in a table, as shown in Table 7.1. We see in the table that activity A is listed as an **immediate predecessor** of activity C. Likewise, both activities D and E must be performed prior to starting activity G.

It is enough to list only the immediate predecessors for each activity.

Note that it is enough to list just the immediate predecessors for each activity. For example, in Table 7.1, because activity A precedes activity C and activity C precedes activity E, the fact that activity A precedes activity E is *implicit*. This relationship need not be explicitly shown in the activity precedence relationships.

Networks consist of nodes that are connected by arcs.

When a project has many activities with fairly complicated precedence relationships, it is difficult for an individual to comprehend the complexity of the project from just the tabular information. In such cases, a visual representation of the project, using a project network, is

TABLE 7.1 Activities and Their Immediate Predecessors for General Foundry

ACTIVITY	DESCRIPTION	IMMEDIATE PREDECESSORS
A	Build internal components	—
B	Modify roof and floor	—
C	Construct collection stack	A
D	Pour concrete and install frame	A, B
E	Build high-temperature burner	C
F	Install pollution control system	C
G	Install air pollution device	D, E
H	Inspect and test	F, G

FIGURE 7.4
Beginning AON Network for General Foundry

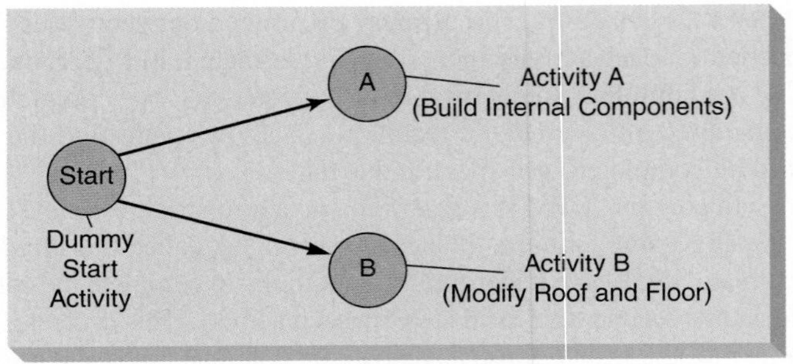

convenient and useful. A **project network** is a diagram of all the activities and the precedence relationships that exist between these activities in a project. We now illustrate how to construct a project network for General Foundry, Inc.

Drawing the Project Network

There are two types of project networks—AON and AOA.

Recall from the discussion in Chapter 5 that a network consists of nodes (or points) and arcs (or lines) that connect the nodes together. There are two approaches to drawing a project network: **activity on node (AON) network** and **activity on arc (AOA) network**. In the AON approach, we denote each activity with a node. Arcs represent precedence relationships between activities. In contrast, in the AOA approach, we represent each activity with an arc. Each node represents an **event**, such as the start or finish of an activity.

Although both approaches are popular in practice, many of the project management software packages, including Microsoft Project, use AON networks. For this reason, we focus only on AON networks in this chapter. For details on AOA project networks, we refer you to a project management textbook.

Nodes denote activities in an AON network.

AON NETWORK FOR GENERAL FOUNDRY In the General Foundry example, two activities (A and B) do not have any predecessors. We draw separate nodes for each of these activities, as shown in Figure 7.4. Although not required, it is usually convenient to have a unique starting activity for a project. We have therefore included a **dummy activity** called Start in Figure 7.4. This dummy activity does not really exist and takes up zero time and resources. Activity Start is an immediate predecessor for both activities A and B, and it serves as the unique starting activity for the entire project.

Arcs denote precedence relationships in an AON network.

We now show the precedence relationships by using arcs (shown with arrow symbols: $\rightarrow$). For example, an arrow from activity Start to activity A indicates that Start is a predecessor for activity A. In a similar fashion, we draw an arrow from Start to B.

Next, we add a new node for activity C. Because activity A precedes activity C, we draw an arc from node A to node C (see Figure 7.5). Likewise, we first draw a node to represent activity D. Then, because activities A and B both precede activity D, we draw arcs from A to D and from B to D (see Figure 7.5).

We proceed in this fashion, adding a separate node for each activity and a separate arc for each precedence relationship that exists. The complete AON project network for the General Foundry project example is shown in Figure 7.6.

FIGURE 7.5
Intermediate AON Network for General Foundry

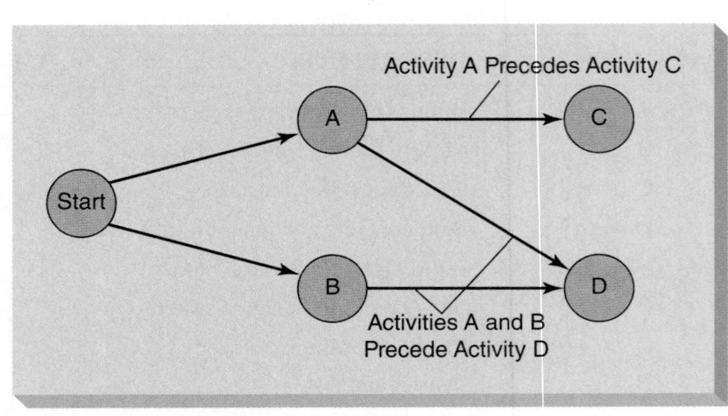

FIGURE 7.6 Complete AON Network for General Foundry

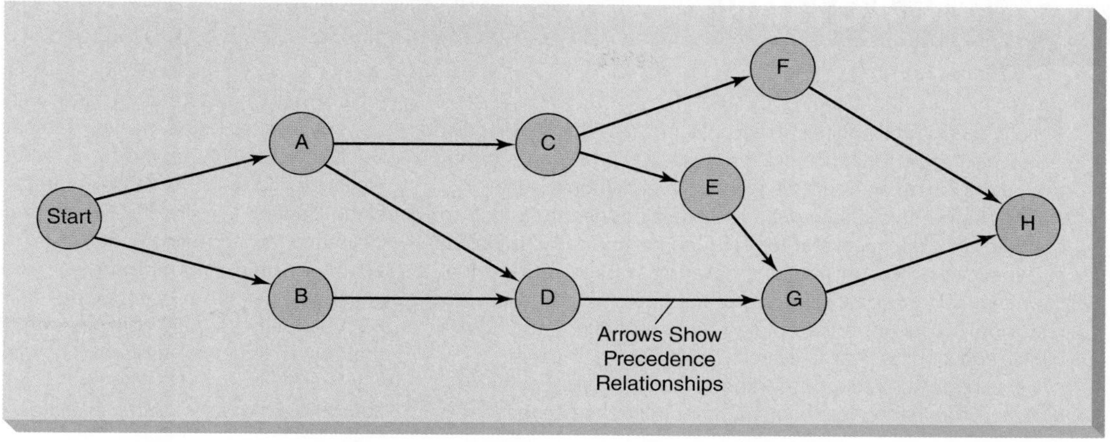

Drawing a project network properly takes some time and experience. When we first draw a project network, it is not unusual that we place our nodes (activities) in the network in such a fashion that the arcs (precedence relationships) are not simple straight lines. That is, the arcs could be intersecting each other and even facing in opposite directions. For example, if we switched the locations of the nodes for activities E and F in Figure 7.6, the arcs from F to H and E to G would intersect. Although such a project network is perfectly valid, it is good practice to have a well-drawn network. One rule that we especially recommend is to place the nodes in such a fashion that all arrows point in the same direction. To achieve this, we suggest that you first draw a rough draft version of the network to make sure all the relationships are shown. Then you can redraw the network to make appropriate changes in the location of the nodes.

It is convenient, but not required, to have unique starting and ending activities in a project.

As with the unique starting node, it is convenient to have the project network finish with a unique ending node. In the General Foundry example, it turns out that a unique activity, H, is the last activity in the project. We therefore automatically have a unique ending node here. However, in situations where a project has multiple ending activities, we include a dummy ending activity. This is an activity that does not exist and takes up zero time or resources. This dummy activity has all the multiple ending activities in the project as immediate predecessors. We illustrate this type of situation in Solved Problem 7-2 at the end of this chapter.

7.3 Determining the Project Schedule

Look back at Figure 7.6 for a moment to see General Foundry's completed AON project network. Once this project network has been drawn to show all the activities and their precedence relationships, the next step is to determine the project schedule. That is, we need to identify the planned starting and ending times for each activity.

Critical path analysis *helps determine the project schedule.*

Let us assume that General Foundry estimates the **activity time** required for each activity, in weeks, as shown in Table 7.2. The table indicates that the total time for all eight of General Foundry's activities is 25 weeks. However, because several activities can take place simultaneously, it is clear that the total project completion time may be much less than 25 weeks. To find out just how long the project will take, we perform **critical path analysis** for the network.

The **critical path** *is the longest path in the network.*

The **critical path** is the *longest* time path through the network. To find the critical path, we calculate two distinct starting and ending times for each activity. These are defined as follows:

Earliest start time (EST) = the earliest time at which an activity can start, assuming all predecessors have been completed

Earliest finish time (EFT) = the earliest time at which an activity can be finished

Latest start time (LST) = the latest time at which an activity can start so as to not delay the completion time of the entire project

Latest finish time (LFT) = the latest time by which an activity has to finish so as to not delay the completion time of the entire project

Delta's Ground Crew Orchestrates a Smooth Takeoff

Flight 199's three engines screech its arrival as the wide-bodied jet lumbers down Orlando's taxiway with 200 passengers arriving from San Juan. In an hour, the plane is to be airborne again.

But before this jet can depart, there is business to attend to: hundreds of passengers and tons of luggage and cargo to unload and load; hundreds of meals, thousands of gallons of jet fuel, countless soft drinks and bottles of liquor to restock; cabin and rest rooms to clean; toilet holding tanks to drain; and engines, wings, and landing gear to inspect.

The 12-person ground crew knows that a miscue anywhere—a broken cargo loader, lost baggage, misdirected passengers—can mean a late departure and trigger a chain reaction of headaches from Orlando to Dallas to every destination of a connecting flight.

Like a pit crew awaiting a race car, trained crews are in place for Flight 199 with baggage carts and tractors, hydraulic cargo loaders, a truck to load food and drinks, another to lift the cleanup crew, another to put fuel on, and a fourth to take water off. The team usually performs so smoothly that most passengers never suspect the proportions of the effort. Gantt charts and PERT aid Delta and other airlines with the staffing and scheduling that are necessary for this symphony to perform.

Source: Based on *New York Times* (January 21, 1998): C1, C20.

TABLE 7.2
Time Estimates for General Foundry

ACTIVITY	DESCRIPTION	TIME (WEEKS)
A	Build internal components	2
B	Modify roof and floor	3
C	Construct collection stack	2
D	Pour concrete and install frame	4
E	Build high-temperature burner	4
F	Install pollution control system	3
G	Install air pollution device	5
H	Inspect and test	2
	Total time (weeks)	25

We use a two-pass procedure to find the project schedule.

We use a two-pass process, consisting of a forward pass and a backward pass, to determine these time schedules for each activity. The earliest times (EST and EFT) are determined during the **forward pass**. The latest times (LST and LFT) are determined during the **backward pass**.

Forward Pass

The forward pass identifies all the earliest times.

To clearly show the activity schedules on a project network, we use the notation shown in Figure 7.7. The EST of an activity is shown in the top-left corner of the node denoting that activity.

FIGURE 7.7
Notation Used in Nodes for Forward and Backward Passes

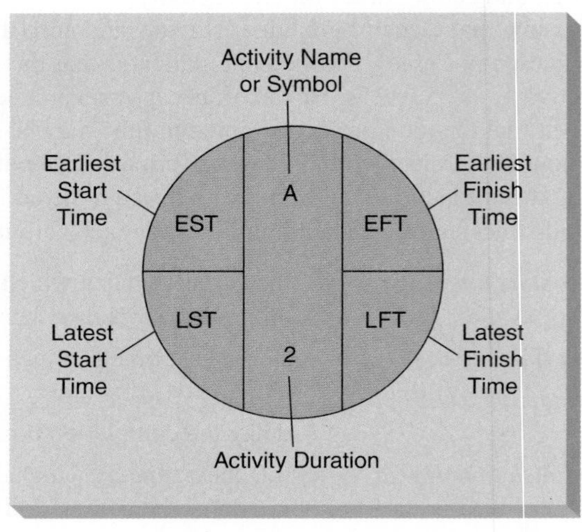

FIGURE 7.8 Earliest Start Times and Earliest Finish Times for General Foundry

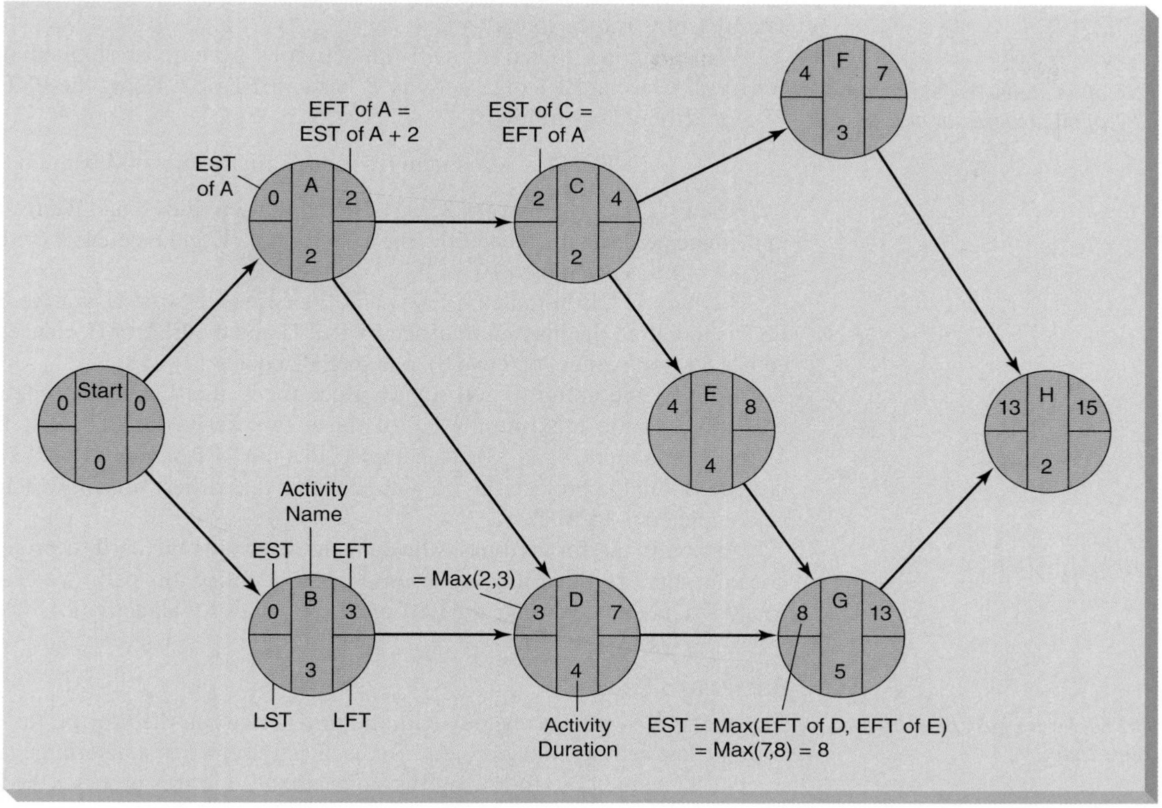

The EFT is shown in the top-right corner. The latest times, LST and LFT, are shown in the bottom-left and bottom-right corners, respectively.

All predecessor activities must be completed before an activity can begin.

EST RULE Before an activity can start, *all* its immediate predecessors must be finished:

- If an activity has only a single immediate predecessor, its EST equals the EFT of the predecessor.
- If an activity has multiple immediate predecessors, its EST is the maximum of all EFT values of its predecessors.

That is,

$$\text{EST} = \text{Maximum}\ \{\text{EFT value of all immediate predecessors}\} \qquad (7\text{-}1)$$

EFT RULE The EFT of an activity is the sum of its EST and its activity time. That is,

$$\text{EFT} = \text{EST} + \text{Activity time} \qquad (7\text{-}2)$$

Figure 7.8 shows the complete project network for General Foundry's project, along with the EST and EFT values for all activities. We next describe how these values have been calculated.

Because activity Start has no predecessors, we begin by setting its EST to 0. That is, activity Start can begin at the *end* of week 0, which is the same as the beginning of week 1.[2] If activity Start has an EST of 0, its EFT is also 0 because its activity time is 0.

Next, we consider activities A and B, both of which have only Start as an immediate predecessor. Using the EST rule, the EST for both activities A and B equals zero, which is the EFT

[2] In writing all earliest and latest times, we need to be consistent. For example, if we specify that the EST value of activity *i* is week 4, do we mean the *beginning* of week 4 or the *end* of week 4? Note that if the value refers to the *beginning* of week 4, it means that week 4 is also available for performing activity *i*. In our discussions, *all* earliest and latest time values correspond to the *end* of a period. That is, if we specify that the EST of activity *i* is week 4, it means that activity *i* starts work only at the beginning of week 5.

EFT = EST + Activity time

of activity Start. Now, using the EFT rule, the EFT for A is 2 (= 0 + 2), and the EFT for B is 3 (= 0 + 3). Because activity A precedes activity C, the EST of C equals the EFT of A (= 2). The EFT of C is therefore 4 (= 2 + 2).

EST of an activity = Maximum EFT of all predecessor activities

We now come to activity D. Both activities A and B are immediate predecessors for D. Whereas A has an EFT of 2, activity B has an EFT of 3. Using the EST rule, we compute the EST of activity D as follows:

$$\text{EST of D} = \text{Maximum (EFT of A, EFT of B)} = \text{Maximum (2, 3)} = 3$$

The EFT of D equals 7 (= 3 + 4). Next, both activities E and F have activity C as their only immediate predecessor. Therefore, the EST for both E and F equals 4 (= EFT of C). The EFT of E is 8 (= 4 + 4), and the EFT of F is 7 (= 4 + 3).

Activity G has both activities D and E as predecessors. Using the EST rule, we know its EST is therefore the maximum of the EFT of D and the EFT of E. Hence, the EST of activity G equals 8 (= maximum of 7 and 8), and its EFT equals 13 (= 8 + 5).

Finally, we come to activity H. Because it also has two predecessors, F and G, the EST of H is the maximum EFT of these two activities. That is, the EST of H equals 13 (= maximum of 7 and 13). This implies that the EFT of H is 15 (= 13 + 2). Because H is the last activity in the project, this also implies that the earliest time in which the entire project can be completed is 15 weeks.

Although the forward pass allows us to determine the earliest project completion time, it does not identify the critical path. In order to identify this path, we need to now conduct the backward pass to determine the LST and LFT values for all activities.

Backward Pass

The backward pass finds all the latest times.

Just as the forward pass begins with the first activity in the project, the backward pass begins with the last activity in the project. For each activity, we first determine its LFT value, followed by its LST value. The following two rules are used in this process: the LFT rule and the LST rule.

LFT RULE This rule is again based on the fact that before an activity can start, all its immediate predecessors must be finished:

- If an activity is an immediate predecessor for just a single activity, its LFT equals the LST of the activity that immediately follows it.
- If an activity is an immediate predecessor to more than one activity, its LFT is the minimum of all LST values of all activities that immediately follow it. That is,

$$\text{LFT} = \text{Minimum \{LST of all immediate following activities\}} \quad \text{(7-3)}$$

LST RULE The LST of an activity is the difference between its LFT and its activity time. That is,

$$\text{LST} = \text{LFT} - \text{Activity time} \quad \text{(7-4)}$$

Figure 7.9 shows the complete project network for General Foundry's project, along with LST and LFT values for all activities. Next, we analyze how these values were calculated.

LST = LFT − Activity time

We begin by assigning an LFT value of 15 weeks for activity H. That is, we specify that the LFT for the entire project is the same as its EFT. Using the LST rule, we calculate that the LST of activity H is equal to 13 (= 15 − 2).

Because activity H is the lone succeeding activity for both activities F and G, the LFT for both F and G equals 13. This implies that the LST of G is 8 (= 13 − 5), and the LST of F is 10 (= 13 − 3).

Proceeding in this fashion, we find that the LFT of E is 8 (= LST of G), and its LST is 4 (= 8 − 4). Likewise, the LFT of D is 8 (= LST of G), and its LST is 4 (= 8 − 4).

LFT of an activity = Minimum LST of all activities that follow

We now consider activity C, which is an immediate predecessor to two activities: E and F. Using the LFT rule, we compute the LFT of activity C as follows:

$$\text{LFT of C} = \text{Minimum (LST of E, LST of F)} = \text{Minimum (4, 10)} = 4$$

The LST of C is computed as 2 (= 4 − 2). Next, we compute the LFT of B as 4 (= LST of D) and its LST as 1 (= 4 − 3).

FIGURE 7.9 Latest Start Times and Latest Finish Times for General Foundry

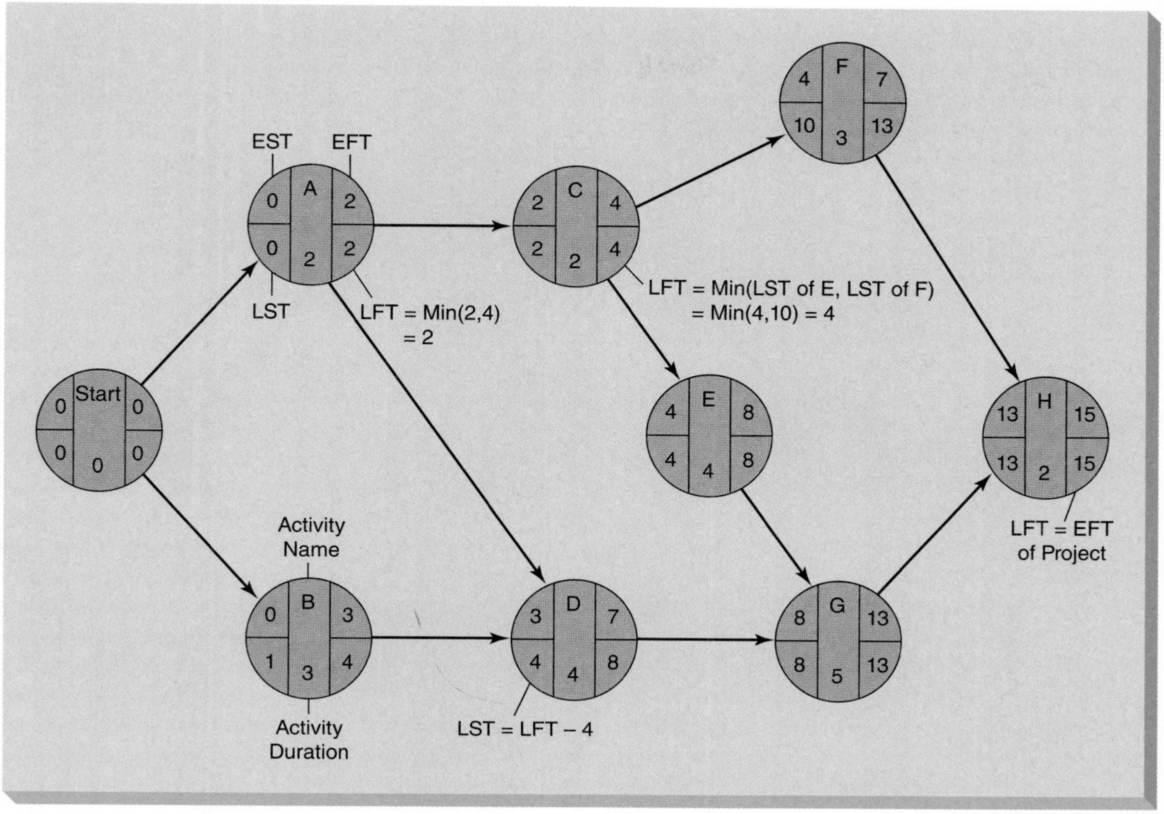

We now consider activity A. We compute its LFT as 2 (= Minimum of LST of C and LST of D). Hence, the LST of activity A is 0 (= 2 − 2). Finally, both the LFT and LST of activity Start are equal to 0.

Calculating Slack Time and Identifying the Critical Path(s)

Slack time *is free time for an activity.*

After we have computed the earliest and latest times for all activities, it is a simple matter to find the amount of **slack time**, or free time, that each activity has. *Slack* is the length of time an activity can be delayed without delaying the entire project. Mathematically,

$$\text{Slack} = \text{LST} - \text{EST} \text{ or Slack} = \text{LFT} - \text{EFT} \quad (7\text{-}5)$$

Table 7.3 summarizes the EST, EFT, LST, LFT, and slack time for all of General Foundry's activities. Activity B, for example, has 1 week of slack time because its LST is 1 and its EST is 0

TABLE 7.3 General Foundry's Project Schedule and Slack Times

ACTIVITY	EST	EFT	LST	LFT	SLACK, LST–EST	ON CRITICAL PATH?
A	0	2	0	2	0	Yes
B	0	3	1	4	1	No
C	2	4	2	4	0	Yes
D	3	7	4	8	1	No
E	4	8	4	8	0	Yes
F	4	7	10	13	6	No
G	8	13	8	13	0	Yes
H	13	15	13	15	0	Yes

FIGURE 7.10 Critical Path and Slack Times for General Foundry

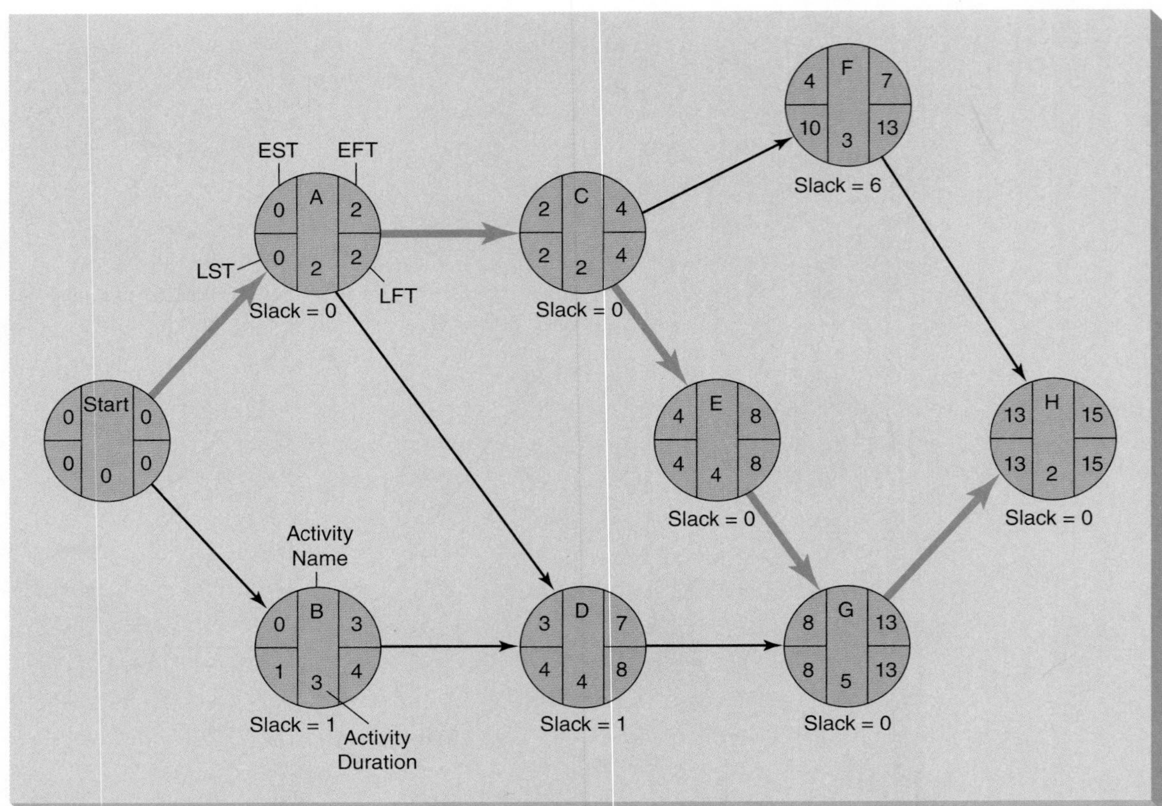

(alternatively, its LFT is 4 and its EFT is 3). This means that activity B can be delayed by up to 1 week, and the whole project can still finish in 15 weeks.

Critical activities have no slack time.

On the other hand, activities A, C, E, G, and H have *no* slack time. This means that none of them can be delayed without delaying the entire project. This also means that if Harky wants to reduce the total project time, he will have to reduce the length of one of these activities. These activities are called *critical activities* and are said to be on the *critical path.* The critical path is a continuous path through the project network that

The critical path is the longest path through the network.

- Starts at the first activity in the project (Start in our example)
- Terminates at the last activity in the project (H in our example)
- Includes only critical activities (i.e., activities with no slack time)

General Foundry's critical path, Start-A-C-E-G-H, is shown in the network in Figure 7.10. The total project completion time of 15 weeks corresponds to the longest path in the network.

A project can have multiple critical paths.

MULTIPLE CRITICAL PATHS In General Foundry's case, there is just a single critical path. Can a project have multiple critical paths? The answer is yes. For example, in General Foundry's case, what if the time required for activity B were estimated as 4 weeks instead of 3 weeks? Due to this change, the earliest and latest times for activities B and D would have to be revised, as shown in Figure 7.11.

Note that in addition to the original critical path (Start-A-C-E-G-H), there is now a second critical path (Start-B-D-G-H). Delaying an activity on either critical path will delay the completion of the entire project.

Total Slack Time versus Free Slack Time

Let us now refer to the project network in Figure 7.10. Consider activities B and D, which have slacks of 1 week each. Does it mean that we can delay *each* activity by 1 week and still complete the project in 15 weeks? The answer is no, as discussed next.

FIGURE 7.11 Modified Network with Multiple Critical Paths for General Foundry

Total slack time is shared among more than one activity.

Let's assume that activity B is delayed by 1 week. It has used up its slack of 1 week and now has an EFT of 4. This implies that activity D now has an EST of 4 and an EFT of 8. Note that these are also its LST and LFT values, respectively. That is, activity D also has no slack time now. Essentially, the slack of 1 week that activities B and D had was *shared* between them. Delaying either activity by 1 week causes not only that activity but also the other activity to lose its slack. This type of a slack time is referred to as *total slack*. Typically, when two or more noncritical activities appear successively in a path, they share total slack.

IN ACTION Project Management and Software Development

Although computers have revolutionized how companies conduct business and allowed some organizations to achieve a long-term competitive advantage in the marketplace, the software that controls these computers is often more expensive than intended and takes longer to develop than expected. In some cases, large software projects are never fully completed. The London Stock Exchange, for example, had an ambitious software project called TAURUS that was intended to improve computer operations at the exchange. The TAURUS project, which cost hundreds of millions of dollars, was never completed. After numerous delays and cost overruns, the project was finally halted. The FLORIDA system, an ambitious software development project for the Department of Health and Rehabilitative Services for the state of Florida, was also delayed, cost more than expected, and didn't operate as everyone had hoped. Although not all software development projects are delayed or over budget, it has been estimated that more than half of all software projects cost more than 189% of their original projections.

To control large software projects, many companies are now using project management techniques. Ryder Systems, Inc., American Express Financial Advisors, and United Air Lines have all created project management departments for their software and information systems projects. These departments have the authority to monitor large software projects and make changes to deadlines, budgets, and resources used to complete software development efforts.

Source: Based on J. King. "Tough Love Reins in IS Projects," *Computerworld* (June 19, 1995): 1–2.

Free slack time is associated with a single activity.

In contrast, consider the slack time of 6 weeks in activity F. Delaying this activity decreases only its slack time and does not affect the slack time of any other activity. This type of a slack time is referred to as *free slack*. Typically, if a noncritical activity has critical activities on either side of it in a path, its slack time is free slack.

7.4 Variability in Activity Times

Activity times are subject to variability.

In identifying all earliest and latest times so far, and the associated critical path(s), we have adopted the CPM approach of assuming that all activity times are known and fixed constants. That is, there is no variability in activity times. However, in practice, it is likely that activity completion times vary depending on various factors.

For example, building internal components (activity A) for General Foundry is estimated to finish in 2 weeks. Clearly, factors such as late arrival of raw materials, absence of key personnel, and so on, could delay this activity. Suppose activity A actually ends up taking 3 weeks. Because activity A is on the critical path, the entire project will now be delayed by 1 week, to 16 weeks. If we had anticipated completion of this project in 15 weeks, we would obviously miss our deadline.

Although some activities may be relatively less prone to delays, others could be extremely susceptible to delays. For example, activity B (modify roof and floor) could be heavily dependent on weather conditions. A spell of bad weather could significantly affect its completion time.

There are three approaches to studying the impact of variability in activity times.

The preceding discussion implies that we cannot ignore the impact of variability in activity times when deciding the schedule for a project. In general, there are three approaches that we can use to analyze the impact of variability in activity times on the completion time of the project:

- The first approach is to provide for variability by building in "buffers" to activity times. For example, if we know based on past experience that a specific activity has exceeded its time estimate by 20% on several occasions, we can build in a 20% time buffer for this activity by inflating its time estimate by 20%. There are, of course, a few obvious drawbacks to this approach. For example, if every activity has inflated time estimates due to these buffers, the entire project duration will be artificially large. Incidentally, practicing project managers will tell you that providing time buffers is not practical because the people concerned with the activity will just proceed more slowly than planned on the activity because they know that the buffer exists (i.e., the duration will stretch to fit the allotted time).
- The second approach, known as PERT analysis, employs a probability-based analysis of the project completion time. A primary advantage of this approach is that it is fairly easy to understand and implement. However, the drawback is that we have to make certain assumptions regarding the probability distributions of activity times. We discuss this approach in detail in this section.
- The third approach uses computer simulation, the topic of Chapter 10. This approach, while typically being the most difficult approach from an implementation point of view, is also likely to be the most comprehensive in terms of its capabilities and analysis. We illustrate this approach for a project management problem in Solved Problem 10-4 at the end of Chapter 10.

PERT Analysis

PERT uses three time estimates for each activity.

Recall that in our study so far, we have estimated the duration for each activity by using a single time estimate (such as 2 weeks for activity A in General Foundry's project). In practice, such durations may be difficult to estimate for many activities. For example, think about the difficulty you would have if someone asked you to estimate exactly how long your next assignment in this course will take to complete. (Remember, your estimate must be guaranteed to be sufficient and should not include any unnecessary buffers.) To correct for this difficulty, in PERT analysis we base the duration of each activity on three separate time estimates:

Optimistic time (a) = The time an activity will take, assuming favorable conditions (i.e., everything goes as planned). In estimating this value, there should be only a small probability (say, 1/100) that the activity time will be a or lower.

Most likely time (m) = The most realistic estimate of the time required to complete an activity.

Pessimistic time (b) = The time an activity will take, assuming unfavorable conditions (i.e., nothing goes as planned). In estimating this value, there should also be only a small probability that the activity time will be b or higher.

The beta probability distribution is often used to describe activity times.

How do we use these three time estimates? It turns out that a probability distribution, known as the **beta probability distribution**, is very appropriate for approximating the distribution of activity times. As shown in Figure 7.12, one way to characterize the beta distribution is to use three parameters—which, in the case of activity durations, correspond to the optimistic, most likely, and pessimistic time estimates we have already defined for each activity.

By using these three parameters for each activity, we can compute its expected activity time and variance. To find the **expected activity time (*t*)**, the beta distribution weights the three time estimates as follows:

$$t = (a + 4m + b)/6 \tag{7-6}$$

The expected activity time is used in the project network to compute all earliest and latest times.

That is, the most likely time (m) is given four times the weight of the optimistic time (a) and pessimistic time (b). It is important to note that this expected activity time, t, computed using Equation 7-6 for each activity, is used in the project network to compute all earliest and latest times.

To compute the **variance of activity completion time**, we use this formula:[3]

$$\text{Variance} = [(b - a)/6]^2 \tag{7-7}$$

The standard deviation of activity completion time is the square root of the variance. Hence,

$$\text{Standard deviation} = \sqrt{\text{Variance}} = (b - a)/6 \tag{7-8}$$

FIGURE 7.12 Beta Probability Distribution with Three Time Estimates

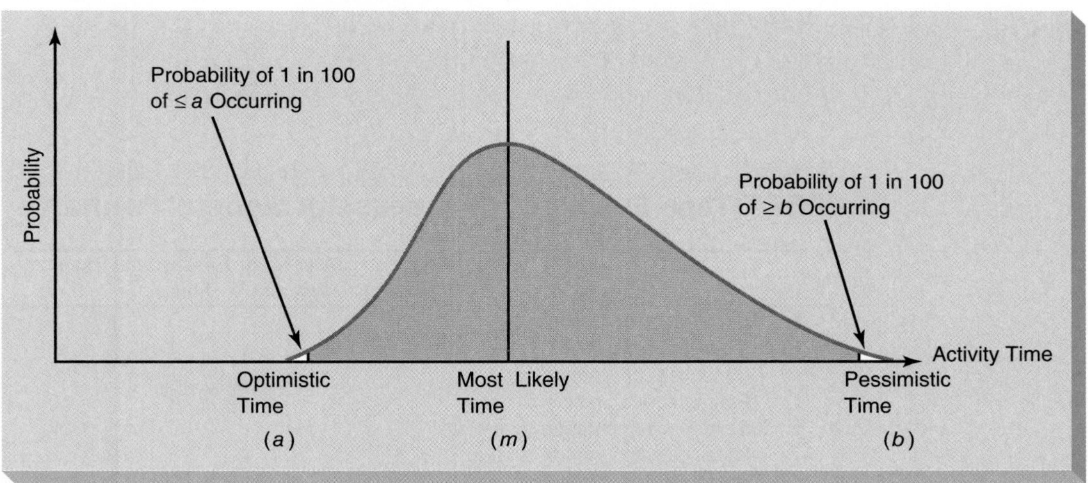

[3]This formula is based on the statistical concept that from one end of the beta distribution to the other is 6 standard deviations (± 3 standard deviations from the mean). Because $(b - a)$ is 6 standard deviations, the variance is $[(b - a)/6]^2$.

Excel Note

The Companion Website for this textbook, at www.pearsonhighered.com/balakrishnan, contains the Excel file for each sample problem discussed here. The relevant file name is shown in the margin next to each example.

File: 7-1.xls

For General Foundry's project, let us assume that Lester Harky has estimated the optimistic, most likely, and pessimistic times for each activity, as shown in columns C, D, and E, respectively, in Screenshot 7-1. Note that some activities (e.g., A, B) have relatively small variability, while others (e.g., F, G) have a large spread between their pessimistic and optimistic time estimates. On occasion, it is possible for an activity to have no variability at all (i.e., the activity's a, m, and b time estimates are all the same).

Using these estimates in Equations 7-6 through 7-8, we compute the expected time, variance, and standard deviation for each activity. These values are shown in columns F, G, and H, respectively, of Screenshot 7-1. Note that the expected times shown in column F are, in fact, the activity times we used in our earlier computation and identification of the critical path. Hence, the earliest and latest times we computed before (see Table 7.3 on page 279) are valid for the PERT analysis of General Foundry's project.

Probability of Project Completion

The critical path analysis helped us determine that General Foundry's expected project completion time is 15 weeks. Lester Harky knows, however, that there is significant variation in the time estimates for several activities. Variation in activities that are on the critical path can affect the overall project completion time, possibly delaying it. This is one occurrence that worries Harky considerably.

We compute the project variance by summing variances of only those activities that are on the critical path.

PERT uses the variance of critical path activities to help determine the variance of the overall project. Project variance is computed by summing variances of critical activities:

$$\text{Project variance} = \sum(\text{Variances of activities on critical path}) \qquad \textbf{(7-9)}$$

From Screenshot 7-1 we know that the variance of activity A is 0.11, variance of activity C is 0.11, variance of activity E is 1.00, variance of activity G is 1.78, and variance of activity H is 0.11. Hence, the total project variance and project standard deviation may be computed as

$$\text{Project variance } (\sigma_P^2) = 0.11 + 0.11 + 1.00 + 1.78 + 0.11 = 3.11$$

SCREENSHOT 7-1 Excel Layout to Compute General Foundry's Expected Times and Variances

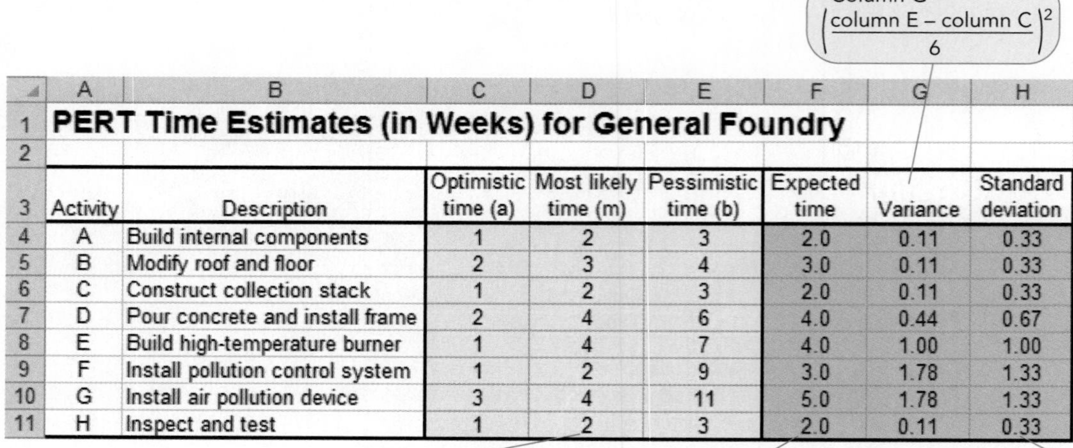

PERT Time Estimates (in Weeks) for General Foundry

Activity	Description	Optimistic time (a)	Most likely time (m)	Pessimistic time (b)	Expected time	Variance	Standard deviation
A	Build internal components	1	2	3	2.0	0.11	0.33
B	Modify roof and floor	2	3	4	3.0	0.11	0.33
C	Construct collection stack	1	2	3	2.0	0.11	0.33
D	Pour concrete and install frame	2	4	6	4.0	0.44	0.67
E	Build high-temperature burner	1	4	7	4.0	1.00	1.00
F	Install pollution control system	1	2	9	3.0	1.78	1.33
G	Install air pollution device	3	4	11	5.0	1.78	1.33
H	Inspect and test	1	2	3	2.0	0.11	0.33

FIGURE 7.13
Probability Distribution for Project Completion Times

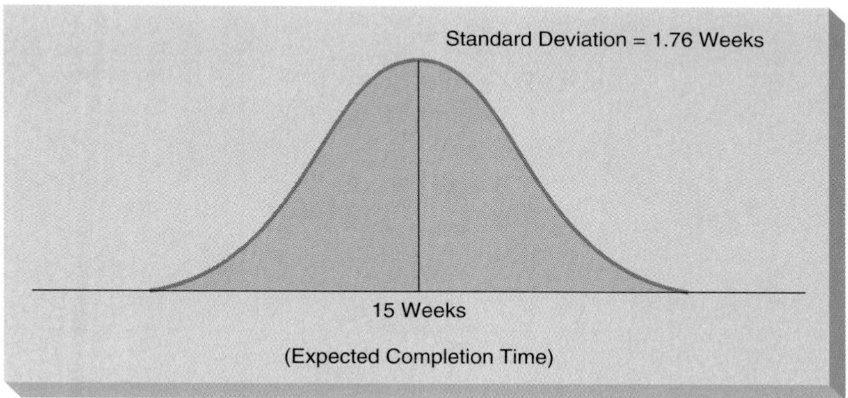

which implies

$$\text{Project standard deviation}(\sigma_p) = \sqrt{\text{Project variance}} = \sqrt{3.11} = 1.76$$

PERT now makes two assumptions: (1) Total project completion times follow a normal probability distribution, and (2) activity times are statistically independent. With these assumptions, the bell-shaped normal curve shown in Figure 7.13 can be used to represent project completion dates. This normal curve implies that there is a 50% chance that the project completion time will be less than 15 weeks and a 50% chance that it will exceed 15 weeks. That is, instead of viewing the computed project completion time as a guaranteed estimate (as we did earlier, when using the CPM approach), the PERT analysis views it as just the expected completion time, with only a 50% probability of completion within that time.

How can this information be used to help answer questions regarding the probability of finishing the project at different times? For example, what is the probability that Harky will finish this project on or before the 16-week deadline imposed by the environmental agency? To find this probability, Harky needs to determine the appropriate area under the normal curve. The standard normal equation can be applied as follows:

$$\begin{aligned} Z &= (\text{Target completion time} - \text{Expected completion time})/\sigma_P \\ &= (16 \text{ weeks} - 15 \text{ weeks})/1.76 \text{ weeks} = 0.57 \end{aligned} \quad \textbf{(7-10)}$$

where Z is the number of standard deviations the target completion time lies from the expected completion time.

Now we compute the probability of project completion.

Referring to the normal probability table in Appendix C (see page 574), we find a probability of 0.7157. Thus, there is a 71.57% chance that the pollution control equipment can be put in place in 16 weeks or less. This is shown in Figure 7.14.

FIGURE 7.14
Probability of General Foundry Meeting the 16-Week Deadline

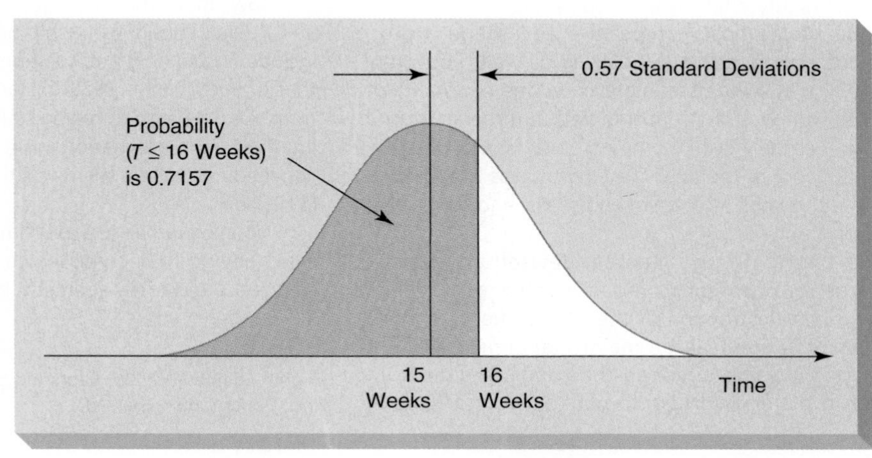

FIGURE 7.15
***Z* Value for 99% Probability of Project Completion**

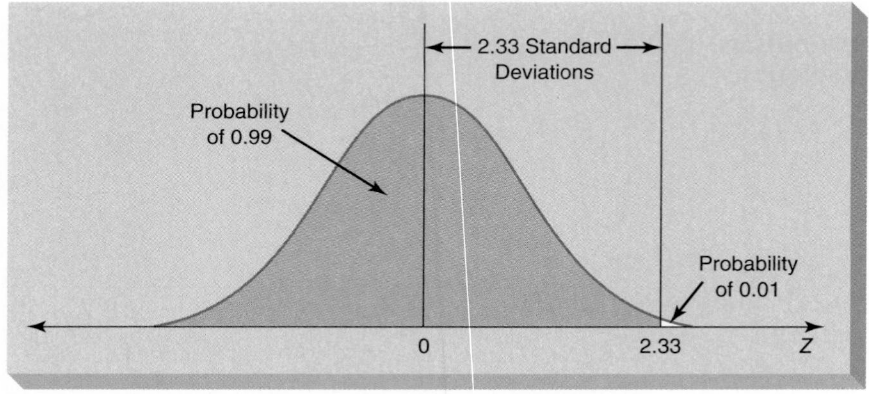

Determining Project Completion Time for a Given Probability

Lester Harky is extremely worried that there is only a 71.57% chance that the pollution control equipment can be put in place in 16 weeks or less. He thinks that it may be possible for him to plead with the environmental agency for more time. However, before he approaches the agency, he wants to arm himself with sufficient information about the project. Specifically, he wants to find the target completion time by which he has a 99% chance of completing the project. He hopes to use his analysis to convince the agency to agree to this extended deadline.

Clearly, this target completion time would be greater than 16 weeks. However, what is the exact value of this new deadline? To answer this question, we again use the assumption that General Foundry's project completion time follows a normal probability distribution, with a mean of 15 weeks and a standard deviation of 1.76 weeks.

For Harky to find the target completion time under which the project has a 99% chance of completion, he needs to determine the *Z* value that corresponds to 99%, as shown in Figure 7.15.

Now we compute the due date for a given probability.

Referring again to the normal probability table in Appendix C, we identify a *Z* value of 2.33 as being closest to the probability of 0.99. That is, Harky's target completion time should be 2.33 standard deviations above the expected completion time. Starting with the standard

IN ACTION Project Management Provides a Competitive Advantage for Bechtel

Now in its second century, the San Francisco–based Bechtel Group is the world's premier manager of massive construction and engineering projects. Known for billion-dollar projects, Bechtel is famous for its construction feats on the Hoover Dam, the Ted Williams Tunnel project, and the rebuilding of Kuwait's oil and gas infrastructure after the invasion by Iraq.

Even for Bechtel, whose competitive advantage is project management, restoring the 650 blazing oil wells lit by Iraqi sabotage in 1990 was a logistical nightmare. The panorama of destruction in Kuwait was breathtaking, with fire roaring out of the ground from virtually every compass point. Kuwait had no water, electricity, food, or facilities. The country was littered with unexploded mines, bombs, grenades, and shells, and lakes of oil covered its roads.

In Phase 1 of the project, Bechtel devised an unprecedented emergency program to regain control of Kuwait's oil fields and to halt destruction of the environment. Phase 2 focused on rehabilitation. With a major global procurement program, Bechtel specialists tapped the company's network of suppliers and buyers worldwide. At the port of Dubai, 550 miles southeast of Kuwait, the firm established a central transshipment point and deployed 125,000 tons of equipment and supplies. Creating a workforce of 16,000, Bechtel mobilized 742 airplanes and ships and more than 5,800 bulldozers, ambulances, and other pieces of operating equipment from 40 countries on five continents.

Now, more than two decades later, the fires are long out, and Kuwait continues to ship oil. Bechtel's more recent projects include (1) building and running a rail line between London and the Channel Tunnel ($7.4 billion); (2) developing an oil pipeline from the Caspian Sea region to Russia ($850 million); (3) expanding the Miami International Airport ($2 billion); and (4) building liquefied natural gas plants on the island of Trinidad, West Indies ($1 billion).

When countries seek out firms to manage these massive projects, they go to Bechtel, which, again and again, through outstanding project management, has demonstrated its competitive advantage.

Source: Adapted from J. Heizer and B. Render. *Operations Management*, Eighth Edition, © 2006. Reprinted by permission of Pearson Education, Inc., Upper Saddle River, NJ.

normal equation (see Equation 7-10), we can solve for the target completion time and rewrite the equation as

$$\begin{aligned}\text{Target completion time} &= \text{Expected completion time} + Z \times \sigma\text{p} \\ &= 15 + 2.33 \times 1.76 = 19.1 \text{ weeks}\end{aligned} \quad (7\text{-}11)$$

Hence, if Harky can get the environmental agency to give him a new target completion time of 19.1 weeks (or more), he can be 99% sure of finishing the project on time.

Variability in Completion Time of Noncritical Paths

Noncritical paths with large variances should be closely monitored.

In our discussion so far, we have focused exclusively on the variability in completion times of activities on the critical path. This seems logical because these activities are, by definition, the more important activities in a project network. However, when there is variability in activity times, it is important that we also investigate the variability in the completion times of activities on *noncritical* paths.

Consider, for example, activity D in General Foundry's project. Recall from Table 7.3 on page 279 that this is a noncritical activity, with a slack time of 1 week. We have therefore not considered the variability in D's time in computing the probabilities of project completion times. We observe, however, that D has a variance of 0.44 (see Screenshot 7-1 on page 284). In fact, the pessimistic completion time for D is 6 weeks. This means that if D ends up taking its pessimistic time to finish, the project will not finish in 15 weeks, even though D is not a critical activity.

For this reason, when we find probabilities of project completion times, it may be necessary for us to not focus only on the critical path(s). We may need to also compute these probabilities for noncritical paths, especially those that have relatively large variances. It is possible for a noncritical path to have a smaller probability of completion within a due date compared with the critical path. In fact, a different critical path can evolve because of the probabilistic situation.

7.5 Managing Project Costs and Other Resources

The techniques discussed so far are very good for planning, scheduling, and monitoring a project with respect to time. We have not, however, considered another very important factor—project *cost*. In this section, we begin by investigating how costs can be planned and scheduled. Then we see how costs can be monitored and controlled.

Planning and Scheduling Project Costs: Budgeting Process

The budgeting process determines the budget per period of the project.

The overall approach in the budgeting process of a project is to determine how much is to be spent every week or month. This is accomplished as follows:

Three Steps of the Budgeting Process

1. Identify all costs associated with each of the activities. Then add these costs together to get one estimated cost or budget for each activity. When dealing with a large project, several activities may be combined into larger work packages. A work package is simply a logical collection of activities. Because the General Foundry project is quite small, each activity can be a work package.
2. Identify when and how the budgeted cost for an activity will actually be spent. In practice, this would be specific to the activity in question. For example, in some cases the entire cost may be spent at the start of the activity. In others, the expense may occur only after the activity has been completed.

   In our discussion here, we assume that the cost of each activity is spent at a linear rate over time. Thus, if the budgeted cost for a given activity is \$48,000, and the activity's expected time is 4 weeks, the budgeted cost per week is \$12,000 (=\$48,000/4 weeks).
3. Using the earliest and latest start and finish times for each activity, find out how much money should be spent during each period of the project to finish it by the target completion time.

TABLE 7.4
Activity Costs for General Foundry

ACTIVITY	EXPECTED TIME (t)	EST	LST	TOTAL BUDGETED COST	BUDGETED COST PER WEEK
A	2	0	0	$22,000	$11,000
B	3	0	1	$30,000	$10,000
C	2	2	2	$26,000	$13,000
D	4	3	4	$48,000	$12,000
E	4	4	4	$56,000	$14,000
F	3	4	10	$30,000	$10,000
G	5	8	8	$80,000	$16,000
H	2	13	13	$16,000	$8,000
				Total $308,000	

BUDGETING FOR GENERAL FOUNDRY Let us apply the three-step budgeting process to the General Foundry problem. Lester Harky has carefully computed the costs associated with each of his eight activities. Assuming that the cost of each activity is spent at a linear rate over time, he has also divided the total budget for each activity by the activity's expected time to determine the weekly budget for the activity. The budget for activity A, for example, is $22,000 (see Table 7.4). Because its expected time (t) is 2 weeks, $11,000 is spent each week to complete the activity. Table 7.4 also provides two pieces of data we found earlier: the EST and LST for each activity.

Looking at the total of the budgeted activity costs, we see that the entire project will cost $308,000. Finding the weekly budget will help Harky determine how the project is progressing on a week-to-week basis.

We can form a weekly budget using EST values.

The weekly budget for the project is developed from the data in Table 7.4. The EST for activity A is 0. Because A takes 2 weeks to complete, its weekly budget of $11,000 should be spent in weeks 1 and 2. For activity B, the EST is 0, the expected completion time is 3 weeks, and the budgeted cost per week is $10,000. Hence, $10,000 should be spent for activity B in each of weeks 1, 2, and 3. Using the EST, we can find the exact weeks during which the budget for each activity should be spent. These weekly amounts can be summed for all activities to arrive at the weekly budget for the entire project. For example, a total of $21,000 each should be spent during weeks 1 and 2. These weekly totals can then be added to determine the total amount that should be spent to date (total to date). All these computations are shown in Table 7.5.

TABLE 7.5 Budgeted Costs (in Thousands) for General Foundry, Using Earliest Start Times

	WEEK															
ACTIVITY	1	2	3	4	5	6	7	8	9	10	11	12	13	14	15	TOTAL
A	$11	$11														$22
B	$10	$10	$10													$30
C			$13	$13												$26
D				$12	$12	$12	$12									$48
E					$14	$14	$14	$14								$56
F					$10	$10	$10									$30
G									$16	$16	$16	$16	$16			$80
H														$8	$8	$16
																$308
Total per week	$21	$21	$23	$25	$36	$36	$36	$14	$16	$16	$16	$16	$16	$8	$8	
Total to date	$21	$42	$65	$90	$126	$162	$198	$212	$228	$244	$260	$276	$292	$300	$308	

TABLE 7.6 Budgeted Costs (in Thousands) for General Foundry, Using Latest Start Times

	WEEK															
ACTIVITY	**1**	**2**	**3**	**4**	**5**	**6**	**7**	**8**	**9**	**10**	**11**	**12**	**13**	**14**	**15**	**TOTAL**
A	$11	$11														$622
B		$10	$10	$10												$630
C			$13	$13												$626
D					$12	$12	$12	$12								$648
E					$614	$614	$614	$614								$656
F											$10	$10	$10			$630
G									$16	$16	$16	$16	$16			$680
H														$8	$8	$616
																$308
Total per week	$11	$21	$23	$23	$26	$26	$26	$26	$16	$16	$26	$26	$26	$8	$8	
Total to date	$11	$32	$55	$78	$104	$130	$156	$182	$198	$214	$240	$266	$292	$300	$308	

We can also form a weekly budget using LST values.

The activities along the critical path must spend their budgets at the times shown in Table 7.5. The activities that are *not* on the critical path, however, can be started at a later date. This concept is embodied in the LST for each activity. Thus, if LST values are used, another budget can be obtained. This budget will delay the expenditure of funds until the last possible moment. The procedures for computing the budget when LST is used are the same as when EST is used. The results of the new computations are shown in Table 7.6.

Compare the budgets given in Tables 7.5 and 7.6. The amount that should be spent to date (total to date) for the budget in Table 7.5 reveals the earliest possible time that funds can be expended. In contrast, the budget in Table 7.6 uses fewer financial resources in the first few weeks because it was prepared using LST values. That is, the budget in Table 7.6 shows the latest possible time that funds can be expended and have the project still finish on time. Therefore, Lester Harky can use any budget between these feasible ranges and still complete the air pollution project on time. These two tables form feasible budget ranges.

The two tables form feasible budget ranges.

This concept is illustrated in Figure 7.16, which plots the total-to-date budgets for EST and LST.

Monitoring and Controlling Project Costs

We can track costs to see if the project is on budget

Budget charts like the ones shown in Figure 7.16 are typically developed before the project is started. Then, as the project is being completed, funds expended should be monitored and controlled. The purpose of monitoring and controlling project costs is to ensure that the project is progressing on schedule and that cost overruns are kept to a minimum. The status of the entire project should be checked periodically.

Lester Harky wants to know how his air pollution project is going. It is now the end of the sixth week of the 15-week project. Activities A, B, and C have been fully completed. These activities incurred costs of $20,000, $36,000, and $26,000, respectively. Activity D is only 10% complete, and so far the cost expended on it has been $6,000. Activity E is 20% complete, with an incurred cost of $20,000. Activity F is 20% complete, with an incurred cost of $4,000. Activities G and H have not been started. Is the air pollution project on schedule? What is the value of work completed? Are there any cost overruns?

We compute the value of work completed for each activity.

One way to measure the value of the work completed (or the cost-to-date) for an activity is to multiply its total budgeted cost by the percentage of completion for that activity.[4]

[4] The percentage of completion for each activity can be measured in many ways. For example, we might use the ratio of labor hours expended to total labor hours estimated.

FIGURE 7.16
Budget Ranges for General Foundry

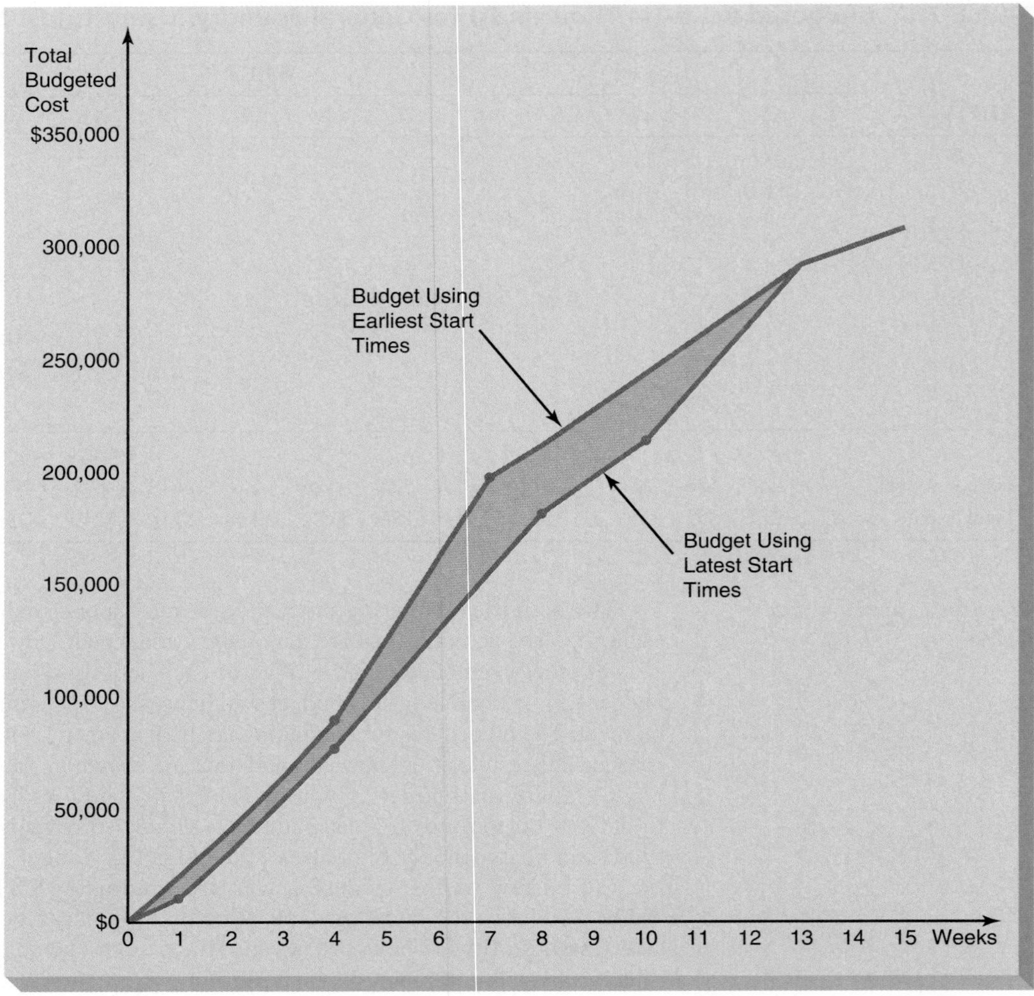

That is,

$$\text{Value of work completed} = \text{Percentage of work completed} \times \text{Total activity budget} \quad \textbf{(7-12)}$$

To determine the cost difference (i.e., the amount of overrun or underrun) for an activity, the value of work completed is subtracted from the actual cost. Hence,

$$\text{Cost difference} = \text{Actual cost} - \text{Value of work completed} \quad \textbf{(7-13)}$$

If a cost difference is negative, it implies that there is a cost underrun. In contrast, if the number is positive, there has been a cost overrun.

Table 7.7 summarizes this information for General Foundry's project. The second column shows the total budgeted cost (from Table 7.4 on page 288), and the third column contains the percentage of completion for each activity. Using these data, and the actual cost expended for each activity, we can compute the value of work completed and the cost difference for every activity.

We compute cost underruns and overruns.

Activity D, for example, has a value of work completed of \$4,800 (=\$48,000 × 10%). The actual cost is \$6,000, implying that there is a cost overrun of \$1,200. The cost difference for all activities can be added to determine the total project overrun or underrun. In General Foundry's case, we can see from Table 7.7 that there is a \$12,000 cost overrun at the end of the sixth week. The total value of work completed so far is only \$100,000, and the actual cost of the project to date is \$112,000.

How do these costs compare with the budgeted costs for week 6? If Harky had decided to use the budget for ESTs (see Table 7.5 on page 288), we can see that \$162,000 should have been spent. Thus, the project is behind schedule, and there are cost overruns. Harky

TABLE 7.7 Monitoring and Controlling Budgeted Costs for General Foundry

ACTIVITY	TOTAL BUDGETED COST	PERCENTAGE COMPLETED		VALUE OF WORK COMPLETED	ACTUAL COST	ACTIVITY DIFFERENCE
A	$22,000	100		$ 22,000	$ 20,000	–$ 2,000
B	$30,000	100		$ 30,000	$ 36,000	$ 6,000
C	$26,000	100		$ 26,000	$ 26,000	$ 0
D	$48,000	10		$ 4,800	$ 6,000	$ 1,200
E	$56,000	20		$ 11,200	$ 20,000	$ 8,800
F	$30,000	20		$ 6,000	$ 4,000	–$ 2,000
G	$80,000	0		$ 0	$ 0	$ 0
H	$16,000	0		$ 0	$ 0	$ 0
			Total	$100,000	$112,000	$12,000 (Overrun)

needs to move faster on this project to finish on time. He must also control future costs carefully to try to eliminate the current cost overrun of $12,000. To monitor and control costs, the budgeted amount, the value of work completed, and the actual costs should be computed periodically.

Managing Other Resources

Other resources can also be planned for and monitored.

So far, we have focused on monitoring and controlling costs. Although this is clearly an important issue, there may be other resources (e.g., labor, machinery, materials) that also need to be carefully planned for and monitored in order for a project to finish on schedule. For example, activity E (build high-temperature burner) may need some specialized equipment in order to be performed. Likewise, installation of the air pollution device (activity G) may require a specialist to be present. It is therefore important that we be aware of such resource requirements and ensure that the right resources are available at the right time.

Just as we constructed a weekly budget using activity schedules and costs (see Tables 7.5 and 7.6), we can construct weekly requirement charts for any resource. Assume that Lester Harky has estimated the support staff requirement for each of the eight activities in the project, as shown in Table 7.8. For example, during each week that activity A is in progress, Harky needs four support staffers to be available.

Table 7.9 shows the weekly support staff needed for General Foundry's project using EST values. A graph that plots the total resource (such as labor) needed per period (Y-axis) versus time (X-axis) is called a **resource loading chart**. Figure 7.17 shows the support staff loading chart for General Foundry's project.

TABLE 7.8 Support Staff Requirements for General Foundry

ACTIVITY	DESCRIPTION	SUPPORT STAFF NEEDED PER WEEK
A	Build internal components	4
B	Modify roof and floor	5
C	Construct collection stack	6
D	Pour concrete and install frame	4
E	Build high-temperature burner	3
F	Install pollution control system	4
G	Install air pollution device	7
H	Inspect and test	2

TABLE 7.9 Support Staff Requirements for General Foundry, Using Earliest Start Times

	WEEK															
ACTIVITY	1	2	3	4	5	6	7	8	9	10	11	12	13	14	15	TOTAL
A	4	4														8
B	5	5	5													15
C			6	6												12
D				4	4	4	4									16
E					3	3	3	3								12
F					4	4	4									12
G									7	7	7	7	7			35
H														2	2	4
																114
Total per week	9	9	11	10	11	11	11	3	7	7	7	7	7	2	2	
Total to date	9	18	29	39	50	61	72	75	82	89	96	103	110	112	114	

FIGURE 7.17 Support Staff Loading Chart for General Foundry

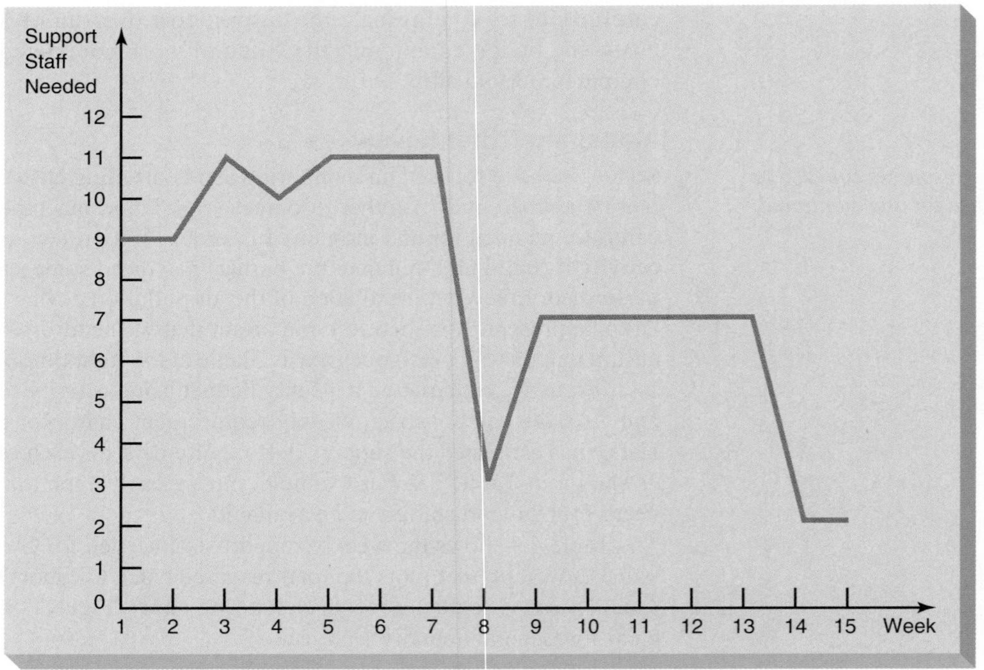

7.6 Project Crashing

Reducing a project's duration is called **crashing.**

While managing a project, it is not uncommon for a project manager to be faced with either (or both) of the following situations: (1) The project is behind schedule, and (2) the scheduled project completion time has been moved forward. In either situation, some or all of the remaining activities need to be speeded up in order to finish the project by the desired due date. The process of shortening the duration of a project in the least expensive manner possible is called **crashing**.

As noted earlier, in section 7.2, CPM is a deterministic technique in which each activity has two estimates of time. The first is the *standard* or *normal* time that we used in our computation of earliest and latest times. Associated with this standard time is the *standard* or *normal cost* of the activity, which we used in section 7.5 to schedule and monitor the cost of the project.

IN ACTION Costing Projects at Nortel

Many companies, including Nortel, a large telecommunications company, are benefiting from project management. With more than 20,000 active projects, worth a total of more than $2 billion, effectively managing projects at Nortel has been challenging. Getting the needed input data, including times and costs, can be difficult.

Like most other companies, Nortel used standard accounting practices to monitor and control costs. This typically involves allocating costs to each department. Most projects, however, span multiple departments. This can make it very difficult to get timely cost information. Project managers often get project cost data later than they want it. Because the cost data are allocated to departments, the data are often not detailed enough to help manage projects and get an accurate picture of true project costs.

To get more accurate cost data for project management, Nortel adopted an activity-based costing (ABC) method that is often used in manufacturing operations. In addition to standard cost data, each project activity was coded with a project identification number and a regional research development location number. This greatly improved the ability of project managers to control costs. Because some of the month-end costing processes were simplified, the approach also lowered project costs in most cases. Project managers also were able to get more detailed costing information. Because the cost data were coded for each project, getting timely feedback was also possible. In this case, getting good input data reduced project costs, reduced the time needed to get critical project feedback, and made project management more accurate.

Source: Based on C. Dorey. "The ABCs of R&D at Nortel," *CMA Magazine* (March 1998): 19–23.

Crash time *is the shortest duration of an activity.*

The second time is the *crash time*, which is defined as the shortest duration required to complete an activity. Associated with this crash time is the *crash cost* of the activity. Usually, we can shorten an activity by adding extra resources (e.g., equipment, people) to it. Hence, it is logical for the crash cost of an activity to be higher than its standard cost.

The amount of time by which an activity can be shortened (i.e., the difference between its standard time and crash time) depends on the activity in question. We may not be able to shorten some activities at all. For example, if a casting needs to be heat-treated in a furnace for 48 hours, adding more resources does not help shorten the time. In contrast, we may be able to shorten some activities significantly (e.g., we may be able to frame a house in 3 days instead of 10 days by using three times as many workers).

We want to find the cheapest way of crashing a project to the desired due date.

Likewise, the cost of crashing (or shortening) an activity depends on the nature of the activity. Managers are usually interested in speeding up a project at the least additional cost. Hence, in choosing which activities to crash, and by how much, we need to ensure that all the following occur:

- The amount by which an activity is crashed is, in fact, permissible.
- Taken together, the shortened activity durations will enable us to finish the project by the due date.
- The total cost of crashing is as small as possible.

In the following pages, we first illustrate how to crash a small project using simple calculations that can even be performed by hand. Then, we describe an LP-based approach that can be used to determine the optimal crashing scheme for projects of any size.

Crashing General Foundry's Project (Hand Calculations)

Suppose that General Foundry has been given only 13 weeks (instead of 16 weeks) to install the new pollution control equipment or face a court-ordered shutdown. As you recall, the length of Lester Harky's critical path was 15 weeks. Which activities should Harky crash, and by how much, in order to meet this 13-week due date? Naturally, Harky is interested in speeding up the project by 2 weeks, at the least additional cost.

Crashing a project using hand calculations involves four steps, as follows:

Four Steps of Project Crashing

1. Compute the crash cost per week (or other time period) for all activities in the network. If crash costs are assumed to be linear over time, the following formula can be used:

$$\text{Crash cost per period} = \frac{(\text{Crash cost} - \text{Standard cost})}{(\text{Standard time} - \text{Crash time})} \qquad \textbf{(7-14)}$$

2. Using the current activity times, find the critical path(s) in the project network. Identify the critical activities.
3. If there is only one critical path, select the activity on this critical path that (a) can still be crashed and (b) has the smallest crash cost per period. Crash this activity by one period.

   If there is more than one critical path, select one activity from each critical path such that (a) each selected activity can still be crashed, and (b) total crash cost per period of all selected activities is the smallest. Crash each activity by one period. Note that a single activity may be common to more than one critical path.
4. Update all activity times. If the desired due date has been reached, stop. If not, return to step 2.

General Foundry's standard and crash times and standard and crash costs are shown in Table 7.10. Note, for example, that activity B's standard time is 3 weeks (the estimate used in computing the current critical path), and its crash time is 1 week. This means that activity B can be shortened by up to 2 weeks if extra resources are provided. The cost of these additional resources is \$4,000 (= Difference between the crash cost of \$34,000 and the standard cost of \$30,000). If we assume that the crashing cost is linear over time (i.e., the cost is the same each week), activity B's crash cost per week is \$2,000 (= \$4,000/2 weeks).

This assumes that crash costs are linear over time.

This calculation is shown in Figure 7.18. Crash costs for all other activities can be computed in a similar fashion.

TABLE 7.10 Standard and Crash Times and Costs for General Foundry

	TIME (WEEKS)		COST		
ACTIVITY	STANDARD	CRASH	STANDARD	CRASH	CRASH COST PER WEEK
A	2	1	\$22,000	\$22,750	\$750
B	3	1	\$30,000	\$34,000	\$2,000
C	2	1	\$26,000	\$27,000	\$1,000
D	4	3	\$48,000	\$49,000	\$1,000
E	4	2	\$56,000	\$58,000	\$1,000
F	3	2	\$30,000	\$30,500	\$500
G	5	2	\$80,000	\$84,500	\$1,500
H	2	1	\$16,000	\$19,000	\$3,000

FIGURE 7.18 Standard and Crash Times and Costs for Activity B

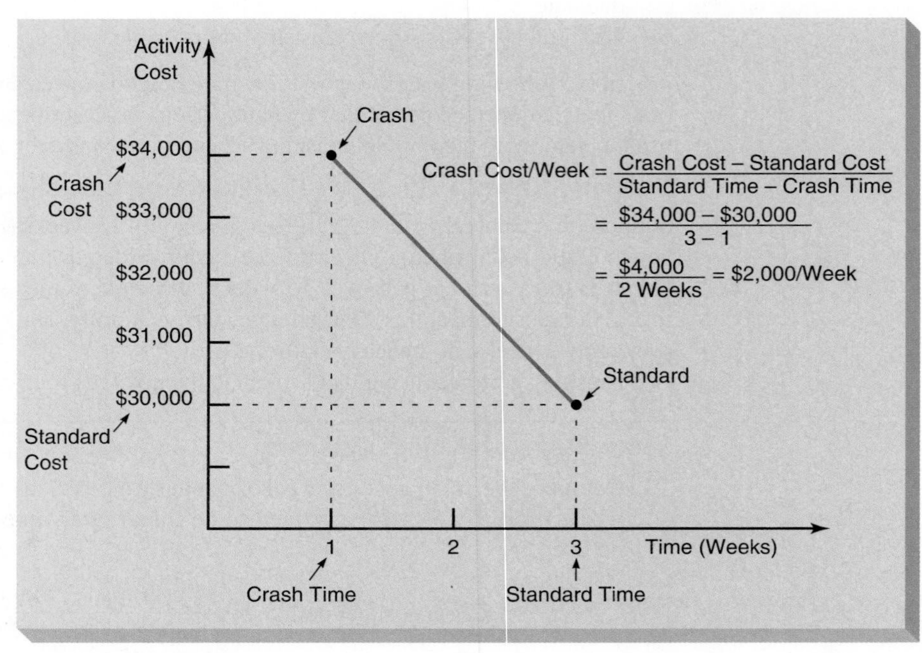

FIGURE 7.19 Critical Path and Slack Times for General Foundry

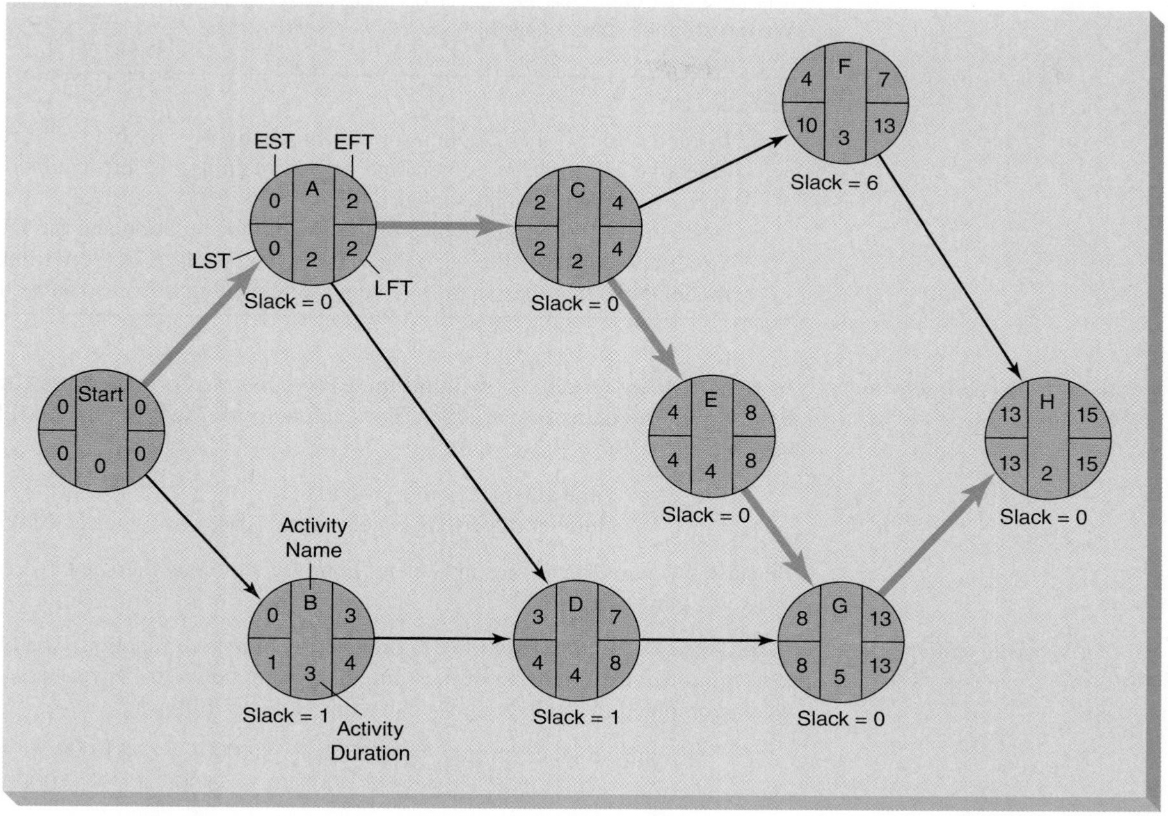

Steps 2, 3, and 4 of the project crashing process can now be applied to reduce General Foundry's project completion time at a minimum cost. For your convenience, we show the project network for General Foundry again in Figure 7.19.

The current critical path (using standard times) is Start-A-C-E-G-H, in which Start is a dummy starting activity. Of these critical activities, activity A has the lowest crash cost per week, at $750. Harky should therefore crash activity A by 1 week to reduce the project completion time to 14 weeks. The cost is an additional $750. Note that activity A cannot be crashed any further because it has reached its crash limit of 1 week.

There are now two critical paths.

At this stage, the original path Start-A-C-E-G-H remains critical, with a completion time of 14 weeks. However, a new path Start-B-D-G-H is also critical now, with a completion time of 14 weeks. Hence, any further crashing must be done to both critical paths.

On each of these critical paths, we need to identify one activity that can still be crashed. We also want the total cost of crashing an activity on each path to be the smallest. We might be tempted to simply pick the activities with the smallest crash cost per period in each path. If we do this, we would select activity C from the first path and activity D from the second path. The total crash cost would then be $2,000 (=$1,000 + $1,000).

Crashing activities common to more than one critical path may be cheapest.

But we spot that activity G is common to both paths. That is, by crashing activity G, we will simultaneously reduce the completion time of both paths. Even though the $1,500 crash cost for activity G is higher than that for activities C or D, we would still prefer crashing G because the total cost is now only $1,500 (compared with the $2,000 if we crash C and D).

Hence, to crash the project down to 13 weeks, Lester Harky should crash activity A by 1 week and activity G by 1 week. The total additional cost is $2,250(=$750 + $1,500).

Crashing General Foundry's Project Using Linear Programming

Although the preceding crashing procedure is simple for projects involving just a few activities, it can become extremely cumbersome to use for larger projects. Linear programming (LP) is an excellent technique for determining the optimal (i.e., least expensive) way to crash even larger projects. Let us examine how this technique may be used here.

The data needed for General Foundry's project crashing LP model are the standard and crash time and cost data (see Table 7.10) and the activity precedence information (see Figure 7.19). We develop the model as follows.

Excel Notes

- In each of our Excel layouts, for clarity, changing variable cells are shaded yellow, the objective cell is shaded green, and cells containing the left-hand-side (LHS) formula for each constraint are shaded blue.
- Also, to make the equivalence of the written formulation and the Excel layout clear, our Excel layouts show the decision variable names used in the written formulation of the model. Note that these names have no role in using Solver to solve the model.

Decision variables are start times and crash amounts.

DECISION VARIABLES As with all the LP models we formulated in Chapters 2–5, we begin by defining the decision variables. For each activity i, we define the following two decision variables:

$$T_i = \text{Time at which activity } i \text{ starts}$$
$$C_i = \text{Number of periods (weeks, in this case) by which activity } i \text{ is crashed}$$

Because there are 8 activities in General Foundry's project, there are 16 decision variables in the project crashing LP model.

The objective is to minimize total crash cost.

OBJECTIVE FUNCTION Next, we formulate the objective function. The objective function here is to minimize the total cost of crashing the project down to 13 weeks. Using the crash cost per week, computed in Table 7.10, we can express this as follows:

$$\text{Minimize total crash cost} = \$750C_A + \$2{,}000C_B + \$1{,}000C_C + \$1{,}000C_D + \$1{,}000C_E + \$500C_F + \$1{,}500C_G + \$3{,}000C_H$$

Constraints define the precedence relationships.

PRECEDENCE CONSTRAINTS Finally, we formulate the constraints. The first set of constraints in this LP model enforces the precedence relationships between activities (shown in the project network in Figure 7.19). We write one constraint for each precedence relationship (i.e., arc) in the project network. In writing these constraints, we must remember that the duration of each activity may be reduced by a crash amount (C_i). For example, consider the precedence relationship between activities A and C. Activity A starts at time T_A, and its duration is $(2 - C_A)$ weeks. Hence, activity A finishes at time $(T_A + 2 - C_A)$. This implies that the earliest start time of activity C (i.e., T_C) can be *no earlier* than $(T_A + 2 - C_A)$. We can express this mathematically as

$$T_C \geq T_A + (2 - C_A) \quad \text{(precedence A} \rightarrow \text{C)}$$

In a similar fashion, we can express all other activity precedence relationships as follows:

$$T_D \geq T_A + (2 - C_A) \quad \text{(precedence A} \rightarrow \text{D)}$$
$$T_D \geq T_B + (3 - C_B) \quad \text{(precedence B} \rightarrow \text{D)}$$
$$T_E \geq T_C + (2 - C_C) \quad \text{(precedence C} \rightarrow \text{E)}$$
$$T_F \geq T_C + (2 - C_C) \quad \text{(precedence C} \rightarrow \text{F)}$$
$$T_G \geq T_D + (4 - C_D) \quad \text{(precedence D} \rightarrow \text{G)}$$
$$T_G \geq T_E + (4 - C_E) \quad \text{(precedence E} \rightarrow \text{G)}$$
$$T_H \geq T_F + (3 - C_F) \quad \text{(precedence F} \rightarrow \text{H)}$$
$$T_H \geq T_G + (5 - C_G) \quad \text{(precedence G} \rightarrow \text{H)}$$

Each activity can be crashed by only a finite amount.

CRASH TIME LIMIT CONSTRAINTS We need a second set of constraints to restrict the number of periods by which each activity can be crashed. Using the crash time limits given in Table 7.10 on page 294, we can write these constraints as

$$C_A \leq 1 \quad C_B \leq 2 \quad C_C \leq 1 \quad C_D \leq 1$$
$$C_E \leq 2 \quad C_F \leq 1 \quad C_G \leq 3 \quad C_H \leq 1$$

The constraint specifies the project due date

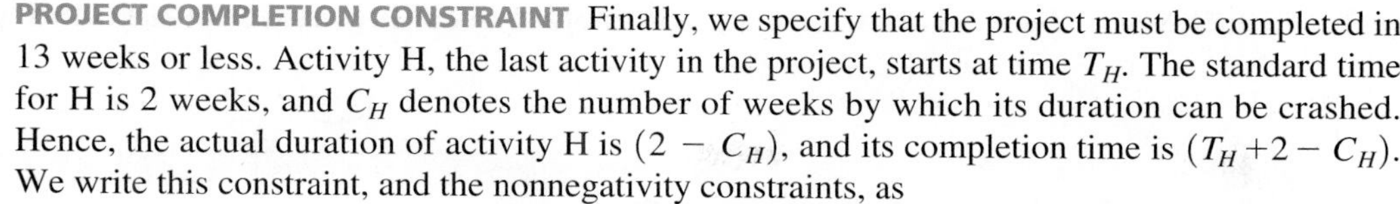

PROJECT COMPLETION CONSTRAINT Finally, we specify that the project must be completed in 13 weeks or less. Activity H, the last activity in the project, starts at time T_H. The standard time for H is 2 weeks, and C_H denotes the number of weeks by which its duration can be crashed. Hence, the actual duration of activity H is $(2 - C_H)$, and its completion time is $(T_H + 2 - C_H)$. We write this constraint, and the nonnegativity constraints, as

$$T_H + 2 - C_H \leq 13$$

$$\text{All } T_i \text{ and } C_i \geq 0$$

File: 7-2.xls, sheet: 7-2A

EXCEL SOLUTION Screenshot 7-2A shows the formula view of the Excel layout for General Foundry's project crashing LP model. This layout follows the same structure and logic we have used in earlier chapters for all LP models. That is, we have modeled all parameters (solution value, objective coefficients, and constraint coefficients) associated with a decision variable in a separate column of the worksheet. We have then computed the objective function and LHS formulas for all constraints, using Excel's SUMPRODUCT function. In implementing this model on Excel, we have algebraically modified each constraint so that all variables are in the LHS of the equation, and only a constant appears on the right-hand side (RHS). For example, the precedence relationship between activities A and C has been modified from $[T_C \geq T_A + (2 - C_A)]$ to $[T_C - T_A + C_A \geq 2]$.

File: 7-2.xls, sheet: 7-2B

Solver entries are objective cell, changing variable cells, and constraints.

INTERPRETING THE RESULTS The Solver entries and solution for this LP model are shown in Screenshot 7-2B. The results show that the General Foundry project can be crashed to 13 weeks, at a cost of $2,250 (cell R6). To do so, activities A (cell J5) and G (cell P5) should be crashed by 1 week each. As expected, this is the same as the result we obtained earlier, using hand calculations. Cells B5:I5 show the revised starting times for activities A through H, respectively.

Using Linear Programming to Determine Earliest and Latest Starting Times

It turns out that we can make minor modifications to the project crashing LP model presented earlier to compute the EST and LST for each activity in a project. However, because the two-pass procedure we discussed in section 7.3 is rather straightforward, LP is seldom used in

SCREENSHOT 7-2A Formula View of Excel Layout for Project Crashing at General Foundry

These variables denote starting times for activities.

These variables denote crash times for each activity.

	A	B	C	D	E	F	G	H	I	J	K	L	M	N	O	P	Q	R	S	T
1	**Project Crashing at General Foundry**																			
2																				
3		T_A	T_B	T_C	T_D	T_E	T_F	T_G	T_H	C_A	C_B	C_C	C_D	C_E	C_F	C_G	C_H			
4		Start A	Start B	Start C	Start D	Start E	Start F	Start G	Start H	Crash A	Crash B	Crash C	Crash D	Crash E	Crash F	Crash G	Crash H			
5	Solution value																			
6	Crash cost									750	2000	1000	1000	1000	500	1500	3000	=SUMPRODUCT(B6:Q6,$B$5:$Q$5)		
7	**Constraints**																			
8	A --> C	-1		1						1								=SUMPRODUCT(B8:Q8,$B$5:$Q$5)	>=	2
9	A --> D	-1			1					1								=SUMPRODUCT(B9:Q9,$B$5:$Q$5)	>=	2
10	B --> D		-1		1						1							=SUMPRODUCT(B10:Q10,$B$5:$Q$5)	>=	3
11	C --> E			-1		1						1						=SUMPRODUCT(B11:Q11,$B$5:$Q$5)	>=	2
12	C --> F			-1			1					1						=SUMPRODUCT(B12:Q12,$B$5:$Q$5)	>=	2
13	D --> G				-1			1					1					=SUMPRODUCT(B13:Q13,$B$5:$Q$5)	>=	4
14	E --> G					-1		1						1				=SUMPRODUCT(B14:Q14,$B$5:$Q$5)	>=	4
15	F --> H						-1		1						1			=SUMPRODUCT(B15:Q15,$B$5:$Q$5)	>=	3
16	G --> H							-1	1							1		=SUMPRODUCT(B16:Q16,$B$5:$Q$5)	>=	5
17	Crash limit A									1								=SUMPRODUCT(B17:Q17,$B$5:$Q$5)	<=	1
18	Crash limit B										1							=SUMPRODUCT(B18:Q18,$B$5:$Q$5)	<=	2
19	Crash limit C											1						=SUMPRODUCT(B19:Q19,$B$5:$Q$5)	<=	1
20	Crash limit D												1					=SUMPRODUCT(B20:Q20,$B$5:$Q$5)	<=	1
21	Crash limit E													1				=SUMPRODUCT(B21:Q21,$B$5:$Q$5)	<=	2
22	Crash limit F														1			=SUMPRODUCT(B22:Q22,$B$5:$Q$5)	<=	1
23	Crash limit G															1		=SUMPRODUCT(B23:Q23,$B$5:$Q$5)	<=	3
24	Crash limit H																1	=SUMPRODUCT(B24:Q24,$B$5:$Q$5)	<=	1
25	Project finish								1								-1	=SUMPRODUCT(B25:Q25,$B$5:$Q$5)	<=	11
26																		LHS	Sign	RHS

Constraints in rows 8–16 enforce precedence relationships.

Constraint ensures that activity H must have a normal starting time of 11 in order for project to finish within 13 weeks.

All entries in column R are computed using the SUMPRODUCT function.

SCREENSHOT 7-2B Solver Entries for Project Crashing at General Foundry

Activity start times

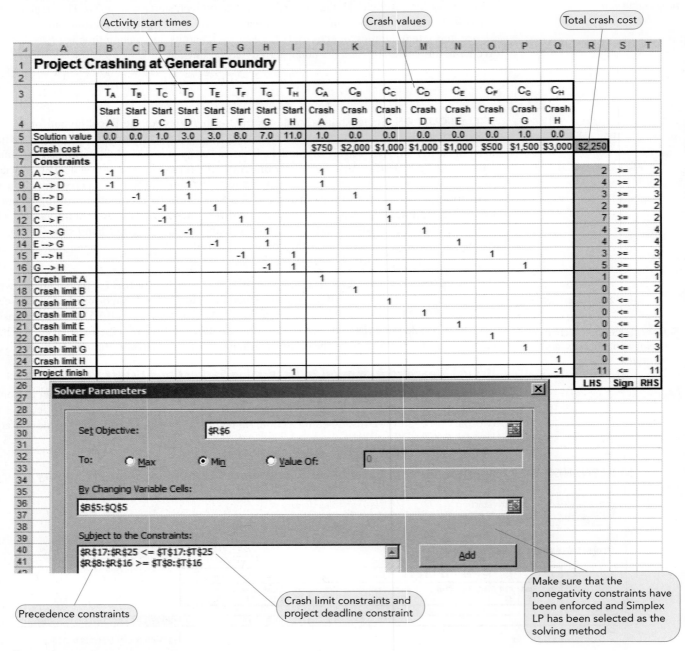

Crash values

Total crash cost

	A	B	C	D	E	F	G	H	I	J	K	L	M	N	O	P	Q	R	S	T
1	**Project Crashing at General Foundry**																			
2																				
3		T_A	T_B	T_C	T_D	T_E	T_F	T_G	T_H	C_A	C_B	C_C	C_D	C_E	C_F	C_G	C_H			
4		Start A	Start B	Start C	Start D	Start E	Start F	Start G	Start H	Crash A	Crash B	Crash C	Crash D	Crash E	Crash F	Crash G	Crash H			
5	Solution value	0.0	0.0	1.0	3.0	3.0	8.0	7.0	11.0	1.0	0.0	0.0	0.0	0.0	0.0	1.0	0.0			
6	Crash cost									$750	$2,000	$1,000	$1,000	$1,000	$500	$1,500	$3,000	$2,250		
7	**Constraints**																			
8	A --> C	-1		1						1								2	>=	2
9	A --> D	-1			1					1								4	>=	2
10	B --> D		-1		1						1							3	>=	3
11	C --> E			-1		1						1						2	>=	2
12	C --> F			-1			1					1						7	>=	2
13	D --> G				-1			1					1					4	>=	4
14	E --> G					-1		1						1				4	>=	4
15	F --> H						-1		1						1			3	>=	3
16	G --> H							-1	1							1		5	>=	5
17	Crash limit A									1								1	<=	1
18	Crash limit B										1							0	<=	2
19	Crash limit C											1						0	<=	1
20	Crash limit D												1					0	<=	1
21	Crash limit E													1				0	<=	2
22	Crash limit F														1			0	<=	1
23	Crash limit G															1		1	<=	3
24	Crash limit H																1	0	<=	1
25	Project finish								1								-1	11	<=	11
26																		LHS	Sign	RHS

Solver Parameters

Set Objective: $R$6

To: Max ⦿ Min Value Of: 0

By Changing Variable Cells: $B$5:$Q$5

Subject to the Constraints:
$R$17:$R$25 <= $T$17:$T$25
$R$8:$R$16 >= $T$8:$T$16

Add

Precedence constraints

Crash limit constraints and project deadline constraint

Make sure that the nonnegativity constraints have been enforced and Simplex LP has been selected as the solving method

practice for this purpose. For this reason, we do not discuss these LP models in detail here and just briefly illustrate their construction.

We first modify the project crashing LP model by removing the project completion constraint and setting all crashing decision variables (C_i) to zero. All precedence constraints in this model remain as is. Then, we solve two LP models in sequence: the first to identify the earliest times and the second to identify the latest times. The additional modifications needed to the project crashing LP model for each of these models are as follows:

- ***LP model for earliest starting times.*** In this LP model, we set the objective function to minimize the sum of all activity starting times. That is, the objective is

$$\text{Minimize sum of activity times} = T_A + T_B + \cdots + T_H$$

- ***LP model for latest starting times.*** In this LP model, we set the objective function to maximize the sum of all activity starting times. That is, the objective is

$$\text{Maximize sum of activity times} = T_A + T_B + \cdots + T_H$$

However, we need to ensure that the entire project finishes at its earliest completion time (as computed by the LP model for the EST). Hence, we add a constraint regarding the starting time of the *last activity* in the project. For example, in General Foundry's project, we set the LST of activity H at 13 weeks (i.e., $T_H = 13$).

7.7 Using Microsoft Project to Manage Projects

The analyses discussed so far in this chapter are effective for managing small projects. However, for managing large, complex projects, using specialized project management software is preferred. In this section, we provide a brief introduction to a popular example of such specialized software, Microsoft Project 2010.

Microsoft Project is useful for project scheduling and control.

We should note that at this introductory level, our intent is not to describe the full capabilities of Microsoft Project. Rather, we illustrate how it can be used to perform some of the basic calculations in managing projects. We leave it to you to explore the advanced capabilities and functions of Microsoft Project (or any other project management software) in greater detail, either on your own or as part of an elective course in project management.

Microsoft Project is extremely useful in drawing project networks (section 7.2), identifying the project schedule (section 7.3), and managing project costs and other resources (section 7.5). It does not, however, perform PERT probability calculations (section 7.4) or have an LP-based procedure built in for project crashing (section 7.6).

File: 7-3.mpp

Creating a Project Schedule Using Microsoft Project

First, we define a new project.

Let us consider the General Foundry project again. Recall from section 7.2 that this project has eight activities. The first step is to define the activities and their precedence relationships. To do so, we start Microsoft Project, click File | New, and select the blank project template. We can now select the Project Information menu command (found within the Project tab) to obtain the window shown in Screenshot 7-3A and enter summary information such as the project start date. Note that dates are referred to by actual calendar dates rather than as day 0, day 1, and so on. For example, we have specified July 1 as our project starting date in Screenshot 7-3A (dates can be shown using several different formats, including showing the year, too, if desired). Microsoft Project automatically updates the project finish date once we have entered all the project information. In Screenshot 7-3A, we have specified the current date as August 12.

Next, we enter the activity information.

ENTERING ACTIVITY INFORMATION After entering the summary information, we use the window shown in Screenshot 7-3B to enter all activity information. For each activity (or task, as Microsoft Project calls it), we enter its name and duration. Microsoft Project identifies tasks by numbers (e.g., 1, 2) rather than letters. Hence, for convenience, we have shown both the letter (e.g., A, B) and the description of the activity in the Task Name column in Screenshot 7-3B. By default, the duration is measured in days. To specify weeks, we include the letter *w* after the duration of each activity. For example, we enter the duration of activity A as 2*w*.

Durations

Activity	*Time (weeks)*
A	2
B	3
C	2
D	4
E	4
F	3
G	5
H	2

As we enter the activities and durations, the software automatically inserts start and finish dates. Note that all activities have the same start date (i.e., July 1) because we have not yet defined the precedence relationships. Also, as shown in Screenshot 7-3B, if the Gantt Chart option is selected in the View menu, a horizontal bar corresponding to the duration of each activity appears on the right pane of the window.

Observe that Saturdays and Sundays are automatically grayed out in the Gantt chart to reflect the fact that these are nonworking days. In most project management software, we can link the entire project to a master calendar (or, alternatively, link each activity to its own specific calendar). Additional nonworking days can be defined using these calendars. For example, we have used the Change Working Time menu command (found within the Project tab) to specify Monday, July 4, as a nonworking day in Screenshot 7-3B. (Note that this day is also grayed out in the Gantt chart.) This automatically extends all activity completion times by one day. Because activity A starts on Friday, July 1, and takes 2 weeks (i.e., 10 working days), its finish time is now Friday, July 15 (rather than Thursday, July 14).

The schedule automatically takes into account nonworking days.

SCREENSHOT 7-3A Project Summary Information in Microsoft Project

Specify current data, if necessary (will automatically show today's date). Used for tracking project status.

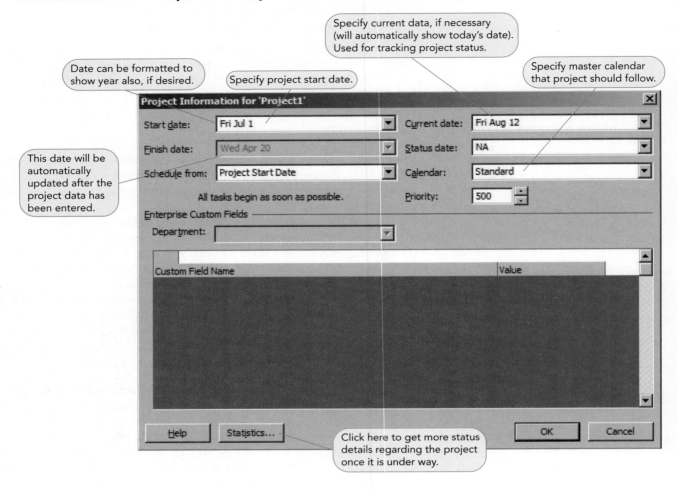

Date can be formatted to show year also, if desired.

Specify project start date.

Specify master calendar that project should follow.

Project Information for 'Project1'

Start date: Fri Jul 1

Current date: Fri Aug 12

Finish date: Wed Apr 20

Status date: NA

Schedule from: Project Start Date

Calendar: Standard

All tasks begin as soon as possible.

Priority: 500

Enterprise Custom Fields

Department:

Custom Field Name

Value

Help

Statistics...

OK

Cancel

This date will be automatically updated after the project data has been entered.

Click here to get more status details regarding the project once it is under way.

SCREENSHOT 7-3B Activity Entry in Microsoft Project for General Foundry

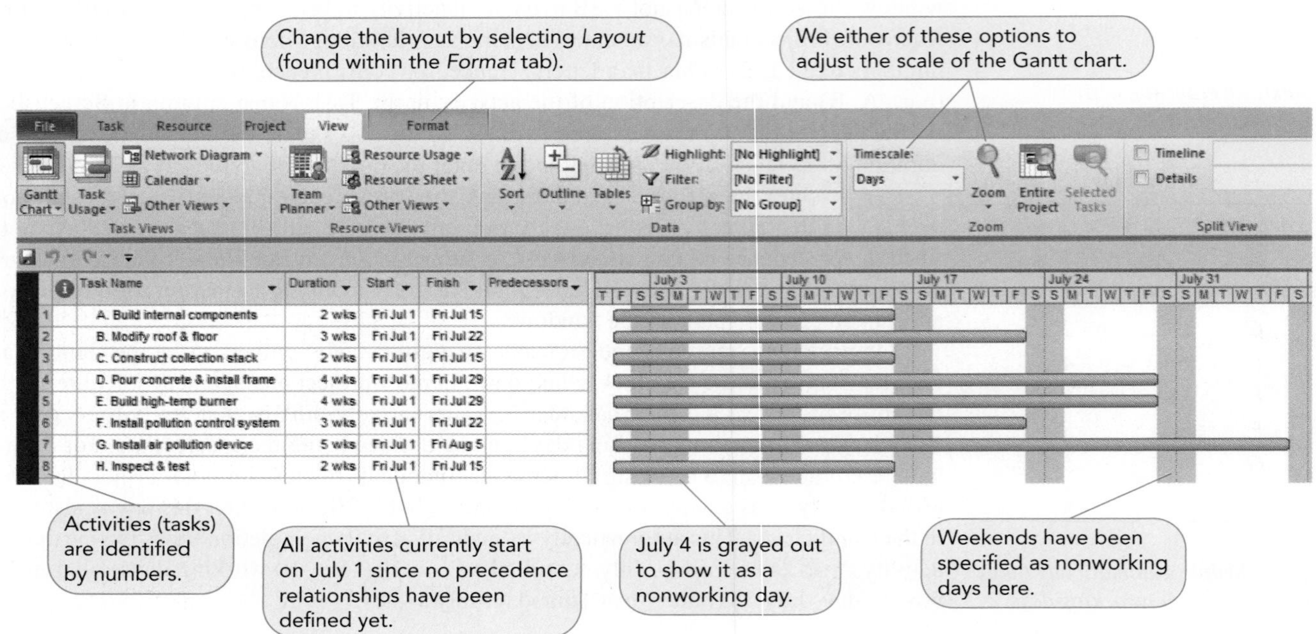

SCREENSHOT 7-3C Defining Links between Activities in Microsoft Project

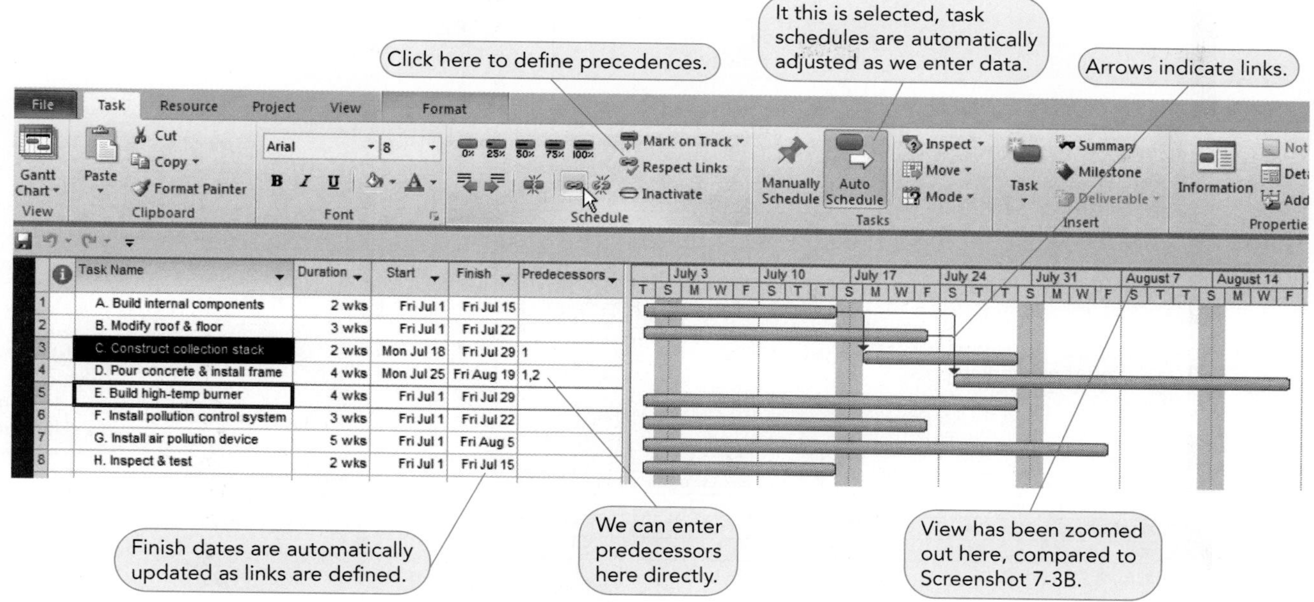

Precedences

Activity	*Predecessors*
A	—
B	—
C	*A*
D	*A, B*
E	*C*
F	*C*
G	*D, E*
H	*F, G*

DEFINING PRECEDENCE RELATIONSHIPS The next step is to define precedence relationships (or links) between the activities. There are two ways of specifying these links. The first is to enter the relevant activity numbers (e.g., 1, 2) in the Predecessor column, as shown in Screenshot 7-3C for activities C and D. The other approach uses the Link icon. For example, to specify the precedence relationship between activities C and E, we click activity C first, hold down the Control (Ctrl) key, and then click activity E. We then click the Link icon (found within the Task tab), as shown in Screenshot 7-3C. As soon as we define a link, the bars in the Gantt chart are repositioned to reflect the new start and finish times for the linked activities if the Auto Schedule mode is enabled (as in Screenshot 7-3C). Further, the link itself is shown as an arrow extending from the predecessor activity.

VIEWING THE PROJECT SCHEDULE When all links have been defined, the complete project schedule can be viewed as a Gantt chart, as shown in Screenshot 7-3D. We can also select Network Diagram (found within the View tab) to view the schedule as a project network (shown

SCREENSHOT 7-3D Gantt Chart in Microsoft Project for General Foundry

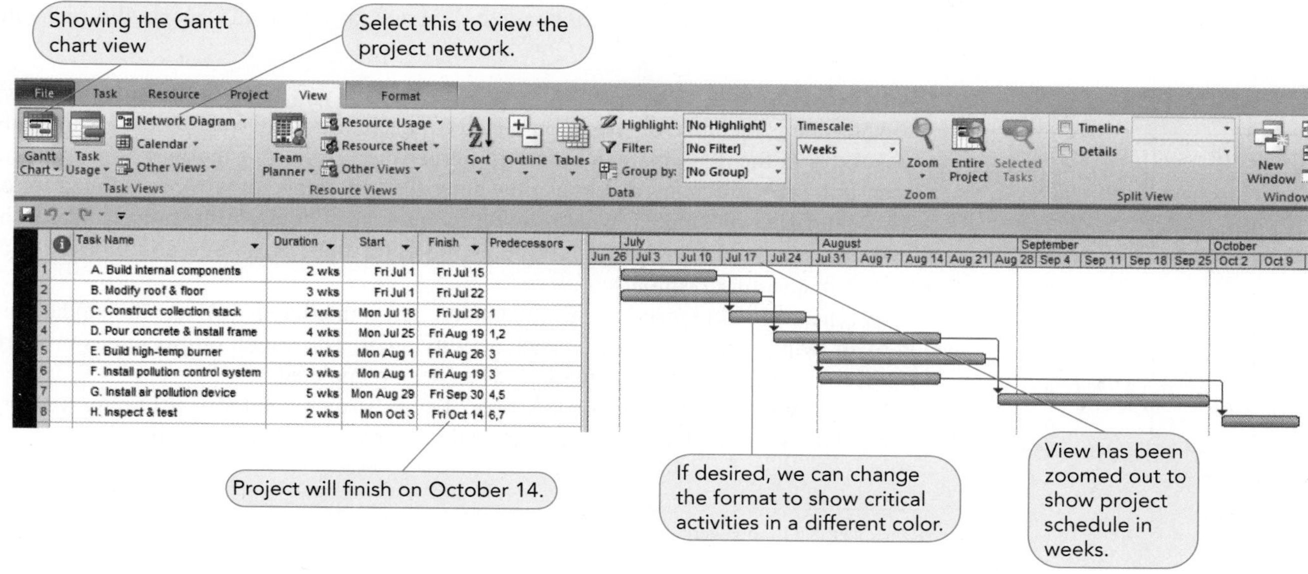

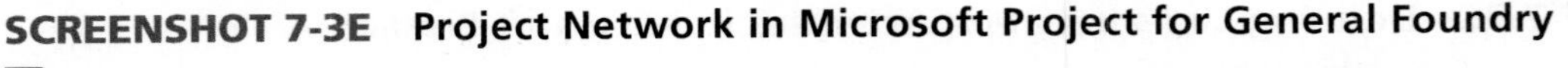

SCREENSHOT 7-3E Project Network in Microsoft Project for General Foundry

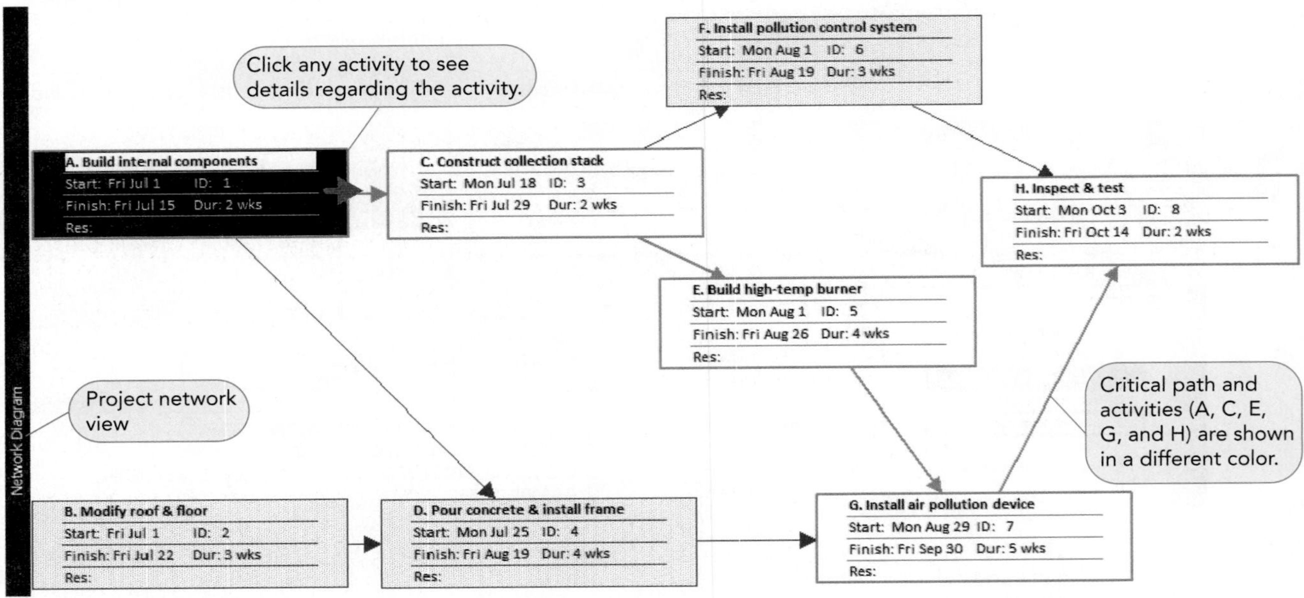

The project can be viewed either as a Gantt chart or as a network.

in Screenshot 7-3E). The critical path is shown in red on the screen in the network diagram. We can click any of the activities in the project network to view details of the activities. Likewise, we can easily add or remove activities and/or links from the project network. Each time we do so, Microsoft Project automatically updates all start dates, all finish dates, and the critical path(s). If desired, we can manually change the layout of the network (e.g., reposition activities) by changing the options in Format|Layout.

Screenshots 7-3D and 7-3E show that if General Foundry's project starts July 1, it can be finished on October 14. The start and finish dates for all activities are also clearly identified. This schedule takes into account the nonworking days on all weekends and on July 4. These screenshots illustrate how the use of specialized project management software can greatly simplify the scheduling procedures discussed in sections 7.2 and 7.3.

The biggest benefit of using software is to track a project.

File: 7-4.mpp

Tracking Progress and Managing Costs Using Microsoft Project

Perhaps the biggest advantage of using specialized software to manage projects is that it can track the progress of the project. In this regard, Microsoft Project has many features available to track individual activities in terms of time, cost, resource usage, and so on. In this section, we first illustrate how we can track the progress of a project in terms of time. We then introduce project costs so that we can compute cost overruns or underruns (as we did in Table 7.7 on page 291).

Percentage Completed

Activity	*Completed*
A	*100*
B	*100*
C	*100*
D	*10*
E	*20*
F	*20*
G	*0*
H	*0*

TRACKING THE TIME STATUS OF A PROJECT An easy way to track the time progress of tasks is to enter the percentage of work completed for each task. One way to do so is to double-click any activity in the Task Name column in Screenshot 7-3D. A window like the one shown in Screenshot 7-4A is displayed. Let us now enter the percentage of work completed for each task (as we did earlier in Table 7.7; also shown in the margin note). For example, Screenshot 7-4A shows that activity A is 100% complete. We enter the percentage completed for all other activities in a similar fashion.

As shown in Screenshot 7-4B, the Gantt chart immediately reflects this updated information by drawing a thick line within each activity's bar. The length of this line is proportional to the percentage of that activity's work that has been completed.

How do we know if we are on schedule? Let us assume that today is Friday, August 12 (i.e., the end of the sixth week in the project schedule).[5] Notice that there is a vertical dashed line shown

[5] Remember that the nonworking day on July 4 has moved all schedules forward by one day.

SCREENSHOT 7-4A Updating Activity Progress in Microsoft Project

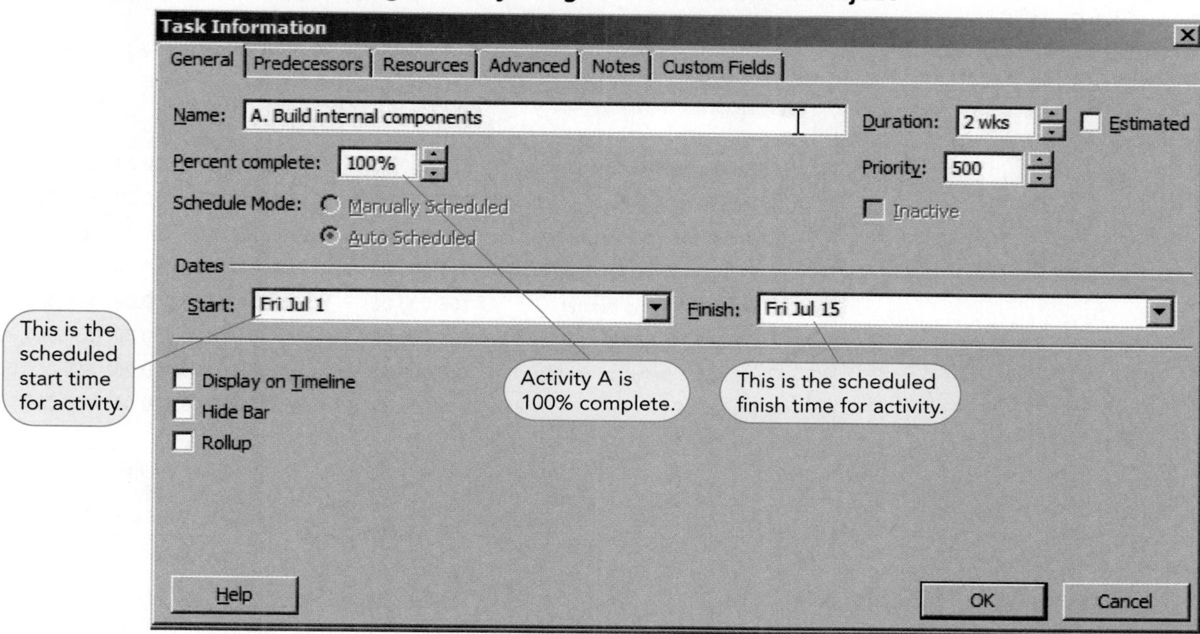

SCREENSHOT 7-4B Tracking Project Progress in Microsoft Project

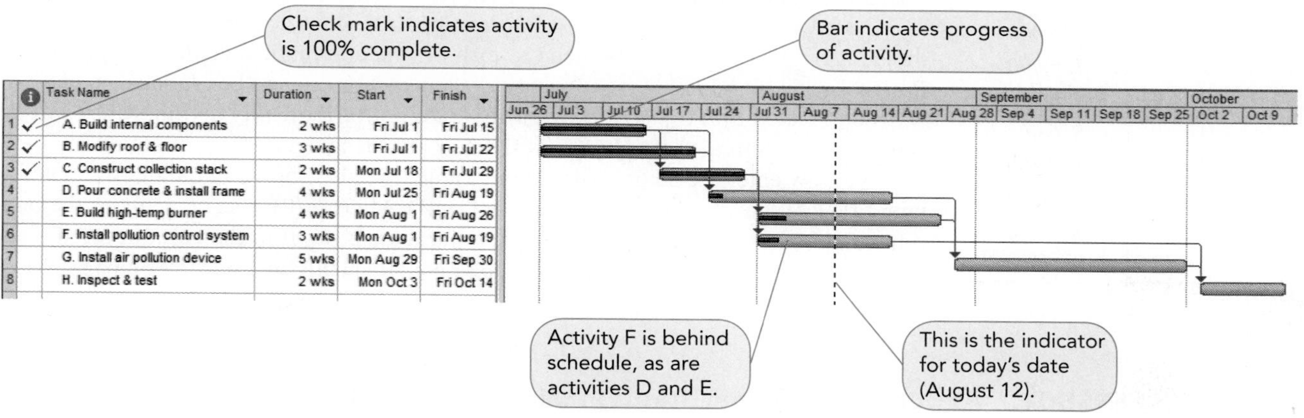

on the Gantt chart corresponding to today's date. Microsoft Project will automatically move this line to correspond with the current date. If the project is on schedule, we should see all bars to the *left* of today's line indicate that they have been completed. For example, Screenshot 7-4B shows that activities A, B, and C are on schedule. In contrast, activities D, E, and F appear to be behind schedule. These activities need to be investigated further to determine the reason for the delay. This type of easy *visual* information is what makes project management software so useful in practice.

We define the costs for each activity.

Budgeted Cost

Activity	*Budget*
A	*$22,000*
B	*$30,000*
C	*$26,000*
D	*$48,000*
E	*$56,000*
F	*$30,000*
G	*$80,000*
H	*$16,000*

TRACKING THE COST STATUS OF A PROJECT Just as we tracked a project's progress with regard to time, we can track its current status with regard to budget. There are several ways to define the cost of an activity. If the total cost consists of both fixed and variable costs, we need to define the resources used in the project, the unit costs of those resources, and the level of usage for each resource by each activity. We can even specify how resources should be charged to an activity (e.g., prorated basis, full billing upon completion). Microsoft Project uses this information to first calculate the variable cost of each activity based on its level of resource usage. This is then added to the fixed costs to find the total cost for each activity.

In the case of General Foundry's project, because we have not specified the fixed and variable costs separately, an alternate way to enter activity costs is to click Tables | Cost (found within the View tab). The window shown in Screenshot 7-4C is displayed. We enter the budgeted cost

SCREENSHOT 7-4C Entering Cost Information in Microsoft Project

Establish baseline by clicking Set Baseline (found within the Project tab).

	Task Name	Fixed Cost	Fixed Cost Accrual	Total Cost	Baseline
1	A. Build internal components	$22,000.00	Prorated	$22,000.00	$22,000.00
2	B. Modify roof & floor	$30,000.00	Prorated	$30,000.00	$30,000.00
3	C. Construct collection stack	$26,000.00	Prorated	$26,000.00	$26,000.00
4	D. Pour concrete & install frame	$48,000.00	Prorated	$48,000.00	$48,000.00
5	E. Build high-temp burner	$56,000.00	Prorated	$56,000.00	$56,000.00
6	F. Install pollution control system	$30,000.00	Prorated	$30,000.00	$30,000.00
7	G. Install air pollution device	$80,000.00	Prorated	$80,000.00	$80,000.00
8	H. Inspect & test	$16,000.00	Prorated	$16,000.00	$16,000.00

In this case, we have entered the activity costs as fixed costs.

Total cost = Fixed cost since no variable costs have been defined.

We compute the variances in activity budgets.

Actual Cost

Activity	*Cost*
A	*$20,000*
B	*$36,000*
C	*$26,000*
D	*$ 6,000*
E	*$20,000*
F	*$ 4,000*
G	*$ 0*
H	*$ 0*

for each activity (see Table 7.7; also shown in the margin note on page 303) in the Fixed Cost column. Microsoft Project automatically copies these values to the Total Cost column. We can now use these total costs to establish the Baseline Cost (or budgeted cost) by clicking Set Baseline (found within the Project tab). This information is also shown in Screenshot 7-4C.

Once we have entered this cost information, how do we compare our current expenses with the budget? To do so, we first need to turn off the automatic calculation option in Microsoft Project by clicking File|Options|Schedule and unchecking the box labeled Actual costs are always calculated by Project. Note that if we do not turn off this option, Microsoft Project assumes that all activities are always working as per the budget.

We now enter the actual costs (from Table 7.7; also shown in the margin note) in the column titled Actual, as shown in Screenshot 7-4D. Microsoft Project calculates the budget overrun or underrun associated with each activity and shows it in the column titled Variance. As expected, these are the same values we computed manually in Table 7.7 on page 291.

SCREENSHOT 7-4D Checking Budget Status in Microsoft Project

Budgeted costs

	Task Name	Fixed Cost	Fixed Cost Accrual	Total Cost	Baseline	Variance	Actual	Remaining
1	A. Build internal components	$20,000.00	Prorated	$20,000.00	$22,000.00	($2,000.00)	$20,000.00	$0.00
2	B. Modify roof & floor	$30,000.00	Prorated	$36,000.00	$30,000.00	$6,000.00	$36,000.00	$0.00
3	C. Construct collection stack	$26,000.00	Prorated	$26,000.00	$26,000.00	$0.00	$26,000.00	$0.00
4	D. Pour concrete & install frame	$48,000.00	Prorated	$49,200.00	$48,000.00	$1,200.00	$6,000.00	$43,200.00
5	E. Build high-temp burner	$56,000.00	Prorated	$64,800.00	$56,000.00	$8,800.00	$20,000.00	$44,800.00
6	F. Install pollution control system	$28,000.00	Prorated	$28,000.00	$30,000.00	($2,000.00)	$5,600.00	$22,400.00
7	G. Install air pollution device	$80,000.00	Prorated	$80,000.00	$80,000.00	$0.00	$0.00	$80,000.00
8	H. Inspect & test	$16,000.00	Prorated	$16,000.00	$16,000.00	$0.00	$0.00	$16,000.00

Total cost values are changed to reflect variances.

Cost overruns and underruns. (Negative values indicate underruns.)

Current expenses. You must turn off automatic calculations in order to enter information here.

As noted earlier, our intent here is to provide just a brief introduction to Microsoft Project. This software (and other specialized project management software) has several other features and capabilities that we have not discussed here. For example, we can use it to associate individual resources with specific activities and establish a separate calendar for each resource. The time schedule of the activity will then be determined based not only on its duration and predecessors but also on the resource calendars. Likewise, we can track each resource and identify possible conflicts (e.g., the same resource being required by two different activities at the same time). Once again, we encourage you to try these procedures on your own to understand the full capabilities of specialized project management software.

Summary

This chapter presents the fundamentals of project management techniques. We discuss two techniques, PERT and CPM, both of which are excellent for controlling large and complex projects.

We first show how to express projects using project networks. Using a two-pass procedure, we can then identify the project schedule and the critical path(s). PERT is probabilistic and allows three time estimates for each activity; these estimates are used to compute the project's expected completion time and variance. We show how to use these parameters to find the probability that the project will be completed by a given date.

We discuss how project management techniques can also be used to plan, schedule, monitor, and control project costs. Using these techniques, we show how to determine whether a project is on schedule at any point in time and whether there are cost overruns or underruns.

Next, we discuss how to crash projects by reducing their completion time through additional resource expenditures. We also illustrate how LP can be used to find the least-cost approach to crashing large projects.

Finally, we provide a brief introduction to Microsoft Project, one of several popular project management software packages.

Glossary

Activity A job or task that consumes time and is a key subpart of a total project.

Activity on Arc (AOA) Network A project network in which arcs denote activities and nodes denote events.

Activity on Node (AON) Network A project network in which nodes denote activities and arcs denote precedence relationships.

Activity Time The duration of an activity.

Backward Pass A procedure that moves from the end of the network to the beginning of the network and is used in determining an activity's LFT and LST.

Beta Probability Distribution A probability distribution that is often used in PERT to compute expected activity completion times and variances.

Crashing The process of reducing the total time it takes to complete a project by expending additional funds.

Critical Path A series of activities that have zero slack. It is the longest time path through the network. A delay for any activity that is on the critical path will delay the completion of the entire project.

Critical Path Analysis An analysis that determines the total project completion time, the critical path for the project, slack, EST, EFT, LST, and LFT for every activity.

Critical Path Method (CPM) A deterministic network technique that is similar to PERT but uses only one time estimate. CPM is used for monitoring budgets and project crashing.

Dummy Activity A fictitious activity that consumes no time and is inserted into an AOA project network to display the proper precedence relationships between activities.

Earliest Finish Time (EFT) The earliest time that an activity can be finished without violation of precedence requirements.

Earliest Start Time (EST) The earliest time that an activity can start without violation of precedence requirements.

Event A point in time that marks the beginning or ending of an activity. It is used in AOA networks.

Expected Activity Time (t) The average time it should take to complete an activity. Expected time $= (a + 4m + b)/6$.

Forward Pass A procedure that moves from the beginning of a network to the end of the network. It is used in determining an activity's EST and EFT.

Gantt Chart An alternative to project networks for showing a project schedule.

Immediate Predecessor An activity that must be completed before another activity can be started.

Latest Finish Time (LFT) The latest time that an activity can be finished without delaying the entire project.

Latest Start Time (LST) The latest time that an activity can be started without delaying the entire project.

Most Likely Time (m) The amount of time that you would expect it would take to complete an activity. Used in PERT.

Optimistic Time (a) The shortest amount of time that could be required to complete an activity. Used in PERT.

Pessimistic Time (b) The greatest amount of time that could be required to complete an activity. Used in PERT.

Program Evaluation and Review Technique (PERT) A probabilistic modeling procedure that allows three time estimates for each activity in a project.

Project Management A decision modeling approach that allows managers to plan, schedule, and control projects.

Project Network A graphical display of a project that shows activities and precedence relationships.

Resource Loading Chart A graph that plots the resource needed per period versus time.

Slack Time The amount of time that an activity can be delayed without delaying the entire project. Slack = LST − EST or LFT − EFT.

Variance of Activity Completion Time A measure of dispersion of the activity completion time. Variance $= [(b - a)/6]^2$.

Work Breakdown Structure (WBS) A plan that details the activities in a project.

Solved Problems

Solved Problem 7-1

To complete the wing assembly for an experimental aircraft, Scott DeWitte has laid out the seven major activities involved. These activities have been labeled A through G in the following table, which also shows their estimated times (in weeks) and immediate predecessors:

ACTIVITY	a	m	b	IMMEDIATE PREDECESSORS
A	1	2	3	—
B	2	3	4	—
C	4	5	6	A
D	8	9	10	B
E	2	5	8	C, D
F	4	5	6	D
G	1	2	3	E

Determine the expected time and variance for each activity.

Solution

For each activity, the expected time and variance can be computed using the formulas presented in Equations 7-6 and 7-7 on page 283, respectively. The results are summarized in the following table:

ACTIVITY	EXPECTED TIME (WEEKS)	VARIANCE
A	2	0.111
B	3	0.111
C	5	0.111
D	9	0.111
E	5	1.000
F	5	0.111
G	2	0.111

Solved Problem 7-2

Referring to Solved Problem 7-1, Scott would now like to determine the critical path for the entire wing assembly project as well as the expected completion time for the total project. In addition, he would like to determine the probability that the project will finish in 21 weeks or less.

FIGURE 7.20 Critical Path for Solved Problem 7-2

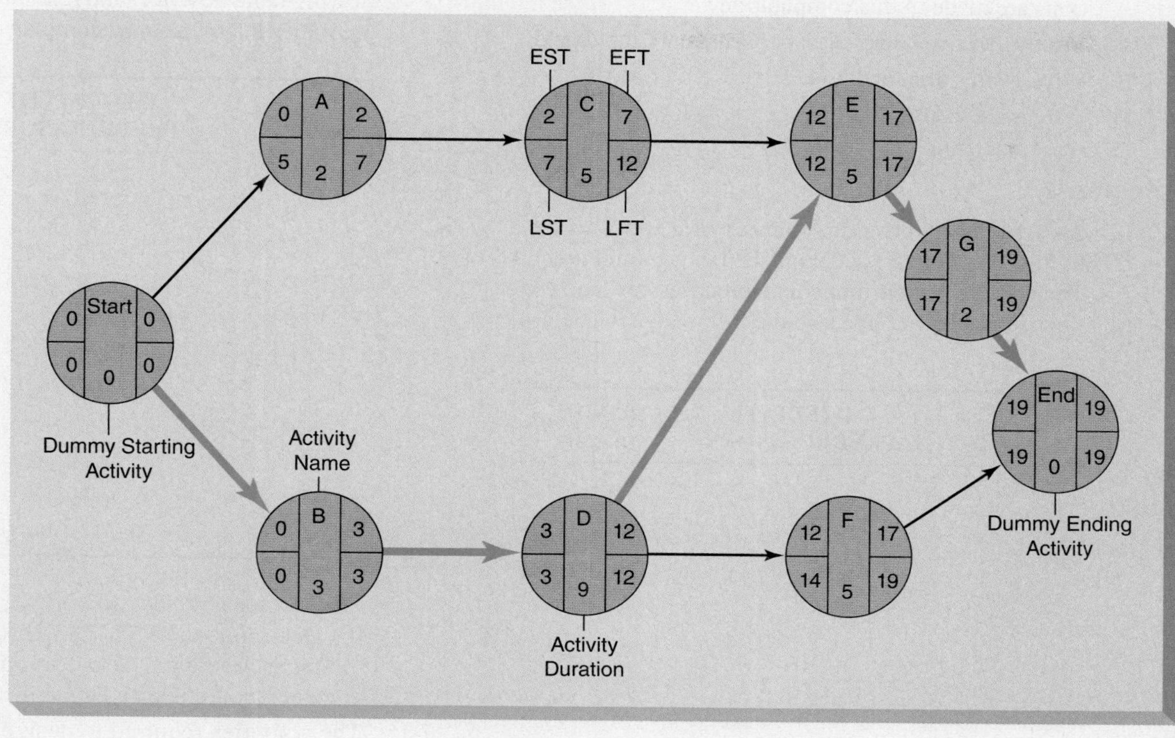

Solution

The AON network for Scott DeWitte's project is shown in Figure 7.20. Note that this project has multiple activities (A and B) with no immediate predecessors and multiple activities (F and G) with no successors. Hence, in addition to a dummy unique starting activity (Start), we have included a dummy unique finishing activity (End) for the project.

Figure 7.20 shows the earliest and latest times for all activities. The activities along the critical path are B, D, E, and G. These activities have zero slack. The expected project completion time is 19 weeks. The sum of the variances of the critical activities is 1.333, which implies that the standard deviation of the project completion time is 1.155 weeks. Hence,

$$P(\text{Completion time} \leq 21 \text{ weeks}) = P(Z \leq (21 - 19)/1.155) = P(Z \leq 1.73)$$
$$= 0.9582 \text{ (from Appendix C)}$$

Discussion Questions and Problems

Discussion Questions

7-1 What are some of the questions that can be answered with project management?

7-2 What are the major differences between PERT and CPM?

7-3 What is an activity? What is an immediate predecessor?

7-4 Describe how expected activity times and variances can be computed in a PERT analysis.

7-5 Briefly discuss what is meant by critical path analysis. What are critical path activities, and why are they important?

7-6 What are the EST and LST? How are they computed?

7-7 Describe the meaning of slack and discuss how it can be determined.

7-8 How can we determine the probability that a project will be completed by a certain date? What assumptions are made in this computation?

7-9 Briefly describe how project budgets can be monitored.

7-10 What is crashing, and how is it done by hand?

7-11 Why is LP useful in project crashing?

Problems

7-12 A certification program consists of a series of activities that must be accomplished in a certain order. The activities, their immediate predecessors, and estimated durations appear in the following table.

ACTIVITY	IMMEDIATE PREDECESSORS	TIME (DAYS)
A	—	2
B	—	5
C	—	1
D	B	10
E	A, D	3
F	C	6
G	E, F	8

(a) Develop a project network for the certification program.
(b) Determine the EST, EFT, LST, LFT, and slack for each activity. Also determine the total program completion time and the critical path(s).

7-13 A local political campaign must coordinate a number of necessary activities to be prepared for an upcoming election. The following table describes the relationships between these activities that need to be completed, as well as estimated times.

ACTIVITY	IMMEDIATE PREDECESSORS	TIME (WEEKS)
A	—	4
B	—	6
C	A	3
D	A	4
E	B, C	8
F	B	7
G	D, E	2
H	F	1

(a) Develop a project network for this problem.
(b) Determine the EST, EFT, LST, LFT, and slack for each activity. Also determine the total project completion time and the critical path(s).

7-14 The Pickett Marketing Firm is developing a new Web-based media campaign for a client. The following table describes the relationships between the activities that need to be completed.

ACTIVITY	IMMEDIATE PREDECESSORS	TIME (DAYS)
A	—	4
B	A	6
C	B	12
D	B	11
E	D	9
F	D	8
G	D	10
H	C	5
I	C	7
J	E, F, G	4
K	H, I	9

(a) Develop a project network for this problem.
(b) Determine the EST, EFT, LST, LFT, and slack for each activity. Also determine the total project completion time and the critical path(s).

7-15 The activities required to design a prototype of an experimental machine are listed in the following table, along with their immediate predecessors and estimated durations.

ACTIVITY	IMMEDIATE PREDECESSORS	TIME (DAYS)
A	—	5
B	—	4
C	A	2
D	A	1
E	B	5
F	B	7
G	C, E	9
H	D, F	6

(a) Develop a project network for this problem.
(b) Determine the EST, EFT, LST, LFT, and slack for each activity. Also determine the total project completion time and the critical path(s).

7-16 An office complex is to be renovated. Before the job can be completed, various tradespeople and skilled workers must install their materials. The table at the top of the next page describes the relationships between the activities that need to be completed.
(a) Develop a project network for this problem.
(b) Determine the EST, EFT, LST, LFT, and slack for each activity. Also determine the total project completion time and the critical path(s).

ACTIVITY	IMMEDIATE PREDECESSORS	TIME (DAYS)
A1	—	5
A2	A1	6
A3	A1	2
A4	A1	9
A5	A2	9
A6	A3, A4	3
A7	A4	7
A8	A4	4
A9	A5, A6, A7	6
A10	A8	5

7-17 An electrical contractor is examining the amount of time his crews take to complete wiring jobs. Some crews seem to take longer than others. For an upcoming job, a list of activities and their optimistic, most likely, and pessimistic completion times are given in the following table.

ACTIVITY	DAYS			IMMEDIATE PREDECESSORS
	a	*m*	*b*	
A	3	6	9	—
B	2	4	6	—
C	1	2	3	—
D	6	7	8	C
E	2	4	6	B, D
F	6	10	14	A, E
G	1	2	6	A, E
H	3	6	9	F
I	10	11	12	G
J	14	16	21	G
K	2	8	11	H, I

(a) Develop a project network for this problem.
(b) Determine the expected duration and variance for each activity.
(c) Determine the EST, EFT, LST, LFT, and slack for each activity. Also determine the total project completion time and critical path(s) for installing electrical wiring and equipment.
(d) What is the probability that this job will finish in 38 days or less?

7-18 A plant engineering group needs to set up an assembly line to produce a new product. The table in the next column describes the relationships between the activities that need to be completed for this product to be manufactured.
(a) Develop a project network for this problem.
(b) Determine the expected duration and variance for each activity.
(c) Determine the EST, EFT, LST, LFT, and slack for each activity. Also determine the total project completion time and the critical path(s).
(d) Determine the probability that the project will be completed in less than 34 days.
(e) Determine the probability that the project will take more than 29 days.

ACTIVITY	DAYS			IMMEDIATE PREDECESSORS
	a	*m*	*b*	
A	3	6	6	—
B	5	8	11	A
C	5	6	10	A
D	1	2	6	B, C
E	7	11	15	D
F	7	9	14	D
G	6	8	10	D
H	3	4	8	F, G
I	3	5	7	E, F, H

7-19 A plant is acquiring new production machinery. Before the machinery can be fully functional, a number of activities must be performed, including roughing out for power, placing the machinery, installing the equipment that will feed product to the machinery, etc. The activities, their precedence relationships, and their durations are shown in the following table.

ACTIVITY	DAYS			IMMEDIATE PREDECESSORS
	a	*m*	*b*	
A	8	10	12	—
B	6	7	8	—
C	3	3	6	—
D	10	20	30	A
E	6	7	8	C
F	9	10	11	B, D, E
G	6	7	11	B, D, E
H	14	15	16	F
I	10	11	12	F
J	6	7	8	G, H
K	4	7	10	I, J
L	1	2	6	G, H

(a) Determine the expected times and variances for each activity.
(b) Construct a project network for this problem.
(c) Determine the EST, EFT, LST, LFT, and slack for each activity. Also determine the critical path and project completion time.
(d) What is the probability that the project will be finished in 70 days?
(e) What is the probability that the project will need at least 75 days?

7-20 A series of activities must be completed in a coordinated fashion to complete a landscaping overhaul. The following table shows the activities; their optimistic, most likely, and pessimistic durations; and their immediate predecessors.

ACTIVITY	DAYS *a*	*m*	*b*	IMMEDIATE PREDECESSORS
A	4	8	12	—
B	4	10	13	A
C	7	14	18	B
D	9	16	20	B
E	6	9	12	B
F	2	4	6	D, E
G	4	7	13	C, F
H	3	5	7	G
I	2	3	4	G, H

(a) Determine the expected times and variances for each activity.
(b) Construct a project network for this problem.
(c) Determine the EST, EFT, LST, LFT, and slack for each activity. Also determine the critical path and project completion time.
(d) What is the probability that the project will be finished in less than 57 days?
(e) What is the probability that the project will need at least 50 days?

7-21 LeBron Woods is responsible for developing a leadership training program for his organization. The following table describes the relationships between the activities that need to be completed.

ACTIVITY	DAYS *a*	*m*	*b*	IMMEDIATE PREDECESSORS
A	3	7	14	—
B	5	10	15	—
C	3	5	10	A, B
D	5	12	13	C
E	2	5	8	C
F	2	5	14	E
G	5	8	11	F
H	6	10	14	D
I	3	4	8	F, H
J	4	7	10	G, I

(a) Determine the expected times and variances for each activity.
(b) Construct a project network for this problem.
(c) Determine the EST, EFT, LST, LFT, and slack for each activity. Also determine the critical path and project completion time.
(d) What is the probability that the project will be finished in less than 49 days?
(e) What is the probability that the project will need at least 54 days?

7-22 The expected project completion time for the construction of a pleasure yacht is 21 months, and the project variance is 6. What is the probability that the project will
(a) require at least 17 months?
(b) be completed within 20 months?
(c) require at least 23 months?
(d) be completed within 25 months?

7-23 The Coogan Construction Company has determined that the expected completion time for its most popular model home follows the normal probability distribution with a mean of 25 weeks and a standard deviation of 4 weeks.
(a) What is the probability that the next home will be completed within 30 weeks?
(b) What is the probability that the next home will be completed within 22 weeks?
(c) Find the number of weeks within which Coogan is 99% sure the next home will be completed.
(d) Find the number of weeks within which Coogan is 85% sure the next home will be completed.

7-24 The General Foundry air pollution project discussed in this chapter has progressed over the past several weeks, and it is now the end of week 8. Lester Harky would like to know the value of the work completed, the amount of any cost overruns or underruns for the project, and the extent to which the project is ahead of schedule or behind schedule by developing a table like the one in Table 7.7 (see page 291). The current project status is shown in the following table.

ACTIVITY	PERCENTAGE COMPLETED	ACTUAL COST
A	100	$20,000
B	100	$36,000
C	100	$26,000
D	100	$44,000
E	55	$29,000
F	55	$12,000
G	10	$5,000
H	13	$1,800

7-25 Fred Ridgeway has been given the responsibility of managing a training and development program. He knows the EST and LST (both in months), and the total costs for each activity. This information is given in the table at the top of the next page.
(a) Using ESTs, determine Fred's total monthly budget.
(b) Using LSTs, determine Fred's total monthly budget.

ACTIVITY	EST	LST	t	TOTAL COST
A	0	0	6	$10,000
B	1	4	2	$14,000
C	3	3	7	$ 5,000
D	4	9	3	$ 6,000
E	6	6	10	$14,000
F	14	15	11	$13,000
G	12	18	2	$ 4,000
H	14	14	11	$ 6,000
I	18	21	6	$18,000
J	18	19	4	$12,000
K	22	22	14	$10,000
L	22	23	8	$16,000
M	18	24	6	$18,000

7-26 Fred Ridgeway's project (see Problem 7-25) has progressed over the past several months, and it is now the end of month 16. Fred would like to know the current status of the project with regard to schedule and budget by developing an appropriate table. The relevant data are shown in the following table.

ACTIVITY	PERCENTAGE COMPLETED	ACTUAL COST
A	100	$13,000
B	100	$12,000
C	100	$6,000
D	100	$6,000
E	60	$9,000
F	10	$800
G	80	$3,600
H	15	$375

Assume that activities not shown in the table have not yet started and have incurred no cost to date. All activities follow their earliest time schedules.

7-27 Susan Roger needs to coordinate the opening of a new office for her company in the city of Denver. The activity time and relationships for this project, as well as the total budgeted cost for each activity, are shown in the following table.

ACTIVITY	IMMEDIATE PREDECESSORS	TIME (WEEKS)	TOTAL COST
A	—	2	$2,200
B	A	3	$5,100
C	A	4	$6,000
D	B, C	2	$3,600
E	C	3	$2,700
F	D, E	3	$1,800

(a) Develop a weekly budget for this project, using the earliest start times.

(b) Develop a weekly budget for this project, using the latest start times.

7-28 Susan Roger's project (see Problem 7-27) has progressed over the past several weeks, and it is now the end of week 8. Susan would like to know the current status of the project with regard to schedule and budget by developing an appropriate table. Assume that all activities follow their earliest time schedules. The relevant data are shown in the following table.

ACTIVITY	PERCENTAGE COMPLETED	ACTUAL COST
A	100	$1,900
B	100	$5,300
C	100	$6,150
D	40	$1,800
E	60	$1,755
F	0	$ 0

7-29 General Foundry's project crashing data are shown in Table 7.10 on page 294. Crash this project by hand to 10 weeks. What are the final times for each activity after crashing, and what is the total cost associated with reducing the duration of this project from 15 to 10 weeks?

7-30 Bowman Builders manufactures steel storage sheds for commercial use. Joe Bowman, president of Bowman Builders, is contemplating producing sheds for home use. The activities necessary to build an experimental model and related data are given in the table on the next page. The project completion time using standard times is 14 weeks.

Set up and solve an LP model using Excel to crash this project to 10 weeks. How much does it cost to reduce the duration of this project from 14 to 10 weeks?

7-31 The table on the next page describes the various activities of a construction project in a chemical plant.

(a) Set up and solve an LP model using Excel to crash this project to 22 days. What is the total crashing cost?

(b) Assuming each activity can only be crashed in whole days, what is the earliest completion of this project? What is the total associated crash cost?

7-32 A new order filling system needs to be installed as soon as possible. The table on the next page lists the project's activities and their predecessors. Also provided is the cost information to reduce the standard activity times.

Set up and solve an LP model using Excel to crash this project to 24 days. What is the total crashing cost?

Table for Problem 7-30

ACTIVITY	IMMEDIATE PREDECESSORS	STANDARD TIME (WEEKS)	STANDARD COST	CRASH TIME (WEEKS)	CRASH COST
A	—	3	$1,000	2	$1,600
B	—	2	$2,000	1	$2,700
C	—	1	$300	1	$300
D	A	7	$1,300	3	$1,600
E	B	6	$850	3	$1,000
F	C	2	$4,000	1	$5,000
G	D, E	4	$1,500	2	$2,000

Table for Problem 7-31

ACTIVITY	IMMEDIATE PREDECESSORS	STANDARD TIME (DAYS)	STANDARD COST	CRASH TIME (DAYS)	CRASH COST
A	—	4	$2,000	2	$2,600
B	A	6	$3,500	5	$4,300
C	A	8	$3,300	6	$3,900
D	B	5	$1,200	4	$1,800
E	C, D	3	$1,700	2	$2,200
F	E	7	$2,200	5	$3,600
G	E	5	$ 900	4	$1,550
H	F, G	4	$1,200	3	$1,700

Table for Problem 7-32

ACTIVITY	IMMEDIATE PREDECESSORS	STANDARD TIME (DAYS)	STANDARD COST	CRASH TIME (DAYS)	CRASH COST
A	—	7	$2,000	5	$ 3,500
B	A	10	$3,000	8	$ 4,700
C	A	8	$3,400	7	$ 3,700
D	C	6	$1,600	4	$ 2,600
E	C	7	$1,900	4	$ 4,000
F	D, E	5	$1,200	3	$ 2,800
G	B, C	11	$8,200	8	$10,900
H	F, G	4	$2,600	3	$ 3,800

7-33 Software Development Specialists (SDS) is involved with developing software for customers in the banking industry. SDS breaks a large programming project into teams that perform the necessary steps. Team A is responsible for going from general systems design all the way through to actual systems testing. This involves 18 separate activities. Team B is then responsible for the final installation.

To determine cost and time factors, optimistic, most likely, and pessimistic time estimates have been made for all of the 18 activities involved for team A. The first step that this team performs is general systems design. The optimistic, most likely, and pessimistic times are 3, 4, and 5 weeks. Following this, a number of activities can begin. Activity 2 is involved with procedures design. Optimistic, most likely, and pessimistic times for completing this activity are 4, 5, and 12 weeks. Activity 3 is developing detailed report designs. Optimistic, most likely, and pessimistic time estimates are 6, 8, and 10 weeks. Activity 4, detailed forms design, has optimistic, most likely, and pessimistic time estimates of 2, 5, and 5 weeks.

Activities 5 and 6 involve writing detailed program specifications and developing file specifications. The three time estimates for activity 5 are 6, 7, and 8 weeks, and the three time estimates for activity 6 are 3, 4, and 5 weeks. Activity 7 involves specifying system test data. Before this is done, activity 6, involving file specifications, must be completed. The time estimates for activity 7 are 2, 3, and 7 weeks. Activity 8 involves reviewing forms. Before activity 8 can be conducted, detailed forms design must be completed. The time estimates for activity 8 are 3, 3, and 9 weeks. The next activity, activity 9, is reviewing the detailed report design. This requires that the detailed report design, activity 3, be completed first. The time estimates for activity 9 are 1, 3, and 5 weeks, respectively.

Activity 10 involves reviewing procedures design. Time estimates are 1, 2, and 9 weeks. Of course, procedures design must be done before activity 10 can be started. Activity 11 involves the system design checkpoint review. A number of activities must be completed before this is done. These activities include reviewing the forms, reviewing the detailed report design, reviewing the procedures design, writing detailed program specs, and specifying system test data. The optimistic, most likely, and pessimistic time estimates for activity 11 are 3, 4, and 5 weeks. Performing program logic design is activity 12. This can be started only after the system design checkpoint review is completed. The time estimates for activity 12 are 4, 5, and 6 weeks.

Activity 13, coding the programs, is done only after the program logic design is completed. The time estimates for this activity are 6, 10, and 14 weeks. Activity 14 is involved in developing test programs. Activity 13 is the immediate predecessor. Time estimates for activity 14 are 3, 4, and 11 weeks. Developing a system test plan is activity 15. A number of activities must be completed before activity 15 can be started. These activities include specifying system test data, writing detailed program specifications, and reviewing procedure designs, the detailed report design, and forms. The time estimates for activity 15 are 3, 4, and 5 weeks.

Activity 16, creating system test data, has time estimates of 2, 4, and 6 weeks. Activity 15 must be done before activity 16 can be started. Activity 17 is reviewing program test results. The immediate predecessor to activity 17 is to test the programs (activity 14). The three time estimates for activity 17 are 2, 3, and 4 weeks. The final activity is conducting system tests. This is activity 18. Before activity 18 can be started, activities 16 and 17 must be complete. The three time estimates for conducting these system tests are 2, 6, and 7 weeks.

How long will it take for team A to complete its programming assignment?

7-34 Bradshaw Construction is involved in constructing municipal buildings and other structures that are used primarily by city and state municipalities. The construction process involves developing legal documents, drafting feasibility studies, obtaining bond ratings, and so forth. Recently, Bradshaw was given a request to submit a proposal for the construction of a municipal building. The first step is to develop legal documents and to perform all steps necessary before the construction contract is signed. This requires more than 20 separate activities that must be completed. These activities, their immediate predecessors, and optimistic (a), most likely (m), and pessimistic (b) time estimates are given in the table on the next page.

Determine the total project completion time for this preliminary step, the critical path, and slack time for all activities involved.

7-35 Getting a degree from a college or university can be a long and difficult task. Certain courses must be completed before other courses may be taken. Develop a network diagram in which every activity is a particular course that you must take for your degree program. The immediate predecessors will be course prerequisites. Don't forget to include all university, college, and departmental course requirements. Then try to group these courses into semesters or quarters for your particular school. How long do you think it will take you to graduate? Which courses, if not taken in the proper sequence, could delay your graduation?

7-36 Dream Team Productions is in the final design phases of its new film, *Killer Worms*, to be released next summer. Market Wise, the firm hired to coordinate the release of *Killer Worms* toys, has identified 16 activities to be completed before the release of the film. These activities, their immediate predecessors, and optimistic (a), most likely (m), and pessimistic (b) time estimates are given in the table on the next page.

(a) How many weeks in advance of the film release should Market Wise start its marketing campaign? What are the critical paths?
(b) If activities I and J were not necessary, what impact would this have on the critical path and the number of weeks needed to complete the marketing campaign?

7-37 Sager Products has been in the business of manufacturing and marketing toys for toddlers for the past two decades. Jim Sager, president of the firm, is considering the development of a new manufacturing line to allow it to produce high-quality plastic toys at reasonable prices. The development process is long and complex. Jim estimates that there are five phases involved and multiple activities for each phase.

Phase 1 of the development process involves the completion of four activities. These activities have no immediate predecessors. Activity A has an optimistic completion time of 2 weeks, a most likely completion time of 3 weeks, and a pessimistic

Table for Problem 7-34

ACTIVITY	WEEKS *a*	*m*	*b*	DESCRIPTION OF ACTIVITY	IMMEDIATE PREDECESSORS
1	1	4	7	Draft legal documents	—
2	2	3	4	Prepare financial statements	—
3	3	4	5	Draft history	—
4	7	8	9	Draft demand portion of feasibility study	—
5	4	4	7	Review and approval of legal documents	1
6	1	2	6	Review and approval of history	3
7	4	5	6	Review feasibility study	4
8	1	2	6	Draft final financial portion of feasibility study	7
9	3	4	5	Draft facts relevant to the bond transaction	5
10	1	1	4	Review and approve financial statements	2
11	18	20	22	Receive firm price of project	—
12	1	2	3	Review and complete financial portion of feasibility study	8
13	1	1	4	Complete draft statement	6, 9, 10, 11, 12
14	0.25	0.50	0.75	Send all materials to bond rating services	13
15	0.20	0.30	0.40	Print statement and distributed it to all interested parties	14
16	1	1	4	Make presentation to bond rating services	14
17	1	2	3	Receive bond rating	16
18	3	5	7	Market bonds	15, 17
19	0.10	0.20	0.30	Execute purchase contract	18
20	0.10	0.15	0.50	Authorize and complete final statement	19
21	2	3	7	Purchase contract	19
22	0.20	0.50	0.80	Make bond proceeds available	20
23	0	0.20	0.40	Sign construction contract	21, 22

Table for Problem 7-36

ACTIVITY	IMMEDIATE PREDECESSORS	WEEKS *a*	*m*	*b*
A	—	1	2	6
B	—	3	3.5	4
C	—	10	12	14
D	—	4	5	9
E	—	2	4	6
F	A	6	7	8
G	B	2	4	6
H	C	5	7	9
I	C	9	10	14
J	C	2	4	6
K	D	2	4	6
L	E	2	4	6
M	F, G, H	5	6	7
N	J, K, L	1	1.5	2
O	I, M	5	7	9
P	N	5	7	9

completion time of 4 weeks. Activity B has estimated values of 5, 6, and 10 weeks for these three completion times. Similarly, activity C has estimated completion times of 1, 1, and 4 weeks; and activity D has expected completion times of 8, 9, and 13 weeks.

Phase 2 involves six separate activities. Activity E has activity A as an immediate predecessor. Time estimates are 1, 1, and 4 weeks. Activity F and activity G both have activity B as their immediate predecessor. For activity F, the time estimates are 3, 4, and 5 weeks. For activity G, the time estimates are 1, 3, and 5 weeks. The only immediate predecessor for activity H is activity C. All three time estimates for activity H are 5 weeks. Activity D must be performed before activity I and activity J can be started. Activity I has estimated completion times of 9, 10, and 11 weeks. Activity J has estimated completion times of 1, 2, and 6 weeks.

Phase 3 is the most difficult and complex of the entire development project. It also consists of six separate activities. Activity K has time estimates of 2, 3, and 4 weeks. The immediate predecessor for this activity is activity E. The immediate predecessor for activity L is activity F. The time estimates for activity L are 3, 4, and 8 weeks. Activity M has 2, 2, and 5 weeks for the estimates of the optimistic, probable, and pessimistic times. The immediate predecessor for activity M is activity G. Activities N and O both have activity I as their immediate predecessor. Activity N has 8, 9, and 10 weeks for its three time estimates. Activity O has 1, 1, and 4 weeks as its time estimates. Finally, activity P has time estimates of 4, 4, and 10 weeks. Activity J is the only immediate predecessor.

Phase 4 involves five activities. Activity Q requires activity K to be completed before it can be started. All three time estimates for activity Q are 6 weeks. Activity R requires that both activity L and activity M be completed first. The three time estimates for activity R are 1, 2, and 3 weeks. Activity S requires activity N to be completed first. Its time estimates are 6, 6, and 9 weeks. Activity T requires that activity O be completed. The time estimates for activity T are 3, 4, and 5 weeks. The final activity for phase 4 is activity U. The time estimates for this activity are 1, 2, and 3 weeks. Activity P must be completed before activity U can be started.

Phase 5 is the final phase of the development project. It consists of only two activities. Activity V requires that activity Q and activity R be completed before it can be started. Time estimates for this activity are 9, 10, and 11 weeks. Activity W is the final activity of the process. It requires three activities to be completed before it can be started: activities S, T, and U. The estimated completion times for activity W are 2, 3, and 7 weeks.

(a) Given this information, determine the expected completion time for the entire process. Also determine which activities are along the critical path.

(b) Jim hopes that the total project will take less than 40 weeks. Is this likely to occur?

(c) Jim has just determined that activities D and I have already been completed and that they do not need to be part of the project. What is the impact of this change on the project completion time and the critical path?

Case Study

Haygood Brothers Construction Company

George and Harry Haygood are building contractors who specialize in the construction of private home dwellings, storage warehouses, and small businesses (less than 20,000 sq. ft. of floor space). Both George and Harry entered a carpenter union's apprenticeship program in the early 1990s and, upon completion of the apprenticeship, became skilled craftsmen in 1996. Before going into business for themselves, they worked for several local building contractors in the Detroit area.

Typically, Haygood Brothers submits competitive bids for the construction of proposed dwellings. Whenever its bids are accepted, various aspects of the construction (e.g., electrical wiring, plumbing, brick laying, painting) are subcontracted. George and Harry, however, perform all carpentry work. In addition, they plan and schedule all construction operations, frequently arrange interim financing, and supervise all construction activities.

The philosophy under which Haygood Brothers has always operated can be simply stated: "Time is money." Delays in construction increase the costs of interim financing and postpone the initiation of their building projects. Consequently, Haygood Brothers deals with all bottlenecks promptly and avoids all delays whenever possible. To minimize the time consumed in a construction project, Haygood Brothers uses PERT.

First, all construction activities and events are itemized and properly arranged (in parallel and sequential combinations) in a network. Then time estimates for each activity are made, the expected time for completing each activity is determined, and the critical (longest) path is calculated. Finally, earliest times, latest times, and slack values are computed. Having made these calculations, George and Harry can place their resources in the critical areas to minimize the time of completing the project.

TABLE 7.11
Project Data for Haygood Brothers Construction Co.

ACTIVITY	IMMEDIATE PREDECESSORS	DAYS		
		a	*m*	*b*
A	—	4	5	6
B	A	2	5	8
C	B	5	7	9
D	B	4	5	6
E	C	2	4	6
F	E	3	5	9
G	E	4	5	6
H	E	3	4	7
I	E	5	7	9
J	D, I	10	11	12
K	F, G, H, J	4	6	8
L	F, G, H, J	7	8	9
M	L	4	5	10
N	K	5	7	9
O	N	5	6	7
P	M, O	2	3	4

The following are the activities that constitute an upcoming project (home dwelling) for Haygood Brothers:

1. Arrange financing (A)
2. Let subcontracts (B)
3. Set and pour foundations (C)
4. Plumbing (D)
5. Framing (E)
6. Roofing (F)
7. Electrical wiring (G)
8. Installation of windows and doors (H)
9. Ductwork and insulation (including heating and cooling units) (I)
10. Sheetrock, paneling, and paper hanging (J)
11. Installation of cabinets (K)
12. Bricking (L)
13. Outside trim (M)
14. Inside trim (including fixtures) (N)
15. Painting (O)
16. Flooring (P)

The immediate predecessors and optimistic (a), most likely (m), and pessimistic (b) time estimates are shown in Table 7.11.

Discussion Questions

1. What is the time length of the critical path? What is the significance of the critical path?
2. Compute the amount of time that the completion of each activity can be delayed without affecting the overall project.
3. The project was begun August 1. What is the probability that the project can be completed by September 30? (*Note:* Scheduled completion time = 60 days.)

Source: Jerry Kinard, Western Carolina University, and Brian Kinard, University of North Carolina - Wilmington.

Case Study

Family Planning Research Center of Nigeria

Dr. Adinombe Watage, deputy director of the Family Planning Research Center in Nigeria's Over-the-River Province, was assigned the task of organizing and training five teams of field workers to perform educational and outreach activities as part of a large project to demonstrate acceptance of a new method of birth control. These workers already had training in family planning education but must receive specific training regarding the new method of contraception. Two types of materials must also be prepared: (1) those for use in training the workers and (2) those for distribution in the field. Training faculty must be brought in, and arrangements must be made for transportation and accommodations for the participants.

Dr. Watage first called a meeting of this office staff. Together they identified the activities that must be carried out, their necessary sequences, and the time they would require. Their results are displayed in Table 7.12.

Louis Odaga, the chief clerk, noted that the project had to be completed in 60 days. Whipping out his solar-powered calculator, he added up the time needed. It came to 94 days. "An

TABLE 7.12
Project Data for Family Planning Research Center

ACTIVITY	IMMEDIATE PREDECESSORS	TIME (DAYS)	STAFFING NEEDED
A. Identify faculty and their schedules	—	5	2
B. Arrange transport to base	—	7	3
C. Identify and collect training materials	—	5	2
D. Arrange accommodations	A	3	1
E. Identify team	A	7	4
F. Bring in team	B, E	2	1
G. Transport faculty to base	A, B	3	2
H. Print program material	C	10	6
I. Have program material delivered	H	7	3
J. Conduct training program	D, F, G, I	15	0
K. Perform fieldwork training	J	30	0

TABLE 7.13
Cost Data for Family Planning Research Center

	STANDARD		CRASH	
ACTIVITY	TIME	COST	TIME	COST
A. Identify faculty and their schedules	5	$ 400	2	$ 700
B. Arrange transport to base	7	$ 1,000	4	$ 1,450
C. Identify and collect training materials	5	$ 400	3	$ 500
D. Arrange accommodations	3	$ 2,500	1	$ 3,000
E. Identify team	7	$ 400	4	$ 850
F. Bring in team	2	$ 1,000	1	$ 2,000
G. Transport faculty to base	3	$ 1,500	2	$ 2,000
H. Print program material	10	$ 3,000	5	$ 4,000
I. Have program material delivered	7	$ 200	2	$ 600
J. Conduct training program	15	$ 5,000	10	$ 7,000
K. Perform fieldwork training	30	$10,000	20	$14,000

impossible task, then," he noted. "No," Dr. Watage replied, "some of these tasks can go forward in parallel." "Be careful, though," warned Mr. Oglagadu, the chief nurse, "There aren't that many of us to go around. There are only 10 of us in this office."

"I can check whether we have enough heads and hands once I have tentatively scheduled the activities," Dr. Watage responded. "If the schedule is too tight, I have permission from the Pathminder Fund to spend some funds to speed it up, just so long as I can prove that it can be done at the least cost necessary. Can you help me prove that? Here are the costs for the activities with the elapsed time that we planned and the costs and times if we shorten them to an absolute minimum." Those data are given in Table 7.13.

Discussion Questions

1. Some of the tasks in this project can be done in parallel. Prepare a diagram showing the required network of tasks and define the critical path. What is the length of the project without crashing?
2. At this point, can the project be done given the personnel constraint of 10 persons?
3. If the critical path is longer than 60 days, what is the least amount that Dr. Watage can spend and still achieve this schedule objective? Assume that crash costs are linear over time.

Source: "Family Planning Research Center of Nigeria" by Curtis P. McLaughlin.

Internet Case Studies

See the Companion Website for this textbook, at www.pearsonhighered.com/balakrishnan, for additional case studies.

CHAPTER 8

Decision Analysis

LEARNING OBJECTIVES

After completing this chapter, students will be able to:

1. List the steps of the decision-making process and describe the different types of decision-making environments.
2. Make decisions under uncertainty and under risk.
3. Use Excel to set up and solve problems involving decision tables.
4. Develop accurate and useful decision trees.
5. Use TreePlan to set up and analyze decision tree problems with Excel.
6. Revise probability estimates using Bayesian analysis.
7. Understand the importance and use of utility theory in decision making.

CHAPTER OUTLINE

8.1 Introduction

Decision analysis is an analytic and systematic way to tackle problems.

To a great extent, the successes and failures that a person experiences in life depend on the decisions that he or she makes. The development of the Mac computer, followed by the iPod, the iPhone, and now the iPad, made Steve Jobs a very wealthy person. In contrast, the person who designed the flawed tires at Firestone (which caused so many accidents with Ford Explorers in the late 1990s) probably did not have a great career at that company. Why and how did these people make their respective decisions? A single decision can make the difference between a successful career and an unsuccessful one. *Decision analysis* is an analytic and systematic approach to the study of decision making. In this chapter, we present decision models that are useful in helping managers make the best possible decisions.

A good decision is based on logic.

What makes the difference between good and bad decisions? In most practical situations, managers have to make decisions without knowing for sure which events will occur in the future. In such cases, a good decision can be defined as one that is based on logic, considers all possible decision alternatives, examines all available information about the future, and applies the decision modeling approach described in this chapter. Occasionally, due to the uncertainty of future events, a good decision could result in an unfavorable outcome. But if a decision is made properly, it is still a good decision.

A bad decision does not consider all alternatives.

In contrast, a bad decision is one that is not based on logic, does not use all available information, does not consider all alternatives, and does not employ appropriate decision modeling techniques. If you make a bad decision but are lucky enough that a favorable outcome occurs, you have still made a bad decision. Although occasionally good decisions yield bad results, in the long run, using decision analysis will result in successful outcomes.

8.2 The Five Steps in Decision Analysis

Whether you are deciding about signing up for next semester's classes, buying a new computer, or building a multimillion-dollar factory, the steps in making a good decision are basically the same:

Five Steps of Decision Making

1. Clearly define the problem at hand.
2. List *all* possible decision alternatives.
3. Identify the possible future outcomes for each decision alternative.
4. Identify the payoff (usually profit or cost) for each combination of alternatives and outcomes.
5. Select one of the decision analysis modeling techniques discussed in this chapter. Apply the decision model and make your decision.

Thompson Lumber Company Example

We use the case of Thompson Lumber Company as an example to illustrate the use of the five decision analysis steps. John Thompson is the founder and president of Thompson Lumber Company, a profitable firm located in Portland, Oregon.

The first step is to define the problem.

STEP 1 In the first step, John identifies his decision-making problem as whether to expand his business by manufacturing and marketing a new product, backyard storage sheds.

The second step is to list alternatives.

STEP 2 The second step is to generate the complete list of decision alternatives available to the decision maker. In decision analysis, a **decision alternative** is defined as a course of action that is available to the decision maker. There is no limit to the number of decision alternatives that a problem can have. The decision maker has total control over which decision alternative he or she chooses and must choose exactly one of the alternatives listed in the problem.

In Thompson Lumber's case, let us assume that John decides that his alternatives are as follows: (1) build a large plant to manufacture the storage sheds, (2) build a small plant to manufacture the storage sheds, or (3) build no plant at all (i.e., not develop the new product line and keep his business at its current size).

One of the biggest mistakes that decision makers make in practice is to leave out important decision alternatives. For example, suppose John had left out the alternative to build no plant at all. It could well turn out that based on all the issues in the decision-making problem, the best decision for him would have been to not expand his business. However, by not including that alternative among his choices, John would have been unable to select that decision. In general, it is important to remember that while a particular decision alternative may sometimes appear to be inappropriate on the surface, it may turn out to be an excellent choice when all issues in the problem are considered.

The third step is to identify possible outcomes.

STEP 3 The third step involves identifying all possible future **outcomes** for each decision alternative. In decision analysis, outcomes are also known as *states of nature*. There is no limit to the number of outcomes that can be listed for a decision alternative, and each alternative can have its own unique set of outcomes. Exactly one of the listed outcomes will occur for a specific decision alternative. However, the decision maker has little or no control over which outcome will occur.

In Thompson Lumber's case, suppose John determines that all three of his decision alternatives have the same three possible outcomes: (1) Demand for the sheds will be high, (2) demand for the sheds will be moderate, or (3) demand for the sheds will be low.

As with decision alternatives, a common mistake in practice is to forget about some of the possible outcomes. Optimistic decision makers may tend to ignore bad outcomes under the mistaken assumption that they will not happen, whereas pessimistic managers may discount a favorable outcome. If we don't consider all possibilities, we will not make a logical decision, and the results may be undesirable.

The fourth step is to list payoffs.

STEP 4 The fourth step is to define the measurable output resulting from each possible combination of decision alternative and outcome. That is, we need to identify the output that will result if we choose a specific decision alternative, and a particular outcome then occurs. In decision analysis, we call these outputs *payoffs*, regardless of whether they denote profit or cost. Payoffs can also be nonmonetary (e.g., number of units sold, number of workers needed).

In Thompson Lumber's case, let us assume that John wants to use net profits to measure his payoffs. He has already evaluated the potential profits associated with the various combinations of alternatives and outcomes, as follows:

- If John decides to build a large plant, he thinks that with high demand for sheds, the result would be a net profit of $200,000 to his firm. The net profit would, however, be only $100,000 if demand were moderate. If demand were low, there would actually be a net loss of $120,000. Payoffs are also called **conditional values** because, for example, John receiving a profit of $200,000 is conditional upon both his building a large factory and having high demand.
- If he builds a small plant, the results would be a net profit of $90,000 if there were high demand for sheds, a net profit of $50,000 if there were moderate demand, and a net loss of $20,000 if there were low demand.
- Finally, doing nothing would result in $0 payoff in any demand scenario.

During the fourth step, the decision maker can construct decision or payoff tables.

The easiest way to present payoff values is by constructing a *payoff table*, or **decision table**. A payoff table for John's conditional profit values is shown in Table 8.1. All the decision alternatives are listed down the left side of this table, and all the possible outcomes are listed across the top. The body of the table contains the actual payoffs (profits, in this case).

The last step is to select and apply a decision analysis model.

STEP 5 The last step is to select a decision analysis model and apply it to the data to help make the decision. The types of decision models available for selection depends on the environment in which we are operating and the amount of uncertainty and risk involved. The model specifies the criteria to be used in choosing the best decision alternative.

TABLE 8.1
Payoff Table for Thompson Lumber

	OUTCOMES		
ALTERNATIVES	HIGH DEMAND	MODERATE DEMAND	LOW DEMAND
Build large plant	$200,000	$100,000	–$120,000
Build small plant	$ 90,000	$ 50,000	–$ 20,000
No plant	$ 0	$ 0	$ 0

8.3 Types of Decision-Making Environments

The types of decisions people make depend on how much knowledge or information they have about the problem scenario. There are three decision-making environments, as described in the following sections.

The consequence of every alternative is known in **decision making under certainty.**

TYPE 1: DECISION MAKING UNDER CERTAINTY In the environment of **decision making under certainty**, decision makers know for sure (i.e., with certainty) the payoff for every decision alternative. Typically, this means that there is only one outcome for each alternative. Naturally, decision makers will select the alternative that will result in the best payoff. The mathematical programming approaches covered in Chapters 2–6 are all examples of decision modeling techniques suited for decision making under certainty.

Let's see how decision making under certainty could affect Thompson Lumber's problem. In this environment, we assume that John knows exactly what will happen in the future. For example, if he knows with certainty that demand for storage sheds will be high, what should he do? Looking at John's conditional profit values in Table 8.1, it is clear in this case that he should build the large plant, which has the highest profit, $200,000.

In real-world cases, however, few managers would be fortunate enough to have complete information and knowledge about the outcomes under consideration. In most situations, managers would either have no information at all about the outcomes, or, at best, have probabilistic information about future outcomes. These are the second and third types of decision-making environments.

Probabilities are not known in **decision making under uncertainty.**

TYPE 2: DECISION MAKING UNDER UNCERTAINTY In **decision making under uncertainty**, decision makers have no information at all about the various outcomes. That is, they do not know the likelihood (or probability) that a specific outcome will occur. For example, it is impossible to predict the probability that the Democratic Party will control the U.S. Congress 25 years from now. Likewise, it may be impossible in some cases to assess the probability that a new product or undertaking will be successful.

There are several decision models available to handle decision-making problems under uncertainty. These are explained in section 8.4.

Probabilities are known in **decision making under risk.**

TYPE 3: DECISION MAKING UNDER RISK In **decision making under risk**, decision makers have some knowledge regarding the probability of occurrence of each outcome. The probability could be a precise measure (e.g., the probability of being dealt an ace from a deck of cards is exactly $\frac{1}{13}$) or an estimate (e.g., the probability that it will rain tomorrow is 0.40). Regardless of how the probabilities are determined, in decision making under risk, decision makers attempt to identify the alternative that optimizes their *expected* payoff.

IN ACTION Decision Analysis Helps American Airlines Assess Uncertainty of Bid Quotes

American Airlines, Inc. (AA) is the world's largest airline in passenger miles transported with annual revenue of over $21 billion. Although its primary goal is to transport passengers, AA has to also manage ancillary functions such as full-truckload (FTL) freight shipment of maintenance equipment and in-flight service items. The inventory value of these goods as they move point to point worldwide can be over $1 billion at any given time.

Each year AA has approximately 500 requests for quotes (RFQs) in the bid process for its FTL point-to-point freight shipment routes. AA needed a should-cost model to assess these quotes to ensure that it does not overpay its FTL suppliers. Working with researchers at North Carolina State University, AA developed a decision tree–based analysis that estimates reasonable costs for these shipments. The fully expanded decision tree for this problem has nearly 60,000 end points.

AA has now used this decision tree model on more than 20 RFQs to prioritize its contractual opportunities and obtain accurate assessments of the FTL costs, thus minimizing the risk of overpaying its FTL suppliers.

Source: Based on M. J. Bailey et al. "American Airlines Uses Should-Cost Modeling to Assess the Uncertainty of Bids for Its Full-Truckload Shipment Routes," *Interfaces* 41, 2 (March–April 2011): 194–196.

Decision analysis models for business problems in this environment typically employ one of two criteria: (1) maximization of expected monetary value or (2) minimization of expected opportunity loss. We study models using both criteria for decision making under risk in section 8.5.

8.4 Decision Making Under Uncertainty

Probabilities of outcomes are not known.

As noted previously, an environment of decision making under uncertainty exists when a manager cannot assess the probabilities of the different outcomes with confidence or when virtually no probability data are available. In this section, we discuss the following five different decision-making criteria to handle such situations:

1. Maximax
2. Maximin
3. Criterion of realism
4. Equally likely
5. Minimax regret

In discussing these criteria here, we assume that all payoffs represent profits. That is, we prefer higher payoffs to smaller ones. If the payoffs represent costs (i.e., we prefer smaller payoffs to higher ones), some of the criteria would need to be used differently. To avoid this confusion, an easy option is to convert costs in a payoff table to profits by multiplying all cost values by –1. This way, we can apply the criteria as discussed here for all problems, regardless of whether the payoffs represent profits or costs.

The first four criteria can be computed directly from the decision (payoff) table, whereas the minimax regret criterion requires use of the opportunity loss table (which we compute subsequently). Let us look at each of the five criteria and apply them to the Thompson Lumber example. Remember that the decision-making environment assumes that John has no probability information about the three outcomes—high demand, moderate demand, and low demand for storage sheds.

Maximax Criterion

Maximax *is an optimistic approach.*

The **maximax** criterion selects the decision alternative that *max*imizes the *max*imum payoff over all alternatives. We first locate the maximum payoff for each alternative and then select the alternative with the highest value among these maximum payoffs. Because this criterion takes an extremely rosy view of the future and locates the alternative with the overall highest possible payoff, it is also called the *optimistic* criterion.

In Table 8.2 we see that John's maximax choice is the first alternative, build large plant. The $200,000 payoff is the maximum of the maximum payoffs (i.e., $200,000, $90,000, and $0) for each decision alternative.

Maximin Criterion

Maximin *is a pessimistic approach.*

The opposite of the maximax criterion is the **maximin** criterion, which takes an extremely conservative view of the future. For this reason, it is also called the *pessimistic* criterion. The maximin criterion finds the alternative that *max*imizes the *min*imum payoff over all decision alternatives. We first locate the minimum payoff for each alternative and then select the alternative with the highest value among those minimum payoffs.

TABLE 8.2 Thompson Lumber's Maximax Decision

	OUTCOMES			
ALTERNATIVES	HIGH DEMAND	MODERATE DEMAND	LOW DEMAND	MAXIMUM FOR ALTERNATIVE
Build large plant	$200,000	$100,000	–$120,000	$200,000 → Maximax
Build small plant	$ 90,000	$ 50,000	–$ 20,000	$ 90,000
No plant	$ 0	$ 0	$ 0	$ 0

TABLE 8.3
Thompson Lumber's Maximin Decision

	OUTCOMES			
ALTERNATIVES	HIGH DEMAND	MODERATE DEMAND	LOW DEMAND	MINIMUM FOR ALTERNATIVE
Build large plant	\$200,000	\$100,000	–\$120,000	–\$120,000
Build small plant	\$ 90,000	\$ 50,000	–\$ 20,000	–\$ 20,000
No plant	\$ 0	\$ 0	\$ 0	\$ 0 → Maximin

John's maximin choice, no plant, is shown in Table 8.3. The \$0 payoff is the maximum of the minimum payoffs (i.e., –\$120,000, –\$20,000, and \$0) for each alternative.

Criterion of Realism (Hurwicz)

The criterion of realism *uses the weighted average approach.*

Decision makers are seldom extreme optimists or extreme pessimists. Because most tend to be somewhere in between the two extremes, the *criterion of realism* (or *Hurwicz*) decision criterion offers a compromise between optimistic and pessimistic decisions. In this criterion, we use a parameter called the **coefficient of realism** to measure the decision maker's level of optimism regarding the future. This coefficient, denoted by α, has a value between 0 and 1. An α value of 0 implies that the decision maker is totally pessimistic about the future, while an α value of 1 implies that the decision maker is totally optimistic about the future. The advantage of this approach is that it allows the decision maker to build in personal feelings about relative optimism and pessimism. The formula is as follows:

$$\text{Realism payoff for alternative} = \alpha \times (\text{Maximum payoff for alternative}) + (1 - \alpha) \times (\text{Minimum payoff for alternative}) \quad \textbf{(8-1)}$$

Because the realism payoff is just a weighted average for the maximum and minimum payoffs (where α is the weight), this criterion is also called the *weighted average* criterion.

Suppose we identify John Thompson's coefficient of realism to be $\alpha = 0.45$. That is, John is a slightly pessimistic person (note that $\alpha = 0.5$ implies a strictly neutral person). Under this situation, his best decision would be to build a small plant. As shown in Table 8.4, this alternative has the highest realism payoff, at \$29,500 [$= 0.45 \times \$90{,}000 + 0.55 \times (-\$20{,}000)$].

Equally Likely (Laplace) Criterion

The equally likely *criterion selects the highest average alternative.*

The **equally likely** (or *Laplace*) criterion finds the decision alternative that has the highest average payoff. We first calculate the average payoff for each alternative and then pick the alternative with the maximum average payoff. Note that the Laplace approach essentially assumes that all the outcomes are equally likely to occur.

The equally likely choice for Thompson Lumber is the first alternative, build a large plant. This strategy, as shown in Table 8.5, has a maximum average payoff of \$60,000 over all alternatives.

Minimax Regret Criterion

Minimax regret *is based on opportunity loss.*

The final decision criterion that we discuss is based on **opportunity loss**, also called *regret*. Opportunity loss is defined as the difference between the optimal payoff and the actual payoff received. In other words, it's the amount lost by *not* picking the best alternative.

TABLE 8.4
Thompson Lumber's Criterion of Realism Decision ($\alpha = 0.45$)

	OUTCOMES			
ALTERNATIVES	HIGH DEMAND	MODERATE DEMAND	LOW DEMAND	WT. AVG. ($\alpha = 0.45$) FOR ALTERNATIVE
Build large plant	\$200,000	\$100,000	–\$120,000	\$24,000
Build small plant	\$ 90,000	\$ 50,000	–\$ 20,000	\$29,500 → Realism
No plant	\$ 0	\$ 0	\$ 0	\$ 0

TABLE 8.5
Thompson Lumber's Equally Likely Decision

ALTERNATIVES	OUTCOMES HIGH DEMAND	MODERATE DEMAND	LOW DEMAND	AVERAGE FOR ALTERNATIVE
Build large plant	$200,000	$100,000	−$120,000	$60,000 → Equally likely
Build small plant	$ 90,000	$ 50,000	−$ 20,000	$40,000
No plant	$ 0	$ 0	$ 0	$ 0

We first develop the opportunity loss table from the payoff table.

Minimax regret finds the alternative that *mini*mizes the *max*imum opportunity loss within each alternative.

To use this criterion, we need to first develop the opportunity loss table. This is done by determining the opportunity loss of not choosing the best alternative for each outcome. To do so, we subtract each payoff for a specific outcome from the *best* payoff for that outcome. For example, the best payoff with high demand in Thompson Lumber's payoff table is $200,000 (corresponding to building a large plant). Hence, we subtract all payoffs for that outcome (i.e., in that column) from $200,000. Likewise, the best payoffs with moderate demand and low demand are $100,000 and $0, respectively. We therefore subtract all payoffs in the second column from $100,000 and all payoffs in the third column from $0. Table 8.6 illustrates these computations and shows John's complete opportunity loss table.

Once the opportunity loss table has been constructed, we locate the maximum opportunity loss (regret) for each alternative. We then pick the alternative with the smallest value among these maximum regrets. As shown in Table 8.7, John's minimax regret choice is the second alternative, build a small plant. The regret of $110,000 is the minimum of the maximum regrets (i.e., $120,000, $110,000, and $200,000) over all three alternatives.

Using Excel to Solve Decision-Making Problems under Uncertainty

File: 8-1.xls

As just demonstrated in the Thompson Lumber example, calculations for the different criteria in decision making under uncertainty are fairly straightforward. In most cases, we can perform these calculations quickly even by hand. However, if we wish, we can easily construct Excel spreadsheets to calculate these results for us. Screenshot 8-1A shows the relevant formulas for the different decision criteria in the Thompson Lumber example. The results are shown in Screenshot 8-1B.

TABLE 8.6 Opportunity Loss Table for Thompson Lumber

ALTERNATIVES	OUTCOMES HIGH DEMAND	MODERATE DEMAND	LOW DEMAND
Build large plant	$200,000 − $200,000 = $ 0	$100,000 − $100,000 = $ 0	$0 − (−$120,000) = $120,000
Build small plant	$200,000 − $ 90,000 = $110,000	$100,000 − $ 50,000 = $ 50,000	$0 − (−$ 20,000) = $ 20,000
No plant	$200,000 − $ 0 = $200,000	$100,000 − $ 0 = $100,000	$0 − $ 0 = $ 0

TABLE 8.7
Thompson Lumber's Minimax Regret Decision

ALTERNATIVES	OUTCOMES HIGH DEMAND	MODERATE DEMAND	LOW DEMAND	MAXIMUM FOR ALTERNATIVE
Build large plant	$ 0	$ 0	$120,000	$120,000
Build small plant	$110,000	$ 50,000	$ 20,000	$110,000 → Minimax
No plant	$200,000	$100,000	$ 0	$200,000

SCREENSHOT 8-1A Formula View of Excel Layout for Thompson Lumber: Decision Making under Uncertainty

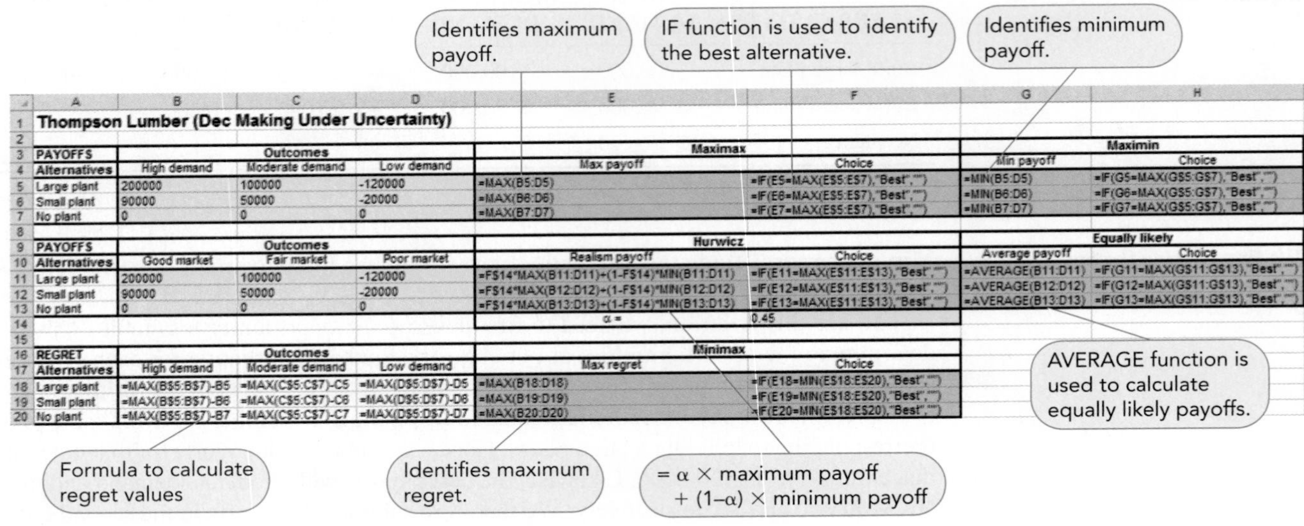
Identifies maximum payoff.
IF function is used to identify the best alternative.
Identifies minimum payoff.
AVERAGE function is used to calculate equally likely payoffs.
Formula to calculate regret values
Identifies maximum regret.
= α × maximum payoff + (1–α) × minimum payoff

SCREENSHOT 8-1B Excel Solution for Thompson Lumber: Decision Making under Uncertainty

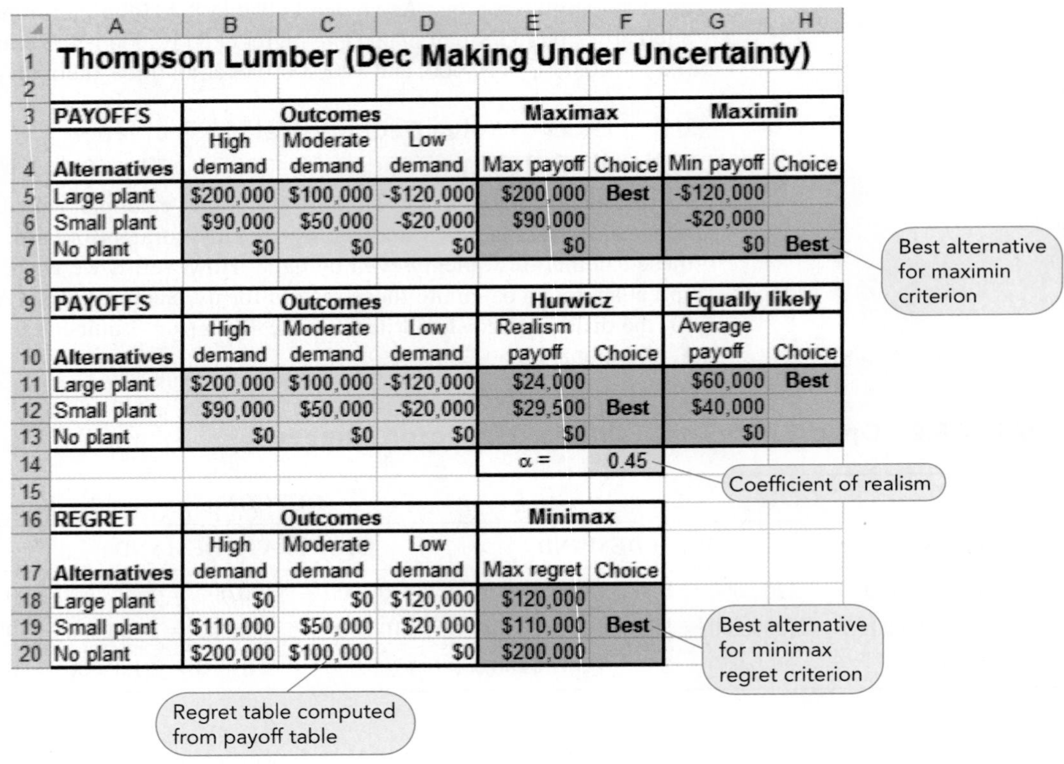
Best alternative for maximin criterion
Coefficient of realism
Best alternative for minimax regret criterion
Regret table computed from payoff table

Excel Notes

- The Companion Website for this textbook, at www.pearsonhighered.com/balakrishnan, contains the Excel file for each sample problem discussed here. The relevant file name is shown in the margin next to each example.
- For clarity, our Excel layouts in this chapter are color coded as follows:
  - *Input cells*, where we enter the problem data, are shaded yellow.
  - *Output cells*, where the results are shown, are shaded green.

Excel worksheets can be created easily to solve decision-making problems under uncertainty.

Note that the number of decision alternatives and the number of outcomes would vary from problem to problem. The formulas shown in Screenshot 8-1A can, however, easily be modified to accommodate any changes in these parameters.

8.5 Decision Making under Risk

In many real-world situations, it is common for the decision maker to have some idea about the probabilities of occurrence of the different outcomes. These probabilities may be based on the decision maker's personal opinions about future events or on data obtained from market surveys, expert opinions, and so on. As noted previously, when the probability of occurrence of each outcome can be assessed, the problem environment is called *decision making under risk.*

In this section we consider one of the most popular methods of making decisions under risk: selecting the alternative with the highest expected monetary value. We also look at the concepts of expected opportunity loss and expected value of perfect information.

Expected Monetary Value

EMV is the weighted average of possible payoffs for each alternative.

Given a decision table with payoffs and probability assessments, we can determine the **expected monetary value (EMV)** for each alternative. The EMV for an alternative is computed as the *weighted average* of all possible payoffs for that alternative, where the weights are the probabilities of the different outcomes. That is,

$$\begin{aligned}\text{EMV (Alternative } i) = {} & \text{(Payoff of first outcome)} \\ & \times \text{(Probability of first outcome)} \\ & + \text{(Payoff of second outcome)} \\ & \times \text{(Probability of second outcome)} \\ & + \cdots + \text{(Payoff of last outcome)} \\ & \times \text{(Probability of last outcome)}\end{aligned} \tag{8-2}$$

In Thompson Lumber's case, let us assume that John has used his knowledge of the storage shed industry to specify that the probabilities of high demand, moderate demand, and low demand are 0.3, 0.5, and 0.2, respectively. Under this scenario, which alternative would give him the greatest EMV? To determine this, we compute the EMV for each alternative, as shown in Table 8.8. The largest EMV, \$86,000, results from the first alternative, build a large plant.

Observe that the EMV represents the long-run *average* payoff, while the *actual* payoff from a decision will be one of the payoffs listed in the decision table. That is, the EMV of \$86,000 does not mean that John will actually realize a profit of \$86,000 if he builds a large plant. Nevertheless, the EMV is widely used as an acceptable criterion to compare decision alternatives in many business decisions because companies make similar decisions on a repeated basis over time.

TABLE 8.8 Thompson Lumber's EMV Decision

	OUTCOMES			
ALTERNATIVES	HIGH DEMAND	MODERATE DEMAND	LOW DEMAND	EMV FOR ALTERNATIVE
Build large plant	\$200,000	\$100,000	–\$120,000	\$200,000 × 0.3 + \$100,000 × 0.5 + (−\$120,000) × 0.2 = \$86,000
Build small plant	\$ 90,000	\$ 50,000	–\$ 20,000	\$90,000 × 0.3 + \$50,000 × 0.5 + (−\$20,000) × 0.2 = \$48,000
No plant	\$ 0	\$ 0	\$ 0	\$0 × 0.3 + \$0 × 0.5 + \$0 × 0.2 = \$ 0
Probabilities	0.3	0.5	0.2	

Expected Opportunity Loss

EOL is the expected cost of not picking the best solution.

An alternative approach in decision making under risk is to minimize **expected opportunity loss (EOL)**. Recall from section 8.4 that opportunity loss, also called regret, refers to the difference between the optimal payoff and the actual payoff received. The EOL for an alternative is computed as the weighted average of all possible regrets for that alternative, where the weights are the probabilities of the different outcomes. That is,

$$\begin{aligned} \text{EOL (Alternative } i) = {} & (\text{Regret of first outcome}) \\ & \times (\text{Probability of first outcome}) \\ & + (\text{Regret of second outcome}) \\ & \times (\text{Probability of second outcome}) \\ & + \cdots + (\text{Regret of last outcome}) \\ & \times (\text{Probability of last outcome}) \end{aligned} \quad \text{(8-3)}$$

Minimum EOL will always result in the same decision as the maximum EMV.

The EOL values for Thompson Lumber's problem are computed as shown in Table 8.9. Using minimum EOL as the decision criterion, the best decision would be the first alternative, build a large plant, with an EOL of $24,000. It is important to note that the minimum EOL will *always* result in the same decision alternative as the maximum EMV.

Expected Value of Perfect Information

John Thompson has been approached by Scientific Marketing, Inc., a market research firm, with a proposal to help him make the right decision regarding the size of the new plant. Scientific claims that its analysis will tell John with *certainty* whether the demand for storage sheds will be high, moderate, or low. In other words, it will change John's problem environment from one of decision making under risk to one of decision making under certainty. Obviously, this information could prevent John from making an expensive mistake. Scientific would charge $30,000 for the information. What should John do? Should he hire Scientific to do the marketing study? Is the information worth $30,000? If not, what is it worth?

EVPI places an upper bound on what to pay for any information.

We call the type of information offered by Scientific *perfect information* because it is certain (i.e., it is never wrong). Although such perfect information is almost never available in practice, determining its value can be very useful because it places an upper bound on what we should be willing to spend on *any* information. In what follows, we therefore investigate two related issues: the **expected value with perfect information (EVwPI)** and the **expected value of perfect information (EVPI)**.

The EVwPI is the expected payoff if we have perfect information *before* a decision has to be made. Clearly, if we knew for sure that a particular outcome was going to occur, we would choose the alternative that yielded the best payoff for that outcome. Unfortunately, until we get

TABLE 8.9 Thompson Lumber's EOL Decision

	OUTCOMES			
ALTERNATIVES	HIGH DEMAND	MODERATE DEMAND	LOW DEMAND	EOL FOR ALTERNATIVE
Build large plant	$ 0	$ 0	$120,000	$0 × 0.3 + $0 × 0.5 + $120,000 × 0.2 = $ 24,000
Build small plant	$110,000	$ 50,000	$ 20,000	$110,000 × 0.3 + $50,000 × 0.5 + $20,000 × 0.2 = $ 62,000
No plant	$200,000	$100,000	$ 0	$200,000 × 0.3 + $100,000 × 0.5 + $0 × 0.2 = $110,000
Probabilities	0.3	0.5	0.2	

this information, we don't know for sure which outcome is going to occur. Hence, to calculate the EVwPI value, we choose the best payoff for each outcome and multiply it by the probability of occurrence of that outcome. That is,

$$\begin{aligned}\text{EVwPI} = &(\text{Best payoff of first outcome})\\ &\times (\text{Probability of first outcome})\\ &+ (\text{Best payoff of second outcome})\\ &\times (\text{Probability of second outcome})\\ &+ \cdots + (\text{Best payoff of last outcome})\\ &\times (\text{Probability of last outcome})\end{aligned} \quad \textbf{(8-4)}$$

EVPI *is the expected value with perfect information minus the maximum EMV.*

We then compute the EVPI as the EVwPI minus the expected value *without* information, namely, the maximum EMV. That is,

$$\text{EVPI} = \text{EVwPI} - \text{Maximum EMV} \quad \textbf{(8-5)}$$

By referring to Table 8.8 on page 327, we can calculate the EVPI for John as follows:

1. The best payoff for the outcome high demand is \$200,000, associated with building a large plant. The best payoff for moderate demand is \$100,000, again associated with building a large plant. Finally, the best payoff for low demand is \$0, associated with not building a plant. Hence,

$$\text{EVwPI} = \$200{,}000 \times 0.3 + \$100{,}000 \times 0.5 + \$0 \times 0.20 = \$110{,}000$$

   That is, if we had perfect information, we would expect an *average* payoff of \$110,000 if the decision could be repeated many times.

2. Recall from Table 8.8 that the maximum EMV, or the best expected value *without* information, is \$86,000. Hence,

$$\text{EVPI} = \text{EVwPI} - \text{Maximum EMV} = \$110{,}000 - \$86{,}000 = \$24{,}000$$

   Thus, the most John should pay for perfect information is \$24,000. Because Scientific Marketing wants \$30,000 for its analysis, John should reject the offer. It is important to note that the following relationship always holds: EVPI = Minimum EOL. Referring to Thompson Lumber's example, we see that EVPI = Minimum EOL = \$24,000.

EVPI = Minimum EOL

Using Excel to Solve Decision-Making Problems under Risk

File: 8-2.xls

Just as with decision making under uncertainty, calculations for finding the EMV, EOL, EVwPI, and EVPI in decision making under risk are also fairly straightforward. In most small cases, we can perform these calculations quickly even by hand. However, if we wish, we can once again easily construct Excel spreadsheets to calculate these values for us. Screenshot 8-2A shows the relevant formulas to solve the Thompson Lumber example. The results are shown in Screenshot 8-2B.

As with Screenshot 8-1A, note that the number of decision alternatives and number of outcomes would vary from problem to problem. The formulas shown in Screenshot 8-2A can, however, be easily modified to accommodate any changes in these parameters.

8.6 Decision Trees

Any problem that can be presented in a decision table can also be graphically illustrated in a *decision tree*. A decision tree consists of nodes (or points) and arcs (or lines), just like a network. (You may recall that we studied several network models in Chapter 5.) We illustrate the construction and use of decision trees using the Thompson Lumber example.

SCREENSHOT 8-2A Formula View of Excel Layout for Thompson Lumber: Decision Making under Risk

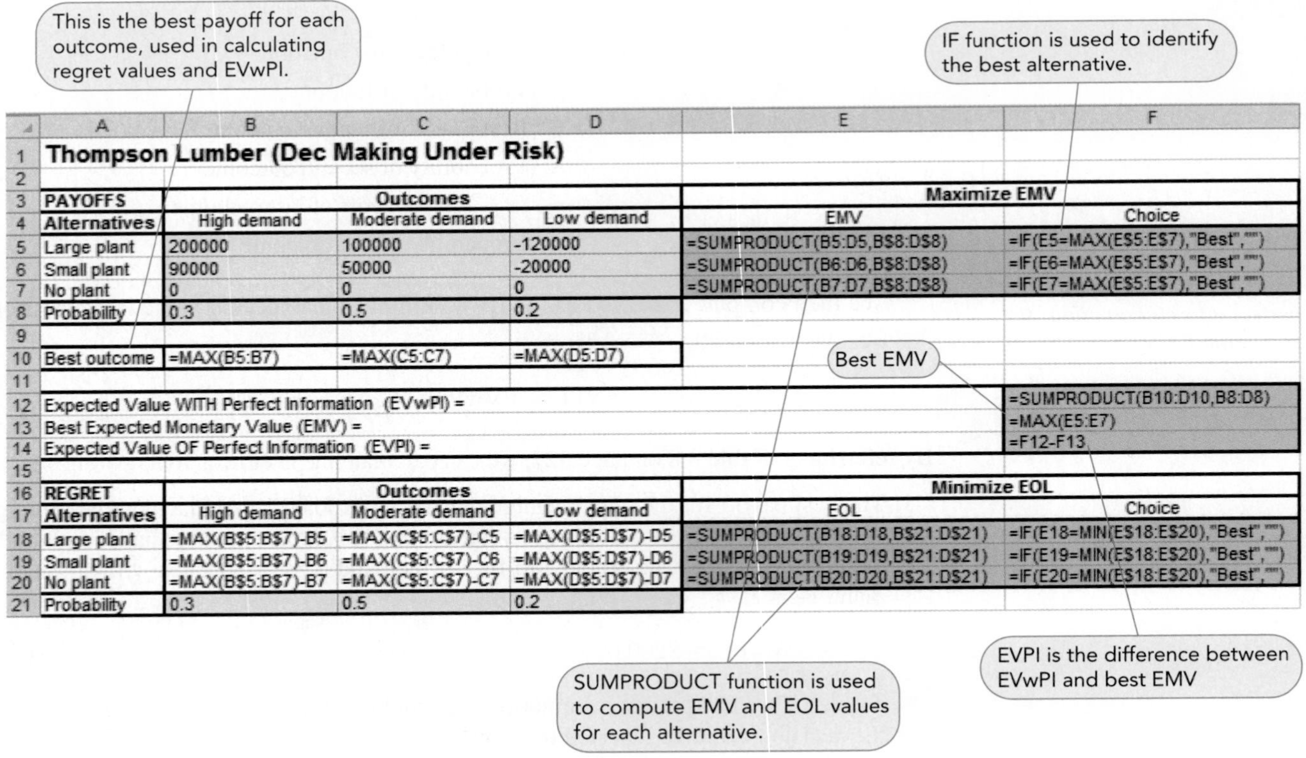

	A	B	C	D	E	F
1	**Thompson Lumber (Dec Making Under Risk)**					
2						
3	**PAYOFFS**		**Outcomes**		**Maximize EMV**	
4	**Alternatives**	High demand	Moderate demand	Low demand	EMV	Choice
5	Large plant	200000	100000	-120000	=SUMPRODUCT(B5:D5,B$8:D$8)	=IF(E5=MAX(E$5:E$7),"Best","")
6	Small plant	90000	50000	-20000	=SUMPRODUCT(B6:D6,B$8:D$8)	=IF(E6=MAX(E$5:E$7),"Best","")
7	No plant	0	0	0	=SUMPRODUCT(B7:D7,B$8:D$8)	=IF(E7=MAX(E$5:E$7),"Best","")
8	Probability	0.3	0.5	0.2		
9						
10	Best outcome	=MAX(B5:B7)	=MAX(C5:C7)	=MAX(D5:D7)		
11						
12	Expected Value WITH Perfect Information (EVwPI) =					=SUMPRODUCT(B10:D10,B8:D8)
13	Best Expected Monetary Value (EMV) =					=MAX(E5:E7)
14	Expected Value OF Perfect Information (EVPI) =					=F12-F13
15						
16	REGRET		**Outcomes**		**Minimize EOL**	
17	**Alternatives**	High demand	Moderate demand	Low demand	EOL	Choice
18	Large plant	=MAX(B$5:B$7)-B5	=MAX(C$5:C$7)-C5	=MAX(D$5:D$7)-D5	=SUMPRODUCT(B18:D18,B$21:D$21)	=IF(E18=MIN(E$18:E$20),"Best","")
19	Small plant	=MAX(B$5:B$7)-B6	=MAX(C$5:C$7)-C6	=MAX(D$5:D$7)-D6	=SUMPRODUCT(B19:D19,B$21:D$21)	=IF(E19=MIN(E$18:E$20),"Best","")
20	No plant	=MAX(B$5:B$7)-B7	=MAX(C$5:C$7)-C7	=MAX(D$5:D$7)-D7	=SUMPRODUCT(B20:D20,B$21:D$21)	=IF(E20=MIN(E$18:E$20),"Best","")
21	Probability	0.3	0.5	0.2		

SCREENSHOT 8-2B Excel Solution for Thompson Lumber: Decision Making under Risk

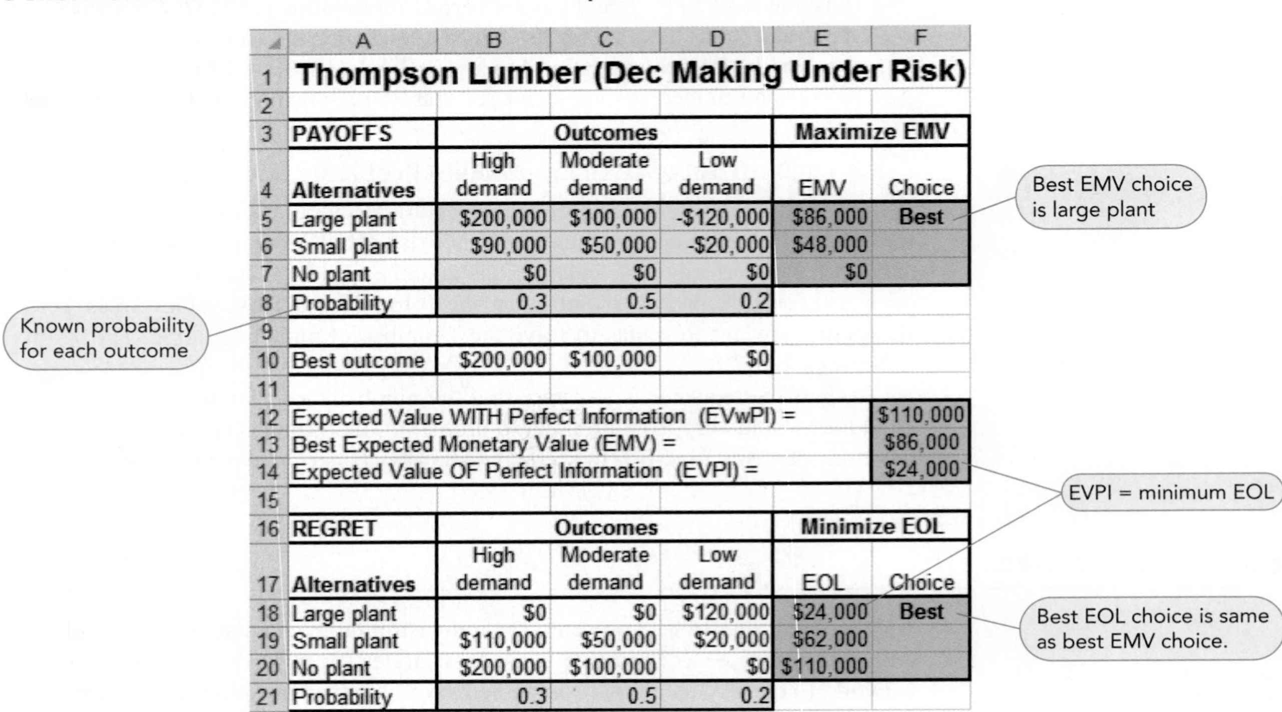

	A	B	C	D	E	F
1	**Thompson Lumber (Dec Making Under Risk)**					
2						
3	**PAYOFFS**		**Outcomes**		**Maximize EMV**	
4	**Alternatives**	High demand	Moderate demand	Low demand	EMV	Choice
5	Large plant	$200,000	$100,000	-$120,000	$86,000	**Best**
6	Small plant	$90,000	$50,000	-$20,000	$48,000	
7	No plant	$0	$0	$0	$0	
8	Probability	0.3	0.5	0.2		
9						
10	Best outcome	$200,000	$100,000	$0		
11						
12	Expected Value WITH Perfect Information (EVwPI) =					$110,000
13	Best Expected Monetary Value (EMV) =					$86,000
14	Expected Value OF Perfect Information (EVPI) =					$24,000
15						
16	**REGRET**		**Outcomes**		**Minimize EOL**	
17	**Alternatives**	High demand	Moderate demand	Low demand	EOL	Choice
18	Large plant	$0	$0	$120,000	$24,000	**Best**
19	Small plant	$110,000	$50,000	$20,000	$62,000	
20	No plant	$200,000	$100,000	$0	$110,000	
21	Probability	0.3	0.5	0.2		

IN ACTION Designing U.S. Army Installations Using Decision Analysis

Prior to 2002, army installations at about 100 major bases in the United States were managed by five U.S. Army organizations. In October 2002, the Installation Management Agency (IMA) was established to centrally manage all installations worldwide. The IMA's objective was to ensure a standard delivery of services and resources to all installations while reducing costs and redundancies.

Within the United States, the IMA was set up to use four regions to manage all continental U.S. installations. Based partly on concerns from Congress, the army wanted an analysis to verify if the IMA's use of four regions was indeed appropriate. Researchers from the U.S. Military Academy used decision analysis to evaluate several regional alternatives (i.e., using anywhere from just 1 up to 8 regions), measuring how well each alternative would perform the functions. The measures captured the effectiveness and efficiency of the regional organization for each function.

The analyses showed that four regions was an appropriate number to manage installations effectively. The use of a decision analysis framework to develop both qualitative and quantitative models of this problem helped provide a sound analysis to senior army decision makers.

Source: Based on T. E. Trainor et al. "The US Army Uses Decision Analysis in Designing Its US Installation Regions," *Interfaces* 37, 3 (May–June 2007): 253–264.

Decision trees contain decision nodes and outcome nodes.

A decision tree presents the decision alternatives and outcomes in a sequential manner. All decision trees are similar in that they contain *decision nodes* and *outcome nodes*. These nodes are represented using the following symbols:

□ = A *decision* node. Arcs (lines) originating from a decision node denote all decision alternatives available to the decision maker at that node. Of these, the decision maker must select only one alternative.

○ = An *outcome* node. Arcs (lines) originating from an outcome node denote all outcomes that could occur at that node. Of these, only one outcome will actually occur.

A decision tree usually begins with a decision node.

Although it is possible for a decision tree to begin with an outcome node, most trees begin with a decision node. In Thompson Lumber's case, this decision node indicates that John has to decide among his three alternatives: building a large plant, a small plant, or no plant. Each alternative is represented by an arc originating from this decision node. Once John makes this decision, one of three possible outcomes (high demand, moderate demand, or low demand) will occur. The simple decision tree to represent John's decision is shown in Figure 8.1.

Observe that all alternatives available to John are shown as arcs originating from a decision node (□). Likewise, at each outcome node (○), all possible outcomes that could occur if John chooses that decision alternative are shown as arcs. The payoffs resulting from each alternative and outcome combination are shown at the end of each relevant path in the tree. For example, if John chooses to build a large plant and demand turns out to be high, the resulting payoff is $200,000.

FIGURE 8.1
Decision Tree for Thompson Lumber

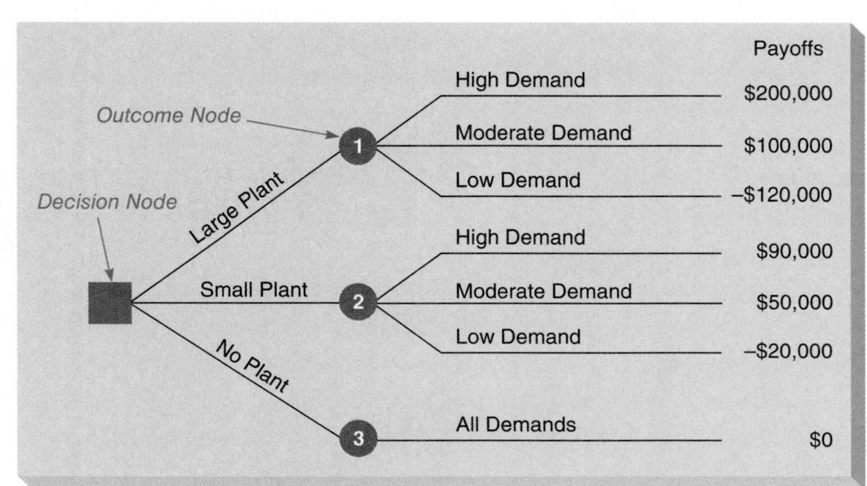

Folding Back a Decision Tree

We fold back a decision tree to identify the best decision.

The process by which a decision tree is analyzed to identify the optimal decision is referred to as *folding back* the decision tree. We start with the payoffs (i.e., the right extreme of the tree) and work our way back to the first decision node. In folding back the decision tree, we use the following two rules:

- At each outcome node, we compute the expected payoff, using the probabilities of all possible outcomes at that node and the payoffs associated with those outcomes.
- At each decision node, we select the alternative that yields the better expected payoff. If the expected payoffs represent profits, we select the alternative with the largest value. In contrast, if the expected payoffs represent costs, we select the alternative with the smallest value.

The EMV is calculated at each outcome node.

The complete decision tree for Thompson Lumber is presented in Figure 8.2. For convenience, the probability of each outcome is shown in parentheses next to each outcome. The EMV at each outcome node is then calculated and placed by that node. The EMV at node 1 (if John decides to build a large plant) is \$86,000, and the EMV at node 2 (if John decides to build a small plant) is \$48,000. Building no plant has, of course, an EMV of \$0.

At this stage, the decision tree for Thompson Lumber has been folded back to just the first decision node and the three alternatives (arcs) originating from it. That is, all outcome nodes and the outcomes from these nodes have been examined and collapsed into the EMVs. The reduced decision tree for Thompson Lumber is shown in Figure 8.3.

The best alternative is selected at a decision node.

Using the rule stated earlier for decision nodes, we now select the alternative with the highest EMV. In this case, it corresponds to the alternative to build a large plant. The resulting EMV is \$86,000.

FIGURE 8.2
Complete Decision Tree for Thompson Lumber

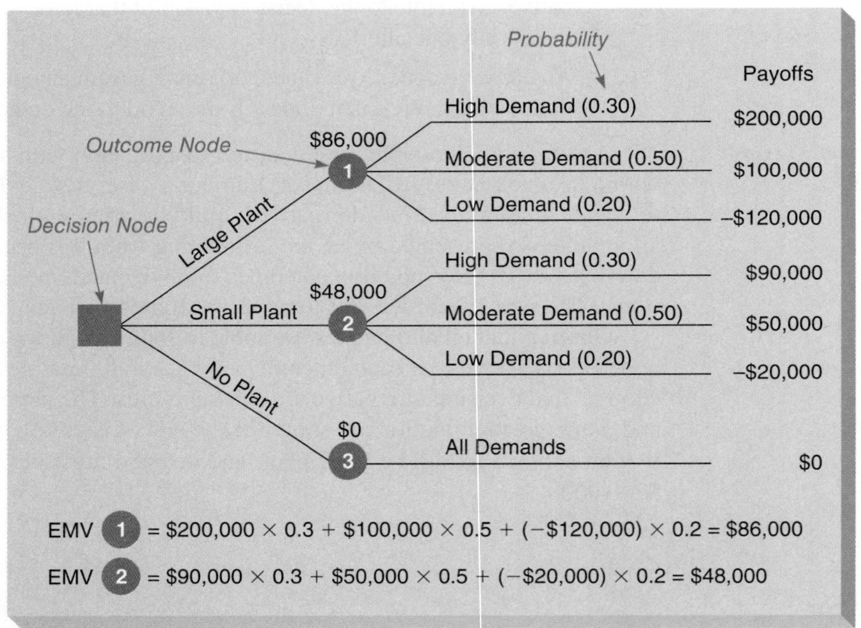

FIGURE 8.3
Reduced Decision Tree for Thompson Lumber

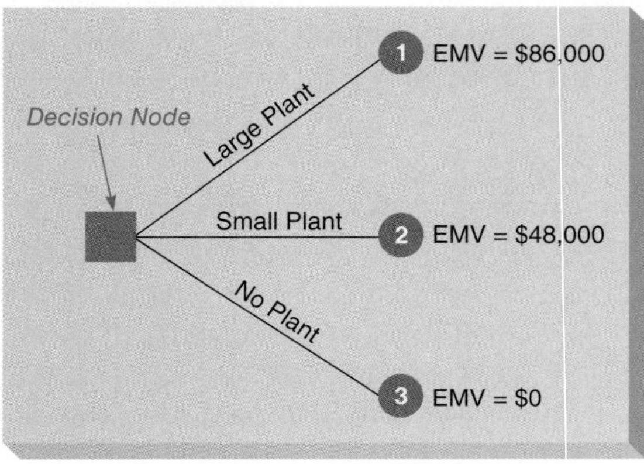

8.7 Using Treeplan to Solve Decision Tree Problems with Excel

TreePlan is an Excel add-in for solving decision tree problems.

We can use TreePlan, an add-in for Excel, to set up and solve decision tree problems. The TreePlan program consists of a single Excel add-in file, *Treeplan.xla*, which can be copied from this textbook's Companion Website to your hard disk.

Loading TreePlan

There are two ways of loading TreePlan in Excel.

To load and enable TreePlan in Excel, you can use either of the two approaches described in the following sections.

LOADING MANUALLY Each time you run Excel, you can load TreePlan manually, as follows:

M1. Click File | Open and use the file browse window to find the *Treeplan.xla* file on your hard disk.
M2. Open the file. Note that you will not see anything new on your Excel spreadsheet at this time. Also, depending on your macro settings for Excel (click File | Help | Options | Trust Center | Trust Center Settings | Macro Settings to see your settings), Excel may ask if you want to enable macros in the file. You must enable macros to use TreePlan.
M3. Under the Add-Ins tab in Excel, you will see a menu command called Decision Tree.

LOADING AUTOMATICALLY You have to load automatically only once, as follows:

A1. Copy the *Treeplan.xla* file to your hard drive.
A2. Open Excel. Click File | Options | Add-Ins. In the Manage window, select Excel Add-Ins and click Go.
A3. Click Browse and use the file browse window to locate and select the *Treeplan.xla* file. Then click OK.
A4. You will see an option named TreePlan Decision Tree in the Add-In list. Make sure the box next to this option is checked. Click OK. *Note:* To subsequently prevent TreePlan from loading automatically, repeat step A2 and uncheck the box next to this add-in.
A5. Under the Add-Ins tab in Excel, you will see a menu command called Decision Tree. *Note:* You must enable macros to use TreePlan (see step M2 for details).

Creating a Decision Tree Using TreePlan

Once you have installed and loaded TreePlan, you can use the following six steps to set up and solve a decision tree problem: (1) start the program; (2) begin a new tree; (3) add nodes and branches; (4) change titles, probabilities, and payoffs; (5) identify the best decision; and (6) make minor formatting changes. On the next several pages, we illustrate these six steps using the Thompson Lumber problem. Recall that we saw the complete decision tree for this problem in Figure 8.2.

Select Add-Ins | Decision Tree in Excel to start TreePlan.

STEP 1: START TREEPLAN Start Excel and open a blank worksheet. Place the cursor in any blank cell (say, cell A1). Select Decision Tree from the Add-Ins tab in Excel. *Note:* If you don't see the Add-Ins tab or the Decision Tree menu command as a choice within this tab, you have to install TreePlan, as discussed in the preceding section.

File: 8-3.xls, sheet: 8-3A

STEP 2: START A NEW TREE Select New Tree. As shown in Screenshot 8-3A, this creates an initial decision tree with a single decision node (in cell B5, if the cursor was placed in cell A1). Two alternatives (named Alternative 1 and Alternative 2) are automatically created at this node.

The TreePlan menu that appears depends on the location of the cursor.

STEP 3: ADD NODES AND BRANCHES We now modify the basic decision tree in Screenshot 8-3A to reflect our full decision problem. To do so, we use TreePlan menus. To bring up the menu, we either select Add-Ins | Decision Tree or press the Control (Ctrl), Shift, and T keys at the same time. The TreePlan menu that is displayed each time depends on the location of the cursor when we bring up the menu, as follows:

- If the cursor is at a node in the tree (such as cell B5 in Screenshot 8-3A), the menu shown in Screenshot 8-3B(a) is displayed.
- If the cursor is at a terminal point in the tree (such as cells F3 and F8 in Screenshot 8-3A), the menu shown in Screenshot 8-3B(b) is displayed.
- If the cursor is at any other location in the spreadsheet, the menu shown in Screenshot 8-3B(c) is displayed.

SCREENSHOT 8-3A
Initial Decision Tree from TreePlan

Invoke this box by clicking Add-Ins | Decision Tree
TreePlan - New Tree
Click here to get initial tree.
New Tree
Cancel
Help
A B C D E F G
Alternative 1
0
0
0
1
0
Alternative 2
0
0
0
Default titles
Initial tree has one decision node with two alternatives.

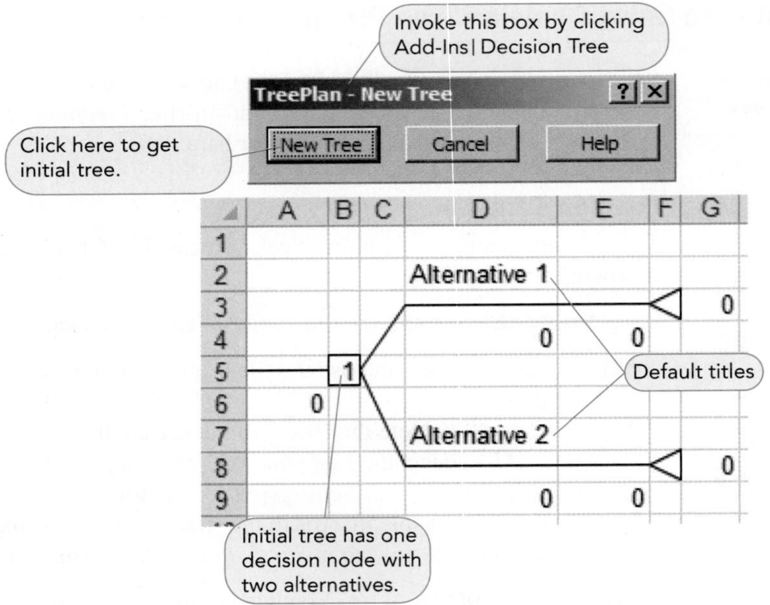

SCREENSHOT 8-3B
TreePlan Menus

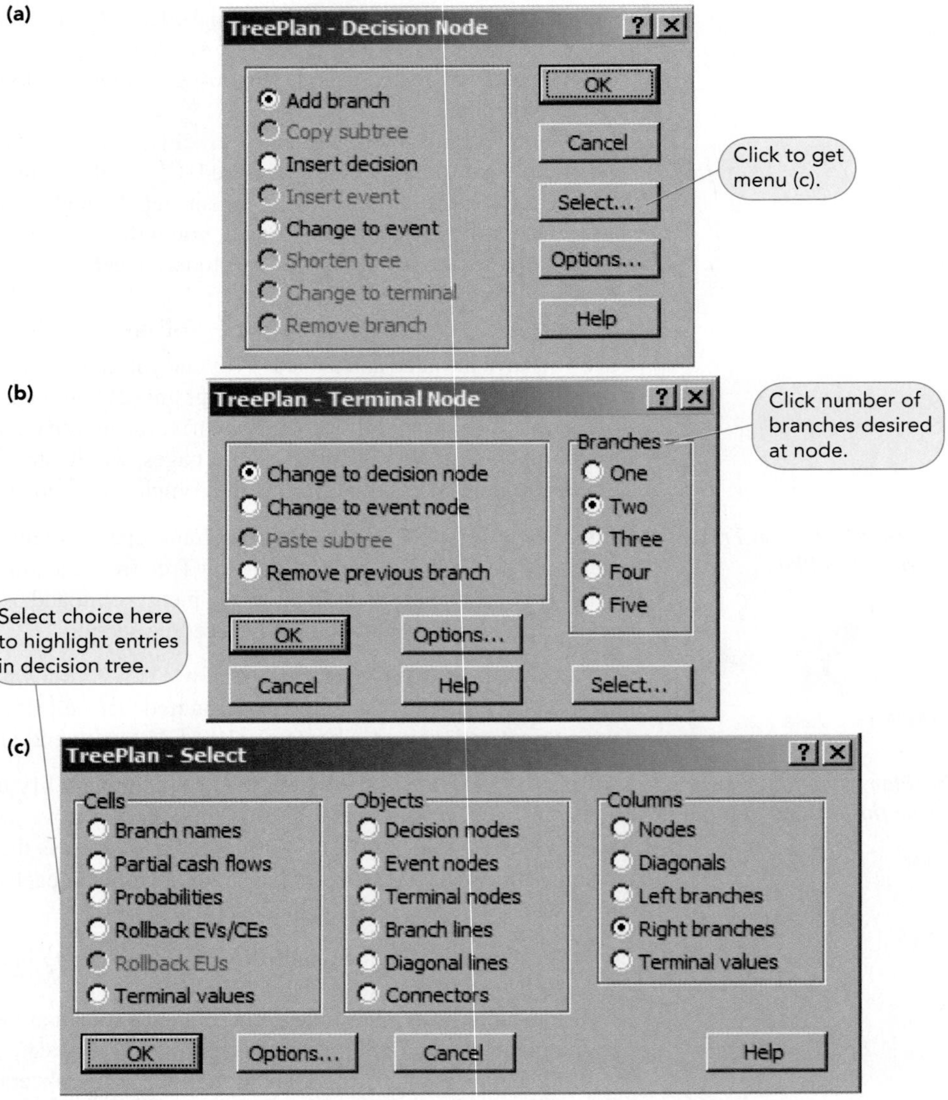

(a)
TreePlan - Decision Node
Add branch
Copy subtree
Insert decision
Insert event
Change to event
Shorten tree
Change to terminal
Remove branch
OK
Cancel
Select...
Options...
Help
Click to get menu (c).
(b)
TreePlan - Terminal Node
Change to decision node
Change to event node
Paste subtree
Remove previous branch
Branches
One
Two
Three
Four
Five
Click number of branches desired at node.
OK
Options...
Cancel
Help
Select...
Select choice here to highlight entries in decision tree.
(c)
TreePlan - Select
Cells
Branch names
Partial cash flows
Probabilities
Rollback EVs/CEs
Rollback EUs
Terminal values
Objects
Decision nodes
Event nodes
Terminal nodes
Branch lines
Diagonal lines
Connectors
Columns
Nodes
Diagonals
Left branches
Right branches
Terminal values
OK
Options...
Cancel
Help

TreePlan refers to outcome nodes as event nodes.

For the Thompson Lumber example, we begin by placing the cursor in cell B5 and bringing up the menu in Screenshot 8-3B(a). We then select Add Branch and click OK to get the third decision branch (named Decision 3).

Next, we move the cursor to the end of the branch for Decision 1 (i.e., to cell F3 in Screenshot 8-3A) and bring up the menu in Screenshot 8-3B(b). We first select Change to Event Node. (Note that TreePlan refers to outcome nodes as *event nodes*.) Then we select Three under Branches to add three outcome arcs to this outcome node. When we click OK, the program creates three arcs, named Event 4, Event 5, and Event 6, respectively. Because these are outcomes, we need to associate probability values with the events. TreePlan automatically assigns equal probability values by default. In this case, because there are three events, the default value assigned is 1/3 (shown as 0.33333).

WWW

File: 8-3.xls, sheet: 8-3C

Each time we add more decision alternatives or outcomes to a decision tree, TreePlan automatically repositions the tree on the Excel worksheet to make it fit better. We next move the cursor to the end of the branch for Decision 2 and repeat the preceding step to create Event 7, Event 8, and Event 9. The structure of the decision tree, shown in Screenshot 8-3C, is now similar to that of the tree in Figure 8.2 (see page 332).

Titles can be changed in TreePlan, if desired.

STEP 4: CHANGE TITLES, PROBABILITIES, AND PAYOFFS We can change the default titles for all arcs in the decision tree to reflect the Thompson Lumber example. For example, we

SCREENSHOT 8-3C Complete Decision Tree Using TreePlan for Thompson Lumber

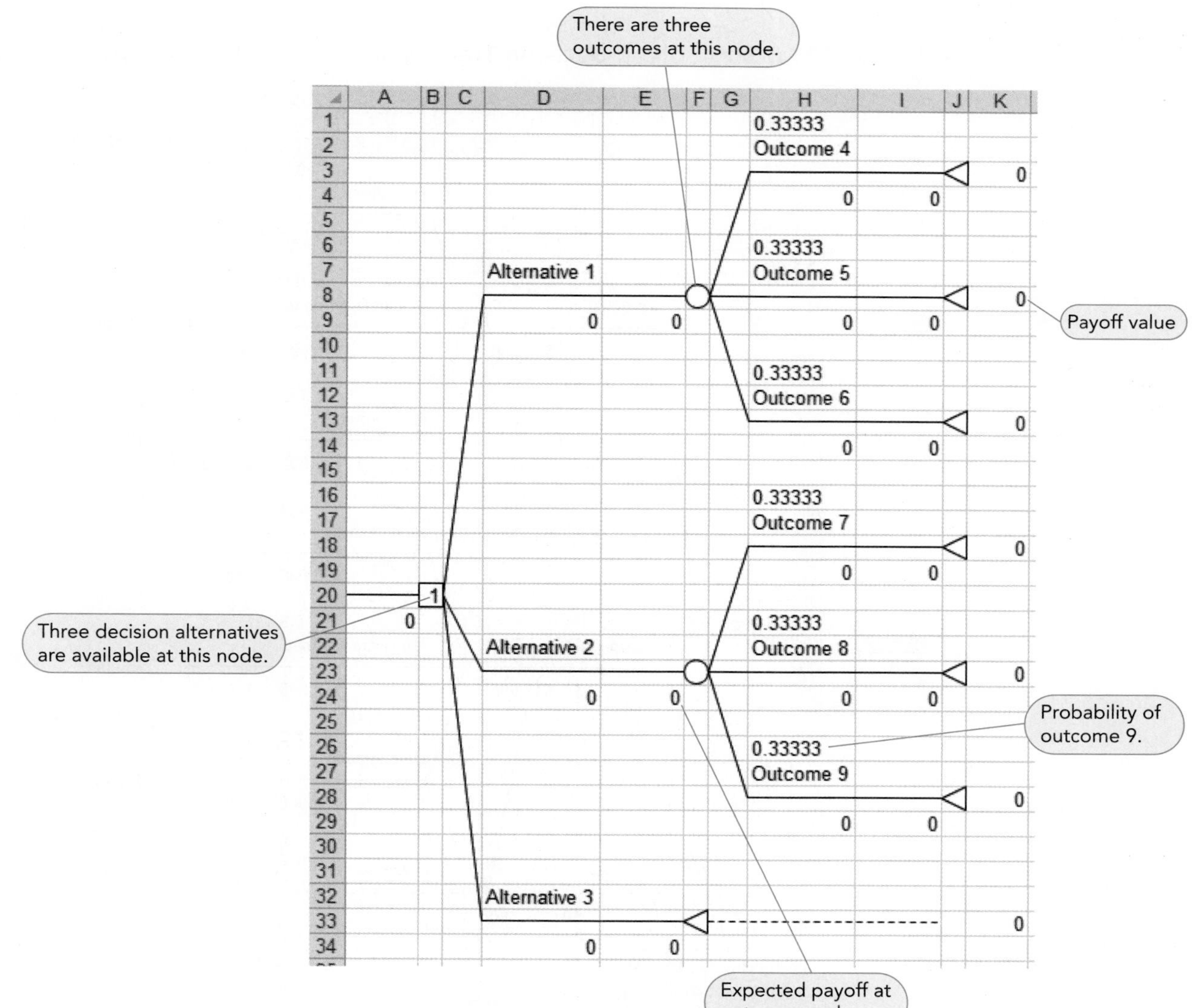

can replace Decision 1 (in cell D7 of Screenshot 8-3C) with Large plant. Likewise, we can replace Event 4 (in cell H2 of Screenshot 8-3C) with High demand. The changes are shown in Screenshot 8-3D.

There are two ways of entering payoffs in TreePlan.

Next, we change the default probability values on the event arcs to the correct values. Finally, we enter the payoffs. TreePlan allows us to enter these values in two ways:

File: 8-3.xls, sheet: 8-3D

- We can directly enter the payoffs at the end of each path in the decision tree. That is, we can enter the appropriate payoff values in cells K3, K8, K13, K18, K23, K28, and K33 (see Screenshot 8-3D).
- We can allow TreePlan to compute the payoffs. Each time we create an arc (a decision alternative or outcome) in TreePlan, it assigns a default payoff of zero to that branch. We can edit these payoffs (or costs) for all alternatives and outcomes. For example, we leave cell D9 at $0 (default value) because there is no cost specified for building a large plant. However, we change the entry in cell H4 to $200,000 to reflect the payoff if demand turns out to be high. TreePlan adds these two entries (in cells D9 and H4) automatically and reports it as the payoff in cell K3. We can do likewise for all other payoffs in John's tree.

TreePlan writes formulas in the appropriate cells as the tree is created.

STEP 5: IDENTIFY THE BEST DECISION TreePlan automatically writes formulas into the appropriate cells as the tree is created and structured. For example, TreePlan writes the following formula in cell E9 (which computes the EMV of building a large plant) of Screenshot 8-3D:

=IF(ABS(1−SUM(H1, H6, H11))<=0.00001, SUM(H1*I4, H6*I9, H11*I14), NA())

SCREENSHOT 8-3D Solved Decision Tree Using TreePlan for Thompson Lumber

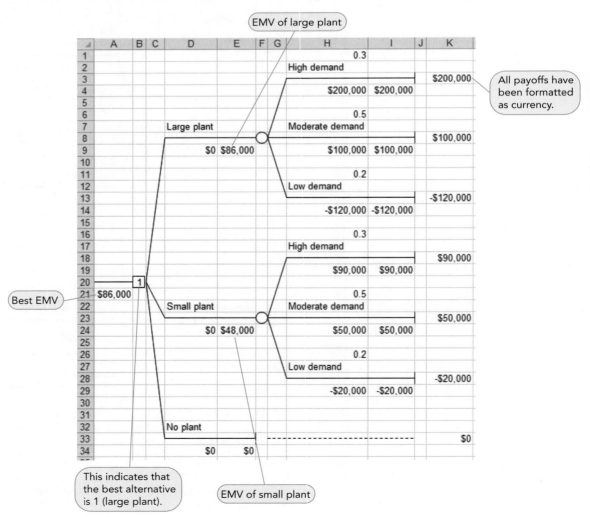

	A	B	C	D	E	F	G	H	I	J	K
1								0.3			
2								High demand			
3											$200,000
4								$200,000	$200,000		
5											
6								0.5			
7				Large plant				Moderate demand			
8											$100,000
9				$0	$86,000			$100,000	$100,000		
10											
11								0.2			
12								Low demand			
13											-$120,000
14								-$120,000	-$120,000		
15											
16								0.3			
17								High demand			
18											$90,000
19								$90,000	$90,000		
20		1									
21	$86,000							0.5			
22				Small plant				Moderate demand			
23											$50,000
24				$0	$48,000			$50,000	$50,000		
25											
26								0.2			
27								Low demand			
28											-$20,000
29								-$20,000	-$20,000		
30											
31											
32				No plant							
33											$0
34				$0	$0						

EMV of large plant

All payoffs have been formatted as currency.

Best EMV

This indicates that the best alternative is 1 (large plant).

EMV of small plant

IN ACTION Decision Analysis Helps Solve Airport Ground Delay Problems

One of the most frustrating aspects of air travel is rushing to the airport only to find out that your flight has been delayed. Often triggered by what is called the Ground-Delay Program (GDP), the Federal Aviation Administration (FAA) keeps flights from departing when the air traffic or weather at the destination is unfavorable.

Decisions involving GDP are classic problems in decision analysis. At the heart of such a problem, there are two decision alternatives: allow the flight to depart or do not allow the flight to depart. In choosing from these alternatives, the decision maker has to consider several unknown future outcomes, such as the weather, expected air traffic, and a variety of other factors that could develop at the destination. These factors could delay or prevent a flight from landing safely.

The original GDP system was administered by the FAA. The FAA monitored existing imbalances between demand and capacity at given airports to determine whether a ground delay was warranted and justified at other airports that fed into it. Some experts, however, claimed that the FAA lacked current and accurate information. In some cases, the FAA relied on the published airline schedules, which were subject to change and inaccuracies. This resulted in the inefficient use of arrival resources and unnecessary ground delays at some airports. To overcome some of these problems, a decision analysis model was developed.

Using decision analysis models can improve not only information flow but also performance. Before the initiative, 51% of flights left on time. Afterward, 66% left on time. In addition to conserving fuel and improving utilization of arrival resources, these types of initiatives can save travelers a tremendous amount of frustration and lost time.

Source: Based on K. Chang, et al. "Enhancements to the FAA Ground-Delay Program Under Collaborative Decision Making," *Interfaces* 31, 1 (January–February 2001): 57–76.

The ABS part of the formula verifies that the sum of probabilities of all outcomes at a given outcome node equals 1. The second part (SUM) computes the EMV using the appropriate payoffs and probability values. The EMVs are shown next to the outcome nodes. For example, cell E9 shows an EMV of $86,000 for the large plant.

Once all expected values have been computed, TreePlan then selects the optimal decision alternative at each decision node. The selection is indicated within that node. For example, the 1 within the decision node in cell B20 indicates that the first alternative (i.e., large plant) is the best choice for Thompson Lumber. The best EMV of $86,000 is shown next to this decision node (in cell A21).

If the payoffs denote costs, we can click Options in any of the TreePlan menus (see Screenshot 8-3B on page 334) to change the selection criterion from maximizing profits to minimizing costs. In this case, TreePlan will select the decision alternative with the smallest expected costs.

STEP 6: MAKE MINOR FORMATTING CHANGES If desired, we can add titles, format payoffs to be shown as dollar values, change number of decimals shown, and make other cosmetic changes to the tree, as shown in Screenshot 8-3D. Appendix B illustrates how to make such formatting changes in Excel.

8.8 Decision Trees for Multistage Decision-Making Problems

The Thompson Lumber problem discussed so far is a single-stage problem. That is, John has to choose a decision alternative, which is followed by an outcome. Depending on the alternative chosen and the outcome that occurs, John gets a payoff, and the problem ends there.

Multistage decision problems involve a sequence of decision alternatives and outcomes.

In many cases, however, the decision-making scenario is a multistage problem. In such cases, the decision maker must evaluate and make a set of **sequential decisions** up front (i.e., before the first decision is implemented). However, the decisions are actually implemented in a sequential manner, as follows. The problem usually begins with the decision maker implementing his or her initial decision. This is followed by an outcome. Depending on the initial decision and the outcome that occurs after it, the decision maker next implements his or her next decision. The alternatives for this follow-up decision may be different for different outcomes of the earlier decision. This decision, in turn, is followed by an outcome. The set of outcomes for this decision may be different from the set of outcomes for the earlier decision. This sequence could continue several more times, and the final payoff is a function of the sequence of decisions made and the outcomes that occurred at each stage of the problem.

It is possible for one outcome (or alternative) to directly follow another outcome (or alternative).

At one or more stages in a problem, it is possible for a specific decision to have no outcomes following it. In such cases, the decision maker is immediately faced with the next decision. Likewise, at one or more stages in the problem, it is possible to have one outcome occur directly after another outcome without the decision maker facing a decision in between the two.

Multistage decision problems are analyzed using decision trees.

For multistage scenarios, decision tables are no longer convenient, and we are forced to analyze these problems using decision trees. Although we can, in theory, extend multistage scenarios to a sequence of as many decisions and outcomes as we wish, we will limit our discussion here to problems involving just two stages. To facilitate this discussion, let us consider an expanded version of the Thompson Lumber problem.

A Multistage Decision-Making Problem for Thompson Lumber

Before deciding about building a new plant, let's suppose John Thompson has been approached by Smart Services, another market research firm. Smart will charge John $4,000 to conduct a market survey. The results of the survey will indicate either positive or negative market conditions for storage sheds. What should John do?

John recognizes that Smart's market survey will not provide him with *perfect* information, but it may help him get a better feel for the outcomes nevertheless. The type of information obtained here is referred to either as *sample* information or *imperfect* information.

EVPI is an upper bound on the value of sample information.

Recall from section 8.5 that we calculated John's EVPI as $24,000. That is, if the results of the market survey are going to be 100% accurate, John should be willing to pay up to $24,000 for the survey. Because Smart's survey will cost significantly less (only $4,000), it is at least worth considering further. However, given that it yields only imperfect information, how much is it actually worth? We determine this by extending the decision tree analysis for Thompson Lumber to include Smart's market survey.

Expanded Decision Tree for Thompson Lumber

All outcomes and alternatives must be considered.

John's new decision tree is represented in Figure 8.4. Let's take a careful look at this more complex tree. Note that all possible alternatives and outcomes are included in their logical sequence. This is one of the strengths of using decision trees in making decisions. The user is forced to examine all possible outcomes, including unfavorable ones. He or she is also forced to make decisions in a logical, sequential manner.

Examining the tree, we see that John's first decision point is whether to conduct Smart's market survey. If he chooses not to do the survey (i.e., the upper part of the tree), he is immediately faced with his second decision node: whether to build a large plant, a small plant, or no plant. The possible outcomes for each of these alternatives are high demand (0.3 probability), moderate demand (0.5 probability), and low demand (0.2 probability). The payoffs for each of the possible consequences are listed along the right side of the tree. As a matter of fact, this portion of John's tree in Figure 8.4 is identical to the simpler decision tree shown in Figure 8.2. Can you see why this is so?

The lower portion of Figure 8.4 reflects the decision to conduct the market survey. This decision has two possible outcomes—positive survey result or negative survey result—each with a specific probability. For now, let us assume that John knows these probabilities to be as follows: probability of 0.57 that the survey will indicate positive market conditions for storage sheds, and probability of 0.43 that the survey will indicate negative market conditions. An explanation of how these probabilities can be calculated in real-world situations is the topic of section 8.9.

Many of the probabilities are conditional probabilities.

Regardless of which survey outcome occurs, John is now faced with his next decision. Although the decision alternatives at this point could be different for different survey outcomes, let us assume in John's case that for both survey outcomes he has the same three alternatives: whether to build a large plant, a small plant, or no plant. Each alternative has the same three outcomes as before: high demand, moderate demand, and low demand. The key difference, however, is that the survey outcome (positive or negative) allows John to update the probabilities of the demand outcomes. For this reason, the probabilities shown in parentheses for these outcomes in Figure 8.4 are called *conditional probabilities*. An explanation of how these probabilities can be calculated in real-world situations is also presented in section 8.9. For now, let us assume that these probabilities have already been calculated and are available to John.

From Figure 8.4, we note, for example, that the probability of high demand for sheds, given a positive survey result, is 0.509. Note that this is higher than the 0.30 probability that John had estimated for high demand before the market survey. This increase in the probability is not surprising because you would, of course, expect a positive survey result to be a stronger

FIGURE 8.4 Expanded Decision Tree with Payoffs and Probabilities for Thompson Lumber

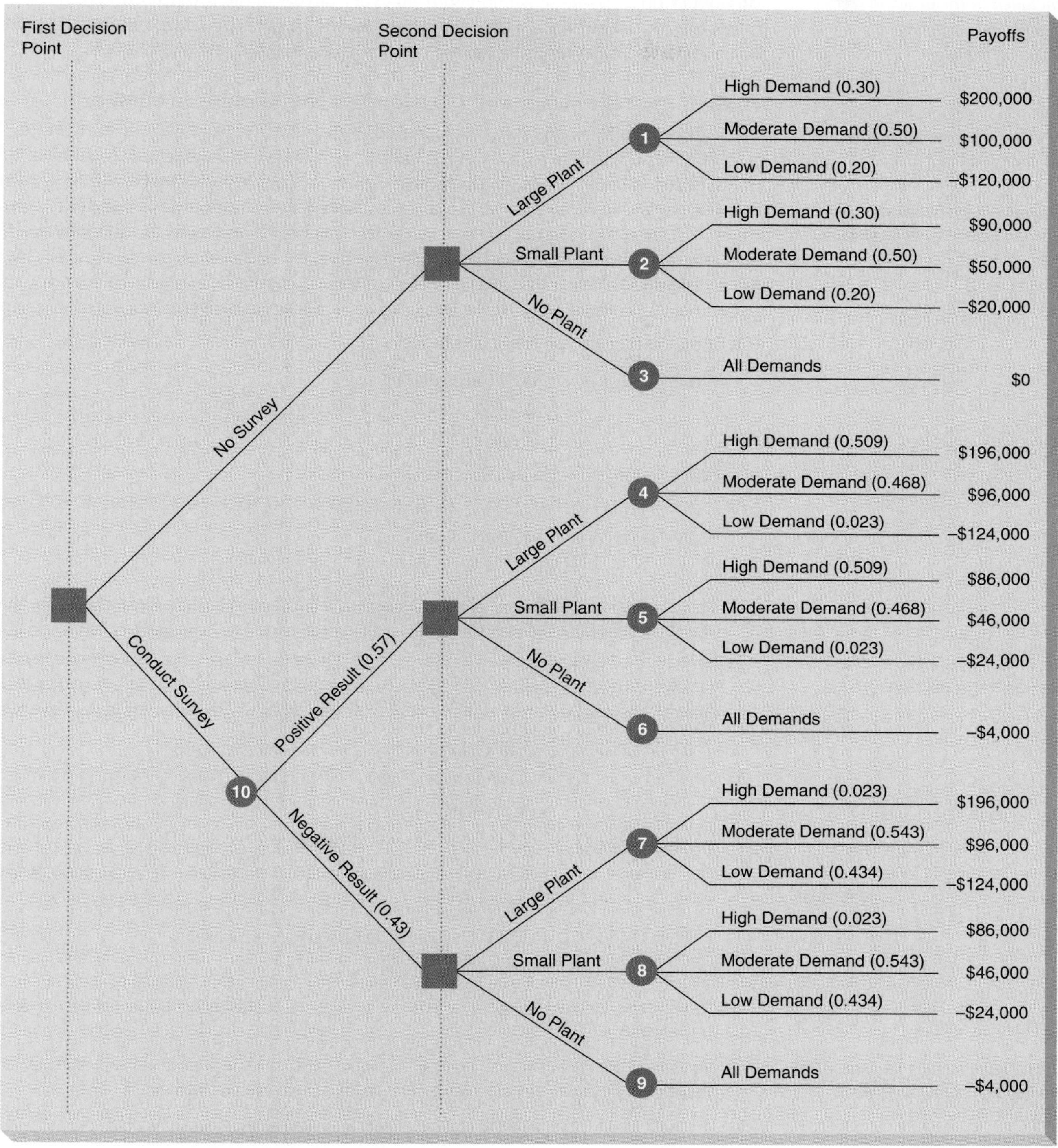

indicator of high demand. Don't forget, however, that any market research study is subject to error. Therefore, it is possible that Smart's market survey didn't result in very reliable information. In fact, as shown in Figure 8.4, demand for sheds could be moderate (with a probability of 0.468) or low (with a probability of 0.023), even if Smart's survey results are positive.

Likewise, we note in Figure 8.4 that if the survey results are negative, the probability of low demand for sheds increases from the 0.20 that John originally estimated to 0.434. However, because Smart's survey results are not perfect, there are nonzero probabilities of moderate and high demand for sheds, even if the survey results are negative. As shown in Figure 8.4, these values are 0.543 and 0.023, respectively.

The cost of the survey has to be included in the decision tree.

Finally, when we look to the payoff values in Figure 8.4, we note that the cost of the market survey ($4,000) has to be subtracted from every payoff in the lower portion of the tree (i.e., the portion with the survey). Thus, for example, the payoff for a large plant followed by high demand for sheds is reduced from the original value of $200,000 to $196,000.

Folding Back the Expanded Decision Tree for Thompson Lumber

We start by computing the EMV of each branch.

With all probabilities and payoffs specified in the decision tree, we can start folding back the tree. We begin with the payoffs at the end (or right side) of the tree and work back toward the initial decision node. When we finish, the sequence of decisions to make will be known.

The alternative that should be chosen is indicated by slashes (//).

For your convenience, we have summarized the computations for John's problem in Figure 8.5. A pair of slashes (//) through a decision branch indicates the alternative selected at a decision node. In Figure 8.5, all expected payoffs have been noted next to the relevant nodes on the decision tree. Although we explain each of these computations in detail below, you may find it easier to do all computations on the tree itself after you have solved several decision tree problems:

1. If the market survey is *not* conducted,

$$\begin{aligned}
\text{EMV (node 1)} &= \text{EMV (Large plant)} \\
&= \$200{,}000 \times 0.30 + \$100{,}000 \times 0.50 + (-\$120{,}000) \times 0.20 \\
&= \$86{,}000 \\
\text{EMV (node 2)} &= \text{EMV (Small plant)} \\
&= \$90{,}000 \times 0.30 + \$50{,}000 \times 0.50 + (-\$20{,}000) \times 0.20 = \$48{,}000 \\
\text{EMV (node 3)} &= \text{EMV (No plant)} \\
&= \$0
\end{aligned}$$

Thus, if the market survey is not conducted, John should build a large plant, for an expected payoff of $86,000. As expected, this is the same result we saw earlier, in Figure 8.2.

EMV calculations for a positive survey result are done first.

2. Now let us examine the portion of the tree where the market survey is conducted. Working backward from the payoffs, we first consider outcome nodes 4, 5, and 6. All calculations at these nodes are conditional on a positive survey result. The calculations are as follows:

$$\begin{aligned}
\text{EMV (node 4)} &= \text{EMV (Large plant} \mid \text{Positive survey result)} \\
&= \$196{,}000 \times 0.509 + \$96{,}000 \times 0.468 + (-\$124{,}000) \times 0.023 \\
&= \$141{,}840 \\
\text{EMV (node 5)} &= \text{EMV (Small plant} \mid \text{Positive survey result)} \\
&= \$86{,}000 \times 0.509 + \$46{,}000 \times 0.468 + (-\$24{,}000) \times 0.023 \\
&= \$64{,}750 \\
\text{EMV (node 6)} &= \text{EMV (No plant} \mid \text{Positive survey result)} \\
&= -\$4{,}000
\end{aligned}$$

Thus, if the survey results are positive, a large plant should be built, for an expected payoff of $141,840.

EMV calculations for a negative survey result are done next.

3. Next, we consider outcome nodes 7, 8, and 9. All calculations at these nodes are conditional on a negative survey result. The calculations are as follows:

$$\begin{aligned}
\text{EMV (node 7)} &= \text{EMV (Large plant} \mid \text{Negative survey result)} \\
&= \$196{,}000 \times 0.023 + \$96{,}000 \times 0.543 + (-\$124{,}000) \times 0.434 \\
&= \$2{,}820 \\
\text{EMV (node 8)} &= \text{EMV (Small plant} \mid \text{Negative survey result)} \\
&= \$86{,}000 \times 0.023 + \$46{,}000 \times 0.543 + (-\$24{,}000) \times 0.434 \\
&= \$16{,}540 \\
\text{EMV (node 9)} &= \text{EMV (No plant} \mid \text{Negative survey result)} \\
&= -\$4{,}000
\end{aligned}$$

Thus, given a negative survey result, John should build a small plant, with an expected payoff of $16,540.

FIGURE 8.5 Thompson Lumber's Expanded Decision Tree, with EMVs Shown

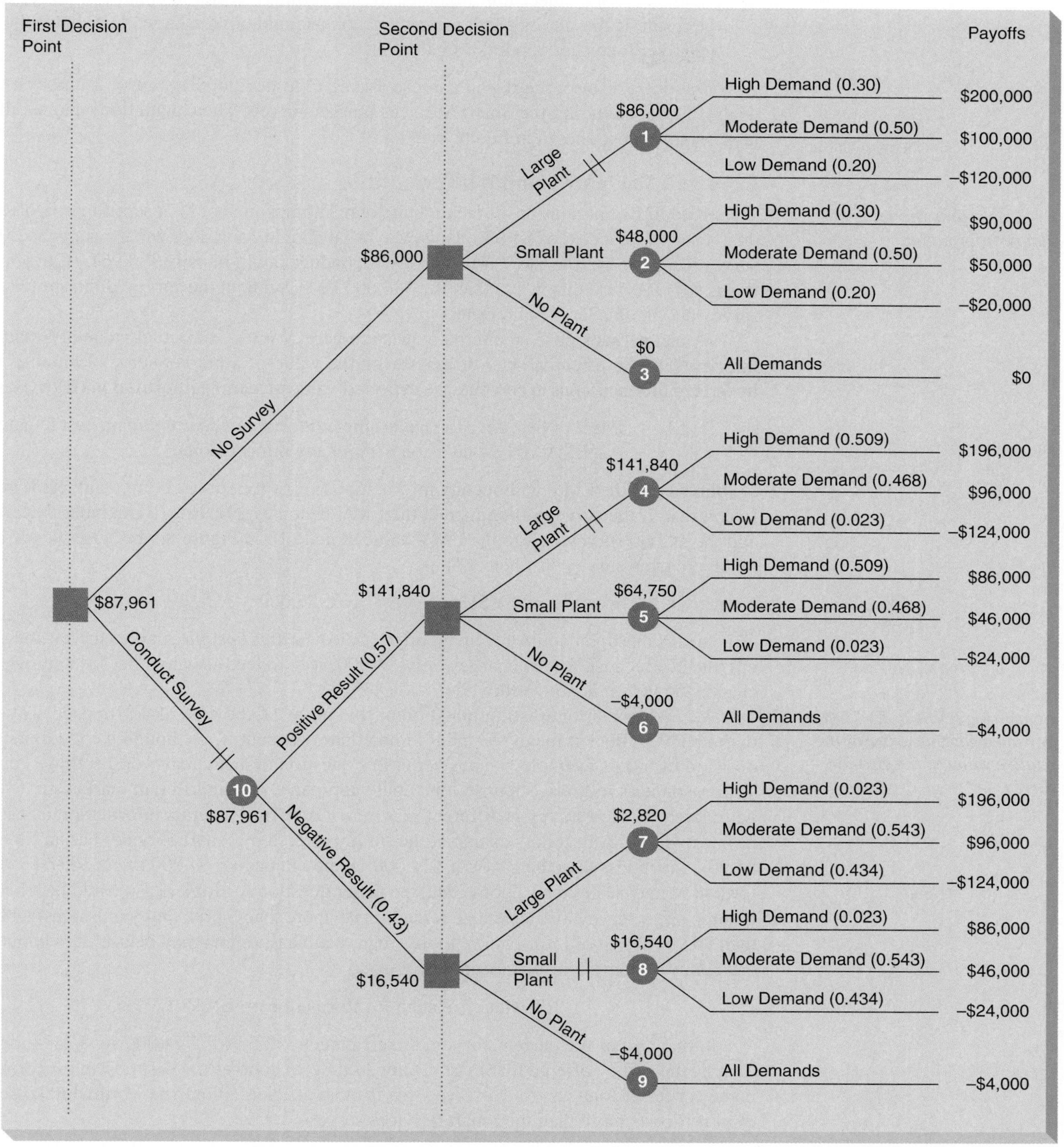

We continue working backward to the origin, computing EMV values.

4. Continuing on the lower portion of the tree and moving backward, we next consider outcome node 10. At this node, we compute the expected value if we conduct the market survey, as follows:

$$\text{EMV (node 10)} = \text{EMV (Conduct survey)}$$
$$= \$141{,}840 \times 0.57 + \$16{,}540 \times 0.43 = \$87{,}961$$

5. Finally, we consider the initial decision node. At this node, we compare the EMV of not conducting the survey with the EMV of conducting the survey. Because the EMV of

$87,961 if we conduct the survey is higher than the $86,000 EMV if the survey is not conducted, John's decision should be to accept Smart's offer to conduct a survey and await the result. If the survey result is positive, John should build a large plant; but if the result is negative, John should build a small plant.

As a practice exercise, see if you can use TreePlan to develop Thompson Lumber's complete decision tree, including the Smart Services market survey. The calculations and results should be similar to those shown in Figure 8.5.

Expected Value of Sample Information

EVSI measures the value of sample information.

The preceding computations indicate that John Thompson should accept Smart's offer to conduct a survey at a cost of $4,000. However, what should John do if Smart wants $6,000 for the survey? In this case, the EMV if the survey is conducted will be only $85,961. (Can you see why this is so?) Because this is less than the $86,000 EMV without the survey, John should reject the survey and build a large plant right away.

We can perhaps pose an alternate question here: What is the actual value of Smart's survey information? An effective way of measuring the value of a market survey (which is typically imperfect information) is to compute the **expected value of sample information (EVSI)**, as follows:

$$\text{EVSI} = (\text{EMV of best decision } \textit{with} \text{ sample information, } \textit{assuming} \text{ no cost to get it}) - (\text{EMV of best decision } \textit{without} \text{ any information}) \quad \text{(8-6)}$$

In John's case, the EMV without any information (i.e., if the survey is not conducted) is $86,000. In contrast, if the survey is conducted, the EMV becomes $91,961. (Remember that we need to add the $4,000 survey cost to the EMV value at node 10 in Figure 8.5 because we are assuming that there is no survey cost here.) Thus,

$$\text{EVSI} = \$91{,}961 - \$86{,}000 = \$5{,}961$$

This means that John could have paid up to $5,961 for this *specific* market survey and still come out ahead. Because Smart charges only $4,000, it is indeed worthwhile. In contrast, if Smart charges $6,000, it is not worthwhile.

Comparing EVSI to EVPI may provide a good measure of the relative value of the current survey.

We address an interesting question at this point: If the cost of a proposed survey is less than its EVSI, does it mean we should immediately accept it? Although we recommended this decision in John's example, the answer to this question in many real-world settings could be no. The reason is as follows. Suppose John could approach *several* different market survey firms for help. Because each survey is different in terms of how imperfect its information is, each survey has its own EVSI. In John's example, the survey offered by Smart Services has an EVSI of only $5,961, much less than the EVPI of $24,000. Although paying $4,000 to get $5,961 worth of information may seem to be a good idea, the better question for John to ask could be whether there is some *other* survey available that perhaps costs more than $4,000 but yields considerably more than $5,961 worth of information. In this regard, a measure that may be useful to compute is the **efficiency of sample information**, as follows:

$$\text{Efficiency of sample information} = \text{EVSI}/\text{EVPI} \quad \text{(8-7)}$$

In the case of the current survey, the efficiency is $\$5{,}961/\$24{,}000 = 0.2484$, or 24.84%. That is, the survey offered by Smart is only 24.84% as good as the best possible information. As noted earlier, if John can find a survey that is more efficient, it may be worthwhile to consider it, even if it costs more than the Smart Services survey.

8.9 Estimating Probability Values Using Bayesian Analysis

Bayes' theorem allows decision makers to revise probability values.

In discussing Thompson Lumber's multistage decision problem (see Figure 8.5), we assumed that the following event and conditional probabilities were available to John with regard to the survey offered by Smart Services:

$$P(\text{Positive survey result}) = P(\text{PS}) = 0.570$$
$$P(\text{Negative survey result}) = P(\text{NS}) = 0.430$$
$$P(\text{High demand} \mid \text{Positive survey result}) = P(\text{HD} \mid \text{PS}) = 0.509$$

$$
\begin{aligned}
&P(\text{Moderate demand} \mid \text{Positive survey result}) &&= P(\text{MD} \mid \text{PS}) &&= 0.468\\
&P(\text{Low demand} \mid \text{Positive survey result}) &&= P(\text{LD} \mid \text{PS}) &&= 0.023\\
&P(\text{High demand} \mid \text{Negative survey result}) &&= P(\text{HD} \mid \text{NS}) &&= 0.023\\
&P(\text{Moderate demand} \mid \text{Negative survey result}) &&= P(\text{MD} \mid \text{NS}) &&= 0.543\\
&P(\text{Low demand} \mid \text{Negative survey result}) &&= P(\text{LD} \mid \text{NS}) &&= 0.443
\end{aligned}
$$

In practice, as illustrated in this section, John would have computed these probabilities using Bayes' theorem on data regarding the performance of Smart Services on past surveys. Bayes' theorem allows decision makers to incorporate additional information (e.g., past performance) to revise their probability estimates of various outcomes. Before continuing further, you may wish to review Bayes' theorem in Appendix A.

Calculating Revised Probabilities

In order to evaluate the reliability of the survey, John asks Smart Services to provide him with information regarding its performance on past surveys. Specifically, he wants to know how many similar surveys the company has conducted in the past, what it predicted each time, and what the actual result turned out to be eventually in each case. Let's assume that Smart has data on 75 past surveys that it has conducted. In these 75 surveys, Smart had predicted high demand in 30 cases, moderate demand in 15 cases, and low demand in 30 cases. These data are summarized in Table 8.10.

Prior probabilities are estimates before the market survey.

Table 8.10 reveals, for example, that in 29 of 30 past cases where a product's demand subsequently turned out to be high, Smart's surveys had predicted positive market conditions. That is, the probability of positive survey results, given high demand, $P(\text{PS} \mid \text{HD})$, is 0.967. Likewise, in 7 of 15 past cases where a product's demand subsequently turned out to be moderate, Smart's surveys had predicted negative market conditions. That is, the probability of negative survey results, given moderate demand, $P(\text{NS} \mid \text{MD})$, is 0.467. How does John use this information to gauge the accuracy of Smart's survey in his specific case?

Revised probabilities are determined using the prior probabilities and the market survey information.

Recall that without any market survey information, John's current probability estimates of high, moderate, and low demand are $P(\text{HD}) = 0.30$, $P(\text{MD}) = 0.50$, and $P(\text{LD}) = 0.20$, respectively. These are referred to as *prior* probabilities. Based on the survey performance information in Table 8.10, we compute John's revised, or *posterior*, probabilities—namely, $P(\text{HD} \mid \text{PS})$, $P(\text{MD} \mid \text{PS})$, $P(\text{LD} \mid \text{PS})$, $P(\text{HD} \mid \text{NS})$, $P(\text{MD} \mid \text{NS})$, and $P(\text{LD} \mid \text{NS})$. This computation, using the formula for Bayes' theorem (see Equation A-7 on page 543 of Appendix A), proceeds as follows:

$$
\begin{aligned}
P(HD|PS) &= \frac{P(PS \text{ and } HD)}{P(PS)} = \frac{P(PS|HD) \times P(HD)}{P(PS)}\\
&= \frac{P(PS|HD) \times P(HD)}{P(PS|HD) \times P(HD) + P(PS|MD) \times P(MD) + P(PS|LD) \times P(LD)}\\
&= \frac{0.967 \times 0.30}{0.967 \times 0.30 + 0.533 \times 0.50 + 0.067 \times 0.20} = \frac{0.290}{0.570} = 0.509
\end{aligned}
$$

We can calculate conditional probabilities using a probability table.

The other five revised probabilities (i.e., $P(\text{MD} \mid \text{PS})$, $P(\text{LD} \mid \text{PS})$, etc.) can also be computed in a similar manner. However, as you can see, Bayes' formula is rather cumbersome and somewhat difficult to follow intuitively. For this reason, it is perhaps easier in practice to compute these revised probabilities by using a probability table. We show these calculations in Table 8.11 for the case where the survey result is positive and in Table 8.12 for the case where the survey result is negative.

TABLE 8.10 Reliability of the Smart Services Survey in Predicting Actual Outcomes

WHEN ACTUAL OUTCOME WAS	SURVEY RESULT WAS: POSITIVE (PS)	NEGATIVE (NS)
High demand (**HD**)	$P(\text{PS} \mid \text{HD}) = 29/30 = 0.967$	$P(\text{NS} \mid \text{HD}) = 1/30 = 0.033$
Moderate demand (**MD**)	$P(\text{PS} \mid \text{MD}) = 8/15 = 0.533$	$P(\text{NS} \mid \text{MD}) = 7/15 = 0.467$
Low demand (**LD**)	$P(\text{PS} \mid \text{LD}) = 2/30 = 0.067$	$P(\text{NS} \mid \text{LD}) = 28/30 = 0.933$

TABLE 8.11 Probability Revisions, Given a Positive Survey Result (PS)

OUTCOME	CONDITIONAL PROB. $P(\text{PS} \mid \text{OUTCOME})$		PRIOR PROB.		JOINT PROB.	REVISED PROB. $P(\text{OUTCOME} \mid \text{PS})$
High demand (**HD**)	0.967	×	0.30	=	0.290	$0.290/0.57 = 0.509$
Moderate demand (**MD**)	0.533	×	0.50	=	0.267	$0.267/0.57 = 0.468$
Low demand (**LD**)	0.067	×	0.20	=	0.013	$0.013/0.57 = 0.023$
	$P(\textbf{PS}) = P(\text{Positive Survey})$			=	0.570	1.000

TABLE 8.12 Probability Revisions, Given a Negative Survey Result (NS)

OUTCOME	CONDITIONAL PROB. $P(\text{NS} \mid \text{OUTCOME})$		PRIOR PROB.		JOINT PROB.	REVISED PROB. $P(\text{OUTCOME} \mid \text{NS})$
High demand (**HD**)	0.033	×	0.30	=	0.010	$0.010/0.43 = 0.023$
Moderate demand (**MD**)	0.467	×	0.50	=	0.233	$0.233/0.43 = 0.543$
Low demand (**LD**)	0.933	×	0.20	=	0.187	$0.187/0.43 = 0.434$
	$P(\textbf{NS}) = P(\text{Negative Survey})$			=	0.430	1.000

The calculations in Table 8.11 are as follows. For any outcome, such as high demand (HD), we know the conditional probability, $P(\text{PS} \mid \text{HD})$, and the prior probability, $P(\text{HD})$. Using Equation A-6 on page 541 of Appendix A, we can compute the joint probability, $P(\text{PS and HD})$, as the product of the conditional and prior probabilities. After we repeat this computation for the other two outcomes (moderate demand and low demand), we add the three joint probabilities—$P(\text{PS and HD}) + P(\text{PS and MD}) + P(\text{PS and LD})$—to determine $P(\text{PS})$. Observe that this computation is the same as that in the denominator of the Bayes' theorem formula. After we have computed $P(\text{PS})$, we can use Equation A-5 on page 540 of Appendix A to compute the revised probabilities $P(\text{HD} \mid \text{PS})$, $P(\text{MD} \mid \text{PS})$, and $P(\text{LD} \mid \text{PS})$. Table 8.12 shows similar calculations when the survey result is negative. As you can see, the probabilities obtained here are the same ones we used earlier in Figure 8.5 on page 341.

IN ACTION Using Utility and Decision Trees in Hip Replacement

Should you or a family member undergo a somewhat dangerous surgery for an illness, or is it better to manage the illness medically by using drugs? Should a health care firm put a new drug on its list of approved medicines? What medical procedures should the government reimburse? Individuals and institutions face medical treatment decision problems from a variety of perspectives. For example, the decision an individual patient faces is driven by the medical treatment that best describes the patient's attitudes about risk (utility) and quality of life over the rest of his or her life.

One common application of utility theory decision tree modeling in medicine is total hip replacement surgery for patients with severe arthritis of the hip. Several hundred thousand hip replacements are performed per year in North America. Although this surgery is mostly successful, the treatment decision for an individual patient can be difficult. Although surgery offers the potential of increased quality of life, it also carries the risk of death.

A decision tree analysis helps define all the time-sequenced outcomes that can occur in dealing with arthritis of the hip. Conservative management using medication is a surgical alternative, but the disease is degenerative, and a worsening condition is inevitable. A successful surgery, which restores full function, is likely, but uncertainty exists even then. First, infection can cause the new prosthetic hip to fail. Or the new hip may fail over time due to breakage or malfunction. Both cases require a revision surgery, whose risks are greater than the first surgery. Decision trees and utility theory help patients first assess their personal risk levels and then allow them to compute life expectancy based on sex and race.

Source: Based on G. Hazen, J. Pellissier, and J. Sounderpandian. "Stochastic Tree Models in Medical Decision Making," *Interfaces* 28, 4 (July–August 1998): 64–80.

Potential Problems in Using Survey Results

In using past performance to gauge the reliability of a survey's results, we typically base our probabilities only on those cases in which a decision to take some course of action is actually made. For example, we can observe demand only in cases where the product was actually introduced after the survey was conducted. Unfortunately, there is no way to collect information about the demand in situations in which the decision after the survey was to not introduce the product. This implies that conditional probability information is not quite always as accurate as we would like it to be. Nevertheless, calculating conditional probabilities helps to refine the decision-making process and, in general, to make better decisions. For this reason, the use of Bayesian analysis in revising prior probabilities is very popular in practice.

8.10 Utility Theory

EMV is not always the best criterion to use to make decisions.

So far we have used monetary values to make decisions in all our examples. In practice, however, using money to measure the value of a decision could sometimes lead to bad decisions. The reason for this is that different people value money differently at different times. For example, having $100 in your pocket may mean a lot to you today, when you are a student, but may be relatively unimportant in a few years, when you are a wealthy businessperson. This implies that while you may be unwilling to bet $100 on a risky project today, you may be more than willing to do so in a few years. Unfortunately, when we use monetary values to make decisions, we do not account for these perceptions of risk in our model.

Here's another example to drive home this point. Assume that you are the holder of a lottery ticket. In a few moments, a fair coin will be flipped. If it comes up tails, you win $100,000. If it comes up heads, you win nothing. Now suppose a wealthy person offers you $35,000 for your ticket before the coin is flipped. What should you do? According to a decision based on monetary values, as shown in the decision tree in Figure 8.6, you should reject the offer and hold on to your ticket because the EMV of $50,000 is greater than the offer of $35,000. In reality, what would *you* do? It is likely that many people would take the guaranteed $35,000 in exchange for a risky shot at $100,000. (In fact, many would probably be willing to settle for a lot less than $35,000.) Of course, just how low a specific individual would go is a matter of personal preference because, as noted earlier, different people value money differently. This example, however, illustrates how basing a decision on EMV may not be appropriate.

One way to get around this problem and incorporate a person's attitude toward risk in the model is through **utility theory**. In the next section we explore first how to measure a person's utility function and then how to use utility measures in decision making.

FIGURE 8.6
Decision Tree for a Lottery Ticket

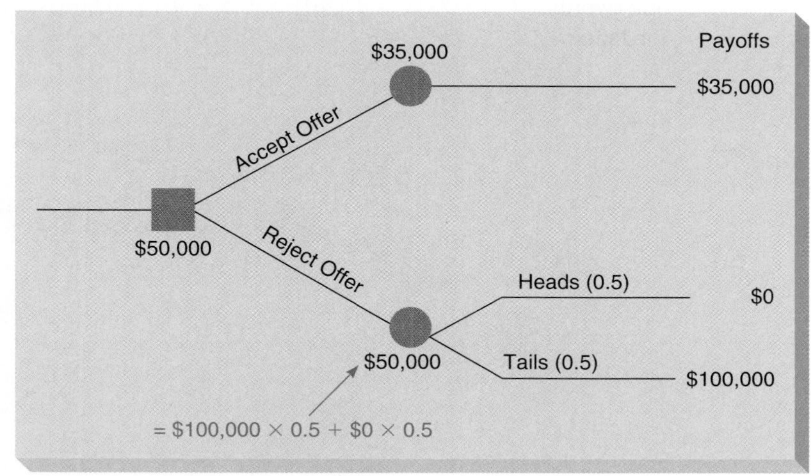

Measuring Utility and Constructing a Utility Curve

Utility function converts a person's value for money and attitudes toward risk into a dimensionless number between 0 and 1.

Using a utility function is a way of converting a person's value for money and attitudes toward risk into a dimensionless number between 0 and 1. There are three important issues to note at this stage:

- Each person has his or her own utility function. It is therefore critical in any problem to determine the utility function for the decision maker in that problem.
- A person's utility function could change over time as his or her economic and other conditions change. Recall the earlier example about how important \$100 is to you today as opposed to how important it may be to you in a few years. A person's utility function should therefore be updated periodically.
- A person may have different utility functions for different magnitudes of money. For example, most people tend to be very willing to take risks when the monetary amounts involved are small. (After all, we're all willing to buy a \$1 lottery ticket, even when we know very well that we're unlikely to win anything.) However, the same people tend to be unwilling to take risks with larger monetary amounts. (Would you be willing to buy a \$1,000 lottery ticket even if the potential top prize were \$1 billion?) This implies that we should consider a person's utility function only over the relevant range of monetary values involved in the specific problem at hand.

Let us use an example to study how we can determine a person's utility function.

We assign the worst payoff a utility of 0 and the best payoff a utility of 1.

JANE DICKSON'S UTILITY FUNCTION Jane Dickson would like to construct a utility function to reveal her preference for monetary amounts between \$0 and \$50,000. We start assessing Jane's utility function by assigning a utility value of 0 to the worst payoff and a utility value of 1 to the best payoff. That is, $U(\$0) = 0$ and $U(\$50{,}000) = 1$. Monetary values between these two payoffs will have utility values between 0 and 1. To determine these utilities, we begin by posing the following gamble to Jane, as outlined in Figure 8.7:

> You have a 50% chance at getting \$0 and a 50% chance at getting \$50,000. That is, the EMV of this gamble is \$25,000. What is the minimum guaranteed amount that you will accept in order to walk away from this gamble? In other words, what is the minimum amount that will make you indifferent between alternative 1 (gamble between \$0 and \$50,000) and alternative 2 (obtain this amount for sure).

***Certainty equivalent** is the minimum guaranteed amount you are willing to accept to avoid the risk associated with a gamble.*

The answer to this question may vary from person to person, and it is called the **certainty equivalent** between the two payoff values (\$0 and \$50,000, in this case). Let's suppose Jane is willing to settle for \$15,000. (Some of you may have settled for less, while others may have wanted more.) That is, Jane is willing to accept a guaranteed payoff of \$15,000 to avoid the risk associated with a potential payoff of \$50,000. The implication is that from a utility perspective (i.e., with respect to Jane's attitudes toward risk and value for money), the expected value between \$0 and \$50,000 is only \$15,000, and not the \$25,000 we calculated in Figure 8.7. In otherwords, $U(\$15{,}000) = U(\$0) \times 0.5 + U(\$50{,}000) \times 0.5 = 0 \times 0.5 + 1 \times 0.5 = 0.5$ for Jane.

FIGURE 8.7
Gamble Posed to Jane for Utility Assessment

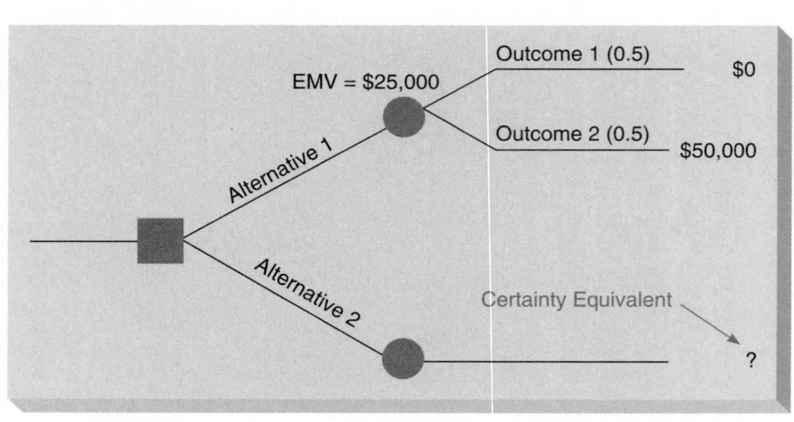

We repeat the gamble in Figure 8.7, except that the two monetary amounts presented to Jane in the gamble are \$15,000 and \$50,000. The EMV is \$32,500. Let's suppose Jane is willing to settle for a certainty equivalent of \$27,000. This implies that for Jane, $U(\$27{,}000) = U(\$15{,}000) \times 0.5 + U(\$50{,}000) \times 0.5 = 0.5 \times 0.5 + 1 \times 0.5 = 0.75$.

We repeat the gamble in Figure 8.7 again, this time with monetary amounts of \$0 and \$15,000. The EMV is \$7,500. Let's suppose Jane is willing to settle for a certainty equivalent of \$6,000. This implies that for Jane, $U(\$6{,}000) = U(\$0) \times 0.5 + U(\$15{,}000) \times 0.5 = 0 \times 0.5 + 0.5 \times 0.5 = 0.25$.

A **utility curve** *plots utility values versus monetary values.*

At this stage, we know the monetary values associated with utilities of 0, 0.25, 0.5, 0.75, and 1 for Jane. If necessary, we can continue this process several more times to find additional utility points. For example, we could present the gamble between \$27,000 (with a utility of 0.75) and \$50,000 (with a utility of 1) to determine the monetary value associated with a utility of $0.875 = (0.75 \times 0.5 + 1 \times 0.5)$. However, the five assessments shown here are usually enough to get an idea of Jane's feelings toward risk. Perhaps the easiest way to view Jane's utility function is to construct a **utility curve** that plots utility values (*Y*-axis) versus monetary values (*X*-axis). This is shown in Figure 8.8. In the figure, the assessed utility points of \$0, \$6,000, \$15,000, \$27,000, and \$50,000 are obtained from the preceding discussion, while the rest of the curve is eyeballed in. As noted earlier, it is usually enough to know five points on the curve in order to get a reasonable approximation.

Jane's utility curve is typical of a risk avoider. A **risk avoider** is a decision maker who gets less utility or pleasure from a greater risk and tends to avoid situations in which high losses might occur. As monetary value increases on her utility curve, the utility increases at a slower rate. Another way to characterize a person's attitude toward risk is to compute the risk premium, defined as

$$\text{Risk premium} = (\text{EMV of gamble}) - (\text{Certainty equivalent}) \qquad \textbf{(8-8)}$$

Risk premium *is the EMV that a person is willing to give up in order to avoid the risk associated with a gamble.*

The **risk premium** represents the monetary amount that a decision maker is willing to give up in order to avoid the risk associated with a gamble. For example, Jane's risk premium in the first gamble between \$0 and \$50,000 is computed as \$25,000 − \$15,000 = \$10,000. That is, Jane is willing to give up \$10,000 to avoid the uncertainty associated with a gamble. Likewise, she is willing to give up \$5,500 (=\$32,500 − \$27,000) to avoid the risk of gambling between \$15,000 and \$50,000.

Clearly, a person who is more averse to risk will be willing to give up an even larger amount to avoid the uncertainty. In contrast, a person who is a risk seeker will insist on getting a certainty

FIGURE 8.8
Utility Curve for Jane Dickson

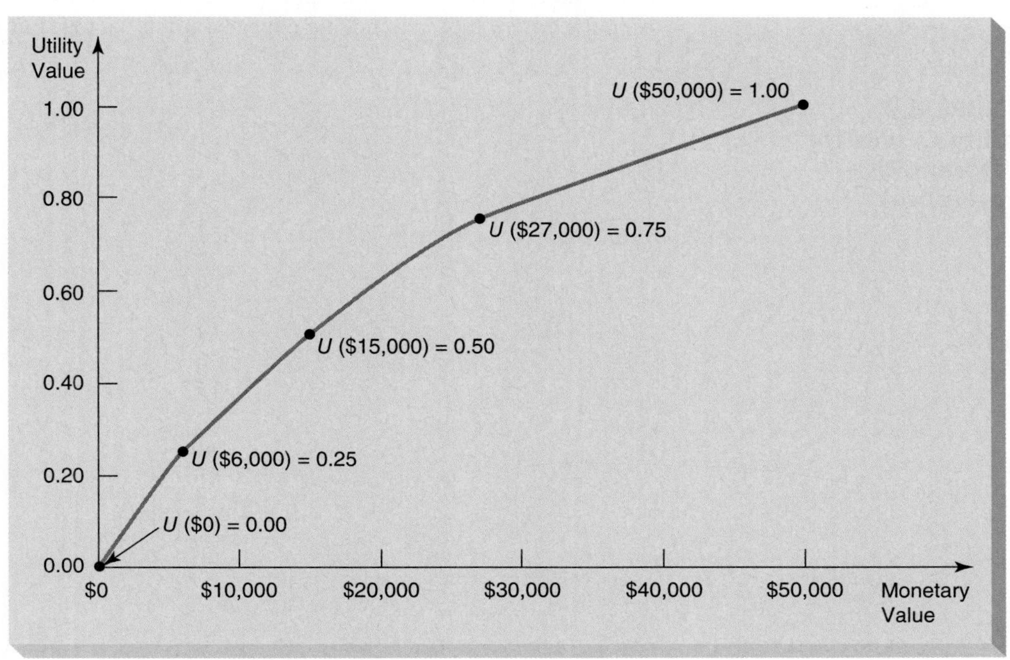

equivalent that is greater than the EMV in order to walk away from a gamble. Such a person will therefore have a negative risk premium. Finally, a person who is risk neutral will always specify a certainty equivalent that is exactly equal to the EMV. Based on the preceding discussion, we can now define the following three preferences for risk:

- Risk avoider or risk-averse person: Risk premium > 0
- Risk indifferent or risk-neutral person: Risk premium $= 0$
- Risk seeker or risk-prone person: Risk premium < 0

*A **risk neutral** person has a utility curve that is a straight line.*

Figure 8.9 illustrates the utility curves for all three risk preferences. As shown in the figure, a person who is a **risk seeker** has an opposite-shaped utility curve to that of a risk avoider. This type of decision maker gets more utility from a greater risk and a higher potential payoff. As monetary value increases on his or her utility curve, the utility increases at an increasing rate. A person who is **risk neutral** has a utility curve that is a straight line.

The shape of a person's utility curve depends on the specific decision being considered, the person's psychological frame of mind, and how the person feels about the future. As noted earlier, it may well be that a person has one utility curve for some situations and a completely different curve for others. In practice, most people are likely to be risk seekers when the monetary amounts involved are small (recall the earlier comment about buying a $1 lottery ticket) but tend to become risk avoiders as the monetary amounts increase. The exact monetary amount at which a specific individual switches from being a risk seeker to a risk avoider is, of course, a matter of personal preference.

EXPONENTIAL UTILITY FUNCTION If a person is a risk avoider, it is possible to use curve-fitting techniques to fit an equation to the utility curve. This makes it convenient to determine the person's utility for any monetary value within the appropriate range. Looking at the utility curve in Figure 8.9 for a risk avoider, it is apparent that the curve can be approximated by an exponential function. The equation would be as follows:

$$U(X) = 1 - e^{-X/R} \tag{8-9}$$

where e is the exponential constant (equal to 2.7182), X represents the monetary value, and R is a parameter that controls the shape of the person's utility curve. As R increases, the utility curve becomes flatter (corresponding to a decision maker who is less risk averse).

Utility as a Decision-Making Criterion

Utility values replace monetary values.

Once we have determined a decision maker's utility curve, how do we use it in making decisions? We construct the decision tree and make all prior and revised probability estimates and computations as before. However, instead of using monetary values as payoffs, we now replace all monetary payoffs with the appropriate utility values. We then fold back the decision tree, using the criterion of maximizing expected utility values. Let's look at an example.

FIGURE 8.9 Utility Curves for Different Risk Preferences

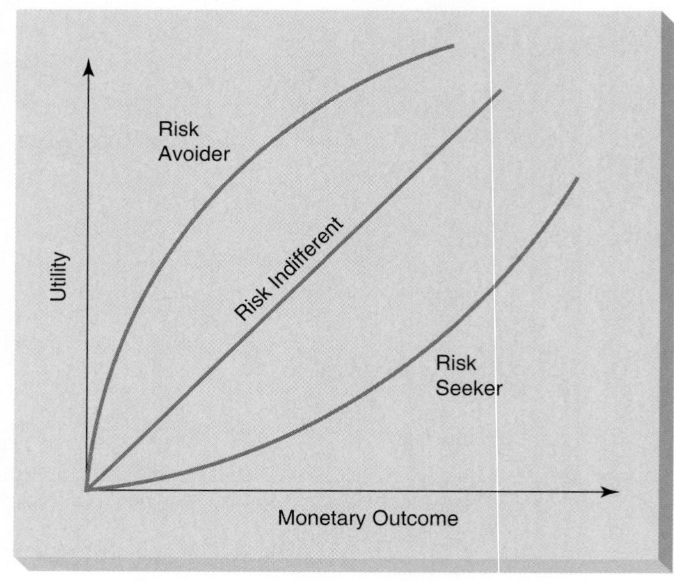

FIGURE 8.10
Decision Tree Using EMV for Mark Simkin

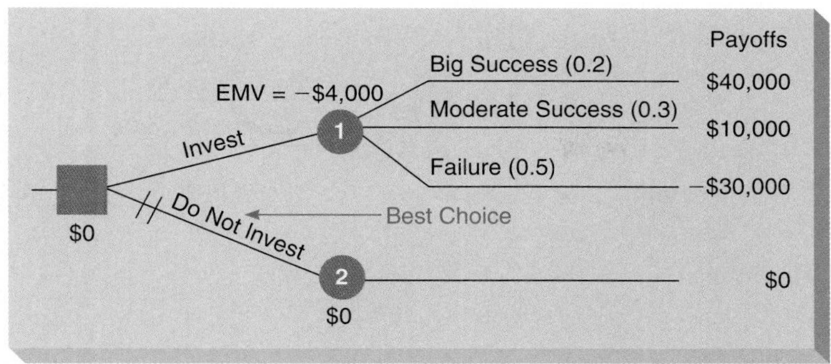

Mark Simkin has an opportunity to invest in a new business venture. If the venture is a big success, Mark will make a profit of $40,000. If the venture is a moderate success, Mark will make a profit $10,000. If the venture fails, Mark will lose his investment of $30,000. Mark estimates the venture's chances as 20% for big success, 30% for moderate success, and 50% for failure. Should Mark invest in the venture?

Mark's alternatives are displayed in the tree shown in Figure 8.10. Using monetary values, the EMV at node 1 is $\$40{,}000 \times 0.2 + \$10{,}000 \times 0.3 + (-\$30{,}000) \times 0.5 = -\$4{,}000$. Because this is smaller than the EMV of $0 at node 2, Mark should turn down the venture and invest his money elsewhere.

Now let's view the same problem from a utility perspective. Using the procedure outlined earlier, Mark is able to construct a utility curve showing his preference for monetary amounts between $40,000 and –$30,000 (the best and worst payoffs in his problem). This curve, shown in Figure 8.11, indicates that within this monetary range Mark is a risk seeker (i.e., a gambler).

Mark's objective is to maximize expected utility.

From Figure 8.11, we note the following utility values for Mark: $U(-\$30{,}000) = 0$, $U(\$0) = 0.15$, $U(\$10{,}000) = 0.30$, and $U(\$40{,}000) = 1$. Substituting these values in the decision tree in Figure 8.10 in place of the monetary values, we fold back the tree to maximize Mark's expected utility. The computations are shown in Figure 8.12.

Using expected utility may lead to a decision that is different from the one suggested by EMV.

Using utility values, the expected utility at node 1 is 0.29, which is greater than the utility of 0.15 at node 2. This implies that Mark should invest his money in the venture. As you can

FIGURE 8.11 Utility Curve for Mark Simkin

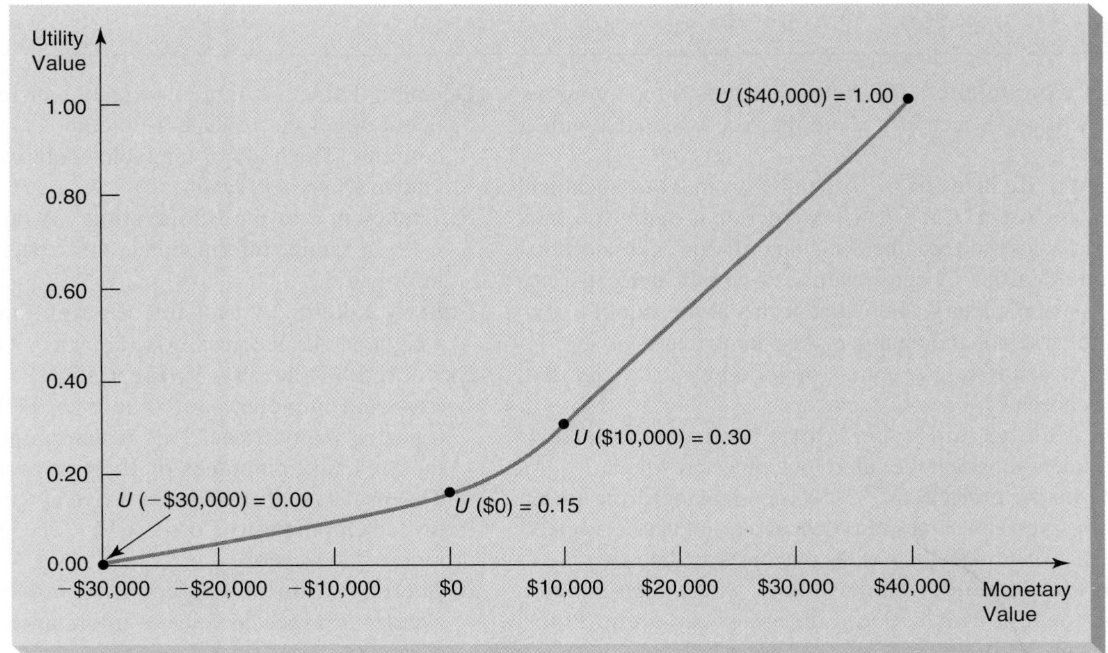

FIGURE 8.12
Decision Tree Using Utility Values for Mark Simkin

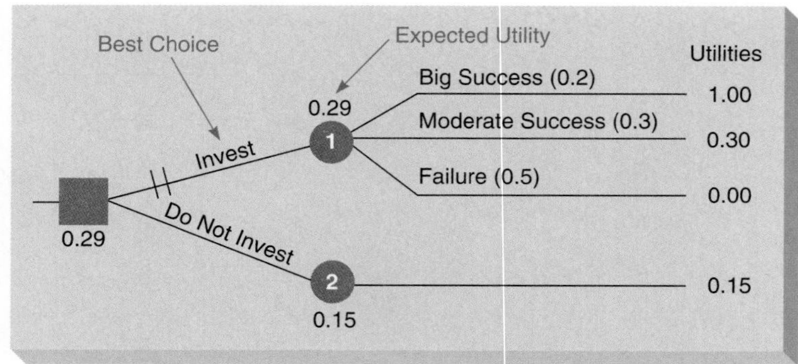

see, this is the opposite of the decision suggested if EMV had been used, and it clearly illustrates how using utilities instead of monetary values may lead to different decisions in the same problem. In Mark's case, the utility curve indicates that he is a risk seeker, and the choice of investing in the venture certainly reflects his preference for risk.

Summary

This chapter introduces the topic of decision analysis, which is an analytic and systematic approach to studying decision making. We first indicate the steps involved in making decisions in three different environments: (1) decision making under certainty, (2) decision making under uncertainty, and (3) decision making under risk. For decision problems under uncertainty, we identify the best alternatives, using criteria such as maximax, maximin, criterion of realism, equally likely, and minimax regret. For decision problems under risk, we discuss the computation and use of the expected monetary value (EMV), expected opportunity loss (EOL), and expected value of perfect information (EVPI). We also illustrate the use of Excel to solve decision analysis problems.

Decision trees are used for larger decision problems in which decisions must be made in sequence. In this case, we compute the expected value of sample information (EVSI). Bayesian analysis is used to revise or update probability values. We also discuss how decision trees can be set up and solved using TreePlan, an Excel add-in.

When it is inappropriate to use monetary values, utility theory can be used to assign a utility value to each decision payoff. In such cases, we compute expected utilities and select the alternative with the highest utility value.

Glossary

Certainty Equivalent The minimum guaranteed amount one is willing to accept to avoid the risk associated with a gamble.

Coefficient of Realism (α). A number from 0 to 1 such that when α is close to 1, the decision criterion is optimistic, and when α is close to zero, the decision criterion is pessimistic.

Conditional Value A consequence or payoff, normally expressed in a monetary value, that occurs as a result of a particular alternative and outcome. Also known as a *payoff.*

Decision Alternative A course of action or a strategy that can be chosen by a decision maker.

Decision Making under Certainty A decision-making environment in which the future outcomes are known.

Decision Making under Risk A decision-making environment in which several outcomes can occur as a result of a decision or an alternative. Probabilities of the outcomes are known.

Decision Making under Uncertainty A decision-making environment in which several outcomes can occur. Probabilities of these outcomes are not known.

Decision Table A table in which decision alternatives are listed down the rows and outcomes are listed across the columns. The body of the table contains the payoffs. Also known as a *payoff table.*

Efficiency of Sample Information A ratio of the expected value of sample information to the expected value of perfect information.

Equally Likely A decision criterion that places an equal weight on all outcomes. Also known as *Laplace.*

Expected Monetary Value (EMV) The average or expected monetary outcome of a decision if it can be repeated many times. This is determined by multiplying the monetary outcomes by their respective probabilities. The results are then added to arrive at the EMV.

Expected Opportunity Loss (EOL) The average or expected regret of a decision.

Expected Value of Perfect Information (EVPI) The average or expected value of information if it is completely accurate.

Expected Value of Sample Information (EVSI) The average or expected value of imperfect or survey information.

Expected Value with Perfect Information (EVwPI) The average or expected value of the decision if the decision maker knew what would happen ahead of time.

Maximax An optimistic decision-making criterion. This is the alternative with the highest possible return.

Maximin A pessimistic decision-making criterion that maximizes the minimum outcome. It is the best of the worst possible outcomes.

Minimax Regret A decision criterion that minimizes the maximum opportunity loss.

Opportunity Loss The amount you would lose by not picking the best alternative. For any outcome, this is the difference between the consequences of any alternative and the best possible alternative. Also called *regret*.

Outcome An occurrence over which a decision maker has little or no control. Also known as a state-of-nature.

Risk Avoider A person who avoids risk. As the monetary value increases on the utility curve, the utility increases at a decreasing rate. This decision maker gets less utility for a greater risk and higher potential returns.

Risk Neutral A person who is indifferent toward risk. The utility curve for a risk-neutral person is a straight line.

Risk Premium The monetary amount that a person is willing to give up in order to avoid the risk associated with a gamble.

Risk Seeker A person who seeks risk. As the monetary value increases on the utility curve, the utility increases at an increasing rate. This decision maker gets more pleasure for a greater risk and higher potential returns.

Sequential Decisions Decisions in which the outcome of one decision influences other decisions.

Utility Curve A graph or curve that illustrates the relationship between utility and monetary values. When this curve has been constructed, utility values from the curve can be used in the decision-making process.

Utility Theory A theory that allows decision makers to incorporate their risk preference and other factors into the decision-making process.

Solved Problems

Solved Problem 8-1

Cal Bender and Becky Addison are undergraduates in business at Central College. In an attempt to make extra money, Cal and Becky have decided to look into the possibility of starting a small company that would provide word-processing services to students who need term papers or other reports prepared in a professional manner. They have identified three strategies. Strategy 1 is to invest in a fairly expensive microcomputer system with a high-quality laser printer. In a good market, they should be able to obtain a net profit of $10,000 over the next two years. If the market is bad, they could lose $8,000. Strategy 2 is to purchase a cheaper system. With a good market, they could get a return during the next two years of $8,000. With a bad market, they could incur a loss of $4,000. Their final strategy, strategy 3, is to do nothing. Cal is basically a risk taker, whereas Becky tries to avoid risk.

a. Which decision criterion should Cal use? What would Cal's decision be?
b. Which decision criterion should Becky use? What decision would Becky make?
c. If Cal and Becky were indifferent to risk, which decision criterion should they use? What would be the decision?

Solution

The problem is one of decision making under uncertainty. To answer the specific questions, it is helpful to construct a decision table showing the alternatives, outcomes, and payoffs, as follows:

ALTERNATIVE	GOOD MARKET	BAD MARKET
Expensive system	$10,000	−$8,000
Cheaper system	$ 8,000	−$4,000
Do nothing	$ 0	$ 0

a. Cal should use the maximax, or optimistic, decision criterion. The maximum payoffs for the three alternatives are $10,000, $8,000, and $0, respectively. Hence, Cal should select the expensive system.

b. Becky should use the maximin, or pessimistic, decision criterion. The minimum payoffs for the three alternatives are –$8,000, –$4,000, and $0, respectively. Hence, Becky should choose to do nothing.

c. If Cal and Becky are indifferent to risk, they should use the equally likely criterion. The average payoffs for the three alternatives are $1,000, $2,000, and $0, respectively. Hence, their decision would be to select the cheaper system.

Solved Problem 8-2

Maria Rojas is considering the possibility of opening a small dress shop on Fairbanks Avenue, a few blocks from the university. She has located a good mall that attracts students. Her options are to open a small shop, a medium-sized shop, or no shop at all. The market for a dress shop can be good, average, or bad. The probabilities for these three possibilities are 0.2 for a good market, 0.5 for an average market, and 0.3 for a bad market. The net profit or loss for the medium-sized and small shops for the various market conditions are given in the following payoff table:

	OUTCOMES		
ALTERNATIVE	GOOD MARKET	AVERAGE MARKET	BAD MARKET
Small shop	$ 75,000	$25,000	–$40,000
Medium-sized shop	$100,000	$35,000	–$60,000
No shop	$ 0	$ 0	$ 0
Probabilities	0.2	0.5	0.3

Building no shop at all yields no loss and no gain. What do you recommend?

Solution

The problem can be solved by computing the EMV for each alternative, as follows:

$$\text{EMV(Small shop)} = \$75{,}000 \times 0.2 + \$25{,}000 \times 0.5 + (-\$40{,}000) \times 0.3 = \$15{,}500$$

$$\text{EMV(Medium shop)} = \$100{,}000 \times 0.2 + \$35{,}000 \times 0.5 + (-\$60{,}000) \times 0.3 = \$19{,}500$$

$$\text{EMV(No shop)} = \$0$$

As can be seen, the best decision is to build the medium-sized shop. The EMV for this alternative is $19,500.

Solved Problem 8-3

Monica Britt has enjoyed sailing small boats since she was 7 years old, when her mother started sailing with her. Today Monica is considering the possibility of starting a company to produce small sailboats for the recreational market. Unlike other mass-produced sailboats, however, these boats will be made specifically for children between the ages of 10 and 15. The boats will be of the highest quality and extremely stable, and the sail size will be reduced to prevent problems with capsizing.

Because of the expense involved in developing the initial molds and acquiring the necessary equipment to produce fiberglass sailboats for young children, Monica has decided to conduct a pilot study to make sure that the market for the sailboats will be adequate. She estimates that the pilot study will cost her $10,000. Furthermore, the pilot study can be either successful or not successful. Her basic decisions are to build a large manufacturing facility, a small manufacturing facility, or no facility at all. With a favorable market, Monica can expect to make $90,000 from the large facility or $60,000 from the smaller facility. If the market is unfavorable, however, Monica estimates that she would lose $30,000 with a large facility, whereas she would lose only $20,000 with the small facility. Monica estimates that the probability of a favorable market, given a successful pilot study result, is 0.8. The probability of an unfavorable market, given an unsuccessful pilot study result, is estimated to be 0.9. Monica feels there is a 50–50 chance that the pilot study will be successful. Of course, Monica could bypass the pilot study and simply make the decision whether to build a large plant, a small plant, or no facility at all. Without doing any testing in a pilot study, she estimates the probability of a successful market is 0.6. What do you recommend?

Solution

The decision tree for Monica's problem is shown in Figure 8.13 on the next page. The tree shows all alternatives, outcomes, probability values, payoffs, and EMVs. The expected value computations at the various nodes are as follows:

$$\begin{aligned}
\text{EMV(Node 1)} &= \$60{,}000 \times 0.6 + (-\$20{,}000) \times 0.4 = \$28{,}000 \\
\text{EMV(Node 2)} &= \$90{,}000 \times 0.6 + (-\$30{,}000) \times 0.3 = \$42{,}000 \\
\text{EMV(Node 3)} &= \$0 \\
\text{EMV(Node 4)} &= \$50{,}000 \times 0.8 + (-\$30{,}000) \times 0.2 = \$34{,}000 \\
\text{EMV(Node 5)} &= \$80{,}000 \times 0.8 + (-\$40{,}000) \times 0.2 = \$56{,}000 \\
\text{EMV(Node 6)} &= -\$10{,}000 \\
\text{EMV(Node 7)} &= \$50{,}000 \times 0.1 + (-\$30{,}000) \times 0.9 = -\$22{,}000 \\
\text{EMV(Node 8)} &= \$80{,}000 \times 0.1 + (-\$40{,}000) \times 0.9 = -\$28{,}000 \\
\text{EMV(Node 9)} &= -\$10{,}000 \\
\text{EMV(Node 10)} &= \$56{,}000 \times 0.5 + (-\$10{,}000) \times 0.5 = \$23{,}000
\end{aligned}$$

Monica's optimal solution is to *not* conduct the pilot study and construct the large plant directly. The EMV of this decision is $42,000.

Solved Problem 8-4

Developing a small driving range for golfers of all abilities has long been a desire of John Jenkins. John, however, believes that the chance of a successful driving range is only about 40%. A friend of John's has suggested that he conduct a survey in the community to get a better feel for the demand for such a facility. There is a 0.9 probability that the survey result will be positive if the driving range will be successful. Furthermore, it is estimated that there is a 0.8 probability that the survey result will be negative if indeed the driving range will be unsuccessful. John would like to determine the chances of a successful driving range, given a positive result from the survey.

Solution

This problem requires the use of Bayes' theorem. Before we start to solve the problem, we will define the following terms:

$$\begin{aligned}
P(\text{S}) &= \text{probability of successful driving range} \\
P(\text{U}) &= \text{probability of unsuccessful driving range} \\
P(\text{P}|\text{S}) &= \text{probability survey result will be positive given a successful driving range} \\
P(\text{N}|\text{S}) &= \text{probability survey result will be negative given a successful driving range} \\
P(\text{P}|\text{U}) &= \text{probability survey result will be positive given an unsuccessful driving range} \\
P(\text{N}|\text{U}) &= \text{probability survey result will be negative given an unsuccessful driving range}
\end{aligned}$$

Now, we can summarize what we know:

$$\begin{aligned}
P(\text{S}) &= 0.4 \\
P(\text{P}|\text{S}) &= 0.9 \\
P(\text{N}|\text{U}) &= 0.8
\end{aligned}$$

FIGURE 8.13 **Complete Decision Tree for Monica Britt**

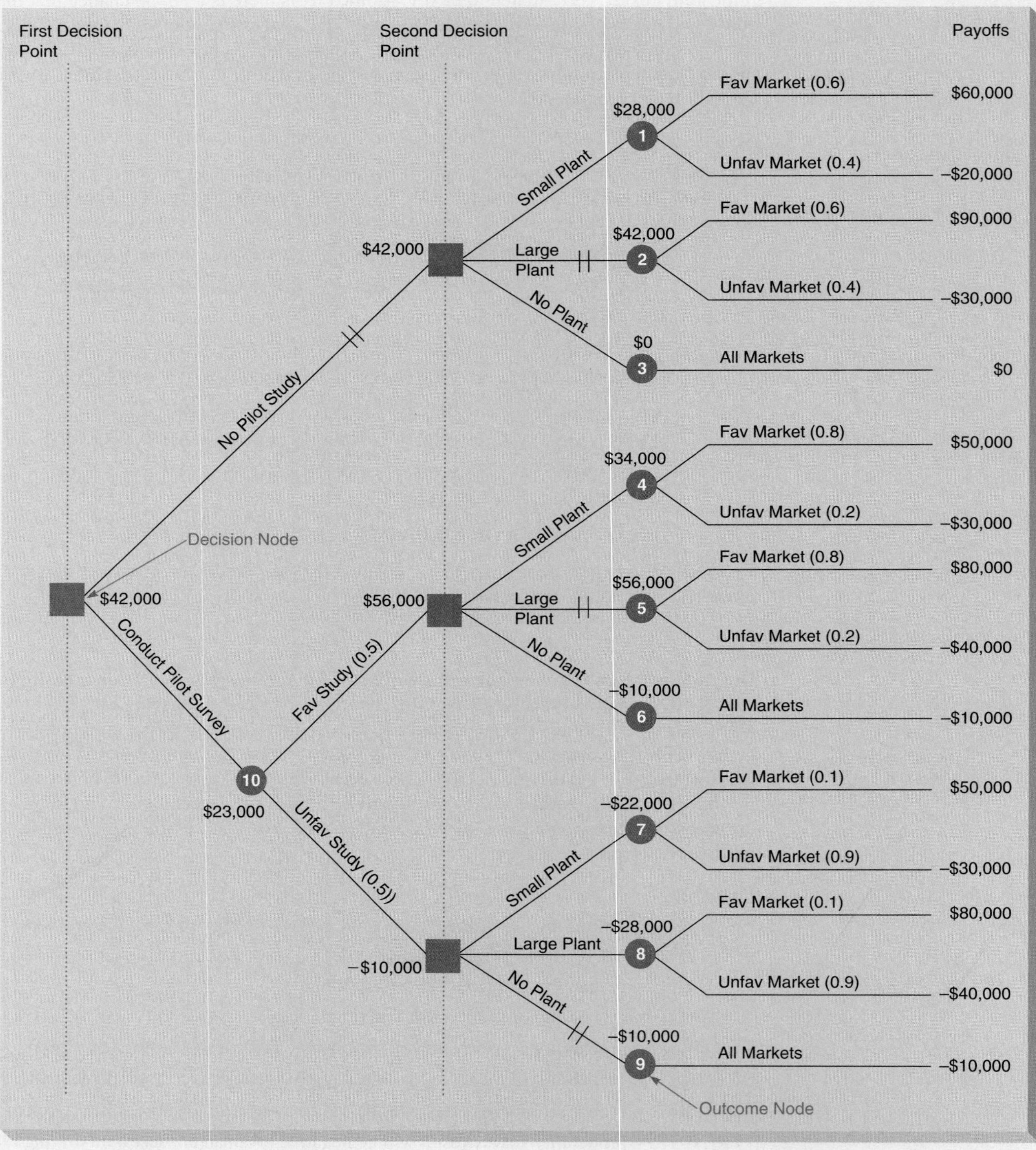

From this information we can compute three additional probabilities needed to solve the problem:

$$P(\text{U}) = 1 - P(\text{S}) = 1 - 0.4 = 0.6$$
$$P(\text{U}|\text{S}) = 1 - P(\text{P}|\text{S}) = 1 - 0.9 = 0.1$$
$$P(\text{P}|\text{U}) = 1 - P(\text{N}|\text{U}) = 1 - 0.8 = 0.2$$

Now we can put these values into Bayes' theorem to compute the desired revised probability given a positive survey result, as shown in the following table:

OUTCOME	CONDITIONAL PROBABILITY P(P | OUTCOME)		PRIOR PROBABILITY OF OUTCOME		JOINT PROBABILITY P(P *and* OUTCOME)	POSTERIOR PROBABILITY
Successful driving range (S)	0.9	×	0.4	=	0.36	0.36/0.48 = 0.75
Unsuccessful driving range (U)	0.2	×	0.6	=	0.12	0.12/0.48 = 0.25
					0.48	

The probability of a successful driving range, given a positive survey result is $P(\text{S}|\text{P}) = P(\text{P and S})/P(\text{S}) = 0.36/0.48$, or 0.75.

Discussion Questions and Problems

Discussion Questions

8-1 Give an example of a good decision that you made that resulted in a bad outcome. Also give an example of a bad decision that you made that had a good outcome. Why was each decision good or bad?

8-2 Describe what is involved in the decision-making process.

8-3 What is an alternative? What is an outcome?

8-4 Discuss the differences between decision making under certainty, decision making under risk, and decision making under uncertainty.

8-5 State the meanings of EMV and EVPI.

8-6 Under what conditions is a decision tree preferable to a decision table?

8-7 What is the difference between prior and posterior probabilities?

8-8 What is the purpose of Bayesian analysis? Describe how you would use Bayesian analysis in the decision-making process.

8-9 What is the purpose of utility theory?

8-10 Briefly discuss how a utility function can be assessed. What is a standard gamble, and how is it used in determining utility values?

8-11 How is a utility curve used in selecting the best decision for a particular problem?

8-12 What is a risk seeker? What is a risk avoider? How do the utility curves for these types of decision makers differ?

Problems

8-13 In the environment of increased competition, a fitness club executive is considering the purchase of additional equipment. His alternatives, outcomes, and payoffs (profits) are shown in the following table:

EQUIPMENT	FAVORABLE MARKET	UNFAVORABLE MARKET
Acme	\$400,000	−\$175,000
Standard	\$280,000	−\$ 90,000
High Pro	\$ 95,000	−\$ 15,000

(a) If the executive is an optimistic decision maker, which alternative will he likely choose?
(b) If the executive is a pessimistic decision maker, which alternative will he likely choose?
(c) Market research suggests the chance of a favorable market for fitness clubs is 76%. If the executive uses this analysis, which alternative will he likely choose?

8-14 Steve's Mountain Bicycle Shop is considering three options for its facility next year. Steve can expand his current shop, move to a larger facility, or make no change. With a good market, the annual payoff would be \$76,000 if he expands, \$90,000 if he moves, and \$40,000 if he does nothing. With an average market, his payoffs will be \$30,000, \$41,000, and \$15,000, respectively. With a poor market, his payoff will be −\$17,000, −\$28,000, and \$4,000, respectively.
(a) Which option should Steve choose if he uses the maximax criterion?
(b) Which option should Steve choose if he uses the maximin criterion?
(c) Which option should Steve choose if he uses the equally likely criterion?

(d) Which option should Steve choose if he uses the criterion of realism with $\alpha = 0.4$?
(e) Which option should Steve choose if he uses the minimax regret criterion?

8-15 Steve (see Problem 8-14) has gathered some additional information. The probabilities of good, average, and poor markets are 0.25, 0.45, and 0.3, respectively.
(a) Using EMVs, what option should Steve choose? What is the maximum EMV?
(b) Using EOL, what option should Steve choose? What is the minimum EOL?
(c) Compute the EVPI and show that it is the same as the minimum EOL.

8-16 Debbie Gibson is considering three investment options for a small inheritance that she has just received—stocks, bonds, and money market. The return on her investment will depend on the performance of the economy, which can be strong, average, or weak. The returns for each possible combination are shown in the following table:

INVESTMENT	STRONG	AVERAGE	WEAK
Stocks	12%	6%	−10%
Bonds	7%	4%	1%
Money market	4%	3%	2%

Assume that Debbie will choose only one of the investment options.
(a) Which investment should Debbie choose if she uses the maximax criterion?
(b) Which investment should Debbie choose if she uses the maximin criterion?
(c) Which investment should Debbie choose if she uses the equally likely criterion?
(d) Which investment should Debbie choose if she uses the criterion of realism with $\alpha = 0.5$?
(e) Which investment should Debbie choose if she uses the minimax regret criterion?

8-17 After reading about economic predictions, Debbie Gibson (see Problem 8-16) has assigned the probability that the economy will be strong, average, and weak at 0.2, 0.35, and 0.45, respectively.
(a) Using EMVs, what option should Debbie choose? What is the maximum EMV?
(b) Using EOL, what option should Debbie choose? What is the minimum EOL?
(c) Compute the EVPI and show that it is the same as the minimum EOL.

8-18 A hospital administrator in Portland is trying to determine whether to build a large wing onto the existing hospital, a small wing, or no wing at all. If the population of Portland continued to grow, a large wing could return $225,000 to the hospital each year. If the small wing were built, it would return $90,000 to the hospital each year if the population continued to grow. If the population of Portland remained the same, the hospital would encounter a loss of $125,000 if the large wing were built. Furthermore, a loss of $65,000 would be realized if the small wing were constructed and the population remained the same. It is unknown whether Portland's population will grow in the near future.
(a) Construct a decision table.
(b) Using the equally likely criterion, determine the best alternative.
(c) The chairman of the hospital's board has advised using a coefficient of realism of 0.7 in determining the best alternative. What is the best decision according to this criterion?

8-19 Shaq Bryant sells newspapers on Sunday mornings in an area surrounded by three busy churches. Assume that Shaq's demand can either be for 100, 300, or 500 newspapers, depending on traffic and weather. Shaq has the option to order 100, 300, or 500 newspapers from his supplier. Shaq pays $1.25 for each newspaper he orders and sells each for $2.50.
(a) How many papers should Shaq order if he chooses the maximax criterion?
(b) How many papers should Shaq order if he chooses the maximin criterion?
(c) How many papers should Shaq order if he chooses the equally likely criterion?
(d) How many papers should Shaq order if he chooses the criterion of realism with $\alpha = 0.45$?
(e) How many papers should Shaq order if he chooses the minimax regret criterion?

8-20 Shaq (see Problem 8-19) has done some research and discovered that the probabilities for demands of 100, 300, and 500 newspapers are 0.4, 0.35, and 0.25, respectively.
(a) Using EMVs, how many papers should Shaq order?
(b) Using EOL, how many papers should Shaq order?
(c) Compute Shaq's EVwPI and EVPI.

8-21 The Boatwright Sauce Company is a small manufacturer of several different sauces to use in food products. One of the products is a blended sauce mix that is sold to retail outlets. Joy Boatwright must decide how many cases of this mix to manufacture each month. The probability that the demand will be six cases is 0.1, for seven cases is 0.5, for eight cases is 0.3, and for nine cases is 0.1. The cost of every case is $55, and the price that Joy gets for each case is $90. Unfortunately, any cases not sold by the end of the month are of no value, due to spoilage. How many cases of sauce should Joy manufacture each month?

8-22 Waldo Books needs to decide how many copies of a new hardcover release to purchase for its shelves. The store has assumed that demand will be 50, 100, 150, or 200 copies next month, and it needs to decide whether to order 50, 100, 150, or 200 books for this period. Each book costs Waldo $20 and can be sold for $30. Waldo can sell any unsold books back to the supplier for $4.

(a) Which option should Waldo choose if it uses the maximax criterion?

(b) Which option should Waldo choose if it uses the maximin criterion?

(c) Which option should Waldo choose if it uses the equally likely criterion?

(d) Which option should Waldo choose if it uses the criterion of realism with $\alpha = 0.7$?

(e) Which option should Waldo choose if it uses the minimax regret criterion?

8-23 After researching the market, Waldo Books (see Problem 8-21) has concluded that the probabilities of selling 50, 100, 150, and 200 books next month are 0.2, 0.35, 0.25, and 0.2, respectively.

(a) Using EMVs, how many books should Waldo order?

(b) Using EOL, how many books should Waldo order?

(c) Compute Waldo's EVwPI and EVPI.

8-24 A souvenir retailer has an opportunity to establish a new location inside a large airport. The annual returns will depend primarily on the size of the space she rents and if the economy will be favorable. The retailer has worked with the airport concession commission, and has projected the following possible annual earnings associated with renting a small, medium, large, or very large space:

SIZE	GOOD ECONOMY	FAIR ECONOMY	POOR ECONOMY
Small	$ 70,000	$28,000	–$ 14,000
Medium	$112,000	$42,000	–$ 28,000
Large	$140,000	$42,000	–$ 56,000
Very large	$420,000	$35,000	–$224,000

(a) What is the souvenir retailer's maximax decision?

(b) What is her maximin decision?

(c) What is her equally likely decision?

(d) What is her criterion of realism decision, using $\alpha = 0.8$?

(e) What is her minimax regret decision?

8-25 An ambulance driver has three major routes from the hospital base station to the university, to which he makes several trips weekly. The traffic patterns are, however, very complex. Under good conditions, Broad Street is the fastest route. When Broad is congested, one of the other routes, either Drexel Avenue or the expressway, is usually preferable. Over the past two months, the driver has tried each route several times, under different traffic conditions. This information is summarized (in minutes of travel time to work) in the following table:

ROUTE	NO CONGESTION	MILD CONGESTION	SEVERE CONGESTION
Broad Street	10	21	30
Drexel Avenue	13	17	23
Expressway	20	21	20

In the past 50 days, the driver has encountered severe traffic congestion 10 days and mild traffic congestion 20 days. Assume that the past 50 days are typical of traffic conditions.

(a) Which route should the driver take? Remember that we want to find the fastest route.

(b) If the ambulance had a traffic scanner to accurately inform the driver of the level of congestion in this part of town, how much time could he potentially save?

8-26 A group of medical professionals is considering constructing a private clinic. If patient demand for the clinic is high, the physicians could realize a net profit of $100,000. If the demand is low, they could lose $40,000. Of course, they don't have to proceed at all, in which case there is no cost. In the absence of any market data, the best the physicians can guess is that there is a 50–50 chance that demand will be good.

(a) Construct a decision tree to help analyze this problem. What should the medical professionals do?

(b) The physicians have been approached by a market research firm that offers to perform a study of the market at a fee of $5,000. The market researchers claim that their experience enables them to use Bayes' theorem to make the following statements of probability:

probability of high demand given a positive study result	= 0.82
probability of low demand given a positive study result	= 0.18
probability of high demand given a negative study result	= 0.11
probability of low demand given a negative study result	= 0.89
probability of a positive study result	= 0.55
probability of a negative study result	= 0.45

Expand the decision tree in part (a) to reflect the options now open with the market study. What should the medical professionals do now?

(c) What is the maximum amount the physicians would be willing to pay for the market study?

(d) What is the efficiency of the market study's information?

8-27 In Problem 8-26, you helped a group of medical professionals analyze a decision, using EMV as the decision criterion. This group has also assessed its utility for money: $U(-\$45{,}000) = 0, U(-\$40{,}000) = 0.1$, $U(-\$5{,}000) = 0.7$, $U(\$0) = 0.9$, $U(\$95{,}000) = 0.99$, and $U(\$100{,}000) = 1$.

(a) Are the medical professionals risk seekers or risk avoiders? Justify your answer.

(b) Use expected utility as the decision criterion and determine the best decision for the medical professionals (including the option to use the market research firm).

8-28 Jerry Young is thinking about opening a bicycle shop in his hometown. Jerry loves to take his own bike on 50-mile trips with his friends, but he believes that any small business should be started only if there is a good chance of making a profit. Jerry can open a small shop, a large shop, or no shop at all. Because there will be a five-year lease on the building that Jerry is thinking about using, he wants to make sure that he makes the correct decision.

Jerry has done some analysis about the profitability of the bicycle shop. If Jerry builds the large bicycle shop, he will earn $60,000 if the market is good, but he will lose $40,000 if the market is bad. The small shop will return a $30,000 profit in a good market and a $10,000 loss in a bad market. At the present time, he believes that there is a 59% chance that the market will be good.

Jerry also has the option of hiring his old marketing professor for $5,000 to conduct a marketing research study. If the study is conducted, the results could be either favorable or unfavorable. It is estimated that there is a 0.6 probability that the survey will be favorable. Furthermore, there is a 0.9 probability that the market will be good, given a favorable outcome from the study. However, the marketing professor has warned Jerry that there is only a probability of 0.12 of a good market if the marketing research results are not favorable.

(a) Develop a decision tree for Jerry and help him decide what he should do.

(b) How much is the marketing professor's information worth? What is the efficiency of this information?

8-29 A manufacturer buys valves from two suppliers. The quality of the valves from the suppliers is as follows:

PERCENTAGE DEFECTIVE	PROBABILITY FOR SUPPLIER A	PROBABILITY FOR SUPPLIER B
1	0.60	0.30
3	0.25	0.40
5	0.15	0.30

For example, the probability of getting a batch of valves that are 1% defective from supplier A is 0.60. Because the manufacturer orders 10,000 valves per order, this would mean that there is a 0.6 probability of getting 100 defective valves out of the 10,000 valves if supplier A is used to fill the order. A defective valve can be repaired for 60 cents. Although the quality of supplier B is lower, it will sell an order of 10,000 valves for $37 less than supplier A.

(a) Develop a decision tree to help the manufacturer decide which supplier it should use.

(b) For how much less would supplier B have to sell an order of 10,000 valves than supplier A for the manufacturer to be indifferent between the two suppliers?

8-30 After observing the heavy snow that his town received the previous winter, Ajay Patel, an enterprising student, plans to offer a snow-clearing service in his neighborhood this winter. If he invests in a new heavy-duty blower, Ajay forecasts a profit of $700 if snowfall this winter is heavy, a profit of $200 if it is moderate, and a loss of $900 if it is light. As per the current weather forecasts, the probabilities of heavy, moderate, and light snowfall this winter are 0.4, 0.3, and 0.3, respectively.

Rather than purchase a new blower, Ajay could get his father's blower repaired and just accept smaller jobs. Under this option, Ajay estimates a profit of $350 for a heavy snowfall, a profit of $100 for a moderate snowfall, and a loss of $150 for a light snowfall. Ajay, of course, has the option of choosing neither of these options.

The local weather expert, Samantha Adams, is Ajay's good friend. For $50, she is willing to run sophisticated weather models on her computer and tell Ajay whether she expects this winter to be unseasonably cold. For the sake of solving this problem, assume that the following information is available. There is a 45% chance that Samantha will predict this winter to be unseasonably cold. If she does say this, the probabilities of heavy, moderate, and light snowfall are revised to 0.7, 0.25, and 0.05, respectively. On the other hand, if she predicts that this winter will not be unseasonably cold, these probabilities are revised to 0.15, 0.33, and 0.52, respectively.

Draw the decision tree for the situation faced by Ajay. Fold back the tree and determine the strategy you would recommend he follow. What is the efficiency of Samantha's information?

8-31 Oscar Weng is planning to raise funds to pay for a scouting trip by running a concession stand during tomorrow's high school soccer game. Oscar needs to decide whether to rent a large insulated thermos from the local rental store and sell cocoa at the game or to rent a large refrigerated container and sell lemonade.

Unfortunately, Oscar does not have the resources to rent both items. Sales depend on whether it is sunny or rainy during the game. If the weather is sunny, Oscar will make a profit of $60 from lemonade but only $20 from cocoa. If, however, it is rainy, Oscar will make a profit of $80 from cocoa but only break even if he brings lemonade. Based on the local newspaper's prediction, Oscar thinks there is a 60% chance of it being sunny tomorrow.

Oscar's older brother Elmo, who has earned the Meteorology Badge, claims he can predict the weather more accurately than the newspaper. For only $4, he offers to study the weather and tell Oscar if there is a "good chance" or "bad chance" of it being sunny tomorrow. Assume that the following data are available about the accuracy of the brother's information:

- The probability that he will say "good chance" is 0.7.
- If he says "good chance," then there is a 0.83 probability that it will actually be sunny tomorrow.
- If he says "bad chance," then there is only a 0.25 probability that it will actually be sunny tomorrow.

(a) Draw the complete decision tree for Oscar's problem and fold it back to help him decide what he should do.

(b) How much is his brother's information actually worth to Oscar?

8-32 You have been hired by the No Flight Golf Company, and your first task is to decide whether to market a new golf ball utilizing breakthrough technology and, if so, determine the price. The payoff of your decision will be affected by whether your competitor will market similar balls and the price of their golf balls after you go to market. The cost to market the golf balls is $80,000, and the probability that your competitor will enter the market is 0.75. The following table describes the payoffs of each pricing combination, assuming that No Flight will have competition:

	COMPETITOR'S PRICE		
OUR PRICE	HIGH	MEDIUM	LOW
High	$400,000	$250,000	$ 25,000
Medium	$475,000	$325,000	$175,000
Low	$350,000	$250,000	$125,000

If No Flight sets its price high, the probability that the competition will set its price high, medium, and low is 0.3, 0.55, and 0.15, respectively. If No Flight sets its price medium, the probability that the competition will set its price high, medium, and low is 0.2, 0.7, and 0.1, respectively. Finally, if No Flight sets its price low, the probability that the competition will set its price high, medium, and low is 0.15, 0.25, and 0.6, respectively.

If No Flight has no competition for its new golf balls, its expected payoff for setting the price high, medium, and low is $600,000, $500,000, and $400,000, respectively, excluding marketing costs. Do you recommend marketing the new golf balls? If so, what is your pricing recommendation?

8-33 Your regular tennis partner has made a friendly wager with you. The two of you will play out one point in which you can serve. The loser pays the winner $100. If your first serve is not in play, you get a second serve. If your second serve is not in play, you lose the point. You have two kinds of serves: a hard one and a soft one. You know that your hard serve is in play 65% of the time and, when it is in play, you win the point 75% of the time. You put your soft serve in play 88% of the time and, when it is in play, you win the point 27% of the time. Should you accept the wager? If so, should you use your hard or soft serve?

8-34 Rob Johnson is a product manager for Diamond Chemical. The firm is considering whether to launch a new product line that will require building a new facility. The technology required to produce the new product is yet untested. If Rob decides to build the new facility and the process is successful, Diamond Chemical will realize a profit of $675,000. If the process does not succeed, the company will lose $825,000. Rob estimates that there is a 0.6 probability that the process will succeed.

Rob can also decide to build a pilot plant for $60,000 to test the new process before deciding to build the full-scale facility. If the pilot plant succeeds, Rob feels the chance of the full-scale facility succeeding is 85%. If the pilot plant fails, Rob feels the chance of the full-scale facility succeeding is only 20%. The probability that the pilot plant will succeed is estimated at 0.6. Structure this problem with a decision tree and advise Rob what to do.

8-35 Rob Johnson (see Problem 8-34) has some revised information concerning the accuracy of the pilot plant probabilities. According to his new information, the probability that the pilot plant will be successful, given that the full-scale facility will work, is 0.8. The probability that the pilot plant will fail, given that the full-scale facility will fail, is 0.85. Calculate the posterior probabilities and reevaluate the decision tree from Problem 8-34. Does this new information affect Diamond Chemical's original decision?

8-36 You are reconsidering your analysis of the tennis wager between you and your partner (see Problem 8-33) and have decided to incorporate utility theory into the decision making process.

The following table describes your utility values for various payoffs:

MONETARY VALUE	UTILITY
–$100	0.00
–$ 50	0.50
$ 0	0.80
$ 50	0.95
$100	1.00

(a) Redo Problem 8-35 using this information.
(b) How can you best describe your attitude toward risk? Justify your answer.

8-37 Shamrock Oil owns a parcel of land that has the potential to be an underground oil field. It will cost $500,000 to drill for oil. If oil does exist on the land, Shamrock will realize a payoff of $4,000,000 (not including drilling costs). With current information, Shamrock estimates that there is a 0.2 probability that oil is present on the site. Shamrock also has the option of selling the land as is for $400,000, without further information about the likelihood of oil being present. A third option is to perform geological tests at the site, which would cost $100,000. There is a 30% chance that the test results will be positive, after which Shamrock can sell the land for $650,000 or drill the land, with a 0.65 probability that oil exists. If the test results are negative, Shamrock can sell the land for $50,000 or drill the land, with a 0.05 probability that oil exists. Using a decision tree, recommend a course of action for Shamrock Oil.

8-38 Shamrock Oil (see Problem 8-37) has some revised information concerning the accuracy of the geological test probabilities. According to this new information, the probability that the test will be positive, given that oil is present in the ground, is 0.85. The probability that the test will be negative, given that oil is not present, is 0.75. Calculate the posterior probabilities and reevaluate the decision tree from Problem 8-37. Does this new information affect Shamrock Oil's original decision?

8-39 Shamrock Oil (see Problem 8-37) has decided to rely on utility theory to assist in the decision concerning the oil field. The following table describes its utility function; all monetary values are in thousands of dollars:

MONETARY VALUE	UTILITY
–$ 600	0.00
–$ 500	0.03
–$ 50	0.10
$ 400	0.15
$ 550	0.17
$3,400	0.90
$3,500	1.00

(a) Redo Problem 8-37 using this information.
(b) How can you best describe Shamrock Oil's attitude toward risk? Justify your answer.

8-40 Jim Sellers is thinking about producing a new type of electric razor for men. If the market is good, he would get a return of $140,000, but if the market for this new type of razor is poor, he would lose $84,000. Because Ron Bush is a close friend of Jim Sellers, Jim is considering the possibility of using Bush Marketing Research to gather additional information about the market for the razor. Ron has suggested two options to Jim. The first alternative is a sophisticated questionnaire that would be administered to a test market. It will cost $5,000. The second alternative is to run a pilot study. This would involve producing a limited number of the new razors and trying to sell them in two cities that are typical of American cities. The pilot study is more accurate but is also more expensive. It will cost $20,000. Ron has suggested that it would be a good idea for Jim to conduct either the questionnaire or the pilot before making the decision concerning whether to produce the new razor. But Jim is not sure if the value of either option is worth the cost.

For the sake of solving this problem, assume that Jim has the following probability estimates available: the probability of a successful market without performing the questionnaire or pilot study is 0.5, the probability of a successful market given a positive questionnaire result is 0.78, the probability of a successful market given a negative questionnaire result is 0.27, the probability of a successful market given a positive pilot study result is 0.89, and the probability of a successful market given a negative pilot study result is 0.18. Further, the probability of a positive questionnaire result is 0.45 and the probability of a positive pilot study result is also 0.45.

(a) Draw the decision tree for this problem and identify the best decision for Jim.
(b) What is the value of the questionnaire's information? What is its efficiency?
(c) What is the value of the pilot study's information? What is its efficiency?

8-41 Jim Sellers (see Problem 8-40) has been able to estimate his utility for a number of different values, and he would like to use these utility values in making his decision. The utility values are $U(-\$104{,}000) = 0$, $U(-\$89{,}000) = 0.5$, $U(-\$84{,}000) = 0.55$, $U(-\$20{,}000) = 0.7$, $U(-\$5{,}000) = 0.8$, $U(\$0) = 0.81$, $U(\$120{,}000) = 0.9$, $U(\$135{,}000) = 0.95$, and $U(\$140{,}000) = 1$.

(a) Solve Problem 8-40(a) again using utility values.
(b) Is Jim a risk avoider or risk seeker? Justify your answer.

8-42 Jason Scott has applied for a mortgage to purchase a house, and he will go to settlement in two months.

His loan can be locked in now at the current market interest rate of 7% and a cost of $1,000. He also has the option of waiting one month and locking in the rate available at that time at a cost of $500. Finally, he can choose to accept the market rate available at settlement in two months at no cost. Assume that interest rates will either increase by 0.5% (0.3 probability), remain unchanged (0.5 probability), or decrease by 0.5% (0.2 probability) at the end one month.

Rates can also increase, remain unchanged, or decrease by another 0.5% at the end on the second month. If rates increase after one month, the probability that they will increase, remain unchanged, and decrease at the end of the second month is 0.5, 0.25, and 0.25, respectively. If rates remain unchanged after one month, the probability that they will increase, remain unchanged, and decrease at the end of the second month is 0.25, 0.5, and 0.25, respectively. If rates decrease after one month, the probability that they will increase, remain unchanged, and decrease at the end of the second month is 0.25, 0.25, and 0.5, respectively.

Assuming that Jason will stay in the house for 5 years, each 0.5% increase in the interest rate of his mortgage will cost him $2,400. Each 0.5% decrease in the rate will likewise save him $2,400. What strategy would you recommend?

8-43 Jason Scott (see Problem 8-42) has decided to incorporate utility theory into his decision with his mortgage application. The following table describes Jason's utility function:

MONETARY VALUE	UTILITY
–$4,800	0.00
–$2,900	0.10
–$2,400	0.12
–$1,000	0.15
–$ 500	0.19
$ 0	0.21
$1,900	0.26
$2,400	0.30
$4,800	1.00

(a) How can you best describe Jason's attitude toward risk? Justify your answer.
(b) Will the use of utilities affect Jason's original decision in Problem 8-42?

8-44 An investor is deciding whether to build a retail store. If she invests in the store and it is successful, she expects a return of $100,000 in the first year. If the store is not successful, she will suffer a loss of $80,000. She guesses that the probability that the store will be a success is 0.6.

To remove some of the uncertainty from this decision, the investor tries to establish more information, but this market research will cost $20,000. If she spends this money, she will have more confidence in her investment. There is a 0.6 probability that this information will be favorable; if it is, the likelihood that the store will be a success increases to 0.9. If the information is not favorable, the likelihood that the store will be a success reduces to only 0.2. Of course, she can elect to do nothing.
(a) What do you recommend?
(b) How much is the information worth? What is its efficiency?

8-45 Replace all monetary values in Problem 8-44 with the following utilities:

MONETARY VALUE	UTILITY
$100,000	1.00
$ 80,000	0.40
$ 0	0.20
–$ 20,000	0.10
–$ 80,000	0.05
–$100,000	0.00

(a) What do you recommend, based on expected utility?
(b) Is the investor a risk seeker or a risk avoider? Justify your answer.

8-46 The Jamis Corporation is involved with waste management. During the past 10 years it has become one of the largest waste disposal companies in the Midwest, serving primarily Wisconsin, Illinois, and Michigan. Bob Jamis, president of the company, is considering the possibility of establishing a waste treatment plant in northern Mississippi. From past experience, Bob believes that a small plant would yield a $500,000 profit, regardless of the demand for the plant. The success of a medium-sized plant would depend on demand. With a low demand for waste treatment, Bob expects a $200,000 profit. A fair demand would yield a $700,000 profit, and a high demand would return $800,000. Although a large plant is much riskier than a medium-sized one, the potential rewards are much greater. With a high demand, a large plant would return $1,000,000. However, the plant would yield a profit of only $400,000 with a fair demand, and it would actually lose $200,000 with a low demand. Looking at the current economic conditions in northern Mississippi, Bob estimates that the probabilities of low, fair, and high demands are 0.15, 0.4, and 0.45, respectively.

Because of the large potential investment and the possibility of a loss, Bob has decided to hire a market research team that is based in Jackson, Mississippi. This team will perform a survey to get a better feel for the probability of a low, medium, or high demand for a waste treatment facility. The cost of the survey is \$50,000, and the survey could result in three possible outcomes—low, fair, and high. To help Bob determine whether to go ahead with the survey, the marketing research firm has provided Bob with the following information regarding the conditional probabilities, i.e., P(Survey results | Possible outcomes):

	SURVEY RESULTS		
POSSIBLE OUTCOME	LOW	FAIR	HIGH
Low demand	0.7	0.2	0.1
Fair demand	0.4	0.5	0.1
High demand	0.1	0.3	0.6

For example, P(Low survey result | Low demand) = 0.7. What should Bob do?

8-47 Before market research was done, Peter Martin believed that there was a 50–50 chance that his food store would be a success. The research team determined that there was a 0.75 probability that the market research would be favorable, given a successful food store. Moreover, there was a 0.65 probability that the market research would be unfavorable, given an unsuccessful food store. This information is based on past experience.

(a) If the market research is favorable, what is Peter's revised probability of a successful food store?

(b) If the market research is unfavorable, what is Peter's revised probability of a successful food store?

8-48 A market research company has approached you about the possibility of using its services to help you decide whether to launch a new product. According to its customer portfolio, it has correctly predicted a favorable market for its clients' products 14 out of the last 16 times. It has also correctly predicted an unfavorable market for its clients' products 9 out of 11 times. Without this research company's help, you have estimated the probability of a favorable market at 0.55. Calculate the posterior probabilities, using the track record of the research firm.

8-49 Lathum Consulting is an econometrics research firm that predicts the direction of the gross national product (GNP) during the next quarter. More specifically, it forecasts whether the GNP will grow, hold steady, or decline. The following table describes Lathum's track record from past predictions by displaying the probabilities of its predictions, given the actual outcome:

	GNP PREDICTION		
ACTUAL GNP	GROWTH	STEADY	DECLINE
Growth	0.75	0.08	0.05
Steady	0.18	0.80	0.12
Decline	0.07	0.12	0.83

For example, the chance that Lathum will predict that the GNP will grow when it actually is steady is 18%. Your company is considering a contract with Lathum Consulting to assist in predicting the direction of next quarter's GNP. Prior to enlisting Lathum's services, you have assessed the probability of the GNP growing, holding steady, and declining at 0.3, 0.45, and 0.25, respectively. Calculate the posterior probabilities, using the services of Lathum Consulting.

8-50 In the past few years, the traffic problems in Lynn McKell's hometown have gotten worse. Now, Broad Street is congested about half the time. The normal travel time to work for Lynn is only 15 minutes when she takes Broad Street and there is no congestion. With congestion, however, it takes Lynn 40 minutes to get to work using Broad Street. If Lynn decides to take the expressway, it takes 30 minutes, regardless of the traffic conditions. Lynn's utility for travel time is U(15 minutes) = 0.9, U(30 minutes) = 0.7, and U(40 minutes) = 0.2.

(a) Which route will minimize Lynn's expected travel time?

(b) Which route will maximize Lynn's utility?

(c) When it comes to travel time, is Lynn a risk seeker or a risk avoider? Justify your answer.

Case Study

Ski Right

After retiring as a physician, Bob Guthrie became an avid downhill skier on the steep slopes of the Utah Rocky Mountains. As an amateur inventor, Bob was always looking for something new. With the recent deaths of several celebrity skiers, Bob knew he could use his creative mind to make skiing safer and his bank account larger. He knew that many deaths on the slopes were caused by head injuries. Although ski helmets have been on the market for some time, most skiers considered them boring and basically ugly. As a physician, Bob knew that some type of new ski helmet was the answer.

Bob's biggest challenge was to invent a helmet that was attractive, safe, and fun to wear. Multiple colors, using the latest fashion designs, would be a must. After years of skiing, Bob knew that many skiers believed that how you looked on the slopes was more important than how you skied. His helmets would have to look good and fit in with current fashion trends. But attractive helmets were not enough. Bob had to make the helmets fun and useful. The name of the new ski helmet, Ski Right, was sure to be a winner. If Bob could come up with a good idea, he believed that there was a 20% chance that the market for the Ski Right helmet would be excellent. The chance of a good market should be 40%. Bob also knew that the market for his helmet could be only average (30% chance) or even poor (10% chance).

The idea of how to make ski helmets fun and useful came to Bob on a gondola ride to the top of a mountain. A busy executive on the gondola ride was on his cell phone, trying to complete a complicated merger. When the executive got off the gondola, he dropped the phone, and it was crushed by the gondola mechanism. Bob decided that his new ski helmet would have a built-in cell phone and an AM/FM stereo radio. All the electronics could be operated by a control pad worn on a skier's arm or leg.

Bob decided to try a small pilot project for Ski Right. He enjoyed being retired and didn't want a failure to cause him to go back to work. After some research, Bob found Progressive Products (PP). The company was willing to be a partner in developing the Ski Right and sharing any profits. If the market was excellent, Bob would net $5,000. With a good market, Bob would net $2,000. An average market would result in a loss of $2,000, and a poor market would mean Bob would be out $5,000.

Another option for Bob was to have Leadville Barts (LB) make the helmet. The company had extensive experience in making bicycle helmets. PP would then take the helmets made by LB and do the rest. Bob had a greater risk. He estimated that he could lose $10,000 in a poor market or $4,000 in an average market. A good market for Ski Right would result in a $6,000 profit for Bob, and an excellent market would mean a $12,000 profit.

A third option for Bob was to use TalRad (TR), a radio company in Tallahassee, Florida. TR had extensive experience in making military radios. LB could make the helmets, and PP could do the rest. Again, Bob would be taking on greater risk. A poor market would mean a $15,000 loss, and an average market would mean a $10,000 loss. A good market would result in a net profit of $7,000 for Bob. An excellent market would return $13,000.

Bob could also have Celestial Cellular (CC) develop the cell phones. Thus, another option was to have CC make the phones and have PP do the rest of the production and distribution. Because the cell phone was the most expensive component of the helmet, Bob could lose $30,000 in a poor market. He could lose $20,000 in an average market. If the market was good or excellent, Bob would see a net profit of $10,000 or $30,000, respectively.

Bob's final option was to forget about PP entirely. He could use LB to make the helmets, CC to make the phones, and TR to make the AM/FM stereo radios. Bob could then hire some friends to assemble everything and market the finished Ski Right helmets. With this final alternative, Bob could realize a net profit of $55,000 in an excellent market. Even if the market were just good, Bob would net $20,000. An average market, however, would mean a loss of $35,000. If the market was poor, Bob would lose $60,000.

Discussion Questions

1. What do you recommend?
2. What is the opportunity loss for this problem?
3. Compute the expected value of perfect information.
4. Was Bob completely logical in how he approached this decision problem?

Case Study

Blake Electronics

In 1969, Steve Blake founded Blake Electronics in Long Beach, California, to manufacture resistors, capacitors, inductors, and other electronic components. During the Vietnam War, Steve was a radio operator, and it was during this time that he became proficient at repairing radios and other communications equipment. Steve viewed his four-year experience with the army with mixed feelings. He hated army life, but that experience gave him the confidence and the initiative to start his own electronics firm.

Over the years, Steve kept the business relatively unchanged. By 1984, total annual sales were in excess of $2 million. In 1988, Steve's son, Jim, joined the company after finishing high school and two years of courses in electronics at Long Beach Community College. Jim had always been aggressive in high school athletics, and he became even more aggressive as general sales manager of Blake Electronics. This aggressiveness bothered Steve, who was more conservative. Jim would make deals to supply companies with electronic components before he bothered to find out if Blake Electronics had the ability or capacity to produce the components. On several occasions, this behavior caused the company some embarrassing moments when Blake Electronics was unable to produce the electronic components for companies with which Jim had made deals.

In 1992, Jim started to go after government contracts for electronic components. By 1994, total annual sales had increased to more than $10 million, and the number of employees exceeded 200. Many of these employees were electronics specialists and graduates of electrical engineering programs from top colleges and universities. But Jim's tendency to stretch Blake Electronics to contracts continued as well, and by 2001, Blake Electronics had a reputation with government agencies as a company that could not deliver what it promised. Almost overnight,

FIGURE 8.14
Master Control Center

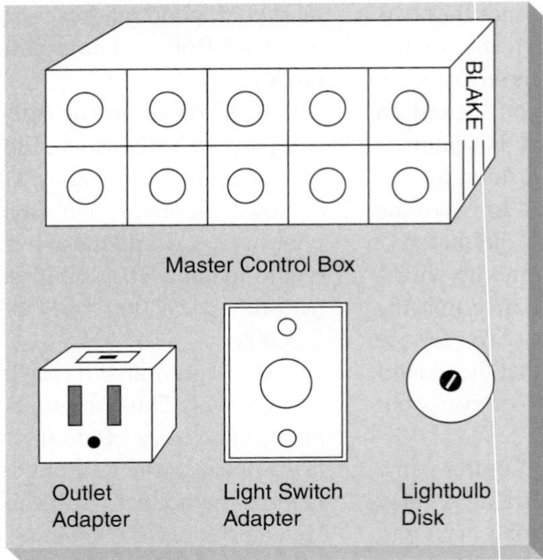

government contracts stopped, and Blake Electronics was left with an idle workforce and unused manufacturing equipment. This high overhead started to melt away profits, and in 2003, Blake Electronics was faced with the possibility of sustaining a loss for the first time in its history.

In 2005, Steve decided to look at the possibility of manufacturing electronic components for home use. Although this was a totally new market for Blake Electronics, Steve was convinced that this was the only way to keep Blake Electronics from dipping into the red. The research team at Blake Electronics was given the task of developing new electronic devices for home use. The first idea from the research team was the Master Control Center. The basic components for this system are shown in Figure 8.14.

The heart of the system is the master control box. This unit, which would have a retail price of $250, has two rows of five buttons. Each button controls one light or appliance and can be set as either a switch or a rheostat. When set as a switch, a light finger touch on the bottom either turns a light or appliance on or off. When set as a rheostat, a finger touching the bottom controls the intensity of the light. Leaving your finger on the button makes the light go through a complete cycle, ranging from off to bright and back to off again.

To allow for maximum flexibility, each master control box is powered by two D-sized batteries that can last up to a year, depending on usage. In addition, the research team has developed three versions of the master control box—versions A, B, and C. If a family wants to control more than 10 lights or appliances, another master control box can be purchased.

The lightbulb disk, which would have a retail price of $2.50, is controlled by the master control box and is used to control the intensity of any light. A different disk is available for each button position for all three master control boxes. By inserting the lightbulb disk between the lightbulb and the socket, the appropriate button on the master control box can completely control the intensity of the light. If a standard light switch is used, it must be on at all times for the master control box to work.

One disadvantage of using a standard light switch is that only the master control box can be used to control the particular light. To avoid this problem, the research team developed a special light switch adapter that would sell for $15. When this device is installed either the master control box or the light switch adapter can be used to control the light.

When used to control appliances other than lights, the master control box must be used in conjunction with one or more outlet adapters. The adapters are plugged in to a standard wall outlet, and the appliance is then plugged in to the adapter. Each outlet adapter has a switch on top that allows the appliance to be controlled from the master control box or the outlet adapter. The price of each outlet adapter would be $25.

The research team estimated that it would cost $500,000 to develop the equipment and procedures needed to manufacture the master control box and accessories. If successful, this venture could increase sales by approximately $2 million. But would the master control boxes be a successful venture? With a 60% chance of success estimated by the research team, Steve has serious doubts about trying to market the master control boxes even though he liked the basic idea. Because of his reservations, Steve decided to send requests for proposals (RFPs) for additional marketing research to 30 marketing research companies in southern California.

The first RFP to come back was from a small company called Marketing Associates, Inc. (MAI), which would charge $100,000 for the survey. According to its proposal, MAI has been in business for about three years and has conducted about 100 marketing research projects. MAI's major strengths appeared to be individual attention to each account, experienced staff, and fast work. Steve was particularly interested in one part of the proposal, which revealed MAI's success record with previous accounts. This is shown in Table 8.13.

The only other proposal to be returned was by a branch office of Iverstine and Kinard, one of the largest marketing research firms in the country. The cost for a complete survey would be $300,000. Although the proposal did not contain the

TABLE 8.13
Success Figures for MAI

OUTCOME	SURVEY RESULTS FAVORABLE	SURVEY RESULTS UNFAVORABLE	TOTAL
Successful venture	35	20	55
Unsuccessful venture	15	30	45

same success record as MAI, the proposal from Iverstine and Kinard did contain some interesting information. The chance of getting a favorable survey result, given a successful venture, was 90%. On the other hand, the chance of getting an unfavorable survey result, given an unsuccessful venture, was 80%. Thus, it appeared to Steve that Iverstine and Kinard would be able to predict the success or failure of the master control boxes with a great amount of certainty.

Steve pondered the situation. Unfortunately, the two marketing research teams gave different types of information in their proposals. Steve concluded that there would be no way that the two proposals could be compared unless he got additional information from Iverstine and Kinard. Furthermore, Steve wasn't sure what he would do with the information and whether it would be worth the expense of hiring one of the marketing research firms.

Discussion Questions

1. Does Steve need additional information from Iverstine and Kinard?
2. What would you recommend?

Internet Case Studies

See the Companion Website for this textbook, at www.pearsonhighered.com/balakrishnan, for additional case studies.

CHAPTER 9

Queuing Models

LEARNING OBJECTIVES

After completing this chapter, students will be able to:

1. Discuss the trade-off curves for cost of waiting time and cost of service.
2. Understand the three parts of a queuing system: the arrival population, the queue, and the service facility.
3. Describe basic queuing system configurations.
4. Understand the assumptions of common queuing models discussed in this chapter.
5. Use Excel to analyze a variety of operating characteristics of queuing systems.
6. Understand more complex queuing systems.

CHAPTER OUTLINE

9.1 Introduction

The study of **queues**,[1] also called *waiting lines*, is one of the oldest and most widely used decision modeling techniques. Queues are an everyday occurrence, affecting people shopping for groceries, buying gasoline, making bank deposits, and waiting on the telephone for the first available customer service person to answer. Queues can also take the form of machines waiting to be repaired, prisoners to be processed in a jail system, or airplanes lined up on a runway for permission to take off.

A primary goal of queuing analysis is to find the best level of service for an organization.

Most queuing problems focus on finding the ideal level of service that a firm should provide. Supermarkets must decide how many cash register checkout positions should be opened. Gasoline stations must decide how many pumps should be available. Manufacturing plants must determine the optimal number of mechanics to have on duty each shift to repair machines that break down. Banks must decide how many teller windows to keep open to serve customers during various hours of the day. In most cases, this level of service is an option over which management has control. An extra teller, for example, can be borrowed from another chore or can be hired and trained quickly if demand warrants it. This may, however, not always be the case. For example, a plant may not be able to locate or hire skilled mechanics to repair sophisticated electronic machinery.

Approaches for Analyzing Queues

In practice, there are two principal approaches that managers can use to analyze the performance of a queuing system and evaluate its cost-effectiveness. The first approach is based on *analytical modeling*. For several different queuing systems that satisfy certain properties, decisions modelers have derived explicit formulas to calculate various performance measures. These formulas, although rather cumbersome in some cases, are quite straightforward to use, especially if they are coded in a computer software program. In this chapter, we discuss analytical models for a few simple queuing systems. Although we show the mathematical equations needed to compute the performance measures of these queuing systems, we will actually use Excel worksheets (included on the Companion Website) to calculate these values in each case. From a managerial perspective, therefore, the use of these analytical models will be very easy and straightforward.

More sophisticated models exist to handle variations of basic assumptions, but when even these do not apply, we can turn to computer simulation, which is the topic of Chapter 10.

Many real-world queuing systems can, however, be so complex that they cannot be modeled analytically at all. When this happens, decision modelers usually turn to the second approach—**computer simulation**—to analyze the performance of these systems. We discuss simulation in Chapter 10 and also illustrate how this technique can be used to analyze queuing systems.

9.2 Queuing System Costs

As noted earlier, a primary goal of queuing analysis is to find the best level of service that a firm should provide. In deciding this ideal level of service, managers have to deal with two types of costs:

1. *Cost of providing the service.* This is also known as the **service cost**. Examples of this type of cost include wages paid to servers, the cost of buying an extra machine, and the cost of constructing a new teller window at a bank. As a firm increases the size of its

HISTORY How Queuing Models Began

Queuing theory began with the research work of a Danish engineer named A. K. Erlang. In 1909 Erlang experimented with fluctuating demand in telephone traffic. Eight years later, he published a report addressing the delays in automatic dialing equipment. At the end of World War II, Erlang's early work was extended to more general problems and to business applications of waiting lines.

[1] The word *queue* is pronounced like the letter Q (i.e., "kew").

FIGURE 9.1
Queuing Costs and Service Levels

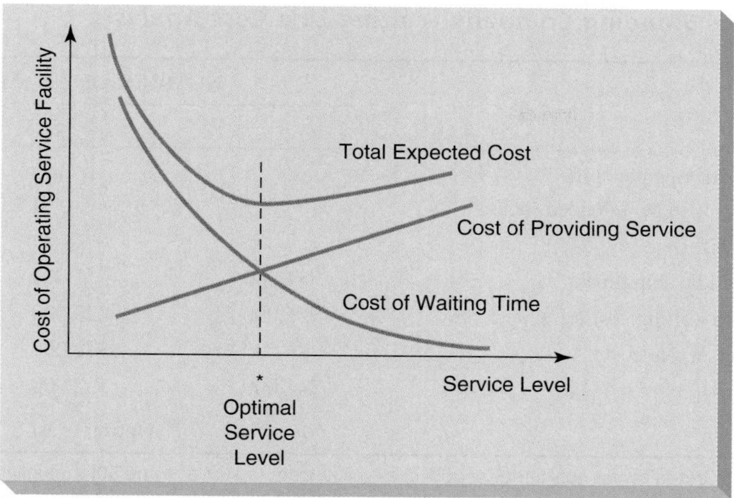

staff and provides added service facilities, the result could be excellent customer service with seldom more than one or two customers in a queue. While customers may be happy with the quick response, the cost of providing this service can, however, become very expensive.

2. *Cost of* not *providing the service.* This is also known as the **waiting cost** and is typically the cost of customer dissatisfaction. If a facility has just a minimum number of checkout lines, pumps, or teller windows open, the service cost is kept low, but customers may end up with long waiting times in the queue. How many times would you return to a large department store that had only one cash register open every time you shop? As the average length of the queue increases and poor service results, customers and goodwill may be lost.

Managers must deal with the trade-off between the cost of providing service and the cost of customer waiting time. The latter may be hard to quantify.

Most managers recognize the trade-off that must take place between the cost of providing good service and the cost of customer waiting time, and they try to achieve a happy medium between the two. They want queues that are short enough so that customers don't become unhappy and either storm out without buying or buy but never return. But they are willing to allow some waiting in line if this wait is balanced by a significant savings in service costs.

Total expected cost is the sum of service plus waiting costs.

One means of evaluating a service facility is thus to look at a total expected cost, a concept illustrated in Figure 9.1. Total expected cost is the sum of expected waiting costs and expected costs of providing service.

Service costs increase as a firm attempts to raise its level of service. For example, if three teams of stevedores, instead of two, are employed to unload a cargo ship, service costs are increased by the additional price of wages. As service improves in speed, however, the cost of time spent waiting in lines decreases. This waiting cost may reflect lost productivity of workers while their tools or machines are awaiting repairs or may simply be an estimate of the costs of customers lost because of poor service and long queues.

THREE RIVERS SHIPPING COMPANY EXAMPLE As an illustration of a queuing system, let's look at the case of the Three Rivers Shipping Company. Three Rivers runs a huge docking facility located on the Ohio River near Pittsburgh. Approximately five ships arrive to unload their cargoes of steel and ore during every 12-hour work shift. Each hour that a ship sits idle in line, waiting to be unloaded, costs the firm a great deal of money, about $1,000 per hour. From experience, management estimates that if one team of stevedores is on duty to handle the unloading work, each ship will wait an average of 7 hours to be unloaded. If two teams are working, the average waiting time drops to 4 hours; for three teams, it is 3 hours; and for four teams of stevedores, only 2 hours. But each additional team of stevedores is also an expensive proposition, due to union contracts.

The goal is to find the service level that minimizes total expected cost.

The Three Rivers superintendent would like to determine the optimal number of teams of stevedores to have on duty each shift. The objective is to minimize total expected costs. This analysis is summarized in Table 9.1. To minimize the sum of service costs and waiting costs, the firm makes the decision to employ two teams of stevedores each shift.

TABLE 9.1 Three Rivers Shipping Company Waiting Line Cost Analysis

	NUMBER OF TEAMS OF STEVEDORES			
	1	**2**	**3**	**4**
(a) Average number of ships arriving per shift	5	5	5	5
(b) Average time each ship waits to be unloaded (hours)	7	4	3	2
(c) Total ship hours lost per shift ($a \times b$)	35	20	15	10
(d) Estimated cost per hour of idle ship time	$1,000	$1,000	$1,000	$1,000
(e) Value of ship's lost time or waiting cost ($c \times d$)	$35,000	$20,000	$15,000	$10,000
(f) Stevedore team salary,* or service cost	$6,000	$12,000	$18,000	$24,000
(g) Total expected cost ($e + f$)	$41,000	$32,000 (Optimal cost)	$33,000	$34,000

*Stevedore team salaries are computed as the number of people in a typical team (assumed to be 50) multiplied by the number of hours each person works per day (12 hours) multiplied by an hourly salary of $10 per hour. If two teams are employed, the rate is just doubled.

9.3 Characteristics of a Queuing System

In this section we discuss the three components of a queuing system that are critical for the development of analytical **queuing models**: (1) the arrivals or inputs to the system (sometimes referred to as the *calling population*), (2) the queue or the waiting line itself, and (3) the service facility. Together, these three components define the type of queuing system under consideration.

Arrival Characteristics

With regard to the input source that generates arrivals or customers for a queuing system, it is important to consider the following: (1) size of the **arrival population**, (2) pattern of arrivals (or the arrival distribution) at the queuing system, and (3) behavior of the arrivals.

Unlimited (or infinite) populations *are assumed for most queuing models.*

SIZE OF THE ARRIVAL POPULATION Population sizes are considered to be either *infinite (unlimited)* or *finite (limited)*. When the number of customers or arrivals on hand at any given moment is just a small portion of potential arrivals, the arrival population is considered an **infinite, or unlimited, population**. For practical purposes, examples of unlimited populations include cars arriving at a highway tollbooth, shoppers arriving at a supermarket, or students arriving to register for classes at a large university. Most queuing models assume such an infinite arrival population. When this is not the case, modeling becomes much more complex. An example of a **finite, or limited, population** is a shop with only eight machines that might break down and require service.

Analytical queuing models typically use the average arrival rate.

ARRIVAL DISTRIBUTION Arrivals can be characterized either by an average *arrival rate* or by an average *arrival time*. Because both measures occur commonly in practice, it is important to distinguish between the two. An average arrival rate denotes the average number of arrivals in a given interval of time. Examples include two customers per hour, four trucks per minute, two potholes per mile of road, and five typing errors per printed page. In contrast, an average arrival time denotes the average time between successive arrivals. Examples include 30 minutes between customers, 0.25 minutes between trucks, 0.5 miles between potholes, and 0.2 pages between typing errors. It is important to remember that for analytical queuing models, we typically use the average arrival *rate*.

Arrivals are random when they are independent of one another and cannot be predicted exactly.

Customers can arrive at a service facility either according to some known constant schedule (e.g., one patient every 15 minutes, one student for advising every half hour), or they can arrive in a random manner. Arrivals are considered random when they are independent of one another and their occurrence cannot be predicted exactly.

It turns out that in many real-world queuing problems, even when arrivals are random, the actual number of arrivals per unit of time can be estimated by using a probability distribution

The **Poisson distribution** *is used in many queuing models to represent arrival patterns.*

known as the **Poisson distribution**. The Poisson distribution is applicable whenever the following assumptions are satisfied: (1) The average arrival rate over a given interval of time is known, (2) this average rate is the same for all equal-sized intervals, (3) the actual number of arrivals in one interval has no bearing on the actual number of arrivals in another interval, and (4) there cannot be more than one arrival in an interval as the size of the interval approaches zero. For a given average arrival rate, a discrete Poisson distribution can be established by using the following formula:[2]

$$P(X) = \frac{e^{-\lambda}\lambda^X}{X!} \text{ for } X = 0, 1, 2, \cdots \tag{9-1}$$

where

X = number of arrivals per unit of time (e.g., hour)

$P(X)$ = probability of exactly X arrivals

λ = average arrival *rate* (i.e., average number of arrivals per unit of time)

e = 2.7183 (known as the exponential constant)

These values are easy to compute with the help of a calculator or Excel. Figure 9.2 illustrates the shape of the Poisson distribution for $\lambda = 2$ and $\lambda = 4$. This means that if the average arrival rate is $\lambda = 2$ customers per hour, the probability of 0 customers arriving in any random hour is 0.1353, the probability of 1 customer is 0.2707, 2 customers is 0.2707, 3 customers is 0.1804, 4 customers is 0.0902 and so on. The chance that 9 or more will arrive in any hour is virtually zero.

All the analytical models discussed in this chapter assume Poisson arrivals. However, in practice, arrivals in queuing systems need not always be Poisson and could follow other probability distributions. The use of statistical goodness of fit tests to identify these distributions and analytical queuing models to analyze such systems are topics discussed in more advanced texts. Of course, as we will discuss in Chapter 10, we can also analyze such queuing systems by using computer simulation.

Balking *refers to customers who do not join a queue.* **Reneging** *customers join a queue but leave before being served.*

BEHAVIOR OF ARRIVALS Most queuing models assume that an arriving customer is a patient customer. Patient customers are people or machines that wait in the queue until they are served and do not switch between lines. Unfortunately, life and decision models are complicated by the fact that people have been known to balk or renege. **Balking** refers to customers refusing to

FIGURE 9.2 Two Examples of the Poisson Distribution for Arrival Times

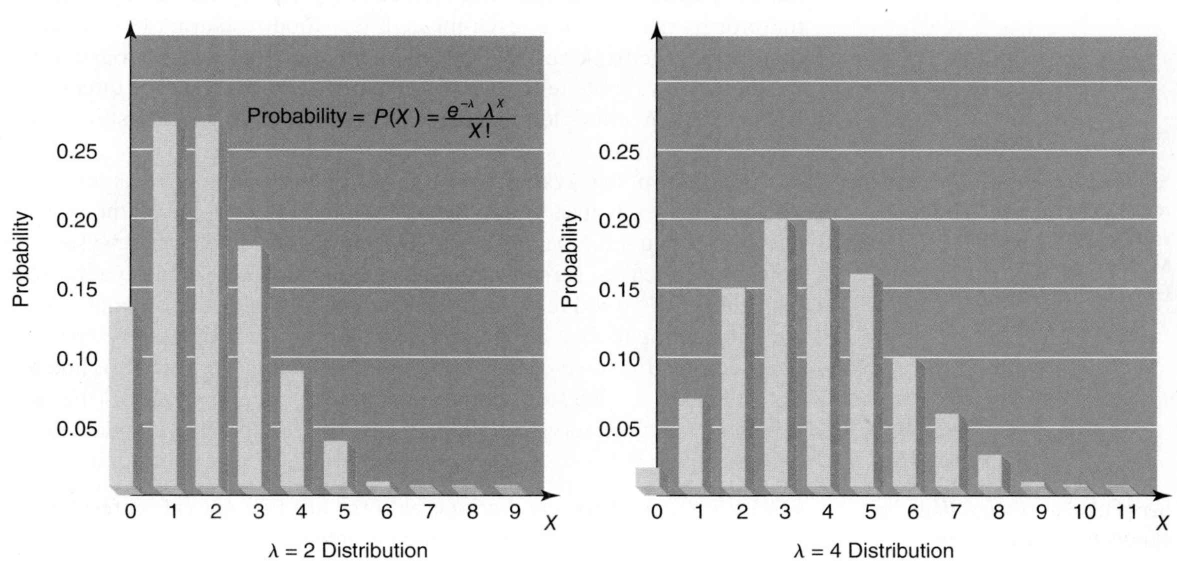

[2]The term $X!$, called *X factorial*, is defined as $(X)(X-1)(X-2)\ldots(3)(2)(1)$. For example, $5! = (5)(4)(3)(2)(1) = 120$. By definition, $0! = 1$.

join a queue because it is too long to suit their needs or interests. **Reneging** customers are those who enter the queue but then become impatient and leave without completing their transaction. Actually, both of these situations serve to accentuate the need for queuing models. How many times have you seen a shopper with a basket full of groceries, including perishables such as milk, frozen food, or meats, simply abandon the shopping cart before checking out because the queue was too long? This expensive occurrence for the store makes managers acutely aware of the importance of service-level decisions.

Queue Characteristics

The models in this chapter assume unlimited queue length.

The queue itself is the second component of a queuing system. The *length* of a queue can be either limited (finite) or unlimited (infinite). A queue is said to be limited when it cannot increase to an infinite length due to physical or other restrictions. For example, the queue at a bank's drive-up window may be limited to 10 cars due to space limitations. Or, the number of people waiting for service in an airline's phone reservation system may be limited to 30 due to the number of telephone lines available. In contrast, a queue is defined as unlimited when its size is unrestricted, as in the case of the tollbooth serving arriving automobiles. In all the analytic queuing models we discuss in this chapter, we assume that queue lengths are *unlimited.*

Most queuing models use the **first-in, first-out** *rule. This is obviously not appropriate in all service systems, especially those dealing with emergencies.*

A second waiting line characteristic deals with **queue discipline**. This refers to the rule by which customers in the line are to receive service. Most systems use a queue discipline known as the **first-in, first-out (FIFO)** rule. However, in places such as a hospital emergency room or an express checkout line at a supermarket, various assigned priorities may preempt FIFO. Patients who are critically injured will move ahead in treatment priority over patients with broken fingers or noses. Shoppers with fewer than 10 items may be allowed to enter the express checkout queue but are then treated as first-come, first-served. Computer programming runs are another example of queuing systems that operate under priority scheduling. In many large companies, when computer-produced paychecks are due out on a specific date, the payroll program has highest priority over other runs.[3]

Service Facility Characteristics

The third part of a queuing system is the service facility itself. It is important to examine two basic properties: (1) the configuration of the service facility and (2) the pattern of service times (or the service distribution) at the facility.

Service facilities can either have a single server or multiple servers.

CONFIGURATION OF THE SERVICE FACILITY Service facilities are usually classified in terms of the number of servers (or channels) and the number of phases (or service stops) that must be made. A **single-server queuing system** is typified by the drive-in bank that has only one open teller or by the type of a drive-through fast-food restaurant that has a similar setup. If, on the other hand, the bank has several tellers on duty and each customer waits in one common line for the first available teller, we would have a **multiple-server queuing system** at work. Many banks today are multiple-server service systems, as are most post offices and many airline ticket counters.

Single-phase *means the customer receives service at only one station before leaving the system.* **Multiphase** *implies two or more stops before leaving the system.*

A **single-phase system** is one in which the customer receives service from only one station and then exits the system. A fast-food restaurant in which the person who takes your order also brings you the food and takes your money is a single-phase system. So is a driver's license bureau in which the person taking your application also grades your test and collects the license fee. But if a fast-food restaurant requires you to place your order at one station, pay at a second, and pick up the food at a third service stop, it is a **multiphase system**. Similarly, if the driver's license bureau is large or busy, you will probably have to wait in line to complete the application (the first service stop), queue again to have the test graded (the second service stop), and finally go to a third service counter to pay the fee. To help you relate the concepts of servers and phases, Figure 9.3 presents four possible service facility configurations.

Service times often follow the **exponential distribution.**

SERVICE DISTRIBUTION Service patterns are like arrival patterns in that they can be either constant or random. If the service time is constant, it takes the same amount of time to take care

[3] The term FIFS (*first-in, first-served*) is often used in place of FIFO. Another discipline, LIFS (*last-in, first-served*), is commonly used when material is stacked or piled and the items on top are used first.

FIGURE 9.3 Four Basic Queuing System Configurations

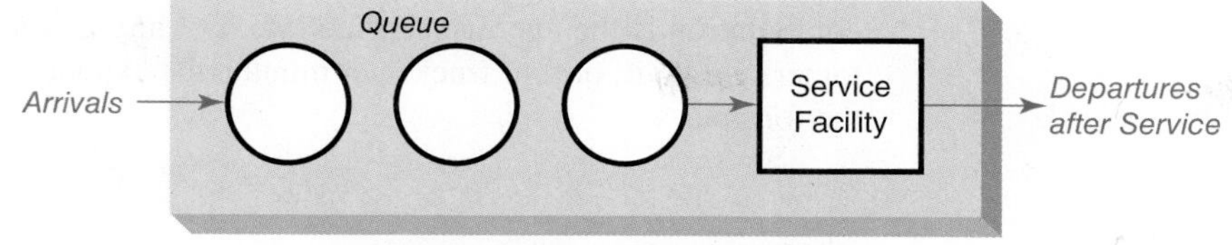

Single-Server, Single-Phase System

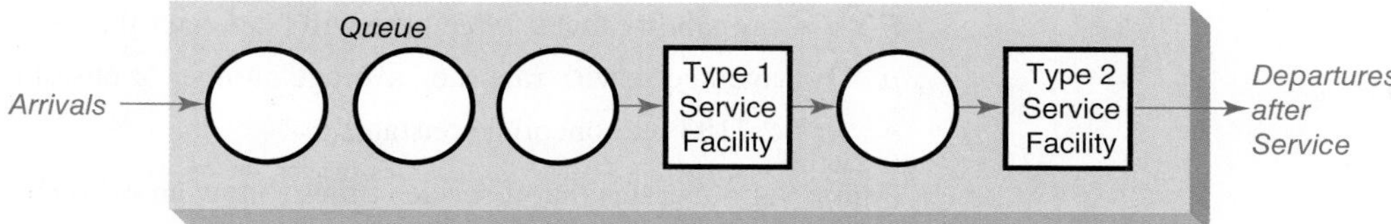

Single-Server, Multiphase System

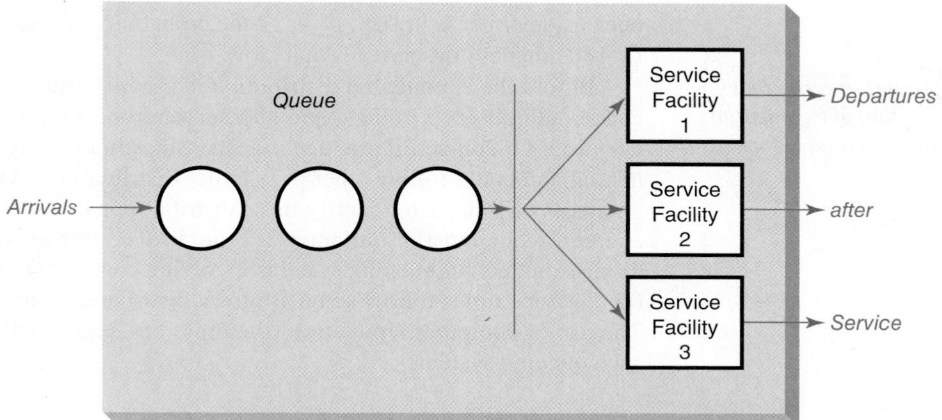

Multiple-Server, Single-Phase System

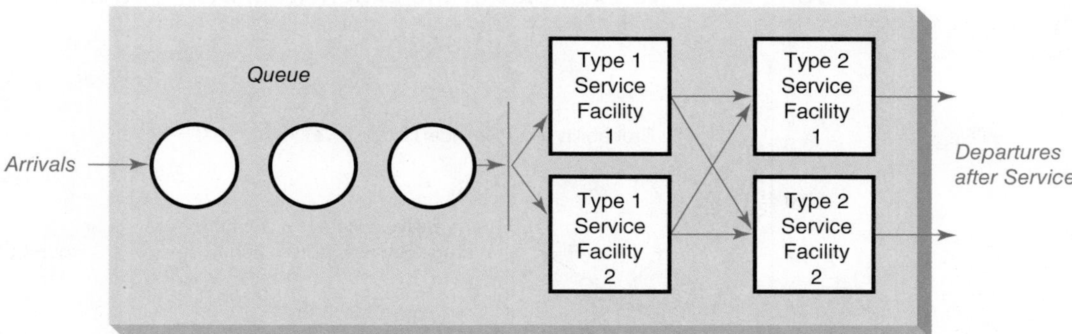

Multiple-Server, Multiphase System

of each customer. This is the case, for example, in a machine-performed service operation such as an automatic car wash. More often, however, service times are randomly distributed. Even in such situations, it turns out that we can estimate service times in many real-world queuing problems by using a probability distribution known as the **exponential distribution**.

The Poisson and exponential probability distributions are directly related to each other. If the number of arrivals follows a Poisson distribution, it turns out that the time between successive arrivals follows an exponential distribution. Processes that follow these distributions are commonly referred to as *Markovian* processes.

Just as we did with arrivals, we need to distinguish here between service rate and service time. While the service rate denotes the number of units served in a given interval of time, the service time denotes the length of time taken to actually perform the service. Although the exponential distribution estimates the probability of service times, the parameter used in this computation is the average service rate. For any given average service rate, such as two customers per hour, or four trucks per minute, the exponential distribution can be established using the formula

$$P(t) = e^{-\mu t} \quad \text{for } t \geq 0 \tag{9-2}$$

where

t = service time

$P(t)$ = probability that service time will be greater than t

μ = average service rate (i.e., average number of customers served per unit of time)

e = 2.7183 (exponential constant)

Figure 9.4 illustrates that if service times follow an exponential distribution, the probability of any very long service time is low. For example, when the average service *rate* is 3 customers per hour (i.e., the average service *time* is 20 minutes per customer), seldom, if ever, will a customer require more than 1.5 hours (= 90 minutes). Likewise, if the average service rate is one customer per hour (i.e., $\mu = 1$), the probability of the customer spending more than 3 hours (=180 minutes) in service is quite low.

It is important to verify that the assumption of exponential service times is valid before applying the model.

Before the exponential distribution is used in a queuing model, the decision modeler can and should observe, collect, and plot service time data to determine whether they fit the distribution. Of course, in practice, service times in queuing systems need not always be exponential and could follow other probability distributions. As with arrivals, the use of statistical goodness of fit tests to identify these distributions is discussed in more advanced texts. In this chapter, while most of our analytical models assume exponential service times, we will also discuss models for queuing systems involving constant service times and general service times (i.e., service times follow some arbitrary distribution with mean μ and standard deviation σ). The use of computer simulation (the topic of Chapter 10) is another approach for analyzing such queuing systems.

FIGURE 9.4 Two Examples of the Exponential Distribution for Service Times

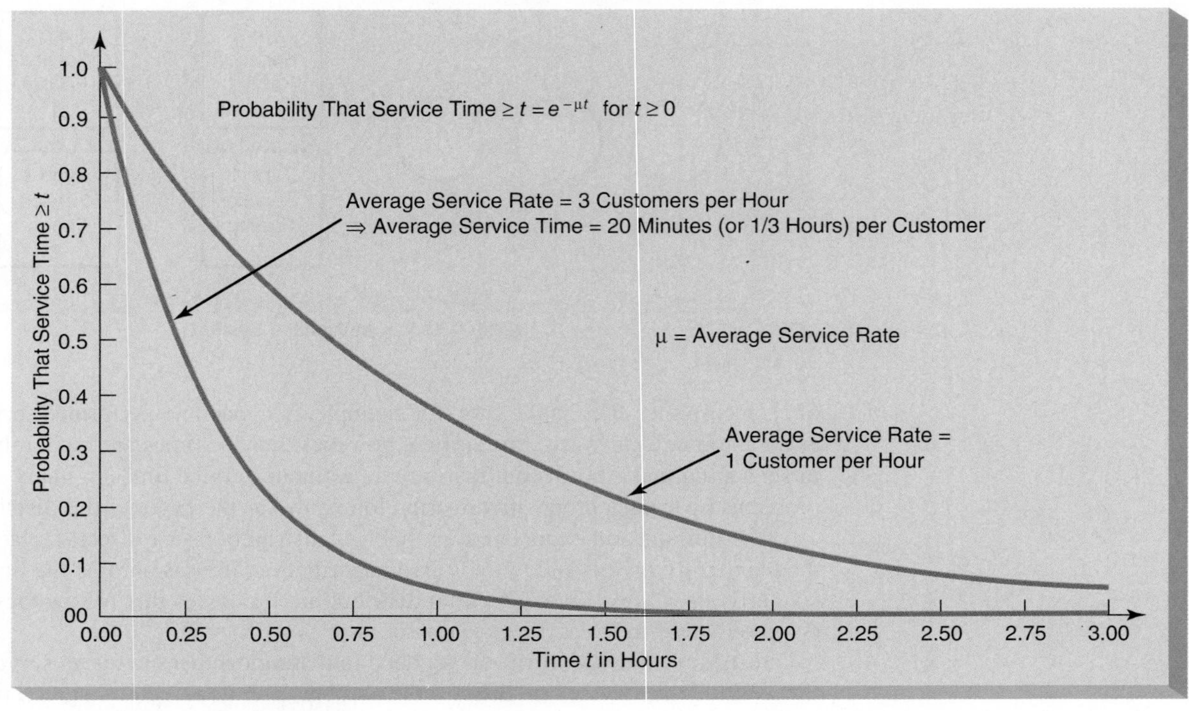

Measuring the Queue's Performance

Queuing models can help a manager obtain many performance measures (also known as **operating characteristics**) of a waiting line system. We list here some of the measures commonly used in practice. For each performance measure, we also list the standard notation that is used:

Here is a list of the key operating characteristics of a queuing system.

- ρ = **utilization factor** of the system (i.e., the probability that all servers are busy)
- L_q = average length (i.e., the number of customers) of the queue
- L = average number of customers in the system (i.e., the number in the queue plus the number being served)
- W_q = average time that each customer spends in the queue
- W = average time that each customer spends in the system (i.e., the time spent waiting plus the time spent being served)
- P_0 = probability that there are no customers in the system (i.e., the probability that the service facility will be idle)
- P_n = probability that there are exactly n customers in the system

Kendall's Notation for Queuing Systems

Kendall's notation is used to classify queuing systems.

In queuing theory we commonly use a three-symbol notation, known as *Kendall's notation*, to classify the wide variety of queuing models that are possible in practice. The three-symbol notation is as follows:

$$A/B/s$$

where

A = the arrival probability distribution. Typical choices are M (Markovian) for a Poisson distribution, D for a constant or deterministic distribution, or G for a general distribution with known mean and variance.

B = the service time probability distribution. Typical choices are M for an exponential distribution, D for a constant or deterministic distribution, or G for a general distribution with known mean and variance.

s = number of servers.

Using Kendall's notation, we would denote a single-server queuing system with Poisson arrival and exponential service time distributions as an M/M/1 system. If this system had two servers, we would then classify it as an M/M/2 system.

Kendall's three-symbol notation is sometimes extended to include five symbols.

Kendall's notation has sometimes been extended to include five symbols. The first three symbols are the same as just discussed. The fourth symbol denotes the maximum allowable length of the queue. It is used in systems in which there is a **finite, or limited, queue length**. The fifth symbol denotes the size of the arrival population. It is used in systems in which the size of the arrival population is finite. By default, if these two symbols are omitted, their values are assumed to be infinity. Hence, the M/M/1 notation discussed previously corresponds to an M/M/1/∞/∞ queuing system.

Variety of Queuing Models Studied Here

We study five commonly used queuing models here.

Although a wide variety of queuing models can be applied in practice, we introduce you to five of the most widely used models in this chapter. These are outlined in Table 9.2, and examples of each follow in the next few sections. More complex models are described in queuing theory textbooks[4] or can be developed through the use of computer simulation (which is the focus of Chapter 10). Note that all five of the queuing models listed in Table 9.2 have five characteristics in common. They all assume the following:

1. Arrivals that follow the Poisson probability distribution.
2. FIFO queue discipline.
3. A single-phase service facility.

[4] See, for example, B. D. Bunday. *An Introduction to Queuing Theory*. New York: Halsted Press, 1996, or C. H. Ng. *Queuing Modeling Fundamentals*. New York: Wiley, 1997.

TABLE 9.2 Queuing Models Described in This Chapter

NAME (KENDALL NOTATION)	EXAMPLE	NUMBER OF SERVERS	NUMBER OF PHASES	ARRIVAL RATE PATTERN	SERVICE TIME PATTERN	POPLN. SIZE	QUEUE DISCIP.
Simple system (M/M/1)	Information counter at department store	Single	Single	Poisson	Exponential	Unlimited	FIFO
Multiple-server (M/M/s)	Airline ticket counter	Multiple	Single	Poisson	Exponential	Unlimited	FIFO
Constant service (M/D/1)	Automated car wash	Single	Single	Poisson	Constant	Unlimited	FIFO
General service (M/G/1)	Auto repair shop	Single	Single	Poisson	General	Unlimited	FIFO
Limited population (M/M/s/∞/N)	Shop with exactly ten machines that might break	Multiple	Single	Poisson	Exponential	Limited	FIFO

4. **Infinite, or unlimited, queue length**. That is, the fourth symbol in Kendall's notation is ∞.
5. Service systems that operate under steady, ongoing conditions. This means that both arrival rates and service rates remain stable during the analysis.

9.4 Single-Server Queuing System with Poisson Arrivals and Exponential Service Times (M/M/1 Model)

In this section we present a decision model to determine the operating characteristics of an **M/M/1** queuing system. After these numeric measures have been computed, we then add in cost data and begin to make decisions that balance desirable service levels with queuing costs.

Assumptions of the M/M/1 Queuing Model

The single-server, single-phase model we consider here is one of the most widely used and simplest queuing models. It assumes that seven conditions exist:

These seven assumptions must be met if the single-server, single-phase model is to be applied.

1. Arrivals are served on a FIFO basis.
2. Every arrival waits to be served, regardless of the length of the line; that is, there is no balking or reneging.

IN ACTION **IBM Uses Queuing Analysis to Improve Semiconductor Production**

IBM's 300 mm fabrication (fab) facility in East Fishkill, New York cost more than $4 billion to build. High capacity utilization and short lead times are keys to reducing the cost per wafer, expediting time to market, and improving profitability and yield. IBM's managers and engineers therefore maintain constant focus on balancing future demand, equipment utilization, bottlenecks, and lead times.

To help in this effort, IBM developed an advanced queuing network model called Enterprise Production Planning and Optimization System (EPOS) to address both short-term tactical capacity planning and long-term strategic capital investment planning. EPOS enhances prior queuing network models by not only adding the ability to model product-specific batch arrivals and service, but also by embedding a linear program to help decide which lot to allocate to which queue when route choices are present.

Since its implementation, EPOS has become an integral part of IBM's efforts to improve factory performance by predicting bottlenecks, managing lead times, prioritizing continuous-improvement efforts, and planning capital equipment investments, thus helping IBM reduce expenses by tens of millions of dollars.

Source: Based on S. M. Brown et al. "Queuing Model Improves IBM's Semiconductor Capacity and Lead-Time Management," *Interfaces* 40, 5 (September–October 2010): 397–407.

3. Arrivals are independent of preceding arrivals, but the average number of arrivals (the arrival rate) does not change over time.
4. Arrivals are described by a Poisson probability distribution and come from an infinite or very large population.
5. Service times also vary from one customer to the next and are independent of one another, but their average rate is known.
6. Service times occur according to the exponential probability distribution.
7. The average service rate is greater than the average arrival rate; that is, $\mu > \lambda$. If this condition does not hold (and $\mu \leq \lambda$), the queue length will grow indefinitely because the service facility does not have the capacity to handle the arriving customers (on average).

When these seven conditions are met, we can develop equations that define the system's operating characteristics. The mathematics used to derive each equation is rather complex and beyond the scope of this textbook, so we will just present the resulting equations here.

We use Excel templates to calculate operating characteristics for our queuing models.

Although we could calculate the operating characteristic equations for *all* the queuing systems discussed in this chapter by hand, doing so can be quite cumbersome. An easier approach is to develop Excel worksheets for these formulas and use them for all calculations. This allows us to focus on what is really important for managers: the interpretation and use of the results of queuing models. Therefore, we adopt this approach in our discussions in this chapter.

Operating Characteristic Equations for an M/M/1 Queuing System

We let

$$\lambda = \text{average number of arrivals per time period (e.g., per hour)}$$

$$\mu = \text{average number of people or items served per time period}$$

λ and μ must both be rates and be defined for the same time interval.

It is very important to note two issues here. First, both λ and μ must be rates. That is, they must denote the average number of occurrences per a given time interval. Second, both λ and μ must be defined for the *same time interval*. That is, if λ denotes the average number of units arriving *per hour*, then μ must denote the average number of units served *per hour*. As noted earlier, it is necessary for the average service rate to be greater than the average arrival rate (i.e., $\mu > \lambda$). The operating characteristic equations for the M/M/1 queuing system are as follows:

These seven queuing equations for the single-server, single-phase model describe the important operating characteristics of the service system.

1. Average server utilization in the system:

$$\rho = \lambda/\mu \tag{9-3}$$

2. Average number of customers or units waiting in line for service:

$$L_q = \frac{\lambda^2}{\mu(\mu - \lambda)} \tag{9-4}$$

3. Average number of customers or units in the system:

$$L = L_q + \lambda/\mu \tag{9-5}$$

4. Average time a customer or unit spends waiting in line for service:

$$W_q = \frac{L_q}{\lambda} = \frac{\lambda}{\mu(\mu - \lambda)} \tag{9-6}$$

5. Average time a customer or unit spends in the system (namely, in the queue or being served):

$$W = W_q + 1/\mu \tag{9-7}$$

6. Probability that there are zero customers or units in the system:

$$P_0 = 1 - \lambda/\mu \tag{9-8}$$

7. Probability that there are n customers or units in the system:

$$P_n = (\lambda/\mu)^n P_0 \tag{9-9}$$

Arnold's Muffler Shop Example

We now apply these formulas to the queuing problem faced by Arnold's Muffler Shop in New Orleans. Customers needing new mufflers arrive at the shop on the average of two per hour. Arnold's mechanic, Reid Blank, is able to perform this service at an average rate of three per hour, or about one every 20 minutes. Larry Arnold, the shop owner, studied queuing models in an MBA program and feels that all seven of the conditions for a single-server queuing model are met. He proceeds to calculate the numeric values of the operating characteristics of his queuing system.

Using ExcelModules for Queuing Model Computations

ExcelModules includes worksheets for all the queuing models discussed in this chapter.

Excel Note

- The Companion Website for this textbook, at www.pearsonhighered.com/balakrishnan, contains a set of Excel worksheets, bundled together in a software package called ExcelModules. The procedure for installing and running this program, as well as a brief description of its contents, is given in Appendix B.
- The Companion Website also provides the Excel file for each sample problem discussed here. The relevant file name is shown in the margin next to each example.
- For clarity, all worksheets for queuing models in ExcelModules are color coded as follows:
  - *Input cells*, where we enter the problem data, are shaded yellow.
  - *Output cells*, which show results, are shaded green.

When we run the ExcelModules program, we see a new tab titled ExcelModules in Excel's Ribbon. We select this tab and then click the Modules icon followed by the Queuing Models menu. The choices shown in Screenshot 9-1A are displayed. From these choices, we select the appropriate queuing model.

When *any* of the queuing models is selected in ExcelModules, we are first presented with an option to specify a title for the problem (see Screenshot 9-1B). The default title is Problem Title.

To analyze M/M/1 systems, we use the M/M/s worksheet in ExcelModules and set s = 1.

EXCELMODULES SOLUTION FOR ARNOLD'S MUFFLER SHOP The M/M/1 queuing model is included in ExcelModules as a special case of the M/M/s model with s = 1. Hence, to analyze Arnold's problem, we select the choice labeled Exponential Service Times (M/M/s), shown in

SCREENSHOT 9-1A Queuing Models Menu in ExcelModules

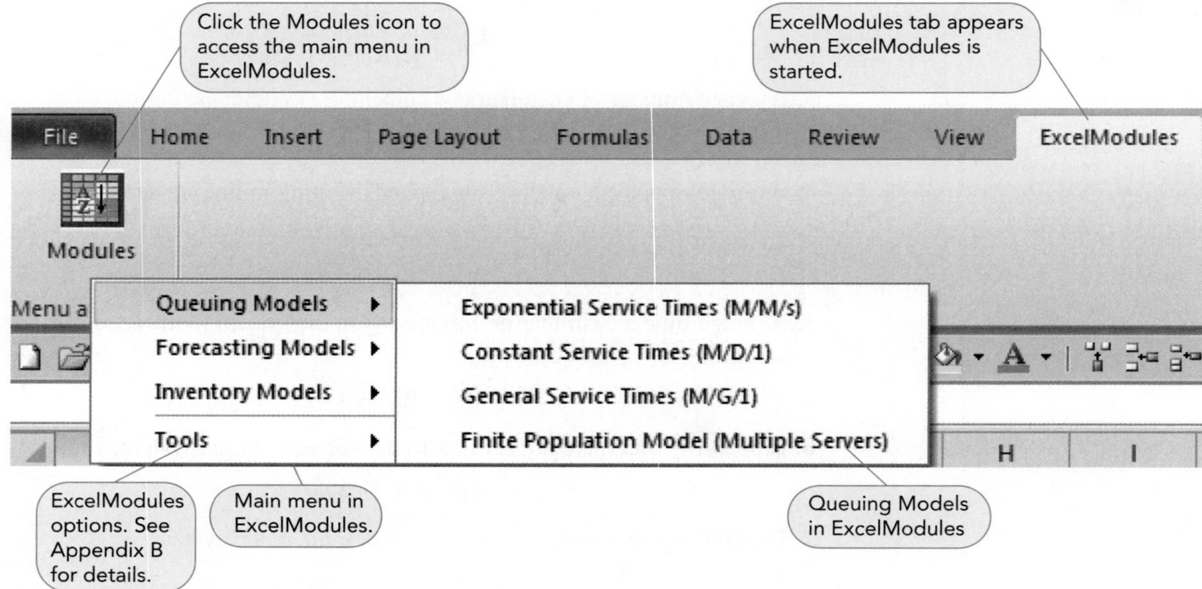

SCREENSHOT 9-1B
Input Window for Optional Problem Title

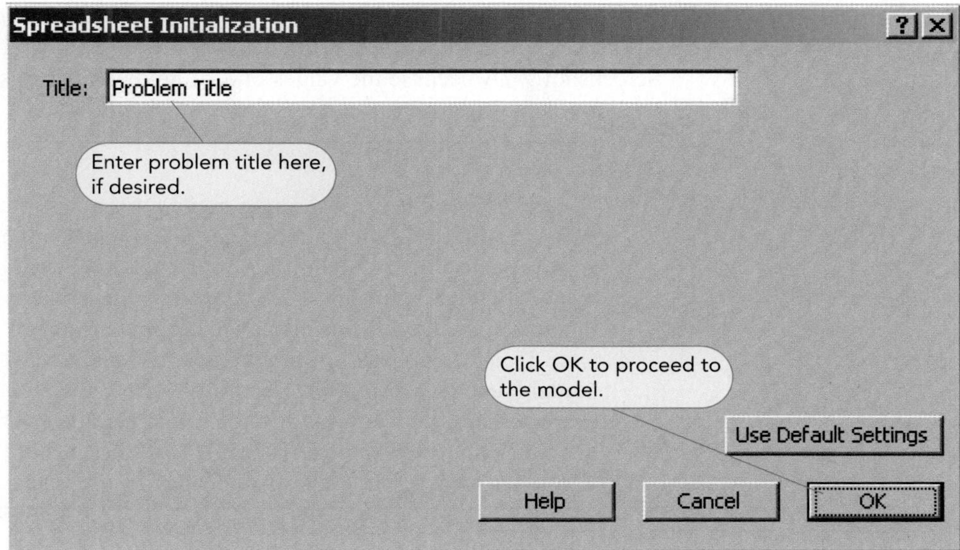

File: 9-2.xls, sheet: 9-2A

Screenshot 9-1A. When we click OK after entering the problem title, we get the screen shown in Screenshot 9-2A. Each queuing worksheet in ExcelModules includes one or more messages specific to that model. It is important to note and follow the messages. For example, the M/M/s worksheet includes the following two messages:

1. Both λ and μ must be RATES and use the same time unit. For example, given a service time such as 10 minutes per customer, convert it to a service rate such as 6 per hour.
2. The total service rate (rate $\times$ servers) must be greater than the arrival rate.

SCREENSHOT 9-2A M/M/s Worksheet in ExcelModules

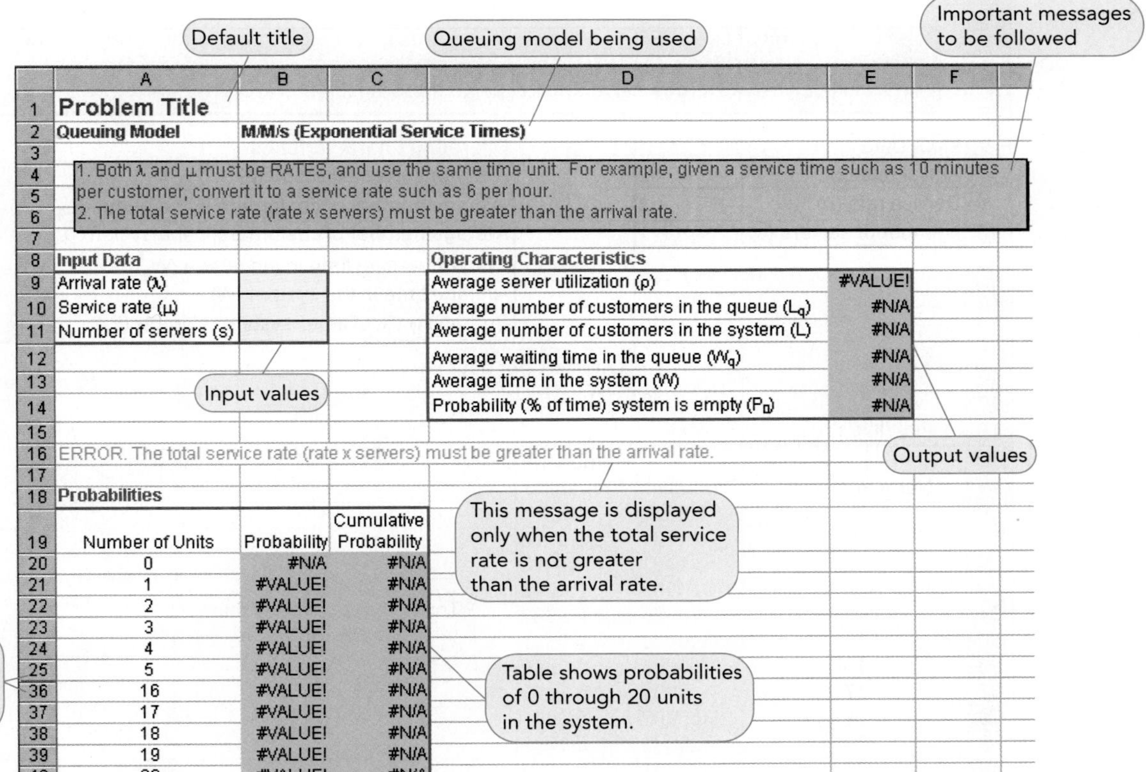

Important: *The total service rate must exceed the arrival rate.*

If the total average service rate ($\mu \times s$) does *not* exceed the average arrival rate (λ), the worksheet will automatically print the error message shown in row 16. This message is seen in Screenshot 9-2A because the values of λ, μ, and number of servers (s) have not been input yet and have defaulted to zero values.

Excel Notes

- The worksheets in ExcelModules contain formulas to compute the operating characteristics for different queuing models. The default values of zero for input data such as λ and μ cause the results of these formulas to initially appear as #N/A, #VALUE!, or #DIV/0! (see Screenshot 9-2A). However, as soon as we enter valid values for these input data, the worksheets display the formula results.
- Once ExcelModules has been used to create an Excel worksheet for a particular queuing model (such as M/M/s), the resulting worksheet can be used to compute the operating characteristics with several different input parameter values. For example, we can enter different input values in cells B9:B11 of Screenshot 9-2A and compute the resulting operating characteristic values without having to create a *new* M/M/s worksheet each time.

File: 9-2.xls, sheet: 9-2B

In Larry Arnold's case, the average arrival rate (λ) is two cars per hour. The average service rate (μ) is three mufflers per hour. We therefore enter these values in cells B9 and B10, respectively, as shown in Screenshot 9-2B. The number of servers (cell B11) equals one here because there is only one mechanic.

SCREENSHOT 9-2B Operating Characteristics with μ = 3 for Arnold's Muffler Shop: M/M/1 Queuing System

Problem title

M/M/s with s = 1 is the M/M/1 model.

Arnold's Muffler Shop

Queuing Model — M/M/s (Exponential Service Times)

1. Both λ and μ must be RATES, and use the same time unit. For example, given a service time such as 10 minutes per customer, convert it to a service rate such as 6 per hour.
2. The total service rate (rate x servers) must be greater than the arrival rate.

Input Data	
Arrival rate (λ)	2
Service rate (μ)	3
Number of servers (s)	1

2 cars per hour

3 mufflers per hour

One mechanic

Operating Characteristics	
Average server utilization (ρ)	0.6667
Average number of customers in the queue (L_q)	1.3333
Average number of customers in the system (L)	2.0000
Average waiting time in the queue (W_q)	0.6667
Average time in the system (W)	1.0000
Probability (% of time) system is empty (P_0)	0.3333

Mechanic is busy 67% of the time.

0.67 hours = 40 minutes

= 60 minutes

Probabilities

Number of Units	Probability	Cumulative Probability
0	0.3333	0.3333
1	0.2222	0.5556
2	0.1481	0.7037
3	0.0988	0.8025
4	0.0658	0.8683
5	0.0439	0.9122
16	0.0005	0.9990
17	0.0003	0.9993
18	0.0002	0.9995
19	0.0002	0.9997
20	0.0001	0.9998

This is the probability that there are ≤ 4 cars in the system.

The worksheet now displays the operating characteristics of this queuing system in cells E9:E14. In addition, the worksheet computes the probability that there are exactly n customers in the system, for $n = 0$ through 20. Cumulative probabilities (i.e., the probability that there are n or *fewer* customers) are also calculated. These values are shown in cells A19:C40.

We get the results for the Arnold's Muffler Shop problem.

The results show that there are, on average, two cars in the system (i.e., $L = 2$), and each car spends an average of one hour in the system (i.e., $W = 1$ hour). The corresponding values for the waiting line alone (not including the server) are $L_q = 1.33$ cars, and $W_q = 0.667$ hours (or 40 minutes). The mechanic (server) is busy 67% of the time (i.e., the utilization factor $\rho = 0.67$). The fact that there is only one mechanic implies that an arriving car has a 33% chance of not having to wait ($P_0 = 0.33$).

Cost Analysis of the Queuing System

Conducting an economic analysis is the next step. It permits cost factors to be included.

Now that the operating characteristics of the queuing system have been computed, Arnold decides to do an economic analysis of their impact. The queuing model was valuable in predicting potential waiting times, queue lengths, idle times, and so on. But it did not identify optimal decisions or consider cost factors. As stated earlier, the solution to a queuing problem may require a manager to make a trade-off between the increased cost of providing better service and the decreased waiting costs derived from providing that service.

Customer waiting time is often considered the most important factor.

Arnold estimates that the cost of customer waiting time, in terms of customer dissatisfaction and lost goodwill, is $10 per hour spent in his shop. Observe that this time includes the time a customer's car is waiting in the queue for service as well as the time when the car is actually being serviced. The only cost of providing service that Arnold can identify is the salary of Reid Blank, the mechanic, who is paid $12 per hour.

Waiting costs plus service costs equal total cost.

The total cost, defined as the sum of the waiting cost and the service cost, is calculated as follows:

$$\text{Total cost} = C_w \times L + C_s \times s \tag{9-10}$$

where

C_w = customer waiting cost per unit time period

L = average number of customers in the system

C_s = cost of providing service per server per unit time period

s = number of servers in the queuing system

In Arnold's case, $C_w = \$10$ per hour, $L = 2$ (see Screenshot 9-2B), $C_s = \$12$ per hour, and $s = 1$ (because there is only one mechanic). Hence, Arnold computes his total cost as $\$10 \times 2 + \$12 \times 1 = \$32$ per hour.

Increasing the Service Rate

Now Arnold faces a decision. He finds out through the muffler business grapevine that Rusty Muffler Shop, a crosstown competitor, employs a mechanic named Jimmy Smith who can install new mufflers at an average rate of four per hour. Larry Arnold contacts Smith and inquires as to his interest in switching employers. Smith says that he would consider leaving Rusty Muffler Shop but only if he were paid a $15 per hour salary. Arnold, being a crafty businessman, decides to check whether it would be worthwhile to fire Blank and replace him with the speedier but more expensive Smith.

File: 9-2.xls, sheet: 9-2C

Arnold first recomputes all the operating characteristics, using a new average service rate (μ) of four mufflers per hour. The average arrival rate (λ) remains at two cars per hour. The revised characteristic values if Smith is employed are shown in Screenshot 9-2C.

It is quite evident that Smith's higher average rate (four mufflers per hour compared to Blank's three mufflers per hour) will result in shorter queues and waiting times. For example, a customer would now spend an average of only 0.5 hours in the system (i.e., $W = 0.5$) and 0.25 hours waiting in the queue ($W_q = 0.25$) as opposed to 1 hour in the system and 0.67 hours in the queue with Blank as the mechanic. The average number of customers in the system (L) decreases from two units to one unit.

SCREENSHOT 9-2C Revised Operating Characteristics with $\mu = 4$ for Arnold's Muffler Shop: M/M/1 Queuing System

	A	B	C	D	E	F
1	Arnold's Muffler Shop					
2	Queuing Model	M/M/s (Exponential Service Times)				
3						
4	1. Both λ and μ must be RATES, and use the same time unit. For example, given a service time such as 10 minutes					
5	per customer, convert it to a service rate such as 6 per hour.					
6	2. The total service rate (rate x servers) must be greater than the arrival rate.					
7						
8	Input Data			Operating Characteristics		
9	Arrival rate (λ)	2		Average server utilization (ρ)	0.5000	
10	Service rate (μ)	4		Average number of customers in the queue (L_q)	0.5000	
11	Number of servers (s)	1		Average number of customers in the system (L)	1.0000	
12				Average waiting time in the queue (W_q)	0.2500	
13				Average time in the system (W)	0.5000	
14				Probability (% of time) system is empty (P_0)	0.5000	
15						
16						
17						
18	Probabilities					
19	Number of Units	Probability	Cumulative Probability			
20	0	0.5000	0.5000			
21	1	0.2500	0.7500			
22	2	0.1250	0.8750			
23	3	0.0625	0.9375			
24	4	0.0313	0.9688			
25	5	0.0156	0.9844			
36	16	0.0000	1.0000			
37	17	0.0000	1.0000			
38	18	0.0000	1.0000			
39	19	0.0000	1.0000			
40	20	0.0000	1.0000			

Here is a comparison of total costs, using the two different mechanics.

Arnold revises his economic analysis with the new information. The revised values are $C_w = \$10$ per hour, $L = 1$ (see Screenshot 9-2C), $C_s = \$15$ per hour, and $s = 1$ (because there is still only one mechanic). Hence, Arnold's revised total cost with Smith as the mechanic is $\$10 \times 1 + \$15 \times 1 = \$25$ per hour. Because the total cost with Blank as the mechanic was \$32 per hour, Arnold may very well decide to hire Smith and reduce his cost by \$7 per hour (or \$56 per 8-hour day).

9.5 Multiple-Server Queuing System with Poisson Arrivals and Exponential Service Times (M/M/S Model)

The next logical step is to look at a multiple-server queuing system, in which two or more servers are available to handle arriving customers. Let us still assume that customers awaiting service form one single line and then proceed to the first available server. An example of such a multiple-server, single-phase waiting line is found in many banks or post offices today. A common line is formed, and the customer at the head of the line proceeds to the first free teller or clerk. (Refer to Figure 9.3 on page for a typical multiple-server configuration.)

The multiple-server model also assumes Poisson arrivals and exponential services.

The multiple-server system presented here again assumes that arrivals follow a Poisson probability distribution and that service times are distributed exponentially. Service is first come, first served, and all servers are assumed to perform at the same average rate.[5] Other assumptions listed earlier for the single-server model apply as well.

[5]Analytical models for multiserver queuing systems where different servers perform at different average rates are beyond the scope of this textbook.

Operating Characteristic Equations for an M/M/s Queuing System

We let

$$\lambda = \text{average number of arrivals per time (e.g., per hour)}$$
$$\mu = \text{average number of customers served per time } \textit{per server}$$
$$s = \text{number of servers}$$

As with the M/M/1 system, with an **M/M/s** system, it is very important that we define both λ and μ for the *same time interval*. It is also important to note that the average service rate μ is defined *per server*. That is, if there are two servers and each server is capable of handling an average of three customers per hour, μ is defined as three per hour, *not* six per hour $(= 2 \times 3)$. Finally, as noted earlier, it is necessary for the average total service rate to be greater than the average arrival rate (that is, $s\mu > \lambda$).

The operating characteristic equations for the M/M/s queuing system are as follows:

1. Average server utilization in the system:

$$\rho = \lambda/(s\mu) \qquad \textbf{(9-11)}$$

2. Probability that there are zero customers or units in the system:

$$P_0 = \frac{1}{\left[\sum_{k=0}^{s-1} \frac{1}{k!}\left(\frac{\lambda}{\mu}\right)^k\right] + \frac{1}{s!}\left(\frac{\lambda}{\mu}\right)^s \frac{s\mu}{(s\mu - \lambda)}} \qquad \textbf{(9-12)}$$

3. Average number of customers or units waiting in line for service:

$$L_q = \frac{(\lambda/\mu)^s \lambda\mu}{(s-1)!(s\mu - \lambda)^2} P_0 \qquad \textbf{(9-13)}$$

4. Average number of customers or units in the system:

$$L = L_q + \lambda/\mu \qquad \textbf{(9-14)}$$

5. Average time a customer or unit spends waiting in line for service:

$$W_q = L_q/\lambda \qquad \textbf{(9-15)}$$

6. Average time a customer or unit spends in the system:

$$W = W_q + 1/\mu \qquad \textbf{(9-16)}$$

7. Probability that there are n customers or units in the system:

$$P_n = \frac{(\lambda/\mu)^n}{n!} P_0 \quad \text{for } n \le s \qquad \textbf{(9-17)}$$

$$P_n = \frac{(\lambda/\mu)^n}{s!s^{(n-s)}} P_0 \quad \text{for } n > s \qquad \textbf{(9-18)}$$

These equations are more complex than the ones used in the single-server model. Yet they are used in exactly the same fashion and provide the same type of information as those in the simpler M/M/1 model.

Arnold's Muffler Shop Revisited

For an application of the multiple-server queuing model, let us return to Arnold's Muffler Shop problem. Earlier, Larry Arnold examined two options. He could retain his current mechanic, Reid Blank, at a total system cost of \$32 per hour, or he could fire Blank and hire a slightly more expensive but faster worker named Jimmy Smith. With Smith on board, the system cost could be reduced to \$25 per hour.

The muffler shop considers opening a second muffler service bay that operates at the same speed as the first one.

Arnold now explores a third option. He finds that at minimal after-tax cost, he can open a second service bay in which mufflers can be installed. Instead of firing his first mechanic, Blank, he would hire a second mechanic, Joel Simpson. The new mechanic would be able to install mufflers at the same average rate as Blank ($\mu = 3$ per hour) and be paid the same salary as Blank ($12 per hour). Customers, who would still arrive at the average rate of $\lambda = 2$ per hour, would wait in a single line until one of the two mechanics became available. To find out how this option compares with the old single-server queuing system, Arnold computes the operating characteristics for the M/M/2 system.

File: 9-3.xls

Remember that in the M/M/s model, the average service rate is μ per server.

EXCELMODULES SOLUTION FOR ARNOLD'S MUFFLER SHOP WITH TWO MECHANICS Once again, we select the choice titled Exponential Service Times (M/M/s) from the Queuing Models menu in ExcelModules (see Screenshot 9-1A on page 378). After entering the optional title, we enter the input data as shown in Screenshot 9-3. For Arnold's problem, observe that the average arrival rate (λ) is two cars per hour. The average service rate (μ) is three mufflers per hour *per mechanic*. We enter these values in cells B9 and B10, respectively. The number of servers (cell B11) is two because there are now two mechanics.

The worksheet now displays the operating characteristics of this queuing system in cells E9:E14. Probabilities of having a specific number of units in the system are shown in cells A19:C40. Arnold first compares these results with the earlier results. The information is summarized in Table 9.3. The increased service from opening a second bay has a dramatic effect on almost all results. In particular, average time spent waiting in line (W_q) drops down from 40 minutes with only Blank working or 15 minutes with only Smith working, to only 2.5 minutes with Blank and Simpson working! Similarly, the average number of cars in the system (L) falls to 0.75.[6] But does this mean that a second bay should be opened?

We dramatically lower waiting time results by opening the second service bay.

SCREENSHOT 9-3 Revised Operating Characteristics for Arnold's Muffler Shop: M/M/2 Queuing System

	A	B	C	D	E
1	Arnold's Muffler Shop				
2	Queuing Model	M/M/s (Exponential Service Times)			
3					
4	1. Both λ and μ must be RATES, and use the same time unit. For example, given a service time such as 10 minutes				
5	per customer, convert it to a service rate such as 6 per hour.				
6	2. The total service rate (rate x servers) must be greater than the arrival rate.				
7					
8	Input Data			Operating Characteristics	
9	Arrival rate (λ)	2		Average server utilization (ρ)	0.3333
10	Service rate (μ)	3		Average number of customers in the queue (L_q)	0.0833
11	Number of servers (s)	2		Average number of customers in the system (L)	0.7500
12				Average waiting time in the queue (W_q)	0.0417
13				Average time in the system (W)	0.3750
14				Probability (% of time) system is empty (P_0)	0.5000
15					
16					
17					
18	Probabilities				
19	Number of Units	Probability	Cumulative Probability		
20	0	0.5000	0.5000		
21	1	0.3333	0.8333		
22	2	0.1111	0.9444		
23	3	0.0370	0.9815		
24	4	0.0123	0.9938		
25	5	0.0041	0.9979		
36	16	0.0000	1.0000		
37	17	0.0000	1.0000		
38	18	0.0000	1.0000		
39	19	0.0000	1.0000		
40	20	0.0000	1.0000		

M/M/*s* with *s* = 2 is the M/M/2 model.

Servers are busy only 33.3% of the time.

Two mechanics on duty

Equal service rate for both mechanics. Rate shown is *per mechanic*.

0.0417 hours = 2.5 minutes

Hidden rows. See Companion Website for full file.

[6] Note that adding a second mechanic cuts queue waiting time and length by more than half; that is, the relationship between the number of servers and queue characteristics is *nonlinear*. This is because of the random arrival and service processes. When there is only one mechanic, and two customers arrive within a minute of each other, the second will have a long wait. The fact that the mechanic may have been idle for 30 minutes before they both arrive does not change the average waiting time. Thus, single-server models often have high wait times compared to multiple-server models.

TABLE 9.3 Effect of Service Level on Arnold's Operating Characteristics

OPERATING CHARACTERISTIC	LEVEL OF SERVICE		
	ONE MECHANIC (μ = 3)	TWO MECHANICS (μ = 3 EACH)	ONE FASTER MECHANIC (μ = 4)
Probability that the system is empty (P_0)	0.33	0.50	0.50
Average number of cars in the system (L)	2 cars	0.75 cars	1 car
Average time spent in the system (W)	60 minutes	22.5 minutes	30 minutes
Average number of cars in the queue (L_q)	1.33 cars	0.083 cars	0.50 cars
Average time spent in the queue (W_q)	40 minutes	2.5 minutes	15 minutes

Cost Analysis of the Queuing System

We do an economic analysis with two service bays.

To complete his economic analysis of the M/M/2 queuing system, Arnold notes that the relevant values are C_w = \$10 per hour, L = 0.75 (see Screenshot 9-3), C_s = \$12 per hour, and s = 2 (because there are two mechanics). The total cost is, therefore, \$10 × 0.75 + \$12 × 2 = \$31.50 per hour.

As you recall, total cost with just Blank as the mechanic was found to be \$32 per hour. Total cost with just the faster but more expensive Smith was \$25 per hour. Although opening a second bay would be likely to have a positive effect on customer goodwill and hence lower the cost of waiting time (i.e., lower C_w), it does mean an increase in the total cost of providing service. Look back to Figure 9.1 on page , and you will see that such trade-offs are the basis of queuing theory. Based on his analysis, Arnold decides to replace his current worker Blank with the speedier Smith and not open a second service bay.

9.6 Single-Server Queuing System with Poisson Arrivals and Constant Service Times (M/D/1 Model)

Constant service rates speed up the process compared to exponentially distributed service times with the same value of μ.

When customers or equipment are processed according to a fixed cycle, as in the case of an automatic car wash or an amusement park ride, constant service rates are appropriate. Because constant service rates are certain, the values for L_q, W_q, L, and W in such a queuing system are always less than they would be in an equivalent M/M/s system, which have variable service

IN ACTION Using Queuing Models in a Hospital Eye Clinic

The hospital outpatient eye clinic at the United Kingdom's Royal Preston Hospital is not unlike other clinics at hospitals throughout the rest of the world: It is regularly overbooked and overrun, and it has excessive patient waiting times. Even though its patient charter states that no one should wait to be seen for more than 30 minutes past their appointment time, patients, on average, waited over 50 minutes.

Many problems in hospital clinics can be explained as a vicious cycle of events: (1) appointments staff overbook every clinic session because of the large patient volume; (2) patients therefore wait in long queues; (3) doctors are overburdened; and (4) when a doctor is ill, the staff spends much time canceling and rescheduling appointments.

To break out of this cycle, the clinic at Royal Preston needed to reduce patient waiting times. This was done by applying computer-driven queuing models and attempting to reduce the patient time variability. The hospital used queuing software to specifically address the 30-minute statistic in the patient charter. Researchers assumed that (1) each patient arrived on time, (2) the service distribution was known from past history, (3) 12% of patients missed their appointments, and (4) 33% of the patients queued for a second consultation.

Making a list of 13 recommendations (many nonquantitative) to the clinic, researchers returned two years later to find that most of their suggestions were followed (or at least seriously attempted), yet performance of the clinic had shown no dramatic improvement. Patient waiting times were still quite long, the clinic was still overbooked, and appointments sometimes had to be canceled. The conclusion: Even though models can often help *understand* a problem, some problems, like those in the outpatient clinic, are messy and hard to fix.

Source: Based on J. C. Bennett and D. J. Worthington. "An Example of a Good but Partially Successful OR Engagement: Improving Outpatient Clinic Operations," *Interfaces* (September–October 1998): 56–69.

times. As a matter of fact, both the average queue length and the average waiting time in the queue are *halved* with the constant service rate model.

Operating Characteristic Equations for an M/D/1 Queuing System

In the *M/D/1* queuing system we let

$$\lambda = \text{average number of arrivals per time (e.g., per hour)}$$
$$\mu = \text{constant number of people or items served per time period}$$

The operating characteristic equations for the M/D/1 queuing system are as follows:

1. Average server utilization in the system:

$$\rho = \lambda/\mu \tag{9-19}$$

2. Average number of customers or units waiting in line for service:

$$L_q = \frac{\lambda^2}{2\mu(\mu - \lambda)} \tag{9-20}$$

3. Average number of customers or units in the system:

$$L = L_q + \lambda/\mu \tag{9-21}$$

4. Average time a customer or unit spends waiting in line for service:

$$W_q = L_q/\lambda = \frac{\lambda}{2\mu(\mu - \lambda)} \tag{9-22}$$

5. Average time a customer or unit spends in the system (namely, in the queue or being served):

$$W = W_q + 1/\mu \tag{9-23}$$

6. Probability that there are zero customers or units in the system:

$$P_0 = 1 - \lambda/\mu \tag{9-24}$$

Garcia-Golding Recycling, Inc.

Garcia-Golding Recycling, Inc., collects and compacts aluminum cans and glass bottles in New York City. Its truck drivers, who arrive to unload these materials for recycling, currently wait an average of 15 minutes before emptying their loads. The cost of the driver and truck time wasted while in queue is valued at $60 per hour. Garcia-Golding is considering purchasing a new automated compactor. The new compactor will be able to process truckloads at a constant rate of 12 trucks per hour (i.e., 5 minutes per truck), and its cost will be amortized at a rate of $3 per truck unloaded. Trucks arrive according to a Poisson distribution at an average rate of 8 per hour. Should Garcia-Golding purchase the new compactor?

File: 9-4.xls

EXCELMODULES SOLUTION FOR GARCIA-GOLDING RECYCLING We select the choice titled Constant Service Times (M/D/1) from the Queuing Models menu in ExcelModules (see Screenshot 9-1A on page 378). After entering the optional title, we enter the input data as shown in Screenshot 9-4. For Garcia-Golding's problem, the average arrival rate (λ) is 8 trucks per hour. The constant service rate (μ) is 12 trucks per hour. We enter these values in cells B9 and B10, respectively. The worksheet now displays the operating characteristics of this queuing system in cells E9:E14.

Cost Analysis of the Queuing System

We do a cost analysis for the recycling example.

The *current* system makes drivers wait an average of 15 minutes before emptying their trucks. The waiting cost per trip is

$$\begin{aligned}\text{Current waiting cost per trip} &= (0.25 \text{ hours waiting}) \times \$60/\text{hour}\\ &= \$15 \text{ per trip}\end{aligned}$$

SCREENSHOT 9-4 Operating Characteristics for Garcia-Golding Recycling: M/D/1 Queuing System

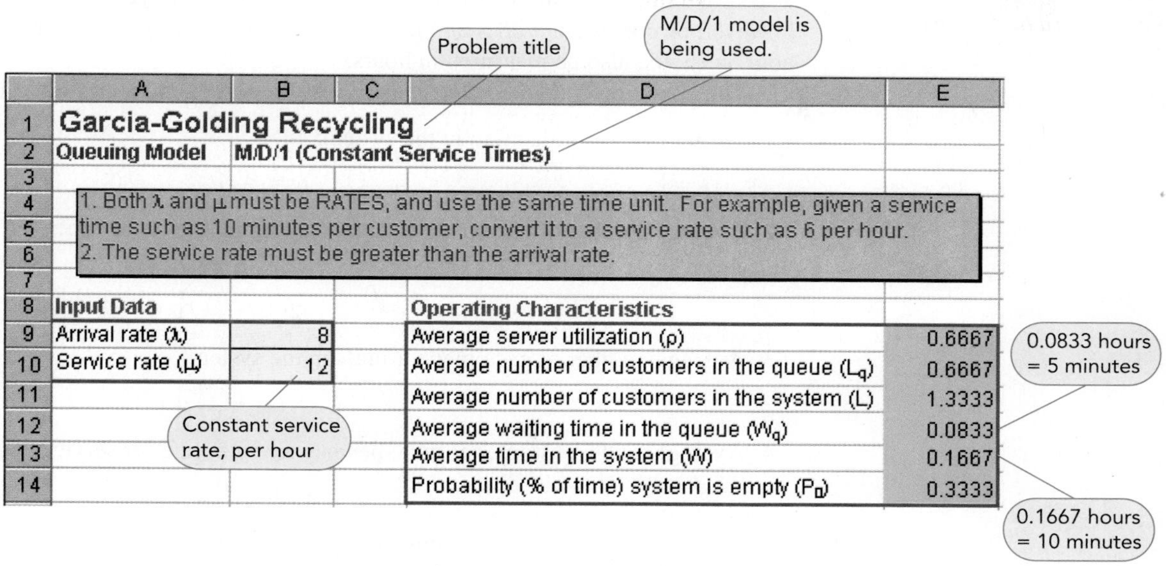

	A	B	C	D	E
1	Garcia-Golding Recycling				
2	Queuing Model	M/D/1 (Constant Service Times)			
3					
4	1. Both λ and μ must be RATES, and use the same time unit. For example, given a service				
5	time such as 10 minutes per customer, convert it to a service rate such as 6 per hour.				
6	2. The service rate must be greater than the arrival rate.				
7					
8	Input Data			Operating Characteristics	
9	Arrival rate (λ)	8		Average server utilization (ρ)	0.6667
10	Service rate (μ)	12		Average number of customers in the queue (L_q)	0.6667
11				Average number of customers in the system (L)	1.3333
12				Average waiting time in the queue (W_q)	0.0833
13				Average time in the system (W)	0.1667
14				Probability (% of time) system is empty (P_0)	0.3333

The average waiting time in the queue (W_q) with the new automated compactor is only 0.0833 hours, or 5 minutes. Therefore, the revised waiting cost per trip is

$$\begin{aligned}\text{Revised waiting cost per trip} &= (0.0833 \text{ hours waiting}) \times \$60/\text{hour}\\ &= \$5 \text{ per trip}\\ \text{Savings with new equipment} &= \$15 - \$5 = \$10 \text{ per trip}\\ \text{Amortized cost of equipment} &= \$3 \text{ per trip}\\ \text{Hence, net savings} &= \$10 - \$3 = \$7 \text{ per trip}\end{aligned}$$

Garcia-Golding should therefore purchase the new compactor.

9.7 Single-Server Queuing System with Poisson Arrivals and General Service Times (M/G/1 Model)

So far, we have studied systems in which service times are either exponentially distributed or constant. In many cases, however, service times could follow some **arbitrary, or general, distribution** with mean μ and standard deviation σ. In such cases, we refer to the model as a *general* service time model. Real-world examples of general service times include time required to service vehicles at an auto repair shop (e.g., an oil change service) and time required by a store clerk to complete a sales transaction.

General service time models assume arbitrary distributions for service times.

The single-server system presented here assumes that arrivals follow a Poisson probability distribution. As in earlier models, with the **M/G/1** model we also assume that (1) service is on a first-come, first-served basis, (2) there is no balking or reneging, and (3) the average service rate is greater than the average arrival rate.

Operating Characteristic Equations for an M/G/1 Queuing System

For the M/G/1 system we let

λ = average number of arrivals per time (e.g., per hour)

μ = average number of people or items served per time period

σ = standard deviation of service time

λ and μ are rates and must be for the same time interval. The standard deviation, σ, must also be measured in the same time unit.

As with the M/M/s models, with the M/G/1 model, λ and μ must be defined for the *same time interval*. Also, it is important to note that while λ and μ are rates (i.e., number of occurrences in a specified time interval), σ is the standard deviation of the service time. The units for σ should, however, be consistent with λ and μ. For example, if λ and μ are expressed as average rates per hour, σ should also be measured in hours.

The operating characteristic equations for the M/G/1 model are as follows:

1. Average server utilization in the system:

$$\rho = \lambda/\mu \tag{9-25}$$

2. Average number of customers or units waiting in line for service:

$$L_q = \frac{\lambda^2\sigma^2 + (\lambda/\mu)^2}{2(1 - (\lambda/\mu))} \tag{9-26}$$

3. Average number of customers or units in the system:

$$L = L_q + \lambda/\mu \tag{9-27}$$

4. Average time a customer or unit spends waiting in line for service:

$$W_q = L_q/\lambda \tag{9-28}$$

5. Average time a customer or unit spends in the system:

$$W = W_q + 1/\mu \tag{9-29}$$

6. Probability that there are zero customers or units in the system:

$$P_0 = 1 - \lambda/\mu \tag{9-30}$$

Meetings with Professor Crino

This is an example of a general service time model.

Professor Michael Crino advises all honors students at Central College. During the registration period, students meet with Professor Crino to decide courses for the following semester and to discuss any other issues they may be concerned about. Rather than have students set up specific appointments to see him, Professor Crino prefers setting aside two hours each day during the registration period and having students drop in on an informal basis. This approach, he believes, makes students feel more at ease with him.

Based on his experience, Professor Crino thinks that students arrive at an average rate of one every 12 minutes (or five per hour) to see him. He also thinks the Poisson distribution is appropriate to model the arrival process. Advising meetings last an average of 10 minutes each; that is, Professor Crino's service rate is six per hour. However, because some students have concerns that they wish to discuss with Professor Crino, the length of these meetings varies. Professor Crino estimates that the standard deviation of the service time (i.e., the meeting length) is 5 minutes.

File: 9-5.xls, sheet: 9-5A

EXCELMODULES SOLUTION FOR PROFESSOR CRINO'S PROBLEM We select the choice titled General Service Times (M/G/1) from the Queuing Models menu in ExcelModules (see Screenshot 9-1A on page 378). After entering the optional title, we enter the input data in the screen as shown in Screenshot 9-5A. For Professor Crino's problem, the average arrival rate (λ) is five students per hour. The average service rate (μ) is six students per hour. Observe that, as required, μ exceeds λ, and both are for the same time interval (per hour, in this case). The standard deviation (σ) of the service time is 5 minutes. However, because λ and μ are expressed per hour, we also express σ in hours and write it as 0.0833 hours (= 5 minutes).

We enter the values of λ, μ, and σ in cells B9, B10, and B11, respectively, as shown in Screenshot 9-5A. The worksheet now displays the operating characteristics of this queuing system in cells E9:E14.

The results indicate that, on average, Professor Crino is busy during 83.3% of his advising period. There are 2.60 students waiting to see him on average, and each student waits an average of 0.52 hours (or approximately 31 minutes).

SCREENSHOT 9-5A Operating Characteristics for Professor Crino's Problem: M/G/1 Queuing System

	A	B	C	D	E
1	Professor Crino's Problem				
2	Queuing Model	M/G/1 (General Service Times)			
3					
4	1. Both λ and μ must be RATES, and use the same time unit. However, the standard deviation (σ)				
5	must be for the service TIME, not the service rate.				
6	2. The service rate must be greater than the arrival rate.				
7					
8	Input Data			Operating Characteristics	
9	Arrival rate (λ)	5		Average server utilization (ρ)	0.8333
10	Service rate (μ)	6		Average number of customers in the queue (L_q)	2.6038
11	Standard deviation (σ)	0.0833		Average number of customers in the system (L)	3.4371
12				Average waiting time in the queue (W_q)	0.5208
13				Average time in the system (W)	0.6874
14				Probability (% of time) system is empty (P_0)	0.1667

Using Excel's Goal Seek to Identify Required Model Parameters

Looking at the results in Screenshot 9-5A, Professor Crino realizes that making students wait an average of 31 minutes is unacceptable. Ideally, he would like to speed up these meetings so that students wait no more than 15 minutes (or 0.25 hours) on average. He realizes that he has little control over the standard deviation of the service time. However, by insisting that students come prepared (e.g., decide ahead of time which courses they want to take) for these meetings, Professor Crino thinks he can decrease the average meeting length. The question is this: What should be the average meeting length that will enable Professor Crino to meet his goal of a 15-minute average waiting time?

Excel's Goal Seek *procedure allows us to find the required value of a queue parameter to achieve a stated goal.*

One way to solve this problem is to plug in different values for the average service rate μ in cell B10 of Screenshot 9-5A and keep track of the W_q value in cell E12 until it drops below 0.25. An alternate, and preferred, approach is to use a procedure in Excel called Goal Seek to automate the search process for the value of μ. You may recall that we used Goal Seek in Chapter 1 to find the break-even point (refer to page 12 for details). The Goal Seek procedure allows us to specify a desired value for a *target cell*. This target cell should contain a formula that involves a different cell, called the *changing cell*. Once we specify the target cell, its desired value, and the changing cell in Goal Seek, the procedure automatically manipulates the changing cell value to try to make the target cell achieve its desired value.

In our model, the changing cell is the average service rate μ (cell B10). The target cell is the average waiting time W_q (cell E12). We want the target cell to achieve a value of 15 minutes (which we specify as 0.25 hours because μ and λ are per hour). After bringing up the General Service Times (M/G/1) worksheet in ExcelModules (see Screenshot 9-5A), we invoke the Goal Seek procedure by clicking the Data tab on Excel's Ribbon, followed by the What-If Analysis button (found in the Data Tools group within the Data tab), and then finally on Goal Seek. The window shown in Screenshot 9-5B is now displayed.

File: 9-5.xls, sheet: 9-5C

We specify cell E12 as the target cell in the Set cell box, a desired value of 0.25 for this cell in the To value box, and cell B10 in the box labeled By changing cell. When we click OK, we get the windows shown in Screenshot 9-5C. The results indicate that if Professor Crino can increase his service rate to 6.92 students per hour, the average waiting time drops to around 15 minutes. That is, Professor Crino needs to reduce his average meeting length to approximately 8.67 minutes (= 6.92 students per 60 minutes).

We can use Goal Seek in any of the queuing models discussed here to determine the value of an input parameter (e.g., μ or λ) that would make an operating characteristic reach a desired value. For example, we could use it in the M/M/1 worksheet (section 9.4) to find the value of

SCREENSHOT 9-5B
Goal Seek Input Window in Excel

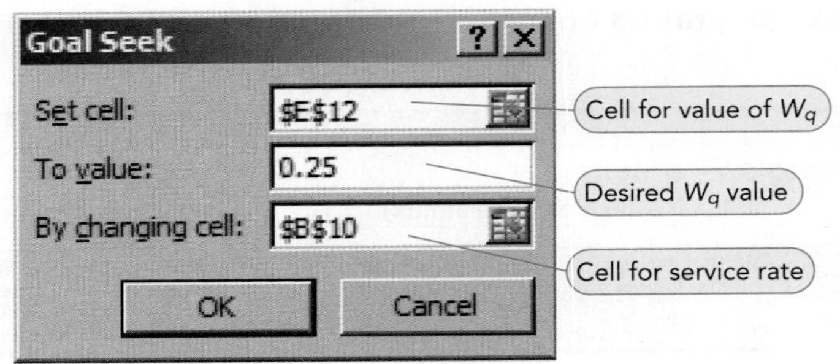

SCREENSHOT 9-5C Goal Seek Status Window and Revised Operating Characteristics for Professor Crino's Problem: M/G/1 Queuing System

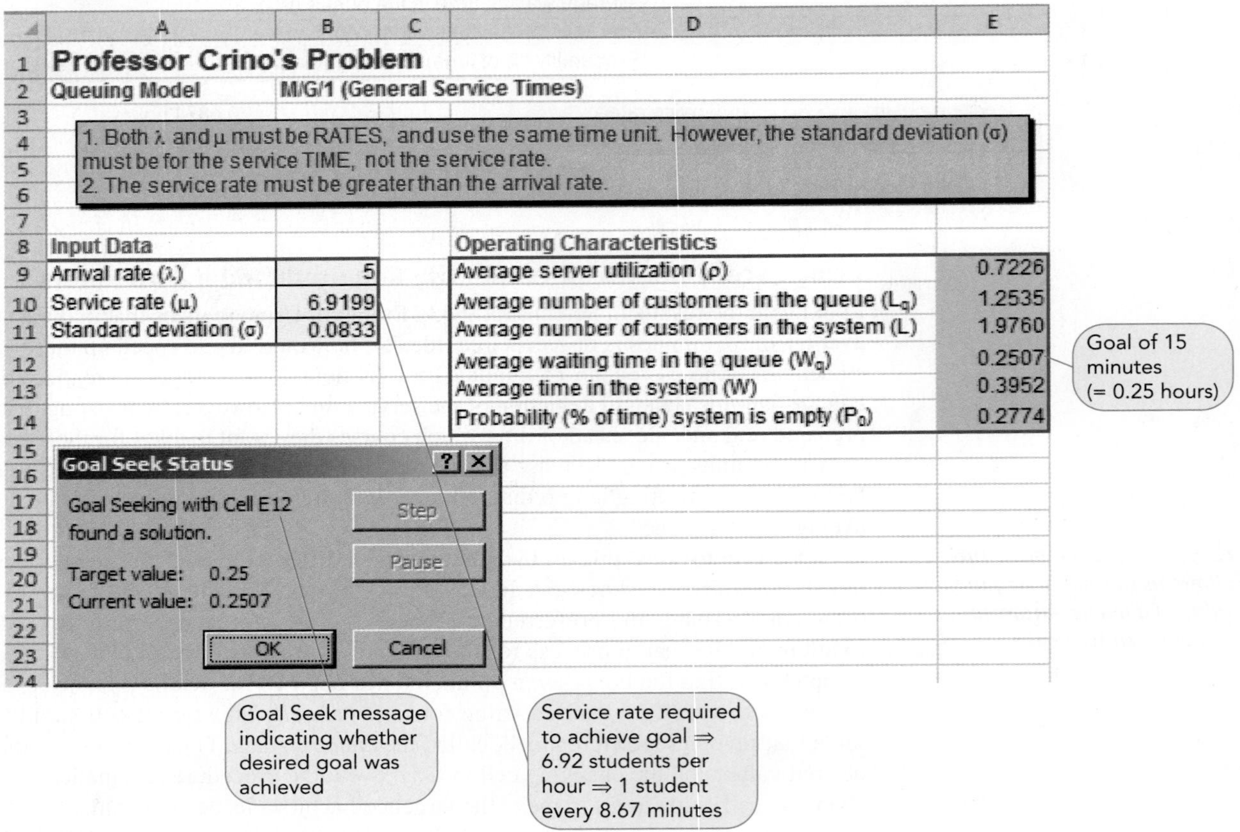

μ that would allow Arnold to offer his customers a guarantee of having to wait no more than 5 minutes (or 0.0833 hours). The answer turns out to be six mufflers per hour. See if you can verify this by using Goal Seek and the Exponential Service Times (M/M/s) queuing model in ExcelModules.

9.8 Multiple-Server Queuing System with Poisson Arrivals, Exponential Service Times, and Finite Population Size (M/M/S/∞/N Model)

All the queuing models we have studied so far have assumed that the size of the calling population is infinite. Hence, as customers arrive at the queuing system, the potential number of customers left in the population is still large, and the average arrival rate does not change. However, when there is a limited population of potential customers for a service facility, we need to consider a different queuing model. This model would be used, for example, if we

IN ACTION Queuing Analysis Helps the Israeli Army Redesign Recruitment Procedures

Israel has compulsory army service starting at age 18. To examine candidates for service, the army was using a two-day process at six recruitment offices located around the country. Even though the staff worked at peak capacity, over 70 percent of candidates did not finish the process within two days and had to be recalled for extra visits. Before building a new recruitment office to meet this growing problem, the army wanted to investigate whether it was possible to improve performance in the recruiting offices.

The research team developed a queuing model to study this problem based on the following parameters: arrival-time distribution, routes, station data, and the order in which rooms are filled. The model helped them arrive at a configuration that processed about 99 percent of candidates completely in just one day with shortened waiting times at various stations, but was still economical in terms of personnel capacity and usage. Savings of over $3.3 million resulted from closed offices as well as decreased costs for personnel, traveling, and office expenses.

Source: Based on O. Shtrichman, R. Ben-Haim, and M. A. Pollatschek. "Using Simulation to Increase Efficiency in an Army Recruitment Office," *Interfaces* 31, 4 (July–August 2001): 61–70.

were considering equipment repairs in a factory that has 5 machines, if we were in charge of maintenance for a fleet of 10 commuter airplanes, or if we ran a hospital ward that has 20 beds. The limited population model permits any number of servers to be considered.

In the finite population model, the arrival rate is dependent on the length of the queue.

The reason the M/M/s/∞/N model differs from the earlier queuing models is that there is now a dependent relationship between the length of the queue and the arrival rate. To illustrate this situation, we can assume that our factory has five machines. If all five are broken and awaiting repair, the arrival rate drops to zero. In general, as the waiting time becomes longer in a limited population queuing system, the arrival rate of customers drops lower.

In this section, we describe a finite arrival population model that has the following assumptions:

Arrival rate, λ is per customer or unit.

1. There are s servers with *identical* service time distributions.
2. The population of units seeking service is finite, of size N.[7]
3. The arrival distribution of *each customer* in the population follows a Poisson distribution, with an average rate of λ.
4. Service times are exponentially distributed, with an average rate of μ.
5. Both λ and μ are specified for the same time period.
6. Customers are served on a first-come, first-served basis.

Operating Characteristic Equations for the Finite Population Queuing System

For the M/M/s/∞/N model we let

$$\lambda = \text{average number of arrivals per time (e.g., per hour)}$$
$$\mu = \text{average number of people or items served per time period}$$
$$s = \text{number of servers}$$
$$N = \text{size of the population}$$

The operating characteristic equations for the M/M/s/∞/N model are as follows:

1. Probability that there are zero customers or units in the system:

$$P_0 = \frac{1}{\displaystyle\sum_{n=0}^{s-1} \frac{N!}{(N-n)!n!}\left(\frac{\lambda}{\mu}\right)^n + \sum_{n=s}^{N} \frac{N!}{(N-n)!s!s^{n-s}}\left(\frac{\lambda}{\mu}\right)^n} \qquad \textbf{(9-31)}$$

[7] Although there is no definite number that we can use to divide finite from infinite arrival populations, the general rule of thumb is this: If the number in the queue is a significant proportion of the arrival population, we should use a finite queuing model.

2. Probability that there are exactly n customers in the system:

$$P_n = \frac{N!}{(N-n)!n!}\left(\frac{\lambda}{\mu}\right)^n P_0, \quad \text{if } 0 \leq n \leq s \tag{9-32}$$

$$P_n = \frac{N!}{(N-n)!s!s^{n-s}}\left(\frac{\lambda}{\mu}\right)^n P_0, \quad \text{if } s < n \leq N \tag{9-33}$$

$$P_n = 0, \quad \text{if } n > N \tag{9-34}$$

3. Average number of customers or units in line, waiting for service:

$$L_q = \sum_{n=s}^{N}(n-s)P_n \tag{9-35}$$

4. Average number of customers or units in the system:

$$L = \sum_{n=0}^{s-1} nP_n + L_q + s\left(1 - \sum_{n=0}^{s-1} P_n\right) \tag{9-36}$$

5. Average time a customer or unit spends in the queue waiting for service:

$$W_q = \frac{L_q}{\lambda(N-L)} \tag{9-37}$$

6. Average time a customer or unit spends in the system:

$$W = \frac{L}{\lambda(N-L)} \tag{9-38}$$

Department of Commerce Example

We look at an example of a finite population model.

The U.S. Department of Commerce (DOC) in Washington, DC, uses five high-speed printers to print all documents. Past records indicate that each of these printers needs repair after about 20 hours of use. Breakdowns have been found to be Poisson distributed. The one technician on duty can repair a printer in an average of 2 hours, following an exponential distribution.

File: 9-6.xls, sheet: 9-6A

EXCELMODULES SOLUTION FOR THE DOC'S PROBLEM We select the choice titled Finite Population Model (Multiple Servers) from the Queuing Models menu in ExcelModules (see Screenshot 9-1A on page 378). After entering the optional title, we get the screen shown in Screenshot 9-6A. For the DOC's problem, the average arrival rate (λ) for *each printer* is $1/20 = 0.05$ per hour. The average service rate (μ) is one every two hours, or 0.50 printers per hour. As before, both μ and λ are expressed for the same time period (per hour, in this case). The number of servers (s) is one because there is only one technician on duty. Finally, the population size (N) is five because there are five printers at the DOC.

We enter the values of λ, μ, s, and N in cells B9, B10, B11, and B12, respectively, as shown in Screenshot 9-6A. The worksheet now displays the operating characteristics of this queuing system in cells E9:E15. Probability values (P_n) are shown in cells B19:B24.

Cost Analysis of the Queuing System

The results indicate that there are 0.64 printers down, on average, in the system. If printer downtime is estimated at \$120 per hour, and the technician is paid \$25 per hour, we can compute the total cost per hour as

This is the total cost computation.

$$\begin{aligned} \text{Total cost} &= (\text{Average number of printers down}) \times (\text{Cost of downtime hour}) \\ &\quad + (\text{Cost of technician hour}) \\ &= 0.64 \times \$120 + \$25 = \$101.80 \text{ per hour} \end{aligned}$$

File: 9-6.xls, sheet: 9-6B

The office manager is willing to consider hiring a second printer technician, provided that doing so is cost-effective. To check this, we compute the DOC queue's operating characteristics again. However, the number of servers this time (cell B11) is two. The results are shown in Screenshot 9-6B on page 394.

SCREENSHOT 9-6A Operating Characteristics for the Department of Commerce Problem: M/M/1 Queuing System with Finite Population

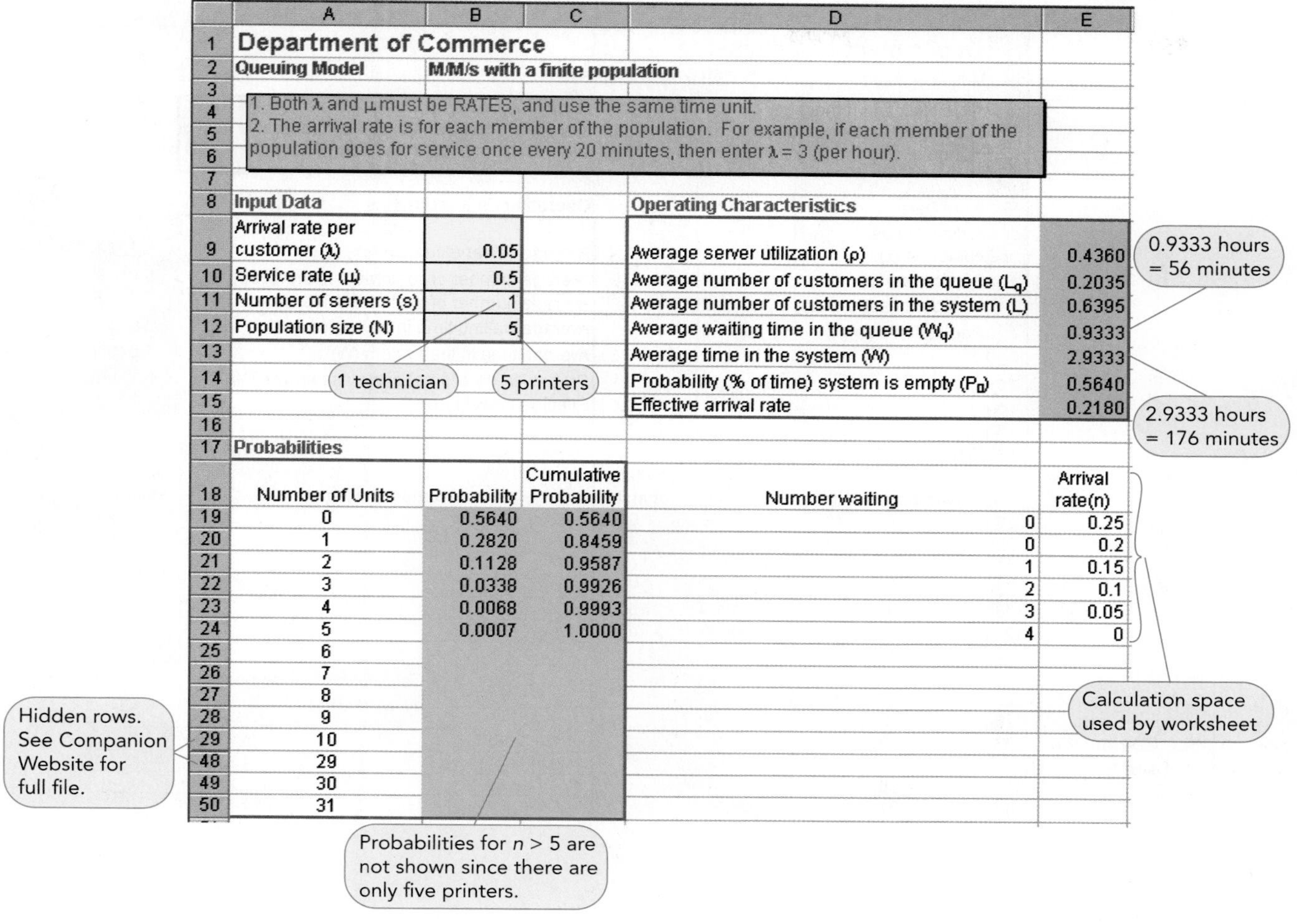

Screenshot 9-6B indicates that there are now only 0.46 printers, on average, in the system. We can compute the revised total cost per hour as

This is the total cost with two technicians.

$$\begin{aligned}\text{Total cost} &= (\text{Average number of printers down}) \times (\text{Cost of downtime hour}) \\ &\quad + (\text{Cost of technician hour}) \times (\text{Number of technicians}) \\ &= 0.64 \times \$120 + \$25 \times 2 = \$105.20 \text{ per hour}\end{aligned}$$

Because the total cost is higher in this case ($105.20 versus $101.80 per hour), the office manager should not hire a second technician.

9.9 More Complex Queuing Systems

Many queuing systems that occur in real-world situations have characteristics like those of Arnold's Muffler Shop, Garcia-Golding Recycling, Inc., Professor Crino's advising meetings, and the Department of Commerce examples. This is true when the situation calls for issues such as (1) single or multiple servers, (2) Poisson arrivals, (3) exponential, constant, or arbitrary service times, (4) a finite or an infinite arrival population, (5) infinite queue length, (6) no balking or reneging, and (7) first-in, first-out service.

SCREENSHOT 9-6B Revised Operating Characteristics for the Department of Commerce Problem: M/M/2 Queuing System with Finite Population

	A	B	C	D	E
1	Department of Commerce				
2	Queuing Model	M/M/s with a finite population			
3–6	1. Both λ and μ must be RATES, and use the same time unit. 2. The arrival rate is for each member of the population. For example, if each member of the population goes for service once every 20 minutes, then enter λ = 3 (per hour).				
7					
8	Input Data			Operating Characteristics	
9	Arrival rate per customer (λ)	0.05		Average server utilization (ρ)	0.2268
10	Service rate (μ)	0.5		Average number of customers in the queue (L_q)	0.0113
11	Number of servers (s)	2		Average number of customers in the system (L)	0.4648
12	Population size (N)	5		Average waiting time in the queue (W_q)	0.0497
13				Average time in the system (W)	2.0497
14				Probability (% of time) system is empty (P_0)	0.6186
15				Effective arrival rate	0.2268
16					
17	Probabilities				
18	Number of Units	Probability	Cumulative Probability	Number waiting	Arrival rate(n)
19	0	0.6186	0.6186	0	0.25
20	1	0.3093	0.9279	0	0.2
21	2	0.0619	0.9897	0	0.15
22	3	0.0093	0.9990	1	0.1
23	4	0.0009	1.0000	2	0.05
24	5	0.0000	1.0000	3	0
25	6				
26	7				
27	8				
28	9				
29	10				
48	29				
49	30				
50	31				

L drops to 0.46 with two technicians.
2 technicians
System is empty 62% of the time—that is, no printers are broken.
Calculation space used by worksheet.
Hidden rows. See Companion Website for full file.

More sophisticated models exist to handle variations of basic assumptions, but when even these do not apply, we can turn to computer simulation, the topic of Chapter 10.

Often, however, *variations* of this specific case are present in a queuing system. Arrival times, for example, may not be Poisson distributed. A college registration system in which seniors have first choice of courses and hours over all other students is an example of a first-come, first-served model with a preemptive priority queue discipline. A physical examination for military recruits is an example of a multiphase system—one that differs from the single-phase models discussed in this chapter. Recruits first line up to have blood drawn at one station, then wait to take an eye exam at the next station, talk to a psychiatrist at the third, and are examined by a doctor for medical problems at the fourth. At each phase, the recruits must enter another queue and wait their turn. An airline reservation system with a finite number of phone lines is an example of a system with a limited queue length.

It turns out that for many of these more complex queuing systems also, decision modelers have developed analytical models to compute their operating characteristics. Not surprisingly, the mathematical expressions for these computations are somewhat more cumbersome than the ones covered in this chapter.[8] However, as noted previously, real-world queuing systems can often be so complex that they cannot be modeled analytically at all. When this happens, decision modelers usually turn to a different approach—*computer simulation*—to analyze the performance of these systems. We discuss simulation in Chapter 10.

[8] Often, the qualitative results of queuing models are as useful as the quantitative results. Results show that it is inherently more efficient to pool resources, use central dispatching, and provide single multiple-server systems rather than multiple single-server systems.

Summary

Queuing systems are an important part of the business world. This chapter describes several common queuing situations and presents decision models for analyzing systems that follow certain assumptions: (1) The queuing system involves just a single phase of service, (2) arrivals are Poisson distributed, (3) arrivals are treated on a first-in, first-out basis and do not balk or renege, (4) service times follow the exponential distribution, an arbitrary distribution, or are constant, and (5) the average service rate is faster than the average arrival rate.

The models illustrated in this chapter are for single-server, single-phase and for multiple-server, single-phase problems. We show how to compute a series of operating characteristics in each case using Excel worksheets and then study total expected costs. Total cost is the sum of the cost of providing service plus the cost of waiting time.

Key operating characteristics for a system are (1) utilization rate, (2) percentage of idle time, (3) average time spent waiting in the system and in the queue, (4) average number of customers in the system and in the queue, and (5) probabilities of various numbers of customers in the system.

We emphasize that a variety of queuing situations exist that do not meet all the assumptions of the traditional models considered here. In such cases, we need to use more complex analytical models or turn to a technique called computer simulation, which is the topic of Chapter 10.

Glossary

Arbitrary, or General, Distribution A probability distribution that is sometimes used to describe random service times in a queuing system.

Arrival Population The population from which arrivals at the queuing system come. Also known as the *calling population*.

Balking The case in which arriving customers refuse to join the waiting line.

Computer Simulation A technique for representing queuing models that are complex and difficult to model analytically.

Exponential Distribution A probability distribution that is often used to describe random service times in a queuing system.

Finite, or Limited, Population A case in which the number of customers in the system is a significant proportion of the calling population.

Finite, or Limited, Queue Length A queue that cannot increase beyond a specific size.

First-In, First-Out (FIFO) A queue discipline in which the customers are served in the strict order of arrival.

Goal Seek A procedure in Excel that can be used to identify the value of a queuing system parameter required to achieve a desired value of an operating characteristic.

Infinite, or Unlimited, Population A calling population that is very large relative to the number of customers currently in the system.

Infinite, or Unlimited, Queue Length A queue that can increase to an infinite size.

M/D/1 Kendall's notation for the constant service time model.

M/G/1 Kendall's notation for the arbitrary, or general, service time model.

M/M/1 Kendall's notation for the single-server model with Poisson arrivals and exponential service times.

M/M/s Kendall's notation for the multiple-server queuing model (with s servers), Poisson arrivals, and exponential service times.

Multiphase System A system in which service is received from more than one station, one after the other.

Multiple-Server Queuing System A system that has more than one service facility, all fed by the same single queue.

Operating Characteristics Descriptive characteristics of a queuing system, including the average number of customers in a line and in the system, the average waiting times in a line and in the system, and the percentage of idle time.

Poisson Distribution A probability distribution that is often used to describe random arrivals in a queue.

Queue One or more customers or units waiting to be served. Also called a *waiting line*.

Queue Discipline The rule by which customers in a line receive service.

Queuing Model A mathematical model that studies the performance of waiting lines or queues.

Reneging The case in which customers enter a queue but then leave before being served.

Service Cost The cost of providing a particular level of service.

Single-Phase System A queuing system in which service is received at only one station.

Single-Server Queuing System A system with one service facility fed by one queue. Servers are also referred to as *channels*.

Utilization Factor (ρ) The proportion of time that a service facility is in use.

Waiting Cost. The cost to a firm of having customers or units waiting in line to be served.

Solved Problems

Solved Problem 9-1

The Maitland Furniture store gets an average of 50 customers per shift. The manager of Maitland wants to calculate whether she should hire one, two, three, or four salespeople. She has determined that average waiting times will be seven minutes with one salesperson, four minutes with two salespeople, three minutes with three salespeople, and two minutes with four salespeople. She has estimated the cost per minute that customers wait at $1. The cost per salesperson per shift (including fringe benefits) is $70. How many salespeople should be hired?

Solution

The manager's calculations are as follows:

	NUMBER OF SALESPEOPLE			
	1	2	3	4
(a) Average number of customers per shift	50	50	50	50
(b) Average waiting time (minutes) per customer	7	4	3	2
(c) Total waiting time (minutes) per shift (a × b)	350	200	150	100
(d) Cost per minute of waiting time (estimated)	$1	$1	$1	$1
(e) Value of lost time per shift (c × d)	$350	$200	$150	$100
(f) Salary cost per shift	$70	$140	$210	$280
(g) Total cost per shift	$420	$340	$360	$380

Because the minimum total cost per shift relates to two salespeople, the manager's optimum strategy is to hire two salespeople.

Solved Problem 9-2

Marty Schatz owns and manages a chili dog and soft drink store near the campus. Although Marty can service 30 customers per hour on the average (μ), he gets only 20 customers per hour (λ). Because Marty could wait on 50% more customers than actually visit his store, it doesn't make sense to him that he should have any waiting lines.

Marty hires you to examine the situation and to determine some characteristics of his queue. After looking into the problem, you make the seven assumptions listed in section 9.4. What are your findings?

Solution

File: 9-7.xls

For this problem, we use the Exponential Service Times (M/M/s) queuing worksheet in ExcelModules. The arrival rate (λ) is 20 customers per hour, the service rate (μ) is 30 customers per hour, and there is one server. We enter these values in cells B9, B10, and B11, respectively, as shown in Screenshot 9-7.

The operating characteristics of this queuing system are displayed in cells E9:E14. The probabilities that there are exactly n customers in the system, for $n = 0$ through 20, are shown in cells B20:B40.

Solved Problem 9-3

Refer to Solved Problem 9-2. Marty agreed that these figures seemed to represent his approximate business situation. You are quite surprised at the length of the lines and elicit from him an estimated value of the customer's waiting time (in the queue, not being waited on) at 10 cents per minute. During the 12 hours that Marty is open, he gets $12 \times 20 = 240$ customers. The average customer is in a queue 4 minutes, so the total customer waiting time is 240×4 minutes $= 960$ minutes. The value of 960 minutes is $\$0.10 \times 960$ minutes $= \$96$.

SCREENSHOT 9-7 Operating Characteristics for Solved Problem 9-2: M/M/1 Queuing System

	A	B	C	D	E	F
1	Solved Problem 9-2					
2	Queuing Model	M/M/s (Exponential Service Times)				
3						
4	1. Both λ and μ must be RATES, and use the same time unit. For example, given a service time such as 10 minutes					
5	per customer, convert it to a service rate such as 6 per hour.					
6	2. The total service rate (rate x servers) must be greater than the arrival rate.					
7						
8	Input Data			Operating Characteristics		
9	Arrival rate (λ)	20		Average server utilization (ρ)	0.6667	
10	Service rate (μ)	30		Average number of customers in the queue (L_q)	1.3333	
11	Number of servers (s)	1		Average number of customers in the system (L)	2.0000	
12				Average waiting time in the queue (W_q)	0.0667	
13				Average time in the system (W)	0.1000	
14				Probability (% of time) system is empty (P_0)	0.3333	
15						
16						
17						
18	Probabilities					
19	Number of Units	Probability	Cumulative Probability			
20	0	0.3333	0.3333			
21	1	0.2222	0.5556			
22	2	0.1481	0.7037			
23	3	0.0988	0.8025			
24	4	0.0658	0.8683			
25	5	0.0439	0.9122			
36	16	0.0005	0.9990			
37	17	0.0003	0.9993			
38	18	0.0002	0.9995			
39	19	0.0002	0.9997			
40	20	0.0001	0.9998			

M/M/s with s = 1

1 server

0.0667 hours = 4 minutes

= 6 minutes

Hidden rows. See Companion Website for full file.

You tell Marty that not only is 10 cents per minute quite conservative, but he could probably save most of that $96 of customer ill will if he hired another salesclerk. After much haggling, Marty agrees to provide you with all the chili dogs you can eat during a week-long period in exchange for your analysis of the results of having two clerks wait on the customers.

Assuming that Marty hires one additional salesclerk whose service rate equals Marty's rate, complete the analysis.

Solution

File: 9-8.xls

We once again use the Exponential Service Times (M/M/s) queuing worksheet in ExcelModules. The arrival rate (λ) is 20 customers per hour, and the service rate (μ) is 30 customers per hour. There are, however, two servers now. We enter these values in cells B9, B10, and B11, respectively, as shown in Screenshot 9-8.

The operating characteristics of this queuing system are displayed in cells E9:E14. The probabilities that there are exactly n customers in the system, for $n = 0$ through 20, are shown in cells B20:B40.

You now have (240 customers) $\times$ (0.0042 hours) $=$ 1 hour total customer waiting time per day. The total cost of 1 hour of customer waiting time is (60 minutes) $\times$ ($0.10 per minute) $=$ $6.

You are ready to point out to Marty that hiring one additional clerk will save $96 $-$ $6 $=$ $90 of customer ill will per 12-hour shift. Marty responds that the hiring should also reduce the number of people who look at the line and leave as well as those who get tired of waiting in line and leave. You tell Marty that you are ready for two chili dogs, extra hot.

SCREENSHOT 9-8 Operating Characteristics for Solved Problem 9-3: M/M/2 Queuing System

	A	B	C	D	E
1	Solved Problem 9-3				
2	Queuing Model	M/M/s (Exponential Service Times)			
3					
4	1. Both λ and μ must be RATES, and use the same time unit. For example, given a service time such as 10 minutes				
5	per customer, convert it to a service rate such as 6 per hour.				
6	2. The total service rate (rate x servers) must be greater than the arrival rate.				
7					
8	Input Data			Operating Characteristics	
9	Arrival rate (λ)	20		Average server utilization (ρ)	0.3333
10	Service rate (μ)	30		Average number of customers in the queue (L_q)	0.0833
11	Number of servers (s)	2		Average number of customers in the system (L)	0.7500
12				Average waiting time in the queue (W_q)	0.0042
13				Average time in the system (W)	0.0375
14				Probability (% of time) system is empty (P_0)	0.5000
15					
16					
17					
18	Probabilities				
19	Number of Units	Probability	Cumulative Probability		
20	0	0.5000	0.5000		
21	1	0.3333	0.8333		
22	2	0.1111	0.9444		
23	3	0.0370	0.9815		
24	4	0.0123	0.9938		
25	5	0.0041	0.9979		
36	16	0.0000	1.0000		
37	17	0.0000	1.0000		
38	18	0.0000	1.0000		
39	19	0.0000	1.0000		
40	20	0.0000	1.0000		

2 servers

W_q drops from 0.0667 hours to 0.0042 hours (= 0.25 minutes) with two servers.

Hidden rows. See Companion Website for full file.

Discussion Questions and Problems

Discussion Questions

9-1 What is a queuing problem? What are the components in a queuing system?

9-2 What are the assumptions underlying common queuing models?

9-3 Describe the important operating characteristics of a queuing system.

9-4 Why must the service rate be greater than the arrival rate in a single-server queuing system?

9-5 Briefly describe three situations in which the FIFO discipline rule is not applicable in queuing analysis.

9-6 Provide examples of four situations in which there is a limited, or finite, waiting line.

9-7 What are the components of the following systems? Draw and explain the configuration of each.
(a) Barbershop
(b) Car wash
(c) Laundromat
(d) Small grocery store

9-8 Do doctors' offices generally have random arrival rates for patients? Are service times random? Under what circumstances might service times be constant?

9-9 Do you think the Poisson distribution, which assumes independent arrivals, is a good estimation of arrival rates in the following queuing systems? Defend your position in each case.
(a) Cafeteria in your school
(b) Barbershop
(c) Hardware store
(d) Dentist's office
(e) College class
(f) Movie theater

Problems

9-10 The Edge Convenience Store has approximately 300 customers shopping in its store between 9 A.M. and 5 P.M. on Saturdays. In deciding how many cash registers to keep open each Saturday, Edge's manager considers two factors: customer waiting time (and the associated waiting cost) and the service costs of employing additional checkout clerks. Checkout clerks are paid an average of \$10 per hour. When only one is on duty, the waiting time per customer is about 10 minutes (or $\frac{1}{6}$ hour); when two clerks are on duty, the average checkout time is 6 minutes per person; 4 minutes when three clerks are working; and 3 minutes when four clerks are on duty.

Edge's management has conducted customer satisfaction surveys and has been able to estimate that the store suffers approximately \$13 in lost sales and goodwill for every *hour* of customer time spent waiting in checkout lines. Using the information provided, determine the optimal number of clerks to have on duty each Saturday to minimize the store's total expected cost.

9-11 From historical data, Harry's Car Wash estimates that dirty cars arrive at a rate of 10 per hour all day Saturday. With a crew working the wash line, Harry figures that cars can be cleaned at a rate of one every five minutes. One car at a time is cleaned in this example of a single-server waiting line. Assuming Poisson arrivals and exponential service times, find the
(a) average number of cars in line
(b) average time a car waits before it is washed
(c) average time a car spends in the service system
(d) utilization rate of the car wash
(e) probability that no cars are in the system

9-12 Rockwell Electronics Corporation retains a service crew to repair machine breakdowns that occur on an average of $\lambda = 3$ per day (approximately Poisson in nature). The crew can service an average of $\mu = 8$ machines per day, with a repair time distribution that resembles the exponential distribution.
(a) What is the utilization rate of this service system?
(b) What is the average downtime for a machine that is broken?
(c) How many machines are waiting to be serviced at any given time?
(d) What is the probability that more than one machine is in the system? What is the probability that more than two machines are broken and waiting to be repaired or being serviced? More than three? More than four?

9-13 The people staffing the ticket booth at an aquarium are able to distribute tickets and brochures to 440 patrons every hour, according to an exponential distribution. On a typical day, an average of 352 people arrive every hour to gain entrance to the aquarium. The arrivals have been found to follow a Poisson distribution. The aquarium's manager wants to make the arrival process as convenient as possible for the patrons and so wishes to examine several queue operating characteristics.
(a) Find the average number of patrons waiting in line to purchase tickets.
(b) What percentage of the time is the ticket window busy?
(c) What is the average time that a visitor to the aquarium spends in the system?
(d) What is the average time spent waiting in line to get to the ticket window?
(e) What is the probability that there are more than two people in the system? More than three people?
(f) What is the probability that there are more than two people in line? More than three people?

9-14 A computer processes jobs on a first-come, first-served basis in a time-sharing environment. The jobs have Poisson arrival rates, with an average of six minutes between arrivals. The objective in processing these jobs is that they spend no more than eight minutes, on average, in the system. How fast does the computer have to process jobs, on average, to meet this objective?

9-15 An agent in a train station sells tickets and provides information to travelers. An average of two travelers approach the agent for assistance each minute. Their arrival is distributed according to a Poisson distribution. The agent is able to meet the travelers' needs in approximately 20 seconds, distributed exponentially.
(a) What is the probability that there are more than two travelers in the system? More than three? More than four?
(b) What is the probability that the system is empty?
(c) How long will the average traveler have to wait before reaching the agent?
(d) What is the expected number of travelers in the queue?
(e) What is the average number in the system?
(f) If a second agent is added (who works at the same pace as the first), how will the operating characteristics computed in parts (b), (c), (d), and (e) change? Assume that travelers wait in a single line and go to the first available agent.

9-16 The wheat harvesting season in the U.S. Midwest is short, and most farmers deliver their truckloads of wheat to a giant central storage bin within a two-week span. Because of this, wheat-filled trucks waiting to unload and return to the fields have been known to back up for a block at the receiving bin. The central bin is owned cooperatively, and it is to every farmer's benefit to make the unloading/storage process as efficient as possible. The cost of grain deterioration caused by unloading delays and the cost of truck rental and idle driver time are significant concerns to the cooperative members. Although farmers have difficulty quantifying crop damage, it is easy to assign a waiting and unloading cost for truck and driver of $18 per hour. The storage bin is open and operated 16 hours per day, seven days per week during the harvest season and is capable of unloading 35 trucks per hour, according to an exponential distribution. Full trucks arrive all day long (during the hours the bin is open), at a rate of about 30 per hour, following a Poisson pattern.

To help the cooperative get a handle on the problem of lost time while trucks are waiting in line or unloading at the bin, find the

(a) average number of trucks in the unloading system
(b) average time per truck in the system
(c) utilization rate for the bin area
(d) probability that there are more than three trucks in the system at any given time
(e) total daily cost to the farmers of having their trucks tied up in the unloading process
(f) The cooperative, as mentioned, uses the storage bin only two weeks per year. Farmers estimate that enlarging the bin would cut unloading costs by 50% next year. It will cost $9,000 to do so during the off-season. Would it be worth the cooperative's while to enlarge the storage area?

9-17 A restaurant's reservation agent takes reservations for dinner by telephone. If he is already on the phone when a patron calls to make a reservation, the incoming call is answered automatically, and the customer is asked to wait for the agent. As soon as the agent is free, the patron who has been on hold the longest is transferred to the agent to be served. Calls for reservations come in at a rate of about 15 per hour. The agent is able to make a reservation in an average of three minutes. Calls tend to follow a Poisson distribution, and the times to make a reservation tend to be exponential. The agent is paid $15 per hour. The restaurant estimates that every minute a customer must wait to speak to the agent costs the restaurant $1.

(a) What is the average time that diners must wait before their calls are transferred to the agent?
(b) What is the average number of callers waiting to make a reservation?
(c) The restaurant is considering adding a second agent to take calls, who would be paid the same $15 per hour. Should it hire another agent? Explain.

9-18 Sal's International Barbershop is a popular haircutting and styling salon near the campus of the University of New Orleans. Four barbers work full time and spend an average of 15 minutes on each customer. Customers arrive all day long, at an average rate of 12 per hour. When they enter, they take a number to wait for the first available barber. Arrivals tend to follow the Poisson distribution, and service times are exponentially distributed.

(a) What is the probability that the shop is empty?
(b) What is the average number of customers in the barbershop?
(c) What is the average time spent in the shop?
(d) What is the average time that a customer spends waiting to be called to a chair?
(e) What is the average number of customers waiting to be served?
(f) What is the shop's utilization factor?
(g) Sal's is thinking of adding a fifth barber. How will this affect the utilization rate?

9-19 Sal (see Problem 9-18) is considering changing the queuing characteristics of his shop. Instead of selecting a number for the first available barber, a customer will be able to select which barber he or she prefers upon arrival. Assuming that this selection does not change while the customer is waiting for his or her barber to become available and that the requests for each of the four barbers are evenly distributed, answer the following:

(a) What is the average number of customers in the barber shop?
(b) What is the average time spent in the shop?
(c) What is the average time a customer spends waiting to be called to a chair?
(d) What is the average number of customers waiting to be served?
(e) Explain why the results from Problems 9-18 and 9-19 differ.

9-20 Carlos Gomez is the receiving supervisor for a large grocery store. Trucks arrive to the loading dock at an average rate of four per hour, according to a Poisson distribution, for 8 hours each day. The cost of operating a truck is estimated to be $80 per hour. Trucks are met by a three-person crew, which is able to unload a truck in an average of 12 minutes, according to an exponential distribution. The payroll cost associated with hiring a crew member, including benefits, is $22 per hour. Carlos is now considering the installation of new equipment to help the crew, which would decrease the average unloading time from 12 minutes to 9 minutes. The cost of this equipment would be about $500 per day. Is the installation of the new equipment economically feasible?

9-21 A local office of the Department of Motor Vehicles (DMV) wishes to overcome the reputation of making citizens wait in line for extremely long times before being able to conduct their business. Accordingly, the DMV is analyzing how best to serve the driving public. Its goal is to make sure that citizens will not have to wait more than five minutes before they are engaged in service with a clerk. The DMV currently has eight clerks to serve people. If a clerk is not busy with customers, he can fill his time with filing or processing mailed-in requests for service. On a typical day, drivers come into the DMV according to the following pattern:

TIME	ARRIVAL RATE (CUSTOMERS/HOUR)
8 A.M.–10 A.M.	20
10 A.M.–2 P.M.	40
2 P.M.–5 P.M.	25

Arrivals follow a Poisson distribution. Service times follow an exponential distribution, with an average of 10 minutes per customer. How many clerks should be on duty during each period to maintain the desired level of service? You may use Excel's Goal Seek procedure to find the answer.

9-22 Julian Argo is a computer technician in a large insurance company. He responds to a variety of complaints from agents regarding their computers' performance. He receives an average of one computer per hour to repair, according to a Poisson distribution. It takes Julian an average of 50 minutes to repair any agent's computer. Service times are exponentially distributed.

(a) Determine the operating characteristics of the computer repair facility. What is the probability that there will be more than two computers waiting to be repaired?

(b) Julian believes that adding a second repair technician would significantly improve his office's efficiency. He estimates that adding an assistant, but still keeping the department running as a single-server system, would double the capacity of the office from 1.2 computers per hour to 2.4 computers per hour. Analyze the effect on the waiting times for such a change and compare the results with those found in part (a).

(c) Insurance agents earn $30 for the company per hour, on average, while computer technicians earn $18 per hour. An insurance agent who does not have access to his computer is unable to generate revenue for the company. What would be the hourly savings to the firm associated with employing two technicians instead of one?

9-23 Julian is considering putting the second technician in another office on the other end of the building, so that access to a computer technician is more convenient for the agents. Assume that the other agent will also have the ability to repair a computer in 50 minutes and that each faulty computer will go to the next available technician. Is this approach more cost-effective than the two approaches considered in Problem 9-22?

9-24 Bru-Thru is a chain of drive-through beer and wine outlets where customers arrive, on average, every five minutes. Management has a goal that customers will be able to complete their transaction, on average, in six minutes with a single server. Assume that this system can be described as an M/M/1 configuration. What is the average service time that is necessary to meet this goal?

9-25 Recreational boats arrive at a single gasoline pump located at the dock at Trident Marina at an average rate of 10 per hour on Saturday mornings. The fill-up time for a boat is normally distributed, with an average of 5 minutes and a standard deviation of 1.5 minutes. Assume that the arrival rate follows the Poisson distribution.

(a) What is the probability that the pump is vacant?

(b) On average, how long does a boat wait before the pump is available?

(c) How many boats, on average, are waiting for the pump?

9-26 A chemical plant stores spare parts for maintenance in a large warehouse. Throughout the working day, maintenance personnel go to the warehouse to pick up supplies needed for their jobs. The warehouse receives a request for supplies, on average, every 2 minutes. The average request requires 1.7 minutes to fill. Maintenance employees are paid $20 per hour, and warehouse employees are paid $12 per hour. The warehouse is open 8 hours each day. Assuming that this system follows the M/M/s requirements, what is the optimal number of warehouse employees to hire?

9-27 During peak times the entry gate at a large amusement park experiences an average arrival of 500 customers per minute, according to a Poisson distribution. The average customer requires four seconds to be processed through the entry gate. The park's goal is to keep the waiting time less than five seconds. How many entry gates are necessary to meet this goal?

9-28 Customers arrive at Valdez's Real Estate at an average rate of one per hour. Arrivals can be assumed to follow the Poisson distribution. Juan Valdez, the agent, estimates that he spends an average of 30 minutes with each customer. The standard deviation of service time is 15 minutes, and the service time distribution is arbitrary.

(a) Calculate the operating characteristics of the queuing system at Valdez's agency.

(b) What is the probability that an arriving customer will have to wait for service?

9-29 If Valdez wants to ensure that his customers wait an average of around 10 minutes, what should be his average service time? Assume that the standard deviation of service time remains at 15 minutes.

9-30 Customers arrive at an automated coffee vending machine at a rate of 4 per minute, following a Poisson distribution. The coffee machine dispenses a cup of coffee at a constant rate of 10 seconds.
(a) What is the average number of people waiting in line?
(b) What is the average number of people in the system?
(c) How long does the average person wait in line before receiving service?

9-31 Chuck's convenience store has only one gas pump. Cars pull up to the pump at a rate of one car every eight minutes. Depending on the speed at which the customer works, the pumping time varies. Chuck estimates that the pump is occupied for an average of five minutes, with a standard deviation of one minute. Calculate Chuck's operating characteristics. Comment on the values obtained. What, if anything, would you recommend Chuck should do?

9-32 Get Connected, Inc., operates several Internet kiosks in Atlanta, Georgia. Customers can access the Web at these kiosks, paying $2 for 30 minutes or a fraction thereof. The kiosks are typically open for 10 hours each day and are always full. Due to the rough usage these PCs receive, they break down frequently. Get Connected has a central repair facility to fix these PCs. PCs arrive at the facility at an average rate of 0.9 per day. Repair times take an average of 1 day, with a standard deviation of 0.5 days.

Calculate the operating characteristics of this queuing system. How much is it worth to Get Connected to increase the average service rate to 1.25 PCs per day?

9-33 A construction company owns six backhoes, which each break down, on average, once every 10 working days, according to a Poisson distribution. The mechanic assigned to keeping the backhoes running is able to restore a backhoe to sound running order in 1 day, according to an exponential distribution.
(a) How many backhoes are waiting for service, on average?
(b) How many are currently being served?
(c) How many are in running order, on average?
(d) What is the average waiting time in the queue?
(e) What is the average wait in the system?

9-34 A technician monitors a group of five computers in an automated manufacturing facility. It takes an average of 15 minutes, exponentially distributed, to adjust any computer that develops a problem. The computers run for an average of 85 minutes, Poisson distributed, without requiring adjustments. Compute the following measures:
(a) average number of computers waiting for adjustment
(b) average number of computers not in working order
(c) probability the system is empty
(d) average time in the queue
(e) average time in the system

9-35 A copier repair person is responsible for servicing the copying machines for seven companies in a local area. Repair calls come in at an average of one call every other day. The arrival rate follows the Poisson distribution. Average service time per call, including travel time, is exponentially distributed, with a mean of two hours. The repair person works an eight-hour day.
(a) On average, how many hours per day is the repair person involved with service calls?
(b) How many hours, on average, does a customer wait for the repair person to arrive after making a call?
(c) What is the probability that more than two machines are out of service at the same time?

9-36 The Johnson Manufacturing Company operates six identical machines that are serviced by a single technician when they break down. Breakdowns occur according to the Poisson distribution and average 0.03 breakdowns per machine operating hour. Average repair time for a machine is five hours and follows the exponential distribution.
(a) What percentage of the technician's time is spent repairing machines?
(b) On average, how long is a machine out of service because of a breakdown?
(c) On average, how many machines are out of service?
(d) Johnson wants to investigate the economic feasibility of adding a second technician. Each technician costs the company $18 per hour. Each hour of machine downtime costs $120. Should a second technician be added?

9-37 A typical subway station in Washington, DC, has six turnstiles, each of which can be controlled by the station manager to be used for either entrance or exit control—but never for both. The manager must decide at different times of the day how many turnstiles to use for entering passengers and how many to use to allow passengers to exit.

At the Washington College Station, passengers enter the station at a rate of about 84 per minute between the hours of 7 and 9 A.M. Passengers exiting trains at the stop reach the exit turnstile area at a rate of about 48 per minute during the same morning rush hour. Each turnstile can allow an average of 30 passengers per minute to enter or exit. Arrival and service times have been thought to follow Poisson and exponential distributions, respectively. Assume that riders form a common queue at both entry and exit turnstile areas and proceed to the first empty turnstile.

The Washington College Station manager does not want the average passenger at his station to have to wait in a turnstile line for more than six seconds, nor does he want more than eight people in any queue at any average time.

(a) How many turnstiles should be opened in each direction every morning?

(b) Discuss the assumptions underlying the solution of this problem, using queuing theory.

9-38 A clerk of court is responsible for receiving and logging legal documents that are to be placed before the various judges to review and sign. She receives these documents on a first-come, first-served basis. Lawyers' couriers arrive before the clerk at an average rate of eight per hour, according to a Poisson distribution. The time it takes the clerk to process the documents is normally distributed, with an average of six minutes and a standard deviation of two minutes.

(a) What is the probability that a courier will have to wait for service?

(b) On average, how many couriers will be waiting for service?

(c) How long is the average wait for service?

9-39 County General Hospital's cardiac care unit (CCU) has seven beds, which are virtually always occupied by patients who have just undergone heart surgery. Two registered nurses are on duty at the CCU in each of the three 8-hour shifts. On average, a patient requires a nurse's attention every 66 minutes. The arrival rate follows a Poisson distribution. A nurse will spend an average of 19 minutes (exponentially distributed) assisting a patient and updating medical records regarding the care provided.

(a) What percentage of the nurses' time is spent responding to these requests?

(b) What is the average time a patient spends waiting for one of the nurses to arrive at bedside?

(c) What is the average number of patients waiting for a nurse to arrive?

(d) What is the probability that a patient will not have to wait for a nurse to arrive?

Case Study

New England Foundry

For more than 75 years, New England Foundry, Inc., has manufactured woodstoves for home use. In recent years, with increasing energy prices, George Mathison, president of New England Foundry, has seen sales triple. This dramatic increase in sales has made it even more difficult for George to maintain quality in all the woodstoves and related products.

Unlike other companies manufacturing woodstoves, New England Foundry is *only* in the business of making stoves and stove-related products. Its major products are the Warmglo I, the Warmglo II, the Warmglo III, and the Warmglo IV. The Warmglo I is the smallest woodstove, with a heat output of 30,000 Btu, and the Warmglo IV is the largest, with a heat output of 60,000 Btu. In addition, New England Foundry, Inc., produces a large array of products that have been designed to be used with their four stoves. These products include warming shelves, surface thermometers, stovepipes, adaptors, stove gloves, trivets, mitten racks, andirons, chimneys, and heat shields. New England Foundry also publishes a newsletter and several paperback books on stove installation, stove operation, stove maintenance, and wood sources. It is George's belief that the company's wide assortment of products is a major contributor to the sales increases.

The Warmglo III outsells all the other stoves by a wide margin. The heat output and available accessories are ideal for the typical home. The Warmglo III also has a number of outstanding features that make it one of the most attractive and heat-efficient stoves on the market. Each Warmglo III also has a thermostatically controlled primary air intake valve that allows the stove to adjust itself automatically to produce the correct heat output for varying weather conditions. A secondary air opening is used to increase the heat output in case of very cold weather. The internal stove parts produce a horizontal flame path for more efficient burning, and the output gases are forced to take an S-shaped path through the stove. The S-shaped path allows more complete combustion of the gases and better heat transfer from the fire and gases through the cast iron to the area to be heated. These features, along with the accessories, resulted in expanding sales and prompted George to build a new factory to manufacture Warmglo III stoves. An overview diagram of the factory is shown in Figure 9.5.

The new foundry uses the latest equipment, including a new Disamatic that helps in manufacturing stove parts. Regardless of new equipment or procedures, casting operations have remained basically unchanged for hundreds of years. To begin with, a wooden pattern is made for every cast iron piece in the stove. The wooden pattern is an exact duplication of the cast iron piece that is to be manufactured. New England Foundry has all its patterns made by Precision Patterns, Inc., and these patterns are stored in the pattern shop and maintenance room. Then a specially formulated sand is molded around the wooden pattern. There can be two or more sand molds for each pattern. Mixing the sand and making the molds are done in the molding room. When the wooden pattern is removed, the resulting sand molds form a negative image of the desired casting. Next, the molds are transported to the casting room, where molten iron is poured into the molds and allowed to cool. When the iron has solidified, the molds are moved into the cleaning, grinding,

FIGURE 9.5 Overview of the Factory

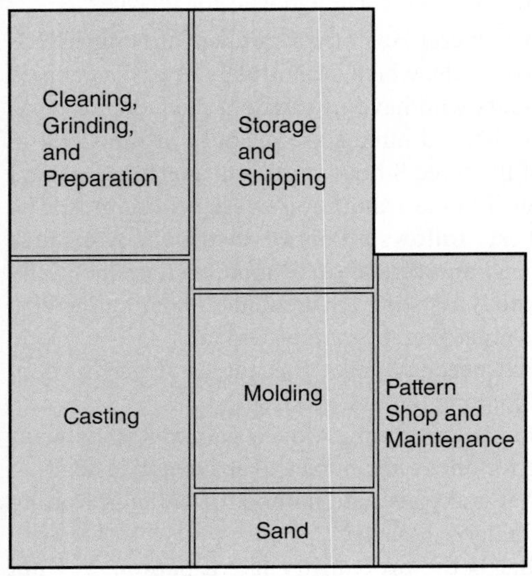

FIGURE 9.6 Overview of the Factory after Changes

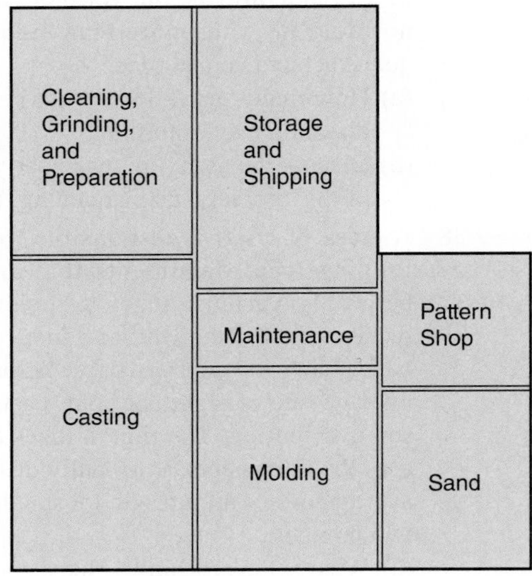

and preparation room. The molds are dumped into large vibrators that shake most of the sand from the casting. The rough castings are then subjected to both sandblasting to remove the rest of the sand and grinding to finish some of the surfaces of the castings. The castings are then painted with a special heat-resistant paint, assembled into workable stoves, and inspected for manufacturing defects that may have gone undetected thus far. Finally, the finished stoves are moved to storage and shipping, where they are packaged and shipped to the appropriate locations.

At present, the pattern shop and the maintenance department are located in the same room. One large counter is used both by maintenance personnel to get tools and parts and by sand molders who need various patterns for the molding operation. Pete Nawler and Bob Bryan, who work behind the counter, are able to service a total of 10 people per hour (or about 5 per hour each). On average, 4 people from maintenance and 3 people from the molding department arrive at the counter per hour. People from the molding department and from maintenance arrive randomly, and to be served, they form a single line. Pete and Bob have always had a first-come, first-served policy. Because of the location of the pattern shop and maintenance department, it takes about three minutes for a person from the maintenance department to walk to the pattern and maintenance room, and it takes about one minute for a person to walk from the molding department to the pattern and maintenance room.

After observing the operation of the pattern shop and maintenance room for several weeks, George decided to make some changes to the layout of the factory. An overview of these changes is shown in Figure 9.6.

Separating the maintenance shop from the pattern shop had a number of advantages. It would take people from the maintenance department only one minute instead of three to get to the new maintenance department. Using time and motion studies, George was also able to determine that improving the layout of the maintenance department would allow Bob to serve 6 people from the maintenance department per hour, and improving the layout of the pattern department would allow Pete to serve 7 people from the molding shop per hour.

Discussion Questions

1. How much time would the new layout save?
2. If maintenance personnel were paid \$9.50 per hour and molding personnel were paid \$11.75 per hour, how much could be saved per hour with the new factory layout?

Case Study

Winter Park Hotel

Donna Shader, manager of the Winter Park Hotel, is considering how to restructure the front desk to reach an optimum level of staff efficiency and guest service. At present, the hotel has five clerks on duty, each with a separate waiting line, during the peak check-in time of 3:00 P.M. to 5:00 P.M. Observation of arrivals during this time shows that an average of 90 guests arrive each hour (although there is no upward limit on the number that could arrive at any given time). It takes an average of 3 minutes for the front-desk clerk to register each guest.

Ms. Shader is considering three plans for improving guest service by reducing the length of time guests spend waiting in line. The first proposal would designate one employee as a quick-service clerk for guests registering under corporate accounts, a market segment that fills about 30% of all occupied rooms. Because corporate guests are preregistered, their registration takes just 2 minutes. With these guests separated from the rest of the clientele, the average time for registering a typical guest would climb to 3.4 minutes. Under plan 1, noncorporate guests would choose any of the remaining four lines.

The second plan is to implement a single-line system. All guests could form a single waiting line to be served by whichever of five clerks became available. This option would require sufficient lobby space for what could be a substantial queue.

The use of an automatic teller machine (ATM) for check-ins is the basis of the third proposal. This ATM would provide approximately the same service rate as would a clerk. Given that initial use of this technology might be minimal, Shader estimated that 20% of customers, primarily frequent guests, would be willing to use the machines. (This might be a conservative estimate if the guests perceive direct benefits from using the ATM, as bank customers do. Citibank reports that some 95% of its Manhattan customers use its ATMs.) Ms. Shader would set up a single queue for customers who prefer human check-in clerks. This queue would be served by the five clerks, although Shader is hopeful that the machine will allow a reduction to four.

Discussion Questions

1. Determine the average amount of time that a guest spends checking in. How would this change under each of the stated options?
2. Which option do you recommend?

Internet Case Studies

See the Companion Website for this textbook, at www.pearsonhighered.com/balakrishnan, for additional case studies.

CHAPTER 10

Simulation Modeling

LEARNING OBJECTIVES

After completing this chapter, students will be able to:

1. Understand the basic steps of conducting a simulation.
2. Explain the advantages and disadvantages of simulation.
3. Tackle a wide variety of problems by using simulation.
4. Set up and solve simulation models by using Excel's standard functions.
5. Use the Crystal Ball add-in for Excel to set up and solve simulation models.
6. Explain other types of simulation models.

CHAPTER OUTLINE

10.1 Introduction

We are all aware to some extent of the importance of simulation models in our world. Boeing Corporation and Airbus Industries, for example, commonly build simulation models of their proposed jet airplanes and then test the aerodynamic properties of the models. Your local civil defense organization may carry out rescue and evacuation practices as it simulates the natural disaster conditions of a hurricane or tornado. The U.S. Army simulates enemy attacks and defense strategies in war games played on computers. Business students take courses that use management games to simulate realistic competitive business situations. And thousands of organizations develop simulation models to assist in making decisions involving their supply chain, inventory control, maintenance scheduling, plant layout, investments, and sales forecasting. Simulation is one of the most widely used decision modeling tools. Various surveys of the largest U.S. corporations reveal that most use simulation in corporate planning.

Simulation sounds like it may be the solution to all management problems. This is, unfortunately, by no means true. Yet we think you may find it one of the most flexible and fascinating of the decision modeling techniques in your studies. Let's begin our discussion of simulation with a simple definition.

What Is Simulation?

To **simulate** *means to duplicate the features of a real system. The idea is to imitate a real-world situation with a mathematical model that does not affect operations.*

To *simulate* is to try to duplicate the features, appearance, and characteristics of a real system. In this chapter we show how to simulate a business or management system by building a *mathematical model* that comes as close as possible to representing the reality of the system. We won't build any *physical* models, as might be used in airplane wind tunnel simulation tests. But just as physical model airplanes are tested and modified under experimental conditions, our mathematical models need to be experimented with to estimate the effects of various actions. The idea behind **simulation** is to imitate a real-world situation mathematically, to then study its properties and operating characteristics, and, finally, to draw conclusions and make action decisions based on the results of the simulation. In this way, the real-life system is not touched until the advantages and disadvantages of what may be a major policy decision are first measured on the system's model.

To use simulation, a manager should (1) define a problem, (2) introduce the variables associated with the problem, (3) construct a mathematical model, (4) set up possible courses of action for testing, (5) run the experiment, (6) consider the results (possibly deciding to modify the model or change data inputs), and (7) decide what course of action to take. These steps are illustrated in Figure 10.1.

The problems tackled by simulation can range from very simple to extremely complex, from bank teller lines to an analysis of the U.S. economy. Although very small simulations can be conducted by hand, effective use of this technique requires some automated means of calculation—namely, a computer. Even large-scale models, simulating perhaps years of business decisions, can be handled in a reasonable amount of time by computer. Though simulation is one of the oldest decision modeling tools (see the *History* box), it was not until the

FIGURE 10.1
Process of Simulation

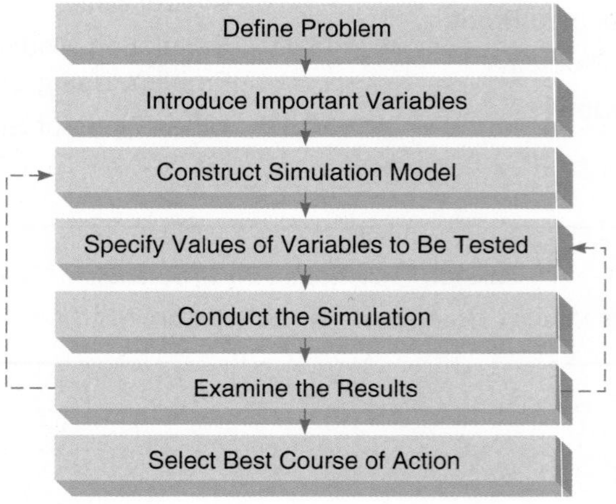

HISTORY Simulation

The history of simulation goes back 5,000 years to Chinese war games, called *weich'i*, and continues through 1780, when the Prussians used the games to help train their army. Since then, all major military powers have used war games to test military strategies under simulated environments.

From military or operational gaming, a new concept, *Monte Carlo simulation*, was developed as a decision modeling technique by the great mathematician John von Neumann during World War II. Working with neutrons at the Los Alamos Scientific Laboratory, von Neumann used simulation to solve physics problems that were too complex or expensive to analyze by hand or with physical models. The random nature of the neutrons suggested the use of a roulette wheel in dealing with probabilities. Because of the gaming nature, von Neumann called it the Monte Carlo model of studying laws of chance.

With the advent and common use of business computers in the 1950s, simulation grew as a management tool. Specialized computer languages (GPSS and SIMSCRIPT) were developed in the 1960s to handle large-scale problems more effectively. In the 1980s, prewritten simulation programs to handle situations ranging from queuing to inventory were developed. A few of them are ProModel, SLAM, and WITNESS.

introduction of computers in the mid-1940s and early 1950s that it became a practical means of solving management and military problems.

In this chapter, we explain the Monte Carlo simulation method and use it to model a variety of problems. For each simulation model, we show how Excel can be used to set up and solve the problem. In this regard, we discuss two approaches in this chapter:

We discuss two ways of using Excel for simulation here: with and without add-ins.

- ***Simulation using Excel's standard built-in functions.*** This approach is adequate for many applications and is especially useful if you are operating in a computer environment, such as in a university network, where the installation of additional software on individual computers is not preferred or convenient.
- ***Simulation using*** **Crystal Ball.** Several add-ins are available that make setting up and solving simulation models on Excel even easier. In this approach, we illustrate the use of one of the more powerful add-ins, Crystal Ball.

We end this chapter by briefly discussing two other types of simulation models besides the Monte Carlo approach.

Advantages and Disadvantages of Simulation

Simulation is a tool that has become widely accepted by managers for several reasons. The main advantages of simulation are as follows:

These advantages of simulation make it one of the most widely used decision modeling techniques in corporations.

1. It is relatively straightforward and flexible. Properly implemented, a simulation model can be made flexible enough to easily accommodate several changes to the problem scenario.
2. It can be used to analyze large and complex real-world situations that cannot be solved by using conventional decision models. For example, it may not be possible to build and solve a purely mathematical model of a city government system that incorporates important economic, social, environmental, and political factors. But simulation has been used successfully to model urban systems, hospitals, educational systems, national and state economies, and even world food systems.
3. Simulation allows what-if types of questions. With a simulation model, a manager can try out several policy decisions within a matter of minutes.
4. Simulations do not interfere with the real-world system. It may be too disruptive, for example, to experiment with new policies or ideas in a hospital, school, or manufacturing plant. With simulation, experiments are done with the model, not on the system itself.
5. Simulation allows us to study the interactive effects of individual components or variables to determine which ones are important. In any given problem scenario, not all inputs are equally important. We can use simulation to selectively vary each input (or combination of inputs) to identify the ones that most affect the results.
6. "Time compression" is possible with simulation. The effects of ordering, advertising, or other policies over many months or years can be obtained by a computer simulation model in a short time.

7. Simulation allows for the inclusion of real-world complications that most decision models cannot permit. For example, some of the queuing models discussed in Chapter 9 require exponential or Poisson distributions; the PERT analysis covered in Chapter 7 requires normal distributions. But simulation can use any probability distribution that the user defines.

The disadvantages of simulation include cost, its trial-and-error nature, and its uniqueness.

The main disadvantages of simulation are as follows:

1. Good simulation models can be very expensive. It is often a long, complicated process to develop a model. A corporate planning model, for example, can take months or even years to develop.
2. Simulation does not generate optimal solutions to problems, as do other decision modeling techniques, such as linear programming or integer programming. It is a trial-and-error approach that can produce different solutions in repeated runs.
3. Managers must generate all the conditions and constraints for solutions that they want to examine. The simulation model does not produce answers by itself.
4. Each simulation model is unique. Its solutions and inferences are not usually transferable to other problems.

10.2 Monte Carlo Simulation

Monte Carlo simulation *can be used with variables that are probabilistic.*

When a problem contains elements that exhibit chance or probability in their behavior, **Monte Carlo simulation** may be applied. The basic idea in Monte Carlo simulation is to randomly generate values for the unknown elements (i.e., variables) in the model through random sampling. The technique breaks down into simple steps. This section examines each of these steps in turn.

Steps of Monte Carlo Simulation

1. Establish a probability distribution for each variable in the model that is subject to chance.
2. Using random numbers, simulate values from the probability distribution for each variable in step 1.
3. Repeat the process for a series of **replications** (also called *runs*, or *trials*).

Step 1: Establish a Probability Distribution for Each Variable

Variables we may want to simulate abound in business problems because very little in life is certain.

Many variables in real-world systems are probabilistic in nature, and we might want to simulate them. A few of these variables are as follows:

- Product demand
- Lead time for orders to arrive
- Time between machine breakdowns
- Time between arrivals at a service facility
- Service time
- Time to complete a project activity
- Number of employees absent from work on a given day
- Stock market performance

To establish a probability distribution for a variable, we often assume that historical behavior is a good indicator of future outcomes.

There are several ways in which we can establish a *probability distribution* for a given variable. One common approach is to examine the historical outcomes of that variable. Then, we can compute the probability of each possible outcome of the variable by dividing the frequency of each observation by the total number of observations. Alternatively, we can use statistical goodness-of-fit tests to identify a commonly known probability distribution (e.g., normal, uniform, exponential, Poisson, binomial) that best characterizes the behavior of the variable. In practice, there are hundreds of probability distributions available to characterize the behavior of the various variables in a simulation model. In our study here, however, we will examine only a few of these probability distributions.

HARRY'S AUTO SHOP EXAMPLE To illustrate how to establish a probability distribution for a variable, let us consider, for example, the monthly demand for radial tires at Harry's Auto Shop over the past 60 months. The data are shown in the first two columns of Table 10.1. If we

TABLE 10.1 Historical Monthly Demand for Radial Tires at Harry's Auto Shop

DEMAND	FREQUENCY	PROBABILITY
300	3	$3/60 = 0.05$
320	6	$6/60 = 0.10$
340	12	$12/60 = 0.20$
360	18	$18/60 = 0.30$
380	15	$15/60 = 0.25$
400	6	$6/60 = 0.10$

assume that past demand rates will hold in the future, we can convert these data to a probability distribution for tire demand. To do so, we divide each demand frequency by the total number of months, 60. This is illustrated in the third column of Table 10.1.

Step 2: Simulate Values from the Probability Distributions

Once we have established the probability distribution for a variable, how do we simulate random values from this distribution? As we shall see shortly, the procedure to do so varies, based on the type of probability distribution. In this section, let us see how we can use the probability distribution identified in Table 10.1 to simulate Harry's tire demand for a *specific* month in the future. Note that in simulating the demand for any given month, we need to ensure the following:

- The actual monthly demand value is 300, 320, 340, 360, 380, or 400.
- There is a 5% chance that the monthly demand is 300, 10% chance that it is 320, 20% chance that it is 340, 30% chance that it is 360, 25% chance that it is 380, and 10% chance that it is 400.

Probabilities reflect long-term behavior.

These probability values, however, reflect only the long-term behavior. That is, if we simulate tire demand for many months (several hundred, or, better yet, several thousand), the demand will be 300 for exactly 5% of the months, 320 for exactly 10% of the months, and so on. Based on our knowledge of probability distributions, we can also use these probability values to compute Harry's expected value (or average) of monthly demand, as follows:

$$\begin{aligned}\text{Expected monthly demand} &= \textstyle\sum_i (i\text{th demand value}) \times (\text{Probability of } i\text{th demand value})\\ &= 300 \times 0.05 + 320 \times 0.10 + 340 \times 0.20 + 360 \times 0.30\\ &\quad + 380 \times 0.25 + 400 \times 0.10\\ &= 358 \text{ tires}\end{aligned}$$

Simulated results can differ from analytical results in a short simulation.

In the short term, however, the occurrence of demand may be quite different from these probability values. For example, if we simulate demand for just five months, it is entirely possible (and logical) for the demand to be 320 tires per month for *all* five months. The average demand for these five months would then be 320 tires per month, which is quite different from the expected value of 358 tires per month we just calculated. Hence, what we need is a procedure that will achieve the following objectives:

- Generate, in the *short term*, random demand values that do not exhibit any specific pattern. The expected value need not necessarily equal 358 tires per month.
- Generate, in the *long term*, random demand values that conform exactly to the required probability distribution. The expected value must equal 358 tires per month.

In simulation, we achieve these objectives by using a concept called *random numbers*.

There are several ways to pick random numbers—using a computer, a table, a roulette wheel, and so on.

RANDOM NUMBERS A **random number** is a number that has been selected through a totally random process. For example, assume that we want to generate a series of random numbers from a set consisting of 100 integer-valued numbers: 0, 1, 2, … , 97, 98, 99. There are several ways to do so. One simple way would be as follows:

1. Mark each of 100 identical balls with a unique number between 0 and 99. Put all the balls in a large bowl and mix thoroughly.
2. Select *any* ball from the bowl. Write down the number.
3. Replace the ball in the bowl and mix again. Go back to step 2.

Instead of balls in a bowl, we could have accomplished this task by using the spin of a roulette wheel with 100 slots, or by using tables of random digits that are commonly available.[1] Also, as we shall see shortly, it turns out that most computer software packages (including Excel) and many handheld calculators have built-in procedures for generating an endless set of random numbers.

Cumulative probabilities are found by summing all the previous probabilities up to the current demand.

USING RANDOM NUMBERS TO SIMULATE DEMAND IN HARRY'S AUTO SHOP How do we use random numbers to simulate Harry's tire demand? We begin by converting the probability distribution in Table 10.1 to a *cumulative probability* distribution. As shown in Table 10.2, the cumulative probability for each demand value is the sum of the probability of that demand and all demands *less than* that demand value. For example, the cumulative probability for a demand of 340 tires is the sum of the probabilities for 300, 320, or 340 tires. Obviously, the cumulative probability for a demand of 400 tires (the maximum demand) is 1.

We create a random number interval for each value of the variable. The specific numbers assigned to an interval are not relevant as long as the right proportion of unique numbers is assigned to the interval.

Consider the set of 100 integer-valued numbers ranging from 0 to 99. We now use the cumulative probabilities computed in Table 10.2 to create *random number intervals* by assigning these 100 numbers to represent the different possible demand values. Because there is a 5% probability that demand is 300 tires, we assign 5% of the numbers (i.e., 5 of the 100 numbers between 0 and 99) to denote this demand value. For example, we could assign the first 5 numbers possible (i.e., 0, 1, 2, 3, and 4) to denote a demand of 300 tires. Every time the random number drawn is one of these five numbers, the implication is that the simulated demand that month is 300 tires. Likewise, because there is a 10% chance that demand is 320 tires, we could let the next 10 numbers (i.e., 5 to 14) represent that demand—and so on for the other demand values. The complete random number intervals for the Harry's Auto Shop problem are shown in Table 10.3. It is important to note that the specific random numbers assigned to denote a demand value are not relevant, as long as the assignment is unique and includes the right proportion of numbers. That is, for example, we can use any set of 5 random numbers between 0 and 99 to denote a demand value of 300 tires, as long as these numbers are not assigned to denote any other demand level.

We simulate values by comparing the random numbers against the random number intervals.

To simulate demand using the random number intervals, we need to generate random numbers between 0 and 99. Suppose we use a computer for this purpose (we will see how to do so

TABLE 10.2 Cumulative Probabilities for Radial Tires at Harry's Auto Shop

DEMAND	PROBABILITY	CUMULATIVE PROBABILITY
300	0.05	0.05
320	0.10	0.05 + 0.10 = 0.15
340	0.20	0.15 + 0.20 = 0.35
360	0.30	0.35 + 0.30 = 0.65
380	0.25	0.65 + 0.25 = 0.90
400	0.10	0.90 + 0.10 = 1.00

TABLE 10.3 Random Number Intervals for Radial Tires at Harry's Auto Shop

DEMAND	PROBABILITY	CUMULATIVE PROBABILITY	RANDOM NUMBER INTERVAL
300	0.05	0.05	0 to 4
320	0.10	0.15	5 to 14
340	0.20	0.35	15 to 34
360	0.30	0.65	35 to 64
380	0.25	0.90	65 to 89
400	0.10	1.00	90 to 99

[1]See, for example, *A Million Random Digits with 100,000 Normal Deviates*. New York: The Free Press, 1955, p. 7.

IN ACTION Simulating a Production Line at Delphi

Delphi Corporation, a major supplier of fuel injectors to automobile manufacturers, was considering a new line that would produce the next generation of fuel injectors. In order for the line to be financially viable, it needed to have a high throughput, be cost effective to build, and be able to fit in the available space. To address this issue, Delphi used a simulation model at a very early design stage to serve as a test bed for several candidate line designs.

Simulating a line design involves fully specifying various details such as which machines to use, in what order, conveyor lengths, machine process rates, failure and repair distributions for each machine, etc. Although such detailed information is typically not available at the concept stage of a line design, this is precisely when simulation helps to assess a line's potential performance characteristics. A major advantage of using simulation at such an early stage is that implementing the model's recommendations is inexpensive because the equipment has not yet been built. In contrast, the model's recommendations may be more difficult to cost justify after the equipment has been built since much of the cost has already been sunk.

The simulation analysis has provided and continues to provide Delphi with valuable guidance for the layout, loading and staffing of the new production line.

Source: Based on M. H. Tongarlak et al. "Using Simulation Early in the Design of a Fuel Injector Production Line," *Interfaces* 40, 2 (March-April 2010): 105–117.

shortly). Assume that the first random number generated is 52. Because this is between 35 and 64, it implies that the simulated demand in month 1 is 360 tires. Now assume that the second random number generated is 6. Because this is between 5 and 14, it implies that the simulated demand in month 2 is 320 tires. The procedure continues in this fashion.

Step 3: Repeat the Process for a Series of Replications

A simulation process must be repeated numerous times to get meaningful results.

As noted earlier, although the long-term average demand is 358 tires per month in Harry's example, it is likely that we will get different average values from a short-term simulation of just a few months. It would be very risky to draw any hard-and-fast conclusion regarding any simulation model from just a few simulation replications. We need to run the model for several thousand replications (also referred to as *runs*, or *trials*) in order to gather meaningful results.

10.3 Role of Computers in Simulation

Although it is possible to simulate small examples such as the Harry's Auto Shop problem by hand, it is easier and much more convenient to conduct most simulation exercises by using a computer. Three of the primary reasons for this follow:

Software packages have built-in procedures for simulating from several different probability distributions.

1. It is quite cumbersome to use hand-based random number generation procedures for even common probability distributions, such as the normal, uniform, and exponential distributions. As noted earlier, most computer software packages (including Excel) have built-in procedures for generation of random numbers. It is quite easy to simulate values from many probability distributions by using a software package's random number generator.
2. In order for the simulation results to be valid and useful, it is necessary to replicate the process hundreds (or even thousands) of times. Doing this by hand is laborious and time-consuming. In contrast, it is possible to simulate thousands of replications for a model in just a matter of seconds by using most software packages.

Software packages allow us to easily replicate a model and keep track of several output measures.

3. During the simulation process, depending on the complexity and scope of the model, we may need to manipulate many input parameters and keep track of several output measures. Here again, doing so by hand could become very cumbersome. Software packages, on the other hand, can be used to easily change multiple input values and track as many output measures as required in any simulation model.

Types of Simulation Software Packages

Three types of software packages are available to help set up and run simulation models on computers, as discussed in the following sections.

The use of simulation has been broadened by the availability of computing technology.

GENERAL-PURPOSE PROGRAMMING LANGUAGES General-purpose programming languages that can be used to set up and run simulation models include standard programming languages such as Visual Basic, C++, and FORTRAN. The main advantage of these languages is that an experienced programmer can use them to develop simulation models for many diverse situations. The big disadvantage, however, is that a program written for a simulation model is specific to that model and is not easily portable. That is, a simulation model developed for one problem or situation may not be easily transferable to a different situation.

Special-purpose simulation languages have several advantages over general-purpose languages.

SPECIAL-PURPOSE SIMULATION LANGUAGES AND PROGRAMS Languages such as GPSS, Simscript III, and Visual SLAM and programs such as Extend, MicroSaint Sharp, BuildSim, AweSim, ProModel, and Xcell can be used to set up and run simulation models. Using such special-purpose languages and programs has three advantages compared with using general-purpose languages: (1) They require less programming time for large simulations, (2) they are usually more efficient and easier to check for errors, and (3) they have built-in procedures to automate many of the tasks in simulation modeling. However, because of the significant learning curve associated with these languages, they are typically likely to be most useful to experienced modelers dealing with extremely complex simulation models.

We focus on building simulation models using Excel in this chapter.

SPREADSHEET MODELS The built-in ability to generate random numbers and use them to select values from several probability distributions makes spreadsheets excellent tools for conducting simple simulations. Spreadsheets are also very powerful for quickly tabulating results and presenting them using graphs. In keeping with the focus of this textbook, we therefore use Excel (and an Excel add-in, Crystal Ball) in the remainder of this chapter to develop several simulation models.

Random Generation from Some Common Probability Distributions Using Excel

In the following pages, we discuss how we can use Excel's built-in functions to generate random values from seven commonly used probability distributions in simulation models: (1) continuous uniform, (2) discrete uniform, (3) normal, (4) exponential, (5) binomial, (6) discrete general with two outcomes, and (7) discrete general with more than two outcomes.

Excel's RAND *function generates random numbers.*

GENERATING RANDOM NUMBERS IN EXCEL Excel uses the RAND function to generate random numbers. The format for using this function is

=RAND()

Note that the = sign before the RAND function implies that the cell entry is a formula. Also, there is no argument within the parentheses; that is, the left parenthesis is immediately followed by the right parenthesis.

If we enter =RAND() in any cell of a spreadsheet, it will return a random value between 0 and 1 (actually, between 0 and 0.9999 ...) *each time you press the calculate key* (i.e., the F9 key). The RAND function can be used either by itself in a cell or as part of a formula. For example, to generate a random number between 0 and 4.9999 ... , the appropriate formula to use would simply be

=5*RAND()

Uniform distributions can be either discrete or continuous.

CONTINUOUS UNIFORM DISTRIBUTION A variable follows a continuous uniform distribution between a lower limit a and an upper limit b if all values between a and b, including fractional values, are equally likely. To simulate a variable that follows this distribution, we use the following formula:

$$=a+(b-a)*\text{RAND}()$$

For example, if $a = 3$ and $b = 9$, we know that =(9 − 3)*RAND() will generate a random value between 0 and 5.9999… . If we add this to 3, we will get a random value between 3 and 8.999 … (which, for all practical purposes, is 9).

DISCRETE UNIFORM DISTRIBUTION If all values between a and b are equally likely, but the variable is allowed to take on only integer values between a and b (inclusive), we refer to this

There are two ways of simulating from a discrete uniform distribution.

as a discrete uniform distribution. To generate values randomly from this distribution, there are two different approaches we can use in Excel. First, we can extend the preceding formula for continuous uniform distributions by including Excel's INT function. The resulting formula is

$$=\text{INT}(a+(b-a+1)*\text{RAND}())$$

Note that we need to add 1 to the $(b - a)$ term in this formula because the INT function always rounds down (that is, it just drops the fractional part from the value).

Alternatively, Excel has a built-in function called RANDBETWEEN that we can use to generate random values from discrete uniform distributions between a and b. The format for this function is

$$=\text{RANDBETWEEN}(a, b)$$

So, for example, if we want to generate random integers between 0 and 99 (as we did in the Harry's Auto Shop example earlier), we can use either of these two Excel formulas:

$$=\text{INT}(100*\text{RAND}()) \quad \text{or} \quad =\text{RANDBETWEEN}(0,99)$$

Excel's NORMINV *function can be used to simulate from a normal distribution.*

NORMAL DISTRIBUTION The normal distribution is probably one of the most commonly used distributions in simulation models. The normal distribution is always identified by two parameters: mean μ and standard deviation σ (or variance σ^2). To simulate a random value from a normal distribution with mean μ and standard deviation σ, we use the NORMINV function in Excel as follows:

$$=\text{NORMINV}(\text{RAND}(),\mu,\sigma)$$

For example, the formula =NORMINV(RAND(),30,5) will generate a random value from a normal distribution with a mean of 30 and a standard deviation of 5. If we repeat this process several thousand times, 50% of the values will be below 30 and 50% will be above 30, 68.26% will be between 25 and 35 (=mean $\pm$ 1 standard deviation), and so on. Note that a normally distributed random value will include fractions because the normal distribution is a continuous distribution. If we need to convert normally distributed random values to integers, we can do so by using Excel's ROUND function as follows:

$$=\text{ROUND}(\text{NORMINV}(\text{RAND}(),\mu,\sigma),0)$$

The argument of 0 in the ROUND function specifies that we want to round off fractional values to the nearest number with zero decimal places (i.e., integer). In this case, fractional values of 0.5 and above are rounded up, while fractional values below 0.5 are rounded down.

In some situations, we may need to truncate the value generated from a normal distribution. For example, if we randomly generate demand values from a normal distribution with a mean of 10 and a standard deviation of 4, it is possible that the generated value is sometimes negative. Because demand cannot be negative, we may need to truncate the generated demand by setting any negative value to zero. A simple way of doing so is to use Excel's MAX function, as follows:

$$=\text{MAX}(0,\text{NORMINV}(\text{RAND}(),10,4))$$

Excel's LN function can be used to simulate from an exponential distribution.

EXPONENTIAL DISTRIBUTION The exponential distribution is commonly used to model arrival and service times in queuing systems. (You may recall that we saw a few examples of this in Chapter 9.) The exponential distribution can be described by a single parameter, μ, which describes the average *rate* of occurrences. (Alternatively, $1/\mu$ describes the mean time between successive occurrences.) To simulate a random value from an exponential distribution with average rate μ, we use the following formula in Excel:

$$=-(1/\mu)*\text{LN}(\text{RAND}())$$

where LN in the formula refers to the natural logarithmic function. For example, if the average service rate in a queuing system is 10 customers per hour, the service *time* (in hours) for a specific customer may be randomly generated by using the following formula:

$$=-(1/10)*\text{LN}(\text{RAND}())$$

Excel's CRITBINOM function can be used to simulate from a binomial distribution.

BINOMIAL DISTRIBUTION The binomial distribution models the probability of the number of successes occurring in n independent events (called trials), where each event has the same two outcomes, which we will label success and failure, and the probability of success in each event is the same value, p. To simulate a random number of successes in the n trials, we use the CRITBINOM function in Excel as follows:[2]

=CRITBINOM(n,p,RAND())

Excel's IF function can be used to select from two possible outcomes.

DISCRETE GENERAL DISTRIBUTION WITH TWO OUTCOMES If the outcomes of a probability distribution are discrete but the probabilities of the various outcomes are *not* the same, we refer to this as a **discrete general distribution** (as opposed to a discrete uniform distribution, where all outcomes have the same probability).

Let us first consider a discrete general distribution with only two outcomes. Suppose we want to randomly select individuals from a population where there are 55% males and 45% females. This implies that in the long term, our selected group will have exactly 55% males and 45% females. However, in the short term, any combination of males and females is possible and logical. To simulate these random draws in Excel, we can use the IF function as follows:

=IF(RAND()<0.55,"Male","Female")

Note that the quotes are needed in the IF function because Male and Female are both text characters. If we use numeric codes (e.g., 1 = Male, 2 = Female) instead of text characters, the formula is then

=IF(RAND()<0.55,1,2)

Random numbers can actually be assigned in many different ways, as long as they represent the correct proportion of the outcomes.

Because RAND() has a 55% chance of returning a value between 0 and 0.55 (which implies it has a 45% chance of returning a value between 0.55 and 0.999 …), the preceding formula is logical. Note that we could have set up the IF function such that *any* 55% of values between 0 and 1 denotes male and the other 45% denotes female. For example, we could have expressed the formula as follows:

=IF(RAND()<0.45,"Female","Male")

If we replicate the simulation enough times, the male-to-female split will be the same (i.e., 55% male and 45% female), regardless of how the IF function is set up.

Distribution of Tire Demand

Demand	*Probability*
300	*0.05*
320	*0.10*
340	*0.20*
360	*0.30*
380	*0.25*
400	*0.10*

DISCRETE GENERAL DISTRIBUTION WITH MORE THAN TWO OUTCOMES Let us now consider a discrete general distribution with more than two outcomes by revisiting the Harry's Auto Shop example. (Table 10.1 is repeated in the margin for your convenience.) The demand for tires is one of six values: 300, 320, 340, 360, 380, or 400. However, unlike with the discrete uniform distribution, in this case the probability of demand for each value is not the same.

We want to use Excel to simulate demands randomly from this distribution, just as we did manually in Table 10.3 (on page 412) using random number intervals. To do so, a more experienced Excel user could use a *nested* IF function (i.e., IF function within IF function). However, it is probably more convenient to use Excel's LOOKUP, VLOOKUP, or HLOOKUP functions to randomly select values from this type of probability distribution. In our discussion here, we illustrate the use of the LOOKUP function.

Excel Notes

- The Companion Website for this textbook, at www.pearsonhighered.com/balakrishnan, contains the Excel file for each sample problem discussed here. The relevant file name is shown in the margin next to each example.
- For clarity, our simulation worksheets are color coded as follows:
  - *Input cells*, where we enter known data, are shaded yellow.
  - *Simulation cells*, which show simulated values, are shaded blue.
  - *Output cells*, where the results are shown, are shaded green.

[2] Excel 2010 includes an additional function called BINOM.INV, which is an improved version of CRITBINOM and uses the same arguments.

File: 10-1.xls, sheet: 10-1A

- When you open any of the Excel files for the examples in this chapter, if the Calculation Options in Excel is set to automatic (click Formulas | Calculation Options | Automatic), Excel will automatically recalculate all random numbers in the model. This, in turn, may cause all simulated values in the worksheet to change. Hence, the values you see in the Excel file may not be the same as those shown in the screenshots included in the textbook.
- *Tip:* After creating a simulation model, if you wish to save your results in such a way that the values do *not* change each time you open the Excel file, you can set the Calculation Options in Excel to manual (click Formulas | Calculation Options | Manual). Alternatively, you can use the Paste Values feature in Excel (see Appendix B for details). You can copy the cells showing the results and use Paste Values to save your answers as values rather than as formulas. Remember, however, that any cell overwritten in this manner will no longer contain the formula.

Excel's LOOKUP function can be used to simulate from a discrete general distribution.

Screenshot 10-1A shows the Excel layout showing the formulas for setting up a LOOKUP function. We begin by arranging all the demand values in a column (say, column A). Titles, like the ones shown in row 1, are optional. We then list the probability of each demand in another column (say, column B). In Screenshot 10-1A, we have shown the demand values in cells A2:A7 and the corresponding probabilities in cells B2:B7.

File: 10-1.xls, sheet: 10-1B

Just as we did in Table 10.3, we now create the *random number intervals*. The only difference is that instead of using two-digit random numbers from 0 to 99, we use continuous-valued random numbers from 0 to 0.9999. The formulas to compute the random number intervals for Harry's example are shown in cells C2:D7 of Screenshot 10-1A. The actual values are shown in Screenshot 10-1B. Notice that the lower-limit numbers in cells C2:C7 are identical to the ones

SCREENSHOT 10-1A
Excel Layout and Formulas for a LOOKUP Function

	A	B	C	D
1	Demand	Probability	Lower limit of random number interval	Upper limit of random number interval
2	300	0.05	0	=C2+B2
3	320	0.1	=D2	=C3+B3
4	340	0.2	=D3	=C4+B4
5	360	0.3	=D4	=C5+B5
6	380	0.25	=D5	=C6+B6
7	400	0.1	=D6	=C7+B7
8				
9	Random number =		=RAND()	
10	Simulated demand =		=LOOKUP(C9,C2:C7,A2:A7)	

Entries in columns A and B are known values.

RAND function generates random number between 0 and 1.

Value of random number

Cell range containing lower limits of random number intervals.

Cell range containing values of simulated variable.

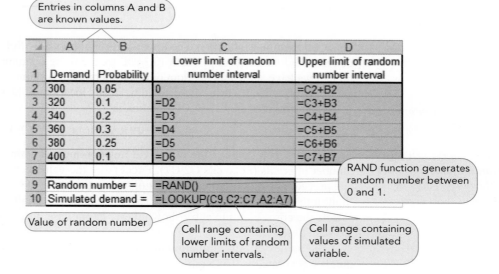

SCREENSHOT 10-1B
Simulation Using a LOOKUP Function

	A	B	C	D
1	Demand	Probability	Lower limit of random number interval	Upper limit of random number interval
2	300	0.05	0.00	0.05
3	320	0.10	0.05	0.15
4	340	0.20	0.15	0.35
5	360	0.30	0.35	0.65
6	380	0.25	0.65	0.90
7	400	0.10	0.90	1.00
8				
9	Random number =		0.715	
10	Simulated demand =		380	

This column has no role in the LOOKUP function and can be dropped if desired.

0.715 is between 0.65 and 0.90 in the RN intervals.

The entry in cell range A2:A7 corresponding to the RN interval 0.65 to 0.90 is 380.

TABLE 10.4 Simulation from Various Probability Distributions Using Excel's Built-in Formulas

TO SIMULATE	USE BUILT-IN EXCEL FORMULA
Random number	=RAND()
Continuous uniform distribution Between a and b	$=a+(b-a)$*RAND()
Discrete uniform distribution Between a and b	=INT($a+(b-a+1)$*RAND()) or =RANDBETWEEN(a, b)
Normal distribution Mean $= \mu$; Standard deviation $= \sigma$	=NORMINV(RAND(), μ, σ)
Exponential distribution Mean rate $= \mu$	$=-(1/\mu)$*LN(RAND())
Binomial distribution Number of events $= n$ Probability of success in each event $= p$	=CRITBINOM(n, p, RAND())
Discrete general distribution with two outcomes only: A and B Probability of outcome $A = p$	=IF(RAND()<p, A, B)
Discrete general distribution with more than two outcomes: *Range*1 = Cell range containing lower limits of the random number intervals *Range*2 = Cell range containing the variable values	=LOOKUP(RAND(), *Range*1, *Range*2)

we developed in Table 10.3. The upper-limit numbers are slightly different because we used discrete random numbers in Table 10.3 and we are using continuous random numbers here. Although we have shown the random number intervals in columns that are adjacent to the demand and probability values here, these could be in any location of the spreadsheet.

We use random number intervals in this simulation.

The format for the LOOKUP function is

=LOOKUP(RAND(),C2:C7,A2:A7)

The first range in the LOOKUP function must contain the lower limits of the random number intervals.

The first cell range in the LOOKUP function must contain the *lower limits* of the random number intervals (i.e., cells C2:C7). Excel takes the value generated by the RAND() function and proceeds down this column to identify the entry where the RAND() value exceeds the lower limit. It then moves to the other range specified in the LOOKUP function (i.e., cells A2:A7) and selects the corresponding entry shown there. In our case, this range has the demand value that we wish to simulate.[3]

The values of this simulation are shown in Screenshot 10-1B. Let's suppose the random number generated is 0.715 (shown in cell C9). Using the preceding logic, the LOOKUP function compares this number to the entries in the cell range C2:C7. Having recognized that 0.715 exceeds the fifth entry (0.65) in the range but not the sixth (0.90), it returns the fifth entry in the cell range A2:A7. This is cell A6 (also shown in cell A10), which corresponds to a demand value of 380 tires.[4]

Summary of some of Excel's built-in functions used in simulation.

For your convenience, Table 10.4 presents a summary of the Excel formulas we have presented so far for simulating random values from various probability distributions. In the following sections, we describe four simulation models that use these formulas for their implementation.

[3] Note that the upper limit of the random number interval (cells D2:D7) play no role in the LOOKUP function. In fact, it is not necessary to even show this column, and we can safely delete it. However, we have included these entries in all our models here to make it easier to understand the use of the LOOKUP function.

[4] In this example, we have shown the value of the random number separately in cell C9 and used this number in the formula in cell C10. Note that the RAND() function could have been directly embedded in the LOOKUP formula itself. Except for the simulation model discussed in section 10.4, we do not show the random number values separately in our models.

10.4 Simulation Model to Compute Expected Profit

Table 10.1 Revisited

Demand	*Probability*
300	*0.05*
320	*0.10*
340	*0.20*
360	*0.30*
380	*0.25*
400	*0.10*

Let us set up the Harry's Auto Shop example as our first simulation model. Recall from Table 10.1 that Harry's monthly demand of tires is 300, 320, 340, 360, 380, or 400, with specific probabilities for each value. Now let us assume that the following additional information is known regarding Harry's operating environment:

Demand, selling price, and profit margin are all probabilistic.

- Depending on competitors' prices and other market conditions, Harry estimates that his average selling price per tire each month follows a discrete uniform distribution between \$60 and \$80 (in increments of \$1).
- Harry's variable cost per tire also varies each month, depending on material costs and other market conditions. This causes Harry's average profit margin per tire (calculated as a percentage of the selling price) to vary each month. Using past data, Harry estimates that his profit margin per tire follows a continuous uniform distribution between 20% and 30% of the selling price.
- Harry estimates that his fixed cost of stocking and selling tires is \$2,000 per month.

Using this information, let us simulate and calculate Harry's *average profit* per month from the sale of auto tires.

Setting Up the Model

The first issue to understand in any simulation model is what we mean by **one replication** *of the model.*

In any simulation model, the first issue we need to understand is what we mean by *one replication* of the model. In Harry's case, each replication corresponds to simulating one month of tire sales. That is, we will set up the model to simulate one month of tire sales at Harry's Auto Shop and then run the model repeatedly for as many replications as desired. The logic of Harry's simulation process is presented in Figure 10.2. Such **flow diagrams**, or **flowcharts**, are very useful in understanding the logical sequence of events in simulation models, especially in complex problem scenarios.

File: 10-2.xls, sheet: 10-2A

Let us now translate the flowchart in Figure 10.2 into a simulation model, using Excel. Screenshot 10-2A shows the formula view of the Excel layout for Harry's model. All titles, like the ones shown in rows 1 and 3, are optional. For a given replication, the spreadsheet is organized as follows:

- Cell A4 generates the random number used to simulate the demand that month. For this model alone, we show the actual value of the random number used to simulate each variable value.
- The random number in cell A4 is used in a LOOKUP function to simulate the monthly demand in cell B4. The data (demands, probabilities, and random number intervals) of the LOOKUP function are shown in cells I4:L9.

FIGURE 10.2 Flowchart for Harry's Auto Shop Simulation Model

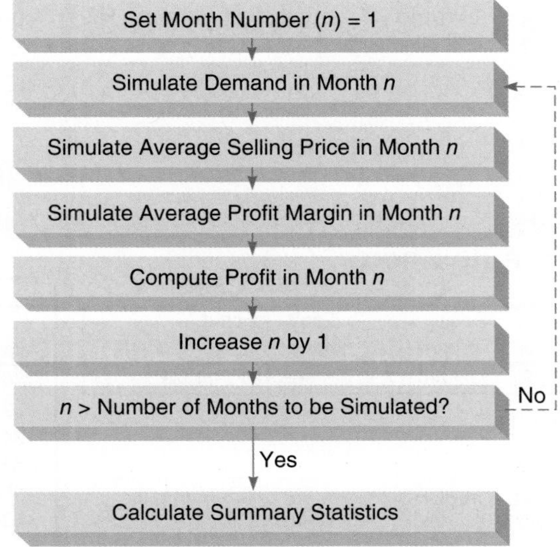

SCREENSHOT 10-2A Excel Layout and Formulas for Harry's Auto Shop

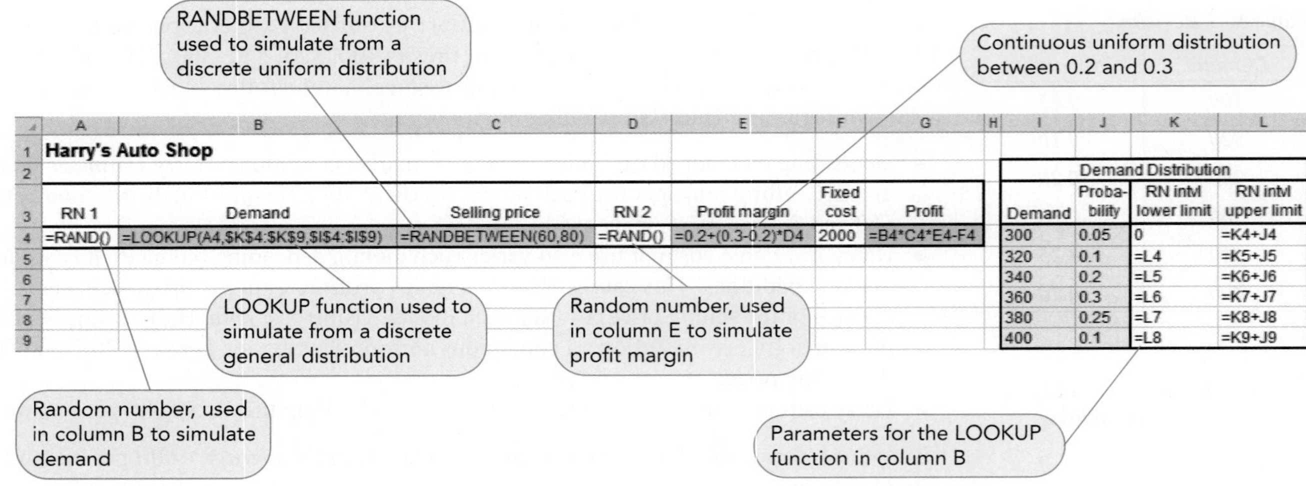

Harry's Auto Shop

RN 1	Demand	Selling price	RN 2	Profit margin	Fixed cost	Profit
=RAND()	=LOOKUP(A4,$K$4:$K$9,$I$4:$I$9)	=RANDBETWEEN(60,80)	=RAND()	=0.2+(0.3-0.2)*D4	2000	=B4*C4*E4-F4

Demand Distribution			
Demand	Proba-bility	RN intvl lower limit	RN intvl upper limit
300	0.05	0	=K4+J4
320	0.1	=L4	=K5+J5
340	0.2	=L5	=K6+J6
360	0.3	=L6	=K7+J7
380	0.25	=L7	=K8+J8
400	0.1	=L8	=K9+J9

- In cell C4, we simulate the average selling price per tire by using the RANDBETWEEN function (with $a = 60$ and $b = 80$). The formula is =RANDBETWEEN(60,80).
- Cell D4 generates the random number used to simulate the average profit margin per tire.
- The random number in cell D4 is used in cell E4 to simulate the average profit margin per tire. For this, we use the continuous uniform distribution formula, with $a = 0.2$ and $b = 0.3$. The formula is =0.2+(0.3−0.2)*D4.
- Cell F4 shows the fixed cost, equal to $2,000 per month.
- Using these simulated values, Harry's monthly profit is calculated in cell G4 as

$$\text{Profit} = (\text{Demand for tires}) \times (\text{Average selling price per tire}) \\ \times (\text{Average profit margin per tire}) - (\text{Monthly fixed cost})$$

That is, the formula in cell G4 is =B4*C4*E4−F4.

File: 10-2.xls, sheet: 10-2B

Screenshot 10-2B shows the result for a single replication of Harry's simulation model. This result indicates that Harry will earn a profit of $4,125.52 per month. It is important to remember, however, that each randomly simulated value only represents something that *could* occur. As such, there is no guarantee that the specific values simulated in Screenshot 10-2B will actually occur. Due to the presence of random numbers, these simulated values will change each time the model is replicated (i.e., they will change each time the F9 key is pressed in Excel). Hence, it would be incorrect to estimate Harry's profit based on just one replication (month).

SCREENSHOT 10-2B Results for the Simulation Model of Harry's Auto Shop

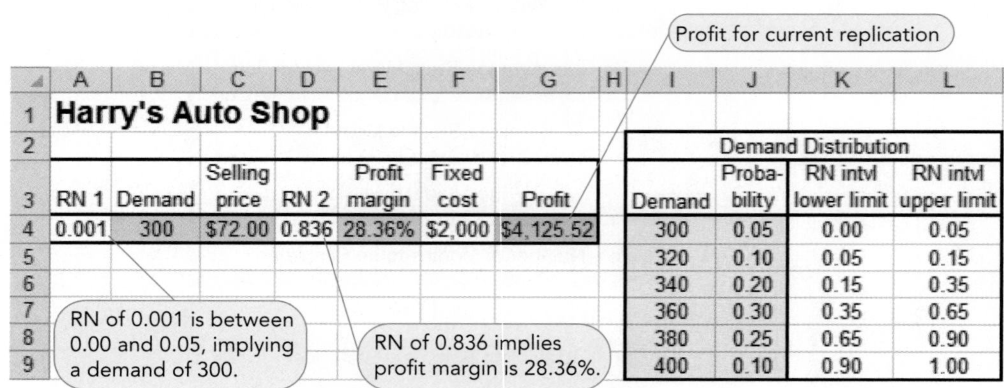

Harry's Auto Shop

RN 1	Demand	Selling price	RN 2	Profit margin	Fixed cost	Profit
0.001	300	$72.00	0.836	28.36%	$2,000	$4,125.52

Demand Distribution			
Demand	Proba-bility	RN intvl lower limit	RN intvl upper limit
300	0.05	0.00	0.05
320	0.10	0.05	0.15
340	0.20	0.15	0.35
360	0.30	0.35	0.65
380	0.25	0.65	0.90
400	0.10	0.90	1.00

We need to replicate a simulation model at least a few thousand times to get consistent summary results.

To calculate Harry's *average* monthly profit, we need to replicate the simulation model several thousand times. However, in order to keep the computation times reasonable (especially in a classroom setting) and to keep the size of the resulting Excel files relatively small, we illustrate only 200 replications in most of our models in this chapter. We then compute summary statistics just from these 200 replications. It is important to note that 200 replications are not enough for a simulation model to yield consistent summary results. That is, an average based on just 200 replications, for example, will be different each time we run the simulation model. Therefore, in practice, we should replicate a model as many times as convenient.

Replication by Copying the Model

If the simulation model is very compact, we can perform replications by simply copying the model several times.

In simulation models where each replication consists of just a single row of computations in Excel (such as in Harry's model), an easy way to perform 200 replications is to copy all formulas and values in that row to 199 other rows. For example, we can copy cells A4:G4 in Screenshot 10-2B to cells A5:G203. (*Note:* For your convenience, a worksheet illustrating this way of replicating Harry's model is included in the Excel file *10-2.xls* on the Companion Website; see the sheet named *10-2B1*.) Due to the use of random numbers in the formulas, the values of the simulated variables will be different in each replication. Hence, each of the 200 entries computed in cells G4:G203, which represents the monthly profit that *could* result in a given month, will be different. Once we have simulated these 200 monthly profit values, we can compute the average monthly profit by using the Excel formula =AVERAGE(G4:G203).

Replicating a model by copying it multiple times could make the Excel file very large.

A clear drawback of this approach for replicating a simulation model is that it could make the resulting Excel file quite large and unwieldy. In fact, for models where each replication consists of computations spanning several rows in Excel (as we will see shortly), it is impractical to even consider copying the entire model 200 or more times. For this reason, we next illustrate a different approach—one that replicates a model multiple times without requiring us to copy the entire model each time.

Replication Using Data Table

Using **Data Table** *in Excel is a convenient way of replicating a large model several times.*

For replicating a simulation model, we can use an Excel procedure called Data Table. The primary use of this procedure in Excel is to plug in different values for a variable in a formula and compute the result each time. For example, if the formula is $(2a + 5)$, we can set up Data Table to plug in several values for the variable a and report the result of the formula each time. In a simulation model, however, we don't really have a "variable" and a "formula" to use in Data Table. So, as explained next, we make Data Table plug in multiple values for a dummy variable in a dummy formula (both of which have nothing to do with the simulation model) and report the "result" each time. The key here is that each time Data Table computes the formula's result, it automatically updates all calculations on the Excel sheet (i.e., it activates the F9 key). As a consequence, all random numbers in the simulation model change, and the result is a new replication of the model, with new values for all simulated entries.

File: 10-2.xls, sheet: 10-2C

We illustrate the use of Data Table to replicate Harry's simulation model 200 times in Screenshot 10-2C. Here again, we have chosen 200 replications just for convenience. The procedure is as follows:

This is how we set up Data Table.

1. We first use 200 cells in an empty column in the spreadsheet to represent the 200 values of the *dummy* variable. If we wish, we can leave these cells blank because they have no real role to play in the simulation model. However, as we have done in cells N4:N203 in Screenshot 10-2C, it is convenient to fill these cells with numbers from 1 to 200, to indicate we are performing 200 replications. If we wish, we can title this column *Replication* or *Run* (as shown in cell N3). *Note:* A convenient way to enter a series of numbers in Excel is to click Fill | Series found within the Home tab.
2. In the cell adjacent to the *first* cell in the range N4:N203 (i.e., in cell O4), we specify the cell reference for the output measure we want replicated 200 times. In Harry's model, this corresponds to cell G4, the monthly profit value. Hence, the formula in cell O4 would be =G4. We can title this column *Profit* if we wish (as shown in cell O3). We leave cells O5:O203 blank. Data Table will fill in these cells automatically when we run it.

SCREENSHOT 10-2C Data Table for Harry's Auto Shop

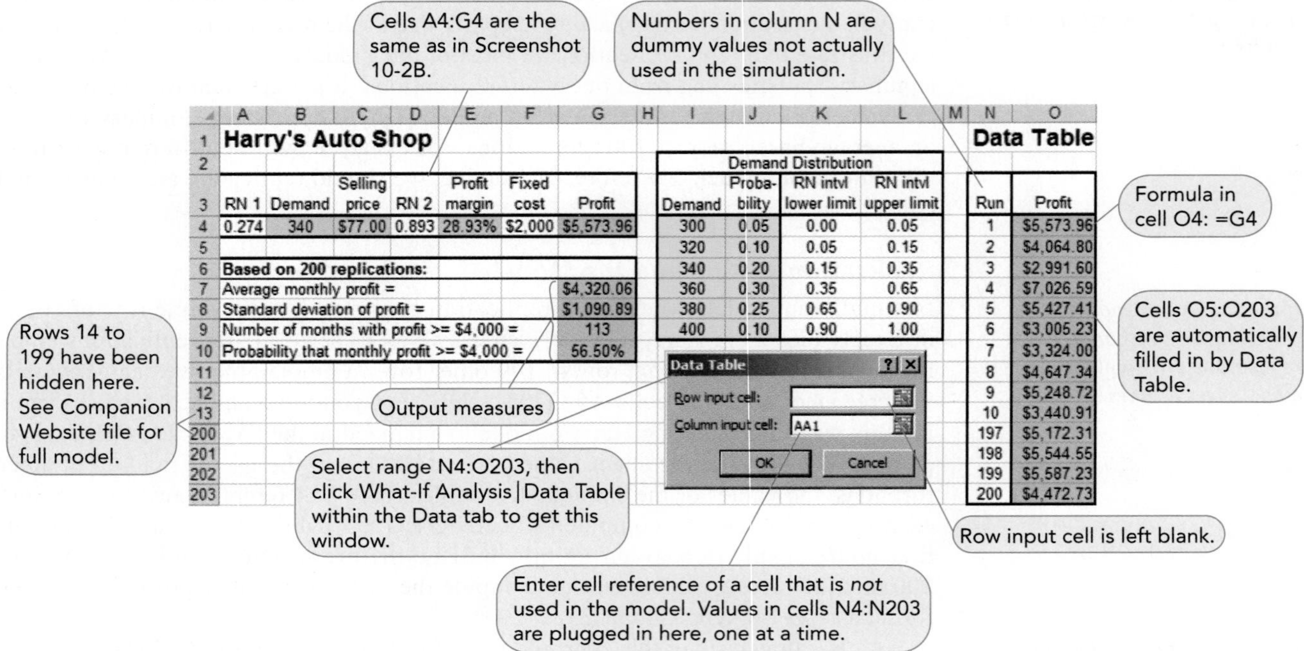

	A	B	C	D	E	F	G
3	RN 1	Demand	Selling price	RN 2	Profit margin	Fixed cost	Profit
4	0.274	340	$77.00	0.893	28.93%	$2,000	$5,573.96
6	Based on 200 replications:						
7	Average monthly profit =						$4,320.06
8	Standard deviation of profit =						$1,090.89
9	Number of months with profit >= $4,000 =						113
10	Probability that monthly profit >= $4,000 =						56.50%

Demand Distribution			
Demand	Probability	RN intvl lower limit	RN intvl upper limit
300	0.05	0.00	0.05
320	0.10	0.05	0.15
340	0.20	0.15	0.35
360	0.30	0.35	0.65
380	0.25	0.65	0.90
400	0.10	0.90	1.00

Run	Profit
1	$5,573.96
2	$4,064.80
3	$2,991.60
4	$7,026.59
5	$5,427.41
6	$3,005.23
7	$3,324.00
8	$4,647.34
9	$5,248.72
10	$3,440.91
197	$5,172.31
198	$5,544.55
199	$5,587.23
200	$4,472.73

3. We now use the mouse or keyboard to select the range N4:O203 (i.e., both columns). *After* selecting this range, we click the Data tab and choose What-If Analysis | Data Table. The window titled Data Table, shown in Screenshot 10-2C, is now displayed.
4. Because our table is arranged in columns, we leave the Row input cell box blank. We then select any arbitrary cell that has nothing to do with the simulation model and enter this cell reference in the Column input cell box. It is important to make sure this selected cell (AA1, in Screenshot 10-2C) has no role to play in the simulation model. In effect, we are telling Data Table that cell AA1 contains our *dummy* formula.
5. Finally, we click OK to run Data Table. The procedure now takes the 200 entries in cells N4:N203, plugs them one at a time in cell AA1, and reports the value of cell G4 each time in cells O4:O203. As noted earlier, even though the variable values in cells N4:N203 and the formula in cell AA1 are dummies, Excel generates new random numbers for each replication of the model. The simulated results in cells O4:O203 are therefore different for each replication.

Excel Notes

- All entries in a simulation model, including columns in Data Table, can be formatted in any manner desired. For example, the profit value can be formatted to display as currency.
- It is usually a good idea to change the Calculation Options in Excel to Manual or Automatic Except for Data Tables when using Data Table (click Calculation Options, found within the Formulas tab). Otherwise, Excel will recalculate the entire Data Table each time we make *any* change in the spreadsheet. Depending on the size of the simulation model and the table, this could be time-consuming.
- For the same reason, it is a good idea to set up each simulation model in a separate Excel file rather than in a different sheet of the same file.
- If we change the Calculation Options to manual, remember that Excel will recalculate values only when we press the F9 key. Likewise, Data Table will initially show the same result value for every replication. We need to press F9 to get the final values.
- Once we have set up and run Data Table, we cannot edit parts of it (if we try to change any entry in the table, Excel will return the message "Cannot change part of a data table.").

To edit a Data Table, we select all cells that were automatically filled in by the Data Table procedure (e.g., cells O5:O203 in Screenshot 10-2C) and delete those cells. Now we make any changes we wish to the table (such as changing the number of replications) and run the Data Table procedure again.

- Although Data Table shows the value of the final output measure for each replication, the simulation model itself does not show details (e.g., monthly demand, selling price) for these replications. If we want to see complete details for each replication, we need to copy the entire model as many times as desired.

Analyzing the Results

Cells O4 to O203 show the monthly profit for 200 replications (months). We can now calculate the following statistics:

Cell G7: =AVERAGE(O41:O203) Average monthly profit = \$4,320.06

Cell G8: =STDEV(O4:O203) Standard deviation of monthly profit = \$1,090.89

Note: Values in your file will be different if you recalculate the model because the random numbers will change, and we are using only 200 replications.

Excel's Descriptive Statistics procedure can also be used to compute summary statistics.

Alternatively, if the Analysis ToolPak add-in is installed and enabled, we can use Excel's Descriptive Statistics procedure to compute these and other statistics, such as confidence intervals. We invoke this procedure by clicking Data Analysis | Descriptive Statistics, found within the Data tab. The window shown in Screenshot 10-2D(a) appears. We enter the information as shown and press OK. The summary statistics shown in Screenshot 10-2D(b) are then displayed. The results indicate, for example, that the 95% confidence interval for the average monthly profit would extend from \$4,167.95 to \$4,472.17 (=\$4,320.06 ± \$152.11).

The simulation results can be used to compute several performance measures.

We can also calculate several other measures of performance. For example, suppose Harry estimates that in order for tire sales to be financially viable, he needs to get a monthly profit of at least \$4,000 from tires. What is the probability that Harry will get this amount of profit? To

SCREENSHOT 10-2D Descriptive Statistics for Harry's Auto Shop

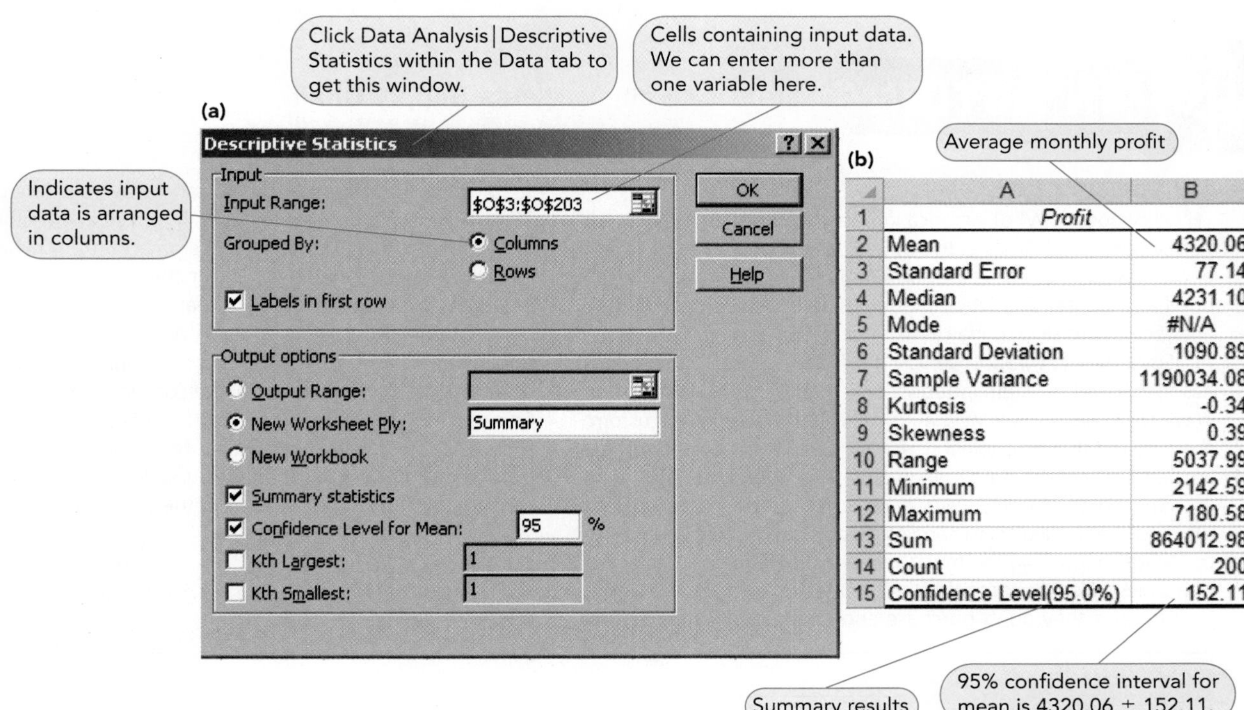

	A	B
1	Profit	
2	Mean	4320.06
3	Standard Error	77.14
4	Median	4231.10
5	Mode	#N/A
6	Standard Deviation	1090.89
7	Sample Variance	1190034.08
8	Kurtosis	-0.34
9	Skewness	0.39
10	Range	5037.99
11	Minimum	2142.59
12	Maximum	7180.58
13	Sum	864012.98
14	Count	200
15	Confidence Level(95.0%)	152.11

answer this question, we first need to count the number of months (of the 200 months) in which Harry's profit exceeds $4,000. We can use Excel's COUNTIF function to do this, as shown in cell G9 of Screenshot 10-2C on page 422. The relevant formula is

Cell G9: =COUNTIF(O4:O203,">=4000") Number of months with profit≥$4,000 = 113

Then, we divide this count by 200 to get the probability value (shown in cell G10). Screenshot 10-2C shows that Harry has a 56.5% chance of getting a monthly profit in excess of $4,000. Here again, the values will be different if you recalculate the model because the random numbers will change, and we are using only 200 replications.

Now suppose Harry decides that if his profit from tire sales is below $3,000 per month, he will stop selling tires. Using an approach similar to the one discussed here, see if you can calculate the probability of this event.

10.5 Simulation Model of an Inventory Problem

Factors in inventory problems include (1) how much to order and (2) when to order.

There are two main factors to consider in most inventory problems: (1) how much to order and (2) when to order. Under specific assumptions, it is possible to develop precise analytical models to answer these questions.[5]

In many real-world inventory situations, though, several inventory parameters are random variables. For example, the demand for an item could be random, implying that the rate at which its inventory is depleted is uncertain. Likewise, the time between when we place an order for an item with our supplier and when we receive it (known as the *lead time*) could be random. This implies that we may run out of inventory for the item before we receive the next consignment, causing a *stockout*.

Although it may be possible for us to express the behavior of parameters such as demand and lead time by using probability distributions, developing analytical models becomes extremely difficult. In such situations, the best means to answer the kind of inventory questions noted here is simulation.

Simulation is useful when demand and lead time are probabilistic.

In Solved Problem 10-1 at the end of this chapter, we simulate a fairly simple inventory problem in which only the demand is random. In the following pages, we illustrate a more comprehensive inventory problem in which both the demand and lead time are random variables.

IN ACTION Simulating Volkswagen's Supply Chain

Volkswagen (VW) of America imports, markets, and distributes Volkswagens and Audis in the United States from its parent company in Germany. As part of a reengineering effort, VW developed a computer simulation model, using ProModel software, to analyze how to save money in its huge supply chain.

Since the early 1900s, vehicle distribution in the United States has followed the system introduced by Ford Motor. This structure, in which manufacturers view auto dealers as their primary customers, is so old that its original performance intentions are rarely examined. Dealers and auto manufacturers are loosely coupled, with each managing its own inventory costs. Like other manufacturers, VW encourages dealers to carry as much stock as possible but understands that having too much inventory could force a dealer out of business. Dealers recognize the threatening inventory costs but know that if they don't purchase enough cars, VW may restrict supply or appoint additional dealers. The average VW dealer sells 30 cars per month and stocks fewer than 100 in inventory.

To better the chances of a customer getting his or her first choice of car, to be able to deliver that car in 48 hours, and to be able to reduce total system (dealers and VW) costs for transportation, financing, and storage, VW considered a new strategy: pooling vehicles in regional depots. Rather than opening these centers and observing how well the concept worked, VW focused on simulating the flow of cars from plants to dealers. The model showed that there would be significant savings by opening its distribution centers. VW managers also learned that supply-chain performance must be viewed from the system level.

Source: Based on N. Karabakal, A. Gunal, and W. Ritchie. "Supply-Chain Analysis at Volkswagen of America," *Interfaces* 30, 4 (July–August 2000): 46–55.

[5] We discuss some of these models in Chapter 12.

Simkin's Hardware Store

Simkin's Hardware Store sells the Ace model electric drill. Daily demand for the drill is relatively low but subject to some variability. Over the past 300 days, Barry Simkin has observed the demand frequency shown in column 2 of Table 10.5. He converts this historical frequency into a probability distribution for the variable daily demand (column 3).

Lead time *is the time between order placement and order receipt.*

When Simkin places an order to replenish his inventory of drills, the time between when he places an order and when it is received (i.e., the *lead time*) is a probabilistic variable. Based on the past 100 orders, Simkin has found that lead time follows a discrete uniform distribution between one and three days. He currently has seven Ace electric drills in stock, and there are no orders due.

Simkin wants to identify the order quantity, Q, and reorder point, R, that will help him reduce his total monthly costs. The *order quantity* is the fixed size of each order that is placed. The *reorder point* specifies the inventory level at which an order is triggered. That is, if the inventory level at the end of a day is at or below the reorder point, an order is placed. The total cost includes the following three components:

There are three components of the total cost.

- A fixed order cost that is incurred each time an order is placed
- A holding cost for each drill held in inventory from one period to the next
- A stockout cost for each drill that is not available to satisfy demand

Simkin estimates that the fixed cost of placing an order with his Ace drill supplier is $20. The cost of holding a drill in stock is $0.02 per drill per day. Each time Simkin is unable to satisfy a demand (i.e., he has a stockout), the customer buys the drill elsewhere, and Simkin loses the sale. He estimates that the cost of a stockout is $8 per drill. Assume that the shop operates 25 days each month on average.

There are two decision variables: order quantity (Q) *and reorder point* (R).

Note that there are two decision variables (order quantity, Q, and reorder point, R) and two probabilistic components (demand and lead time) in Simkin's inventory problem. Using simulation, we can try different (Q, R) combinations to see which combination yields the lowest total cost. As an illustration, let us first examine a policy that has $Q = 10$ and $R = 5$; that is, each time the inventory at the end of a day drops to 5 or less, we place an order for 10 drills with the supplier.

Setting Up the Model

A replication here corresponds to one month of operations at Simkin's store.

In Simkin's problem, each replication corresponds to tracking the inventory position and orders for electric drills over a month (i.e., 25 days), on a day-by-day basis. Hence, unlike Harry's Auto Shop problem in section 10.4, where we could model each replication by using just a single row in Excel, Simkin's simulation model will be much larger. If we represent the inventory operations of each day as a single row, the model will consist of 25 rows.

The Excel layout for Simkin's problem is shown in Screenshot 10-3A. Wherever necessary, we have shown the Excel formula used in a column.

File: 10-3.xls, sheet: 10-3A

In Screenshot 10-3A, all input parameters for the simulation model (e.g., the order quantity, reorder point, lead time range, all unit costs) are shown in separate cells (in column T). All formulas in the model use these cell references, rather than the values directly. This is a good

TABLE 10.5
Distribution of Daily Demand for Ace Electric Drills

DEMAND	FREQUENCY	PROBABILITY
0	15	$15/300 = 0.05$
1	30	$30/300 = 0.10$
2	60	$60/300 = 0.20$
3	120	$120/300 = 0.40$
4	45	$45/300 = 0.15$
5	30	$30/300 = 0.10$

SCREENSHOT 10-3A Excel Layout and Results for Simkin's Hardware Store

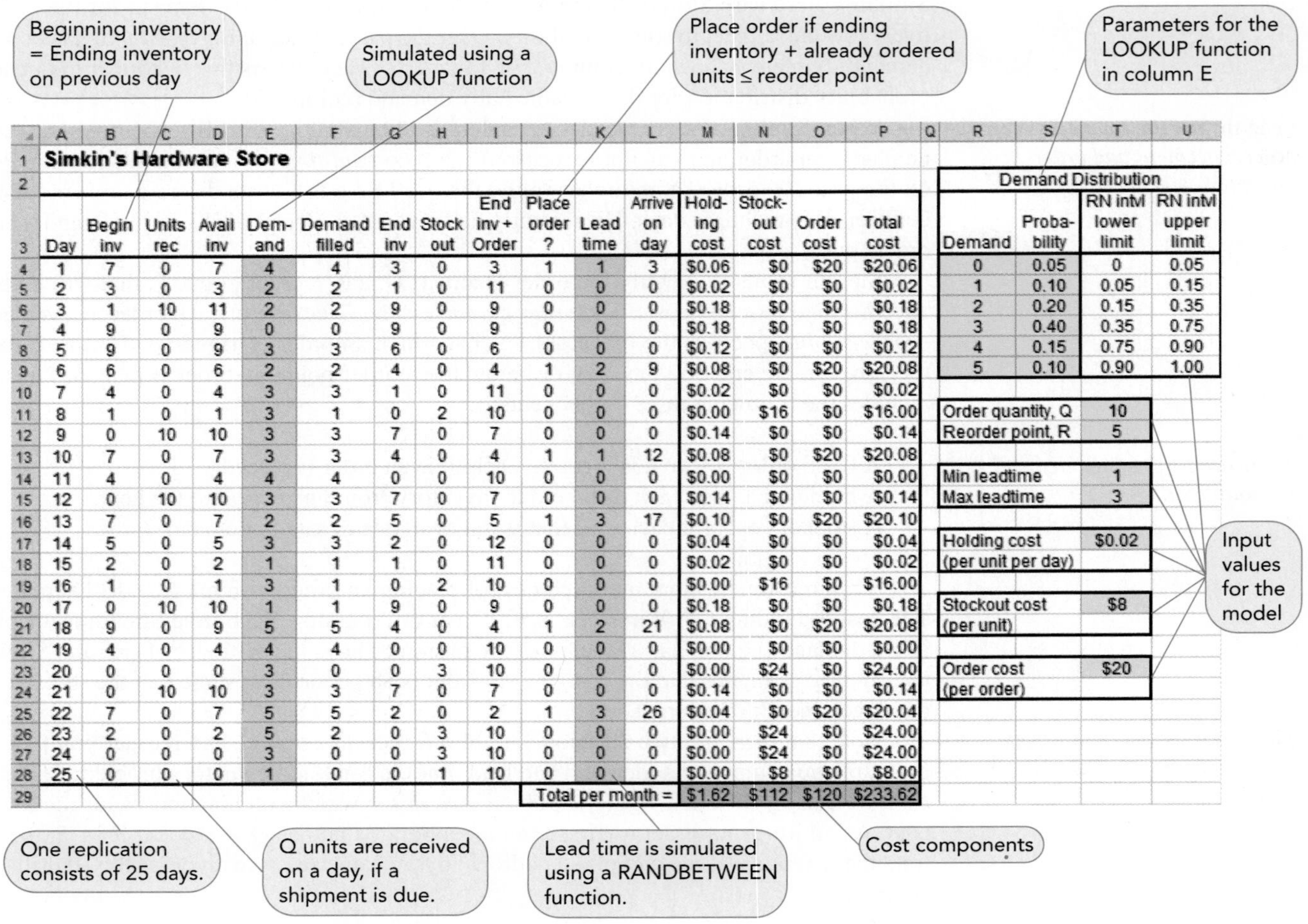

Beginning inventory = Ending inventory on previous day

Simulated using a LOOKUP function

Place order if ending inventory + already ordered units ≤ reorder point

Parameters for the LOOKUP function in column E

Simkin's Hardware Store

Day	Begin inv	Units rec	Avail inv	Dem-and	Demand filled	End inv	Stock out	End inv + Order	Place order ?	Lead time	Arrive on day	Hold-ing cost	Stock-out cost	Order cost	Total cost
1	7	0	7	4	4	3	0	3	1	1	3	$0.06	$0	$20	$20.06
2	3	0	3	2	2	1	0	11	0	0	0	$0.02	$0	$0	$0.02
3	1	10	11	2	2	9	0	9	0	0	0	$0.18	$0	$0	$0.18
4	9	0	9	0	0	9	0	9	0	0	0	$0.18	$0	$0	$0.18
5	9	0	9	3	3	6	0	6	0	0	0	$0.12	$0	$0	$0.12
6	6	0	6	2	2	4	0	4	1	2	9	$0.08	$0	$20	$20.08
7	4	0	4	3	3	1	0	11	0	0	0	$0.02	$0	$0	$0.02
8	1	0	1	3	1	0	2	10	0	0	0	$0.00	$16	$0	$16.00
9	0	10	10	3	3	7	0	7	0	0	0	$0.14	$0	$0	$0.14
10	7	0	7	3	3	4	0	4	1	1	12	$0.08	$0	$20	$20.08
11	4	0	4	4	4	0	0	10	0	0	0	$0.00	$0	$0	$0.00
12	0	10	10	3	3	7	0	7	0	0	0	$0.14	$0	$0	$0.14
13	7	0	7	2	2	5	0	5	1	3	17	$0.10	$0	$20	$20.10
14	5	0	5	3	3	2	0	12	0	0	0	$0.04	$0	$0	$0.04
15	2	0	2	1	1	1	0	11	0	0	0	$0.02	$0	$0	$0.02
16	1	0	1	3	1	0	2	10	0	0	0	$0.00	$16	$0	$16.00
17	0	10	10	1	1	9	0	9	0	0	0	$0.18	$0	$0	$0.18
18	9	0	9	5	5	4	0	4	1	2	21	$0.08	$0	$20	$20.08
19	4	0	4	4	4	0	0	10	0	0	0	$0.00	$0	$0	$0.00
20	0	0	0	3	0	0	3	10	0	0	0	$0.00	$24	$0	$24.00
21	0	10	10	3	3	7	0	7	0	0	0	$0.14	$0	$0	$0.14
22	7	0	7	5	5	2	0	2	1	3	26	$0.04	$0	$20	$20.04
23	2	0	2	5	2	0	3	10	0	0	0	$0.00	$24	$0	$24.00
24	0	0	0	3	0	0	3	10	0	0	0	$0.00	$24	$0	$24.00
25	0	0	0	1	0	0	1	10	0	0	0	$0.00	$8	$0	$8.00
									Total per month =			$1.62	$112	$120	$233.62

Demand Distribution

Demand	Proba-bility	RN intvl lower limit	RN intvl upper limit
0	0.05	0	0.05
1	0.10	0.05	0.15
2	0.20	0.15	0.35
3	0.40	0.35	0.75
4	0.15	0.75	0.90
5	0.10	0.90	1.00

Order quantity, Q	10
Reorder point, R	5
Min leadtime	1
Max leadtime	3
Holding cost (per unit per day)	$0.02
Stockout cost (per unit)	$8
Order cost (per order)	$20

Input values for the model

One replication consists of 25 days.

Q units are received on a day, if a shipment is due.

Lead time is simulated using a RANDBETWEEN function.

Cost components

To run several what-if scenarios using the same model, it is good to make parameter values cell references in all formulas.

practice to follow, especially if we want to use the simulation model to run several what-if scenarios using different values for these parameters (as we shall see shortly). The model in Screenshot 10-3A is organized as follows:

Here is how we simulate the inventory example.

- Column A shows the day number (1 to 25).
- Column B shows the beginning inventory at the start of a day. On day 1, this equals 7 (given). On all other days, the beginning inventory equals the ending inventory of the previous day. For example, cell B5 = cell G4, cell B6 = cell G5, and so on.
- Column C shows the units received (if any) that day from a prior order. Because there are no outstanding orders on day 1, cell C4 shows a value of 0. The formula for the remaining cells in this column uses Excel's COUNTIF function. In column L (discussed shortly), we simulate the arrival day for each order that is placed. We use the COUNTIF formula to check the number of times the current day number matches the arrival day number. The formula used to calculate the number of units arriving each day is then as follows:

  Units received = Number of orders due that day × Order size

  For example, the formula in cell C5 is

  =COUNTIF($L$4:L4,A5)*$T$11

We use a $ symbol to anchor cell references while copying formulas in Excel.

  The COUNTIF portion of the formula checks to see how many orders are due for arrival on day 2 (specified by cell A5). This number is then multiplied by the order quantity, Q, specified in cell T11. Note that the use of a $ to anchor cell references in this formula allows us to directly copy it to cells C6:C28.

- The total *available* inventory each day, shown in column D, is then the sum of the values in columns B and C:

$$\text{Column D} = \text{Column B} + \text{Column C}$$

Demand is simulated by using a LOOKUP function.

- Column E shows the demand each day. These values are simulated from a discrete general probability distribution shown in Table 10.5, using Excel's LOOKUP function. The parameters (demands, probabilities, and random number intervals) of the LOOKUP function are shown in cells R4:U9. Hence, the formula in cells E4:E28 is

=LOOKUP(RAND(),$T$4:$T$9,$R$4:$R$9)

Here again, the use of $ to anchor cell references in the formula allows us to create it in cell E4 and then copy it to cells E5:E28.

- Column F shows the actual demand filled. If the demand is less than or equal to the available inventory, the entire demand is satisfied. In contrast, if the demand exceeds the available inventory, then only the demand up to the inventory level is satisfied. We can use Excel's MIN function to model this, as follows:

$$\text{Demand satisfied} = \text{MIN (Available inventory, Demand)}$$

Hence, column F = MIN(column D, column E).

If demand is less than available inventory, there is some ending inventory.

- Column G calculates the ending inventory. If the demand is less than the available inventory, there is some ending inventory. However, if the demand is greater than or equal to the available inventory, the ending inventory is zero. We can use Excel's MAX function to model this, as follows:

$$\text{Ending inventory} = \text{MAX (Available inventory} - \text{Demand, 0)}$$

Hence, column G = MAX(column D − column E, 0).

A stockout occurs when demand exceeds available inventory.

- We now calculate the stockout (or lost sales) in column H. If the demand exceeds the available inventory, there is a stockout. However, if the demand is less than or equal to the available inventory, there is no stockout. Once again, we can use the MAX function to model this, as follows:

$$\text{Stockout} = \text{MAX (Demand} - \text{Available inventory, 0)}$$

Hence, column H = MAX(column E − column D, 0).

We need to check for outstanding orders before placing a new order.

- If the ending inventory is at or below the reorder point, an order needs to be placed with the supplier. Before we place an order, however, we need to check whether there are outstanding orders. The reason for this is as follows. If the ending inventory level has already triggered an order on an earlier day, but that order has not yet been received due to the delivery lead time, a duplicate order should not be placed. Hence, in column I, we calculate the *apparent* ending inventory; that is, we add the *actual* ending inventory (shown in column G) and any orders that have already been placed. The logic behind the formula in column I is as follows:

$$\begin{aligned}&\text{Apparent inventory at end of period } t = \\ &\quad \text{Apparent inventory at end of period } (t-1) \\ &\quad - \text{Demand satisfied in period } t + \text{Order size, if} \\ &\quad \text{an order was placed at the end of period } (t-1)\end{aligned}$$

For example, the formula in cell I5 is

=I4−F5+IF(J4=1,$T$11,0)

- If the apparent inventory at the end of any day is at or below the reorder point (cell T12), an order is to be placed that day. We denote this event in column J by using an IF function (1 implies place an order, 0 implies don't place an order). For example, the formula in cell J5 is

=IF(I5<=$T$12,1,0)

Lead time is simulated by using a RANDBETWEEN function.

- If an order is placed, the delivery lead time for this order is simulated in column K by using a RANDBETWEEN function (between 1 and 3). For example, the formula in cell K5 is

  =IF(J5=1,RANDBETWEEN($T$14,$T$15),0)

- Finally, in column L, we calculate the arrival day of this order as follows:

  Arrive on day = Current day + Lead time + 1

  For example, the formula in cell L5 is

  =IF(J5=1,A5+K5+1,0)

  Note that this formula includes +1 because the order is actually placed at the end of the current day (or, equivalently, the start of the next day).

Computation of Costs

Columns M through P show the cost computations for Simkin's inventory model each day of the month. The relevant formulas are as follows:

We compute the costs.

Column M:	Holding Cost	= $T$17 × Ending inventory in column G
Column N:	Stockout Cost	= $T$20 × Shortage in Column H
Column O:	Order Cost	= $T$23 (if value in Column J = 1)
Column P:	Total Cost	= Column M + Column N + Column O

The totals for each cost component for the entire month are shown in row 29 (cells M29:P29). For instance, the replication in Screenshot 10-3A shows a holding cost of $1.62 (cell M29), stockout cost of $112 (cell N29), order cost of $120 (cell O29), and total cost of $233.62 (cell P29).

Replication Using Data Table

To compute Simkin's average monthly cost, we need to replicate the model as many times as possible. Each time, due to the presence of random variables, all simulated values in the spreadsheet will change. Hence, the inventory costs will change.

File: 10-3.xls, sheet: 10-3B

We have already seen how we can use Data Table to easily replicate a simulation model multiple times. In Harry's Auto Shop example, we replicated only a single output measure (i.e., monthly profit) by using Data Table (see Screenshot 10-2C on page 422). In contrast, suppose we would like to replicate each of the four costs—holding cost, stockout cost, order cost, and total cost—in Simkin's example. It turns out that we can expand the use of Data Table to replicate all four measures at the same time. The procedure, illustrated in Screenshot 10-3B, is as follows:

This is how we set up Data Table to replicate more than one output measure.

1. Here again, we illustrate only 200 replications of the model. We first enter numbers 1 to 200 in cells W4:W203, corresponding to these 200 replications.
2. In cells X4 to AA4 (i.e., adjacent to the *first* cell in the range W4:W203), we specify the cell references for the four output measures we want replicated. Hence, the formula in cell X4 is =M29, in cell Y4 is =N29, in cell Z4 is =O29, and in cell AA4 is =P29. We leave cells X5:AA203 blank. As before, Data Table will fill in these cells when we run it.
3. We now use the mouse or keyboard to select the entire range W4:AA203 (i.e., all five columns). *After* selecting this range, we choose Data | What-If Analysis | Data Table from Excel's menu.
4. We leave the row input cell box blank and enter some arbitrary cell reference in the column input box. As before, we need to make sure the selected cell (AA1, in this case) is not used anywhere in the simulation model.
5. Finally, we click OK to run Data Table. The procedure computes and displays 200 simulated values of the monthly holding, stockout, order, and total costs in columns X, Y, Z, and AA, respectively.

SCREENSHOT 10-3B Data Table for Simkin's Hardware Store

Columns A through P are the same as in Screenshot 10-3A.

Values in cells W5:AA203 are automatically filled in by Data Table.

Formula in cell AA4: =P29

Simkin's Hardware Store

Day	Begin inv	Units rec	Avail inv	Dem-and	Demand filled	End inv	Stock out	End inv + Order	Place order ?	Lead time	Arrive on day	Hold-ing cost	Stock-out cost	Order cost	Total cost
1	7	0	7	0	0	7	0	7	0	0	0	$0.14	$0	$0	$0.14
2	7	0	7	5	5	2	0	2	1	1	4	$0.04	$0	$20	$20.04
3	2	0	2	4	2	0	2	10	0	0	0	$0.00	$16	$0	$16.00
4	0	10	10	3	3	7	0	7	0	0	0	$0.14	$0	$0	$0.14
5	7	0	7	4	4	3	0	3	1	3	9	$0.06	$0	$20	$20.06
6	3	0	3	0	0	3	0	13	0	0	0	$0.06	$0	$0	$0.06
7	3	0	3	2	2	1	0	11	0	0	0	$0.02	$0	$0	$0.02
8	1	0	1	4	1	0	3	10	0	0	0	$0.00	$24	$0	$24.00
9	0	10	10	5	5	5	0	5	1	3	13	$0.10	$0	$20	$20.10
10	5	0	5	3	3	2	0	12	0	0	0	$0.04	$0	$0	$0.04
11	2	0	2	2	2	0	0	10	0	0	0	$0.00	$0	$0	$0.00
12	0	0	0	3	0	0	3	10	0	0	0	$0.00	$24	$0	$24.00
13	0	10	10	2	2	8	0	8	0	0	0	$0.16	$0	$0	$0.16
14	8	0	8	3	3	5	0	5	1	2	17	$0.10	$0	$20	$20.10
15	5	0	5	5	5	0	0	10	0	0	0	$0.00	$0	$0	$0.00
16	0	0	0	2	0	0	2	10	0	0	0	$0.00	$16	$0	$16.00
17	0	10	10	4	4	6	0	6	0	0	0	$0.12	$0	$0	$0.12
18	6	0	6	5	5	1	0	1	1	1	20	$0.02	$0	$20	$20.02
19	1	0	1	4	1	0	3	10	0	0	0	$0.00	$24	$0	$24.00
20	0	10	10	5	5	5	0	5	1	1	22	$0.10	$0	$20	$20.10
21	5	0	5	4	4	1	0	11	0	0	0	$0.02	$0	$0	$0.02
22	1	10	11	3	3	8	0	8	0	0	0	$0.16	$0	$0	$0.16
23	8	0	8	2	2	6	0	6	0	0	0	$0.12	$0	$0	$0.12
24	6	0	6	3	3	3	0	3	1	3	28	$0.06	$0	$20	$20.06
25	3	0	3	3	3	0	0	10	0	0	0	$0.00	$0	$0	$0.00
									Total per month =			$1.46	$104	$140	$245.46

Hidden rows

Results based on current replication

Demand Distribution			
Demand	Proba-bility	RN intvl lower limit	RN intvl upper limit
0	0.05	0	0.05
1	0.10	0.05	0.15
2	0.20	0.15	0.35
3	0.40	0.35	0.75
4	0.15	0.75	0.90
5	0.10	0.90	1.00

Order quantity, Q	10
Reorder point, R	5
Min leadtime	1
Max leadtime	3
Holding cost (per unit per day)	$0.02
Stockout cost (per unit)	$8
Order cost (per order)	$20

Based on 200 replications:	
Average holding cost =	$1.79
Average stockout cost =	$98.64
Average order cost =	$122.20
Average total cost =	$222.63

Results based on 200 replications

Data Table

Run	Hold-ing cost	Stock-out cost	Order cost	Total cost
1	$1.46	$104	$140	$245.46
2	$2.46	$16	$140	$158.46
3	$1.28	$128	$120	$249.28
4	$1.90	$56	$140	$197.90
5	$1.46	$120	$120	$241.46
6	$1.72	$88	$120	$209.72
7	$1.58	$96	$120	$217.58
8	$1.88	$96	$120	$217.88
9	$1.58	$128	$120	$249.58
10	$2.18	$48	$140	$190.18
11	$1.90	$88	$120	$209.90
12	$1.76	$136	$120	$257.76
13	$1.70	$112	$120	$233.70
14	$1.90	$24	$120	$145.90
15	$1.12	$168	$140	$309.12
16	$1.74	$40	$140	$181.74
17	$1.88	$80	$120	$201.88
18	$1.44	$152	$120	$273.44
19	$1.40	$104	$140	$245.40
20	$1.46	$168	$120	$289.46
21	$1.78	$112	$120	$233.78
22	$1.80	$96	$140	$237.80
23	$2.04	$80	$120	$202.04
24	$1.94	$56	$120	$177.94
25	$1.84	$168	$120	$289.84
26	$2.00	$80	$120	$202.00
27	$1.86	$64	$120	$185.86
199	$1.56	$152	$100	$253.56
200	$1.84	$80	$140	$221.84

Select cells W4:AA203 before clicking Data | What-If Analysis | Data Table.

Analyzing the Results

We can conduct statistical analyses on the replicated values.

We can now use the 200 cost values to conduct statistical analyses, as before. For example, if $Q = 10$ and $R = 5$, Screenshot 10-3B indicates that Simkin's average monthly costs of holding, stockout, and order are \$1.79 (cell U27), \$98.64 (cell U28), and \$122.20 (cell U29), respectively. The average total cost, shown in cell U30, is \$222.63.

As an exercise, see if you can set up Data Table to calculate Simkin's average demand fill rate per month. That is, what percentage of monthly demand received does Simkin satisfy on average? *Hint:* The fill rate for each replication is the ratio of demand satisfied (sum of entries in column F) to demand received (sum of entries in column E).

Using Scenario Manager to Include Decisions in a Simulation Model

In simulating Simkin's inventory model so far, we have assumed a fixed order quantity, Q, of 10, and a fixed reorder point, R, of 5. Recall, however, that Simkin's objective was to identify the Q and R values that will help him reduce his total monthly costs. To achieve this objective, suppose Simkin wants to try four different values for Q (i.e., 8, 10, 12, and 14) and two different values for R (i.e., 5 and 8). One approach to run this extended simulation would be to run the model and Data Table (see Screenshot 10-3B) eight times—once for each combination of Q and R values. We could then compare the average total cost (cell U30) in each case to determine which combination of Q and R is best. This approach, of course, could become quite cumbersome, especially if we wanted to vary several different input parameters and try multiple values for each parameter.

We use Scenario Manager when we want to try several values for one or more input parameters in a model.

It turns out that we can use an Excel procedure called Scenario Manager to automatically run a simulation model for several combinations of input parameter values. To do so, we first assume *any* combination of values for the input parameters and set up the complete simulation model (including Data Table) to replicate the desired output measures. After we have done so, we next define multiple scenarios—one for each combination of input parameter values. When we then run Scenario Manager, Excel will automatically run the model and the Data Table replications for each scenario and report the desired results.

We illustrate the construction and use of Scenario Manager by using the simulation model we have already constructed for Simkin (shown in Screenshot 10-3B for $Q = 10$ and $R = 5$). The procedure is as follows:

This is how we set up Scenario Manager.

1. Invoke Scenario Manager by clicking What-If Analysis | Scenario Manager, found within the Data tab. The window shown in Screenshot 10-3C(a) is displayed.
2. Click Add to create a new scenario. The Add Scenario window shown in Screenshot 10-3C(b) is displayed. In the box titled Scenario name, enter any name of your choice for the scenario. (In Simkin's model, we have used names such as Q8R5, Q8R8, and Q12R5 to make the scenarios self-explanatory.) In the Changing cells box, enter the cell references for the cells whose values you wish to change. In Simkin's model, these would be cells T11 and T12, corresponding to the input parameters Q and R, respectively. If the changing cells are not contiguous in the model, separate the cell references with commas. Next, if desired, enter a comment to describe the scenario. Checking the Prevent changes option protects the scenario from being accidentally edited or deleted, while the Hide option hides the scenario.

SCREENSHOT 10-3C Setting Up Scenario Manager in Excel

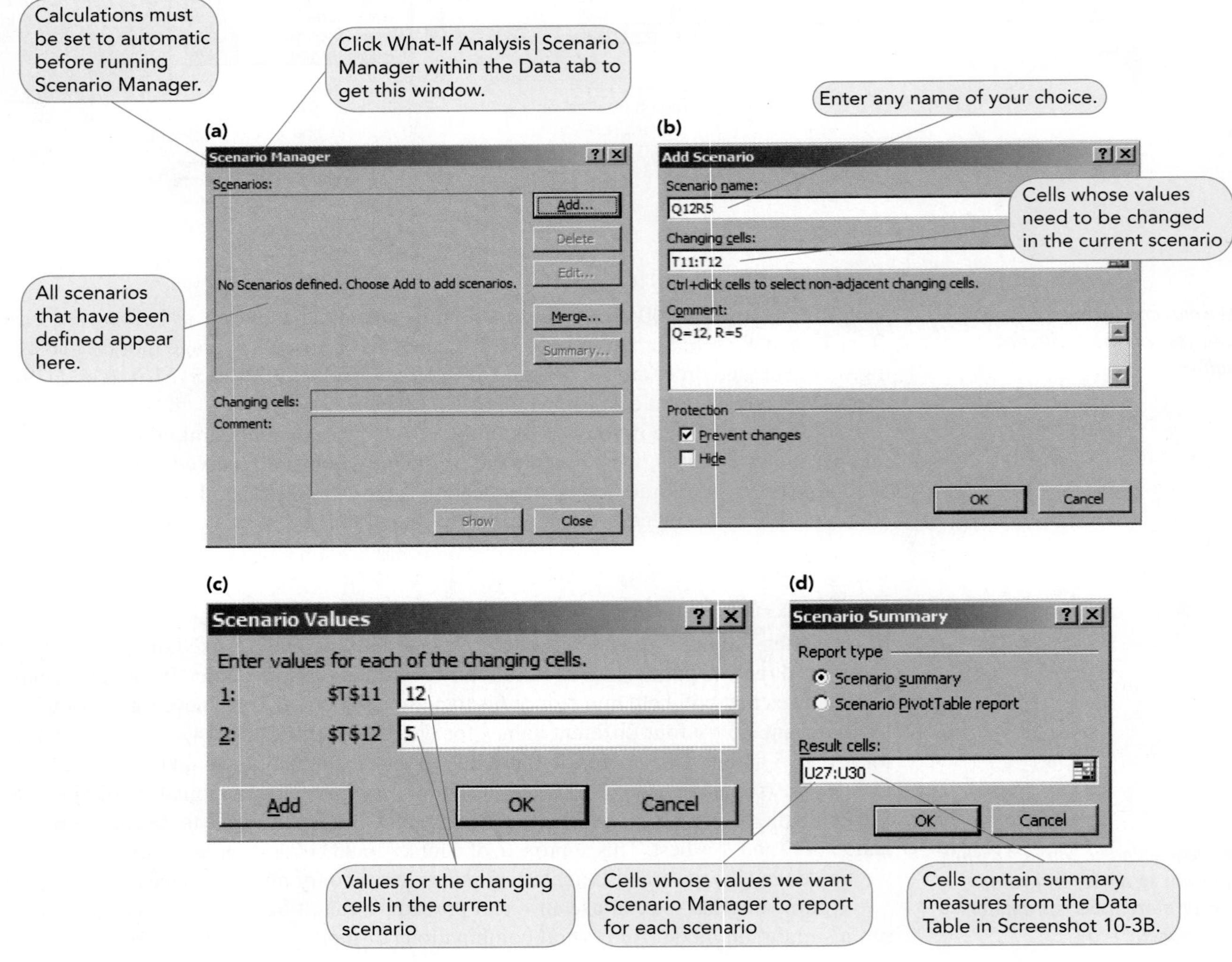

Click OK to get the Scenario Values window, as shown in Screenshot 10-3C(c). For each changing cell, enter the appropriate value. For example, for the scenario shown in Screenshot 10-3C(c), the values of Q and R are 12 and 5, respectively.

3. Repeat step 2 for as many scenarios as desired. In Simkin's model, you define eight scenarios corresponding to the eight combinations $(Q, R) - (8, 5), (8, 8), (10, 5), (10, 8), (12, 5), (12, 8), (14, 5)$, and $(14, 8)$. You can also edit or delete a scenario after it has been created (assuming that the Prevent changes option is unchecked).

Scenario Manager's results can be shown either as a scenario summary table or as a PivotTable.

4. When all scenarios have been defined, click Summary (see Screenshot 10-3C(a)) to run Scenario Manager. The Scenario Summary window shown in Screenshot 10-3C(d) appears. In the box titled Result cells, enter the cell references for the output measures you would like Scenario Manager to report for each scenario. In Simkin's model, these would be cells U27:U30, corresponding to the four average cost measures—holding cost, stockout cost, order cost, and total cost (see Screenshot 10-3B on page 429). Here again, use commas to separate cell references that are not contiguous.

   The results can be shown either as a Scenario summary table (preferred in most cases) or as a PivotTable report. (Choose the latter option if there are many changing cells and scenarios, and if you are comfortable analyzing results using PivotTables in Excel.)

5. Click OK. Scenario Manager runs the simulation model (including Data Table) for each scenario and presents the results in a separate worksheet, as shown in Screenshot 10-3D. (We have added grid lines to the summary table to make it clearer.)

WWW

File: 10-3.xls, sheet: 10-3D

Excel Notes

- The Calculation Options in Excel must not be set to Manual *before* you run Scenario Manager. If this option is set to Manual, Scenario Manager will report the same summary results for all scenarios.
- The standard version of Excel can accommodate up to 32 changing cells for each scenario.
- Although the number of scenarios allowed in Excel is limited only by your computer's memory, note that Scenario Manager may take a long time to execute if you include too many scenarios, especially if running each scenario involves running Data Table with many replications.

Analyzing the Results

For each combination of order quantity and reorder point, Screenshot 10-3D shows the average monthly holding, stockout, order, and total costs. Note that because all these values are based on only 200 replications of the simulation model, they could change each time we run Scenario Manager.

SCREENSHOT 10-3D Scenario Manager Results for Simkin's Hardware Store

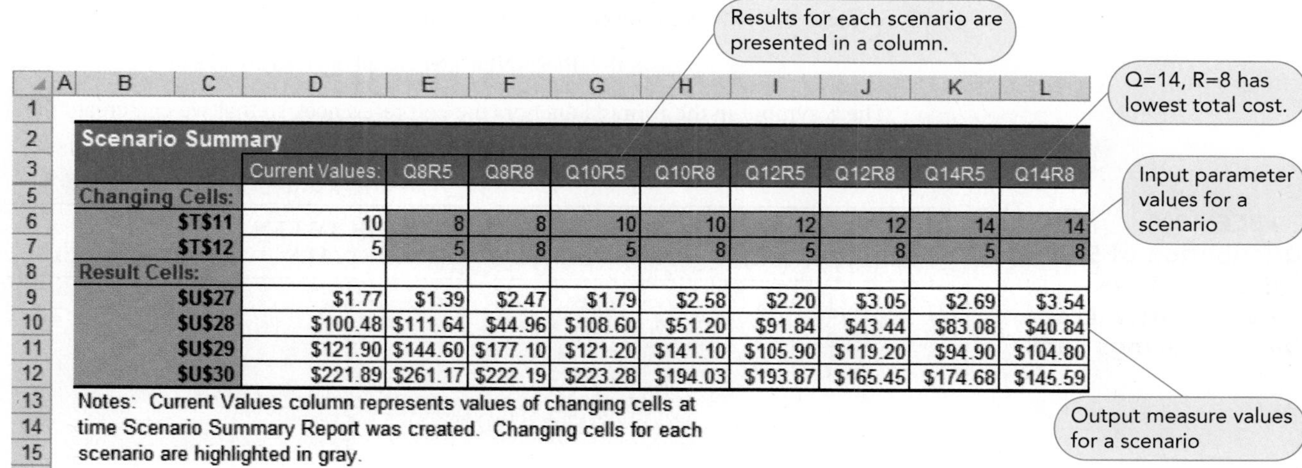

	Scenario Summary	Current Values:	Q8R5	Q8R8	Q10R5	Q10R8	Q12R5	Q12R8	Q14R5	Q14R8
5	Changing Cells:									
6	\$T\$11	10	8	8	10	10	12	12	14	14
7	\$T\$12	5	5	8	5	8	5	8	5	8
8	Result Cells:									
9	\$U\$27	\$1.77	\$1.39	\$2.47	\$1.79	\$2.58	\$2.20	\$3.05	\$2.69	\$3.54
10	\$U\$28	\$100.48	\$111.64	\$44.96	\$108.60	\$51.20	\$91.84	\$43.44	\$83.08	\$40.84
11	\$U\$29	\$121.90	\$144.60	\$177.10	\$121.20	\$141.10	\$105.90	\$119.20	\$94.90	\$104.80
12	\$U\$30	\$221.89	\$261.17	\$222.19	\$223.28	\$194.03	\$193.87	\$165.45	\$174.68	\$145.59

Notes: Current Values column represents values of changing cells at time Scenario Summary Report was created. Changing cells for each scenario are highlighted in gray.

Results for each scenario are presented in a column.
Q=14, R=8 has lowest total cost.
Input parameter values for a scenario
Output measure values for a scenario

Looking at the values in Screenshot 10-3D, it appears that Simkin's lowest total cost of $145.59 per month is obtained when he uses an order quantity of 14 units and a reorder point of 8 units.

As an exercise, see if you can compute other output measures (e.g., demand fill rate, probability that total monthly cost exceeds $200) in the simulation model. Then, include these measures also in the Results cell for each scenario and run Scenario Manager. Likewise, see if you can analyze the impact on total cost when you vary the values of other input parameters, such as the minimum and maximum delivery lead times.

10.6 Simulation Model of a Queuing Problem

Simulation is an effective technique for modeling many real-world queuing systems that cannot be analyzed analytically.

In Chapter 9, we computed performance measures for several simple queuing systems, using analytical models. However, as noted in that chapter, many real-world queuing systems can be difficult to model analytically. In such cases, we usually turn to simulation to analyze the performance of these systems. To study this issue, in this section we illustrate an example of a queuing model in which both the arrival times of customers and the service times at the facility follow discrete general distributions. Then, in Solved Problem 10-2 at the end of this chapter, we discuss the simulation of another queuing model in which arrival times are exponentially distributed and service times are normally distributed.

Denton Savings Bank

Sanjay Krishnan, manager at the Denton Savings Bank, is attempting to improve customer satisfaction by offering service such that (1) the average customer waiting time does not exceed 2 minutes and (2) the average queue length is 2 or fewer customers. The bank gets an average of 150 customers each day. Given the existing situation for service and arrival times, as shown in Table 10.6, does the bank meet Sanjay's criteria?

In discrete-event simulation models, we need to keep track of the passage of time by using a simulation clock.

Note that in simulating this queuing model, we need to keep track of the passage of time to record the specific arrival and departure times of customers. We refer to such models, in which events (e.g., customer arrivals and departures) occur at discrete points in time, as **discrete-event simulation** models.

Setting Up the Model

File: 10-4.xls

Each replication of this simulation model corresponds to a day's operation at the bank (i.e., the arrival and service of 150 customers). The Excel layout for this problem is presented in Screenshot 10-4. To keep track of the passage of time in this model, we monitor a clock that starts at zero and continually counts time (in minutes, in Denton's model). Observe that in row 4, we have included customer number 0, with zero values for all columns, to *initialize* this simulation clock. This is a good practice in all discrete-event simulation models. Rows 5 through 154 in the spreadsheet are organized as follows:

Time between successive arrivals follows a discrete general distribution.

- Column A lists the customer number (1 through 150).
- Column B shows the time between arrivals of successive customers, simulated using a LOOKUP function. The parameters (i.e., arrival times, probabilities, and random number intervals) for this LOOKUP function are shown in cells J6:M11. The formula in cells B5:B154 is

  =LOOKUP(RAND(),$L$6:$L$11,$J$6:$J$11)

  The $ symbol in the formula anchors the cell references so that we can create the formula in cell B5 and then copy it to cells B6:B154.

TABLE 10.6 Distribution of Service Times and Time between Arrivals at Denton Savings Bank

SERVICE TIME	PROBABILITY	TIME BETWEEN ARRIVALS	PROBABILITY
1	0.25	0	0.10
2	0.20	1	0.15
3	0.40	2	0.10
4	0.15	3	0.35
		4	0.25
		5	0.05

SCREENSHOT 10-4 Excel Layout and Results for Denton Savings Bank

Simulated using a LOOKUP function

= Start time + Service time

Length of queue, including current patient

Denton Savings Bank

Row	Customer #	Time between arrivals	Arrival time	Start service	Service time	End service	Wait time	Queue length
4	0	0	0	0	0	0	0	0
5	1	3	3	3	2	5	0	0
6	2	2	5	5	3	8	0	0
7	3	4	9	9	2	11	0	0
8	4	3	12	12	3	15	0	0
9	5	3	15	15	3	18	0	0
10	6	4	19	19	3	22	0	0
11	7	4	23	23	3	26	0	0
12	8	2	25	26	1	27	1	1
13	9	4	29	29	3	32	0	0
14	10	0	29	32	3	35	3	1
15	11	5	34	35	3	38	1	1
16	12	3	37	38	4	42	1	1
17	13	3	40	42	2	44	2	1
18	14	1	41	44	1	45	3	2
19	15	4	45	45	3	48	0	0
20	16	3	48	48	1	49	0	0
21	17	3	51	51	3	54	0	0
22	18	3	54	54	4	58	0	0
23	19	3	57	58	3	61	1	1
24	20	4	61	61	3	64	0	0
25	21	3	64	64	4	68	0	0
26	22	1	65	68	1	69	3	1
153	149	4	413	413	2	415	0	0
154	150	3	416	416	1	417	0	0

Hidden rows

= Start time – Arrival time

Time	Probability	RN intvl lower limit	RN intvl upper limit
Arrival Distribution			
0	0.10	0.00	0.10
1	0.15	0.10	0.25
2	0.10	0.25	0.35
3	0.35	0.35	0.70
4	0.25	0.70	0.95
5	0.05	0.95	1.00
Service Time Distribution			
1	0.25	0.00	0.25
2	0.20	0.25	0.45
3	0.40	0.45	0.85
4	0.15	0.85	1.00

Based on 1 replication:	
Average wait time =	1.64
Average queue length =	0.86

Based on 200 replications:	
Average wait time =	4.82
Average queue length =	2.14

Summary measures from Data Table

Data Table

Run	Avg wait time	Avg queue length
1	1.64	0.86
2	1.37	0.71
3	3.86	1.76
4	4.94	2.20
5	2.53	1.18
6	2.53	1.24
7	3.09	1.47
8	3.45	1.56
9	3.60	1.66
10	13.33	5.57
11	6.66	2.85
12	1.83	0.96
13	2.42	1.27
14	3.88	1.82
15	2.73	1.28
16	1.31	0.65
17	6.99	2.87
18	1.99	0.93
19	3.11	1.49
20	1.34	0.72
21	3.21	1.49
22	3.61	1.59
23	4.21	1.82
150	7.88	3.29
151	5.46	2.47
152	17.02	6.70
199	5.31	2.41
200	4.82	2.11

=M20

=M21

Data Table replicates both output measures 200 times each.

- Column C calculates the actual arrival time of the current customer as the sum of the arrival time of the previous customer and the time between arrivals (simulated in column B). This type of computation is an example of the use of the simulation clock, which records the actual elapsed clock time in a simulation model. For example, the formula in cell C5 is

  =C4+B5

- The actual time at which this customer starts service is calculated in column D as the maximum of the customer's arrival time and the time the previous customer finishes service. For example, the formula in cell D5 is

  =MAX(C5,F4)

Service time also follows a discrete general distribution.

- Column E shows the service time for this customer, simulated using a LOOKUP function. The parameters of this LOOKUP function are shown in cells J14:M17. The formula in cells E5:E154 is

  =LOOKUP(RAND(),$L$14:$L$17,$J$14:$J$17)

- The clock time at which this customer ends service is shown in column F as the sum of the start time (shown in column D) and the service time (shown in column E). For example, the formula in cell F5 is

  =D5+E5

- Column G calculates the wait time of this customer as the difference between the customer's start time (shown in column D) and arrival time (shown in column C). For example, the formula in cell G5 is

  =D5−C5

We use Excel's MATCH function to calculate the queue length.

- Finally, column H calculates the queue length by using Excel's MATCH function. The MATCH function is used to determine how many customers (up to the current customer) have start times that are smaller than the arrival time of the current customer. Clearly, all customers (including the current one) who do not meet this criterion are in the queue. For example, the formula in cell H5 is

=A5−MATCH(C5,$D$5:D5,1)

Using the wait times and queue lengths shown in cells G5:H154 for the 150 customers, we can determine the following two performance measures for the bank each day: (1) average wait time per customer (shown in cell M20) and (2) average queue length (shown in cell M21).

Replication Using Data Table

Data Table is used here to replicate both performance measures.

Based on the average wait time and queue length values in cells M20 and M21, respectively, of Screenshot 10-4, it may seem to appear that Denton is meeting both of Sanjay's desired targets. The average wait time is only 1.64 minutes, and there are only 0.86 customers on average in the queue. However, note that these values are based on just one replication and will change each time we recalculate the model. Hence, to determine more precise values for these averages, we now replicate each performance measure 200 times. Screenshot 10-4 shows how we can use Data Table to do so, in columns O through Q. Note that Data Table has been used here to replicate both performance measures at the same time.

Analyzing the Results

Based on the average values computed from 200 replications in Screenshot 10-4, it appears that the system does *not* meet either criterion. The average wait time of 4.82 minutes per customer (cell M24) is more than double Sanjay's desired target of 2 minutes per customer. The average queue length of 2.14 customers (cell M25) is, however, close to Sanjay's desired target of 2 customers. Sanjay should, perhaps, focus on initiating training programs to improve the average service rate of his tellers.

IN ACTION Using Simulation to Facilitate Better Healthcare

A healthcare–associated infection (HAI) occurs when there is no evidence of patient infection at the time of hospital admission. There are about 2 million annual incidents of HAIs in the United States, resulting in over 100,000 deaths. Although HAIs cost hospitals more than $30 billion per year, hospitals typically have a financial and legal incentive to conceal HAIs, making it difficult to study the problem. Hospitals, however, are very interested in studying various issues such as whether greater compliance with hand-hygiene measures reduce costs, the relative merits of isolation versus hand hygiene, and how infection-control measures impact costs.

To address these questions, researchers developed a simulation model to track HAIs in an intensive care unit (ICU). The discrete-event simulation model used data from Cook County Hospital in Chicago, Illinois, to model the entire process and its associated costs. The process includes the following steps: pathogens, patients, and visitors enter an ICU, interact with health care workers and with each other, infect or become infected, get cured of both primary disease and additional infections, and are finally discharged.

A Cook County Hospital spokesperson notes that the "model was useful and has caused us to develop two more infection control interventions."

Source: Based on R. Hagtvedt et al. "A Simulation Model to Compare Strategies for the Reduction of Health-Care–Associated Infections," *Interfaces* 39, 3 (May-June 2009): 256–270.

10.7 Simulation Model of a Revenue Management Problem

Revenue management *problems are popular in the airline and hotel industries.*

Another popular application of simulation is in *revenue management* problems, first introduced by the airline and hotel industries as *yield management* problems. This type of problem focuses on trying to identify the most efficient way of using an existing capacity (usually fixed) to manage revenues in situations where customer demand and behavior are uncertain.[6] To study this type of problem, in this section we consider an example in which the owner of a limousine service wants to find the optimal number of reservations she should accept for a trip. Then, in Solved Problem 10-3 at the end of this chapter, we illustrate the simulation of another revenue management problem, involving room reservations at a hotel.

Judith's Airport Limousine Service

Judith McKnew is always on the lookout for entrepreneurial opportunities. Living in Six Mile, South Carolina, she recognizes that the nearest airport is 50 miles away. Judith estimates that, on average, there are about 45 people from Six Mile (and its vicinity) who need rides to or from the airport each day. To help them, Judith is considering leasing a 10-passenger van and offering a limousine service between Six Mile and the airport. There would be four trips per day: a morning trip and an evening trip to the airport, and a morning trip and an evening trip from the airport.

After researching the issue carefully, Judith sets some operating guidelines for her problem and estimates the following parameters for each trip:

- Reservations for a trip can be made up to 12 hours in advance, by paying a nonrefundable $10 deposit. Judith will accept reservations up to her reservation limit (which this simulation model will help her decide).
- The ticket price is $35 per passenger per trip. Passengers with reservations must pay the $25 balance at the start of the trip.

The number of reservations is probabilistic.

- The number of reservations requested each trip follows a discrete uniform distribution between 7 and 14. Judith will, of course, reject a reservation request if she has reached her reservation limit.

The number of show-ups is also probabilistic.

- The probability that a person with a reservation shows up for the trip is 0.80. In other words, 20% of people with reservations do not show up. Anyone who does not show up forfeits the $10 deposit.
- If the number of passengers who show up exceeds 10 (the passenger capacity of the van), alternate arrangements must be made to get these extra people to the airport. This will cost Judith $75 per person. That is, Judith will lose $40 (= $75 − $35) per overbooked person.

Finally, the number of walk-ups is also probabilistic.

- The number of walk-up passengers (i.e., passengers without reservations) for a trip has the following discrete general distribution: probability of zero walk-ups is 0.30, probability of one walk-up is 0.45, and probability of two walk-ups is 0.25. Judith does not anticipate that there will ever be more than two walk-ups per trip.
- Walk-up passengers pay $50 per trip. However, Judith does not have to make alternate arrangements for these passengers if her van is full.
- The total cost per trip (to or from the airport) to Judith is $100. Note that due to the possibility of walk-up passengers on the return trip, Judith has to make a trip to the airport even if she has no passengers on that trip.

Judith wants to find out how many reservations she should accept in order to maximize her average profit per trip. Specifically, she is considering accepting 10, 11, 12, 13, or 14 reservations.

Setting Up the Model

File: 10-5.xls, sheet: 10-5A

Each replication in Judith's problem corresponds to one trip. The Excel layout for this problem, shown in Screenshot 10-5A, is organized as follows:

Each replication here corresponds to one trip.

- Cell B3 shows the number of reservations accepted for the trip. Note that this is a decision that is specified by Judith. Let us first set up the model assuming that Judith accepts 14 reservations for each trip. Later, we will use Scenario Manager to run this model automatically for all reservation limits (i.e., 10 to 14).

---

[6] A good description of *yield management* can be found in B. C. Smith, J. F. Leimkuhler, and R. M. Darrow. "Yield Management at American Airlines," *Interfaces* 22, 1 (January-February 1992): 8–31.

SCREENSHOT 10-5A Excel Layout and Results for Judith's Limousine Service

Computed using the CRITBINOM function.

=RANDBETWEEN(G4,G5).

Judith's Limousine Service

Row	A	B
3	Judith's reservation limit	14
4	Reservations requested	7
5	Reservations accepted	7
6	Number show up	6
7	Number overbook	0
8	Seats remaining	4
9	Number walk-up	2
10	Walk-up accepted	2
11	Total seats occupied	8
12	Revenue	$320
13	Cost	$100
14	Profit	$220
15	Occupancy rate	80.0%

=B11/G3

D–F	G
Van's passenger capacity =	10
Minimum reservation request =	7
Maximum reservation request =	14
Probability person shows up	0.80
Reservation deposit amount =	$10
Balance of ticket price =	$25
Walk-up ticket price =	$50
Cost per overbooked person =	$75
Fixed cost per trip =	$100

Walk-up Distribution			
Number	Probability	RN intvl LL	RN intvl UL
0	0.30	0.00	0.30
1	0.45	0.30	0.75
2	0.25	0.75	1.00

Based on 200 replications:	
Average profit =	$221.53
Average occupancy rate =	89.1%

Data Table

=B14

=B15

Run	Profit	Occ rate
1	$220	80.0%
2	$180	100.0%
3	$180	100.0%
4	$170	60.0%
5	$170	60.0%
6	$180	70.0%
7	$305	100.0%
8	$170	70.0%
9	$140	100.0%
10	$200	80.0%
11	$265	90.0%
12	$240	90.0%
13	$275	100.0%
14	$145	60.0%
15	$250	100.0%
16	$230	100.0%
17	$275	100.0%
18	$295	90.0%
19	$275	100.0%
199	$275	100.0%
200	$220	80.0%

Hidden rows.

Parameters for LOOKUP function in cell B9.

Summary measures from Data Table.

Data Table replicates both output measures 200 times each.

- Cell B4 shows the number of reservations requested for a trip. We simulate this value from a discrete uniform distribution by using the RANDBETWEEN function with parameters $a = 7$ (specified in cell G4) and $b = 14$ (specified in cell G5). The formula in cell B4 is

=RANDBETWEEN(G4,G5)

- In cell B5, we set the actual number of reservations accepted by Judith for the trip as the *smaller* of Judith's reservation limit (cell B3) and the number of reservations requested (cell B4). The formula in cell B5 is

=MIN(B3,B4)

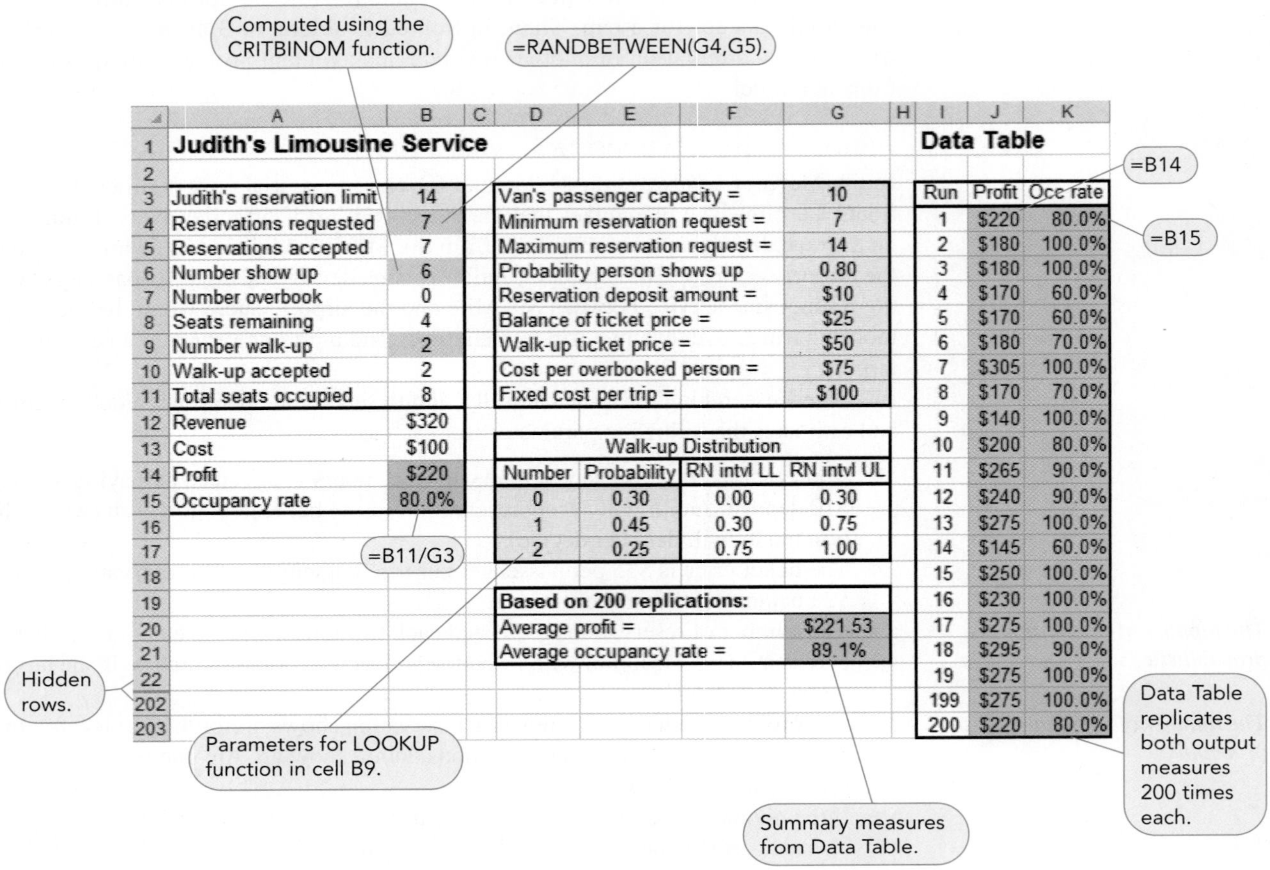

The number of people showing up is simulated using a CRITBINOM function.

- Next, we simulate the number of people with reservations who actually show up. This can be modeled as a binomial distribution (see page 416) where the number of independent events (n) corresponds to the number of people with reservations (i.e., cell B5), and the probability of success in each event (p) is the probability the person will actually show up (0.80 here, shown in cell G6). The relevant formula in cell B6 is[7]

=CRITBINOM(B5,G6,RAND())

- If the number of passengers showing up (cell B6) exceeds the van's passenger capacity (specified in cell G3), we have overbooked passengers. Otherwise, we have no overbooked passengers. In cell B7, we calculate the number of overbooked passengers by using the MAX function, as follows:

=MAX(B6−G3,0)

[7] As noted previously, we can use either the CRITBINOM function or the BINOM.INV function in Excel 2010.

- Likewise, if the van capacity exceeds the number of passengers showing up, we have some seats remaining. Otherwise, we are full. In cell B8, we calculate this number as follows:

=MAX(G3−B6,0)

The number of walk-up passengers is simulated by using a LOOKUP function.

- Next, in cell B9, we simulate the number of walk-up passengers by using a LOOKUP function. The parameter values for this function are specified in cells D15:G17. The formula in cell B9 is

=LOOKUP(RAND(),F15:F17,D15:D17)

- The number of walk-ups who can be accommodated in the van is obviously limited by the seats remaining (cell B8). Hence, in cell B10, we calculate the number of walk-ups accepted by using a MIN function, as follows:

=MIN(B8,B9)

- In cell B11, we compute the total number of seats occupied for the trip. The formula is

=G3−B8+B10

- The total revenue and cost for the trip are now calculated in cells B12 and B13, respectively, as

Revenue = \$10 × Reservations accepted + \$25 × Number of people who show up + \$50 × Walk-ups accepted

= G7*B5 + G8*B6 + G9*B10

Cost = \$75 × Number overbooked + \$100

= G10*B7 + G11

The **load factor** *defines the percentage of capacity that is occupied.*

- In cell B14, we calculate the trip profit as (Revenue − Cost).
- Another performance measure that is popular in many revenue management problems is the percentage of capacity that has been actually utilized. Airlines and hotels refer to this measure as the *load factor*. To illustrate this measure, we compute Judith's occupancy rate for the trip in cell B15 as

=B11/G3

Replicating the Model Using Data Table and Scenario Manager

We use Data Table to replicate Judith's model.

The profit of \$220 (shown in cell B14) and occupancy rate of 80% (shown in cell B15) in Screenshot 10-5A are based on just one replication of the model. Hence, they should not be used to make any conclusive statements about Judith's problem. To determine more precise values, we now replicate each performance measure 200 times. Columns I through K show how we can use Data Table to do so. The formula in cell J4 is =B14, while the formula in cell K4 is =B15. Cells J5:K203 are left blank and will be automatically filled in by the Data Table procedure when it is run. Based on these 200 replicated values, we calculate the average values of both measures (shown in cells G20 and G21, respectively). With a reservation limit of 14, Screenshot 10-5A indicates that Judith can expect a profit of \$221.53 per trip and an occupancy rate of 89.1%.

Next, we use Scenario Manager to try different values for the reservation limit.

Now that we have set up Judith's simulation model and Data Table for a specific reservation limit, we can use Scenario Manager to try different values for this parameter. The procedure is as follows (here again, remember to make sure that the Calculations Options is set to Automatic in Excel before running Scenario Manager):

1. Invoke Scenario Manager by clicking Data | What-If Analysis | Scenario Manager.
2. Define five scenarios, corresponding to the five reservation limits that Judith wants to try (i.e., 10 to 14). For each scenario, specify cell B3 as the cell reference in the Changing cells box and enter the appropriate reservation limit in the Scenario Values window.
3. Once all scenarios have been defined, click Summary. In the box titled Result cells, specify cells G20 and G21 as the cells to track.
4. Click OK to run Scenario Manager. The results appear in a separate worksheet, as shown in Screenshot 10-5B.

File: 10-5.xls, sheet: 10-5B

SCREENSHOT 10-5B Scenario Manager Results for Judith's Limousine Service

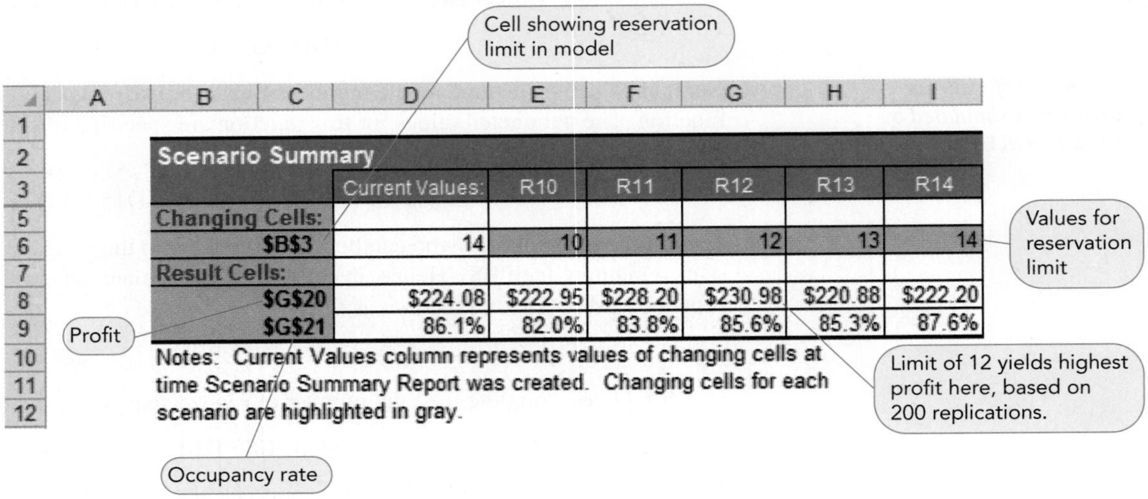

Scenario Summary	Current Values:	R10	R11	R12	R13	R14
Changing Cells:						
$B$3	14	10	11	12	13	14
Result Cells:						
$G$20	$224.08	$222.95	$228.20	$230.98	$220.88	$222.20
$G$21	86.1%	82.0%	83.8%	85.6%	85.3%	87.6%

Notes: Current Values column represents values of changing cells at time Scenario Summary Report was created. Changing cells for each scenario are highlighted in gray.

Analyzing the Results

Comparing the profit values in Screenshot 10-5B, it appears that Judith's best choice would be to accept 12 reservations per trip. (Remember that this result is based on only 200 replications.) The resulting average profit is $230.98 per trip. Not surprisingly, the occupancy rate is highest when Judith accepts 14 reservations, even though the rate does not seem to exceed 90% in any scenario.

So far, we have developed four simulation models using only Excel's built-in functions. We have also used Data Table to replicate the output measures in each model and Scenario Manager to automatically try different values for one or more input parameters. Solved Problems 10-1 to 10-3 at the end of this chapter discuss three additional simulation models using only Excel's built-in functions.

There are, however, several add-in programs available that make it even easier to develop and replicate simulation models using Excel. Hence, in the next two sections (and in Solved Problem 10-4 at the end of this chapter, in which we simulate a project management problem), we illustrate the use of one of the more powerful Excel add-ins for simulation, Crystal Ball.

10.8 Simulation Model of an Inventory Problem Using Crystal Ball

Crystal Ball *is an Excel add-in used for simulation.*

Crystal Ball, an add-in for Excel, is published by Oracle, Inc. (For more information, please refer to www.oracle.com.)

Reasons for Using Add-in Programs

From a logic and appearance point of view, a simulation model that is set up in Excel with Crystal Ball (or any other add-in) will look very similar to one that is set up without an add-in. Hence, any of the simulation models that we have created so far (using only Excel's built-in functions) can also be used with Crystal Ball. There are, however, three main features that add-ins such as Crystal Ball offer over Excel's built-in functions and procedures. As we will see shortly, these features are worthwhile enough to make the use of such add-in programs very useful in simulation modeling. The three features that add-ins such as Crystal Ball offer are as follows:

These three features of add-ins make them useful tools for developing simulation models on spreadsheets.

1. They have built-in functions to simulate not only from the simple probability distributions discussed so far but also from many other distributions that are commonly encountered in practice (e.g., binomial, triangular, lognormal). Further, the formulas to simulate from these distributions are simple, intuitive, and easy to use. For example, to simulate a random value in Crystal Ball from a normal distribution with mean and standard deviation σ, we use the following formula =CB.NORMAL(μ,σ). As you can see, this formula is much more intuitive than the formula we used earlier for simulating from a normal distribution: =NORMINV(RAND(),μ,σ).
2. They have built-in procedures that make it very easy to replicate the simulation model several hundred (or even several thousand) times. This means we will not have to set up and use Data Table.

3. They have built-in procedures that make it easy to collect and present information on various output measures. These measures can also be displayed graphically, if desired.

We should note that our intent here is to only provide a brief introduction to Crystal Ball and not to describe every aspect or capability of this add-in program. Once you have completed this section and the next, however, you should have sufficient knowledge about this add-in to explore some of its other options and procedures. Many of these are self-explanatory, and we strongly encourage you to try these out on your own.

Simulation of Simkin's Hardware Store Using Crystal Ball

Here we revisit Simkin's Hardware Store example.

To illustrate the use of Crystal Ball, let us revisit the inventory problem of Simkin's Hardware Store. Recall from section 10.5 that Simkin wants to test four different values (8, 10, 12, and 14) for the order quantity, Q, and two different values (5 and 8) for the reorder point, R, to see which combination of values for these two input parameters minimizes his monthly total cost. The total cost includes the following components: holding cost, stockout cost, and order cost. (At this time, we recommend that you refer to section 10.5 for a quick refresher on this problem and the simulation model we developed for it.)

File: 10-6.xls

STARTING CRYSTAL BALL If you have installed Crystal Ball on your PC, you can start the program (and Excel) by clicking Crystal Ball in the Windows Start menu.

Once the add-in has been loaded in Excel, you will see a new tab called Crystal Ball in Excel, with several menu commands, as shown in the top part of Screenshot 10-6A.

SCREENSHOT 10-6A Excel Layout and Results Using Crystal Ball for Simkin's Hardware Store

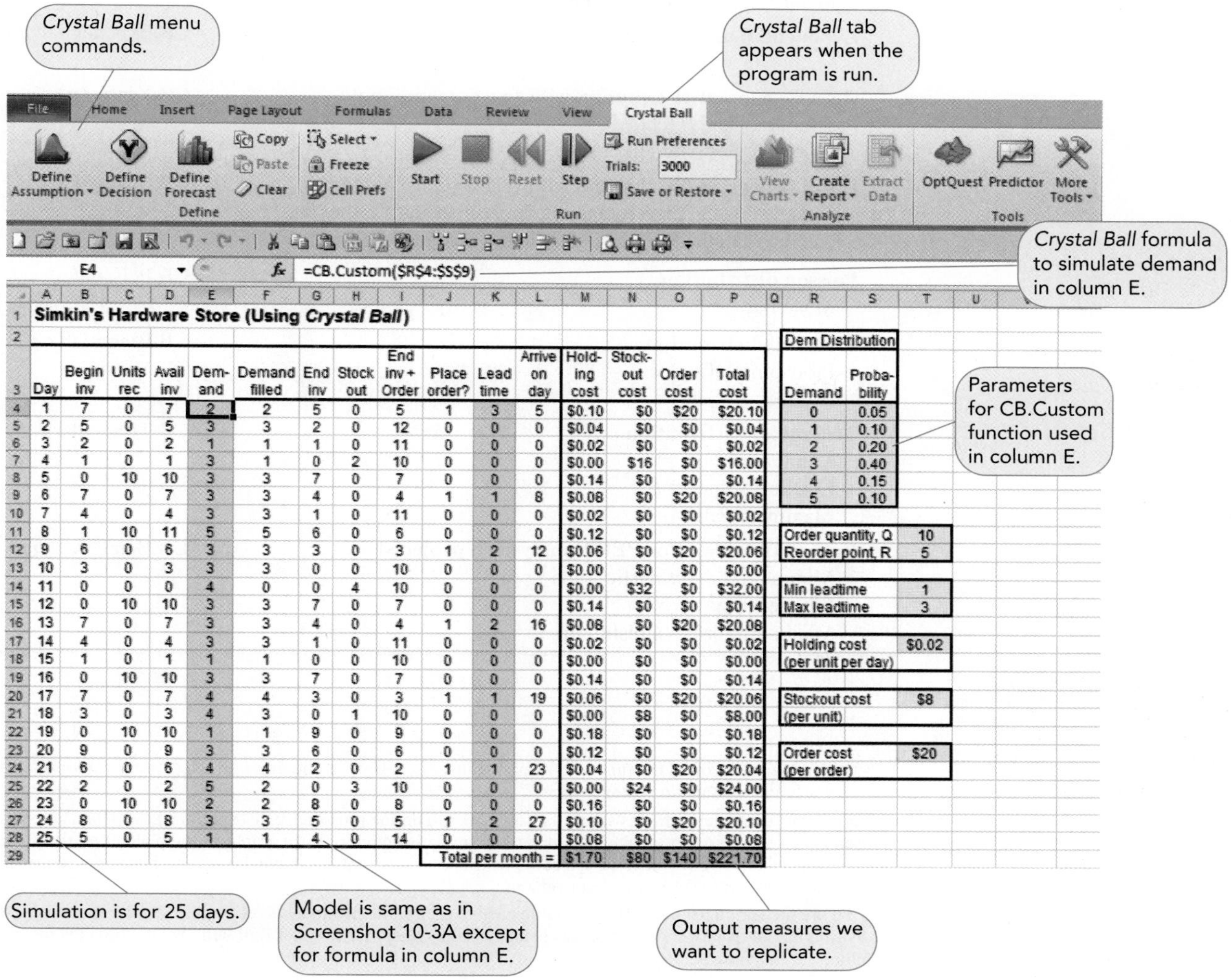

Crystal Ball menu commands.

Crystal Ball tab appears when the program is run.

File | Home | Insert | Page Layout | Formulas | Data | Review | View | Crystal Ball

Define Assumption · Define Decision · Define Forecast · Copy · Paste · Clear · Select · Freeze · Cell Prefs (Define) | Start · Stop · Reset · Step · Run Preferences · Trials: 3000 · Save or Restore (Run) | View Charts · Create Report · Extract Data (Analyze) | OptQuest · Predictor · More Tools (Tools)

E4 | =CB.Custom($R$4:$S$9)

Crystal Ball formula to simulate demand in column E.

Simkin's Hardware Store (Using *Crystal Ball*)

Day	Begin inv	Units rec	Avail inv	Dem-and	Demand filled	End inv	Stock out	End inv + Order	Place order?	Lead time	Arrive on day	Hold-ing cost	Stock-out cost	Order cost	Total cost
1	7	0	7	2	2	5	0	5	1	3	5	$0.10	$0	$20	$20.10
2	5	0	5	3	3	2	0	12	0	0	0	$0.04	$0	$0	$0.04
3	2	0	2	1	1	1	0	11	0	0	0	$0.02	$0	$0	$0.02
4	1	0	1	3	1	0	2	10	0	0	0	$0.00	$16	$0	$16.00
5	0	10	10	3	3	7	0	7	0	0	0	$0.14	$0	$0	$0.14
6	7	0	7	3	3	4	0	4	1	1	8	$0.08	$0	$20	$20.08
7	4	0	4	3	3	1	0	11	0	0	0	$0.02	$0	$0	$0.02
8	1	10	11	5	5	6	0	6	0	0	0	$0.12	$0	$0	$0.12
9	6	0	6	3	3	3	0	3	1	2	12	$0.06	$0	$20	$20.06
10	3	0	3	3	3	0	0	10	0	0	0	$0.00	$0	$0	$0.00
11	0	0	0	4	0	0	4	10	0	0	0	$0.00	$32	$0	$32.00
12	0	10	10	3	3	7	0	7	0	0	0	$0.14	$0	$0	$0.14
13	7	0	7	3	3	4	0	4	1	2	16	$0.08	$0	$20	$20.08
14	4	0	4	3	3	1	0	11	0	0	0	$0.02	$0	$0	$0.02
15	1	0	1	1	1	0	0	10	0	0	0	$0.00	$0	$0	$0.00
16	0	10	10	3	3	7	0	7	0	0	0	$0.14	$0	$0	$0.14
17	7	0	7	4	4	3	0	3	1	1	19	$0.06	$0	$20	$20.06
18	3	0	3	4	3	0	1	10	0	0	0	$0.00	$8	$0	$8.00
19	0	10	10	1	1	9	0	9	0	0	0	$0.18	$0	$0	$0.18
20	9	0	9	3	3	6	0	6	0	0	0	$0.12	$0	$0	$0.12
21	6	0	6	4	4	2	0	2	1	1	23	$0.04	$0	$20	$20.04
22	2	0	2	5	2	0	3	10	0	0	0	$0.00	$24	$0	$24.00
23	0	10	10	2	2	8	0	8	0	0	0	$0.16	$0	$0	$0.16
24	8	0	8	3	3	5	0	5	1	2	27	$0.10	$0	$20	$20.10
25	5	0	5	1	1	4	0	14	0	0	0	$0.08	$0	$0	$0.08
											Total per month =	$1.70	$80	$140	$221.70

Dem Distribution	
Demand	Proba-bility
0	0.05
1	0.10
2	0.20
3	0.40
4	0.15
5	0.10

Order quantity, Q	10
Reorder point, R	5
Min leadtime	1
Max leadtime	3
Holding cost (per unit per day)	$0.02
Stockout cost (per unit)	$8
Order cost (per order)	$20

Parameters for CB.Custom function used in column E.

Simulation is for 25 days.

Model is same as in Screenshot 10-3A except for formula in column E.

Output measures we want to replicate.

The Crystal Ball menus and toolbar are shown when the program is run.

As noted earlier, add-ins such as Crystal Ball include an extensive set of built-in functions to simulate from many probability distributions. For your convenience, Table 10.7 presents a list of some of the functions available in Crystal Ball to generate random values from some of the distributions commonly used in simulation.[8, 9]

The model with Crystal Ball looks very similar to the model that uses only Excel's built-in functions.

EXCEL LAYOUT USING CRYSTAL BALL FOR SIMKIN'S HARDWARE STORE We begin by setting up Simkin's inventory simulation model for any combination of Q and R values. (Let's use $Q = 10$ and $R = 5$, as we did in section 10.5.) Notice that the Excel layout in Screenshot 10-6A is very similar to the one we developed in section 10.5 for this problem using only Excel's built-in functions (refer to Screenshot 10-3A on page 426). In fact, the only change here is in column E, where we simulate the demand each day. Recall that we simulated these values in Screenshot 10-3A by using Excel's LOOKUP function. In Screenshot 10-6A, however, we use the CB.Custom function that is available in Crystal Ball to simulate from discrete general distributions (see Table 10.7 for details). The parameters for this function are shown in cells R4:S9 in Screenshot 10-6A. The formula for the demand in cells E4:E28 is[10]

We use the CB.Custom function to simulate demand here.

=CB.Custom($R$4:$S$9)

TABLE 10.7 Simulating from Various Probability Distributions Using Crystal Ball

TO SIMULATE FROM	CRYSTAL BALL FORMULA
Continuous uniform distribution Between a and b	=CB.Uniform(a,b)
Discrete uniform distribution Between a and b	=CB.DiscreteUniform(a,b)
Normal distribution Mean = μ; standard deviation = σ	=CB.Normal(μ,σ)
Exponential distribution Mean rate = μ	=CB.Exponential(μ)
Discrete general distribution with two outcomes only A (code 1) and B (code 0) Probability of outcome $A = p$	=CB.YesNo(p)
Discrete general distribution with two or more outcomes *Range* = Cell range containing variable values (in the first column) and their probabilities (in the second column)	=CB.Custom(*Range*)
Poisson distribution Mean rate = μ	=CB.Poisson(μ)
Binomial distribution Probability of success = p Number of trials = n	=CB.Binomial(p,n)
Triangular distribution Minimum value = a Likeliest value = b Maximum value = c	=CB.Triangular(a,b,c)
Beta distribution (for PERT analysis in projects) Minimum (or Optimistic) time = a Likeliest time = b Maximum (or Pessimistic) time = c	=CB.BetaPert(a,b,c)

[8] You can see a list of all the functions available in Crystal Ball by clicking f_x in Excel's standard toolbar and selecting Crystal Ball in the function category.

[9] Instead of using the formulas shown in Table 10.7 to define probability distributions in Crystal Ball, we could have used the Define Assumption menu command. Using this option opens a graphical template of all the probability distributions available, from which we select the distribution we want. We have, however, chosen to use the formulas here because we find them to be more convenient.

[10] To see the simulated value for a variable change each time the model is recomputed, make sure the Set cell value to distribution mean box under Cell Prefs is unchecked. Otherwise, Crystal Ball will always show the mean of the distribution for the variable.

The rest of the formulas in Screenshot 10-6A are the same as in Screenshot 10-3A. Cells M29:P29 show the four total monthly cost measures—holding cost, stockout cost, order cost, and total cost.

Replicating the Model

Once we have set up Simkin's simulation model, we want to replicate it several thousand times and keep track of the cost measures (cells M29:P29) each time. Instead of using Data Table (as we did in Screenshot 10-3B), we replicate the model in Crystal Ball, using the following two-step procedure: (1) define forecasts and (2) run replications.

Output measures are called forecasts in Crystal Ball.

DEFINING FORECASTS First, we define the cells that we want to replicate. This is done as follows:

1. Select cell M29. This cell *must* contain the formula for an output measure (forecast) we want to replicate.
2. Click Define Forecast, found within the Crystal Ball tab. The window shown in Screenshot 10-6B is displayed.
3. If desired, specify the name and units of the output measure, as shown in Screenshot 10-6B. Click OK.
4. Repeat this procedure for the other three output measures (forecasts) in cells N29, O29, and P29.

We can track several forecasts at the same time.

RUNNING REPLICATIONS Once all forecasts have been defined, click Run Preferences, found within the Crystal Ball tab. The Run Preferences window shown in Screenshot 10-6C is

SCREENSHOT 10-6B Defining a Forecast Cell in Crystal Ball

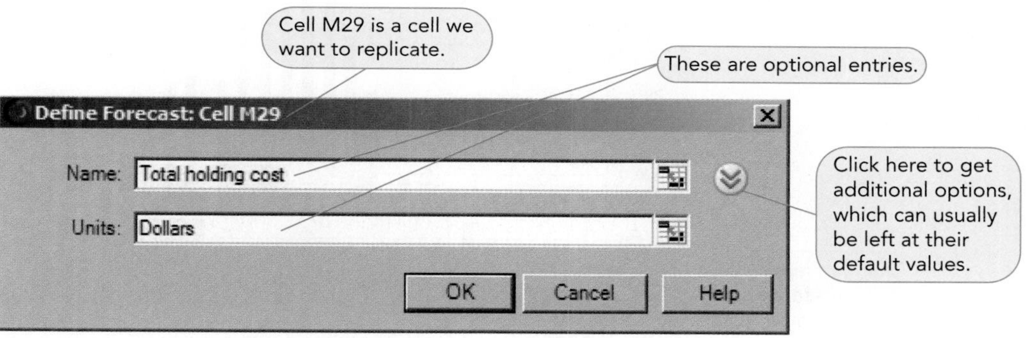

SCREENSHOT 10-6C Setting Run Preferences in Crystal Ball

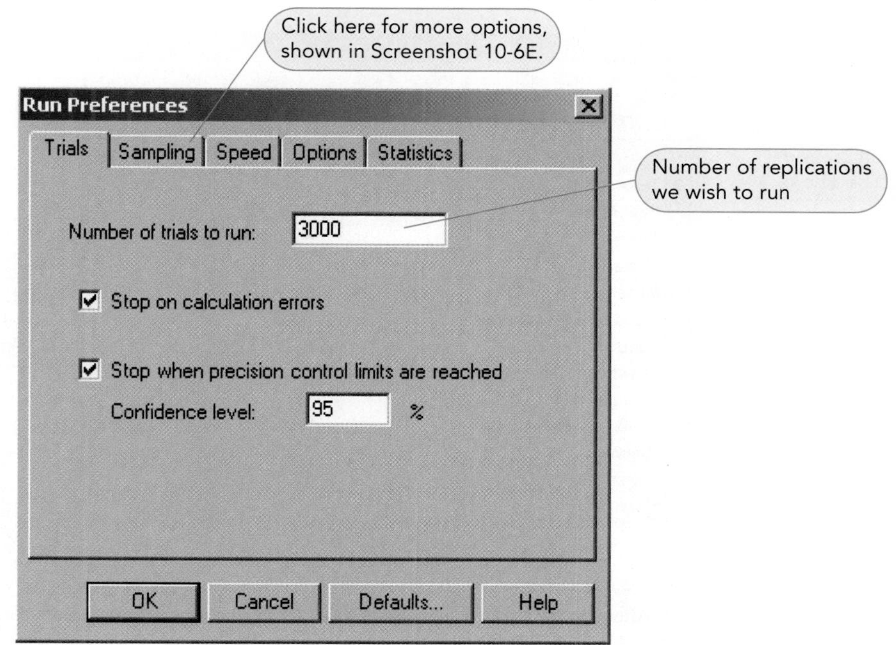

We can specify a larger number of replications here without worrying about the Excel file becoming too large.

displayed. Specify the number of trials (replications) desired and click OK. Note that because Crystal Ball is not going to show each replication's cost values in the spreadsheet (unlike Data Table in section 10.5), we do not have to be concerned about the Excel file getting too large. Hence, we can ask for a much larger number of replications here. For our discussion here, let us simulate the model 3,000 times. All other options in the window can be left at their defaults.

The results can be viewed in either graphical or tabular form.

To now run the model, click Start, found within the Crystal Ball tab.[11] Crystal Ball runs the model for the specified number of replications, keeping track of forecast cells M29:P29 for each replication. When finished, the results of the simulation are presented in a separate window for each output measure. As shown in Screenshot 10-6D for the total cost (cell P29), we can view the results for each output measure either in graphical form or as a summary statistics table. To switch from the graphical view to the table, click View | Statistics on the window shown in Screenshot 10-6D.

SCREENSHOT 10-6D Graphical and Tabular Results from Crystal Ball for Simkin's Hardware Store

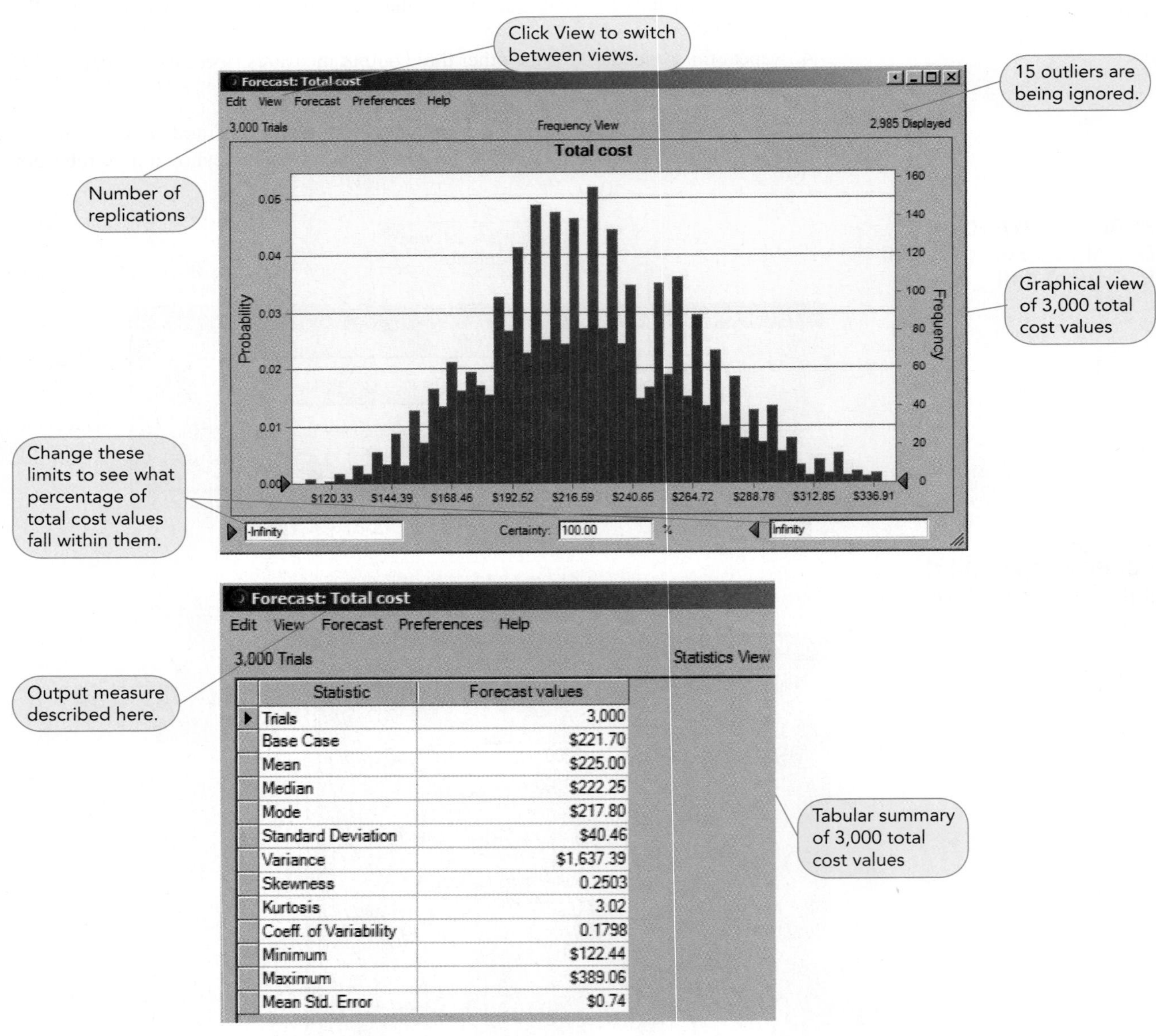

Statistic	Forecast values
Trials	3,000
Base Case	$221.70
Mean	$225.00
Median	$222.25
Mode	$217.80
Standard Deviation	$40.46
Variance	$1,637.39
Skewness	0.2503
Kurtosis	3.02
Coeff. of Variability	0.1798
Minimum	$122.44
Maximum	$389.06
Mean Std. Error	$0.74

[11] After completing a simulation run, you may need to reset the run count (click Reset, found with the Crystal Ball tab) before running the model again.

Screenshot 10-6D indicates that if $Q = 10$ and $R = 5$, Simkin's average monthly total cost is \$225. Note that this value is a more precise estimate of the average cost than the \$222.63 value we computed in section 10.5 using 200 replications with Data Table. Can you see why?

As an exercise, see if you can set up Crystal Ball to run 3,000 replications and compute Simkin's average fill rate per month with $Q = 10$. *Hint:* The answer should be around 82%.

We use Decision Table *in Crystal Ball to try several values automatically for an input parameter.*

Using Decision Table in Crystal Ball

The model discussed so far allows us to determine Simkin's average monthly cost for an inventory policy with $Q = 10$, and $R = 5$. However, recall that Simkin wants to test four different values (8, 10, 12, and 14) for Q and two different values (5 and 8) for R to see which combination of values is best for his inventory system. Just as we used Scenario Manager in section 10.5 to get Excel to try these values of Q and R automatically in the simulation model, we use a procedure called Decision Table in Crystal Ball for this purpose.

Crystal Ball also includes a procedure called OptQuest that can be used to automatically search for the best combination of decision variable values (within preset bounds) that optimizes a defined output measure.

It is a good idea to use the same series of random numbers each time we run a simulation model with different values for input parameters.

USING THE SAME SEQUENCE OF RANDOM NUMBERS Before we describe the Decision Table and OptQuest procedures, we note an important issue. Whenever we run a simulation model multiple times with different values for input parameters, and then compare the results, it is a good idea to run the model using the same series of random numbers. By doing so, we are sure that any observed differences in output measures are due to differences in the input parameter values and not due to the randomness of the simulation process. Although Excel's RAND function does not allow us to fix the sequence of random numbers generated in the examples we discussed in sections 10.4 to 10.7, Crystal Ball permits us to do so here. To enable this feature, we first click Run Preferences to get the window shown in Screenshot 10-6C on page 441. We then click the tab titled Sampling on this window to get the window shown in Screenshot 10-6E. Finally, we check the Use same sequence of random numbers option and specify any number of our choice for the Initial seed value. (We use the same number each time.)

This is how we set up the Decision Table procedure.

SETTING UP THE DECISION TABLE PROCEDURE IN CRYSTAL BALL The steps to set up and run the Decision Table procedure for Simkin's simulation model are as follows:

1. As before, define cells M29:P29 as forecast cells by using the Define Forecast menu command.
2. Select cell T11 (i.e., a cell in which we want different values to be plugged in). Click Define Decision, found within the Crystal Ball tab. The Define Decision Variable window

SCREENSHOT 10-6E Using the Same Sequence of Random Numbers in Crystal Ball

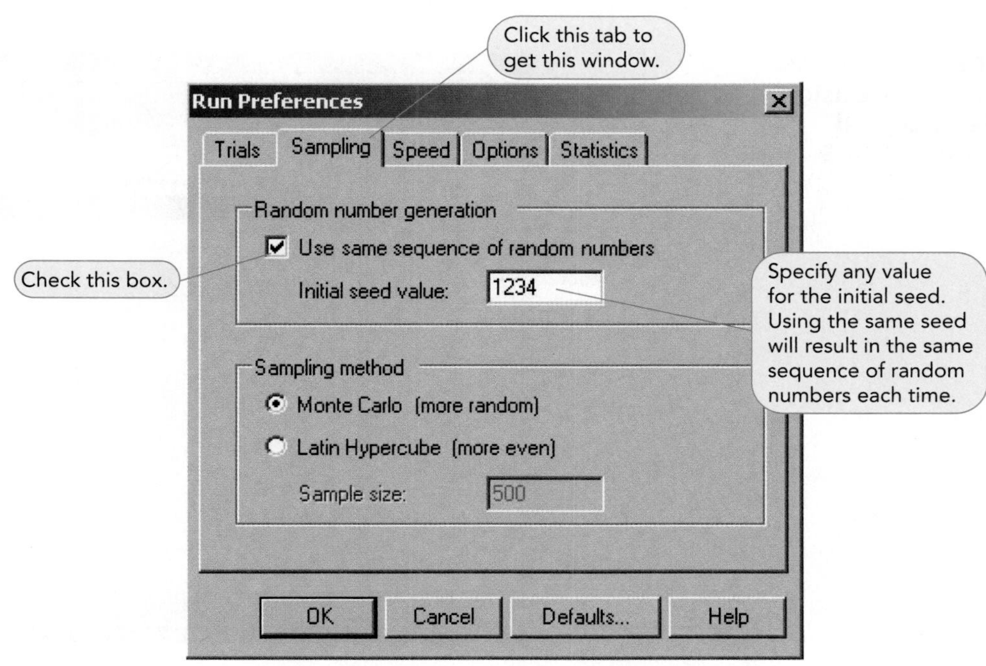

SCREENSHOT 10-6F Defining a Decision Variable Cell in Crystal Ball

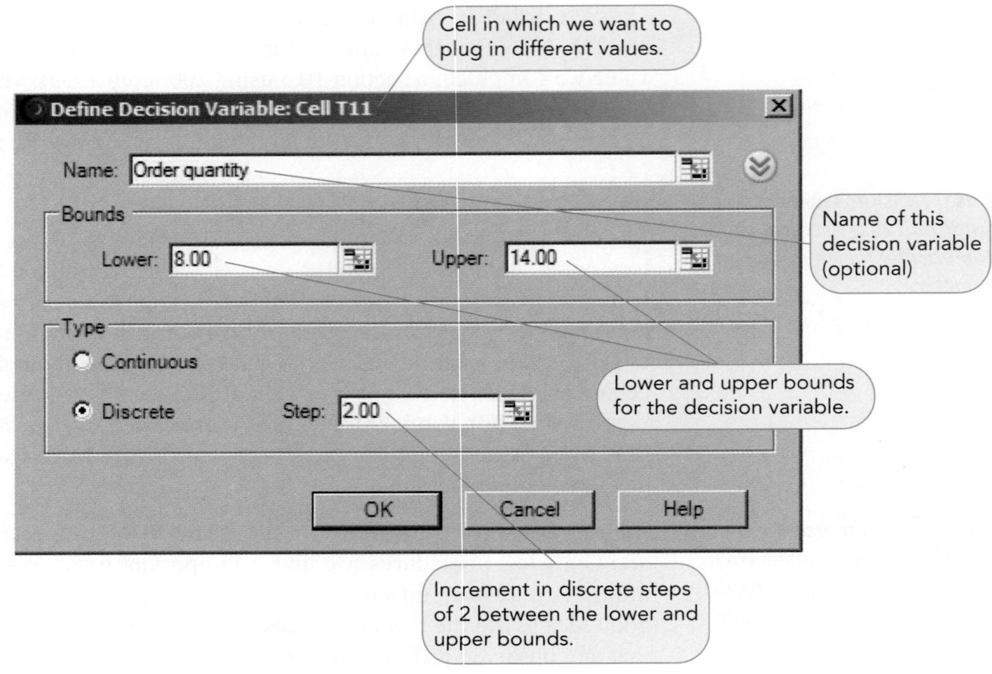

shown in Screenshot 10-6F is displayed. Name the decision variable (if desired). Enter the lower and upper bounds (i.e., 8 and 14, respectively) for the order quantity. Specify a discrete step size of 2 to analyze Q values of 8, 10, 12, and 14 only. Click OK.

Repeat this step after selecting cell T12. In this case, the lower and upper bounds are 5 and 8, respectively, and the discrete step size is 3 (because we want to analyze R values of 5 and 8 only).

We should run Decision Table separately for each output measure that we wish to analyze.

3. Click More Tools, found within the Crystal Ball tab, and then select Decision Table from the choices that are presented. The window shown in Screenshot 10-6G is displayed. From the list of defined forecasts, select the forecast that you want Decision Table to track. In Screenshot 10-6G, we have selected the total cost (cell P29) as the target cell. *Note:* Because Decision Table presents detailed results for each combination of decision values, it should be run separately for each forecast. Hence, if we wish to also analyze holding cost, stockout cost, and order cost, we should run Decision Table separately for each forecast.

SCREENSHOT 10-6G Setting Up Decision Table in Crystal Ball—Step 1 of 3

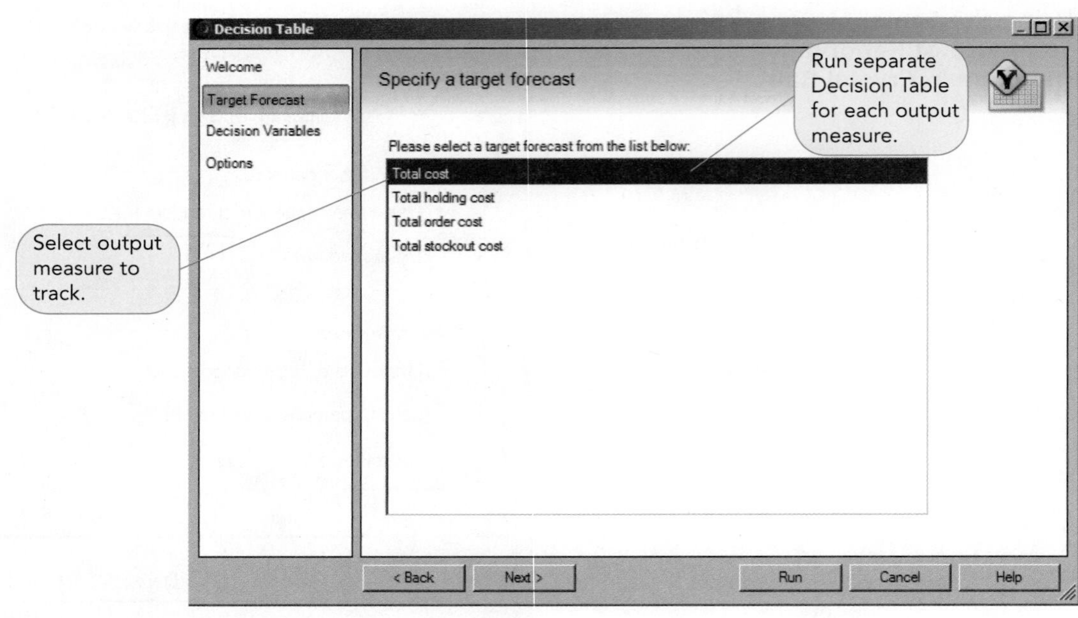

SCREENSHOT 10-6H Setting Up Decision Table in Crystal Ball—Step 2 of 3

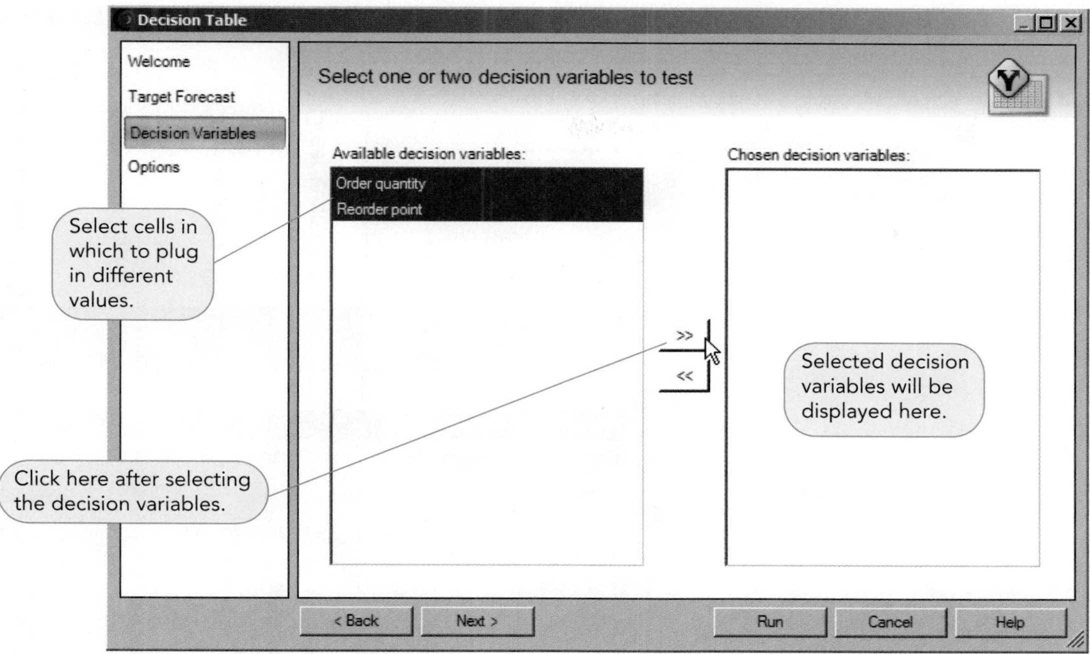

4. Click Next. The window shown in Screenshot 10-6H is displayed. From the window on the left, select the one or two decision variables (input parameters) whose values you wish to vary. In Simkin's model, these are the order quantity (cell T11) and reorder point (cell T12). Click the button marked >>. The selected decision variables are now displayed in the window on the right.
5. Click Next. The window shown in Screenshot 10-6I is displayed. Make sure the appropriate number of values are shown for the order quantity (four values) and reorder point (two values). Enter the desired number of replications. Although we have specified 3,000 replications in Screenshot 10-6I, it is a good idea to run Decision Table with just a few replications first to verify that everything has been set up properly before running it with a larger number. Click Run.

SCREENSHOT 10-6I Setting Up Decision Table in Crystal Ball—Step 3 of 3

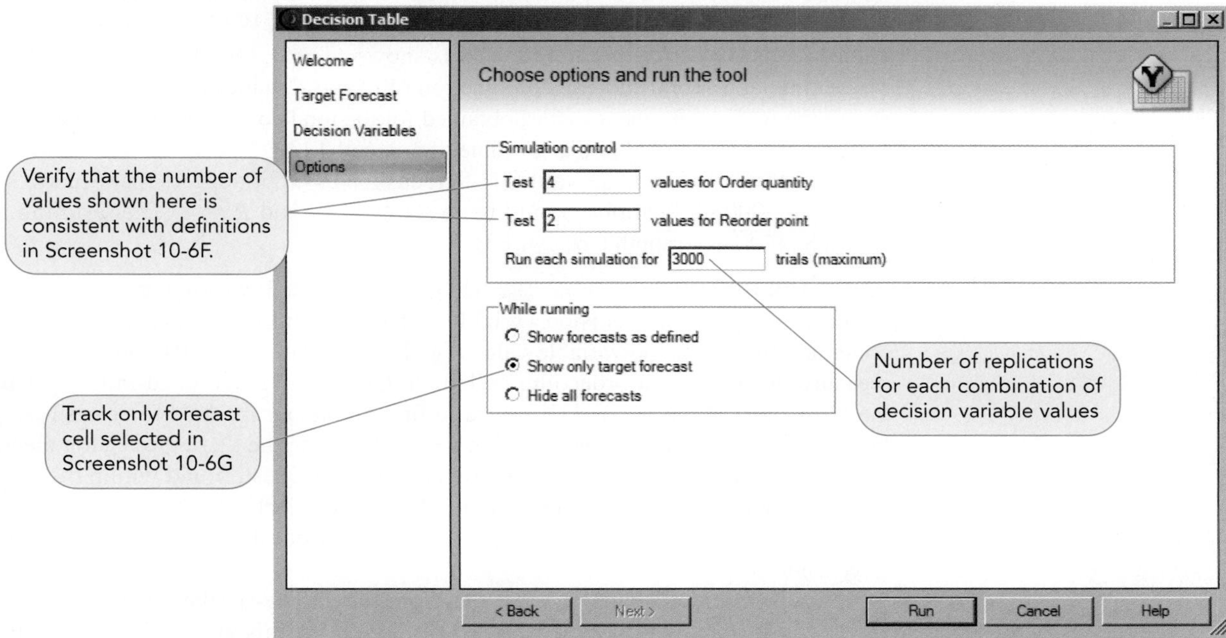

SCREENSHOT 10-6J Results from Decision Table in Crystal Ball for Simkin's Hardware Store

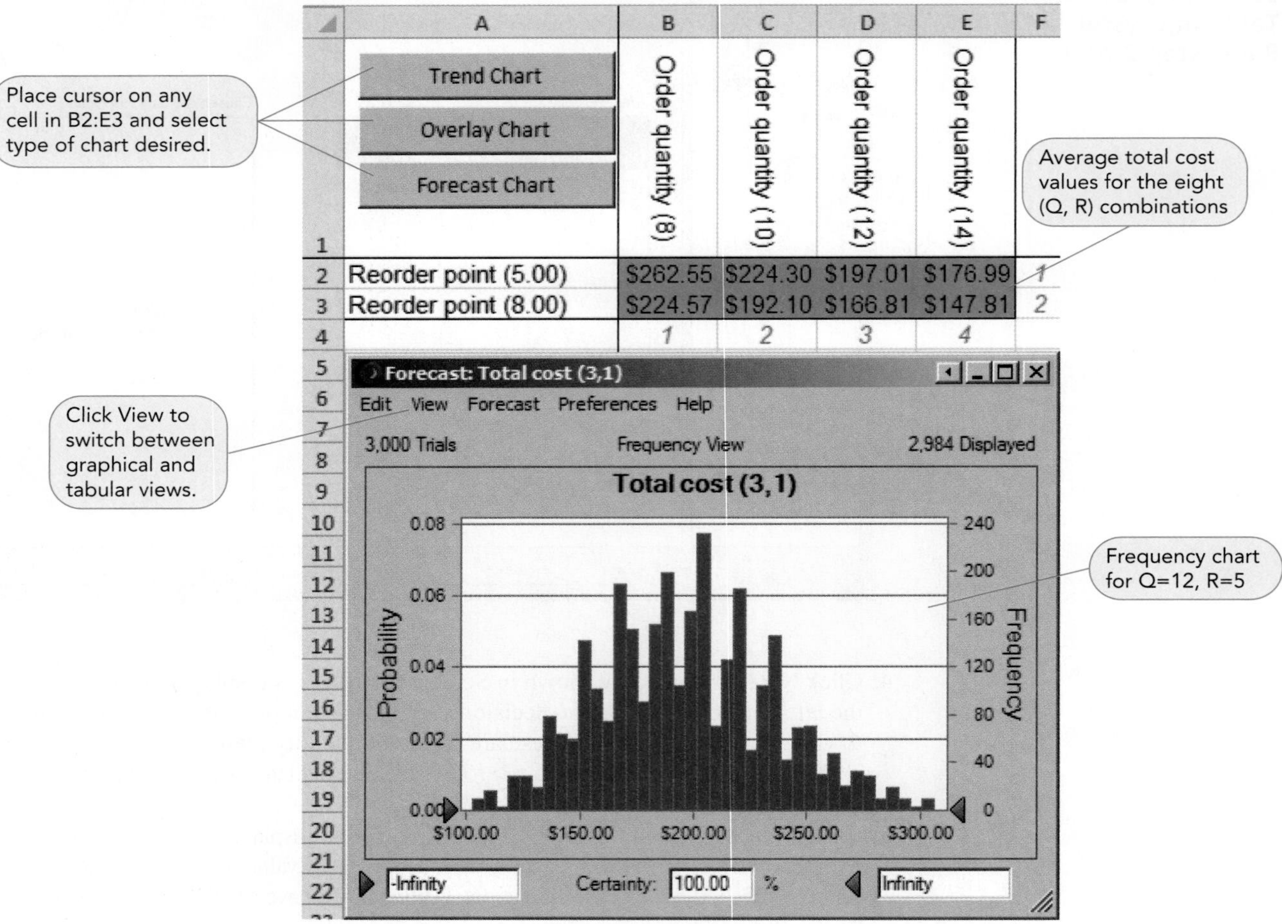

Decision Table plugs in each value of Q and R in cells T11 and T12 (see Screenshot 10-6A on page 439), respectively, and runs 3,000 replications in each case. The results, shown in Screenshot 10-6J, are displayed in a separate workbook. We can click any of these total cost values (cells B2:E3) and select the charts shown (Trend, Overlay, or Forecast) to see details of the simulation for a specific combination of Q and R values. For example, Screenshot 10-6J shows the forecast frequency chart obtained for the total cost in cell D2, which corresponds to a Q value of 12 in cell T11 and an R value of 5 in cell T12.

Comparing the average values in Screenshot 10-6J, it appears that Simkin's best choice, based on 3,000 replications, would be to set $Q = 14$ and $R = 8$. The resulting average total cost is $147.81 per month (see cell E3).

USING THE OPTQUEST PROCEDURE IN CRYSTAL BALL If we are unsure of the specific values we want to try for the decision variables, or if we want to automatically search for the best combination of decision variable values (within preset bounds) that optimizes a defined output measure, we can use a procedure called OptQuest that is included in Crystal Ball. As with the Decision Table procedure, we need to first define our model's forecasts (using the Define Forecast menu command) and decision variables (using the Define Decision menu command). We then run the OptQuest procedure by clicking OptQuest, found within the Crystal Ball tab to get the window shown in Screenshot 10-6K. We select Objectives from the choices in the left window, and then click Add Objective to specify our desired objective as illustrated in the screenshot.

Next, we select Decision Variables from the choices in the left window to get the OptQuest window shown in Screenshot 10-6L. Note that this window automatically shows the

SCREENSHOT 10-6K Setting Up the Objective in Crystal Ball's OptQuest Procedure

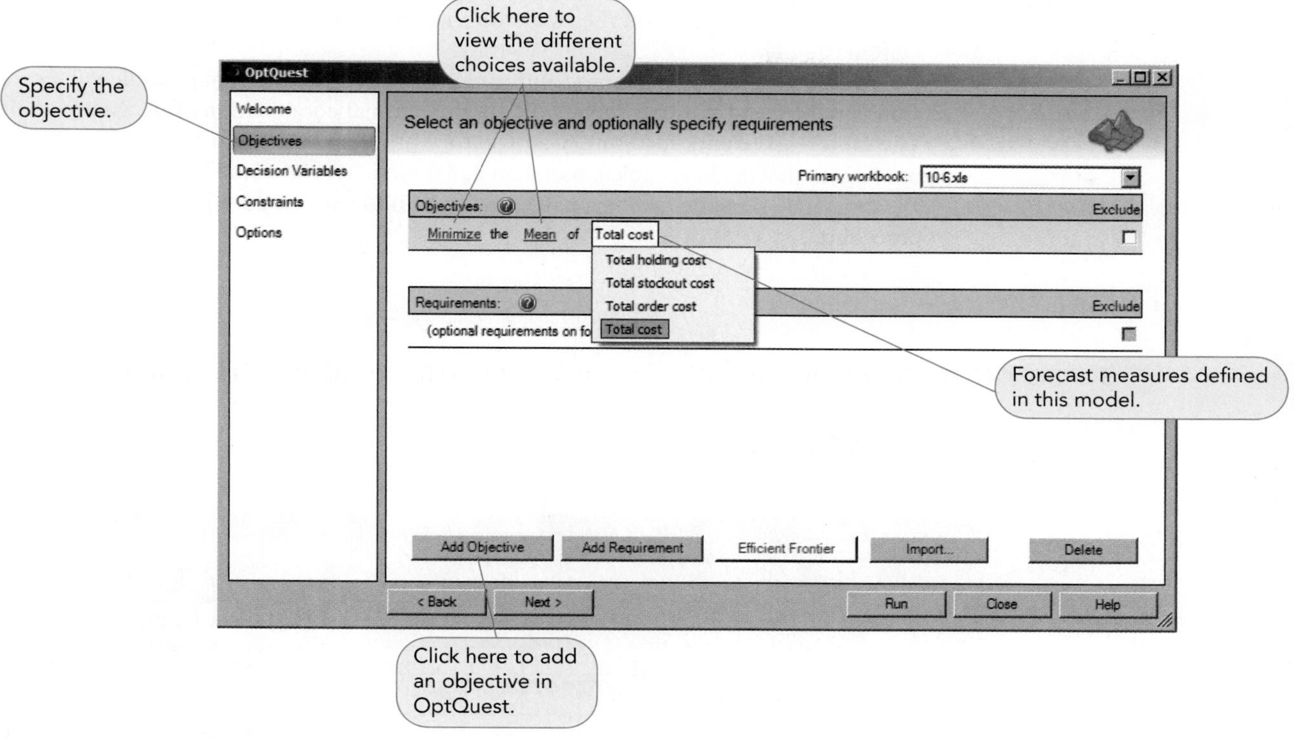

SCREENSHOT 10-6L Setting Up the Decision Variables in Crystal Ball's OptQuest Procedure

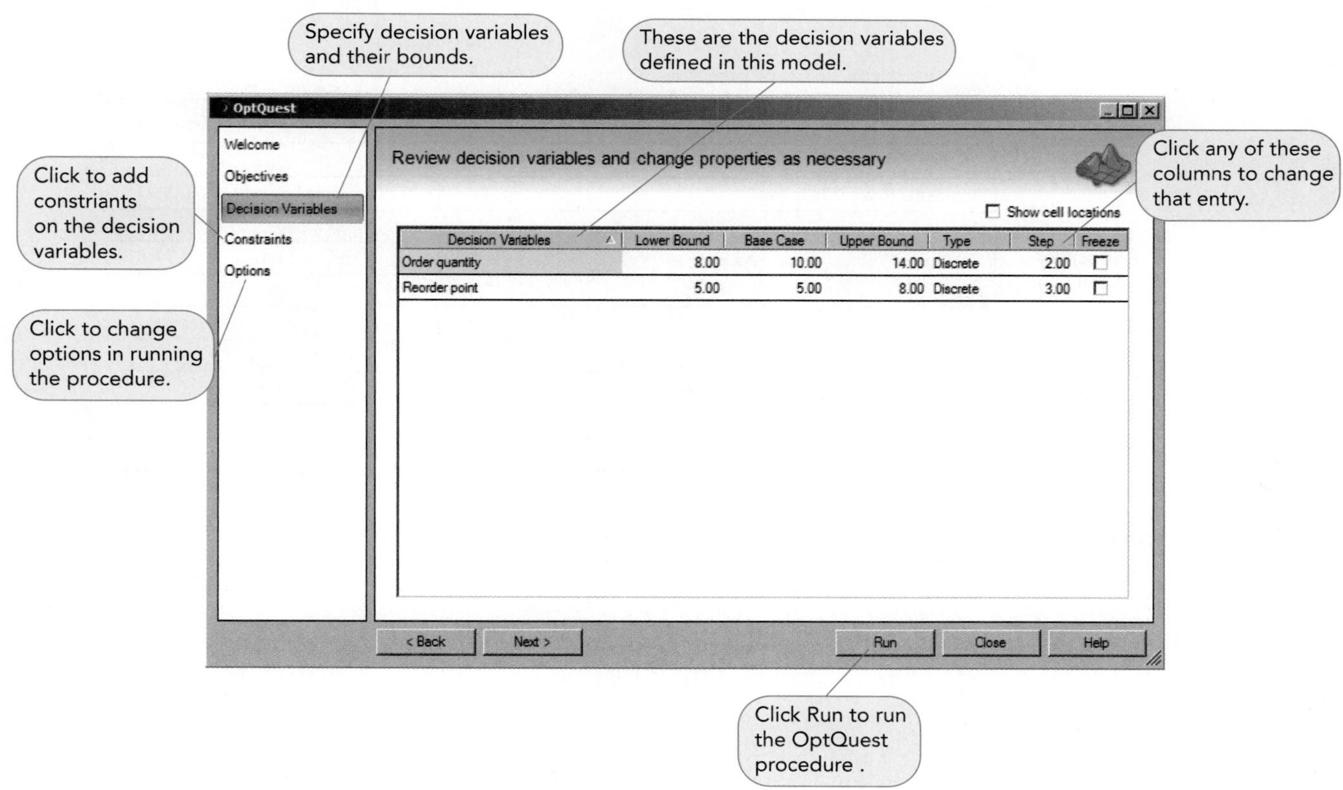

decision variables that have already been defined for this model. We can click on any of the columns (e.g., Lower Bound, Upper Bound, Step, etc.) to modify that parameter. If desired, we can add constraints on the decision variables as well as change the default options in OptQuest.

When we click Run, the procedure automatically tries different possible values for the decision variables and presents the results for the optimal combination of decision variable values. The OptQuest results for Simkin's inventory problem, shown in Screenshot 10-6M, indicate once again that the best choice, based on 3,000 replications, would be to set $Q = 14$ and $R = 8$. We can click View or Analyze in the results window to see additional results of the OptQuest procedure.

SCREENSHOT 10-6M Results Window in Crystal Ball's OptQuest Procedure

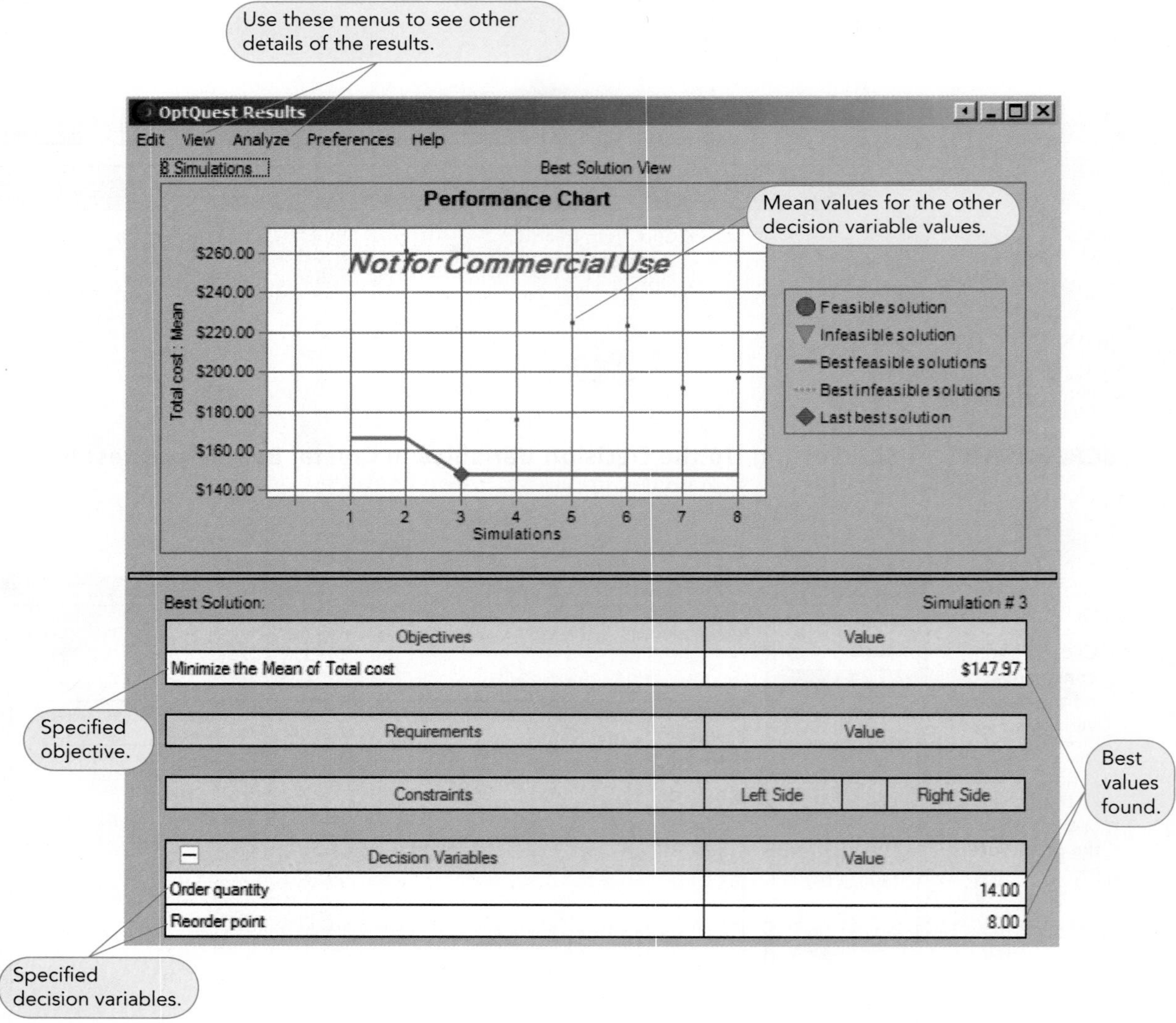

IN ACTION Simulating Taco Bell's Restaurant Operation

Determining how many employees to schedule each 15 minutes to perform each function in a Taco Bell restaurant is a complex and vexing problem. So Taco Bell, the $5 billion giant with 6,500 U.S. and foreign locations, decided to build a simulation model. In selected MODSIM as its software to develop a new labor-management system called LMS.

To develop and use a simulation model, Taco Bell had to collect quite a bit of data. Almost everything that takes place in a restaurant, from customer arrival patterns to the time it takes to wrap a taco, had to be translated into reliable, accurate data. Just as an example, analysts had to conduct time studies and data analysis for every task that is part of preparing every item on the menu. To the researchers' surprise, the hours devoted to collecting data greatly exceeded those it took to actually build the LMS model.

Inputs to LMS include staffing, such as the number of people and positions. Outputs are performance measures, such as mean time in the system, mean time at the counter, people utilization, and equipment utilization. The model paid off. More than $53 million in labor costs were saved in LMS's first four years of use.

Sources: Based on J. Hueter and W. Swart. "An Integrated Labor-Management System for Taco Bell," *Interfaces* 28, 1 (January–February 1998): 75–91 and L. Pringle. "Productivity Engine," *OR/MS Today* 27, 3 (June 2000): 30.

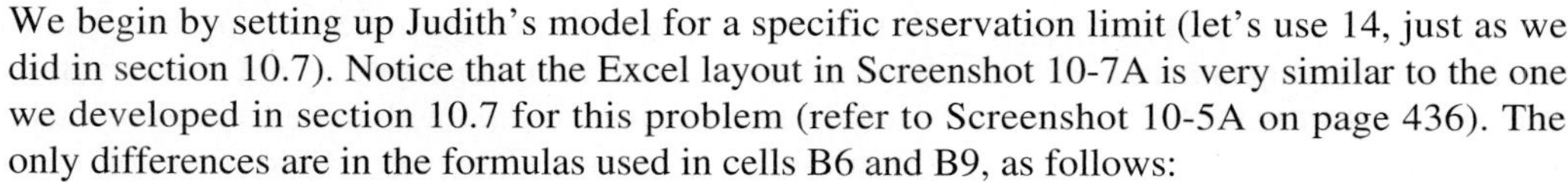

10.9 Simulation Model of a Revenue Management Problem Using Crystal Ball

We revisit the Judith's Limousine Service example.

In this section, we illustrate the use of Crystal Ball to simulate the revenue management problem we discussed in section 10.7. Recall that the problem involves an entrepreneur, Judith McKnew, who is trying to decide how many reservations (10, 11, 12, 13, or 14) she should accept per trip for her 10-passenger airport limousine service. (At this time, we recommend that you refer to section 10.7 for a quick refresher on this problem and the simulation model we developed for it.)

Setting Up the Model

File: 10-7.xls

We begin by setting up Judith's model for a specific reservation limit (let's use 14, just as we did in section 10.7). Notice that the Excel layout in Screenshot 10-7A is very similar to the one we developed in section 10.7 for this problem (refer to Screenshot 10-5A on page 436). The only differences are in the formulas used in cells B6 and B9, as follows:

The number of people showing up is simulated here using Crystal Ball's CB.Binomial function.

- Cell B6 simulates the number of passengers with reservations who actually show up for the trip. In section 10.7, we simulated this using Excel's CRITBINOM function. In Crystal Ball, we can simulate this using the CB.BINOMIAL function with parameters $p = 0.8$ (specified in cell G6) and $n =$ number of reservations accepted (cell B5). The formula in cell B6 (refer to Table 10.7 on page 440 for details if necessary) is

  =CB.BINOMIAL(G6,B5)

- In cell B9, we simulate the number of walk-up passengers. In section 10.7, we simulated this using Excel's LOOKUP function. In Crystal Ball, we can simulate this using the custom distribution function. The range of values and probabilities has been specified in cells D15:E17 in Screenshot 10-7A. The formula in cell B9 is

  =CB.Custom(D15:E17)

  The two desired output measures—profit and occupancy rate—are computed in cells B14 and B15, respectively.

We use Decision Table to test different values for the reservation limit.

USING DECISION TABLE TO IDENTIFY THE BEST RESERVATION LIMIT In Judith's problem, we want to try out five different values (10, 11, 12, 13, and 14) for the reservation limit. To do so using Decision Table in Crystal Ball, we use the following steps, just as we did in section 10.8 for Simkin's inventory model. Let us run Decision Table to track the profit (cell B14):

1. Specify that Crystal Ball should use the same sequence of random numbers in each case (refer to Screenshot 10-6E on page 443 for details).

SCREENSHOT 10-7A Excel Layout and Results Using Crystal Ball for Judith's Limousine Service

B6 =CB.Binomial(G6,B5)

	A	B	C	D	E	F	G
1	**Judith's Limousine Service (Using *Crystal Ball*)**						
2							
3	Judith's reservation limit	14		Van's passenger capacity =			10
4	Reservations requested	11		Minimum reservation request =			7
5	Reservations accepted	11		Maximum reservation request =			14
6	Number show up	8		Probability person shows up			0.80
7	Number overbook	0		Reservation deposit amount =			$10
8	Seats remaining	2		Balance of ticket price =			$25
9	Number walk-up	1		Walk-up ticket price =			$50
10	Walk-up accepted	1		Cost per overbooked person =			$75
11	Total seats occupied	9		Fixed cost per trip =			$100
12	Revenue	$360					
13	Cost	$100		Walk-up Distribution			
14	Profit	$260		Number	Probability		
15	Occupancy rate	90.0%		0	0.30		
16				1	0.45		
17				2	0.25		

We want to try different values for this limit.

CB.Binomial function is used to simulate number showing up in cell B6.

Input values for the model

Output measures that we want to replicate

Range for CB.Custom function used to simulate walk-ups in cell B9

Model is same as in Screenshot 10-5A except for formulas in cells B6 and B9.

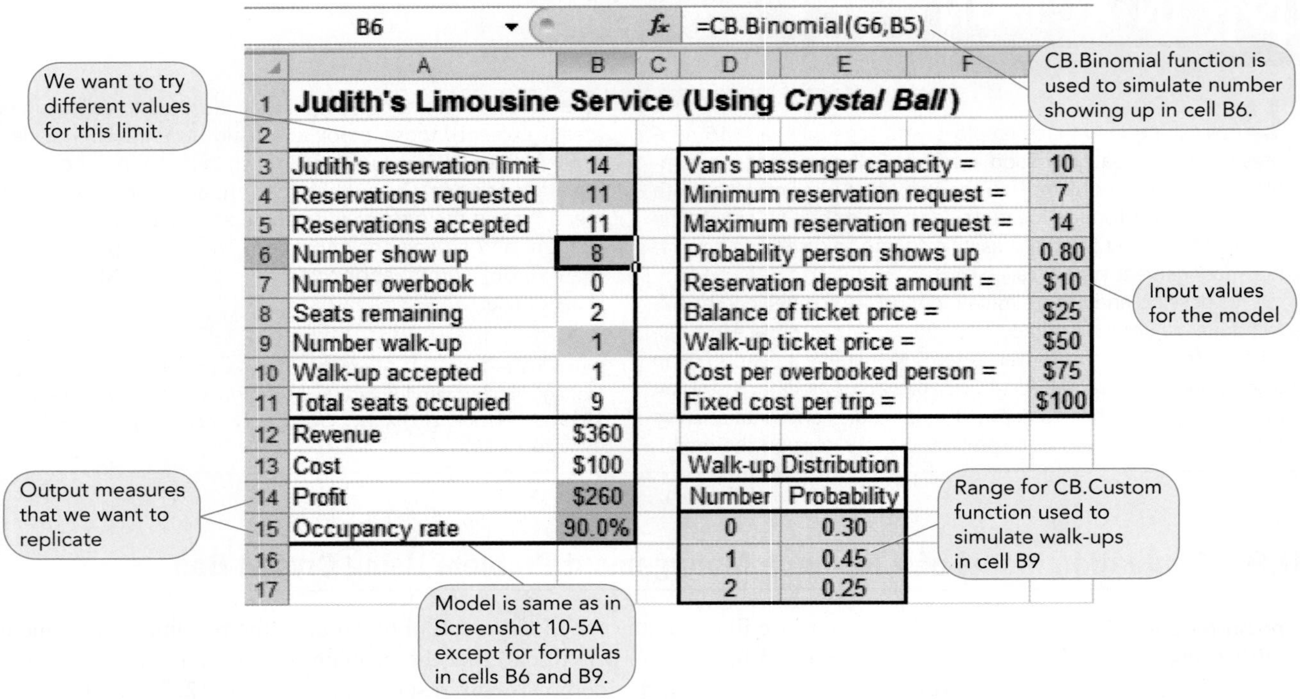

We define the forecast cells that we want to track.

2. Select cell B14, which contains the formula for the output measure (i.e., profit) that we want to track. Click Define Forecast, found within the Crystal Ball tab. If desired, specify the name and units of the output measure in the window that is displayed (refer to Screenshot 10-6B on page 441 for a sample view of this window). Click OK.

We define the input parameter cells that we want to vary automatically.

3. Select cell B3 (the cell in which you want the reservation limit values to be plugged in). Click Define Decision, found within the Crystal Ball tab. In the window that is displayed (refer to Screenshot 10-6F on page 444 for a sample view of this window), enter a lower value of 10 and an upper value of 14. The discrete step size is 1 because we want to study all reservations limits between 10 and 14. Click OK.
4. Click More Tools, found within the Crystal Ball tab, and then select Decision Table from the choices that are presented. Make sure the desired forecast cell (cell B14, in Judith's problem) is shown as the target cell in the window that is displayed. Click Next.
5. Select the decision variable cell (B3) and click the button marked >>> in the window that is displayed. Click Next.
6. In the final window (refer to Screenshot 10-6I on page 445 for a sample view of this window), make sure the appropriate number of values is shown for cell B3 (five values in Judith's problem). Enter the desired number of replications (such as 3,000) for each choice. Click Run.

We can see details for any of the simulation results.

Decision Table plugs in each value (i.e., 10 to 14) of the decision variable (reservation limit) in cell B3 (see Screenshot 10-7A) and runs 3,000 replications in each case. The results, shown in Screenshot 10-7B, are displayed in a separate workbook. We can click on any of these profit values (in cells B2:F2) and select the charts shown to see details for that simulation. For example, Screenshot 10-7B shows the tabular summary obtained for the profit when the reservation limit is 11.

Comparing the profit values in Screenshot 10-7B, it appears that based on 3,000 replications, Judith's best choice would be to accept 12 reservations per trip. The resulting average profit is $226.69 per trip.

At this stage, see if you can set up and run Decision Table to track the occupancy rate (cell B15) for the five reservation limits. For your reference, Screenshot 10-7C shows a tabular summary of the occupancy rates obtained by running the OptQuest procedure in Crystal Ball (click

SCREENSHOT 10-7B Results from Decision Table in Crystal Ball for Judith's Limousine Service

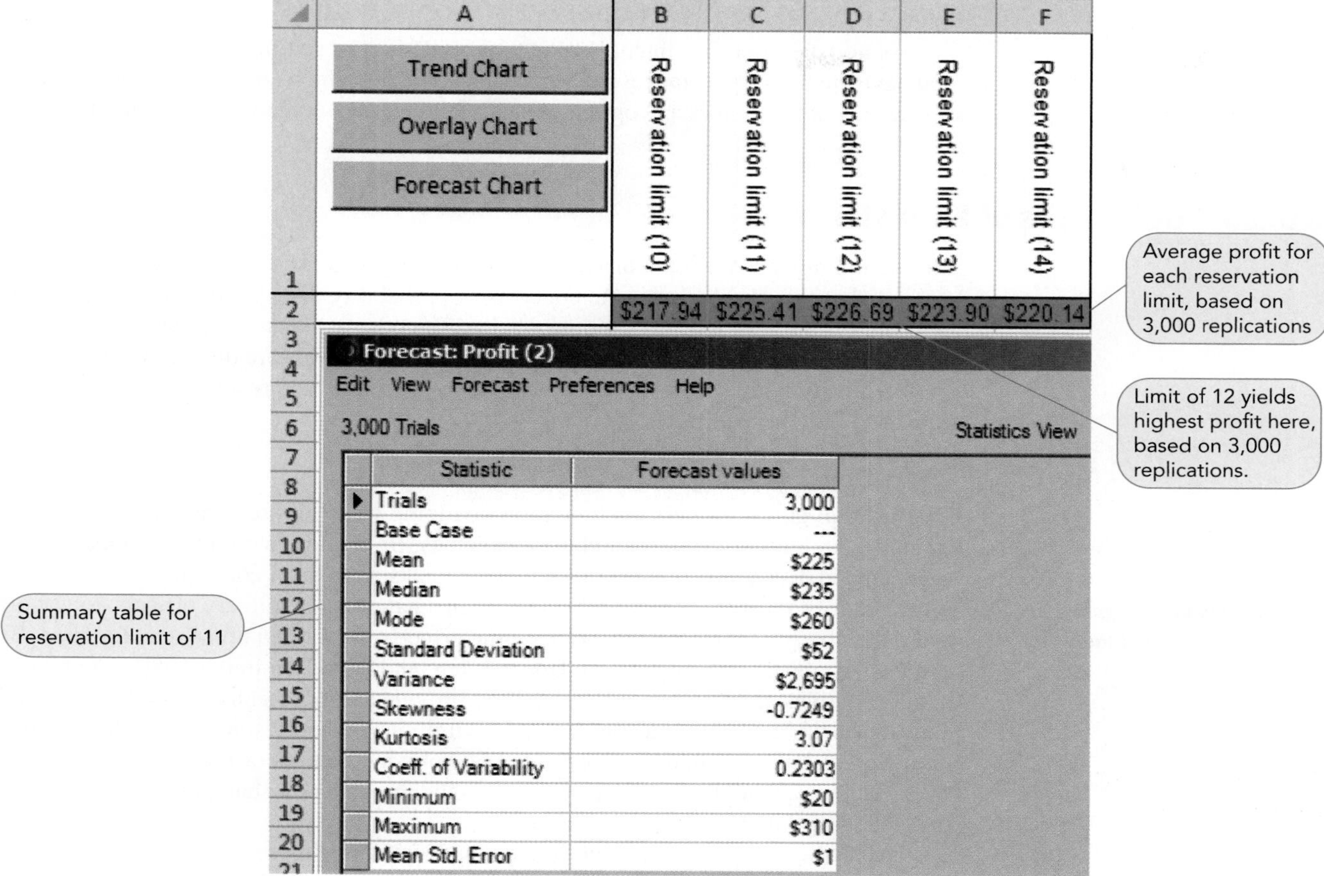

Statistic	Forecast values
Trials	3,000
Base Case	---
Mean	$225
Median	$235
Mode	$260
Standard Deviation	$52
Variance	$2,695
Skewness	-0.7249
Kurtosis	3.07
Coeff. of Variability	0.2303
Minimum	$20
Maximum	$310
Mean Std. Error	$1

SCREENSHOT 10-7C Results from OptQuest in Crystal Ball for Judith's Limousine Service

Click View|Solution Analysis to get this table.

OptQuest Results

Edit View Analyze Preferences Help

5 Total Solutions

Solution Analysis View

		Objective	Decision Variables
Rank	Solution #	Maximize Mean Occupancy rate	Reservation limit
1	5	86.7%	13.00
2	1	86.6%	12.00
3	3	86.4%	14.00
4	4	85.3%	11.00
5	2	81.9%	10.00

Objective specified in OptQuest.

Rank order of the five reservation limits with respect to occupancy rates.

View|Solution Analysis in the OptQuest Results window to get this table). The results seem to indicate that the average occupancy rate does not change appreciably between reservation limits of 12 to 14.

As noted earlier, our intent here is to provide just a brief introduction to Crystal Ball. As you navigate the various menus in the package (some of which are discussed here), you may notice several other choices and options. Once again, we encourage you to try out these procedures on your own.

10.10 Other Types of Simulation Models

Simulation models are often broken into three categories. The first, the Monte Carlo method discussed in this chapter, uses the concepts of probability distribution and random numbers to evaluate system responses to various policies. The other two categories are operational gaming and systems simulation. Although in theory the three methods are distinctly different from one another, the growth of computerized simulation has tended to create a common basis in procedures and blur these differences.[12]

Operational Gaming

Operational gaming refers to simulation involving two or more competing players. The best examples are military games and business games. Both allow participants to match their management and decision-making skills in hypothetical situations of conflict.

Business simulation games are popular educational tools in many colleges.

Military games are used worldwide to train a nation's top military officers, to test offensive and defensive strategies, and to examine the effectiveness of equipment and armies. Business games, first developed by the firm Booz, Allen, and Hamilton in the 1950s, are popular with both executives and business students. They provide an opportunity to test business skills and decision-making ability in a competitive environment. The person or team that performs best in the simulated environment is rewarded by knowing that his or her company has been most successful in earning the largest profit, grabbing a high market share, or perhaps increasing the firm's trading value on the stock exchange.

During each period of competition, be it a week, month, or quarter, teams respond to market conditions by coding their latest management decisions with respect to inventory, production, financing, investment, marketing, and research. The competitive business environment is simulated using a computer, and a new printout summarizing current market conditions is presented to players. This allows teams to simulate years of operating conditions in a matter of days, weeks, or a semester.

Systems Simulation

Systems simulation is similar to business gaming in that it allows users to test various managerial policies and decisions to evaluate their effect on the operating environment. This variation of simulation models the dynamics of large systems. Such systems are corporate operations,[13] the national economy, a hospital, or a city government system.

In a corporate operating system, sales, production levels, marketing policies, investments, union contracts, utility rates, financing, and other factors are all related in a series of mathematical equations that are examined through simulation. In a simulation of an urban government, systems simulation could be employed to evaluate the impact of tax increases, capital expenditures for roads and buildings, housing availability, new garbage routes, immigration and out-migration, locations of new schools or senior citizen centers, birth and death rates, and many more vital issues. Simulations of *economic systems*, often called *econometric* models, are used by government agencies, bankers, and large organizations to predict inflation rates, domestic and foreign money supplies, and unemployment levels. Inputs and outputs of a typical economic system simulation are illustrated in Figure 10.3.

---

[12] Theoretically, random numbers are used only in Monte Carlo simulation. However, in some complex gaming or systems simulation problems in which relationships cannot be defined exactly, it may be necessary to use the probability concepts of the Monte Carlo method.

[13] This is sometimes referred to as *industrial dynamics*, a term coined by Jay Forrester. Forrester's goal was to find a way "to show how policies, decisions, structure, and delays are interrelated to influence growth and stability" in industrial systems. See J. W. Forrester. *Industrial Dynamics*. Cambridge, MA: MIT Press, 1961.

FIGURE 10.3
Inputs and Outputs of a Typical Economic System Simulation

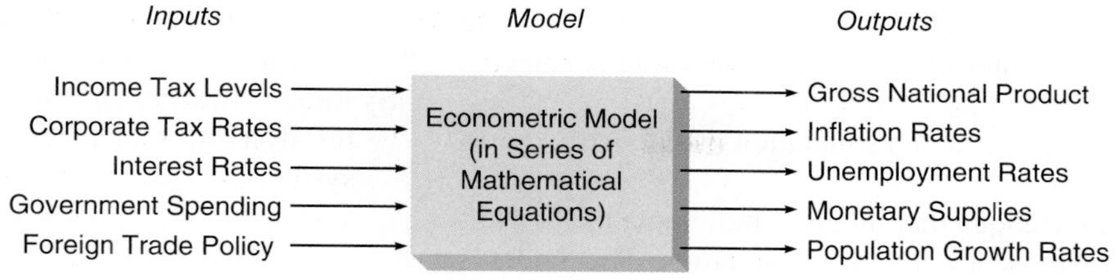

Inputs
Income Tax Levels
Corporate Tax Rates
Interest Rates
Government Spending
Foreign Trade Policy

Model
Econometric Model (in Series of Mathematical Equations)

Outputs
Gross National Product
Inflation Rates
Unemployment Rates
Monetary Supplies
Population Growth Rates

Econometric models are huge simulations involving thousands of regression equations tied together by economic factors. They use what-if questions to test various policies.

The value of systems simulation lies in its allowance of what-if questions to test the effects of various policies. A corporate planning group, for example, can change the value of any input, such as an advertising budget, and examine the impact on sales, market share, or short-term costs. Simulation can also be used to evaluate different research and development projects or to determine long-range planning horizons.

Summary

This chapter discusses the concept and approach of simulation as a problem-solving tool. Simulation involves building a mathematical model that attempts to describe a real-world situation. The model's goal is to incorporate important variables and their interrelationships in such a way that we can study the impact of managerial changes on the total system. The approach has many advantages over other decision modeling techniques and is especially useful when a problem is too complex or difficult to solve by other means.

The Monte Carlo method of simulation uses random numbers to generate random variable values from probability distributions. The simulation procedure is conducted for many time periods to evaluate the long-term impact of each policy value being studied.

We first illustrate how to set up Monte Carlo simulations by using Excel's built-in functions. We also show how Excel's Data Table can be used to run several replications of simulation models and how Scenario Manager can be used to try different values for input parameters. Then, we show how Crystal Ball, an Excel add-in for simulation, can be used to develop and run simulation models. The major advantages of using add-ins are (1) the availability of easy formulas for many common probability distributions, (2) the ability to quickly set up and run many replications of the model, and (3) the ability to easily collect statistical information on many different output measure.

We conclude this chapter with a brief discussion of operational gaming and systems simulation, two other categories of simulation.

Glossary

CRITBINOM An Excel function that can be used to randomly generate values from binomial probability distributions. Excel 2010 includes an improved version of this function, called BINOM.INV.

Crystal Ball An add-in for Excel that simplifies the implementation and solution of simulation models.

Data Table A procedure in Excel that allows simulation models to be replicated several times.

Decision Table A procedure in Crystal Ball that is used to automatically try different values for a decision variable in the simulation model.

Discrete-Event Simulation A simulation model in which we need to keep track of the passage of time by using a simulation clock.

Discrete General Distribution A distribution in which a variable can take on one of several discrete values, each with its own probability.

Flow Diagram, or Flowchart A graphical means of presenting the logic of a simulation model. It is a tool that helps in writing a simulation computer program.

LOOKUP An Excel function that can be used to randomly generate values from discrete general probability distributions.

Monte Carlo simulation A simulation that experiments with probabilistic elements of a system by generating random numbers to create values for those elements.

NORMINV An Excel function that can be used to randomly generate values from normal probability distributions.

Operational Gaming The use of simulation in competitive situations such as military games and business or management games.

OptQuest A procedure in Crystal Ball that is used to automatically identify the best combination of values for decision variables that optimizes a desired output measure in the simulation model.

RAND An Excel function that generates a random number between 0 and 1 each time it is computed.

RANDBETWEEN An Excel function that can be used to randomly generate values from discrete uniform probability distributions.

Random Number A number (typically between zero and one in most computer programs) whose value is selected completely at random.

Replication A single run of a simulation model. Also known as a *run* or *trial*.

Simulation A technique that involves building a mathematical model to represent a real-world situation. The model is then experimented with to estimate the effects of various actions and decisions.

Systems Simulation A simulation model that deals with the dynamics of large organizational or governmental systems.

Solved Problems

Solved Problem 10-1

Higgins Plumbing and Heating maintains a supply of eight water heaters in any given week. Owner Jerry Higgins likes the idea of having this large supply on hand to meet customer demand but also recognizes that it is expensive to do so. He examines water heater sales over the past 50 weeks and notes the following data:

WATER HEATER SALES PER WEEK	NUMBER OF WEEKS THIS NUMBER WAS SOLD
4	6
5	5
6	9
7	12
8	8
9	7
10	3

a. Set up a model to simulate Higgins' weekly sales over a 2-year (104-week) period and compute the following measures (based on a single replication):

- Average weekly sales
- Number of weeks with stockouts over a two-year period

Replicate your model 200 times, using Data Table, to determine the (1) average weekly sales and (2) probability that Higgins will have more than 20 weeks with stockouts over a 2-year period.

b. Use the probability distribution for sales to determine the expected value of sales. Explain any differences between this value and the average value computed using Data Table in part (a).

File: 10-8.xls

Solution

The Excel layout to answer all the questions in this problem is presented in Screenshot 10-8. The spreadsheet is organized as follows:

- Column A shows the week number.
- We use a LOOKUP function to simulate the weekly sales in column B. The parameters (random number intervals, sales, and probabilities) for the LOOKUP function are shown in cells E4:H10.
- In column C, we use an IF function to determine the occurrence of a stockout (0 = no stockout, 1 = stockout). For example, the formula in cell C4 is =IF(B4>$H$12,1,0).

a. The average sales over the 2-year period is the average of the sales values in cells B4:B107. This value, shown in cell H16 in Screenshot 10-8, is 7.14 units per week. Next, we can add the 104 stockout indicators in cells C4:C107 to determine the number of

SCREENSHOT 10-8 Excel Layout and Results for Higgins Plumbing and Heating

Higgins Plumbing and Heating

Row	Week	Sales	Stockout? (1 = Yes)
4	1	8	0
5	2	8	0
6	3	4	0
7	4	9	1
8	5	6	0
9	6	7	0
10	7	8	0
11	8	7	0
12	9	7	0
13	10	7	0
14	11	9	1
15	12	9	1
16	13	8	0
17	14	9	1
18	15	8	0
19	16	8	0
20	17	9	1
21	18	9	1
22	19	7	0
23	20	9	1
24	21	8	0
25	22	7	0
106	103	7	0
107	104	6	0

Sales Distribution

Sales	Prob-ability	RN intvl lower limit	RN intvl upper limit
4	0.12	0.00	0.12
5	0.10	0.12	0.22
6	0.18	0.22	0.40
7	0.24	0.40	0.64
8	0.16	0.64	0.80
9	0.14	0.80	0.94
10	0.06	0.94	1.00

Supply each week = 8

(a)

Based on 1 replication:

Average sales = 7.14

No. of stockout weeks = 24

Based on 200 replications:

Average sales = 6.90

P(>20 stockout weeks) = 54.5%

(b)

Expected sales = 6.88

Data Table

Run	Avg sales	Stockout weeks
1	7.14	24
2	6.81	21
3	7.14	23
4	6.94	22
5	6.75	21
6	6.88	23
7	6.83	21
8	7.03	23
9	6.84	17
10	6.76	23
11	6.76	18
12	6.76	21
13	6.95	23
14	6.80	18
15	6.77	21
16	7.12	25
17	6.93	20
18	6.77	22
19	7.01	20
20	6.65	19
21	6.95	27
22	6.88	20
103	6.99	22
104	6.92	26
105	7.08	21
199	6.84	19
200	6.94	23

Parameters for LOOKUP function used to simulate sales

=H16

=H17

Hidden rows

COUNTIF function is used to count number of weeks with >20 stockouts.

Data Table used to replicate both output measures 200 times each.

stockouts over the 2-year period. This value, shown in cell H17, is 24 stockout weeks. (Remember that these values will change each time you recalculate the model.)

We now set up Data Table to run 200 replications of the values in cells H16 and H17. The table is shown in columns J to L in Screenshot 10-8. From the 200 replicated values in cells K4:K203, we compute the average sales to be 6.90 units per week (shown in cell H20). We then use Excel's COUNTIF function on the 200 replicated values in cells L4:L203 to compute the probability that Higgins will have more than 20 weeks with stockouts over a 2-year period. The formula used is =COUNTIF(L4:L203,">20")/200. The value, shown in cell H21, indicates there is a 54.5% chance that this event will occur.

b. Using expected values, we find the following:

$$\text{Expected heater sales} = 0.12 \times 4 + 0.10 \times 5 + 0.18 \times 6 + 0.24 \times 7 + 0.16 \times 8 + 0.14 \times 9 + 0.06 \times 10$$

$$= 6.88 \text{ heaters}$$

We can compute this value by using the following formula:

=SUMPRODUCT(E4:E10,F4:F10)

This value is shown in cell H24 in Screenshot 10-8. The simulated average (6.90 in Screenshot 10-8) is based on just 200 replications of the model. Hence, although this value is close to the expected value of 6.88, the two values need not necessarily be the same. With a longer simulation, the two values will become even closer.

Solved Problem 10-2

Norris Medical Clinic is staffed by a single physician who, on average, requires 15 minutes to treat a patient. The distribution of this service time follows a truncated normal distribution with a standard deviation of 4 minutes and a minimum value of 5 minutes. Patients arrive at an average rate of 2.5 customers per hour, according to the exponential distribution. Simulate 100 patient arrivals and replicate the model 200 times, using Data Table, to answer the following questions:

a. What percentage of time is the queue empty?
b. How many patients, on average, are in the queue?
c. What is the average wait time per patient in the queue?

Solution

File: 10-9.xls

This is an example of a discrete-event simulation model. The model simulates a queuing system in which arrival times follow an exponential distribution and service times follow a normal distribution. Each replication of the model corresponds to the arrival and service of 100 patients at the clinic. The Excel layout for this problem is presented in Screenshot 10-9. We

SCREENSHOT 10-9 Excel Layout and Results for Norris Medical Clinic

Simulated using LN function

Simulated using NORMINV function. Set to minimum of 5 minutes.

Norris Medical Clinic

Patient #	Time between arrivals	Arrival time	Start service	Service time	End service	Wait time	Queue length
0	0.0	0	0	0.0	0	0	0
1	4.0	4.0	4.0	18.0	22.0	0.0	0
2	49.6	53.5	53.5	6.2	59.7	0.0	0
3	5.1	58.7	59.7	20.7	80.5	1.1	1
4	8.0	66.7	80.5	13.8	94.3	13.8	1
5	6.9	73.6	94.3	21.0	115.3	20.7	2
6	5.0	78.6	115.3	17.1	132.4	36.7	3
7	41.7	120.3	132.4	14.6	146.9	12.1	1
8	8.5	128.8	146.9	15.8	162.8	18.2	2
9	28.7	157.4	162.8	16.4	179.2	5.4	1
10	12.6	170.0	179.2	16.4	195.6	9.2	1
11	3.5	173.5	195.6	17.9	213.5	22.1	2
12	90.5	264.0	264.0	17.8	281.8	0.0	0
13	36.2	300.2	300.2	10.4	310.7	0.0	0
14	2.0	302.2	310.7	16.8	327.5	8.5	1
15	1.9	304.1	327.5	18.3	345.8	23.4	2
16	20.9	325.0	345.8	13.5	359.3	20.8	2
17	1.9	326.9	359.3	13.9	373.3	32.4	3
18	19.2	346.1	373.3	18.7	392.0	27.1	2
19	15.5	361.6	392.0	12.0	404.0	30.3	2
20	19.7	381.3	404.0	12.2	416.2	22.7	2
99	24.6	1965.7	2054.4	17.1	2,071.4	88.6	6
100	1.3	1967.0	2071.4	14.1	2,085.6	104.4	7

Hidden rows

= Start time + Service time

Arrival Distribution	
Exponential	
Average arrival rate (per hour)	2.5

Service Time Distribution	
Normal	
Mean service time (minutes)	15
Std dev of service time (minutes)	4
Minimum service time (minutes)	5

Based on 1 replication:	
Percent of time the queue is empty =	21.0%
Average number of patients in the queue =	1.90
Average wait time per patient in the queue =	23.71

Based on 200 replications:	
Percent of time the queue is empty =	38.7%
Average number of patients in the queue =	1.13
Average wait time per patient in the queue =	12.66

Summary results from Data Table

Data Table

=K15 =K16 =K17

Run	% empty queue	Avg # patients	Avg wait time
1	0.21	1.90	23.71
2	0.22	2.32	30.05
3	0.46	0.66	5.50
4	0.51	0.87	9.72
5	0.41	1.17	13.39
6	0.45	0.72	6.21
7	0.53	0.65	6.71
8	0.37	0.90	9.55
9	0.51	0.70	6.60
10	0.29	1.48	17.16
11	0.34	1.01	11.13
12	0.54	0.53	4.36
13	0.43	0.95	10.83
14	0.42	1.05	12.79
15	0.30	1.71	20.56
16	0.40	0.90	9.31
17	0.38	1.03	11.20
18	0.41	0.86	8.82
19	0.38	1.13	12.94
20	0.37	0.88	8.15
21	0.41	1.03	11.35
100	0.40	1.30	15.94
101	0.46	0.77	7.55
102	0.51	0.85	10.72
103	0.37	1.01	10.12
199	0.23	2.62	35.11
200	0.30	1.49	16.96

Data Table used to replicate all three output measures 200 times each.

have included patient number 0, with zero values for all columns, to *initialize* the simulation clock that keeps track of the passage of time. Rows 5 through 104 in the spreadsheet are organized as follows:

- Column A shows the patient number (1 through 100).
- Column B shows the time between arrivals of successive patients, simulated from an exponential distribution by using the LN function. From Table 10.4 on page 418, the Excel formula is $=-(1/\mu)$*LN(RAND()). Note that the average arrival rate, μ, in this case is 2.5 patients per hour. However, because all other times in this problem are counted in minutes, we convert the interarrival time between successive patients to minutes also. The formula in cells B5:B104 is therefore

  =−60*(1/$K$6)*(LN(RAND()))

- In column C, we calculate the arrival time of the current patient as the sum of the arrival time of the previous patient and the time between arrivals (column B). For example, the formula in cell C5 is

  =C4+B5

- The time this patient actually starts service is calculated in column D as the maximum of the arrival time and the time the previous patient finishes service. For example, the formula in cell D5 is

  =MAX(C5,F4)

- Column E shows the service time for this patient, simulated using a NORMINV function. The parameters of this NORMINV function are shown in cells K10:K11. We use a MAX function to ensure that the minimum service time per patient is 5 minutes. The formula in cells E5:E104 is

  =MAX($K$12,NORMINV(RAND(),$K$10,$K$11))

- The time at which this patient ends service is shown in column F as the sum of the start time (shown in column D) and the service time (shown in column E).
- In column G, we calculate the wait time of this patient as the difference between the patient's start time (shown in column D) and arrival time (shown in column C).
- Finally, in column H, we calculate the queue length, using Excel's MATCH function. For example, the formula in cell H5 is

  =A5−MATCH(C5,$D$5:D5,1)

Using the 100 wait time and queue length values in cells G5:H104, we determine the following three performance measures for the queuing system each day:

a. Percentage of time the queue is empty (cell K15) =COUNTIF(H5:H104,"=0")/100 = 21%

b. Average number of patients in the queue (cell K16) =AVERAGE(H5:H104) = 1.90

c. Average wait time per patient in the queue (cell K17) =AVERAGE(G5:G104) = 23.71 minutes

The values in cells K15:K17 represent results from just one replication of the model. To determine more precise values for these measures, we now replicate all three measures 200 times each. The Data Table procedure to do so is shown in columns M through P in Screenshot 10-9. Based on the 200 replicated values in this Data Table procedure, the queue at the clinic is empty 36.7% of the time, there are 1.13 patients on average in the queue at any time, and each patient in the queue waits for an average of 12.66 minutes.

Solved Problem 10-3

Heartbreak Hotel routinely experiences no-shows (people who make reservations for a room and don't show up) during the peak season when the hotel is always full. No-shows follow the distribution shown in the following table:

NO-SHOWS	PROBABILITY
0	0.10
1	0.13
2	0.31
3	0.16
4	0.21
5	0.09

To reduce the number of vacant rooms, the hotel overbooks three rooms; that is, the hotel accepts three more reservations than the number of rooms available. On a day when the hotel experiences fewer than three no-shows, there are not enough rooms for those who have reservations. The hotel's policy is to send these guests to a competing hotel down the street, at Heartbreak's expense of $125. If the number of no-shows is more than three, the hotel has vacant rooms, resulting in an opportunity cost of $50 per room.

a. Simulate 1 month (30 days) of operation to calculate the hotel's total monthly cost due to overbooking and opportunity loss. Replicate this cost 200 times to compute the average monthly cost.

b. Heartbreak Hotel would like to determine the most desirable number of rooms to overbook. Of these six choices—0, 1, 2, 3, 4, or 5 rooms—what is your recommendation? Why?

Solution

File: 10-10.xls, sheet: 10-10A

This is an example of a revenue management problem where the number of no-shows follows a discrete general distribution. Each replication of the simulation model corresponds to 30 days of operations at the hotel. The Excel layout for this model is presented in Screenshot 10-10A. The spreadsheet is organized as follows:

- Column A shows the day number (1 through 30).
- In column B, we use a LOOKUP function to simulate the number of no-shows. The parameters for this LOOKUP function are shown in cells I4:L9.
- In column C, we compute the number of short rooms (i.e., rooms that are unavailable for guests) by comparing the number of no-shows with the number of rooms we decide to overbook (shown in cell K11). For example, the formula in cell C4 is

=MAX($K$11−B4,0)

- Short cost in column D = $K$13 × column C.
- In column E, we compute the number of vacant rooms by once again comparing the number of no-shows with the number of rooms we decide to overbook (shown in cell K11). For example, the formula in cell E4 is

=MAX(B4−$K11,0)

- Vacant cost in column F = $K$14 × column E.
- Total cost in column G = column D + column E.

SCREENSHOT 10-10A Excel Layout and Results for Heartbreak Hotel

Parameters for LOOKUP function in column B

Heartbreak Hotel

Row	Day	No-shows	Short rooms	Short cost	Vacant rooms	Vacant cost	Total cost
4	1	5	0	$0.00	2	$100.00	$100.00
5	2	4	0	$0.00	1	$50.00	$50.00
6	3	4	0	$0.00	1	$50.00	$50.00
7	4	2	1	$125.00	0	$0.00	$125.00
8	5	1	2	$250.00	0	$0.00	$250.00
9	6	4	0	$0.00	1	$50.00	$50.00
10	7	1	2	$250.00	0	$0.00	$250.00
11	8	3	0	$0.00	0	$0.00	$0.00
12	9	2	1	$125.00	0	$0.00	$125.00
13	10	2	1	$125.00	0	$0.00	$125.00
14	11	5	0	$0.00	2	$100.00	$100.00
15	12	1	2	$250.00	0	$0.00	$250.00
16	13	2	1	$125.00	0	$0.00	$125.00
17	14	5	0	$0.00	2	$100.00	$100.00
18	15	2	1	$125.00	0	$0.00	$125.00
19	16	3	0	$0.00	0	$0.00	$0.00
20	17	0	3	$375.00	0	$0.00	$375.00
21	18	2	1	$125.00	0	$0.00	$125.00
22	19	4	0	$0.00	1	$50.00	$50.00
23	20	2	1	$125.00	0	$0.00	$125.00
24	21	1	2	$250.00	0	$0.00	$250.00
25	22	2	1	$125.00	0	$0.00	$125.00
26	23	4	0	$0.00	1	$50.00	$50.00
27	24	0	3	$375.00	0	$0.00	$375.00
28	25	5	0	$0.00	2	$100.00	$100.00
29	26	3	0	$0.00	0	$0.00	$0.00
30	27	1	2	$250.00	0	$0.00	$250.00
31	28	0	3	$375.00	0	$0.00	$375.00
32	29	4	0	$0.00	1	$50.00	$50.00
33	30	2	1	$125.00	0	$0.00	$125.00

Simulated using LOOKUP function

Total cost is sum of short cost and vacant cost.

No-Shows Distribution

No-shows	Probability	RN intvl lower limit	RN intvl upper limit
0	0.10	0.00	0.10
1	0.13	0.10	0.23
2	0.31	0.23	0.54
3	0.16	0.54	0.70
4	0.21	0.70	0.91
5	0.09	0.91	1.00

Rooms overbooked	3
Cost per room short	$125
Cost per room vacant	$50
Based on 1 replication:	
Average daily cost =	$140.00
Based on 200 replications:	
Average daily cost =	$130.35

We want to try different values here.

Data Table

Run	Cost
1	$140.00
2	$122.50
3	$94.17
4	$140.00
5	$101.67
6	$103.33
7	$79.17
8	$135.83
9	$104.17
10	$125.00
11	$108.33
12	$126.67
13	$142.50
14	$137.50
15	$115.00
16	$134.17
17	$94.17
18	$100.00
19	$133.33
20	$134.17
21	$143.33
22	$120.83
23	$152.50
24	$131.67
25	$121.67
26	$125.83
27	$140.83
28	$145.00
29	$109.17
30	$129.17
31	$148.33
199	$141.67
200	$154.17

=K17

a. The average total cost of $140 per day shown in cell K17 is based on only 1 replication. Hence, to get a more precise estimate of this average, we replicate this measure by using Data Table, as shown in column N and O in Screenshot 10-10A. Based on 200 replications, the average total cost at Heartbreak Hotel appears to be $130.35 per day (shown in cell K20).

b. To determine the number of rooms that Heartbreak Hotel should overbook each day, we set up Scenario Manager to automatically try the six choices—0, 1, 2, 3, 4, and 5. For each scenario, cell K11 is the changing cell and cell K20 is the result cell. The results of the Scenario Manager procedure, shown in Screenshot 10-10B, indicate that Heartbreak Hotel should overbook two rooms each day. The total cost of $83.55 at this level is the lowest among all scenarios.

SCREENSHOT 10-10B Scenario Manager Results for Heartbreak Hotel

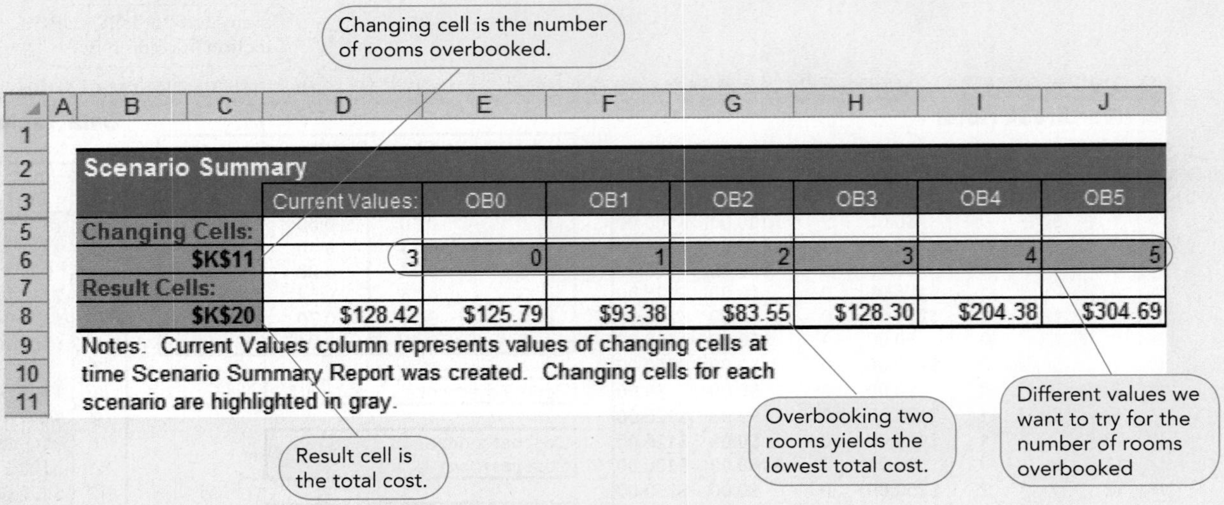

Changing cell is the number of rooms overbooked.

Scenario Summary							
	Current Values:	OB0	OB1	OB2	OB3	OB4	OB5
Changing Cells:							
$K$11	3	0	1	2	3	4	5
Result Cells:							
$K$20	$128.42	$125.79	$93.38	$83.55	$128.30	$204.38	$304.69

Notes: Current Values column represents values of changing cells at time Scenario Summary Report was created. Changing cells for each scenario are highlighted in gray.

Result cell is the total cost.

Overbooking two rooms yields the lowest total cost.

Different values we want to try for the number of rooms overbooked

Solved Problem 10-4

General Foundry, Inc., a metalworks plant in Milwaukee, has long been trying to avoid the expense of installing air pollution control equipment. The local environmental protection agency (EPA) has recently given the foundry 16 weeks to install a complex air filter system on its main smokestack. General Foundry has been warned that it may be forced to close unless the device is installed in the allotted period. Lester Harky, the managing partner, wants to make sure that installation of the filtering system progresses smoothly and on time. General Foundry has identified the eight activities that need to be performed in order for the project to be completed. For each activity, the following table shows the immediate predecessors and three times estimates—optimistic, most likely, and pessimistic:

ACTIVITY	DESCRIPTION	IMMEDIATE PREDECESSORS	OPTIMISTIC TIME (a)	MOST LIKELY TIME (m)	PESSIMISTIC TIME (b)
A	Build internal components	—	1	2	3
B	Modify roof and floor	—	2	3	4
C	Construct collection stack	A	1	2	3
D	Pour concrete and install frame	A, B	2	4	6
E	Build high-temperature burner	C	1	4	7
F	Install pollution control system	C	1	2	9
G	Install air pollution device	D, E	3	4	11
H	Inspect and test	F, G	1	2	3

Lester wants to find the probability that the project will meet the EPA's 16-week deadline. Round off all activity times to two decimal places.[14]

[14] Current versions of Crystal Ball include a function called CB.BetaPert that can be used to simulate activity times using a beta distribution and the three time estimates. Prior versions did not include this function and the easy option there is to use a triangular distribution, which also uses three time estimates and is commonly used to model project activity times.

FIGURE 10.4 Project Network for General Foundry

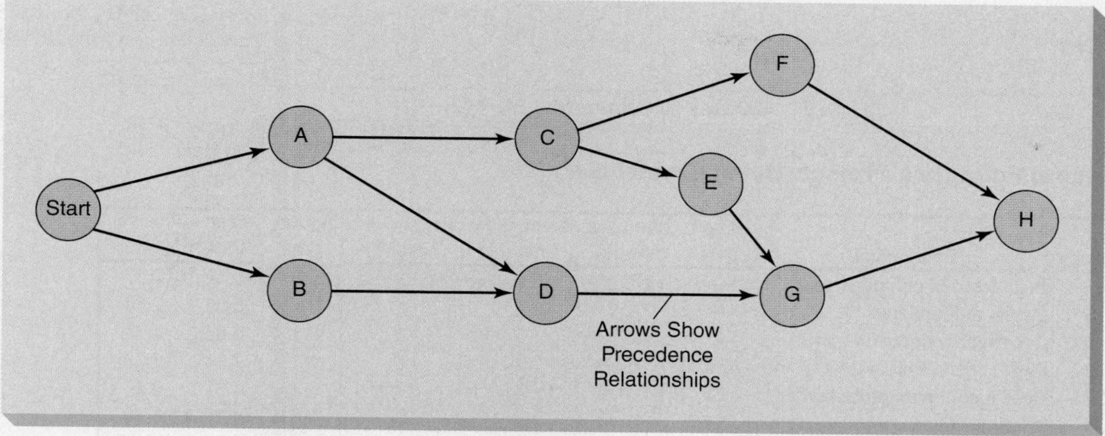

Solution

Simulation is a popular technique for analyzing uncertainty in projects.

This is an example of analyzing uncertainty in a project management problem. Recall that in Chapter 7, we studied this issue analytically, using probability distributions. In that analysis, we first computed the expected value and variance of the project completion time, assuming that the activity time of each activity followed a beta distribution. We then used a normal distribution to compute various probabilities for the project completion time (see section 7.4 for details). As noted in that chapter, another popular way to analyze uncertainty in projects is by using simulation. Let us simulate General Foundry's project here.

Before simulating a project, it is convenient to draw the project network.

It is convenient to first express the activities in the project as a project network. We show this in Figure 10.4, where the nodes represent the activities and the arcs represent the precedence relationships between activities.

The Excel layout for this simulation model is presented in Screenshot 10-11. The spreadsheet is organized as follows:

File: 10-11.xls

- Columns A through F show the name, description, immediate predecessors, and three time estimates for each activity (activities A through H).
- In column G, we simulate the actual duration of each activity by using the CB.BetaPert function in Crystal Ball. We then round this value to two decimal places, using the ROUND function. For example, the formula in cell G4 is

  =ROUND(CB.BetaPert(D4,E4,F4),2)

- In column H, we calculate the actual start time for each activity. In computing this time, we need to ensure that all predecessors for an activity have been completed before that activity can begin. For example, both activities A and B have to finish before activity D can start. Hence, the start time for activity D is set equal to the maximum of the finish times of activities A and B. That is, the formula in cell H7 is

  =MAX(I4,I5)

- In column I, we compute the finish time of each activity as the sum of the start time of that activity (column H) and the actual duration of that activity (column G).

In General Foundry's project, the project completion time is the completion time of activity H, shown in cell I11. Based on the single replication shown in Screenshot 10-11, it appears that the project will finish in only 15.26 weeks. However, in order to get a more precise value of this output measure, we use Crystal Ball to replicate the model 3,000 times. Cell I11 is defined as the forecast cell.

SCREENSHOT 10-11 Excel Layout and Results Using Crystal Ball for General Foundry

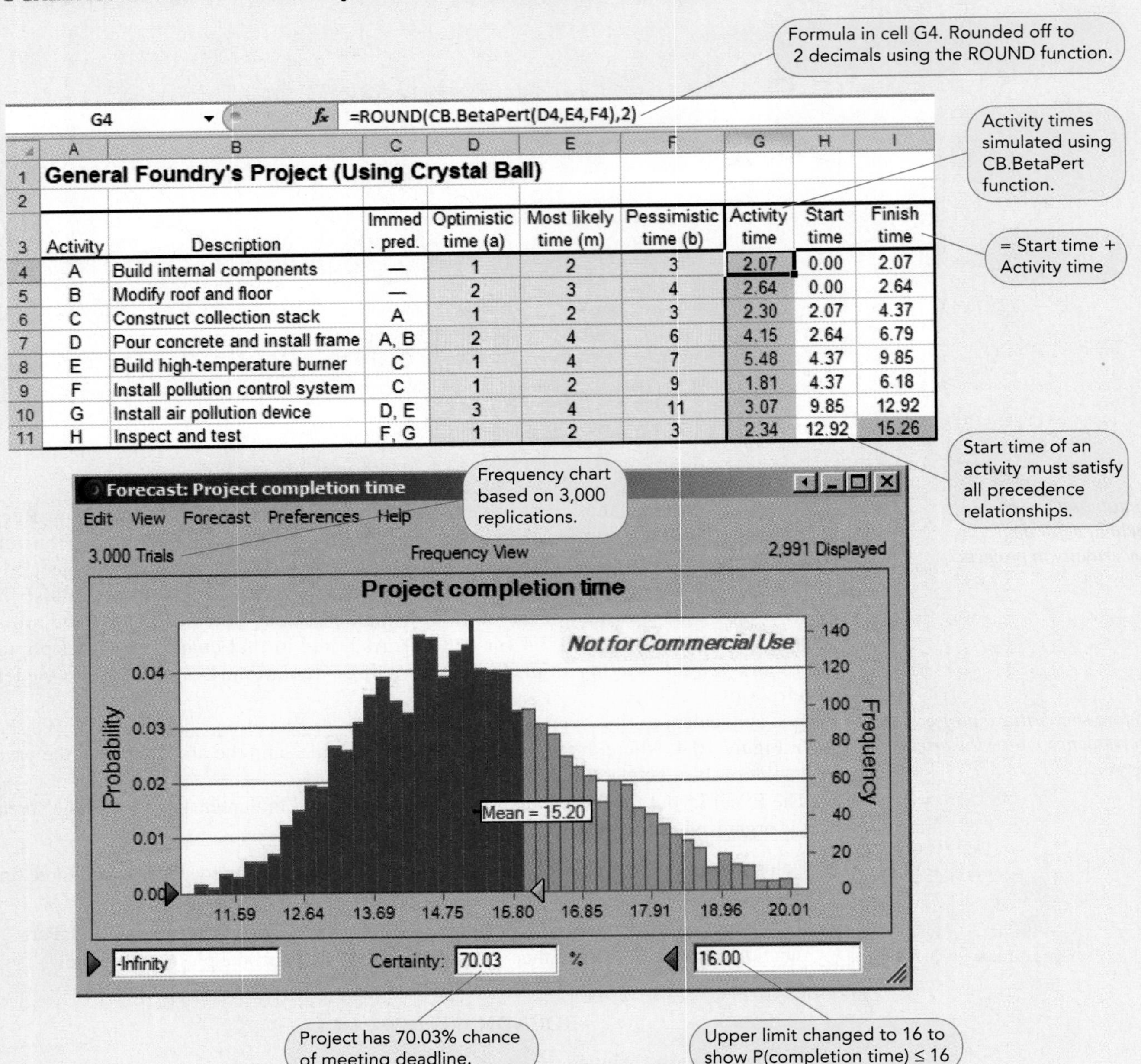

Formula in cell G4. Rounded off to 2 decimals using the ROUND function.
G4
=ROUND(CB.BetaPert(D4,E4,F4),2)
Activity times simulated using CB.BetaPert function.
General Foundry's Project (Using Crystal Ball)
Activity
Description
Immed. pred.
Optimistic time (a)
Most likely time (m)
Pessimistic time (b)
Activity time
Start time
Finish time
= Start time + Activity time
A Build internal components — 1 2 3 2.07 0.00 2.07
B Modify roof and floor — 2 3 4 2.64 0.00 2.64
C Construct collection stack A 1 2 3 2.30 2.07 4.37
D Pour concrete and install frame A, B 2 4 6 4.15 2.64 6.79
E Build high-temperature burner C 1 4 7 5.48 4.37 9.85
F Install pollution control system C 1 2 9 1.81 4.37 6.18
G Install air pollution device D, E 3 4 11 3.07 9.85 12.92
H Inspect and test F, G 1 2 3 2.34 12.92 15.26
Start time of an activity must satisfy all precedence relationships.
Forecast: Project completion time
Edit View Forecast Preferences Help
Frequency chart based on 3,000 replications.
3,000 Trials
Frequency View
2,991 Displayed
Project completion time
Not for Commercial Use
Probability
Frequency
Mean = 15.20
11.59 12.64 13.69 14.75 15.80 16.85 17.91 18.96 20.01
-Infinity
Certainty: 70.03 %
16.00
Project has 70.03% chance of meeting deadline.
Upper limit changed to 16 to show P(completion time) ≤ 16

The frequency chart obtained from Crystal Ball is also shown in Screenshot 10-11. Based on this chart, it appears that the average completion time of the project is 15.20 weeks. (To show the mean, click on the graph to get an options window where you can enable this feature.) More importantly for General Foundry, the chart indicates that there is a 70.03% chance that the project will finish in less than 16 weeks. Note that this probability is consistent with the analytical result we obtained in section 7.4 (see page 285) using normal probability analysis.

Discussion Questions and Problems

Discussion Questions

10-1 What are the advantages and limitations of simulation models?

10-2 Why might a manager be forced to use simulation instead of an analytical model in dealing with a problem of
  (a) inventory ordering policy?
  (b) ships docking in a port to unload?
  (c) bank teller service windows?
  (d) the U.S. economy?

10-3 What types of management problems can be solved more easily by using decision modeling techniques other than simulation?

10-4 What are the major steps in the simulation process?

10-5 What is Monte Carlo simulation? What principles underlie its use, and what steps are followed in applying it?

10-6 Why is a computer necessary in conducting a real-world simulation?

10-7 What is operational gaming? What is systems simulation? Give examples of how each may be applied.

10-8 Do you think the application of simulation will increase strongly in the next 10 years? Why or why not?

10-9 Would the average output value in a simulation problem change appreciably if a longer period were simulated? Why or why not?

10-10 How might drawing a flow diagram help in developing a simulation model?

10-11 List the advantages of using an Excel add-in program rather than using Excel's built-in functions to develop a simulation model.

10-12 What does Scenario Manager allow you to accomplish in an Excel-based simulation model?

10-13 Do you think we can use Excel's Solver to solve simulation models? Why or why not?

Problems

Notes:

- *Simulation models for all the following problems can be set up by using Excel.*
- *Wherever necessary, replications can be done either using Data Table or using Crystal Ball.*
- *In all problems, we have specified the number of replications to use simply as **N**. Your instructor may specify the actual value of **N** that he or she wants you to use. If not, we recommend that you try to replicate each simulation model as many times as is convenient. If you are using Data Table, 200 to 300 replications should be appropriate to keep the computation time reasonable and the resulting Excel file relatively small (even though the average values may vary from simulation to simulation). However, if you are using Crystal Ball, you should try 3,000 or more replications.*
- *Wherever a decision is involved, you can use Scenario Manager in Excel and Decision Table or OptQuest if you are using Crystal Ball.*

10-14 Weekly demand for tennis balls at The Racquet Club is normally distributed, with a mean of 35 cases and a standard deviation of 5 cases. The club gets a profit of $50 per case.
  (a) Simulate 52 weeks of demand and calculate the average weekly profit. Make all demand values integers in your model.
  (b) What is the probability that weekly profit will be $2,000 or more?

10-15 Edward Owen is responsible for the maintenance, rental, and day-to-day operation of several large apartment complexes on the upper-east side of New York City. Owen is especially concerned about the cost projections for replacing air conditioner (A/C) compressors. He would like to simulate the number of A/C failures each month. Using data from similar apartment buildings he manages in a New York City suburb, Clark establishes the probability of failures during a month as follows:

NUMBER OF A/C FAILURES	PROBABILITY
0	0.10
1	0.17
2	0.21
3	0.28
4	0.16
5	0.07
6	0.01

  (a) Simulate Owen's monthly A/C failures for a period of three years. Compute the average number of failures per month.
  (b) Explain any difference between the simulated average failures and the expected value of failures computed by using the probability distribution.

10-16 Jay's Appliances sells micro-fridges according to the monthly demand distribution shown in the table at the top of the next page. Simulate 6 years of demand and compare theoretical and simulated results for the following measures:
  (a) Average demand.
  (b) Probability that demand will be less than or equal to 30 micro-fridges.

Table for Problem 10-16

DEMAND	PROBABILITY
10	0.02
15	0.07
20	0.11
25	0.12
30	0.21
35	0.18
40	0.21
45	0.06
50	0.02

10-17 Shawn Bishop, a neuroscience PhD student at Clarksville University, has been having problems balancing his checkbook. His monthly income is derived from a graduate research assistantship; however, he also makes extra money in most months by tutoring undergraduates in their introductory neurobiology course. His chances of various income levels are shown here (assume that this income is received at the beginning of each month):

MONTHLY INCOME	PROBABILITY
$ 850	0.35
$ 900	0.25
$ 950	0.25
$1,000	0.15

Bishop has expenditures that vary from month to month, and he estimates that they will follow this distribution:

MONTHLY EXPENSES	PROBABILITY
$ 800	0.05
$ 900	0.20
$1,000	0.40
$1,100	0.35

Bishop begins his final year with $1,500 in his checking account. Simulate the cash flow for 12 months and replicate your model *N* times to identify Bishop's (a) ending balance at the end of the year and (b) probability that he will have a negative balance in any month.

10-18 Chelsea Truman sells celebrity magazines on Sunday morning in an area surrounded by three busy shopping centers. Demand for the magazines is distributed as shown in the following table:

DEMAND	PROBABILITY
50	0.05
75	0.10
100	0.25
125	0.30
150	0.20
175	0.10

Chelsea has decided to order 100 magazines from her supplier. Chelsea pays $2 for each magazine she orders and sells each magazine for $3. Unsold magazines can be returned to the supplier for $0.75.

(a) Simulate 1 year (52 Sundays) of operation to calculate Chelsea's total yearly profit. Replicate this calculation *N* times. What is the average yearly profit?

(b) Chelsea would like to investigate the profitability of ordering 50, 100, 150, and 175 magazines at the start of each Sunday. Which order quantity would you recommend? Why?

10-19 The Paris Bakery has decided to bake 30 batches of its famous beignets at the beginning of the day. The store has determined that daily demand will follow the distribution shown in the following table:

DAILY DEMAND	PROBABILITY
15	0.08
20	0.12
25	0.25
30	0.20
35	0.20
40	0.15

Each batch costs the Paris Bakery $50 and can be sold for $100. The Paris Bakery can sell any unsold batches for $25 the next day.

(a) Simulate 1 month (25 days) of operation to calculate the bakery's total monthly profit. Replicate this calculation *N* times to compute the average total monthly profit.

(b) The Paris Bakery would like to investigate the profitability of baking 25, 30, 35, or 40 batches at the start of the day. Which quantity would you recommend? Why?

10-20 Lionel's Life Jacket Rentals leases life jackets each day from a supplier and rents them to customers who use them when they raft down the Delaware River. Each day, Lionel leases 30 life jackets from his supplier, at a cost of $4 per life jacket. He rents them to his customers for $15 per day. Rental demand follows the normal distribution, with a mean of 30 life jackets and a standard deviation of 6 life jackets. (In your model use integers for all demands.)

(a) Simulate this leasing policy for a month (30 days) of operation to calculate the total monthly profit. Replicate this calculation N times. What is the average monthly profit?

(b) Lionel would like to evaluate the average monthly profit if he leases 25, 30, 35, and 40 life jackets. What is your recommendation? Why?

10-21 Kirkpatrick Aircrafts operates a large number of computerized plotting machines. For the most part, the plotting devices are used to create line drawings of complex wing airfoils and fuselage part dimensions. The engineers operating the automated plotters are called loft lines engineers.

The computerized plotters consist of a minicomputer system connected to a 4- by 5-foot flat table with a series of ink pens suspended above it. When a sheet of clear plastic or paper is properly placed on the table, the computer directs a series of horizontal and vertical pen movements until the desired figure is drawn.

The plotting machines are highly reliable, with the exception of the four sophisticated ink pens that are built in. The pens constantly clog and jam in a raised or lowered position. When this occurs, the plotter is unusable.

Currently, Kirkpatrick Aircrafts replaces each pen as it fails. The service manager has, however, proposed replacing all four pens every time one fails. This should cut down the frequency of plotter failures. At present, it takes one hour to replace one pen. All four pens could be replaced in two hours. The total cost of a plotter being unusable is \$500 per hour. Each pen costs \$80. The following breakdown data are thought to be valid:

ONE PEN REPLACED	
HOURS BETWEEN FAILURES	PROBABILITY
10	0.05
20	0.15
30	0.15
40	0.20
50	0.20
60	0.15

FOUR PENS REPLACED	
HOURS BETWEEN FAILURES	PROBABILITY
70	0.10
100	0.15
110	0.25
120	0.35
130	0.20
140	0.05

(a) For each option (replacing one pen at a time and replacing all four pens at a time), simulate the average total time a plotter would operate before it would have 20 failures. Then compute the total cost per hour for each option to determine which option Kirkpatrick Aircrafts should use. Use N replications.

(b) Compute the total cost per hour analytically for each option. How do these results compare to the simulation results?

10-22 A high school guidance counselor has scheduled one-on-one meetings today with 10 seniors to discuss their college plans. Each meeting is scheduled for 20 minutes, with the first meeting set to start at 9:00 A.M. Due to their hectic class and extra-curricular schedules, not every student arrives on time, and not every meeting lasts exactly 20 minutes. The counselor knows the following from past experience: A student will be 10 minutes early 5% of the time, 5 minutes early 20% of the time, exactly on time 35% of the time, 5 minutes late 30% of the time, and 10 minutes late 10% of the time. The counselor further estimates that there is a 15% chance that a meeting will take only 15 minutes, 50% chance it will take exactly the planned time, 25% chance it will take 25 minutes, and 10% chance it will take 30 minutes.

Students are seen in the order in which they have been scheduled, regardless of when they arrive. However, a student arriving early can see the counselor as soon as the previous meeting ends. Use N replications to determine when the counselor will complete the last meeting.

10-23 Dr. Carter Logue practices dentistry in Santa Fe, New Mexico. Logue tries hard to schedule appointments so that patients do not have to wait beyond their appointment time. His October 20 schedule is shown in the following table:

PATIENT	SCHEDULED APPOINTMENT	TIME NEEDED (MIN.)
Adams	9:30 A.M.	20
Brown	9:45 A.M.	15
Crawford	10:15 A.M.	15
Dannon	10:30 A.M.	10
Erving	10:45 A.M.	20
Fink	11:15 A.M.	15
Graham	11:30 A.M.	30
Hinkel	11:45 A.M.	15

Unfortunately, not every patient arrives exactly on schedule. Also, some examinations take longer than planned, and some take less time than planned. Logue's experience dictates the following: 20% of the patients will be 20 minutes early, 10% of the patients will be 10 minutes early, 40% of the patients will be on time, 25% of the patients will be 10 minutes late, and 5% of the patients will be 20 minutes late.

He further estimates that there is a 15% chance that an appointment will take 20% less time than planned, 50% chance it will take exactly the planned time, 25% chance it will take 20% more time than planned, and 10% chance it will take 40% more time than planned.

Dr. Logue has to leave at 12:15 P.M. on October 20 to catch a flight to a dental convention in Rio de Janerio. Assuming that he is ready to start his workday at 9:30 A.M. and that patients are treated in order of their scheduled exam (even if one late patient arrives after an early one), will he be able to make the flight? Use *N* replications.

10-24 Lee Appliances knows that weekly demand for high-end microwaves is normally distributed, with a mean of 25 units and a standard deviation of 7 units. (In your model use integers for all demands.) Lee replenishes its inventory by ordering 300 units from the distributor whenever its current inventory reaches 70 units. The lead time (in weeks) to receive an order from the distributor follows the distribution shown in the following table:

LEAD TIME	PROBABILITY
1	0.15
2	0.25
3	0.30
4	0.15
5	0.10
6	0.10

The cost to hold 1 unit in inventory for 1 week is \$20. The cost to place an order with the factory is \$300. Stockout costs are estimated at \$100 per unit. The initial inventory level is 140 units.

(a) Simulate 52 weeks of operation to calculate the total semiannual cost and the percentage of stockouts for the period. Replicate these calculations *N* times each to calculate the average values for these measures.

(b) Lee would like to evaluate the economics of ordering 250, 275, 300, 325, and 350 units, with a reorder point of 70 units. Based on the average total semiannual cost, which order quantity would you recommend?

(c) Lee would like to evaluate the economics of ordering 300 units, with reorder points of 60, 70, 80, 90, and 100 tires. Based on the average total semiannual cost, which reorder point would you recommend?

10-25 Mattress Heaven orders a certain brand of mattress from its supplier and sells the mattresses at its retail location. The store currently orders 400 mattresses whenever the inventory level drops to 200. The cost to hold 1 mattress in inventory for one day is \$0.75. The cost to place an order with the supplier is \$75, and stockout costs are \$150 per mattress. Beginning inventory is 150 mattresses. The daily demand probabilities are shown in the following table:

DAILY DEMAND	PROBABILITY
20	0.08
30	0.14
40	0.20
50	0.26
60	0.22
70	0.10

Lead time follows a discrete uniform distribution between 2 and 5 days (both inclusive). Simulate this inventory policy for a quarter (90 days) and calculate the total quarterly cost. Also calculate the percentage of stockouts for the quarter. Replicate these calculations *N* times each to calculate the average values for these measures.

10-26 Consider the Mattress Heaven problem described in Problem 10-25.

(a) Mattress Heaven would like to evaluate ordering 350, 400, 450, and 500 mattresses when the reorder point of 200 is reached. Based on the average total quarterly cost, which order quantity would you recommend?

(b) Mattress Heaven would like to evaluate reorder points of 150, 200, 250, and 300 mattresses, with an order quantity of 400 mattresses. Based on the average total quarterly cost, which reorder point would you recommend?

10-27 Music Mania sells MP3 players to its customers. Music Mania orders 300 MP3 players from its supplier when its inventory reaches 80 units. Daily demand for MP3 players is discrete, uniformly distributed between 30 and 60 (both inclusive). The lead time from the supplier also varies for each order and is discrete, uniformly distributed between 1 and 3 days (both inclusive). The cost to hold 1 unit in inventory for one day is \$0.50. The cost to place an order is \$100. Stockout cost per unit is estimated at \$20. Initial inventory is 300 units.

Simulate this inventory policy for a quarter (90 days) and calculate the total quarterly cost. Also calculate the percentage of stockouts for the quarter. Replicate these calculations *N* times each to calculate the average values for these measures.

10-28 Consider the Music Mania problem described in Problem 10-27.

(a) Music Mania would like to evaluate ordering 250, 300, 350, and 400 MP3 players when the reorder point of 80 is reached. Based on the average total quarterly cost, which order quantity would you recommend?

(b) Music Mania would like to evaluate reorder points of 60, 80, and 100 MP3 players, with an order quantity of 300 players. Based on the average total cost for the quarter, which reorder point would you recommend?

10-29 Troy's Tires sells a certain brand tire which has a daily demand that is normally distributed, with a mean of 15 tires and a standard deviation of 4 tires. (In your model use integers for all demands.) Troy's Tires replenishes its inventory by ordering 250 tires from the factory whenever its current inventory reaches 40 tires. The lead time (in days) to receive an order from the factory follows the distribution shown in the following table:

LEAD TIME	PROBABILITY
1	0.10
2	0.22
3	0.28
4	0.15
5	0.15
6	0.10

The cost to hold 1 tire in inventory for one day is \$0.20. The cost to place an order with the factory is \$100. Stockout costs are estimated at \$10 per tire. The initial inventory level is 100 tires.

(a) Simulate 6 months (180 days) of operation to calculate the total semiannual cost and the percentage of stockouts for the period. Replicate these calculations N times each to calculate the average values for these measures.

(b) Troy's Tires would like to evaluate the economics of ordering 150, 200, 250, 300, and 350 tires, with a reorder point of 40 tires. Based on the average total semiannual cost, which order quantity would you recommend?

(c) Troy's Tires would like to evaluate the economics of ordering 250 tires, with reorder points of 40, 50, 60, 70, and 80 tires. Based on the average total semiannual cost, which reorder point would you recommend?

10-30 Ashcroft Airlines flies a six-passenger commuter fight once a day to Gainesville, Florida. A nonrefundable one-way fare with a reservation costs \$129. The daily demand for this flight is given in the following table, along with the probability distribution of no-shows (where a no-show has a reservation but does not arrive at the gate and forfeits the fare):

DEMAND	PROBABILITY	NO-SHOWS	PROBABILITY
5	0.05	0	0.15
6	0.11	1	0.25
7	0.20	2	0.26
8	0.18	3	0.23
9	0.16	4	0.11
10	0.12		
11	0.10		
12	0.08		

Ashcroft currently overbooks three passengers per flight. If there are not enough seats for a passenger at the gate, Ashcroft Airlines refunds his or her fare and also provides a \$150 voucher good on any other trip. The fixed cost for each flight is \$450, regardless of the number of passengers.

(a) Set up a simulation model and calculate Ashcroft's profit per flight. Replicate the calculation N times each to calculate the average profit per flight.

(b) Ashcroft Airlines would like to investigate the profitability of overbooking 0, 1, 2, 3, 4, and 5 passengers. What is your recommendation? Why?

10-31 Winston-Salem's general hospital has an emergency room that is divided into six departments: (1) the initial exam station, to treat minor problems and make diagnoses; (2) an x-ray department; (3) an operating room; (4) a cast-fitting room; (5) an observation room for recovery and general observation before final diagnosis or release; and (6) an out-processing department, where clerks check out patients and arrange for payment or insurance forms. The probabilities that a patient will go from one department to another are presented in the following table. (See Table for Problem 10-31 on page 468.)

Simulate the trail followed by 200 emergency room patients. Process 1 patient at a time, from entry at the initial exam station until leaving through out-processing. Note that a patient can enter the same department more than once. Based on your simulation, what is the probability that a patient enters the x-ray department more than once?

10-32 Management of Charlottesville Bank is concerned about a loss of customers at its main office downtown. One solution that has been proposed is to add one or more drive-through teller windows to make it easier for customers in cars to obtain quick service without parking. Neha Patel, the bank president, thinks the bank should only risk the cost of installing one drive-through window. She is

Table for Problem 10-31

FROM	TO	PROBABILITY
Initial exam station	X-ray department	0.45
	Operating room	0.15
	Observation room	0.10
	Out-processing clerk	0.30
X-ray department	Operating room	0.10
	Cast-fitting room	0.25
	Observation room	0.35
	Out-processing clerk	0.30
Operating room	Cast-fitting room	0.25
	Observation room	0.70
	Out-processing clerk	0.05
Cast-fitting room	Observation room	0.55
	X-ray department	0.05
	Out-processing clerk	0.40
Observation room	Operating room	0.15
	X-ray department	0.15
	Out-processing clerk	0.70

informed by her staff that the cost (amortized over a 20-year period) of building a drive-through window is $36,000 per year. It also costs $48,000 per year in wages and benefits to staff each new drive-through window.

The director of management analysis, Robyn Lyon, believes that two factors encourage the immediate construction of two drive-through windows, however. According to a recent article in *Banking Research* magazine, customers who wait in long lines for drive-through service will cost banks an average of $3 per minute in loss of goodwill. Also, adding a second drive-through window will cost an additional $48,000 in staffing, but amortized construction costs can be cut to a total of $60,000 per year if the two drive-through windows are installed together instead of one at a time. To complete her analysis, Lyon collected arrival and service rates at a competing downtown bank's drive-through windows for one month. These data are shown in the following table:

TIME BETWEEN ARRIVALS (MIN.)	OCCURRENCES
1	200
2	250
3	300
4	150
5	100

SERVICE TIME (MIN.)	OCCURRENCES
1	100
2	150
3	350
4	150
5	150
6	100

(a) Simulate a 1-hour time period for a system with one drive-through window. Replicate the model N times.

(b) Simulate a 1-hour time period for a system with two drive-through windows. Replicate the model N times.

(c) Conduct a cost analysis of the two options. Assume that the bank is open 7 hours per day and 200 days per year.

10-33 Erik Marshall owns and operates one of the largest BMW auto dealerships in St. Louis. In the past 36 months, his weekly sales of Z3s have ranged from a low of 6 to a high of 12, as reflected in the following table:

Z3 SALES PER WEEK	FREQUENCY
6	3
7	4
8	6
9	12
10	9
11	1
12	1

Erik believes that sales will continue during the next 24 months at about the same rate and that delivery lead times will also continue to follow this pace (stated in probability form):

DELIVERY TIME (WEEKS)	PROBABILITY
1	0.44
2	0.33
3	0.16
4	0.07

Erik's current policy is to order 14 autos at a time (two full truckloads, with 7 autos on each truck) and to place a new order whenever the stock on hand reaches 12 autos. Beginning inventory is 14 autos. Erik establishes the following relevant costs: (i) The carrying cost per Z3 per week is $400, (ii) the cost of a lost sale averages $7,500, and (iii) the cost of placing an order is $1,000.

(a) Simulate Erik's inventory policy for the next two years. What is the total weekly cost of this policy? Also, what is the average number of stockouts per week? Use N replications of your model.

(b) Erik wishes to evaluate several different ordering quantities—12, 14, 16, 18, and 20. Based on the total weekly cost, what would you recommend? Why? Set $R = 12$ in each case.

10-34 Jesse's Plumbing Service's monthly demand follows a discrete uniform distribution between 40 and 55 jobs. The probability that a specific job will be for minor service (e.g., clogged sink) is 0.65, and the probability that it will be for a major service (e.g., flooded basement) is 0.35. Revenues for minor service follow a normal distribution, with a mean of \$100 and a standard deviation of \$15. For major projects, Jesse estimates that revenues will be \$600 with 30% chance, \$900 with 40% chance, or \$1,200 with 30% chance. Set up a simulation model for Jesse's problem and replicate it *N* times to calculate his average monthly revenue.

10-35 Sydney Garner is considering building a 300-seat amphitheater in a popular park. After studying the market, Sydney has drawn the following conclusions:

- There will be one show every night during summer months
- The theater will make a profit of \$1 on each occupied seat and suffer a loss of \$0.25 on each unoccupied seat.
- The probability that it rains on any given night is 0.2.
- The number of customers on a dry night is normally distributed, with a mean of 275 and a standard deviation of 30.
- The number of customers on a cold night is normally distributed, with a mean of 200 and a standard deviation of 50.

Set up Sydney's problem and simulate total profit for 1 month (30 days). In your model use integers for all demands. Replicate your model *N* times and calculate Sydney's average monthly profit.

10-36 Wang's Concrete Service notes that the number of jobs each month follows the following distribution: 10 with probability 0.15, 11 with probability 0.20, 12 with probability 0.20, 13 with probability 0.20, 14 with probability 0.15, and 15 with probability 0.10. The probability that a specific job will be for a residential driveway is 70%, and the probability that it will be for a commercial project is 30%. Revenues for residential driveways follow a normal distribution, with a mean of \$500 and a standard deviation of \$50. Commercial projects, although more lucrative, also have larger variability. Wang estimates that revenues here follow a normal distribution, with a mean of \$1,500 and a standard deviation of \$400. Set up a simulation model for Wang's problem and replicate it *N* times to calculate the average monthly revenue.

10-37 The Decatur Fire Department makes annual door-to-door solicitations for funds. Residents of each visited house are asked to contribute \$15 (and receive a free family portrait package), \$25 (and receive two free family portrait packages), or \$35 (and receive three free family portrait packages). An analysis from previous years' solicitations indicates that the following:

- Only 80% of the homes visited have someone at home.
- When someone is at home, there is only a 40% chance that he or she will make a donation.
- Of the people making donations, there is a 50% chance they will contribute \$15, a 25% chance they will contribute \$25, and a 15% chance they will contribute \$35. Occasionally (10% chance), a person makes a donation in excess of \$35. Such distributions follow a discrete uniform distribution between \$40 and \$50 (in increments of \$1).

The fire chief plans to visit 30 houses tomorrow. Set up a simulation model and replicate it *N* times to determine the probability that the chief will receive more than \$300 in donations from these 30 houses.

10-38 A local bank has a single drive-through window with arrival times and service times that follow the distributions from the following table:

TIME BETWEEN ARRIVALS (MIN.)	PROBABILITY	SERVICE TIME (MIN.)	PROBABILITY
1	0.15	1	0.15
2	0.24	2	0.35
3	0.27	3	0.22
4	0.22	4	0.28
5	0.12		

Simulate the arrival of 200 customers to compute each of the following measures: (a) average time a customer waits for service, (b) average time a customer is in the system (wait plus service time), and (c) percentage of time the server is busy with customers. Replicate each measure *N* times to compute the average.

10-39 Colin sells pretzels at the local high school basketball games. For an upcoming game, Colin has to decide how many pretzels to order (170, 190, or 210), at a cost of \$0.50 each. Colin sells pretzels for \$1.50 each. However, any unsold pretzels must be thrown away.

If the game is interesting, Colin thinks that fewer people will visit his stand. In such a case, Colin estimates that demand will be normally distributed, with a mean of 140 and a standard deviation of 20. However, if the game is a blowout, he expects more people to visit the stand. Demand in this case follows a discrete uniform distribution between 180 and 200. Based on his familiarity with the two teams, he estimates that there is only a 40% chance that the game will be a blowout.

Set up a simulation model and replicate it N times for each order size to determine Colin's expected profit and expected percentage of unsold pretzels. What do you recommend that Colin do?

10-40 The Diego Street Convenience Store has a single checkout register, with customer arrival distribution shown in the following table:

TIME BETWEEN ARRIVALS (MIN.)	PROBABILITY
1	0.18
2	0.20
3	0.22
4	0.25
5	0.15

Service time follows a discrete uniform distribution between 1 and 4 minutes. Simulate the arrival of 200 customers to compute the average time a customer waits for service and the probability that a customer waits 3 minutes or longer for service.

Replicate each measure N times to compute its average.

10-41 Zodiac Chemical manufactures chlorine gas by passing electricity through saltwater in a diaphragm cell. The plant has 88 diaphragm cells that operate in parallel. Each cell can produce 5 tons of chlorine gas per day, and each ton of chlorine gas has a profit contribution of $15. Due to the harsh environment, cell failures occur, causing the cell to be taken offline for maintenance. A cell fails, on average, every 30 hours, according to the exponential probability distribution. Only one cell can be repaired at any given time. Using the current maintenance procedure, the repair time follows a truncated normal probability distribution, with a mean of 21 hours, a standard deviation of 6 hours, and a minimum value of 5 hours. A new maintenance procedure is being considered that will require a significant capital investment. If this new procedure is implemented, the repair time will still follow a truncated normal distribution, but the mean time will be 14 hours, the standard deviation will be 4 hours, and the minimum time will be 3 hours. Simulate 200 failures to determine the annual savings in downtime with the new method.

10-42 Make a Splash T-Shirts is planning to print and sell specially designed tee shirts for the upcoming World Series. The shirts will cost $12 each to produce and can be sold for $30 each until the World Series. After the World Series, the price will be reduced to $20 per shirt. The demand at the $30 price is expected to be normally distributed, with a mean of 12,000 shirts and a standard deviation of 2,500 shirts. The demand for the $20 price is expected to be normally distributed, with a mean of 5,000 shirts and a standard deviation of 1,000 shirts. Any shirts left over will be discarded. Because of the high setup costs, Make a Splash T-Shirts is planning on producing one run of 17,000 shirts. In your model use integers for all demands.

(a) Simulate N setups to calculate the average profit for this quantity of shirts.
(b) Make a Splash T-Shirts would like to evaluate producing 16,000, 17,000, 18,000, 19,000, and 20,000 shirts. Which would you recommend? Why?

10-43 Phillip Florrick is responsible for the warehouse operation for a local discount department store chain. The warehouse has only one unloading dock that is currently operated by a single three-person crew. Trucks arrive at an average rate of five per hour and follow the exponential probability distribution. The average time for one of the crews to unload a truck tends to follow a normal distribution, with a mean of 9 minutes and standard deviation of 3 minutes (minimum time is 1 minute). Phillip has estimated the cost of operating a truck at $40 per hour. Phillip pays each person on the unloading crew $11 per hour. The unloading dock operates 8 hours each day. Simulate 100 days of this operation to calculate the total daily cost. Replicate this calculation N times to compute the expected total cost per day of this operation.

10-44 A customer service counter at a local bookstore is normally staffed by a single employee. The probabilities of arrival times and service times are shown in the following table:

TIME BETWEEN ARRIVALS (MIN.)	PROBABILITY	SERVICE TIME (MIN.)	PROBABILITY
1	0.07	1	0.07
2	0.25	2	0.24
3	0.23	3	0.28
4	0.26	4	0.28
5	0.19	5	0.13

Simulate the arrival of 100 customers to compute the average number of customers in line and the probability that a customer will have to wait 3 or more minutes for service to begin. Replicate each measure N times to compute its average.

10-45 Timberwolves Electric and Wiring Company installs wiring and electrical fixtures in residential construction. Andrew Dickel, the owner of Timberwolves, has been concerned with the amount of time it takes to complete wiring jobs because some of his workers are very unreliable. For each wiring job, a list of activities, their mean duration times, standard deviation of duration times, and immediate predecessors are given in the following table:

ACTIVITY	DAYS MEAN	DAYS STANDARD DEVIATION	IMMEDIATE PREDECESSORS
A	5.83	0.83	—
B	3.67	0.33	—
C	2.00	0.33	—
D	7.00	0.33	C
E	4.00	0.67	B, D
F	10.00	1.33	A, E
G	2.17	0.50	A, E
H	6.00	1.00	F
I	11.00	0.33	G
J	16.33	1.00	G
K	7.33	1.33	H, I

Assume that all activity durations follow a normal distribution, with the means and standard deviations shown. Use simulation to determine the probability that Timberwolves will finish the project in 40 days or less.

10-46 A plant engineering group needs to set up an assembly line to produce a new product. The following table describes the relationships between the activities that need to be completed for this product to be manufactured:

ACTIVITY	DAYS *a*	DAYS *m*	DAYS *b*	IMMEDIATE PREDECESSORS
A	3	6	8	—
B	5	8	10	A
C	5	6	8	A
D	1	2	4	B, C
E	7	11	17	D
F	7	9	12	D
G	6	8	9	D
H	3	4	7	F, G
I	3	5	7	E, F, H

If using Crystal Ball, assume that the duration of each activity follows a BetaPert distribution, with the three time estimates shown for that activity. Otherwise, assume that each activity time is normally distributed with expected time and standard deviation computed as shown in equations 7-6 and 7-8, respectively, on page 283. Round off all activity times to two decimal places.

(a) Use simulation to determine the probability that the project will finish in 37 days or less.

(b) Use simulation to determine the probability that the project will take more than 32 days.

10-47 Luna Martinez, director of personnel at Management Resources, Inc., is in the process of designing a program that its customers can use in the job-finding process. Some of the activities include preparing résumés, writing letters, making appointments to see prospective employers, researching companies and industries, and so on. Information on the activities is shown in the following table:

ACTIVITY	DAYS MEAN	DAYS STANDARD DEVIATION	IMMEDIATE PREDECESSORS
A	10.00	0.67	—
B	7.17	0.50	—
C	3.17	0.17	—
D	20.00	3.33	A
E	7.00	0.33	C
F	10.00	0.33	B, D, E
G	7.33	0.67	B, D, E
H	15.00	0.33	F
I	11.17	0.50	F
J	7.00	0.33	G, H
K	6.67	0.67	I, J
L	2.17	0.50	G, H

Assume that all activity durations follow a normal distribution, with the means and standard deviations shown. Round off all activity times to two decimal places. Use simulation to determine the average project completion time and the probability that the project will take at least 75 days.

10-48 Lamont Henri needs to plan and manage a local construction project. The following table describes the relationships between the activities that need to be completed:

ACTIVITY	DAYS *a*	DAYS *m*	DAYS *b*	IMMEDIATE PREDECESSORS
A	4	8	13	—
B	4	10	15	A
C	7	14	20	B
D	9	16	19	B
E	6	9	11	B
F	2	4	5	D, E
G	4	7	11	C, F
H	3	5	9	G
I	2	3	4	G, H

If using Crystal Ball, assume that the actual duration of each activity follows a BetaPert distribution, with the three time estimates shown for that activity. Otherwise, assume that each activity time is normally distributed with expected time and standard deviation computed as shown in equations 7-6 and 7-8, respectively, on page 283. Round off all activity times to one decimal place. Use simulation to determine the probability that the project will take at least 50 days.

10-49 Elena Wilhelm is responsible for developing a comprehensive sales training program for her organization. The following table describes the relationships between the activities that need to be completed:

ACTIVITY	DAYS MINIMUM	DAYS MAXIMUM	IMMEDIATE PREDECESSORS
A	7	13	—
B	5	11	—
C	3	8	A, B
D	5	9	C
E	2	9	C
F	3	5	E
G	5	12	F
H	9	12	D
I	6	8	F, H
J	7	10	G, I

Assume that the actual duration of each activity follows a discrete uniform distribution between the minimum and maximum times shown for that activity. Use simulation to determine the probability that the project will be finished in less than 49 days. Round off each activity time to the nearest whole number.

10-50 Lynn Rogers (who just turned 30) currently earns \$60,000 per year. At the end of each calendar year, she plans to invest 10% of her annual income in a tax-deferred retirement account. Lynn expects her salary to grow between 0% and 8% each year, following a discrete uniform distribution between these two rates. Based on historical market returns, she expects the tax-deferred account to return between –5% and 20% in any given year, following a continuous uniform distribution between these two rates. Use N replications of a simulation model to answer each of the following questions.

(a) What is the probability that Lynn will have in excess of \$1 million in this account when she turns 60 (i.e., in 30 years)?

(b) If Lynn wants this probability to be over 95%, what should be her savings rate each year?

10-51 Adams College has a self-insured employee health care plan. Each employee pays a monthly premium of \$100. Adams pays the rest of the health care costs. The number of covered employees is 1,000 this year. Each year, the number of employees who have major health claims follows a continuous uniform distribution between 10% and 15%, and the number of employees who have minor health claims follows a continuous uniform distribution between 60% and 65%. The rest have no health claims. Round off all numbers of claims to integers.

For this year, major health claims are expected to follow a normal distribution, with a mean of \$5,000 and a standard deviation of \$1,000. Minor health claims are expected to follow a normal distribution, with a mean of \$1,500 and a standard deviation of \$300. For purposes of simulating this model, assume that every minor health claim is the same amount simulated above. Assume likewise for major health clams. Use N replications of a simulation model to answer each of the following questions.

(a) What is the probability that Adams College's total out-of-pocket cost will exceed \$300,000 this year?

(b) The number of employees from year to year follows a continuous uniform distribution between a 3% decrease and a 4% increase. Round off all numbers of employees to integers. Also, due to rising health costs, the mean of minor health claims is expected to rise in a discrete uniform manner between 2% and 5% each year, and the mean of major health claims is expected to rise in a discrete uniform manner between 4% and 7% each year. What is the probability that Adams College's total out-of-pocket cost will exceed \$2,000,000 over the next five years?

Case Study

Alabama Airlines

Alabama Airlines opened its doors in June 2011 as a commuter service, with its headquarters and only hub located in Birmingham. A product of airline deregulation, Alabama Air joined the growing number of successful short-haul, point-to-point airlines, including Lone Star, Comair, Atlantic Southeast, Skywest, and Business Express.

Alabama Air was started and managed by two former pilots, David Douglas (formerly with the defunct Eastern Airlines) and Michael Hanna (formerly with Pan Am). It acquired a fleet of 12 used prop-jet planes and the airport gates vacated by Sprint Airlines when it downsized in 2010.

With business growing quickly, Douglas turned his attention to Alabama Air's toll-free reservations system. Between midnight and 6:00 A.M., only one telephone reservations agent had been on duty. The time between incoming calls during this period is distributed as shown in Table 10.8. Douglas carefully observed and timed the agent and estimated that the time taken to process passenger inquiries is distributed as shown in Table 10.9.

TABLE 10.8 Current Incoming Call Distribution

TIME BETWEEN CALLS (MIN.)	PROBABILITY
1	0.11
2	0.21
3	0.22
4	0.20
5	0.16
6	0.10

TABLE 10.9 Service Time Distribution

TIME TO PROCESS ENQUIRIES (MIN.)	PROBABILITY
1	0.20
2	0.19
3	0.18
4	0.17
5	0.13
6	0.10
7	0.03

All customers calling Alabama Air go on hold and are served in the order of the calls unless the reservations agent is available for immediate service. Douglas is deciding whether a second agent should be on duty to cope with customer demand. To maintain customer satisfaction, Alabama Air does not want a customer on hold for more than three to four minutes and also wants to maintain a "high" operator utilization.

Further, the airline is planning a new TV advertising campaign. As a result, it expects an increase in toll-free line phone enquiries. Based on similar campaigns in the past, the incoming call distribution from midnight to 6 A.M. is expected to be as shown in Table 10.10. (The same service time distribution will apply.)

TABLE 10.10 Revised Incoming Call Distribution

TIME BETWEEN CALLS (MIN.)	PROBABILITY
1	0.22
2	0.25
3	0.19
4	0.15
5	0.12
6	0.07

Discussion Questions

1. What would you advise Alabama Air to do for the current reservation system, based on the original call distribution? Create a simulation model to investigate the scenario. Describe the model carefully and justify the duration of the simulation, assumptions, and measures of performance.
2. What are your recommendations regarding operator utilization and customer satisfaction if the airline proceeds with the advertising campaign?

Source: © Zbigniew H. Przasnyski. Used with permission.

Case Study

Abjar Transport Company

In 2011, Samir Khaldoun, after receiving an MBA degree from a leading university in the United States, returned to Jeddah, Saudi Arabia, where his family has extensive business holdings. Samir's first assignment was to stabilize and develop a newly formed, family-owned transport company—Abjar Transport.

An immediate problem Samir faces is the determination of the number of trucks needed to handle the forecasted freight volume. Before now, trucks were added to the fleet on an "as-needed" basis, without comprehensive capacity planning. This approach has created problems of driver recruitment, truck service and maintenance, and excessive demurrage (i.e., port fees) because of delays at unloading docks and retention of cargo containers.

Samir forecasts that Abjar's freight volume should average 160,000 tons per month, with a standard deviation of 30,000 tons. Freight is unloaded on a uniform basis throughout the month. Based on past experience, the amount handled per month is assumed to be normally distributed.

After extensive investigation, Samir concludes that the fleet should be standardized to 40-foot Mercedes 2624 2 × 4 tractor-trailer rigs, which are each suitable for carrying two 20-foot containers, or one 40-foot container cargo capacity is approximately 60 tons per rig. Each tractor-trailer unit is estimated to cost 240,000 riyals. Moreover, they must meet Saudi Arabian specifications—double cooling fans, oversized radiators, and special high-temperature tires. Historical evidence suggests that these Mercedes rigs will operate 96% of the time.

Approximately 25% of the freight handled by these tractor-trailer rigs is containerized in container lengths of 20, 30, and 40 feet. (The balance of the freight—75%—is not containerized.) The 20-foot containers hold approximately 20 tons of cargo, the 30-foot containers hold 45 tons, and the 40-foot containers hold 60 tons of freight. Approximately 60% of the containerized freight is shipped in 40-foot units, 20% is shipped in 30-foot units, and 20% is transported in 20-foot units.

Abjar Transport picks up freight at the dock and delivers it directly to customers or to warehouses for later delivery. Based on his study of truck routing and scheduling patterns, Samir concludes that each rig should pick up freight at the dock three times each day.

Discussion Questions

1. How many tractor-trailer rigs should make up the Abjar Transport fleet?

Internet Case Studies

See the Companion Website for this textbook, at www.pearsonhighered.com/balakrishnan, for additional case studies

CHAPTER 11

Forecasting Models

LEARNING OBJECTIVES

After completing this chapter, students will be able to:

1. Understand and know when to use various types of forecasting models.
2. Compute a variety of forecasting error measures.
3. Compute moving averages, weighted moving averages, and exponential smoothing time-series models.
4. Decompose time-series data to identify and analyze trends and seasonality.
5. Identify variables and use them in causal simple and multiple linear regression models.
6. Use Excel to analyze a variety of forecasting models.

CHAPTER OUTLINE

11.1 Introduction

Every day, managers make decisions without knowing exactly what will happen in the future. Inventory is ordered even though no one knows what sales will be, new equipment is purchased even though no one knows the demand for products, and investments are made even though no one knows what profits will be. Managers are always trying to reduce this uncertainty and to make better estimates of what will happen in the future. Accomplishing this objective is the main purpose of forecasting.

There are many ways to try to forecast the future. In many firms (especially small ones), the forecasting models may be qualitative or subjective, involving "expert" opinions based on intuition and years of experience. The more reliable forecasting models, however, are usually *quantitative* models, such as moving averages, exponential smoothing, trend analysis, seasonality analysis, decomposition models, and causal regression analysis, that rely on numeric data.

No single forecasting method is superior; whatever works best should be used.

There is seldom a single superior forecasting model. One firm may find regression models effective, another firm may use several quantitative models, and a third may combine both quantitative and qualitative techniques. Whichever model works best for a firm is the one that should be used. In this chapter, we discuss several different forecasting models that are commonly used in practice. For each model, we show the equations needed to compute the forecasts and provide examples of how they are analyzed.

Regardless of the model used to make the forecast, the following steps that present a systematic overall way of initiating, designing, and implementing a forecast system are used:

There are seven steps in forecasting.

Steps to Forecasting

1. Determine the use of the forecast; what is the objective we are trying to obtain?
2. Identify the items that need to be forecasted.
3. Determine the time horizon of the forecast: Is it 1 to 30 days (short time horizon), 1 month to 1 year (medium time horizon), or more than 1 year (long time horizon)?
4. Select the forecasting model or models.
5. Gather the data needed to make the forecast.
6. Validate the forecasting model.
7. Make the forecast and implement the results.

When the forecasting model is to be used to generate forecasts regularly over time, data must be collected routinely, and the actual computations must be repeated. In this age of technology and computers, however, forecast calculations are seldom performed by hand. Computers and forecasting software packages simplify these tasks to a great extent. Numerous statistical programs, such as SAS, SPSS, and Minitab, are readily available to handle various forecasting models. However, in keeping with the spreadsheet focus of this textbook, we use Excel add-ins such as Analysis ToolPak and worksheets (included on this textbook's Companion Website) to actually calculate the forecast values for each model. Several other spreadsheet-based forecasting software programs (such as Crystal Ball Predictor by Oracle Corp. and StatPro by Palisade Corporation) are also popular in practice.

11.2 Types of Forecasts

The three categories of models are qualitative, time-series, and causal models.

The forecasting models we consider here can be classified into three categories. These categories, shown in Figure 11.1, are qualitative models, time-series models, and causal models. Although we provide a brief description of a few qualitative models in section 11.3, the focus of this chapter is on time-series and causal models.

Qualitative Models

Qualitative models *incorporate subjective factors.*

Qualitative models attempt to incorporate judgmental or subjective factors into the forecasting model. Opinions by experts, individual experiences and judgments, and other subjective factors may be considered. Qualitative models are especially useful when subjective factors are

FIGURE 11.1
Forecasting Models Discussed

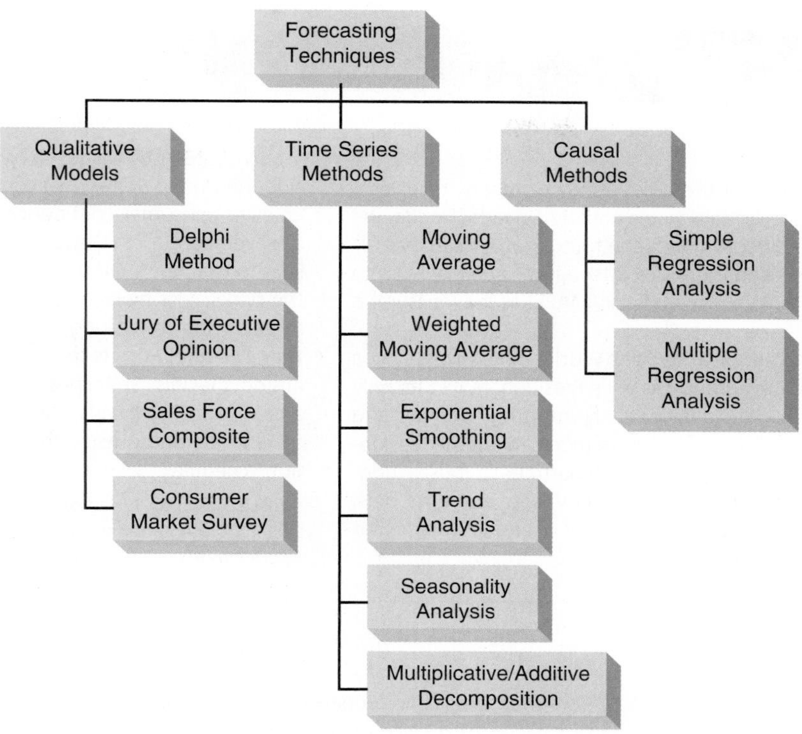

expected to be very important or when accurate quantitative data are difficult to obtain. Qualitative models are also useful for long-term forecasting.

Time-Series Models

Time-series models *assume that the past is an indication of the future.*

Whereas qualitative models rely on judgmental or subjective data, **time-series models** rely on quantitative data. Time-series models attempt to predict the future by using historical data. These models make the assumption that what happens in the future is a function of what has happened in the past. In other words, time-series models look at what has happened over a period of time and use a series of past data to make a forecast. Thus, if we are forecasting weekly sales for lawn mowers, we use the past weekly sales for lawn mowers in making the forecast. The time-series models we examine in this chapter are (1) moving averages, (2) weighted moving averages, (3) exponential smoothing, (4) linear trend analysis, (5) seasonality analysis, and (6) multiplicative and additive decomposition.

Causal Models

Causal models *incorporate factors that influence the quantity being forecasted.*

Like time-series models, **causal models** also rely on quantitative data. Causal models incorporate the variables or factors that might influence the quantity being forecasted into the forecasting model. For example, daily sales of a cola drink might depend on the season, the average temperature, the average humidity, whether it is a weekend or a weekday, and so on. Thus, a causal model would attempt to include factors for temperature, humidity, season, day of the week, and so on. Causal models can also include past sales data as time-series models do.

11.3 Qualitative Forecasting Models

Here is a brief overview of four different qualitative forecasting techniques commonly used in practice:

Four qualitative or judgmental approaches are Delphi, jury of executive opinion, sales force composite, and consumer market survey.

1. *Delphi method.* The **Delphi** iterative group process allows experts, who may be located in different places, to make forecasts. There are three different types of participants in the Delphi process: decision makers, staff personnel, and respondents. The **decision-making group** usually consists of 5–10 experts who will be making the actual forecast. The *staff*

IN ACTION Forecasting at Disney World

When the President of the Walt Disney Company receives a daily report from Disney's main theme parks in Orlando, Florida, the report contains only two numbers: the forecast of yesterday's attendance at the parks and the actual attendance. An error close to zero (using mean absolute percent error [MAPE] as the measure) is expected.

The forecasting team at Disney World doesn't just do a daily prediction, however, and Disney's President is not its only customer. It also provides daily, weekly, monthly, annual, and five-year forecasts to the labor management, maintenance, operations, finance, and park scheduling departments. It uses judgmental models, econometric models, moving average models, and regression analysis. The team's forecast of annual volume has resulted in a MAPE of zero.

With 20% of Disney World's customers coming from outside the United States, its econometric model includes such variables as consumer confidence and the gross domestic products of seven countries. Disney also surveys one million people each year to examine their future travel plans and their experiences at the parks. This helps forecast not only attendance but behavior at each ride (how long people will wait and how many times they will ride). Inputs to the monthly forecasting model include airline specials, speeches by the chair of the Federal Reserve, and Wall Street trends. Disney even monitors 3,000 school districts inside and outside the United States for holiday and vacation schedules.

Source: Based on J. Newkirk and M. Haskell. "Forecasting in the Service Sector," presentation at the *12th Annual Meeting of the Production and Operations Management Society*, Orlando, FL, April 1, 2001.

personnel assist the decision makers by preparing, distributing, collecting, and summarizing a series of questionnaires and survey results. The *respondents* are a group of people whose judgments are valued and are being sought. This group provides inputs to the decision makers before the forecast is made.

2. *Jury of executive opinion.* This method begins with the opinions of a small group of high-level managers, often in combination with statistical models, and results in a group estimate of demand.
3. *Sales force composite.* In this approach, each salesperson estimates what sales will be in his or her region; these forecasts are reviewed to ensure that they are realistic and are then combined at the district and national levels to reach an overall forecast.
4. *Consumer market survey.* This method solicits input from customers or potential customers regarding their future purchasing plans. It can help not only in preparing a forecast but also in improving product design and planning for new products.

11.4 Measuring Forecast Error

The overall accuracy of a forecasting model can be determined by comparing the forecasted values with the actual or observed values. If F_t denotes the forecast in period t and A_t denotes the actual value in period t, the **forecast error** (or forecast deviation) is defined as

$$\begin{aligned}\text{Forecast error} &= \text{Actual value} - \text{Forecast value}\\ &= A_t - F_t \end{aligned} \tag{11-1}$$

The **forecast error** *tells us how well the model performed against itself using past data.*

Several measures are commonly used in practice to calculate the overall forecast error. These measures can be used to compare different forecasting models as well as to monitor forecasts to ensure that they are performing well. Three of the most popular measures are covered in the following sections.

MEAN ABSOLUTE DEVIATION **Mean absolute deviation (MAD)** is computed as the average of the *absolute* values of the individual forecast errors. That is, if we have forecasted and actual values for T periods, MAD is calculated as

$$\text{MAD} = \sum_{t=1}^{T} |\text{Forecast error}|/T = \sum_{t=1}^{T} |A_t - F_t|/T \tag{11-2}$$

MEAN SQUARED ERROR The **mean squared error (MSE)** is computed as the average of the *squared* values of the individual forecast errors. That is, if we have forecasted and actual values for T periods, MSE is calculated as

$$\text{MSE} = \sum_{t=1}^{T} (\text{Forecast error})^2/T = \sum_{t=1}^{T} (A_t - F_t)^2/T \tag{11-3}$$

MSE accentuates large deviations.

A drawback of using MSE is that it tends to accentuate large deviations due to the squared term. For example, if the forecast error for period 1 is twice as large as the error for period 2, the squared error in period 1 is four times as large as that for period 2. Hence, using MSE as the measure of forecast error typically indicates that we prefer to have several smaller deviations rather than even one large deviation.

MAPE expresses the error as a percentage of the actual values.

MEAN ABSOLUTE PERCENT ERROR A problem with both MAD and MSE is that their values depend on the magnitude of the item being forecast. If the forecast item is measured in thousands, the MAD and MSE values can be very large. To avoid this problem, we can use the **mean absolute percent error (MAPE)**. This is computed as the average of the absolute difference between the forecasted and actual values, expressed as a percentage of the actual values. That is, if we have forecasted and actual values for T periods, MAPE is calculated as

$$\text{MAPE} = 100 \sum_{t=1}^{T} [\,|A_t - F_t|/A_t\,]/T \tag{11-4}$$

MAPE is perhaps the easiest measure to interpret. For example, a result that MAPE is 2% is a clear statement that is not dependent on issues such as the magnitude of the input data. For this reason, although we calculate all three measures in our analyses, we focus primarily on MAPE in our discussions.

11.5 Basic Time-Series Forecasting Models

A time series is based on a sequence of evenly spaced (e.g., weekly, monthly, quarterly) data points. Examples include weekly sales of Dell personal computers, quarterly earnings reports of Cisco Systems stock, daily shipments of Energizer batteries, and annual U.S. consumer price indices. Forecasting time-series data implies that future values are predicted *only* from past values. Other variables, no matter how potentially valuable, are ignored.

Components of a Time Series

We can view a long-term time series (i.e., data for over one year) as being made up of four distinct components. Analyzing a time series means breaking down the data to identify these four components and then projecting them forward. The process of identifying the four components is referred to as *decomposition*. The four components are as follows:

Four components of a time series are trend, seasonality, cycles, and random variations.

1. *Trend.* A **trend** is the upward or downward movement of data over time. For example, prices for many consumer goods exhibit an upward trend over time due to the presence of inflation. Although it is possible for the relationship between time and the data to have any form (linear or nonlinear), we focus only on linear trend relationships in this chapter.
2. *Seasonality.* **Seasonality** is the pattern of demand fluctuations that occurs every year above or below the average demand. That is, the same seasonal pattern repeats itself every year over the time horizon. For example, lawn mower sales are always above average each year in spring and below average in winter.
3. *Cycles.* Just as seasonality is the pattern that occurs each year, **cycles** are patterns that occur over several years. Cycles are usually tied to the business cycle. For example, the economies

FIGURE 11.2
Components of a Time Series (Charted over Four Years)

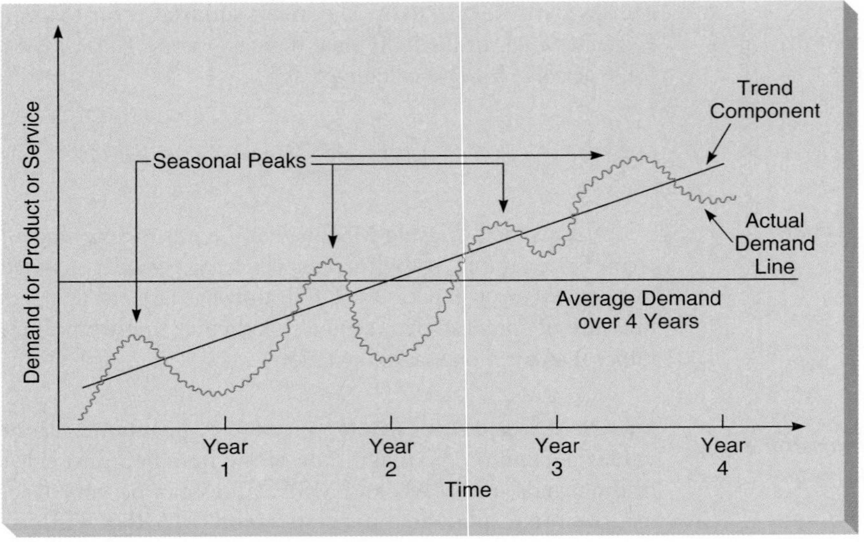

of most countries experience cycles of high growth followed by a period of relatively low growth or even recession.

4. *Random variations.* **Random variations** are "blips" in the data caused by chance and unusual situations. They follow no discernible pattern. For this reason, we cannot really capture this component and use it to forecast future values.

Figure 11.2 shows a time series and its components.

This is the form of a multiplicative decomposition model.

There are two general approaches to decomposing a time series into its components. The most widely used is a **multiplicative decomposition model**, which assumes that the forecasted value is the product of the four components. It is stated as

$$\text{Forecast} = \text{Trend} \times \text{Seasonality} \times \text{Cycles} \times \text{Random variations} \tag{11-5}$$

This is the form of an additive decomposition model.

An **additive decomposition model** that adds the components together to provide an estimate is also available. It is stated as

$$\text{Forecast} = \text{Trend} + \text{Seasonality} + \text{Cycles} + \text{Random variations} \tag{11-6}$$

We study the multiplicative model in section 11.7 and the additive model in Solved Problem 11-4 at the end of this chapter. As noted earlier, the random variations follow no discernible pattern. In most real-world models, forecasters assume that these variations are averaged out over time. They then concentrate on only the seasonal component and a component that is a combination of the trend and cyclical factors.

Stationary and Nonstationary Time-Series Data

Stationary data *have no trend, while* **nonstationary data** *exhibit trend.*

Time-series data are said to be **stationary data** if there is no significant upward or downward movement (or trend) in the data over time. That is, the average value for the time-series data remains constant over the time horizon considered in the model. Stationary time-series data are typically encountered when the time horizon is short term (1–30 days) or medium term (1 month to 1 year). For time horizons that are long term (1 year or greater), time-series data tend to typically exhibit some trend. In such cases, we refer to the data as *nonstationary*.

In the remainder of this section, we discuss three popular forecasting models used for stationary time-series data: (1) moving averages, (2) weighted moving averages, and (3) exponential smoothing. Although we show the equations needed to compute the forecasts for each model, we use Excel worksheets (included on this textbook's Companion Website) to actually calculate these values.

TABLE 11.1 Three-Month Moving Averages Forecast for Wallace Garden Supply

MONTH	ACTUAL SALES	THREE-MONTH MOVING AVERAGES
January	10	
February	12	
March	16	
April	13	$(10 + 12 + 16)/3 = 12.67$
May	17	$(12 + 16 + 13)/3 = 13.67$
June	19	$(16 + 13 + 17)/3 = 15.33$
July	15	$(13 + 17 + 19)/3 = 16.33$
August	20	$(17 + 19 + 15)/3 = 17.00$
September	22	$(19 + 15 + 20)/3 = 18.00$
October	19	$(15 + 20 + 22)/3 = 19.00$
November	21	$(20 + 22 + 19)/3 = 20.33$
December	19	$(22 + 19 + 21)/3 = 20.67$

Moving Averages

Moving averages *smooth out variations when forecasting demands are fairly steady.*

Moving averages are useful if we can assume that the item we are trying to forecast will stay fairly steady over time. We calculate a three-period moving average by summing the actual value of the item for the past three periods and dividing the total by 3. This three-period moving average serves as the forecast for the next period. With each passing period, the most recent period's actual value is added to the sum of the previous two periods' data, and the earliest period is dropped. This tends to smooth out short-term irregularities in the time series.

The moving average for the preceding k periods (where k can be any integer > 2) serves as the forecast for the following period. Mathematically, the k-period moving average can be expressed as

$$k\text{-period moving average} = \Sigma\ (\text{Actual values in previous } k \text{ periods})/k \qquad \textbf{(11-7)}$$

WALLACE GARDEN SUPPLY EXAMPLE Monthly sales of storage sheds at Wallace Garden Supply are shown in the middle column of Table 11.1. A three-month moving average is shown on the rightmost column. As discussed next, we can also use the ExcelModules program to calculate these moving averages.

Using ExcelModules for Forecasting Model Computations

Excel Notes

- The Companion Website for this textbook, at www.pearsonhighered.com/balakrishnan, contains a set of Excel worksheets, bundled together in a software package called ExcelModules. The procedure for installing and running this program, as well as a brief description of its contents, is given in Appendix B.
- The Companion Website also provides the Excel file for each sample problem discussed here. The relevant file name is shown in the margin next to each example.
- For clarity, all worksheets for forecasting models in ExcelModules are color coded as follows:
  - *Input cells*, where we enter the problem data, are shaded yellow.
  - *Output cells*, which show forecasts and measures of forecast error, are shaded green.

When we run the ExcelModules program, we see a new tab titled ExcelModules in Excel's Ribbon. We select this tab and then click the Modules icon followed by the Forecasting Models menu. The choices shown in Screenshot 11-1A are displayed. From these choices, we select the appropriate forecasting model.

SCREENSHOT 11-1A Forecasting Models Menu in ExcelModules

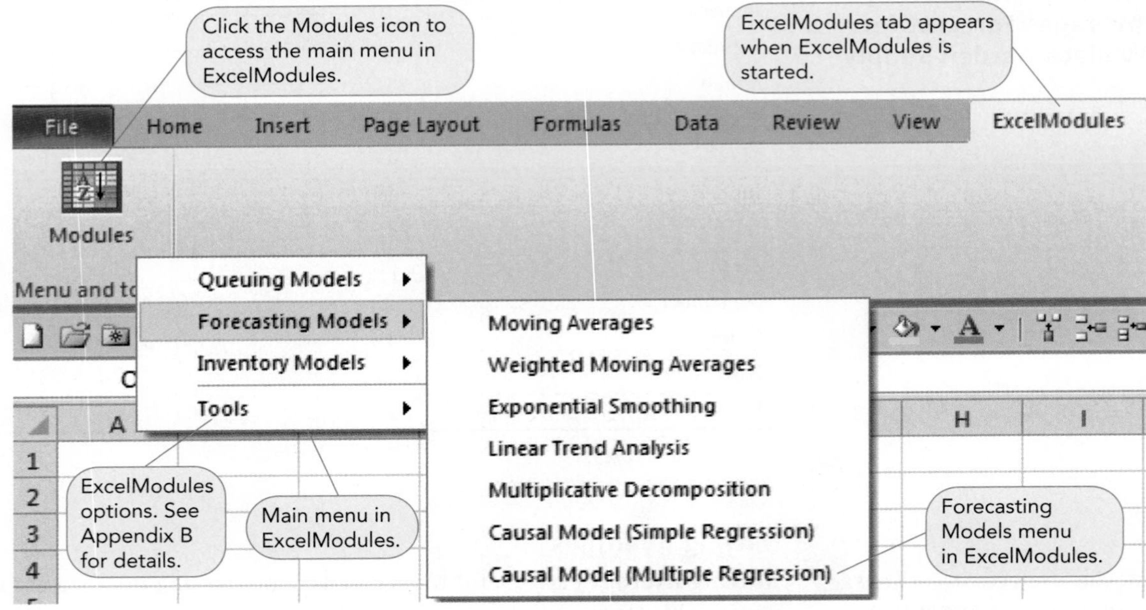

When *any* of the forecasting models is selected in ExcelModules, we are first presented with a window that allows us to specify several options. Some of these options are common for all models, whereas others are specific to the forecasting model selected. For example, Screenshot 11-1B shows the Spreadsheet Initialization window when we select the Moving Averages forecasting model. The options here include the following:

1. The title of the problem. The default value is Problem Title.
2. The number of past periods for which we have data regarding the item (e.g., demand, sales) being forecast. The default value is 3.
3. The name for the period (e.g., Week, Month). The default value is Period.
4. The number of periods to average (i.e., the value of k in Equation 11-7). The default value is 2.
5. Graph. Checking this box results in line graphs of the actual and forecast values.

SCREENSHOT 11-1B Sample Options Window for Forecasting Models in ExcelModules

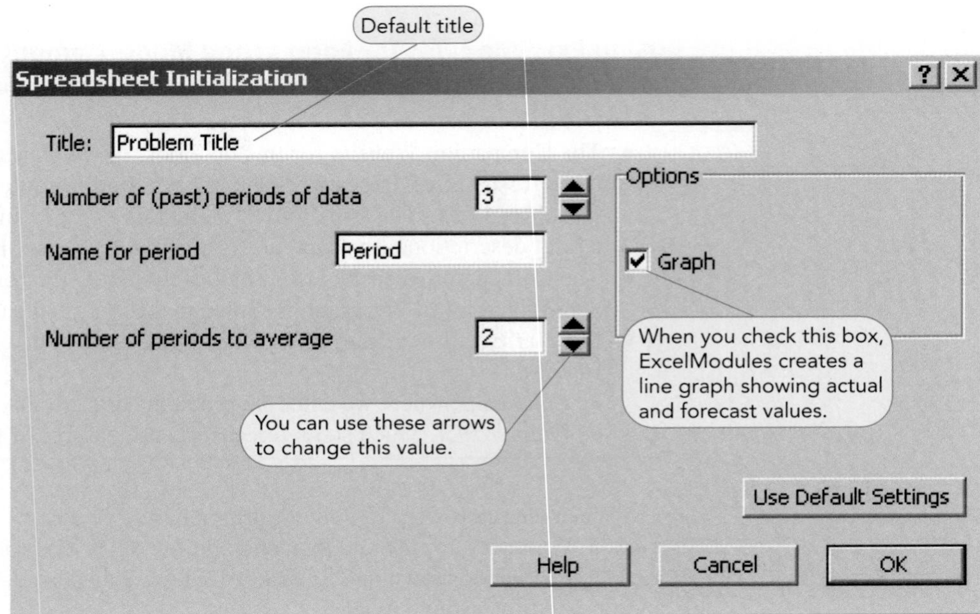

IN ACTION Forecasting Sales at Sun Microsystems

Sun Microsystems Inc., a worldwide supplier of enterprise computing products, employs about 33,500 people and has revenues of over $14 billion. Although Sun's products range from microprocessors to information technology services, the bulk of its income is from the sales of computer servers and storage systems.

Sun's strategy involves extensive outsourcing, which presents significant supply chain management challenges due to the short life cycle of its computer products. Sun therefore relies on accurate demand forecasts over a quarterly time horizon to effectively manage its supply chain. Sun's sales forecasting had historically relied on judgmental forecasts which are subject to distortion.

To address this deficiency, Sun's supply chain managers worked with researchers to develop statistical forecasting techniques that could be used to enhance—but not supplant—the company's judgmental forecasts. The result of this project was a suite of software called the Sun Labs Forecasting System.

This forecasting system operates almost entirely unattended and provides an effective combination of judgmental and statistical forecasting information that consistently improves upon the forecast accuracy of both constituents. The system has been received very favorably by Sun's supply chain managers.

Source: Based on P. M. Yelland, S. Kim, and R. Stratulate. "A Bayesian Model for Sales Forecasting at Sun Microsystems," *Interfaces* 40, 2 (March–April 2010): 118–129.

File: 11-2.xls, sheet: 11-2B

USING EXCELMODULES FOR MOVING AVERAGES Screenshot 11-2A shows the options we select for the Wallace Garden Supply example.

When we click OK on this screen, we get the screen shown in Screenshot 11-2B, where we enter the actual shed sales for the 12 months (see Table 11.1) in cells B7:B18.

Excel Notes

- The worksheets in ExcelModules contain formulas to compute the forecasts and forecast errors for different forecasting models. The default zero values for the input data cause the results of these formulas to initially appear as #N/A, #VALUE!, or #DIV/0!. However, as soon as we enter valid values for the input data, the worksheets will display the formula results.
- Once ExcelModules has been used to create the Excel worksheet for a particular forecasting model (e.g., a three-period moving averages model), the resulting worksheet can be used to compute the forecasts with several different input data. For example, we can enter different input data in cells B7:B18 of Screenshot 11-2B and compute the results without having to create a new three-period moving averages worksheet each time.

SCREENSHOT 11-2A Options Window for Moving Averages Worksheet in ExcelModules

We have data for 12 months.

Spreadsheet Initialization

Title: Wallace Garden Supply

Number of (past) periods of data: 12

Name for period: Month

Options: ☑ Graph

Number of periods to average: 3

We want to compute a 3-month moving average.

Use Default Settings

Help | Cancel | OK

SCREENSHOT 11-2B Moving Averages Model for Wallace Garden Supply

	A	B	C	D	E	F	G	H
1	**Wallace Garden Supply**							
2	Forecasting		3 period moving average					
3	Enter the data in the cells shaded YELLOW.							
4								
5	Input Data			Forecast Error Analysis				
6	Period	Actual Value		Forecast	Error	Absolute error	Squared error	Absolute % error
7	Month 1	10						
8	Month 2	12						
9	Month 3	16						
10	Month 4	13		12.667	0.333	0.333	0.111	2.56%
11	Month 5	17		13.667	3.333	3.333	11.111	19.61%
12	Month 6	19		15.333	3.667	3.667	13.444	19.30%
13	Month 7	15		16.333	-1.333	1.333	1.778	8.89%
14	Month 8	20		17.000	3.000	3.000	9.000	15.00%
15	Month 9	22		18.000	4.000	4.000	16.000	18.18%
16	Month 10	19		19.000	0.000	0.000	0.000	0.00%
17	Month 11	21		20.333	0.667	0.667	0.444	3.17%
18	Month 12	19		20.667	-1.667	1.667	2.778	8.77%
19				**Average**		**2.000**	**6.074**	**10.61%**
20	**Next period**	**19.667**				**MAD**	**MSE**	**MAPE**

Average of 3 previous months $= \frac{10 + 12 + 16}{3} = 12.667$

Forecast value for month 13

Input data for past 12 months

Measures of forecast error

The worksheet now displays the three-month moving averages (shown in cells D10:D18), and the forecast for the next month (i.e., January of the next year), shown in cell B20. In addition, the following measures of forecast error are also calculated and reported: MAD (cell F19), MSE (cell G19), and MAPE (cell H19).

File: 11-2.xls, sheet: 11-2C

The output indicates that a three-month moving average model results in a MAPE of 10.61%. The forecast for the next period is 19.667 storage sheds. The line graph (if Graph is checked in the options in Screenshot 11-2A) is shown in a separate worksheet. We show the graph for the Wallace Garden Supply example in Screenshot 11-2C.

Forecast error measures permit comparison of different models.

INTERPRETING FORECAST ERRORS As noted earlier, the measures of forecast error allow us to compare different forecasting models to see which one provides the best forecast. For example, instead of a three-month moving average, we can try a four-month moving average for the Wallace Garden Supply example. See if you can repeat the procedure described in Screenshots 11-2A and 11-2B for a four-month moving average. You should see that the MAPE with $k = 4$ is 14.22%. This implies that, at least in this example, the three-month moving average model provides a better forecast than the four-month model. We can try other values for k in a similar fashion.

Weighted Moving Averages

In the regular moving average approach, all the input data are assumed to be equally important. For example, in a three-period model, data for all three previous periods are given equal importance, and a simple average of the three values is computed. In some cases, however, data for some periods (e.g., recent periods) may be more important than data for other periods (e.g., earlier periods). This is especially true if there is a trend or pattern in the data. In such cases, we can use weights to place more emphasis on some periods and less emphasis on others.

SCREENSHOT 11-2C Chart of Three-Period Moving Averages Forecast for Wallace Garden Supply

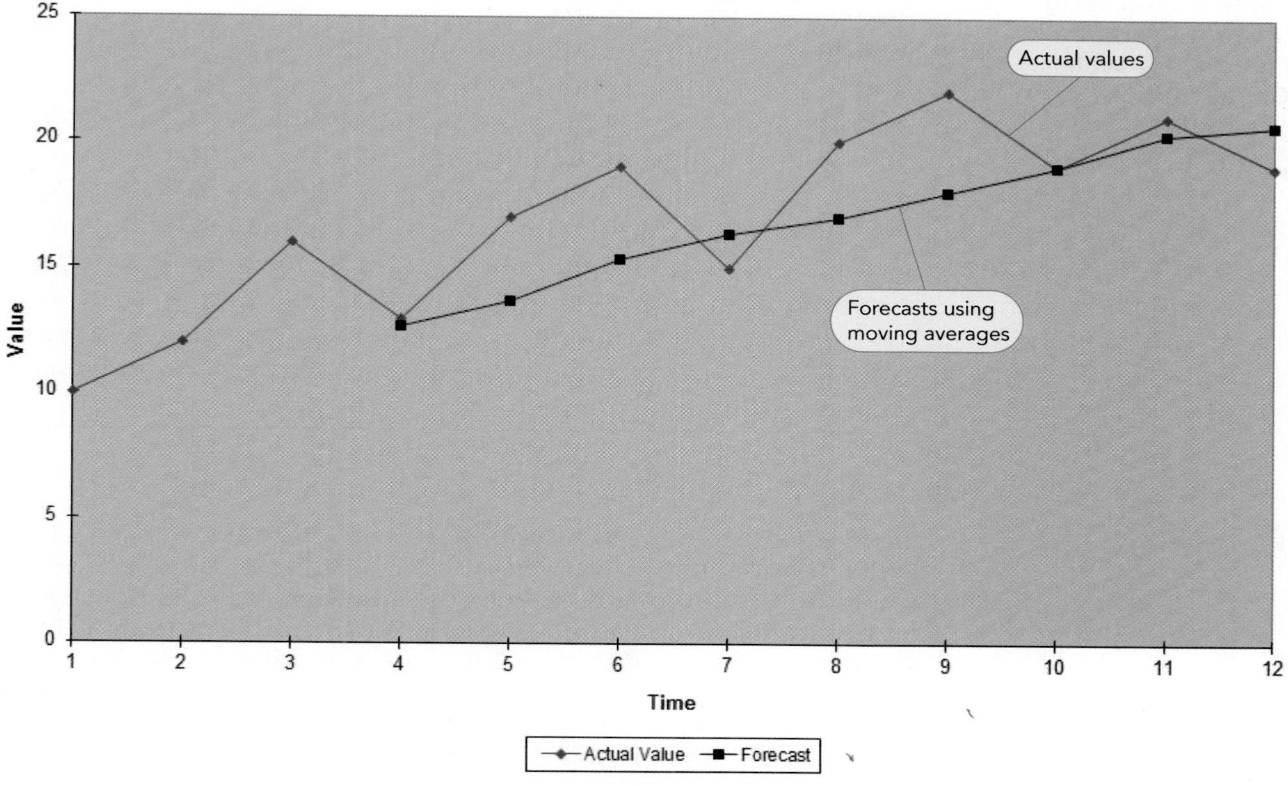

Weights can be used to put more emphasis on some periods.

The choice of weights is somewhat arbitrary because there is no set formula to determine them. Therefore, deciding which weights to use requires some experience and a bit of luck. For example, if the latest period is weighted too heavily, the model might reflect a large unusual change in the forecast value too quickly.

Mathematically, the k-period **weighted moving average**, which serves the forecast for the next period, can be expressed as

$$k\text{-period weighted moving average} = \frac{\sum_{i=1}^{k} (\text{Weight for period } i) \times (\text{Actual value in period } i)}{\sum_{i=1}^{k} (\text{Weights})} \qquad \textbf{(11-8)}$$

WALLACE GARDEN SUPPLY REVISITED—PART I Instead of using a three-month moving average, let us assume that Wallace Garden Supply would like to forecast sales of storage sheds by weighting the past three months, as follows:

PERIOD	WEIGHT
Last month	3
Two months ago	2
Three months ago	1

The results of Wallace Garden Supply weighted average forecast using these weights are shown in Table 11.2. Let us now see how we can also use ExcelModules to compute these weighted moving averages.

TABLE 11.2
Three-Month Weighted Moving Averages Forecast for Wallace Garden Supply

MONTH	ACTUAL SALES	WEIGHTED MOVING AVERAGES
January	10	
February	12	
March	16	
April	13	$(1 \times 10 + 2 \times 12 + 3 \times 16)/6 = 13.67$
May	17	$(1 \times 12 + 2 \times 16 + 3 \times 13)/6 = 13.83$
June	19	$(1 \times 16 + 2 \times 13 + 3 \times 17)/6 = 15.50$
July	15	$(1 \times 13 + 2 \times 17 + 3 \times 19)/6 = 17.33$
August	20	$(1 \times 17 + 2 \times 19 + 3 \times 15)/6 = 16.67$
September	22	$(1 \times 19 + 2 \times 15 + 3 \times 20)/6 = 18.17$
October	19	$(1 \times 15 + 2 \times 20 + 3 \times 22)/6 = 20.17$
November	21	$(1 \times 20 + 2 \times 22 + 3 \times 19)/6 = 20.17$
December	19	$(1 \times 22 + 2 \times 19 + 3 \times 21)/6 = 20.50$

Weights usually add up to 1.

USING EXCELMODULES FOR WEIGHTED MOVING AVERAGES When we select the choice titled Weighted Moving Averages from the Forecasting Models menu in ExcelModules (see Screenshot 11-1A on page 482), the window shown in Screenshot 11-3A is displayed. The option entries in this window are similar to those for moving averages (see Screenshot 11-2A). The only additional choice is the box labeled Weights sum to 1. Although not required (note, for example, that the sum of weights in the Wallace Garden Supply example is 6), it is common practice to assign weights to various periods such that they sum to one. Our specific entries for Wallace Garden Supply's problem are shown in Screenshot 11-3A.

When we click OK on this screen, we get the screen shown in Screenshot 11-3B, where we enter the actual shed sales for the 12 months (see Table 11.2) in cells B7:B18 and the weights for the past 3 months in cells C7:C9.

File: 11-3.xls, sheet: 11-3B

The worksheet now displays the 3-month weighted moving averages (shown in cells E10:E18) and the forecast for the next month (i.e., January of the next year), shown in cell B20. In addition, the following measures of forecast error are also calculated and reported: MAD (cell G19), MSE (cell H19), and MAPE (cell I19). The line graph, if asked for, is shown on a separate worksheet.

SCREENSHOT 11-3A
Options Window for Weighted Moving Averages Worksheet in ExcelModules

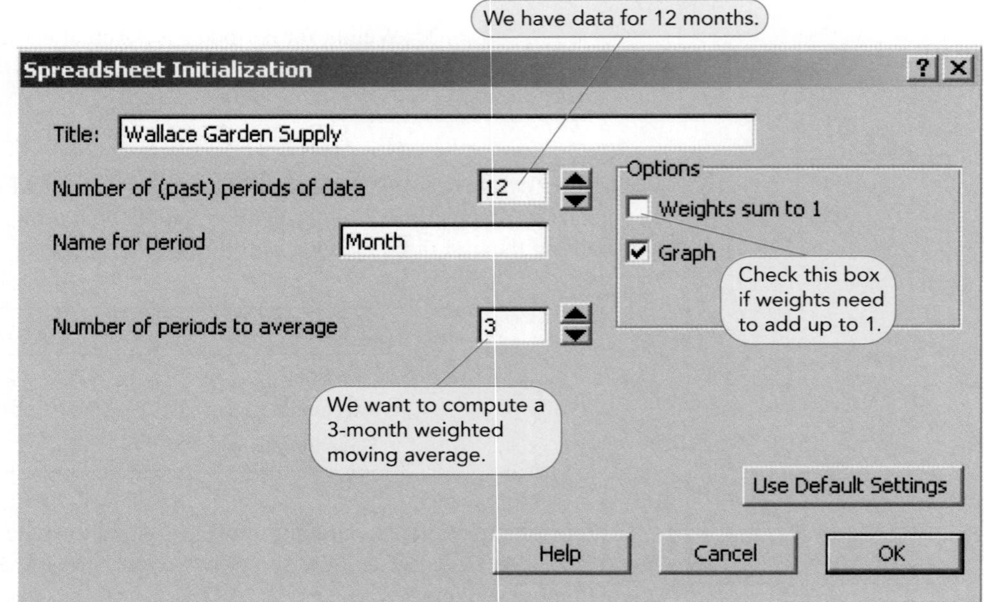

SCREENSHOT 11-3B Weighted Moving Averages Model for Wallace Garden Supply

	A	B	C	D	E	F	G	H	I
1	Wallace Garden Supply								
2	Forecasting		3 period weighted moving average						
3	Enter the data in the cells shaded YELLOW.								
4									
5	Input Data				Forecast Error Analysis				
6	Period	Actual value	Weights		Forecast	Error	Absolute error	Squared error	Absolute % error
7	Month 1	10	1						
8	Month 2	12	2						
9	Month 3	16	3						
10	Month 4	13			13.667	-0.667	0.667	0.444	5.13%
11	Month 5	17			13.833	3.167	3.167	10.028	18.63%
12	Month 6	19			15.500	3.500	3.500	12.250	18.42%
13	Month 7	15			17.333	-2.333	2.333	5.444	15.56%
14	Month 8	20			16.667	3.333	3.333	11.111	16.67%
15	Month 9	22			18.167	3.833	3.833	14.694	17.42%
16	Month 10	19			20.167	-1.167	1.167	1.361	6.14%
17	Month 11	21			20.167	0.833	0.833	0.694	3.97%
18	Month 12	19			20.500	-1.500	1.500	2.250	7.89%
19					Average		2.259	6.475	12.20%
20	Next period	19.667					MAD	MSE	MAPE

Weighted average of the 3 previous months = $\frac{3 \times 16 \times 2 \times 12 + 1 \times 10}{6} = 13.667$

Weights for the 3 previous months

Measures of forecast error

In this particular example, you can see that weighting the latest month more heavily actually provides a less accurate forecast. That is, the MAPE value is now 12.20%, compared with a MAPE value of only 10.61% for the 3-month simple moving average.

USING SOLVER TO DETERMINE THE OPTIMAL WEIGHTS As noted earlier, the choice of weights is somewhat arbitrary because there is no set formula to determine them. However, for a specified value of k (i.e., number of periods to use in computing the weighted moving average), we can use Excel's Solver to find the optimal weights to use in the forecasting model.

Solver can be used to determine the optimal weights.

Recall that we used Solver to solve linear, integer, and nonlinear programming problems in Chapters 2 through 6. Setting up a problem in Solver requires three components:

- ***Changing variable cells.*** These cells denote the decision variables for which we are trying to identify optimal values.
- ***Objective cell.*** This cell contains the formula for the measure we are trying to either maximize or minimize.
- ***Constraints.*** These are one or more restrictions on the values that the decision variables are allowed to take.

In our case, the decision variables are the weights to be used in computing the weighted moving average. Hence, we specify cells C7:C9 as our changing variable cells. The objective is to minimize some measure of forecast error, such as MAD, MSE, or MAPE. Let us assume that we want to minimize the MAPE here. Cell I19 is, therefore, the objective cell.

This problem is a nonlinear program.

If we want to specify that the weights must add up to one, we must include this as a constraint in the model. The only other constraint is the nonnegativity constraint on the decision variables (weights). Recall that we can easily enforce this constraint by checking the Make Unconstrained Variable Non-Negative box in the Solver Parameters window. It is important to note that we should select GRG Nonlinear as the solving method to solve this problem because the formula for the objective function (MAPE, in this case) is *nonlinear*.

SCREENSHOT 11-3C Optimal Weights, Using Solver, for Wallace Garden Supply

	A	B	C	D	E	F	G	H	I
1	**Wallace Garden Supply**								
2	**Forecasting**		3 period weighted moving average						
3	Enter the data in the cells shaded YELLOW.								
4									
5	**Input Data**				**Forecast Error Analysis**				
6	Period	Actual value	Weights		Forecast	Error	Absolute error	Squared error	Absolute % error
7	Month 1	10	0.2218						
8	Month 2	12	0.5927						
9	Month 3	16	0.1855						
10	Month 4	13			12.298	0.702	0.702	0.492	5.40%
11	Month 5	17			14.556	2.444	2.444	5.971	14.37%
12	Month 6	19			14.407	4.593	4.593	21.093	24.17%
13	Month 7	15			16.484	-1.484	1.484	2.202	9.89%
14	Month 8	20			17.814	2.186	2.186	4.776	10.93%
15	Month 9	22			16.815	5.185	5.185	26.889	23.57%
16	Month 10	19			19.262	-0.262	0.262	0.069	1.38%
17	Month 11	21			21.000	0.000	0.000	0.000	0.00%
18	Month 12	19			20.036	-1.036	1.036	1.074	5.45%
19					**Average**		**1.988**	**6.952**	**10.57%**
20	**Next period**	**20.185**					**MAD**	**MSE**	**MAPE**
21									
22	**Sum of weights =**		**1.000**						

Optimal weights are displayed here.
Objective is to minimize MAPE.
=SUM(C7:C9)
Solver Parameters
Set Objective: $I$19
To: Max Min Value Of:
By Changing Variable Cells:
$C$7:$C$9
Subject to the Constraints:
$C$22 = 1
Changing variable cells are the weights.
Constraint specifies that weights must sum to 1.
Ensure that the non-negativity constraints are enforced. Select GRG Nonlinear as the solving method.

File: 11-3.xls, sheet: 11-3C

Screenshot 11-3C shows the Solver entries and results for the Wallace Garden Supply problem. For illustration purposes, we have chosen to include the constraint that the sum of weights must equal one. The formula to model this constraint is shown in Screenshot 11-3C.

The same weights need not minimize both MAPE and MSE.

The results indicate that MAPE decreases to 10.57% when weights of 0.185, 0.593, and 0.222 are associated with the latest period, the period before that, and two periods before that, respectively. Observe that MSE actually increases from 6.475 in Screenshot 11-3B to 6.952 in Screenshot 11-3C. That is, the weights that minimize MAPE need not necessarily minimize the MSE value also.

Exponential Smoothing

Both moving averages and weighted moving averages are effective in smoothing out sudden fluctuations in the demand pattern in order to provide stable estimates. In fact, increasing the size of k (i.e., the number of periods averaged) smoothes out fluctuations even better. However, doing so requires us to keep extensive records of past data.

Exponential smoothing *is a type of moving averages model.*

An alternate forecasting approach that is also a type of moving average technique, but requires little record keeping of past data, is called **exponential smoothing**. Let F_t denote the forecast in period t and A_t denote the actual value in period t. The basic exponential smoothing formula is as follows:

$$\text{Forecast for period}(t + 1) = \text{Forecast for period } t + \alpha \times (\text{Actual value in period } t - \text{Forecast for period } t)$$

or

$$F_{t+1} = F_t + \alpha \times (A_t - F_t) \quad \textbf{(11-9)}$$

where α is a weight (called a **smoothing constant**) that has a value between 0 and 1, inclusive. The forecast for a period is equal to the forecast for the previous period, adjusted by a fraction (specified by α) of the forecast error in the previous period. Observe that in Equation 11-9, F_t can be written as

$$F_t = F_{t-1} + \alpha \times (A_{t-1} - F_{t-1})$$

Likewise, F_{t-1} can be expressed in terms of F_{t-2} and A_{t-2}, and so on. Substituting for F_t, F_{t-1}, F_{t-2}, and so on in Equation 11-9, we can show that

$$F_{t+1} = \alpha A_t + \alpha(1 - \alpha)A_{t-1} + \alpha(1 - \alpha)^2 A_{t-2} + \alpha(1 - \alpha)^3 A_{t-3} + \cdots \quad \textbf{(11-10)}$$

That is, the forecast in period $(t + 1)$ is just a weighted average of the actual values in period t, $(t - 1)$, $(t - 2)$, and so on. Observe that the weight associated with a period's actual value decreases exponentially over time. For this reason, the term *exponential smoothing* is used to describe the technique.

The smoothing constant, α, allows managers to assign weight to recent data.

The actual value of α can be changed to give more weight to recent periods (when α is high) or more weight to past periods (when α is low). For example, when $\alpha = 1$, the forecast in period $t + 1$ is equal to the actual value in period t. That is, the entire new forecast is based just on the most recent period. When $\alpha = 0.5$, it can be shown mathematically that the new forecast is based almost entirely on values in just the past three periods. When $\alpha = 0.1$, the forecast places relatively little weight on recent periods and takes many periods of values into account.

WALLACE GARDEN SUPPLY REVISITED—PART II Suppose Wallace Garden Supply would like to forecast sales of storage sheds by using an exponential smoothing model. To get the model started, we need to know the forecast for the first period, January. In Wallace's problem, let us assume that the forecast for sales of storage sheds in January equals the actual sales that month (i.e., 10 sheds). The exponential smoothing forecast calculations are shown in Table 11.3 for $\alpha = 0.1$ and $\alpha = 0.9$. Next, we show how we can use ExcelModules to do these calculations.

USING EXCELMODULES FOR EXPONENTIAL SMOOTHING When we select the choice titled Exponential Smoothing from the Forecasting Models menu in ExcelModules (see Screenshot 11-1A on page 482), the window shown in Screenshot 11-4A is displayed. The option entries in this window are similar to those for moving averages (as we saw in Screenshot 11-2A).

WWW

File: 11-4.xls, sheet: 11-4B

When we click OK on this screen, we get the screen shown in Screenshot 11-4B on page 491. We now enter the actual shed sales for the 12 months (see Table 11.3) in cells B7:B18 and the value of α in cell B20. We use $\alpha = 0.1$ for this sample computer run. By default, ExcelModules assumes that the forecast for the first period equals the actual sales in that period (i.e., cell D7 = cell B7). In cases where this forecast is a different value, we can just type that entry in cell D7.

The worksheet now displays the exponential smoothing forecasts (shown in cells D7:D18) and the forecast for the next month (i.e., January of the next year), shown in cell B22. In addition, the following measures of forecast error are also calculated and reported: MAD (cell F19), MSE (cell G19), and MAPE (cell H19). The line graph, if asked for, is shown on a separate worksheet.

TABLE 11.3 Exponential Smoothing Forecasts for Wallace Garden Supply ($\alpha = 0.1$ and $\alpha = 0.9$)

MONTH	ACTUAL SALES	FORECAST ($\alpha = 0.1$)	$\alpha = 0.9$
January	10	10.0 (assumed value)	10.0
February	12	$10.0 + 0.1(10 - 10.0) = 10.0$	10.0
March	16	$10.0 + 0.1(12 - 10.0) = 10.2$	11.8
April	13	$10.2 + 0.1(16 - 10.2) = 10.8$	15.6
May	17	$10.8 + 0.1(13 - 10.8) = 11.0$	13.3
June	19	$11.0 + 0.1(17 - 11.0) = 11.6$	16.6
July	15	$11.6 + 0.1(19 - 11.6) = 12.3$	18.8
August	20	$12.3 + 0.1(15 - 12.3) = 12.6$	15.4
September	22	$12.6 + 0.1(20 - 12.6) = 13.4$	19.5
October	19	$13.4 + 0.1(22 - 13.4) = 14.2$	21.7
November	21	$14.2 + 0.1(19 - 14.2) = 14.7$	19.3
December	19	$14.7 + 0.1(21 - 14.7) = 15.3$	20.8

SCREENSHOT 11-4A Options Window for Exponential Smoothing Worksheet in ExcelModules

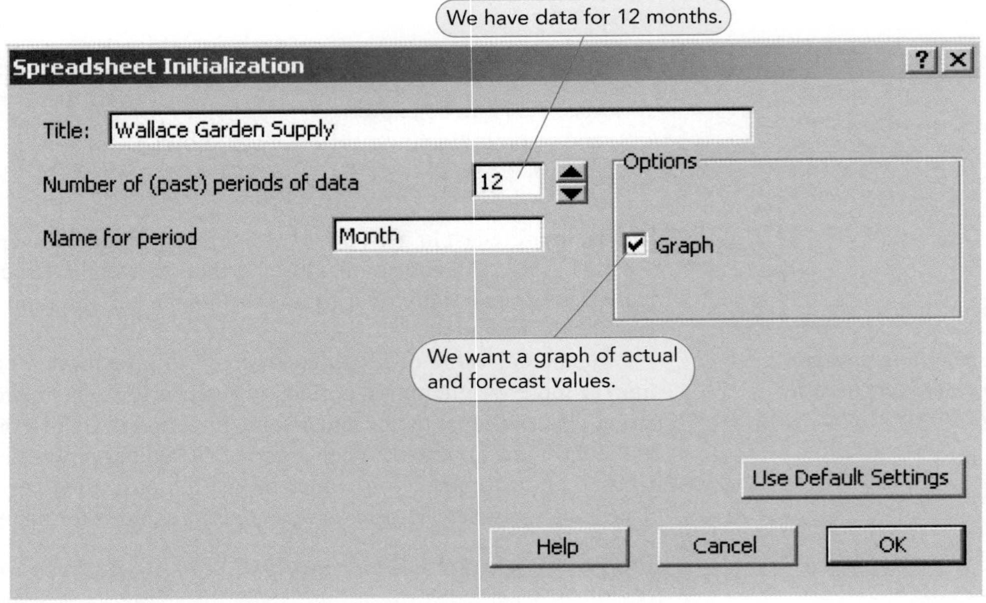

With $\alpha = 0.1$, MAPE turns out to be 28.44%. Note that all error values here have been computed using months 2 through 12, compared to earlier cases (see Screenshots 11-2B and 11-3B) where only months 4 through 12 were used.

See if you can repeat the exponential smoothing calculations for $\alpha = 0.9$ and obtain a MAPE of 17.18%.

File: 11-4.xls, sheet: 11-4C

USING SOLVER TO DETERMINE THE OPTIMAL VALUE OF α Just as we used Solver to find the optimal weights in the weighted moving average technique, we can use it to find the optimal smoothing constant in the exponential smoothing technique. The lone changing variable cell here is the value of α (cell B20, as shown in Screenshot 11-4C on page 492). The objective cell is the measure of forecast error (i.e., MAD, MSE, or MAPE) that we want to minimize. In Screenshot 11-4C, we have chosen to minimize the MAPE (cell H19). The only constraint (other than the nonnegativity constraint) is that the value of α must be less than or equal to one. Here again, the solving method selected in Solver should be GRG Nonlinear.

This nonlinear program has only one constraint.

Screenshot 11-4C shows the Solver entries and results for the Wallace Garden Supply problem. The optimal value of α turns out to be 0.419, yielding a MAPE value of 14.70%. Compare this with a MAPE of 28.44% when $\alpha = 0.1$ and a MAPE of 17.18% when $\alpha = 0.9$.

SCREENSHOT 11-4B Exponential Smoothing Model for Wallace Garden Supply, Using a Smoothing Constant of $\alpha = 0.1$

	A	B	C	D	E	F	G	H
1	**Wallace Garden Supply**							
2	**Forecasting**		Exponential smoothing					
3	Enter the data in the cells shaded YELLOW.							
4								
5	**Input Data**			**Forecast Error Analysis**				
6	Period	Actual value		Forecast	Error	Absolute error	Squared error	Absolute % error
7	Month 1	10		10.000				
8	Month 2	12		10.000	2.000	2.000	4.000	16.67%
9	Month 3	16		10.200	5.800	5.800	33.640	36.25%
10	Month 4	13		10.780	2.220	2.220	4.928	17.08%
11	Month 5	17		11.002	5.998	5.998	35.976	35.28%
12	Month 6	19		11.602	7.398	7.398	54.733	38.94%
13	Month 7	15		12.342	2.658	2.658	7.067	17.72%
14	Month 8	20		12.607	7.393	7.393	54.650	36.96%
15	Month 9	22		13.347	8.653	8.653	74.879	39.33%
16	Month 10	19		14.212	4.788	4.788	22.925	25.20%
17	Month 11	21		14.691	6.309	6.309	39.806	30.04%
18	Month 12	19		15.322	3.678	3.678	13.529	19.36%
19				**Average**		**5.172**	**31.467**	**28.44%**
20	**Alpha**	0.1				**MAD**	**MSE**	**MAPE**
21								
22	**Next period**	**15.690**						

The value of MSE is 9.842 when $\alpha = 0.419$. However, the minimum value of MSE is 8.547 and is obtained when $\alpha = 0.646$. (See if you can verify this for yourself by using Solver.) That is, the same value of α need not necessarily minimize both the MAPE and MSE measures.

IN ACTION New-Product Forecasting at Intel

When a new product is introduced, its adoption rate can be severely impacted by any production shortage. In contrast, excess inventory of the product erodes profits and wastes production capacity that could have been better used elsewhere. Since this capacity is often shared by many products, life-cycle forecasting is critical not only for demand management but also for effective operations management.

Intel's microprocessor marketing and business planning (MMBP) team is responsible for forecasting demand for critical products in the desktop, mobile, and server markets. Each month, the team generates updated 12-month demand forecasts for each active product using historical data, collective mental models, and current market news. These forecasts serve as crucial inputs to Intel's three-month production cycle, as well as to production, materials, inventory, and logistics planning activities in later months.

Working with researchers from Lehigh University, Intel's MMBP team tested a new integrated forecasting model that perpetually reduces forecast variance as new market information is acquired over time. The new method shows a 9.7 percent reduction in MAPE over the 12-month horizon on average and an impressive 33 percent reduction in the MAPE for the fourth month (which Intel views as a critical month for production planning purposes). The new process also generates the forecast in about two hours, far less than the three days needed by the old process.

Source: Based on S. D. Wu et al. "Improving New-Product Forecasting at Intel Corporation," *Interfaces* 40, 5 (September–October 2010): 385–396.

SCREENSHOT 11-4C Optimal Smoothing Constant, Using Solver, for Wallace Garden Supply

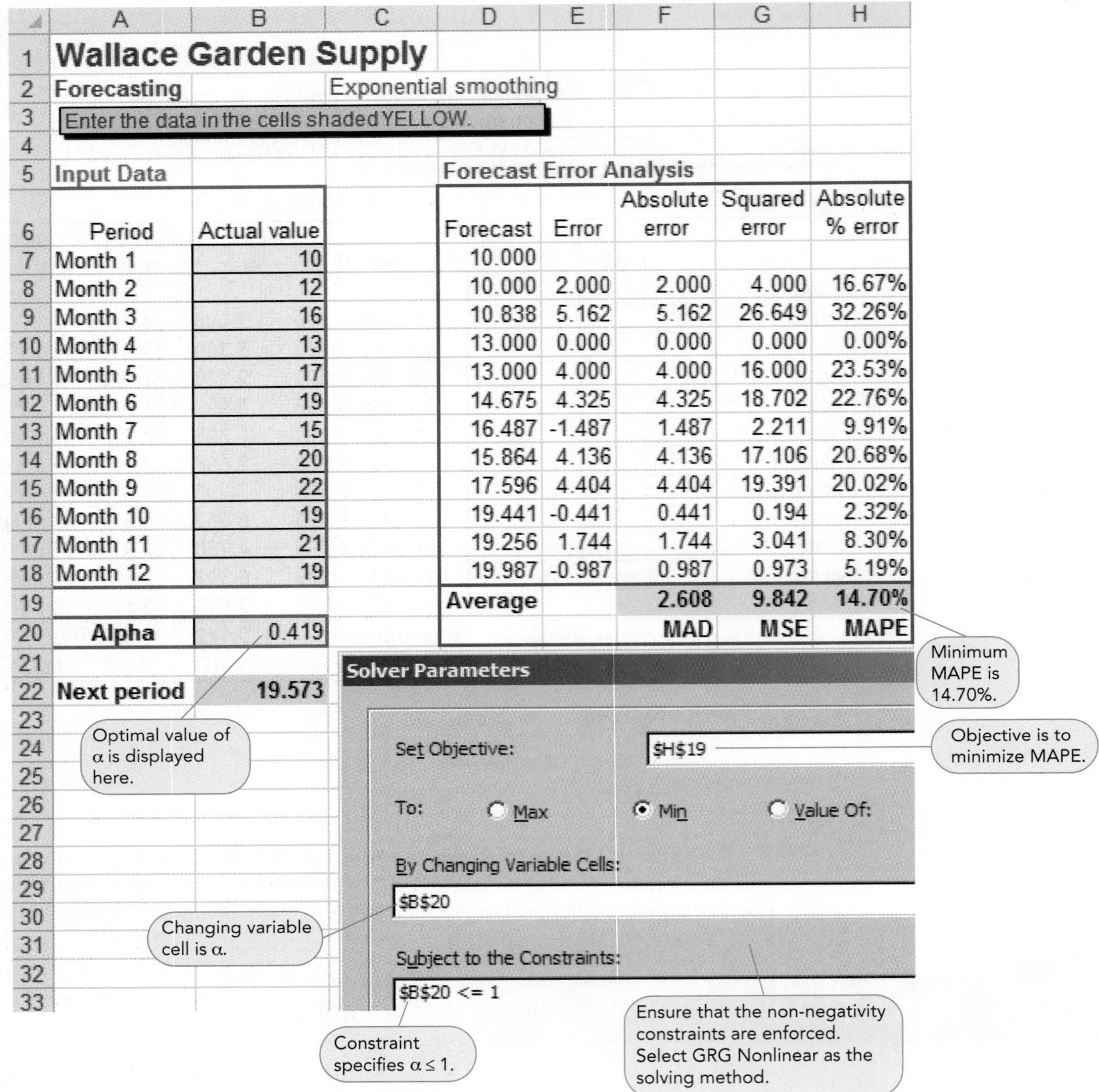

Wallace Garden Supply

Forecasting — Exponential smoothing

Enter the data in the cells shaded YELLOW.

Period	Actual value	Forecast	Error	Absolute error	Squared error	Absolute % error
Month 1	10	10.000				
Month 2	12	10.000	2.000	2.000	4.000	16.67%
Month 3	16	10.838	5.162	5.162	26.649	32.26%
Month 4	13	13.000	0.000	0.000	0.000	0.00%
Month 5	17	13.000	4.000	4.000	16.000	23.53%
Month 6	19	14.675	4.325	4.325	18.702	22.76%
Month 7	15	16.487	-1.487	1.487	2.211	9.91%
Month 8	20	15.864	4.136	4.136	17.106	20.68%
Month 9	22	17.596	4.404	4.404	19.391	20.02%
Month 10	19	19.441	-0.441	0.441	0.194	2.32%
Month 11	21	19.256	1.744	1.744	3.041	8.30%
Month 12	19	19.987	-0.987	0.987	0.973	5.19%
		Average		2.608	9.842	14.70%
				MAD	MSE	MAPE

Alpha	0.419
Next period	19.573

11.6 Trend and Seasonality in Time-Series Data

Linear trend analysis fits a straight line to time-series data.

Although moving average models smooth out fluctuations in a time series, they are not very good at picking up trends in data. Likewise, they are not very good at detecting seasonal variations in data. In this section, we discuss how trend and seasonal variations can be detected and analyzed in time-series data. Here again, although we show the equations needed to compute the forecasts for each model, we use worksheets (included in ExcelModules) to actually calculate these values.

Linear Trend Analysis

The *trend analysis* technique fits a trend equation (or curve) to a series of historical data points. It then projects the curve into the future for medium- and long-term forecasts. Several mathematical trend equations can be developed (e.g., linear, exponential, quadratic equations). However,

TABLE 11.4 Demand at Midwestern Electric

YEAR	DEMAND
2002	64
2003	68
2004	72
2005	74
2006	79
2007	80
2008	90
2009	105
2010	142
2011	122

in this section, we discuss only linear trends. In other words, the mathematical trend equation we develop will be a straight line.

MIDWESTERN ELECTRIC COMPANY EXAMPLE Let us consider the case of Midwestern Electric Company. The firm's demand for electrical generators over the period 2002–2011 is shown in Table 11.4.

The goal here is to identify a straight line that describes the relationship between demand for generators and time. The variable to be forecasted or predicted (demand, in this case) is called the **dependent variable** and is denoted by Y. The variable used in the prediction (year, in this case) is called the **independent variable**, and is denoted by X.

Scatter Chart

A scatter chart helps obtain ideas about a relationship.

To quickly get an idea whether any relationship exists between two variables, a **scatter chart** (also called a scatter diagram or plot) can be drawn on a two-dimensional graph. The independent variable (e.g., time) is usually measured on the horizontal (X) axis, and the dependent variable (e.g., demand) is usually measured on the vertical (Y) axis.

SCATTER CHART USING EXCEL Although we can draw a scatter chart by using ExcelModules (discussed shortly), we can also use Excel's built-in charting capabilities to draw such charts. The input data for Midwestern Electric's problem is shown in Screenshot 11-5A. The steps for creating a scatter chart in Excel are as follows:

File: 11-5.xls

1. Enter the time (year) and demand data in two columns (preferably adjacent, with the year in the first column), as shown in Screenshot 11-5A.
2. Highlight the two columns of data (i.e., cells A3:B12). Select the Insert tab in Excel's Ribbon and then select the desired option among the different Scatter charts that are available (see Screenshot 11-5A). Excel will immediately draw the selected scatter chart using

SCREENSHOT 11-5A Creating a Scatter Chart in Excel

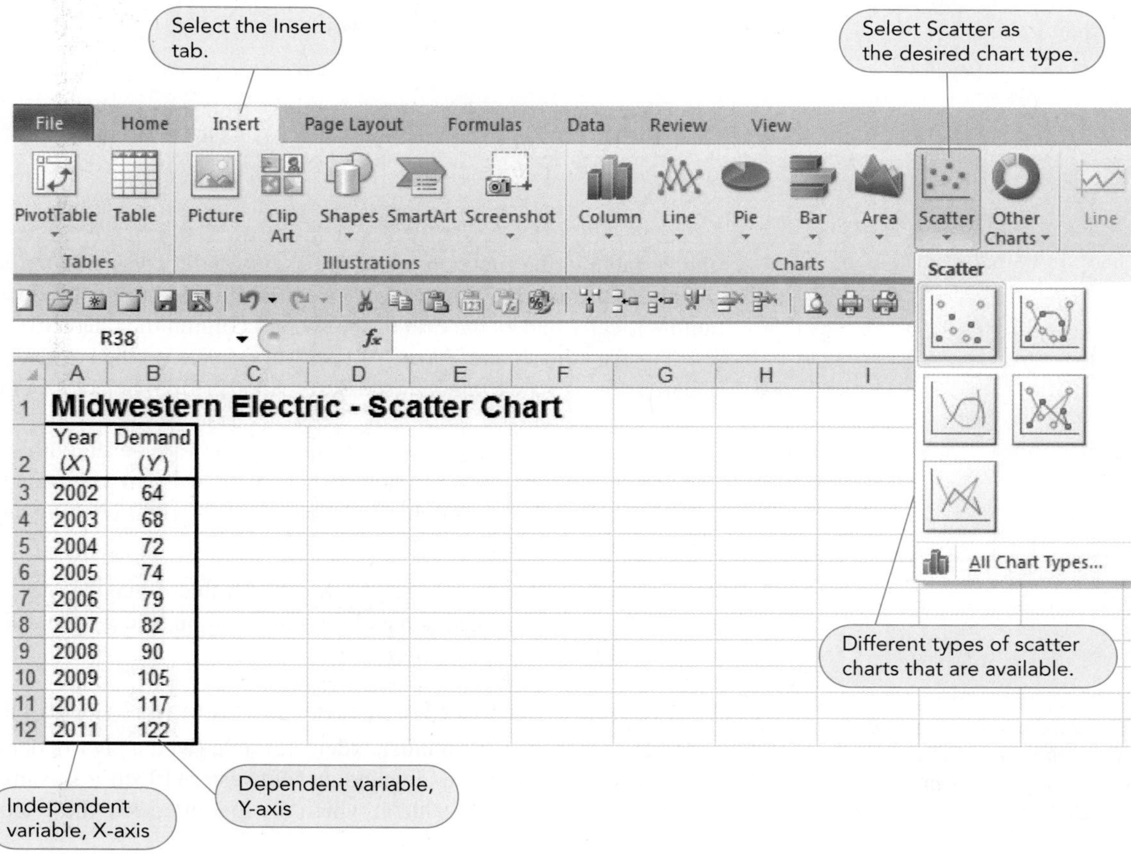

SCREENSHOT 11-5B Scatter Chart for Midwestern Electric

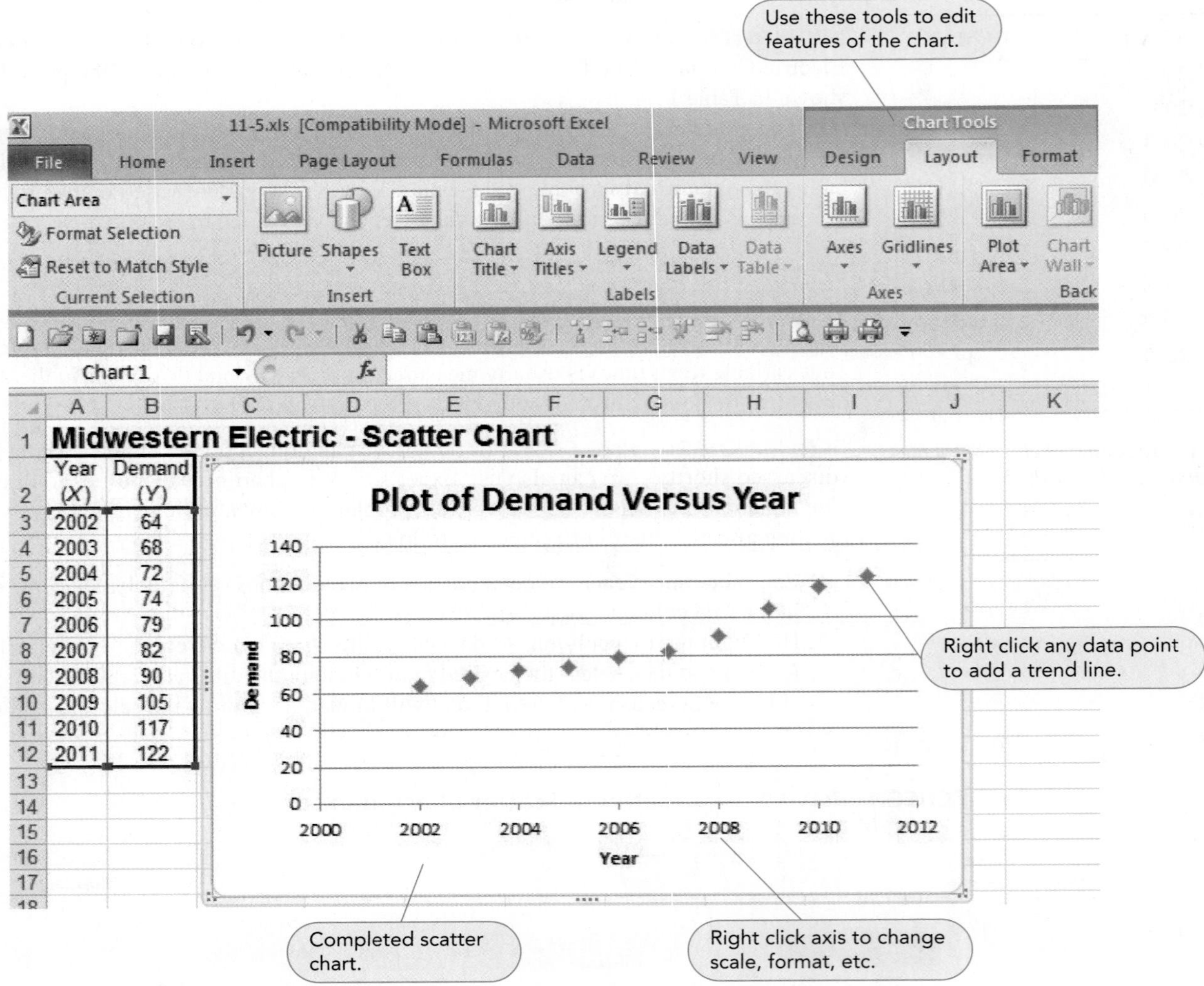

the variable in the first column as the X-axis and the variable in the second column as the Y-axis. If the column titles (row 2) were highlighted prior to selecting the chart, Excel automatically makes the title of the second column the chart title.

To swap the X- and Y-axes (if necessary), click on the scatter chart. A new tab titled Chart Tools is now available (see Screenshot 11-5B). Select Design and then select Switch Row/Column.

3. To further customize the scatter chart, select the Layout tab within Chart Tools to reveal the various options shown in Screenshot 11-5B. Also, if you want to display a linear trend line directly on the scatter chart, you can do so by right-clicking any of the data points on the chart and selecting the option Add Trendline.

It appears from the chart in Screenshot 11-5B that it may be reasonable to approximate the relationship between time and demand for generators in Midwestern Electric's problem by using a linear trend line.

Least-Squares Procedure for Developing a Linear Trend Line

The slope of a linear trend line is the average change in Y *for a unit increase in the value of time* (X).

A linear trend line between an independent variable (which always denotes time in a trend analysis) and a dependent variable (demand, in Midwestern Electric's example) is described in terms of its Y-intercept (i.e., the Y value at which the line intersects the Y-axis) and its slope (i.e., the angle of the line). The slope of a linear trend line can be interpreted as the average change in Y for a unit increase in the value of time (X). The line can be expressed by using the following equation:

$$\hat{Y} = b_0 + b_1 X \qquad \textbf{(11-11)}$$

where

$\hat{Y}$ = forecasted average value of the dependent variable (demand) (pronounced "Y-hat")

X = value of the independent variable (time)

b_0 = Y- intercept of the line, based on the current sample

b_1 = slope of the line, based on the current sample

Note that we refer to $\hat{Y}$ as the forecasted *average* value because it is, in fact, the average (or expected value) of a probability distribution of possible values of Y for a given value of X.

To develop a linear trend line between Y and X, there are essentially an infinite number of values that we could assign to b_0 and b_1. Therefore, we cannot determine the best values for b_0 and b_1 either by eyeballing the scatter chart or by manually trying out different values. Note that we want to find values of b_0 and b_1 that make the forecasted demand (estimated from the trend line) for a specific year as close as possible to the actual demand that year. For example, if we had used the linear trend line to forecast demand for 2011, we would have wanted its forecast to be as close to 122 as possible. To achieve this objective, we use a precise statistical method known as the **least-squares procedure**. The goal of this procedure is to identify the linear trend line that minimizes the sum of the squares of the vertical differences from the line to each of the actual observations. That is, it minimizes the sum of the squared errors between the forecasted and actual values. Figure 11.3 illustrates the error terms.

The least-squares method finds a straight line that minimizes the sum of the vertical differences from the line to each of the data points.

Mathematically, we can express the least-squares procedure as follows: Find the values of b_0 and b_1 that minimizes the sum of squared errors (SSE), defined as

$$SSE = \sum_{i=1}^{n}(Y_i - \hat{Y}_i)^2 = \sum_{i=1}^{n}[\,Y_i - (b_0 + b_1 X_i)\,]^2 \qquad \textbf{(11-12)}$$

where n = number of observations (10, in Midwestern Electric's example).

FIGURE 11.3
Least-Squares Method for Finding the Best-Fitting Straight Line

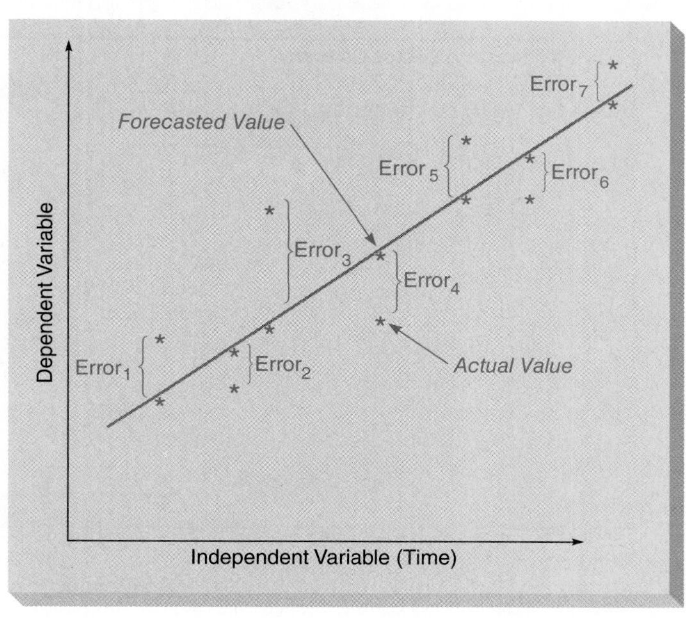

We need to solve for the Y-intercept and the slope to find the equation of the least-squares line.

We can use calculus to solve Equation 11-12 and develop the following equations to compute the values of b_0 and b_1 and minimize SSE:[1]

$$b_1 = \frac{\sum XY - n\overline{XY}}{\sum X^2 - n\overline{X}^2} \tag{11-13}$$

and

$$b_0 = \overline{Y} - b_1\overline{X} \tag{11-14}$$

where

$\overline{X}$ = average of the values of the Xs

$\overline{Y}$ = average of the values of the Ys

Even though the formulas for b_0 and b_1 may look somewhat cumbersome, they are fairly easy to use. In fact, most handheld calculators today have built-in functions to compute these values for a given data set. Of course, in keeping with our focus on using spreadsheets in this textbook, we will use Excel for these computations. There are two approaches available in Excel for this purpose:

- *Least-squares procedure using ExcelModules.* We will discuss this approach in the following pages.
- *Least-squares procedure using Excel's Analysis ToolPak add-in.* We will discuss this approach in detail in section 11.8.

TRANSFORMING TIME VALUES Recall that the independent variable X in linear trend analysis always denotes time. Depending on the manner in which this time is measured, the independent variable can be stated in months, such as January, February, etc., or in years, such as 2002, 2003, etc. (as in Midwestern Electric's example). Hence, in order to facilitate the trend line computations, we may need to transform the time values to a simpler numeric scheme. In the case of Midwestern Electric's data, a convenient way to do so would be to code the year 2002 as $X = 1$, the year 2003 as $X = 2$, and so on.

USING EXCELMODULES FOR LINEAR TREND ANALYSIS Equations 11-13 and 11-14 have been coded in ExcelModules, along with formulas for computing the usual measures of forecast error. To run these computations, we select the choice titled Linear Trend Analysis from the Forecasting Models menu in ExcelModules (see Screenshot 11-1A on page 482). The window shown in Screenshot 11-6A is displayed. The option entries in this window are similar to those

SCREENSHOT 11-6A Options Window for Linear Trend Analysis Worksheet in ExcelModules

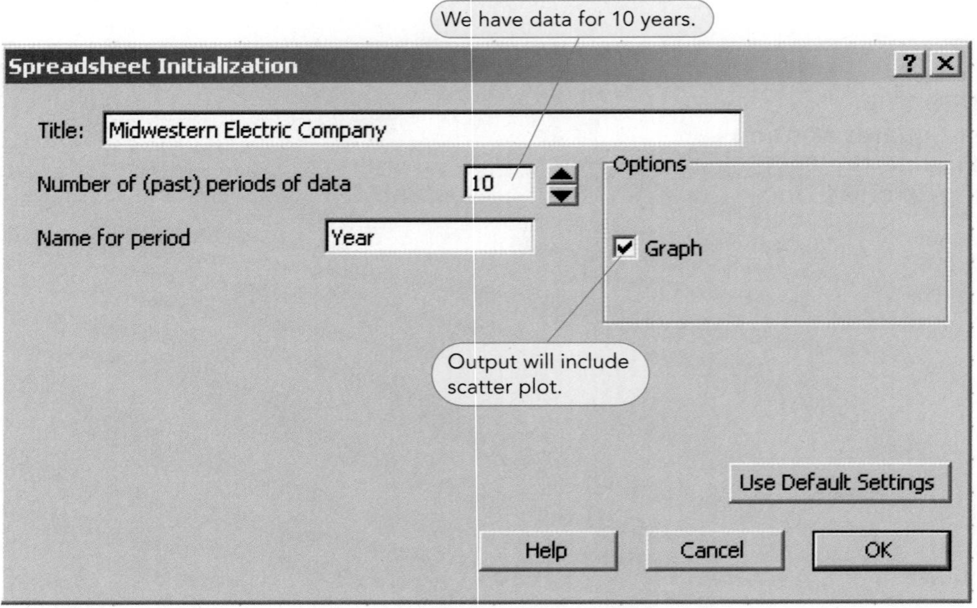

[1] Essentially, we take the first derivative of Equation 11-12 with respect to b_0 and b_1, set both equations equal to zero, and solve for b_0 and b_1. See a statistics textbook such as D. F. Groebner, P. W. Shannon, P. C. Fry, and K. D. Smith. *Business Statistics*, 8th ed. Upper Saddle River, NJ: Prentice Hall, 2011, for more details.

SCREENSHOT 11-6B Linear Trend Analysis Model for Midwestern Electric

	A	B	C	D	E	F	G	H	I
1	**Midwestern Electric Company**								
2	**Forecasting**		Linear trend analysis						
3	Enter the actual values in cells shaded YELLOW. Enter new time period at the bottom to forecast Y.								
4									
5	**Input Data**				**Forecast Error Analysis**				
6	Period	Actual value (or) Y	Period number (or) X		Forecast	Error	Absolute error	Squared error	Absolute % error
7	Year 2002	64	1		57.818	6.182	6.182	38.215	9.66%
8	Year 2003	68	2		64.370	3.630	3.630	13.179	5.34%
9	Year 2004	72	3		70.921	1.079	1.079	1.164	1.50%
10	Year 2005	74	4		77.473	-3.473	3.473	12.060	4.69%
11	Year 2006	79	5		84.024	-5.024	5.024	25.243	6.36%
12	Year 2007	82	6		90.576	-8.576	8.576	73.544	10.46%
13	Year 2008	90	7		97.127	-7.127	7.127	50.798	7.92%
14	Year 2009	105	8		103.679	1.321	1.321	1.746	1.26%
15	Year 2010	117	9		110.230	6.770	6.770	45.829	5.79%
16	Year 2011	122	10		116.782	5.218	5.218	27.229	4.28%
17					**Average**		**4.840**	**28.901**	**5.72%**
18	Intercept	**51.267**					**MAD**	**MSE**	**MAPE**
19	Slope	**6.552**							
20									
21	**Next period**	123.333	11						

Callouts: Forecasts are computed using the trend equation. / Trend equation coefficients / Measures of forecast error / Forecast for 2012 / Input value of X = 11 corresponds to year 2012.

for moving averages (as we saw in Screenshot 11-2A on page 483). Note that if we check Graph in the options shown in Screenshot 11-6A, ExcelModules will automatically draw a scatter chart, along with the linear trend line, as part of the output.

When we click OK on this screen, we get the screen shown in Screenshot 11-6B. We now enter the actual demand for generators in 2002 to 2011 (refer to Table 11.4 on page 493) in cells B7:B16 (Y values). The corresponding values for the time periods (X) are automatically input by ExcelModules in cells C7:C16. We also enter the time period for the forecast needed ($X = 11$, corresponding to the year 2012) in cell C21. Finally, if desired, we can enter the actual names of the periods (i.e., the years 2002 to 2011) in cells A7:A16.

File: 11-6.xls, sheet: 11-6B

The worksheet now computes and reports the values of b_0 and b_1 (shown in cells B18 and B19, respectively, in Screenshot 11-6B) for the least-squares linear trend line between time and demand. In Midwestern Electric's case, the equation of this relationship is

$$\text{Forecasted demand} = 51.267 + 6.552 \times \text{year}$$

Based on this equation, demand forecasts for 2002 through 2011 are displayed in cells E7:E16. The forecast for 2012 (i.e., time $X = 11$) is shown in cell B21 to be 123 generators (rounded). In addition, the following measures of forecast error are also calculated and reported: MAD (cell G17), MSE (cell H17), and MAPE (cell I17).

File: 11-6.xls, sheet: 11-6C

If specified in the options (see Screenshot 11-6A), ExcelModules shows the scatter chart between X and Y on a separate worksheet, along with the least-squares linear trend line. We show this chart in Screenshot 11-6C. We can compare the chart of actual demand values and the trend line to check the validity of the trend line model. In Midwestern Electric's case, the linear trend line seems to approximate the demand values reasonably well. The relatively low MAPE value of 5.72% also supports this conclusion.

Seasonality Analysis

Seasonal variations occur annually.

Time-series forecasting such as that in the example of Midwestern Electric involves looking at the *trend* of data over a series of time observations. Sometimes, however, recurring variations at certain periods (i.e., months) of the year make a seasonal adjustment in the time-series

SCREENSHOT 11-6C Chart of Linear Trend Analysis Forecast for Midwestern Electric

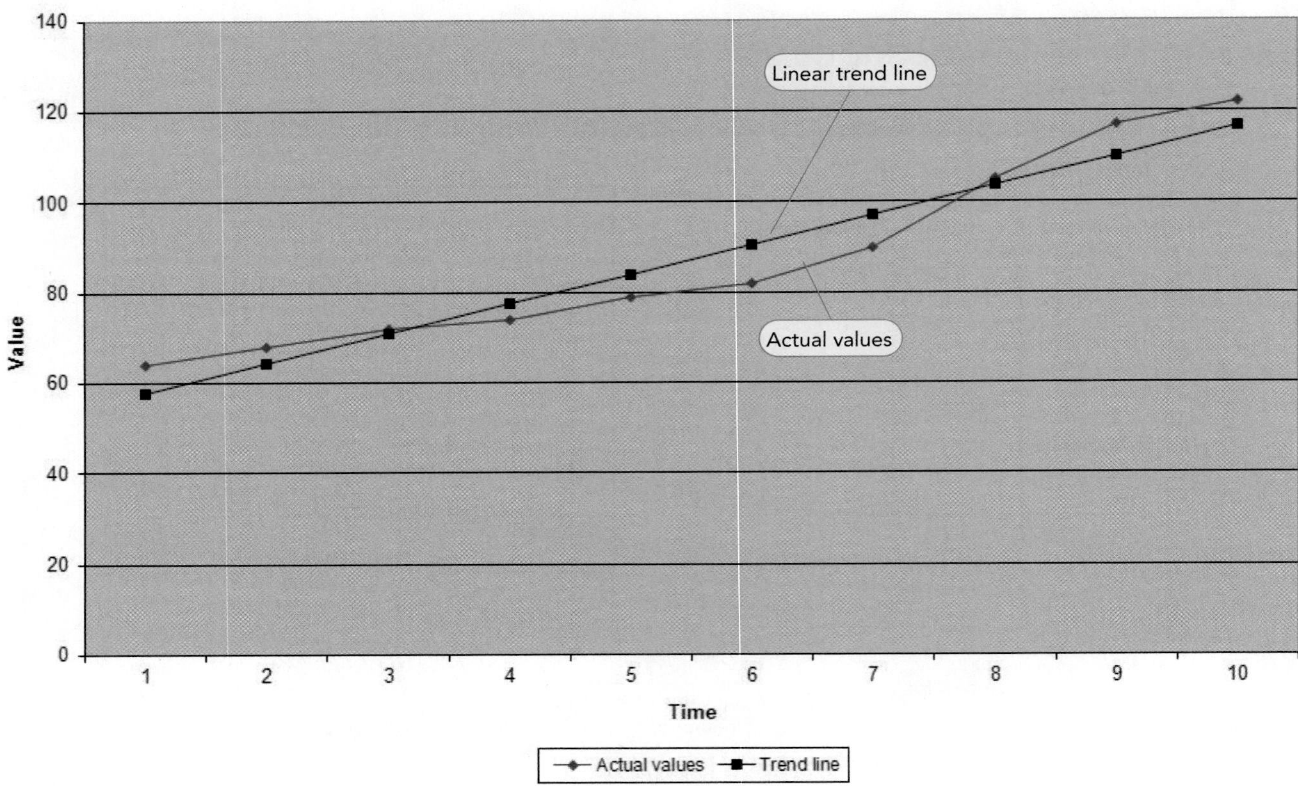

forecast necessary. Demand for coal and oil fuel, for example, usually peaks during cold winter months. Demand for golfing equipment and sunscreen may be highest in summer.

Analyzing time-series data in monthly or quarterly terms usually makes it easy to spot seasonal patterns. A seasonal *index*, which can be defined as the ratio of the average value of the item in a season to the overall annual average value, can then be computed for each season.

Several methods are available for computing seasonal indices. One such method, which bases these indices on the *average* value of the item over all periods (e.g., months, quarters) is illustrated in the following example. A different method, which uses a concept called *centered moving average* to compute seasonal indices, is illustrated in section 11.7.

File: 11-7.xls

EICHLER SUPPLIES EXAMPLE Monthly demands of a brand of telephone answering machines at Eichler Supplies are shown in cells C3:C26 of Screenshot 11-7 for the two most recent years.

To compute the monthly seasonal indices, using the average demand value over the two years, we can create an Excel worksheet, as follows:

1. *Column D.* Compute the average monthly demand, using all the available data. In Eichler's case, we do this by taking the average of the demand values for all 24 months. The formula is =AVERAGE(C3:C26).
2. *Column E.* Compute the seasonal ratio for each month by dividing the actual demand that month by the average demand (i.e., column E = column C/column D). For example, the seasonal ratio for January of year 1 is $80/94 = 0.851$.
3. *Column F.* Observe that because we have two years of time-series data, we have two seasonal ratios for each month. For example, January has ratios of 0.851 and 1.064, as shown in cells E3 and E15, respectively. We compute the seasonal index for January as the average of these two ratios. Hence, the seasonal index for January is equal to $(0.851 + 1.064)/2 = 0.957$. Similar computations for all 12 months of the year are shown in column F of Screenshot 11-7.

A seasonal index with value below 1 indicates that demand is below average that month, and an index with value above 1 indicates that demand is above average that month. Using these

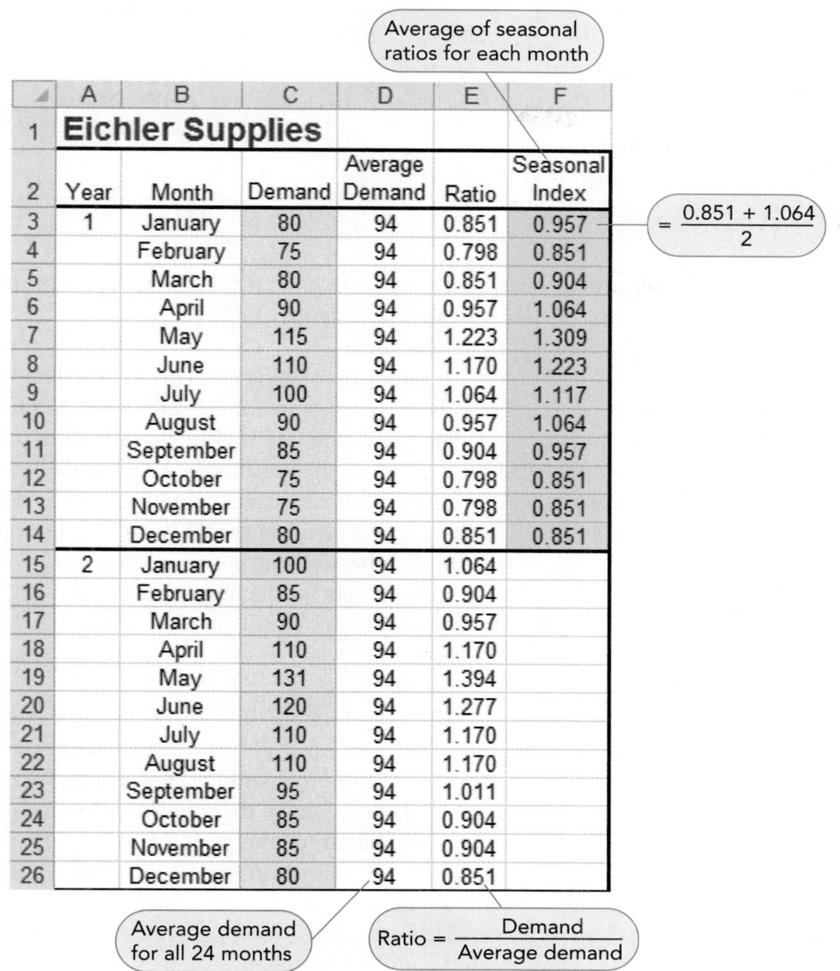

	A	B	C	D	E	F
1	Eichler Supplies					
2	Year	Month	Demand	Average Demand	Ratio	Seasonal Index
3	1	January	80	94	0.851	0.957
4		February	75	94	0.798	0.851
5		March	80	94	0.851	0.904
6		April	90	94	0.957	1.064
7		May	115	94	1.223	1.309
8		June	110	94	1.170	1.223
9		July	100	94	1.064	1.117
10		August	90	94	0.957	1.064
11		September	85	94	0.904	0.957
12		October	75	94	0.798	0.851
13		November	75	94	0.798	0.851
14		December	80	94	0.851	0.851
15	2	January	100	94	1.064	
16		February	85	94	0.904	
17		March	90	94	0.957	
18		April	110	94	1.170	
19		May	131	94	1.394	
20		June	120	94	1.277	
21		July	110	94	1.170	
22		August	110	94	1.170	
23		September	95	94	1.011	
24		October	85	94	0.904	
25		November	85	94	0.904	
26		December	80	94	0.851	

SCREENSHOT 11-7 Computation of Seasonal Indices for Eichler Supplies

seasonal indices, we can adjust the monthly demand for any future month appropriately. For example, if we expect the third year's average demand for answering machines to be 100 units per month, we can forecast January's monthly demand as $100 \times 0.957 \approx 96$ units, which is below average. Likewise, we can forecast May's monthly demand as $100 \times 1.309 \approx 131$ units, which is above average.

11.7 Decomposition of a Time Series

Decomposition breaks down a time series into its components.

Now that we have analyzed both trend and seasonality, we can combine these two issues to decompose time-series data. Recall from section 11.5 that a time series is composed of four components: trend, seasonality, cycles, and random variations. Recall also that we defined two types of time-series decomposition models in that section: (1) multiplicative models and (2) additive models. In this section, we use an example to illustrate how we can use a multiplicative decomposition model to break down a time series into two components: (1) a seasonal component and (2) a combination of the trend and cycle components (we refer to this combined component simply as *trend*). In Solved Problem 11-4 at the end of this chapter, we use the same example to illustrate how an additive decomposition model would break down the data. As discussed earlier, it is not possible to discern the random component in any decomposition model.

Multiplicative Decomposition Example: Sawyer Piano House

Sandy Sawyer's family has been in the piano business for three generations. The Sawyers stock and sell a wide range of pianos, from console pianos to grand pianos. Sandy's father, who currently runs the business, forecasts sales for different types of pianos each year by using his experience. Although his forecasts have been reasonably good, Sandy (who has recently completed

TABLE 11.5
Sales of Grand Pianos at Sawyer Piano House

	2007	2008	2009	2010	2011
Quarter 1	4	6	10	12	18
Quarter 2	2	4	3	9	10
Quarter 3	1	4	5	7	13
Quarter 4	5	14	16	22	35

her undergraduate degree in management) is highly skeptical of such a seat-of-the-pants approach. She feels confident that she can develop a quantitative model that will do a much better job of forecasting piano sales.

To convince her father that she is correct, Sandy decides to develop a model to forecast sales for grand pianos. She hopes to show him how good the model could be in capturing patterns in past sales. For this purpose, she collects sales data for the past five years, broken down by quarters each year. That is, she collects data for the past 20 quarters, as shown in Table 11.5. Because sales of grand pianos are seasonal and there has been an upward trend in sales each year, Sandy believes a decomposition model would be appropriate here. More specifically, she decides to use a multiplicative decomposition model.

Although the computations for decomposing a time series using a multiplicative model are fairly simple, we illustrate them by using an Excel worksheet that is included for this purpose in ExcelModules.

Using ExcelModules for Multiplicative Decomposition

When we select the choice titled Multiplicative Decomposition from the Forecasting Models menu in ExcelModules (see Screenshot 11-1A on page 482), the window shown in Screenshot 11-8A is displayed. We specify the number of periods for which we have past data (20, in Sandy's example), the name for the period (Quarter, because we have quarterly data), and the number of seasons each year (4, in Sandy's example). In addition, we see an option for the procedure to use in computing the seasonal indices.

The Average ALL Data option uses the procedure discussed in section 11.6 to compute the seasonal indices. In Sandy's example, this implies that we would first compute the average sales

SCREENSHOT 11-8A Options Window for Multiplicative Decomposition Worksheet in ExcelModules

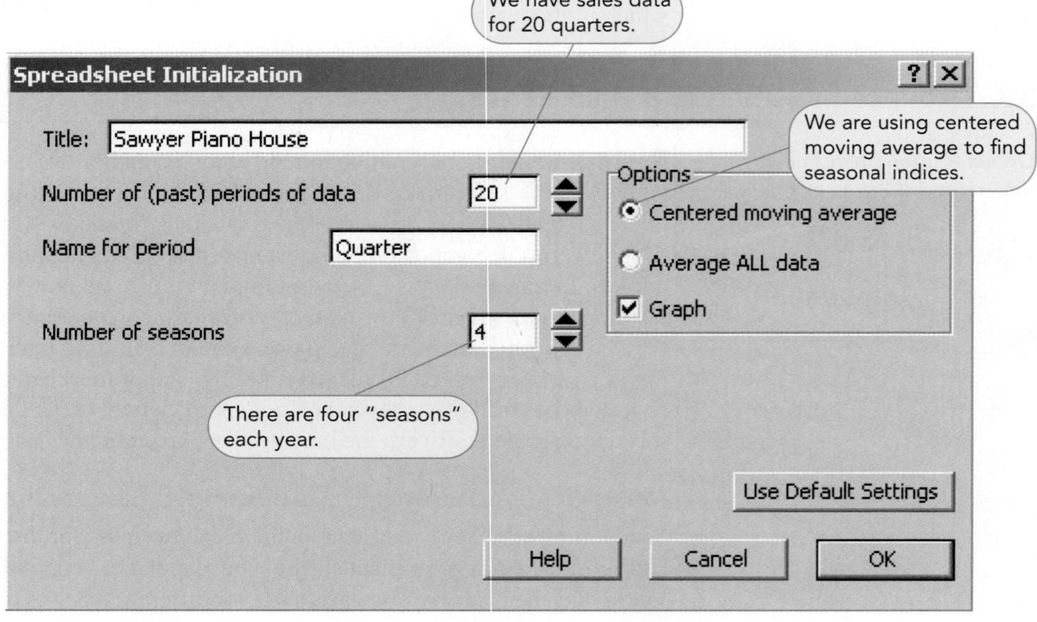

for all 20 quarters for which we have data. We would then divide the sales each quarter by the average sales to compute that quarter's seasonal ratio. Note that this will yield five ratios for each quarter (one for each year). Finally, we would average the five ratios for each quarter to compute that quarter's seasonal index.

The centered moving average approach helps smooth out fluctuations in the data.

The Centered Moving Average option uses a slightly more complicated procedure to compute the seasonal indices. Recall from section 11.5 that moving averages smooth out fluctuations in a time series. Hence, using this option could help us obtain more precise estimates of the seasonal indices. In the following pages, we illustrate this procedure for computing seasonal indices, using Sandy's example.

File: 11-8.xls, sheet: 11-8B

When we click OK on the screen in Screenshot 11-8A, we get the screen shown in Screenshot 11-8B. We now enter the actual pianos sold during the past 20 quarters (see Table 11.5) in cells B7:B26. The corresponding time periods (i.e., the X variable values) are automatically specified in cells C7:C26 by the worksheet.

The worksheet now displays the results shown in Screenshot 11-8B. The calculations are as follows:

We compute the seasonal indices first.

1. *Computation of the seasonal indices, columns D–G.* First we compute the seasonal indices:
   - In column D, we first smooth out fluctuations in each quarter's sales data by computing the moving average sales for k quarters, centered on that quarter. Because there are four seasons (quarters) in Sandy's time-series data, we use $k = 4$ here. Then, in cell D9 (for example), we compute the average sales for four quarters, where these four quarters are centered on the third quarter of year 1 (i.e., quarter number 3). *Note:* In cases in which k is even (such as here, in which $k = 4$), it is not possible to directly center k quarters of data around a quarter. We therefore modify the computations as follows (e.g., when $k = 4$):

$$\begin{aligned}\text{Centered average for quarter } t = \big[&0.5 \times \text{Sales in quarter } (t-2)\\ &+ \text{Sales in quarter } (t-1) + \text{Sales in quarter } t\\ &+ \text{Sales in quarter } (t+1) + 0.5 \times \text{Sales in quarter } (t+2)\big]/4\end{aligned}$$

   - Next, we compute the seasonal ratio for each quarter by dividing the actual sales (column B) in that quarter by its centered average (column D). That is, column E = column B/column D.
   - The seasonal ratios for each quarter (five for each quarter, in Sandy's case) are collected in cells B33:E37. The seasonal index for each quarter is computed as the average of all the ratios for that quarter. These seasonal indices are shown in cells B38:E38 and repeated in column F, next to the appropriate quarters each year.
   - Finally, in column G, we compute the unseasonalized sales in each quarter as the actual sales (column B) in that quarter divided by the seasonal index (column F) for that quarter. That is, column G = column B/column F.

The seasonalized time-series data are converted to unseasonalized data.

We then compute the linear trend equation.

2. *Computation of the trend equation.* Now that we have the unseasonalized sales data, we can analyze the trend. Because the purpose of the linear trend equation is to minimize the least-squares error (as shown in section 11.6), it is important to remove the seasonal effects from the data before we develop the trend line. Otherwise, the presence of seasonal variations may severely affect the linear trend equation.

   Using the unseasonalized sales in column G as the dependent variable (Y) and the time period number in column C as the independent variable (X), we compute the linear trend equation. The resulting Y-intercept (a) and slope (b) for this straight line are shown in cells G28 and G29, respectively. In Sandy's case, the linear trend equation is

$$\text{Unseasonalized sales forecast} = -0.365 + 1.023 \times \text{Quarter number}$$

3. *Computation of forecast, columns H and I.* The forecast is now calculated as the product of the composite trend and seasonality components. The computations are as follows:

We now compute the forecasts.

   - In column H, we use the trend equation to compute the unseasonalized forecast for each quarter. For example, for the fourth quarter of year 2 (i.e., quarter number 8), this value is computed in cell H14 as $[-0.365 + 1.023 \times 8] = 7.816$. These values are also computed for the next year (i.e., quarters 21 to 24, denoting the four quarters in year 2012) in cells B42:B45.

SCREENSHOT 11-8B Multiplicative Decomposition Model for Sawyer Piano House

= Actual value / Centered moving average

= Actual value / Seasonal index

	A	B	C	D	E	F	G	H	I	J	K	L	M
1	**Sawyer Piano House**												
2	**Forecasting**		Multiplicative decomposition										
3	4 seasons		Enter the actual values in the cells shaded YELLOW. Do not change the time period numbers!										
4													
5	**Input Data**			**Seasonal Index Computation**				**Forecast Error analysis**					
6	Period	Actual value (Y)	Time period (X)	Centered average	Seasonal ratio	Seasonal index	Unseasonalized value	Unseasonalized Forecast	Seasonalized Forecast	Error	Absolute error	Squared error	Absolute % error
7	Quarter 1	4	1			1.239	3.227	0.658	0.815	3.185	3.185	10.144	79.62%
8	Quarter 2	2	2			0.596	3.353	1.680	1.002	0.998	0.998	0.996	49.89%
9	Quarter 3	1	3	3.250	0.308	0.485	2.061	2.703	1.311	-0.311	0.311	0.097	31.13%
10	Quarter 4	5	4	3.750	1.333	1.577	3.170	3.725	5.876	-0.876	0.876	0.768	17.53%
11	Quarter 5	6	5	4.375	1.371	1.239	4.841	4.748	5.884	0.116	0.116	0.013	1.93%
12	Quarter 6	4	6	5.875	0.681	0.596	6.706	5.770	3.442	0.558	0.558	0.311	13.95%
13	Quarter 7	4	7	7.500	0.533	0.485	8.244	6.793	3.296	0.704	0.704	0.496	17.60%
14	Quarter 8	14	8	7.875	1.778	1.577	8.875	7.816	12.328	1.672	1.672	2.795	11.94%
15	Quarter 9	10	9	7.875	1.270	1.239	8.069	8.838	10.954	-0.954	0.954	0.910	9.54%
16	Quarter 10	3	10	8.250	0.364	0.596	5.029	9.861	5.882	-2.882	2.882	8.305	96.06%
17	Quarter 11	5	11	8.750	0.571	0.485	10.305	10.883	5.280	-0.280	0.280	0.079	5.61%
18	Quarter 12	16	12	9.750	1.641	1.577	10.143	11.906	18.780	-2.780	2.780	7.730	17.38%
19	Quarter 13	12	13	10.750	1.116	1.239	9.682	12.928	16.023	-4.023	4.023	16.186	33.53%
20	Quarter 14	9	14	11.750	0.766	0.596	15.088	13.951	8.322	0.678	0.678	0.460	7.54%
21	Quarter 15	7	15	13.250	0.528	0.485	14.427	14.973	7.265	-0.265	0.265	0.070	3.78%
22	Quarter 16	22	16	14.125	1.558	1.577	13.947	15.996	25.232	-3.232	3.232	10.447	14.69%
23	Quarter 17	18	17	15.000	1.200	1.239	14.523	17.019	21.093	-3.093	3.093	9.564	17.18%
24	Quarter 18	10	18	17.375	0.576	0.596	16.765	18.041	10.761	-0.761	0.761	0.580	7.61%
25	Quarter 19	13	19			0.485	26.794	19.064	9.249	3.751	3.751	14.067	28.85%
26	Quarter 20	35	20			1.577	22.188	20.086	31.684	3.316	3.316	10.994	9.47%
27									**Average**		**1.722**	**4.751**	**23.74%**
28						**Intercept**	**-0.365**				**MAD**	**MSE**	**MAPE**
29						**Slope**	**1.023**						

Input data for 20 quarters.

Regression (trend line) parameters

Measures of forecast error

	A	B	C	D	E
30					
31	**Seasonal Ratios**				
32		Season 1	Season 2	Season 3	Season 4
33				0.308	1.333
34		1.371	0.681	0.533	1.778
35		1.270	0.364	0.571	1.641
36		1.116	0.766	0.528	1.558
37		1.200	0.576		
38	**Average**	1.239	0.596	0.485	1.577
39					
40	**Forecasts for future periods**				
41	Period	Unseasonalized forecast	Seasonal index	Seasonalized forecast	
42	21.000	21.109	1.239	**26.162**	
43	22.000	22.131	0.596	**13.201**	
44	23.000	23.154	0.485	**11.234**	
45	24.000	24.176	1.577	**38.136**	

Seasonal ratios in column E have been collected here.

Seasonal indices, also shown in column F

Forecast using trend equation

Forecasts multiplied by seasonal index

We seasonalize the forecasts.

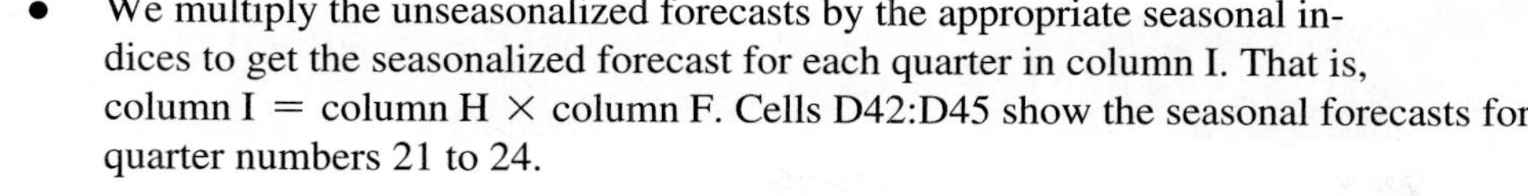

- We multiply the unseasonalized forecasts by the appropriate seasonal indices to get the seasonalized forecast for each quarter in column I. That is, column I = column H × column F. Cells D42:D45 show the seasonal forecasts for quarter numbers 21 to 24.

Finally, we compute measures of forecast error.

4. *Computation of forecast error measures, columns J through M.* As with all the other forecasting models in ExcelModules discussed so far, we compute the forecast error (i.e., Actual value – Forecast value) in column J, the absolute error in column K, the squared error in column L, and the absolute percentage error in column M for each quarter. We then use these error values to compute the MAD (cell K27), MSE (cell L27), and MAPE (cell M27) values.

File: 11-8.xls, sheet: 11-8C

USING CHARTS TO CHECK THE VALIDITY OF THE MODEL How good is Sandy's multiplicative decomposition model at forecasting piano sales? One approach, of course, is to use the measures of forecasting error we have computed as indicators. As discussed earlier, however, these measures are difficult to interpret by themselves and are better suited for purposes of comparing different models. An alternative approach is to draw line charts of the actual and forecast values (columns B and I, respectively, in Screenshot 11-8B) against the quarter number. These line charts are automatically drawn by ExcelModules and presented on a separate worksheet. The graph is shown in Screenshot 11-8C.

We use line charts of the actual and forecast values to check the validity of the model.

The line charts show that there are a few quarters (e.g., quarters 1, 10, 13, 19, and 20) in which there are sizable errors in the forecast. Overall, however, Sandy's decomposition model seems to do a good job of replicating the pattern of piano sales over the past few years. There is no consistent under- or overforecast seen, and the forecast errors appear to be randomly distributed.

Using this analysis as evidence, it looks like Sandy will be able to convince her father that such quantitative forecasting decision models are the way to go in the future.

SCREENSHOT 11-8C Chart of Multiplicative Decomposition Forecast for Sawyer Piano House

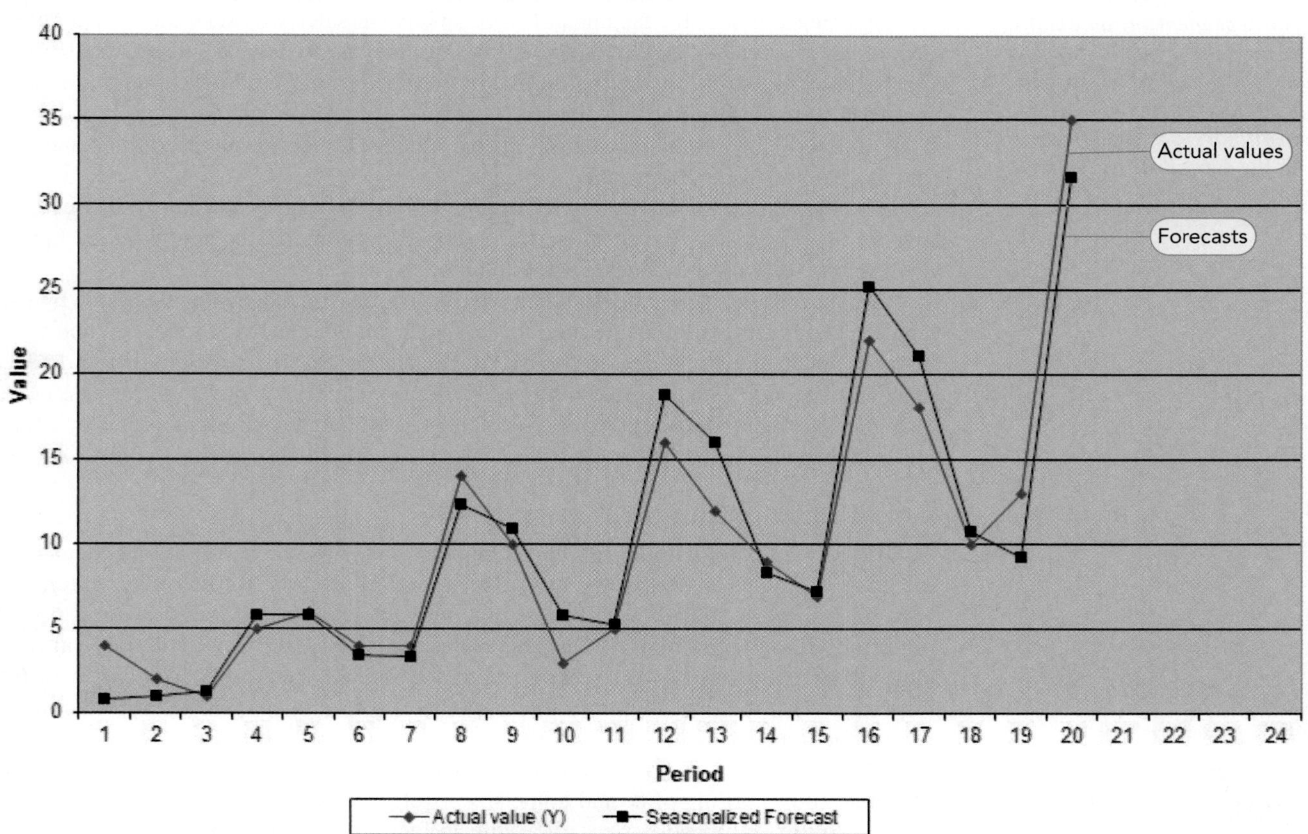

IN ACTION Predicting Advertising Demand at NBC-Universal

NBC Universal (NBCU), a world leader in the production, distribution, and marketing of entertainment, news, and information, had revenues of over $14 billion in 2005. NBCU owns a television network and several stations in the United States, an impressive portfolio of cable networks, a major motion picture company, and very popular theme parks. Over 60 percent of NBCU's revenues are from the sales of on-air advertising time on its television networks and stations.

Each year, the upfront market is a brief period in late May when the television networks sell a majority of their on-air advertising inventory, right after announcing their program schedules for the upcoming broadcast year. To address the challenging problem of forecasting upfront market demand, NBCU initially relied primarily on judgment models and then tried time-series forecasting models. These models proved, however, to be rather unsatisfactory due to the unique nature of the demand population. NBCU now estimates upfront demand using a novel procedure that combines the Delphi forecasting method with grass roots forecasting.

The system, which has been in place since 2004, has been used to support sales decisions each year worth over $4.5 billion. The system enables NBCU to easily analyze pricing scenarios across all of its television properties, while predicting demand with a high level of accuracy. NBCU's sales leaders have credited the forecast system with giving them a unique competitive advantage over its competitors.

Source: Based on S. Bollapragada et al. "NBC-Universal Uses a Novel Qualitative Forecasting Technique to Predict Advertising Demand," *Interfaces* 38, 2 (March–April, 2008): 103–111.

11.8 Causal Forecasting Models: Simple and Multiple Regression

Consider an apparel firm that wishes to forecast the sales of its line of swimwear. It is likely that sales are related to variables such as the selling price, competitors' prices, average daily temperature, whether schools are in session, and advertising budgets. The purpose of a *causal forecasting model* is to develop the best statistical relationship between one or more of these variables and the variable being forecast (swimwear sales, in this case).

The dependent variable is the item we are trying to forecast, and the independent variable is an item (or items) we think might have a causal effect on the dependent variable.

In a causal model for the apparel firm, swimwear sales would be the *dependent* (predicted or forecasted) variable, and the variables used to forecast swimwear sales would be *independent* (or predictor) variables. Note that unlike in the linear trend model we studied in section 11.6, there can be more than one independent variable in a causal model. Further, although time could be an independent variable in a causal model, it does not necessarily need to be one. That is, the data need not be time-series data.

The most common causal model used in practice is **regression analysis**. Several types of regression equations can be developed (e.g., linear, quadratic, cubic, logarithmic). In this section, however, we discuss only linear regression models.

In causal forecasting models, when we try to forecast the dependent variable by using just a single independent variable, the model is called a *simple* regression model. When we use more than one independent variable to forecast the dependent variable, the model is called a *multiple* regression model. We illustrate both types of models in the following sections, using simple examples. As with all models so far in this chapter, although we present a few key equations, we perform the actual calculations by using worksheets provided in ExcelModules.

Causal Simple Regression Model

Sue Taylor works for a home appraisal company that is used by several local banks to appraise the price of homes as part of the mortgage approval process. Based on her extensive experience with home appraisals, Sue knows that one factor that has a direct relationship to the selling price of a home is its size. Sue therefore wants to establish a mathematical relationship that will help her forecast the selling price of a home, based on its size. Table 11.6 provides information on the last 12 homes that have been sold in a specific neighborhood in the city where Sue lives.

We can use a scatter chart to check the relationship.

As a first step toward developing this mathematical relationship, we should draw a scatter chart that shows selling price and home size. (Refer to section 11.6 to see how this chart can be drawn using Excel, if necessary.) We will, in fact, draw such a chart by using ExcelModules

TABLE 11.6 Home Sales Data for the Simple Regression Model

HOME	SELLING PRICE (THOUSANDS)	HOME SIZE (THOUSANDS OF SQ. FT.)
1	\$182.5	2.01
2	\$227.3	2.65
3	\$251.9	2.43
4	\$325.2	2.89
5	\$225.1	2.55
6	\$315.0	3.00
7	\$367.5	3.22
8	\$220.8	2.37
9	\$266.5	2.91
10	\$261.0	2.56
11	\$177.5	2.25
12	\$235.9	3.41

shortly. For now, let us proceed under the assumption that the scatter chart reveals a linear relationship between a home's selling price and its size. That is, the mathematical equation between these variables denotes a straight line.

We use the least-squares procedure here.

Just as we did with linear trend analysis, we use the least-squares procedure here to establish the equation of this straight line. Once again, we let Y represent the dependent variable that we want to forecast (selling price, in this example). But unlike in the trend models, here the independent variable, X, is not time; instead, it is the size of each home. The same basic model discussed in section 11.6 applies. That is,

$$\hat{Y} = b_0 + b_1X$$

where

$\hat{Y}$ = forecasted average value of the dependent variable, based on the current sample

X = value of the independent variable

b_0 = Y-intercept of the line, based on the current sample

b_1 = slope of the line, based on the current sample

We determine the Y-intercept (b_0) and slope (b_1) by using the least-squares formulas.

Recall from section 11.6 that the objective of the least-squares procedure is to determine the values of b_0 and b_1 that minimize the sum of the squared errors between the forecasted ($\hat{Y}$) and actual (Y) values. The formulas to compute these values were given in Equations 11-13 and 11-14 on page 496. However, rather than manually use these formulas, we next discuss the following two approaches to using Excel to develop this regression equation, as well as accompanying statistical measures:

We describe two approaches in Excel for regression: using ExcelModules and Analysis ToolPak.

- *Regression using ExcelModules.* In addition to computing the regression equation, ExcelModules computes the forecast for each observation and the three usual measures of forecast error (i.e., MAD, MSE, and MAPE).
- *Regression using Excel's Analysis ToolPak add-in.* An advantage of using this procedure is that it provides detailed information regarding the significance of the regression equation.

Causal Simple Regression Using ExcelModules

When we select the choice titled Causal Model (Simple Regression) from the Forecasting Models menu in ExcelModules (see Screenshot 11-1A on page 482), the window shown in Screenshot 11-9A is displayed. The option entries in this window are similar to those for earlier procedures. If we check the Graph option, ExcelModules draws the scatter chart as part of the results, along with the least-squares regression line.

File: 11-9.xls, sheet: 11-9B

When we click OK on this screen, we get the screen shown in Screenshot 11-9B. We now enter the selling prices (dependent variable, Y) for the 12 homes in cells B7:B18 and the corresponding sizes (independent variable, X) in cells C7:C18.

The worksheet now computes and displays the regression equation. For Sue's problem, the Y-intercept (b_0) is shown in cell B20, and the slope (b_1) is shown in cell B21. The causal simple regression model is

$$\text{Forecasted average selling price} = -8.125 + 97.789 \times \text{Home size}$$

SCREENSHOT 11-9A Options Window for Causal Model (Simple Regression) Worksheet in ExcelModules

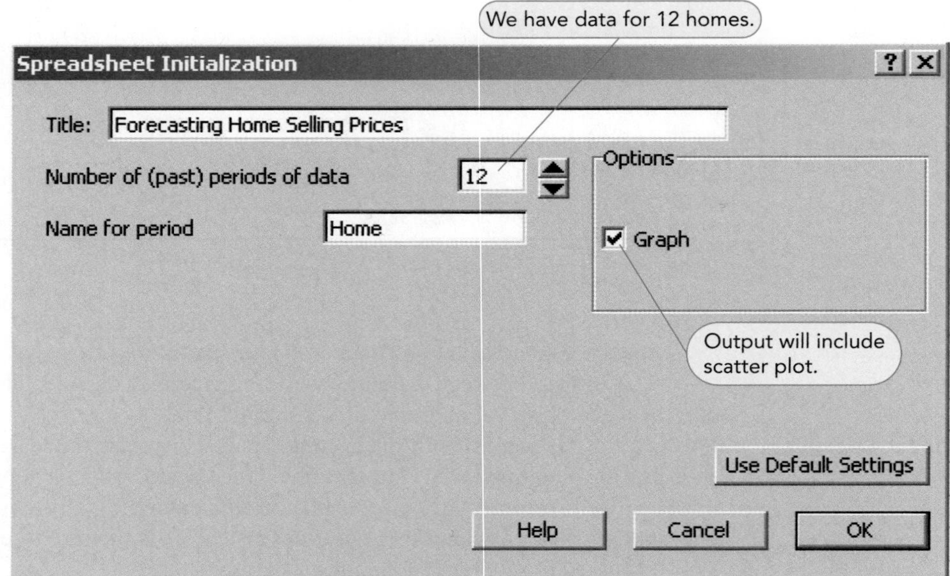

SCREENSHOT 11-9B Causal Model (Simple Regression) for Forecasting Home Selling Prices

	A	B	C	D	E	F	G	H	I
1	**Forecasting Home Selling Prices**								
2	**Forecasting**		Causal regression analysis						
3	Enter the (Y,X) pairs in cells shaded YELLOW. Enter new value of X at the bottom to forecast Y.								
4									
5	**Input Data**				**Forecast Error Analysis**				
6	Period	Dep Variable (or) (Y)	Indep Variable (or) (X)		Forecast	Error	Absolute error	Squared error	Absolute % error
7	Home 1	182.5	2.01		188.431	-5.931	5.931	35.178	3.25%
8	Home 2	227.3	2.65		251.016	-23.716	23.716	562.460	10.43%
9	Home 3	251.9	2.43		229.503	22.397	22.397	501.644	8.89%
10	Home 4	325.2	2.89		274.486	50.714	50.714	2571.944	15.59%
11	Home 5	225.1	2.55		241.237	-16.137	16.137	260.413	7.17%
12	Home 6	315.0	3.00		285.242	29.758	29.758	885.510	9.45%
13	Home 7	367.5	3.22		306.756	60.744	60.744	3689.818	16.53%
14	Home 8	220.8	2.37		223.635	-2.835	2.835	8.039	1.28%
15	Home 9	266.5	2.91		276.441	-9.941	9.941	98.832	3.73%
16	Home 10	261.0	2.56		242.215	18.785	18.785	352.869	7.20%
17	Home 11	177.5	2.25		211.901	-34.401	34.401	1183.396	19.38%
18	Home 12	235.9	3.41		325.336	-89.436	89.436	7998.816	37.91%
19					**Average**		**30.400**	**1512.410**	**11.73%**
20	Intercept	**-8.125**					**MAD**	**MSE**	**MAPE**
21	Slope	**97.789**							
22							**SE**	**42.602**	
23	**Forecast**	295.0	3.10				**Correlation**	**0.702**	
24							**r-squared**	**0.493**	

Forecasts are computed using the regression equation.

Regression coefficients

Measures of forecast error

Standard error of the regression estimate

Forecasted average selling price for house size of 3,100 square feet

49.3% of variability in selling prices is explained by home size.

The Y-intercept may not have a practical meaning in many causal models. The slope indicates the average change in Y for a unit increase in X.

Typically, we can interpret the Y-intercept as the forecasted value of the dependent variable when the independent variable has a value of zero. However, in Sue's example, the Y-intercept of -8.125 has no practical meaning because a home with size zero does not exist. Further, because the data set does not include observations with $X = 0$, it would be inappropriate to interpret the Y-intercept at this X value. On the other hand, the slope of 97.789 implies that the average selling price of a home increases by \$97,789 for every 1,000 square feet increase in size. (Remember that the selling price is in thousands of dollars and the sizes are in thousands of square feet.)

In addition to computing the regression equation, ExcelModules plugs the size values for all homes into this equation to compute the forecasted selling price for each home. These forecasts are shown in cells E7:E18. The following measures of forecast error are then calculated and reported: MAD (30.40, in cell G19), MSE (1,512.41, in cell H19), and MAPE (11.73%, in cell I19).

File: 11-9.xls, sheet: 11-9C

REGRESSION CHARTS Now that we have identified the equation for the causal simple regression model, how do we determine its validity and accuracy? One way to do so is to use the scatter chart of selling price versus size. Recall from section 11.6 that we can draw scatter chart using Excel. However, ExcelModules automatically provides this chart if specified in the options (see Screenshot 11-9A). The scatter chart for Sue's example is shown in Screenshot 11-9C, along with the linear regression line, so we can see how well the model fits the data. From this chart, it appears that while there is a reasonable linear relationship between selling price and size, there are sizable differences between the actual values and the fitted line (forecast values) in a few cases.

An alternative way to check the validity and accuracy of the causal model is to draw line charts of the actual and forecasted values (cells B7:B18 and E7:E18, respectively, in Screenshot 11-9B) against the observation number. If the Graph option is checked in Screenshot 11-9A, ExcelModules automatically draws these line charts also (in addition to the scatter chart) and presents them on a separate worksheet. The line charts for Sue's example, shown in Screenshot 11-9D, indicate that the causal model she has developed does replicate the pattern of selling prices. However, these charts also confirm the presence of a few sizable forecast errors (e.g., homes 4, 7, 11, and 12). Sue may therefore want to consider including other independent variables in her causal model to improve the forecast accuracy.

File: 11-9.xls, sheet: 11-9D

SCREENSHOT 11-9C Scatter Chart with Regression Line for Forecasting Home Selling Prices

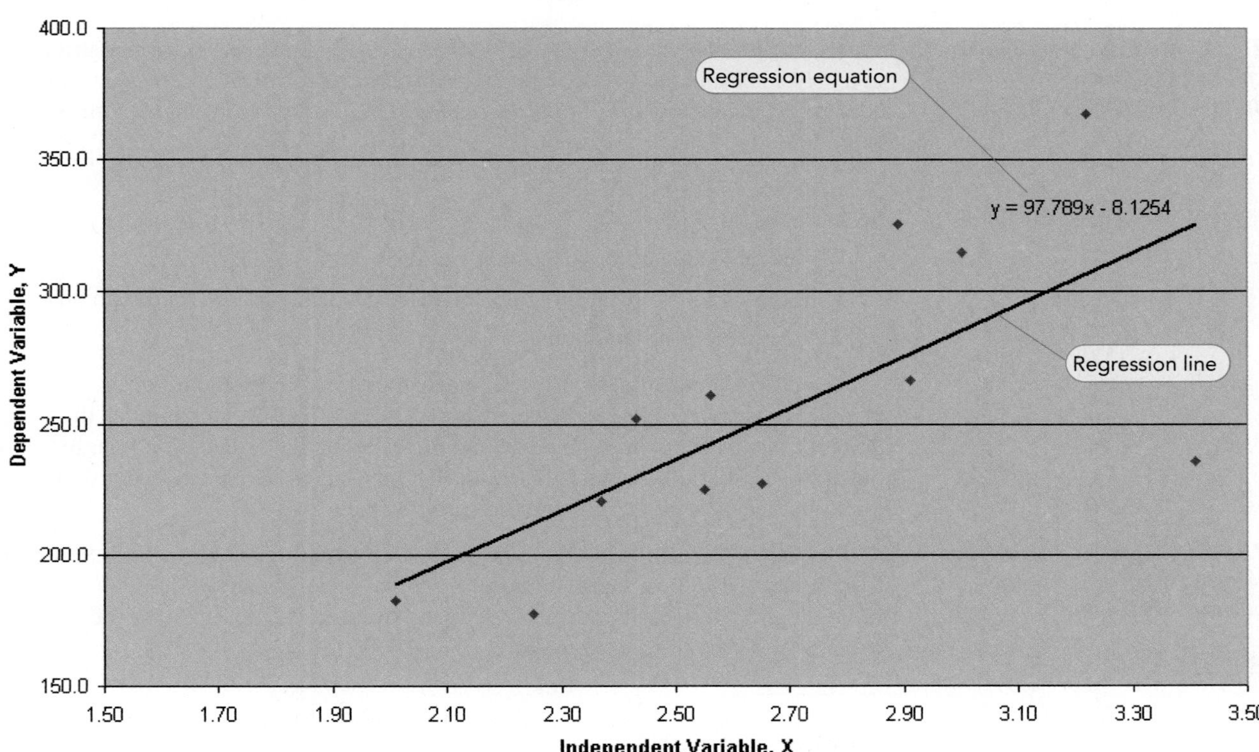

SCREENSHOT 11-9D Chart of Causal Model (Simple Regression) Forecast for Forecasting Home Selling Prices

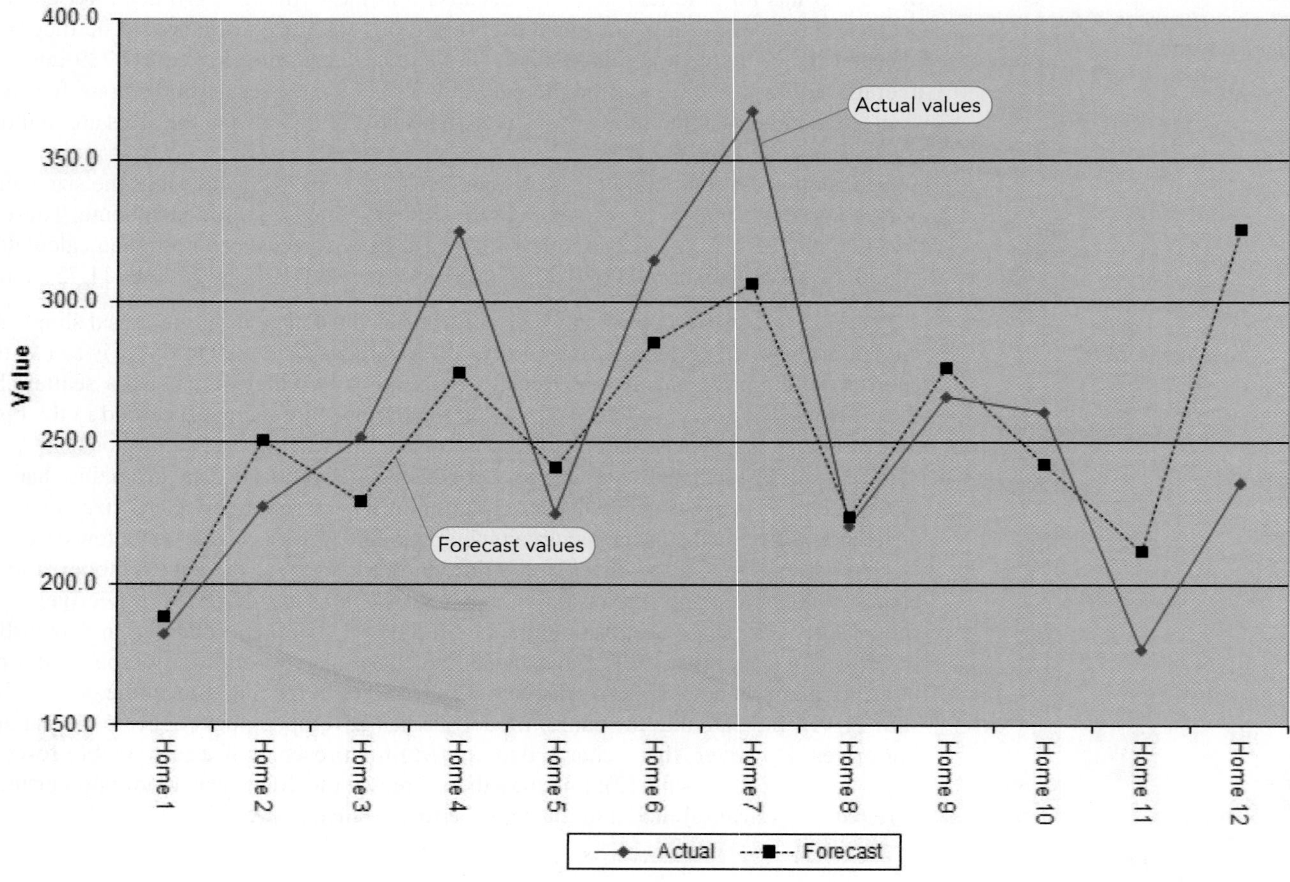

The standard error is useful in creating confidence intervals around the regression line.

STANDARD ERROR OF THE REGRESSION ESTIMATE Another way of measuring the accuracy of the regression estimates is to compute the **standard error of the regression estimate,** $S_{Y.X}$, also called the *standard deviation of the regression*. The equation for computing the standard error is

$$S_{Y.X} = \sqrt{\sum (Y_i - \hat{Y}_i)^2/(n-2)} \tag{11-15}$$

where

Y_i = actual value of the dependent variable for the ith observation

$\hat{Y}_i$ = regression (forecasted) value of the dependent variable for the ith observation

n = number of observations

ExcelModules automatically computes and reports the standard error. The value for Sue's example, shown in cell H22 of Screenshot 11-9B, is 42.602. This implies that the standard deviation of the distribution of home selling prices around the regression line, for a given value of home size, is \$42,602. As we will see shortly, the standard error can be used in setting up confidence intervals around the average forecasted values.

The correlation coefficient *helps measure the strength of the linear relationship.*

CORRELATION COEFFICIENT (r) The regression equation is one way of expressing the nature of the relationship between two variables.[2] The equation shows how one variable relates to the value and changes in another variable. Another way to evaluate the linear relationship

[2] Regression lines do not always show cause-and-effect relationships. In general, they describe the relationship between the movement of variables.

FIGURE 11.4
Four Values of the Correlation Coefficient

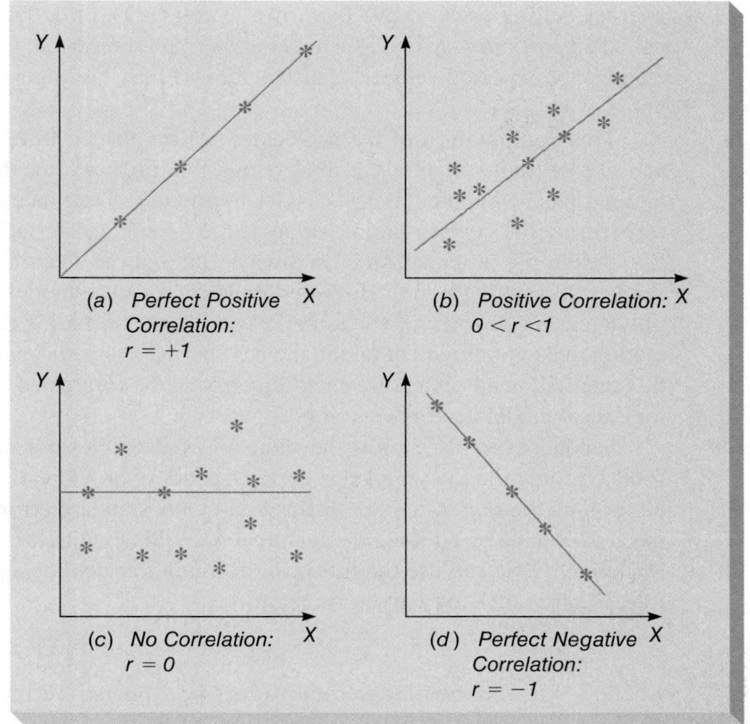

between two variables is to compute the **correlation coefficient**. This measure expresses the degree or strength of the linear relationship. It is usually denoted by r and can be any number between and including $+1$ and -1. Figure 11.4 illustrates what different values of r might look like for different types of relationships between an independent variable X and a dependent variable Y.

The rather cumbersome equation for the correlation coefficient r is

$$r = \frac{n\sum XY - \sum X \sum Y}{\sqrt{[n\sum X^2 - (\sum X)^2][n\sum Y^2 - (\sum Y)^2]}} \tag{11-16}$$

ExcelModules, however, also calculates and reports the value of the correlation coefficient. Although there is no specific rule to decide when two variables can be deemed to be highly correlated, in general, correlation coefficient magnitudes of 0.6 and greater are indicative of a strong relationship. In Sue's example, therefore, the r value of 0.702 (shown in cell H23 of Screenshot 11-9B) indicates the presence of a strong positive linear relationship between selling price and home size.

The **coefficient of determination** *tells us how much of the variability in the depended variable is explained by the independent variable.*

COEFFICIENT OF DETERMINATION (R^2) Another measure that is used often to describe the strength of the linear relationship between two variables is the **coefficient of determination**. This is simply the square of the coefficient of correlation and is denoted by R^2. The value of R^2 will always be a positive number in the range $0 \leq R^2 \leq 1$. The coefficient of determination is defined as the amount of the variability in the dependent variable (Y) that is explained by the regression equation. In Sue's example, the value of R^2 is 0.493 (shown in cell H24 in Screenshot 11-9B on page 506), which is just the square of 0.702, the correlation coefficient. This indicates that only 49.3% of the total variation in home selling prices is explained by size, leaving 51.7% unexplained (or explained by other variables). For this reason, as noted earlier, Sue may want to consider including other independent variables in her causal model.

USING THE CAUSAL SIMPLE REGRESSION MODEL Suppose Sue wants to estimate the average selling price of a home that is 3,100 square feet in size. We enter this value in cell C23 as shown in Screenshot 11-9B (note that we should enter 3,100 as 3.10). The model forecasts an average selling price of 295.0 (shown in cell B23), or \$295,000. This forecast of \$295,000 is called a *point estimate* of Y. As noted earlier, the forecasted value (point estimate) is actually the average, or expected value, of a distribution of possible values of home selling prices for a given value of size.

One weakness of regression is that we need to know the values of the independent variable.

This computation of the forecasted selling price illustrates two potential weaknesses of causal forecasting methods such as regression. First, we see that even after the regression equation has been computed, it is necessary to provide an estimate of the independent variable before forecasting the corresponding value of the dependent variable. This may not be a problem in Sue's example (after all, she can always find out the size of any home for which she wants to forecast the selling price). However, consider a causal model that uses, for example, the unemployment rate to forecast stock market performance. In this case, imagine the difficulty of estimating the unemployment rate in the next period. As you can clearly see, any error in estimating this rate will result in a corresponding error in the forecasted stock market performance, even if the causal model itself is very good.

A second weakness of regression is that individual values of Y can be quite far from the forecasted average value.

Second, even if we know the value of X for which we want to forecast Y, the regression line forecasts only the *average* value of Y. Depending on the variability of the distribution of Y values around the regression line (measured by the standard error of the regression estimate, $S_{Y.X}$), the actual value of Y for a given value of X could be quite far from the forecasted average value. Statistically, we can use the following formula to calculate an approximate confidence interval for *all* values of Y for a given value of X[3]:

$$\hat{Y} \pm Z_{\alpha/2} \times S_{Y.X} \quad \text{(or)} \quad (b_0 + b_1X) \pm Z_{\alpha/2} \times S_{Y.X} \qquad \textbf{(11-17)}$$

where $Z_{\alpha/2}$ is the standard normal value (see Appendix C on page 574) for a confidence level of $(1 - \alpha)\%$. For example, an approximate 95% confidence interval for the selling price of *all* homes of size 3,100 square feet can be computed to be $295.0 \pm 1.96 \times 42.602 = 211.5$ to 378.5, or \$211,500 to \$378,500. As you can see, this is a fairly broad interval, which is consistent with the fact that the size of a home is able to explain only 49.3% of the variability in its selling price.

A causal model is typically valid only for the range of X values in the data set for which it was developed.

Would it be logical to use the causal model developed here to forecast the average selling price of a home of size 5,000 square feet? What about a home of size 1,400 square feet? We note that the sizes of both these homes are not within the range of sizes for the homes in Sue's data set (see Table 11.6 on page 505). It is entirely possible, for example, that the relationship between selling price and home size follows a different causal relationship for large homes (i.e., home sizes in excess of 4,500 square feet). Hence, we cannot guarantee the validity of the causal model developed here in forecasting the selling prices of these homes.

Causal Simple Regression Using Excel's Analysis ToolPak (Data Analysis)

Excel's Analysis ToolPak add-in includes a procedure for regression.

As noted earlier, Excel's Analysis ToolPak add-in includes a procedure for regression. (See section B.6 in Appendix B for details on how to install and enable this add-in in Excel.) When enabled, this add-in is called Data Analysis and appears as part of the Analysis group within the Data tab in Excel's Ribbon. To invoke the regression procedure, we click Data | Data Analysis and then select Regression from the list of choices, as shown in Screenshot 11-9E(a). The window shown in Screenshot 11-9E(b) is displayed.

RUNNING THE REGRESSION PROCEDURE IN DATA ANALYSIS We need to specify the cell ranges for the selling prices (Y) and sizes (X), and indicate where we want the output of the regression to be displayed. For example, in Screenshot 11-9E(b), we have specified the Y-range as cells B6:B18 (from the Excel worksheet shown in Screenshot 11-9B on page 506) and the X-range as cells C6:C18. We have asked for the output of the regression analysis to be presented in a new worksheet named *11-9F*. If we check the box named Labels, the first entry in the cell

[3] We refer to this as an *approximate* formula for the confidence interval because the exact formula varies slightly, depending on the value of X for which the interval is computed. Also, when the sample size is large ($n > 30$), the confidence interval can be computed using normal (Z) tables. However, when the number of observations is small, the t-distribution is appropriate. For details, see any forecasting or statistics textbook, such as J. E. Hanke and D. W. Wichern. *Business Forecasting*, 9th ed. Upper Saddle River, NJ: Prentice Hall, 2009.

SCREENSHOT 11-9E Simple Regression Using Excel's Analysis ToolPak

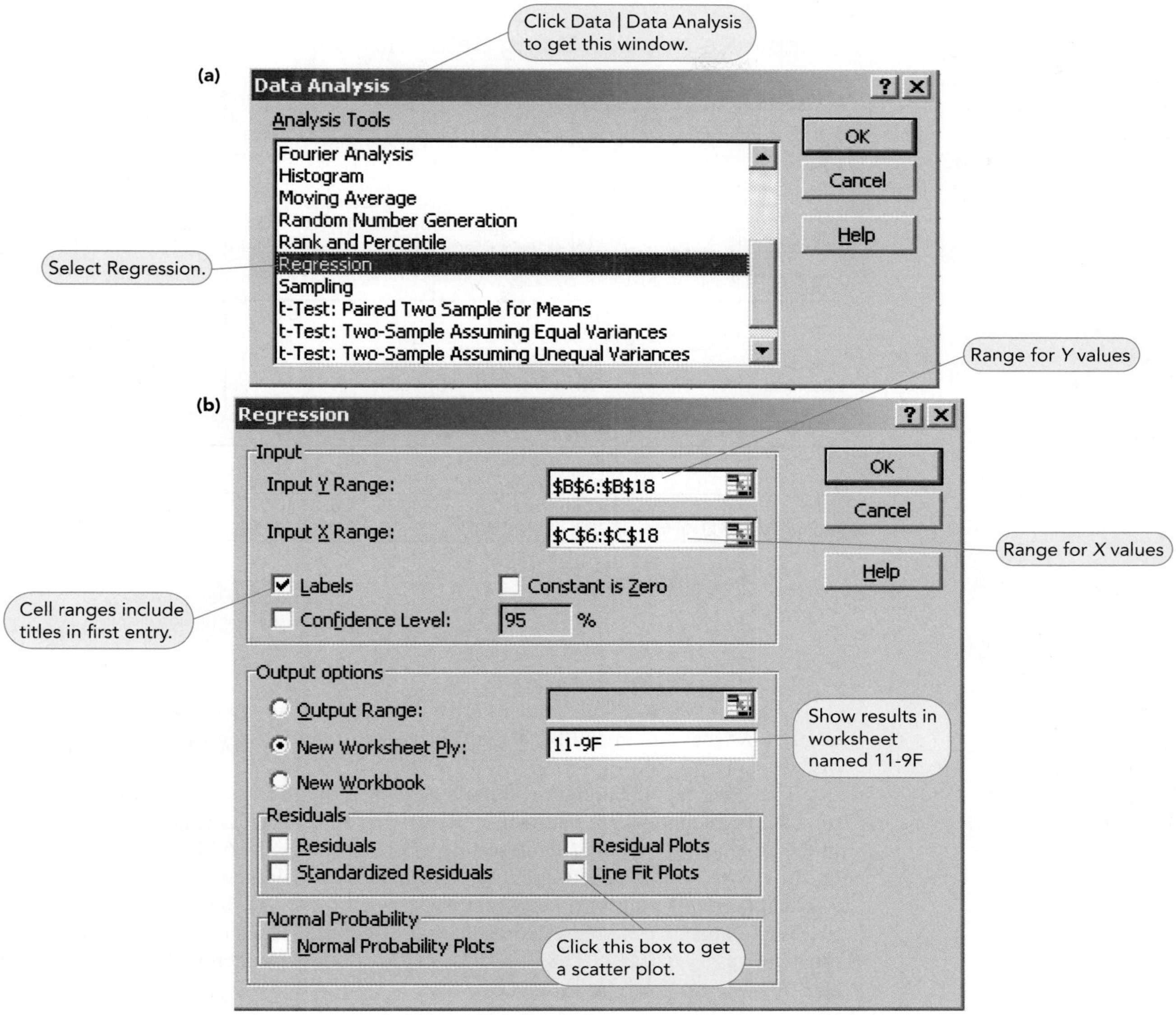

Click Data | Data Analysis to get this window.

(a)

Data Analysis

Analysis Tools

Fourier Analysis
Histogram
Moving Average
Random Number Generation
Rank and Percentile
Regression
Sampling
t-Test: Paired Two Sample for Means
t-Test: Two-Sample Assuming Equal Variances
t-Test: Two-Sample Assuming Unequal Variances

OK
Cancel
Help

Select Regression.

Range for Y values

(b)

Regression

Input
Input Y Range: $B$6:$B$18
Input X Range: $C$6:$C$18
Labels
Constant is Zero
Confidence Level: 95 %

OK
Cancel
Help

Range for X values

Cell ranges include titles in first entry.

Output options
Output Range:
New Worksheet Ply: 11-9F
New Workbook

Show results in worksheet named 11-9F

Residuals
Residuals
Residual Plots
Standardized Residuals
Line Fit Plots

Normal Probability
Normal Probability Plots

Click this box to get a scatter plot.

range for a variable should include the name of that variable. Checking the box named Line Fit Plots will result in a scatter chart like the one in Screenshot 11-9C.

Residual plots and the normal probability plot are used to verify the validity of assumptions in a regression model.

All other options (i.e., Residuals, Standardized Residuals, Residual Plots, and Normal Probability Plot) deal with verifying the validity of assumptions made when using the least-squares procedures to develop a regression model. These options are usually more relevant for *explanatory* models, where the intent is to explain the variability in the dependent variable using the independent variable. Although still relevant, they are relatively less important in *predictive* regression models (such as in causal forecasting models), where the objective is mainly to obtain a good forecast of the dependent variable using the independent variable. For this reason, we do not discuss these topics here and refer you to any statistics textbook for a detailed discussion.

File: 11-9.xls, sheet: 11-9F

RESULTS OF THE REGRESSION PROCEDURE When we click OK, Data Analysis runs the regression procedure, and the results shown in Screenshot 11-9F are displayed. Just as in the earlier results we obtained using ExcelModules (see Screenshot 11-9B on page 506), the results here too show a Y-intercept of -8.125 (cell B18), slope of 97.989 (cell B19), correlation coefficient of 0.702 (cell B5; named Multiple R by Data Analysis), coefficient of determination

SCREENSHOT 11-9F Simple Regression Output from Excel's Analysis ToolPak

	A	B	C	D	E	F	G
1	**Simple Regression Using Data Analysis**						
2							
3	**SUMMARY OUTPUT**						
4	*Regression Statistics*						
5	Multiple R	0.702					
6	R Square	0.493					
7	Adjusted R Square	0.443					
8	Standard Error	42.602					
9	Observations	12					
10							
11	**ANOVA**						
12		*df*	*SS*	*MS*	*F*	*Signific-ance F*	
13	Regression	1	17670.281	17670.281	9.736	0.011	
14	Residual	10	18148.916	1814.892			
15	Total	11	35819.197				
16							
17		*Coeffi-cients*	*Standard Error*	*t Stat*	*P-value*	*Lower 95%*	*Upper 95%*
18	Intercept	-8.125	85.119	-0.095	0.926	-197.781	181.531
19	Home size ('000 sq ft)	97.789	31.340	3.120	0.011	27.960	167.619

Correlation coefficient

17,670.281 of the total sum of squares of 35,819.197 is explained here.

P-value of 0.011 indicates that regression is significant at the 5% level.

Regression coefficients

95% confidence interval for the population slope

R^2 of 0.493 (cell B6), and standard error of the regression estimate of 42.602 (cell B8). The adjusted R^2 measure in cell B7 is relevant only for multiple regression models, which we will discuss shortly.

The table labeled ANOVA details how well the regression equation fits the data. The total sum of squares (SS) value of 35,819.197 (cell C15) is a measure of the total variability in the dependent variable (home selling prices). Of this, 17,670.281 (cell C13) is explained by the regression equation, leaving 18,148.916 unexplained (cell C14, also known as the residual sum of squares). Recall that we defined the R^2 as the percentage of variation in Y that is explained by the regression equation. From the values in the ANOVA table, R^2 can be computed as $17{,}670.281/35{,}819.197 = 0.493$, or 49.3%, which is the same value reported in cell B6.

Statistical significance tests check whether the regression relationship really exists for the entire population or whether it is just a random occurrence based on the current sample.

STATISTICAL SIGNIFICANCE OF THE REGRESSION EQUATION The output from Data Analysis also provides information on the statistical significance of the regression equation. That is, it indicates whether the linear relationship obtained between Y and X is, in fact, a true reflection of the real situation or whether it is just a random occurrence based on this specific data set. Recall from Equation 11-11 that we expressed the regression equation as $\hat{Y} = b_0 + b_1X$. Note that the two coefficients b_0 and b_1 are sample statistics because they are both estimated based on a specific sample. In Sue's model, for example, b_0 and b_1 have been estimated based on just 12 homes. Now suppose the true population relationship between Y and X (i.e., the relationship if our data set consisted of *all* homes in the population) can be expressed as follows:

$$\mu_{Y|X} = \beta_0 + \beta_1 X \qquad \textbf{(11-18)}$$

where

$\mu_{Y|X}$ = forecasted average value of Y for a given value of X, based on the entire population

β_0 = Y-intercept of the line, based on the entire population

β_1 = slope of the line, based on the entire population

Does a nonzero value of the slope b_1 based on a specific sample immediately imply that the true population slope β_1 is also nonzero? That is, is the slope between Y and X significantly different from zero, from a statistical perspective? To test this issue, we set up the following null and alternate hypothesis:

$$H_0 : \beta_1 = 0 \text{ (i.e., the regression between } Y \text{ and } X \text{ is not statistically significant)}$$
$$H_1 : \beta_1 \neq 0 \text{ (i.e., the regression between } Y \text{ and } X \text{ is statistically significant)}$$

There are two tests for testing statistical significance in simple regression models: F*-test and* t*-test.*

Using the information provided in the Data Analysis regression output, there are two ways to conduct this hypothesis test: (1) *F*-test and (2) *t*-test. We refer you to any statistics textbook for the details and rationale behind these tests. In our discussion here, we simply interpret the test results provided in the Data Analysis output.

The result of the *F*-test is included in the ANOVA table. The computed *F*-statistic of 9.736, shown in cell E13 in Screenshot 11-9F, is *F*-distributed with 1 numerator degrees of freedom (cell B13) and 10 denominator degrees of freedom (cell B14). The *P*-value associated with this *F*-statistic is shown in cell F13 (Data Analysis labels this *P*-value as Significance *F*). In Sue's case, the *P*-value of the test is 0.011, implying that the null hypothesis can be rejected at the 5% significance level but not at the 1% level. Another way of stating this is that we are 98.9% (= 1 − *P*-value) confident that the relationship between *Y* and *X* is statistically significant.

The result of the *t*-test is included in the regression coefficients table. The computed *t*-statistic of 3.12, shown in cell D19 in Screenshot 11-9F, is *t*-distributed with 10 degrees of freedom (cell B14). The *P*-value associated with this *t*-statistic is 0.011, shown in cell E19. Note that this is the same *P*-value we obtained in the *F*-test, which leads to the same conclusion as in that test. In fact, in simple regression models, the *P*-value will always be the same for both the *F*-test and the *t*-test. It is therefore not necessary to conduct both tests, although all statistical software packages, including Data Analysis, automatically report the results for both tests.

Significance tests involving the Y-intercept are often not relevant and are ignored.

Data Analysis also provides information regarding the statistical significance of the *Y*-intercept. The computed *t*-statistic is shown in cell D18, and the associated *P*-value is shown in cell E18 in Screenshot 11-9F. However, as noted earlier, the *Y*-intercept does not have a practical meaning in many causal regression models. For example, it is meaningless in Sue's model because a home cannot have a size of zero. For this reason, it is quite common for the result of this significance test to be ignored, even though most statistical software packages report it by default.

CONFIDENCE INTERVALS FOR THE POPULATION SLOPE In addition to testing for the statistical significance of the slope, we can also compute confidence intervals for the population slope (i.e., β_1). By default, Data Analysis always reports a 95% confidence interval for this parameter (shown in cells F19:G19 in Screenshot 11-9F). The interval implies that while we have obtained a point estimate of 97.989 for the regression slope based on the current sample of 12 homes, we are 95% confident that the true population slope between home selling prices and sizes is somewhere between 27.960 and 167.619. Here again, the interval is fairly broad because the R^2 value of the regression model is only 49.3%.

We can also obtain intervals for other confidence levels by checking the appropriate option (see Screenshot 11-9E) and specifying the desired confidence level. By the way, note that Data Analysis also reports the confidence interval for the *Y*-intercept. However, for the same reasons discussed previously, we typically ignore these types of computations regarding the *Y*-intercept.

Causal Multiple Regression Model

Adding additional independent variables turns a simple regression model into a multiple regression model.

A *multiple regression* model is a practical extension of the simple regression model. It allows us to build a model with more than one independent variable. The general form of the multiple regression equation is

$$\hat{Y} = b_0 + b_1X_1 + b_2X_2 + \ldots + b_pX_p \quad \textbf{(11-19)}$$

where

b_0 = *Y*-axis intercept, based on the current sample

b_i = slope of the regression for the *i*th independent variable (X_i), based on the current sample

p = number of independent variables in the model

Calculations in multiple regression are very complex and best left to a computer.

The mathematics of multiple regression becomes quite complex, based on the number of independent variables, and the computations are therefore best left to a computer. As with simple regression, we discuss two approaches here. The first approach uses a worksheet included

TABLE 11.7
Home Sales Data for the Multiple Regression Model

HOME	SELLING PRICE (THOUSANDS)	HOME SIZE (THOUSANDS SQ. FT.)	LAND AREA (ACRES)
1	$182.5	2.01	0.40
2	$227.3	2.65	0.60
3	$251.9	2.43	0.65
4	$325.2	2.89	1.10
5	$225.1	2.55	0.75
6	$315.0	3.00	1.50
7	$367.5	3.22	1.70
8	$220.8	2.37	0.45
9	$266.5	2.91	0.80
10	$261.0	2.56	1.00
11	$177.5	2.25	0.50
12	$235.9	3.41	0.70

in ExcelModules, and the second approach uses the regression procedure in Excel's Analysis ToolPak. Next, we illustrate both approaches for causal multiple regression models, using an expanded version of Sue Taylor's home selling price example.

FORECASTING HOME SELLING PRICES—REVISITED Sue Taylor is not satisfied with the R^2 value of 0.493 obtained from her causal simple regression model. She thinks she can forecast home selling prices more precisely by including a second independent variable in her regression model. In addition to the size of a home, she believes that the area of the land (in acres) would also be a good predictor of selling prices. Sue has updated the information for the 12 homes in her input data, as shown in Table 11.7. What is the effect of including this additional independent variable?

Causal Multiple Regression Using ExcelModules

ExcelModules includes a worksheet for causal forecasting models using multiple regression.

Let us first use ExcelModules to develop a regression model to predict the selling price of a home based both on its size and land area. When we select the choice titled Causal Model (Multiple Regression) from the Forecasting Models menu in ExcelModules (see Screenshot 11-1A on page 482), the window shown in Screenshot 11-10A is displayed. The option entries in this window are similar to those for the simple regression model, with the additional choice to specify the number of independent variables. The entries for Sue's example are shown in Screenshot 11-10A.

SCREENSHOT 11-10A
Options Window for Causal Model (Multiple Regression) Worksheet in ExcelModules

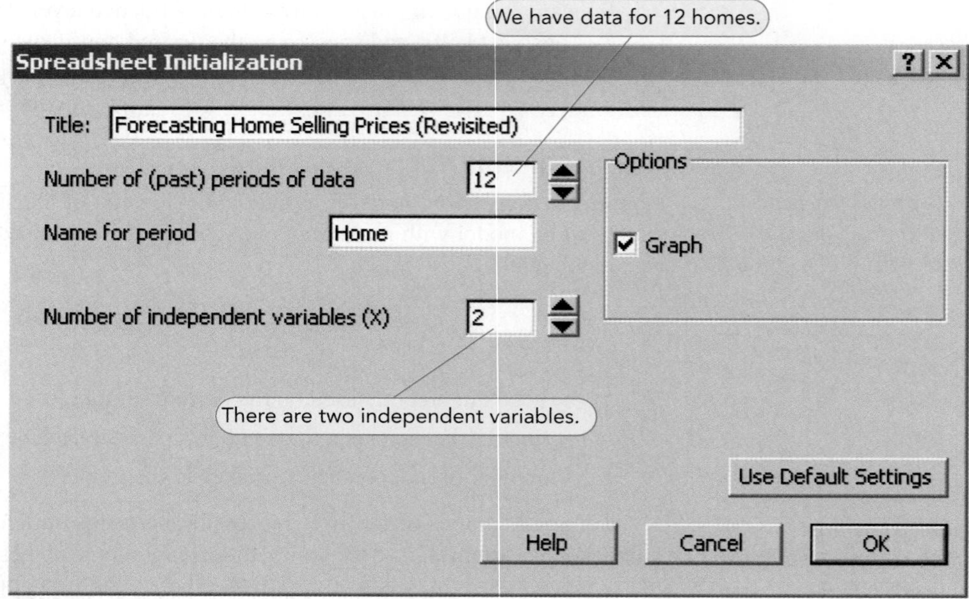

SCREENSHOT 11-10B Causal Model (Multiple Regression) for Forecasting Home Selling Prices

	A	B	C	D	E	F	G	H	I	J
1	**Forecasting Home Selling Prices (Revisited)**									
2	Forecasting		Multiple regression							
3	Enter the data in the shaded area. To get a forecast use the shaded data area at the bottom left of the sheet.									
4										
5										
6	Input Data					Forecasts Error Analysis				
7		Y	x 1	x 2		Forecast	Error	Absolute error	Squared error	Absolute % error
8	Home 1	182.5	2.01	0.40		188.912	-6.412	6.412	41.113	3.51%
9	Home 2	227.3	2.65	0.60		225.603	1.697	1.697	2.879	0.75%
10	Home 3	251.9	2.43	0.65		226.650	25.250	25.250	637.540	10.02%
11	Home 4	325.2	2.89	1.10		288.250	36.950	36.950	1365.287	11.36%
12	Home 5	225.1	2.55	0.75		240.719	-15.619	15.619	243.966	6.94%
13	Home 6	315.0	3.00	1.50		336.614	-21.614	21.614	467.178	6.86%
14	Home 7	367.5	3.22	1.70		364.325	3.175	3.175	10.083	0.86%
15	Home 8	220.8	2.37	0.45		202.361	18.439	18.439	339.979	8.35%
16	Home 9	266.5	2.91	0.80		254.169	12.331	12.331	152.055	4.63%
17	Home 10	261.0	2.56	1.00		269.691	-8.691	8.691	75.528	3.33%
18	Home 11	177.5	2.25	0.50		205.547	-28.047	28.047	786.632	15.80%
19	Home 12	235.9	3.41	0.70		253.358	-17.458	17.458	304.771	7.40%
20						Average		16.307	368.918	6.65%
21	Regression Line							MAD	MSE	MAPE
22	Intercept	99.919								
23	Slopes		21.383	115.030				SE	22.179	
24								multiple-r	0.936	
25	Forecast	269.735	3.10	0.90				r-squared	0.876	

Land area
Home size
Selling price
Regression coefficients
Forecast computed using the multiple regression line.
Measure of forecast error.
Forecasted average selling price for house with 3,100 square feet and 0.9 acres of land.
87.6% of the variability in selling price is explained by this model.

File: 11-10.xls, sheet: 11-10B

When we click OK on this screen, we get the screen shown in Screenshot 11-10B. We now enter the selling prices (dependent variable, Y) for the past 12 years in cells B8:B19 and the corresponding home sizes (independent variable X_1) and land areas (independent variable X_2) in cells C8:C19 and D8:D19, respectively. Note that the values in cells B3:B19 and C3:C19 are the same as the ones we entered in the simple regression model earlier.

The worksheet computes the multiple regression equation and displays the results. For Sue's example, the Y-intercept (b_0) is shown in cell B22, and the slopes b_1 for home size and b_2 for land area are shown in cells C23 and D23, respectively. The causal regression model is

$$\text{Forecasted average selling price} = 99.919 + 21.383 \times \text{Home size} + 115.030 \times \text{Land area}$$

The effect of each independent variable in a multiple regression model is affected by all the other independent variables in the model.

Note the huge difference between the regression coefficients here and the coefficients obtained in the simple regression model between selling price and home size. That is, the addition of the third variable in the model completely changes the regression equation, even though the data remain unchanged for selling price and home size. As it turns out, this is a fairly common occurrence in regression models.

The home size and land area values for the 12 homes in the sample are now plugged in to this regression equation to compute the forecasted selling prices. These forecasts are shown in cells F8:F19. The following measures of forecast error are then calculated and reported: MAD (cell H20), MSE (cell I20), and MAPE (cell J20).

File: 11-10.xls, sheet: 11-10C

If the Graph option is checked in Screenshot 11-10A, ExcelModules creates line charts of the actual and forecasted values against the observation number, and shows the chart on a separate worksheet. We present the chart for Sue's example in Screenshot 11-10C.

SCREENSHOT 11-10C Chart of Causal Model (Multiple Regression) Forecast for Forecasting Home Selling Prices

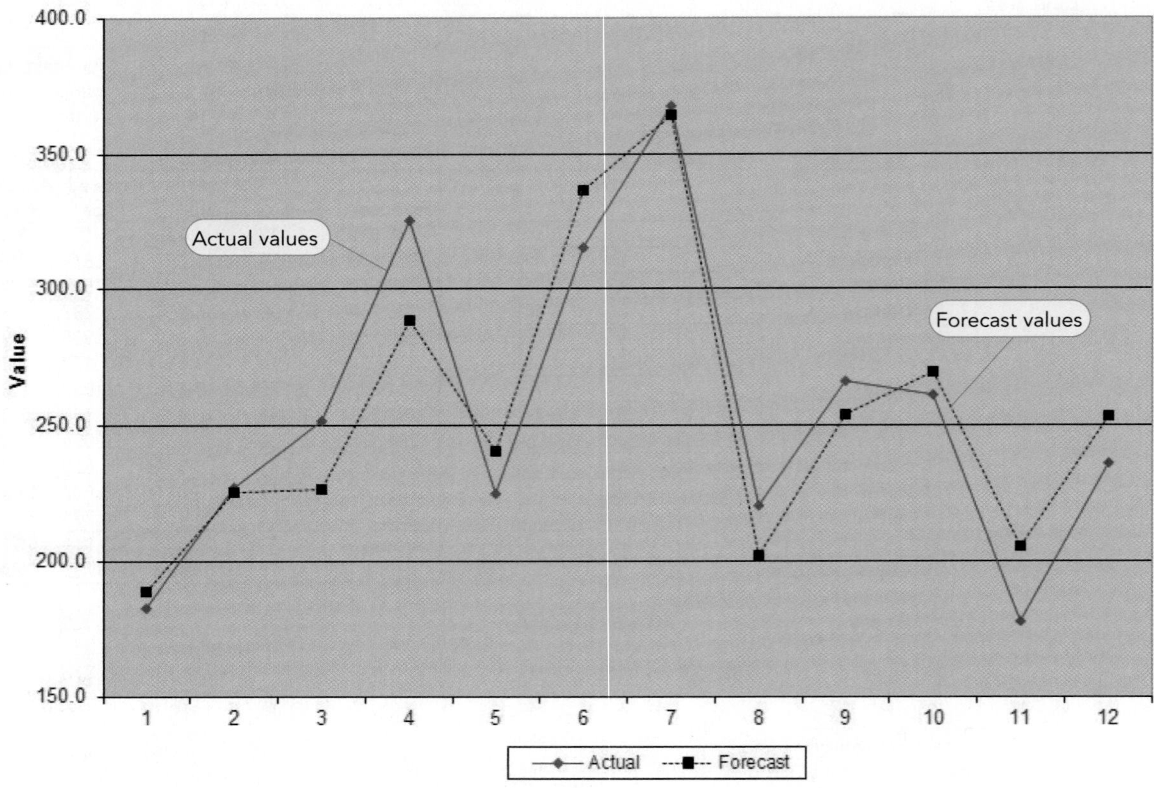

Forecast measures will typically improve in multiple regression models when compared to a simple regression model.

ANALYZING THE RESULTS Is this multiple regression model better than the original simple regression model? The R^2 value increases from just 0.493 in the simple regression model to 0.876 with the addition of the second variable, land area. That is, home size and land area together are able to explain 87.6% of the variability in home selling prices. In addition, all three measures of forecast error show sizable drops in magnitude. For example, the MAPE decreases from 11.73% in the simple regression model to just 6.65% in the multiple regression model. Likewise, the MAD decreases from 30.40 in the simple regression model to just 16.307 with the second independent variable.

To further study the effect of adding land area as an independent variable, let us compare the multiple regression model's line chart (shown in Screenshot 11-10C) with the simple regression model's chart (shown in Screenshot 11-9D on page 508). It appears that most of the points in Screenshot 11-10C (especially homes 2, 6, 7, and 12) show a sizable improvement in terms of the forecast error.

All these issues seem to indicate that the addition of the second independent variable does help Sue in being able to forecast home selling prices more accurately. However, as we will see shortly when we study multiple regression analysis using Data Analysis, we need to be cautious in deciding which independent variable to add in a multiple regression model.

USING THE CAUSAL MULTIPLE REGRESSION MODEL Recall that we used the simple regression model to forecast the average selling price of a 3,100 square foot home. Now suppose this home has a land area of 0.90 acres. We enter these values in cells C23 and D23, respectively, as shown in Screenshot 11-10B (recall that we should enter 3,100 as 3.10). The model forecasts an average selling price of 269.735 (shown in cell B25), or $269,735.

We can use the standard error of the regression estimate to construct confidence intervals around the regression line.

As with the simple regression model, we can use this point estimate in conjunction with the standard error of the regression estimate (given in cell I23 in Screenshot 11-10B) to calculate an approximate 95% confidence interval for the selling price of *all* homes of size 3,100 square feet and with a land area of 0.9 acres. This confidence interval turns out to be

269.733 ± 1.96 × 22.179 = 226.262 to 313.204, or \$226.262 to \$313,204. Because the standard error here is smaller than the corresponding value in the simple regression model, the width of this confidence interval is also narrower. However, while the confidence interval computed in the simple regression model was for *all* homes of size 3,100 square feet, the interval here is relevant only for those homes that also have a land area of 0.9 acres.

Causal Multiple Regression Using Excel's Analysis ToolPak (Data Analysis)

Just as we did in simple regression, we can also use Excel's Analysis ToolPak for multiple regression. To invoke the procedure, we once again click Data | Data Analysis and select Regression from the list of choices. The window shown in Screenshot 11-10D is displayed.

Independent variables must be arranged adjacently in order to use the regression procedure in Data Analysis for multiple regression.

Before we use Data Analysis for multiple regression, we need to ensure that the independent variables in the model are adjacent to each other in an Excel worksheet. In Sue's case, for example, we have entered the selling prices in cells B7:B19, as shown in Screenshot 11-10B, and the two independent variables (home size and land area) in adjacent columns in cells C7:C19 and D7:D19, respectively. We now specify these cell ranges in the appropriate boxes, as shown in Screenshot 11-10D. (Note that the cell ranges for both independent variables are specified as one entry: C7:D19.) The Labels box is checked to indicate that the cell ranges include the name of each variable as the first entry. We then indicate that we want the output of the regression to be displayed in a new worksheet named *11-10E*. The rest of the entries and their implications are the same as in the simple regression procedure.

File: 11-10.xls, sheet: 11-10E

RESULTS OF THE REGRESSION PROCEDURE When we click OK, Data Analysis runs the multiple regression procedure, and the results shown in Screenshot 11-10E are displayed. Here again, just as in the earlier results we obtained using ExcelModules (Screenshot 11-10B), the results show a *Y*-intercept of 99.919 (cell B18), slope of 21.383 for home size (cell B19), slope of 115.030 for land area (cell B20), coefficient of determination R^2 of 0.876 (cell B6), and standard error of the regression estimate of 22.179 (cell B8). The *adjusted* R^2 value in cell B7 is an empirical measure that applies a correction factor to the R^2 value based on the number of independent variables and the number of observations. It is commonly used to compare

SCREENSHOT 11-10D Multiple Regression Using Excel's Analysis ToolPak

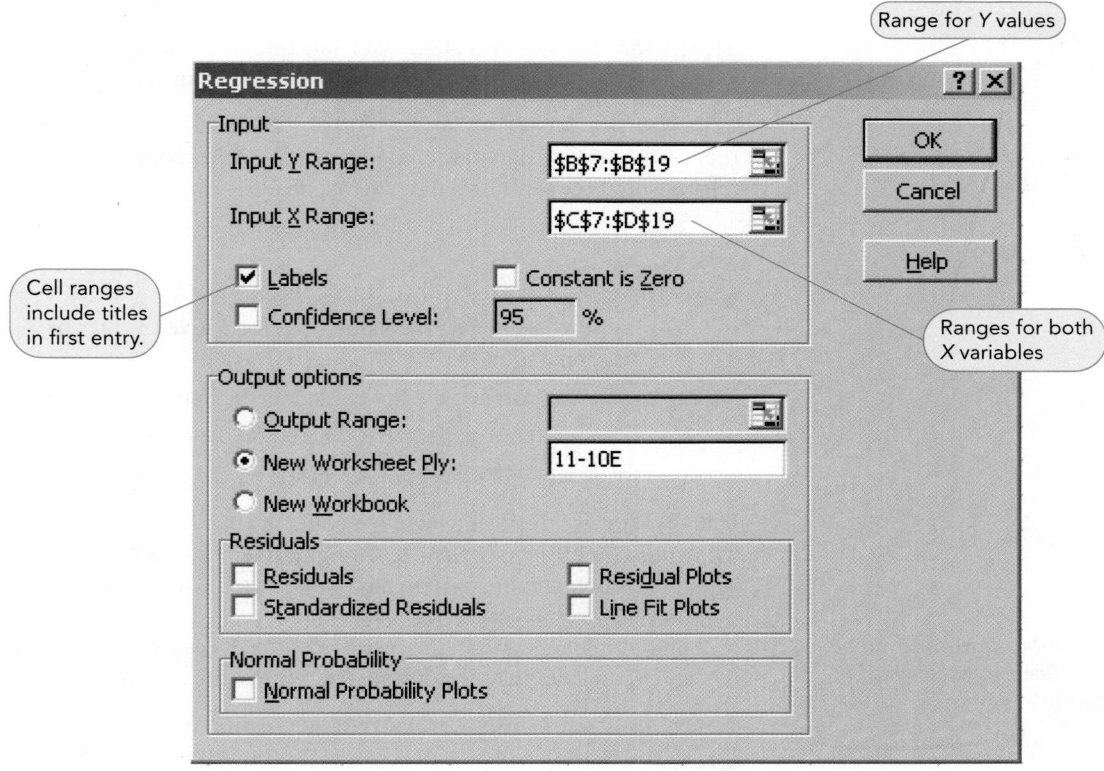

SCREENSHOT 11-10E Multiple Regression Output from Excel's Analysis ToolPak

	A	B	C	D	E	F	G
1	**Multiple Regression Using Data Analysis**						
2							
3	**SUMMARY OUTPUT**						
4	*Regression Statistics*						
5	Multiple R	0.936					
6	R Square	0.876					
7	Adjusted R Square	0.849					
8	Standard Error	22.179					
9	Observations	12					
10							
11	**ANOVA**						
12		*df*	*SS*	*MS*	*F*	*Significance F*	
13	Regression	2	31392.185	15696.093	31.910	0.000	
14	Residual	9	4427.011	491.890			
15	Total	11	35819.197				
16							
17		*Coefficients*	*Standard Error*	*t Stat*	*P-value*	*Lower 95%*	*Upper 95%*
18	Intercept	99.919	48.807	2.047	0.071	-10.490	210.329
19	(X1) Home size ('000 sq ft)	21.383	21.805	0.981	0.352	-27.944	70.710
20	(X2) Land area (acres)	115.030	21.779	5.282	0.001	65.762	164.297

= 31,392.185 / 35,819.197
Overall model is significant.
95% confidence intervals for population slopes
Regression coefficients
P-value of 0.352 indicates that home size is not significant given presence of land area in the model.

multiple regression models with different numbers of independent variables (as opposed to the original R^2 value, which will always be higher for a model with a larger number of independent variables).

Notice that the total SS value of 35,819.197 (in cell C15 of the ANOVA table) is the same value we saw in the simple regression model. Of this, the multiple regression model explains 31,382.185, leaving only 4,427.011 unexplained. The R^2 value can therefore be computed as $31{,}382.185/35{,}819.197 = 0.876$, or 87.6%, which is the same value reported in cell B6.

STATISTICAL SIGNIFICANCE OF THE REGRESSION EQUATION Just as we did in simple regression, if our data set consists of the entire population of homes, the true population relationship between Y and the two independent variables X_1 and X_2 can be expressed as

$$\mu_{\mathrm{Y|Xs}} = \beta_0 + \beta_1 X_1 + \beta_2 X_2 \tag{11-20}$$

where

$\mu_{\mathrm{Y|Xs}}$ = forecasted average value of Y for a given values of X_1 and X_2, based on the entire population

β_0 = Y-intercept of the line, based on the entire population

β_1 = slope with respect to X_1, based on the entire population

β_2 = slope with respect to X_2, based on the entire population

Unlike simple regression, where we could test the significance of the regression relationship by using either the F-test or the t-test, in multiple regression these two tests deal with different issues. As before, we refer you to any statistics textbook for the details of these tests, and we only interpret their results in our discussion here.

The F-test tests the overall significance of the model in multiple regression.

In multiple regression, the F-test tests the overall significance of the regression model. That is, the null and alternate hypotheses for this test are as follows:

$H_0: \beta_1 = \beta_2 = 0$ (i.e., the overall regression model is not significant)
$H_1:$ At least one of β_1 and $\beta_2 \neq 0$ (i.e., at least one variable in the model is significant)

In Sue's example, the computed F-statistic for this test is 31.910, as shown in cell E13 in Screenshot 11-10E. This statistic is F-distributed with 2 numerator degrees of freedom (cell B13) and 9 denominator degrees of freedom (cell B14). The P-value associated with this F-statistic, shown in cell F13, is essentially zero, implying that the null hypothesis can be rejected at virtually any level of significance. That is, we can clearly conclude that there is a statistically significant relationship between Y and at least one of the two X variables. It is important to note that this result of the F-test should not be interpreted as an indication that both X variables are significant.

The t*-test tests the significance of an individual independent variable in the model, given the presence of all the other independent variables.*

The t-test, in contrast, tests the significance of each of the regression slopes, given the presence of all the other independent variables. This previous condition illustrates an important issue about multiple regression: The relationship of each independent variable with the dependent variable in a multiple regression model is affected by all the other independent variables in the model. To illustrate this issue, let us first test the slope for the land area. The null and alternate hypotheses for this test are as follows:

$H_0 : \beta_2 = 0$ (i.e., the slope of land area is not significant, given the presence of home size)
$H_1 : \beta_2 \neq 0$ (i.e., the slope of land area is significant, given the presence of home size)

The computed t-statistic for this test is 5.282, as shown in cell D20 in Screenshot 11-10E. This statistic is t-distributed with 9 degrees of freedom (cell B14). The P-value associated with this t-statistic, shown in cell E20, is 0.001, implying that there is a statistically significant relationship between Y and X_2 (land area), given the presence of the independent variable X_1 (home size) in the model.

Now let us test the slope for the home size. The null and alternate hypotheses for this test are as follows:

$H_0 : \beta_1 = 0$ (i.e., the slope of home size is not significant, given the presence of land area)
$H_1 : \beta_1 \neq 0$ (i.e., the slope of home size is significant, given the presence of land area)

Home size is not significant in the model, given the presence of land area.

The computed t-statistic for this test is 0.981, as shown in cell D19 in Screenshot 11-10E. This statistic is also t-distributed with 9 degrees of freedom (cell B14). The P-value for this test, shown in cell E20, is 0.352, implying that there is *no* statistically significant relationship between Y and X_1 (home size), given the presence of the independent variable X_2 (land area) in the model. Are we concluding here that home size is not a relevant variable to predict home selling prices? The answer is an emphatic no. In fact, recall from the simple regression model that we did establish a statistically significant relationship between home selling prices and home size. All we are concluding in the multiple regression model is that home size adds little incremental value to the model when land area has already been included. In other words, when land area has been included in the regression model, we should perhaps not include home size in the model also, and we should possibly look for other independent variables.

Multicollinearity *exists when two or more independent variables in a multiple regression model are highly correlated with each other.*

MULTICOLLINEARITY If home size was a statistically significant predictor in the simple regression model, why did it become nonsignificant when we added land area as a second independent variable? One possible explanation for this could be a phenomenon called *multicollinearity*. This occurs whenever two or more independent variables in a model are highly correlated with each other. When this happens, the relationship between each independent variable and the dependent variable is affected in an unpredictable manner by the presence of the other highly correlated independent variable.

We can detect pairwise multicollinearity by using correlation analysis.

How can we detect multicollinearity? We can use a simple correlation analysis to detect highly correlated pairs of independent variables.[4] To invoke the procedure in the Analysis ToolPak add-in, we click Data | Data Analysis and select Correlation from the list of choices that is presented. The window shown in Screenshot 11-10F(a) is displayed. We enter the cell ranges for all variables, which must be arranged in adjacent columns or rows. (In Sue's example, we

[4] Multicollinearity can also exist between more than just a pair of variables. For example, independent variables X_1 and X_2 may together be highly correlated with a third independent variable, X_3. We can detect such situations by using a measure called the variance inflationary factor. We refer to you any statistics textbook for details on this measure and its use.

SCREENSHOT 11-10F Correlation Analysis Using Excel's Analysis ToolPak

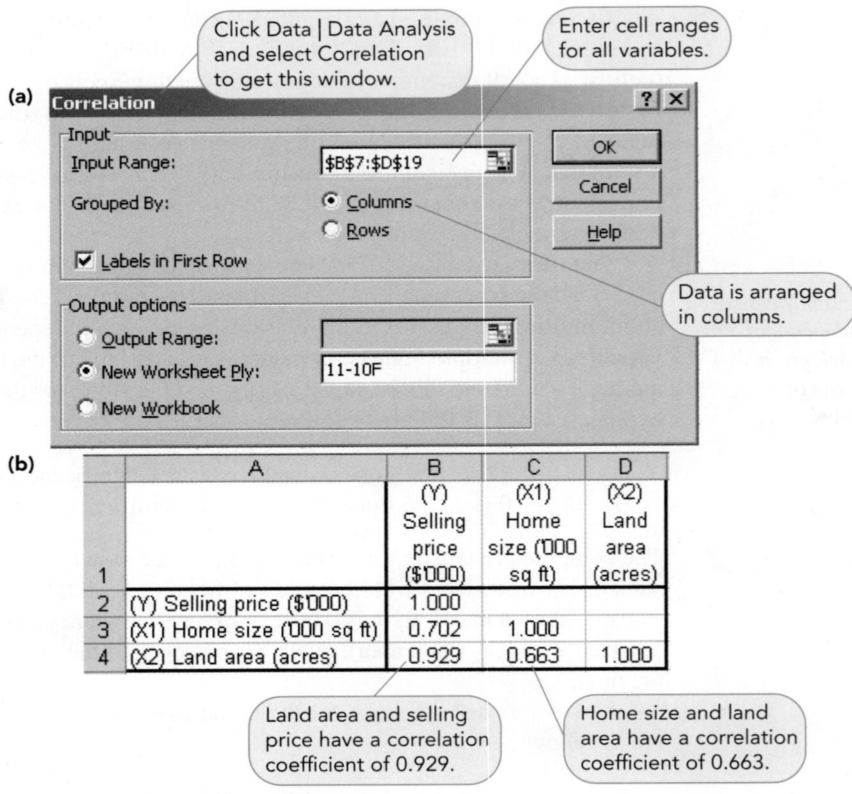

	A	B	C	D
1		(Y) Selling price ($'000)	(X1) Home size ('000 sq ft)	(X2) Land area (acres)
2	(Y) Selling price ($'000)	1.000		
3	(X1) Home size ('000 sq ft)	0.702	1.000	
4	(X2) Land area (acres)	0.929	0.663	1.000

File: 11-10.xls, sheet: 11-10F

have included the cell ranges for Y, X_1, and X_2 from the worksheet shown in Screenshot 11-10B on page 515.) When we now run the procedure, the results shown in Screenshot 11-10F(b) are displayed.

The results indicate that both independent variables are individually highly correlated with the dependent variable. The correlation coefficient between Y and X_1 is 0.702 (cell B3), and it is 0.929 (cell B4) between Y and X_2. This explains why each variable, by itself, is significantly related to Y. However, the results also indicate the X_1 and X_2 are correlated at a level of 0.663 (cell C4). As noted earlier, while there is no clear cut-off to decide when two variables are highly correlated, in general, correlation coefficient magnitudes of 0.6 or greater are indicative of a strong relationship. If two independent variables exhibit this level of relationship, they should not be included in a multiple regression model at the same time. If they are both included, the effect of each independent variable on the other can be unpredictable, as we saw in Sue's example in Screenshot 11-10E.

We can construct various confidence intervals for the population slopes.

CONFIDENCE INTERVALS FOR THE POPULATION SLOPES Just as we did in simple regression, we can compute intervals at various levels of confidence for each population slope (i.e., β_1 and β_2). By default, Data Analysis always reports 95% confidence intervals for both these parameters (shown in cells F19:G19 and F20:G20, respectively, in Screenshot 11-10E). Note that the confidence interval for β_1 extends from a negative value to a positive value (i.e., it spans a value of zero). This is consistent with our earlier finding that the slope of home size is not significantly different from zero, given the presence of land area in the model.

In this model also, the Y-intercept is not relevant for any practical interpretation. (After all, we cannot have a home of size zero with no land area.) For this reason, we ignore the hypothesis test and confidence interval information for the Y-intercept, even though Data Analysis provides that information by default.

Summary

Forecasts are a critical part of a manager's function. Demand forecasts drive the production, capacity, and scheduling systems in a firm and affect the financial, marketing, and personnel planning functions.

This chapter introduces three types of forecasting models: judgmental, time series, and causal. Four qualitative models are discussed for judgmental forecasting: Delphi method, jury of executive opinion, sales force composite, and consumer market survey. We then discuss moving averages, weighted moving averages, exponential smoothing, trend projection, seasonality, and multiplicative decomposition models for time-series data. Finally, we illustrate a popular causal model, regression analysis. In addition, we discuss the use of scatter charts and provide an analysis of forecasting accuracy. The forecast measures discussed includes mean absolute deviation (MAD), mean squared error (MSE), and mean absolute percent error (MAPE).

As we demonstrate in this chapter, no forecasting method is perfect under all conditions. Even when management has found a satisfactory approach, it must still monitor and control its forecasts to make sure errors do not get out of hand. Forecasting can be a very challenging but rewarding part of managing.

Glossary

Additive Decomposition Model A decomposition model in which the forecasted value is the sum of the four components: trend, seasonality, cycles, and random variations.

Causal Models Models that forecast using variables and factors, in addition to time.

Correlation Coefficient A measure of the strength of the linear relationship between two variables.

Coefficient of Determination A measure that indicates what percentage of the variability in the dependent variable is explained by the independent variables.

Cycles Patterns that occur over several years. Cycles are usually tied to the business cycle.

Decision-Making Group A group of experts in a Delphi technique who have the responsibility of making the forecast.

Delphi A judgmental forecasting technique that uses decision makers, staff personnel, and respondents to determine a forecast.

Dependent Variable The variable to be forecasted or predicted. Denoted by Y.

Exponential Smoothing A forecasting technique that is a combination of the last forecast and the last actual value.

Forecast Error The difference between the actual and forecasted values. Also known as *forecast deviation.*

Independent Variable A variable used in a prediction. Denoted by X.

Least-Squares Procedure A procedure used in trend projection and regression analysis to minimize the squared distances between the estimated straight line and the actual values.

Mean Absolute Deviation (MAD) The average of the absolute forecast errors.

Mean Absolute Percent Error (MAPE) The average of the absolute forecast errors as a percentage of the actual values.

Mean Squared Error (MSE) The average of the squared forecast errors.

Moving Average A forecasting technique that averages past values in computing the forecast.

Multiplicative Decomposition Model A decomposition model in which the forecasted value is the product of the four components trend, seasonality, cycles, and random variation.

Qualitative Models Models that forecast using judgments, experience, and qualitative and subjective data.

Random Variations "Blips" in the data that are caused by chance and unusual situations. They follow no discernible pattern.

Regression Analysis A forecasting procedure that uses the least-squares procedure on one or more independent variables to develop a forecasting model.

Scatter Chart A chart or diagram of the variable to be forecasted or predicted, drawn against another variable, such as time. Also called a *scatter diagram* or *plot.*

Seasonality A pattern of demand fluctuations above or below the trend line that occurs every year.

Smoothing Constant A value between 0 and 1 that is used in an exponential smoothing forecast.

Standard Error of the Regression Estimate A measure of the accuracy of regression estimates. Also called *standard deviation of the regression.*

Stationary Data Time-series data in which there is no significant upward or downward movement (or trend) over time.

Time-Series Models Models that forecast by using historical data.

Trend The upward or downward movement of the data over time.

Weighted Moving Average A moving average forecasting method that places different weights on different past values.

Solved Problems

Solved Problem 11-1

Demand for outpatient surgery at Washington General Hospital has increased steadily in the past few years, as shown in the following table:

YEAR	SURGERIES
1	45
2	50
3	52
4	56
5	58

We can construct intervals of various confidence levels for the population slope.

The director of medical services predicted six years ago that demand in year 1 would be 42 surgeries. Using exponential smoothing with $\alpha = 0.20$, develop forecasts for years 2 through 6. What is the MAD value?

Solution

File: 11-11.xls

To solve this problem, we use the Forecasting Models | Exponential Smoothing choice in ExcelModules. Screenshot 11-11 shows the computations. The input entries are shown in cells B7:B11, and the α value is shown in cell B13. The MAD value is calculated to be 8.98 (cell F12). The rounded forecast for year 6 is 50 (cell B15).

SCREENSHOT 11-11 Exponential Smoothing Model for Solved Problem 11-1

	A	B	C	D	E	F	G	H
1	Solved Problem 11-1							
2	Forecasting		Exponential smoothing					
3	Enter the data in the cells shaded YELLOW.							
4								
5	Input Data			Forecast Error Analysis				
6	Period	Actual value		Forecast	Error	Absolute error	Squared error	Absolute % error
7	Year 1	45		42.000				
8	Year 2	50		42.600	7.400	7.400	54.760	14.80%
9	Year 3	52		44.080	7.920	7.920	62.726	15.23%
10	Year 4	56		45.664	10.336	10.336	106.833	18.46%
11	Year 5	58		47.731	10.269	10.269	105.448	17.70%
12				Average		8.981	82.442	16.55%
13	Alpha	0.2				MAD	MSE	MAPE
14								
15	Next period	49.785						

Given forecast for year 1

Value of the smoothing constant

Solved Problem 11-2

Room registrations (in thousands) at the Toronto Towers Plaza Hotel for the past nine years are as follows (earliest year is shown first): 17, 16, 16, 21, 20, 20, 23, 25, and 24. Management would like to determine the mathematical trend of guest registration in order to project future occupancy. This estimate would help the hotel determine whether a future expansion will be needed. Develop the linear trend equation and forecast year 11's registrations.

Solution

File: 11-12.xls

To solve this problem, we use the Forecasting Models | Linear Trend Analysis choice in ExcelModules. Screenshot 11-12 shows the computations. The input entries are shown in cells B7:B15. The period values are automatically entered by ExcelModules in cells C7:C15.

SCREENSHOT 11-12 Trend Analysis Model for Solved Problem 11-2

Solved Problem 11-2

Forecasting Linear trend analysis

Enter the actual values in cells shaded YELLOW. Enter new time period at the bottom to forecast Y.

Input Data			Forecast Error Analysis				
Period	Actual value (or) Y	Period number (or) X	Forecast	Error	Absolute error	Squared error	Absolute % error
Year 1	17	1	15.689	1.311	1.311	1.719	7.71%
Year 2	16	2	16.822	-0.822	0.822	0.676	5.14%
Year 3	16	3	17.956	-1.956	1.956	3.824	12.22%
Year 4	21	4	19.089	1.911	1.911	3.652	9.10%
Year 5	20	5	20.222	-0.222	0.222	0.049	1.11%
Year 6	20	6	21.356	-1.356	1.356	1.838	6.78%
Year 7	23	7	22.489	0.511	0.511	0.261	2.22%
Year 8	25	8	23.622	1.378	1.378	1.898	5.51%
Year 9	24	9	24.756	-0.756	0.756	0.571	3.15%
			Average		**1.136**	**1.610**	**5.88%**
					MAD	**MSE**	**MAPE**
Intercept	**14.556**						
Slope	**1.133**						
Next period	27.022	11					

Regression coefficients

Forecast for year 11, in thousands

The regression equation is Registrants = 14.556 + 1.133 × Year number. MAPE is calculated to be 5.88% (cell I16). The projected average registration for year 11 is 27,022 guests (cell B20).

Solved Problem 11-3

Quarterly demand for Jaguar XJ8s at a New York auto dealership is forecast using the equation

$$\hat{Y} = 10 + 3X$$

where X = quarter number ($X = 1$ is quarter 1 of year 2011, $X = 2$ is quarter 2 of year 2011, and so on), and $\hat{Y}$ = quarterly demand. The demand for luxury sedans is seasonal, and the indices for quarters 1, 2, 3, and 4 of each year are 0.80, 1.00, 1.30, and 0.90, respectively. Forecast the seasonalized demand for each quarter of year 2013.

Solution

Using the coding scheme for X, quarters 1 to 4 of year 2013 are coded $X = 9$ to 12, respectively. Hence,

$$\hat{Y}(\text{quarter 1 of year 2013}) = 10 + 3 \times 9 = 37 \quad \text{Seasonalized forecast} = 37 \times 0.80 = 29.6$$
$$\hat{Y}(\text{quarter 2 of year 2013}) = 10 + 3 \times 10 = 40 \quad \text{Seasonalized forecast} = 40 \times 1.00 = 40.0$$
$$\hat{Y}(\text{quarter 3 of year 2013}) = 10 + 3 \times 11 = 43 \quad \text{Seasonalized forecast} = 43 \times 1.30 = 55.9$$
$$\hat{Y}(\text{quarter 4 of year 2013}) = 10 + 3 \times 12 = 46 \quad \text{Seasonalized forecast} = 40 \times 0.90 = 41.0$$

Solved Problem 11-4

In section 11.7, we helped Sandy Sawyer decompose Sawyer Piano House's time-series data using a multiplicative decomposition model. Repeat the computations now, using an additive decomposition model. For your convenience, the data for this model (showing grand piano sales for the past 20 quarters) are repeated in Table 11.8.

TABLE 11.8
Sales of Grand Pianos at Sawyer Piano House

	2007	2008	2009	2010	2011
Quarter 1	4	6	10	12	18
Quarter 2	2	4	3	9	10
Quarter 3	1	4	5	7	13
Quarter 4	5	14	16	22	35

Solution

Recall from Equation 11-6 that the additive decomposition model can be specified as

$$\text{Forecast} = \text{Trend} + \text{Seasonality} + \text{Cycles} + \text{Random variations}$$

File: 11-13.xls

Although ExcelModules does not include a worksheet for additive decomposition, the worksheet provided for multiplicative decomposition can easily be modified to suit an additive model. We first select the choice titled Multiplicative Decomposition from the Forecasting Models menu in ExcelModules. Then, as we did in Screenshot 11-8A on page 500, we specify the number of periods for which we have past data (20), the name for the period (Quarter), and the number of seasons each year (4). In addition, we select the Centered Moving Average option to compute seasonal indices. We click OK, and in the resulting screen, we enter the actual number of pianos sold during the past 20 quarters in cells B7:B26. The corresponding time periods (i.e., the X variable values) are automatically specified in cells C7:C26 by the worksheet.

The worksheet displays the results of the multiplicative decomposition model. We now modify this worksheet as follows to transform it to an additive mode (unless specified here, the computations in a column are the same as in the multiplicative model. The results for the additive model are shown in Screenshot 11-13):

1. *Computation of the seasonal indices, Columns D–G.* We compute the following:

   - In column D we compute the centered moving average sales for each quarter.
   - Next, we compute the seasonal difference for each quarter by *subtracting* from the actual sales (column B) in that quarter its centered average (column D). That is, column E = column B − column D. Note that instead of dividing by the centered moving average (as in a multiplicative model), we subtract it in an additive model.
   - The seasonal differences for each quarter are collected in cells B33:E37, and we compute the seasonal index for each quarter as the average of all the differences for that quarter. These seasonal indices are shown in cells B38:E38 and repeated in column F, next to the appropriate quarters each year. Seasonal index values in an additive model are positive or negative. A positive index indicates that the actual value in that period is above average, while a negative index indicates that the actual value is below average.
   - Finally, in column G, we compute the unseasonalized sales in each quarter as the actual sales (column B) in that quarter minus the seasonal index (column F) for that quarter. That is, column G = column B − column F.

We subtract the seasonal indices from the seasonalized data in an additive model.

2. *Computation of the trend equation.* Using the unseasonalized sales in column G as the dependent variable (Y) and the time period number in column C as the independent variable (X), we compute the linear trend equation. The resulting Y-intercept (a) and slope (b) for this straight line are shown in cells G28 and G29, respectively. In Sandy's case, the linear trend equation for the additive model is

$$\text{Unseasonalized sales forecast} = 0.149 + 0.959 \times \text{Quarter number}$$

3. *Computation of forecast, columns H and I.* We now calculate the forecast by adding the appropriate seasonal indices to the unseasonalized sales forecasts. Note that instead of multiplying by the seasonal index (as in a multiplicative model), we add it in an additive model. The computations are as follows:

   - In column H, we use the trend equation to compute the unseasonalized forecast for each quarter. For example, for the fourth quarter of year 2 (i.e., quarter 8), this value

SCREENSHOT 11-13 Additive Decomposition Model for Sawyer Piano House

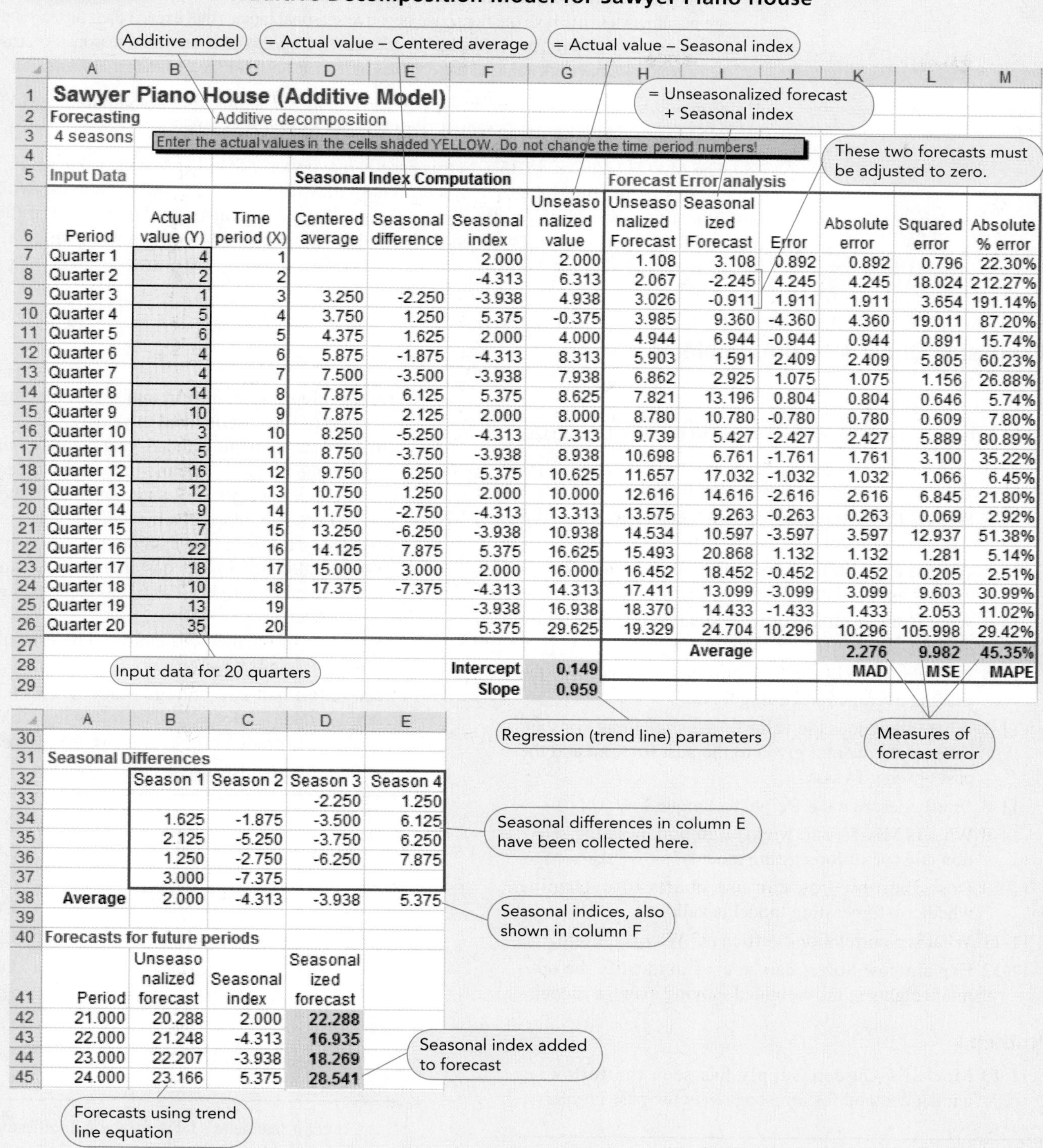

Sawyer Piano House (Additive Model)

Forecasting — Additive decomposition

4 seasons — Enter the actual values in the cells shaded YELLOW. Do not change the time period numbers!

Input Data			Seasonal Index Computation				Forecast Error analysis					
Period	Actual value (Y)	Time period (X)	Centered average	Seasonal difference	Seasonal index	Unseasonalized value	Unseasonalized Forecast	Seasonalized Forecast	Error	Absolute error	Squared error	Absolute % error
Quarter 1	4	1			2.000	2.000	1.108	3.108	0.892	0.892	0.796	22.30%
Quarter 2	2	2			-4.313	6.313	2.067	-2.245	4.245	4.245	18.024	212.27%
Quarter 3	1	3	3.250	-2.250	-3.938	4.938	3.026	-0.911	1.911	1.911	3.654	191.14%
Quarter 4	5	4	3.750	1.250	5.375	-0.375	3.985	9.360	-4.360	4.360	19.011	87.20%
Quarter 5	6	5	4.375	1.625	2.000	4.000	4.944	6.944	-0.944	0.944	0.891	15.74%
Quarter 6	4	6	5.875	-1.875	-4.313	8.313	5.903	1.591	2.409	2.409	5.805	60.23%
Quarter 7	4	7	7.500	-3.500	-3.938	7.938	6.862	2.925	1.075	1.075	1.156	26.88%
Quarter 8	14	8	7.875	6.125	5.375	8.625	7.821	13.196	0.804	0.804	0.646	5.74%
Quarter 9	10	9	7.875	2.125	2.000	8.000	8.780	10.780	-0.780	0.780	0.609	7.80%
Quarter 10	3	10	8.250	-5.250	-4.313	7.313	9.739	5.427	-2.427	2.427	5.889	80.89%
Quarter 11	5	11	8.750	-3.750	-3.938	8.938	10.698	6.761	-1.761	1.761	3.100	35.22%
Quarter 12	16	12	9.750	6.250	5.375	10.625	11.657	17.032	-1.032	1.032	1.066	6.45%
Quarter 13	12	13	10.750	1.250	2.000	10.000	12.616	14.616	-2.616	2.616	6.845	21.80%
Quarter 14	9	14	11.750	-2.750	-4.313	13.313	13.575	9.263	-0.263	0.263	0.069	2.92%
Quarter 15	7	15	13.250	-6.250	-3.938	10.938	14.534	10.597	-3.597	3.597	12.937	51.38%
Quarter 16	22	16	14.125	7.875	5.375	16.625	15.493	20.868	1.132	1.132	1.281	5.14%
Quarter 17	18	17	15.000	3.000	2.000	16.000	16.452	18.452	-0.452	0.452	0.205	2.51%
Quarter 18	10	18	17.375	-7.375	-4.313	14.313	17.411	13.099	-3.099	3.099	9.603	30.99%
Quarter 19	13	19			-3.938	16.938	18.370	14.433	-1.433	1.433	2.053	11.02%
Quarter 20	35	20			5.375	29.625	19.329	24.704	10.296	10.296	105.998	29.42%
								Average		2.276	9.982	45.35%
					Intercept	0.149				MAD	MSE	MAPE
					Slope	0.959						

Seasonal Differences

	Season 1	Season 2	Season 3	Season 4
			-2.250	1.250
	1.625	-1.875	-3.500	6.125
	2.125	-5.250	-3.750	6.250
	1.250	-2.750	-6.250	7.875
	3.000	-7.375		
Average	2.000	-4.313	-3.938	5.375

Forecasts for future periods

Period	Unseasonalized forecast	Seasonal index	Seasonalized forecast
21.000	20.288	2.000	22.288
22.000	21.248	-4.313	16.935
23.000	22.207	-3.938	18.269
24.000	23.166	5.375	28.541

is computed in cell H14 as $(0.149 + 0.959 \times 8) = 7.821$. These values are also computed for the next year (i.e., quarters 21 to 24, denoting the four quarters in year 2012) in cells B42:B45.

We seasonalize forecasts by adding the appropriate seasonal indices.

- The appropriate seasonal indices are added to the unseasonalized forecasts to get the seasonalized forecast for each quarter in column I. That is, column I = column H + *column F*. Cells D42:D45 show the seasonal forecasts for quarters 21 to 24.

Notice that the seasonal forecasts for quarters 2 and 3, shown in cells I8 and I9, respectively, are negative (because both quarters have negative seasonal indices that exceed their unseasonalized sales forecasts). Clearly, this is illogical in practice, and we should adjust these seasonal forecasts to zero. Note: We have not adjusted these values in Screenshot 11-13 to facilitate this discussion.

Finally, we compute measures of forecast error.

4. *Computation of forecast error measures, columns J through M.* We compute the MAD, MSE, and MAPE values in cells K27, L27, and M27, respectively.

File: 11-13.xls

The MAPE value of 45.35% in this case is much worse than the MAPE value of 23.74% obtained using the multiplicative model. Sandy may therefore be better off staying with the multiplicative model. If desired, we can ask ExcelModules to also draw line charts of the actual and forecasted values for the additive model. Although this chart is not shown here, it is included in the Excel file *11-13.xls* on this textbook's Companion Website.

Discussion Questions and Problems

Discussion Questions

11-1 Briefly describe the steps used to develop a forecasting system.

11-2 What is a time-series forecasting model?

11-3 What is the difference between a causal model and a time-series model?

11-4 What is a qualitative forecasting model, and when is using it appropriate?

11-5 What is the meaning of least squares in a regression model?

11-6 What are some of the problems and drawbacks of the moving average forecasting model?

11-7 What effect does the value of the smoothing constant have on the weight given to the past forecast and the past observed value?

11-8 Briefly describe the Delphi technique.

11-9 What is MAPE, and why is it important in the selection and use of forecasting models?

11-10 Describe how you can use charts to determine whether a forecasting model is valid.

11-11 What is a correlation coefficient? Why is it useful?

11-12 Explain how Solver can be used to identify the optimal weights in the weighted moving average model.

Problems

11-13 McCall's Garden Supply has seen the following annual demand for lime bags over the past 11 years:

YEAR	BAGS (THOUSANDS)	YEAR	BAGS (THOUSANDS)
1	4	7	7
2	8	8	9
3	6	9	13
4	6	10	14
5	9	11	16
6	8		

(a) Develop 2-year, 3-year, and 4-year moving averages to forecast demand in year 12.

(b) Forecast demand with a 3-year weighted moving average in which demand in the most recent year is given a weight of 2 and demands in the other two years are each given a weight of 1.

(c) Forecast demand by using exponential smoothing with a smoothing constant of 0.4. Assume that the forecast for year 1 is 6,000 bags to begin the procedure.

(d) Which of the methods analyzed here would you use? Explain your answer.

11-14 Jeannette Phan is a college student who has just completed her junior year. The following table summarizes her grade point average (GPA) for each of the past nine semesters:

YEAR	SEMESTER	GPA
Freshman	Fall	2.4
	Winter	2.9
	Spring	3.1
Sophomore	Fall	3.2
	Winter	3.0
	Spring	2.9
Junior	Fall	2.8
	Winter	3.6
	Spring	3.2

(a) Forecast Jeannette's GPA for the fall semester of her senior year by using a three-period moving average.

(b) Forecast Jeannette's GPA for the fall semester of her senior year by using exponential smoothing with $\alpha = 0.3$.

(c) Which of the two methods provides a more accurate forecast? Justify your answer.

(d) If you decide to use a three-period weighted moving average, find the optimal weights that would minimize MAPE. Is this method an improvement over the previous two methods?

11-15 Daily sales volume for Nilgiris Convenience Store is shown in the following table:

DAY	SALES	DAY	SALES
1	\$622	6	\$656
2	\$418	7	\$689
3	\$608	8	\$675
4	\$752	9	\$706
5	\$588	10	\$725

Develop two-day, three-day, and four-day moving averages to forecast the sales for each day. What is the forecast for day 11 in each case?

11-16 Consider the data given in Problem 11-15 for Nilgiris Convenience Store.

(a) If the store wants to use exponential smoothing to forecast the sales volume, what is the optimal value of α that would minimize MAPE? What is the forecast for day 11 using this model?

(b) If the store wants to use linear trend analysis to forecast the sales volume, what is the linear equation that best fits the data? What is the forecast for day 11 using this model?

(c) Which of the methods analyzed here and in Problem 11-15 would you use? Explain your answer.

11-17 The following table shows the number of Blu-ray DVD players that Electronic Depot has sold during the past 12 weeks:

WEEK	SALES	WEEK	SALES
1	22	7	24
2	27	8	25
3	30	9	22
4	21	10	30
5	33	11	38
6	28	12	37

Develop 2-week, 3-week, and 4-week moving averages to forecast the sales for each week. What is the forecast for week 13 in each case?

11-18 Consider the data given in Problem 11-17 for Blu-ray DVD player sales at Electronic Depot.

(a) If Electronic Depot decides to forecast sales by using a three-period weighted moving average, what are the optimal weights that minimize MAPE? What would be the week 13 forecast using these weights?

(b) If Electronic Depot decides to forecast sales by using exponential smoothing, what is the optimal value of α that minimizes MAPE? What would be the week 13 forecast using this procedure?

(c) Which of the methods analyzed here and in Problem 11-17 would you use? Explain your answer.

11-19 Sales of Hot-Blast heaters have grown steadily during the past five years, as shown in the following table:

YEAR	SALES
1	480
2	525
3	548
4	593
5	614

(a) Using exponential smoothing constants of 0.35, 0.65, and 0.95, develop forecasts for years 2 through 6. The sales manager had predicted, before the business started, that year 1's sales would be 440 air conditioners. Which smoothing constant gives the most accurate forecast?

(b) Use a three-year moving average forecasting model to forecast sales of heaters.

(c) Using linear trend analysis, develop a forecasting model for the sales of heaters.

(d) Which of the methods analyzed here would you use? Explain your answer.

11-20 Highland Automotive wishes to forecast the number of new cars that will be sold next week. The following table summarizes the number of new cars sold during each of the past 12 weeks:

WEEK	NUMBER SOLD	WEEK	NUMBER SOLD
1	22	7	28
2	26	8	26
3	23	9	29
4	27	10	29
5	21	11	27
6	25	12	31

(a) Provide a forecast by using a 3-week weighted moving average technique with weights 5, 3, and 1 (5 = most recent).

(b) Forecast sales by using an exponential smoothing model with $\alpha = 0.45$.

(c) Highland would like to forecast sales by using linear trend analysis. What is the linear equation that best fits the data?

(d) Which of the methods analyzed here would you use? Explain your answer.

11-21 The operations manager of a musical instrument distributor feels that demand for bass drums may be related to the number of television appearances by the popular rock group Green Shades during the preceding month. The manager has collected the data shown in the following table:

DEMAND	TV APPEARANCES
3	4
6	5
7	8
5	7
10	9
9	6
8	6

(a) Graph these data to see whether a linear equation might describe the relationship between the group's television shows and bass drum sales.
(b) Use the least-squares regression method to derive a forecasting equation.
(c) What is your estimate for bass drum sales if Green Shades performed on TV four times last month?

11-22 Sales of industrial vacuum cleaners at Overholt Supply Co. over the past 13 months were as follows:

MONTH	SALES (THOUSANDS)	MONTH	SALES (THOUSANDS)
January	9	August	12
February	12	September	15
March	14	October	10
April	8	November	12
May	13	December	14
June	15	January	9
July	9		

(a) Using a moving average with three periods, determine the demand for vacuum cleaners for next February.
(b) Using a three-period weighted moving average with weights 3, 2, and 1 (3 = most recent), determine the demand for vacuum cleaners for February.
(c) Evaluate and comment on the accuracy of each of these models.

11-23 Calls to a college emergency hotline for the past 29 months are as follows (with the earliest month shown first): 50, 35, 25, 40, 45, 35, 20, 30, 35, 20, 15, 40, 55, 35, 25, 55, 55, 40, 35, 60, 75, 50, 40, 42, 51, 22, 38, 45, and 65.
(a) Assuming an initial forecast of 55 calls for month 1, use exponential smoothing with $\alpha = 0.15$, 0.65, and 0.95 to forecast calls for each month. What is the forecast for the 30th month in each case?
(b) Actual calls during the 30th month were 85. Which smoothing constant provides a superior forecast?

11-24 Passenger miles flown on I-Go Airlines, a commuter firm serving the Boston hub, are as follows for the past 12 weeks:

WEEK	MILES (THOUSANDS)	WEEK	MILES (THOUSANDS)
1	21	7	24
2	25	8	22
3	23	9	26
4	27	10	24
5	22	11	19
6	20	12	26

(a) Assuming an initial forecast of 22,000 miles for week 1, use exponential smoothing with $\alpha = 0.3$, 0.6, and 0.8 to forecast miles for weeks 2 through 12. What is the forecast for week 13 in each case?
(b) Evaluate and comment on the accuracy of each of these models.

11-25 Rental income at the Walsh Real Estate Company for the period February–July has been as follows:

MONTH	INCOME (THOUSANDS)
February	\$83.0
March	\$81.5
April	\$77.8
May	\$84.7
June	\$84.3
July	\$85.8

(a) Use exponential smoothing with $\alpha = 0.2$ and 0.4 to forecast August's income. Assume that the initial forecast for February is \$78,000.
(b) Which smoothing constant provide a better forecast? Justify your answer.
(c) Determine the optimal value of α that minimizes MAPE.

11-26 Commuter ridership in Athens, Greece, during the summer months is believed to be heavily tied to the number of tourists visiting the city. During the past 12 years, the data in the table at the top of the next page have been obtained.
(a) Use trend analysis to forecast ridership in years 13, 14, and 15. How well does the model fit the data?
(b) Draw the relationship between the number of tourists and ridership. Is a linear model reasonable?
(c) Develop a linear regression relationship between the number of tourists and ridership.
(d) What is the expected ridership if 10 million tourists visit the city next year?

YEAR	NUMBER OF TOURISTS (MILLIONS)	RIDERSHIP (HUNDREDS OF THOUSANDS)
1	11	14
2	6	9
3	10	12
4	8	14
5	18	24
6	19	26
7	20	23
8	16	19
9	18	26
10	24	43
11	19	33
12	11	16

11-27 Becky Schalkoff, a New Orleans criminal psychologist, specializes in treating patients who are phobic, afraid to leave their homes. The following table indicates how many patients Dr. Schalkoff has seen each year for the past 10 years. It also indicates the crime rate (robberies per 1,000 population) in New Orleans during each year:

YEAR	NUMBER OF PATIENTS	CRIME RATE
1	30	67.3
2	27	70.6
3	34	82.4
4	35	84.7
5	34	90.1
6	49	98.0
7	54	110.1
8	48	103.8
9	52	112.3
10	55	125.2

Using trend analysis, how many patients do you think Dr. Schalkoff will see in years 11, 12, and 13? How well does the model fit the data?

11-28 Consider the patient data for Dr. Schalkoff given in Problem 11-27.

(a) Draw the relationship between the crime rate and Dr. Schalkoff's patient load. Is a linear model between these two variables reasonable?

(b) Apply linear regression to study the relationship between the crime rate and Dr. Schalkoff's patient load.

(c) If the crime rate increases to 140.2 in year 11, how many patients will Dr. Schalkoff treat?

(d) If the crime rate drops to 98.6, what is the patient projection?

11-29 In the past two years at William Middleton's tire dealership, 125 and 175 high-performance radials, respectively, were sold in fall, 225 and 275 were sold in winter, 75 and 90 were sold in spring, and 210 and 225 were sold in summer. With a major expansion planned, Mr. Middleton projects sales next year to increase to 900 high-performance radials. What will the seasonalized demand be each season for these tires?

11-30 Management of Remington's Department Store has used time-series extrapolation to forecast retail sales for the next four quarters. The sales estimates are \$130,000, \$150,000, \$170,000, and \$190,000 for the respective quarters. Seasonal indices for the four quarters have been found to be 1.25, 0.95, 0.75, and 1.05, respectively. Compute the seasonalized sales forecast for each quarter.

11-31 Charles Brandon is thinking about investing in the Purple Arrow Company, which makes central air conditioning units. The company has been in business for over 50 years, and Charles believes it is very stable. Based on his investing knowledge and experience, Charles believes that the dividend paid out by the company is a function of earnings per share (EPS). Using the Internet, Charles has been able to find the EPS and dividend per share paid by Purple Arrow for each of the past 10 years, as shown in the following table:

YEAR	EPS	DIVIDEND PER SHARE
1	\$2.34	\$0.29
2	\$1.70	\$0.14
3	\$1.89	\$0.19
4	\$1.94	\$0.16
5	\$1.51	\$0.05
6	\$2.04	\$0.39
7	\$1.72	\$0.11
8	\$1.98	\$0.27
9	\$1.89	\$0.19
10	\$1.57	\$0.09

(a) Develop a regression model to predict the dividend per share based on EPS.

(b) Identify and interpret the R^2 value.

(c) The EPS next year is projected be \$1.33. What is the expected dividend?

11-32 Thirteen students entered the undergraduate business program at Longstreet College two years ago. The table near the top of the next column indicates what their GPAs were after they were in the program for two years and what each student scored on the SAT math exam when he or she was in high school.

(a) Is there a meaningful relationship between GPAs and SAT math scores? Justify your answer.

(b) If Gwen gets a 490 SAT math score, what is her predicted GPA?

(c) If Jarvis gets a perfect 800 SAT math score, what is his predicted GPA? Is it appropriate to use this model to predict Jarvis's score? Why or why not?

STUDENT	SAT MATH	GPA
A	460	3.00
B	440	3.03
C	630	3.10
D	730	3.55
E	650	3.76
F	430	3.98
G	460	2.25
H	520	2.63
I	770	3.32
J	540	2.09
K	650	2.85
L	750	4.00
M	410	1.70

11-33 Sruti Singh is shopping for a used Volkswagen Golf and feels that there is a relationship between the mileage and market value of the car. The following table provides data on previous car sales from the local area:

CAR	MILEAGE	MARKET VALUE	AGE (YEARS)
1	11,600	$14,200	1
2	22,800	$14,000	1
3	35,000	$10,500	3
4	42,700	$ 9,300	3
5	54,500	$12,800	4
6	58,200	$10,900	5
7	66,800	$ 9,500	7
8	73,100	$ 7,900	6
9	77,500	$ 6,200	8
10	85,700	$ 7,500	9

(a) Develop a simple regression model to predict the market value of a Volkswagen Golf based on its mileage.

(b) What percentage of the market value variation is explained by the mileage variable?

(c) Sruti has found a car with 46,700 miles. Construct a 95% confidence interval for the market value of this car.

11-34 Sruti Singh (see Problem 11-33) would like to investigate the effect of adding the age of the car (in years) to the regression model. The table in Problem 11-33 includes the ages of the original 10 cars.

(a) Develop a multiple regression model to predict the market value of a Volkswagen Golf based on its mileage and age.

(b) What percentage of the selling price variation is explained by this expanded model?

(c) The car that Sruti found with 46,700 miles is 5 years old. What is the revised 95% confidence interval for the market value of this car? Explain why this interval is different from the one in Problem 11-33(c).

11-35 Callaway College is a small business school that offers an MBA program. The main entrance criterion for admission to the MBA program is the Common Business Admission Test (CBAT) score. The following table provides the GPAs of 12 students who have graduated recently, along with their CBAT scores and ages:

STUDENT	GPA	CBAT	AGE
1	3.70	690	34
2	3.00	610	29
3	3.25	480	24
4	4.00	740	39
5	3.52	580	30
6	2.83	460	27
7	3.80	570	35
8	4.00	620	42
9	3.65	750	24
10	3.47	510	30
11	3.33	550	27
12	3.75	700	28

(a) Develop a simple regression model to predict the GPA of a student based on his or her CBAT score.

(b) Identify and interpret the R^2 value.

(c) A new graduate student has a CBAT score of 630. Construct a 90% confidence interval for this student's predicted GPA.

11-36 Callaway College (see Problem 11-35) would like to investigate the effect of adding the age of the student to the regression model. The table in Problem 11-35 includes the ages of the original 12 students.

(a) Develop a multiple regression model to predict the GPA of a student based on his or her CBAT score and age.

(b) Identify and interpret the R^2 value for this expanded regression model.

(c) The new student with a CBAT score of 630 is 29 years old. What is the revised 90% confidence interval for this student's predicted GPA? Explain why this interval is different from the one in Problem 11-35(c).

11-37 Kurt's Hardware Store advertises and sells snow blowers each season. The following table provides the annual demand, level of advertising, in dollars, and snowfall, in inches, for the past eight years:

YEAR	DEMAND (UNITS)	ADVERTISING	SNOWFALL (INCHES)
1	41	$4,000	82
2	38	$3,500	64
3	26	$1,800	52
4	43	$2,800	60
5	33	$3,000	58
6	30	$2,400	50
7	34	$2,600	60
8	37	$2,200	53

(a) Develop a simple regression model to predict the demand for snow blowers based on the number of advertising dollars spent.
(b) What percentage of the demand variation is explained by the level of advertising?
(c) Next year's advertising budget is $2,600. What is the predicted demand for snow blowers?

11-38 Kurt's Hardware Store (see Problem 11-37) would like to investigate the effect of adding annual snowfall to the regression model. The table in Problem 11-37 includes the annual snowfall (in inches) for the past eight years.
(a) Develop a multiple regression model to predict the demand for snow blowers based on the advertising budget and the amount of snowfall.
(b) What percentage of the demand variation is explained by this expanded model?
(c) What is the predicted demand for snow blowers with an advertising budget of $2,600 and expected snowfall of 65 inches?

11-39 The Fowler Martial Arts Academy trains young boys and girls in self-defense. Joan Fowler, the owner of the academy, notes that monthly revenue is higher when school is in session but quite low when school is out (because many children are away on vacation or at summer camp). She has researched revenues for the past four years and obtained the information shown in the Table for Problem 11-39.

Decompose Joan's data by using a multiplicative model. Use the model to forecast revenues for year 5. Comment on the validity of the model.

11-40 In addition to his day job as an engineer, Luis Garcia runs a small ethnic grocery store. The shop stocks food items from southeast Asian countries and caters to the large population of people from this region who live in Luis's community. Luis wants to develop a quantitative model to forecast sales. His sales data (in thousands) for the past 16 quarters are as shown in the Table for Problem 11-40.

Table for Problem 11-39

MONTH	YEAR 1	YEAR 2	YEAR 3	YEAR 4
January	$59,042	$57,495	$56,583	$55,658
February	$62,659	$62,622	$66,438	$67,164
March	$22,879	$24,273	$27,766	$27,795
April	$29,946	$30,492	$31,600	$30,667
May	$26,839	$28,237	$29,589	$31,962
June	$19,134	$17,893	$20,115	$21,096
July	$20,051	$21,126	$19,324	$22,778
August	$19,625	$22,876	$23,486	$23,144
September	$19,925	$22,641	$24,719	$26,601
October	$58,435	$60,796	$60,666	$61,385
November	$87,705	$87,815	$86,693	$88,581
December	$77,430	$78,711	$80,056	$81,048

Table for Problem 11-40

QUARTER	YEAR 1	YEAR 2	YEAR 3	YEAR 4
Quarter 1	$42.9	$43.8	$49.0	$51.3
Quarter 2	$48.5	$50.3	$54.2	$58.2
Quarter 3	$54.1	$57.8	$59.3	$62.9
Quarter 4	$74.1	$79.8	$83.3	$88.5

Develop a multiplicative decomposition model for Luis's sales data. Use the model to forecast revenues for year 4. Comment on the validity of the model.

11-41 The GNP for each quarter of the past four years is shown in the following table:

YEAR	QUARTER	GNP (BILLIONS)
1	1	$ 9,027
	2	$ 9,092
	3	$ 9,194
	4	$ 9,367
2	1	$ 9,505
	2	$ 9,588
	3	$ 9,726
	4	$ 9,938
3	1	$10,063
	2	$10,238
	3	$10,285
	4	$10,375
4	1	$10,430
	2	$10,473
	3	$10,501
	4	$10,580

(a) Find the optimal value of α that would minimize MAPE for the exponential smoothing model.
(b) What is the linear trend equation that best fits the data? Forecast the GNP for the first quarter of year 5 by using this equation.
(c) Forecast the GNP for the first quarter of year 5 by using a four-period moving average.
(d) Which of these methods is most appropriate to use? Justify your answer.

11-42 Using the data from Problem 11-41, forecast the GNP for each quarter of year 5 by using the multiplicative decomposition model. What is the MAPE value for this model?

11-43 The average price per gallon of gasoline in major U.S. cities for each month during a three-year period are shown in the following table:

MONTH	YEAR 1	YEAR 2	YEAR 3
January	$2.972	$3.301	$3.472
February	$2.955	$3.369	$3.484
March	$2.991	$3.541	$3.447
April	$3.117	$3.506	$3.564
May	$3.178	$3.498	$3.729
June	$3.148	$3.617	$3.640
July	$3.189	$3.593	$3.482
August	$3.255	$3.510	$3.427
September	$3.280	$3.582	$3.531
October	$3.274	$3.559	$3.362
November	$3.264	$3.555	$3.263
December	$3.298	$3.489	$3.131

(a) Using exponential smoothing with $\alpha = 0.45$, what is the gasoline price forecast for January of year 4?
(b) What is the linear trend equation that best fits the data? Forecast the average gasoline price for January of year 4 by using this equation.
(c) Which method is more accurate?

11-44 Using the data from Problem 11-43, forecast the average gasoline price for each month in year 4 by using the multiplicative decomposition model. What is the MAPE value for this model?

11-45 Quarterly sales figures for the Cavill Pump Company, in thousands, for the past four years are shown in the following table:

QUARTER	YEAR 1	YEAR 2	YEAR 3	YEAR 4
1	$263	$312	$283	$319
2	$300	$323	$320	$303
3	$245	$298	$365	$339
4	$381	$390	$398	$368

(a) Forecast the demand for the first quarter of year 5 by using a four-period moving average model.
(b) What is the linear trend equation that best fits the data? Forecast the demand for the first quarter of year 5 by using this equation.
(c) Which method is more accurate?

11-46 Consider the data from Problem 11-45.
(a) Develop a sales forecast for each quarter in year 5 by using the multiplicative decomposition model.
(b) Repeat the computations by using an additive decomposition model.
(c) Which decomposition model is more accurate? Explain your answer.

11-47 The following table shows the quarterly demand, in thousands of cases, for a national beer distributor over the past 4 years:

QUARTER	YEAR 1	YEAR 2	YEAR 3	YEAR 4
1	294	335	433	280
2	499	507	516	524
3	437	529	501	515
4	344	285	482	530

(a) Forecast the demand for the first quarter of year 5 by using a four-period moving average model.
(b) Forecast the demand for the first quarter of year 5 by using an exponential smoothing model with $\alpha = 0.4$.
(c) Which method is more accurate?

11-48 Consider the data from Problem 11-47.
(a) Forecast the demand for beer for each quarter in year 5 by using the multiplicative decomposition model.
(b) Repeat the computations by using an additive decomposition model.
(c) Which decomposition model is more accurate? Explain your answer.

Case Study

North-South Airline

In January 2011, Northern Airlines merged with Southeast Airlines to create the fourth-largest U.S. carrier. The new North-South Airline inherited both an aging fleet of Boeing 727–300 aircraft and Stephen Ruth. Ruth was a tough former secretary of the Navy who stepped in as new president and chairman of the board.

Ruth's first concern in creating a financially solid company was maintenance costs. It was commonly surmised in the airline industry that maintenance costs rise with the age of the aircraft. Ruth quickly noticed that historically there had been a significant difference in the reported B727–300 maintenance costs both in the airframe and engine areas between Northern Airlines and Southeast Airlines, with Southeast having the newer fleet.

On February 7, 2011, Ruth called Peg Young, vice president for operations and maintenance, into his office and asked her to study the issue. Specifically, Ruth wanted to know whether the average fleet age was correlated to direct airframe maintenance costs and whether there was a relationship between average fleet age and direct engine maintenance costs. Young was to report back by February 21 with the answer, along with quantitative and graphical descriptions of the relationship.

Young's first step was to have her staff construct the average age of Northern and Southeast B727–300 fleets, by quarter, since the introduction of that aircraft to service by each airline in late 2003 and early 2004. The average age of each fleet was calculated by first multiplying the total number of calendar days each aircraft had been in service at the pertinent point in time by the average daily utilization of the respective fleet to total fleet hours flown. The total fleet hours flown was then divided by the number of aircraft in service at that time, giving the age of the "average" aircraft in the fleet.

The average utilization was found by taking the actual total fleet hours flown at September 30, 2010, from Northern and Southeast data, and dividing by the total days in service for all aircraft at that time. The average utilization for Southeast was 8.3 hours per day, and the average utilization for Northern was 8.7 hours per day. Because the available cost data were calculated for each yearly period ending at the end of the first quarter, average fleet age was calculated at the same points in time. The fleet data are shown in the table below.

Discussion Questions

Prepare Peg Young's response to Stephen Ruth.

Note: Dates and names of airlines and individuals have been changed in this case to maintain confidentiality. The data and issues described here are actual.

	NORTHERN AIRLINE DATA			SOUTHEAST AIRLINE DATA		
YEAR	AIRFRAME COST PER AIRCRAFT (THOUSANDS)	ENGINE COST PER AIRCRAFT (THOUSANDS)	AVERAGE AGE (HOURS)	AIRFRAME COST PER AIRCRAFT (THOUSANDS)	ENGINE COST PER AIRCRAFT (THOUSANDS)	AVERAGE AGE (HOURS)
2004	$51.80	$43.49	6,512	$13.29	$18.86	5,107
2005	$54.92	$38.58	8,404	$25.15	$31.55	8,145
2006	$69.70	$51.48	11,077	$32.18	$40.43	7,360
2007	$68.90	$58.72	11,717	$31.78	$22.10	5,773
2008	$63.72	$45.47	13,275	$25.34	$19.69	7,150
2009	$84.73	$50.26	15,215	$32.78	$32.58	9,364
2010	$78.74	$79.60	18,390	$35.56	$38.07	8,259

Case Study

Forecasting Football Game Attendance at Southwestern University

Southwestern University (SWU), a large state college in Stephenville, Texas, 30 miles southwest of the Dallas/Fort Worth metroplex, enrolls close to 20,000 students. In a typical town–gown relationship, the school is a dominant force in the small city, with more students during fall and spring than permanent residents.

A longtime football powerhouse, SWU is a member of the Big Eleven conference and is usually in the top 20 in college football rankings. To bolster its chances of reaching the elusive and long-desired number-one ranking, in 2006 SWU hired the legendary Bo Pitterno as its head coach. Although the number-one ranking remained out of reach, attendance at the five Saturday home games each year increased. Prior to Pitterno's arrival, attendance generally averaged 25,000 to 29,000 per game. Season ticket sales bumped up by 10,000 just with the announcement of the new coach's arrival. Stephenville and SWU were ready to move to the big time!

The immediate issue facing SWU, however, was not NCAA ranking; it was capacity. The existing SWU stadium, built in 1953, has seating for 54,000 fans. The table on the next page indicates attendance at each game for the past six years:

	2006		2007		2008	
GAME	ATTENDEES	OPPONENT	ATTENDEES	OPPONENT	ATTENDEES	OPPONENT
1	34,200	Baylor	36,100	Oklahoma	35,900	TCU
2*	39,800	Texas	40,200	Nebraska	46,500	Texas Tech
3	38,200	LSU	39,100	UCLA	43,100	Alaska
4**	26,900	Arkansas	25,300	Nevada	27,900	Arizona
5	35,100	USC	36,200	Ohio State	39,200	Rice

	2009		2010		2011	
GAME	ATTENDEES	OPPONENT	ATTENDEES	OPPONENT	ATTENDEES	OPPONENT
1	41,900	Arkansas	42,500	Indiana	46,900	LSU
2*	46,100	Missouri	48,200	North Texas	50,100	Texas
3	43,900	Florida	44,200	Texas A&M	45,900	Prairie View A&M
4**	30,100	Miami	33,900	Southern	36,300	Montana
5	40,500	Duke	47,800	Oklahoma	49,900	Arizona State

* Homecoming games.
** During the fourth week of each season, Stephenville hosted a hugely popular Southwestern crafts festival. This event brought tens of thousands of tourists to the town, especially on weekends, and had an obvious negative impact on game attendance.

Source: J. Heizer and B. Render. *Operations Management*, 10th ed., © 2011. Reprinted by permission of Pearson Education, Inc., Upper Saddle River, NJ.

One of Pitterno's demands upon joining SWU had been a stadium expansion, or possibly even a new stadium. With attendance increasing, SWU administrators began to face the issue head-on. Pitterno had wanted dormitories in the stadium, solely for his athletes, as an additional feature of any expansion.

SWU's president, Dr. Marty Starr, decided it was time for his vice president of development to forecast when the existing stadium would "max out." He also sought a revenue projection, assuming an average ticket price of $20 in 2012 and a 5% increase each year in future prices.

Discussion Questions

1. Develop a forecasting model and justify its selection over other techniques. Project attendance through 2013.
2. What revenues are to be expected in 2012 and 2013?
3. Discuss the school's options.

Internet Case Studies

See the Companion Website for this textbook, at www.pearsonhighered.com/balakrishnan, for additional case studies.

APPENDICES

APPENDIX A: PROBABILITY CONCEPTS AND APPLICATIONS

A.1 Fundamental Concepts

People often misuse the two basic rules of probabilities by making such statements as "I'm 110% sure we're going to win the big game."

There are two basic statements about the mathematics of *probability*:

1. The probability, P, of any event or state of nature occurring is greater than or equal to 0 and less than or equal to 1. That is,

$$0 \leq P(\text{event}) \leq 1 \quad \text{(A-1)}$$

A probability of 0 indicates that an event is never expected to occur. A probability of 1 means that an event is always expected to occur.

2. The sum of the simple probabilities for all possible outcomes of an activity must equal 1.

Both of these concepts are illustrated in Example 1.

EXAMPLE 1: TWO LAWS OF PROBABILITY Demand for white latex paint at Diversey Paint and Supply has always been 0, 1, 2, 3, or 4 gallons per day. (There are no other possible outcomes, and when one occurs, no other can.) Over the past 200 working days, the owner notes the following frequencies of demand:

DEMAND (GALLONS)	NUMBER OF DAYS
0	40
1	80
2	50
3	20
4	10
	Total 200

If this past distribution is a good indicator of future sales, we can find the probability of each possible outcome occurring in the future by converting the data into percentages of the total:

DEMAND	PROBABILITY
0	0.20 (= 40/200)
1	0.40 (= 80/200)
2	0.25 (= 50/200)
3	0.10 (= 20/200)
4	0.05 (= 10/200)
	Total 1.00 (= 200/200)

Thus the probability that sales are 2 gallons of paint on any given day is $P(2 \text{ gallons}) = 0.25 = 25\%$. The probability of any level of sales must be greater than or equal to 0 and less than or equal to 1. Since 0, 1, 2, 3, and 4 gallons exhaust all possible events or outcomes, the sum of their probability values must equal 1.

Types of Probability

There are two different ways to determine probability: the *objective approach* and the *subjective approach*.

OBJECTIVE PROBABILITY Example 1 provides an illustration of objective probability assessment. The probability of any paint demand level is the *relative frequency* of occurrence of that demand in a large number of trial observations (200 days, in this case). In general:

$$P(\text{event}) = \frac{\text{Number of occurrences of the event}}{\text{Total number of trials or outcomes}}$$

Objective probability can also be set using what is called the *classical, or logical, approach*. Without performing a series of trials, we can often logically determine what the probabilities of various events should be. For example, the probability of tossing a fair coin once and getting a head is

$$P(\text{head}) = \frac{1}{2} \quad \begin{matrix} \leftarrow \textit{number of ways of getting a head} \\ \leftarrow \textit{number of possible outcomes (head or tail)} \end{matrix}$$

Similarly, the probability of drawing a spade out of a deck of 52 playing cards can be logically set as

$$P(\text{spade}) = \frac{13}{52} \quad \begin{matrix} \leftarrow \textit{number of chances of drawing a spade} \\ \leftarrow \textit{number of possible outcomes} \end{matrix}$$

$$= \frac{1}{4} = 0.25 = 25\%$$

Where do probabilities come from? Sometimes they are subjective and based on personal experiences. Other times they are objectively based on logical observations such as the roll of a die. Often, probabilities are derived from historical data.

SUBJECTIVE PROBABILITY When logic and past history are not appropriate, probability values can be assessed *subjectively*. The accuracy of subjective probabilities depends on the experience and judgment of the person making the estimates. A number of probability values cannot be determined unless the subjective approach is used. What is the probability that the price of gasoline will be more than $4 in the next few years? What is the probability that the U.S. economy will be in a severe depression in 2013? What is the probability that you will be president of a major corporation within 20 years?

There are several methods for making subjective probability assessments. Opinion polls can be used to help in determining subjective probabilities for possible election returns and potential political candidates. In some cases, experience and judgment must be used in making subjective assessments of probability values. A production manager, for example, might believe that the probability of manufacturing a new product without a single defect is 0.85. In the Delphi method, a panel of experts is assembled to make their predictions of the future. This approach is discussed in Chapter 11.

A.2 Mutually Exclusive and Collectively Exhaustive Events

Events are said to be *mutually exclusive* if only one of the events can occur on any one trial. They are called *collectively exhaustive* if the list of outcomes includes every possible outcome. Many common experiences involve events that have both of these properties. In tossing a coin, for example, the possible outcomes are a head or a tail. Because both of them cannot occur on any one toss, the outcomes head and tail are mutually exclusive. Since obtaining a head and a tail represent every possible outcome, they are also collectively exhaustive.

EXAMPLE 2: ROLLING A DIE Rolling a die is a simple experiment that has six possible outcomes, each listed in the following table with its corresponding probability:

OUTCOME OF ROLL	PROBABILITY
1	1/6
2	1/6
3	1/6
4	1/6
5	1/6
6	1/6
	Total 1

These events are both mutually exclusive (on any roll, only one of the six events can occur) and also collectively exhaustive (one of them must occur and hence they total in probability to 1).

EXAMPLE 3: DRAWING A CARD You are asked to draw one card from a deck of 52 playing cards. Using a logical probability assessment, it is easy to set some of the relationships, such as

$$P(\text{drawing a 7}) = \frac{4}{52} = \frac{1}{13}$$

$$P(\text{drawing a heart}) = \frac{13}{52} = \frac{1}{4}$$

We also see that these events (drawing a 7 and drawing a heart) are *not* mutually exclusive because a 7 of hearts can be drawn. They are also *not* collectively exhaustive because there are other cards in the deck besides 7s and hearts.

You can test your understanding of these concepts by going through the following cases:

This table is especially useful in helping to understand the difference between mutually exclusive and collectively exhaustive.

DRAWS	MUTUALLY EXCLUSIVE?	COLLECTIVELY EXHAUSTIVE?
1. Draw a spade and a club	Yes	No
2. Draw a face card and a number card	Yes	Yes
3. Draw an ace and a 3	Yes	No
4. Draw a club and a nonclub	Yes	Yes
5. Draw a 5 and a diamond	No	No
6. Draw a red card and a diamond	No	No

Adding Mutually Exclusive Events

Often we are interested in whether one event *or* a second event will occur. When these two events are mutually exclusive, the law of addition is simply as follows:

$$P(\text{event } A \text{ or event } B) = P(\text{event } A) + P(\text{event } B)$$

or, more briefly,

$$P(A \text{ or } B) = P(A) + P(B) \tag{A-2}$$

For example, we just saw that the events of drawing a spade or drawing a club out of a deck of cards are mutually exclusive. Since $P(\text{spade}) = \frac{13}{52}$ and $P(\text{club}) = \frac{13}{52}$, the probability of drawing either a spade or a club is

$$\begin{aligned} P(\text{spade or club}) &= P(\text{spade}) + P(\text{club}) \\ &= \frac{13}{52} + \frac{13}{52} \\ &= \frac{26}{52} = \frac{1}{2} = 0.50 = 50\% \end{aligned}$$

The *Venn diagram* in Figure A.1 depicts the probability of the occurrence of mutually exclusive events.

FIGURE A.1
Addition Law for Events that Are Mutually Exclusive

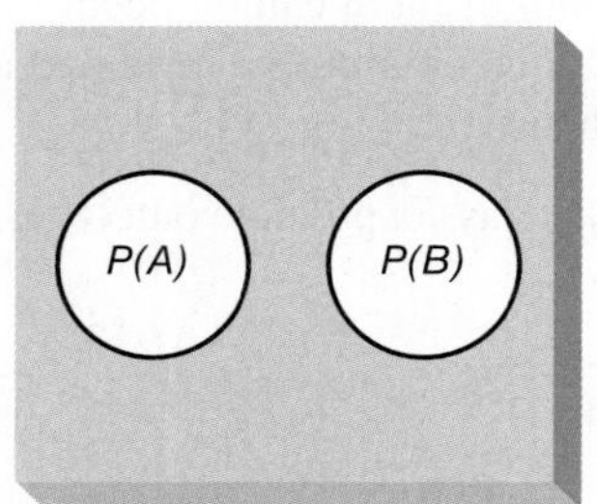

P(A or B) = P(A) + P(B)

Law of Addition for Events that Are Not Mutually Exclusive

When two events are not mutually exclusive, Equation A-2 must be modified to account for double counting. The correct equation reduces the probability by subtracting the chance of both events occurring together:

$$\begin{aligned} P(\text{event } A \text{ or event } B) = &\; P(\text{event } A) + P(\text{event } B) \\ &- P(\text{event } A \text{ and event } B \text{ both occurring}) \end{aligned}$$

The formula for adding events that are not mutually exclusive is $P(A \text{ or } B) = P(A) + P(B) - P(A \text{ and } B)$. *Do you understand why we subtract P(A and B)?*

This can be expressed in shorter form as

$$P(A \text{ or } B) = P(A) + P(B) - P(A \text{ and } B) \tag{A-3}$$

FIGURE A.2
Addition Law for Events that Are Not Mutually Exclusive

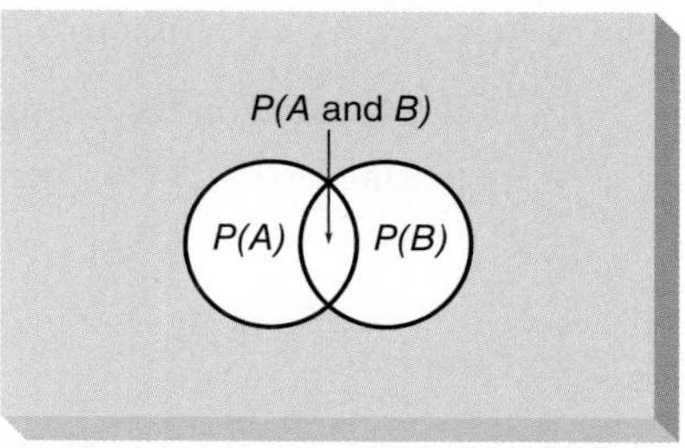

$P(A \text{ or } B) = P(A) + P(B) - P(A \text{ and } B)$

Figure A.2 illustrates this concept of subtracting the probability of outcomes that are common to both events. When events are mutually exclusive, the area of overlap, called the *intersection*, is 0, as shown in Figure A.1.

Let us consider the events drawing a 5 and drawing a diamond out of the card deck. These events are not mutually exclusive, so Equation A-3 must be applied to compute the probability of either a 5 or a diamond being drawn:

$$\begin{aligned} P(\text{five } \textit{or} \text{ diamond}) &= P(\text{five}) + P(\text{diamond}) - P(\text{five } \textit{and} \text{ diamond}) \\ &= \frac{4}{52} + \frac{13}{52} - \frac{1}{52} \\ &= \frac{16}{52} = \frac{4}{13} \end{aligned}$$

A.3 Statistically Independent Events

Events can either be *independent events* or *dependent events*. When they are *independent*, the occurrence of one event has no effect on the probability of occurrence of the second event. Let us examine four sets of events and determine which are independent:

1. **(a)** Your education
   (b) Your income level
   } *Dependent events.* Can you explain why?
2. **(a)** Draw a jack of hearts from a full 52-card deck
   (b) Draw a jack of clubs from a full 52-card deck
   } *Independent events*
3. **(a)** Chicago Cubs win the National League pennant
   (b) Chicago Cubs win the World Series
   } *Dependent events*
4. **(a)** Snow in Santiago, Chile
   (b) Rain in Tel Aviv, Israel
   } *Independent events*

The three types of probability under both statistical independence and statistical dependence are (1) marginal, (2) joint, and (3) conditional. When events are independent, these three are very easy to compute, as we shall see.

A **marginal probability** *is the probability of an event occurring.*

A *marginal* (or a *simple*) *probability* is just the probability of an event occurring. For example, if we toss a fair die, the marginal probability of a 2 landing face up is $P(\text{die is a 2}) = \frac{1}{6} = 0.166$. Because each separate toss is an independent event (i.e., what we get on the first toss has absolutely no effect on any later tosses), the marginal probability for each possible outcome is $\frac{1}{6}$.

A **joint probability** *is the product of marginal probabilities*

The *joint probability* of two or more independent events occurring is the product of their marginal or simple probabilities. This can be written as

$$P(AB) = P(A) \times P(B) \qquad \textbf{(A-4)}$$

where

$P(AB)$ = joint probability or events A and B occurring together, or one after the other
$P(A)$ = marginal probability of event A
$P(B)$ = marginal probability of event B

The probability, for example, of tossing a 6 on the first roll of a die and a 2 on the second roll is

$$\begin{aligned} &P(6 \text{ on first and 2 on second roll}) \\ &= P(\text{tossing a } 6) \times P(\text{tossing a } 2) \\ &= \frac{1}{6} \times \frac{1}{6} = \frac{1}{36} \\ &= 0.028 \end{aligned}$$

A **conditional probability** *is the probability of an event occurring given that another event has taken place.*

The third type, *conditional probability*, is expressed as $P(B|A)$, or "the probability of event B, given that event A has occurred." Similarly, $P(A|B)$ would mean "the conditional probability of event A, given that event B has taken place." Since events are independent, the occurrence of one in no way affects the outcome of another, $P(A|B) = P(A)$ and $P(B|A) = P(B)$.

EXAMPLE 4: PROBABILITIES WHEN EVENTS ARE INDEPENDENT A bucket contains three black balls and seven green balls. We draw a ball from the bucket, replace it, and draw a second ball. We can determine the probability of each of the following events occurring:

1. A black ball is drawn on the first draw:

$$P(B) = 0.30$$

(This is a marginal probability.)

2. Two green balls are drawn:

$$P(GG) = P(G) \times P(G) = (0.7)(0.7) = 0.49$$

(This is a joint probability for two independent events.)

3. A black ball is drawn on the second draw if the first draw is green:

$$P(B|G) = P(B) = 0.30$$

(This is a conditional probability but equal to the marginal probability because the two draws are independent events.)

4. A green ball is drawn on the second draw if the first draw was green:

$$P(G|G) = P(G) = 0.70$$

(This is a conditional probability as above.)

A.4 Statistically Dependent Events

When events are statistically dependent, the occurrence of one event affects the probability of occurrence of some other event. Marginal, conditional, and joint probabilities exist under dependence as they did under independence, but the form of the latter two are changed.

A marginal probability is computed exactly as it was for independent events. Again, the marginal probability of the event A occurring is denoted as $P(A)$.

Calculating a conditional probability under dependence is somewhat more involved than it is under independence. The formula for the conditional probability of A, given that event B has taken place, is now stated as

$$P(A|B) = \frac{P(AB)}{P(B)} \qquad \textbf{(A-5)}$$

A Presbyterian minister, Thomas Bayes (1702–1761), did the work leading to this theorem.

The use of this important formula, often referred to as *Bayes' law*, or *Bayes' theorem*, is best defined by an example.

EXAMPLE 5: PROBABILITIES WHEN EVENTS ARE DEPENDENT Assume that we have an urn containing 10 balls, as follows

4 are white (*W*) and lettered (*L*).

2 are white (*W*) and numbered (*N*).

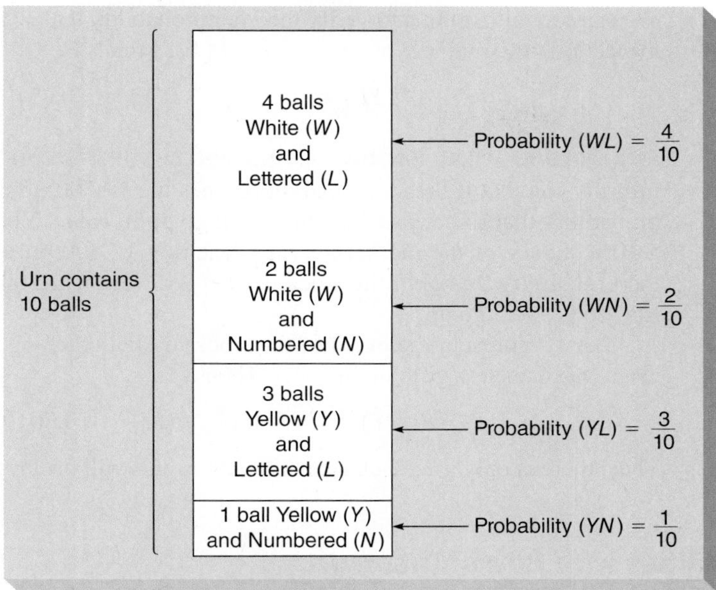

FIGURE A.3
Dependent Events of Example 5

3 are yellow (*Y*) and lettered (*L*).

1 is yellow (*Y*) and numbered (*N*).

You randomly draw a ball from the urn and see that it is yellow. What, then, we may ask, is the probability that the ball is lettered? (See Figure A.3.)

Because there are 10 balls, it is a simple matter to tabulate a series of useful probabilities:

$$P(WL) = \frac{4}{10} = 0.4 \qquad P(YL) = \frac{3}{10} = 0.3$$

$$P(WN) = \frac{2}{10} = 0.2 \qquad P(YN) = \frac{1}{10} = 0.1$$

$$P(W) = \frac{6}{10} = 0.6, \text{ or } P(W) = P(WL) + P(WN) = 0.4 + 0.2 = 0.6$$

$$P(L) = \frac{7}{10} = 0.7, \text{ or } P(L) = P(WL) + P(YL) = 0.4 + 0.3 = 0.7$$

$$P(Y) = \frac{4}{10} = 0.4, \text{ or } P(Y) = P(YL) + P(YN) = 0.3 + 0.1 = 0.4$$

$$P(N) = \frac{3}{10} = 0.3, \text{ or } P(N) = P(WN) + P(YN) = 0.2 + 0.1 = 0.3$$

We can now apply Bayes' law to calculate the conditional probability that the ball drawn is lettered, given that it is yellow:

$$P(L|Y) = \frac{P(YL)}{P(Y)} = \frac{0.3}{0.4} = 0.75$$

This equation shows that we divided the probability of yellow and lettered balls (3 out of 10) by the probability of yellow balls (4 out of 10). There is a 0.75 probability that the yellow ball that you drew is lettered.

Recall that the formula for a joint probability under statistical independence was simply $P(AB) = P(A) \times P(B)$. When events are *dependent*, however, the joint probability is derived from Bayes' conditional formula. Equation A-6 reads "the joint probability of events *A* and *B* occurring is equal to the conditional probability of event *A*, given that *B* occurred, multiplied by the probability of event *B*":

$$P(AB) = P(A|B) \times P(B) \qquad \textbf{(A-6)}$$

We can use this formula to verify the joint probability that $P(YL) = 0.3$, which was obtained by inspection in Example 5 by multiplying $P(L|Y)$ times $P(Y)$:

$$P(YL) = P(L|Y) \times P(Y) = (0.75)(0.4) = 0.3$$

EXAMPLE 6: JOINT PROBABILITIES WHEN EVENTS ARE DEPENDENT Your stockbroker informs you that if the stock market reaches the 12,500-point level by January, there is a 0.70 probability that Tubeless Electronics will go up in value. Your own feeling is that there is only a 40% chance of the market average reaching 12,500 points by January. Can you calculate the probability that *both* the stock market will reach 12,500 points *and* the price of Tubeless Electronics will go up?

Let M represent the event of the stock market reaching the 12,500 level, and let T be the event that Tubeless goes up in value. Then

$$P(MT) = P(T|M) \times P(M) = (0.70)(0.40) = 0.28$$

Thus, there is only a 28% chance that *both* events will occur.

A.5 Revising Probabilities with Bayes' Theorem

Bayes' theorem can also be used to incorporate additional information as it is made available and help create *revised,* or *posterior, probabilities*. This means that we can take new or recent data and then revise and improve upon our *prior probability* estimates for an event (see Figure A.4). Let us consider the following example.

EXAMPLE 7: POSTERIOR PROBABILITIES A cup contains two dice that are identical in appearance. One, however, is fair (unbiased) and the other is loaded (biased). The probability of rolling a 3 on the fair die is $\frac{1}{6}$, or 0.166. The probability of tossing the same number on the loaded die is 0.60.

We have no idea which die is which but select one by chance and toss it. The result is a 3. Given this additional piece of information, can we find the (revised) probability that the die rolled was fair? Can we determine the probability that it was the loaded die that was rolled?

The answer to these questions is yes, and we do so by using the formula for joint probability under statistical dependence and Bayes' theorem. First, we take stock of the information and probabilities available. We know, for example, that because we randomly selected the die to roll, the probability of it being fair or loaded is 0.50:

$$P(\text{fair}) = 0.50 \qquad P(\text{loaded}) = 0.50$$

We also know that

$$P(3|\text{fair}) = 0.166 \qquad P(3|\text{loaded}) = 0.60$$

Next, we compute joint probabilities $P(3 \text{ and fair})$ and $P(3 \text{ and loaded})$ using the formula $P(AB) = P(A \mid B) \times P(B)$:

$$\begin{aligned} P(3 \text{ and fair}) &= P(3|\text{fair}) \times P(\text{fair}) \\ &= (0.166)(0.50) = 0.083 \end{aligned}$$

FIGURE A.4
Using Bayes' Process

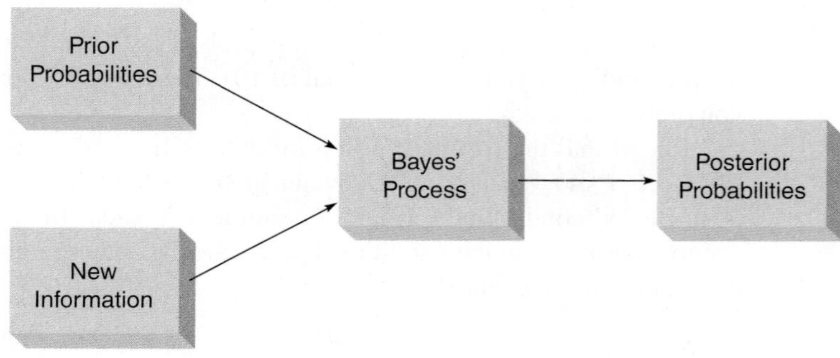

$$\begin{aligned} P(3 \text{ and loaded}) &= P(3|\text{loaded}) \times P(\text{loaded}) \\ &= (0.60)(0.50) = 0.300 \end{aligned}$$

A 3 can occur in combination with the state "fair die" or in combination with the state "loaded die." The sum of their probabilities gives the unconditional or marginal probability of a 3 on the toss, namely, $P(3) = 0.083 + 0.300 = 0.383$.

If a 3 does occur, and if we do not know which die it came from, the probability that the die rolled was the fair one is

$$P(\text{fair}|3) = \frac{P(\text{fair and } 3)}{P(3)} = \frac{0.083}{0.383} = 0.22$$

The probability that the die rolled was loaded is

$$P(\text{loaded}|3) = \frac{P(\text{loaded and } 3)}{P(3)} = \frac{0.300}{0.383} = 0.78$$

These two conditional probabilities are called the *revised*, or *posterior*, *probabilities* for the next roll of the die.

Before the die was rolled in the preceding example, the best we could say was that there was a 50–50 chance that it was fair (0.50 probability) and a 50–50 chance that it was loaded. After one roll of the die, however, we are able to revise our prior probability estimates. The new posterior estimate is that there is a 0.78 probability that the die rolled was loaded and only a 0.22 probability that it was not.

General Form of Bayes' Theorem

Another way to compute revised probabilities is with Bayes' theorem.

Revised probabilities can also be computed in a more direct way using a general form for Bayes' theorem. Recall from Equation A-5 that Bayes' law for the conditional probability of event A, given event B, is

$$P(A|B) = \frac{P(AB)}{P(B)}$$

However, we can show that

$$P(A|B) = \frac{P(B|A)P(A)}{P(B|A)P(A) + P(B|\bar{A})P(\bar{A})} \quad \text{(A-7)}$$

where

$\bar{A}$ = the complement of the event A; for example, if A is the event "fair die," then $\bar{A}$ is "unfair" or "loaded die"

Now let's return to Example 7.

Although it may not be obvious to you at first glance, we used this basic equation to compute the revised probabilities. For example, if we want the probability that the fair die was rolled given the first toss was a 3, namely, P (fair die | 3 rolled), we can let

event "fair die" replace A in Equation A-7.

event "loaded die" replace $\bar{A}$ in Equation A-7.

event "3 rolled" replace B in Equation A-7.

We can then rewrite Equation A-7 and solve as follows:

$$\begin{aligned} &P(\text{fair die}|3 \text{ rolled}) \\ &= \frac{P(3|\text{fair})P(\text{fair})}{P(3|\text{fair})P(\text{fair}) + P(3|\text{loaded})P(\text{loaded})} \\ &= \frac{(0.166)(0.50)}{(0.166)(0.50) + (0.60)(0.50)} \\ &= \frac{0.083}{0.383} = 0.22 \end{aligned}$$

This is the same answer that we computed in Example 7. Can you use this alternative approach to show the $P(\text{loaded die} \mid 3 \text{ rolled}) = 0.78$? Either method is perfectly acceptable when we deal with probability revisions in Chapter 8.

A.6 Further Probability Revisions

Although one revision of prior probabilities can provide useful posterior probability estimates, additional information can be gained from performing the experiment a second time. If it is financially worthwhile, a decision maker may even decide to make several more revisions.

EXAMPLE 8: A SECOND PROBABILITY REVISION Returning to Example 7, we now attempt to obtain further information about the posterior probabilities as to whether the die just rolled is fair or loaded. To do so, let us toss the die a second time. Again, we roll a 3. What are the further revised probabilities?

To answer this question, we proceed as before, with only one exception. The probabilities $P(\text{fair}) = 0.50$ and $P(\text{loaded}) = 0.50$ remain the same, but now we must compute $P(3{,}3 \mid \text{fair}) = (0.166)(0.166) = 0.027$ and $P(3{,}3 \mid \text{loaded}) = (0.6)(0.6) = 0.36$. With these joint probabilities of two 3s on successive rolls, given the two types of dice, we can revise the probabilities:

$$\begin{aligned} P(3{,}3 \text{ and fair}) &= P(3{,}3 \mid \text{fair}) \times P(\text{fair}) \\ &= (0.027)(0.5) = 0.013 \\ P(3{,}3 \text{ and loaded}) &= P(3{,}3 \mid \text{loaded}) \times P(\text{loaded}) \\ &= (0.36)(0.5) = 0.18 \end{aligned}$$

Thus, the probability of rolling two 3s, a marginal probability, is $0.013 + 0.18 = 0.193$, the sum of the two joint probabilities:

$$\begin{aligned} P(\text{fair} \mid 3{,}3) &= \frac{P(3{,}3 \text{ and fair})}{P(3{,}3)} \\ &= \frac{0.013}{0.193} = 0.067 \\ P(\text{loaded} \mid 3{,}3) &= \frac{P(3{,}3 \text{ and loaded})}{P(3{,}3)} \\ &= \frac{0.18}{0.193} = 0.933 \end{aligned}$$

What has this second roll accomplished? Before we rolled the die the first time, we knew only that there was a 0.50 probability that it was either fair or loaded. When the first die was rolled in Example 7, we were able to revise these probabilities:

$$\begin{aligned} \text{probability the die is fair} &= 0.22 \\ \text{probability the die is loaded} &= 0.78 \end{aligned}$$

Now, after the second roll in Example 8, our refined revisions tell us that

$$\begin{aligned} \text{probability the die is fair} &= 0.067 \\ \text{probability the die is loaded} &= 0.933 \end{aligned}$$

This type of information can be extremely valuable in business decision making.

A.7 Random Variables

The preceding section discusses various ways of assigning probability values to the outcomes of an experiment. Let us now use this probability information to compute the expected outcome, variance, and standard deviation of the experiment. This can help select the best decision among a number of alternatives.

A *random variable* assigns a real number to every possible outcome or event in an experiment. It is normally represented by a letter such as X or Y. When the outcome itself is numerical or quantitative, the outcome numbers can be the random variable. For example, consider refrigerator sales at an appliance store. The number of refrigerators sold during a given day can be the random variable. Using X to represent this random variable, we can express this relationship as follows:

$$X = \text{number of refreigerators sold during the day}$$

In general, whenever the experiment has quantifiable outcomes, it is beneficial to define these quantitative outcomes as the random variable. Examples are given in Table A.1.

When the outcome itself is not numerical or quantitative, it is necessary to define a random variable that associates each outcome with a unique real number. Several examples are given in Table A.2.

There are two types of random variables: *discrete random variables* and *continuous random variables*. Developing probability distributions and making computations based on these distributions depends on the type of random variable.

Try to develop a few more examples of discrete random variables to be sure you understand this concept.

A random variable is a *discrete random variable* if it can assume only a finite or limited set of values. Which of the random variables in Table A.1 are discrete random variables? Looking at Table A.1, we can see that stocking 50 Christmas trees, inspecting 600 items, and sending out 5,000 letters are all examples of discrete random variables. Each of these random variables can assume only a finite or limited set of values. The number of Christmas trees sold, for example, can only be integer numbers from 0 to 50. There are 51 values that the random variable X can assume in this example.

A *continuous random variable* is a random variable that has an infinite or an unlimited set of values. Are there any examples of continuous random variables in Tables A.1 or A.2? Looking at

TABLE A.1 Examples of Random Variables

EXPERIMENT	OUTCOME	RANDOM VARIABLES	RANGE OF RANDOM VARIABLES
Stock 50 Christmas trees	Number of Christmas trees sold	X = number of Christmas trees sold	0, 1, 2, . . . , 50
Inspect 600 items	Number of acceptable items	Y = number of acceptable items	0, 1, 2, . . . , 600
Send out 5,000 sales letters	Number of people responding to the letters	Z = number of people responding to the letters	0, 1, 2, . . . , 5,000
Build an apartment building	Percent of building completed after 4 months	R = percent of building completed after 4 months	$0 \le R \le 100$
Test the lifetime of a lightbulb (minutes)	Length of time the bulb lasts up to 80,000 minutes	S = time the bulb burns	$0 \le S \le 80{,}000$

TABLE A.2 Random Variables for Outcomes that Are Not Numbers

EXPERIMENT	OUTCOME	RANDOM VARIABLES	RANGE OF RANDOM VARIABLES
Students respond to a questionnaire	Strongly agree (SA) Agree (A) Neutral (N) Disagree (D) Strongly disagree (SD)	$X = \begin{cases} 5 \text{ if SA} \\ 4 \text{ if A} \\ 3 \text{ if N} \\ 2 \text{ if D} \\ 1 \text{ if SD} \end{cases}$	1, 2, 3, 4, 5
One machine is inspected	Defective Not defective	$Y = \begin{cases} 0 \text{ if defective} \\ 1 \text{ if not defective} \end{cases}$	0, 1
Consumers respond to how they like a product	Good Average Poor	$Z = \begin{cases} 3 \text{ if good} \\ 2 \text{ if average} \\ 1 \text{ if poor} \end{cases}$	1, 2, 3

Table A.1, we can see that testing the lifetime of a lightbulb is an experiment that can be described with a continuous random variable. In this case, the random variable, S, is the time the bulb burns. It can last for 3,206 minutes, 6,500.7 minutes, 251.726 minutes, or any other value between 0 and 80,000 minutes. In most cases, the range of a continuous random variable is stated as: lower value $\leq S \leq$ upper value, such as $0 \leq S \leq 80{,}000$. The random variable R in Table A.1 is also continuous. Can you explain why?

A.8 Probability Distributions

Earlier we discussed the probability values of an event. We now explore the properties of *probability distributions*. We see how popular distributions, such as the normal, Poisson, and exponential probability distributions, can save us time and effort. Since selection of the appropriate probability distribution depends partially on whether the random variable is *discrete* or *continuous*, we consider each of these types separately.

Probability Distribution of a Discrete Random Variable

When we have a *discrete random variable*, there is a probability value assigned to each event. These values must be between 0 and 1, and they must sum to 1. Let's look at an example.

The 100 students in Pat Shannon's statistics class have just completed the instructor evaluations at the end of the course. Dr. Shannon is particularly interested in student response to the textbook because he is in the process of writing a competing statistics book. One of the questions on the evaluation survey was: "The textbook was well written and helped me acquire the necessary information."

5. Strongly agree
4. Agree
3. Neutral
2. Disagree
1. Strongly disagree

The students' response to this question in the survey is summarized in Table A.3. Also shown is the random variable X and the corresponding probability for each possible outcome. This *discrete probability distribution* was computed using the relative frequency approach presented previously.

The distribution follows the three rules required of all probability distributions: (1) the events are mutually exclusive and collectively exhaustive, (2) the individual probability values are between 0 and 1 inclusive, and (3) the total of the probability values sum to 1.

Although listing the probability distribution as we did in Table A.3 is adequate, it can be difficult to get an idea about characteristics of the distribution. To overcome this problem, the probability values are often presented in graph form. The graph of the distribution in Table A.3 is shown in Figure A.5.

The graph of this probability distribution gives us a picture of its shape. It helps us identify the central tendency of the distribution, called the *expected value*, and the amount of variability or spread of the distribution, called the *variance*.

TABLE A.3
Probability Distribution for Textbook Question

OUTCOME	RANDOM VARIABLE (X)	NUMBER RESPONDING	PROBABILITY $P(X)$
Strongly agree	5	10	$0.1 = 10/100$
Agree	4	20	$0.2 = 20/100$
Neutral	3	30	$0.3 = 30/100$
Disagree	2	30	$0.3 = 30/100$
Strongly disagree	1	10	$0.1 = 10/100$
		Total 100	$1.0 = 100/100$

FIGURE A.5
Probability Function for Dr. Shannon's Class

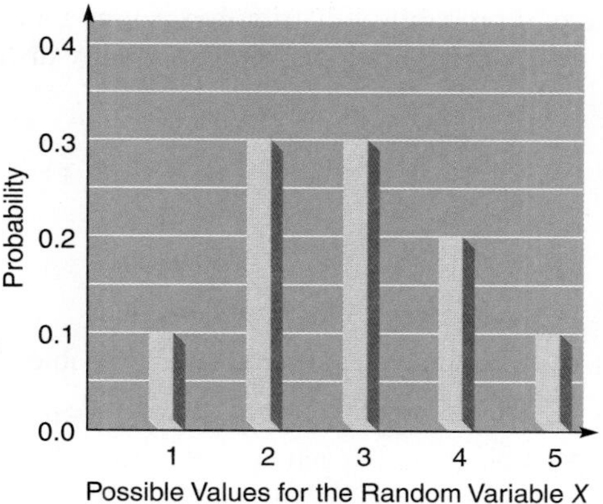

Expected Value of a Discrete Probability Distribution

Once we have established a probability distribution, the first characteristic that is usually of interest is the *central tendency*, or average of the distribution. The *expected value*, a measure of central tendency, is computed as a weighted average of the values of the random variable:

The expected value *of a discrete distribution is a weighted average of the values of the random variable.*

$$E(X) = \sum_{i=1}^{n} X_i P(X_i)$$
$$= X_1P(X_1) + X_2P(X_2) + \cdots + X_nP(X_n) \quad \text{(A-8)}$$

where

X_i = random variable's possible values
$P(X_i)$ = probability of each of the random variable's possible values
$\sum_{i=1}^{n}$ = summation sign indicating we are adding all n possible values
$E(X)$ = expected value of the random variable

The expected value of any discrete probability distribution can be computed by multiplying each possible value of the random variable, X_i, times the probability, $P(X_i)$, that outcome will occur, and summing the results, Σ. Here is how the expected value can be computed for the textbook question:

$$E(X) = \sum_{i=1}^{5} X_i P(X_i)$$
$$= X_1P(X_1) + X_2P(X_2) + X_3P(X_3) + X_4P(X_4) + X_5P(X_5)$$
$$= (5)(0.1) + (4)(0.2) + (3)(0.3) + (2)(0.3) + (1)(0.1)$$
$$= 2.9$$

The expected value of 2.9 implies that the mean response is between disagree (2) and neutral (3), and that the average response is closer to neutral, which is 3. Looking at Figure A.5, this is consistent with the shape of the probability function.

Variance of a Discrete Probability Distribution

In addition to the central tendency of a probability distribution, most people are interested in the variability or the spread of the distribution. If the variability is low, it is much more likely that the outcome of an experiment will be close to the average or expected value. On the other hand, if the variability of the distribution is high, which means that the probability is spread out over the various random variable values, there is less chance that the outcome of an experiment will be close to the expected value.

A probability distribution is often described by its mean and variance.

The *variance* of a probability distribution is a number that reveals the overall spread or dispersion of the distribution. For a discrete probability distribution, it can be computed using the following equation:

$$\text{Variance} = \sum_{i=1}^{n} [X_i - E(X)]^2 P(X_i) \qquad \textbf{(A-9)}$$

where

X_i = random variable's possible values
$E(X)$ = expected value of the random variable
$[X_i - E(X)]$ = difference between each value of the random variable and the expected value
$P(X_i)$ = probability of each possible value of the random variable

To compute the variance, denoted by σ^2, each value of the random variable is subtracted from the expected value, squared, and multiplied times the probability of occurrence of that value. The results are then summed to obtain the variance. Here is how this procedure is done for Dr. Shannon's textbook question:

$$\begin{aligned}
\text{Variance} &= \sum_{i=1}^{5} [X_i - E(X)]^2 P(X_i) \\
\text{Variance} &= (5 - 2.9)^2(0.1) + (4 - 2.9)^2(0.2) + (3 - 2.9)^2(0.3) + (2 - 2.9)^2(0.3) \\
&\quad + (1 - 2.9)^2\,(0.1) \\
&= (2.1)^2(0.1) + (1.1)^2(0.2) + (0.1)^2(0.3) + (-0.9)^2(0.3) + (-1.9)^2(0.1) \\
&= 0.441 + 0.242 + 0.003 + 0.243 + 0.361 \\
&= 1.29
\end{aligned}$$

A related measure of dispersion or spread is the *standard deviation*. This quantity is also used in many computations involved with probability distributions. The standard deviation, denoted by σ, is just the square root of the variance:

$$\sigma = \sqrt{\text{variance}} \qquad \textbf{(A-10)}$$

The standard deviation for the textbook question is

$$\sigma = \sqrt{1.29} = 1.14$$

Probability Distribution of a Continuous Random Variable

There are many examples of *continuous random variables*. The time it takes to finish a project, the number of ounces in a barrel of butter, the high temperature during a given day, the exact length of a given type of lumber, and the weight of a railroad car of coal are all examples of continuous random variables. Since random variables can take on an infinite number of values, the fundamental probability rules for continuous random variables must be modified.

As with discrete probability distributions, the sum of the probability values must equal 1. Because there are an infinite number of values of the random variables, however, the probability of each value of the random variable must be 0. If the probability values for the random variable values were greater than 0, the sum would be infinitely large.

A probability density function $f(X)$*, is a mathematical way of describing the probability distribution.*

With a *continuous probability distribution*, there is a continuous mathematical function that describes the probability distribution. This function is called the *probability density function* or simply the *probability function*. It is usually represented by $f(X)$.

We now look at the sketch of a sample density function in Figure A.6. This curve represents the probability density function for the weight of a particular machined part. The weight could vary from 5.06 to 5.30 grams, with weights around 5.18 grams being the most likely. The shaded area represents the probability the weight is between 5.22 and 5.26 grams.

If we wanted to know the probability of a part weighing exactly 5.1300000 grams, for example, we would have to compute the area of a slice of width 0. Of course, this would be 0. This result may seem strange, but if we insist on enough decimal places of accuracy, we are bound to find that the weight differs from 5.1300000 grams *exactly*, be the difference ever so slight.

FIGURE A.6
Sample Density Function

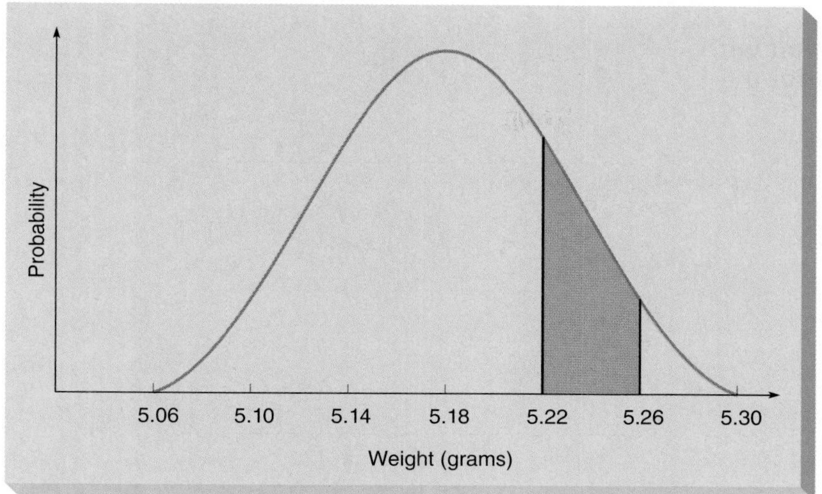

In this section we investigate the fundamental characteristics and properties of probability distributions in general. In the next three sections we introduce two important continuous distributions—the normal distribution and the exponential distribution—and a useful discrete probability distribution—the Poisson distribution.

A.9 The Normal Distribution

The normal distribution affects a large number of processes in our lives (e.g., filling boxes of cereal with 32 ounces of corn flakes). Each normal distribution depends on the mean and standard deviation.

One of the most popular and useful continuous probability distributions is the *normal distribution*. The probability density function of this distribution is given by the rather complex formula

$$f(X) = \frac{1}{\sigma\sqrt{2\pi}} e^{\left[\frac{-(X-\mu)^2}{2\sigma^2}\right]} \quad \textbf{(A-11)}$$

The normal distribution is specified completely when values for the mean, μ, and the standard deviation, σ, are known. Figure A.7 shows several different normal distributions with the same standard deviation and different means. As shown, differing values of μ will shift the average or center of the normal distribution. The overall shape of the distribution remains the same. On the other hand, when the standard deviation is varied, the normal curve either flattens out or becomes steeper. This is shown in Figure A.8.

FIGURE A.7
Normal Distribution with Different Values for μ

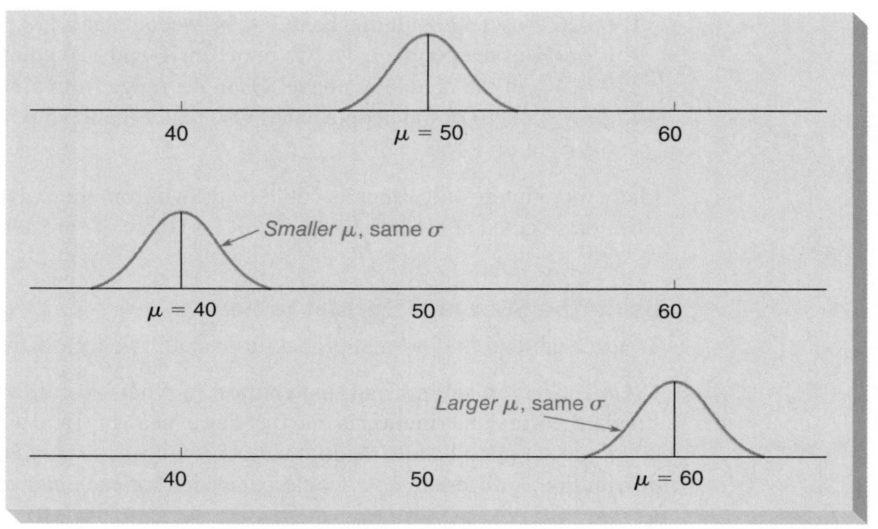

FIGURE A.8
Normal Distribution with Different Values for σ

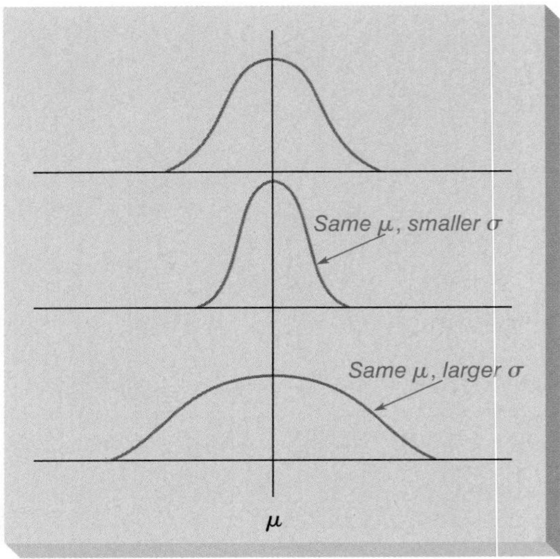

As the standard deviation, σ, becomes smaller, the normal distribution becomes steeper. When the standard deviation becomes larger, the normal distribution has a tendency to flatten out or become broader.

Area under the Normal Curve

Because the normal distribution is symmetrical, its midpoint (and highest point) is at the mean. Values on the X axis are then measured in terms of how many standard deviations they lie from the mean. Recall that the area under the curve (in a continuous distribution) describes the probability that a random variable has a value in a specified interval. The normal distribution requires mathematical calculations beyond the scope of this book, but tables that provide areas or probabilities are readily available. For example, Figure A.9 illustrates three commonly used relationships that have been derived from standard normal tables (discussed in the next section). The area from point a to point b in the first drawing represents the probability, 68.26%, that the random variable will be within 1 standard deviation of the mean. In the middle graph, we see that about 95.44% of the area lies within ± 2 standard deviations of the mean. The third figure shows that 99.74% lies between $\pm 3\sigma$.

95% confidence is actually ± 1.96 standard deviations, whereas ± 3 standard deviations is actually a 99.74% spread.

Translating Figure A.9 into an application implies that if the mean IQ in the United States is $\mu = 100$ points and if the standard deviation is $\sigma = 15$ points, we can make the following statements:

1. 68.26% of the population have IQs between 85 and 115 points ($\pm 1\sigma$).
2. 95.44% of the people have IQs between 70 and 130 points ($\pm 2\sigma$).
3. 99.74% of the population have IQs in the range from 55 to 145 points ($\pm 3\sigma$).
4. Only 15.87% of the people have IQs greater than 115 points (from first graph, the area to the right of $+1\sigma$).

Many more interesting remarks could be drawn from these data. Can you tell the probability that a person selected at random has an IQ of less than 70? greater than 145? less than 130?

Using the Standard Normal Table

To use a table to find normal probability values, we follow two steps.

STEP 1 Convert the normal distribution to what we call a *standard normal distribution*. A standard normal distribution is one that has a mean of 0 and a standard deviation of 1. All normal tables are set up to handle random variables with $\mu = 0$ and $\sigma = 1$. Without a standard normal distribution, a different table would be needed for each pair of μ and σ values. We call the new

FIGURE A.9
Three Common Areas under Normal Curves

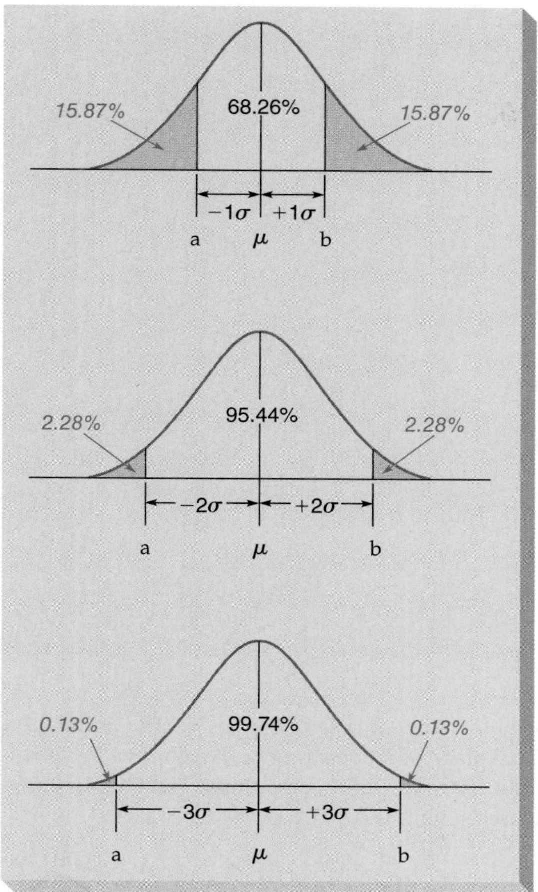

Figure A.9 is very important, and you should comprehend the meaning of ±1, 2, and 3 standard deviation symmetrical areas. Managers often speak of 95% and 99% confidence interval, which roughly refer to ±2 and 3 standard deviation graphs.

standard random variable Z. The value for Z for any normal distribution is computed from this equation:

$$Z = \frac{X - \mu}{\sigma} \quad \textbf{(A-12)}$$

where

X = value of the random variable we want to measure
μ = mean of the distribution
σ = standard deviation of the distribution
Z = number of standard deviations from X to the mean, μ

For example, if $\mu = 100$, $\sigma = 15$, and we are interested in finding the probability that the random variable X is less than 130, we want $P(X < 130)$:

$$Z = \frac{X - \mu}{\sigma} = \frac{130 - 100}{15}$$

$$= \frac{30}{15} = 2 \text{ standard deviations}$$

This means that the point X is 2.0 standard deviations to the right of the mean. This is shown in Figure A.10.

STEP 2 Look up the probability from a table of normal curve areas. Appendix C on page 574 is such a table of areas for the standard normal distribution. It is set up to provide the area under the curve to the left of any specified value of Z.

FIGURE A.10
Normal Distribution Showing the Relationship between Z Values and X Values

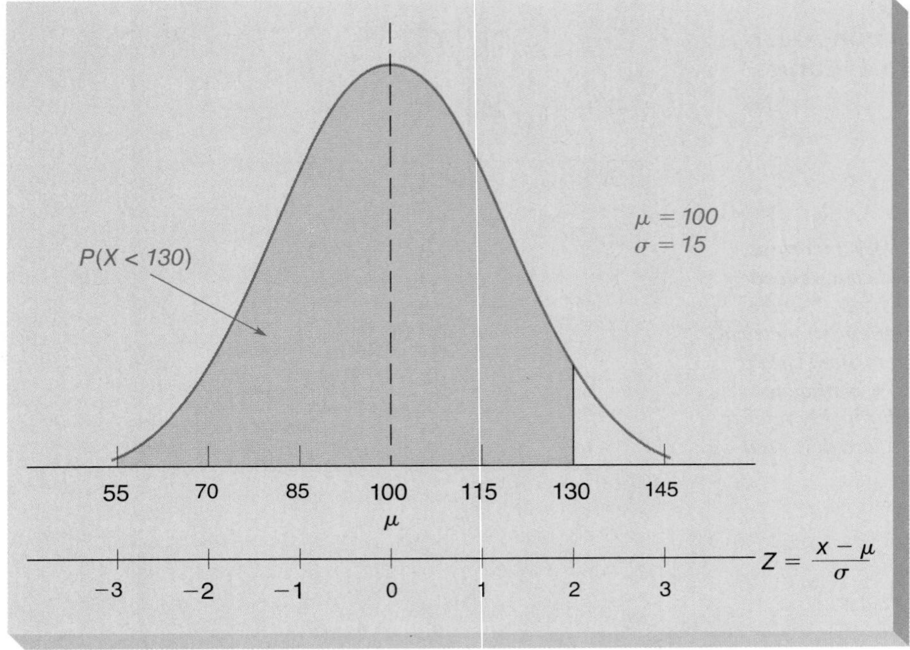

To be sure you understand the concept of symmetry in Appendix C, try to find the probability, such as $P(X < 85)$*. Note that the standard normal table shows only right-hand-side Z values.*

Let's see how Appendix C can be used. The column on the left lists values of Z, with the second decimal place of Z appearing in the top row. For example, for a value of $Z = 2.00$ as just computed, find 2.0 in the left-hand column and 0.00 in the top row. In the body of the table, we find that the area sought is 0.9772, or 97.72%. Thus,

$$P(X < 130) = P(Z < 2.00) = 0.9772$$

This suggests that if the mean IQ score is 100, with a standard deviation of 15 points, the probability that a randomly selected person's IQ is less than 130 is 0.9772. By referring back to Figure A.9, we see that this probability could also have been derived from the middle graph. (Note that $1.0 - 0.9772 = 0.0228 = 2.28$, which is the area in the right-hand tail of the curve.)

To feel comfortable with the use of the standard normal probability table, we need to work a few more examples. We now use the Haynes Construction Company as a case in point.

Haynes Construction Company Example

Haynes Construction Company builds primarily three- and four-unit apartment buildings (called triplexes and quadraplexes) for investors, and it is believed that the total construction time in days follows a normal distribution. The mean time to construct a triplex is 100 days, and the standard deviation is 20 days. Recently, the president of Haynes Construction signed a contract to complete a triplex in 125 days. Failure to complete the triplex in 125 days would result in severe penalty fees. What is the probability that Haynes Construction will not be in violation of their construction contract? The normal distribution for the construction of triplexes is shown in Figure A.11.

FIGURE A.11
Normal Distribution for Haynes Construction

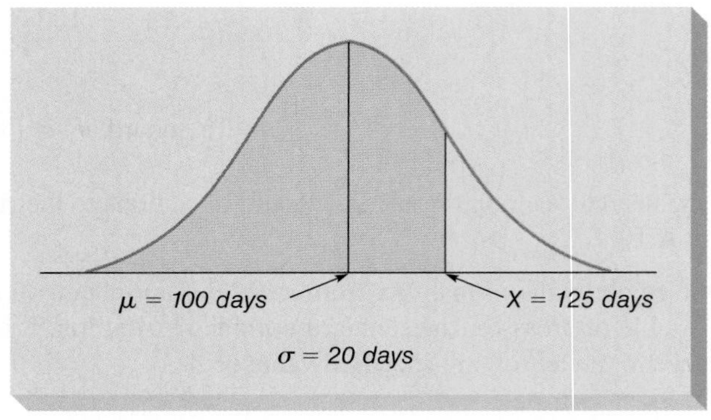

To compute this probability, we need to find the shaded area under the curve. We begin by computing Z for this problem:

$$Z = \frac{X - \mu}{\sigma} = \frac{125 - 100}{20} = \frac{25}{20} = 1.25$$

Looking in Appendix C for a Z value of 1.25, we find an area under the curve of 0.8944. (We do this by looking up 1.2 in the left-hand column of the table and then moving to the 0.05 column to find the value of $Z = 1.25$.) Therefore, the probability of not violating the contract is 0.8944, or an 89.44% chance.

Now let us look at the Haynes problem from another perspective. If the firm finishes this triplex in 75 days or less, it will be awarded a bonus payment of $5,000. What is the probability that Haynes will receive the bonus?

Figure A.12 illustrates the probability we are looking for in the shaded area. The first step is again to compute the Z value:

$$Z = \frac{X - \mu}{\sigma} = \frac{75 - 100}{20} = \frac{-25}{20} = -1.25$$

This Z value indicates that 75 days is -1.25 standard deviations to the left of the mean. But the standard normal table is structured to handle only positive Z values. To solve this problem, we observe that the curve is symmetric. The probability that Haynes will finish in *less than 75 days is equivalent* to the probability that it will finish in *more than 125 days*. In Figure A.11 we found that the probability that Haynes will finish in less than 125 days was 0.8944. So the probability that it takes more than 125 days is

$$P(X > 125) = 1.0 - P(X < 125) = 1.0 - 0.8944 = 0.1056$$

Thus, the probability of completing the triplex in 75 days or less is 0.1056, or 10.56%.

One final example: What is the probability that the triplex will take between 110 and 125 days? We see in Figure A.13 that

$$P(110 < X < 125) = P(X < 125) - P(X < 110)$$

That is, the shaded area in the graph can be computed by finding the probability of completing the building in 125 days or less *minus* the probability of completing it in 110 days or less.

FIGURE A.12
Probability that Haynes Will Receive the Bonus by Finishing in 75 Days

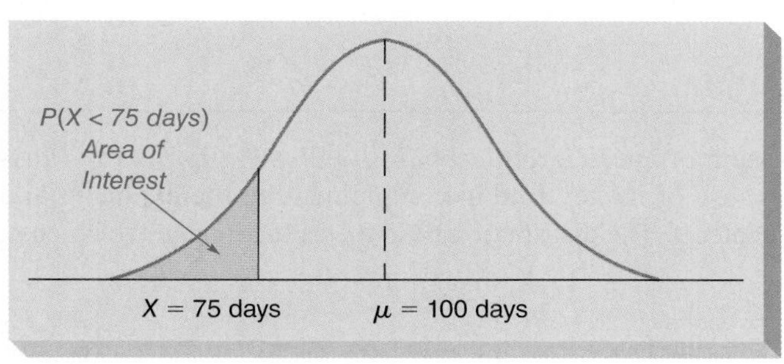

FIGURE A.13
Probability of Haynes' Finishing in 110 to 125 Days

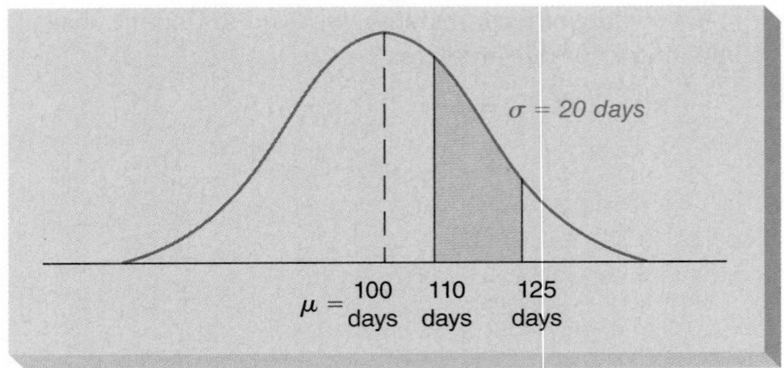

Recall that $P(X < 125 \text{ days})$ is equal to 0.8944. To find $P(X < 110 \text{ days})$, we follow the two steps developed earlier:

1. $Z = \dfrac{X - \mu}{\sigma} = \dfrac{110 - 100}{20} = \dfrac{10}{20}$

   $= 0.5$ standard deviations

2. From Appendix C, we find that the area for $Z = 0.50$ is 0.6915. So the probability that the triplex can be completed in less than 110 days is 0.6915. Finally,

$$P(110 < X < 125) = 0.8944 - 0.6915 = 0.2029$$

The probability that it will take between 110 and 125 days is 0.2029.

A.10 The Exponential Distribution

The *exponential distribution*, also called the *negative exponential distribution*, is used in dealing with queuing models. The exponential distribution describes the number of customers serviced in a time interval. The exponential distribution is a continuous distribution. Its probability function is given by

$$f(X) = \mu e^{-\mu x} \qquad \textbf{(A-13)}$$

where

X = random variable (service times)

μ = average number of units the service facility can handle in a specific period of time

e = 2.718, the base of natural logarithms

The general shape of the exponential distribution is shown in Figure A.14. Its expected value and variance can be shown to be

$$\text{Expected value} = \frac{1}{\mu} \qquad \textbf{(A-14)}$$

$$\text{Variance} = \frac{1}{\mu^2} \qquad \textbf{(A-15)}$$

The exponential distribution is illustrated in Chapter 9.

A.11 The Poisson Distribution

An important *discrete probability distribution* is the *Poisson distribution*.[1] We examine it because of its key role in complementing the exponential distribution in queuing models in Chapter 9. The distribution describes situations in which customers arrive independently during

[1] This distribution, derived by Simeon Poisson in 1837, is pronounced "pwah-sahn."

FIGURE A.14
Negative Exponential Distribution

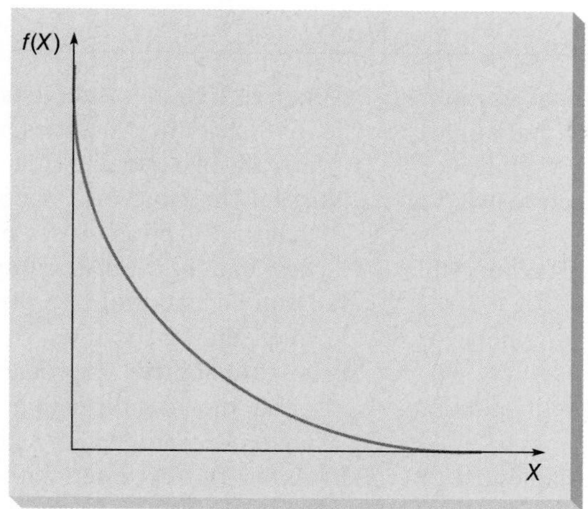

a certain time interval, and the number of arrivals depends on the length of the time interval. Examples are patients arriving at a health clinic, customers arriving at a bank window, passengers arriving at an airport, and telephone calls going through a central exchange.

The formula for the Poisson distribution is

$$P(X) = \frac{\lambda^x e^{-\lambda}}{X!} \tag{A-16}$$

where

$P(X)$ = probability of exactly X arrivals or occurrences

λ = average number of arrivals per unit of time (the mean arrival rate), pronounced "lambda"

e = 2.718, the base of the natural logarithms

X = specific value (0, 1, 2, 3, and so on) of the random variable

The mean and variance of the Poisson distribution are equal and are computed simply as

$$\text{expected value} = \lambda \tag{A-17}$$

$$\text{variance} = \lambda \tag{A-18}$$

A sample distribution for $\lambda = 2$ arrivals is shown in Figure A.15.

FIGURE A.15
Sample Poisson Distribution with $\lambda = 2$

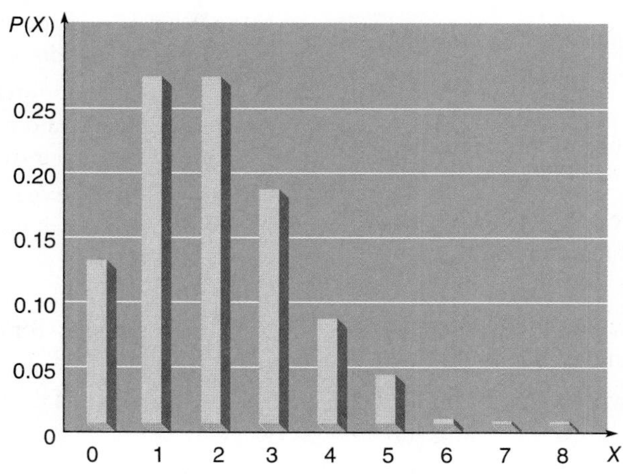

Glossary

Bayes' Theorem A formula that allows us to compute conditional probabilities when dealing with statistically dependent events.

Classical, or Logical, Approach An objective way of assessing probabilities based on logic.

Collectively Exhaustive Events A collection of all possible outcomes of an experiment.

Conditional Probability The probability of one event occurring given that another has taken place.

Continuous Probability Distribution A probability distribution with a continuous random variable.

Continuous Random Variable A random variable that can assume an infinite or unlimited set of values.

Dependent Events The situation in which the occurrence of one event affects the probability of occurrence of some other event.

Discrete Probability Distribution A probability distribution with a discrete random variable.

Discrete Random Variable A random variable that can only assume a finite or limited set of values.

Expected Value The (weighted) average of a probability distribution.

Independent Events The situation in which the occurrence of one event has no effect on the probability of occurrence of a second event.

Joint Probability The probability of events occurring together (or one after the other).

Marginal Probability The simple probability of an event occurring.

Mutually Exclusive Events A situation in which only one event can occur on any given trial or experiment.

Negative Exponential Distribution A continuous probability distribution that describes the time between customer arrivals in a queuing situation.

Normal Distribution A continuous bell-shaped distribution that is a function of two parameters, the mean and standard deviation of the distribution.

Poisson Distribution A discrete probability distribution used in queuing theory.

Prior Probability A probability value determined before new or additional information is obtained. It is sometimes called an *a priori* probability estimate.

Probability A statement about the likelihood of an event occurring. It is expressed as a numeric value between 0 and 1, inclusive.

Probability Density Function The mathematical function that describes a continuous probability distribution. It is represented by $f(X)$.

Probability Distribution The set of all possible values of a random variable and their associated probabilities.

Random Variable A variable that assigns a number to every possible outcome of an experiment.

Relative Frequency Approach An objective way of determining probabilities based on observing frequencies over a number of trials.

Revised, or Posterior, Probability A probability value that results from new or revised information and prior probabilities.

Standard Deviation The square root of the variance.

Subjective Approach A method of determining probability values based on experience or judgment.

Variance A measure of dispersion or spread of the probability distribution.

Discussion Questions and Problems

Discussion Questions

A-1 What are the two basic laws of probability?

A-2 What is the meaning of mutually exclusive events? What is meant by collectively exhaustive? Give an example of each.

A-3 Describe the various approaches used in determining probability values.

A-4 Why is the probability of the intersection of two events subtracted in the sum of the probability of two events?

A-5 What is the difference between events that are dependent and events that are independent?

A-6 What is Bayes' theorem, and when can it be used?

A-7 How can probability revisions assist in managerial decision making?

A-8 What is a random variable? What are the various types of random variables?

A-9 What is the difference between a discrete probability distribution and a continuous probability distribution? Give your own example of each.

A-10 What is the expected value, and what does it measure? How is it computed for a discrete probability distribution?

A-11 What is the variance, and what does it measure? How is it computed for a discrete probability distribution?

A-12 Name three business processes that can be described by the normal distribution.

A-13 After evaluating student response to a question about a case used in class, the instructor constructed the following probability distribution:

RESPONSE	RANDOM VARIABLE, X	PROBABILITY
Excellent	5	0.05
Good	4	0.25
Average	3	0.40
Fair	2	0.15
Poor	1	0.15

What kind of probability distribution is it?

Problems

A-14 A student taking Management Science 301 at East Haven University will receive one of five possible grades for the course: A, B, C, D, or E. The distribution of grades over the past two years is shown in the following table.

GRADE	NUMBER OF STUDENTS
A	80
B	75
C	90
D	30
F	25
	Total 300

If this past distribution is a good indicator of future grades, what is the probability of a student receiving a C in the course?

A-15 A silver dollar is flipped twice. Calculate the probability of each of the following occurring:
(a) A head on the first flip
(b) A tail on the second flip given that the first toss was a head
(c) Two tails
(d) A tail on the first and a head on the second
(e) A tail on the first and a head on the second or a head on the first and a tail on the second
(f) At least one head on the two flips

A-16 An urn contains 8 red chips, 10 green chips, and 2 white chips. A chip is drawn and replaced, and then a second chip drawn. What is the probability of
(a) a white chip on the first draw?
(b) a white chip on the first draw and a red on the second?
(c) two green chips being drawn?
(d) a red chip on the second, given that a white chip was drawn on the first?

A-17 Evertight, a leading manufacturer of quality nails, produces 1-, 2-, 3-, 4-, and 5-inch nails for various uses. In the production process, if there is an overrun or if the nails are slightly defective, they are placed in a common bin. Yesterday, 651 of the 1-inch nails, 243 of the 2-inch nails, 41 of the 3-inch nails, 451 of the 4-inch nails, and 333 of the 5-inch nails were placed in the bin.
(a) What is the probability of reaching into the bin and getting a 4-inch nail?
(b) What is the probability of getting a 5-inch nail?
(c) If a particular application requires a nail that is 3 inches or shorter, what is the probability of getting a nail that will satisfy the requirements of the application?

A-18 Last year, at Northern Manufacturing Company, 200 people had colds during the year. One hundred fifty-five people who did no exercising had colds, whereas the remainder of the people with colds were involved in a weekly exercise program. Half of the 1,000 employees were involved in some type of exercise.
(a) What is the probability that an employee will have a cold next year?
(b) Given that an employee is involved in an exercise program, what is the probability that he or she will get a cold?
(c) What is the probability that an employee who is not involved in an exercise program will get a cold next year?
(d) Are exercising and getting a cold independent events? Explain your answer.

A-19 The Springfield Kings, a professional basketball team, has won 12 of its last 20 games and is expected to continue winning at the same percentage rate. The team's ticket manager is anxious to attract a large crowd to tomorrow's game but believes that depends on how well the Kings perform tonight against the Galveston Comets. He assesses the probability of drawing a large crowd to be 0.90 should the team win tonight. What is the probability that the team wins tonight and that there will be a large crowd at tomorrow's game?

A-20 David Mashley teaches two undergraduate statistics courses at Kansas College. The class for Statistics 201 consists of 7 sophomores and 3 juniors. The more advanced course, Statistics 301, has 2 sophomores and 8 juniors enrolled. As an example of a business sampling technique, Professor Mashley randomly selects, from the stack of Statistics 201 registration cards, the class card of one student and then places that card back in the stack. If that student was a sophomore, Mashley draws another card from the Statistics 201 stack; if not, he randomly draws

a card from the Statistics 301 group. Are these two draws independent events? What is the probability of
(a) a junior's name on the first draw?
(b) a junior's name on the second draw, given that a sophomore's name was drawn first?
(c) a junior's name on the second draw, given that a junior's name was drawn first?
(d) a sophomores' name on both draws?
(e) a junior's name on both draws?
(f) one sophomore's name and one junior's name on the two draws, regardless of order drawn?

A-21 The oasis outpost of Abu Ilan, in the heart of the Negev desert, has a population of 20 Bedouin tribesmen and 20 Farima tribesmen. El Kamin, a nearby oasis, has a population of 32 Bedouins and 8 Farima. A lost Israeli soldier, accidentally separated from his army unit, is wandering through the desert and arrives at the edge of one of the oases. The soldier has no idea which oasis he has found, but the first person he spots at a distance is a Bedouin. What is the probability that he wandered into Abu Ilan? What is the probability that he is in El Kamin?

A-22 The lost Israeli soldier mentioned in Problem A-21 decides to rest for a few minutes before entering the desert oasis he has just found. Closing his eyes, he dozes off for 15 minutes, wakes, and walks toward the center of the oasis. The first person he spots this time he again recognizes as a Bedouin. What is the posterior probability that he is in El Kamin?

A-23 Ace Machine Works estimates that the probability their lathe tool is properly adjusted is 0.8. When the lathe is properly adjusted, there is a 0.9 probability that the parts produced pass inspection. If the lathe is out of adjustment, however, the probability of a good part being produced is only 0.2. A part randomly chosen is inspected and found to be acceptable. At this point, what is the posterior probability that the lathe tool is properly adjusted?

A-24 The Boston South Fifth Street Softball League consists of three teams: Mama's Boys, team 1; the Killers, team 2; and the Machos, team 3. Each team plays the other teams just once during the season. The win–loss record for the past five years is as follows:

WINNER	(1)	(2)	(3)
Mama's Boys (1)	X	3	4
The Killers (2)	2	X	1
The Machos (3)	1	4	X

Each row represents the number of wins over the past five years. Mama's Boys beat the Killers three times, beat the Machos four times, and so on.
(a) What is the probability that the Killers will win every game next year?
(b) What is the probability that the Machos will win at least one game next year?
(c) What is the probability that Mama's Boys will win exactly one game next year?
(d) What is the probability that the Killers will win less than two games next year?

A-25 The schedule for the Killers next year is as follows (refer to Problem A-24):
Game 1: The Machos
Game 2: Mama's Boys
(a) What is the probability that the Killers will win their first game?
(b) What is the probability that the Killers will win their last game?
(c) What is the probability that the Killers will break even—win exactly one game?
(d) What is the probability that the Killers will win every game?
(e) What is the probability that the Killers will lose every game?
(f) Would you want to be the coach of the Killers?

A-26 The Northside Rifle team has two markspersons, Dick and Sally. Dick hits a bull's-eye 90% of the time, and Sally hits a bull's-eye 95% of the time.
(a) What is the probability that either Dick or Sally or both will hit the bull's-eye if each takes one shot?
(b) What is the probability that Dick and Sally will both hit the bull's-eye?
(c) Did you make any assumptions in answering the preceding questions? If you answered yes, do you think that you are justified in making the assumption(s)?

A-27 In a sample of 1,000 representing a survey from the entire population, 650 people were from Laketown, and the rest of the people were from River City. Out of the sample, 19 people had some form of cancer. Thirteen of these people were from Laketown.
(a) Are the events of living in Laketown and having some sort of cancer independent?
(b) Which city would you prefer to live in, assuming that your main objective was to avoid having cancer?

A-28 Compute the probability of "loaded die, given that a 3 was rolled," as shown in Example 7, this time using the general form of Bayes' theorem from Equation A-7.

A-29 Which of the following are probability distributions? Why?

(a)

RANDOM VARIABLE X	PROBABILITY
−2	0.1
−1	0.2
0	0.3
1	0.25
2	0.15

(b)

RANDOM VARIABLE Y	PROBABILITY
1	1.1
1.5	0.2
2	0.3
2.5	0.25
3	−1.25

(c)

RANDOM VARIABLE Z	PROBABILITY
1	0.1
2	0.2
3	0.3
4	0.4
5	0.0

A-30 Harrington Health Food stocks 5 loaves of Neutro-Bread. The probability distribution for the sales of Neutro-Bread is listed in the following table:

NUMBER OF LOAVES SOLD	PROBABILITY
0	0.05
1	0.15
2	0.20
3	0.25
4	0.20
5	0.15

How many loaves will Harrington sell, on average?

A-31 What are the expected value and variance of the following probability distribution?

RANDOM VARIABLE X	PROBABILITY
1	0.05
2	0.05
3	0.10
4	0.10
5	0.15
6	0.15
7	0.25
8	0.15

A-32 Sales for Fast Kat, a 16-foot catamaran sailboat, have averaged 250 boats per month over the past five years, with a standard deviation of 25 boats. Assuming that the demand is about the same as past years and follows a normal curve, what is the probability sales will be less than 280 boats?

A-33 Refer to Problem A-32. What is the probability that sales will be more than 265 boats during the next month? What is the probability that sales will be less than 250 boats next month?

A-34 Precision Parts is a job shop that specializes in producing electric motor shafts. The average shaft size for the E300 electric motor is 0.55 inch, with a standard deviation of 0.10 inch. It is normally distributed. What is the probability that a shaft selected at random will be between 0.55 and 0.65 inch?

A-35 Refer to Problem A-34. What is the probability that a shaft size will be greater than 0.65 inch? What is the probability that a shaft size will be between 0.53 and 0.59 inch? What is the probability that a shaft size will be under 0.45 inch?

A-36 An industrial oven used to cure sand cores for a factory manufacturing engine blocks for small cars is able to maintain fairly constant temperatures. The temperature range of the oven follows a normal distribution with a mean of 450°F and a standard deviation of 25°F. Leslie Larsen, president of the factory, is concerned about the large number of defective cores that have been produced in the last several months. If the oven gets hotter than 475°F, the core is defective. What is the probability that the oven will cause a core to be defective? What is the probability that the temperature of the oven will range from 460° to 470°F?

A-37 Steve Goodman, production foreman for the Florida Gold Fruit Company, estimates that the average sale of oranges is 4,700 and the standard deviation is 500 oranges. Sales follow a normal distribution.

(a) What is the probability that sales will be greater than 5,500 oranges?

(b) What is the probability that sales will be greater than 4,500 oranges?

(c) What is the probability that sales will be less than 4,900 oranges?

(d) What is the probability that sales will be less than 4,300 oranges?

A-38 Susan Williams has been the production manager of Medical Suppliers, Inc., for the past 17 years. Medical Suppliers, Inc., is a producer of bandages and arm slings. During the past 5 years, the demand for No-Stick bandages has been fairly constant. On the average, sales have been about 87,000 packages of No-Stick. Susan has reason to believe that the distribution of No-Stick follows a normal curve, with a standard deviation of 4,000 packages. What is the probability that sales will be less than 81,000 packages?

A-39 Armstrong Faber produces a standard number two pencil called Ultra-Lite. Since Chuck Armstrong started Armstrong Faber, sales had grown steadily. With the increase in the price of wood products, however, Chuck has been forced to increase the price of the Ultra-Lite pencils. As a result, the demand for Ultra-Lite has been fairly stable over the past six years. On the average, Armstrong Faber has sold 457,000 pencils each year. Furthermore, 90% of the time sales have been between 454,000 and 460,000 pencils. It is expected that the sales follow a normal distribution with a mean of 457,000 pencils. Estimate the standard deviation of this distribution. (*Hint:* Work backward from the normal table to find Z. Then apply Equation A-12.)

A-40 Patients arrive at the emergency room of Costa Valley Hospital at an average of 5 per day. The demand for emergency room treatment at Costa Valley follows a Poisson distribution.

(a) Compute the probability of exactly 0, 1, 2, 3, 4, and 5 arrivals per day.

(b) What is the sum of these probabilities, and why is the number less than 1?

A-41 Using the data in Problem A-40, determine the probability of more than 3 visits for emergency room service on any given day.

A-42 Cars arrive at Carla's Muffler shop for repair work at an average of 3 per hour, following an exponential distribution.

(a) What is the expected time between arrivals?

(b) What is the variance of the time between arrivals?

APPENDIX B: USEFUL EXCEL 2010 COMMANDS AND PROCEDURES FOR INSTALLING EXCELMODULES

B.1 Introduction

Excel is Microsoft Office's spreadsheet application program. A *spreadsheet* lets us embed hidden formulas that perform calculations on visible data. The main document (or file) used in Excel to store and manipulate data is called a *workbook*. A workbook can consist of a number of worksheets, each of which can be used to list and analyze data. Excel allows us to enter and modify data on several worksheets simultaneously. We can also perform calculations based on data from multiple worksheets and/or workbooks.

This appendix provides a brief overview of some basic Excel commands and procedures, as applied to Excel 2010. It also discusses how add-ins, such as Solver and Data Analysis, can be installed and enabled in Excel. We should note that while the fundamental appearance of a workbook as well as the syntax and use of functions and many menu commands has remained the same across different versions of Excel, the interface (in terms of the appearance of toolbars, menus, etc.) has changed significantly in Excel 2007 and Excel 2010 compared to Excel 2003 and prior versions. Likewise, as illustrated in this textbook, Solver's appearance and menu options have changed significantly in Excel 2010 compared to previous versions of Excel.

Finally, this appendix describes the installation and usage procedures for ExcelModules, a software package provided on the Companion Website for this textbook.[1] We use this software to develop and solve decision models for queuing (Chapter 9), forecasting (Chapter 11), and inventory control (Chapter 12).

In addition to the extensive help features built into Excel, there are thousands of online tutorials available to help us learn Excel. Many of these are quite comprehensive in their content. To get a current listing of these online tutorials, simply type "Excel tutorial" in the search box of any Web browser.

B.2 Getting Started

When we start Excel, it opens an empty file (called a workbook) named Book1, as shown in Screenshot B-1. We can also start Excel by directly clicking on any Excel file accessible on the computer. In that case, Excel opens that file when it starts.

A workbook consists of a number of pages called *worksheets*. The number of blank worksheets in a new workbook is set in Excel's main options (click File | Options | General to view and/or change this number). We can easily insert more worksheets or delete existing ones, as illustrated later in this appendix. The sheet tabs at the bottom of each worksheet help us identify and move to each worksheet in the workbook. We can rename any sheet by double-clicking its tab and typing in the new name.

Organization of a Worksheet

A worksheet consists of columns and rows, as shown in Screenshot B-1. Columns are identified by headers with letters (e.g., A, B, C), and rows are identified by headers with numbers (e.g., 1, 2, 3). Excel files stored in Excel 2007/2010 format (with the file extension *.xlsx*) have 1,048,576 rows by 16,384 columns per worksheet. In contrast, files stored under prior versions of Excel (with the file extension *.xls*) are restricted to only 65,536 rows and 256 columns. Where a row and a column intersect is known as a cell. Each cell has a reference based on the intersection of the row and column. For example, the reference of the cell at the intersection of column B and row 7 is referred to as cell B7 (as shown in Screenshot B-1).

A *cell* is the fundamental storage unit for Excel data, including both values and labels. A *value* is a number or a hidden formula that performs a calculation, and a *label* is a heading or some explanatory text. We can enter different types of entries (e.g., text, numbers, formulas, dates, and times) into cells.

[1]The Companion Website for this textbook is at www.pearsonhighered.com/balakrishnan.

SCREENSHOT B-1 General Layout of an Excel Worksheet

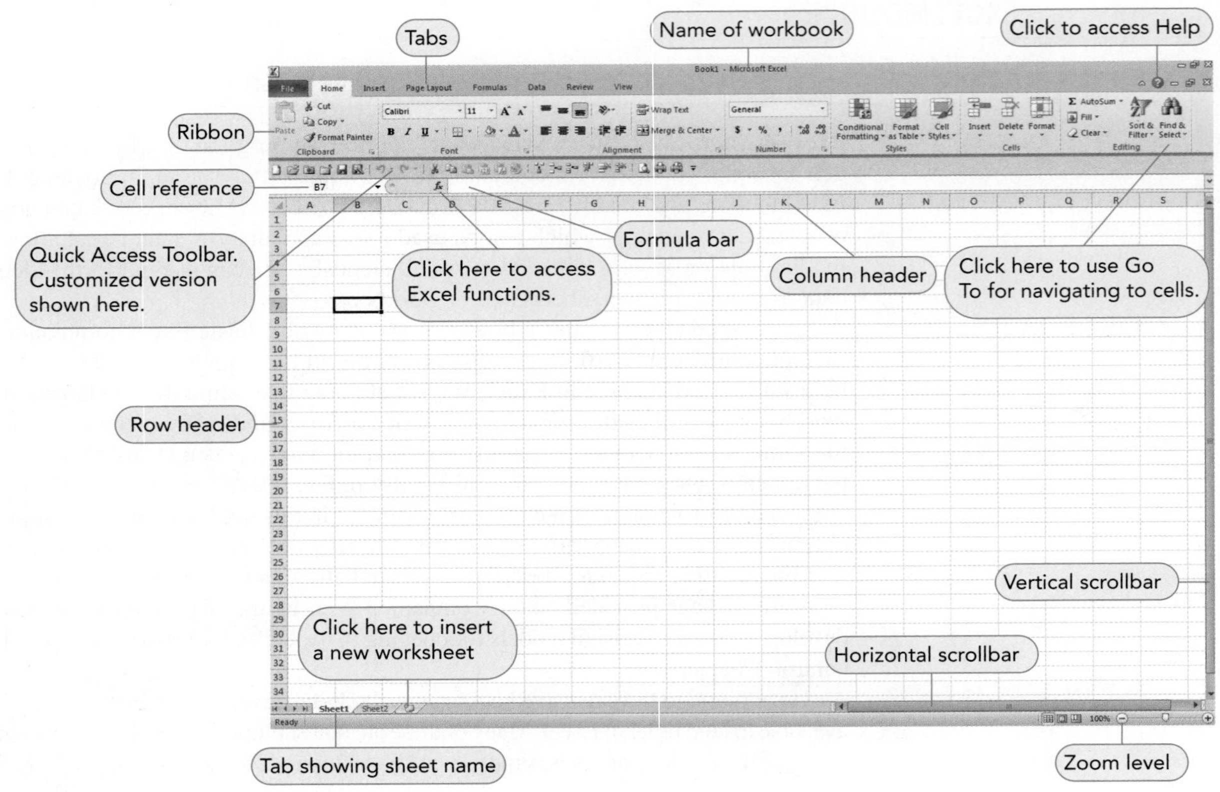

Navigating through a Worksheet

We can navigate through a worksheet by using either the mouse or the keys on the keyboard. To select a cell by using the mouse, click the cell (e.g., B7, as shown in Screenshot B-1). To move anywhere on a worksheet, we can also use the arrow keys or the Page Up and Page Down keys on the keyboard.

We can also use the Go To menu option to navigate between cells. This option is useful if we want to modify the contents of a cell. To go to a specific cell, click Find & Select | Go To (see Screenshot B-1). In the Go To dialog box, we can even click the Special button to go to cells with special features. For example, we can choose to go to cells with comments, to blank cells, or to the last cell in the worksheet.

B.3 The Ribbon, Toolbars, and Tabs

A toolbar consists of commands (usually represented by icons) that provide shortcuts to common tasks. Unlike Excel 2003, which has several toolbars available for use, Excel 2010 has a single supersized toolbar called the Ribbon (see Screenshot B-1). The Ribbon consists of the following default tabs: File, Home, Insert, Page Layout, Formulas, Data, Review, and View. Additional tabs may be present in the Ribbon if we have installed additional add-ins (e.g., Crystal Ball, ExcelModules), as illustrated later in this appendix.

As with previous versions of Microsoft Office, many of the commands (and associated icons) in Excel's tabs are identical to the ones in other Microsoft Office programs such as PowerPoint and Word. We can customize any of the tabs in the Ribbon by right-clicking anywhere on it and selecting Customize the Ribbon or through Excel's options settings (illustrated later in this appendix).

FILE TAB The File tab, shown in Screenshot B-2A, includes commands for many file-related tasks such as saving and printing. It also provided access to the numerous default options that may be set in Excel.

The following list indicates the menu commands available on this tab, along with brief descriptions of each command. Many of the menu commands in this tab (as well as in other tabs) can be added to the Quick Access Toolbar for ease of access and use. This toolbar can be

SCREENSHOT B-2A Menu Commands in the File Tab in Excel 2010

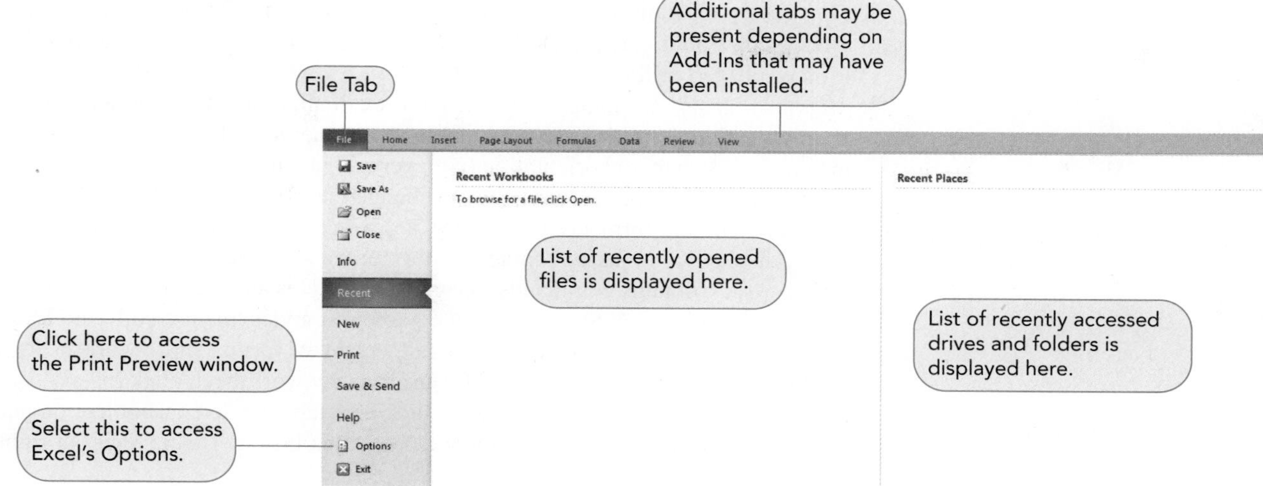

placed either above or below the Ribbon and customized as desired. For example, a customized version of the Quick Access Toolbar in shown below the Ribbon in Screenshot B-1.

1. *Save.* Save the current workbook (or file).
2. *Save As.* Save the current workbook under a different name or file type (e.g., .xls, .txt, .pdf).
3. *Open.* Open an existing workbook.
4. *Close.* Close the current workbook.
5. *Info.* Display information about the current workbook (e.g., properties, permissions, revision history).
6. *Recent.* Display a list of recently opened workbooks and places (folders). This is illustrated in Screenshot B-2A.
7. *New.* Open a new blank workbook or other templates available in Microsoft Office.
8. *Print.* Print part or all of the current worksheet. This feature is discussed in more detail in section B.6.
9. *Save & Send.* Save the current workbook and send using e-mail, to the Web, etc.
10. *Help.* Access the extensive help built into Microsoft Excel. More detail on this feature is provided later in this appendix.
11. *Options.* Change default workbook and worksheet options (e.g., font, number of worksheets). This feature is discussed in more detail in section B.7.
12. *Exit.* Exit Microsoft Excel.

HOME TAB The Home tab, shown in Screenshot B-2B, includes commands for many editing and formatting related tasks. By default, this is the tab that is visible when Excel starts. The following list describes the primary menu commands on this tab. Note that on this tab (and all other tabs) in the Ribbon, icons representing commands associated with similar tasks are typically located together to form groups. For example, the groups in the Home tab are called Clipboard, Font, Alignment, Number, Styles, etc.

1. *Clipboard group.* Contains the standard editing tools Cut, Copy, and Paste. Click the arrow under the Paste command to access specialized paste options such as Paste Values, Paste Formats, Paste Formulas, Paste Comments, Transpose, etc. Click the arrow next to

SCREENSHOT B-2B Menu Commands in the Home Tab in Excel 2010

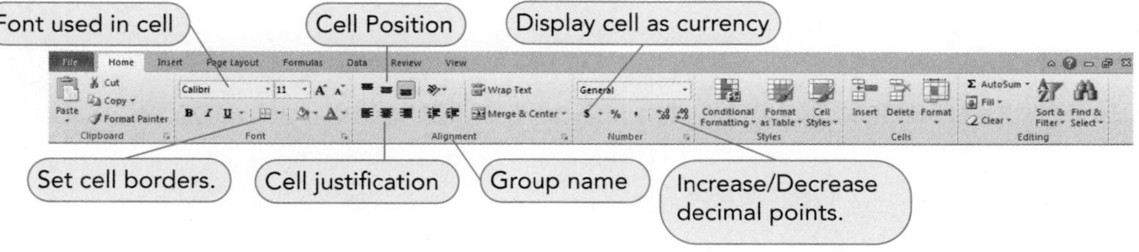

Copy to copy the entire selected contents as a picture rather than as individual formulas, values, or text.

2. *Font group.* Contains commands to set the font type and size, as well as formatting features such as bold, italic, underline, font color, and fill color. We can also define borders for the selected cell(s).
3. *Alignment group.* Contains commands to set cell alignment features such as justification, position within the cell, wrap text, merge (or un-merge) cells, increase (or decrease) cell indent, and change text orientation (e.g., vertical, angular).
4. *Number group.* Contains commands to change the display mode (e.g., number, text, date, time, custom) and format (e.g., number of decimal points shown, display values as currency, display values as percentage) of the contents of a cell (or multiple cells).
5. *Style group.* Contains commands to change cell styles and set conditional formatting rules for cells. Click on Cell Styles to see the numerous styles that are built into Excel.
6. *Cells group.* Contains commands to insert, delete, or format entire worksheets, as well as individual cells, rows, or columns. To insert a new worksheet, click Insert | Insert Sheet or click the Insert Worksheet icon next to the Sheet tab (see Screenshot B-1 on page 562 for illustration). To delete an existing worksheet, click Delete | Delete Sheet or right-click on the Sheet tab and select Delete.

   To insert new row(s), click on the row header(s) above where we want the new row(s) to be inserted. Then click Insert | Insert Sheet Rows. To delete row(s), select the row(s) that we want to delete. Then click Delete | Delete Sheet Rows.

   To change the height of a row, move the mouse to the bottom edge of the row heading. The cursor will change to a plus sign with arrows on the top and bottom. Click and drag to the new desired height. Double-clicking will automatically adjust the row height to the tallest entry in the row. Alternatively, click Format | Row Height or Format | AutoFit Row Height.

   To hide a row(s), first select the row(s) to hide. Then click Format | Hide & Unhide | Hide Rows (or right-click the mouse and select the Hide option). To unhide hidden row(s), first select the row before and after the hidden row(s). Then click Format | Hide & Unhide | Unhide Rows (or right-click the mouse and select the Unhide option).

   All of these actions (insert, delete, hide, unhide, and change column width) can also be done for columns, using similar procedures.
7. *Editing group.* Contains commands to perform editing tasks such as search, replace, sort, filter, etc. This group also includes the Fill command that can be used to automatically enter a series in a worksheet (e.g., numbers from 1 to 100, days of the week, months of the year) rather than typing these entries manually.

INSERT TAB The Insert tab, shown in Screenshot B-2C, includes commands for creating and/or inserting different objects such as tables, charts, pictures, clip art, hyperlinks (to other documents or Web links), text boxes, headers and/or footers, equations, symbols, etc. As with the Home tab, similar commands are arranged together within groups, such as Tables, Illustrations, Charts, Text, etc. Chapter 11 provides a detailed explanation of how to create a scatter chart in Excel.

PAGE LAYOUT TAB The Page Layout tab, shown in Screenshot B-2D, includes commands for setting print options such as margins, page orientation, size, print area, titles, page breaks, etc. In addition, it includes commands for display options such as view gridlines, view row and column headings, and themes. We discuss some of these commands in greater detail in section B.6.

SCREENSHOT B-2C
Menu Commands in the Insert Tab in Excel 2010

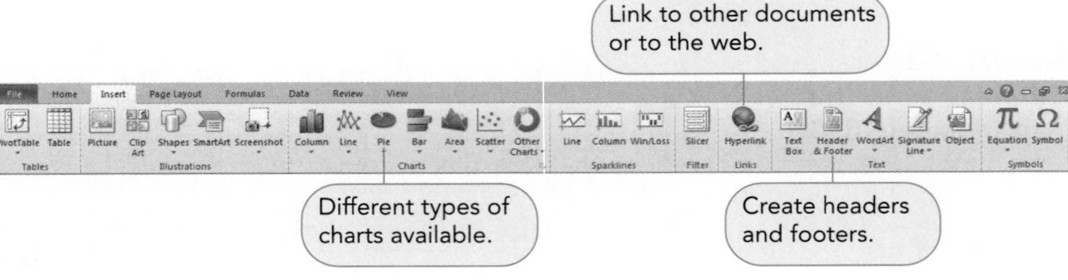
Link to other documents or to the web.
Different types of charts available.
Create headers and footers.

SCREENSHOT B-2D
Menu Commands in the Page Layout Tab in Excel 2010

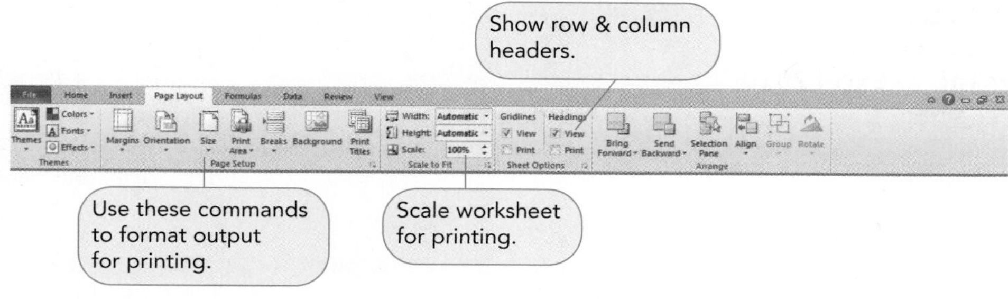
Show row & column headers.
Use these commands to format output for printing.
Scale worksheet for printing.

SCREENSHOT B-2E
Menu Commands in the Formulas Tab in Excel 2010

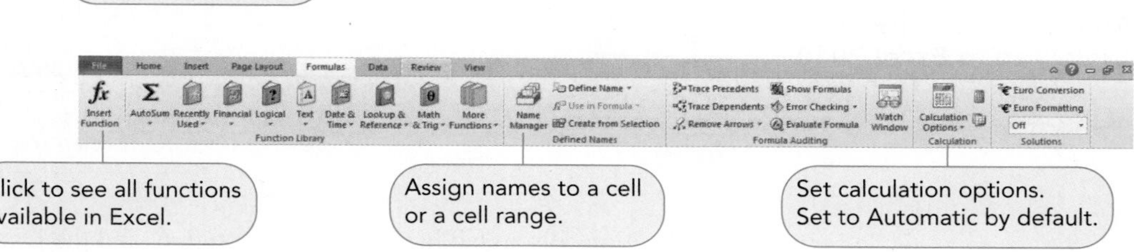
Click to see all functions available in Excel.
Assign names to a cell or a cell range.
Set calculation options. Set to Automatic by default.

FORMULAS TAB The Formulas tab, shown in Screenshot B-2E, includes commands to access and select the numerous mathematical functions that are built into Excel for computational purposes.

The icons representing these commands are arranged in the following default groups.

1. *Function Library group.* Click the Insert Function icon (represented by f_x) to access all functions available in Excel. Alternatively, click any of the other icons in this group (e.g., Financial, Logical, Math & Trig) to access only the functions under that subcategory.
2. *Defined Names group.* Use these commands to define names for an individual cell or a cell range. For example, if we define cell range B5:D10 using the name Table1, we can then refer to this cell range as Table1 in all formulas.
3. *Formula Auditing group.* These commands are useful for tracing and verifying cell relationships in formulas. They are especially useful when we encounter formula errors such as circular references.
4. *Calculation group.* Microsoft Excel 2010 has three different options available for how it performs calculations:

   - *Automatic (default).* All calculations in all open worksheets and workbooks are performed automatically as soon as a cell entry is completed.
   - *Manual.* All calculations in the workbook are performed only when the F9 key is pressed.
   - *Automatic Except for Data Tables.* All calculations are performed automatically except for data tables, which are executed only when the F9 key is pressed. As discussed in Chapter 10, this option is very useful when running large simulation models.

DATA TAB The Data tab, shown in Screenshot B-2F, includes commands to access data from external sources as well as several data tools to organize, manipulate, and analyze data. Of special interest in this textbook are the following: (1) the sort and filter options which allow us to sort data using multiple criteria, or filter it so that only selected entries are displayed, (2) the What-If Analysis command that includes three procedures (Scenario Manager, Goal Seek, and Data Table) that are discussed in this textbook, and (3) Excel add-ins such as Data Analysis and Solver found in the Analysis group. The Solver add-in forms the basis for all modeling

SCREENSHOT B-2F
Menu Commands in the Data Tab in Excel 2010

Click to access Scenario Manager, Goal Seek, and Data Table procedures.
Excel Add-Ins that have been enabled for use.

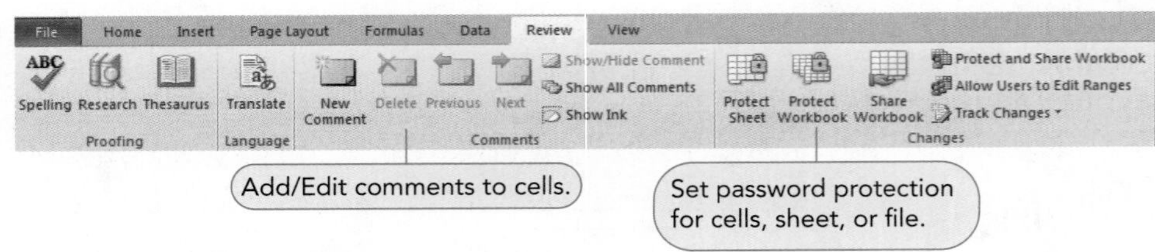

SCREENSHOT B-2G
Menu Commands in the Review Tab in Excel 2010

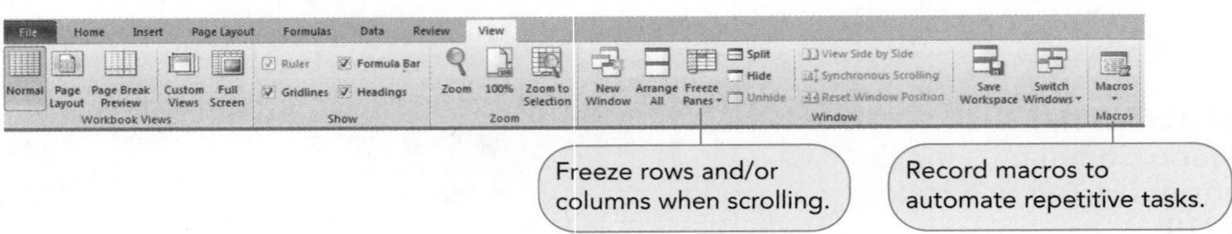

SCREENSHOT B-2H
Menu Commands in the View Tab in Excel 2010

applications discussed in Chapters 2 through 6, and the Data Analysis statistical tool is used in Chapters 10 and 11.

REVIEW TAB The Review tab, shown in Screenshot B-2G, includes commands for proofing text (e.g., spell check, thesaurus), creating and editing comments in cells, and using password options to protect individual cells, worksheets, or workbooks to prevent changes to their contents.

VIEW TAB The View tab, shown in Screenshot B-2H, includes various options to view the current worksheet, freeze rows and/or columns when scrolling, zoom in or out to specific content, and arrange multiple workbooks when more than one workbook is open. We can also record macros to automate repetitive tasks.

Excel Help

If we are unsure about how to perform any action in Excel (or any other Microsoft Office program), we can use the extensive built-in help feature to get assistance. The help feature can display tips and detailed instructions (including examples) on how to use different Excel functions and procedures or provide help on the specific task we are performing. To start this feature, click the Help icon (which looks like a question mark) on the top-right side of the Ribbon (see Screenshot B-1 on page 562) or click Help | Microsoft Excel Help, found within the File tab.

We can use common constructions to query the help database. For example, we can type "How do I format a cell?" and click the Search button. The program then responds with links to various help topics. If none of the suggestions match the query, click Next. When the response that best matches the query has been located, click that item. The help text is then displayed.

B.4 Working with Worksheets

To enter data or information in a worksheet, we first click the cell in which we want to enter the data. Then, we simply type in the data. We can enter numbers, text, dates, times, or formulas. (These are discussed in section B.5.) When we are done, we press the Enter key, and the next cell in the column is automatically selected.

SELECTING A GROUP OF ADJACENT CELLS Click the first cell to be selected. Hold down the Shift key and click the last cell to be selected. All cells in between these two cells will automatically be selected. Alternatively, after clicking the first cell, hold the left mouse button down and drag until we have selected all the cells needed.

SELECTING A GROUP OF NONADJACENT CELLS Left-click the first cell to be selected. Hold down the Ctrl key and click each of the other cells to be selected. Only the cells clicked will be selected.

SELECTING AN ENTIRE ROW OR COLUMN Click the header (number) of the row that we want to select in its entirety. To select more than one entire row, keep either the Shift or the Ctrl key pressed (as discussed in the preceding item for selecting cells), depending on whether the rows are adjacent or nonadjacent. We can use a similar procedure to select one or more columns in their entirety.

EDITING DATA To edit the existing information in a cell, double-click the cell to be edited (or click once on the cell and press the F2 function key on the keyboard). We can now simply type over or modify the contents as desired.

CLEARING DATA To clear the data in selected cells, first select the cells that we want to clear. Next, press the Delete key on the keyboard.

B.5 Using Formulas and Functions

Formulas allow us to perform calculations on our worksheet data. A formula must start with an "equal to" (=) sign in Excel. To enter a formula, we click the cell where we want to enter the formula. Next type an = sign, followed by the formula. A formula can consist of mathematical operations involving numbers or cell references that point to cells with numerical values. After typing in a formula, press Enter to perform the calculation. If the Formulas | Calculation Options setting is set to Automatic (the default; see Screenshot B-2E on page 565), Excel will automatically recalculate the formula when we change any of the input values used in the formula.

Functions are formulas that are already built into Excel. As noted in section B.3, to see the full list of built-in functions in Excel, click the Insert Function command, found within the Formulas tab (or the f_x icon next to the formula bar on a worksheet, as shown in Screenshot B-1 on page 562). A partial list is shown in Screenshot B-3. We can view subsets of these functions by selecting the category (e.g., Statistical, Financial) or click the appropriate category in the Function Library group.

When we select a specific function, the syntax for that function is displayed at the bottom of the window. For example, Screenshot B-3 shows the syntax for the SUMPRODUCT function that is used extensively in Chapters 2 through 6. For more detailed help on the selected function, click on Help on this function, in the bottom left of the window.

When using functions in Excel, we can prefix the function with an = sign and directly type in the function using the required syntax. Alternatively, we can select the cell in which we want to use a particular function. Then, we can call up the list of available functions (as described previously) and select the desired function. A window that shows the required input entries

SCREENSHOT B-3 Functions Available in Excel

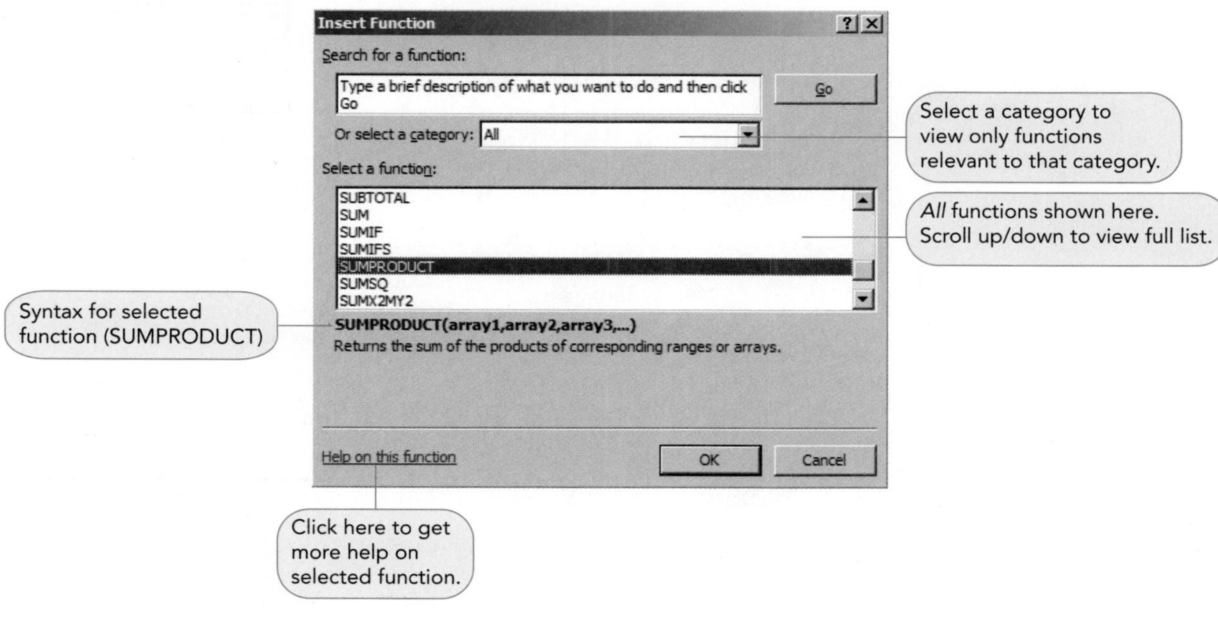

for the selected function is now displayed to guide us through the creation of the cell entry using the function.

Errors in Using Formulas and Functions

Sometimes, when we use a function or formula, the resulting output indicates an error in the entry. The following is a list of common errors when using formulas or functions and their possible causes:

1. #DIV/0! indicates that the formula or function involves division by zero.
2. #Name? indicates that the formula or function is not recognized by Excel. This is usually caused by a typographical error.
3. #VALUE indicates that one or more cell references used in a formula or function are invalid.
4. #### indicates that the cell is not wide enough to display the number. This can be easily remedied by increasing the width of the cell.

B.6 Printing Worksheets

If we wish to print the part or all of a worksheet, we can go directly to the print menu by clicking either File | Print (see Screenshot B-2A on page 563) or the Print icon on the Quick Access Toolbar (see Screenshot B-1 on page 562). The print interface window shown in Screenshot B-4 is displayed. A preview of the printed output is shown in the right side window. Before clicking Print, it is a good idea to verify that the output appears exactly the way we want it to print.

SCREENSHOT B-4
Options Available in the Print Preview Window

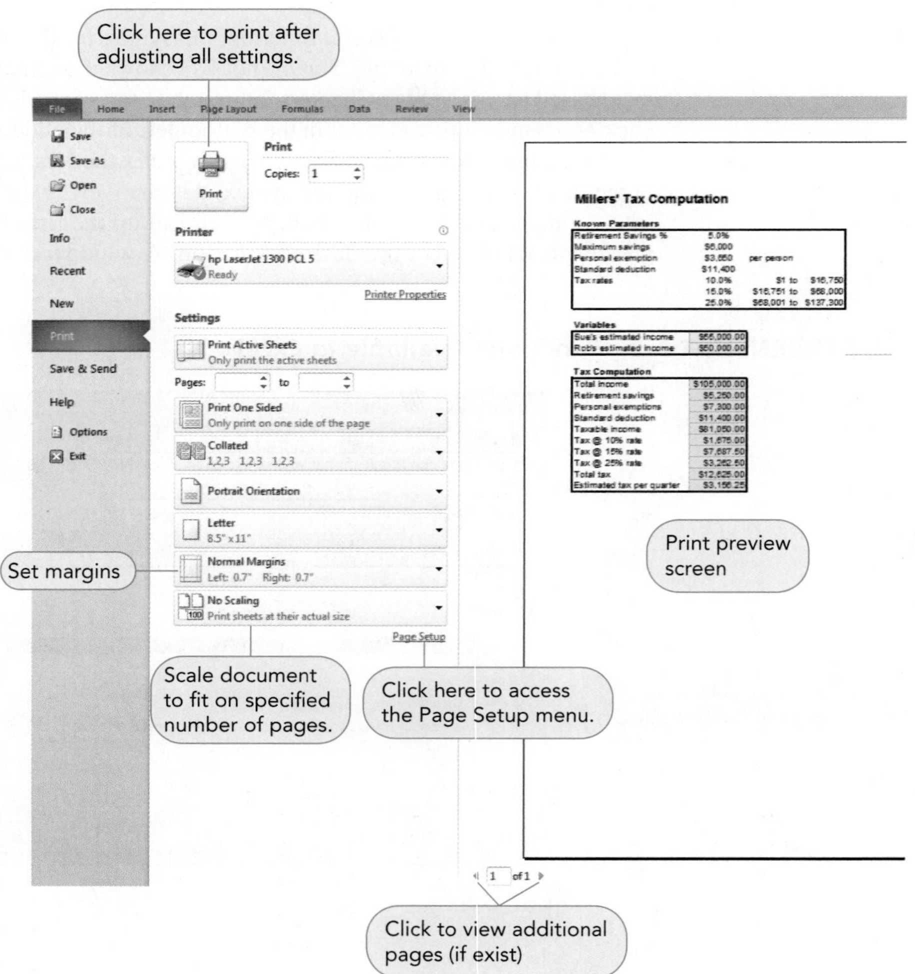

Excel has numerous options available to make modifications to the printed output, as discussed in the following sections.

SETTING THE NUMBER OF COPIES, PAPER SIZE, ORIENTATION, AND SCALING We can change the number of copies, paper size, page orientation, and print mode (one-sided or two-sided) using the options shown in Screenshot B-4. We can also scale the output so that the entire contents can be made to fit within a specified number of printed pages.

SETTING THE PRINT AREA If we wish to print only a portion of the current worksheet, first select the desired region of cells to print. Then click Print Area|Set Print Area, found in the Page Setup group within the Page Layout tab. We can clear a selected print area by clicking Print Area|Clear Print Area.

SETTING PRINT MARGINS To change the print margins, click the arrow next to Normal Margins in Screenshot B-4 (or, alternatively, click Margins, found within the Page Layout tab) and adjust the margins as desired

PAGE BREAKS To insert a page break, first click on the row or column where we want the page break to be. For rows, the break will be above the selected row. For columns, it will be to the left of the selected column. Then click Breaks|Insert Page Break, found within the Page Layout tab. To remove an existing page break, first select the rows (or columns) on either side of the page break. Then click Breaks|Remove Page Break.

CENTERING DATA ON A PAGE To center data on a page, click Page Setup, as shown on Screenshot B-4 (or click Print Titles, found within the Page Layout tab). Select the tab named Margin and then check the boxes corresponding to whether we want the data centered horizontally, vertically, or both.

INSERTING A HEADER OR FOOTER To add a header and/or a footer, click Page Setup, as shown on Screenshot B-4 (or click Print Titles, found within the Page Layout tab). Then select the tab named Header/Footer and enter the text and format the header or footer.

PRINTING THE WORKSHEET After making all adjustments, to print the worksheet click Print from within the Print Preview window in Screenshot B-4.

B.7 Excel Options and Add-Ins

As noted in section B.3, Excel has numerous options available with regards to how worksheets and workbooks are managed. To access these options, click Options, found within the File tab. The window shown in Screenshot B-5A is displayed.

As shown on the left pane of this screenshot, there are several categories of options available. Most are self-explanatory, and almost all can be left at their default values for most users. Note that two of the choices available here deal with customizing the Ribbon and Quick Access Toolbar, which we have already addressed. In the remainder of this section, we discuss in a bit more detail the last two option categories—Add-Ins and Trust Center—since they are of particular relevance in this textbook. Screenshot B-5A shows the contents of the right window pane when we select Add-Ins from the option categories.

ADD-INS Add-ins are special programs that are designed to perform specific tasks in Excel. Typically, an add-in has the file extension *.xla*. Although Excel includes several add-ins, we focus here on only two, Solver and Data Analysis, that are useful in decision modeling.

Both Solver and Data Analysis are included with all recent versions of Excel. However, if we choose to install Excel using the default options, only Data Analysis may be installed during the installation process. To ensure that Solver is also installed, we need to change the installation defaults for Excel by clicking on the Excel options during the installation process and then choosing Add-Ins. Make sure the box next to the Solver option is checked.

Even after these add-ins have been installed, they need to be enabled (or switched on) in order for them to be available in Excel. To check if these add-ins have been enabled, start Excel and select the Data tab. If Data Analysis and/or Solver are seen as menu options in the Analysis

SCREENSHOT B-5A Excel Options and Managing Add-ins

Excel Options

General
Formulas
Proofing
Save
Language
Advanced
Customize Ribbon
Quick Access Toolbar
Add-Ins
Trust Center

View and manage Microsoft Office Add-ins.

Add-ins

Name	Location	Type
Active Application Add-ins		
Acrobat PDFMaker Office COM Addin	C:\....0\PDFMaker\Office\PDFMOfficeAddin.dll	COM Add-in
Analysis ToolPak	C:\...ce\Office14\Library\Analysis\ANALYS32.XLL	Excel Add-in
Analysis ToolPak - VBA	C:\...Office14\Library\Analysis\ATPVBAEN.XLAM	Excel Add-in
Euro Currency Tools	C:\... Office\Office14\Library\EUROTOOL.XLAM	Excel Add-in
Solver Add-in	C:\...ce\Office14\Library\SOLVER\SOLVER.XLAM	Excel Add-in
Inactive Application Add-ins		
Crystal Ball	C:\...Oracle\Crystal Ball\Bin\SecureCBAddin.dll	COM Add-in
Custom XML Data	C:\...es\Microsoft Office\Office14\OFFRHD.DLL	Document Inspector
Date (XML)	C:\...iles\microsoft shared\Smart Tag\MOFL.DLL	Action
Financial Symbol (XML)	C:\...iles\microsoft shared\Smart Tag\MOFL.DLL	Action
Headers and Footers	C:\...es\Microsoft Office\Office14\OFFRHD.DLL	Document Inspector
Hidden Rows and Columns	C:\...es\Microsoft Office\Office14\OFFRHD.DLL	Document Inspector
Hidden Worksheets	C:\...es\Microsoft Office\Office14\OFFRHD.DLL	Document Inspector
Invisible Content	C:\...es\Microsoft Office\Office14\OFFRHD.DLL	Document Inspector
Microsoft Actions Pane 3		XML Expansion Pack
Treeplan-Addin-Classic-177	D:\...ents\Book\TreePlan-Addin-Classic-177.xla	Excel Add-in
Document Related Add-ins		
No Document Related Add-ins		
Disabled Application Add-ins		

Add-in: Acrobat PDFMaker Office COM Addin
Publisher: Adobe Systems, Incorporated
Compatibility: No compatibility information available
Location: C:\Program Files\Adobe\Acrobat 9.0\PDFMaker\Office\PDFMOfficeAddin.dll

Description: Acrobat PDFMaker Office COM Addin

Manage: Excel Add-ins Go...

OK Cancel

Click here to customize the Ribbon and/or Quick Access Toolbar.

Click here to set security settings for macros.

Select this to manage Excel's built-in Add-Ins.

This list will vary depending on specific Add-Ins installed in the computer.

group, the add-in has been enabled on that personal computer. However, if we do not see either (or both) add-ins, click File | Add-Ins to get the window shown in Screenshot B-5A. Select Excel Add-Ins in the box labeled Manage and click Go.

The list of available Excel add-ins is now displayed, as shown in Screenshot B-5B. To enable Data Analysis, make sure the boxes next to Analysis ToolPak and Analysis ToolPak – VBA are both checked. Likewise, to enable Solver, make sure the box next to Solver Add-In is checked. Screenshot B-5B also shows the TreePlan add-in that is used in Chapter 8. If we want TreePlan to start automatically each time we start Excel, make sure its box is also checked.

SCREENSHOT B-5B List of Available Excel Add-ins

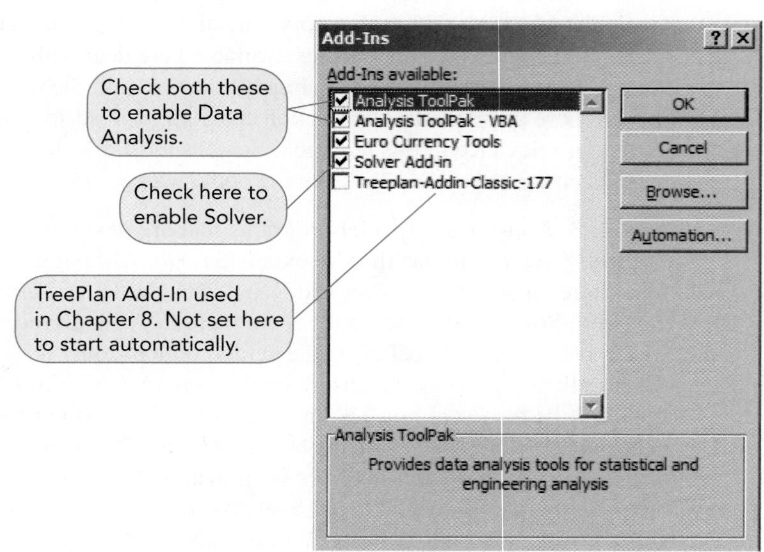

Depending on the boxes checked, the corresponding add-in should now be shown as an option under the Analysis group within the Data tab. For example, Screenshot B-2F on page 565 shows that both Data Analysis and Solver add-ins have been enabled. From here onward, these add-ins will be available each time we start Excel on that computer. To access either add-in, simply click the Data tab and select the appropriate choice in the menu.

TRUST CENTER Some add-ins (such as ExcelModules that we use in Chapters 9, 11, and 12) involve macros. By default, macros are disabled in Excel to prevent unauthorized programs for corrupting documents. To ensure that these add-ins function properly, we need to ensure that the macros embedded in them are enabled. To do so, click Trust Center in Excel's options window (see Screenshot B-5A). Then click Trust Center Settings and select Macro Settings from the choices in the left side window. If we select Disable All Macros with Notification, Excel will ask for permission to run the macros each time the add-in is started. However, if we select Disable All Macros Without Notification, the add-in may not function properly since the macros are automatically disabled. As noted in Excel itself, selecting Enable All Macros is not recommended (unless we are sure of all the programs with macros that are being run).

B.7 ExcelModules

This Companion Website for this textbook contains a customized Excel add-in called ExcelModules. This program has been designed to help us better learn and understand decision models in queuing (Chapter 9), forecasting (Chapter 11), and inventory control (Chapter 12).

Installing ExcelModules

To install the current version (i.e., version 3) of ExcelModules on a computer, locate and click the file named *ExcelModules3.exe* on the Companion Website. Then follow the setup instructions on the screen. Alternatively, download this executable file to the computer and install the program from there.

Default values have been assigned for most installation parameters in the setup program, but these can be changed as needed. For example, the program will be installed by default to a directory on the C: drive named *C:\Program Files\ExcelModules3*. Generally speaking, it is only necessary to simply click Next each time that the installation program asks a question. The program automatically creates a shortcut called *ExcelModules v3* on the desktop.

Running ExcelModules

Once the program has been installed, we can start it by clicking the *ExcelModules v3* shortcut on the desktop. When ExcelModules is started, it automatically also starts Excel. Alternatively, if Excel is already open, we can add ExcelModules to it by clicking the *ExcelModules v3* icon on the desktop or by clicking the file named *ExcelModules3.xla*, which is located in the directory where the software was installed. (The default is *C:\Program Files\ExcelModules3* if this was not changed at the time of installation.)

It is also possible to set ExcelModules to load automatically each time we start Excel. To do this, we follow the process described for add-ins in section B.6 and select the file named *ExcelModules3.xla*.

As noted previously, ExcelModules requires the use of macros in Excel. Depending on how the computer has been set to handle macros, Excel will generate a security notice, shown in Screenshot B-6A, asking for permission to enable macros each time we start ExcelModules. We must allow macros to be enabled in order for the program to function properly.

When the program starts, a new tab named ExcelModules appears on Excel's Ribbon. When we click this tab, we see a group named Menus and tools containing a single icon named Modules. When we click this icon, we see the various decision models that are included in ExcelModules, as shown in Screenshot B-6B. The screenshot also lists the specific forecasting models that are included in the program. Instructions for using each decision model in ExcelModules are provided at appropriate places in Chapters 9, 11, and 12 of this textbook.

SCREENSHOT B-6A Security Notice Regarding Macros in Excel

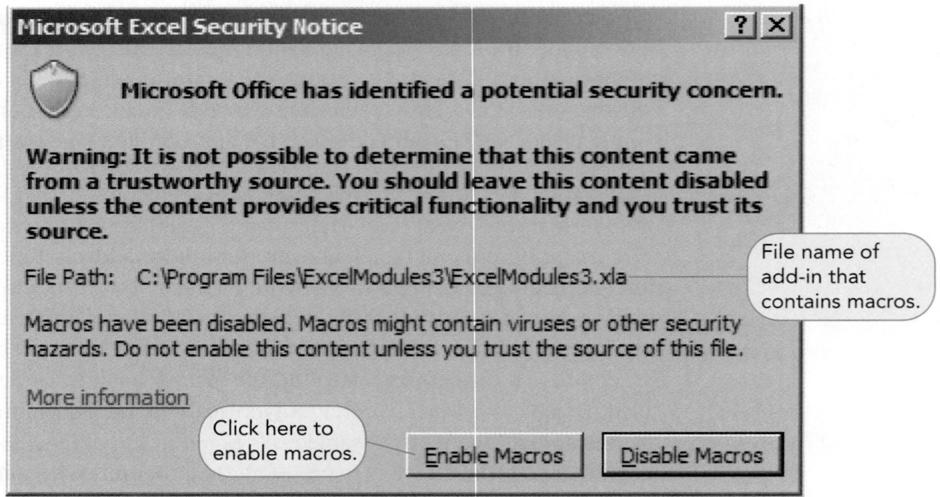

ExcelModules Options and Help

As shown in Screenshot B-6B, ExcelModules also includes a menu item named Tools. If we select this item, we are presented with the choices shown in Screenshot B-6C. The specific action associated with each of these choices is as follows:

1. *Print on 1 page.* Formats the model's output to print on one page.
2. *Display Type.* Change the appearance of the spreadsheet by toggling headers and grid lines on/off.
3. *Instruction.* Remove the instruction textbox that is at generated at the top of each worksheet.
4. *Clear Sheet.* Erase the current worksheet (use with caution).
5. *eMail Pearson.* Contact the software developer for technical user support if needed.
6. *Pearson Web Site.* Open the web page for this textbook.
7. *Unload.* Unload the ExcelModules add-in (but not Excel).
8. *About.* An about screen for this software.
9. *Help.* Detailed help file for ExcelModules.

If there are technical problems with ExcelModules that the instructor cannot resolve, please send an e-mail message to the program's developer, Professor Howard Weiss, at hweiss@sbm.temple.edu or click ExcelModules | Modules | Tools | eMail Pearson. Be sure to include the name

SCREENSHOT B-6B Menu Commands Available in ExcelModules

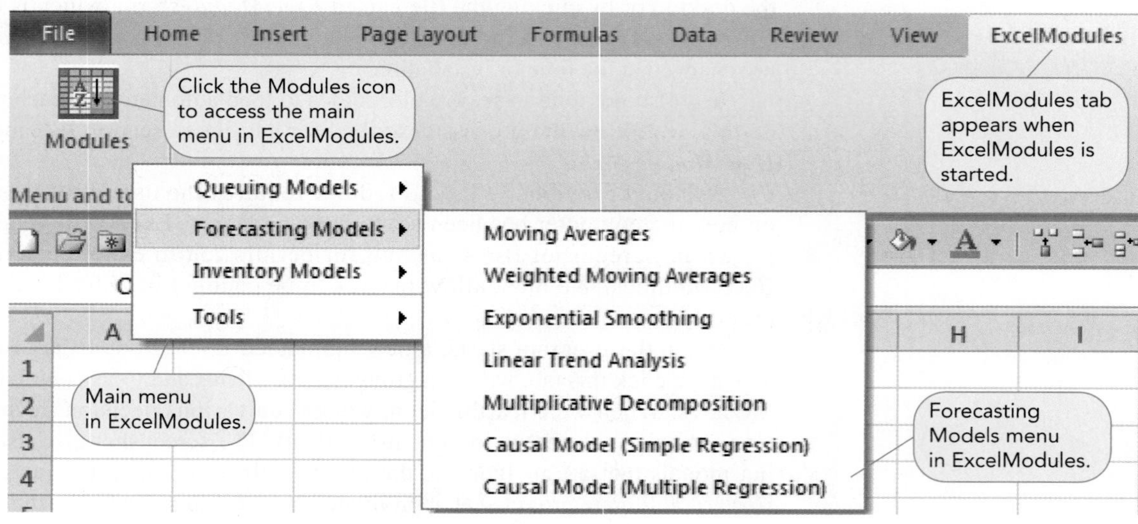

SCREENSHOT B-6C Tools Menu in ExcelModules

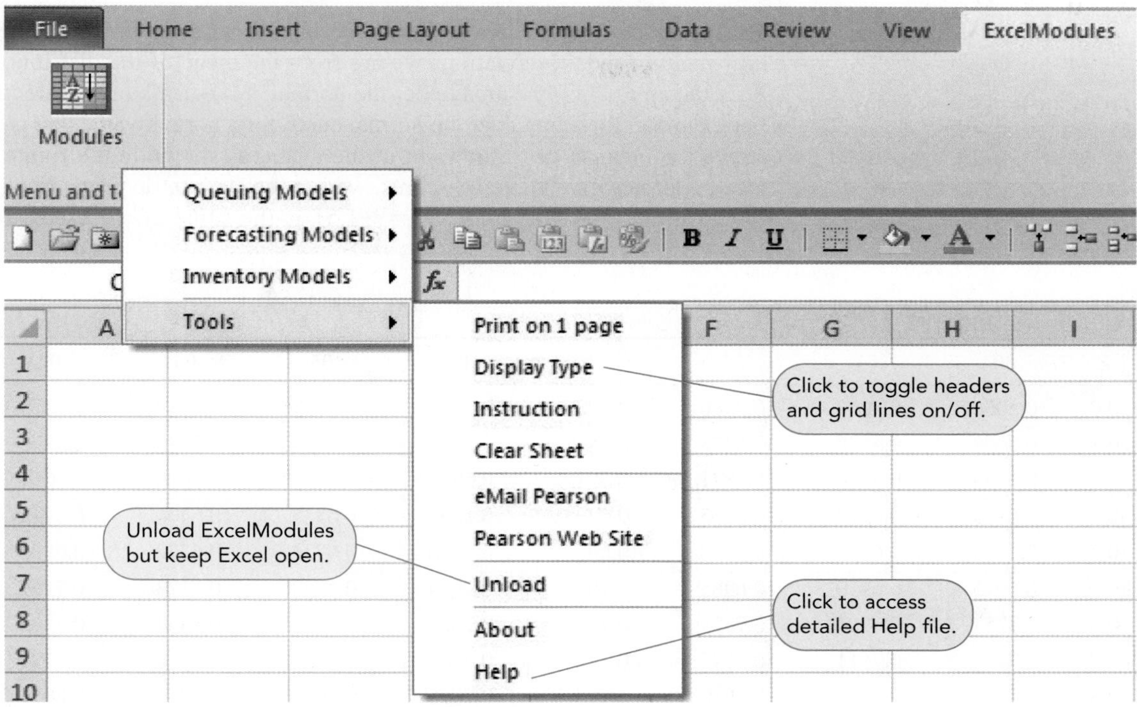

and version number of the program (i.e., *ExcelModules v3*), the specific model in which the problem is occurring, and a detailed explanation of the problem. Attach the data file for which the problem occurs (if appropriate).

ExcelModules serves two purposes in the learning process. First, it can help us solve homework problems. We enter the appropriate data, and the program provides numerical solutions. In addition, ExcelModules allows us to note the Excel formulas used to develop solutions and modify them to deal with a wider variety of problems. This "open" approach allows us to observe, understand, and even change the formulas underlying the Excel calculations, conveying Excel's power as a decision modeling tool.

APPENDIX C: AREAS UNDER THE STANDARD NORMAL CURVE

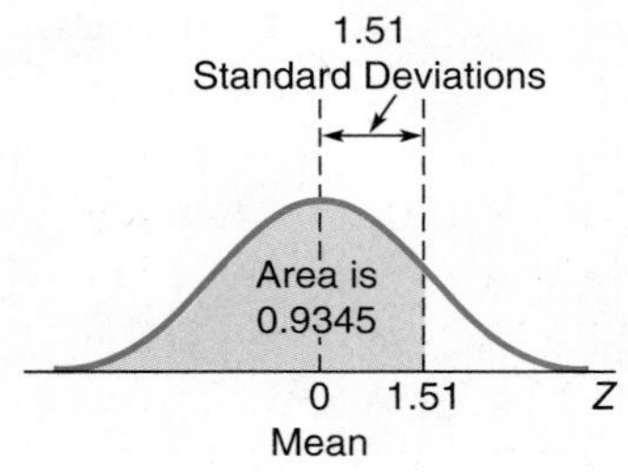

Example: To find the area under the normal curve, we must know the Z score, which defines how many standard deviations we are from the mean of the distribution. For positive valued Z scores up to 3.59, the area under the normal curve can be read directly from the table below. For example, the area under the normal curve for a normal value that is 1.51 standard deviations above the mean (i.e., to the right of the mean, as shown in the figure) is 0.9345. To find the area under negative valued Z scores, we use the symmetric property of the normal distribution. For example, the area under $Z = -1.51$ is the same as the area *above* $Z = 1.51$, equal to $1 - 0.9345 = 0.0655$.

Z	00	.01	.02	.03	.04	.05	.06	.07	.08	.09
0.0	0.5000	0.5040	0.5080	0.5120	0.5160	0.5199	0.5239	0.5279	0.5319	0.5359
0.1	0.5398	0.5438	0.5478	0.5517	0.5557	0.5596	0.5636	0.5675	0.5714	0.5753
0.2	0.5793	0.5832	0.5871	0.5910	0.5948	0.5987	0.6026	0.6064	0.6103	0.6141
0.3	0.6179	0.6217	0.6255	0.6293	0.6331	0.6368	0.6406	0.6443	0.6480	0.6517
0.4	0.6554	0.6591	0.6628	0.6664	0.6700	0.6736	0.6772	0.6808	0.6844	0.6879
0.5	0.6915	0.6950	0.6985	0.7019	0.7054	0.7088	0.7123	0.7157	0.7190	0.7224
0.6	0.7257	0.7291	0.7324	0.7357	0.7389	0.7422	0.7454	0.7486	0.7517	0.7549
0.7	0.7580	0.7611	0.7642	0.7673	0.7704	0.7734	0.7764	0.7794	0.7823	0.7852
0.8	0.7881	0.7910	0.7939	0.7967	0.7995	0.8023	0.8051	0.8078	0.8106	0.8133
0.9	0.8159	0.8186	0.8212	0.8238	0.8264	0.8289	0.8315	0.8340	0.8365	0.8389
1.0	0.8413	0.8438	0.8461	0.8485	0.8508	0.8531	0.8554	0.8577	0.8599	0.8621
1.1	0.8643	0.8665	0.8686	0.8708	0.8729	0.8749	0.8770	0.8790	0.8810	0.8830
1.2	0.8849	0.8869	0.8888	0.8907	0.8925	0.8944	0.8962	0.8980	0.8997	0.9015
1.3	0.9032	0.9049	0.9066	0.9082	0.9099	0.9115	0.9131	0.9147	0.9162	0.9177
1.4	0.9192	0.9207	0.9222	0.9236	0.9251	0.9265	0.9279	0.9292	0.9306	0.9319
1.5	0.9332	0.9345	0.9357	0.9370	0.9382	0.9394	0.9406	0.9418	0.9429	0.9441
1.6	0.9452	0.9463	0.9474	0.9484	0.9495	0.9505	0.9515	0.9525	0.9535	0.9545
1.7	0.9554	0.9564	0.9573	0.9582	0.9591	0.9599	0.9608	0.9616	0.9625	0.9633
1.8	0.9641	0.9649	0.9656	0.9664	0.9671	0.9678	0.9686	0.9693	0.9699	0.9706
1.9	0.9713	0.9719	0.9726	0.9732	0.9738	0.9744	0.9750	0.9756	0.9761	0.9767
2.0	0.9772	0.9778	0.9783	0.9788	0.9793	0.9798	0.9803	0.9808	0.9812	0.9817
2.1	0.9821	0.9826	0.9830	0.9834	0.9838	0.9842	0.9846	0.9850	0.9854	0.9857
2.2	0.9861	0.9864	0.9868	0.9871	0.9875	0.9878	0.9881	0.9884	0.9887	0.9890
2.3	0.9893	0.9896	0.9898	0.9901	0.9904	0.9906	0.9909	0.9911	0.9913	0.9916
2.4	0.9918	0.9920	0.9922	0.9925	0.9927	0.9929	0.9931	0.9932	0.9934	0.9936
2.5	0.9938	0.9940	0.9941	0.9943	0.9945	0.9946	0.9948	0.9949	0.9951	0.9952
2.6	0.9953	0.9955	0.9956	0.9957	0.9959	0.9960	0.9961	0.9962	0.9963	0.9964
2.7	0.9965	0.9966	0.9967	0.9968	0.9969	0.9970	0.9971	0.9972	0.9973	0.9974
2.8	0.9974	0.9975	0.9976	0.9977	0.9977	0.9978	0.9979	0.9979	0.9980	0.9981
2.9	0.9981	0.9982	0.9982	0.9983	0.9984	0.9984	0.9985	0.9985	0.9986	0.9986
3.0	0.9987	0.9987	0.9987	0.9988	0.9988	0.9989	0.9989	0.9989	0.9990	0.9990
3.1	0.9990	0.9991	0.9991	0.9991	0.9992	0.9992	0.9992	0.9992	0.9993	0.9993
3.2	0.9993	0.9993	0.9994	0.9994	0.9994	0.9994	0.9994	0.9995	0.9995	0.9995
3.3	0.9995	0.9995	0.9995	0.9996	0.9996	0.9996	0.9996	0.9996	0.9996	0.9997
3.4	0.9997	0.9997	0.9997	0.9997	0.9997	0.9997	0.9997	0.9997	0.9997	0.9998
3.5	0.9998	0.9998	0.9998	0.9998	0.9998	0.9998	0.9998	0.9998	0.9998	0.9998

APPENDIX D: BRIEF SOLUTIONS TO ALL ODD-NUMBERED END-OF-CHAPTER PROBLEMS

Chapter 1

1-19 (a) 375,000. (b) $22,500.

1-21 (a) Make major modifications. (b) $45,500.

1-23 $10,500.

1-25 10,550 units.

1-27 Yes. The profit will increase by $1,000.

1-29 (a) $BEP_A = 6{,}250$. $BEP_B = 7{,}750$. (b) Choose A. (c) 3,250 widgets, but both machines lose money at this production level.

Chapter 2

2-13 X = 2.3, Y = 3.9, Objective = 8.50.

2-15 X = 22.50. Y = 6.75, Objective = 110.25.

2-17 X = 3, Y = 5.6, Objective = 48.20.

2-19 A = 3.33, B = 1.67, C = 1.67, Objective = 158.33.

2-21 Painting = 624, Glazing = 300, Revenue = $3,858.

2-23 Internet = 10, Print = 50, Exposure = 6 million people.

2-25 Make 24 A motors and 84 B motors. Profit = $1,572.

2-27 Invest $401.72 in Carolina Solar and $2,750.79 in South West. Total investment = $3,152.52.

2-29 Regular = 52, Low Fat = 48, Profit = $161.36.

2-31 Build 344 small boxes and 80 large boxes. Profit = $13,520.

2-33 Make 175 benches and 50 tables. Profit = $2,575.

2-35 Schedule 35 core courses and 25 electives. Faculty salaries = $166,000.

2-37 16 pounds of Feed Mix X and 16 pounds of Feed Mix Y. Total cost = $112 per day.

2-39 Build 284 small boxes, 80 large boxes, and 100 mini boxes. Profit = $13,420.

2-41 EC221 = 20,650, EC496 = 100, NC455 = 2,750 and NC791 = 400. Profit = $232,700.

2-43 Invest $2,555.25 in BBC and $1,139.50 in CBC Total investment = $3,694.75

Chapter 3

3-1 Make 20 canvas, 40 plastic, 25 nylon, and 40 leather backpacks. Profit = $2,483.58.

3-3 Make 1,200 Junior, 750 Travel, and 300 Deluxe pillows. Profit = $3,340.50.

3-5 Make 116.67 Italian, 60 French, and 350 Caribbean. Profit = $39,600.

3-7 In-house: W111 = 1,864, W222 = 2,250, W333 = 1,020. Out-source: W111 = 136, W222 = 1,500, W333 = 680. Total cost = $150,964.20.

3-9 Interview 1,175 male Democrats and 525 female Democrats; 1,125 male Republicans and 675 female Republicans; and 450 male independents and 550 female independents. Total cost to poll = $49,100.

3-11 Issue 4,000 $1 coupons, 6,500 $0.85 coupons, 1,500 $0.70 coupons, 1,500 $0.55 coupons, and 1,500 $0.40 coupons. Total cost = $37,234.50.

3-13 Invest $100,000 in Miami, $191,666.67 in American Smart Car, $75,000 in Green Earth Energy, $50,000 in Rosslyn Drugs, and $83,333.33 in RealCo. Total Return = $38,708.33.

3-15 Invest $30,000 in T-bills, $60,000 in international mutual funds, $20,000 in school bonds, $20,000 in certificates of deposit, $30,000 in tax-free municipal bonds, and $40,000 in the stock market. Total return = $19,075.

3-17 Have 4 nurses begin work at 1 A.M., 9 at 5 A.M., 8 at 9 A.M., 7 at 1 P.M., 5 at 5 P.M., and none at 9 P.M. Total nurses needed is 33. Alternate solutions may exist.

3-19 Assign 12 nurses each to A and A(alt), 4 nurses each to B and B(alt), 10 nurses each to C and C(alt), and no nurses to either D or D(alt). Cost for each half shift = $21,252. Total cost = $42,504.

3-21 Ship 210 pounds of Cargo A, 150 pounds of B, 125.45 pounds of E, and 250 pounds of G. Freight = $5,921.82

3-23 Ship 10 tons of A, 12 tons of B, and 5.78 tons of C. Revenue = $19,657.78.

3-25 Plant 32.5 acres of corn and 25 acres of okra. Total revenue = $151,775.

3-27 Plant 2,200 acres of wheat, 165.52 acres of alfalfa, and 1,000 acres of barley. Profit = $339,931.03.

3-29 Hire 15 union, 12 non-union, and 3 temporary workers. Total cost = $4,218.

3-31 Each pound of feed is comprised of 0.167 pounds of beef, 0.459 pounds of lamb, 0.066 pounds of rice, and 0.309 pounds of chicken. Cost = $0.40 per pound.

3-33 The diet should include 1.655 servings of chicken patty, 2.077 cups of milk, 9.348 cups of fruit cocktail, and 7.892 cups of orange juice. Cost = $8. *Note:* Alternate optimal solutions may exist.

3-35 The hotdog is comprised of 0.0313 pounds of beef, 0.0313 pounds of pork, and 0.0625 pounds of turkey. Cost = $0.086.

3-37 *Tuffcoat:* Base A = 320 gallons, Base B = 1,280 gallons, Cost = $6.10 per gallon. *Satinwear:* Base A = 625 gallons, Base B = 625 gallons, Cost = $5.50 per gallon. Total Cost = $16,635.

3-39 Feed A = 8 lb., Feed B = 2 lb., Feed C = 2 lb., Feed D = 12 lb., Feed E = 16 lb. Cost = $22.33 per bag.

3-41 *Unrounded solution: IC341:* September = 1,525, October = 0, November = 1,690, December = 1,000. IC256: September = 900, October = 1,989.42, November = 460.58, December = 1,250. Total cost: $12,429. Alternate solutions may exist.

3-43 *Unrounded solution:* January: 175 agents and 9.39 trainees; February: 175.64 agents and 21.28 trainees; March: 189.90 agents and 16.79 trainees; April: 200.99 agents and 2.68 trainees; May: 199.65 agents, 0 trainees. Salary = $3,236,250.53.

3-45 Total cost = $16,420.

3-47 Each school will have 1,120 students. Total mileage = 20,114.

Chapter 4

4-11 Solution to original problem: (24,4) $124: (a) No change in corner point; objective = $132. (b) New corner point: (24,14); objective increases to $194. (c) New corner point (15,10); objective = $130.

4-13 (a) Total audience would increase by 406. (b) No. They are already over this contract level. (c) No. Need to increase exposure to at least 3,144.83 for optimal solution to change. (d) 0 to 6,620.69.

4-15 (a) Total cost decreases by $0.0038. (b) 100% rule satisfied, same mix, total cost is $0.0529. (c) 100% rule satisfied, total cost decreases by $0.0038.

4-17 (a) Alternate optimal solutions exist. (b) Profit increases by $3,758.60, to $341,620.67. (c) Profit increases by $20.69 for each additional acre-foot of water.

4-19 (a) Cost decreases by $0.007 for each additional gram of carbohydrates allowed in the meal. Cost increases by $0.074 for each additional mg of iron required in the diet. (b) Cost increases by $0.148 for each pound of milk. (c) $0.319. (d) Unique optimal solution.

4-21 (a) Optimal solution = (15,10), profit = $125. (b) $\{3.33 \leq C_X \leq 10\}$, $\{2.5 \leq C_Y \leq 7.5\}$. (c) Profit would increase by $1.25; between 48 and 120. (d) Profit would decrease by $0.63; between 40 and 88. (e) Same corner point, new profit = $185. (f) Same corner point, new profit = $105. (g) No change. (h) No. The shadow price is zero. (i) Same corner point, new profit = $145. (j) Yes. Profit increases by $12.50.

4-23 Compact model is not attractive. Kiddo model is attractive.

4-25 (a) $0 to $7.33. (b) No.

4-27 No. Profit would decrease by $3.225 for each TwinTote made if TwinTotes are not included in the 40% limit for ToddleTotes. If it is included in the 40% limit, profit would decrease by $1.685.

4-29 (a) New production plan and increased profit unknown from current report. New plan would include more oak tables. (b) Production plan would not change. Profit decreases by $231.56. (c) Production plan would not change. Profit increases by $845.20. (d) Same production plan, profit decreases by $15. (e) No impact. Already making 33.08. (f) Currently making 85.56. Profit would decrease.

4-31 (a) Production plan will not change. Profit decreases by $90. (b) Production plan will not change. Profit increases by $1,946.80. (c) 100% rule not satisfied. New production plan and profit unknown from current report. (d) Production plan will not change. Profit increases by $514.40. (e) 100% rule not satisfie(d) New production plan and profit unknown from current report.

4-33 (a) Cost = $176.42, tuna = 10, tuna/cheese = 30, ham = 10, ham/cheese = 12, cheese = 8. (b) *Binding:* bread, tuna, minimum total, minimum tuna, minimum ham, and minimum ham/cheese. (c) Between $2.12 and $3.02. (d) Between 124 and 154 ounces. (e) No. (f) 2.4 hours.

4-35 (a) New production plan with higher cost. (b) No change. Current plan uses only 76 ounces. (c) New production plan with higher cost. (d) New production plan with higher cost. (e) No impact. Currently delivering 30 tuna and cheese. (f) Cost will decrease; currently delivering 70 sandwiches.

4-37 (a) No. This purchase would increase cost by $0.22. (b) Substitute at most 3.5 ham-type sandwiches. (c) 4 jars.

Chapter 5

Note: Alternate optimal solutions could exist for some of the problems.

5-13 (a) Total cost = $52,200. (b) Total cost with transshipment = $51,450.

5-15 Total interest = $28,300, or an average rate of 9.43%.

5-17 Cost with New Orleans = $20,000, Cost with Houston = $19,500. Houston should be selected.

5-19 Cost with Brevard = $17,400, Cost with Laurens = $17,250. Laurens should be selected. (b) Maximum shipped on any route = 100, Cost = $18,650.

5-21 Total cost = \$11,740.

5-23 Assign Job A to Machine Y, B to Z, C to W, and D to X. Total hours = 50.

5-25 Assign Morris to Cardiology, Richards to Orthopedics, Cook to Urology, and Morgan to Pediatrics. Total index = 86.

5-27 Assign Squad 1 to Case C, 2 to B, 3 to D, 4 to E, and 5 to A. Total days = 28.

5-29 Total length = 4,500 feet (use 1-2, 1-3, 1-4, 3-6, 4-5, 6-7, 7-9, 8-9, 9-10, 9-12, 10-11, 11-13, 12-14); Other solutions are available.

5-31 1–3–5–7–10–13, Distance = 430 miles.

5-33 (a) 167 widgets. (b) 140 widgets.

5-35 3 million gallons per hour.

5-37 Shortest distance = 74. The path is 1-5-9-12-14.

5-39 Distance = 2,100 yards (use 1-2, 1-3, 3-7, 4-5, 5-6, 6-7, 6-8, 8-9); Other solutions are available.

5-41 Load on each machine = 68.22 hours.

Chapter 6

6-13 Clean 8 houses and 10 lawyer offices. Profit = \$2,050.

6-15 (a) Total workers = 27. (b) Total pay = \$12,345.

6-17 Need 10 coins.

6-19 Include all but investment A. Total return will be \$3,580.

6-21 Sign pitchers B, C, D, F, and H. Total value = 25.

6-23 Select Atlanta and Los Angeles. Alternate solutions are possible.

6-25 Choose Philadelphia and Denver. Total cost = \$4,390.

6-27 (a) Locations 1 and 3; 130 miles total. (b) Open trauma centers at locations 2 and 4.

6-29 Publish 8,000 copies of Book 2, 5,000 copies of Book 3, and 7,000 copies of Book 5. Profit = \$487,000.

6-31 TV = 10, Newspaper = 35. Goals R1 and R2 fully satisfied. Goal R3 underachieved by 750,000 people.

6-33 *Unrounded Solution:* Make 1,938.67 coils, 350.94 shafts, and 3,267.46 housings. Buy 61.33 coils, 1,649.06 shafts, and no housings. Goals R1 and R2 are fully satisfied. Goal R3 is underachieved by 138.67 coils.

6-35 Invest \$1,650 in investment B, \$600 in investment C, \$4,500 in investment E and \$2,250 in investment F. Return is \$583.50. Goals 1, 3, 5 and 7 are fully met. Goal 2 is underachieved by \$416.50. Goal 4 is overachieved by \$1,350. Goal 6 is overachieved by \$2,250.

6-37 $X_1 = 2.80, X_2 = 4.92, X_3 = 3.37$. Objective = 186.07 Solution appears to be global optimal.

6-39 Produce 38.46 six-cylinder engines. Profit = \$89,615.38. Solution appears to be global optimal.

6-41 Invest 21% of funds in A, 33% of funds in B, and 46% of funds in G. Solution appears to be global optimal.

6-43 Load on each machine = 68.56 hours.

Chapter 7

7-13 Critical path = A–C–E–G, Project length = 17 weeks.

7-15 Critical path B–E–G, Project length = 18 days.

7-17 (c) Critical path = C–D–E–F–H–K, Project length = 36.5 days. (d) 0.7352.

7-19 (c) Critical path = A–D–F–H–J–K, Project length = 69 days. (d) 0.6097. (e) 0.0473.

7-21 (c) Critical path = B–C–D–H–I–J, Project length = 48 days. (d) 0.6279. (e) 0.0251.

7-23 (a) 0.8944. (b) 0.2266. (c) 34.31 weeks. (d) 29.15 weeks.

7-25 (a) *EST totals for months* 1–36: \$1,667, \$8,667, \$8,667, \$2,381, \$4,381, \$4,381, \$4,114, \$2,114, \$2,114, \$2,114, \$1,400, \$1,400, \$3,400, \$3,400, \$3,127, \$3,127, \$1,727, \$1,727, \$10,727, \$10,727, \$10,727, \$10,727, \$10,442, \$10,442, \$4,442, \$2,714, \$2,714, \$2,714, \$2,714, \$2,714, \$714, \$714, \$714, \$714, \$714, and \$714. (b) *LST totals for months* 1–36: \$1,667, \$1,667, \$1,667, \$2,381, \$9,381, \$9,381, \$2,114, \$2,114, \$2,114, \$4,114, \$3,400, \$3,400, \$1,400, \$1,400, \$1,945, \$3,127, \$1,727, \$1,727, \$3,727, \$6,727, \$4,727, \$7,727, \$8,442, \$7,442, \$10,442, \$9,896, \$8,714, \$5,714, \$5,714, \$5,714, \$2,714, \$714, \$714, \$714, \$714, and \$714.

7-27 (a) *EST totals for weeks* 1–12: \$1,100, \$1,100, \$3,200, \$3,200, \$3,200, \$1,500, \$2,700, \$2,700, \$900, \$600, \$600, and \$600. (b) *LST totals for weeks* 1–12: \$1,100, \$1,100, \$1,500, \$1,500, \$3,200, \$3,200, \$2,600, \$2,700, \$2,700, \$600, \$600, and \$600.

7-29 Total crash cost = \$7,250. New durations for A = 1, C = 1, D = 3, and G = 2.

7-31 (a) Crash A by 2, D by 1, E by 1, F by 2, and H by 1. Total crash cost = \$3,600. (b) Possible to crash project to 21 days. Total cost = \$4,400.

7-33 Critical path = 1–3–9–11–12–13–14–17–18. Completion time = 47.5 weeks.

7-35 Answer will vary based on student. First list all courses including electives to get a degree. Then list all prerequisites for every course. Develop network diagram. Potential difficulties include incorporating min/max number of courses to take during a given semester, and scheduling electives.

7-37 (a) Critical path = D–I–N–S–W. Project length = 38.5 weeks. (b) Probability = 0.8642.

(c) Critical path = B–F–L–R–V. Project length = 27 weeks.

Chapter 8

8-13 (a) Maximax; Acme; \$400,000. (b) Maximin; High Pro; −\$15,000. (c) Acme, EMV = \$262,000.

8-15 (a) Move shop, EMV = \$32,550. (b) Move shop, EOL = \$7,200. (c) EVPI = \$7,200.

8-17 (a) Bonds, EMV = 3.25%. (b) Bonds, EOL = 2.15%. (c) EVPI = 2.15%.

8-19 (a) 500. (b) 100. (c) 300. (d) 100. (e) 300.

8-21 7 cases.

8-23 (a) 100. (b) 100. (c) EVwPI = \$1,225. EVPI = \$485.

8-25 (a) Drexel. (b) 0.60 minutes.

8-27 (a) Risk avoiders. (b) Expected utility = 0.90.

8-29 (a) Supplier A, Expected cost = \$126. (b) \$54.

8-31 (a) Expected profit = \$50.36. Hire Elmo. (b) \$10.36.

8-33 Expected payoff = \$31.63. Accept wager.

8-35 Expected profit = \$246,000. Build pilot.

8-37 Expected payoff = \$565,000. Test land.

8-39 (a) Expected utility = 0.246. Test land. (b) Risk seeker.

8-41 (a) Expected utility = 0.823. Conduct questionnaire. (b) Risk avoider.

8-43 (a) Risk seeker. (b) No. Expected utility = 0.261.

8-45 (a) Expected utility = 0.62. Get information. (b) Risk seeker.

8-47 (a) 0.682. (b) 0.278.

8-49 Given growth prediction: 0.696, 0.250, 0.054. Given steady prediction: 0.058, 0.870, 0.072. Given decline prediction: 0.054, 0.195, 0.751.

Chapter 9

9-11 (a) 4.1667. (b) 25 minutes. (c) 30 minutes. (d) 0.8333. (e) 0.1667.

9-13 (a) 3.2 patrons. (b) 0.8. (c) 0.0114 hours. (d) 0.0091 hours. (e) 0.5120, 0.4096,

9-15 (a) 0.2963, 0.1975, 0.1317. (b) 0.3333. (c) 0.6667 minutes. (d) 1.333 travelers. (e) 2 travelers. (f) P_0 = 0.5, W_q = 0.0417 minutes, L_q = 0.08333 travelers, L = 0.75 travelers.

9-17 (a) 0.15 hours (9 minutes). (b) 2.25. (c) Do not add second server. Costs increase by \$6.49 per hour.

9-19 (a) 12 total (3 per queue). (b) 1 hour. (c) 0.75 hours. (d) 9 total (2.25 per queue). (e) Single M/M/4 system is more efficient than 4 parallel independent M/M/1 systems.

9-21 8 A.M.–10 A.M.: 5 clerks, 10 A.M.–2 P.M.: 8 clerks, 2 P.M.–5 P.M.: 6 clerks.

9-23 Cost is \$8.82 higher than the single-server system with two servers.

9-25 (a) 0.1667. (b) 0.2271 hours. (c) About 2 boats.

9-27 7 gates.

9-29 About 23 minutes per customer.

9-31 L_q = 0.5417 cars, L = 1.1667 cars, W_q = 4.33 minutes, W = 9.33 minutes. Consider adding a second pump.

9-33 (a) 0.3297. (b) 0.8431. (c) 5.1569. (d) 0.6395 days. (e) 1.6355 days.

9-35 (a) 5.53 hours. (b) 2.236 hours. (c) 0.22.

9-37 4 entry, 2 exit.

9-39 (a) 71.90%. (b) 0.1249 hours. (c) 0.5673 patients. (d) 57.79%.

Chapter 10

Note: **All answers given here are based on only 200 replications of the simulation model and are, hence, rather approximate. Your answers may therefore vary.**

10-15 Expected failures = 2.48 per month. Simulation average is around the same value. Difference is due to small number of replications in simulation.

10-17 (a) \$359. (b) 0.0204.

10-19 (a) \$30,649. (b) Order 35.

10-21 (a) 1 pen = \$14 per hour; 4 pens = \$11.25 per hour. (b) 1 pen = \$13.81 per hour; 4 pens = \$11.23 per hour. Compares very favorably.

10-23 Average time needed = 175 minutes, Probability finish in ≤ 165 minutes = 0.135.

10-25 \$49,229; 5.51%.

10-27 \$15,271; 10.67%.

10-29 (a) \$6,899; 7.15%. (b) 200. (c) 70.

10-31 0.056.

10-33 \$28,664 per month; 3.67 cars. (b) 20 cars.

10-35 \$7,368.

10-37 0.14.

10-39 Order 190 pretzels. Profit = \$145. Unsold = 16%.

10-41 \$23,960.

10-43 \$1,054.

10-45 0.94.

10-47 0.035.

10-49 0.45.

10-51 (a) 0.62. (b) 0.88.

Chapter 11

11-13 (a) $\text{MAPE}_{2-\text{MA}}$ = 18.87%, $\text{MAPE}_{3-\text{MA}}$ = 19.18%, $\text{MAPE}_{4-\text{MA}}$ = 23.75%. (b) $\text{MAPE}_{3-\text{WMA}}$ = 17.76%. (c) MAPE_{EXP} = 20.57%. (d) Three-period WMA seems to be best.

11-15 $\text{MAPE}_{2-\text{MA}}$ = 10.29%, 715.5, $\text{MAPE}_{3-\text{MA}}$ = 6.6%, 702, $\text{MAPE}_{4-\text{MA}}$ = 5.27%, 698.75.

11-17 $\text{MAPE}_{2-\text{MA}}$ = 18.41%, 37.5, $\text{MAPE}_{3-\text{MA}}$ = 18.11%, 35, $MAPE_{4-MA}$ = 18.27%, 31.75.

11-19 (a) $MAPE_{0.35} = 13.56\%$, $MAPE_{0.65} = 9.06\%$, $MAPE_{0.95} = 6.29\%$. (b) $MAPE_{3-MA} = 11.13\%$. (c) $Y = 451.2 + 33.60X$ if years are coded 1 to 5. MAPE = 1.02%. (d) Linear trend analysis.

11-21 (a) Graph indicates an approximate linear relationship. (b) $Y = 0.352 + 0.971X$. (c) 4.

11-23 $Forecast_{0.15} = 49$, $Forecast_{0.65} = 58$, $Forecast_{0.95} = 64$. (b) 0.95.

11-25 (a) $MAPE_{0.2} = 4.42\%$, $MAPE_{0.4} = 3.70\%$. (b) 0.4 (c) 0.7, MAPE = 3.08%.

11-27 Average patients = 23.733 + 3.285 × Year. 60 in year 11, 63 in year 12, and 66 in year 13. Fits very well.

11-29 193, 321, 106, and 280.

11-31 (a) Average dividend = −0.464 + 0.351 × EPS. (b) $R^2 = 0.69$. (c) Average dividend = $0.003.

11-33 (a) Average value = 15,322.82 − 0.096 × Mileage. (b) 72.2%. (c) $8,342 to $13,382.

11-35 (a) Average GPA = 2.019 + 0.002 × CBAT. (b) 43.9%. (c) 3.22 to 3.96.

11-37 (a) Average demand = 29.351 + 0.003 × Advertising. (b) 18.4%. (c) 36.

11-39 Demand for periods 49 to 60 = 60,493, 69,902, 28,402, 33,014, 31,973, 21,062, 22,124, 24,141, 24,595, 96,132, and 86,586, respectively. The model fits the data very well.

11-41 (a) 1.0. (b) Average GNP = 8,942.825 + 112.476 × Quarter; 10,855. (c) 10,496.

11-43 (a) $3.259. (b) Average price = 3.156 + 0.012 × Month; $3.598. (c) Exponential smoothing has a lower MAPE.

11-45 (a) 332. (b) Average Sales = 288.775 + 4.313 × Quarter; 362. (c) Four-period moving average has a lower MAPE.

11-47 (a) 462.25. (b) 482.88. (c) Four-period moving average has a lower MAPE.

Chapter 12

12-15 (a) 38,730. (b) 6,000. (c) $52.62; no effect on ROP. (d) 44,721; 50,000; 54,772.

12-17 45,000 loads.

12-19 (a) 956 units, 11,250 units, 84 orders. (b) 676 units, 15,750 units, 118 orders.

12-21 Expand to 20,000 cu. ft. to hold 200 motors; expansion worth $22,500 per year.

12-23 EOQ varies between 1,342 (at OC = $45) and 1,414 (at OC = $50). Expected OC = $47.13; EOQ at this OC = 1,373.

12-25 3,849 bearings.

12-27 30 units.

12-29 Closely control X4; do not closely control U1, W3, and Z6.

12-31 (a) 548 tripods. (b) 718 tripods. (c) 852 tripods. (d) Five-week delivery option; Cost = $176.04.

12-33 Order 158 sheets each time.

12-35 1,501 discs, total cost = $30,850.03.

12-37 Safety stock = 51 units; ROP = 301 units.

12-39 A: items 5 and 9; B: items 2 and 7; C: rest of the items.

12-41 A: items I, A, and H; B: items J and F; C: rest of the items.

Appendix A

A-15 (a) 0.5. (b) 0.5. (c) 0.25. (d) 0.25. (e) 0.50. (f) 0.75.

A-17 (a) 0.26. (b) 0.19. (c) 0.54.

A-19 0.54.

A-21 0.385, 0.615.

A-23 0.947.

A-25 (a) 0.2. (b) 0.4. (c) 0.44. (d) 0.08. (e) 0.48. (f) Not a good team.

A-27 (a) No. (b) River City.

A-29 (a) and (c).

A-31 $E(X) = 5.45$, $\sigma^2 = 4.047$.

A-33 0.2743, 0.5.

A-35 0.1587, 0.2347, 0.1587.

A-37 (a) 0.0548. (b) 0.6554. (c) 0.6554. (d) 0.2120.

A-39 1829.27 ≈ 1,830.

A-41 0.7365.

INDEX

Note: Any page number with an "n" after it means that topic can be found in a footnote.